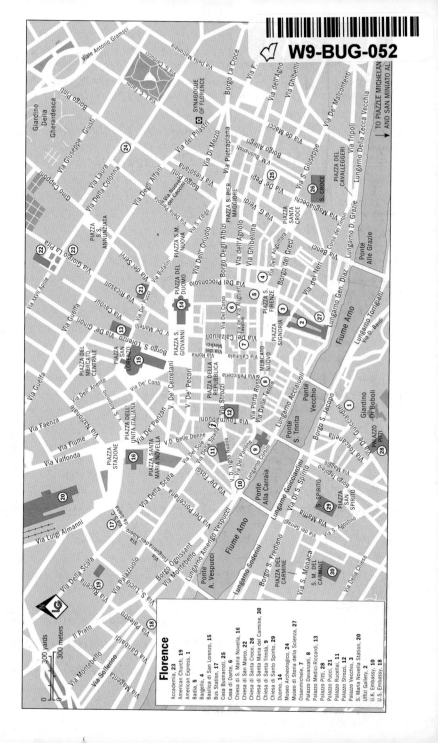

W9-BUG-052

Florence

Accademia, 23
American Church, 19
American Express, 1
Badia, 4
Bargello, 4
Basilica di San Lorenzo, 15
Bus Station, 17
Casa Buonarroti, 25
Casa di Dante, 6
Chiesa di S. Maria Novella, 16
Chiesa di San Marco, 22
Chiesa di Santa Croce, 26
Chiesa di Santa Maria del Carmine, 30
Chiesa di Santa Trinità, 12
Chiesa di Santo Spirito, 29
Duomo, 14
Museo Archeologico, 24
Museo di Storia della Scienza, 27
Orsanmichele, 7
Palazzo Davanzati, 8
Palazzo Medici-Riccardi, 13
Palazzo Pitti, 28
Palazzo Pucci, 21
Palazzo Ruccellai, 11
Palazzo Strozzi, 12
Palazzo Vecchio, 3
S. Maria Novella Station, 20
Uffizi Gallery, 2
U.K. Embassy, 10
U.S. Embassy, 18

TO PIAZZLE MICHELAN
AND SAN MINIATO AL

300 yards
300 meters

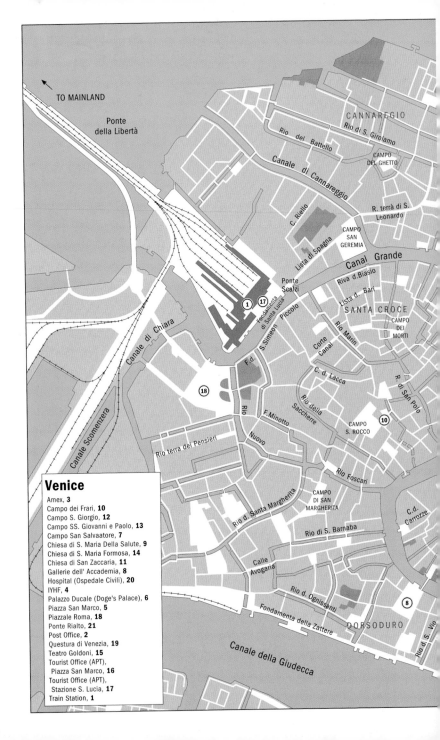

TO MAINLAND

Ponte
della Libertà

CANNAREGIO

Rio di S. Girolamo

Rio del Battello

Canale di Cannareggio

CAMPO
DEL GHETTO

R. terrà di S.
Leonardo

CAMPO
SAN
GEREMIA

Lista di Spagna

C. Riello

Canal Grande

Ponte
Scalzi

Riva d.Biasio

Lista d. Bari

SANTA CROCE

CAMPO
DEI
MORTI

Fondamenta
di Santa Lucia

F.d. S.Simeon Piccolo

Rio Marin

Corte
Canal

C. d. Lacca

R. di San Polo

Canale di Chiara

Rio della
Sacchere

CAMPO
S. ROCCO

Canale Scomenzera

Rio terra dei Pensieri

F.Minotto

Nuovo

Rio Foscari

CAMPO
DI SAN
MARGHERITA

C.d.
Carrozze

Rio d. Santa Margherita

Rio di S. Barnaba

Calle
Avogaria

Rio d. Ognissanti

Rio d. S. Vio

Fondamenta della Zattere

DORSODURO

Canale della Giudecca

Venice

Amex, **3**
Campo dei Frari, **10**
Campo S. Giorgio, **12**
Campo SS. Giovanni e Paolo, **13**
Campo San Salvaatore, **7**
Chiesa di S. Maria Della Salute, **9**
Chiesa di S. Maria Formosa, **14**
Chiesa di San Zaccaria, **11**
Gallerie dell' Accademia, **8**
Hospital (Ospedale Civili), **20**
IYHF, **4**
Palazzo Ducale (Doge's Palace), **6**
Piazza San Marco, **5**
Piazzale Roma, **18**
Ponte Rialto, **21**
Post Office, **2**
Questura di Venezia, **19**
Teatro Goldoni, **15**
Tourist Office (APT),
  Piazza San Marco, **16**
Tourist Office (APT),
  Stazione S. Lucia, **17**
Train Station, **1**

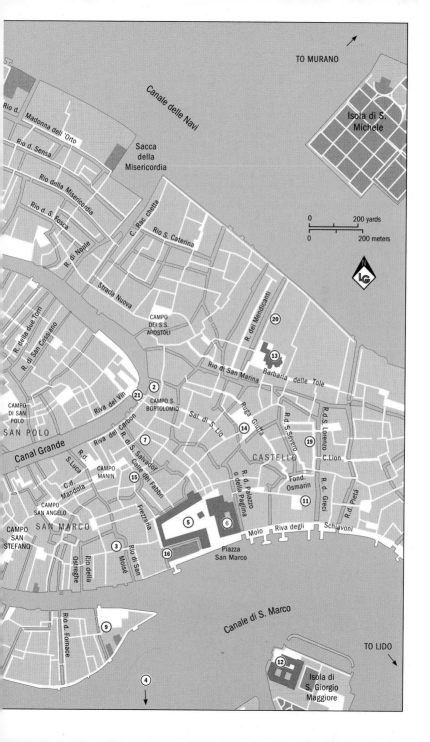

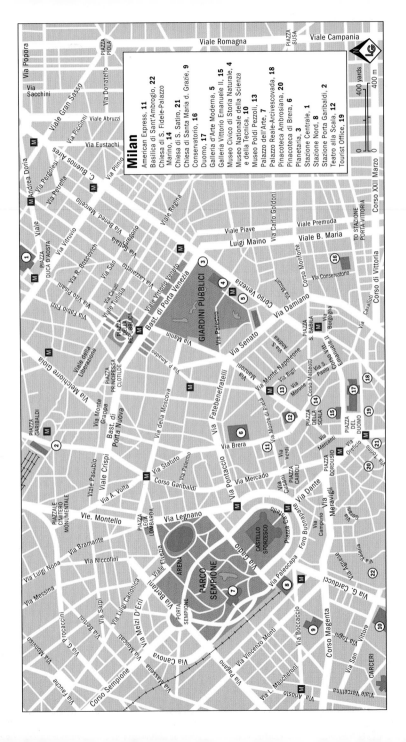

Milan

American Express, **11**
Basilica di Sant'Ambrogio, **22**
Chiesa di S. Fidele-Palazzo Marino, **14**
Chiesa di S. Satiro, **21**
Chiesa di Santa Maria d. Grazie, **9**
Conservatorio, **16**
Duomo, **17**
Galleria d'Arte Moderna, **5**
Galleria Vittorio Emanuele II, **15**
Museo Civico di Storia Naturale, **4**
Museo Nazionale della Scienza e della Tecnica, **10**
Museo Poldi Pezzoli, **13**
Palazzo dell'Arte, **7**
Palazzo Reale-Arcivescovada, **18**
Pinacoteca Ambrosiana, **20**
Pinacoteca di Brera, **6**
Planetaria, **3**
Stazione Centrale, **1**
Stazione Nord, **8**
Stazione Porta Garibaldi, **2**
Teatro alla Scala, **12**
Tourist Office, **19**

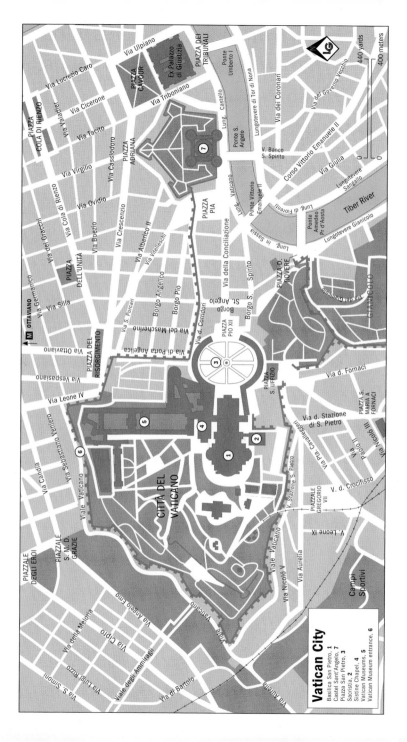

Vatican City

Basilica San Pietro, **1**
Castel Sant'Angelo, **7**
Piazza San Pietro, **3**
Sacristia, **2**
Sistine Chapel, **4**
Vatican Museums, **5**
Vatican Museum entrance, **6**

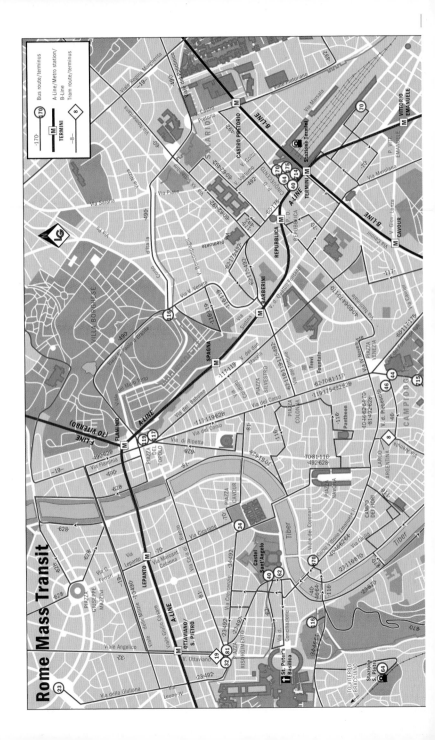

Rome Mass Transit

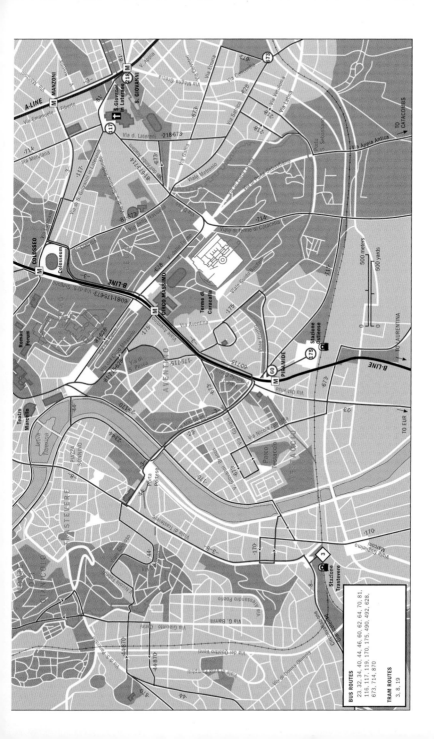

BUS ROUTES
23, 32, 34, 40, 44, 46, 60, 62, 64, 70, 81, 116, 117, 119, 170, 175, 490, 492, 628, 673, 714, 870

TRAM ROUTES
3, 8, 19

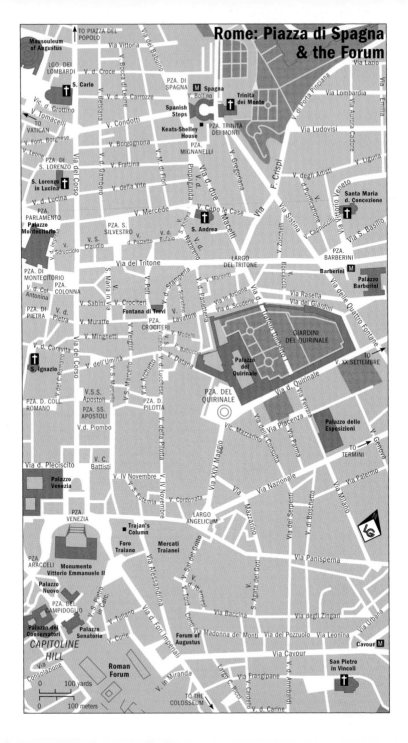

Rome: Piazza di Spagna & the Forum

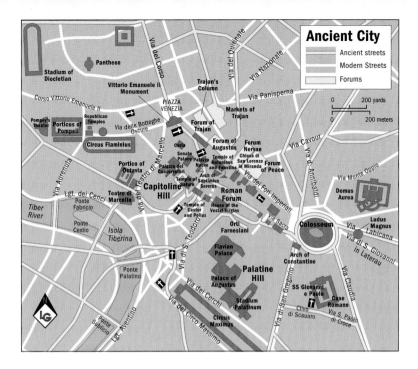

Ancient City

Ancient streets
Modern Streets
Forums

0 200 yards
0 200 meters

Stadium of Diocletian

Pantheon

Via del Corso

Via del Quirinale

Via Nazionale

Vittorio Emanuele II Monument

Trajan's Column

Via Panisperna

Corso Vittorio Emanuele II

PIAZZA VENEZIA

Markets of Trajan

Pompey's Theater

Porticus of Pompeii

Republican Temples

Via delle Botteghe Oscure

Forum of Trajan

Via Cavour

Circus Flaminius

Curia

Forum of Augustus

Forum Nerva

Via d. Annibaldi

Senate Palace

Palazzo Nuovo

Temple of Antoninus and Faustina

Chiesa di San Lorenzo id Miranda

Forum of Peace

Portico of Octavia

Palazzo dei Conservatori

Via Monte Oppio

Arch of Septimus Sererus

Capitoline Hill

Roman Forum

Via dei Fori Imperiali

Domus Aurea

Lgt. dei Cenci

Temple of Saturn

Via Aurentia

Tiber River

Ponte Fabricio

Teatro di Marcello

Temple of Castor and Pollux

House of the Vestal Virgins

Via Sacra

Ludus Magnus

Via di S. Giovanni in Laterau

Ponte Cestio

Isola Tiberina

Orti Farnesiani

Colosseum

Via

Via del Teatro di Marcello

Via di S. Teodoro

Flavian Palace

Palatine Hill

Arch of Constantine

Via Claudia

Ponte Palatino

Palace of Augustus

SS Giovanni e Paolo

Case Romane

Ponte Subiclio

Lgt. Aventino

Via dei Cerchi

Stadium Palatinum

Via di San Gregorio

Clivo di Scauaro

Via S. Paolo di Croce

Ponte Subiclio

Via dei Circo Massimo

Circus Maximus

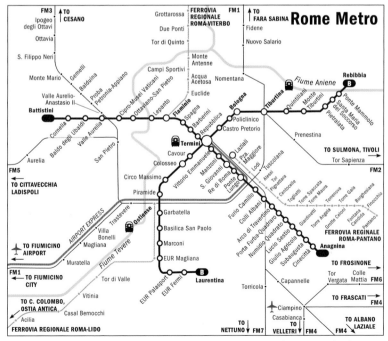

Rome Metro

FM3 TO CESANO

Ipogeo degli Ottavi

Grottarossa

FERROVIA REGIONALE ROMA-VITERBO

FM1

TO FARA SABINA

Ottavia

Due Ponti

Fidene

S. Filippo Neri

Tor di Quinto

Nuovo Salario

Monte Antenne

Campi Sportivi

Monte Mario

Gemelli

Balduina

Acqua Acetosa

Nomentana

Fiume Aniene

Rebibbia

B

Valle Aurelio-Anastasio II

Proba Petronia-Appiano

Cipro-Musei Vaticani

Ottaviano-San Pietro

Euclide

Bologna

Tiburtina

Quintiliani

Monte Tiburtini

Santa Maria del Soccorso

Ponte Mammolo

Battistini

Lepanto

Flaminio

Spagna

Barberini

Repubblica

Policlinico

Castro Pretorio

Pietralata

Cornelia

Baldo degli Ubaldi

Valle Aurelia

San Pietro

Termini

Prenestina

TO SULMONA, TIVOLI

Aurelia

Cavour

Lazio

Pza Maggiore

Tor Sapienza

FM5

Colosseo

Vittorio Emanuele

Manzoni

S. Giovanni

Re di Roma

Lodi

Tuscolana

Alessi

FM2

TO CITTAVECCHIA LADISPOLI

Circo Massimo

Ponte Lungo

Tor Pignattara

Centocelle

Togliatti

Torre Spaccata

Torre Maura

Torrenova

Giardinetti

Torre Gaia

Piramide

Furio Camillo

Colli Albani

Arco di Travertino

Torre Angela

Grotte Celoni

Finocchio

Borghesiana

Pantano

AIRPORT EXPRESS

Trastevere

Ostiense

Garbatella

Porta Furba-Quadraro

Numidio Quadrato

Giulio Agricola

Lucio Sestio

Subaugusta

Cinecittà

Anagnina

FERROVIA REGINALE ROMA-PANTANO

TO FIUMICINO AIRPORT

Villa Bonelli

Magliana

Basilica San Paolo

Marconi

TO FROSINONE

Muratella

EUR Magliana

Tor Vergata

Colle Mattia

FM6

Fiume Tevere

FM1

TO FIUMICINO CITY

Tor di Valle

EUR Palasport

EUR Fermi

Laurentina

B

Torricola

Capannelle

TO FRASCATI

FM4

TO C. COLOMBO, OSTIA ANTICA

Vitinia

Ciampino

Casabianca

TO ALBANO LAZIALE

Casal Bernocchi

Acilia

FERROVIA REGIONALE ROMA-LIDO

TO NETTUNO FM7

TO VELLETRI FM4

FM4

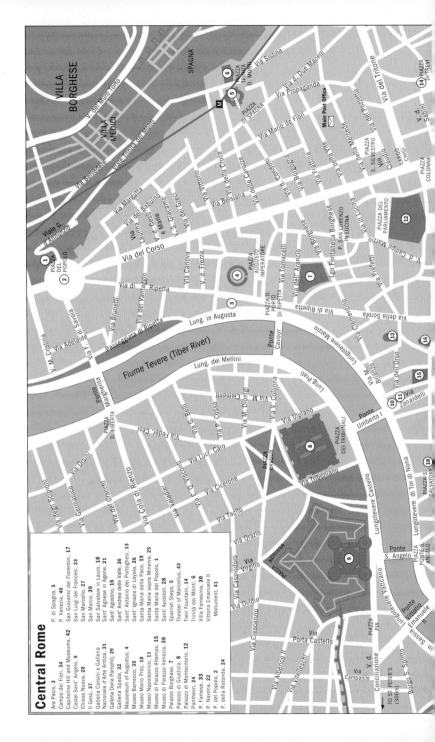

Central Rome

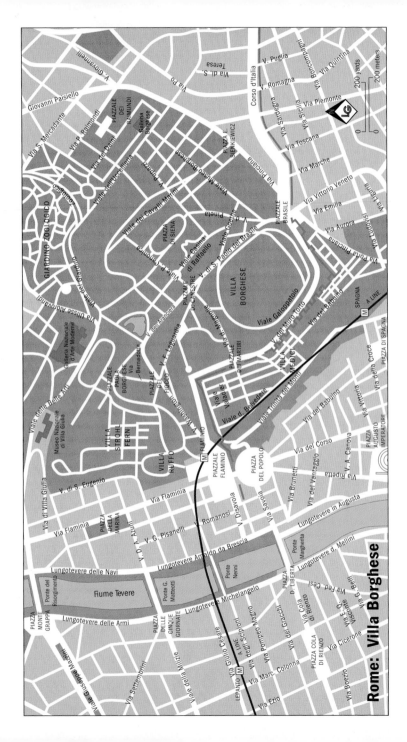

Rome: Villa Borghese

LET'S GO

■ PAGES PACKED WITH ESSENTIAL INFORMATION

"Value-packed, unbeatable, accurate, and comprehensive."

—*The Los Angeles Times*

"The guides are aimed not only at young budget travelers but at the independent traveler; a sort of streetwise cookbook for traveling alone."

—*The New York Times*

"Unbeatable; good sight-seeing advice; up-to-date info on restaurants, hotels, and inns; a commitment to money-saving travel; and a wry style that brightens nearly every page."

—*The Washington Post*

■ THE BEST TRAVEL BARGAINS IN YOUR BUDGET

"All the dirt, dirt cheap."

—*People*

"Let's Go follows the creed that you don't have to toss your life's savings to the wind to travel—unless you want to."

—*The Salt Lake Tribune*

■ REAL ADVICE FOR REAL EXPERIENCES

"The writers seem to have experienced every rooster-packed bus and lunar-surfaced mattress about which they write."

—*The New York Times*

"[Let's Go's] devoted updaters really walk the walk (and thumb the ride, and trek the trail). Learn how to fish, haggle, find work—anywhere."

—*Food & Wine*

"A world-wise traveling companion—always ready with friendly advice and helpful hints, all sprinkled with a bit of wit."

—*The Philadelphia Inquirer*

■ A GUIDE WITH A SPIRIT AND A SOCIAL CONSCIENCE

"Lighthearted and sophisticated, informative and fun to read. [Let's Go] helps the novice traveler navigate like a knowledgeable old hand."

—*Atlanta Journal-Constitution*

"The serious mission at the book's core reveals itself in exhortations to respect the culture and the environment—and, if possible, to visit as a volunteer, a student, or a teacher rather than a tourist."

—*San Francisco Chronicle*

LET'S GO PUBLICATIONS

TRAVEL GUIDES

Australia 9th edition
Austria & Switzerland 12th edition
Brazil 1st edition
Britain 2008
California 10th edition
Central America 9th edition
Chile 2nd edition
China 5th edition
Costa Rica 3rd edition
Eastern Europe 13th edition
Ecuador 1st edition
Egypt 2nd edition
Europe 2008
France 2008
Germany 13th edition
Greece 9th edition
Hawaii 4th edition
India & Nepal 8th edition
Ireland 13th edition
Israel 4th edition
Italy 2008
Japan 1st edition
Mexico 22nd edition
Middle East 4th edition
New Zealand 8th edition
Peru 1st edition
Puerto Rico 3rd edition
South Africa 5th edition
Southeast Asia 9th edition
Spain & Portugal 2008
Thailand 3rd edition
Turkey 5th edition
USA 24th edition
Vietnam 2nd edition
Western Europe 2008

ROADTRIP GUIDE

Roadtripping USA 2nd edition

ADVENTURE GUIDES

Alaska 1st edition
Pacific Northwest 1st edition
Southwest USA 3rd edition

CITY GUIDES

Amsterdam 5th edition
Barcelona 3rd edition
Boston 4th edition
London 16th edition
New York City 16th edition
Paris 14th edition
Rome 12th edition
San Francisco 4th edition
Washington, D.C. 13th edition

POCKET CITY GUIDES

Amsterdam
Berlin
Boston
Chicago
London
New York City
Paris
San Francisco
Venice
Washington, D.C.

LET'S GO

ITALY

2008

VINNIE CHIAPPINI EDITOR
STEFAN ZEBROWSKI-RUBIN ASSOCIATE EDITOR
CAITLIN MARQUIS ASSOCIATE EDITOR

RESEARCHER-WRITERS
DANNY BILOTTI
EMILY CUNNINGHAM
LEE ANN CUSTER
KYLE LEINGANG
JOHN MISTOVICH
ODEVIZ SOTO

MAISIE CLARK MAP EDITOR
ANNE BENSSON MANAGING EDITOR

ST. MARTIN'S PRESS ✹ NEW YORK

Maps by David Lindroth copyright © 2008 by St. Martin's Press.

Distributed outside the USA and Canada by Macmillan.

ISBN-13: 978-0-312-37451-8
ISBN-10: 0-312-37451-8
First edition
10 9 8 7 6 5 4 3 2 1

Let's Go: Italy is written by Let's Go Publications, 67 Mount Auburn St., Cambridge, MA 02138, USA.

Let's Go® and the LG logo are trademarks of Let's Go, Inc.

HOW TO USE THIS BOOK

COVERAGE LAYOUT. Welcome to *Let's Go: Italy 2008*. Our book begins in Rome, once the center of the world and still a thriving arena of global commerce. From there, towns are grouped in chapters by political boundaries except in the Lake Country where the northern Italy's lakes are conveniently grouped. The book flows from north to south—from the snow-capped mountaintops of Valle d'Aosta to sunny Sicily—and finally to the island of Sardinia. Black tabs on the side of each page and our extensive Index (p. 773) will help you navigate Italy's regions.

TRANSPORTATION INFO. Sections on intercity transportation generally list all major destinations, followed by trip duration, frequency, time range of departures, and price. A typical listing: Trains to **Rome** (1hr., 13 per day 4:30am-7pm, €10). For more general information on travel, consult the Essentials (p. 9) section.

COVERING THE BASICS. Discover Italy (p. 1), contains **Let's Go Picks** (our favorite places in Italy) and **Suggested Itineraries** to help you plan your trip. **Essentials** (p. 9) provides logistical information and useful tips for travelers in Italy. **Life and Times** (p. 63) explains Italy's 3000 years of history, culture, and customs. Along your Italian trek, reference the **Appendix's** (p. 760) useful Italian phrasebook and menu reader. For information on study abroad, volunteer, and work opportunities in Italy, consult **Beyond Tourism** (p. 95).

SCHOLARLY ARTICLES. To help travelers understand their destinations in a more in-depth fashion, Let's Go solicits experts for in-depth treatments of country-specific topics. Our extended articles discuss the cultural institution of *calcio* (soccer; p. 90), the emotional entanglement behind the influential *Laocoön* sculpture (p. 149), the role of tourism in southern Italy (p. 105), and a program in Rome that intends to resurrect Latin, Italian's long-dead ancestor (p. 158).

PRICE DIVERSITY. Our researchers list establishments in order of value from best to worst, with absolute favorites denoted by the Let's Go thumbs-up (🖑). Since the cheapest price does not always mean the best value, we have incorporated a system of price ranges for food and accommodations (p. 84).

LANGUAGE AND OTHER QUIRKS. The English translations for cities are listed when applicable, followed by their Italian name. For pronunciation help, consult the phonetic spelling in each city introduction, or the **Appendix** (p. 760). In text and on maps, the names of streets and *piazze* have been shortened to the standardized abbreviations chart on the inside back cover.

PHONE CODES AND TELEPHONE NUMBERS. Phone codes for each city appear opposite the name of the city and are denoted by the ☎ icon. Phone numbers in text are also preceded by the ☎ icon. To save space, the city phone codes have been omitted in our listings. **Emergency phone numbers** have not been listed in every city but more accessibly and conveniently on the inside back cover.

A NOTE TO OUR READERS. The information for this book was gathered by *Let's Go* researchers from May through August of 2007. Each listing is based on one researcher's opinion, formed during his or her visit at a particular time. Those traveling at other times may have different experiences since prices, dates, hours, and conditions are always subject to change. You are urged to check the facts presented in this book beforehand to avoid inconvenience and surprises.

RESEARCHER-WRITERS

Danny Bilotti *Sicily, Calabria*

While airport bungles and wild dogs plagued his first days in Sicily, Danny valiantly used the little Italian he knew to combat trying transportation and tiny towns. The LG virgin mastered his research and even found time to conquer Mt. Etna. The stoic Econ major finished his route in his native (but yet-undiscovered) Calabria, finding his namesake *piazza* in Cosenza, trying out a wild white-water excursion, and adding the heaven-on-earth town of Praia a Mare.

Emily Cunningham *Veneto, Trentino, Fruili, Emilia-Romagna, Le Marche*

Although mistaken for Jennifer Lopez on the Spanish Steps and dubbed *bellissima* by more than a few restaurant owners, Emily forsook romance, choosing instead to keep track of her beloved Boston Red Sox and find every hotel that included breakfast. She seamlessly switched between finding Trieste's classiest cafes, admiring art in Venice's Guggenheim, and raging in Rimini.

Lee Ann Custer *Liguria, Tuscany, Umbria*

Excited to return to her old home base of Siena for the Palio, this fluent Italian speaker conscientiously breezed through her route. Although fresh to LG, Cincinnati-native Lee Ann wrote like a well-traveled vet, flashing her press pass in Umbria, tackling the Tuscan titans, and finishing up early in sun-soaked Liguria. The Italophile with a weak spot for Giotto made especially sure that both personality and architectural particularities shone through in her writing.

Kyle Leingang *Piedmont, Valle d'Aosta, The Lake Country, Lombardy*

This recent college graduate, armed with can-do enthusiasm and a California-cool attitude, never felt alone on his route. Refusing to allow both gruff conductors and too-cool bouncers to spoil his research, Kyle tackled transportation hubs with the same gusto as flashy Milan. This tireless researcher found the hottest big city nightlife and the best views in the Lake Country. Next year he'll be attending a Boston-area law school.

John Mistovich *Rome, Sardinia*

Considering that John had already crossed the continental US by rail on a diet of canned tuna and crackers, it's not surprising that he took budget travel to a whole new level in his research. Despite setbacks like a drive-by dog food attack and spending a night on a beach, this student of global commerce never lost his love for making three wishes in every church and asking *belle donne* to apply his sunscreen.

Odeviz Soto *Campania, Puglia, Basilicata, Abruzzo, Molise*

This well-traveled quadrilingual Floridian, who recently graduated with a History degree, wasted no time in exchanging the garbage-filled streets of Naples for nearby beaches and islands. Despite the Mediterranean heat, Odeviz kept his cool and charmed every Italian he met. He was rewarded with the local inside scoop—plus free homemade wine. Odeviz arrived on a one-way ticket to Europe; after traipsing around Italy, he plans to spend a year teaching in Austria, as he did in Poland and China in past summers.

CONTRIBUTING WRITERS

Alexander Bevilacqua was born in Milan and has lived in Germany, Australia, and the United States, but his heart remains in the wheat fields of southern Italy. He is a 2006 graduate in History at Harvard University and was a Researcher-Writer for *Let's Go: Germany 2005* in Bavaria.

Dr. Laura Flusche teaches art history at the University of Dallas's Rome campus. She is the founder of Friends of Rome (www.friendsofrome.org), a nonprofit dedicated to the preservation of Roman monuments. She's also president of The Institute of Design & Culture in Rome (www.idcrome.org).

Edoardo Gallo, from Cuneo, Italy, is currently working as a consultant in New York after researching for *Let's Go: Central America* in El Salvador, Nicaragua, and Honduras. He is a 2004 graduate in Physics and Mathematics of Harvard University and is also a passionate, lifelong fan of Juventus.

Clem Wood has spent summers in both Florence and Rome. He will graduate from Harvard in the spring of 2008 with an A.B. in Classics and plans to return to Italy for further adventures and studies in the near future.

CONTENTS

ACKNOWLEDGMENTS

LET'S GO

TEAM ITALY THANKS: Anne for being the best ME ever (period). Maisie for collapsing on our couch every time she dropped off presents. *What's it Like to Live in Italy?* for unity, France for laying down the romance (not the drama), Lauren for her hair-raising winning joke, and all our RWs for living the Three Ps.

VINNIE THANKS: Caitlin for outperforming my ghost intern. Stefan for also talking to himself. Anne for all your help. Maisie! Belissima & Mistomagic for keeping it classy. Inés for being my summer mom. Ma & Pops for everything. Jack, Moxie, & PBR for good times. TB for being Army Strong. Woo for FIFA, throwing down, and 1/3 of our chats. Red Velvet Cake for obvious reasons. 6 Exeter. DBAB.

STEFAN THANKS: *Mille grazie* to Vinnie for keeping things light with clipart, Anne for constant guidance, and Caitlin for editing like a Milanese bouncer. Thank you Sara for good mornings, Dre for thoughtful advice; ✪FRITA love always (that's you too Victoria). *Baci* to Paula for making a summer sublet a beautiful home; Hezzy and Parker for hanging out and sharing life. And, of course, *ti amo mamma*.

CAITLIN THANKS: Vinnie, for never taking himself seriously. Stefan, for being Italian at heart. Odeviz, for making me smile. Dre, for being incredible; Sara, for songs and stories. Victoria, for tolerating us. FRITA, for no-strings-attached dates. Susan and Ez, for understanding that life gets crazy. Hope, for giving me a reason to commute. Sheena, for life support. M&D, for everything.

MAISIE THANKS: The Team Italy RWs for writing me nice notes on their map corrections. Danny for calling me from Italy even though it was expensive. The editors of Team Italy for always being kind. The FRITA pod. Mapland.

Editor
Vinnie Chiappini
Associate Editors
Stefan Zebrowski-Rubin
Caitlin Marquis
Managing Editor
Anne Bensson
Map Editor
Maisie Clark
Typesetter
Alexandra Hoffer

Publishing Director
Jennifer Q. Wong
Editor-in-Chief
Silvia Gonzalez Killingsworth
Production Manager
Victoria Esquivel-Korsiak
Cartography Manager
Thomas MacDonald Barron
Editorial Managers
Anne Bensson, Calina Ciobanu, Rachel Nolan
Financial Manager
Sara Culver
Business and Marketing Manager
Julie Vodhanel
Personnel Manager
Victoria Norelid
Production Associate
Jansen A. S. Thurmer
Director of E-Commerce & IT
Patrick Carroll
Website Manager
Kathryne A. Bevilacqua
Office Coordinators
Juan L. Peña, Bradley J. Jones

Director of Advertising Sales
Hunter McDonald
Senior Advertising Associate
Daniel Lee

President
William Hauser
General Managers
Bob Rombauer, Jim McKellar

Italy: Chapters

② PRICE RANGES ③ ④
① ITALY ⑤

Our researchers list establishments in order of value from best to worst; our favorites are denoted by the Let's Go thumbs-up (🖒). However, because the best value is not always the cheapest price, we have also incorporated a system of price ranges, based on a rough expectation of what you'll spend. For **accommodations**, we base our range on the cheapest price for which a single traveler can stay for one night. For **restaurants** and other dining establishments, we estimate the average amount a traveler will spend. The table tells you what you'll *typically* find in Italy at the corresponding price range; keep in mind that no system can allow for every individual establishment's quirks, and you'll typically get more for your money in larger cities. In other words: expect anything.

ACCOMMODATIONS	RANGE	WHAT YOU'RE *LIKELY* TO FIND
❶	under €20	Campgrounds, dorm rooms, or dorm-style rooms. Expect bunk beds and a communal bath; you may have to provide or rent towels and sheets.
❷	€20-29	Upper-end hostels or lower-end *pensioni*. You may have a private bathroom, or there may be a sink in your room and a communal shower in the hall.
❸	€30-40	A small room with a private bath, probably in a budget hotel or *pensione*. Should have decent amenities, such as phone and TV. Breakfast may be included in the price of the room.
❹	€41-60	Similar to ❸, but may have more amenities or be in a more highly-touristed or conveniently-located area.
❺	above €60	Large hotels or upscale chains. If it's a ❺ and it doesn't have the perks you want, you've paid too much.

FOOD	RANGE	WHAT YOU'RE *LIKELY* TO FIND
❶	under €7	Probably a fast-food stand, *gelateria*, *bar*, cafe, or a pizzeria. Rarely ever a sit-down meal.
❷	€7-15	Sit-down pizzerias and most affordable *trattorie*. Should include mid-priced *primi* and *secondi*.
❸	€16-22	Similar to ❷, but nicer setting and a more elaborate menu. May offer a cheaper lunch *menù*, and pizza could be a less expensive alternative to a *primo* and *secondo* combination.
❹	€23-30	As in ❸, higher prices are likely related to better service, but in these restaurants, the food will tend to be fancier or more elaborate, or the location will be especially convenient or historic. While few restaurants in this price range will have a dress code, T-shirts, jeans, or shorts may be frowned upon.
❺	above €30	Venerable reputation, a 90-page wine list, or the freshest seafood with a harbor view. Elegant attire may be expected.

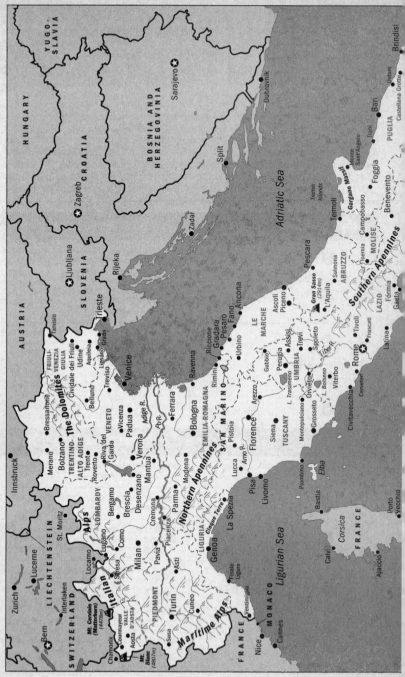

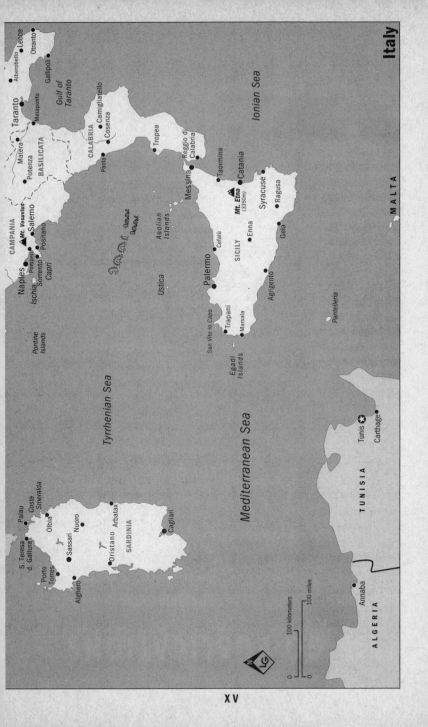

Italy

XV

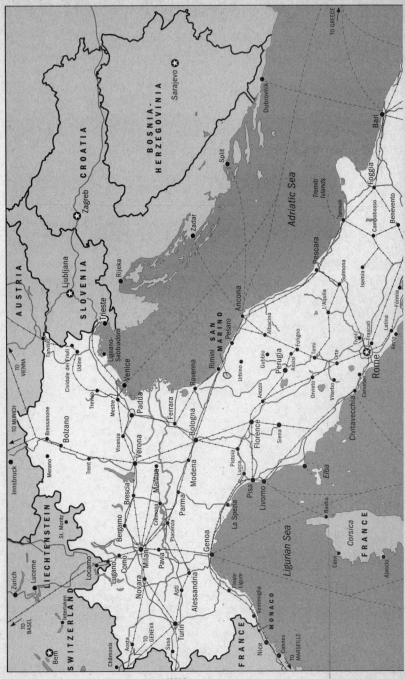

XVI

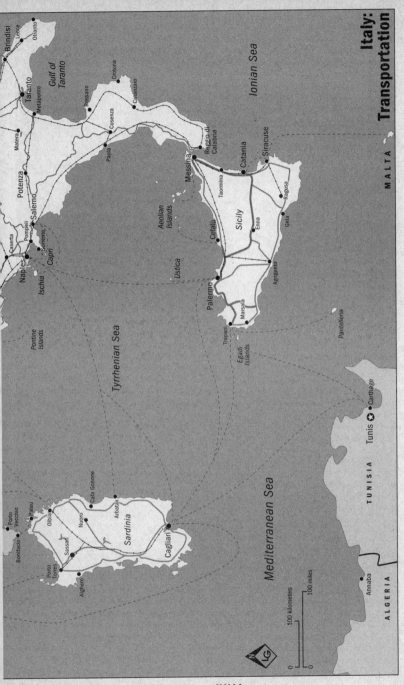

Italy:
Transportation

DISCOVER ITALY

The classic images of Italy—the vespas, the Vatican, the *vino*—are all enjoyable, but don't let them define your experience. Instead, learn how to lounge, to embrace delays, and to saunter down cobblestone pavements—in stilettos, of course. Slap on your Frauda sunglasses, slip into a D&G outfit, douse yourself in Gucci perfume, and indulge in some good ol' Italian elegance. Meet those eccentric restaurant owners, learn Italy's local secrets, and explore her untainted nature. And during your most action-packed adventures, don't forget to step back, as Italians often do, and experience *la dolce far niente* (literally, the sweetness of doing nothing). Don't just come to Italy to confirm the spaghetti-and-meatballs image you already have; come to discover something you can't send home on a postcard. Discover the chaos, serenity, energy, and allure. Discover Italy.

FACTS AND FIGURES

ITALY 2007 POPULATION: 58 million	**REGULAR CHURCHGOERS:** 18 million
NUMBER OF CELL PHONES: 63 million	**REGULAR SOCCER FANS:** 30 million
NUMBER OF VESPA SALES IN 2005: 395,000	**VATICAN CITY:** World's richest institution; world's smallest country
ANNUAL PASTA CONSUMPTION PER PERSON: 59 lb.	**DAILY BREAD CONSUMPTION PER PERSON:** ½ lb.

READY, SET...DON'T GO YET!

Tourism enters overdrive in June, July, and August. Hotels are booked solid, prices skyrocket, and rows of lounge chairs take over pristine beaches. Around *Ferragosto*, a national holiday on August 15, Italians head to the coast, leaving a flood of closed businesses in their wake. Some larger cities avoid this summer hibernation and remain enjoyable in August, but late May through July make for a livelier trip. Traveling to Italy in early May or early September assures a calmer, cooler, cheaper vacation. The temperature drops to a comfortable average of 25°C (77°F) with regional variations. Depending on the region, a trip in April or October often has the advantages of lower prices and smaller crowds. The best weather for hiking in the Alps is from June to September; ski season generally lasts from December through late March, but continues all year in some locations.

MOSAICS TO MODERNISM

Unsurprisingly, Italy, the birthplace of the Renaissance, is also home to impressive art collections. The most important, such as the museums listed below, are found in the country's largest cities; however, virtually every small town has its own *museo archeologico* or *pinacoteca* (art gallery) showcasing collections that range from Greek pottery shards and Roman mosaics to contemporary art. Don't head to these if you're looking for a high concentration of famous works, but avoiding the crowds and seeking out that lone Caravaggio or da Messina in a regional museum can offer more rewarding experience than a constant barrage of masterworks. Also, keep in mind that some of Italy's greatest artwork is held within the sacred walls of her many churches.

DISCOVER

CITY	PRINCIPAL ART COLLECTIONS
Florence	Uffizi Gallery (p. 439)
	Galleria dell'Accademia (p. 444)
	Museo dell'Opera del Duomo (p. 438)
Milan	Pinacoteca di Brera (p. 249)
	Galleria d'Arte Moderna (p. 251)
Naples	Museo Archeologico Nazionale (p. 568)
	Museo di Capodimonte (p. 570)
Rome	Sistine Chapel (p. 147)
	Vatican Museums (p. 148)
	Galleria Borghese (p. 148)
	Museo Nazionale d'Arte Antica (p. 151)
Reggio di Calabria	Museo Nazionale (p. 638)
Rovereto	Museo d'Arte Moderna e Contemporanea—"Il Mart" (p. 360)
Siena	Pinacoteca Nazionale (p. 459)
	Museo dell'Opera Metropolitana (p. 459)
Trieste	Museo Revoltella (p. 372)
Turin	Museo Egizio (p. 173)
	Galleria Sabauda (p. 173)
Venice	Collezione Peggy Guggenheim (p. 327)
	Gallerie dell'Accademia (p. 327)

SO MUCH MORE THAN PIZZA

Pizza, beloved internationally as a quick takeout meal, is much more than fast food when enjoyed on its native soil. Originating in Naples (p. 555) in the 1800s after introduction of tomatoes, pizza has evolved beyond the basic Margherita. The pizzerias of Italy may be good, but if you grant them more than a cursory visit, you're missing something great: true Italian cuisine. Even pasta, an integral part of the Italian diet for thousands of years, faces competition for its claim as the Italian carb of choice. Italy's famous creamy rice dish, *risotto*, incorporates local specialties: wine and truffles in Piedmont, seafood in the Veneto, and saffron in Milan. In northern in regions such as Trentino-Alto Adige (p. 356), polenta and *gnocchi* (potato and flour dumplings) enjoy popularity. To go beyond these nationwide staples, begin your regional tour of Italian cuisine with Piedmont's (p. 164) white truffles; watch your wallet, though, because these 'white diamonds' go for US$850-1500 per lb. This region also saw the invention of Nutella, which now enjoys international consumption exceeding that of all peanut butter brands combined. Genoa (p. 200) flaunts colorful pesto, which gets its name from *pestatura* (a method of grinding using a mortar and pestle); imitations are marketed worldwide, but the best basil leaves—and therefore the best pesto—hail from Liguria. The Friuli-Venezia Giulia region (p. 368) has a subtle Slavic flair, apparent in ingredients like yogurt, fennel, cumin, and paprika. Treviso (p. 351), in the Veneto region, is famous for its tiramisu, a heavenly espresso-and-rum-soaked cake layered with mild *mascarpone* cheese. Its name, which literally means "pick me up," is rumored to have originated from its use by tired prostitutes. Check out Tuscany's (p. 421) bread, but only as intended: with food. By itself, this saltless bread comes as a surprise; several theories explain the lack of salt, including a 12th-century salt price-hike protest that changed from boycott to tradition after prices came back down. Centuries ago, Florence (p. 421) birthed *gelato*, a milk-based frozen treat now available throughout the country. In the heart of Emilia-Romagna, Bologna (p. 382), birthplace of *tortellini* and *bolognese* sauce, reigns as culinary capital of Italy, while Modena (p. 395) is famous for its balsamic vinegar, and Parma (p. 400) boasts tender prosciutto. The region is perhaps most famous, however, for its *parmigiano-reggiano* cheese. Besides Naples's (p. 555) pizza, southern Italy offers seafood, olive oil, and *granita*, a slushy Sicilian (p. 648) version of *gelato*, and *cipolle rosse* (red onions) from Tropea (p. 639). To find the perfect wine to compliment your meal, see In Vino Veritas (p. 88).

BICEP CURLS GET THE GIRLS

Sandwiched between the Mediterranean and Adriatic Seas, the Italian coastline stretches over 2000 mi. In the northwest, the famous beaches of **Liguria** (p. 200) form the Italian Riviera, home to the picturesque fishing villages of **Cinque Terre** (p. 213) and the glitterati-packed resorts of **San Remo** (p. 228). Farther down, the hidden gem of **Sperlonga** (p. 159) provides a relaxing daytrip from sweaty Rome. Some of Italy's best beaches farther down the coast: swing south along the Amalfi Coast to beach towns like **Positano** (p. 595) and **Capri** (p. 589) that offer sparkling waters, lapping against cliffs and lemon groves. After getting your dose of high culture in Venice's art museums, don't miss the nearby beach towns like **Caorle** (p. 348), **Lignano** (p. 376), and **Grado** (p. 374). On the Salento Peninsula, **Otranto** (p. 626) and **Gallipoli's** (p. 628) emerald waters entice visitors. In Abruzzo and Molise, the **Tremiti Islands** (p. 554) are home to rocky coves and secluded beaches, good for swimming and snorkeling. Also on the east coast, **Rimini** (p. 411) attracts a large student population with its hot beaches during the day and hotter club scene at night. Calabria and Sicily offer visitors enormous variety, from the untouristed, dark stone coasts of **Pantelleria** (p. 716) to the resort towns of **Cefalù** (p. 659).

TAKE A HIKE!

Italy presents plenty of opportunities for the outdoor adventurer, whether you get your kicks staring into the fiery mouth of a volcano or strolling through the Tuscan countryside. The **Aeolian Islands** (p. 662) are home to both active and inactive volcanoes; **Mt. Etna** (p. 688) offers prime volcanic terrain and far-reaching views. Hike, bike, or ski through **Abruzzo National Park** (p. 548) in the southern Apennines, the northeastern **Dolomites** (p. 356), or Calabria's **Sila Massif** (p. 644). Enjoy the hiking and beaches of Liguria's **Cinque Terre** (p. 213), a young backpacker's paradise. Slow things down by taking Grandma on a walk through the **Chianti region** (p. 452) of Tuscany, which offers travelers a less strenuous outdoor experience; walk along country roads past vineyards, olive groves, and ancient castles, all while enjoying panoramic views of the surrounding hills and valleys.

TAKE A BREAK ON A LAKE

Northern Italy is home to the gorgeous Lake Country. Quaint towns and breathtaking panoramas surround abound. You can enjoy them by strolling through citrus groves in **Limone** (p. 283), paddleboating in **Riva del Garda** (p. 280), or windsurfing in **Domaso** (p. 290). De-stress in **Stresa** (p. 299) while hiking or biking scenic trails. Dance in **Desenzano** (p. 278), reportedly home of the best nightclubs on Lake Garda. *Mangia* in **Menaggio** (p. 293) to get a taste of some authentic regional cuisine. Be prepared to shell out a few extra euro for this paradise; however, the lakeside view from your balcony will remind you that it's worth it.

HOW TO RUIN A PERFECTLY GOOD TRIP

The Roman Empire may have fallen 1500 years ago, but it continues to bring global commerce into Rome. Both crumbling and wonderfully preserved arches, aqueducts, and amphitheaters give a sense of majesty, mystery, and poetry to Italy. Although many Italian cities, including **Spoleto** (p. 517), **Rimini** (p. 411), **Aquileia** (p. 374), **Aosta** (p. 192), and **Acqui Terme** (p. 186) boast some sort of Roman relic, the most impressive ruins are scattered through the streets of **Rome** (p. 106), where travelers can admire the famous Colosseum, Pantheon, and Roman Forum. Daytrips from Rome lead to the extravagant **Villa Adriana** in Tivoli (p. 160). Farther south, **Naples** (p. 555) boasts a world-renowned archaeological museum and miles of subterranean Roman aqueducts open for exploration. Near Naples, **Pompeii** (p. 573) is a city caught in AD 79, having been covered in lava from an eruption of Mt. Vesuvius. A neighboring excavation site, **Herculaneum** (p. 576), features another surprisingly intact 2000-year-old town. Across the peninsula, **Brindisi** (p. 618) is home to the column marking the end of the Appian Way, an ancient road that led to Rome. Italy also has numerous relics of pre-Roman inhabitants. Etruscan artifacts can be found in many Tuscan towns like **Fiesole** (p. 451). Sicily's proximity to Greece led to the establishment of many Greek colonies, which were the first great civilizations in Italy, including **Segesta** (p. 712), **Agrigento** (p. 701), and **Syracuse** (p. 693). On the mainland, **Paestum** (p. 608) is home to both Doric temples and Roman forums. Evidence of more ancient civilizations can be found in Matera's *sassi* (p. 632), **Alberobello's** *trulli* (p. 614), and in **Sardinia's** *nuraghi* (p. 722).

▧ LET'S GO PICKS

BEST PLACE TO SHOW UP BACCHUS HIMSELF: In the vineyards of the **Chianti** region (p. 452).

BEST PLACE TO SAY A HAIL MARY TO ATONE FOR BACCHANALIAN EXCESS: The **Vatican** (p. 139) offers confession in numerous languages.

BEST PLACE TO SLEEP LIKE A ROCK: Matera's sassy 7000-year-old *sassi*, homes carved into the mountainside (p. 632). The white-washed, conical *trulli* of **Alberobello** (p. 614) are mortarless abodes used as residences, churches, and restaurants. **Pantelleria's** domed *dammusi* (p. 716) are constructed from petrified lava.

BEST PLACE TO REVEL IN INSOMNIA: Wild bars and raging, themed clubs dominate the beachside party town of Rimini (p. 411) and nearby Riccione (p. 417).

BEST PLACE TO PEOPLE-WATCH: Check out the well-dressed glitterati in **Milan** (p. 237) or the fashionable beachgoers in classy **Capri** (p. 589).

BEST PLACE TO CORPSE-WATCH: Pace through the huge **Cappuchin Catacombs** (p. 656) in Palermo, where 8000 bodies rest in their moth-eaten Sunday best. Or check out the partially decayed body of **Ötzi** (p. 361), a 5000-year-old Iceman in Bolzano.

SUGGESTED ITINERARIES

EATALY (4 WEEKS)

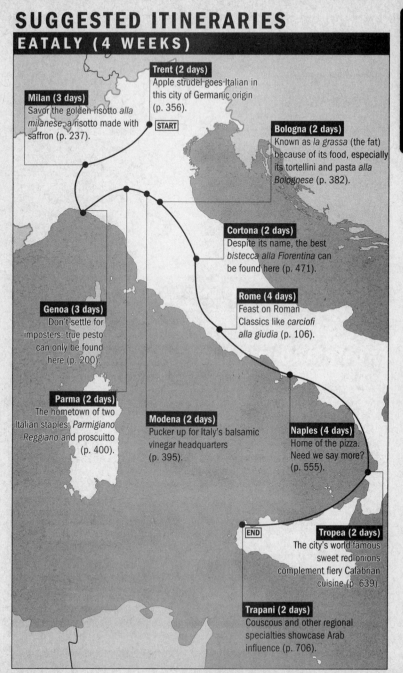

Milan (3 days)
Savor the golden risotto *alla milanese*, a risotto made with saffron (p. 237).

Trent (2 days)
Apple strudel goes Italian in this city of Germanic origin (p. 356).

START

Bologna (2 days)
Known as *la grassa* (the fat) because of its food, especially its tortellini and pasta *alla Bolognese* (p. 382).

Cortona (2 days)
Despite its name, the best *bistecca alla Fiorentina* can be found here (p. 471).

Genoa (3 days)
Don't settle for imposters; true pesto can only be found here (p. 200).

Rome (4 days)
Feast on Roman Classics like *carciofi alla giudia* (p. 106).

Parma (2 days)
The hometown of two Italian staples: *Parmigiano Reggiano* and proscuitto (p. 400).

Modena (2 days)
Pucker up for Italy's balsamic vinegar headquarters (p. 395).

Naples (4 days)
Home of the pizza. Need we say more? (p. 555).

END

Tropea (2 days)
The city's world-famous sweet red onions complement fiery Calabrian cuisine (p. 639).

Trapani (2 days)
Couscous and other regional specialties showcase Arab influence (p. 706).

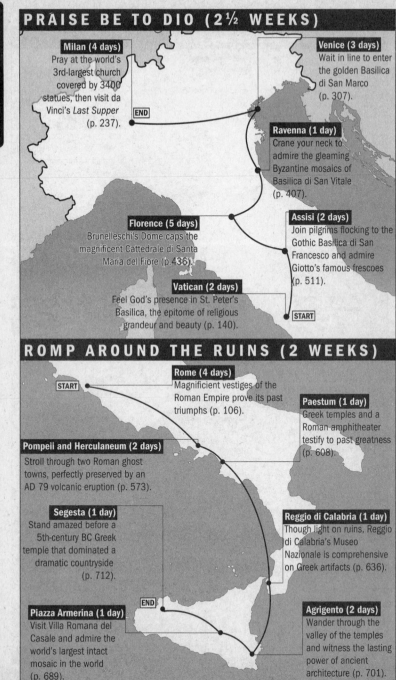

PRAISE BE TO DIO (2½ WEEKS)

Milan (4 days)
Pray at the world's 3rd-largest church covered by 3400 statues, then visit da Vinci's *Last Supper* (p. 237).

END

Venice (3 days)
Wait in line to enter the golden Basilica di San Marco (p. 307).

Ravenna (1 day)
Crane your neck to admire the gleaming Byzantine mosaics of Basilica di San Vitale (p. 407).

Florence (5 days)
Brunelleschi's Dome caps the magnificent Cattedrale di Santa Maria del Fiore (p.436).

Assisi (2 days)
Join pilgrims flocking to the Gothic Basilica di San Francesco and admire Giotto's famous frescoes (p. 511).

Vatican (2 days)
Feel God's presence in St. Peter's Basilica, the epitome of religious grandeur and beauty (p. 140).

START

ROMP AROUND THE RUINS (2 WEEKS)

START

Rome (4 days)
Magnificient vestiges of the Roman Empire prove its past triumphs (p. 106).

Paestum (1 day)
Greek temples and a Roman amphitheater testify to past greatness (p. 608).

Pompeii and Herculaneum (2 days)
Stroll through two Roman ghost towns, perfectly preserved by an AD 79 volcanic eruption (p. 573).

Segesta (1 day)
Stand amazed before a 5th-century BC Greek temple that dominated a dramatic countryside (p. 712).

Reggio di Calabria (1 day)
Though light on ruins, Reggio di Calabria's Museo Nazionale is comprehensive on Greek artifacts (p. 636).

END

Piazza Armerina (1 day)
Visit Villa Romana del Casale and admire the world's largest intact mosaic in the world (p. 689).

Agrigento (2 days)
Wander through the valley of the temples and witness the lasting power of ancient architecture (p. 701).

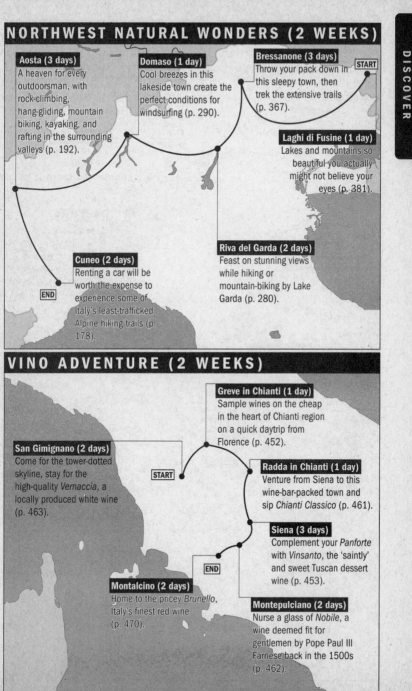

DISCOVER

NORTHWEST NATURAL WONDERS (2 WEEKS)

Aosta (3 days)
A heaven for every outdoorsman, with rock-climbing, hang-gliding, mountain biking, kayaking, and rafting in the surrounding valleys (p. 192).

Domaso (1 day)
Cool breezes in this lakeside town create the perfect conditions for windsurfing (p. 290).

Bressanone (3 days)
Throw your pack down in this sleepy town, then trek the extensive trails (p. 367).

START

Laghi di Fusine (1 day)
Lakes and mountains so beautiful you actually might not believe your eyes (p. 381).

Cuneo (2 days)
Renting a car will be worth the expense to experience some of Italy's least-trafficked Alpine hiking trails (p. 178).

END

Riva del Garda (2 days)
Feast on stunning views while hiking or mountain-biking by Lake Garda (p. 280).

VINO ADVENTURE (2 WEEKS)

Greve in Chianti (1 day)
Sample wines on the cheap in the heart of Chianti region on a quick daytrip from Florence (p. 452).

San Gimignano (2 days)
Come for the tower-dotted skyline, stay for the high-quality *Vernaccia*, a locally produced white wine (p. 463).

START

Radda in Chianti (1 day)
Venture from Siena to this wine-bar-packed town and sip *Chianti Classico* (p. 461).

Siena (3 days)
Complement your *Panforte* with *Vinsanto*, the 'saintly' and sweet Tuscan dessert wine (p. 453).

END

Montalcino (2 days)
Home to the pricey *Brunello*, Italy's finest red wine (p. 470).

Montepulciano (2 days)
Nurse a glass of *Nobile*, a wine deemed fit for gentlemen by Pope Paul III Farnese back in the 1500s (p. 462).

DISCOVER

BEST OF ITALY (4 WEEKS)

Turin (3 days)
Enjoy the cultural offerings, hot nightlife, and nearby outdoor adventures in this rising star of the North (p. 164).

Milan (3 days)
Party it up in this fast-paced financial and fashion center that hasn't forgotten its past (p. 237).

Trieste (2 days)
Sample sapphire seas and sauerkraut in this multicultural hidden gem (p. 368).

START

Venice (5 days)
Dreams come true when drifting down Venice's romantic canals (p. 307).

Florence (5 days)
This Renaissance Mecca has more world-class art, awe-inpiring churches, and high-class shopping than you can shake a stick at (p. 421).

Cinque Terre (2 days)
Hike among five colorful towns and lounge on the beach in this backpacker's mainstay (p. 213).

Rome (5 days)
After more than 2700 years, powerful history and lively nightlife still echo in *la città eterna* (p. 106).

Naples (3 days)
Grab a slice in pizza's hometown and don't miss nearby Herculaeum and Pompeii (p. 555).

END

Catania (2 days)
Climb Mt. Etna and discover this Sicilian treasure's mixed architecture and lively student population (p. 683).

ESSENTIALS

PLANNING YOUR TRIP

 ENTRANCE REQUIREMENTS
Passport (p. 10). Required for citizens of Australia, Canada, Ireland, New Zealand, the UK, and the US.
Visa (p. 11). Required only for citizens of Australia, Canada, Ireland, New Zealand, the UK, and the US for stays over 90 days.
Work Permit (p. 12). Required for all foreigners planning to work in Italy.

EMBASSIES AND CONSULATES

ITALIAN CONSULAR SERVICES ABROAD

Australia: 12 Grey St., Deakin, Canberra ACT 2600 (☎61 26 2733 333; www.ambcanberra.esteri.it/Ambasciata_Canberra). **Consulates:** 509 St. Kilda Rd., Melbourne VIC 3004 (☎61 03 9867 5744; www.consmelbourne.esteri.it); The Gateway, Level 45, 1 Macquarie Pl., Sydney NSW 2000 (☎61 02 9392 7900; www.conssydney.esteri.it).

Canada: 275 Slater St., 21st fl., Ottawa, ON K1P 5H9 (☎613-232-2401; www.ambottawa.esteri.it). **Consulate:** 3489 Drummond St., Montreal, QC H3G 1X6 (☎514-849-8351; www.consmontreal.esteri.it).

Ireland: 63/65 Northumberland Rd., Dublin (☎353 166 017 44; www.ambdublino.esteri.it).

New Zealand: 34-38 Grant Rd., PO Box 463, Thorndon, Wellington (☎644 473 5339; www.italy-embassy.org.nz). **Consulates:** 102 Kitchener Rd., PO Box 31 121 Auckland (☎649 489 9632).

UK: 14 Three Kings Yard, London W1K 4EH (☎44 20 731 222 00; www.embitaly.org.uk). **Consulates:** 32 Melville Street, Edinburgh EH3 7HA (☎44 131 226 3631; www.consedimburgo.esteri.it); Rodwell Tower, 111 Piccadilly, Manchester M1 2HY (☎44 161 236 9024; www.consmanchester.esteri.it).

US: 3000 Whitehaven St., N.W., Washington, D.C. 20008 (☎202-612-4400; www.ambwashingtondc.esteri.it). **Consulates:** 600 Atlantic Ave., Boston, MA 02110-2206 (☎617-722-9201; www.consboston.esteri.it); 500 N. Michigan Ave., Ste. #1850, Chicago, IL 60611 (☎312-467-1550; www.conschicago.esteri.it); 690 Park Ave., New York, NY 10021 (☎212-737-9100; www.consnewyork.esteri.it).

CONSULAR SERVICES IN ITALY

Australia: V. Antonio Bosio 5, Rome 00161 (☎06 85 27 21, emergency 800 877 790; www.italy.embassy.gov.au). Open M-F 8:30am-5pm.

Canada: V. Zara 30, Rome 00198 (☎06 85 44 41; www.dfait-maeci.gc.ca/canada-europa/italy/menu-en.asp). Open M-Th 8:30-11:30am.

Ireland: P. di Campitelli 3, Rome 00186 (☎06 69 79 121; www.ambasciata-irlanda.it). Open M-F 10am-1pm.

New Zealand: V. Zara 28, Rome 00198 (☎06 44 17 171; www.nzembassy.com). Open M-F 8:30am-12:45pm and 1:45-5pm. **Consulate:** V. Guido d'Arezzo 6, Milan 20145 (☎02 48 01 25 44). Open M-F 8:30am-5pm.

UK: V. XX Settembre 80a, Rome 00187 (☎06 42 20 00 01; www.britain.it). Open autumn-spring M-F 9am-5pm; summer 8am-2pm. Closed UK and Italian holidays.

US: V. Vittorio Veneto 121, Rome 00187 (☎06 46 741; www.usembassy.it). Consular services open M-F 8:30am-12:30pm. Closed US and Italian holidays. **Consulate:** V. Principe Amedeo 2/10, Milan 20121 (☎02 29 03 51). Open M-F 8:30am-noon.

TOURIST OFFICES

Italian Government Tourist Board (ENIT) provides useful info about many aspects of the country, including the arts, nature, history, and leisure activities. Visit their website, www.italiantourism.com, for info. Call ☎212-245-4822 for a free copy of *General Information for Travelers to Italy.* The main office in Rome (☎06 49 71 11; sedecentrale@cert.enit.it) can help locate any local office not listed online.

Australia: Level 26, 44 Market St., Sydney NSW 2000 (☎29 26 21 666; enitour@ihug.com.au).

Canada: 175 E. Bloor St., Ste. 907 South Tower, Toronto, ON M4W 3R8 (☎416-925-4882; enit.canada@on.aibn.com).

UK: 1 Princes St., London, W1B 2AY (☎20 7408 1254; www.italiantouristboard.co.uk).

US: 630 5th Ave., Ste. 1565, New York, NY 10111 (☎212-245-5618; www.italiantourism.com).

DOCUMENTS AND FORMALITIES

PASSPORTS

REQUIREMENTS

Citizens of Australia, Canada, Ireland, New Zealand, the UK, and the US need valid passports to enter Italy and to re-enter their home countries. Returning home with an expired passport is illegal and may result in a fine.

NEW PASSPORTS

Citizens of Australia, Canada, Ireland, New Zealand, the UK, and the US can apply for a passport at any passport office or at selected post offices and courts of law. Citizens of these countries may also download passport applications from the official website of their country's government or passport office. Any new passport or renewal applications must be filed well in advance of the departure date, though most passport offices offer rush services for a very steep fee. Note, however, that "rushed" passports still take up to two weeks to arrive.

PASSPORT MAINTENANCE

Photocopy the page of your passport with your photo, as well as your visas, traveler's check serial numbers, and any other important documents. Carry one set of copies in a safe place, apart from the originals, and leave another set at home. Consulates also recommend that you carry an expired passport or an official copy of your birth certificate in a part of your baggage separate from other documents.

If you lose your passport, immediately notify the local police and the nearest embassy or consulate of your home country. To expedite its replacement, you must show ID and proof of citizenship; it also helps to know all information previously recorded in the passport. In some cases, a replacement may take weeks to

ONE EUROPE. European unity has come a long way since 1958, when the European Economic Community (EEC) was created to promote European solidarity and cooperation. Since then, the EEC has become the European Union (EU), a mighty political, legal, and economic institution. On May 1, 2004, ten South, Central, and Eastern E.ropean countries—Cyprus, the Czech Republic, Estonia, Hungary, Latvia, Lithuania, Malta, Poland, Slovakia, and Slovenia—were admitted to the EU, joining 15 other member states: Austria, Belgium, Denmark, Finland, France, Germany, Greece, Ireland, Italy, Luxembourg, the Netherlands, Portugal, Spain, Sweden, and the UK. On January 1, 2007, Romania and Bulgaria were admitted.

What does this have to do with the average non-EU tourist? The EU's policy of **freedom of movement** means that border controls between the first 15 member states (minus Ireland and the UK, but plus Norway and Iceland) have been abolished, and visa policies harmonized. Under this treaty, formally known as the **Schengen Agreement,** you're still required to carry a passport (or government-issued ID card for EU citizens) when crossing an internal border, but once you've been admitted into one country, you're free to travel to other participating states. On June 5, 2005, Switzerland ratified the treaty but has yet to implement it. The 10 of the newest member states of the EU are anticipated to implement the policy in October of 2007. Britain and Ireland have also formed a **common travel area,** abolishing passport controls between the UK and the Republic of Ireland.

For more important consequences of the EU for travelers, see **The Euro** (p. 14) and **European Customs** and **EU customs regulations** (p. 14).

process, and may be valid only for a limited time. Any visas stamped in your old passport will be irretrievably lost. In an emergency, ask for immediate temporary traveling papers that will permit you to re-enter your home country.

VISAS AND WORK PERMITS

VISAS

EU citizens do not need a visa. Citizens of Australia, Canada, New Zealand, and the US do not need a visa for stays of up to 90 days, though this three-month period begins upon entry into any of the countries that belong to the EU's **freedom of movement** zone. For more information, see **One Europe** above. Those staying longer than 90 days may purchase a visa, which costs €60, at the Italian consulate or embassy in their home country.

Double-check entrance requirements at the nearest Italian embassy or consulate (see **Embassies and Consulates Abroad,** on p. 9) for up-to-date info before departure. US citizens can also consult http://travel.state.gov.

Foreign nationals planning to stay in Italy over 90 days should apply within eight working days of arrival for a **permesso di soggiorno** (permit of stay). Generally, non-EU tourists are required to get a permit at a police station or foreign office (*questura*) if staying longer than 20 days or taking up residence in a location other than a hotel, official campsite, or boarding house. If staying in a hotel or hostel, the staff will fulfill registration requirements for you and the fee is waived. There are steep fines for a failure to comply. Double-check entrance requirements at the nearest embassy or consulate (p. 9) before departure. For more info, consult http://amb-washingtondc.esteri.it or www.stranieriinitalia.it (click on left side bar under heading *Per vivere in Italia*).

Entering Italy to study requires a student visa. For more info, see **Beyond Tourism** (p. 95) or visit www.ambwashingtondc.esteri.it.

WORK PERMITS

Admission as a visitor from a non-EU country does not include the right to work, which is authorized only by a work permit. For more information, see the **Beyond Tourism** chapter (p. 95).

IDENTIFICATION

When you travel, always carry at least two forms of identification on your person, including a photo ID. A passport and either a driver's license or birth certificate is an adequate combination. Never carry all your IDs together; split them up in case of theft or loss, and keep photocopies of all of them in your luggage and at home.

STUDENT, TEACHER, AND YOUTH IDENTIFICATION

The **International Student Identity Card (ISIC),** the most widely accepted form of student ID, provides discounts on some sights, accommodations, food, and transportation; access to a 24hr. emergency helpline; and insurance benefits for US cardholders (see **Insurance,** p. 22). Applicants must be full-time secondary or post-secondary school students at least 12 years of age. Because of the proliferation of fake ISICs, some services require additional proof of student identity.

The **International Teacher Identity Card (ITIC)** offers teachers the same insurance coverage as the ISIC and similar but limited discounts. To qualify for the card, teachers must be currently employed and have worked a minimum of 18hr. per week for at least one school year. For travelers who are under 26 years old but are not students, the **International Youth Travel Card (IYTC)** also offers many of the same benefits as the ISIC.

Each of these identity cards costs US$22. ISICs, ITICS, and IYTCs are valid for one year from the date of issue. To learn more about ISICs, ITICs, and IYTCs, try www.myisic.com. Many student travel agencies (p. 26) issue the cards; for a list of issuing agencies or more information, see the **International Student Travel Confederation (ISTC)** website (www.istc.org).

The **International Student Exchange (ISE) Card** is a similar identification card available to students, faculty, and youths aged 12 to 26. The card provides discounts, medical benefits, access to a 24hr. emergency helpline, and the ability to purchase student airfares. An ISE Card costs US$25; call ☎800 255 8000 in North America or ☎480 951 1177 from all other continents for more info, or visit www.isecard.com.

CUSTOMS

Upon entering Italy, you must declare certain items from abroad and pay a duty on the value of those articles if they exceed the allowance established by Italy's customs service. Note that goods and gifts purchased at **duty-free** shops abroad are not exempt from duty or sales tax; "duty-free" merely means that you need not pay a tax in the country of purchase. Duty-free allowances were abolished for travel between EU member states on June 30, 1999, but still exist for those arriving from outside the EU. Upon returning home, you must likewise declare all articles acquired abroad and pay a sales tax on the value of articles in excess of your home country's allowance (see p. 17 on taxes). In order to expedite your return, make a list of any valuables brought from home and register them with customs before traveling abroad, and be sure to keep receipts for all goods acquired abroad.

MONEY

CURRENCY AND EXCHANGE

The currency chart below is based on August 2007 exchange rates between local currency and Australian dollars (AUS$), Canadian dollars (CDN$), European

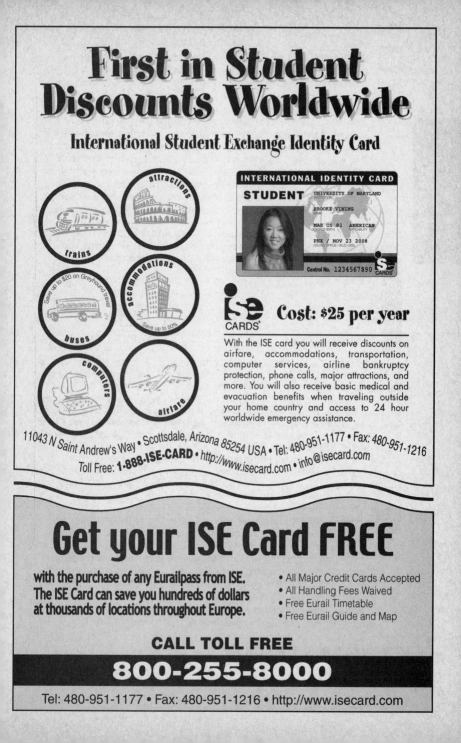

> **CUSTOMS IN THE EU.** As well as freedom of movement of people within the EU (or see **One Europe**, p. 11), travelers in the 15 original EU member countries (Austria, Belgium, Denmark, Finland, France, Germany, Greece, Ireland, Italy, Luxembourg, the Netherlands, Portugal, Spain, Sweden, and the UK) can also take advantage of the freedom of movement of goods. This means that there are no customs controls at internal EU borders (i.e., you can take the blue customs channel at the airport), and travelers are free to transport whatever legal substances they like as long as it is for their own personal (non-commercial) use—up to 800 cigarettes, 10L of spirits, 90L of wine (including up to 60L of sparkling wine), and 110L of beer. Duty-free allowances were abolished on June 30, 1999 for travel between the original 15 EU member states; this now also applies to Cyprus and Malta. However, travelers between the EU and the rest of the world still get a duty-free allowance when passing through customs.

Union euro (EUR€), New Zealand dollars (NZ$), British pounds (UK£), and US dollars (US$). Check the currency converter on websites like www.xe.com or www.bloomberg.com, or a large newspaper for the latest exchange rates.

EURO (€)		
AUS$1 = €0.62	€1 = AUS$1.61	
CDN$1 = €0.69	€1 = CDN$1.45	
NZ$1 = €0.55	€1 = NZ$1.80	
UK£1 = €1.47	€1 = UK£0.68	
US$1 = €0.73	€1 = US$1.38	

As a general rule, it's cheaper to convert money in Italy than at home. While currency exchange will probably be available in your arrival airport, it's wise to bring enough foreign currency to last for the first 24 to 72hr. of your trip.

When changing money abroad, try to go only to banks or money changers *(cambio)* that have at most a 5% margin between their buy and sell prices. Since you lose money with every transaction, **convert large sums,** but **no more than you'll need.**

If you use traveler's checks or bills, carry some in small denominations (the equivalent of US$50 or less) for times when you are forced to exchange money at disadvantageous rates, but bring bills in a range of denominations since charges may be levied per check cashed. Store your money in a variety of forms; ideally, at any given time you will be carrying some cash, some traveler's checks, and an ATM and/or credit card.

> **THE EURO.** The official currency of 13 members of the European Union—Austria, Belgium, Finland, France, Germany, Greece, Ireland, Italy, Luxembourg, the Netherlands, Portugal, Spain, and Slovenia—is now the euro.
>
> The currency has some important—and positive—consequences for travelers hitting more than one euro-zone country. For one thing, money-changers across the euro-zone are obliged to exchange money at the official, fixed rate (see above), and at no commission (though they may still charge a small service fee). Second, euro-denominated traveler's checks allow you to pay for goods and services across the euro-zone, again at the official rate and commission-free.

TRAVELER'S CHECKS

Traveler's checks are one of the safest and least troublesome means of carrying funds. However, they can also be one of the most frustrating means of spending money since fewer and fewer shops accept traveler's checks. If you do choose to purchase them, it is best to buy them in euro, so that you will not lose money in a conversion rate. American Express and Visa are the most recognized brands, and many banks and agencies sell them for a small commission. Check issuers provide refunds if the checks are lost or stolen, and many provide additional services, such as toll-free refund hotlines abroad, emergency message services, and assistance with lost and stolen credit cards or passports. Ask about toll-free refund hotlines and the location of refund centers when purchasing checks.

American Express: Checks available with commission at select banks, at all AmEx offices, and online (www.americanexpress.com; US residents only). American Express cardholders can also purchase checks by phone (☎800 528 4800). Checks available in Australian, British, Canadian, European, Japanese, and US currencies, among others. Also offers the Travelers Cheque Card, a prepaid reloadable card. Checks for Two can be signed by either of two people traveling together. For purchase locations or more information, contact AmEx service centers: in Australia ☎61 29 271 8666, in Italy 39 06 72 282, in New Zealand 649 367 4567, in the UK 44 1273 696 933, in the US and Canada 800-221-7282; elsewhere, call the US collect at 1 336 393 1111.

Travelex: Visa TravelMoney prepaid cash card and Visa traveler's checks available. For information about Thomas Cook MasterCard in Canada and the US call ☎800-223-7373, in the UK 0800 622 101; elsewhere call the UK collect at +44 1733 318 950. For information about Interpayment Visa in the US and Canada call ☎800-732-1322, in the UK 0800 515 884; elsewhere call the UK collect at +44 1733 318 949. For more information, visit www.travelex.com.

Visa: Checks available (generally with commission) at banks worldwide. For the location of the nearest office, call the Visa Travelers Cheque Global Refund and Assistance Center: in the UK ☎0800 895 078, in the US 800-227-6811; elsewhere, call the UK collect at 44 2079 378 091. Checks available in British, Canadian, European, Japanese, and US currencies, among others. Visa also offers TravelMoney, a prepaid debit card that can be reloaded online or by phone. For more information on Visa travel services, see http:/ /usa.visa.com/personal/using_visa/travel_with_visa.html.

CREDIT, DEBIT, AND ATM CARDS

Where they are accepted, credit cards often offer superior exchange rates—up to 5% better than the retail rate used by banks and other currency exchange establishments. Credit cards may also offer services such as insurance or emergency help, and are sometimes required to reserve hotel rooms or rental cars. **MasterCard** and **Visa** are the most frequently accepted; **American Express** cards work at some ATMs and at major airports.

The use of ATM cards is widespread in Italy. Depending on the system that your home bank uses, you can most likely access your personal bank account from abroad. **Cirrus** and **BankMate** are two of the most common financial networks. ATMs get the same wholesale exchange rate as credit cards, but there is often a limit on the amount of money you can withdraw per day (usually around US$500). There is also typically a surcharge of US$1-5 per withdrawal.

Debit cards are as convenient as credit cards but withdraw money directly from the holder's checking account. A debit card can be used wherever its associated credit card company (usually MasterCard or Visa) is accepted. Debit cards often also function as ATM cards and can be used to withdraw cash from associated banks and ATMs throughout Italy.

The two major international money networks are **MasterCard/Maestro/Cirrus** (for ATM locations ☎800 424 7787 or www.mastercard.com) and **Visa/PLUS** (for ATM locations ☎ 800 847 2911 or www.visa.com). Most ATMs charge a transaction fee that is paid to the bank that owns the ATM.

> **PINS AND ATMS.** To use a cash or credit card to withdraw money from a cash machine (ATM) in Europe, you must have a four-digit **Personal Identification Number (PIN).** If your PIN is longer than four digits, ask your bank whether you can just use the first four, or whether you'll need a new one. **Credit cards** don't usually come with PINs, so if you intend to hit up ATMs in Europe with a credit card to get cash advances, call your credit card company before leaving to request one.
>
> Travelers with alphabetic, rather than numerical, PINs may also be thrown off by the lack of letters on European cash machines. The following are the corresponding numbers to use: 1=QZ; 2=ABC; 3=DEF; 4=GHI; 5=JKL; 6=MNO; 7=PRS; 8=TUV; and 9=WXY. Note that if you mistakenly punch the wrong code into the machine three times, it will swallow your card for good.

GETTING MONEY FROM HOME

If you run out of money while traveling, the easiest and cheapest solution is to have someone back home make a deposit to your bank account. Failing that, consider one of the following options.

WIRING MONEY

It is possible to arrange a **bank money transfer,** which means asking a bank back home to wire money to a bank in Italy. This is the cheapest way to transfer cash, but it's also the slowest, usually taking several days or more. Note that some banks may only release your funds in local currency, potentially sticking you with a poor exchange rate; inquire about this in advance. Money transfer services like **Western Union** are faster and more convenient than bank transfers—but also much pricier. Western Union has many locations worldwide. To find one, visit www.westernunion.com, or call in Australia ☎ 800 173 833, in Canada and the US 800-325-6000, in the UK 0800 833 833, or in Italy ☎ 17 75 332 7900. To wire money using a credit card (Discover, MasterCard, Visa), call in Canada and the US ☎ 800-CALL-CASH, in the UK 0800 833 833. Money transfer services are also available to **American Express** cardholders and at selected **Thomas Cook** offices.

US STATE DEPARTMENT (US CITIZENS ONLY)

In serious emergencies only, the US State Department will forward money within hours to the nearest consular office, which will then disburse it according to instructions for a US$30 fee. If you wish to use this service, you must contact the Overseas Citizens Service division of the US State Department (☎ 202-647-5225, toll-free 888-407-4747).

COSTS

The cost of your trip will vary considerably, depending on where you go, how you travel, and where you stay. The most significant expenses will probably be your round-trip **airfare** to Italy (see **Getting to Italy: By Plane,** p. 25) and a **railpass** (p. 29). Before you go, spend some time calculating a reasonable daily **budget.**

STAYING ON A BUDGET

To give you a general idea, a bare-bones day in Italy (camping or sleeping in hostels/guesthouses, buying food at supermarkets) would cost US$35-55 (€25-40); a slightly more comfortable day (sleeping in hostels/guesthouses and the occasional budget hotel, eating one meal per day at a restaurant, going out at night) would cost US$75-95 (€55-70); and for a luxurious day, the sky's the limit. Don't forget to factor in emergency reserve funds (at least US$200) when planning how much money you'll need.

TIPS FOR SAVING MONEY

Some simpler ways include searching out opportunities for free entertainment, splitting accommodation and food costs with trustworthy fellow travelers, and buying food in supermarkets rather than eating out. Bring a **sleepsack** (p. 18) to save on sheet charges in European hostels, and do your **laundry** in the sink (unless you're explicitly prohibited from doing so). Museums often have certain days once a month or once a week when admission is free; plan accordingly. If you are eligible, consider getting an ISIC or an IYTC (p. 12); many sights and museums offer reduced admission to students and youths. For getting around quickly, bikes are the most economical option. Renting a bike is cheaper than renting a moped or scooter. Don't forget about walking, though; you can learn a lot about a city by seeing it on foot. Drinking at bars and clubs quickly becomes expensive. It's cheaper to buy alcohol at a supermarket and drink (responsibly, of course) before going out. That said, don't go overboard. Though staying within your budget is important, don't do so at the expense of your health or a great travel experience.

TIPPING AND BARGAINING

At many Italian restaurants, a service charge (*servizio*) or cover (*coperto*) is included in the bill. Locals sometimes do not give tips, but it is appropriate for foreign visitors to leave an additional 5-10% at restaurants for the waiter. Taxi drivers expect about a 5-10% tip, though Italians rarely tip them. Bargaining is common in Italy, but use discretion. Haggling is appropriate at markets, with vendors, and unmetered taxi fares (settle the price before getting in), but elsewhere, it is usually inappropriate. Hotel negotiation is more successful in uncrowded *pensioni*. To get lower prices, show little interest. Don't offer what you can't pay; you're expected to buy once the merchant accepts your price.

TAXES

The **Value Added Tax** (**VAT**; *imposto sul valore aggiunta*, or **IVA**) is a sales tax levied in the EU. Foreigners making any purchase over €155 are entitled to an additional 20% VAT refund. Some stores take off 20% on-site; or, fill out forms at the customs upon leaving the EU and send receipts from home within six months. The refund will be

TOP TEN WAYS TO SAVE IN ITALY

Homeland of Gucci, Prada, and Armani, Italy doesn't always cater to the frugal-minded, starving-artist types. But that doesn't mean that if you're going to shell the dough out, you can't spend it wisely. Keeping in mind that safety should always be a top priority when traveling, consider the following tips for saving money while living well:

1. For best **exchange rates**, use your ATM card instead of exchanging money.

2. Fly through London on Ryanair for the cheapest rates to Italy if you're traveling from the US or Canada.

3. Register with **Hostelling International,** and save on hostels in Italy and around the world.

4. Be on the lookout for days when you can **get into sights and museums for free.**

5. Buy food at **open-air markets** and grocery stores instead of restaurants.

6. To avoid an extra service charge in a bar, **drink and eat at the counter** instead of sitting down at a table.

7. Find **free Internet** access in most libraries and tourist offices.

8. Swim and lounge at **public beaches** to avoid the cover charge at many private beaches.

9. Look for cafes and restaurants on **side streets** rather than in main squares.

10. Bring a **sleepsack** to avoid paying extra for linen in hostels.

mailed to you. Not all storefront "Tax-Free" stickers imply an immediate, on-site refund; ask before making a purchase.

PACKING

PACK LIGHTLY: Lay out only what you absolutely need, then take half the clothes and twice the money. The Travelite FAQ (www.travelite.org) is a good resource for tips on traveling light. The online Universal Packing List (http://upl.codeq.info) will generate a customized list of suggested items based on your trip length, the expected climate, your planned activities, and other factors. If you plan to do a lot of hiking, also consult our section on The Great Outdoors (p. 53). Some savvy travelers keep a bag packed with all the essentials: passport, money belt, hat, socks, etc. Then, when they decide to leave, they know they haven't forgotten anything.

Luggage: If you plan to cover most of your itinerary by foot, a sturdy **frame backpack** is unbeatable. (For the basics on buying a pack, see p. 55.) Toting a **suitcase** or **trunk** is fine if you plan to live in one or two cities and explore from there, but not a great idea if you plan to move around frequently. In addition to your main piece of luggage, a **daypack** (a small backpack or courier bag) is useful.

Clothing: No matter when you're traveling, it's a good idea to bring a warm jacket or wool sweater, a rain jacket (Gore-Tex® is both waterproof and breathable), sturdy shoes or hiking boots, and thick socks. Flip-flops or waterproof sandals are must-haves for grubby hostel showers, and extra socks are always a good idea. You may also want one outfit for going out, and maybe a nicer pair of shoes. If you plan to visit religious or cultural sites, remember that you will need modest and respectful dress. Women traveling alone, especially in Southern Italy, should dress modestly to avoid unwanted attention. Consult the table of Italy's average temperatures (p. 760) to determine what other clothes would be best suited for your trip.

Sleepsack: Some hostels require that you either provide your own linen or rent sheets from them. Save cash by making your own sleepsack: fold a full-size sheet in half the long way, then sew it closed along the long side and one of the short sides.

Converters and Adapters: In Italy, electricity is **230Volts AC,** enough to fry any 120V North American appliance. Americans and Canadians should buy an adapter (which changes the shape of the plug; US$5) and a converter (which changes the voltage; US$20-30). Don't make the mistake of using only an adapter unless appliance instructions explicitly state otherwise. Travelers from NZ, Australia, and the UK (who use 230V at home) won't need a converter, but will need a set of adapters to use anything electrical. For more on all things adaptable, check out www.kropla.com/electric.htm.

Toiletries: Condoms, deodorant, razors, tampons, and toothbrushes are often available, but it may be difficult to find your preferred brand; bring extras. Contact lenses are likely to be expensive and difficult to find, so bring enough extra pairs and solution for your entire trip. Also bring your glasses and a copy of your prescription in case you need emergency replacements.

First-Aid Kit: For a basic first-aid kit, pack bandages, a pain reliever, antibiotic cream, a thermometer, a multifunction pocketknife, tweezers, moleskin, decongestant, motion-sickness remedy, diarrhea or upset-stomach medication (Pepto Bismol® or Imodium®), an antihistamine, sunscreen, insect repellent, and burn ointment.

Film: Film and developing in Italy can be expensive, so consider bringing along enough film for your entire trip and developing it at home. If you don't want to bother with film, consider using a digital camera. Although it requires a steep initial investment, a digital camera means you never have to buy film again. Just be sure to bring along a large enough memory card and extra (or rechargeable) batteries. Less serious photographers may want to bring a disposable camera or two. Airport security X-rays can fog film, so buy a lead-lined pouch at a camera store or ask security to hand-inspect it. Always pack film in your carry-on luggage, since higher-intensity X-rays are used on checked luggage.

Other Useful Items: For safety purposes, you should bring a **money belt** and a small **padlock.** Basic **outdoors equipment** (plastic water bottle, compass, waterproof matches, pocketknife, sunglasses, sunscreen, hat) may also prove useful. Quick repairs of torn garments can be done on the road with a needle and thread; also consider bringing electrical tape for patching tears. If you want to do laundry by hand, bring detergent, a small rubber ball to stop up the sink, and string for a makeshift clothes line. Other things you might forget include: an umbrella, sealable plastic bags (for damp clothes, soap, food, shampoo, and other spillables), an alarm clock, safety pins, rubber bands, a flashlight, earplugs, garbage bags, and a small calculator. A cell phone can be a life-saver (literally) on the road; see p. 44 for information on getting one that will work in Italy.

Important Documents: Don't forget your passport, traveler's checks, ATM and/or credit cards, adequate ID, and photocopies of all of the aforementioned in case these documents are lost or stolen (p. 10). Also check that you have any of the following that might apply to you: a hosteling membership card (p. 47); driver's license (p. 12); travel insurance forms (p. 22); ISIC (p. 12); and/or rail or bus pass (p. 29).

SAFETY AND HEALTH

GENERAL ADVICE

In any type of crisis situation, the most important thing to do is **stay calm.** Your country's embassy abroad (p. 9) is usually your best resource when things go wrong; registering with that embassy upon arrival in the country is often a good idea. The government offices listed in the **Travel Advisories** box (p. 20) can provide information on the services they offer their citizens in case of emergencies abroad.

LOCAL LAWS AND POLICE

In Italy you will mainly encounter two types of police: the *polizia* (☎113) and the *carabinieri* (☎112). The *polizia* are a civil force under the command of the Ministry of the Interior, whereas the *carabinieri* fall under the auspices of the Ministry of Defense and are considered a military force. Both, however, generally serve the same purpose—to maintain security and order in the country. In the case of attack or robbery both will respond to inquiries for help.

DRUGS AND ALCOHOL

Needless to say, **illegal drugs** are best avoided altogether. In Italy, drugs including marijuana, cocaine, and heroin are illegal. An increase in cocaine and heroin addiction and trafficking have led Italian authorities to respond harshly to drug-related offenses. If you carry **prescription drugs,** bring copies of the prescriptions and a note from a doctor, and have them accessible at international borders. The drinking age in Italy is 16. Drinking and driving is prohibited and can result in a prison sentence. The legal blood alcohol content (BAC) for driving is less than 0.05%, significantly lower than US standards, which limit BAC to 0.08%.

SPECIFIC CONCERNS

NATURAL DISASTERS

EARTHQUAKES. Italy is crossed by several fault lines, the chief one running from Sicily to Friuli-Venezia Giulia in the northeast. The country's principal cities do not lie near these faults, though smaller tourist towns like Assisi do and thus may experience earthquakes (most recently in 1997).

DEMONSTRATIONS AND POLITICAL GATHERINGS

Americans should be mindful while traveling in Italy, as there is some anti-American sentiment. No matter where you travel in Italy, you will likely encounter some sort of anti-American or, more likely, anti-Bush statements. It is best to err on the side of caution and sidestep these discussions. In general, use discretion and avoid being too vocal about your citizenship.

TERRORISM

Terrorism has not been as serious a problem in Italy as in other European countries, though the general threat of terrorism still exists. Exercise common sense and caution when in crowded, public areas like train or bus stations and open spaces like *piazze* in larger cities. The box on **travel advisories** below lists offices to contact and webpages to visit to get the most updated list of your home country's government's advisories about travel.

TRAVEL ADVISORIES. The following government offices provide travel information and advisories by telephone, by fax, or via the web:

Australian Department of Foreign Affairs and Trade: ☎612 6261 1111; www.dfat.gov.au.

Canadian Department of Foreign Affairs and International Trade (DFAIT): Call ☎800-267-8376; www.dfait-maeci.gc.ca. Call for their free booklet, *Bon Voyage...But.*

New Zealand Ministry of Foreign Affairs: ☎044 398 000; www.mfat.govt.nz.

United Kingdom Foreign and Commonwealth Office: ☎020 7008 1500; www.fco.gov.uk.

US Department of State: ☎888-407-4747; http://travel.state.gov. Visit the website to read the pamphlet *A Safe Trip Abroad.*

PERSONAL SAFETY

EXPLORING AND TRAVELING

To avoid unwanted attention, try to blend in as much as possible. Respecting local customs (in many cases, dressing more conservatively than you would at home) may placate would-be hecklers. Familiarize yourself with your surroundings before setting out, and carry yourself with confidence. Check maps in shops and restaurants rather than on the street. If you are traveling alone, be sure someone at home knows your itinerary, and never tell anyone you meet that you're by yourself. When walking at night, stick to busy, well-lit streets and avoid dark alleyways. If you ever feel uncomfortable, leave the area as quickly and directly as you can.

There is no sure-fire way to avoid all the threatening situations you might encounter while traveling, but a good **self-defense course** will give you concrete ways to react to unwanted advances. **Model Mugging** can refer you to local self-defense courses in Australia, Canada, Switzerland and the US. Visit the website at www.modelmugging.org for a list of nearby chapters.

If you are using a **car,** learn local driving signals and wear a seatbelt. Children under 40 lb. should ride only in specially designed carseats, available for a small fee from most car rental agencies. Study route maps before you hit the road, and if you plan on spending a lot of time driving, consider bringing spare parts. For long drives in desolate areas, invest in a cellular phone and a roadside assistance program (see p. 36). Park your vehicle in a garage or well-traveled area, and use a steering wheel locking device in larger cities. **Sleeping in your car** is the most dangerous way to get your rest. For info on the perils of **hitchhiking,** see p. 40.

POSSESSIONS AND VALUABLES

Never leave your belongings unattended; crime can occur even in hostels and hotels, which appear to be very safe. Bring your own padlock for hostel lockers, and don't ever store valuables in a locker. Be particularly careful on **buses** and **trains;** there are many horror stories about determined thieves who wait for travelers to fall asleep. Carry your bag or purse in front of you where you can see it. When traveling with others, sleep in alternate shifts. When alone, use good judgment in selecting a train compartment: never stay in an empty one, and use a lock to secure your pack to the luggage rack. Use extra caution if traveling at night or on overnight trains. Try to sleep on top bunks with your luggage stored above you (if not in bed with you), and keep important documents and other valuables on you at all times.

There are a few steps you can take to minimize the financial risk associated with traveling. First, **bring as little with you as possible.** Second, buy a few combination **padlocks** to secure your belongings either in your pack or in a hostel or train station locker. Third, **carry as little cash as possible.** Keep your traveler's checks and ATM/credit cards in a **money belt**—not a "fanny pack"—along with your passport and ID cards. Fourth, **keep a small cash reserve separate from your primary stash.** This should be about €50 sewn into or stored in the depths of your pack, along with your traveler's check numbers and photocopies of your passport, your birth certificate, and other important documents.

In large cities **con artists** often work in groups and may involve children. Beware of certain classics: sob stories ending in pleas for money, mustard spilled (or saliva spit) onto your shoulder to distract you while they snatch your bag. **Never let your passport and your bags out of your sight.** Hostel workers will sometimes stand at bus and train station arrival points trying to recruit tired and disoriented travelers to their hostel; never believe strangers who tell you that theirs is the only hostel open. Beware of **pickpockets** in city crowds, especially on public transportation. Also, be alert in public telephone booths: if you must say your calling card number, do so quietly; if you punch it in, make sure no one can look over your shoulder.

If you will be traveling with electronic devices, such as a laptop computer or a PDA, check whether your homeowner's insurance covers loss, theft, or damage when you travel. If not, you might consider purchasing a low-cost separate insurance policy. **Safeware** (☎800-800-1492; www.safeware.com) specializes in covering computers and charges $90 for 90-day comprehensive international travel coverage up to $4000.

PRE-DEPARTURE HEALTH

In your **passport,** write the names of any people you wish to be contacted in case of a medical emergency, and list any allergies or medical conditions. Matching a prescription to a foreign equivalent is not always easy, safe, or possible, so if you take prescription drugs, consider carrying up-to-date prescriptions or a statement from your doctor stating the medication's trade name, manufacturer, chemical name, and dosage. While traveling, be sure to keep all medication with you in your carry-on luggage. For tips on packing a **first-aid kit** and other health essentials, see p. 18. While it may be difficult to find brand-name medications like Tylenol or Advil, these products can be easily identified by their drug names (such as acetaminophen or paracetamol and ibuprofen).

ESSENTIALS

IMMUNIZATIONS AND PRECAUTIONS

Although no immunizations are required, travelers over two years old should make sure that the following vaccines are up to date: MMR (for measles, mumps, and rubella); DTaP or Td (for diphtheria, tetanus, and pertussis); IPV (for polio); Hib (for *Haemophilus influenzae* B); and HepB (for Hepatitis B). For recommendations on immunizations and prophylaxis, consult the Centers for Disease Control and Prevention (CDC; see p. 22) in the US or the equivalent in your home country, and check with a doctor for guidance. Meningitis shots are advisable, especially for college-age backpackers staying in hostels.

INSURANCE

Travel insurance covers four basic areas: medical/health problems, property loss, trip cancellation/interruption, and emergency evacuation. Though regular insurance policies may well extend to travel-related accidents, you may consider purchasing separate travel insurance if the cost of potential trip cancellation, interruption, or emergency medical evacuation is greater than you can absorb. Prices for travel insurance purchased separately generally run about US$50 per week for full coverage, while trip cancellation/interruption may be purchased separately at a rate of US$3-5 per day depending on length of stay.

Medical insurance (especially university policies) often covers costs incurred abroad; check with your provider. **US Medicare** does not cover foreign travel. **Canadian** provincial health insurance plans increasingly do not cover foreign travel; check with the provincial Ministry of Health or Health Plan Headquarters for details. **Australians** traveling in Italy are entitled to many of the services that they would receive at home as part of the Reciprocal Health Care Agreement. **Homeowners' insurance** (or your family's coverage) often covers theft during travel and loss of travel documents (passport, plane ticket, railpass, etc.) up to US$500.

ISIC and **ITIC** (see p. 12) provide basic insurance benefits to US cardholders, including US$100 per day of in-hospital sickness for up to 100 days and US$10,000 of accident-related medical reimbursement (see www.isicus.com). Cardholders have access to a toll-free 24hr. helpline for medical, legal, and financial emergencies overseas. **American Express** (☎800 338 1670) grants most cardholders automatic collision and theft car rental insurance on rentals made with the card.

USEFUL ORGANIZATIONS AND PUBLICATIONS

The American **Centers for Disease Control and Prevention** (**CDC;** ☎877-FYI-TRIP; www.cdc.gov/travel) maintains an international travelers' hotline and an informative website. Consult the appropriate government agency of your home country for consular information sheets on health, entry requirements, and other issues for various countries (see the listings in the box on **Travel Advisories,** p. 20). For quick information on health and other travel warnings, call the **Overseas Citizens Services** (M-F 8am-8pm from US ☎888-407-4747, from overseas 202-501-4444), or contact a passport agency, embassy, or consulate abroad. For information on medical evacuation services and travel insurance firms, see the US government's website at http://travel.state.gov/travel/abroad_health.html or the **British Foreign and Commonwealth Office** (www.fco.gov.uk). For general health information, contact the **American Red Cross** (☎202-303-4498; www.redcross.org).

STAYING HEALTHY

Common sense is the simplest prescription for good health while you travel. Drink lots of fluids to prevent dehydration and constipation, and wear sturdy, broken-in shoes and clean socks.

ONCE IN ITALY

ENVIRONMENTAL HAZARDS

Arid summer weather in the south creates prime conditions for heat exhaustion and dehydration. Be especially careful at Pompeii; there may no longer be a threat of volcanic eruption, but a lack of water fountains and shade create new dangers. Trekking at high altitudes in the Dolomites, the Alps, and on Mt. Vesuvius and Mt. Etna should not be done too hastily; be especially careful in winter to protect yourself against hypothermia and frostbite.

Heat exhaustion and dehydration: Heat exhaustion leads to nausea, excessive thirst, headaches, and dizziness. Avoid it by drinking plenty of fluids, eating salty foods (e.g., crackers), abstaining from dehydrating beverages (e.g., alcohol and caffeinated beverages), and wearing sunscreen. Continuous heat stress can eventually lead to heatstroke, characterized by a rising temperature, severe headache, delirium and cessation of sweating. Victims should be cooled off with wet towels and taken to a doctor.

Sunburn: Always wear sunscreen (SPF 30 or higher) when spending time outdoors. If you get sunburned, drink more fluids than usual and apply an aloe-based lotion. Severe sunburns can lead to sun poisoning, a condition that can cause fever, chills, nausea, and vomiting. Sun poisoning should always be treated by a doctor.

Hypothermia and frostbite: A rapid drop in body temperature is the clearest sign of overexposure to cold. Victims may also shiver, feel exhausted, have poor coordination or slurred speech, hallucinate, or suffer amnesia. *Do not let hypothermia victims fall asleep.* To avoid hypothermia, keep dry, wear layers, and stay out of the wind. When the temperature is below freezing, watch out for frostbite. If skin turns white or blue, waxy, and cold, do not rub the area. Drink warm beverages, stay dry, and slowly warm the area with dry fabric or steady body contact until a doctor can be found.

High Altitude: Allow your body a couple of days to adjust to less oxygen before exerting yourself. Note that alcohol is more potent and UV rays are stronger at high elevations.

INSECT-BORNE DISEASES

Many diseases are transmitted by insects—mainly mosquitoes, fleas, ticks, and lice. Be aware of insects in wet or forested areas, especially while hiking and camping; wear long pants and long sleeves, tuck your pants into your socks, and use a mosquito net. Use insect repellents such as DEET and soak or spray your gear with permethrin (licensed in the US only for use on clothing). **Mosquitoes**—responsible for malaria, dengue fever, and yellow fever—can be particularly abundant in wet, swampy, or wooded areas like those found in Liguria and Trentino-Alto Adige. **Ticks,** which can carry Lyme and other diseases, can be particularly dangerous in rural and forested regions, especially in Friuli-Venezia Giulia, the Veneto, and Trentino-Alto Adige.

Lyme disease: A bacterial infection carried by ticks and marked by a circular bull's-eye rash of 2 in. or more. Later symptoms include fever, headache, fatigue, and aches and pains. Antibiotics are effective if administered early. Left untreated, Lyme can cause problems in joints, the heart, and the nervous system. If you find a tick attached to your skin, grasp the head with tweezers as close to your skin as possible and apply slow, steady traction. Removing a tick within 24hr. greatly reduces the risk of infection. Do not try to remove ticks with petroleum jelly, nail polish remover, or a hot match. Ticks usually inhabit moist, shaded environments and heavily wooded areas. If you are going to be hiking in these areas, wear long clothes and DEET.

FOOD- AND WATER-BORNE DISEASES

Prevention is the best cure: be sure that your food is properly cooked and the water you drink is clean. If the region's tap water is known to be unsanitary, peel fruits and vegetables before eating them and avoid tap water (including ice cubes and anything washed in tap water, like salad). Watch out for food from markets or street vendors that may have been cooked in unhygienic conditions. Other culprits are raw shellfish, unpasteurized milk, and sauces containing raw eggs (like *carbonara*). Buy bottled water, or purify your own water by bringing it to a rolling boil or treating it with **iodine tablets;** note, however, that some parasites, such as *giardia*, have exteriors that resist iodine treatment, so boiling is more reliable. Always wash your hands before eating or bring a quick-drying purifying liquid hand cleaner. While Italy's water is relatively clean (the ancient Roman aqueduct water still provides Rome with a reliable water source), it is important to be wary in places like some campgrounds and trains where water is not clean. The sign *"acqua non potabile"* means the water is not drinkable; the sign *"acqua potabile"* means the water is sanitary. Even as a developed nation, Italy experienced an outbreak of stomach flu due to contaminated drinking water in Taranto in 2006.

> **Giardiasis:** Transmitted through parasites and acquired by drinking untreated water from streams or lakes. Symptoms include diarrhea, cramps, bloating, fatigue, weight loss, and nausea. If untreated, it can lead to severe dehydration. Giardiasis occurs worldwide.

OTHER INFECTIOUS DISEASES

The following diseases exist in every part of the world. Travelers should know how to recognize them and what to do if they suspect they have been infected.

> **Rabies:** Transmitted through the saliva of infected animals; fatal if untreated. By the time symptoms (thirst and muscle spasms) appear, the disease is in its terminal stage. If you are bitten, wash the wound, seek immediate medical care, and try to have the animal located. A rabies vaccine, which consists of 3 shots given over a 21-day period, is available and recommended for developing world travel, but is only semi-effective.

> **Hepatitis B:** A viral infection of the liver transmitted via blood or other bodily fluids. Symptoms, which may not surface until years after infection, include jaundice, appetite loss, fever, and joint pain. It is transmitted through unprotected sex and unclean needles. A 3-shot vaccination sequence is recommended for sexually-active travelers and anyone planning to seek medical treatment abroad; it must begin 6 months before traveling.

> **AIDS and HIV:** For detailed information on Acquired Immune Deficiency Syndrome (AIDS) in Italy, call the 24hr. National AIDS Hotline at ☎800-342-2437.

> **Sexually transmitted infections (STIs):** Gonorrhea, chlamydia, genital warts, syphilis, herpes, HPV, and other STIs are easier to catch than HIV and can be just as serious. Though condoms may protect you from some STIs, oral or even tactile contact can lead to transmission. If you think you may have contracted an STI, see a doctor immediately.

OTHER HEALTH CONCERNS

MEDICAL CARE ON THE ROAD

Although quality of care varies by region, Italy overall conforms to standards of modern health care. Health care tends to be better in the north and in private hospitals and clinics. Doctors speak English in most large cities; if they don't, they may be able to arrange for a translator. Let's Go lists info on how to access medical help in the Practical Information sections of most cities.

 NO IV WITHOUT ID. If you must make a trip to a **hospital** while in Italy, don't forget your **passport**—if your case is not an emergency, you might encounter bureaucratic barriers to receiving treatment.

If you are concerned about obtaining medical assistance while traveling, you may wish to employ special support services. The *MedPass* from **GlobalCare, Inc.,** 6875 Shiloh Rd. East, Alpharetta, GA 30005, USA (☎800-860-1111; www.globalcare.net), provides 24hr. international medical assistance, support, and medical evacuation resources. The **International Association for Medical Assistance to Travelers (IAMAT;** US ☎716-754-4883, Canada 519-836-0102; www.iamat.org) has free membership, lists English-speaking doctors worldwide, and offers detailed info on immunization requirements and sanitation. If your regular **insurance** policy does not cover travel abroad, you may wish to purchase additional coverage (see p. 22).

Those with medical conditions (such as diabetes, allergies to antibiotics, epilepsy, or heart conditions) may want to obtain a **MedicAlert** membership (US$40 per year), which includes among other things a stainless steel ID tag and a 24hr. collect-call number. Contact the MedicAlert Foundation International, 2323 Colorado Ave., Turlock, CA 95382, USA (☎888-633-4298, outside US 209-668-3333; www.medicalert.org).

WOMEN'S HEALTH

Women traveling in unsanitary conditions are vulnerable to **urinary tract (including bladder and kidney) infections.** Over-the-counter medicines can sometimes alleviate symptoms, but if they persist, see a doctor. **Vaginal yeast infections** may flare up in hot and humid climates. Wearing loosely fitting trousers or a skirt and cotton underwear will help, as will over-the-counter remedies like Monistat or Gynelotrimin. Bring supplies from home if you are prone to infection, as they may be difficult to find on the road. **Tampons, pads,** and **contraceptive devices** are widely available, though your favorite brand may not be stocked—bring extras of anything you can't live without. Pharmacies refill empty **birth control** packages even without Italian-issued prescriptions. The morning-after pill is extremely difficult to find in Italy. **Abortion** (*aborto* or *interruzione volontaria di gravidanza;* abortion/miscarriage or voluntary interruption of pregnancy) is legal and may be performed in the first 90 days of pregnancy for free in a public hospital or for a fee in an authorized private facility. Except in urgent cases, a week-long reflection period is required. Women under 18 must obtain parental permission or a judge's decision. Availability may be limited in some areas, especially in the south, due to a "conscience clause:" physicians who oppose abortion can opt out of performing the procedure. The election of Pope Benedict XVI has sparked controversy over abortion, but no immediate policy changes are expected.

GETTING TO ITALY

BY PLANE

When it comes to airfare, a little effort can save you a bundle. Courier fares are the cheapest options for travelers whose plans are flexible enough to deal with the restrictions. Tickets sold by consolidators and standby seating are also good deals, but last-minute specials, airfare wars, and charter flights often beat these fares. The key is to hunt around, be flexible, and ask about discounts. Students, seniors, and those under 26 should never pay full price for a ticket.

AIRFARES

Airfares to Italy peak between April and **early September;** holidays are also expensive. The cheapest times to travel are from late September to mid-December and January to March. Midweek (M-Th morning) round-trip flights run US$40-50 cheaper than weekend flights, but they are generally more crowded and less likely to permit frequent-flier upgrades. Not fixing a return date ("open return") or arriving in and departing from different cities ("open-jaw") can be pricier than round-trip flights. Flights into Rome and Milan tend to be cheaper.

If Italy is only one stop on a more extensive globe-hop, consider a round-the-world (RTW) ticket. Tickets usually include at least five stops and are valid for about a year; prices range US$1200-5000. Try **Northwest Airlines/KLM** (☎800-225-2525; www.nwa.com) or **Star Alliance,** a consortium of 16 airlines including **United Airlines** (www.staralliance.com).

Fares for round-trip flights to Rome and Milan from the US or Canadian east coast cost US$700-1200, US$500-700 in the low season (mid-Sept. to mid-Dec. and Jan.-Mar.); from the US or Canadian west coast US$800-1600/US$600-1000; from the UK, UK£175-300/UK£125-200; from Australia AUS$1700-2600/AUS$1320-2000; from New Zealand NZ$2000-3000/NZ$1800-2400.

BUDGET AND STUDENT TRAVEL AGENCIES

While knowledgeable agents specializing in flights to Italy can make your life easy and help you save, they may not spend the time to find you the lowest possible fare—they get paid on commission. Travelers holding **ISICs** and **IYTCs** (p. 12) qualify for big discounts from student travel agencies. Most flights from budget agencies are on major airlines, but in peak season some may sell seats on less reliable chartered aircraft.

STA Travel, 5900 Wilshire Blvd., Ste. 900, Los Angeles, CA 90036, USA (24hr. reservations and info ☎800-781-4040; www.statravel.com). A student and youth travel organization with over 150 offices worldwide (check their website for a listing of all their offices), including US offices in Boston, Chicago, Los Angeles, New York, Seattle, San Francisco, and Washington, D.C. Ticket booking, travel insurance, railpasses, and more. Walk-in offices are located throughout Australia (☎03 9207 5900), New Zealand (☎09 309 9723), and the UK (☎08701 630 026).

Travel CUTS (Canadian Universities Travel Services Limited), 187 College St., Toronto, ON M5T 1P7, Canada (☎888-592-2887; www.travelcuts.com). Offices across Canada and the US, including Los Angeles, New York, Seattle, and San Francisco.

USIT, 19-21 Aston Quay, Dublin 2, Ireland (☎01 602 1904; www.usit.ie). Ireland's leading student/budget travel agency has 20 offices throughout Northern Ireland and the Republic of Ireland. Offers programs to work, study, and volunteer worldwide.

Wasteels, Skoubogade 6, 1158 Copenhagen K., Denmark (☎3314 4633; www.wasteels.com). A huge chain with 180 locations across Europe. Sells Wasteels BIJ tickets discounted 30-45% off regular fare, 2nd-class international point-to-point train tickets with unlimited stopovers for those under 26 (sold only in Europe).

COMMERCIAL AIRLINES

The commercial airlines' lowest regular offer is the **APEX** (Advance Purchase Excursion) fare, which provides confirmed reservations and allows "open-jaw" tickets. Generally, reservations must be made seven to 21 days ahead of departure, with seven- to 14-day minimum-stay and up to 90-day maximum-stay restrictions. These fares carry hefty cancellation and change penalties (fees rise in summer). Book peak-season APEX fares early. Use **Expedia** (www.expedia.com) or **Travelocity** (www.travelocity.com) to get an idea of the lowest published fares, then use the resources outlined here to try to beat those fares. Low-season fares should be markedly cheaper than the **high-season** (mid-June to early Sept.) ones listed here.

TRAVELING FROM NORTH AMERICA

Standard commercial carriers like **American** (☎800-433-7300; www.aa.com), **United** (☎800-538-2929; www.ual.com), and **Northwest** (☎800-225-2525; www.nwa.com) will offer the most convenient flights, but they may not be the cheapest, unless you

✈ **FLIGHT PLANNING ON THE INTERNET.** The Internet may be the budget traveler's dream when it comes to finding and booking bargain fares, but the array of options can be overwhelming. Many airline sites offer special last-minute deals on the Web. Look for occasional sale fares on **www.alitalia.com** and **www.flyairone.it.**

STA (www.statravel.com) and **StudentUniverse** (www.studentuniverse.com) provide quotes on student tickets, while **Orbitz** (www.orbitz.com), **Opodo** (www.opodo.com), **Expedia** (www.expedia.com), and **Travelocity** (www.travelocity.com) offer full travel services. **Priceline** (www.priceline.com) lets you specify a price, and obligates you to buy any ticket that meets or beats it; **Hotwire** (www.hotwire.com) offers bargain fares, but won't reveal the airline or flight times until you buy. Other sites that compile deals include www.bestfares.com, www.flights.com, www.kayak.com, www.lowestfare.com, www.onetravel.com, and www.travelzoo.com.

SideStep (www.sidestep.com) and **Booking Buddy** (www.bookingbuddy.com) are online tools that can help sift through multiple offers; these two let you enter your trip information once and search multiple sites.

Air Traveler's Handbook (www.faqs.org/faqs/travel/air/handbook) is an indispensable resource on the Internet; it has a comprehensive listing of links to everything you need to know before you board a plane.

snag a special promotion or airfare war ticket. Check **Lufthansa** (☎866-583-8932; www.lufthansa.com), **British Airways** (☎800-247-9297; www.britishairways.com), **Air France** (☎800-237-2747; www.airfrance.us), and **Alitalia** (☎800-223-5730; www.alitaliausa.com) for tickets from destinations throughout the US. **Finnair** (☎800-950-5000; www.finnair.com) often offers cheap tickets from San Francisco, New York, and Toronto to Helsinki, with connections to Rome and Milan. Cheap flights out of New York to Rome are offered by **eurofly** (www.euroflyusa.com/US).

TRAVELING FROM IRELAND AND THE UK

Many carriers fly from the British Isles to the continent, so *Let's Go* only lists discount airlines or those with cheap specials. **Cheapflights** (www.cheapflights.co.uk) publishes airfare bargains. Prices listed are for one-way flights.

Aer Lingus: Ireland ☎0818 365 000; www.aerlingus.ie. Flights from Dublin, Cork, Galway, Kerry, and Shannon to Bologna, Milan, Naples, Rome, and Venice (EUR€30-150).

bmibaby: UK ☎0871 224 0224; www.bmibaby.com. Departures from throughout the UK. Round-trip London to Naples (UK£35-130) and Venice (UK£30-80).

easyJet: UK ☎0871 244 2366; www.easyjet.com. London to Bologna, Milan, Naples, Pisa, Rome, Turin, and Venice (UK£30-150).

KLM: UK ☎0870 24 29 242; www.klmuk.com. Cheap tickets between UK airports and over 23 Italian destinations (UK£49-200).

Ryanair: Ireland ☎0818 303 030, UK 0871 246 0000; www.ryanair.com. The cheapest flights (from £10 with taxes) from Dublin, Glasgow, Liverpool, London, and Shannon to over a dozen destinations throughout Italy.

TRAVELING FROM AUSTRALIA AND NEW ZEALAND

Flights from Australia and New Zealand to Italy usually involve at least 20hr. of travel time and at least one stopover. **Zuji** (www.zuji.com) helps find cheap flights to Rome through an Asian or European city.

Qantas Air: Australia ☎9691 3636, New Zealand 61 2 9691 3636; www.qantas.com.au. Flights from Australia and New Zealand to Rome.

Singapore Air: Australia ☎13 10 11, New Zealand 0800 808 909; www.singaporeair.com. Flies from Auckland, Christchurch, Melbourne, Perth, and Sydney.

AIR COURIER FLIGHTS

Those who travel light should consider courier flights. Couriers help transport cargo on international flights by using their checked luggage space for freight. Generally, couriers are limited to carry-ons and must deal with complex flight restrictions. Most flights are round-trip only, with short fixed-length stays (usually one week) and a limit of a one ticket per issue. Most of these flights also operate only out of major gateway cities, mostly in North America. Round-trip courier fares from the US to Italy run about US$150-600. Most flights leave Los Angeles, Miami, New York, or San Francisco in the US; and Montreal, Toronto, or Vancouver in Canada. Generally, you must be over 18 (in some cases 21). In summer, popular destinations usually require an advance reservation of about two weeks (you can usually book up to two months ahead). Super-discounted fares are common for "last-minute" flights (three to 14 days ahead).

Air Courier Association, 1767 A Denver West Blvd., Golden, CO 80401 (☎800-461-8556; www.aircourier.org). Ten departure sites throughout the US and Canada to Rome (US$ 150-400). One-year membership US$49.

International Association of Air Travel Couriers (IAATC; www.courier.org). Flights from 7 North American cities to Rome. One-year membership US$45.

Courier Travel (www.couriertravel.org). Searchable online database. Available flights to Italy are usually from New York to **Rome.**

FROM THE UK, AUSTRALIA, AND NEW ZEALAND

The minimum age for couriers from the **UK** is usually 18. The **International Association of Air Travel Couriers** (see above) often offers courier flights from New York and London to **Rome and from Auckland to Frankfurt and London. Courier Travel** (see above) also offers flights from London and Sydney to Italy.

STANDBY FLIGHTS

Traveling standby requires considerable flexibility in arrival and departure dates. Companies dealing in standby flights sell vouchers rather than tickets, along with the promise to get you to your destination (or near your destination) within a certain window of time (typically 1-5 days). You call in before your window of time to hear your flight options and the probability that you will be able to board each flight. You can then decide which flights you want to try to catch, show up at the appropriate airport at the appropriate time, present your voucher, and board if space is available. Vouchers can be bought for both one-way and round-trip travel. You may receive a monetary refund only if every available flight within your date range is full; if you opt not to take an available flight, you can only get credit for future travel. Read agreements with any company offering standby flights with care, as tricky fine print can leave you in the lurch. To check on a company's service record in the US, contact the Better Business Bureau (☎703-276-0100; www.bbb.org). It is difficult to receive refunds, and clients' vouchers will not be honored when an airline fails to receive payment in time.

TICKET CONSOLIDATORS

Ticket consolidators, or **"bucket shops,"** buy unsold tickets in bulk from commercial airlines and sell them at discounted rates. The best place to look is in the Sunday travel section of any major newspaper (such as *The New York Times*), where many bucket shops place tiny ads. Call quickly, as availability is extremely limited. Not all bucket shops are reliable, so insist on a receipt that gives full details of restrictions, refunds, and tickets. Pay by credit card (in spite of the 2-5% fee) so you can stop payment if you never receive your tickets. For more info, see www.travel-library.com/air-travel/consolidators.html.

TRAVELING FROM CANADA AND THE US

A few consolidators worth trying are **Rebel** (☎800-732-3588; www.rebeltours.com), **Cheap Tickets** (www.cheaptickets.com), **Flights.com** (www.flights.com), and **Travel-HUB** (www.travelhub.com). *Let's Go* does not endorse any of these agencies. Always be cautious and research companies before handing over your credit card.

CHARTER FLIGHTS

Tour operators contract charter flights with airlines in order to fly extra loads of passengers during peak season. These flights are far from hassle free. They occur less frequently than major airlines, make refunds particularly difficult, and are almost always fully booked. Their scheduled times may change and they may be cancelled at the last moment (as late as 48hr. before the trip, and without a full refund). And check-in, boarding, and baggage claim for them are often much slower. They can be, however, much cheaper.

Discount clubs and fare brokers offer members savings on last-minute charter and tour deals. Study contracts closely; you don't want to end up with an unwanted overnight layover. **Travelers Advantage** (☎800-835-8747; www.travelersadvantage.com; US$90 annual fee includes discounts and cheap flight directories) specializes in **European** travel and tour packages.

BY TRAIN

Traveling to Italy by train from within Europe can be as expensive as a flight, but allows travelers to watch the country unfold before them, and for the possibility of spontaneous stopovers before reaching their ultimate destination. For info on traveling within Italy by rail, see **By Train**, p. 32.

MULTINATIONAL RAILPASSES

EURAIL PASSES. Eurail is **valid** in most of Western Europe but **not** the UK. Standard **Eurail Passes,** valid for a consecutive number of days, are best for those planning to spend an extended period of time on trains. **Eurail Pass,** valid for any 10 or 15 (not necessarily consecutive) days in a two-month period, is more cost-effective for those traveling long distances less frequently. **Eurail Pass Saver** provides first-class travel for travelers in groups of two to five. **Eurail Pass Youth** provides parallel second-class perks for 11- to 26-year-olds.

EURAIL PASSES	15 DAYS	21 DAYS	1 MONTH	2 MONTHS	3 MONTHS
1st class Eurail Pass	US$675	US$879	US$1089	US$1539	US$1899
Eurail Pass Saver	US$569	US$745	US$925	US$1309	US$1615
Eurail Pass Youth	US$439	US$569	US$709	US$999	US$1235
EURAIL SELECTPASS		10 DAYS IN 2 MONTHS		15 DAYS IN 2 MONTHS	
1st class Eurail Pass Flexi		US$799		US$1049	
Eurail Pass Saver Flexi		US$6798		US$805	
Eurail Pass Youth Flexi		US$279		US$619	

Passholders receive a timetable for routes and a map with details on possible bike rental, car rental, hotel, and museum discounts, as well as reduced fares or free passage on many boat, bus, and private railroad lines.

The **Eurail Selectpass** is a slimmed-down version of the Eurail Pass: it allows five to 15 days of unlimited travel in any two-month period within three to five bordering countries of 22 European countries. Eurail Selectpasses (for individuals) and **Eurail Selectpass Savers** range from US$365-449 per person (5 days) to US$805 (15 days). The **Eurail Selectpass Youth** (2nd-class), for those under 26, costs US$279-

619. You are entitled to the same **freebies** as the Eurail Pass, but only when they are within or between countries that you selected with your purchase.

Eurail Regional Passes are valid in specific countries (Youth and Saver options also available). The **France-Italy pass** is available for four to 10 days in a two-month period, and costs €305 (4 days) to €589 (10 days), €269-509 for the Saver pass, and €229-385 for the Youth pass. The **Greece-Italy pass** is also valid for four to 10 days in a 2-month period. The cost is €275-549/235-459/235-359. Though sold at some Italian and Greek train stations, it's cheaper to purchase in advance.

FURTHER READING AND RESOURCES ON TRAIN TRAVEL
Info on rail travel and railpasses: www.raileurope.com.
Point-to-point fares and schedules: www.raileurope.com/us/rail/fares_schedules/index.htm. Allows you to calculate whether buying a railpass would save you money.
Railsaver: www.railpass.com/new. Uses your itinerary to calculate the best rail-pass for your trip.
European Railway Server: www.railfaneurope.net. Links to rail servers through-out Europe.
Independent Travellers Europe by Rail 2006: The Inter-railer's and Eurailer's Guide. Thomas Cook Publishing (US$23).

SHOPPING FOR A EURAIL. Passes are designed by the EU itself, and non-Europeans can only buy them from non-European agents before they leave. The passes must be sold at uniform prices determined by the EU. Some agents tack on a US$10 handling fee, and others offer certain bonuses, so shop around. Prices usually go up each year, so if you're planning to travel early in the year, save cash by purchasing before January 1 (you'll have 3 months to validate your pass).

Eurail passes should be bought before leaving; only a few places in major European cities sell them, usually at marked-up prices. You can get a replacement for a lost pass if you have purchased insurance under the Pass Security Plan (US$10-17). Eurail Passes are available through travel agents, student travel agencies like STA (p. 25), **Rail Europe** (US ☎888-382-7245, Canada 800-361-7245; www.raileurope.com), or **Flight Centre** (US ☎866-967-5351, Canada 877-965-5302; www.flightcentre.com). You can also buy directly from Eurail's website, www.eurail.com, but the company doesn't ship to Europe.

INTERRAIL PASS. If you have lived for at least six months in one of the European countries where **InterRail Global Pass** is valid, it provides an economical option. The InterRail Global Pass allows for travel within 30 European countries (excluding the country of residence). Passes may be purchased for five days within a 10-day period, 10 days within a 22-day period, 22 continuous days or one continuous month. The five-day pass (€249, under 26 €159) must be used within 10 days, the 10-day pass (€359, under 26 €239) must be used within 22 days, the 22-day pass (€469, under 26 €309) is valid only for a 22-day period, and the one-month pass (€599, under 26 €399) is similarly valid only for a one-month period. Passholders receive **discounts** on many ferries to various European destinations. Passes can be purchased online at www.interrailnet.com.

BY BUS AND BOAT

Though European trains are popular and buses can be unreliable, in some cases buses prove a better option. Often cheaper than railpasses, **international bus passes** allow unlimited travel on a hop-on, hop-off basis between major European cities. In Italy, bus travel is more of a gamble; scattered offerings from private companies are often cheap, but sometimes unreliable. Amsterdam, Athens, Istanbul, London,

Munich, and Oslo are centers for lines that offer long-distance rides across Europe. The prices below are based on high-season travel.

Eurolines, 4 Vicarage Rd., Edgbaston, Birmingham B15 3ES, UK (☎08705 143 219; www.eurolines.com). The largest operator of Europe-wide coach services. Unlimited 15-day (high season UK£195, under 26 and over 60 UK£165; low season UK£149/129); 30-day (high season UK£290/235; low season UK£209/169); or 60-day (high season UK£333/259; low season UK£265/211) travel passes that offer unlimited transit between 35 major European cities.

Busabout, 258 Vauxhall Bridge Rd., London SW1V 1BS, UK (☎0207 950 1661; www.busabout.com). Offers 5 interconnecting bus circuits covering 60 cities and towns in Europe. Unlimited (consecutive-day) Passes, Flexipasses, and Add On Passes are available. Unlimited standard/student passes are valid for 2 weeks (US$469/419), 4 weeks (US$739/659), 6 weeks (US$919/819), 8 weeks (US$1049/939), 12 weeks (US$1319/1179), or for the season (US$1649/1469).

Most European ferries are quite comfortable; the cheapest ticket typically still includes a reclining chair or couchette. Fares jump sharply in July and August. Ask for discounts; ISIC holders can often get student fares, and Eurail Pass holders get many reductions and free trips (for examples of popular freebies, also see p. 29). You'll occasionally have to pay a port tax (under US$10). Schedules are erratic, and different companies offer similar routes at varying prices. Shop around, and be wary of dinky, unreliable companies that don't take reservations. **Mediterranean** ferries may be the most glamorous, but they can also be the most rocky. Ferries run from Sicily to Tunisia and Malta, and from Sardinia to Tunisia and Corsica. Ferries float across the **Adriatic** from Ancona and Bari, Italy, to Split and Dubrovnik, Croatia, respectively. Ferries also run across the **Aegean Sea,** from Ancona, Italy, to Patras, Greece, and from Bari, Italy, to Igoumenitsa and Patras, Greece. **Eurail** is valid on certain ferries between Brindisi, Italy, and Corfu, Igoumenitsa, and Patras, Greece. Countless ferry companies operate these routes simultaneously; see the **transportation** sections of individual cities and towns for more specific info.

BORDER CROSSINGS

The surrounding countries of France, Switzerland, and Austria sometimes make great daytrips from Italy's border cities. Multiple-country rail passes are available through **RailEurope** (www.raileurope.com). See p. 29 for more info on cross-border transportation. The following cities are not far across the borders of Austria, France, and Switzerland:

FROM	DEPARTS	TO	ARRIVES
Venice	1:33pm	Innsbruck, Austria	6:33pm
Turin	7:35am	Nice, France (via Ventimiglia)	12:01pm
Como	hourly 9am-5pm at seven past the hour	Lugano, Switzerland	hourly 9am-5pm at 53 past the hour

As a part of the EU, Italy only requires that travelers present a valid passport and ID to travel between EU nations. When traveling to France and Austria, no currency exchange is necessary; yet, Switzerland still uses the Swiss franc (SFr).

GETTING AROUND ITALY

Fares are either **one-way** or **round-trip.** "Period returns" require you to return within a specific number of days; "day return" means you must return on the same day. Unless stated otherwise, *Let's Go* always lists single fares. Round-trip fares on trains and buses in Italy can be simply double the one-way fare.

BY PLANE

With 14 major airports throughout Italy, there is no excuse for not making that hop, skip, and jump up to Venice to rendezvous with your newfound Italian lover. The main Italian hubs are Rome, Milan, Bergamo, Verona, Bologna, Genoa, Pisa, Florence, Turin, Venice, Naples, Bari, and Palermo. The recent emergence of no-frills airlines has made hop scotching around Europe by air increasingly affordable and convenient. Though these flights often feature inconvenient hours or serve less-popular regional airports, with one-way flights averaging about US$80, it's never been faster or easier to jet set across the Continent. **Ryanair** (p. 27) and **easyjet** (p. 27) are two among many cheap airlines that fly throughout Italy and outwards. The **Star Alliance European Airpass** offers economy class fares as low as US$65 for travel within Europe to more than 200 destinations in 42 countries. The pass is available to non-European passengers on Star Alliance carriers, including Air Canada, Austrian Airlines, BMI British Midland, Lufthansa, Scandinavian Airlines System, Thai International, and United Airlines, as well as on certain partner airlines. See www.staralliance.com for more information. In addition, a number of European airlines offer discount coupon packets. Most are only available as tack-ons for transatlantic passengers, but some are stand-alone offers. Most must be purchased before departure, so research in advance.

BY TRAIN

Trenitalia (☎89 20 21; www.trenitalia.com) is the main provider of railway transportation throughout Italy. Trenitalia is owned by **Ferrovie dello Stato** (FS), which is owned by the Italian government. Other (somewhat less reliable) companies include **Ferrovia Nord,** which runs a line between Milan and Como, and **Ferrovie Sud-Est (FSE),** which runs mainly in Puglia. The local rail in some of Italy shuts down on Sunday, leaving buses as the only weekend transportation option.

Several types of trains ride the Italian rails. The **locale** stops at every station along a particular line, often taking twice as long. The **diretto** makes fewer stops than the *locale*, while the **espresso** just stops at major stations. The air-conditioned, more expensive, **InterCity (IC)**, or **rapido**, train travels only to the largest cities; a few routes may require reservations. Tickets for the fast, comfy, and pricey **Eurostar** trains (1st- and 2nd-class trains) require reservations. Eurail passes are valid without a supplement on all trains except the Eurostar. All InterRail holders must also purchase supplements (€2-20) for trains like Eurostar and InterCity. Train tickets may be purchased from *bigletterie* and automated ticket machines, which have instructions in English. There are often discounts for those under 26 who are traveling in groups of six.

> ┏━ **EASY COME, EASILY MISSED.** Trenitalia stations are poorly labeled. Ask the conductor which is your stop to avoid missing it entirely.

Trains are not always safe. For long trips make sure you are on the correct car, as trains sometimes split at crossroads. For more specific travel safety concerns see **Personal Safety** (p. 20). Towns listed in parentheses on European schedules require a train switch at the town listed immediately before the parentheses. Note that unless stated otherwise, *Let's Go* lists one-way fares.

TRAIN TRAVEL DISTANCES AND TIMES

	Bari	Bologna	Bolzano	Florence	Genoa	Milan	Naples	Rome	Trieste	Turin	Venice
Bari	km\hr.	6	11	7	10½	8½	4½	5	10½	10	8½
Bologna	681		3½	1	3	2	5	3	4	3½	2
Bolzano	950	291		5	5	3½	10	7	5½	5½	3½
Florence	784	106	397		4	3	4	2	5	5	3
Genoa	966	285	399	268		2	7½	5	7	1½	5
Milan	899	218	276	324	156		6½	5	5	1½	3
Naples	322	640	931	534	758	858		2	9	9	7
Rome	482	408	90	302	526	626	232		6½	7	5
Trieste	955	308	338	414	535	420	948	715		7	2
Turin	1019	338	408	442	174	139	932	699	551		5
Venice	806	269	225	265	387	284	899	567	165	414	

NATIONAL PASSES. In general, trains in Italy are cheap enough not to warrant buying a national pass. **Eurail** sells a **National Pass** for Italy (Youth and Saver options also available). The **Italy pass** is available for three to 10 days in a two-month period, and costs €195 (3 days) to €449 (10 days), €169-389 for the Saver pass, and €165-299 for the Youth pass. The Euro Domino pass became the Inter-Rail One Country Pass in 2007 and is available to anyone who has lived in Europe for at least six months; it is only valid in one country (designated when bought), and is not valid in the country of residence (e.g., Italians cannot buy the InterRail One Country Pass for Italy). Passes can be bought for three to eight days within one month. A three-day pass is €109, under 26 €71; an eight-day pass costs €229/149. Reservations must be paid for separately. Supplements are included for many high-speed trains. As of 2007, the pass can be purchased online at www.interrailnet.com. In addition to simple railpasses, many countries (as well as Eurail) offer **rail-and-drive passes**, which combine car rental with rail travel—a good option for travelers who wish both to visit cities accessible by rail and to make trips into the surrounding areas. Prices range US$330-768 per person, depending on the type of pass, car, and the number of people included. Children under the age of 11 cost $95-150, and adding more days costs $29-104 per day. For price estimates, contact Rail Europe (p. 29).

> **⚡TIP** **NEED VALIDATION?** Always validate your train ticket before boarding in the validation machines, colored yellow or orange. Failure to validate may result in steep fines, and train operators do not accept ignorance as an excuse.

RESERVATIONS. Seat reservations are rarely required, but you are not guaranteed a seat without one (€2.50 and up, depending on the ticket). Reservations are available up to two months in advance on major trains (IC and Eurostar), and Italians often reserve far ahead; strongly consider reserving during peak holiday and tourist seasons (at the very latest a few hours ahead). If someone occupies your seat, be prepared to say politely, *"Mi scusi, ma ho prenotato questo posto"* (Excuse me, but I have

ESSENTIALS

reserved this seat). Purchase a **supplement** (€3-15.50) or special fare for faster or higher-quality trains. Eurail passes do not include reservations.

OVERNIGHT TRAINS. Night trains have their advantages: you don't waste daylight hours traveling, and you can forego the hassle and expense of securing a night's accommodation. However, they have their drawbacks, namely discomfort and sleeplessness. Consider paying extra for a **cuccetta,** one of six fold-down bunks in a compartment (around €20); private **sleeping cars** offer more comfort, but are considerably more expensive and not always available. Even if you're not willing to spend the money, some trains have more comfortable seating compartments with fold-out seats. If you are using a restricted-day railpass, inspect train schedules to maximize the use of your pass: a direct overnight train or boat journey uses up only one of your travel days if it departs after 7pm (you only write in the next day's date on your pass).

SHOULD YOU BUY A RAILPASS? Railpasses were conceived to allow you to jump on any train in Europe, go wherever you want whenever you want, and change your plans at will. In practice, it's not so simple. You still must stand in line to validate your pass, pay for supplements, and fork over cash for seat and couchette reservations. More importantly, railpasses don't always pay off. If you are planning to spend extensive time on trains, hopping between big cities, a railpass will probably be worth it. But in many cases, especially if you are under 26, point-to-point tickets may prove a cheaper option.

You may find it tough to make your railpass pay for itself in Italy where train fares are reasonable, distances short, or buses preferable. If, however, the total cost of your trips nears the price of the pass, the convenience of avoiding ticket lines may be worth the difference.

BY FERRY

The islands of Sicily and Sardinia, as well as the smaller islands along the coasts, are connected to the mainland and each other by **ferries** *(traghetti)* and the more expensive **hydrofoils** *(aliscafi);* international trips are generally made by ferries. Italy's largest private ferry service, **Tirrenia** (www.gruppotirrenia.it), runs ferries to Sardinia, Sicily, and Tunisia. Other major ferry companies **(Siremar, Usitca, Toremar, Saremar, Caremar, Moby Lines,** and **Grandi Navi Veloci)** and the **SNAV** (www.snav.it) hydrofoil services travel between major ports like Ancona, Bari, Brindisi, Genoa, La Spezia, Naples, and Trapani. Ferry services also depart for the Tremiti, Pontine, and Aeolian Islands.

Ferry service is also prevalent in the Lake Country. These ferries can be expensive and time-consuming, but sometimes they are the best way to go from city to city around the lakes, and many carry cars as well. Pick up a schedule brochure at the tourist office upon arrival at each lake. Some cities act as major hubs (e.g., Desenzano on Lake Garda) and require you to stop there between cities in order to catch a ferry to your next destination. Ferry times and fares vary, so check the major hub cities in your area.

For major trips reserve tickets at least one week in advance. Schedules change unpredictably—confirm your departure one day in advance. Some ports require check-in two hours before departure, or your reservation will be cancelled. **Posta ponte** (deck class; preferable in warm weather) is cheapest but is often only available when the **poltrona** (reclining cabin seats) are full. Port taxes often apply.

BY BUS AND METRO

Though notoriously unreliable and uncomfortable, **buses** *(autobus)* are often cheaper than trains. Two bus systems exist within Italy: intercity, which run

Experience Europe by Eurail!

It's not just the Best Way to See Europe, it's also the cleanest, greenest and smartest

enjoy

experience

explore

If you believe the journey's as important as the destination then rail's clearly the best way to experience the real Europe. Fast, sleek trains get you where you want to go when you want to go and - mile for mile - do less damage to the environment than cars or planes. Even better, you don't have to navigate unfamiliar roads, pay for gas (it's not cheap in Europe!) or find parking - leaving you more time and money to spend simply enjoying your travel.

Eurail has created a range of passes to suit every conceivable itinerary and budget. So whether you want to discover the whole continent, or focus on just one or two countries, you'll find Eurail the smartest way to do Europe, all around.

Welcome to Europe by Eurail!

EURAIL® *The best way to see Europe*

DON'T TRASH IT! Hold on to your (validated!) bus, metro, and train tickets throughout your entire journey. Auditors will spontaneously board at any given time to check for freeloaders and dole out hefty fines.

ESSENTIALS

between towns and regions, and intra-city, which provide local transportation. Intercity buses, or *pullman*, tend to go on strike much less frequently than trains. Tickets can generally be purchased at private bus company offices near the bus station or departure point, or onboard the bus. In many rural areas, where stops are unmarked, it is crucial to find out exactly where to stand to flag down the bus. On rare occasions, the tickets are actually sold by the side of the road out of a salesperson's car near where the bus will stop. Intra-city bus tickets are usually sold at any *tabaccheria*, and must be validated using the orange machines immediately upon entering the bus. Failure to do so will result in fines up to US$140 upon inspection. The websites www.bus.it and www.italybus.it are both helpful resources for finding bus companies in specific regions and routes to small towns.

Most large cities, including Rome, Naples, and Milan, have **metro systems** that connect major tourist destinations. Fast and cheap, these are the best forms of local transportation along with local buses. The metro usually operates from 6am until midnight, and tickets usually cost approximately €1. The cabins and stations get packed during rush hour, so guard personal belongings carefully, as theft is rampant. Tickets are sold in stations at counters or from automated machines. Remember to validate them, or risk getting heavily fined.

 FERMATA FRENZY. Taking the bus in Italy is easy, affordable, and a great way to get around, but most bus stops that aren't in major *piazze* are only "fermata prenotata" stops. The bus driver won't stop there unless he/she sees somebody waiting or someone onboard requests a stop. Drivers often miss travelers waiting quietly on the side of the road, so make your presence known. Wave your hands, step out on the curb, and make eye contact; you might feel silly but you'll feel a lot worse if the bus drives right by.

BY CAR

While the Italian bus and train systems are quite effective in negotiating travel between the major cities, travelers looking to explore smaller cities and rural villages might find renting a **car** to be a more viable option. A single traveler won't save by renting a car (especially considering the high gasoline prices), but four usually will. If you can't decide between train and car travel, you may benefit from a combination of the two; RailEurope and other railpass vendors offer **rail-and-drive** packages. **Fly-and-drive** packages are often available from travel agents or airline-rental agency partnerships.

RENTING

You can generally make reservations before you leave by calling major international offices in your home country. It is always significantly less expensive to reserve a car from the US than from Europe. Reserve ahead and pay in advance if at all possible. Sometimes the price and availability information from the offices in your home country does not agree with what the local offices in Italy will tell you. Try checking with both numbers to make sure you get the best price and the most accurate information possible. Local desk numbers are included in town listings; for home-country numbers, call your toll-free directory.

Though the minimum age to rent a car in Italy is 18, most companies will only rent cars to those over 21, or even 25, depending on the type of car being rented. Drivers under 25 should expect to pay a surcharge of approximately €12 per day (though most companies have a maximum total surcharge in the case of long rental periods). Policies and prices vary from agency to agency. Small local operations occasionally rent to people under 21, but be sure to ask about the insurance coverage and deductible, and always check the fine print. At most agencies, all that's needed to rent a car is a license from home and proof that you've had it for a year. Some agencies require international driving permits, see p. 38. Rental agencies in Italy include:

Auto Europe (☎Italy 800 12 37 04, Canada and the US 888-223-5555; www.autoeurope.com).

Avis (Australia ☎136 333, Canada and the US 800-352-7900, Italy 19 91 00 133, New Zealand 0800 655 111, UK 08700 100 287; www.avis.com).

Budget (Canada ☎800-268-8900, UK 8701 565 656, US 800-472-3325, www.budgetrentacar.com).

Europe by Car (US ☎800-223-1516; www.europebycar.com).

Europcar International (Italy ☎19 93 07 030; www.europcar.com).

Hertz (Australia ☎9698 2555; Canada 800-654-3001; UK 08708 44 88 44; US 800-654-3001; www.hertz.com).

COSTS AND INSURANCE

Expect to pay US$200-600 per week for a two- to four-door economy car with manual transmission and A/C. Automatic cars cost at least an extra US$100 per week, and are hard to find. Expect to pay more for larger cars and for 4WD.

Many rental packages offer unlimited kilometers, while others offer a limited number of kilometers per day with a surcharge per kilometer after that. Return the car with a full tank of gasoline (a.k.a. petrol) to avoid high fuel charges at the end. Be sure to ask whether the price includes **insurance** against theft and collision. Remember that if you are driving a conventional rental vehicle on an **unpaved road** in a rental car, you are almost never covered by insurance; ask about this before leaving the rental agency. Be aware that cars rented on an **American Express** or **Visa/MasterCard Gold** or **Platinum** credit card in Italy might *not* carry the automatic insurance that they would in some other countries; check with your credit card company. If you rent, lease, or borrow a car, you will need a **Green Card,** or **International Insurance Certificate,** to certify that you have liability insurance and that it applies abroad. Green cards can be obtained at car rental agencies, car dealers (for those leasing cars), some travel agents, and some border crossings.

All rental companies in Italy require you to buy a **Collision Damage Waiver (CDW),** which will waive the excess in the case of a collision. **Loss Damage Waivers (LDWs),** also required by rental companies in Italy, do the same in the case of theft or vandalism. Insurance plans from rental companies almost always come with an **excess** of around US$5000 for conventional vehicles. With the purchase of a CDW and LDW, the excess can be reduced to US$400-700. This means that the insurance bought from the rental company only applies to damages over the excess; damages up to that amount must be covered by your existing insurance plan.

National chains often allow one-way rentals (picking up in one city and dropping off in another). There is usually a minimum hire period and sometimes an extra drop-off charge of several hundred dollars.

INTERNATIONAL DRIVING PERMIT (IDP)

If you plan to drive a car while in Italy, you must **be over 18 and** have an International Driving Permit (IDP). Even though an IDP is usually not required to rent a car, it may be a good idea to get one anyway, in case you're in a situation (e.g., an accident, being stranded in a small town) **where the police do not know English; info on the IDP is printed in 11 languages, including Italian.**

Your IDP, valid for one year, must be issued in your own country before you depart. An application for an IDP usually requires one or two photos, a current local license, an additional form of identification, and a fee (up to US$20). To apply, contact your home country's automobile association. Be careful when purchasing an IDP online or anywhere other than your home automobile association. Many vendors sell permits of questionable legitimacy for higher prices.

ON THE ROAD

Driving in Italy is very similar to driving in the rest of Europe: vehicles drive on the right, pass on the left, and follow international rules and road signs established by the Geneva Convention. The roads in Italy range from the *autostrade*—superhighways with 130kph (80 mph) speed limit, increased to 150kph (93 mph) in some areas—to the narrow and sometimes unpaved *strade comunali* (local roads). Mountain roads can have steep cliffs and narrow curves, exercise caution if you must drive in the Dolomites or the Apennines. Highways usually charge expensive tolls, often best paid with a credit card. In cities the speed limit is usually 50kph (31 mph). Headlights must be on when driving on the *autostrada*. For more driving rules and regulations, consult *Moto Europa* (www.ideamerge.com/motoeuropa) or *In Italy Online* (www.initaly.com/travel/info/driving.htm). Gasoline *(benzina)* prices vary little because prices are regulated by the government. Prices average about US$1.75 per liter. Unleaded gasoline is called *benzina sensa piombo;* diesel is called *gasolio.* Credit cards are accepted at most stations. Take note that it's illegal to carry spare fuel.

> **!** **DRIVING PRECAUTIONS.** When traveling in the summer or in the desert, bring substantial amounts of water (a suggested five liters of **water** per person per day) for drinking and for the radiator. For long drives to unpopulated areas, register with police before beginning the trek and again upon arrival at the destination. Check with the local automobile club for details. When traveling for long distances, make sure tires are in good repair and have enough air, and get good maps. A **compass** and a **car manual** can also be very useful. You should always carry a **spare tire** and **jack, jumper cables, extra oil, flares,** a **flashlight,** and **heavy blankets** (in case your car breaks down at night or in the winter). If you don't know how to **change a tire,** learn before heading out, especially if you are planning on traveling in deserted areas. Blowouts on dirt roads are very common. If your car breaks down, **stay in your vehicle;** if you wander off, there's less likelihood that trackers will find you.

CAR ASSISTANCE

The **Automobile Club d'Italia (ACI)** is at the service of all drivers in Italy, with offices located throughout the country (www.aci.it). In case of breakdown, call ☎ 116 for assistance from the nearest ACI. On superhighways use the emergency telephones placed every 2km. For long drives in desolate areas, invest in a roadside assistance program and a cell phone, but be aware that use of **phones** en route is only permitted with a hands-free device.

LEASING A CAR

For longer than 17 days, leasing can be cheaper than renting; it is often the only option for those ages 18 to 21. The cheapest leases are agreements to buy the car and then sell it back to the manufacturer at a prearranged price. As far as you're concerned, though, it's a lease and doesn't entail enormous financial transactions. Leases generally include insurance coverage and are not taxed. Expect to pay around US$1100-1800 (depending on size of car) for 60 days. Contact **Auto Europe** or **Europe by Car** (p. 38) before you go.

BY BICYCLE, MOPED, AND FOOT

Renting a **bike** is easy in Italy; look for *noleggio* signs. If you want to bring your own, many airlines will count a bike as your second piece of luggage; a few charge extra (one-way US$50-110). Bikes must be packed in a cardboard box with the pedals and front wheel detached; many airlines sell bike boxes at the airport (US$10). Most ferries let you take your bike for free or for a nominal fee, and you can always ship your bike on trains. Renting a bike beats bringing your own if you plan to stay in one or two regions, and some hostels rent bicycles for low prices. *Let's Go* lists bike rental stores in the **Transportation** section of towns and cities when available. **Ciclismo Classico,** 30 Marathon St., Arlington, MA 02474, USA (☎800-866-7314; www.ciclismoclassico.com), offers beginner to advanced level trips across Italy, including Sardinia, the Amalfi Coast, Southern Italy, Sicily, Piedmont, and the Veneto.

   Scooters or **mopeds** are available for rent in major cities, as well as in smaller or rural locations. Often a *motorino* (scooter) is the most convenient method of transportation to reach sights in places with unreliable bus or train connections. Rental companies are required by law to provide a helmet, which the driver must wear. Gas and insurance may or may not be included in the rental price. Even if riding a scooter is exhilarating, always be careful; practice first in empty streets and learn to keep with the flow of traffic rather than just following street signs. Drivers in Italy—especially in the south—are notorious for ignoring traffic laws.

   Some of Italy's grandest scenery can be seen only by **foot.** *Let's Go* features many daytrips, but native inhabitants and fellow travelers are the best source for tips. Professionally run hiking and walking tours are often your best bet for navigating *la bell'Italia.* Hiking tours generally range from six to nine days long and cost from US$2700-3000. Check out Ciclismo Classico (see above) for hiking options along the Amalfi Coast, and through Tuscany or the Cinque Terre. The **Backpack Europe** website (www.backpackeurope.com) provides links to great hiking, walking, and kayaking options throughout Italy.

BY THUMB

! *Let's Go* never recommends hitchhiking as a safe means of transportation, and none of the information presented here is intended to do so.

Let's Go strongly urges you to consider the risks before you choose to hitchhike. Hitching means entrusting your life to a stranger and risking assault, sexual harassment, theft, and unsafe driving. For women traveling alone (or even in pairs), hitching is just too dangerous. A man and a woman are a less dangerous combination; two men will have a harder time getting a lift, while three men will go nowhere. Because hitchhiking can be difficult in Italy, travelers usually pick a well-lit spot outside of urban areas, where drivers can stop, return to the road without causing an accident, and have time to look over potential passengers as they approach. Note that it is illegal to walk along the highway. Some travelers head to service areas *(le aree di servizio)* to get rides. Italian speakers will have an easier time getting where they want to go; knowing the Italian name of the destination is essential. Keep luggage on the seat next to you, instead of in the trunk, to facilitate a quick exit. Most Western European countries, including Italy, offer a ride service which pairs drivers with riders; the fee varies by destination. **Eurostop International** (www.eurostop.be) is one of the largest. Or try **Via-vai** (fax 044 51 92 01 44; www.viavai.com/autostop). Not all organizations screen drivers; ask in advance. Request the ID number from the ride service of the driver you are paired with and give it to someone you trust; when you get picked up, make sure your driver confirms the ID number.

KEEPING IN TOUCH

BY EMAIL AND INTERNET

Internet is a growing phenomenon in Italy, and is therefore not as accessible in rural areas as it is in cities. Rates range from €1.50-6 per hour. Check http://cafe.ecs.net for regional listings of Internet access points in Italy.

Although it is possible in some places to forge a remote link with your home server, in most cases this is a much slower (and more expensive) option than taking advantage of free **web-based email accounts** (e.g., www.gmail.com and www.hotmail.com). **Internet cafes** and the occasional free Internet terminal at a public library or university are listed in the **Practical Information** sections of cities. For lists of additional cybercafes in Italy, check out www.cybercaptive.com.

Increasingly, travelers find that taking their **laptop computers** on the road with them can be a convenient option for staying connected. Laptop users can call an Internet service provider via a modem using long-distance phone cards specifically intended for such calls. They may also find Internet cafes that allow them to connect their laptops to the Internet. And most excitingly, travelers with Wi-Fi-enabled computers may be able to take advantage of an increasing number of Internet "hot spots," where they can get online for free or for a small fee. Newer computers can detect these hot spots automatically; otherwise, websites like www.jiwire.com, and www.wi-fihotspotlist.com can help you find them. For information on insuring your laptop while traveling, see p. 21.

WARY WI-FI. Wi-Fi hot spots make Internet access possible in public and remote places. Unfortunately, they also pose **security risks.** Hot spots are public, open networks that use unencrypted, unsecured connections. They are susceptible to hacks and "packet sniffing"—ways of stealing passwords and other private information. To prevent problems, disable ad hoc mode, turn off file sharing, turn off network discovery, encrypt your e-mail, turn on your firewall, beware of phony networks, and watch for over-the-shoulder creeps. Ask the establishment whose Wi-Fi you're using for the name of the network so you know you're on the right one. If you are in the vicinity and do not plan to access the Internet, turn off your Wi-Fi adapter completely.

Another option in Italy is to buy a stored-value card from the **Internet Train** network. Swipe it like a credit card and you can surf the web at Internet Train outlets wherever you go. Locations in cities such as Florence, Siena, Rome, and Naples can be found online (www.internettrain.it).

BY TELEPHONE

CALLING HOME FROM ITALY

Italians love their cell phones, so public phones and land lines are hard to come by. If you find one, you can usually make **direct international calls,** but if you aren't using a phone card, you may need to feed the machine regularly. **Prepaid phone**

cards are a common and relatively inexpensive means of calling abroad. Each one comes with a Personal Identification Number (PIN) and a toll-free access number. You call the access number and then follow the directions for dialing your PIN. To purchase prepaid phone cards, check online for the best rates; www.calling-cards.com is a good place to start. Online providers generally send your access number and PIN via email, with no actual "card" involved. You can also call home with prepaid phone cards purchased in Italy (see **Calling Within Italy,** p. 42).

PLACING INTERNATIONAL CALLS. To call Italy from home or to call home from Italy, dial:

1. The **international dialing prefix.** To call from **Australia,** dial 0011; **Canada** or the **US,** 011; **Ireland, New Zealand,** or the **UK,** 00; **Italy,** 00.
2. The **country code** of the country you want to call. To call **Australia,** dial 61; the **US** or **Canada,** 1; **Ireland,** 353; **New Zealand,** 64; the **UK,** 44; **Italy,** 39.
3. The **city/area code.** *Let's Go* lists the city/area codes for cities and towns in Italy opposite the city or town name, next to a ☎.
4. The **local number.**

Another option is to purchase a **calling card,** linked to a major national telecommunications service in your home country. Calls are billed collect or to your account. To obtain a calling card, contact the appropriate company listed below. Where available, there are often advantages to purchasing calling cards online, including better rates and immediate access to your account. To call home with a calling card, contact the operator for your service provider in Italy by dialing the appropriate toll-free access number (listed below in the third column).

COMPANY	TO OBTAIN A CARD:	TO CALL ABROAD:
AT&T (US)	800-364-9292 or www.att.com	800 17 24 44
Canada Direct	800-561-8868 or www.infocanadadirect.com	800 17 22 13
MCI (US)	800-777-5000 or www.minutepass.com	800 90 58 25
Telecom New Zealand Direct	www.telecom.co.nz	800 17 26 41
Telstra Australia	1800 676 638 or www.telstra.com	800 17 26 10

Placing a **collect call** through an international operator can be expensive, but may be necessary in case of an emergency. You can frequently call collect without even possessing a company's calling card just by calling its access number and following the instructions.

CALLING WITHIN ITALY

The simplest, though not always the most convenient, way to call within Italy is to use a pay phone. *Scheda,* or **prepaid phone cards** are available at newspaper kiosks, *tabaccherie,* Internet cafes, and post offices; these cards carry a certain amount of phone time depending on the their denomination and usually save time and money in the long run. The computerized phone will tell you how much time, in units, you have left on your card. Italian phone cards are a little tricky to maneuver; rip off the perforated corner and insert the card in the slot of the phone, usually stripe-up. For instructions in a different language, push the silver button with two flags on it. Another kind of prepaid telephone card comes with a PIN and a toll-free access number. Instead of inserting the card into the phone, you call the access number and follow the directions on the card. These cards can be used to make international and domestic calls. Phone rates typically tend to be highest in the morning, lower in the evening, and lowest on Sunday and late at night. Rates are significantly higher when dialing from pay phones, so use a private line when you can.

CELLULAR PHONES

Cellular phones *(telefonini)* are a convenient and inexpensive option for longer visits. Given the prevalence of cell phones in Italy, pay phones are hard to come by, making cell phones a good alternative for tourists. This thankfully doesn't mean dealing with cell phone plans and bills; prepaid minutes are widely available and phones can be purchased cheaply or even rented.

The international standard for cell phones is **Global System for Mobile Communication (GSM).** To make and receive calls in Italy you will need a **GSM-compatible phone** and a **SIM (Subscriber Identity Module) card** by TIM (Telecom Italia Mobile), WIND, 3, and Vodafone in Italy, a country-specific, thumbnail-sized chip that gives you a local phone number and plugs you into the local network. Many SIM cards are **prepaid:** they come with calling time included and you don't need to sign up for a monthly service plan. Incoming calls are generally free on Italian SIM cards. When you use up the prepaid time, you can buy additional cards or vouchers (usually available at *tabaccherie*) to "top up" your phone. For more information on SIM cards and buying or renting GSM phones, check out www.telestial.com, www.roadpost.com, www.planetomni.com, or www.cellularabroad.com.

> **TIP** **GSM PHONES.** Just having a GSM phone doesn't mean you're necessarily good to go when you travel abroad. The majority of GSM phones sold in the United States operate on a different **frequency** (1900) than international phones (900/1800) and will not work abroad. Tri-band phones work on all three frequencies (900/1800/1900) and will operate through most of the world. Additionally, some GSM phones are **SIM-locked** and will only accept SIM cards from a single carrier. You'll need a **SIM-unlocked** phone to use a SIM card from a local carrier when you travel.

TIME DIFFERENCES

Italy is on Central European Time, one hour ahead of Greenwich Mean Time (GMT). Daylight Saving Time starts on the last Sunday in March, when clocks are moved ahead one hour, so Italy is two hours ahead of GMT. Clocks are put back one hour on the last Sunday of October. The following table applies from late October to early April.

4AM	5AM	6AM	7AM	8AM	NOON	1PM	10PM
Vancouver Seattle San Francisco Los Angeles	Denver	Chicago	New York Toronto	New Brunswick	GMT London	**ROME**	Sydney Canberra Melbourne

BY MAIL

SENDING MAIL HOME FROM ITALY

Airmail is the best way to send mail home from Italy. **Aerogrammes,** printed sheets that fold into envelopes and travel via airmail, are available at post offices. Write "airmail," "par avion," or "per posta aerea" on the front. Most post offices will charge exorbitant fees or simply refuse to send aerogrammes with enclosures. **Surface mail** is by far the cheapest and slowest way to send mail. It takes one to two months to cross the Atlantic and one to three to cross the Pacific—good for heavy items you won't need for a while, such as souvenirs that you've acquired along the way. Delivery times and package shipping costs vary; inquire at the post office.

SENDING MAIL TO ITALY

To ensure timely delivery, mark envelopes "airmail," "par avion," or "per posta aerea." In addition to the standard postage system whose rates are listed below, **Federal Express** (Australia ☎ 13 26 10, Canada and the US 800-463-3339, Ireland 1800 535 800, New Zealand 0800 733 339, the UK 08456 070 809; www.fedex.com) handles express mail services from most countries to Italy. Sending a postcard within Italy costs €0.60, while sending letters (up to 20g) domestically also costs €0.60. Note that in general the postal service is more efficient in urban areas.

There are several ways to arrange pick up of letters sent to you while you are abroad. Mail can be sent via **Fermo Posta** (General Delivery) to almost any city or town in Italy with a post office, **but don't be surprised if it takes its time arriving at its destination.** Address these letters like so:

Dante ALIGHIERI

c/o Ufficio Postale Centrale

FERMO POSTA

48100 Ravenna

Italy

The mail will go to a special desk in the central post office, unless you specify a post office by street address or postal code. It's best to use the largest post office, since mail may be sent there regardless. It is usually safer and quicker, though more expensive, to send mail express or registered. If the clerks insist that there is nothing for you, ask them to check under your first name as well. *Let's Go* lists post offices in the **Practical Information** section for each city and town if available.

American Express's travel offices throughout the world offer a free **Client Letter Service** (mail held up to 30 days and forwarded upon request) for cardholders who contact them in advance. Some offices provide these services to non-cardholders (especially AmEx Travelers Cheque holders), but call ahead to make sure. *Let's Go* lists AmEx locations for most large cities in **Practical Information** sections; for a complete list, call ☎ 800-528-4800 or visit www.americanexpress.com/travel.

ACCOMMODATIONS

HOSTELS

Many hostels are laid out dorm-style, often with large single-sex rooms and bunk beds, although private rooms that sleep two to four are becoming more common. They sometimes have kitchens and utensils for public use, bike or moped rentals, storage areas, transportation to airports, breakfast and other meals, laundry facilities, and Internet access. There can be drawbacks: some hostels close during certain daytime "lockout" hours, have a curfew, don't accept reservations, impose a maximum stay, or, less frequently, require that you do chores. In Italy, a dorm bed in a hostel will average around €15-25 and a private room around €25-30. A great source of budget accommodations can be found at www.hostelz.com, which offers regional lists of hostels, guesthouses, hotels, apartments and more.

 A HOSTELER'S BILL OF RIGHTS. There are certain standard features that we do not include in our hostel listings. Unless we state otherwise, you can expect that every hostel has no lockout, no curfew, free sheets, free hot showers, some system of secure luggage storage, and no key deposit.

ESSENTIALS

HOSTELLING INTERNATIONAL

Joining the youth hostel association in your own country (listed below) automatically grants you membership privileges in **Hostelling International (HI)**, a federation of national hosteling associations. Non-HI members may be allowed to stay in some hostels, but will have to pay extra to do so. HI hostels are scattered throughout Italy, and **are typically less expensive than private hostels.** HI's umbrella organization's website (www.hihostels.com), which lists the web addresses and phone numbers of all national associations, can be a great place to begin researching hosteling in a specific region. Other comprehensive hosteling websites include www.hostels.com, www.hostelplanet.com and www.eurotrip.com.

Most HI hostels also honor **guest memberships**—you'll get a blank card with space for six validation stamps. Each night you'll pay a nonmember supplement (€3) and earn one guest stamp; get six stamps and you're a member. A new membership benefit is the FreeNites program, which allows hostelers to gain points toward free stays. Most student travel agencies (see p. 26) sell HI cards, as do all of the national hosteling organizations listed below. All prices listed below are valid for **one-year memberships** unless otherwise noted.

Associazione Italiana Alberghi per la Gioventù (AIG), Via Cavour 44, 00184 Roma (☎06 48 71 152; www.ostellionline.org). Search hostels in desired region of Italy and find general information.

Australian Youth Hostels Association (AYHA), 422 Kent St., Sydney, NSW 200 (☎02 9261 1111; www.yha.com.au). AUS\$52, under 18 AUS\$19.

ESSENTIALS

Hostelling International-Canada (HI-C), 205 Catherine St. Ste. 400, Ottawa, ON K2P 1C3 (☎613-237-7884; www.hihostels.ca). CDN$35, under 18 free.

An Óige (Irish Youth Hostel Association), 61 Mountjoy St., Dublin 7 (☎830 4555; www.irelandyha.org). €20, under 18 €10.

Hostelling International Northern Ireland (HINI), 22-32 Donegall Rd., Belfast BT12 5JN (☎02890 32 47 33; www.hini.org.uk). UK£15, under 25 UK£10.

Youth Hostels Association of New Zealand Inc. (YHANZ), Level 1, 166 Moorhouse Ave., P.O. Box 436, Christchurch (☎0800 278 299 (NZ only) or 03 379 9970; www.yha.org.nz). NZ$40, under 18 free.

Scottish Youth Hostels Association (SYHA), 7 Glebe Crescent, Stirling FK8 2JA (☎01786 89 14 00; www.syha.org.uk). UK£8, under 18 £4.

Youth Hostels Association (England and Wales), Trevelyan House, Dimple Rd., Matlock, Derbyshire DE4 3YH (☎08707 708 868; www.yha.org.uk). UK£16, under 26 UK£10.

Hostelling International-USA, 8401 Colesville Rd., Ste. 600, Silver Spring, MD 20910 (☎301-495-1240; www.hiayh.org). US$28, under 18 free.

BOOKING HOSTELS ONLINE. One of the easiest ways to ensure you've got a bed for the night is by reserving online. Click to the **Hostelworld** booking engine through **www.letsgo.com**, and you'll have access to bargain accommodations from Argentina to Zimbabwe with no added commission.

HOTELS, GUESTHOUSES, PENSIONS

Hotels, or *alberghi,* offer singles *(singola)* for €20-50 per night and doubles *(doppia* or *matrimoniale)* €40-100. Some hotels offer *pensione completa* (full pen-

Marta Guest House is situated in an elegant building in the Prati district (Castel Sant'Angelo), only a few stops from PIAZZA NAVONA, SPANISH STEPS and VATICAN CITY. Our beautiful rooms are spacious and luminous (with some of the furniture dating back to the 1900's), all with private bath, TV, safe and AC.

For a great family atmosphere and magnificent accomodation at low prices, come stay with us at Marta Guest House!

Marta Guest House
Via Tacito 41
00193 Roma, Italy

Phone: 39 06 6889 2992
Fax: 39 06 6821 7474
Email: martaguesthouse@iol.it

Book rooms online at
http://marta.hotelinroma.com
http://www.martaguesthouse.com

ESSENTIALS

sion; all meals) and *mezza pensione* (half pension; breakfast only). You'll usually share a hall bathroom; a private bathroom will cost extra, as may hot showers. Smaller **guesthouses** and **pensions** (hotels that have earned 1-3 stars on the Italian scale of 1-5) are often cheaper than fancier hotels. If you make **reservations** in writing, indicate your night of arrival and the number of nights you plan to stay. The hotel will send you a confirmation and may request payment for the first night. Often it is easiest to make reservations over the phone with a credit card. Upon arrival, confirm nightly charges as Italian hotels are notorious for tacking on additional costs at check-out time. The best offerings in each town are listed under the **Accommodations** section; to find hotels elsewhere in Italy, try http://en.venere.com/italy, www.alberghieturismo.it, www.itwg.com, or the local tourist office.

OTHER TYPES OF ACCOMMODATIONS

BED & BREAKFASTS

For a cozy alternative to impersonal hotel rooms, B&Bs (private homes with rooms available to travelers) range from acceptable to sublime. Rooms in Italian B&Bs generally cost €20-50 for a single and €70-90 for a double. Any number of websites provide listings for B&Bs; check out **Bed & Breakfast Inns Online** (www.bbonline.com), **InnFinder** (www.inncrawler.com), **InnSite** (www.innsite.com), **BedandBreakfast.com** (www.bedandbreakfast.com), **Pamela Lanier's Bed & Breakfast Guide Online** (www.lanierbb.com), or **BNBFinder.com** (www.bnbfinder.com).

AGRITURISMO

Frequently omitted by mainstream travel guides and ignored by local tourist offices, *agriturismo* is a pleasurable, leisurely, and inexpensive way to become acquainted

Over 12,000 hostels in 165 countries

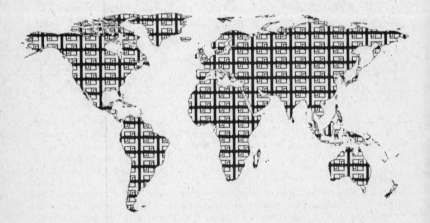

 HOSTELWORLD

with the Italian countryside. Local families open their homes to guests and provide meals for reasonable prices. The host family and guests gather around the same table each night, sharing bottles of homemade wine, fresh vegetables from the garden, and stories that last far into the night. These houses, however, are usually only accessible by car—a tranquil remoteness that simply adds to their charm, provided that it doesn't prevent you from staying altogether. If you're looking to truly experience the laid-back Italian lifestyle, hearty cuisine, local wines, and sweeping countryside vistas, *agriturismo* is the best way to spend your time and money. To find *agriturismo* options in your region, consult local tourist offices or check out the **Associazione Nazionale per l'Agriturismo, l'Ambiente e il Territorio** (www.agriturist.it).

UNIVERSITY DORMS

Many **colleges** and **universities** open their residence halls to travelers when school is not in session; some do so even during term-time. Getting a room may take a couple of phone calls and require advanced planning, but rates tend to be low and many offer free local calls and Internet access. For a list of student housing opportunities in Italian cities, write asking for a "Guide for Foreign Students" to **The Italian Ministry of Education,** Vle. Trastevere 76/A, 00153 Rome (☎06 5 84 91; www.pubblica.istruzione.it).

HOME EXCHANGES AND HOSPITALITY CLUBS

Home exchanges offer travelers various types of homes (houses, apartments, condominiums, villas, even castles in some cases), plus the opportunity to live like a native and to cut down on accommodation fees. For more information, contact HomeExchange.com Inc., P.O. Box 787, Hermosa Beach, CA 90254, USA (☎310 798 3864 or toll free 800-877-8723; www.homeexchange.com), **or** Intervac International Home Exchange (☎**051 91 78 41;** www.intervac.com).

Hospitality clubs link their members with individuals or families abroad who are willing to host travelers for free or for a small fee to promote cultural exchange and general good karma. In exchange, members usually must be willing to host travelers in their own homes; a small membership fee may also be required. **The Hospitality Club** (www.hospitalityclub.org) is a good place to start. **Servas** (www.servas.org) is an established, more formal, peace-based organization, and requires a fee and an interview to join. An Internet search will find many similar organizations, some of which cater to special interests (e.g., women, GLBT travelers, or members of certain professions). As always, use common sense when planning to stay with or host someone you do not know.

LONG-TERM ACCOMMODATIONS

Travelers planning to stay in Italy for extended periods of time may find it most cost-effective to rent an **apartment** *(affittasi)*. A basic one-bedroom (or studio) apartment in Rome will range €500-2000 per month, but will likely be in the €750-1000 range. Besides the rent itself, prospective tenants are often also required to front a security deposit (frequently one month's rent) and the last month's rent.

A good place to check for apartments is **craigslist** (www.craigslist.org), a forum for renters and rentees where you can see others' listings or post your own housing needs. For regional listings, try http://affittistudenti.studenti.it and www.secondamano.it. If it's Rome you're after, look at http://liveinrome.com; for listings in Rome, Florence, and Venice, check www.romepower.com.

CAMPING

Over 2000 campgrounds in Italy are designated between 1 and 4 stars; a 4-star campground includes amenities such as a market, swimming pool, and a bar. Costs vary, but are generally under €10 per person. Some campgrounds offer bungalows as a cheap alternative for travelers without tents; others even have tents to rent. Camping is illegal unless done at designated sites. A regional guide can be found through **Easy Camping** (☎33 96 09 41 04; easycamping.it). Reservations are recommended at some sites. Campgrounds are listed in the **Accommodations** section when available. More information can be found through the following source:

> **Confederazione Italiana Campeggiatori (Federcampeggio),** Via Vittorio Emanuele 11, 50041 Calenzano, FI (☎055 88 23 91; www.campeggio.com). General information and a regional guide to campgrounds. International Camping Cards providing discounts available at Federcampeggio centres.

Renting an RV costs more than tenting or hosteling but less than staying in hotels while renting a car (see **By Car,** p. 36). The convenience of bringing along your own bedroom, bathroom, and kitchen makes RVing an attractive option, especially for older travelers and families with children. Rates vary widely by region, season (**July and August** are the most expensive months), and type of RV. Rental prices for a standard RV are around **€700 per week.**

Hikers might also be interested in the mountain refuges of the **Club Alpino Italiano,** P. Savonarola 3, I-48022 Lugo di Romagna, Ravenna (☎/fax 05 45 30 541; www.racine.ravenna.it/cailugo). These often hard-to-reach shelters and bivouacs range in price from €17 (€8.50 for members) to €26 (€13) per night, depending on accessibility and services.

THE GREAT OUTDOORS

The **Great Outdoor Recreation Page** (www.gorp.com) provides general information for travelers planning on camping or spending time in the outdoors.

> **LEAVE NO TRACE.** *Let's Go* encourages travelers to embrace the "Leave No Trace" ethic, minimizing their impact on natural environments and protecting them for future generations. Trekkers and wilderness enthusiasts should set up camp on durable surfaces, use cookstoves instead of campfires, bury human waste away from water supplies, bag trash and carry it out with them, and respect wildlife and natural objects. For more detailed information, contact the **Leave No Trace Center for Outdoor Ethics,** P.O. Box 997, Boulder, CO 80306 (☎800-332-4100 or 303-442-8222; www.lnt.org).

USEFUL RESOURCES

A variety of publishing companies offer hiking guidebooks to meet the educational needs of the novice or the expert. For information about camping, hiking, and biking, write or call the publishers listed below to receive a free catalog. Campers heading to Italy should consider buying an **International Camping Carnet.** Similar to a hostel membership card, it's required at a few campgrounds and sometimes provides discounts. It is available in North America from the **Family Campers and RVers Association** and in the UK from **The Caravan Club** (see below). For Italian information, consult the **Touring Club Italiano (TCI), C. Italia 10, Milan** (☎**02 85 261; www.touringclub.com).**

Cicerone Press, 2 Police Sq., Milnthorpe, Cumbria UK LA7 7PY, (☎44 1539 562 069; www.ciceroneguides.com). Walking, trekking, and climbing guides, including *Walking in Tuscany* (2006; UK£14), *Walking in Sicily* (2006; UK£12), and *Through the Italian Alps* (2005; UK£12).

Automobile Association, Contact Centre, Lambert House, Stockport Road, Cheadle SK8 2DY, UK (☎08706 000 371; www.theAA.com). Publishes *Caravan and Camping Europe* and *Britain & Ireland* (UK£10) as well as road atlases for Europe, Britain, France, Germany, Ireland, Italy, Spain, and the US.

The Caravan Club, East Grinstead House, East Grinstead, West Sussex, RH19 1UA, UK (☎01342 326 944; www.caravanclub.co.uk). For UK£34, members receive access to sites, insurance services, equipment discounts, maps, and a monthly magazine.

The Mountaineers Books, 1001 SW Klickitat Way, Ste. 201, Seattle, WA 98134, USA (☎206-223-6303; www.mountaineersbooks.org). Over 600 titles on hiking, biking, mountaineering, natural history, and conservation.

NATIONAL PARKS

With 21 national parks (and counting), over 150 regional parks, and countless national, regional, and marine reserves, Italy protects approximately 10% of its land. Whether you seek mountains, lakes, forests, or oceans, Italy's national parks have something to offer. Bears and lynxes inhabit the **Parco Nazionale d'Abruzzo, Lazio e Molise** (www.parcoabruzzo.it; see p. 548), accessible by both car and train from Rome. The beautiful coast of the **Parco Nazionale delle Cinque Terre** (www.parconazionale5terre.it; see p. 213) can be reached by bus, train, and boat. For a list of all the parks, consult **Federparchi.** (☎06 51 60 49 40; www.parks.it.)

WILDERNESS SAFETY

Staying **warm, dry,** and **well hydrated** is key to a happy and safe wilderness experience. For any hike, prepare yourself for an emergency by packing a first-aid kit, a reflector, a whistle, high-energy food, extra water, raingear, a hat, mittens, and extra socks. For warmth, wear wool or insulating synthetic materials designed for the outdoors. Cotton is a bad choice as it dries painfully slowly.

Check **weather forecasts** often and pay attention to the skies when hiking, as weather patterns can change suddenly. Always let someone—a friend, your hostel, a park ranger, or a local hiking organization—know when and where you are going. Know your physical limits and do not attempt a hike beyond your ability.

CAMPING AND HIKING EQUIPMENT

WHAT TO BUY

Good camping equipment is both sturdy and light. North American suppliers tend to offer the most competitive prices.

Sleeping Bags: Most sleeping bags are rated by season; "summer" means 30-40°F (around 0°C) at night; "four-season" or "winter" often means below 0°F (-17°C). Bags are made of down (warm and light, but expensive, and miserable when wet) or of synthetic material (heavy, durable, and warm when wet). Prices range US$50-250 for a summer synthetic to US$200-300 for a good down winter bag. **Sleeping bag pads** include foam pads (US$10-30), air mattresses (US$15-50), and self-inflating mats (US$30-120). Bring a **stuff sack** to store your bag and keep it dry.

Tents: The best tents are free-standing (with their own frames and suspension systems), set up quickly, and only require staking in high winds. Low-profile dome tents are the best all-around. Worthwhile 2-person tents start at US$100, 4-person tents start at US$160. Make sure your tent has a rain fly and seal its seams with waterproofer. Other useful accessories include a **battery-operated lantern,** a plastic **groundcloth,** and a nylon **tarp.**

Backpacks: Internal-frame packs mold well to your back, keep a lower center of gravity, and flex adequately to allow you to hike difficult trails, while external-frame packs are more comfortable for long hikes over even terrain, as they carry weight higher and distribute it more evenly. Make sure your pack has a strong, padded hip-belt to transfer weight to your legs. There are models designed specifically for women. Any serious backpacking requires a pack of at least 4000 cu. in. (16,000cc), plus 500 cu. in. for sleeping bags in internal-frame packs. Sturdy backpacks cost anywhere from US$125 to 420—your pack is an area where it doesn't pay to save. On your hunt for the perfect pack, fill up prospective models with something heavy, strap it on correctly, and walk around the store to get a sense of how the model distributes weight. Either buy a **rain cover** (US$10-20) or store all of your belongings in plastic bags inside your pack.

Boots: Be sure to wear hiking boots with good **ankle support.** They should fit snugly and comfortably over 1-2 pairs of **wool socks** and a pair of thin **liner socks.** Break in boots over several weeks before you go to spare yourself blisters.

Other Necessities: Synthetic layers, like those made of polypropylene or polyester, and a pile jacket will keep you warm even when wet. A **space blanket** (US$5-15) will help you to retain body heat and doubles as a groundcloth. Plastic **water bottles** are vital; look for shatter- and leak-resistant models. Carry **water-purification tablets** for when you can't boil water. Although most campgrounds provide campfire sites, you may want to bring a small **metal grill.** For those places (including virtually every organized campground in Europe) that forbid fires or the gathering of firewood, you'll need a **camp stove** (the classic Coleman starts at US$50) and a propane-filled **fuel bottle** to operate it. While packing these supplies, be sure to plan around flight restrictions. Also bring a **first-aid kit, pocketknife, insect repellent,** and **waterproof matches** or a **lighter.**

WHERE TO BUY IT

The online and mail-order companies listed below offer lower prices than many retail stores. A visit to a local camping or outdoors store will give you a good sense of the look and weight of certain items before you buy.

Campmor, 400 Corporate Dr., PO Box 680, Mahwah, NJ 07430, USA (☎800-525-4784; www.campmor.com).

Cotswold Outdoor, Unit 11 Kemble Business Park, Crudwell, Malmesbury Wiltshire, SN16 9SH, UK (☎08704 427 755; www.cotswoldoutdoor.com).

Discount Camping, 833 Main North Rd., Pooraka, South Australia 5095, Australia (☎618 8262 3399; www.discountcamping.com.au).

Eastern Mountain Sports (EMS), 1 Vose Farm Rd., Peterborough, 03458 NH, USA (☎888-463-6367; www.ems.com).

Gear-Zone, 8 Burnet Rd., Sweetbriar Rd. Industrial Estate, Norwich, NR3 2BS, UK (☎1603 410 108; www.gear-zone.co.uk).

L.L. Bean, Freeport, ME 04033, USA (US and Canada ☎800-441-5713; UK 0800 891 297; www.llbean.com).

Mountain Designs, 443a Nudgee Rd., Hendra, Queensland 4011, Australia (☎617 3114 4300; www.mountaindesigns.com).

Recreational Equipment, Inc. (REI), Sumner, WA 98352, USA (US and Canada ☎800-426-4840, elsewhere 253-891-2500; www.rei.com).

ORGANIZED ADVENTURE TRIPS

Organized adventure tours offer another way of exploring the wild. Activities include hiking, biking, skiing, canoeing, kayaking, rafting, climbing, photo safaris, and archaeological digs. Tourism bureaus often can suggest parks, trails, and outfitters. Organizations that specialize in camping and outdoor equipment like REI and EMS (see p. 56) also are good sources for information.

Specialty Travel Index, P.O. Box 458, San Anselmo, CA 94979, USA (US ☎888-624-4030, elsewhere 415-455-1643; www.specialtytravel.com). Provides links to organized travel tours providing adventure tours as well as art, cultural, special needs, and other special interest tours.

Ecotravel (www.ecotravel.com). Online directory of various programs in Italy and throughout the world.

La Boscaglia (☎05 16 26 41 69; www.boscaglia.it). Offers walking tours and treks throughout Italy.

NatureTrek, Cheriton Mill, Cheriton, Alresford, Hampshire, SO24 0NG (☎01962 733051; www.naturetrek.co.uk). Offers responsible travel opportunities worldwide, including many in Italy.

SPECIFIC CONCERNS

SUSTAINABLE TRAVEL

In Italy, attention is often given to cultural restoration while natural resources are overlooked and under appreciated. Italy's mountains, lakes, and marine environments have been enjoyed for longer than its temples and villas. As the number of travelers on the road continues to rise, however, the detrimental effect they can have on nature becomes an increasing concern. The once-pristine Mediterranean, home to 20% of the world's marine species, receives especially high tourist traffic. With this in mind, *Let's Go* promotes the philosophy of **sustainable travel.** Through a sensitivity to issues of ecology and sustainability, today's travelers can be a powerful force in preserving as well as restoring the places they visit. **Sustainable Travel International,** 3250 O'Neal Circle Ste. H-11, Boulder CO 80301, USA (☎720-273-2975; www.sustainabletravelinternational.org), provides information on sustainable travel in Italy and general info on topics such as carbon offsets.

Ecotourism, a rising trend in sustainable travel, focuses on the conservation of natural habitats and how to use them to build up the economy without exploitation or overdevelopment. Travelers can make a difference by doing research in advance and by supporting organizations and establishments that pay attention to their impact on their natural surroundings and that strive to be environmentally friendly. Opportunities in Italy can be found at www.ecoturismo-italia.it, an Italian nonprofit that works in conjunction with international organizations. For information on getting involved in environmental conservation, see the resources below or the **Beyond Tourism** (p. 95) section of this book.

> **ECOTOURISM RESOURCES.** For more information on environmentally responsible tourism, contact one of the organizations below:
>
> **Conservation International,** 2011 Crystal Dr., Ste. 500, Arlington, VA 22202, USA (☎800-406-2306 or 703-341-2400; www.conservation.org).
>
> **Green Globe 21,** Green Globe vof, Verbenalaan 1, 2111 ZL Aerdenhout, The Netherlands (☎31 23 544 0306; www.greenglobe.com).
>
> **International Ecotourism Society,** 1333 H St. NW, Ste. 300E, Washington, D.C. 20005, USA (☎202-347-9203; www.ecotourism.org).
>
> **United Nations Environment Program (UNEP),** 39-43 Quai André Citroën, 75739 Paris Cedex 15, France (☎33 1 44 37 14 50; www.uneptie.org/pc/tourism).

RESPONSIBLE TRAVEL

The impact of tourist euro on the destinations you visit should not be underestimated. The choices you make during your trip can have powerful effects on local communities—for better or for worse. Travelers who care about the destinations and environments they explore should make themselves aware of the social, cultural and political implications of the choices they make when they travel. Simple decisions such as buying local products instead of globally available ones, paying fair prices for products or services, and attempting to say a few words in the local language can have a strong, positive effect on the community.

Community-based tourism aims to channel tourist euro into the local economy by emphasizing tours and cultural programs that are run by members of the host community and that often benefit disadvantaged groups. This type of tourism also benefits the tourists themselves, as it often takes them beyond the traditional tours of the region. The *Ethical Travel Guide* (UK£13), a project of **Tourism Concern** (☎44 020 7133 3330; www.tourismconcern.org.uk), is an excellent resource for information on community-based travel with a directory of 300 establishments in 60 countries. For information on the role of tourism in Southern Italy, see the article "Saving Alta Irpinia" (p. 105).

TRAVELING ALONE

There are many benefits to traveling alone, including independence and a greater opportunity to connect with locals. On the other hand, solo travelers are more vulnerable targets for harassment and street theft. If you are traveling alone, look confident, try not to stand out as a tourist, and be especially careful in deserted or very crowded areas. Stay away from areas that are not well lit. If questioned, never admit that you are traveling alone. Maintain regular contact with someone at home who knows your itinerary, and always research your destination before traveling. For more tips, pick up *Traveling Solo* by Eleanor Berman (Globe Pequot Press, US$18), visit www.travelaloneandloveit.com, or subscribe to **Connecting: Solo Travel Network**, 689 Park Rd., Unit 6, Gibsons, BC V0N 1V7, Canada (☎604-886-9099; www.cstn.org; membership US$30-48).

WOMEN TRAVELERS

Women exploring on their own inevitably face some additional safety concerns, but it's easy to be adventurous without taking undue risks. If you are concerned, consider staying in hostels which offer single rooms that lock from the inside or in religious organizations with single-sex rooms. Stick to centrally located accommodations and avoid solitary late-night treks or metro rides.

Always carry extra cash for a phone call, bus, or taxi. **Hitchhiking** is never safe for lone women, or even for two women traveling together. Look as if you know where you're going, avoid the heckles and stares of Italian men, and approach older women or couples for directions if you're lost or uncomfortable.

Generally, the less you look like a tourist, the better off you'll be. Dress conservatively, especially in rural areas. Wearing a conspicuous **wedding band** sometimes helps to prevent unwanted advances.

Your best answer to verbal harassment is to do as the Italian women do and give no answer at all; feigning deafness, sitting motionless, and staring straight ahead at nothing in particular will usually do the trick. The extremely persistent can sometimes be dissuaded by a firm, loud, and very public "Vai via" or "Vattene" (Go away!) in Italian. Don't hesitate to seek out a *poliziotto* (police officer) or a passerby if you are being harassed. Memorize the emergency numbers in places you visit, and consider carrying a whistle on your keychain. A self-defense course will both prepare you for a potential attack and raise your level of awareness of your surroundings (see **Personal Safety,** p. 20).

GLBT TRAVELERS

It is difficult to characterize the Italian attitude toward gay, lesbian, bisexual, and transgendered (GLBT) travelers. Homophobia is still an issue in some regions. Rome, Florence, Milan, and Bologna all have easily accessible gay scenes. Away from the larger cities, however, gay social life may be difficult to find. The monthly **Babilonia** and the annual **Guida Gay Italia** can be found at newsstands, and the free **Pride and GayClubbing** can be found at most gay venues. Travelers can also expect the larger cities to have gay discoteche and bars (listed by Let's Go). Listed below are contact organizations, mail-order catalogs, and publishers that offer materials addressing some specific concerns. **Planet Out** (www.planetout.com) offers a comprehensive site addressing gay travel concerns. The online newspaper **365gay.com** also has a travel section (www.365gay.com/travel/travelchannel.htm).

Gay.It, V. Ravizza, 22/E, 56121 Pisa (www.gay.it). Provides info on gay life in Italy. Associated website in English (www.gayfriendlyitaly.com) gives regional info on nightlife, homophobia, gay events and more.

International Lesbian and Gay Association (ILGA), Ave. des Villas 34, 1060 Brussels, Belgium (☎32 2 502 2471; www.ilga.org). Provides political information, such as homosexuality laws of individual countries.

Arcigay, V. Don Minzoni 18, 40100 Bologna (☎051 64 93 0555; www.arcigay.it). National organization for homosexuals. Holds group discussions, dances, and many special events. Their website contains addresses and phone numbers of city centers.

> **ADDITIONAL RESOURCES: GLBT**
> *Spartacus 2005-2006: International Gay Guide.* Bruno Gmunder Verlag (US$33).
> *The Gay Vacation Guide: The Best Trips and How to Plan Them,* Mark Chesnut.
> Kensington Books (US$15).

TRAVELERS WITH DISABILITIES

Those with disabilities should inform airlines and hotels of their disabilities when making reservations; some time may be needed to prepare special accommodations. Call ahead to restaurants, museums, and other facilities to find out if they are wheelchair-accessible. There is no quarantine for a **guide dog** to enter Italy, but a valid certificate from the Health Authorities in its country of origin is required. Guide dogs are allowed into public places and shops, and travel free of charge on public transport.

Rail is probably the most convenient form of travel for disabled travelers in Europe: many stations have ramps, and some trains have wheelchair lifts, special seating areas, and specially equipped toilets. All Eurostar, some InterCity (IC) and some EuroCity (EC) trains are **wheelchair-accessible.** For those who wish to rent cars, some major **car rental** agencies offer hand-controlled vehicles. Look for pamphlets on accessibility from local tourist offices; a list of publications and where to find them can be found at www.coinsociale.it/tourism/services/guide.php.

USEFUL ORGANIZATIONS

Accessible Italy, Via C. Manetti 34, 47891 Dogana, Repubblica di San Marino (☎378 94 11 11; www.accessibleitaly.com). Provides tours to Italy for travelers with disabilities. Proceeds go towards improving handicap-access to attractions in Italy. Also organizes handicap-accessible weddings in Italy.

Accessible Journeys, 35 West Sellers Ave., Ridley Park, PA 19078, USA (☎800-846-4537; www.disabilitytravel.com). Designs tours for wheelchair users and slow walkers. The site has tips and forums for all travelers.

CO.IN. Cooperative Integrate, (☎067 12 90 11; www.coinsociale.it). "Roma per tutti" (Rome for everyone) provides information in Italian, English, Spanish, and French on accessibility of sites, hotels, restaurants, etc. in Rome and other Italian and European cities. "Italia per tutti" provides accessibility information on 7000 structures in Italy.

Flying Wheels Travel, 143 W. Bridge St., Owatonna, MN 55060, USA (☎507-451-5005; www.flyingwheelstravel.com). Specializes in escorted trips to Europe for people with physical disabilities; plans custom trips worldwide.

The Guided Tour, Inc., 7900 Old York Rd., Ste. 114B, Elkins Park, PA 19027, USA (☎800-783-5841; www.guidedtour.com). Organizes travel programs for persons with developmental and physical challenges.

Mobility International USA (MIUSA), P.O. Box 10767, Eugene, OR 97440, USA (☎541-343-1284; www.miusa.org). Provides a variety of books and other publications containing information for travelers with disabilities.

Society for Accessible Travel and Hospitality (SATH), 347 Fifth Ave., Ste. 610, New York, NY 10016, USA (☎212-447-7284; www.sath.org). An advocacy group that publishes free online travel information. Annual membership US$49, students US$29.

MINORITY TRAVELERS

Particularly in southern Italy, racial minority travelers or members of non-Christian religions may feel unwelcome. In terms of safety, there is no easy answer. Men and women should always travel in groups and avoid unsafe parts of town. The best answer to verbal harassment is often not to acknowledge it.

DIETARY CONCERNS

With delicious carnivorous offerings, vegetarians may feel there's nothing for them in Italy. While there are only a few strictly vegetarian restaurants in Italy, it is not difficult to find vegetarian meals. To avoid confusion in restaurants, make sure you tell your waiter "Non mangio carne" (I don't eat meat) or say that you would like your pizza or pasta sauce "senza carne, per favore" (without meat, please). Before you head to Italy, check out the Italian Vegetarian Association (AVI), V. XXV Aprile, 41 - 20026 Novate Milanese, Milano (www.vegetariani.it).

The travel section of The Vegetarian Resource Group's website, at www.vrg.org/travel, has a comprehensive list of organizations and websites that are geared toward helping vegetarians and vegans traveling abroad; the site also offers *Good Vegetarian Food*, an Italy-specific guide (Italian Vegetarian Association, 2004; UK£8). For more information, visit your local bookstore or health food store, and consult *The Vegetarian Traveler: Where to Stay if You're Vegetarian, Vegan, Environmentally Sensitive*, by Jed and Susan Civic (Larson Publications; US$16). Vegetarians will also find numerous resources on the web; try www.happycow.net and www.vegetariansabroad.com for starters.

Lactose intolerance also does not have to be an obstacle to eating well. Though it may seem like everybody in Italy but you is devouring pizza and *gelato*, there are ways for even the lactose intolerant to indulge in local cuisine. In restaurants ask for items without *latte* (milk), *formaggio* (cheese), *burro* (butter), or *crema* (cream). Or order the cheeseless delicacy, *pizza marinara*.

Travelers who keep kosher should contact synagogues in larger cities for information on kosher restaurants. Your own synagogue or college Hillel should have access to lists of Jewish institutions across Italy. If you are strict in your observance, you may have to prepare your own food on the road. A good resource is the *Jewish Travel Guide*, edited by Michael Zaidner (Vallentine Mitchell; US$18). For listings of kosher restaurants in Italy, visit www.jewishitaly.org or http://shamash.org/kosher, a kosher restaurant database. Travelers looking for halal restaurants may find www.zabihah.com useful.

OTHER RESOURCES

Let's Go tries to cover all aspects of budget travel, but we can't put *everything* in our guides. Listed below are books and websites that can serve as jumping-off points for your own research.

USEFUL PUBLICATIONS

Culture Shock!: Italy, Alessandro Falassi and Raymond Flower. Helpful tips for travelers about Italian life and culture. Graphic Arts Center Publishing Company, 2005 (US$13).

Italy: The Best Travel Writing from the New York Times, Umberto Eco and *New York Times* writers. With stunning photographs, this anthology shows and tells the wonders of each town and city of Italy. Harry N. Abrams, Inc., 2005 (US$50).

Living, Studying, and Working in Italy: Everything You Need to Know to Live la Dolce Vita, Monica Larner and Travis Ward. A comprehensive guide for an extended stay or permanent Italian move. Henry Holt and Co., 2003 (US$17).

Touring Club Italiano (TCI), C. Italia 10, Milan (☎02 85 261; www.touringclub.com). Detailed maps and road atlases, as well as guides on the food, heritage, and nature of Italy's regions.

WORLD WIDE WEB

Almost every aspect of budget travel is accessible via the web. In 10min. at the keyboard, you can make a hostel reservation, get advice on travel hot spots from other travelers, or find out when your trains leaves from Rome to Vienna.

Listed here are some regional and travel-related sites to start off your surfing; other relevant websites are listed throughout the book. Because website turnover is high, use search engines (e.g., www.google.com) to strike out on your own.

 WWW.LETSGO.COM Our website features extensive content from our guides; a community forum where travelers can connect with each other, ask questions or advice, and share stories and tips; and expanded resources to help you plan your trip. Visit us to browse by destination and to find information about ordering our titles.

THE ART OF TRAVEL

Backpacker's Ultimate Guide: www.bugeurope.com. Tips on packing, transportation, and where to go. Also tons of country-specific travel information.

BootsnAll.com: www.bootsnall.com. Numerous resources for independent travelers, from planning your trip to reporting on it when you get back.

Expats in Italy: www.expatsinitaly.com. Offers advice from non-Italians living in Italy.

How to See the World: www.artoftravel.com. A compendium of great travel tips, from cheap flights to self defense to interacting with local culture.

Slow Travel Italy: www.slowtrav.com/italy. Mission includes promoting longer stays at each destination with quality over quantity. Provides comprehensive instructions on navigating Italian roads, railways, customs, and much more. Includes numerous links to helpful websites. Also posts personal blogs and travel stories.

Travel Intelligence: www.travelintelligence.net. A large collection of travel writing by distinguished travel writers.

Travel Library: www.travel-library.com. A fantastic set of links for general information and personal travelogues.

World Hum: www.worldhum.com. An independently produced collection of "travel dispatches from a shrinking planet."

INFORMATION ON ITALY

CIA World Factbook: www.odci.gov/cia/publications/factbook/index.html. Tons of vital statistics on Italy's geography, government, economy, and people.

Geographia: www.geographia.com. Highlights, culture, and people of Italy.

TravelPage: www.travelpage.com. Links to official tourist office sites in Italy.

PlanetRider: www.planetrider.com. A subjective list of links to the "best" websites covering the culture and tourist attractions of Italy.

World Travel Guide: www.travel-guides.com. Helpful practical info.

ESSENTIALS

LIFE AND TIMES

From da Vinci to Gucci, Italy has consistently set the world standard for innovation and elegance. Defined by the legacy of the Roman Empire and the prominence of the Catholic Church, its artistic, intellectual, and cultural developments have survived the centuries and today form the foundation of modern civilization. Although Italy has the most UNESCO World Heritage Sites, its history has been marked as much by unresolved conflict as by accomplishment. Haunted by centuries of foreign rule, fragmented governments, and regional disputes, Italy's allegiances are often torn between past and present, local and national. Italy's continued reliance upon past traditions is evident even in the last century in its struggle to overcome the vestiges of fascism, its delayed passage of women's suffrage until 1945, and its continuously strict observance of Catholic customs. Though both Roman rule and the Risorgimento came close to uniting the country's varied regions, distinct regional identities and continuing tensions between North and South persist. Italy's present is a constant negotiation between tradition and progress, unity and independence, as it endeavors to transform its triumphant past into an equally glorious future.

HISTORY AND POLITICS

ITALY BEFORE ROME (UNTIL 753 BC)

Archaeological excavations at Isernia date Italy's earliest inhabitants to the Paleolithic Era (100,000-70,000 BC). Perhaps the most important find has been Ötzi, a 5000-year-old iceman (p. 361) found in 1991 encased deep inside the icy Dolomites. The Bronze Age also brought more sophisticated settlements, and by the 7th century BC, the **Etruscans** had established their stronghold in present-day Tuscany and conquered much of Italy. Their growth was checked by increasing Greek influence along the Mediterranean coast. Forming what the Romans would later call **Magna Graecia,** the Greeks began to establish colonies, which were for the most part autonomous, along the coast of Puglia, at Cumae in Campania, and throughout Calabria and Sicily. These city-states gradually gained naval supremacy over their Etruscan competitors, but by the 3rd century BC, the power of both Greeks and Etruscans declined as another force swelled in the central mainland—the Romans. As they conquered *Magna Graecia*, the Romans inherited their predecessors' rich cultural history.

ANCIENT ROME (753 BC-AD 476)

THE MONARCHY (753-509 BC)

Although various stories recount the founding of Rome, the tale of Romulus and Remus is the most famous. According to

3000 BC
Ötzi, the prehistoric hunter, goes on his last hunt.

1600 BC
Paintings of bikini-like garments are drawn on cave walls. Who knew cave-women could be so scandalous?!

734 BC
The Corinthians send a boatload of ancient adventurers to found Syracuse on the island of Sicily.

753 BC
Romulus and Remus found Rome, but brotherly love soon deteriorates to fratricide.

616 BC
The Etruscan kings come to power in Rome and become known for tyranny.

509 BC
The Roman Republic is established.

legend, one of the seven Vestal Virgins, priestesses who protect Rome's Eternal Flame, conceived the twins **Romulus** and **Remus** when she lost her virginity to Mars, the god of war. In a fury over the shame his niece brought to the family name, her royal uncle ordered the infants killed. They were instead laid by the Tiber River; various accounts describe their rescue, though one of the most common depictions is of Romulus and Remus suckling at the teats of a she-wolf who adopted them (an excellent example can be found in a sculpture dating to 500 BC, in the Musei Capitolini; p. 150). In 753 BC, the brothers founded Rome together on the Palatine Hill. While Romulus was building the wall around the Palatine, however, Remus insulted the height of the wall by showing he could jump over it. Angered by this insult, Romulus killed his brother and became the first king of Rome, which was named in his honor. Eventually, the Etruscan kings forced themselves into power, and by 616 BC, their **Tarquin dynasty** was infamous for its tyranny. After Prince Sextus Tarquinius raped **Lucretia** in 509 BC, her husband Lucius Brutus expelled the Tarquins and established the **Roman Republic.** Although it is likely that Rome was ruled by kings and may have overthrown a tyrant, all of the story's details are a first-century BC invention.

THE REPUBLIC (509-27 BC)

The end of the monarchy and the foundation of the Republic led to new questions about equality and rights. The Republic faced social struggles between upper-class patricians, who enjoyed full participation in the Senate, and middle- and lower-class plebeins, who were denied political involvement. In 450 BC, the **Laws of the Twelve Tables,** the first codified Roman laws, made a slight concession by at least making the law public and allowing some political liberties, which created a class of plebeian elites. The defeat of Tarentum (modern day Taranto) in 272 BC completed the Roman conquest of mainland Italy.

450 BC
Roman Law is codified in the Twelve Tables.

390 BC
In one of the most recent military triumphs for the French, the Gauls sack Rome.

Never satisfied, the Romans went on to conquer **Sicily** in 241 BC and to wrest **Sardinia** in 238 BC from the **Carthaginians,** an extremely successful Phoenician colony. With the conquest of Sardinia, the Romans controlled all of modern-day Italy.

The spoils of war that enriched Rome actually undermined its stability by creating further class inequality. In 133 BC Tiberius Gracchus, the first of the two **Gracchi brothers,** attempted to push through land reforms, but was assassinated. Ten years later his brother Gaius again attempted reforms with the same results. Demands for land redistribution led to riots against the patrician class and then to the **Social War** in 91 BC. The patrician general **Sulla** saw his chance for glory in the social and political unrest, defeated his rivals in 82 BC, and quickly reorganized the constitution to name himself dictator.

91 BC
Riots against the patrician class lead to the Social War.

In 73 BC, **Spartacus,** an escaped gladiatorial slave, led an army of 70,000 slaves and impoverished farmers on a two-year rampage around the Italian peninsula. Sulla's close associates **Marcus Crassus** and **Pompey the Great** quelled the uprising and took power in Rome. One can see a gaudy Marxist version of the events, starring a buff Kirk Douglass and a creepy Laurence Olivier, in the anachronistic 1960 film *Spartacus*.

Rich Crassus and arrogant Pompey joined forces with ambitious **Julius Caesar,** the conqueror of Gaul, but their alliance rapidly fell apart. By 45 BC, Caesar had defeated his "allies" and emerged as the Republic's leader, naming himself Dictator for Life. Angered by Caesar's pandering to the poor, an aristocratic coalition, led by **Brutus,** assassinated the reform-oriented leader on the Ides (15th) of March, 44 BC. Caesar's death created yet another power vacuum as would-be successors struggled for the helm. In 31 BC, Octavian, Caesar's adopted heir, emerged victorious over the decadent Marc Antony and his exotic mistress Cleopatra, and was granted the title of **Augustus,** which means "majestic," in 27 BC.

THE EMPIRE (27 BC-AD 476)

As the center of the world's largest and most powerful empire, Rome eventually reached as far as modern Britain in the north and Iran in the east. Political power and economic prosperity brought about great cultural achievement, and Roman civilization and language made a lasting impact on even the farthest territories.

Augustus was the first of the Empire's **Julio-Claudian** rulers (27 BC-AD 68). Superficially following Republican traditions, he did not call himself *rex* (king), but *princeps* (first citizen). His principate (27 BC-AD 14) is considered the Golden Age of Rome, and this period of (relative) stability and prosperity, the *Pax Romana* (Roman Peace), continued until 180 AD. During this time, Augustus extended Roman law and civic culture, beautified Rome, and reorganized its administration. For all of his excellent reforms, Augustus ran a tight ship. He even exiled his own daughter, **Julia,** possibly for promiscuity.

The Empire continued to expand despite the fact that two of its emperors, **Caligula** (AD 37-41) and **Nero** (AD 54-68), during this time were mad. Following a series of civil wars after Nero's death in 68 AD, the **Flavian** dynasty (AD 69-96 AD) ushered in a period of prosperity, extended to new heights by **Trajan** (AD 98-117), who conquered the regions at the borders of the Black Sea. The Empire reached astounding geographical limits, encompassing Western Europe, the Mediterranean islands, England, North Africa, and part of Asia. Following Trajan, **Hadrian** (AD 117-130) established the **Antonine** dynasty (AD 117-193). The Antonines, especially philosopher-emperor **Marcus Aurelius,** were known for their enlightened leadership. When **Septimius Severus** (AD 146-211) won the principate after yet another civil war, he founded the **Severan** dynasty (AD 193-235).

Weak governments and rapid inflation led to near anarchy in the 3rd century. Then a formerly obscure general, **Diocletian** (AD 284-305), divided the empire into two eastern and two western regions, each with its own ruler. Diocletian's administrative system fell apart under **Constantine** (AD 272-337), who changed religion perhaps more than anyone since Jesus Christ himself. Before the Battle of the Milvian Bridge in AD 312, he

73 BC
Spartacus leads a revolt of 70,000 slaves.

49 BC
Caesar and Cleopatra get it on.

45 BC
Julius Caesar names himself Dictator for Life.

44 BC
Caesar is assassinated on the Ides of March.

27 BC
Augustus becomes the first Roman emperor.

19 BC
Virgil finishes his *Aeneid.* After 2,000 years, we're still not really sure what he meant.

3 BC
Jesus happens.

AD 37
Emperor Caligula tries to make his horse a senator.

AD 64
Nero plays his fiddle while Rome burns.

AD 79
Mount Vesuvius erupts and destroys Pompeii and Herculaneum.

LIFE AND TIMES

AD 80
The Colosseum hosts its inaugural games.

AD 190
Emperor Commodus calls himself Hercules and fights in the arena as a gladiator.

AD 313
The Edict of Milan grants all, though particularly Christians, freedom to worship.

AD 380
Christianity becomes the official religion of the Roman Empire.

AD 476
The last western Roman Emperor abdicates.

1088
The Bologna School of Law becomes Europe's first university.

1266-1273
Thomas Aquinas writes the *Summa Theologica.*

1285
Pope Martin IV, immortalized as a glutton in Dante's *Inferno,* dies of indigestion.

Mid-13th century
Eyeglasses are invented in Italy

1314
Dante's *Inferno* is published.

claimed he saw a cross of light in the sky, emblazoned with the words "by this sign you shall conquer." When victory followed, he converted to Christianity and issued the **Edict of Milan** in AD 313 abolishing religious discrimination. In 330 AD he began the process of moving the capital to Byzantium, renaming the city **Constantinople** (present-day Istanbul) in his honor. These changes split the Empire permanently into the stronger and wealthier Byzantine Empire and the down-sized Roman Empire, which struggled to integrate a large barbarian immigrant population. **Alaric,** king of the Visigoths, sacked Rome in AD 410, dealing a crushing blow to Roman morale. The Roman Emperor **Honorius** was so delirious that he thought the imminent fall of Rome referred to the death of his pet rooster, Roma. The final symbolic blow came in AD 476 when the German chief **Odoacer** crowned himself king after putting the last western emperor, Romulus Augustulus, under house arrest.

MIDDLE AGES (476-1375 AD)

Though sometimes called the "Dark Ages," the near millennium between the fall of Rome and the emergence of the Renaissance was not a cultural wasteland. Instead, this complex period of secular and religious power struggles resulted in the establishment of institutions like the royal court and feudal society. External influences from barbarian tribes, Arabic kingdoms, and the Germanic empire brought a blast of fresh air to counteract the former empire's decay.

While the East continued to thrive as the **Byzantine Empire,** the fall of the Roman Empire in the West left room for the growing strength of the papacy. **Pope Gregory I** (the Great; also known for the Gregorian chant; see p. 80) began to negotiate treaties independent of the Emperor instead of relying upon him for protection. With Arabs and Byzantines advancing on Italian territory, the Pope called upon the barbarian chieftain **Charlemagne** to uphold **Roman Catholicism.** Adding Italy to the Holy Roman Empire (not to be confused with the fallen Roman Empire), Charlemagne was crowned emperor of Christian Europe by Pope Leo III on Christmas Day, AD 800. Pope Urban II further increased the Church's strength by launching the **First Crusade** to liberate the Holy Land in 1095.

Charlemagne's successors were unable to maintain the new Empire, and in the following centuries, Italy became a playing field for petty wars. The instability of the 12th, 13th, and 14th centuries resulted in a division of power between city-states and rival families, leading to intense regional divisions that still exist today. Both European ruling houses and the Vatican enjoyed setting Italians, most notably the **Guelphs** and **Ghibellines** in the 12th and 13th centuries against each other. The pro-papal Guelphs managed to expel the imperial-minded Ghibellines from major northern cities by the mid-13th century. The victorious Guelphs then split into two rival factions, the **Blacks** and the **Whites,** and battled for power, exiling each other every few years. After the Whites exiled the Blacks from Florence in 1300, the Blacks came back with a vengeance in 1302 and rid the city of the Whites. The politically minded Florentine poet **Dante Alighieri** (1265-1321) was permanently exiled to Ravenna for his allegiance to the Whites, and wrote *La Divina Commedia* (p. 79) as an attempt to justify himself in the eyes of his fellow Florentines.

Church separated from state when Holy Roman Emperor **Henry IV** (1084-1105) denounced **Pope Gregory VII** (1073-1085) as a "false monk." Gregory in turn threatened the Emperor's nobles with excommunication. The terrified Emperor gave in to the Pope, but then came back with an army that defeated the Church's forces. The destabilization of Church power reached its zenith during the **Babylonian Captivity** (1309-1377), when the papacy was moved from Rome to Avignon and was supposedly held "captive" by the French kings. The disorder and confusion sparked the **Great Schism** (1378-1417), when three popes simultaneously claimed the holy title. The conflict was overshadowed by an outbreak of the **Black Death,** also called the bubonic plague, in 1347 which killed one-third of Europe's population, and recurred in Italy every July over the next two centuries.

RENAISSANCE (1375-1540)

After the Middle Ages came the great rebirth, or **Rinascimento** (Renaissance), growing out of a rediscovery of Greek and Latin texts and new emphasis on high culture. Pinpointing its origins has always been problematic, though historian Hans Baron has argued that the Italian tendency toward friendly competition spurred the rise of **civic humanism** by compelling city officials to bid for the best minds of the era, creating a market for intelligence.

Rising out of the obscurity of the Middle Ages were the exalted **Medici** clan in Florence, the **Visconti** in Milan, and the **House of Este** in Ferrara. When not stabbing each other in cathedrals, these ruling families instituted a series of humanist-minded economic and social reforms. **Cosimo** and **Lorenzo (Il Magnifico)** consolidated power and broadened the scope of the Medici family's activities from banking and warring to patronizing the arts. They engaged in a high-stakes political battle with sword-wielding **Pope Julius II** to bring Michelangelo to Florence and would have prevailed were it not for his Sistine Chapel commission (p. 147).

Just as things were getting interesting, an ascetic Dominican friar set out to spoil the fun. Infamous **Girolamo Savonarola** was ferociously opposed to what he perceived as the excesses of the Church. In 1497, Savonarola's followers did the deranged priest's bidding by collecting and burning thousands of "immoral" books and other objects of vanity, including cosmetics, fine dresses and musical instruments. The event became known as **The Bonfire of the Vanities,** and participants ranged from enraged Florentine clergy to a reformed Botticelli, who even threw several of his own paintings of mythological figures onto the pyre. Savonarola's power over the Florentine public pushed him into such great criticism of the clergy that a furious **Pope Alexander VI** tried to silence the pesky friar by excommunicating him. Savonarola persevered until the fickle Florentines—tired of his nagging—tortured and hanged him from the top of the **Palazzo Vecchio,** then finally burned him at the stake.

Princes hungry for power continued the Italian tradition of petty warfare, leaving the door open for foreign invasion. The

1347-1349
"Bring out your dead! Bring out your dead!" The Black Death sweeps through Europe.

1420
Brunelleschi begins a lifetime of work on the *duomo* in Florence.

1492
In fourteen-hundred-and-ninety-two Columbus sailed the ocean blue.

1504
Michelangelo sculpts *David.*

1505
Machiavelli writes *The Prince.*

1506
Mona Lisa Gherardini sits for Leonardo da Vinci's *Mona Lisa.*

1512
Michelangelo finishes frescoing the Sistine Chapel.

1564
Gabriele Fallopio invents the condom.

LIFE AND TIMES

1612
Santorio Santorio invents the first thermometer.

1633
Galileo is condemned for heresy by papal authorities.

1662
The Church of Rome declares that chocolate should not be considered food and can therefore be consumed in liquid form during fasting.

1725
Vivaldi writes *The Four Seasons*.

1748
The first excavations begin at Pompeii.

1797
Napoleon invades. "Who's short now?" he allegedly demanded.

1804
Napoleon declares himself the monarch of the Kingdom of Italy.

1815
The Congress of Vienna breaks up the Kingdom of Italy.

1848-1860
Camillo Cavour struggles to unify the peninsula.

1861
Italy's first parliament meets in Turin.

1883
Carlo Collodi writes *Pinocchio*.

weakened cities yielded in the 16th century to the invading Spanish armies of **Charles V.** The fighting continued until 1559 when Spain finally gained control over all Italian cities except Venice. Despite the political unrest plaguing Italy at the time, several prominent Italians embarked to make a splash on the world scene. **Christopher Columbus,** a native of Genoa funded by Queen Isabella of Spain, set sail to discover a faster route to Asia and opened the door to a whole New World of exploration with his 1492 discovery of the Caribbean. The Florentine **Amerigo Vespucci** made his own expeditions across the Atlantic, leaving his name on both Americas, and **Galileo Galilei,** despite the Church's opposition, suggested that the Earth spins around the sun. During his trail for heresy, he recanted, but mumbled "*eppur si muove*" ("but it does move") after the Inquisition ruled him guilty. He died under house arrest in 1642.

FOREIGN RULE (1540-1815)

Once the seat of the mightiest empire of the Western world, the Italian peninsula could no longer support the economic demands placed upon it by the Holy Roman Empire. **Charles II,** the last Spanish Habsburg ruler, died in 1700, sparking the War of the Spanish Succession. Italy, weak and decentralized, became the booty in battles between the Austrian Habsburgs and the French and Spanish Bourbons.

A century later, **Napoleon** decided to solve the disputes by taking all the spoils for himself. In the course of his 19th-century march through Europe, the little emperor with big hopes united much of Italy into the Italian Republic and incidentally fostered national sovereignty. Napoleon declared himself the monarch of the newly united **Kingdom of Italy** in 1804. After Napoleon's fall in 1815 at the **Battle of Waterloo,** the **Congress of Vienna** carved up Italy, unsurprisingly granting considerable control to Austria. Exiled, Napoleon spent his last days amidst the charms of tiny Elba (p. 493), an island off the Tuscan coast.

THE ITALIAN NATION (1815-PRESENT)

UNIFICATION

Following the Congress of Vienna, a long-standing grudge against foreign rule sparked the **Risorgimento,** a nationalist movement that culminated in political unification in 1860. **Giuseppe Mazzini, Giuseppe Garibaldi,** and **Camillo Cavour,** the movement's leaders, are honored on innumerable street signs. **Vittorio Emanuele II,** whose name also crowds Italian maps, was crowned as the first ruler of the independent Kingdom of Italy in 1860. He expanded the nation by annexing the north and central regions with Rome and the Veneto joining in 1870.

Though Italy was unified under a single name, tensions arose between the different regions. The north wanted to protect its money from the needs of the agrarian south, and cities were wary of surrendering power to a central administration. The defiant **Pope Pius IX** (1846-1878), who had lost power to the kingdom, refused to acknowledge Italian acquisition of Rome and began calling himself a prisoner in the Vatican. During **World War I,** nationalism increased as Italy fought against Austria, having been promised territory for its alliance with Russia, Britain, and France.

THE FASCIST REGIME

WWI's chaotic aftermath paved the way for fascism under **Benito Mussolini,** *Il Duce* ("the leader"), who promised strict order and stability for the young nation. He established the world's first fascist regime in 1919 and expelled all opposing parties. As Mussolini initiated domestic development programs and aggressive foreign policies, sentiments toward the fascist leader ran from intense loyalty to belligerent discontent. In 1940, Italy entered **World War II** on the side of its **Axis** ally, Hitler's Nazi Germany. Success for the Axis powers came quickly but was short-lived: the Allies landed in Sicily in 1943, pushing Mussolini from power. Later that year, Mussolini established the **Republic of Salò,** a Nazi puppet state based in Salò (p. 285). As a final indignity, he and his mistress, **Claretta Petacci,** were captured in Milan and executed by infuriated citizens, their naked bodies hung upside-down in public. In 1945, after nearly three years of occupation, Italy was finally completely freed from Nazi control, but tension persisted between those supporting the monarchy and those favoring a return to fascism.

POST-WAR POLITICS

The end of WWII did little but highlight the Italian peninsula's intense factions. In the 62 years since the end of the war, Italy has changed governments more than 60 times. The **Constitution,** adopted in 1948, established a democratic Republic, with a president, a prime minister, a bicameral parliament, and an independent judiciary. The **Christian Democratic Party (DC)** soon triumphed over the **Socialists (PSI)** as the primary player in the government of the Republic. Over 300 parties fought for supremacy in parliament; unsuprisingly, none could claim a majority. Ultimately, tenuous party coalitions formed instead.

Italian economic recovery began with industrialization in the 1950s—Lamborghini billboards and factory smokestacks quickly appeared alongside old cathedral spires and large glowing crucifixes on northern cities' skylines. Despite the **Southern Development Fund,** which was established to build roads, construct schools, and finance industry, the traditionally agrarian south lagged behind the more industrial north; this economic inequality contributed to much of the regional strife that persists today. Economic success gave way to violence in the late 1960s, especially the *autunno caldo* (hot autumn) of 1969, a season of strikes, demonstrations, and riots by university students and factory workers, which foreshadowed greater violence in the 70s. During the period of *Strategia della Tensione* (Strategy of Tension) in the early 70s, right-wing terrorists detonated bombs as public manifestations of political discontent, typically trying to blame them on political opponents. The most shocking episode was the 1978 kidnapping and murder of ex-Prime Minister **Aldo Moro** by a group of left-wing terrorists, the

1896
Italo Marcioni invents the ice cream cone.

1915
Italy enters WWI.

1919
Mussolini heads the world's first fascist regime.

1938
Enrico Fermi wins the Nobel Prize for Physics for directing the first controlled nuclear chain reaction.

1946
The Vespa Scooter is invented by Corradino d'Ascanio, so named for its resemblance to a wasp (*vespa* in Italian).

1948
Italy adopts a constitution, establishing a democratic Republic.

1957
European Economic Community (EEC) founded. Italy, charter member: "Our economy will be stable forever!" to riotous laughter from England.

1969
Riots shake Italian streets.

1972
Francis Ford Coppola directs *The Godfather.*

LIFE AND TIMES

1975
The Giorgio Armani
Company is
founded.

1978
Aldo Moro, a five-
time Italian Prime
Minister, is kid-
napped and mur-
dered by left-wing
terrorists.

1982
Italian soccer team
wins the World Cup
in Spain.

1994
Berlusconi
becomes prime
minister, but is
forced to resign
eight months later.

1999
Roberto Benigni
wins three Oscars
for *La Vita è Bella*.

1999
Italy enters the
European Mone-
tary Union and
adopts the euro.

2001
Berlusconi
becomes Prime
Minister (again).

April 2, 2005
Pope John Paul II
dies after a 26-year
reign.

April 19, 2005
Pope Benedict XVI
is elected.

April 20, 2005
Berlusconi resigns
as Prime Minister.

Brigate Rosse (Red Brigades). The demonstrations and violence of the 70s challenged the conservative Social Democrats. In 1983, **Bettino Craxi** became Italy's first Socialist prime minister, but fell from grace in a corruption scandal, avoiding jail time by fleeing to Tunisia, where he died in 2000.

RECENT DEVELOPMENTS

Italians have always been enamored with powerful, charismatic leaders. Living up to expectations, Italian government officials have rarely shied away from questionable maneuvers intended to bring them more power. Recognizing corruption in his own government, **Luigi Scalfaro**, elected in 1992, launched the *Mani Pulite* (Clean Hand) campaign. With the help of anti-corruption judge **Antonio di Pietro,** he uncovered the *Tangentopoli* (Bribesville) scandal. This unprecedented political crisis found over 1200 officials guilty of bribery. Fallout from the investigation included the 1993 bombing of the Uffizi Gallery in Florence, the suicides of 10 indicted officials, and the murders of anti-Mafia investigators.

ENTER BERLUSCONI. The election of media tycoon **Silvio Berlusconi** as prime minister in 1994 raised eyebrows. The self-made billionaire's empire included three private TV channels, political influence over three state-run channels, a major newspaper, and the AC Milan soccer team. The fragile web of coalitions that enabled Berlusconi's election collapsed after just eight months, forcing him to resign.

Shortly after the collapse of Berlusconi's government, the platform of the reactionary Northern League became separatist under the extremist (and some say racist) **Umberto Bossi.** Aiming to push the economy to meet the European Union's economic standards, the Northern League called for a split from the south in order to create the **Republic of Padania,** a nation for northerners only. The 1996 elections brought the center-left coalition, the **l'Ulivo** (Olive Tree), to power, with **Romano Prodi,** a Bolognese professor, economist, and non-politician, serving as prime minister. Ultimately, Prodi helped stabilize Italian politics. For the first time in modern history, Italy was run by two equal coalitions: the center-left l'Ulivo and the center-right **Il Polo** (Berlusconi's Freedom Alliance, without the Northern League). Despite the optimism of Prodi's government, his coalition lost a vote of confidence in October 1998.

Prodi was succeeded by former communist **Massimo D'Alema.** D'Alema and **Carlo Ciampi** introduced fiscal reforms and pushed a "blood and tears" budget that qualified Italy for entrance into the European Monetary Union in January 1999. Despite D'Alema's successes, he stepped down in May 2000 and was replaced by former Treasury Minister **Giuliano Amato.** Nicknamed "Dr. Subtle," Amato is one of the people credited with the institution of 1999's budget reforms. Perhaps the nickname also derives from Amato's ability to avoid scandal; he was one of few to emerge unscathed from corruption crack-downs in the early 90s, which led to late Socialist Party leader Bettino Craxi's flight to Tunisia.

BERLUSCONI: TAKE TWO. Somehow or another Italy's richest man, Berlusconi, secured his re-election as prime minister again in May 2001. Downplaying corruption charges, he won 30% of the popular vote to head Italy's 59th government since WWII with his Forza Italia party. Berlusconi reaffirmed his commitment to the US, courting President George W. Bush in several meetings and sending 2700 troops to Iraq; left-wing opposition has consistently urged withdrawal of these troops. In European foreign policy, the Prime Minister has focused more on domestic than on European issues, creating some tension between Italy and its neighbors. Most notable is Berlusconi's 2004 comparison of one German European Parliament member to a guard in a Nazi concentration camp, a comment which caused considerable discord between the governments of Italy and Germany, and caused a miffed Chancellor Gerhard Schroeder to cancel his summer holiday in Italy. Other scandals also marred Berlusconi's tenure, including proposed bills in favor of laxer corruption laws. In fact, Berlusconi himself came under investigation with respect to corruption in the 1980s, but courts cleared him of all charges in December 2004.

PRODI: THERE'S A NEW SHERIFF IN TOWN. Berlusconi's unpopularity mounted as a result of troop deployment in Iraq, and an economic recession caused some to call for the reinstitution of *lire*. Berlusconi resigned again as Prime Minister in April 2005, only to form a new coalition several days later. History repeated itself as Romano Prodi won over Berlusconi in the national elections of April 2006, much like he did 10 years earlier. Prodi has not found ruling the Italians to be any easier. A controversy over funding the Italian troops in Afghanistan in early 2007, followed by a dispute over expanding the US Army Base in Vicenza (p. 339), pushed Prodi to the limit. He offered his resignation to President Giorgio Napolitano in February 2007. Napolitano did not accept the resignation enthusiastically and called for a vote of confidence in the legislature. After a clear showing of confidence from both houses, Prodi decided to remain; however, considering Italy's aversion to stability, no one can get too comfortable.

April 23, 2005
Berlusconi's Back! The embattled ruler becomes Prime Minister once again.

2006
Turin hosts Winter Olympics.

May 2, 2006
Berlusconi begrudgingly resigns as Prime Minister, leaving Romano Prodi in his place for the second time.

July 9, 2006
Italy defeats a gaggle of cheating Frenchmen to win World Cup.

February 21, 2007
Frustrated by his opposition, Romano Prodi attempts to resign.

PEOPLE

DEMOGRAPHICS

Despite the stereotype of large families, Italian women today have an average of only 1.3 babies each. With a death rate that narrowly outstrips its birth rate and increasing immigration, Italy's population is holding approximately steady at its current 58 million. Immigration from China, Africa, Eastern Europe, and Middle Eastern countries functions to counteract the dwindling number of

Italians in the workforce. Although some consider immigration to be necessary for the economy, many Italians associate undocumented migrant labor with sex work or drug trafficking, despite efforts by the government to eliminate illegal immigration. The situation is only made worse by Italy's aging population distribution.

LANGUAGE

A descendant of Latin, Italian is part of the family of Romance languages, which includes French, Spanish, Portuguese, and Romanian. Many Italians, especially those in the South, will claim that the first foreign language they learn is Italian; spoken dialects and other variants still exist in various regions, a vestige of Italy's past division into city-states. The throaty **Neapolitan** of southern Italy can be difficult for a northerner to understand. Ligurians use a mix of Italian, Catalan, and French. Many Tuscan dialects substitute an "h" for every "c," so you might be called an "Amerihano" if you hail from the States. **Sardo,** spoken in Sardinia, bears little resemblance to standard Italian, constituting a separate language in itself. In the region of Friuli-Venezia Giulia, there can be as many as four languages spoken in one place—Slovene, Italian, German, and Friulian coexist in Canale. Conversely, citizens of some Italian regions do not speak any Italian at all: the population of Valle d'Aosta speaks mainly French, and Trentino-Alto Adige harbors a German-speaking minority. Standard Italian, developed in the 13th and 14th centuries as a literary dialect, today serves as the language used by schools, media, and literature. North of Rome, dialects are dying out in favor of this standard language, but accents still persist. Locals do their best to employ standard Italian with foreigners, although some may be hesitant to do so. Many Italians, especially older people or those living in rural areas, do not speak English, but most young people, big city dwellers, and those in the tourist industry do.

TALK TO THE HAND. Italians don't just talk with their mouths, they also use hand gestures. When dialects (or basic language skills) fall short, these are universal and instantly understood. To express frustration, as in, "Mamma mia, are you seriously going to fine me even though the signs says I can park here on Sundays?" put your hands together in a prayer-like position and shake them down and up, imploringly. Indignant? Hold all your fingers together, point them upward, and shake your wrist lightly back and forth. Don't care? Point your palm downwards and drag your fingers outwards from where your chin and neck meet. Ask around for more gems. But be sure not to get them confused, because in this context, actions really do speak louder than words.

LISTEN WITH YOUR EYES. First published in 1958 and re-released in 2005 by Chronicle Books, Bruno Munari's **Speak Italian: The Fine Art of the Gesture** waves its hands in every conceivable Italian way and provides a 'supplement to the Italian dictionary' by demystifying Italian hand gestures. A fun collection of black-and-white photos accompanied by explanations in Italian and English, this book will give you 'words' when you find yourself speechless.

RELIGION

As the home of the pope, the successor of the apostle St. Peter, Italy has been the center of the Roman Catholic faith for almost 2000 years. The **Lateran Pacts,** a treaty in 1929 between Pope Pius XI and Benito Mussolini, made the Vatican City a sovereign state within the city of Rome. It is the traditional and administrative capital of the Catholic Church. The treaty also made Catholicism the official religion of Italy, which it remained until 1984. Unsurprisingly, more than 90% of Italians identify themselves as Catholic. Nevertheless, the country is home to a substantial number of Protestants and nearly a million Muslims.

The death of Pope John Paul II in April 2005 stirred Catholics around the globe. Tens of thousands flooded the square in front of St. Peter's Basilica (p. 140) as the College of Cardinals gathered in the Sistine Chapel (p. 147) to elect a new Pope. Sworn to secrecy (a full transcript of the voting will not be made public for 100 years), the Cardinals locked inside the chapel cast four votes per day until a two-thirds majority was reached. After each round of voting, smoke from the chimneys of the Sistine Chapel signaled the results—gray smoke for failure to reach a consensus, and white smoke for a successful election. The process could have taken up to three and a half months (as it did in AD 180), but Cardinal Ratzinger of Munich (now Pope Benedict XVI) was elected on the second day of voting. At 78, Cardinal Ratzinger became the oldest elected pope since Clement XII in 1730. Although his past career indicated he might be overly dogmatic, Benedict has in fact displayed a noticeably softer touch. His first encyclical, *Deus Caritas Est* (God is Love), stressed that the love of God and neighbor as the core Christian life. However, he has also placed a great emphasis on opposing what he calls "the dictatorship of relativism" in the West and advocating the Church's conservative position on social issues like abortion, birth control and same-sex marriage, putting the Church at odds with many opposing activists.

The Church continues to play a substantial role in the lives of ordinary Italians. Most Italians continue to celebrate the feast day of their town's patron saint in annual celebrations, but church attendance is declining. Currently about one-third of the nation attends services weekly. Nevertheless, Italians are very conscientious about respecting churches, cathedrals, and other religious domains. In general, tourists are not allowed in religious spaces unless dressed modestly: covered shoulders for women and long pants for men. Furthermore, some churches do not allow visitors to take photographs because camera flashes damage fragile paintings and mosaics. When visiting churches, remember that the buildings are places of worship first and tourist attractions second.

ART AND ARCHITECTURE

In Italy, great works of art and architecture seem to spring from every street corner. In Rome, the Colosseum (p. 132) hovers above a city bus stop; in Florence, couples flirt in front of the *duomo* (p. 436); in Sicily, diners sit beneath Greek columns. Modern Italians may seem immune to this stunning visual history, but to anyone who hasn't grown up amid ancient columns and medieval fortresses, it's a feast for the senses.

ANCIENT ITALIAN ART

GREEKS. In the 8th century BC, the Greeks established colonies in southern Italy, peppering the region with magnificent **temples** and **theaters.** The best-preserved examples of Greek ruins are in Sicily—not Greece!—in the Valle dei Templi at Agrigento (p. 704) and Taormina (p. 679). Italy is also home to Roman copies of Greek **statues** and original Greek **bronzes;** the prized *Bronzi di Riace*, recovered from the Ionian Sea in 1972 after nearly 2500 years underwater, are now in Reggio di Calabria's Museo Nazionale della Magna Grecia (p. 636).

ETRUSCANS. Native Italian art history begins with the Etruscans, a people who lived on the Italian peninsula before the Romans. Loosely influenced by Greek art and inspired by both the everyday and the afterlife, Etruscan artwork is best known for its narrative quality. The Etruscan works that remain today include decorated **funeral statues, tomb paintings,** and **ceramic ash burial urns,** all of which depict Etruscan scenes and legends. However, because the Romans either destroyed or melted down a large proportion of Etruscan sculptures and bronzes, our modern perception of Etruscan art as solely funerary is skewed. Just like their art, the Etruscans mysteriously disappeared in the 3rd century BC. The Museum at the Villa Giulia in Rome (p. 151) houses many of the remaining Etruscan gems.

AND ROMANS (OH MY!). Roman art (200 BC-AD 500) is known for its vivid portrayal of the political aims and cultural values of Imperial Rome. **Sculptures, architecture,** and other masterpieces fall mainly into two categories: private household art and art in service of the state. Although art historians have traditionally used Greek statues as benchmarks for beauty and artistic skill, the sculpted portraiture developed by the Romans deserves separate recognition. Portraits of the **Republican period** (510-27 BC) were brutally honest, immortalizing wrinkles, scars, and even warts. The later **Imperial sculpture** (27 BC-AD 476) tended to blur the distinction between mortal and god in powerful, idealized images like *Augustus of Prima Porta* (Vatican Museums; p. 147). Later in the period, Roman art developed a flattened style of **portraiture,** with huge eyes looking out in an "eternal stare." The government sponsored **statues, monuments,** and **literary narratives** to commemorate leaders, heroes, and victories. Augustus was perhaps the best master of this form of self-promotion, as evidenced by his impressive **mausoleum** and **Ara Pacis** (Altar of Peace), both gracing the Piazza Augusto Imperatore in Rome (p. 153). Roman monuments evolved into decorated, concrete forms with numerous arches and columns, like the **Colosseum** (p. 132) and the **Pantheon** (p. 129).

Upper-class Romans had an appetite for sumptuous interior decoration. Scenes depicting gods and goddesses, exotic beasts, and street entertainers decorated sprawling villas, courtyards, and fancy shops. Some affluent patrons had their walls adorned with **frescoes,** which used the Greek technique of painting onto wet plaster walls to form a unique, time-resistant effect. It was also popular to hire craftsmen to fashion wall and floor **mosaics,** works of art created using thousands of finely shaded *tesserae* (geometrically-shaped fragments of colored pottery, tile or glass) cemented with mortar. The luxurious **Villa Romana del Casale** (p. 689), just outside Piazza Armerina, holds 40 rooms of stone mosaics, making it the world's largest work of intact artistic mosaics of the Late Roman period.

EARLY CHRISTIAN AND BYZANTINE ART

Fearing persecution, early Christians in Rome, Naples, and Syracuse hid inside haunting **catacombs** to worship their Christian God. But following Emperor Constantine's **Edict of Milan** in AD 313, which made Christianity legal in the declining Empire, the religion quickly became Rome's faith *du jour.* Even the Roman magistrate's basilica was altered to accommodate Christian services. **Transepts** were added to many Roman churches, creating crucifix-shaped architecture. Except for a few **sarcophagi** and **ivory reliefs,** Christian art slowly transitioned from sculpture to pictorial forms in order to depict religious narratives for the illiterate. Ravenna (p. 407) is a veritable treasure trove of the first Byzantine Golden Age, which ran from AD 526 to 726. Examples of these "instructional" mosaics can be seen in Ravenna's octagonal **Basilica of San Vitale** (AD 526-547), which is also one of the first churches to boast a free-standing *campanile* (bell tower).

MIDDLE AGES

ROMANESQUE. Although true classical Roman style would not be revived until the Renaissance, rounded Roman arches, heavy columns, and windowless churches came back into style in the period from AD 800 to 1200. The earliest Italian example of Romanesque architecture is **Basilica di Sant'Ambrogio** in Milan (p.

249), notable for its squat nave and groin vaults. In Tuscany, competition among Italian cities (particularly Florence and Pisa) to outdo their neighbors resulted in great architectural feats, most notably **San Miniato al Monte** (p. 448) and the **Duomo** in Pisa with its famously leaning *campanile* (p. 490). In the south, most notably in **Cattedrale di Monreale** (p. 655), sculptural detailings and intricate mosaics reflect Arab, Byzantine, and Norman influences on the Romanesque style.

GOTHIC. Beginning in the late 13th century, the Gothic movement filtered into Italy from France. Artists and architects rejoiced at the fantastic spaces and light created by the new vaulted technology and giant, multi-colored rose windows. The most impressive Gothic cathedrals include the **Basilica di San Francesco** in Assisi (p. 515), the **Basilica di Santa Maria Gloriosa dei Frari** in Venice (p. 326), and the **Santa Maria Novella** in Florence (p. 436). Secular structures like the **Ponte Vecchio** in Florence (p. 441) followed this stylistic trend too. The **Palazzo Ducale** in Venice (p. 323), spanning several canals with ornate bridges, represents the brilliant marriage of airy, lace-like Islamic stonework and Gothic style. In sculpture, **Nicola Pisano** (c. 1220-1278) created pulpits at both Pisa and Siena that combined Roman reliefs, Gothic form, and early Byzantine mosaics. By the end of the 13th century, Italians were bored by the emaciated torsos of suffering martyrs. **Cimabue** (c. 1240-1302) and **Duccio** (c. 1255-1318) introduced a second dimension and brighter colors, though bleeding Christians remained their subject of choice. Straddling the late Gothic and early Renaissance, **Giotto** (c. 1267-1337) is credited with noting that humans—not giants—look at pictures. He placed his work at eye level, putting the viewer on equal footing with his realistically rendered holy subjects. His frescoed masterpieces are on display at the Basilica di San Francesco in Assisi and the **Scrovegni Chapel** in Padua (p. 336).

RENAISSANCE

EARLY RENAISSANCE. Donatello's (1386-1466) *David* (c. 1430; at the **Bargello** in Florence; p. 442), the first free-standing nude since antiquity, marked the "rebirth" of sculpture without boundaries. His wooden *Mary Magdalene* in Florence (p. 438) similarly represents a departure from earlier, restrained traditions by emphasizing the woman's fallen and repentant side, depicting her in rags and with a sorrowful facial expression. Unlike Donatello's expressive portraiture, **Brunelleschi's** (1377-1446) mathematical studies of ancient Roman architecture became the cornerstone of Renaissance building. His engineering talent allowed him to raise the dome over **Santa Maria del Fiore** (p. 436) and showcase his mastery of proportions in the **Pazzi Chapel** (p. 446). **Lorenzo Ghiberti** (c. 1381-1455) designed two sets of bronze doors for the baptistry in Florence (p. 437), defeating Brunelleschi's doors in the contest of 1401. **Leon Battista Alberti** (1404-1472), a champion of visual perspective, designed Florence's **Santa Maria Novella** (p. 443) and Rimini's **Tempio Malatestiano** (p. 415), prototypes for future Renaissance palaces and churches. In painting, **Sandro Botticelli** (1444-1510) and his *The Birth of Venus* (p. 439), depicting the goddess floating on her tidal foam, epitomize the Italian Renaissance. **Masaccio** (1401-28) filled chapels with angels and gold-leaf and is credited with the first use of the mathematical laws of perspective. His figures in the **Brancacci Chapel** of Florence (p. 448) served as models for Michelangelo and Leonardo. An unlikely artist, **Fra Angelico** (c. 1400-1455) personified the tension between medieval and Renaissance Italy. Though a member of a militant branch of Dominican friars which opposed humanism on principle, Fra Angelico's works, seen at the **Museo della Chiesa di San Marco** in Florence (p. 445), exhibit the techniques of space and perspective endorsed by humanistic artists.

HIGH RENAISSANCE. From 1450 to 1520, the torch of distinction passed between two of art's greatest figures: da Vinci and Michelangelo. Branching out from the disciplines of sculpture and painting, **Leonardo da Vinci** (1452-1519) brilliantly excelled in subjects ranging from geology, engineering, and musical composition to human dissection and armaments design. *The Last Supper*, or *Il Cenacolo*, in Milan (p. 249), preserves the individuality of its figures despite its group context. His experimentations with *chiaroscuro*, or contrasts between light and shadow that highlight contours, and *sfumato*, which is a smoky or hazy effect of brush-work, secured his place as the century's great artistic innovator.

Michelangelo Buonarroti (1475-1564) was a jack of all trades in the art world, despite what he told Julius II after painting the Sistine Chapel ceiling: "I am not a painter!" Julius was so fond of the ceiling (p. 147) that he commissioned *The Last Judgment* for the wall above the chapel's altar. Michelangelo painted like a sculp-tor, boldly emphasizing musculature and depth, and sculpted like a painter, with lean, smooth strokes. Michelangelo's architectural achievements include his designs for the **Laurentian Library** in Florence (p. 445) and the dome on **St. Peter's Basilica** in Rome (p. 140). Classic examples of his sculpture include the *Pietà* in St. Peter's, the *David*, and the unfinished *Slaves* in Florence's Accademia (p. 444).

Other prominent Renaissance artists include **Raffaello** (1483-1520), a draftsman who created technically perfect figures. His frescoes in the papal apartments of the Vatican, including the *School of Athens* (p. 148), show his debt to classical standards. In addition to Michelangelo, the Venetian Renaissance school of artistic thought produced **Giorgione,** known as "The Great" (1478-1510), **Giovanni Bellini** (c. 1430-1516), the pre-eminent teacher within the school, and Bellini's protégé, the prolific **Titian** (1488-1576). Titian's works, including *Venus of Urbino* (1538), are notable for their realistic facial expressions and rich colors. In the **High Renais-sance,** the greatest architect after Michelangelo was **Donato Bramante** (1444-1514), famed for his work on the Tempietto of St. Peter in Rome.

MANNERISM

A heightened sense of aestheticism led to Mannerism, the style that dominated the High Renaissance from the 1520s until the birth of the Baroque style around 1590. Starting in Rome and Florence, Mannerist artists experimented with juxtaposi-tions of color and scale. For example, **Parmigianino** (1503-1540) and his *Madonna of the Long Neck* are emblematic of the movement's self-conscious distortions. Another painter, **Jacopo Tintoretto** (1518-1594), a Venetian Mannerist, was the first to paint multiple light sources within a single composition. The Mannerist period is also known for its architecture by designers such as **Giulio Romano** (c. 1499-1546) who rejected the Renaissance ideal of harmony. The villas and churches of archi-tect **Andrea Palladio** (1508-1580) were also remarkably innovative, particularly the **Villa Rotonda** outside Vicenza (p. 341). His other lasting contribution, the *Four Books of Architecture*, promoted his work and influenced countless architects, especially those of the Baroque movement.

BAROQUE AND ROCOCO

A 17th-century stylistic hybrid born of the Counter-Reformation and absolute monarchy, Baroque composition combined Mannerism's intense emotion with the Renaissance's grandeur to achieve a new expressive theatricality. Heavy on drama, emotion, and richness, Baroque art attempted to inspire faith in the Catho-lic Church and respect for earthly power. Painters of this era favored naturalism, a commitment to portraying nature in its raw state. **Caravaggio** (1573-1610), the epit-ome of Baroque painters, relied heavily on *chiaroscuro* and naturalism to create dramatically unsettling images. It is even rumored that he used the corpse of a prostitute recovered from Rome's Tiber River as a model for the Virgin Mary's body in *Death of the Virgin* (1606). **Gianlorenzo Bernini** (1598-1680), a prolific **High**

Baroque sculptor and architect, designed the overwhelming colonnade of St. Peter's Piazza and the awesome *baldacchino* inside. Drawing inspiration from Hellenistic works, Bernini's sculptures were orgies of movement, interacting violently with light and space. **Francesco Borromini** (1599-1667), Bernini's rival, was even more adept than his rival at shaping the walls of his buildings into lively, serpentine architectural masterpieces, as in his **San Carlo alle Quattro Fontane** (p. 139). Toward the end of the Baroque period, however, this grand style began to give way to the delicacy and elaborate ornamentation of **Rococo,** a light and graceful method originating in 18th-century France. Rococo motifs include seashells, clouds, flowers, and vines carved into woodwork and stone edifices. **Giovanni Battista Tiepolo** (1696-1770), with his brilliant palette and vibrant frescoes, was a prolific Venetian painter of allegories and the premier exemplar of the Italian Rococo style.

NINETEENTH-CENTURY ART

With the decline of Rococo came French-influenced **Neoclassicism,** which abandoned the overly detailed Rococo and dramatic Baroque methods in favor of a purer, more ancient construction. At first, the shift was almost too subtle to notice, primarily because the Neoclassical artists had no new materials on which they could base their Neotraditional works. With the early 17th-century discovery and excavation of Herculaneum and Pompeii, however, Neoclassical artists quickly found their ancient muses in the forms of recovered artifacts. One such Neoclassical artist was the sculptor **Antonio Canova** (1757-1822) who explored the formal Neoclassical style in his giant statues and bas-reliefs. His most famous work is the statue of Pauline Borghese (p. 148), which displays Neoclassical grace and purity of contour. Rebelling against the strict Neoclassical style, **Telemaco Signorini** (1835-1901), **Giovanni Fattori** (1825-1908), and **Silvestro Lega** (1826-1895) spearheaded the **Macchiaioli** group in Florence (c. 1855-65)—a group anticipating French Impressionism that believed a painting's meaning lay in its *macchie* (spots) of color rather than a narrative meaning. A technique called "blotting," which abruptly juxtaposed patches of color, was used to depict politicized scenes of battle and responses to everyday life.

TWENTIETH-CENTURY ART

The Italian **Futurist** painters, sculptors, and architects of the early 20th-century brought Italy to the cutting edge of art. Inspired by **Filippo Tommaso Marinetti's** (1876-1944) *Futurist Manifesto* of 1909, these Italian artists loved to glorify danger, war, and the 20th-century machine age. With pieces displayed in 1912's major Futurist exhibition in Paris, painters **Gino Severini** (1883-1966) and **Carlo Carrà** (1881-1966) and sculptor **Umberto Boccioni** (1882-1916) went beyond Cubism to celebrate the dynamism and energy of modern life by depicting several aspects of moving forms. The work of **Giorgio de Chirico** (1888-1978), some of which is currently on display at the Collezione Peggy Guggenheim in Venice (p. 327), depicts eerie scenes dominated by mannequin figures, empty space, and steep perspective. Although his mysterious and disturbing style, called *Pittura Metafisica*, was never successfully imitated, de Chirico inspired early Surrealist painters. Other 20th-century Italian artists include **Amadeo Modigliani** (1884-1920), a sculptor and painter who was highly influenced by African art and Cubism, and **Marcello Piacentini** (1881-1960) who created fascist architecture that imposed sterility upon classical motifs. In 1938, Piacentini designed the looming **EUR** in Rome (*Esposizione Universale Roma*) as an impressive reminder of the link between Mussolinian fascism and Roman imperialism.

In the Postwar Era, Italian art lacked unity but still produced noteworthy artists. **Lucio Fontana** (1899-1968) started **Spatialism,** a movement to bring art beyond the canvas towards a synthesis of color, sound, movement, time and space. His *taglio* (slash) canvases of the mid-1950s created a new dimension for the 2D surface with a simple linear cut. Conceptual artist **Piero Manzoni** (1933-1963) created a scandal in 1961 when he put his feces in 90 small cans labeled *Artist's Shit*, setting the price of the excrements at their weight in gold. In May 2007 Sotheby's sold a can for €124,000. In the late 1960s **Arte Povera** bridged the gap between art and life by integrating cheap everyday materials into pieces of art. **Michelangelo Pistoletto** (1933-) caused a clamor with his *Venus in Rags* (1967), a plaster cast of a classical Venus facing a pile of old rags, on display at the **Castello di Rivoli Museo d'Arte Contemporanea** in Turin (p. 173). While eclipsed by its Renaissance past, contemporary art in Italy thrives in select museums and at the bi-annual **Venice Biennale** (p. 332) showcasing the recent work of artists from Italy and around the world.

LIFE AND TIMES

LITERATURE

SEX, DRUGS, AND ROMAN MYTHOLOGY

The Romans stole their religion and mythology from anyone and everyone. Although much of their folklore comes from their own early traditions and Etruscan beliefs, much more of their mythology is a filtered form of Greek mythology. It is important to remember that Greek civilization across the Mediterranean flourished centuries before Rome. When Greek poets were reciting the *Odyssey* and *Iliad*, Rome was still an obscure farming village. During the last two centuries of the Roman Republic, roughly the last two centuries BC, interaction between the Greeks and Romans increased because the Romans were conquering the Greeks. When they were not forcing the city-states into submission, they took the time to embrace the Greek mythological system in the form of beautiful poems typically depicting lustful and petty gods. Previously, the Romans mostly had only boring and ambiguous agricultural gods, as well as the famous story of Romulus and Remus (p. 63).

LATIN LOVERS

ET IN ARCADIA EGO. As they gained dominance over the Hellenized Mediterranean, the Romans discovered the refined joys of literature. Plautus (c. 259-184 BC) and Terrence (d. 159 BC), for example, adapted Greek comedies into Latin while giving them their own Roman flair. The lyric, though occasionally obscene, poetry of Catullus (84-54 BC) demonstrates the complex relationship between Greece and Rome. Cicero (106-43 BC), a fiery and complicated Roman politician, orator, and author, whose prose has been central to Latin education since ancient times, is the definitive example of classical Latin. History buffs should check out the writing of Julius Caesar (100-44 BC), who gave a first-hand account of the expansion of Rome's empire in his *Gallic Wars*.

WHEN IN ROME... As a result of Augustus's patronage and the relative peace and prosperity of the time, Augustan Rome produced an array of literary talents. **Livy** (c. 59 BC-AD 17) wrote a mammoth history of Rome from the city's founding to his own time in *Ab Urbe Condita* ("From the Founding of the City"). Coining the phrase *"carpe diem,"* **Horace** (65-8 BC) wrote on love, wine, service to the state, hostile critics, and the pleasure of pastoral life in his *Odes*. **Ovid** (43 BC-AD 17) gave the world the *Metamorphoses*, a beautiful and sometimes racy collection of poetry. For unknown reasons, he angered Augustus so much that he was eventually exiled to modern-day Romania where he eventually died a broken man. **Suetonius's** (c. AD 69-130) *De Vita Caesarum* presents tabloid biographies of the first twelve Emperors, and **Tacitus's** (c. AD 55-116) *Histories* offers a biting synopsis of Roman war, diplomacy, scandal, and rumor during AD 69, the year of notorious Emperor Nero's death. It is widely considered stylistically the greatest work of history in Latin.

DARK AGES TO CULTURAL REBIRTH

DARK TIMES. Between classical antiquity and the Renaissance, authors usually remained anonymous, with the exception of notable religious figures like St. Thomas Aquinas (1225-1274). By the 13th century, Christianity had become the uniting factor of much of chaotic Europe. While this religious zeal was sometimes oppressive, it also ensured the survival of ancient texts and ideas, since monks of this period typically spent their days and nights copying ancient texts. Despite this tendency to preserve ancient thoughts, writers of the Dark Ages also began using a degraded form of Latin. Adding to this evolution of literature were troubadour songs (usually detailing romance at court) and Carolingian and Arthurian adventure stories which developed at the intersection of northern Italy, southern France, and northern Spain. These served as models for the medieval verses delivered by singers and poets who traveled throughout Europe. The invasion of Norman and Arab rulers into Sicily (1091-1224) and southern Italy also introduced diverse literary traditions.

ABANDON ALL HOPE, YE WHO ENTER HERE! Although the tumult of medieval life discouraged most literary musing in the late 13th century, three Tuscan writers, known as the *Tre Corone* (Three Crowns), resuscitated the written art: **Dante, Petrarch,** and **Boccaccio.** Although scholars do not agree on the precise dates of the literary Renaissance, many argue that the work of Dante Alighieri (1265-1321) marked its inception. Considered the father of modern Italian literature, Dante was one of the first poets in all of Europe to write using the *volgare* (common vernacular; Florentine, in Dante's case) instead of Latin. In his epic poem *La Divina Commedia*, he roams the three realms of the afterlife (*Inferno, Purgatorio, Paradiso*) with Virgil as his guide, meeting famous historical and mythological figures and his true love, Beatrice. In the work, Dante calls for social reform and indicts all those who contributed to Florence's moral downfall, including Popes and political figures—especially those who ordered his own political exile. **Petrarch** (1304-74), the second titan of the 13th century, more clearly belongs to the literary Renaissance. A scholar of classical Latin and a key proponent of humanist thought, he wrote sonnets to a married woman named Laura, collected in *Il Canzoniere*. The third member of this literary triumvirate, **Giovanni Boccaccio** (1313-1375), wrote the *Decameron*, a collection of 100 stories that range in tone from suggestive to vulgar. In one, a gardener has his way with an entire convent.

RENAISSANCE MEN. The 14th century saw the rise of **la Commedia dell'Arte,** a form of improvised theater with a standard plot structure and characters. Each character had its own mask and costume and a few fixed personality traits. The most famous character, *Arlecchino* (Harlequin), was easily identified by his diamond-patterned costume. By the 15th and 16th centuries, Italian authors were reviving classical sources in new ways. **Alberti** (1404-1472) and **Palladio** (1508-1580) wrote treatises on architecture and art theory. In 1528 **Baldassare Castiglione** (1478-1529) wrote *Il Cortegiano*, which instructed the Renaissance man on etiquette and other fine points of behavior. At the pinnacle of the Renaissance, **Ludovico Ariosto's** (1474-1533) *Orlando Furioso* (1516) described a whirlwind of military victories and unrequited love, and **Niccolò Machiavelli** (1469-1527) wrote *Il Principe* (The Prince), a grim assessment of what it takes to gain political power. In the spirit of the Renaissance, specialists in other fields tried writing: **Giorgio Vasari** (1511-1574) stopped redecorating Florence's churches to produce the ultimate primer on art history and criticism, *The Lives of the Artists*; **Benv-**

enuto **Cellini** (1500-1571) wrote about his art in *The Autobiography;* and **Michelangelo** (1475-1564) proved to be a prolific composer of sonnets.

MODERN TIMES

The 19th century brought Italian unification and the need for one language. Nationalistic "Italian" literature, an entirely new concept, grew slowly. *Racconti* (short stories) and poetry became popular in the 1800s. **Giovanni Verga's** (1840-1922) brutally honest depiction of destitute Italians ushered in a new tradition of portraying the common man in art and literature, a movement known as *verismo* (contemporary, all-too-tragic realism). In 1825, **Alessandro Manzoni's** (1785-1873) historical novel, *I Promessi sposi*, established the Modernist novel as a major avenue of Italian literary expression. **Carlo Collodi's** (1826-1890) *Storia di un burattino* (Adventures of a Marionette), also called *Le avventure di Pinocchio*, continues to enchant children, now in its innocuous Disney classic format, with the precocious and sometimes diabolic antics of an animated puppet.

ITALY SEEN THROUGH FOREIGN EYES

Shakespeare, William. *Romeo and Juliet; Othello; Julius Caesar; Merchant of Venice.* Fun and games and death all over.

Eliot, George. *Romola.* Deception, politics, and martyrdom in Savonarola's Florence.

Forster, E.M. *A Room with a View.* Victorian coming-of-age in scenic Florence.

Hemingway, Ernest. *A Farewell to Arms.* American soldier learns to love in WWI Italy.

James, Henry. *The Wings of the Dove.* Unscrupulous seduction in Venice's canals.

Lawrence, D.H. *Twilight in Italy.* An intimate connection with sun-soaked Italy.

Mann, Thomas. *Death in Venice.* A writer's obsession with a beautiful boy.

Mayes, Francis. *Under the Tuscan Sun.* A woman's soul-searching in the heart of Italy, which inspired the 2003 movie by the same name.

Stone, Irving. *The Agony and the Ecstasy.* More of the latter than the former in this biography of Michelangelo.

POSTMODERNISM. Twentieth-century Italian writers sought to undermine the concept of objective truth. Nobel Prize winner **Luigi Pirandello** (1867-1936) advanced postmodernism and shook the foundations of theater with his play, *Sei personaggi in cerca d'autore*. Allied victory in WWII spawned anti-fascist fiction, through which post-war authors related their horrific personal and political experiences. The most prolific of these writers, **Alberto Moravia** (1907-1990), wrote the ground-breaking *Gli indifferenti*, which launched an attack on the fascist regime and was promptly censored. **Primo Levi** (1919-1987) wrote *Se questo è un uomo* about his experience in Auschwitz. Several female writers also emerged, including **Natalia Ginzburg** (1916-1991) with *Lessico famigliare*, the story of a quirky middle-class Italian family. **Italo Calvino** (1923-1985) exemplified the postmodern era by creating new worlds in *Il barone rampante* and questioning the act of reading and writing in *Se una notte d'inverno un viaggiatore*. In 1997, the playwright **Dario Fo's** (b. 1926) dramatic satires brought him both a denunciation by the Roman Catholic Church and the Nobel Prize for Literature.

MUSIC

GREGORY'S FAMOUS CHANTING MONKS

Since the echoes of ancient Greek and Roman music have been drowned by the passage of time, Biblical psalms of the Old Testament constitute some of the earliest known songs of both Italian and Western culture. With origins in the Jewish liturgy, the Roman and Ambrosian rites (Italy's medieval liturgies) were characterized by monophonic vocal **plainchant,** also known as plainsong. Although the Ambrosian chant can still be heard in Milan, it is the Roman (now know as the Gregorian) chant that prevails, thanks to the work of its namesake **Pope Gregory I** (pope during AD 590-604), who codified the music he had heard during his days as pope. The **Gregorian Chant,** which regained popularity in the mid-19th century, is characterized by a repeated reciting note interrupted only by periodic deviations. Further advancements were made by Italian monk **Guido d'Arezzo** (AD 995-1050), who originated musical notation and explored the emerging concept of polyphony. Lyricism is largely attributed to **Francesco Landini** (1325-1397), a blind organist of the 14th century **Ars nova** period. This era also brought *madrigales*, musical poems, and *caccia*, musical narratives. Finally, revered Renaissance composer **Giovanni Pierluigi da Palestrina's** (1525-94) masses, hymns, and madrigals were performed in the newly-painted Sistine Chapel (p. 147).

OPERA LIRICA: THE FAT LADY SINGS

Italy's most cherished musical art form was born in Florence, nurtured in Venice and Naples, and revered in Milan. Conceived by the **Camerata,** a circle of Florentine writers, noblemen, and musicians including Vincenzo Galilei (father of the famed Galileo), **opera lirica** originated as an attempt to recreate the dramas of ancient Greece by setting lengthy poems to music. The earliest surviving opera is *Euridice* (1600), performed as a collage of compositions by **Jacobo Peri** (1561-1633) and **Giulio Caccini** (1546-1618). Opera found a perfect equilibrium between music and poetry for the first time in *L'Orfeo* (1607), a breakthrough piece by **Claudio Monteverdi** (1567-1643), who drew freely from history and juxtaposed high drama, love scenes, and uncouth humor (see Cremona, p. 272). Still-popular **Alessandro Scarlatti** (1660-1725) was arguably the most talented composer of Italian operas, pioneering the *overture*, which eventually inspired the classical symphony. Meanwhile, the simple and toneful aria became the dominant form of opera, and castrated men the singers of choice. These *castrati*, thanks to their masculine strength of voice and feminine tone, became the most celebrated and envied group of singers in Italy and all of Europe.

BAROQUE: THE BIRTH OF VIVALDI AND THE VIOLIN

The Baroque period, known for its heavy ornamentation, saw the birth of the string orchestra. The violin's modern form was perfected by **Antonio Stradivari** (1644-1737) and became popular in pieces by fellow Cremonese Monteverdi and his contemporaries (visit the Museo Stradivariano, p. 273). The pianoforte emerged around 1709 thanks to Florentine **Bartolomeo Cristofori.** Violinist **Antonio Vivaldi** (1675-1741), who composed over 600 concertos, continues to awe contemporary audiences with *The Four Seasons* (1725). Most importantly, he established the concerto's present form, in which a full orchestra accompanies a soloist in a three-movement piece.

VIVA VERDI!

LAYING THE GROUNDWORK. With convoluted plots and powerful, dramatic music, 19th-century Italian opera had not yet adopted the French tradition of visual spectacle. A famous composer of tragedies and comedies and master of the *bel canto* (beautiful song), **Gioacchino Rossini** (1792-1868) counts the 1817 *Cinderella* among his famous works. The rhythms and harmonies of Rossini and his contemporaries would inspire the early, more conventional works of Verdi.

LIFE AND TIMES

TOP TEN CINEMATIC ITALY

Picturesque Italy has provided a backdrop for artistic genius, breathtaking romance and feature films. Relive the cinematic moments of the following movies by visiting their original settings.

1. La Dolce Vita (1960): Since it is now illegal, imagine yourself dancing like Sylvia in Rome's Trevi Fountain (p. 138) to recreate Fellini's Oscar-winning feature.

2. The Italian Job (2003): Innocently stand by and see the peaceful Venetian canals where the opening scene's high-speed boat chase took place (p. 307).

3. The Godfather III (1990): Escape Michael Corleone's fate by visiting Palermo's Teatro Massimo (p. 654) and going home unscathed.

4. The Passion of the Christ (2004): Crawl around the 2000-year-old *sassi* of Matera (p. 632) and picture yourself in ancient Italy or Jerusalem. These cave dwellings were used as the backdrop in Mel Gibson's feature.

5. Star Wars Episode II: Attack of the Clones (2002): Re-enact Anakin and Princess Padmé's wedding, which took place at the Villa del Balbianello in Lenno, on Lake Como (p. 292).

AND, OF COURSE, THE MAN HIMSELF. Giuseppe Verdi (1813-1901), whose lyrical half-century domination of Italian opera emphasized human themes and the human voice, remains the crowning musical figure of 19th-century Italy and, along with his German contemporary Wagner, all of opera. *Nabucco*, a pointed and powerful *bel canto*, typifies Verdi's early works. This opera's chorus, *Va pensiero*, became the hymn of Italian freedom and unity during the Risorgimento. Verdi also produced the touching, personal dramas and memorable melodies of *Rigoletto*, *La Traviata*, and *Il Trovatore* in the 1850s. Later work brought the grand and heroic conflicts of *Aïda* (1871), the dramatic thrust of *Otello* (1887), and the mercurial comedy of *Falstaff* (1893). Because Verdi's name served as a convenient acronym for "Vittorio Emanuele, *Re d'Italia*" (King of Italy), *"Viva Verdi!"* became a popular battle cry of the Risorgimento.

TWENTIETH-CENTURY OPERA. In the 20th century, **Ottorino Respighi** (1879-1936) explored his fascination with orchestral color in the popular *Roman Trilogy* (1915-28). Another composer, **Gian Carlo Menotti** (1911-2007) wrote Pulitzer Prize-winning operas *The Consul* (1950) and *The Saint of Bleecker Street* (1955). **Luigi Dallapiccola** (1904-1975) achieved success with surrealist choral works including *Songs of Prison* (1938-41), which protested fascism in Italy. His student, avant-garde composer **Luciano Berio** (1925-2003), pioneered the composition of electronic music and combined opera and drama under the creative title "Music Theatre." Grammy-winning tenor **Luciano Pavarotti** (b. 1935) debuted in the 60s in Italy and around the world, and brought about an opera renaissance with his televised operas in the 1990s. **Andrea Bocelli** (b. 1958), blinded as a child, has bridged the expanse between opera and pop with popular songs such as chart-topping "Con Te Partirò" in 1995. Visitors looking to experience Italian opera firsthand can visit Milan's Teatro alla Scala (p. 251), Rome's Teatro dell'Opera (p. 153), and Palermo's Teatro Massimo (p. 654), or one of Italy's countless other opulent opera houses.

ARRIVEDERCI, VERDI

More recent Italian music has reversed its centuries-long role as a groundbreaker, drawing inspiration instead from American pop culture. Melodic rockers of the 60s included **Enzo Iannacci**, a dentist-turned-musician, the crooning Sardinian **Fabrizio De Andre**, and **Adriano Celentano**, who enjoyed a 40-year-long career. Having emerged in the 60s and 70s, **Lucio Battisti** enjoys popularity comparable to that of the Beatles elsewhere. In the 70s and 80s, **Eduardo Bennato** used rock to generate a political message; his successor **Vasco Rossi** drew an unprecedented crowd to his free 2004 concert. Crooning **Eros Ramazzotti** gained universal appeal by recording every album in Spanish as well as Italian and teaming up with Cher and Tina Turner; similarly, Andrea Bocelli (see Twentieth-Century Opera, above) joined Celine Dion for "The Prayer." Italians **Laura Pausini, Elisa,** and **L'Aura** have followed suit by recording English albums. More recently, **Jovanotti's** rap has entered the scene, along with socially conscious **Frankie-Hi-NRG** and **99 Posse.** For a more relaxed beat, try **Lucio Dalla's** internationally popular *Caruso.*

FILM

OLDIES AND GOLDIES

Italy's golden position within the film industry began in 1905, when the nation released the historical and somewhat flamboyant *La Presa di Roma.* With this movie, the Italian "super-spectacle," an extravagant recreation of historical events through film, was born. Throughout the early 20th century, Italy's films tended to follow this melodramatic pattern, and Italian film stars were often consequently thought of as superhuman. Before WWI, celebrated divas like **Francesca Bertini** (1881-1985) and **Lyda Borelli** (1897-1959) epitomized the Italian *diva* (star).

SEEING IS BELIEVING

No one ever accused Benito Mussolini of missing out on an opportunity. Recognizing film's potential as propaganda in the late 1930s, he created the *Centro Sperimentale della Cinematografia,* a national film school, and the gargantuan **Cinecittà Studios,** Rome's answer to Hollywood. Nationalizing the industry "for the good of the state," Mussolini enforced a few "imperial edicts," one forbidding laughing at the Marx Brothers and another censoring shows that were overly critical of the government. Films created under fascist rule glorified Italian military conquests (alluding to Classical Roman success) and portrayed comfortable middle class life. Films from 1936 to 1943 are often referred to as *telefoni bianchi* (white telephones) in reference to their common prop. Rare compared to black telephones, these phones were a symbol of prosperity that indicated the films' bourgeois quality.

NEOREALISM

The fall of fascism brought the explosion of **neorealist cinema** (1943-50), which rejected contrived sets and

6. Under the Tuscan Sun (2003): Soak up Tuscany's luscious landscape and stunning sunsets in Cortona and wonder if you too can purchase a villa like divorcee Frances Mayes.

7. The Talented Mr. Ripley (1999): Dive into the to-die-for crystal waters that surround the beautiful Ischia on the Amalfi Coast (p. 584) where Jude Law's Dickie Greenleaf was murdered by Matt Damon's Mr. Ripley.

8. La Vita è Bella (1997): Visit the picturesque Arezzo (p. 477), hometown to actor/director Roberto Benigni, who chose the town as the backdrop for many key scenes of his touching and Oscar-winning WWII drama.

9. Ocean's Twelve (2004): Find Villa Erba, the Night Fox's mansion, on the shores of Lake Como in Bellagio (p. 285) and start scheming to compete with mastermind and thief Danny Ocean. This villa was also the vacation home for Italian director Luchino Visconti's family.

10. Romeo and Juliet (1968): Although the Shakespearean original was set in fair Verona, director Franco Zeffirelli filmed in locales across Italy. Challenge your enemy to a duel in the streets of Gubbio (p. 510) where the director set the fatal fight between Romeo and Tybalt.

professional actors, emphasizing instead on-location shooting and "authentic" drama based in reality. These low-budget productions created a film revolution and brought Italian cinema international prestige. Neorealists first gained attention in Italy with **Luchino Visconti's** (1906-1976) French-influenced *Ossessione* (1942). Because fascist censors suppressed this so-called "resistance" film, it wasn't until **Roberto Rossellini's** (1906-1977) film *Roma, città aperta* (1945) that neorealist films gained international exposure. The film began his Neorealistic Trilogy which also included *Paisà* (1946) and *Germania anno zero* (1948). **Vittorio De Sica's** 1948 *Ladri di biciclette* was perhaps the most successful neorealist film. Described by De Sica as a "dedica[tion] to the suffering of the humble," the work explored the human struggle against fate. A demand for Italian comedy gave birth to **neorealismo rosa,** a more comic version of the intense and all-too-authentic glimpse into daily Italian life. Actor **Totò** (1898-1967), the illegitimate son of a Neapolitan duke, was Italy's version of Charlie Chaplin. With his dignified antics and clever lines, Totò charmed audiences and provided subtle commentary on Italian society.

THE GOLDEN AGE

The golden age of Italian cinema, 1958-1968, ushered in **la commedia all'italiana,** during which the prestige and economic success of Italian movies was at its height. **Mario Monicelli** (*I Soliti Ignoti*, 1958; *La Grande guerra*, 1959) brought a darker, more cynical tone to the portrayal of daily Italian life, which was in a stage of rapid transformation and social unease. Italian comedy struggled to portray cultural stereotypes with as much wit as its public demanded. Actors **Marcello Mastroianni, Vittorio Gassman,** and **Alberto Sordi** gained fame portraying self-centered characters lovable for their frailties.

By the 1960s, post-neorealist directors like **Federico Fellini** (1920-1993) and **Michelangelo Antonioni** (1912-2007) valued careful cinematic construction over mere real world experience. With the Oscar-winning *La Strada*, Fellini went beyond neorealism, scripting the vagabond life of two street performers Gelsomina and Zampanò. Self-indulgent and autobiographical, Fellini's *8½* interwove dreams with reality and earned a place in the international cinematic canon. Pope Blessed John XXIII condemned Fellini's *La Dolce Vita* (1960) for its portrayal of decadently stylish celebrities in 1950s Rome. The film coined the term *paparazzi* and glamorized dancing in the Trevi Fountain (p. 138), an act that is now illegal. Antonioni's haunting trilogy, *L'Avventura* (1959), *La Notte* (1960), and *L'Eclisse* (1962) presents a stark world of estranged couples and isolated aristocrats. His *Blow-Up* was a 1966 English-language hit about miming, murder, and mod London. Controversial **Pier Paolo Pasolini** (1922-1975) may have spent as much time on trial for his politics as he did making films. An ardent Marxist, he set his films in the underworld of shanty neighborhoods, poverty, and prostitution. His later films include scandalous adaptations of famous literary works including *Decameron* (1971) and *Arabian Nights* (1974).

INTROSPECTION

Aging directors and a lack of funds led Italian film into an era characterized by nostalgia and self-examination. **Bernardo Bertolucci's** (b. 1940) *Il conformista* (1970) investigates fascist Italy by focusing on one "comrade" struggling to be normal. Other major Italian films of this era include **Vittorio de Sica's** (1901-1974) *Il Giardino dei Finzi-Contini* (1971) and **Francesco Rosi's** *Cristo si è fermato a Eboli* (1979), both films based on prestigious post-war, anti-fascist novels. In the 1980s, the **Taviani** brothers catapulted to fame with *Kaos* (1984), a film based on stories by Pirandello, and *La notte di San Lorenzo* (1982), which depicted an

Italian village during the last days of WWII. Inheriting the *commedia all'italiana* tradition of the golden age, actor-directors like **Nanni Moretti** (b. 1953) and **Maurizio Nichetti** (b. 1948) delighted audiences with macabre humor in the 1980s and early 90s. Both men usually chose projects that required them to play neurotic, introspective, or ridiculous characters. In his psychological comedy-thriller *Bianca* (1983), Nichetti stars as the slightly deranged protagonist, and in *Volere Volare* (1991), he plays a confused cartoon sound designer who turns into a cartoon.

BUONGIORNO, PRINCIPESSA!

Oscar-winners **Gabriele Salvatore** (for *Mediterraneo*, 1991) and **Giuseppe Tornatore** (for *Nuova Cinema Paradiso*, 1998) have earned the attention and affection of audiences worldwide. The golden statue has also shone on other Italian filmmakers. In 1995 Massimo Troisi's *Il Postino* was nominated for a Best Picture Academy Award, and three years later **Roberto Benigni** drew international acclaim for *La vita è bella* (Life is Beautiful). Juxtaposing the tragedy of the Holocaust with a father's love for his son, *La vita è bella* won Oscars for Best Actor (for Benigni), Best Music and Best Foreign Film, as well as a Best Picture nomination at the 1998 American Academy Awards. More recently, Nanni Moretti snagged the Palm D'Or at Cannes in 2001 for *La Stanza del Figlio*, and **Leonardo Pieraccioni** released *Il Paradiso all'improvviso* to much acclaim in 2003.

MEDIA

PRINT

Although newspapers in English can be found at any Italian newsstand, news is typically more interesting in Italian. The media in Italy is anything but impartial and often lambastes everyone from public officials to popular actresses. The most prevalent national daily papers are *Il Corriere della Sera*, a conservative publication based in Milan, and *La Repubblica*, a somewhat liberal paper based in Rome. Other popular papers include *La Stampa* (conservative, based in Turin), *Il Messaggero* (liberal, based in Rome), and *Il Giornale* (based in Milan and owned by ex-Prime Minister Silvio Berlusconi's brother). The pink *La Gazzetta dello Sport* is the true mainstay, covering soccer victories and losses, which cause more of a ruckus than elections. For weekly entertainment listings, large cities have their own magazines, including *Roma C'è; TrovaMilano; Firenze Spettacolo; Milano Where, When, How;* and *Qui Napoli*. English-language Italian papers include *Italy Daily*, an insert in the *International Herald Tribune*, the monthly *talk ABout* and the weekly newsletter *Wanted in Rome*.

TELEVISION

Italian television offers three state-owned channels, RAI1, RAI2, and RAI3, and a handful of cable options from Italy and abroad. It is important to note, however, that everyone's favorite ex-Prime Minister, Silvio Berlusconi, owns all three of the RAI channels and is in control of three others. Television in Italy is a flashy affair. Whether they are game shows or the nightly news, Italian shows overwhelm viewers with disco balls, scantily-clad women, hit Europop songs, and general frivolity. In addition to its domestic sensational spectacles, Italian TV also incorporates international flair in its programming. The evening news reports on domestic and international issues, dubbed re-runs of American shows figure prominently, and bad 80s movies play late into the night.

DESIGN

From the Roman aqueducts to da Vinci's flying machine to Dolce & Gabbana's spacesuit-inspired winter 2008 line, Italians have always had a penchant for design. Compare **Enzo Ferrari's** original 1929 cars to Ford's Model T's, **Bialetti's** 1930 art deco **Moka Express** coffeemaker to one by Mr. Coffee, or a Gucci leather shoe to the American sneaker, and it's evident that Italians designers deserve the prestige they enjoy. Aside from cars and appliances that achieve statuesque beauty, Italian design produced the **Vespa**—still adored by Italians and hated by fearful tourists—in 1946, and the 1957 **Fiat**, a tiny 2-door car. Before the days of sleek laptops, Olivetti's 1969 **Valentine typewriter** by designer **Ettore Sottass** was unique in its combination of style and practicality. This combination of streamlined beauty and simple functionality frequently characterizes Italian design.

Equally stunning and more widely recognized is Italian fashion design. Italian domination began in 1881 when **Cerruti** opened his doors and began his lasting impact on Italian fashion, serving as a mentor and teacher for later designers such as Giorgio Armani. Still-famous **Ferragamo**, whose love affair with shoes would later produce Dorothy's ruby slippers in *The Wizard of Oz* (1939), began designing in 1914. The illustrious **Fendi** line began as a fur business in Rome at the end of WWI, but was revolutionized by the five Fendi sisters who took control after WWII. Two years later, **Guccio Gucci** opened a leather store in Florence that would much later become an international powerhouse of fashion. The 1952 fashion show organized by Gian Battista Giorgini in Florence re-introduced the phrase "Made in Italy," as a universally accepted indication of quality. Italy soon became host to now-famous designers such as **Max Mara** (1951), **Valentino** (1962), the **Giorgio Armani Company** (1975), **Versace** (1978), **Dolce & Gabbana** (1985), all of whose designs litter the red carpet and often overshadow the stars they adorn. To become a star for the day, go shopping in **Milan** (see **Milan: Shopping**, p. 252), and find out what makes this the fashion capital of the world. Take notes on the classic cuts, quality fabrics, and liberal use of black that make Italians so effortlessly stylish, just don't tell any Parisians or Londoners that your visit convinced you that fashion begins and ends in Milan. If you have assimilated to Italian culture and decided that soccer (p. 91) is your passion, take a look at Dolce & Gabbana's AC Milan uniforms (see **Milan: Sports**, p. 252) or their 2006 men's underwear campaign featuring well-cut *calcio* stars.

 FASHION FOR POCKET CHANGE. Save 25-75% at end-of-season sales. These happen in January and July and last until the collection sells out. Many stores also offer previews of the next collection at this time.

FOOD AND WINE: LA DOLCE VITA

MANGIAMO!

In Italy, food preparation is an art form, and food-related traditions constitute a crucial part of the culture. Along with a separate personality, each region of Italy has a distinct culinary identity and even a locally made, distinctively shaped pasta. The words *"Buon appetito!"* and *"Cin cin!"* chime around the table as people sit down to eat. As much an institution as the meal itself, the after-dinner *passeggiata* (promenade) brings Italians strolling into the main square post-dinner. Small portions and leisurely paced meals help keep Italians looking svelte despite the rich foods they savor.

Breakfast is the least elaborate meal in Italy; at most, *la colazione* consists of a quick coffee and a *cornetto* (croissant). For *il pranzo* (lunch), people usually grab a *panino* (sandwich) or salad. It is important to note, however, that lunch is usually the most important meal of the day in rural regions where daily work comes in two shifts and is separated by a long lunch and *pisolino* (nap). More common in northern cities, Italians will end a none-too-stressful day at work with an *aperitivo* (aperitif) around 5 or 6pm. Try a *spritz*, a northern specialty made with *prosecco*, *campari*, or *aperol* and a splash of mineral water. *La cena* (dinner) usually begins at 8pm; in Naples it's not unusual to go for a midnight pizza. Traditionally, dinner is the longest meal of the day, usually lasting much of the evening and consisting of an *antipasto* (appetizer), a *primo piatto* (starch-based first course like pasta or *risotto*), a *secondo piatto* (meat or fish), and a *contorno* (vegetable side dish). Finally, comes the *dolce* (dessert), then *caffè* (espresso), and often an after-dinner liqueur. Many restaurants offer a fixed-price *menù turistico* including *primo*, *secondo*, bread, water, and wine. While food varies regionally, the importance of relaxing over an extended meal does not. For example, restaurants in Bologna do not see more than one seating in a night and dinners anywhere can run for hours. It is not hard to see why Italians championed the Slow Food movement to promote local cuisine and combat fast food.

FOOD ON THE GO

In Italian, *"un bar"* refers to a plain place for a quick, inexpensive meal. Calm dining can be found at a *tavola calda* (cafeteria-style snack bar), *rosticceria* (grill), or *gastronomia* ("food shop" which prepares hot dishes for takeout). While fast-food chains have permeated Italy, the ample seafood, salad, beer, and espresso offerings at most **McDonald's** demonstrate that Italians do fast food their own way. The typical *bar* sells hot and cold *panini*, *gelato*, and coffee. Any *bar* on a major tourist thoroughfare will have prices that reflect location and not necessarily service or quality. In small towns, the *bar* is a social center; children come to meet playmates and eat *gelato*, young adults to sip beer and flirt, and older men to drink wine and talk. In crowded *bars*, clients pay for food at the cashier's desk and take the *scontrino* (receipt) to a bartender for service. Sitting down at a table costs more than standing at the counter. A *salumeria* or *alimentari* (meat and grocery shop) or the popular STANDA or Coop supermarkets sell food basics, while open-air markets have fresher produce and negotiable prices. Customers must carry receipts for 100m after making a purchase to avoid accusations of theft.

 SO A GUY WALKS INTO A BAR... In Italy a *bar* doesn't refer to a beer-serving nightspot but to an establishment where you can get a quick coffee and a bite to eat. For alcohol, one would go to *un bar americano* or a *discoteca*.

WAKE UP AND SMELL THE CAFFÈ!

THE ART OF ESPRESSO. Italians drink coffee at breakfast, lunch, dinner, and any time in between—and still manage to close shop in the afternoon for a snooze. But espresso in Italy isn't merely a beverage; it's an experience, from the harvesting of the beans to the enjoyment of the drink. High altitude *Arabica* beans compose 60-90% of most Italian blends, while the remaining 10-40% is made of woody-flavored *robusta* beans. Italians prefer a higher concentration of *robusta* beans because they emit oils that produce a thick, foamy *crema* under the heat and pressure of the espresso machine. Espresso beans are roasted longer than other coffee beans, giving the drink its full body. The beans are then ground, tapped into a basket, and barraged with hot, pressurized water. In a good cup of espresso, the foamy *crema* should be caramel-colored and thick enough to support a spoonful of sugar for a few long seconds. The thick *crema* prevents the drink's rich aroma from dispersing into the air and is indicative of a well-brewed beverage.

 COFFEE STAINED. While Italians drink coffee with every meal, they do not drink cappuccino after 10am. If you order a cappuccino after lunch or dinner, you might as well open your map on the table and wave your country's flag; every Italian in the surrounding area will know you're a tourist.

HOW TO ORDER. For a standard cup of espresso, request a *caffè*. Stir in sugar and down it in one gulp like the locals. For a spot of milk in it, ask for *caffè macchiato* (*macchia* means stain or spot). Cappuccino, which Italians drink only before lunch, is espresso and steamed milk "capped" by frothed milk; *caffè latte* or *latte macchiato* is heavier on the milk, lighter on the coffee. Note that good espresso is supposed to have a layer of foam on the top due to the high-pressure compression process. For coffee with a kick, try a *caffè corretto* (corrected), which is espresso with a drop of strong liqueur (usually *grappa* or brandy). *Caffè americano*, scorned by Italians, is watery espresso served in a large cup. *Caffè freddo* is a refreshing chilled coffee. For dessert, the *caffè affogato* (drowned coffee) is a scoop of vanilla *gelato* drenched in espresso.

IN VINO VERITAS

Despite living in the shadow of her wine-loving French neighbors, Italy is the world's leading exporter of wine. The ancient Greeks named Dionysus their god of wine, the Romans later worshipped him as Bacchus, and today's Italians, young and old, have a relationship with wine that transcends consumption to become part of their lifestyle. Today, over 2000 varieties of grapes are nurtured in Italy's warm climate and rocky hills before *la vendemmia* (the grape harvest) in September or October. To make red wine, *rosso*, vintners then pump the juice and skins into glass, oak, or steel fermentation vats; white wines, *biancos*, are made from skinless grapes. Whether a wine is *dolce* (sweet) or *secco* (dry) is largely determined by the ripeness and sugar content of its grape. After fermentation, the wine is racked and clarified, a procedure which removes any sediment. The wine is then stored in barrels or vats until bottling.

IT'S ALL IN THE NAME. Look for one of four classifications on your bottle to determine the wine's quality. Independently tested wine will bear the label DOCG (*Denominazione di Origine Controllata e Garantita*); wines that follow regional regulations are labeled DOC (*Denominazione di Origine Controllata*); the label IGT (*Indicazione Geografica*) simply means that a wine has been produced in a specific area; and *Vino da Tavola* is a catch-all term for otherwise unclassifiable table wines.

Wine tasting is made easy by *enoteche* (wine bars), especially government-run ones which serve as regional exhibition and tasting centers to promote local vineyards and sponsor educational events. *Cantine* (wine cellars) do not typically offer tastings unless accompanied by a wine bar. If touring by car, ask the local tourist office about *Strade del Vino* (wine roads). Tuscany, birthplace of the *Mov-*

CORK YOUR WALLET! Wine snobs may spend upward of €50 on a bottle of aged *riserva*, but wines in the €6-12 range can be sublime (or barely drinkable). The most respected wine stewards in the nation regularly rank inexpensive wines above their costly cousins. Expense can equal quality, but it's wiser to go for the high end of a lower-grade wine than the low end of a higher-grade wine.

imento del Turismo del Vino (wine tourism), is especially accessible for wine tasting. Reservations are recommended if visiting a vineyard.

REGIONAL WINES

WINE FROM WINE LAND. Piedmont (p. 164) is Italy's most distinguished wine region (followed closely by Tuscany), producing the touted (and expensive) *barolo*, a full-bodied red made from the region's *nebbiolo* grapes. *Barolo* is aged for as many as twenty years, longer than its lighter cousin, *Barbaresco*. Celebrate Piedmont's lighter side with the sparkling and sweet *asti spumante* after biking through vineyards. The **Veneto** (p. 307) region yields everyday wines such as *bianco di custoza*, a dry *Soave* white, and *Valpolicella*, a sweet dessert wine. Go to **Friuli** (p. 368) for smooth merlots and good whites such as *Tocai Friulano*. Prepare for the *parmigiano-reggiano* and *parma ham* of **Emilia-Romagna** (p. 382) with the red *Sauvignon*, or *Frizzantino Malvasia*, both typical aperitifs or dessert wines. *Lambrusco*, known elsewhere as a cheap export, is enjoyed in Emilia-Romagna as a refreshing red. The *Sangiovese* grapes of **Tuscany** (p. 421) are crushed to make the region's popular *Chianti Classici*, the 'noble' red *vino Nobile di Montepulciano*, and the white *Trebbiano*.

MOVING SOUTH. When in **Rome** (p. 106), drink cold *Frascati*, a clean white wine which owes its invention to the ancient Romans over 2000 years ago. In **Umbria** (p. 499), where wine production dates back to the Etruscans, the world-famous *Orvieto* is a golden white whose versatility is still being explored, as evidenced by the incorporation of French chardonnay grapes to produce the world-class *Cervaro della Sala*. **Naples** (p. 555) boasts *Lacryma Cristi* (Christ's Tear), an overrated tourist favorite, while the red *Aglianico* hails from neighboring **Basilicata** (p. 630. The hotter climate and longer growing season of Southern Italy and the islands produces fruitier, more sugary wines. Try the versatile **Sicilian** (p. 648) *Marsala*, excellent as an aperitif between *primi* and *secondi piatti*, served with Parmesan cheese, or as a dessert wine.

REGIONAL LIQUEURS

DOPO LA CENA. Liqueurs are often enjoyed at the end of the meal as palate-cleansing *digestivi*. Don't pass up the ubiquitous *limoncello*, a heavy lemon liqueur especially famous in Sorrento (p. 579), which also features the walnut-flavored *nocino*. *Amari* cordials, served after festival meals, are often infused with so much sugar that they contradict their name, which means "bitter." Unusual wild fruit and nut essences found in Italian liqueurs include blueberry (in *mirto*), artichoke (in *cynar*), and melon (in *mellone*). Other Italian specialties include almond-flavored *amaretto* (originally made from apricot pits), hazelnut-flavored *frangelico*, and licorice *sambuca*, often served with three coffee beans to represent health, happiness, and prosperity. Once known as "firewater" (or, to some Italians, a morning boost), *grappa* is traditionally unfettered by sugars and leaves

calcio
An Italian Religion

Calcio, known to English-speakers as football or soccer, isn't just a sport in Italy; it's a religion. If culture is what people identify with most strongly, then *calcio* is arguably the most important aspect of Italian culture. *La Gazzetta dello Sport* is by far the most popular Italian daily. The ten most-watched TV broadcasts include ten *calcio* matches, most of them featuring a match of the Italian national team.

The *azzurri* (or Blues, the traditional name of the Italian national team derived from their jersey color) are famous worldwide, and one of the few elements uniting Italians under the same flag. Watching locals cheer the *azzurri* to victory in a local bar is an indescribable show. After every victory, street parades go on for hours with cars full of Italian flags honking throughout the *piazze* and impromptu pool parties in public fountains.

However, the *azzurri* are an exception to the daily *calcio* environment, typically characterized by undestroyable affiliations with one team and profound rivalries with all the others. The main competition is the *Serie A*, the Italian championship that assigns the *scudetto*, the title of Italian Champion, every year. The matches take place every Sunday at 3pm, and to many Italians this time is as sacred as Holy Mass. Recently the Champions' League, with matches on Tuesday and Wednesday nights, has become more prestigious as the best teams in Europe compete for the title of European champion.

Like every estimable religion, *calcio* has its temples with their traditions. Here is a brief guide to the most famous stadiums in Italy:

—*Home of the Best*—Delle Alpi, Turin (71,000). Juventus, the most successful team in Italian history, with 27 Italian Championship wins, plays here. They have the highest number of supporters of any team in Europe, and their black and white jerseys are a universally respected symbol of nobility.

—*La Scala of calcio*—San Siro, Milan (84,000). One of the most beautiful stadiums in Italy, with a perfect view of the field from any seat. Home to AC Milan, the team owned by Berlusconi that has won many titles in the last two decades, and Inter, the only team that has never been in the second division.

—*Best Choreography*—Olimpico, Rome (83,000). The *tifosi* (fans) in Rome are the loudest and most creative. The main team is Roma, but Lazio is almost at the same level and their rivalry permeates every Roman conversation.

—*Southern Passion*—fans in the south are the most passionate. Every game is a matter of life or death, and regional matches often lead to street fights. San Paolo (Naples; 80,000) is as respectable a stadium as San Siro and for several years has been the home of Maradona, the greatest *calcio* player of all time. The arenas La Favorita (Palermo; 50,000) and San Nicola (Bari; 58,000) are always feared by the home team's opponents.

"*Calcio* ... isn't just a sport in Italy; it's a religion."

A tip for first-time match-goers: don't sit in the *curve*, the curved sides of the stadium where the very hot *tifosi* are. Overly zealous fans are often nerve-wrackingly active, waving giant flags, brandishing flares, and chanting insults at the opposing team. By no means wear any other jersey except the home team's while watching a match from this section.

Now that you know about the *calcio* world, buy *La Gazzetta*, purchase your ticket and a *sciarpa* (scarf), and be ready for the time of your life.

A CLOSER LOOK

Edoardo Gallo, from Cuneo, Italy, is currently working as a consultant in New York after researching for Let's Go: Central America in El Salvador, Nicaragua, and Honduras. He is a 2004 graduate in Physics and Mathematics of Harvard University and is also a passionate, lifelong fan of Juventus.

the palate disinfected, if not shocked. After grapes are pressed for wine, the remaining *pomace* (seeds, stalks, and stems) is used for this national favorite.

SPORTS AND RECREATION

ANCIENT TIMES. The Romans liked their athletic spectacles fast and violent. Gladiatorial combat, likely originating as part of a funeral custom offering a gift to the dead, took place in amphitheaters constructed around the Empire. Examples can be seen in Pompeii (p. 573) and of course at the Roman Colosseum (p. 132). They also hosted *venationes* (wild beast hunts), and even giant mock naval battles. Greek athletics, like wrestling, running, and javelin throwing, were slower to catch on in Rome perhaps because there just wasn't enough killin'.

SOCCER. Slightly less violent, today's *calcio* (soccer to Americans, football to everyone else) surpasses all other sports in popularity and competes with politics and religion as a defining aspect of national identity (see "An Italian Religion," p. 91). **La Squadra Azzurra** (The Blue Team) is a source of national pride, substantiating claims that Italy's **1982 World Cup** victory inspired more national unity than any political movement. However, Italian *calcio* fans, or *tifosi*, are divided by their undying devotion to local teams, which heightens in June for the **Coppa Italia** final. During games between inter-urban rivals such as Naples, Milan, and Rome, don't be surprised to find streets hauntingly empty and bars stiflingly full as fans either commiserate or celebrate in communal agony or ecstasy. To become one with the mob, see a game in Rome's Stadio Olimpico (p. 155) or Milan's San Siro (p. 252).

WORLD CUP 2006. Veni, Vidi, Vici: Italy came. Italy saw. Italy conquered. Despite French player Zinedine Zidane's "head-butt felt 'round the world" in the final game, the Italian national team was able to keep its eye on the ball to become ▓the world's best soccer team in 2006. The victory served as a saving grace for Italian soccer since *Calciopoli*, or the Serie A scandal, which occurred around the same time as the World Cup, incriminated Juventus and other teams in Italy's top professional soccer league for fixing match results.

CYCLING. Home to both cyclists and cycling fans, Italy hosts the annual **Giro d'Italia**, a 21-stage cross-country race, in May. Second only to the Tour de France, this race started in 1909 and has since been interrupted only by WWI and WWII. Unlike the Tour de France, in which a yellow jersey signifies victory, the leader in the Giro receives the **maglia rosa,** whose pink hue represents the color of paper used by *La Gazzetta dello Sport*.

SKIING. From December to April, skiers flock to parts of the Italian Alps and Apennines. Head to resorts near Turin (p. 164), host of the 2006 Winter Olympics, or to the Aosta Valley (p. 189) for summer skiing, helicopter skiing, and other exciting possibilities. Annual World Cup competitions at Italian ski slopes appeal to less adventurous ski fans.

FESTIVALS AND HOLIDAYS

Though most Italians work 35hr. per week, take 2hr. lunch breaks, close some businesses on Mondays, and take elaborate month-long coastal vacations each August, they still enjoy a seemingly constant stream of festivals. Many celebrations have religious origins, but aren't necessarily pious. Revelry during **Carnevale** prepares Italian towns for Lent with 10 days of celebration. At **Scoppio del Carro,** held in Florence on Easter Sunday, Florentines set off a cart of explosives in keeping with medieval tradition (except for the addition of a mechanical dove used to light the cart). Countless other quirky local festivals also keep medieval customs alive, often in the form of jousts and period costumes. For a complete list of festivals, write to the **Italian Government Tourist Board** (p. 10).

DATE	FESTIVAL	LOCATION
Jan. 1	**Capodanno (New Year's Day)**	**National Holiday**
Jan. 6	**Epifania (Epiphany)**	**National Holiday**
Jan. 30-31	Fiera di Sant'Orso	Aosta (p. 195)
Feb.-March	Carnevale; see www.carnivalofvenice.it or www.viareggio.ilcarnevale.it	Venice (p. 333); Viareggio (p. 492)
Apr.-June	Verdi Opera Festival	Parma (p. 404)
Palm Su to Easter Su (Mar. 16-23, 2008)	Settimana Santa (Holy Week)	Nationwide
Mar. 21, 2008	Venerdi Santo (Good Friday)	Nationwide
Easter Sunday (Mar. 23, 2008)	**Pasqua (Easter)**	**National Holiday**
Easter M (Mar. 24, 2008)	**Pasquetta (Easter Monday)**	**National Holiday**
Apr. 25	**Festa della Liberazione (Liberation Day)**	**National Holiday**
Late Apr.-June	Maggio Musicale (May of Music)	Florence (p. 449)
May	Land of Motors Festival	Modena (p. 399)
May-June	Monteverdi Opera Festival	Cremona (p. 274)
May 1	**Festa del Lavoro (Labor Day)**	**National Holiday**
May 1	Primo Maggio Concert	Rome (p. 159)
May 1	Sagra di Sant'Efisio	Cagliari (p. 730)
1st Sa in May (May 3, 2008) and Sept. 19	Festa di San Gennaro	Naples (p. 571)
Su after Ascension Day (4 May, 2008)	Festa del Grillo (Festival of the Cricket)	Florence (p. 449)
May 7-9	Festa di San Nicola	Bari (p. 609)
May 15	Corsa dei Ceri (Race of the Candles)	Gubbio (p. 510)
3rd week in May	Calvacata Sarda (Sardinian Cavalcade)	Sassari (p. 732)
Last Su in May (May 25, 2008)	Palio di San Giorgio	Ferrara (p. 395)
Last Su in May (May 25, 2008)	Palio dei Balestrieri (Crossbow Competition between Gubbio and Sansepolcro)	Gubbio (p. 510) Sansepolcro (p. 478)
50 days after Easter	Festa della Palombella (Pentecostal Festival of the Dove, or Holy Spirit)	Orvieto (p. 526)
June	Calcio Storico (old-fashioned soccer)	Florence (p. 449)
Early June	Giostra dell'Archidado (Crossbow Contest)	Cortona (p. 474)
June-July	Festival di Ravenna (classical music)	Ravenna (p. 411)
June-July	Festival dei Due Mondi (2 week Spoleto arts festival)	Spoleto (p. 522)
June-July	Mostra Internazionale del Nuovo Cinema (International New Cinema)	Pesaro (p. 530)
June-Sept.	Verona Opera Festival	Verona (p. 348)
June-Oct.	International Sculpture Exhibition	Matera (p. 633)
June 2	**Festa della Repubblica (Republic Day)**	**National Holiday**
June 3	Festa della Madonna della Lettera	Messina (p. 678)
June 16-17	Regata e Luminara di San Ranieri	Pisa (p. 492)
3rd Su in June (June 15, 2008) and 1st Su in Sept.	Giostra del Saracino (Joust of the Saracen)	Arezzo (p. 477)

DATE	FESTIVAL	LOCATION
June 20 to early-July	Festa della Madonna della Bruna (Feast of the Dark Madonna)	Matera (p. 633)
June 24	Festa di San Giovanni Battista (Feast of St. John)	Florence (p. 449)
Late June-Oct. 2007	Taormina Arte	Taormina (p. 682)
Last Su in June (June 29, 2008)	Gioco del Ponte (Battle of the Bridge)	Pisa (p. 492)
July	Festival di Musica Antica	Urbino (p. 534)
July	Umbria Jazz Festival	Perugia (p. 505)
July	Luglio Musicale Trapanese (July of Music in Trapani)	Trapani (p. 710)
July 2 and Aug. 16	Corsa del Palio	Siena (p. 460)
July 2	Festa della Madonna (Feast of the Virgin Mary)	Enna (p. 692)
2nd weekend in July	Pistoia Blues Festival	Pistoia (p. 481)
July 12 and Sept. 14	Palio della Balestra (Crossbow Contest)	Lucca (p. 487)
Mid-July	ArezzoWave Love Festival	Arezzo (p. 477)
Mid-July	International Jazz Festival	Pescara (p. 552)
3rd Su in July (July 20, 2008)	Festa del Redentore (Feast of the Redeemer)	Venice (p. 333)
July 25	Giostra del Orso (Joust of the Bear)	Pistoia (p. 481)
Last week of July	Giostra Cavalleresca di Sulmona (Horse Joust)	Sulmona (p. 547)
Last Su of July (July 27, 2008)	Festa di Sant'Anna	Enna (p. 692)
Early Aug. to Sept.	Rossini Opera Festival	Pesaro (p. 530)
1st Su in Aug. (Aug. 3, 2008)	Torneo della Quintana (Joust of the Quintana)	Ascoli Piceno (p. 540)
Aug. 13-15	Ferragosto Messinese, Processione dei Giganti	Messina (p. 678)
Aug. 13-15	Festa dei Martiri d'Otranto	Otranto (p. 628)
Aug. 14	Processione dei Candelieri (Procession of Candle Holders)	Sassari (p. 732)
Aug. 14-15	Sagra della Bistecca (Steak Feast)	Cortona (p. 487)
Aug. 15	**Ferragosto (Feast of the Assumption)**	**National Holiday**
Aug. 16 and July 2	Corsa del Palio	Siena (p. 460)
3rd Su of Aug. (Aug. 17, 2008)	Ceremonia della Rievocazione (Ceremony of the Revocation)	Urbino (p. 534)
Aug. 18-19	Festa dei Porcini (Porcini Mushroom Festival)	Cortona (p. 474)
Aug. 24	Festa di San Bartolomeo	Lipari (p. 667)
Last Su of Aug. (Aug. 31, 2008)	Festa della Madonna di Valverde	Enna (p. 692)
Late Aug.-Early Sept.	Venice International Film Festival	Venice (p. 332)
Sept.	Sagra Musicale Umbria (Umbrian Classical Music Festival)	Perugia (p. 505)
Early Sept.	Palio delle Balestre	San Marino (p. 420)
Sept. 3	San Marino Independence Day	San Marino (p. 420)
1st 2 weekends in Sept.	Festival del Prosciutto	Parma (p. 404)
1st Su in Sept. (Sept. 7, 2008)	Festa della Madonna dell'Altomare (Festival of the Virgin of the High Seas)	Otranto (p. 628)
1st Su in Sept.	Festa dell'Aquilone (Kite-flying Competition)	Urbino (p. 534)
1st Su in Sept.	Regata storica (Historical Regatta)	Venice (p. 333)
1st Su in Sept.; also 3rd Su in June	Giostra del Saracino (Joust of the Saracen)	Arezzo (p. 477)
2nd week of Sept.	Annuale della morte di Dante Alighieri (Dante Festival)	Ravenna (p. 411)

LIFE AND TIMES

DATE	FESTIVAL	LOCATION
2nd and 3rd week of Sept.	D'ouja d'Or (Wine Festival)	Asti (p. 185)
Mid-Sept. (4 days)	Festa della Madonna della Consolazione	Reggio di Calabria (p. 638)
Sept. 13-22	Settembre Lucchese (Procession of the Holy Cross)	Lucca (p. 487)
Sept. 14; also July 12	Palio della Balestra (Crossbow Contest)	Lucca (p. 487)
Sept. 19	Festa di San Gennaro	Naples (p. 571)
3rd Su in Sept. (Sept. 21, 2008)	Palio di Asti	Asti (p. 185)
Early Oct.	Sagra dell'Anguilla (Festival of the Eel)	Ferrara (p. 395)
Oct. 4	Festa di San Francesco	Assisi (p. 516)
Late Oct.	EuroChocolate Festival	Perugia (p. 505)
Nov. 1	**Ognissanti (All Saints' Day)**	**National Holiday**
Nov. 2	Giorno dei Morti (All Souls' Day)	Nationwide
Nov. 21	Festa della Salute	Venice (p. 333)
Dec. 8	**Immacolata (Day of Immaculate Conception)**	**National Holiday**
Dec. 13	Festa di Santa Lucia	Syracuse (p. 698)
Dec. 24	Le Farchie di Natale (Christmas Eve)	Nationwide
Dec. 25	**Natale (Christmas Day)**	**National Holiday**
Dec. 26	Festa di Santo Stefano (Saint Stephen's Day)	Nationwide
Dec. 29-Jan. 1	Umbria Jazz Winter	Orvieto (p. 526)
Dec. 31	**Festa di San Silvestro (New Year's Eve)**	**National Holiday**

BEYOND TOURISM

A PHILOSOPHY FOR TRAVELERS

HIGHLIGHTS OF BEYOND TOURISM IN ITALY

TEACH theater and arts to schoolchildren on the coast of **southern Italy.** (p. 103).

ANALYZE rock art from as far back as the Neolithic age in the **Italian Alps** (p. 97).

SPEAK LATIN in **Rome** with Father Reginald Foster *et carpe diem* (p. 101).

COOK like an Italian after attending a culinary school in **Florence** (p. 101).

As a tourist, you are always a foreigner. While hostel-hopping and sightseeing can be great fun, you may want to consider going *beyond* tourism. Experiencing a foreign place through studying, volunteering, or working can help reduce that touristy stranger-in-a-strange-land feeling. Furthermore, travelers can make a positive impact on the natural and cultural environments they visit. With this Beyond Tourism chapter, *Let's Go* hopes to promote a better understanding of Italy and to provide suggestions for those who want to get more than a photo album out of their travels. The "Giving Back" sidebar features (p.222, p. 637) also highlight regional Beyond Tourism opportunities.

There are several options for those who seek Beyond Tourism activities. Opportunities for **volunteerism** abound, with both local and international organizations. **Studying** in a new environment can be enlightening, whether through direct enrollment in a local university or in an independent research project. **Working** is a way to immerse yourself in local culture while financing your travels.

As a **volunteer** in Italy you can participate in projects from maintaining the beautiful Abruzzo National Park to planning cultural festivals, either on a short-term basis or as the main component of your trip. Later in this chapter, we recommend organizations that can help you find the opportunities that best suit your interests, whether you're looking to get involved for a day or for a year.

Studying at a college or in a language program is another option. Many foreign students travel to Italy each year to learn the language, the history, and the culture. In addition to having some of the oldest universities in Europe, Italy also hosts world-renowned fine arts and culinary schools.

Many travelers structure their trips by the **work** available to them along the way ranging from odd jobs on the go to full-time, long-term stints in cities. Opportunities in Italy include interning at a museum in Venice or teaching English in schools around the country. Remember that in order to work in Italy in either a short- or long-term capacity, you must have a work permit.

VOLUNTEERING

Volunteering can be a powerful and fulfilling experience, especially when combined with the thrill of traveling in a new place. Whether you chose to restore medieval villas for future tourists to enjoy or preserve the ocean for future dolphins to live, volunteering in Italy can make your stay more meaningful.

Most people who volunteer in Italy do so on a short-term basis, at organizations that make use of drop-in or once-a-week volunteers. The best way to find opportunities that match up with your interests and schedule may be to check with local or national volunteer centers similar to the ones listed below, which organize workcamps devoted to community development and helping the environment. Numerous organizations seek volunteers for ecological and historical preservation, and opportunities in community development are also available.

> ↳ **WHY PAY MONEY TO VOLUNTEER?** Many volunteers are surprised to learn that some organizations require large fees or "donations." While this may seem ridiculous at first glance, such fees often keep the organization afloat, in addition to covering airfare, room, board, and administrative expenses for the volunteers. (Other organizations must rely on private donations and government subsidies.) If you're concerned about how a program spends its fees, request an annual report or finance account. A reputable organization won't refuse to inform you of how volunteer money is spent.
>
> Pay-to-volunteer programs might be a good idea for young travelers who are looking for more support and structure (such as pre-arranged transportation and housing), or anyone who would rather not deal with the uncertainty implicit in creating a volunteer experience from scratch.

Those looking for longer, more intensive volunteer opportunities usually choose to go through a parent organization that takes care of logistical details and often provides a group environment and support system—for a fee. There are two main types of organizations—religious and non-sectarian—although there are rarely restrictions on participation for either.

Service Civil International, 5505 Walnut Level Rd., Crozet, VA 22932, USA (☎206-350-6585; www.sci-ivs.org). Places volunteers in small, 2- to 3-week, primarily summer, work-camps that range from festival assistance to social work to environmental or historical restoration. 18+. Program fee US$195.

Volunteers for Peace, 1034 Tiffany Rd., Belmont, VT 05730, USA (☎802-259-2759; www.vfp.org). Provides info on over 50 volunteer programs in Italy. Program fee US$250, under 18 $500.

ECOVOLUNTEERISM

Italy's expansive coastline and mild mainland environment play host to thousands of visitors annually. As a result, it is important for tourists to understand the role they play in preserving the environment that has made Italy such a popular tourist destination. Opportunities to work with wildlife and restore local habitats can be a great way to experience Italian culture at its best.

Canadian Alliance for Development Initiatives and Projects (CADIP), 129-1271 Howe St., Vancouver, British Columbia, V6Z 1R3, Canada (☎604-628-7400; www.cadip.org). Offers over 100 short 2-3 week projects in Italy with an emphasis on environmental and historical preservation. Room and board provided by the program. Most projects 18+. US$235; some projects have extra fees.

Parco Nazionale d'Abruzzo, Lazio e Molise, V. Roma s.n.c., 67030 Villetta Barrea, AQ (☎08 64 89 102; www.parcoabruzzo.it). Hosts over 1000 summer volunteers for 1-3 weeks. Responsibilities range from park maintenance to visitor assistance. 18+. Program fee 1 week €110, 2 weeks €170, 3 weeks €230.

Ecovolunteer: Common Dolphin Research, CTS-Centro Turistico Studentesco e Giovanile, Dept. Ambiente, V. Albalonga 3, 00183 Rome (☎06 64 96 03 27; www.ecovolunteer.org). Volunteers in the Gulf of Naples live and eat on a research boat while tracking dolphins and other marine mammals. 1-week programs June-Oct. 18+. Program fee €720-820 per week depending on season. Discount for second week.

Lega Italiana Protezione Uccelli (LIPU), LIPU Sede Nazionale, V. Trento 49, 43100 Parma (☎05 21 27 30 43; www.lipu.it/tu_volontario.htm). Volunteers at this bird sanctuary help with grounds maintenance and do some work with animals.

World-Wide Opportunities on Organic Farms, WWOOF Italia, V. Casavecchia 109, 57022 Castagneto Carducci, Livorno (www.wwoof.it). Provides a list of organic farms that introduce volunteers to tasks like harvesting olives, grapes, and even bamboo. Knowledge of farming not necessary, although volunteers should be physically capable and willing to work hard. Required €25 membership fee.

ART, CULTURE, AND RESTORATION

Italy's rich cultural heritage, which dates back to the Roman times, is increasingly in danger of crumbling or being overrun by modern life. Volunteers looking for a labor-intensive way to engage with Italy's rich cultural heritage should research groups specializing in landmark preservation. Check out the organizations listed below, and **CADIP** above.

Gruppi Archeologici d'Italia, V. Baldo degli Ubaldi 168, 00165 Rome (☎06 39 37 67 11; www.gruppiarcheologici.org). Organizes 1- to 2-week volunteer programs during the summer at archaeological digs throughout Italy. Offers links to various programs that promote cultural awareness about archaeological preservation. All programs 15+, some 17+. Program fee €220-430, depending on program and length of participation.

Footsteps of Man, Ple. Donatori di Sangue 1, 25040 Cerveno, BS, Italy (☎03 64 43 39 83; www.rupestre.net/field/index.html). Accepts 25 volunteers for a minimum stay of 7 days to analyze rock art in the Italian Alps, dating from the Neolithic era to the Middle Ages. Training provided. 16+. €370 per week.

Responsible Travel.com, 3rd Floor, Pavilion House, 6 Old Steine, Brighton BN1 1EJ, UK (☎12 73 60 00 30; www.responsibletravel.com). Various volunteer opportunities, including cultural preservation projects. Length varies. Program fee US$305-1357, depending on project.

Archeo Venezia, Cannaregio 1376/a, 30121 Venezia (☎41 71 05 15; www.provincia.venezia.it/archeove). Offers 1-week programs in archeological field work, including ceramics, metalwork, and painting. €350 program fee includes room and board.

YOUTH AND THE COMMUNITY

Community-based projects are among the most rewarding volunteer experiences. Programs listed below promote close work with the disadvantaged of Italy's population. Due to their one-on-one nature, knowledge of Italian is often necessary.

United Planet, 11 Arlington St., Boston, MA 02116, USA (☎617-267-7763; www.unitedplanet.org). Places volunteers in 6-month to 1-year programs worldwide, including many aimed at helping children, the elderly, and the disabled in Italy. Ages 18-30. Tax-deductible fee of US$5000 for 6 months and $8000 for 1 year includes local transportation costs, training, a monthly stipend and room and board with a host family.

Agape Centro Ecumenico, Segreteria di Agape, Borgata Agape 1, 10060 Prali, TO (☎0121 80 75 14; www.agapecentroecumenico.org). Help maintain this international Protestant conference center in the Italian Alps. Clean and cook for the center from 2 days to 5 weeks in return for free room and board during spring and summer. Knowledge of Italian useful. 18+.

Global Volunteers, 375 East Little Canada Rd., St. Paul, MN 55117, USA (☎800-487-1074; www.globalvolunteers.org). Teach English in southern Italy to children aged 8 to 14. 2-week sessions available throughout the year. Program fee US$1995-2695.

Pueblo Inglés, Rafael Calvo 18, 4A, Madrid 28010, Spain (☎34 913 913 400; www.puebloingles.com). Week-long program in a Tuscan village hires native English-speaking volunteers to provide English-language immersion for Italians. Room and board provided. Ages 22-80; alternative opportunities for ages 14-21. Free.

STUDYING

VISA INFORMATION. Italian bureaucracy often gives international visitors the run-around, but there are ways to minimize paperwork confusion. Just remember that all **non-EU citizens** are required to obtain a visa for any stay longer than three months. For info and applications, contact the Italian embassy or consulate in your country. Before applying for a student visa, however, be sure to obtain the following documentation: valid passport, visa application form (available from most embassy websites), four passport-size photographs, proof of residency, complete documentation on the course or program in which you are participating, affidavit of financial support from parents, and your parents' most recent bank statement. All non-EU citizens are also required to register with the *Ufficio degli Stranieri* (Foreigners' Bureau) at the *questura* (local police headquarters) to receive a *permesso di soggiorno* (permit of stay) within eight days of arriving in Italy. The same documentation is necessary for the *permesso di soggiorno* as for the visa; additionally, applicants must have the required permit of stay form and a *Marca da Bollo,* which costs €14.62 and is available at an Italian *tabaccheria*. **EU citizens** must apply for a *permesso di soggiorno* within three months, but they do not need a visa to study in Italy. Once you find a place to live, bring your permit of stay (it must have at least one year's validity) to a records office. This certificate will both confirm your registered address and expedite travel into and out of Italy.

Study abroad programs range from basic language and culture courses to college-level classes, often for credit. In order to choose a program that best fits your needs, research as much as you can before making your decision—determine costs and duration, as well as what kind of students participate in the program and what sort of accommodations are provided.

In programs that have large groups of students who speak the same language, there is a trade-off. You may feel more comfortable in the community, but you will not have the same opportunity to practice a foreign language or to befriend other international students. For accommodations, dorm life provides a better opportunity to mingle with fellow students, but there is less of a chance to experience Italian cultural immersion. If you live with an Italian host family, there is a potential to build lifelong friendships with natives and to experience day-to-day life in more depth, but conditions can vary greatly from family to family.

UNIVERSITIES

Most university-level study-abroad programs are conducted in Italian, although many programs offer classes in English and beginner- and lower-level language courses. Those who are relatively fluent in Italian may find it cheaper to enroll directly in a university abroad, although getting college credit may be more difficult. You can search **www.studyabroad.com** for various semester-abroad programs that meet your criteria, including your desired location and focus of study. The following is a list of organizations that can help place students in university programs abroad, or have their own branch in Italy.

AMERICAN SCHOOLS

American Field Service (AFS): Intercultura, 71 W. 23rd St., 17th fl., New York, NY 10010 USA (☎212-807-8686; www.afs.org). Operating in Italy since 1955, AFS now leads the country in educational exchanges for high school students between Italy and over 54 countries worldwide. Offers language-based homestays. Ages 16-18. Prices and programs vary.

American Institute for Foreign Study, College Division, River Plaza, 9 W. Broad St., Stamford, CT 06902, USA (☎800-727-2437; www.aifsabroad.com). Term-time programs in Florence and Rome. Mandatory Italian-language class; internships available. Meals, excursions, and homestay or student apartment included. 9-13 credits. Semester US$14,495; year US$26,590. Scholarships and summer sessions also available.

CET Academic Programs: Italian Studies Program in Siena, Florence, and Sicily, 1920 N St. NW, Ste. 200, Washington, D.C. 20036, USA (☎800-225-4262; www.cetacademicprograms.com). Only open to the public for the summer term, this Vanderbilt University program offers art history courses and traveling seminars. Italian-language course mandatory. Summer US$7290-7820; semester US$15,000-16,000. Includes medical insurance and housing.

Council on International Educational Exchange (CIEE), 7 Custom House St., 3rd fl., Portland, ME 01401, USA (☎800-407-8839; www.ciee.org/study). Fall, spring, and year-long college study abroad program in Ferrara. Courses taught in English and Italian. Housing in residence halls or limited homestays. Semester US$12,000.

BEYOND TOURISM

The Experiment in International Living, Kipling Rd., P.O. Box 676, Brattleboro, VT 05302, USA (☎800-345-2929; www.usexperiment.org). 5-week summer programs offer high-school students homestays, cooking, and language training in Italy and cost US$6100-6200.

LANGUAGE SCHOOLS

Language schools can be independently run by international or local organizations or divisions of foreign universities. They rarely offer college credit. They are a good alternative to university study if you desire a deeper focus on the language or a slightly less rigorous courseload. These programs are also good for younger high school students who might not feel comfortable with older students in a university program. Some worthwhile programs include:

Centro Culturale Giaccomo Puccini, V. Vespucci 173, 55049 Viareggio (☎05 84 43 0253; www.centropuccini.it). 2-12 week language courses at all levels. Professional Italian and cultural courses available. Additional accommodations fee for apartment or homestay. Program costs €250-1260. €70 registration fee.

Centro Fiorenza, V. S. Spirito 14, 50125 Florence (☎05 52 39 82 74; www.centrofiorenza.com). Students live in private homes or apartments in Florence and are immersed in Italian. Program also offers courses on the island of Elba, although hotel accommodations there are expensive. Courses (20 lessons per week) 1-5 weeks, from €180. Enrollment fee €55.

Eurocentres, 56 Eccleston Sq., UK-London SW1V 1PH (☎44 02 07 96 38 450; www.eurocentres.com) or Seestr. 247, CH-8038 Zürich, Switzerland (☎41 04 44 85 50 40). Language programs from beginner to advanced levels with homestays in Florence. 2-13 week programs starting at $886. Costs vary with housing and meal options.

Istituto Venezia, Campo S. Margherita 3116/a, Dorsoduro, 30123 Venice (☎041 52 24 331; www.istitutovenezia.com). Language and art history classes at all levels,

taught in small groups. Courses 1-4 weeks. Language classes also taught in Trieste. Accommodation arrangements upon request; costs and housing types vary.

Italiaidea, V. dei Due Macelli 47, 1st fl., 00187 Rome (☎06 69 94 13 14; www.italiaidea.com). 1- to 10-week Italian language and culture courses near the Spanish Steps for groups of 10 or fewer. Courses qualify for credit at most American universities. Students live in private homes, homestay, or apartments; reserve ahead. Program costs €300-600. €50 registration fee.

Koinè, V. de' Pandolfini 27, I-50122 Florence (☎05 52 13 881; www.koine-center.com). Language lessons (group and individual), cultural lessons, wine tastings, and cooking lessons. Courses offered in Florence, Lucca, Bologna, Cortona, and Elba. 1-4 week courses €215-4780. Deposit €150.

Language Immersion Institute, SCB 106, SUNY-New Paltz, 1 Hawk Dr., New Paltz, NY 12561, USA (☎845-257-3500; www.newpaltz.edu/lii). Italian language courses taught in Florence, Milan, Rome, and Siena. 2-24 weeks €370-3830.

ITALIAN SCHOOLS: SPECIAL INTEREST

FINE ARTS

Aegean Center for the Fine Arts, Paros 84400, Cyclades, Greece (☎30 22 84 02 32 87; www.aegeancenter.org). Italian branch located in Pistoia. Instruction in arts, literature, creative writing, voice, and art history. Classes taught in English. Fees cover housing in 16th-century villa, meals, and excursions to Rome, Venice, and Greece. University credit on individual arrangement. 14-week program in the fall €8800.

Art School in Florence, Studio Art Centers International, 50 Broad St., Ste. 1617, New York, NY 10004, USA (☎212-248-7225; www.saci-florence.org). Affiliated with Bowling Green State University. Studio arts, art history, Italian studies. Apartment housing. 6 credits summer US$5850; 15 credits semester US$14,900.

Scuola Arte del Mosaico, V. Francesco Negri 14, 48110 Ravenna (☎349 60 14 566; www.sira.it/mosaic/studio.htm). Participants learn the history and techniques of making ancient and modern mosaics and create their own. 5-day course (40hr.) for beginner, intermediate and professional levels conducted in English. Program fee €660.

COOKING IN LA CUCINA

Apicius, The Culinary Institute of Florence, V. Guelfa 85, Florence 50129 (☎055 26 58 135; www.apicius.it). Professional and non-professional food and wine studies in historic Florence. Cooking courses in English; Italian language classes available. Prices for weekly, non-professional programs €65-1150. Masters in Italian cuisine €10,550.

Cook Italy (☎34 90 07 82 98; www.cookitaly.com). Region- or dish-specific cooking classes. Venues include Lucca, Bologna, Cortona, and Sicily. Courses 3 nights to 2 weeks from €790. Housing, meals, and recipes included.

The International Kitchen, 1 IBM Plaza, 330 N. Wabash #2613, Chicago, IL 60611, USA (☎800-945-8606; www.theinternationalkitchen.com). A leading provider of cooking school vacations to Italy. Traditional cooking instruction in beautiful settings for groups of 6-12 people. Program locations include Tuscany, Liguria, and Amalfi Coast. Courses 1-10 nights. US$20-3500.

ROCKIN' RELICS

🗟 **Aestiva Romae Latinitatis, Summer Latin in Rome,** P. Reginald Foster OCD, Teresianum, P. San Pancrazio 5A, I-00152 Rome. Free 6-week summer Latin program in Rome with legendary Father Reginald Foster, an American priest who works in the "Latin Letters" section of the Vatican's Secretariat of State. Foster has taught this program for over 35 years. Lessons in written and conversational Latin for intermediate and advanced students. Optional lesson "sub arboribus" (under the trees in the monastery garden) given in the evenings. Write for info and application materials.

ArchaeoSpain, PO Box 1331, Farmington, CT 06034, USA (☎866-932-0003; www.archaeospain.com). Archaeology buffs help out at an Italian archaeological site in Rome at Monte Testaccio, once an ancient pottery dump and now the best record of Roman commerce. English speakers and all ages welcome. University credit on individual arrangement. 2-week program $2745. Housing and meals included.

WORKING

As with volunteering, work opportunities tend to fall into two categories. Some travelers want long-term jobs that allow them to integrate into a community, while others seek out short-term jobs to finance the next leg of their travels. In Italy, travelers usually find jobs in the service sector or in agriculture, working for a few weeks at a time.

Listed below are specific jobs for long- and short-term stays, as well as agencies that can provide useful info regarding work opportunities. Note that working abroad requires a special work visa; see the box below for information about obtaining one.

VISA INFORMATION. EU passport holders do not require a visa to work in Italy. They must have a worker's registration book *(libretto di lavoro)*, available at no extra cost upon presentation of the *permesso di soggiorno*. Children of EU citizens may be able to claim dual citizenship or the right to a work permit. **Non-EU citizens** seeking work in Italy must possess an Italian work permit *(autorizzazione al lavoro in Italia)* before entering the country. Only a prospective employer can begin the process, guaranteeing that the individual has been offered a position. Permits are authorized by the Provincial Employment Office and approved by the police headquarters *(questura)* before being forwarded to the employer and prospective employee. The prospective employee must then present the document, along with a valid passport, in order to obtain a work visa. Normally a 3-month tourist permit is granted, and upon presentation of an employer's letter the permit can be extended for a period specified by the employment contract. See www.italyemb.org for further details.

LONG-TERM WORK

If you're planning on spending a substantial amount of time (more than three months) working in Italy, search for a job well in advance. International placement agencies are often the easiest way to find employment abroad, especially for those interested in teaching English. Although they are often only available to college students, **internships** are a good way to segue into working abroad; while they are often un- or underpaid, many say the experience is well worth it. Be wary of advertisements for companies claiming to be able get you a job abroad for a fee—often the same listings are available online or in newspapers. Some reputable organizations include:

Center for Cultural Interchange, 746 N. LaSalle Dr., Chicago, IL 60610, USA (☎312-944-2544; www.cci-exchange.com/intern.htm). 3-5 month volunteer internships with companies in Florence. Opportunities in business, accounting and finance, tourism, and social services. At least 2 years of college-level Italian required. US$6,450-9,650. Tuition includes Italian language course, health insurance, and homestay with half-board.

Global Experiences, 1010 Pendleton St., Alexandria, VA 22314, USA (☎888-247-3552; www.globalexperiences.com). Arranges internships with companies based in

BEYOND TOURISM

Florence, Rome, Verona and Milan. Interns receive intensive language training prior to placement. Fields include law, international business, travel and tourism, graphic design, fashion, and journalism.

Institute for the International Education of Students, 33 N. LaSalle St., 15th fl., Chicago, IL 60602, USA (☎800-995-2300; www.iesabroad.org). Intern placements in Rome and Milan based on availability, background, skills, and language ability. Past placements include assignments with fashion designers, photographers, and political parties. Must be for academic credit.

Peggy Guggenheim Collection, Palazzo Venier dei Leoni, Dorsoduro 701, 30123 Venice (☎041 24 05 401; www.guggenheim-venice.it). Interns assist museum operations such as gallery preparation, tour guidance, and administrative matters for 1-3 months.

TEACHING ENGLISH

Teaching jobs abroad are rarely well-paid, although some elite private American schools offer competitive salaries. Volunteering as a teacher in lieu of getting paid is a popular option; even then, teachers often receive some sort of a daily stipend to help with living expenses. In almost all cases, you must have at least a bachelor's degree to be a full-fledged teacher, although college undergraduates can often get summer positions teaching or tutoring. English-language schools abound in Italy, but the supply of applicants is also plentiful, and positions are competitive. Finding a teaching job is even harder for non-EU citizens, as some schools prefer, or in some cases even require, EU citizenship.

Many schools require teachers to have a **Teaching English as a Foreign Language (TEFL)** certificate. You may still be able to find a teaching job without certification, but certified teachers often find higher-paying jobs. Native English speakers working in private schools are most often hired for English-immersion classrooms. Those volunteering or teaching in public schools are more likely to be working in both English and Italian. Placement agencies or university fellowship programs are the best resources for finding teaching jobs. The alternative is to contact schools directly or to try your luck once you arrive in Italy. If you are going to try the latter, the best time to look is several weeks before the start of the school year. The following organizations are extremely helpful in placing teachers in Italy.

International Schools Services (ISS), 15 Roszel Rd., P.O. Box 5910, Princeton, NJ 08543, USA (☎609-452-0990; www.iss.edu). Hires teachers for more than 200 overseas schools, including several in Italy; candidates should have experience teaching or with international affairs. 2-year commitment expected.

Associazione Culturale Linguista Educational (ACLE), V. Roma 54, 18038 San Remo, Imperio, Italy (☎0184 50 60 70; www.acle.org). Non-profit association working to bring theater, arts, and English language instruction to Italian schools. Employees create theater programs in schools, teach English at summer camps, and help convert a medieval home into a student art center. Knowledge of Italian useful. On-site accommodations and cooking facilities included. Ages 20-30. Sept.-June. 2-week minimum with a weekly salary of €190-200.

Office of Overseas Schools, US Department of State, 2201 C St. NW, Washington, D.C. 20520, USA (☎202-647-4000; www.state.gov/m/a/os). Provides an extensive list of general info about teaching overseas. See also the **Office of English Language Programs** (http://exchanges.state.gov/education/engteaching).

AU PAIR WORK

Au pairs are typically women (although sometimes men), aged 18-27, who work as live-in nannies, caring for children and doing light housework in foreign countries in exchange for room, board, and a small spending allowance or stipend. One perk of the job is that it allows you to get to know Italy without the high expenses of traveling. Drawbacks, however, can include mediocre pay and long hours. In Italy, average weekly pay for au pair work is about €65/US$82. Much of the au pair experience depends on the family with whom you are placed. The agencies below are a good starting point for looking for employment.

Childcare International, Ltd., Trafalgar House, Grenville Pl., London NW7 3SA (☎44 020 89 06 31 16; www.childint.com). Matches prospective au pairs with families. Participants should have some experience in childcare. Ages 18-27.

Roma Au Pair, Via L. Bellotti Bon, 15 Rome, Italy 00197. (☎39 339 77 94 126; www.romaaupair.it) Provides information on au pair placement throughout Italy.

SHORT-TERM WORK

Traveling for long periods of time can be hard on the finances; therefore, many travelers try their hand at odd jobs for a few weeks at a time to help pay for another month or two of touring around. Romantic images of cultivating the land in a sun-soaked vineyard may dance in your head, but in reality, casual agricultural jobs are hard to find in Italy due to foreign migrant workers who are often willing to work for less pay. Your best bet for agricultural jobs is to look in the northwest during the annual fall harvest or volunteer with WWOOF (p. 97). Another popular option is to work several hours a day at a hostel in exchange for free or discounted room and/or board. Most often, these short-term jobs are found by word of mouth, or by expressing interest to the owner of a hostel or restaurant. Due to high turnover in the tourism industry, many places are eager for help, even if it is only temporary. *Let's Go* lists temporary jobs of this nature whenever possible; look in the practical information sections of larger cities or check out the list below for some of the available short-term jobs in popular destinations.

Ostello La Primula (HI), V. IV Novembre 106, Menaggio 22017 (☎/fax 0344 32 356; www.menaggiohostel.com). Work in return for room and board (p. 294).

Youth Info Center (Informagiovani), with multiple locations in every Italian region (www.informagiovani-italia.com). Each center has its own website. Each regional office provides varying amounts of free info on logistics like work regulations, employment trends, volunteer programs, and study opportunities in the area. *Let's Go* lists local offices in their corresponding chapters.

FURTHER READING ON BEYOND TOURISM

Back Door Guide to Short-Term Job Adventures: Internships, Extraordinary Experiences, Seasonal Jobs, Volunteering, Working Abroad, by Michael Landes. Ten Speed Press, 2002 (US$22).

Green Volunteers: The World Guide to Voluntary Work in Nature, ed. Fabio Ausenda. Universe, 2003 (US$15).

How to Get a Job in Europe, by Cheryl Matherly and Robert Sanborn. Planning Communications, 2003 (US$23).

How to Live Your Dream of Volunteering Overseas, by Joseph Collins, Stefano DeZerega, and Zahara Heckscher. Penguin Books, 2002 (US$18).

International Job Finder: Where the Jobs Are Worldwide, by Daniel Lauber and Kraig Rice. Planning Communications, 2002 (US$20).

Live and Work Abroad: A Guide for Modern Nomads, by Huw Francis and Michelyne Callan. Vacation-Work Publications, 2001 (US$16).

Overseas Summer Jobs 2002. Peterson's Guides and Vacation Work, 2002 (US$18).

Volunteer Vacations: Short-term Adventures That Will Benefit You and Others, by Doug Cutchins and Anne Geissinger. Chicago Review Press, 2003 (US$18).

Work Abroad: The Complete Guide to Finding a Job Overseas, by Clayton Hubbs. Transitions Abroad Publishing, 2002 (US$16).

Work Your Way Around the World, by Susan Griffith. Vacation-Work Publications, 2005 (US$22).

BEYOND TOURISM

saving alta irpinia

How ecotourism might save one of Italy's poorest regions.

Anywhere but these rolling hills of wheat. Such a thought is not uncommon in Alta Irpinia, a region in Campania. Here, the problems that mark the entire South are exacerbated by the mountainous terrain that makes agriculture unprofitable, unlike in the fertile Puglian plains. Modern industry and economy have failed here, and the few factories that once provided jobs are moving overseas. Unemployment is around 20%. In addition, Irpinia is at high seismic risk. The effects of the terrible earthquake of November 1980, which claimed 5000 lives and completely destroyed 30 towns, are still visible. While government subsidies flowed in to revitalize the region, there was little long-term success. In recent years, Irpinia's best and brightest have migrated to Naples or north to Turin or Milan. Those who remain are faced with an obsolete traditional lifestyle and continued, ineffective attempts to adopt more modern ways.

Some Irpinians believe that their traditional culture is worth fighting for. A new buzzword, *agriturismo*, or ecotourism, denotes this push to save Irpinia by moving closer to nature and to rural ways of life. The region's riches include beautiful mountains, famous wines, archaeological sites, and ancient castles and churches. Not all was destroyed by earthquakes or by building speculation, although often the potential of a site is wasted because of a lack of resources to develop it. A number of castles dot a region once ruled by the medieval court of Frederick II. The medieval period also left behind many churches and monasteries, but archaeological sites are Irpinia's real hidden treasure. Prior to the Roman invasion, a local population of Sannites flourished here. Little is known about them, as there have never been funds to excavate the region properly. The situation is a vicious circle: without fully developed cultural sites,

there will be no tourism; yet without a tourist industry, there will never be money to excavate ruins or restore churches.

The Zampaglione family is a good example of a business that has completely embraced the *agriturismo* ethos. Their farm near Calitri has produced organic wheat since 1990, which is then made into organic pasta. In 1998 they transformed their old barns into a guesthouse. A visit to the Zampaglione farm presents northern Italians with the chance to connect to the rural culture of their grandparents. The Zampagliones also hope to attract international travelers who already know Italy and wish to see the country from a different angle. However, often weeks pass when no one ventures to the farm, and the post-9/11 tourism slump has not helped.

Ethnographic museums have been more successful in taking root and matching the ideals of *agriturismo*. Museums attempt to preserve and present what is known of traditional village culture. Visitors are fascinated

"A new buzzword, *agriturismo*, or ecotourism, denotes [a] push to save Irpinia"

by the handicrafts, such as ceramics, still practiced in Irpinia. Yet, industrial procedures threaten to replace these ancient crafts. The last original practitioners of Irpinian pottery fire their pots only once a year in a large, purpose-built oven, which is then destroyed. Local cuisine, fortunately, does not face the same risk, as the healthy, rural diet strong in fresh pastas and cheeses continues to thrive.

Agriturismo is still the work of individuals, and does not reflect a greater policy on the part of the Avellino province. Nonetheless, *agriturismo* is an important validation for those who refuse to modernize or leave.

A DIFFERENT PATH

Alexander Bevilacqua was born in Milan and has lived in Germany, Australia, and the United States, but his heart remains in the wheat fields of southern Italy. He is a 2006 graduate in History at Harvard University and was a Researcher-Writer for Let's Go: Germany 2005 in Bavaria.

ROME

ROME (ROMA)　　　　　　　　　☎06

Rome (RO-ma; pop. 2.8 million), *la città eterna*, is a concentrated expression of Italian spirit. Whether flaunting their 2006 World Cup victory or retelling the mythical story of the city's founding, Romans exude a fierce pride for the Rome that was and the Rome that will be. Crumbling pagan ruins form the backdrop for the center of Christianity's largest denomination, and hip clubs and bars border grand cathedrals. Although the city cannot separate itself from its past, it still very much lives in the present. The aroma of homemade pasta, the pop of opening wine bottles, and the rumble of city buses will greet you at every turn on Rome's labyrinthine cobblestone streets. Augustus once boasted that he found Rome a city of brick and left it one of marble. No matter how you find it, you'll undoubtedly leave it with a smile and a new appreciation for *la dolce vita*.

HIGHLIGHTS OF ROME

CHANNEL Rome's Golden Age with a trip to the **Ancient City** (p. 122).

SURVEY Rome's art scene, and let collections from the **Vatican Museums** (p. 147) to the **Galleria Borghese** (p. 148) prove the city deserving of its reputation.

TOSS a coin into the **Trevi fountain** for a speedy return to the Eternal City (p. 138).

EVADE the temptations of Circe on the **Pontine Islands,** where the likes of Mussolini, Nero, and even Odysseus were reputedly held captive (p. 163).

✈ INTERCITY TRANSPORTATION

FLIGHTS

Most international flights arrive at **Da Vinci International Airport,** known as **Fiumicino** (☎65 21 01). After exiting customs, follow the signs for **Stazione Trenitalia/Railway Station.** The **Termini line** (Leonardo Express) runs nonstop to Rome's main train station, **Termini** (30min.; 2 per hr. 5 and 35min. past the hour, 6:35am-11:35pm; €11). Buy a ticket at the Trenitalia ticket counter, the *tabaccheria* on the right, or from one of the machines in the station. Beware of scam artists attempting to sell fake tickets. A train leaves Termini for Fiumicino from track #24 (30min.; 2 per hr. 22 and 52min. past the hr., 5:52am-10:52pm; €12). Buy tickets at the Railway Information Center (open 7am-9:45pm), by track #4, at the Leonardo Express kiosk on track #24, or from other designated areas in the station. Failure to validate your ticket in one of the yellow machines before boarding could lead to a €50 fine.

EARLY AND LATE FLIGHTS. For flights that arrive after 10:30pm or leave before 8am, the most reliable option to go between Rome and the airport is a **taxi.** (Request one at the kiosk in the airport or call ☎49 94 or 66 45.) **Decide upon a price with the driver before getting into the cab**—it should be around €40. Factors such as the amount of luggage and the time of day will affect the price. The cheapest option is to take the blue **COTRAL bus** (☎80 01 50 008) outside the main exit doors after customs to Tiburtina (1:15, 2:15, 3:30, 5am; €5 onboard). From Tiburtina, take buses #492 or 175 or Metro B to Termini. To get to Fiumicino from Rome late at night or early in the morning, take bus #492 or 40N (which takes over for Metro B at night) from Termini to Tiburtina (every 20-30min.), then catch the blue

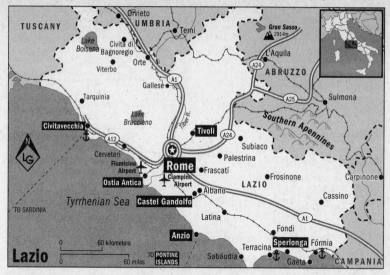

COTRAL bus to Fiumicino from the *piazza* (12:30, 1:15, 2:30, 3:45am; €5). The 24hr. **airport shuttle** service (☎47 40 451 or 42 01 34 69; www.airportshuttle.it) is a good deal for two or more. Call or visit the website to reserve a spot. (€28, each additional passenger €6; early mornings, nights, and holidays prices rise 30%.)

CIAMPINO AIRPORT. Most charter flights and a few domestic ones, including **Ryanair,** arrive at **Ciampino Airport** (☎79 49 41). To get to Rome from Ciampino, take the **COTRAL bus** (every 30min. 6:10am-11:40pm, €1) to Anagnina station on Metro A. The public shuttle buses (☎59 16 826; www.sitbusshuttle.com) or the **Terravision Shuttle** (☎79 34 17 22; www.terravision.it) are slightly more convenient options, especially for late or early flights. They both go to V. Marsala, outside Termini, at the Hotel Royal Santina (40min.; 25 per day per carrier, first shuttles to Ciampino 4:30am, last shuttles to Rome around midnight; public shuttle €6, Terravision €8). Schedules are online and at the Hotel. After 11pm and before 7am, take a **taxi** (€35-40) from the arrivals area.

TRAINS

Stazione Termini is the hub for most train and subway lines, even though it's closed between midnight and 5:30am. Trains arriving in Rome during this time usually arrive at Stazione Tiburtina or Stazione Ostiense; both connect to Termini at night by bus #175. Station services include: shopping; **ATMs;** hotel reservations, across from track #13; **luggage storage,** underneath track #24; **police,** track #13, make a report at track #1. Termini's **bathrooms** (€0.70) beneath track #1 are a surreal black-lit wonderland. Trains (Direct, or D, is the slowest; IC is the intercity train; ES, or Eurostar, is the fastest and most expensive) leave Termini for: **Bologna** (IC 3¾hr., €33; ES 2½hr., €42); **Florence** (D 3¾hr., €14; IC 2½hr., €24; ES 1½hr., €33); **Milan** (D 8hr., €30; IC 6hr., €41; ES 4½hr., €50); **Naples** (D 2½hr., €10; IC 2hr., €19; ES 1¾hr., €25); **Venice** (D overnight, €33; IC 5½hr., €39; ES 4½hr., €50). Hours and prices are updated every six months; check www.trenitalia.it for the most up-to-date schedules and prices.

▄ ORIENTATION

Because Rome's narrow, winding streets are difficult to navigate, it's helpful to orient yourself to major landmarks and main streets. The **Tiber River,** which snakes north-

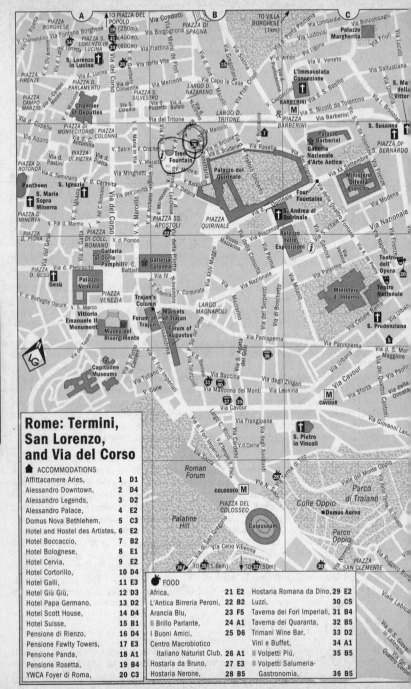

ROME

Rome: Termini, San Lorenzo, and Via del Corso

🏠 ACCOMMODATIONS

Affittacamere Aries,	1	D1
Alessandro Downtown,	2	D4
Alessandro Legends,	3	D2
Alessandro Palace,	4	E2
Domus Nova Bethlehem,	5	C3
Hotel and Hostel des Artistes,	6	E2
Hotel Boccaccio,	7	B2
Hotel Bolognese,	8	E1
Hotel Cervia,	9	E2
Hotel Cortorillo,	10	D4
Hotel Galli,	11	E3
Hotel Giù Giù,	12	D3
Hotel Papa Germano,	13	D2
Hotel Scott House,	14	D4
Hotel Suisse,	15	B1
Pensione di Rienzo,	16	D4
Pensione Fawlty Towers,	17	E3
Pensione Panda,	18	A1
Pensione Rosetta,	19	B4
YWCA Foyer di Roma,	20	C3

🍴 FOOD

Africa,	21	E2	Hostaria Romana da Dino,	29	E2
L'Antica Birreria Peroni,	22	B2	Luzzi,	30	C5
Arancia Blu,	23	F5	Taverna dei Fori Imperiali,	31	B4
Il Brillo Parlante,	24	A1	Taverna dei Quaranta,	32	B5
I Buoni Amici,	25	D6	Trimani Wine Bar,	33	D2
Centro Macrobiotico			Vini e Buffet,	34	A1
Italiano Naturist Club,	26	A1	Il Volpetti Piú,	35	B5
Hostaria da Bruno,	27	E3	Il Volpetti Salumeria-		
Hostaria Nerone,	28	B5	Gastronomía,	36	B5

TO [M] (500m)

PIAZZALE D.
PORTA PIA

🌙 NIGHTLIFE
Alien,   42 E1

☕ CAFES
Enoteca Cavour 313,   37 B4
Il Gelato di San Crispino,   38 B2
Il Gelatone,   39 B4
L'Impiccione Viaggiatore,   40 B4
Lion Bookshop & Café,   41 A1

PIAZZA
D. CROCE
ROSSA

Viale di Villa

PIAZZALE
G. FABRIZIO

POLICLINICO
[M]

Via G. M. Lancisi

PIAZZA
SASSARI

Ministeri del
Bilancio e del Tesoro

Via Nomentana

Via Bellssiario

Via Collina

Via S. Tullo

Via Piave

Via Carducci

V. Flavia

Via XX Settembre

Via Quintino Sella

Via Piemonte

Viale del
Policlinico

Castro
Praetorio

Viale Castro Pretorio

CASTRO
[M] PRETORIO

Biblioteca
Nazionale

Viale Policlinico

CITTÀ
UNIVERSITARIA

Musei Nazionali Romani

Terme di
Diocleziano

S. Maria
d. Angeli

REPUBBLICA
PIAZZA D.
EPUBBLICA

arner
illage
loderno

Via Cernaia

Via Montebello

Via Gaeta

Via Goito

Via Calatalimi

Via Gaeta

Via Volturno

Via Solferino

Via S. Martino d. Battaglia

PIAZZA
INDIPENDENZA

Via Marghera

PIAZZA
D. CROCE
ROSSA

Viale dell'Università

Min. D.festa
Aeronautica

CITTÀ
UNIVERSITARIA

Viale delle Scienze

Enjoy
Rome ℹ

PIAZZA DEI
CINQUECENTO

Via Vicenza

Via Magenta

Via Marsala

TERMINI
[M]

Termini
Station [M]

TERMINI

ℹ

Via Milazzo

Via Castro Pretorio

Splashnet
Internet,
Laundry,
and
Luggage
Storage

Viale dell'Università

Viale Piero Gobetti

PIAZZALE
ALDO MORO

Via d. Frentani

Via Cesare de Lollis

Via dei Marmici

PIAZZA
ELL'ESQUILINO

S. Maria
Maggiore

Via Gioberti

Via Carlo Cattaneo

PIAZZA
M. FANTI

Via Filippo Turati

Via Giovanni Giolitti

Via Marsala

Viale Pretoriano

Via Porta Tiburtina

Via dei Ramni

Via di Tizi

Via dei Dalmati

Prassede

ESQUILINO

Via Carlo Alberto

Via Rattazzi

Via Principe Amedeo

Via T. Mamiani

LARGO
D. FALISCI

Via Tiburtina
Antica

PIAZZALE
TIBURTINO

LARGO
D. OSCHI

SAN
LORENZO

Disfunzioni
Musicali

Via degli Ausoni

Museo
azionale
d'Arte
rientale

Auditorium of
Maecenas

PIAZZA
VITTORIO
EMANUELE II

VITTORIO
EMANUELE [M]

Via La Marmora

Via B. Ricasoli

Via
G. Pepe

S. Bibiana 🕇

Via Bibiana

Via degli Equi

Via dei Sabelli

Via dei Marsi

Via degli Apuli

Via di Campani

Via dei Lucani

LARGO
E. TALAMO

PIAZZA
DANTE

Via Alfieri

Via Tasso

Via Galilei

Via Nino Bixio

Via Emanuele Filiberto

Via Conte Verde

Via Cairoli

Via Principe Umberto

Via Pianciani

Via di Porta Maggiore

Via Giovanni Giolitti

Viale Alessandro Manzoni [M] MANZONI

Viale dello Scalo
di S. Lorenzo

PIAZZA DI
PORTA
MAGGIORE

Via Prenestina

Tomb of
the Baker

TO S. GIOVANNI
IN LATERANO
🕇 (300m)

Via Aleardi

Via Statilia

0   200 meters
0   200 yards

[M] ROME

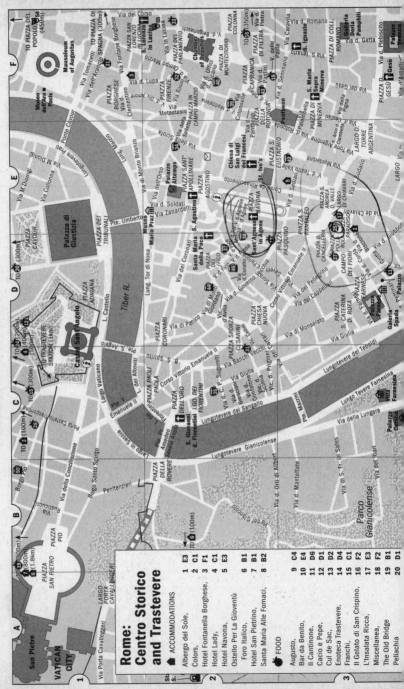

Rome: Centro Storico and Trastevere

▲ ACCOMMODATIONS	
Albergo del Sole,	1 E3
Colors,	2 C1
Hotel Fontanella Borghese,	3 F1
Hotel Lady,	4 C1
Hotel Navona,	5 E3
Ostello Per La Gioventù	
Foro Italico,	6 B1
Hotel San Pietrino,	7 B1
Santa Maria Alle Fornaci,	8 B2

● FOOD	
Augusto,	9 C4
Bar da Benito,	10 E4
Il Cantinone,	11 D6
Cacio e Pepe,	12 D1
Cul de Sac,	13 D2
Enoteca Trastevere,	14 D4
Franchi,	15 C1
Il Gelato di San Crispino,	16 F2
L'Insalata Ricca,	17 E3
Miscellanea,	18 F2
The Old Bridge	19 B1
Pellachia	20 D1

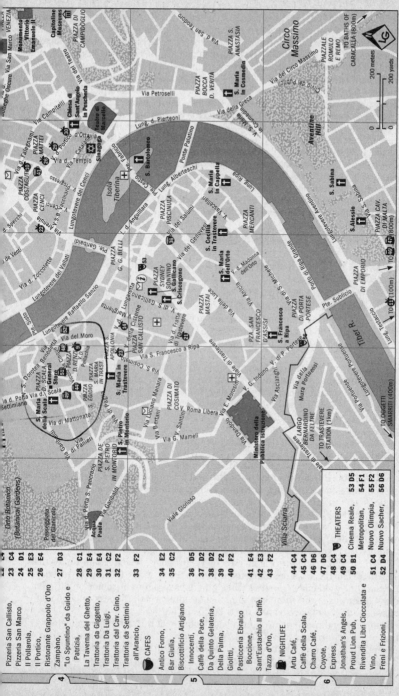

Pizzeria San Callisto,	23	C4
Pizzeria San Marco	24	D1
Il Pollarola,	25	E3
Il Portico,	26	E4
Ristorante Grappolo d'Oro		
Zampàno,	27	D3
"Lo Spuntino" da Guido e		
Patrizia,	28	C1
La Taverna del Ghetto,	29	E4
Trattoria da Giggetto,	30	E4
Trattoria Da Luigi,	31	D2
Trattoria dal Cav. Gino,	32	F2
Trattoria da Settimio		
all'Arancio,	33	F2
CAFES		
Antico Forno,	34	E2
Bar Giulia,	35	C2
Biscottificio Artigiano		
Innocenti,	36	D5
Caffè della Pace,	37	D2
Da Quinto Gelateria,	38	D2
Della Palma,	39	F2
Giolitti,	40	F2
Pasticceria Ebraico		
Boccione,	41	E4
Sant'Eustachio Il Caffè,	42	E3
Tazza d'Oro,	43	F2
NIGHTLIFE		
Artu Café,	44	C4
Caffè della Scala,	45	C4
Charro Café,	46	D6
Coyote,	47	D6
Express,	48	C4
Jonathan's Angels,	49	C4
Proud Lion Pub,	50	B1
Rivendita Libri Cioccolata e		
Vino,	51	C4
Freni e Frizioni,	52	D4
THEATERS		
Cinema Reale,	53	D5
Metropolitan,	54	F1
Nuovo Olimpia,	55	F2
Nuovo Sacher,	56	D6

4

5

6

south through the city, is also a useful reference point. Most trains arrive at **Stazione Termini** east of Rome's historical center. **Termini** and neighboring **San Lorenzo** to the east are home to the city's largest university and most budget accommodations. **Via Nazionale** originates two blocks northwest of Termini Station in **Piazza della Repubblica** and leads to **Piazza Venezia,** the city's focal point, recognizable by the immense white **Vittorio Emanuele II monument.** From P. Venezia, **Via dei Fori Imperiali** runs southeast to the Ancient City, where the **Colosseum** and the **Roman Forum** speak of former glory. **Via del Corso** stretches north from P. Venezia to **Piazza del Popolo,** which has an obelisk in its center. The **Trevi Fountain, Piazza Barberini,** and the fashionable streets around **Piazza di Spagna** lie to the east of V. del Corso. **Villa Borghese,** with its impressive gardens and museums, is northeast of the Spanish Steps. West of V. del Corso is the **centro storico,** the tangle of streets around the **Pantheon, Piazza Navona, Campo dei Fiori,** and the old **Jewish Ghetto. Largo Argentina,** west of P. Venezia, marks the start of **Corso Vittorio Emanuele II,** which runs through the *centro storico* to the Tiber River. Across the river to the northwest is **Vatican City** and the **Borgo-Prati** neighborhood. South of the Vatican are **Trastevere** and residential **Testaccio.** Be sure to pick up a free color map in English at the tourist office (**Practical Information,** p. 113).

▐ LOCAL TRANSPORTATION

SUBWAY (METROPOLITANA) AND BUSES

> **MI SCUSI! MI SCUSI!** Romans often prepare for their descent from the bus or subway well in advance. If you are not getting off at the next stop, step away from the doors and allow people to move to the front as early as the preceding stop. They may ask you, "*Scende la prossima fermata?*" (Are you getting off at the next stop?) to which you should respond "*si*" or "*no.*"

Rome's subway, the **Metropolitana** (www.metroroma.it), has two lines, A and B, which intersect at Termini. Station entrances are marked by poles with a white "M" on a red square. The subway runs daily 5:30am to 11:30pm. At night, bus #55N takes over for Metro A and 40N or 80N take over for Metro B.

Although the network of routes may seem daunting, Rome's buses are an efficient means of getting around the city, especially since the subway does not go into the *centro storico*. The **ATAC** transportation company has many booths, including one in Termini. (☎800 43 17 84; www.atac.roma.it. Open daily 7:30am-8pm.) Pick up a map at **biglietteria ATAC,** V. Gaeta 78 (€1; open daily 7am-7pm). ATAC tickets (€1) are valid for the Metro and buses and can be bought at *tabaccherie,* newsstands, vending machines, and some *bars.* Vending machines are in stations, on street corners, and at major bus stops; look for the ATAC label. Tickets are valid for one Metro ride or unlimited bus travel within 1¼hr. of validation. A BIG daily ticket (€4) covers unlimited bus or train travel in the metropolitan area (including Ostia but not Fiumicino) until midnight the day of purchase; a CIS ticket (€16) is good for a week; a three-day tourist ticket is €11.

Each bus stop *(fermata)* is marked by yellow signs, which list all routes that stop there and the key stops along those routes. Some buses run only on weekdays *(feriali)* or weekends *(festive)* while others have different routes on different days. Most buses run from 5am to midnight, after which the less reliable night buses *(notturni)* take over and run at 30-60min. intervals.

Enter buses through the front and back doors; exit through the middle door. A few useful bus routes are: **#40/64,** Vatican area, C. Vittorio Emanuele, Largo Argentina, P. Venezia, Termini; **#81,** P. Malatesta, San Giovanni, Colosseo, Bocca della Verità, P. Venezia, Largo Argentina, V. del Corso, P. Cavour, V. Cola di Rienzo, Vatican; **#170,** Termini, V. Nazionale, P. Venezia, Bocca della Verità,

Testaccio, Stazione Trastevere, V. Marconi, P. Agricoltura; **#492,** Tiburtina, Termini, P. Barberini, P. Venezia, C. Rinascimento, P. Cavour, P. Risorgimento; **#175,** Termini, P. Barberini, V. del Corso, P. Venezia; **tram 8,** Largo di Torre d'Argentina to Trastevere; **Linea H,** Termini to Trastevere; **#910,** Termini to Villa Borghese.

TAXIS, BIKES, AND MOPEDS

Taxis in Rome are expensive. Try to flag down a stray cab, head to stands near Termini, or find one in the major *piazze*. Ride only in yellow or white taxis, and make sure the taxi has a meter. If it doesn't, settle on a price before getting in the car. Expect to pay around €10-12 for a ride from Termini to the Vatican during the day; prices rise significantly at night. The meter starts at €2.33 (M-Sa 7am-10pm), €3.36 (Su and holidays 7am-10pm), or €4.91 (daily 10pm-7am). Surcharges are levied when heading to or from Fiumicino (€7.23) and Ciampino (€5.50), with a €1 charge per suitcase larger than 35cm by 25cm by 50cm. Standard tip is 10%. **RadioTaxi** (☎06 35 70) responds to calls, but be aware that the meter starts the moment the taxi is dispatched.

Rome's cobblestone streets, dense traffic, and reckless drivers make the city a challenge for bikes and mopeds. **Bikes** cost around €5 per hr. or €10 per day. The price of **scooters** changes based on their size, but is around €35-55 per day. Be aware that the length of a "day" sometimes depends on the shop's closing time. In summer, try the stands (open daily 10am-7pm) on V. del Corso, at P. di San Lorenzo and V. Pontifici, or Treno e Scooter, Termini. (☎48 90 58 23; www.trenoescooter.191.it. Open daily 9am-2pm and 4pm-7pm; AmEx/MC/V). Bici & Baci, V. del Viminale 5, is in front of Termini (☎48 28 443 or 48 98 61 62; www.bicibaci.com; open daily 8am-7pm. AmEx/MC/V). The minimum rental age is 16. Helmets, included with rental, are strictly required by law. Prices often include a 20% sales tax. For those just interested in an afternoon on a bike, Enjoy Rome offers an informative, if harrowing, tour of the city. Villa Borghese is another popular destination for biking. Recently, Segways, P. Popolo, have made an appearance on Rome's labyrinthine streets. (☎38 03 01 29 13 www.segway-roma.ne. €8 per half hour, €15 per hour.)

❼ PRACTICAL INFORMATION

TOURIST AND FINANCIAL SERVICES

Tourist Offices:

Enjoy Rome, V. Marghera 8/A (☎44 56 890; www.enjoyrome.com). From the middle concourse of Termini (between the trains and the ticket booths), exit right. Cross V. Marsala. The office is 3 blocks down V. Marghera on the left. Helpful, English-speaking staff makes reservations at museums and shows, books accommodations, orients travelers in the city, and leads walking tours (€25, under 26 €20). Along with info on excursions and bus lines, the office also provides 2 useful publications: a detailed and accurate map and a *When in Rome* booklet, with practical info and insider tips for making the most of a trip to Rome. Open Apr.-Oct. M-F 8:30am-7pm, Sa 8:30am-2pm; Nov.-Mar. M-F 9am-6pm, Sa 9am-2pm.

> **ROME FOR POCKET CHANGE.** Want a tour of the city without selling your soul to get it? The city-run bus **#110** (departs every 30min. from P. dei Cinquecento outside Termini; in summer 9:30am-7:30pm; €16 or save 10% at www.trambusopen.com.) is an open-top bus that goes to all the major sights in Rome—you'll see everything you would on an expensive tour, but with a whole lot less walking.

PIT Info Points (☎48 90 63 00). Run by the city, these round green kiosks provide limited info on events, hotels, restaurants, and transportation, as well as brochures and a basic map of sights. Open daily 8am-9pm. **Branches:** Castel Sant'Angelo, Trevi Fountain, Fori Imperiali, P. di Spagna, P. Navona, Trastevere, Santa Maria Maggiore, P. San Giovanni in Laterano, V. del Corso, V. Nazionale, and Termini. The same

C LINE TO COME ONLINE

It's difficult to miss the Metro's gaping hole in the *centro storico*. Currently, the A and B lines create an "X" at Termini, ignoring Piazza Venezia and its surroundings. Recently, officials have announced an ambitious plan to add a new C line, linking Grottarossa in the northern suburbs and Pantano southeast of the city. The high-tech system will include 30 trains, 39 new stations, and 34km of track, costing an estimated €4.2 billion. Ideally, the new line would be operational by 2015, but impediments abound.

While the actual tracks will be 100 ft. underground, well below anything of historical value, the escalators, elevators, and stations will certainly encounter artifacts. Each time a site is unearthed, archaeologists jump for joy while project managers shake their heads in dismay. Already, a 15th-century glass factory has been discovered beneath Piazza Venezia, necessitating the relocation of the stop.

Rome continues to struggle to preserve its rich history while also alleviating its congested streets and catch up with the public transportation systems of other major cities. As the C line snakes its way around excavation sites, the lofty goal of 2015 seems more and more unattainable, so plan on getting jostled on the 64 bus down Via Nazionale for at least another decade.

info is available by phone from the **Call Center Comune di Roma** (☎36 00 43 99), which operates daily 9am-7pm.

Embassies:

Australia: V. Antonio Bosio 5 (☎85 27 21, emergency 800 877 790; www.italy.embassy.gov.au). Open M-F 8:30am-5pm.

Canada: V. Zara 30 (☎85 44 41; www.dfait-maeci.gc.ca/canada-europa/italy/menu-en.asp). Open M-Th 8:30-11:30am.

Ireland: P. di Campitelli 3 (☎69 79 121; www.ambasciata-irlanda.it). Open M-F 10am-1pm.

New Zealand: V. Zara 28 (☎44 17 171; www.nzembassy.com). Open M-F 8:30am-12:45pm and 1:45-5pm.

UK: V. XX Settembre 80a (☎42 20 00 01; www.britain.it). Consular services open autumn, winter, spring M-F 9am-5pm; summer 8am-2pm. Closed UK and Italian holidays.

US: V. Vittorio Veneto 121 (☎46 741; www.usembassy.it). Consular services open M-F 8:30am-12:30pm. Closed US and Italian holidays.

Currency Exchange: Banca di Roma and **Banca Nazionale del Lavoro** have good rates, and **ATMs** are readily available all over town. Open M-F 8:30am-1:30pm.

American Express, P. di Spagna 38 (☎67 641; for lost or stolen cards and checks, 80 08 72 000). Open M-F 9am-5:30pm, Sa 9am-12:30pm.

LOCAL SERVICES

Luggage Storage: Splashnet, V. Varese 33. €2 per day. In Termini Station, underneath Track #24. Open daily 6am-midnight. €3.80 1st 5hr., €0.60 per hr. up to 12hrs., €0.20 per hr. thereafter.

Lost Property: Oggetti Smarriti, V. Nicolo Bettoni 1 (☎58 16 040), at Termini, at the glass booth in main passageway. Open M and W 8:30am-1pm and 2:30-6pm, Tu and F 8:30am-1pm, Th 8:30am-6pm. **Lost property on buses:** ☎58 16 040; **Metro A** 48 74 309, call M, W, and F 9am-12:30pm; **Metro B** 57 53 22 65, call F 8am-6:30pm.

Bookstores:

🔲 **The Lion Bookshop and Café,** V. dei Greci 33-36 (☎32 65 40 07 or 32 65 04 37), off V. del Corso. Open M 3:30-7:30pm and Tu-Sa 10am-7:30pm.

Libreria Feltrinelli International, V. Vittorio Emanuele Orlando 84/86 (☎48 27 878), near P. della Repubblica. Open M-Sa 9am-8pm, Su 10am-1:30pm and 4-8pm.

Anglo-American Bookshop, V. della Vite 102 (☎67 95 222; www.aab.it), off V. del Corso near the Spanish Steps. Open M-F 10am-7:30pm, Sa 10am-2pm; closed mid-Aug. AmEx/MC/V.

Mel Bookstore, V. Nazionale 252-255 (☎48 85 405). Open in summer M-Sa 9am-8pm, Su 10am-1:30pm and 4:30-8:30pm; in winter M-Sa 9am-8pm, Su 10am-1:30pm and 4-8pm.

GLBT Resources:

ARCI-GAY, V. Goito 35/B (☎64 50 11 02 or 349 19 76 191; www.arcigayroma.it), holds discussions, dances, and special events. Welcome group every Th 7-9pm. Open M-F 4-8pm. Helpline ☎80 07 13 713. M and W 5-9pm, Sa 4-8pm.

Circolo Mario Mieli di Cultura Omosessuale, V. Efeso 2/A (☎54 13 985; www.mariomieli.org). M: B-San Paolo. Walk 1 block to Largo Beato Placido Riccardi, turn right and walk 1½ blocks to V. Corinto. Turn right, and walk to V. Efeso. Promotes GLBT rights and holds cultural activities. AIDS activists offer psychological and legal assistance. Open daily 10am-7pm.

Libreria Babele, V. dei Banchi Vecchi (☎68 76 628; www.libreriababeleroma.it), across from Castel Sant'Angelo. Library focusing on gay literature. Open M-Sa 11am-7pm.

Laundromats:

Splashnet, V. Varese 33 (☎49 38 04 50; www.splashnetrome.com), 3 blocks north of Termini. Wash €3 per 6kg., dry €3 per 7kg. Internet access €1.50 per hr. Free maps and helpful staff. Ask for the *Let's Go* discount. Open in summer 8:30am-1am; in winter 8:30am-11pm.

BollaBlu, V. Milazzo 20/B (☎44 70 30 96; www.romefriendship.com), near Termini. Wash, dry, and detergent for medium load approx. €10, includes 15min. of free Internet access. Open daily 8am-midnight.

OndaBlu, V. Pricipe Armideo 70B (info ☎80 08 61 346). 17 locations throughout the city. Wash €3.50 per 6.5kg, dry €3.50 per 6.5kg. Detergent €1. Open daily 8am-10pm.

Supermarkets: Three main chains, Standa, Di per Di, and Despar, have stores scattered throughout Rome. AmEx/MC/V.

Standa: V. Cola di Rienzo 71/73, in Borgo Prati, open daily 8am-9pm; V. Trastevere 62, in Trastevere, open M-Sa 8:30am-8pm, Su 9:30am-1:30pm and 4-8pm.

Di Per Di: V. del Gesu 58, in *centro storico*, open M-Sa 8am-9pm, Su 9am-8pm; V. Carlo Tavolacci 1-7, in Trastevere, open M-Sa 8am-8pm, Su 8:30am-1:30pm; V. S. S. Quattro 53/54, near the Colosseum, open M-Sa 8am-9pm, Su 9am-7:30pm.

Despar: V. del Pozzetto 119 , in P. di Spagna and environs, open M-Sa 9am-9pm, Su 10am-9pm; V. Nazionale 211/213, open daily 8:30am-9pm.

Supermercato SMA Rocca, P. Santa Maria Maggiore 1-5, open daily 8am-9pm.

Conad, P. dei Cinquecento, lower level of Termini, open daily 6am-midnight.

EMERGENCY AND COMMUNICATIONS

Rape Crisis Line: Centro Anti-Violenza, V. di Torrespaccata 157 (☎23 26 90 49 or 23 26 90 53). Branches throughout city. Open 24hr. **Samaritans,** V. San Giovanni 250 (☎70 45 44 44), in Laterano. Native English speakers. Counseling available. Call ahead. Open daily 1-10pm.

Counseling Hotlines: Alcoholics Anonymous (☎47 42 913); **Narcotics Anonymous** (www.na.org); **Refugee Center** (☎47 45 603).

Pharmacies: Farmacia Internazionale, P. Barberini 49 (☎48 71 195). M: A-Barberini. Open daily 9am-12:30pm and 3-9pm. Termini Station, Track 1 (☎48 80 776). Open daily 7:30am-10pm. MC/V. **Farmacia Piram,** V. Nazionale 228 (☎48 80 754). Open 24hr. MC/V.

Hospitals:

International Medical Center, V. Firenze 47 (24hr. ☎48 82 371; www.imc84.com). Prescriptions filled. Paramedic crew on call. Referral service to English-speaking doctors. General visit €100, house visits at night €150. Call ahead. Open M-F 9am-8pm; house calls after hours.

Rome-American Hospital, V. Emilio Longoni 69 (24hr. ☎22 551, appointments 22 55 290; www.rah.it). Private emergency and laboratory services, HIV tests, and pregnancy tests. Visits average €100-200. Doctors on call 24hr.

Policlinico Umberto I, Vle. del Policlinico 155 (emergency ☎49 911, automated phone line for first aid and appointments 49 971). M: B-Policlinico or #649 bus. Emergency room *(pronto soccorso)*. Open 24hr.

THE BLOOD OF THE ROMANS. When it is hot and humid outside, mosquitoes swarm Rome. While the nasty little buggers love feasting upon foreign blood, Romans seem to avoid the pestilent attacks. Consequently, insect repellents are extremely overpriced in the city. If you are prone to allergic reactions, bring antihistamine cream and bug spray.

Internet Access: Caffè Tazza d'Oro (see p. 127). **Splashnet** (see Laundromats, p. 115). **Padma Internet Point,** V. Cavour 131 (☎48 93 03 80). 10 computers. €2 per hr. Printing €0.20 per page, graphics €0.75 per page. Open daily 8am-midnight.

Post Office: V. Giolotti 14, in Termini, and P. San Silvestro 19 (☎69 73 72 13) Both open M-F 8am-7pm, Sa 8am-1:15pm. Dozens of locations throughout the city; see www.poste.it/online/cercaup for a full listing. **Postal Codes:** 00100 to 00200; V. Giolotti 00185; P. San Silvestro 00187.

ACCOMMODATIONS

Rome swells with tourists around Easter, from May to July, and in September; be sure to book well in advance for those times. Many establishments also raise their prices during long weekends and holidays. In general prices vary widely with the time of year, and a proprietor's willingness to negotiate increases with length of stay, number of vacancies, and group size. Termini swarms with hotel scouts. Many are legitimate and have IDs issued by tourist offices; however, some impostors have fake badges and direct travelers to run-down locations with exorbitant rates, especially at night. In some neighborhoods, like Trastevere, hotels are pricey, but good deals on apartments can still sometimes be found.

ACCOMMODATIONS BY PRICE

€20-29 (❷)		€41-60 (❹)	
Ostello Per La Gioventù Foro Italico (HI)		Pensione Panda (117)	PS
(118)	VC	Hotel Boccaccio (117)	PS
Alessandro Palace (118)	TE	Pensione Fawlty Towers (119)	SL
Alessandro Downtown (118)	TE	Affittacamere Aries (119)	VIA
Alessandro Legends (118)	TE	Pensione di Rienzo (120)	ES
Hostel Des Artistes (118)	SL	Santa Maria Alle Fornaci (121)	AA
Hotel Papa Germano (119)	VIA	**OVER €60 (❺)**	
€30-40 (❸)		Pensione Rosetta (116)	CS
Colors (117)VC	VC	Albergo del Sole (116)	CS
Hotel San Pietrino (117)	VC	Hotel Navona (116)	CS
Hotel Cervia (119)	SL	Hotel Fontanella Borghese (117)	CS
Hotel Bolognese (119)	VIA	Hotel Suisse (117)	PS
Hotel Scott House (120)	ES	Hotel Lady (118)	VC
Hotel Giù Giù (120)	ES	Hotel Des Artistes (118)	SL
YWCA Foyer di Roma (118)	AA	Hotel Galli (119)	SL
		Hotel Cortorillo (120)	ES
		Domus Nova Bethlehem (120)	AA

CS Centro Storico and Ancient City **ES** Esquilino and West of Termini **PS** Piazza di Spagna and Environs **RH** Religious Housing **SL** San Lorenzo and East of Termini **TE** Termini and Environs **VIA** Via XX Settembre and North of Termini **VC** Vatican City

CENTRO STORICO AND ANCIENT CITY

Because of their proximity to the major sites, these small *alberghi* (hotels) charge a lot more than their Termini counterparts.

Pensione Rosetta, V. Cavour 295 (☎47 82 30 69; www.rosettahotel.com), a few blocks past the Fori Imperiali. Buzz to get through large doors on street and walk straight through courtyard. Extremely affordable for location. 18 tidy, spacious rooms have bath, TV, phone, and fan. A/C €10. Reservations recommended 2 months in advance in high season. Singles €60; doubles €85; triples €95; quads €110. AmEx/MC/V. ❺

Albergo del Sole, V. del Biscione 76 (☎68 80 68 73; www.solealbiscione.it), off Campo dei Fiori. 61 clean, comfortable, modern rooms with phone, TV, and fittingly antique furniture. Common rooms on each floor and fragrant courtyard. Elevator from 2nd to 5th fl. Parking €18-21. Reception 24hr. Check-in and check-out 11am. Reserve 2 months in advance in high season. Singles €65, with bath €90; small doubles €95, with shower €110-160; triples €185; quads €220. Discount for groups of 10+; 10-15% off for large groups with long stay or during low season. Cash or checks only. ❺

Hotel Navona, V. dei Sediari 8, 1st fl. (☎68 64 203; www.hotelnavona.com). Bus #64 to C. Vittorio Emanuele II or #70 to C. del Rinascimento. Take V. de Canestrari from P.

Navona, cross C. del Rinascimento, and go straight; outdoor marking is very small. Keats and Shelley have both stayed here. English-speaking staff. A/C, TV, luggage storage, and breakfast included. Reception 24hr. Check-out 11am. Reservations with credit card and 1st night deposit. Singles €90-110; doubles €130-150; triples €150-200; quads €190-235. Occasional Sa-Su discount offered on-line; *Let's Go* discount 5%; cash discount for singles, doubles, and stays longer than 5 days. D/MC/V. ❺

Hotel Fontanella Borghese, Largo Fontanella Borghese 84, 2nd fl. (☎68 80 95 04; www.fontanellaborghese.com). Heading north from P. Venezia, take a left on Largo Fontanella Borghese. Once owned by the Borghese princes, this hotel now features 29 comfy rooms with A/C, minibar, phone, and satellite TV. Centrally located between P. di Spagna, Trevi fountain, Pantheon, and P. Navona. Singles €130; doubles €205; triples €250; quads €265. AmEx/MC/V. ❺

PIAZZA DI SPAGNA AND ENVIRONS

Though prices near P. di Spagna can be very steep, the accommodations are closer to the Metro and often newer than in the *centro storico;* higher prices translate into lusher fabrics and more amenities.

Pensione Panda, V. della Croce 35, 2nd fl. (☎67 80 179; www.hotelpanda.it). M: A-Spagna. Between P. di Spagna and V. del Corso. 28 spotless rooms with faux marble statues and frescoed ceilings on a quiet street. English spoken. A/C €6. Free Wi-Fi. Reservations recommended. Singles €68, with bath €80; doubles €78/108; triples €140; quads €180. 5% discount when paying with cash. AmEx/MC/V. ❹

Hotel Suisse, V. Gregoriana 54, 3rd fl. (☎67 83 649 or 67 86 172; www.hotelsuisserome.com). M: A-Spagna. At the top of the Spanish Steps, face away from P. di Spagna and take the right fork. The charming antique furniture, huge rooms, and opulent sitting room with a new flatscreen TV make for a pleasant stay. Phone, TV, and bath in all rooms. Breakfast in bed included. Elevator. A/C €10. Free Wi-Fi. 1 single €100; doubles €165; triples €210; quads €230. Look for low-season (Jan. 11-Mar. 13, July-Aug., Nov. 11-Dec. 20) specials on website. MC/V. ❺

Hotel Boccaccio, V. del Boccaccio 25, 1st fl. (☎48 85 962; www.hotelboccaccio.com). M: A-Barberini. Off V. del Tritone near P. Barberini. 8 simple rooms and a cozy terrace in a homey and very quiet hotel. No A/C or TV. Elevator. Singles without bath €45; doubles €80, with bath €100; triples €108/135. Low-season discount depending on length of stay. AmEx/MC/V. ❹

VATICAN CITY

Pensioni near the Vatican offer some of the best deals in Rome as well as extensive amenities. Few places in the city rival the level of sobriety, thanks to the area's high nun-to-tourist ratio.

▨ **Colors,** V. Boezio 31 (☎68 74 030; www.colorshotel.com). M: A-Ottaviano. Take a right on V. Terenzio, off V. Cola di Rienzo, then left on V. Boezio. As the name suggests, a variety of colorful rooms are available. 2 hostel floors and a newly renovated 3rd floor with private rooms. A/C and English-speaking staff. Terraces and kitchens on all floors. Breakfast included. Internet access €2 per hr. Reserve dorms by 9pm night before. Dorms €27; singles €90, with bath 105; doubles €100/130; triples €120. Low season discount up to 30%. Cash only. ❸

▨ **Hotel San Pietrino,** V. Giovanni Bettolo 43, 3rd fl. (☎37 00 132; www.sanpietrino.it). M: A-Ottaviano. Exit on V. Barletta, walk 3 blocks, and turn left on V. Bettolo. A distinct amphibian motif emerges from the small frog statues, stuffed frogs, and other frog trinkets in the hallways. Spacious rooms are simple and clean with A/C, TV, and DVD players. Internet access available. Laundry €8. Two bicycles available for rent (€5 per day). In high season, reserve 2-3 months ahead. Singles €35-45; doubles €70-93; triples €120; family quad €135. Negotiable discount for stays over 1 week. Check website for low-season specials. AmEx/MC/V. ❸

ROME

■ **Ostello Per La Gioventù Foro Italico (HI),** V. delle Olimpiadi 61 (☎32 36 267; www.hihostels.com or www.ostellionline.org). M: A-Ottaviano, then bus #32 from P. del Risorgimento to the 2nd "LGT Cadorna Ostello Gioventù" stop (10-15min.); hostel is the enormous, barracks-style building behind the bushes across the street. Common area. Single-sex floors with giant communal baths. Gargantuan lockers. English-speaking staff. No A/C. Breakfast included. Laundry available. Internet access €5 per hr. Reception 7am-11pm. Curfew 1-1:30am. Dorms €18. Non-member fee €5. AmEx/MC/V. ❷

■ **Hotel Lady,** V. Germanico 198, 4th fl. (☎32 42 112; www.hotelladyroma.it), between V. Fabbio Massimo and V. Paolo Emilio. This cozy hotel's dimly lit hallways accentuate the ceiling's rich wooden beams. Antique furniture, desks, phones, and fans in rooms. Full bath and shower options. No A/C. Singles €80; doubles €100, with bath €145; triples without bath €130. Low-season rates vary; check website. AmEx/MC/V. ❺

⬛TIP **MO' MONEY, NO PROBLEMS.** Most independently run hostels and hotels will offer discounts if you pay in cash in order to avoid a 10% tax from credit companies. Put Daddy's credit card away and hit up the ATMs.

TERMINI AND ENVIRONS

Welcome to budget traveler central. Any of the hostels that make up Alessandro's empire are your best bet—if you can get a reservation. While Termini is chock-full of services for travelers, use caution when walking in the area, especially at night. Pay particular attention to your purse and pockets.

■ **Alessandro Palace,** V. Vicenza 42 (☎44 61 958; www.hostelalessandropalace.com). Exit Termini from track #1. Turn left on V. Marsala, then right on V. Vicenza. Recently renovated dorms, all with bath and A/C. Fun, guests-only bar with flatscreen TV. English-speaking staff. Breakfast included; free pizza party nightly with the purchase of any drink (€3). Lockers available. Towels €2; included with doubles, triples, and quads. Internet access €2 per hr. Check-in 3pm. Check-out 10am. Co-ed and all-female dorms €25-30; doubles €90; triples €120; quads €140. AmEx/MC/V. ❷

Alessandro Downtown, V. Carlo Cattaneo 23 (☎44 34 01 47; www.hostelalessandro-downtown.com). Exit Termini by track #22, make a left on V. Giolitti, then a right onto V. C. Cattaneo. Cheap and worthwhile alternative when the Palace is full, with the same fun service and social environment. Brand-new kitchen, dining room, and sitting room with widescreen TV. Breakfast included; free pasta party weeknights. Locks available for fee. Towels €2. Internet €2 per hr. Check-in 3pm. Check-out 10am. Co-ed and all-female dorms €24-25; doubles €70, with bath €90; quads €120/140. AmEx/MC/V. ❷

Alessandro Legends, V. Curtatone 12 (☎44 70 32 17; www.hostelalessandroleg-ends.com). Pop in a DVD from the hostel's collection and enjoy a free cup of OJ, coffee, or hot chocolate. All rooms have fan. Kitchen. Breakfast included; free pasta party dinner weeknights. Lockers free. Towels €2. Internet access available. Reception 24hr. 10-bed dorms with bath €21; 8-bed single sex dorms €20-25; 6-bed dorms with bath €29.50; quads €126. AmEx/MC/V. ❷

YWCA Foyer di Roma, V. Cesare Balbo 4 (☎48 80 460 or 48 83 917; foyer.roma@ywca-ucdg.it). From Termini, take V. Cavour. Turn right on V. Torino; then take 1st left on V. C. Balbo. The YWCA (pronounced EEV-kah and known as the Casa per Studentesse) has a pretty courtyard and spotless rooms. All rooms come with fan and towels. Singles with private bath have minifridge. Breakfast included; lunch €12. Reception 7am-midnight. Check-out 10am. Curfew midnight. Some rooms wheelchair-accessible. Private rooms open to men, but dorms are all-female. Dorms €28; singles €40, with bath €50; doubles €66/80. Stays longer than 1wk. require €10 membership fee. AmEx/MC/V. ❸

SAN LORENZO AND EAST OF TERMINI

Hotel and Hostel Des Artistes, V. Villafranca 20, 5th fl. (☎44 54 365; www.hotelde-sartistes.com). From Termini's middle concourse, exit right, turn left on V. Marsala, right on V. Vicenza, then take 5th left. Rooftop terrace and small bar. 24hr. English-speaking reception. Check-out 10:30am. Hotel: Private bath, A/C, TV, safe, fan, and hairdryer. Breakfast included. Double €100, with bath €146. Rates vary seasonally. Discount when paying cash. AmEx/MC/V. Hostel: Pastel-colored walls, common room with TV, and free Internet access (15min. limit) at a local cafe. Lockers and luggage storage. €10 key deposit. €20-26 per person depending on availability. 3-day cancellation policy. Cash only. Hotel ❺/hostel ❷

Hotel Cervia, V. Palestro 55, 2nd fl. (☎49 10 57; www.hotelcerviaroma.it). From Termini, exit on V. Marsala, head down V. Marghera and take the 4th left. Clean rooms with fans. English-speaking staff. Also try Cervia's identical sister hotel, **Restino,** on the 5th fl. Breakfast €3. Towels included. Reception 24hr. Check-out 11am. Reserve via email to guarantee room. Occasional 4- and 5-bed dorm setups €20; singles €40, with bath €70; doubles €70/90; triples €90/110; quads €100/135. 5% *Let's Go* discount when paying in cash; discounts also negotiable for longer stays. AmEx/MC/V. ❸

Hotel Galli, V. Milazzo 20 (☎44 56 859; www.albergogalli.com). From Termini's middle concourse, exit right; turn right on V. Marsala and left on V. Milazzo. Take the 2-person elevator to reception on 2nd fl. English-speaking owners manage 12 clean rooms with bath, minifridge, phone, TV, and safe. A/C €5. Check-in noon. Check-out 10am. Singles €65; doubles €95; triples €120; quads €140. Reserve via fax or email. Check on-line for specials and low-season discounts. 3-day cancellation policy. AmEx/MC/V. ❺

Pensione Fawlty Towers, V. Magenta 39, 5th fl. (☎44 50 374; www.fawltytowers.org). From Termini, cross V. Marsala onto V. Marghera, and turn right on V. Magenta. Brightly colored rooms and English-speaking staff. Social terrace with lots of flowers. Full kitchen available. Comfortable common room with satellite TV, A/C, DVD player, VCR, library, refrigerator, lockers, microwave, and free Internet access. Check-out 9:30am for dorms, 10am for private rooms. Reserve by fax for private rooms; no reservations for dorms—arrive as early as possible. Singles €58, with shower €63; doubles €80/89; triples with shower €93, with full bath €99; quads without bath €100. Cash in advance only. Check website for seasonal specials. ❹

I SAY TOMATO, YOU SAY TOMAHTO. In Italy, the 1st floor is actually counted as floor zero (known as *pianterreno*). Consequently, every floor thereafter is numbered one less than you might expect.

VIA XX SETTEMBRE AND NORTH OF TERMINI

Dominated by government ministries and private apartments, this area is less noisy and touristy than nearby Termini.

Hotel Papa Germano, V. Calatafimi 14/A (☎48 69 19; www.hotelpapagermano.com). From Termini, exit right; turn left on V. Marsala, which becomes V. Volturno, and take the 4th right onto V. Calatafimi. Clean, simple rooms with TV, sink, and hairdryer. Mini-fridge in rooms with private bath. English spoken. Breakfast included. A/C €5. Internet access €2 per hr. Check-out 11am. Dorms €26; singles €38; doubles €70, with bath €90; triples €83/108; quads €110/130. Check website for specials and low-season discounts. AmEx/MC/V. ❷

Hotel Bolognese, V. Palestro 15, 2nd fl. (☎/fax 49 00 45; hbolognese@tiscalinet.it). From Termini, exit right; walk down V. Marghera and take the 4th left onto V. Palestro. The proud artist-owner's impressive paintings set this hotel apart. Newly renovated rooms, all with private bath. Breakfast included. Check-out 11am. Singles €30-60; doubles €50-90; triples €90-120. AmEx/MC/V. ❸

Affittacamere Aries, V. XX Settembre 58/A (☎42 02 71 61; www.affittacamerearies.com). From Termini, exit right, and turn left onto V. Marsala, which becomes V. Volturno. Make a right onto V. Cernia and then a left on V. Goito. Follow to its end on V. XX Settembre. Comfortable, basic rooms with fridge, sink, TV, towels, and A/C. English spoken. Breakfast €2.50. Singles €60; doubles €60, with bath €75; triples €105/135. *Let's Go* discount, depending on season. Check website for low-season prices. MC/V. ●

ESQUILINO AND WEST OF TERMINI

Esquilino, south of Termini, has tons of cheap hotels close to the major sights. The area west of Termini is also inviting, with busy streets and lots of shopping.

Hotel Scott House, V. Gioberti 30 (☎44 65 379; www.scotthouse.com). Colorful, modern rooms have private bath, A/C, phone, safebox, and satellite TV. Helpful, English-speaking staff. Breakfast included. Check-out 11am. Singles €35-68; doubles €63-98; triples €75-114; quads €88-129. Check website for low-season specials. €5 off per night per room if paying cash. AmEx/MC/V. ●

Hotel Giù Giù, V. del Viminale 8, 2nd fl. (☎48 27 734; www.hotelgiugiu.com). This elegant but fading *palazzo* filled with porcelain knick-knacks makes guests feel like they're vacationing at Grandma's. 9 rooms with A/C and security box. English spoken. Check-out 10am. Singles €45; doubles with bath €80; triples with bath €120; quads with bath €160. Check website for low-season specials. Cash only. ●

Pensione di Rienzo, V. Principe Amedeo 79/A, 2nd fl. (☎44 67 131; www.hoteldirienzo.it). A tranquil, family-run retreat. Rooms come with fan, TV, and small table and chairs. English spoken. Check-out 10am. Singles €40, with bath €50-60; doubles €60/80; triples with bath €90. AmEx/MC/V. ●

Hotel Cortorillo, V. Principe Amedeo 79/A, 5th fl. (☎44 66 934; www.hotelcortorillo.it). Renovated hotel has bath, TV, minifridge, digital deposit box, and A/C in all 14 spacious rooms. Guests praise the neat rooms and super-friendly staff. Breakfast included. Check-in noon. Check-out 10am. Singles €60; doubles €80; triples €95; quads €105. Check website for low-season discounts. AmEx/MC/V. ●

ALTERNATIVE ACCOMMODATIONS

BED AND BREAKFASTS

B&Bs in Rome differ from their American counterparts. Some are private homes with guest rooms; generous owners typically provide breakfast. Others are apartments with kitchens that clients can use. The rooms and apartments vary in quality, location, and size. The **Bed and Breakfast Association of Rome,** V. Antonio Pacinotti 73, offers advice. (☎55 30 22 48; www.b-b.rm.it. Call M-F 9am-1pm or 3-7pm for an appointment.) **Your Flat in Rome/Byba Appartamenti,** Borgo Pio 160, also rents spacious, short-term apartments in the Borgo area to individuals or groups for as little as €25 per person per night and a 30% deposit. (☎338 95 60 061; www.yourflatinrome.com.) **Hotel Trastevere,** V. Luciano Manara 25 (☎58 14 713; fax 58 81 016), in Trastevere, also has affordable short-term apartments available in this lively neighborhood. **Short Let's Assistance,** Via Zucchelli 26 (☎48 90 58 97; www.shortletsassistance.com), by P. Barberini, oversees 120 apartments and helps find accommodations for stays longer than one month.

RELIGIOUS HOUSING

Don't automatically think religious housing is cheap and nun-filled; it can cost up to €155 for a single. While a few establishments require letters of introduction from local, Catholic dioceses, most are open to people of all denominations. Just don't expect quaint rooms in cloisters. The rooms in religious housing are similar to hotel rooms in terms of amenities; the only difference is that the profits go toward church missions and not the management. Do think sober: early curfews or chores are standard. Check www.santasusanna.org/comingtorome/convents.html for a comprehensive listing of religious housing.

Domus Nova Bethlehem, V. Cavour 85/A (☎47 82 44 14; www.suorebambinogesu.it). Take V. Cavour from Termini, past P. dell'Esquilino, on the right. Modern, central hotel with religious icons throughout. Rooms have A/C, bath, and TV. Breakfast room, courtyard, and expansive rooftop terrace. Breakfast included. Safe-deposit boxes and Internet access available. Parking €15.50 per day. Curfew in summer 2am; in winter 1am. Singles €78; doubles €114; triples €140; quads €150; quints €170. AmEx/MC/V. ❺

Santa Maria Alle Fornaci, P. Santa Maria alle Fornaci 27 (☎39 36 76 32; www.trinitaridematha.it). Facing St. Peter's, turn left through a gate in the basilica walls onto P. del Uffizio. Take 3rd right onto V. Alcide De Gasperi, which leads to P. S. Maria alle Fornaci. Go down the steps immediately to the left of the church. 54 rooms with bath and phone. Religious prints throughout the hotel. Large common room with TV and Internet. Conference room. Breakfast included. Reception 24hr. Singles €60; doubles €90; triples €125. Discounts for groups larger than 25. AmEx/MC/V. ❹

▟ FOOD

While food is an integral part of all cultures, it is absolutely paramount to Romans. Eat until you're full, loosen your belt a notch, and scarf down some more. Traditional Roman cuisine includes *spaghetti alla carbonara* (egg and cream sauce sprinkled with bacon), *spaghetti all'amatriciana* (spicy, with thin tomato sauce, chilies, and bacon), *carciofi alla giudeia* (deep-fried artichokes, found most commonly in the Jewish Ghetto), and *fiori di zucca* (stuffed, fried zucchini flowers—unexpectedly delicious). Pizza is unsurprisingly popular in Rome and is eaten with a fork and knife. Try the *pizza romana*, a focaccia-like flatbread rubbed with olive oil, sea salt, and rosemary that sometimes has toppings. Rome's proximity to the sea makes shellfish and other *pesce* (fish) plates popular as well. Expect to pay an extra €1-1.50 for bread and *coperto* (service), whether you eat the bread or not.

FOOD BY PRICE

UNDER €7(❶)		L'Insalata Ricca (123)	CF
▨ Miscellanea (121)	CS	Il Pollarola (123)	CF
Pizza Art (122)	CS	Vini e Buffet (123)	PS
Trattoria dal Cav. Gino (122)	CS	Il Brillo Parlante (123)	PS
Luzzi (122)	AC	Cacio e Pepe (124)	VC
L'Antica Birreria Peroni (122)	AC	Paninoteca da Guido e Patrizia (124)	VC
Franchi (124)	VC	Africa (124)	TER
Hosteria Romana da Dino (124)	TER	Arancia Blu (124)	TER
Hostaria da Bruno (124)	TER	Pizzeria San Marco (125)	TRA
▨ Pizzeria San Callisto (125)	TRA	La Piazzetta (125)	PS
Augusto (125)	TRA	Trattoria da Giggetto (125)	JG
▨ Bar Da Benito (125)	JG	La Taverna del Ghetto (125)	JG
Il Portico (125)	JG	Il Cantinone (126)	TES
▨ Il Volpetti Pù (126)	TES	Volpetti Salumeria-Gastronomia (126)	TES
€7-15 (❷)		€16-22 (❸)	
▨ Buoni Amici (122)	AC	Trattoria da Settimio all'Arancio (123)	PS
Taverna dei Fori Imperiali (122)	AC	Centro Macrobiotico Italiano Naturist Club	
Hostaria Nerone (122)	AC	(123)	PS
Taverna dei Quaranta (123)	AC		
Ristorante Grappolo d' Oro Zampanò (123)	CF		

AC Ancient City **CF** Campo dei Fiori **CS** *Centro Storico* **JG** Jewish Ghetto **PS** Piazza di Spagna and Environs **TRA** Trastevere **TER** Termini and Environs **TES** Testaccio **VC** Vatican City

CENTRO STORICO

▨ **Miscellanea,** V. delle Paste 110a (☎67 80 983). Around the corner from the Pantheon. A proven student and local favorite, this restaurant and pub's dedicated owner, ▨ **Mickey,** will make sure your meal is memorable. Priding itself on fresh food, gigantic portions, low prices, and above all else, *"simpatia and respetto"* for their customers, Miscellanea exemplifies what a true *ristorante* should be. Customers rave about the sweet *fragoli*, a free "sexy wine" (as the owner calls it), included with every meal. Salads (€6), *antipasto* (€6-7), and *panini* the size of the Pantheon (€3) are the best values in town. Drinks €2-4. Delicious desserts €2-3. Open daily 11am-2am. AmEx. ❶

Pizza Art, V. Arenula 76 (☎68 73 16 03 78). From C. Vittorio Emanuele II, cut through Largo di Torre Argentina. Serves delicious slices of thick focaccia bread pizza, priced per kg. Unusual toppings include arugula, goat cheese, and tomato salmon. Try the candy-like *pizza con nutella.* From €2.50 per slice. Open M-Su 8am-10:30pm. Cash only. ❶

Trattoria dal Cav. Gino, V. Rosini 4 (☎68 73 434), small red and white sign, off V. di Campo Marzio, across from P. del Parlamente. Affable owner Gino greets people at the door and announces the house special, *tonnarelli alla ciociala* (€8). Dine under the blue sky, grape vines, and birds painted on the ceiling. *Primi* €5-8, *secondi* €7-12. Open M-Sa 1-2:30pm and 8-10:30pm. Closed Aug. Cash only. ❶

ANCIENT CITY

The area around the Fora and the Colosseum is home to some of Italy's finest tourist traps. Avoid streets directly surrounding the sights and head to side streets where outposts of cheap food are oases in a desert of color-photograph menus.

▨ I Buoni Amici, V. Aleardo Aleardi 4 (☎70 49 19 93). M: B-Colosseo. From the Colosseum, take V. Labicana, then take a right on V. Merulana and a left on V. A. Aleardi. Look for a blue *osteria* sign. Worth the walk. Exceptional service complements popular *linguine alle vongole* (pasta with clams in the shell; €8), and the self-serve *antipasto* bar. *Primi* €7-8, *secondi* €8-12. Fish €10-12. Wine €8-15. Homemade dessert €4. Cover €1. Open M-Sa 12:30-3pm and 7-11pm. AmEx/MC/V. ❷

▨ Luzzi, V. San Giovanni in Laterano 88 (☎70 96 332), 3 blocks past the Colosseum from V. dei Fori Imperiali. This no-fuss corner *osteria* is always packed with locals. Paintings give you a tour of all the major sights. Daily specials like the *trippa alla romana* and *penne con salmone* (€7) will leave your taste buds wanting more. House wine (€2.50 per ½L; €4 per L), dessert €3-4. *Primi* €5-7, *secondi* €7-11. Open M-Tu and Th-Su noon-3pm and 7pm-midnight. AmEx/MC/V. ❶

Taverna dei Fori Imperiali, V. della Madonna dei Monti 16 (☎67 98 643). M: B-Colosseo. Walk up V. dei Fori Imperiali, and turn right through the park at the beginning of V. Cavour. V. della Madonna dei Monti runs parallel to V. Cavour on the left. Only steps away from Trajan's Forum. Offers creative twists on dishes like *tagliolini cacio e pepe e zafferano* (traditional cheese and pepper sauce infused with saffron; €7.50). Ask about seasonal dishes. *Secondi* €11-14. Desserts €6. Cover €1.50. Open M and W-Su 12:30-3:30pm and 7-10:30pm. Reservations recommended. AmEx/MC/V. ❷

L'Antica Birreria Peroni, V. San Marcello 19 (☎67 95 310; www.anticabirreriaperoni.it). Facing away from the monument, turn right on V. Cesare Battisti and left into P. dei S. S. Apostoli. 1 block down on the left. This energetic *enoteca* has a strong Italian vibe with a German twist. Wash down a *wurstel* (€6-7) with one of the 4 delicious beers on tap (€2-4.50). Fantastic *fiori di zucca* (€1). *Primi* €5-7. Cover €1. Open M-Sa noon-midnight. AmEx/MC/V. ❶

Hostaria Nerone, V. delle Terme di Tito 96 (☎48 17 952). M: B-Colosseo. Take V. Nicola Salvi, turn right, and then left on V. delle Terme di Tito. Indoor/outdoor dining near the Colosseum and the Domus Aurea. Traditional specialties like *spaghetti all'amatriciana* (€8) and *pollo alla romano con peperoni* (€9). House wine €2 per ¼L. Self-serve *antipasto* €8. *Primi* €8-9, *secondi* €9-13. Cover €1.50. Open M-Sa noon-3pm and 7-11pm. Closed Aug. AmEx/MC/V. ❷

Taverna dei Quaranta, V. Claudia 24 (☎70 00 550). M: B-Colosseo. Up the hill past P. del Colosseo. Cozy taverna serves delicious dishes in the quiet shade ascending the Caelian Hill. Try the *oliva ascolane* (fried olives stuffed with meat; €4). 20 types of pizza, along with calzones (€6-8), available only for dinner. House wine €11 per L. *Primi* €8-9, *secondi* €7-12.50. No pizza on M. Cover €1. Open daily 12:15-3:30pm and 7:30pm-11:30pm. AmEx/D/MC/V. ❷

CAMPO DEI FIORI

Ristorante Grappolo d'Oro Zampanò, P. della Cancelleria 80/84 (☎ 68 97 080), between C. V. Emanuele II and the Campo. This upscale *osteria* serves delicious home-made pastas along with a variety of other seasonal dishes. Eat outside and listen to the soothing sound of water from the fountain across the street. *Primi* €8-10, *secondi* €14-15. Cover €1.50. Open M, W-F noon-4:30pm and 7:30-11pm, Sa noon-4:30pm and 7:30pm-11:30pm, Su noon-3pm and 7:30-11pm. MC/V. ❷

L'Insalata Ricca, Largo dei Chiavari 85-6 (☎68 80 36 56; www.linsalataricca.it), off C. V. Emanuele II near P. S. Andrea della Valle. 9 locations throughout Rome. Friendly servers bring mammoth salads (€7-8), including honey salad (beef, cheese, walnuts, and honey), Parma ham, and *pantesca* (tomatoes, capers, and potatoes). Pastas €7-8. Desserts €4. Cover €1.10. Open daily noon-4pm and 8pm-midnight. AmEx/D/MC/V. ❷

Il Pollarola, P. Pollarola 25/27 (☎68 80 16 54), just behind the Campo dei Fiori. Exquisite renditions of traditional dishes. Try the house special *cannelloni specialista* (pasta filled with meat, tomato, and mozzarella cheese; €8). Daily specials €8-12. *Primi* €7-9, *secondi* €9-13. Dessert €5. Cover €1. Open M-Sa 12:30-3pm and 5:30-11pm. AmEx/D/MC/V. ❷

PIAZZA DI SPAGNA AND ENVIRONS

Ditch the area around the tourist traps and investigate the nooks and crannies of the alleyways. You will be rewarded with both superior food and better value.

Trattoria da Settimio all'Arancio, V. dell'Arancio 50-52 (☎68 76 119). Take V. dei Condotti from P. di Spagna; bear right after V. del Corso on V. Tomacelli, then take 1st left. Portions are generous and dishes decadent. Try the handmade *ravioli all'arancio* (large cheese-filled ravioli covered with white cream sauce with a hint of orange). *Primi* €8-15, *secondi* €8-20. Open M-Sa 12:30-3pm and 7pm-midnight. Reservations recommended. AmEx/MC/V. ❸

Vini e Buffet, V. della Torretta 60 (☎68 71 445), near P. di Spagna. From V. del Corso, turn on P. di San Lorenzo in Lucina. Turn left on V. Campo Marzio and right on V. della Torretta. A favorite among local wine enthusiasts. Walls lined with bottles and other vine decor. *Pâté* (€4-4.50) and *scarmorze* (smoked mozzarella with meat or vegetables; €8-9). Crepes €7.50-8. Wide variety of salads €7.50-11. Regional wines €10-24. Open M-Sa 12:30-3pm and 7:30-11pm. Reservations recommended. Cash only. ❷

Centro Macrobiotico Italiano Naturist Club, V. della Vite 14, 4th fl. (☎67 92 509). Heading toward P. del Popolo on V. del Corso, make a right on V. della Vite. All organic vegan-vegetarian menu. "Natural snacks" €8-10. Lunch *menù* €14. Dinner *menù* €20-25. Open M-F 12:30-3pm and 7:30-11pm, Sa 7:30-11pm. Reservations required for dinner. AmEx/MC/V. ❸

Il Brillo Parlante, V. della Fontanella 12 (☎32 43 334; www.ilbrilloparlante.com). Take V. del Corso away from P. del Popolo, then turn left on V. Fontanella. Although the wood-burning pizza oven cooks perfect pizzas (€9), handmade pasta and small dishes like the *pecorino* cheese, honey, and walnuts (€8.50) set this place apart. Outdoor seating available. Open M 5pm-1am, Tu-Su 12:30pm-1am. Bar open 5-7:30pm. Reservations suggested. MC/V. ❷

VATICAN CITY

For food a cut above that of the touristy bars and pizzerias, venture down V. Cola di Rienzo towards P. Cavour and explore the residential side streets.

Cacio e Pepe, V. Giuseppe Avezzana 11 (☎32 17 268). From P. Mazzini, turn right on V. Settembrini, and again at P. dei Martiri di Belfiore before taking a left on V. Giuseppe Avezzana (about a 20min. walk from P. del Risorgimento). Worth the walk from the Vatican area—in the summer, outdoor tables are filled with locals. 3 hearty *primi* prepared daily. Its specialty is the perfect *al dente* pasta piled high with olive oil, grated cheese, and fresh-ground pepper (€6). Full lunch €5-10. Open M-F 12:30-3pm and 7:30-11pm, Sa 12:30-3pm. Cash only. ❷

Paninoteca da Guido e Patrizia, Borgo Pio 13 (☎68 75 491), near Castel Sant'Angelo. Casual atmosphere and homey decor. Popular with lunching locals. Owner Guido holds court behind a well-stocked *tavola calda.* Full meal (*primo, secondo,* and drink) runs around €11. Open M-Sa 8am-6pm. Cash only. ❷

Franchi, V. Cola di Rienzo 200-204 (☎ 68 74 651; www.franchi.it). To be frank, Franchi ("Frankie") has been selling luxurious picnic supplies for nearly 50 years. Cheaper and better quality than most Vatican-area snack bars. Eat at counter or take your food to go. Try the *fritti misti* (deep-fried zucchini flowers, artichoke hearts, and zucchini; €22.50 per kilo) or the house ravioli. A snack-size Napoleon pizza (€2.60) is easy to munch on while standing in line for the Vatican Museums. Stuff yourself for around €8 total. Open M-Sa 9am-8:30pm. AmEx/MC/V. ❶

TERMINI AND ENVIRONS

A well-stocked **Conad** supermarket is on the lower floor of the Termini Station, just inside the V. Marsala entrance. (Open daily 8am-midnight.) An abundance of budget-conscious students with discriminating palates in San Lorenzo makes for inexpensive food with local character.

 TRAIN TO DANGERVILLE. While Termini and the surrounding areas serve as a major train and metro hub, the neighborhoods aren't exactly the safest you'll ever visit. In order to avoid a nighttime mugging, plan your Termini route beforehand and avoid walking alone at night in this area.

Africa, V. Gaeta 26-28 (☎49 41 077), near P. Indipendenza. Decked out in orange, yellow, and black, Africa continues its unique 32-year tradition of Eritrean and Ethiopian food amidst wooden giraffes and handmade lampshades. Meat-filled *sambusas* (€3) and a vegetarian menu. *Secondi* €8-11. Cover €1. Open Tu-Su 8am-2am. MC/V. ❷

Arancia Blu, V. dei Latini 65 (☎44 54 105), off V. Tiburtina. This elegant and popular vegetarian restaurant greets you with 3 wine glasses (white, red, and sparkling wine) and an affordable yet adventurous menu. Enjoy the phenomenal warm pesto salad (€7.50) in the softly lit setting. English menu available. Dessert €7.50. Extensive wine list (€12-130 per bottle). Open daily 8:30pm-midnight. Cash only. ❶

Hostaria da Bruno, V. Varese 29 (☎49 04 03). From V. Marsala, take V. Milazzo, and turn right on V. Varese. Locals on lunch break relax at this bastion of authentic food amid tourist traps. Savor the *tortellini al sugo* (tortellini with meat; €7) or try the chocolate crepes (€4). Open M-F noon-3pm and 7-10pm; Sa 7-10pm. AmEx/MC/V. ❶

Hostaria Romana da Dino, V. dei Mille 10 (☎49 14 25). Exit Termini near track 1, take a left on V. Marsala, a right on V. Vicenza, and a left on V. dei Mille. Look for the vertical blue Pizzaria sign. This humble *hostaria* provides ample seating and delicious dishes for dirt-cheap prices. Delectable pizzas (€5-7) and pastas (€4.50-5). Try the house wine for a mere €1.10 per ¼L. ❶

TRASTEVERE

The winding, cobblestone side streets across the Tiber offers a Rome far removed from the tourist-packed areas around the Colosseum and ruins. No slick, English-speaking proprietors will beckon you to enter their establishment here—in fact you will be hard-pressed to find anyone who speaks much English at all.

Pizzeria San Callisto, P. S. Callisto 9/A (☎58 18 256), off P. S. Maria. Don't mind the creepy statue of a cellist in the doorway. Simply the best pizza in Rome. Gorgeous thin-crust pizzas so large they hang off the plates (€4-8). Open Tu-Su 6:30pm-midnight. AmEx/MC/V. ❶

Pizzeria San Marco, V. Plinio 2 (☎32 35 398), off V. Cola di Rienzo. Incredible, if pricey, 30cm pizzas drenched in toppings with crispy crust and tasty dough bubbles. Over 25 *bianche* (white) pizzas (€8.50-10) and an even larger selection of *rosse* (red) pizzas (€7-9). Toppings include fried egg, tuna, and seasonal vegetables. Calzones €9. *Primi* €8-14, *secondi* €15-25. Open daily noon-1am. AmEx/MC/V. ❷

Augusto, P. dei Renzi 15 (☎58 03 798), before P. Santa Maria in Trastevere when coming from the river. Serves daily pasta specials (from €5) with speedy service to a young crowd in a hip neighborhood. *Secondi* €5.50-8. Bread €0.80. Open M-F 12:30-3pm and 8-11pm, Sa 12:30-3pm. Closed Aug. Cash only. ❶

La Piazzetta, V. Cardinale Merry del Val 16B (☎58 06 241; www.paginegialle.it/piazzetta). Take V. Trastevere away from the Tiber and turn right on V. Cardinale Merry del Val. Eat outside under the trees or inside under the discerning eyes of the dead fish on ice. Try the *fettucini asparagi e porcini* (fettucini with asparagus and mushrooms in cream sauce). Cover €2. Pizzas €5-9. Salads €7-8. *Primi* €7-12. Open daily noon-midnight. AmEx/MC/V. ❷

JEWISH GHETTO

The Jewish Ghetto, about a 10min. walk south of the Campo dei Fiori, serves kosher and traditional Jewish dishes, in addition to traditional Italian specialities. Going kosher for a meal can be a welcome break from pasta and pizza. Keep in mind that much of the Ghetto is closed on Saturdays for the Jewish Sabbath.

Bar Da Benito, V. dei Falegnami 14 (☎68 61 508), easiest to approach from V. del Portico d'Ottavia or V. Arenula. Try timing the lightning-quick bus boys as they clear tables faster than a NASCAR pit crew. Enjoy your fresh and delicious food at the tables in back, at the bar, or takeout. *Primi* €4.50, *secondi* €4.50-7.50. Dessert €2-3.50. Open M-Sa 6:30am-7pm. Closed Aug. Cash only. ❶

Trattoria da Giggetto, V. del Portico d'Ottavia 21-22 (☎68 61 105; www.giggettoalportico.com). Sit next to the ruins of the Portico d'Ottavia at the trattoria. No animal parts go to waste here. In the Roman tradition, *fritto misto* (lamb brains with vegetables; €12) are served alongside standard Italian fare and Jewish delicacies. *Primi* €8.50-14, *secondi* €9-20. Dessert €5-6. Cover €1.50. Open Tu-Su 12:30-3:30 pm and 7:30-11pm. Closed last 2 weeks of July. Dinner reservations required. AmEx/MC/V. ❷

La Taverna del Ghetto, V. del Portico d'Ottavia 8. (☎68 80 97 71; www.latavernadelghetto.com). Lively kosher taverna prides itself on its homemade pasta and delicacies like *lingua all'ebraica* (veal tongue). The *stracotto di manzo* (braised beef; €13.50) goes nicely with red wine. *Primi* €10.50, *secondi* €13.50-16.50. Open M-Th and Sa-Su noon-3pm and 6:30-11pm, F noon-3pm. Cover €1.50. AmEx/MC/V. ❷

Il Portico, V. del Portico D'Ottavia 1/D (☎68 64 642). Pleasant outdoor patio and plentiful pizza toppings like prosciutto and mushrooms (€6.50) separate Il Portico from unworthy impostors. Filling portions. Salads €5-8. *Primi* €5.50-8, *secondi* €7-14. Open daily noon-3:30pm and 7pm-midnight. MC/V. ❶

TESTACCIO

This residential neighborhood is the seat of many excellent restaurants serving traditional meat-heavy fare.

Il Volpetti Più, V. Alessandro Volta 8 (☎57 44 306; www.volpetti.com). Turn left on V. A. Volta, off V. Marmorata. Relive your high school days sliding down the lunch line—but replace the day-old sloppy joes with authentic Italian cuisine. Menu rotates weekly and seasonally. Salads, pasta salads, pizza, and daily specials from €4. Open M-Sa 10:30am-3:30pm and 5:30-9:30pm. AmEx/MC/V. ❶

Il Cantinone, P. Testaccio 31/32 (☎57 46 253). M: B-Piramide. Go up V. Marmorata and turn left on V. Giovanni Batista Bodoni; P. Testaccio is just past V. Luca della Robbia. Massive portions of pasta (*pappardelle* with boar sauce; €8), hearty meat-and-gravy dishes (€10-20), and a terrific house white wine (€6 per L). Check out the enormous brick oven, which pumps out cheap but high-quality pizzas (€5-7). Open M and W-Su noon-3pm and 7pm-midnight. AmEx/MC/V. ❷

Volpetti Salumeria-Gastronomia, V. Marmorata 47 (☎57 42 352), right around the corner from its sister store, Il Volpetti Più. Duck to avoid the hanging shanks of meat at this spiffy shop. Battle locals at the counter for an assortment of fresh gourmet cheeses, homemade pastas, fish, breads, and pastries, all priced by the kg. Open M-Sa 8am-2pm and 5-10:15pm. AmEx. ❷

GELATERIE AND PASTICCERIE

While *gelato* is everywhere in Rome, good *gelato* is not. And lest you think that *gelato* is Rome's only sweet snack, numerous bakeries sell cookies, small cakes, pastries, and other sumptuous sweets, all priced by the *etto* (100g).

Pellachia, Vatican, V. C. di Rienzo 103 (☎32 10 807; www.pellachia.com). Serves dozens of simple, fresh flavors with a finesse that has locals filling up the sidewalk's blue chairs. When out for a treat with your sweetie, ask for the "kiss" *gelato* (chocolate with nuts), or if you're feeling particularly decadent, indulge in the *fragole con panna e gelato* (strawberries with *gelato* and fresh cream; €4.50). Cones €1.50-3. *Granita* €2-3. Open Tu-Su 6am-1:30am. AmEx/MC/V. ❶

The Old Bridge, Vatican, V. dei Bastioni di Michelangelo 5 (☎39 72 30 26). Off P. del Risorgimento, across the street from the bend in the Vatican museum's outside wall. Your wait in line for the Vatican will seem much shorter if you're slurping on a heaping portion of this *gelato.* 20 homemade flavors; fruit flavors are especially refreshing (cup or cone €1.30-3). Cash only. Open M-Sa 10am-2am, Su 3pm-2am. ❶

Pasticceria Ebraico Boccione, Jewish Ghetto, V. del Portico d'Ottavia 1 (☎68 78 637), on the corner of P. Costaguti under the white awning. This tiny family-run bakery makes only about 8 items, including delicious Shabbat challah twisted into croissants and filled with custard (€0.60) and sugar-dusted *ciambelle* (doughnuts; €0.80). Open M-Th and Su 8am-7:30pm, F 8am-3:30pm. Closed in summer Su 2-4pm. ❶

Biscottificio Artigiano Innocenti, Trastevere, V. della Luce 21 (☎57 03 926). From P. Sonnino, take V. Giulio Cesare Santina and turn left on V. della Luce. Sells a dizzying number of cookies and biscuits and has been featured in countless international culinary magazines. Stock up on hazelnut, almond, chocolate, and jam cookies (sold by weight; 10 cookies about €2.50). Open Tu-Sa 8am-8pm, Su 9:30am-2pm. ❶

Il Gelato di San Crispino, Piazza di Spagna and Environs, V. della Panetteria 42 (☎67 93 924; www.ilgelatodisancrispino.com). 2nd left off V. del Lavatore, coming from the Trevi fountain. *Miele* (honey) flavor, the house specialty, is heaven in a spoon, but if you order it *affogato* (drowned) with one of their gourmet liquors, it might be just a little devilish, too. Cones €2-5, "Craziness Cone" €7.50. Open M, W-Th, Su noon-12:30am; F-Sa noon-1:30am. Cash only. ❶

Giolitti, *centro storico,* V. degli Uffici del Vicario 40 (☎69 91 243; www.giolitti.it). From the Pantheon, follow V. del Pantheon, then take V. della Maddalena to its end; turn right on V. degli Uffici del Vicario. Always crowded, this cafe serves more than 50 unique flavors of *gelato,*

ROME

such as *limoncello,* champagne, and *crema* (€2-4), along with several flavors of *granita* (€2.50). Make your order and pay at the cash register before stepping up to the counter. Open daily 7am-1am. AmEx/MC/V. ❶

Rivendita Libri Cioccolata e Vino, Trastevere, Vicolo del Cinque 11a (☎58 30 18 68 www.cioccolataevino.com), on the corner before it intersects with P. di Sant'Egidio. Though this *gelateria* might look like your grandparents' attic, the piano, wine books, ancient velvet chair, and masquerade mask create a charming atmosphere. *Caffè con chicco di cioccolato* €0.80. *Cioccalato freddo* (cold) or *caldo* (hot) €4. *Apertivo al cioccolato* €4-6. Try the sinfully delicious *bottarella* (a tiny chocolate shot glass filled with Bailey's, whipped cream, sprinkles, and cocoa; €2). Open M-F 6pm-2am, Sa 2pm-2am, Su 1pm-2am. MC/V. ❶

Il Gelatone, Ancient City, V. dei Serpente 28 (☎48 20 187). From V. dei Fori Imperiali, take a left on V. Cavour, then left on V. dei Serpente. Neon-colored *gelateria* with creamy, smooth *gelato.* Try the specialty *gelatone,* a blend of chocolate and vanilla with chocolate chips. The cool and refreshing *pompelmo rosa* (pink grapefruit) complements *limoncello* nicely. Over 65 flavors, including soy-based *gelato.* Cones €1.50-3, 4-flavor cone-bowls €4. Open daily 9:30am-midnight. Cash only. ❶

Da Quinto Gelateria, *centro storico,* V. di Tor Millina 15 (☎68 65 657), off P. Navona, on the long side, on the side street next to the church. Walls plastered with pictures of the hot-pink-aproned owner posing with her most famous clientele, including Ben Stiller and various cardinals. Fresh fruit *frulatti* (smoothies) made to order. *Gelato* €1.50-3. *Gelato affogato* (drenched in whiskey, brandy, or rum) €3.50. Open in summer daily 11am-3am. Cash only. ❶

Della Palma, *centro storico,* V. della Maddalena 20/23 (☎68 80 67 52), just steps from the Pantheon, with another location near the Trevi Fountain. Over 100 flavors of *gelato,* including meringue and spicy dark chocolate. Best known for its mousse. Several lactose- and sugar-free soy *gelato* flavors. Pay at the register before ordering at the counter with the receipt. Small (two flavors; €2), medium (4 flavors; €3); more elaborate bowls €6-10. Open daily 8am-1:30am. Cash only for *gelato.* ❷

CAFFÈ

Caffè Tazza d'Oro, *centro storico,* V. degli Orfani 84 (☎67 92 768 or 67 89 792; www.tazzadorocoffee-shop.com). Facing away from the Pantheon's *portico,* the yellow sign is on the right. This famous *caffè* shop makes Rome's highest quality coffee and has an extensive collection of teas. Try the signature *regina arabica* or the summer favorite, *granita di caffè con*

TOP TEN LIST

TOP TEN PLACES TO SMOOCH IN ROMA

While you may be close enough to pucker up with strangers on the subway, save your saliva for these dreamy destinations.

1. Stroll through **Villa Borghese** (p. 139), find a secluded, shady spot, and go in for the kill.
2. Bottle of red. Bottle of white. **Trevi Fountain** (p. 138) at night.
3. With the sun setting behind St. Peter's and the swirling Tiber beneath you, **Ponte Sisto** is the perfect place to lay it on. Hard.
4. **St. Peter's Square** (p. 140). Just keep it PG with His Holiness watching.
5. Survey **Circus Maximus** (p. 131) from Palatine Hill and imagine 300,000 fans cheering you on.
6. The terrace of the **Vittorio Emanuele II monument** (p. 129). It's nicknamed the "wedding cake" for a reason.
7. Top of **the Spanish Steps** (p. 138). If it fails, you can always push the person down them.
8. Waiting for the **Metro.** You'd be surprised. It gets pretty steamy.
9. **Chiesa di Santa Maria in Cosmedin** (p. 138). Forget chocolates and roses; the skull and relics of St. Valentine are the key ingredient in any love potion.
10. Over a shared bowl of spaghetti, *Lady and the Tramp* style.

panna (with fresh whipped cream; €2). Espresso €0.80. Cappuccino €1. Internet access €1 per 15min. Open M-Sa 7am-8pm. ❶

Sant'Eustachio Il Caffè, *centro storico,* P. di Sant'Eustachio 82 (☎68 80 20 48). Turn right on V. Palombella behind the Pantheon. Since 1938, this cafe has built a reputation as one of Rome's finest. Muscle your way to the front of the line for its signature *gran caffè speciale* (€2.20 standing; €4.20 table service). Chocolates, pastries, and ground coffee (€22 per kg) also available. Open M-Th 8:30am-1:30am, F and Su 8:30am-1am, Sa 8:30am-2am. Cash only.❶

Caffè della Pace, *centro storico,* V. della Pace 3-7 (☎68 61 216; www.caffedella-pace.it), off P. Navona. This laid-back spot looks more like a low-lit, swanky *enoteca* than a cafe. Patrons drink their espresso (€3), *prosecco* (€8), or mixed drinks (€10) at tables outside. Open M 4pm-2am, Tu-Su 9am-2am. ❷

ENOTECHE (WINE BARS)

The tinkling of crystal and intimate atmosphere differentiate *enoteche* from the more rough-and-tumble pubs. *Enoteche* usually serve a variety of small dishes and plates, like cheese selections, smoked meats, *antipasto,* and salads. Romans like to eat dinner around 9pm, so they either go to *enoteche* beforehand for a small bite to eat, or stay for the entire evening, sipping and nibbling the night away.

Cul de Sac, P. Pasquino 73 (☎68 80 10 94), off P. Navona. One of Rome's first wine bars. Extensive wine list (from €2 per glass) and outdoor tables. Specialty homemade *pâtés* (including boar and chocolate, and pheasant with truffle) are exquisite, as is the *escargot alla bourguigonne* (€6.40). Desserts €4. *Primi* €7-8, *secondi* €7-9. Open daily noon-4pm and 6pm-12:30am. MC/V. ❷

Enoteca Cavour 313, Ancient City, V. Cavour 313 (☎67 85 496). A short walk from M: B-Cavour; a few blocks from the Colosseum. Sip wine from crystal glasses in this French wine bar's intimate booths. Try a *misto di formaggi* (mixed cheese plate; €8-10). Meats (mixed plate €7-14) listed by region or type. Massive Italian wine list (€3-8 per glass, from €12.50 per bottle). Check the chalkboard on the left for featured wines. Rich desserts €4-6. Open M-Sa 12:30-2:30pm and 7:30pm-12:30am, Su 7:30pm-12:30am. Closed Aug. AmEx/MC/V. ❷

Enoteca Trastevere, Trastevere, V. della Lungaretta 86 (☎58 85 659). A block off P. Santa Maria. Staff helps you choose from their small but high-caliber wine list. Arrive after 10pm as things pick up around midnight. Wine €3.50-5 per glass. Meat and cheese plates €9-12. Desserts €3-5. Open M-Sa 6pm-2:30am, Su 6pm-1am. ❷

Trimani Wine Bar, V. Cernaia 37/B (☎44 69 630), near Termini, perpendicular to V. Volturno. Shop is around the corner at V. Goito 20. Escape the summertime heat in this chilled haven of fine wines. Look to the menu for suggested wines to complement mixed meat plates (€9-13.50) and the exceedingly popular house special, chocolate mousse (€6.50). Wines from €3-15 per glass. Happy hour 11:30am-12:30pm and 5:30-7pm. Open M-Sa 11:30am-3pm and 5:30pm-12:30am. AmEx/MC/V. ❷

⊙ SIGHTS

CENTRO STORICO

VIA DEL CORSO AND PIAZZA VENEZIA. Following the ancient V. Lata, Via del Corso began as Rome's premier race course and now plays host to many parades, including **Carnevale.** Running between P. del Popolo and P. Venezia, it is home to restaurants, hotels, and affordable fashion boutiques (see **Shopping,** p. 155). From P. del Popolo, take V. del Corso to **Piazza di Colonna Romana** where **Palazzo Wedekind,** home to the newspaper *Il Tempo,* was built in 1838 with columns from the

Etruscan city of Veio. Running south from P. del Popolo, V. del Corso ends at P. Venezia, home of the huge white marble **Vittorio Emanuele II Monument.** Referred to as "the wedding cake" and "Mussolini's typewriter," the monolithic monument makes for a good reference point. At the top of the staircase on the exterior is the **Altare della Patria,** which has two eternal flames guarded night and day by members of the Italian Navy in remembrance of the Unknown Soldier. Walk up the stairs to the **Museo Centrale del Risorgimento** for a comprehensive exhibit about Italian unification. *(Open daily 9:30am-6:30pm. Free.)* The **Palazzo Venezia,** right of P. Venezia, was one of Rome's first Renaissance structures. Mussolini used it as an office and delivered some of his most famous speeches from its balcony.

PANTHEON AND PIAZZA DELLA ROTONDA. With granite columns, bronze doors, and a soaring domed interior, the Pantheon has changed little since it was built nearly 2000 years ago. Architects still puzzle over how it was erected; its dome, a perfect half-sphere constructed from poured concrete without the support of vaults, arches, or ribs, is the largest of its kind. It was constructed under Hadrian from AD 118 to 125 over the site of the original Pantheon, destroyed in AD 80. The light entering the roof through the 9m oculus served as a sundial. In AD 608 the Pantheon was consecrated as the **Chiesa di Santa Maria ad Martyres.** Several noteworthy figures are buried within: Renaissance painter Raphael; King Vittorio Emanuele II, the first king of united Italy; his son, Umberto I, second king of Italy; and finally, Umberto's wife, Queen Margherita, after whom the margherita pizza was named in the 19th century. *(Open M-Sa 8:30am-7:30pm, Su 9am-6pm, holidays 9am-1pm. Closed Jan. 1, May 1, Dec. 25. Free. 20 min. audio tour €3.)*

In front of the Pantheon, an **Egyptian obelisk** dominates the P. della Rotonda. Around the left side of the Pantheon and down the street, another obelisk, supported by Bernini's curious **elephant statue,** marks the center of tiny P. Minerva. Behind the obelisk is Rome's only example of a Gothic-style church: **Chiesa di Santa Maria Sopra Minerva.** Built on the site of an ancient Roman temple, this hidden gem has an unassuming exterior but hides some Renaissance masterpieces, including Michelangelo's *Christ Bearing the Cross,* Antoniazzo Romano's *Annunciation,* and a statue of St. Sebastian recently attributed to Michelangelo. The **Cappella Carafa** in the southern transept boasts a brilliant series of Fra Filippo Lippi frescoes. A decapitated St. Catherine of Siena (1347-80) is reportedly buried under the altar; her head rests in Siena's *duomo. (Open daily 7am-1pm and 3-7pm.)* From the upper left corner of P. della Rotonda, V. Giustiniani heads north to V. della Scrofa and V. della Dogana Vecchia. Here stands **Chiesa di San Luigi dei Francesi,** France's national church in Rome, and home to three of Caravaggio's most famous paintings: *The Calling of St. Matthew, St. Matthew and the Angel,* and *The Crucifixion. (P. San Luigi dei Francesi 5. 1 block down V. di Salvatore from C. del Rinascimento, opposite P. Navona. Open daily 7:30am-12:30pm and 3:30-7pm.)*

IMBIBE THIS! Remember that Rome's water is *potabile* (drinkable), and many fountains or spigots run throughout the city. Take a drink, or fill up your water bottle from these free sources of cold, refreshing *acqua naturale.*

PIAZZA NAVONA. Originally a stadium built by Domitian in AD 86, P. Navona is now filled with artists, puppeteers, and mimes peddling their trades. Bernini's **Fontana dei Quattro Fiumi** (Fountain of the Four Rivers) commands the *piazza's* center. Each river god represents a continent: the Ganges for Asia, the Danube for Europe, the Nile for Africa (veiled because the source of the river was then unknown), and the Rio de la Plata for the Americas. At opposite ends of the *piazza* are the **Fontana del Moro** and the **Fontana di Nettuno,** designed by Giacomo della Porta in the 16th century. The **Chiesa di Sant'Agnese in Agone** holds the tiny skull of its namesake saint. It is said that on this very spot, Agnes was condemned to death for refusing to marry the son of a Roman prefect. To circumvent the law against executing virgins, she was dragged naked to a brothel, but her hair miraculously grew to such an extent that it covered her body. Then, when they tried to burn her alive, she would not light, causing a Roman soldier to strike off her head. *(West side of P. Navona, opposite Fontana dei Quattro Fiumi. Open daily 9am-noon and 4-7pm.)* West of P. Navona, where V. di Tor Millina intersects V. della Pace, the semicircular porch of the **Chiesa di Santa Maria della Pace** houses Raphael's gentle *Sibyls* in its Chigi Chapel. *(Open M-F 10am-noon and 3-6pm, Sa 10am-10pm, Su 10am-1pm.)* On nearby C. del Rinascimento, the **Chiesa di Sant'Ivo's** ■**corkscrew cupola** hovers over the Palazzo della Sapienza, the original home of the University of Rome before Mussolini had a larger one built in the 1930s to house more students. *(Open M-Sa 9am-6pm; Chiesa di S. Ivo alla Sapienza services Su 9am-noon.)* C. V. Emanuele II leads to **Il Gesu,** mother church of the Jesuit order. Inside, Andrea Pozzo's *Chapel of S. Ignazio* and Bernini's *Monument to S. Bellarmino* should not be missed. *(Open daily 6:45am-12:45pm and 4-7:45pm.)*

CAMPO DEI FIORI. Campo dei Fiori lies across C. V. Emanuele I from P. Navona. It is home to a bustling morning **market** and a hip, tightly policed, nightlife hot spot. *(Market open daily 9am-1:30pm.)* During papal rule, the area was the site of many executions; the eerie statue of Giordano Bruno is a tribute to one of the deceased. South of the Campo, the Renaissance **Palazzo Farnese** dominates P. Farnese. To the east of the *palazzo* is the **Palazzo Spada** and its **art gallery.**

LARGO DI TORRE ARGENTINA. This busy square is named for the **Torre Argentina** that dominates its southeast corner. The sunken area in the center of the Largo is a complex of four Republican temples unearthed in 1926 during Mussolini's project for demolishing the medieval city. The site is now a cat shelter, and dozens of felines patrol its grounds, providing photo opportunities for cat calendar photographers everywhere. The shelter welcomes donations and volunteers to help take care of the cats. *(At the intersection of C. V. Emanuele II and V. di Torre Argentina. Shelter ☎ 45 42 52 40; www.romancats.com.)*

MUSEI NAZIONALI ROMANI. The fascinating Museo Nazionale Romano Palazzo Massimo alle Terme is devoted to the history of art during the Roman Empire, including the Lancellotti *Discus Thrower*, a rare mosaic of Nero's time, as well as ancient coins and jewelry. *(Largo di Villa Peretti 1. In the left corner of P. dei Cinquecento. ☎ 48 90 35 00, reservations 39 96 77 00. Open Tu-Su 9am-7:45pm. Last entry 45min. before closing. €9, includes admission to Diocleziano, Crypta Balbi, and Palazzo Altemps; EU citizens 18-24 €6; EU citizens under 18 or over 65 free. Audio tour €4; €2.50 with archaeology card. Cash only.)* Nearby, the **Museo Nazionale Romano Terme di Diocleziano,** a beautifully renovated complex partly housed in the huge Baths of Diocletian (p. 142), has exhibits devoted to ancient writing and Latin history through the 6th century BC, as well as a beautiful cloister by Michelangelo. *(V. Enrico de Nicola 78. ☎ 39 96 77 00. Open Tu-Su 9am-7:45pm. Last entry 45min. before closing. €9. Cash only.)* The **Aula Ottogonale,** in another wing, holds 19 Classical sculptures in a gorgeous octagonal space. *(V. Romita 8. ☎ 48 70 690. Open daily 9am-1pm. Free.)*

ANCIENT CITY

PALATINE HILL

South of the Roman Forum, this hill served as the home for every Roman emperor. Purchase tickets or Archeologica Card at the biglietteria 100m down V. di San Gregorio from the Colosseum. Open daily Mar.-Aug. 8:30am-7:15pm; Sept. 9am-7pm; Oct. 9am-6:30pm; Nov. to mid-Feb. 9am-4:30pm; mid-Feb. to Mar. 9am-5pm. Last entry 1hr. before closing. Combined ticket with the Colosseum €11, EU citizens 18-24 €6.50, EU citizens under 18 or over 65 free. Must see both sights in one day. Tickets purchased after 1:30pm are valid until 1:30pm the following day. Cash only.

Legend has it that the Palatine Hill, a plateau between the Tiber River and the Roman Forum, was home to *la lupa*, the she-wolf that suckled Romulus and Remus. During the Republic, the Palatine was the most fashionable residential quarter, where aristocrats and statesmen, including Cicero and Marc Antony, built their homes. Augustus lived here in a modest house, but later emperors capitalized on the hill's prestige and built gargantuan quarters. By the end of the first century AD, the imperial residence covered the entire hill, whose Latin name, *Palatium*, became synonymous with the palace.

The best way to approach the Palatine is from the northeast via the stairs near the **Arch of Titus** in the Forum. The path ascends to the **Farnese Gardens Orti Farnesiani,** the world's oldest botanical gardens, dating back to 1625. Views of the Roman Forum make the gardens perfect for a picnic, and signs marked *"Affacciata sul Foro"* point to a lookout on the reflecting pools at the **House of Vestal Virgins.**

On the southwest side of the hill directly below the Farnese Gardens lie the remains of an ancient village featuring the **Casa di Romulo,** the alleged home of Romulus, and the **Temple of Cybele.** The remains of this area can be dated to roughly the same time as those found in the Forum's Archaic necropolis, which supports the theory that Rome was founded in the 8th century BC. To the left of Casa di Romulo is the **Casa di Livia,** where Augustus's wife Livia resided. The house used to connect to the **Casa di Augusto** (not to be confused with Domus Augustana) next door. Around the corner to the left, stretching along the Farnese Gardens is the mosaic-tiled **Cryptoporticus,** a tunnel which connected Tiberius's palace with nearby buildings and was used by slaves and couriers as a secret passage.

⚡TIP | **PALATINE PROBLEMS.** While there are English audio tours available for most Roman ruins, there is not one offered for the Palatine Hill. Be sure to catch the 🎧 **guided English tour** daily 4:15pm, €3.50; with Archeologica Card €2.50. Also, don't forget that the combined entrance for the Palatine Hill and the Colosseum (€11), purchased at the Palatine's V. di San Gregorio entrance, requires you to see both sites in one day, unless you purchase the tickets after 1:30pm, in which case the tickets are valid until 1:30pm the next day.

To the left of the Casa di Livia at the center of the hill is the sprawling **Domus Flavia,** the site of an octagonal fountain that occupied almost the entire courtyard. Romans have traditionally associated octagons with power; you will see many octagonal rooms in places of important significance, such as the Vatican and at the bases of important statues. To the left of the Domus Flavia stands the solemn **Domus Augustana,** the emperor's private space. Visitors are only allowed on the upper level, from which they can make out the shape of two courtyards down below. The palace's east wing contains the curious **Stadium Palatinum,** a sunken oval space used as a riding school.

Visitors can also see the **Circus Maximus,** which lies right behind the hippodrome. The fire of AD 64 started from there and spread to the Palatine, causing everything in the residences, except for the marble and stone constructions, to burn. The **Museo Palatino,** between the Domus Flavia and the Domus Augustana, displays archaeological artifacts from the early Archaic period on the lower level. The upper floor of the museum displays sculptures of well-to-do Romans and their deities. (Open daily 9:10am-6:20pm. Visiting slots every 20min.; only 30 people per fl. per slot. Free with admission to the Palatine.)

COLOSSEUM

☎ 70 05 469. M: B-Colosseo. Open daily 8:30am-7:15pm. Last entry 6:15pm. Combined ticket with Palatine Hill €11, EU citizens 18-24 €6.50, EU citizens under 18 or over 65 free. Tickets purchased after 1:30pm are valid until 1:30pm the following day. ▓Tours with archaeologist in Italian Sa-Su, English and Spanish daily every 30-45min. from 9:45am-1:45pm and 3-5:15pm. The same sticker you get for the Palatine/Roman Forum will get you an English tour at the Colosseum as well. Tours €3.50. Audio tour €4.50 in Dutch, English, French, Italian, Japanese, and Spanish. Video tour €5.50. Cash only.

 CUT THE LINE. To avoid waiting up to 20min. in line for tickets to the Colosseum, purchase your ticket from the less-crowded *biglietteria* on V. di San Gregorio. The same sticker for the archaeologist tour will work at the Palatine/Colosseum/Roman Forum.

The Colosseum—a hollowed-out ghost of travertine marble that once held more than 50,000 crazed spectators and now dwarfs every other ruin in Rome—stands as an enduring symbol of Rome as the Eternal City. The arena's name comes from the legendary 35m statue of Nero that used to stand beside it. The gilded bronze statue was referred to as "The Colossus," and hence the building became known as the Colosseum. The gaping holes in the bricks are the only signs left of where the brilliant marble ornamentation used to lie. Romans repeatedly stripped monuments of their marble to re-use in new monuments, a process called spoilage. You can see signs of spoilage throughout the ancient city's ruins—look for the holes where the iron hooks were ripped out of the wall.

Within 100 days of the Colosseum's AD 80 opening, some 5000 wild beasts perished in its bloody arena, and the slaughter went on for three more centuries. The wooden floor underneath the sand once covered a labyrinth of cells, ramps, and elevators used to transport exotic animals from cages to arena level where they would suddenly emerge, surprising spectators and hunters alike. Animals weren't the only beings killed for sport; men were also pitted against men. Though these gladiators were often slaves and prisoners, if they won their fights, they were idolized more than soccer players today. Contrary to popular belief, not all gladiator matches ended in death. Fights could stop after the first knockdown, or the loser could ask the emperor, who would defer to the rest of the crowd, for mercy.

A section of marble seating has been reconstructed using original Roman marble to give an idea of what the stands used to look like. Women and men would sit within a hierarchy of social classes and genders, with senators, knights, and vestal virgins closest to the arena and women of lower classes on the highest tier.

Next to the Colosseum, on the corner with V. di San Gregorio, stands the **Arco di Costantino,** one of the best preserved Imperial monuments in the area. The arch commemorates Constantine's victory at the Battle of the Milvian Bridge in AD 312 using fragments from monuments to Trajan, Hadrian, and Marcus Aurelius.

ROMAN FORUM

Main entrance: V. dei Fori Imperiali, at Largo Corrado Ricci, halfway between P. Venezia and the Colosseum. Other entrances are opposite the Colosseum, at the start of V. Sacra, and at the Clivus Capitolinus, near P. del Campidoglio. M: B-Colosseo, or bus to P. Venezia. Access to the Forum is unpredictable, as areas are sometimes fenced off for excavation or restoration. Open daily in summer 8:30am-7:15pm; in winter 9am-4:15pm. Last entry 1hr.

before closing. Free. Guided tour in English with archaeologist daily 12:30pm. €3.50. Inquire at Biglietteria Palatino, at the end of V. Nova past the Arch of Titus, for the audio tour in Dutch, English, French, German, Italian, and Japanese. €4. Cash only.

Because this valley between two of Rome's most famous hills—the Palatine and Capitoline—was originally a marshland prone to flooding, Rome's Iron Age inhabitants (1000-900 BC) avoided it in favor of the Palatine Hill, descending only to bury their dead. In the 8th-7th centuries BC, Etruscans and Greeks used the Forum as a marketplace. The Romans founded a thatched-hut shanty-town here in 753 BC, when Romulus and Sabine leader Titus Tatius joined forces to end the war triggered by the infamous rape of the Sabine women. Today the Forum bears witness to centuries of civic building.

From the Arch of Constantine by the Colosseum, take V. Sacra, the oldest street in Rome, to the **Arch of Titus.** On the left as you approach the arch lie the **Thermae** (Baths) and the **Temple of Jupiter Stator.** On the right is a series of 10 columns, all that remain of Hadrian's **Temple of Venus and Rome.** Built in AD 81 by Domitian, the Arch of Titus stands in the area of the Forum called the **Velia** and celebrates Jerusalem's sack by Domitian's brother Titus. The right panel shows a triumphal Titus on a quadriga chariot, while his soldiers carry back the spoils of war on the left panel. It is missing the two-sided arches typical of a triumphal arch (two lower arches flanking a taller middle arch) because they were damaged when it was removed from its original location in front of a fortress.

Turn right to face the Baroque facade of the **Chiesa della Santa Francesca Romana** (or **Santa Maria Nova**) built over Hadrian's Temple of Venus and Rome. It hides the entrance to the **Antiquarium Forense,** a museum (closed indefinitely) displaying necropolis urns and skeletons. Turn left, and as you pass the Upper Forum, check out the giant ruins of the **Basilica of Maxentius and Constantine** on the right. Emperor Maxentius began construction in AD 308, but Constantine deposed him and completed the project himself. Farther down you pass the **Temple of Romulus,** named for the son of Maxentius (not the legendary founder of Rome), on the right. The original bronze doors have a 4th-century AD working lock.

Just after the Temple of Romulus on the right is the **Archaic Necropolis,** a flat platform where Iron Age graves lend credibility to Rome's legendary founding in 753 BC. Farther down on the right is the **Temple of Antoninus and Faustina,** whose columns and rigid lattice ceiling kept it well preserved. In the AD 7th-8th centuries, after numerous unsuccessful attempts to tear it down, confirmed by the gashes near the top of the columns made by tow cables, the **Chiesa di San Lorenzo in Miranda** was built in the temple's interior. The church is an example of the Renaissance approach to the pagan ruins—either tear down the temples or convert them into churches.

Continuing down V. Sacra's right fork, on the left lie the remains of the **Regia,** which once served as the office of the Pontifex Maximus, Rome's high priest and the titular ancestor of the pope. Next on the left is the **Temple of the Deified Julius,** a shrine built by Augustus in 29 BC to honor the great leader and proclaim himself the inheritor of Julius Caesar's divine spirit. This is believed to be the site of Caesar's cremation, where he was burned in a funeral pyre with a piece of wood, flowers, and a cage with an eagle over his body. As the fire was started, the eagle was released from the cage, a symbol of the soul of the dead emperor flying away towards the heavens. Every year on July 12, Caesar's alleged birthday, people bring flowers to the shrine.

Back on V. Sacra, the **Basilica Aemilia** is on the right as you enter the area called the **Civic Forum.** Built in 179 BC, the Basilica housed the guild of the *argentarii* (money changers). It was rebuilt several times after fires until one started by Alaric and his merry band of Goths in AD 410 left it in its current state. Melted coins are now shiny studs in the pavement. On the left is the Forum's central section, **Market Square.** The **Column of Phocas** in the square was erected in AD 608 for the visiting Byzantine

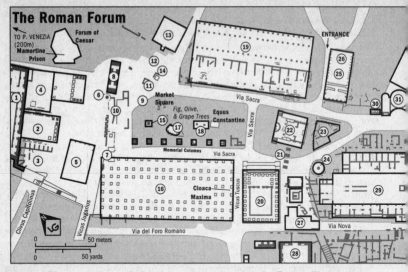

The Roman Forum

TO P. VENEZIA (200m)
Mamertine Prison

Forum of Caesar

13

19

ENTRANCE

26

25

12

14

8

11

1

4

6

Market Square

9

10

Fig, Olive, & Grape Trees

Equus Constantine

Via Sacra

30

31

2

15

17

18

Via Sacra

22

23

Memorial Columns

7

Via Sacra

21

24

3

5

16

Cloaca Maxima

Vicus Tuscus

20

29

Clivus Capitolinus

Vicus Iugarius

27

Via Nova

Via del Foro Romano

28

0   50 meters

0   50 yards

emperor, Phocas, and was the last monument erected in the Forum. The **Lacus Curtius** to its left is marked by concentric marble semicircles in the ground and a small frieze of a man on horseback; it commemorates the heroism of the legendary Roman warrior Marcus Curtius, who threw himself into a deep chasm in 362 BC to save the city from collapse. In the middle of the square, **Three Sacred Trees of Rome**—olive, fig, and grape—were planted by the Italian state in honor of his remarkable heroism. Off V. Sacra to the right is one of the Forum's oldest buildings, the **Curia** (Senate House). Contrary to popular belief, it was not in the square outside the Curia where the group of back-stabbing (literally) senators murdered Julius Caesar in 44 BC. Caesar was actually murdered in the Theater of Pompey in the Campus Martius.

The area in front of the Curia holds several noteworthy ruins. The **Imperial Rostra,** now a single, right angle of stone, was once a speaker's platform erected by Julius Caesar just before his death. The **Comitium,** now a marble semicircle in the ground, was the assembly place where citizens voted, where representatives gathered for public discussion, and where Rome's first laws, the Twelve Tables, were first inscribed on bronze tablets. The **Lapis Niger** (black stone) is the volcanic rock that marks the location of the underground 6th-century BC altar to the god Vulcan, where archaeologists discovered the oldest-known Latin inscription, which warns against defiling the shrine.

Back on V. Sacra, the **Arch of Septimius Severus** is straight ahead, built in AD 203 to celebrate Septimus's victories in the Middle East. Next to it stands the **Umbilicus Romae,** a circular solid brick structure marking the mythological center of Rome. Turn left to reach the **Temple of Saturn** in the **Lower Forum.** Though built in the early 5th century BC, the Temple of Saturn achieved larger-than-life status during the Golden Age of Rome (AD 1st-3rd centuries). The temple became the site of Saturnalia, a raucous Roman winter party where class and social distinctions were forgotten and anything was permitted. The **Tabularium** is the structure built into the rock face which forms the base of the **Campidoglio.** Turn left in front of the Temple of Saturn on the other branch of V. Sacra. To the right is the large **Basilica Julia,** where the well-preserved floor plan supports the intact bases of the columns of the former courthouse. To appreciate the luxury that is modern plumbing, view the remains of **Cloaca Maxima,** Rome's first

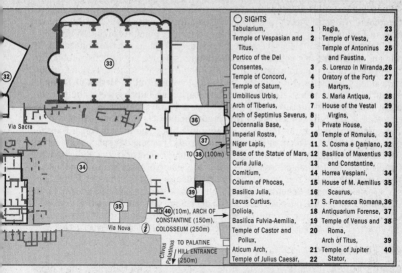

sewer, by taking a right on the Vicus Tuscus and looking right. Then check out the remains of the **Temple of Castor and Pollux,** on the right when facing the Basilica Aemelia at the end of Vicus Tuscus. According to legend, the twin gods Castor and Pollux helped Romans defeat the Etruscans at the Battle of Lake Regillus in 499 BC. Immediately after the battle, the twins appeared in the Forum to water their horses at the nearby **Basin of Juturna,** one of the only springs in ancient Rome.

Once again on V. Sacra, the column base of the former **Arch of Augustus,** built by Augustus to honor himself, stands in the middle of the path. Uphill from the arch, the **Temple of Vesta,** once circular, is now just a vaguely curved wall next to the **House of the Vestal Virgins.** The Vestal Virgins were female priests who were among the most respected people in ancient Rome. The six Virgins were chosen by the Pontifex Maximus from the daughters of the most important families; they had to be between the ages of six and ten and without physical imperfections. A virgin had to serve for 30 years, after which they could choose whether to continue in the priesthood or leave, but as the average lifespan was 35 years old, many never made it to the end of their term. The Virgins could walk unaccompanied in the Forum, pardon prisoners, move about in private chariots, and sit in special reserved seats at gladiatorial games and theatrical shows. They were responsible for the city's sacred eternal flame, keeping it lit for over 1000 years. A small statue of Minerva, which Aeneas took from Troy, occupies the **Palladium,** a secret room accessible only to the Virgins. This esteem had its price: a virgin who strayed from celibacy was buried alive (so that no sacred blood would be spilled).

FORI IMPERIALI. The sprawling Imperial Forums lie on along V. dei Fori Imperiali, a boulevard Mussolini paved to connect the old empire to his new one in P. Venezia, destroying a third of the ruins in the process. The temples, basilicas, and public squares that make up the Imperial Forums were constructed between the first century BC and AD 2nd century in response to increasing congestion in the old Forum. Much of the area is currently being excavated and is closed to the public, but visitors can peer over the railing of V. dei Fori Imperiali and side street V. Alessandrina, or take a ☒**guided archaeological tour** to get closer to the ruins. *(Reservations ☎ 67 97 702. English tour given Su at 4:30pm. €7.)*

Built between AD 107-113, the **Forum of Trajan** celebrated Trajan's victorious campaign in Dacia (mostly present-day Romania). Its creation turned the older Roman Forum into a tourist attraction of sorts. The complex included practical functions as well as a colossal equestrian statue of Trajan and a triumphal arch. At one end stands **Trajan's Column,** an extraordinary specimen of Roman relief-sculpture depicting 2500 legionnaires. In 1588 Pope Sextus V replaced Trajan's statue with one of St. Peter. Nearby, the three-floor, semicircular **Market of Trajan** is essentially Rome's first shopping mall, featuring an impressive—albeit crumbling—display of sculpture. A bit farther down V. Alessandrina stands the gray tufa wall of the **Forum of Augustus,** which commemorates Augustus's victory over Caesar's murderers at the Battle of Philippi in 42 BC. The nearby **Forum Transitorium** (also called the **Forum of Nerva**) was a narrow, rectangular space connecting the Forum of Augustus with the Republican Forum. Emperor Nerva dedicated the temple in 97 BC to the goddess Minerva. In the shade of the Vittorio Emanuele II monument, the paltry remains of the **Forum of Caesar** hold the ruins of Julius Caesar's **Temple to Venus Genetrix** (Mother Venus, to whom he claimed ancestry). In **Vespatian's Forum,** the mosaic-filled **Chiesa della Santi Cosma e Damiano** is across V. Cavour, near the Roman Forum. *(Closed indefinitely for excavations. Tourist office on V. dei Fori Imperiali has maps, guidebooks, and small exhibition about the Imperial Forum. Free.)*

OTHER SIGHTS

DOMUS AUREA. From P. Venezia, follow V. dei Fori Imperiale past the Colosseum; the park is on the left. Take a break from the relentless sun and enjoy the cacophony of chirping birds in the shade. Joggers, wild flowers, and ruins now occupy the Oppian Hill. The park houses a portion of Nero's "Golden House," his 80 acre palace, which covered a substantial chunk of Ancient Rome. An enclosed lake used to be at the base of the hill, and the hill itself was a private garden. The Forum was reduced to a vestibule of the palace; Nero crowned it with a colossal statue of himself as the sun. He also pillaged all of Greece to find works of art worthy of his abode, including the famous *Laocoön* now held in the Vatican's collections (see "The Agony and the Ecstasy," p. 149). Apparently, decadence didn't buy happiness: the megalomaniacal Nero committed suicide five years after building his hedonistic pad. *(Open daily 6:30am-9pm. Free.)*

CHIESA DI SAN PIETRO IN VINCOLI. This 4th-century church is named for the sacred *vincoli* (chains) that bound St. Peter in prison. The two chains were separated for more than a century in Rome and Constantinople, brought back together in the 5th century, and now lie beneath the altar. Michelangelo's ◪**statue of Moses** is tucked in the back right corner. The two horns on his head are actually supposed to be beams of light, indications of wisdom. *(M: B-Cavour. Walk along V. Cavour toward the Forum and take the seemingly endless stairs on the left to P. San Pietro in Vincoli. Open daily 8am-12:30pm and 3-6pm. Modest dress required.)*

CIRCUS MAXIMUS AND BATHS OF CARACALLA. Today's Circus Maximus is only a grassy shadow of its former glory as Rome's largest stadium. After its construction in 600 BC, the circus held more than 300,000 Romans who came to watch chariots careen around the track. Today the ruins are all but gone, and the Circus is mainly a concert venue. The mosaic-coated Baths of Caracalla, about a 10min. walk down V. dei Terme di Caracalla, are the largest and best-preserved in Rome. *(M: B-Circo Massimo, bus #118, or walk down V. di San Gregorio from the Colosseum. Circus open ☎39 96 77 00. 24hr. Baths open Apr.-Oct. M 9am-2pm, Tu-Su 9am-7:15pm; Nov.-Mar. M 9am-2pm, Tu-Su 9am-3:30pm. Last entry 1hr. before closing. €6, EU residents ages 18-24 €3, EU residents under 18 and over 65 free. Audio tour €4.)*

CAPITOLINE HILL. Home to the original "capital," the Monte Capitolino still houses the city's government, topped by Michelangelo's spacious **Piazza di Campidoglio.** *(To get* to the Campidoglio, take bus to P. Venezia, face the Vittorio Emanuele II monument, and walk around to the right to P. d'Aracoeli. Take the stairs up the hill.) At the far end of the *piazza*, the turreted **Palazzo dei Senatori** houses the Roman mayor's offices. Pope Paul III moved the famous **statue of Marcus Aurelius** here from the Palazzo dei Conservatori and then asked Michelangelo to fashion the imposing statues of Castor and Pollux. Framing the *piazza* are the twin Palazzo dei Conservatori to the right and Palazzo Nuovo on the left, home of the **Capitoline Museums** (p. 150). From the Palazzo Nuovo, stairs lead up to the rear entrance of the 7th-century **Chiesa di Santa Maria in Aracoeli.** Its stunning **Cappella Bufalini** to the left of the altar is home to the *Santo Bambino*, a cherubic statue that receives letters from sick children. *(Santa Maria open daily 9am-12:30pm and 3-6:30pm. Donation requested.)* The gloomy **Mamertine Prison,** consecrated as the **Chiesa di San Pietro in Carcere,** lies downhill from the back of the Aracoeli. St. Peter baptized his captors here with water that flooded his cell. *(Entrance underneath the church of S. Giuseppe dei Falegnamis. ☎ 67 92 902. Open daily in summer 9am-7pm; in winter 9am-12:30pm and 2-5pm. Donation requested.)*

CAELIAN HILL. The Caelian and the Esquiline are the biggest of Rome's seven original hills. In ancient times Nero built his decadent Domus Aurea (p. 136) between them. **San Clemente** consists of a 12th-century addition on top of a 4th-century church, with an ancient **mithraeum** and sewers at the bottom. The upper church holds mosaics of the Crucifixion, saints, and apostles, and a 13th-century Masolino fresco cycle graces the **Chapel of Santa Caterina.** The 4th-century level contains the tomb of St. Cyril, a pagan sarcophagus, and a series of frescoes depicting Roman generals. Farther underground is a dank 2nd-century *mithraeum*, below which is the **insulae,** a series of brick and stone rooms where Nero is said to have played his lyre while Rome burned in AD 64. In summer, the **New Opera Festival of Rome** performs abridged productions in the church's outdoor courtyard. *(M: B-Colosseo. Bus #85, 87, 810. Tram #3. Turn left down V. Labicana, away from the Forum, then turn right into P. San Clemente. From M: A-Manzoni, walk west on V. A. Manzoni; turn left into P. San Clemente. ☎ 77 40 021. Open M-Sa 9am-12:30pm and 3-6pm, Su and holidays 10am-12:30pm and 3-6pm. Last entry 20min. before closing. Lower basilica and mithraeum €5, students €3.50. Cash only. For New Opera Festival of Rome, ticket reservations ☎ 77 07 27 68; visit www.newoperafestivaldiroma.com.)*

THE VELABRUM. The Velabrum lies in a flat, flood plain of the Tiber, south of the Jewish Ghetto. At the bend of V. del Portico d'Ottavia, a shattered pediment and a few columns are all that remain of the once magnificent **Portico d'Ottavia.** The 11 BC **Teatro di Marcello**

THE LOCAL STORY

THE LIES OF MARCH

"Beware the Ides of March"—more like, "beware the *lies* of March." After all, our dear friend Shakespeare fictionalized the setting of the toga gang stabbing in his famous play, *Julius Caesar.* As a result, centuries of Roman travelers have mistakenly made pilgrimages to the Roman Forum's *curia* (senate house) instead of the Theater of Pompey. Shocker, huh?

On the Ides of March in 44 BC, Caesar was slated to address the senate near the Theater of Pompey. Despite bloody omens from a soothsayer and his wife, he was coerced into attending the meeting. Senator Casca made the first move and stabbed Caesar in the neck. The senatorial snake pit grew chaotic, and following a mass stabbing, Caesar looked into the eyes of his close aide, Brutus, and gasped "Et tu Brute?".

1600 years later, Shakespeare rewrote the event. History buffs who would like to see the actual site of Caesar's assassination should look no farther than the basements around Rome's Palazzo Pio, off Campo dei Fiori. While the theater is now ruined, remnants of the assassination site still exist underground. When visiting the Palazzo Pio area, be sure to check the cellars of nearby buildings. But beware the Ides of March—the 2000-year-old ghost of Julius Caesar might be lurking there.

next door bears the name of Augustus's nephew; the Colosseum was modeled after its facade. One block south along V. Luigi Petroselli is the P. della Bocca della Verità, the site of the ancient Foro Boario (cattle market). Across the street, the **Chiesa di Santa Maria in Cosmedin** harbors lovely medieval decor. The portico's **Bocca della Verità,** a drain cover with a river god's face, was made famous by Audrey Hepburn in 1953's *Roman Holiday.* But beware, medieval legend has it that the "mouth of truth" bites any liar's hand. Inside, perhaps St. Valentine's skull and bones will ignite your romantic side. Nothing says *amore* like centuries-old relics. *(Chiesa ☎ 67 81 419. Currently undergoing restorations, but still open to public daily 9:30am-5:50pm.)*

WHEN NATURE CALLS. It's hard to find public restrooms without buying anything. Duck into a department store, such as **La Rinascente** or **COIN,** or a large bookstore, such as **Feltrinelli,** to use a free restroom.

PIAZZA DI SPAGNA AND ENVIRONS

FONTANA DI TREVI. Nicolo Salvi's (1697-1751) bombastic Fontana di Trevi has enough presence and grace to turn even the most jaded jerk into a sighing, romantic mush. A fantastic place to people-watch, the fountain's name refers to its location at the intersection of three streets *(tre vie).* Neptune, in the center, stands in front of the goddesses of abundance and good health; the two horsemen in the water represent the mercurial sea, either covered by rough waves or in placid ripples. Although you should hold back to avoid a steep fine, actress Anita Ekberg couldn't resist taking a dip in the fountain's cool waters in the famous scene from Frederico Fellini's *La Dolce Vita.* Legend has it that a traveler who throws a coin into the fountain is ensured a speedy return to Rome, and one who tosses two will fall in love while there. Three coins ensure that wedding bells will soon be ringing. On a less poetic note, the crypt of the **Chiesa dei Santi Vincenzo e Anastasio,** opposite the fountain, preserves the hearts and lungs of popes from 1590 to 1903. Sadly, the crypt is not open for public viewing. *(Church open daily 7am-noon and 4-7pm.)*

SPANISH STEPS. Designed by an Italian, paid for by the French, named for the Spaniards, occupied by the British, and currently featuring American greats like Ronald McDonald, the **Scalinata di Spagna** are, to say the least, multicultural. P. di Spagna is also home to designer boutiques like Fendi, Gucci, Prada, and Valentino, and is a great spot for people-watching or socializing. John Keats died in 1821 in the pink-orange house by the Steps; it's now the small **Keats-Shelley Memorial Museum,** displaying several documents and memoirs of the Romantic poet and his contemporaries, including Lord Byron, Percy Bysshe Shelley, and his wife Mary Shelley. *(☎ 67 84 235; www.keats-shelley-house.org. Open M-F 9am-1pm and 3-6pm, Sa 11am-2pm and 3-6pm. €3.50.)*

PIAZZA DEL POPOLO. Once a favorite venue for the execution of heretics, this is now the "people's square." In the center is the 3200-year-old Obelisk of Pharaoh Ramses II, which Augustus brought from Egypt in AD 10. Climb the hill on the east side of the *piazza* for a spectacular view of the city. **Santa Maria del Popolo** holds Renaissance and Baroque masterpieces, as well as tourists searching for writer Dan Brown's clues from his novel *Angels and Demons.* Two exquisite Caravaggios, *The Conversion of St. Paul* and *Crucifixion of St. Peter,* are in the Cappella Cerasi, next to the altar. The Cappella Chigi was designed by Raphael for the Sienese banker Agostino Chigi, reputedly once the world's richest man. Niches on either side of the altar house sculptures by Bernini and Lorenzetto. With so much artwork, an exquisite portrait of the late Pope John Paul II seems orphaned, leaning against a chapel wall. *(☎ 36 10 836. Open M-Sa 7am-noon and 4-7pm, Su and holidays*

8am-1:30pm and 4:30-7:30pm.) At the southern end of the *piazza* are Carlo Rinaldi's 17th-century twin churches, **Santa Maria di Montesano** and **Santa Maria dei Miracoli.** *(☎ 36 10 250. Open M-Sa 6:30am-1:30pm and 4-7:30pm, Su 8am-1:30pm and 5-7pm.)*

VILLA BORGHESE

VILLA BORGHESE. To celebrate becoming a cardinal, Scipione Borghese financed construction of the **Villa Borghese,** now home to three art museums—the world-renowned **Galleria Borghese** (p. 148); the intriguing **Museo Nazionale Etrusco di Villa Giulia** (p. 151); and the lovely **Galleria Nazionale d'Arte Moderna,** which is actually a Vatican Museum located in the park. *(M: A-Spagna and follow the signs. Or, from the A: Flaminio stop, take V. Washington under the archway. From P. del Popolo, climb the stairs to the right of Santa Maria del Popolo, cross the street, and climb the small path. ☎ 32 16 564. Free.)*

THE GLOBE THEATER. This circular, wooden structure is an exact replica of the 16th-century Elizabethan theater. Presents Shakespearean plays performed in Italian on the outdoor stage. *(Reservations ☎ 82 05 91 27; www.globetheatreroma.com. M-F 1-7pm, Sa-Su 10am-1pm and 3-7pm. July-Sept. tickets, starting from standing room only, €7-18.)*

QUIRINAL HILL. At the southeast end of V. del Quirinale, the ⬛Piazza del Quirinale occupies the summit of the tallest of Rome's seven hills. In the center the statues of Castor and Pollux (Roman copies of the Greek originals) stand on either side of an obelisk from the Mausoleum of Augustus. The president of the Republic resides in the Palazzo del Quirinale, a Baroque architectural collaboration by Bernini, Maderno, and Fontana. Farther along the street lies the facade of Borromini's pulsating **Chiesa di San Carlo alle Quattro Fontane.** Bernini's ⬛Four Fountains are built into the corners of the intersection of V. delle Quattro Fontane and V. del Quirinale. Sidewalks are nonexistent, so be careful when viewing the fountain. *(Palazzo closed to the public. Chiesa open M-F 10am-1pm and 3-6pm, Sa 10am-1pm.)*

PIAZZA BARBERINI. Though the busy traffic circle at V. del Tritone feels more like a modern thoroughfare than a Baroque square, P. Barberini features two Bernini fountains, **Fontana Tritone** and **Fontana delle Api.** Maderno, Bernini, and rival Borromini are responsible for the **Palazzo Barberini,** home to the Galleria Nazionale d'Arte Antica. The severe **Chiesa della Immaccolata Consezione** houses the macabre ⬛Capuchin Crypt decorated with hundreds of human skulls and bones. *(V. V. Veneto 27. www.cappucciniviaveneto.it. Open daily 9am-noon and 3-6pm. Cash donation requested.)*

VATICAN CITY

☎ 69 81 662. M: A-Ottaviano; bus #40, 64, 271, or 492 from Termini or Largo Argentina; or tram #19 from P. Risorgimento, 62 from P. Barberini, or 23 from Testaccio. The official Comune di Roma tourism kiosk has helpful English staff who will provide free maps, brochures, hours, location, and ticket info for any of the sites related to the Vatican or Rome. Located at Castel Sant'Angelo, P. Pia (☎ 58 33 34 57). Open daily 8:30am-7pm. 10 other locations in the city around the major tourist sites.

The foothold of the Roman Catholic Church, once the mightiest power in Europe, occupies 108½ independent acres within Rome. The Lateran Treaty of 1929 allows the Pope to maintain legislative, judicial, and executive powers over this tiny theocracy, but also requires the Church to remain neutral in national politics and municipal affairs. The Vatican has historically and symbolically preserved its independence by minting coins (Italian *lire* and euros with the Pope's face), running a separate press and postal system, maintaining an army of Swiss Guards, and hoarding fine art in the **Musei Vaticani.** Devout pilgrims and atheists alike are awed by the stunning beauty of its two famous churches, the Sistine Chapel and St. Peter's Basilica, and the Vatican Museums are arguably some of Italy's best.

BASILICA DI SAN PIETRO (ST. PETER'S BASILICA)

Multilingual confession available. The multilingual staff of the Pilgrim Tourist Information Center, located on the left between the rounded colonnade and the basilica, provides Vatican postage, free brochures, and currency exchange. A first-aid station and free bathrooms are next to the tourist office. Open daily Apr.-Sept. 7am-7pm; Oct.-Mar. 7am-6pm. Mass M-Sa 8:30, 10, 11am, noon, 5pm; Su and holidays 9, 10:30, 11:30am, 12:15, 1, 4, 5:30pm. Vespers 5pm. Free guided tours Tu and Th 9:45am and W 3pm; meet at Info Center. Modest attire strictly enforced: no shorts, short skirts, or exposed shoulders allowed.

PIAZZA AND FACADE. The famous artist Bernini's colonnade around **Piazza San Pietro,** lined with the statues of 140 saints, was designed to provide a long, impressive vista to pilgrims after their tiring journey through the tiny, winding streets of Borgo and the *centro storico*. Mussolini's broad V. della Conciliazione, built in the 30s to connect the Vatican to the rest of the city, opened a broader view of the church than Bernini ever intended. Round disks mark where to stand so that the quadruple rows of colonnades seem to merge into one perfectly aligned row. Statues of Christ, John the Baptist, and all the apostles except Peter are on top of the basilica. In warm months, the Pope holds papal audiences on a platform in the *piazza* on Wednesday mornings. *(To attend an audience, contact the Prefettura della Casa Pontificia ☎ 69 88 46 31 or stop by the Bronze Door, located on the right after you pass through security. Ascend the steps and ask the Swiss Guard for a ticket.)*

> ⭐**TIP** **COLOR-CODED.** The Virgin Mary can usually be recognized in art by her red dress and bright blue mantle. Blue became her trademark color because the pigment was made from *lapis lazuli*, the most expensive of all paint.

INTERIOR. The basilica rests on the reputed site of St. Peter's tomb. In Holy Years the Pope opens the **Porta Sancta** (Holy Door)—the last door on the right side of the entrance porch—by knocking in the bricks with a silver hammer. The interior of St. Peter's Cathedral measures 187m by 137m along the transepts. Metal lines on the marble floor mark the lengths of other major world churches. To the right, Michelangelo's repaired *Pietà* has been encased in bullet-proof glass since 1972, when an axe-wielding fanatic attacked it, smashing Christ's nose and breaking Mary's hand.

Bernini's **baldacchino** (canopy) rises on spiraling columns over the marble altar, reserved for the Pope's use. The Baroque structure, cast in bronze pillaged from the Pantheon, was unveiled on June 28, 1633, by Pope Urban VIII, a member of the wealthy Barberini family. Bees, the family symbol, buzz here and there, and vines climb toward Michelangelo's cavernous **cupola.** Seventy oil lamps glow in front of the *baldacchino* and illuminate Maderno's sunken *Confessio*, a 17th-century chapel. Two staircases directly beneath the papal altar descend to St. Peter's tomb. The staircases are closed to the public, but the underground **grottoes** offer a better view of the tomb. *(Open daily Apr.-Sept.7am-6pm and Oct.-Mar 7am-5pm. Free.)*

High above the *baldacchino* and the altar rises **Michelangelo's dome,** designed as a circular dome like that of the Pantheon (p. 129). Out of reverence for that ancient architectural wonder, Michelangelo is said to have made this cupola a meter shorter in diameter than the Pantheon's; the difference is not noticeable, however, as the dome towers 120m high and 42.3m across. When Michelangelo died in 1564, only the drum of the dome had been completed. Work remained at a standstill until 1588, when 800 laborers were hired to complete it. Toiling round the clock, they finished the dome on May 21, 1590.

BASILICA ENVIRONS

To the left of the basilica is a courtyard protected by Swiss Guards. The **Ufficio Scavi,** administrative center for the Pre-Constantinian Necropolis, is here. Ask Swiss Guards for permission to enter. To the right of the basilica, at the end of the colonnade, the **Prefettura della Casa Pontifica** gives free tickets to papal audiences in the morning on Wednesdays when the Pope is speaking.

CUPOLA. The cupola entrance is near the Porta Sancta. Ascend 551 stairs to the top or take an elevator to the walkway around the dome's interior. Beware, even if you use the elevator, you will still have to climb 320 steps to see the top ledge's panorama. *(Open daily Apr.-Sept. 8am-5pm; Oct.-Mar. 8am-4pm. Stairs €4, elevator €7.)*

TREASURY OF ST. PETER. The Treasury contains gifts bestowed upon St. Peter's tomb. At the entrance, look for a list of all the popes beginning with St. Peter. Highlights include the dalmatic of Charlemagne (the Holy Roman Emperor's intricately designed robe), a Bernini angel, and the magnificent bronze tomb of Sixtus IV. *(Inside the basilica on the left. Open daily Apr.-Sept. 9am-6:15pm; Oct.-Mar. 9am-5:15pm. Last entry 30min. before closing. Closed when the Pope is celebrating mass in the basilica and on Christmas and Easter. Wheelchair-accessible. Photographs forbidden. €6, under 13 €4.)*

TOMB OF ST. PETER AND PRE-CONSTANTINIAN NECROPOLIS. After converting to Christianity, Constantine built the first basilica directly over the tomb of St. Peter, who had been crucified for preaching the Gospel. In order to build on that exact spot, the emperor had to level a hill and destroy the first-century necropolis that stood there before. The story was merely legend until 1939, when workers came across ancient ruins beneath the basilica. Unsure of finding anything, the Church secretly set about looking for St. Peter's tomb. Twenty-one years later, the saint's tomb was identified under a small temple directly beneath the altars of the Constantinian basilica. The saint's bones, however, were not found in the crude grave. A hollow wall nearby held what the church later claimed to be the holy remains. Some believe that the bones were displaced from the tomb during the Saracens' sack of Rome in AD 849 or during another barbarian sacking. Multilingual tour guides will take you around the streets of the necropolis, which hold several well-preserved pagan and Christian mausolea, funerary inscriptions, mosaics, and sarcophagi. *(Entrance to the necropolis is on the left side of P. S. Pietro, beyond the info office. ☎69 88 53 18; scavi@fsp.va. Office open M-Sa 9am-5pm. To request a tour, arrange in person or write to: The Delegate of the Fabbrica di San Pietro, Excavations Office, 00120 Vatican City. Give a preferred range of times and languages. Phone calls only accepted for reconfirmations. Reserve as far ahead as possible. €10.)*

CASTEL SANT'ANGELO

☎68 19 111, reservations 39 96 76 00. Along the Tiber River on the Vatican side when going from St. Peter's toward the Tiber River. From centro storico, cross Ponte Sant'Angelo. Bus #40, 62, 64, 271, 280 to Ponte V. Emanuele or P. Pia. Dungeon. Open in summer Tu-Su 9am-7:30pm; in winter daily 9am-7pm. Last entry 1hr. before closing. Tours Su 12:30pm in Italian, 2:30pm in English. €5, EU students 18-25 €2.50, EU citizens under 18 or over 65 free. Additional €2 fee for traveling exhibits. Audio tour €4.

Built by Hadrian (AD 76-138) as a mausoleum for himself and his family, this brick and stone mass has served as a fortress, prison, and palace. When a plague struck in AD 590, Pope Gregory the Great saw an angel sheathing his sword at the top of the complex; the plague abated soon thereafter, and the building was rededicated to the angel. The fortress hosts an armory on the one of the top floors and offers an incomparable view of Rome and the Vatican. Outside, the marble **Ponte Sant'Angelo,** lined with statues by Bernini, is the beginning of the traditional pilgrimage route from St. Peter's to the church of **San Giovanni in Laterano** (p. 145).

TERMINI AND ENVIRONS

▨**BASILICA DI SANTA MARIA MAGGIORE.** One of the four "Patriarchal" churches in Rome granted extraterritoriality, this basilica crowns the **Esquiline Hill** and is officially part of Vatican City. In AD 352 Pope Sixtus III commissioned it when he noticed that Roman women were still visiting a temple dedicated to the pagan mother-goddess, Juno Lucina. He tore down the pagan temple and built a basilica in celebration of the Council of Ephesus's recent ruling that Mary was the mother of God. Set in the floor to the right of the altar, a marble slab marks **Bernini's tomb.** Don't miss the **baptistery,** featuring a magnificent statue of St. John the Baptist covered with animal skins and holding a clam shell. The glorious 14th-century mosaics in the church's **loggia** recount the story of the August snowfall that showed the Pope, who had dreamed of snow brought by the Virgin Mary, where to build the church; every mid-August this miracle is re-enacted as priests sprinkle white flower petals from the top of the church. Below the altar are what some believe to be relics from Jesus's manger. *(From Termini, exit right down on V. Giolitti, and walk down V. Cavour. Tickets in souvenir shop. Open daily 7am-7pm. Loggia only accessible with guided tour daily 1pm. Multilingual confession available. Modest dress required. Loggia tour €3; audio tour €4. Cash only.)*

BATHS OF DIOCLETIAN. From AD 298 to 306, 40,000 Christian slaves built these 3000-person-capacity public baths, the largest in Rome. They contained a marble public toilet with seats for 30 people, several pools, gymnasiums, art galleries, gardens, brothels, sports facilities, libraries, and concert halls. The AD 4th-century rotunda displays statues from the baths, and the entrance holds gorgeous, stained-glass windows. In 1561 Michelangelo undertook his last architectural work and converted the ruins into a church, **Chiesa di Santa Maria degli Angeli.** On the bronze door to the left, a startling cross cuts deeply into Christ's body, symbolizing His resurrection. *(Baths on V. Enrico De Nicola 79, in P. dei Cinquecento, across the street from Termini. ☎ 39 96 77 00. Closed for restoration. Church is in P. della Repubblica. ☎ 48 80 812; www.santamariadegliangeliroma.it. Open M-Sa 7am-6:30pm, Su and holidays 7am-7:30pm.)*

VIA XX SETTEMBRE. V. del Quirinale becomes V. XX (pronounced "VEN-tee") Settembre at its intersection with V. delle Quattro Fontane, where a spectacular Bernini fountain sits in each of the four corners. A few blocks down, the colossal **Fontana dell'Acqua Felice** graces P. San Bernardo. Opposite, **Chiesa di Santa Maria della Vittoria** houses an icon of Mary that accompanied the Catholics to victory in a 1620 battle near Prague. Bernini's fantastically controversial **Ecstasy of Saint Theresa of Ávila** amazes visitors in the Cornaro Chapel. At the time of its creation, people were outraged by the depiction of the dart-pierced saint in a pose resembling sexual climax. Many viewers insist, however, that they didn't see all the scandal until told of the controversy. The statue illustrates St. Theresa's heart being pierced by an angel's arrow, filling her with ardent love for God. *(Open daily 7am-noon and 3:30-7pm. Modest dress required.)*

VIA NOMENTANA. This road runs northeast from Michelangelo's **Porta Pia** out of the city. Hop on bus #36 in front of Termini or head back to V. XX Settembre and catch bus #60. A 2km walk from Pta. Pia past villas, embassies, and parks leads to **Chiesa di Sant'Agnese Fuori le Mura** on the left. Its apse displays a Byzantine-style mosaic of St. Agnes. Underneath the church wind some of Rome's most impressive **catacombs.** While St. Agnes's body is buried here, her head resides in the church bearing her name in P. Navona, the location of her beheading. *(V. Nomentana 349. ☎ 86 10 840 to reach the tour guide service. Open M-Sa 9am-noon and 4-6pm, Su 4-6pm. Modest dress required. Catacombs €5, under 16 €3.)*

TRASTEVERE
Take bus #75 or 170 or tram #8 to V. Trastevere.

ISOLA TIBERINA. According to Roman legend, Isola Tiberina emerged with the Roman Republic. After the Etruscan tyrant Tarquin raped the virtuous Lucretia, her outraged family killed him and then tossed his body into the Tiber; so much muck and silt collected around his corpse that an island eventually formed. For centuries the river's fast flowing water was harnessed by mills, which were destroyed by the great flood of 1870. Home to the Fatebenefratelli Hospital since AD 154, the island has long been associated with cures. The Greek god of healing, Aesclepius, appeared to the Romans as a snake and slithered from the river. The eclectic 10th-century **Basilica di San Bartolomeo** has a Baroque facade, a Romanesque tower, and 14 antique columns. (☎68 77 973. Open M-Sa 9am-12:30pm and 3:30-6pm. Free.) The **Ponte Fabricio** (62 BC), known as the **Ponte dei Quattro Capi** (Bridge of Four Heads), is the oldest in the city.

CENTRAL TRASTEVERE. Off Ponte Garibaldi stands the statue of poet G. G. Belli in his own *piazza*, which borders P. Sonnino and marks the beginning of Vle. di Trastevere. Follow V. Giulio Cesane Santina, which turns into V. dei Genovesi, and take a right on V. di Santa Cecilia. Beyond the courtyard is the **Basilica di Santa Cecilia** in Trastevere and its fantastic mosaic above the altar. (Open daily 9:30am-12:30pm and 4-6:30pm. Donation requested. Crypt €2.50. See Cavallini's frescoes M-F 10:15am-12:15pm, Sa-Su 11:15am-12:15pm. €2.50.) From P. Sonnino, V. della Lungaretta leads west to P. di Santa Maria in Trastevere, home to the Chiesa di Santa Maria in Trastevere, built in the AD 4th century by Pope Julius II. The mosaics and the chancel arch are quite impressive. What appears to be a trash heap around the statue of the friar and the infant at the entrance is actually a pile of prayers written on anything from Metro tickets to napkins. (Open M-Sa 9am-5:30pm, Su 8:30-10:30am and noon-5:30pm.)

GIANICOLO HILL. At the top of the hill, the **Chiesa di San Pietro** in Montorio stands on what is believed to be the site of St. Peter's upside-down crucifixion. The church contains del Piombo's *Flagellation*, from designs by Michelangelo. (Open daily May-Oct. Tu-Su 9:30am-12:30pm and 4-6pm; Nov.-Apr. 9:30am-12:30pm and 2-4pm. Free.) Next door in a small courtyard behind locked gates is Bramante's tiny ⊠**Tempietto.** A combination of ancient and Renaissance architecture, the Tempietto was constructed to commemorate the site of St. Peter's martyrdom, and it provided the inspiration for the dome of St. Peter's in Vatican City. (Courtyard open in summer Tu-Sa 9:30am-12:30pm and 4-6pm; in winter Tu-Sa 9:30am-12:30pm and 2-4pm. Free.) Check out an aerial view of Rome from a viewing spot in front of **Acqua Paolo.** The sprawling public gardens behind Acqua Paolo continue up V. Garibaldi. Rome's botanical gardens lie at the bottom of Gianicolo and contain a garden for the blind as well as a rose garden that holds the bush from which all the world's roses are supposedly descended. (Reach the summit on bus #41 from the Vatican, 115 from Trastevere, 870 from P. Fiorentini, where C. V. Emanuele meets the Tiber, or walk up the medieval V. Garibaldi, from V. della Scala in Trastevere for 10min. Botanical Gardens, Largo Cristina di Svezia 24, at the end of V. Corsini, off V. della Lungara. ☎49 91 71 06. Open Apr.-Oct. M-Sa 9:30am-6:30pm; Oct.-Mar. M-Sa 9:30am-5:30pm. Closed holidays. Guided tours Sa 10:30am-noon. Comes with leaflet and audio tour in Italian, English, or French. Call for reservations and more info. €4, ages 6-11 and over 60 €2, under 6 free.)

THE JEWISH GHETTO

Rome's Jewish community is the oldest in Western Europe—Israelites came in 161 BC as ambassadors of Judas Maccabee, asking for Imperial help against invaders. The Ghetto, the tiny area to which Pope Paul IV confined the Jews in 1555, was dissolved in 1870, but it is still the center of Rome's Jewish population of 16,000. Take bus #64; the Ghetto is across V. Arenula from Campo dei Fiori. The Ghetto's main street is V. del Portico d'Ottavia.

PIAZZA MATTEI. This square, centered on Taddeo Landini's 16th-century **Fontana delle Tartarughe,** marks the Ghetto's center. Nearby is the **Chiesa di Sant'Angelo in Pescheria,** installed inside the Portico d'Ottavia in AD 755 and named after the fish market that flourished there. Jews were forced to attend mass here, an act of evange-

ROME

lism that they quietly resisted by stuffing their ears with wax. *(V. dei Funari. Heading toward the Theater of Marcellus on V. del Teatro Marcello, go right on V. Montavara, which becomes V. dei Funari after P. Campitelli. The church is under restoration indefinitely.)*

SINAGOGA ASHKENAZITA. Built between 1901 and 1904 at the corner of Lungotevere dei Cenci and V. Catalana, this temple incorporates Persian and Babylonian architectural techniques. The dome's rainbow colors are a sign of peace. Notice the stained glass high up on the right hand side of the synagogue. Terrorists bombed the building in 1982, killing a small child; the broken glass was replaced by clear glass, in honor of the victim. Guards now search all visitors, and *carabinieri* patrol the vicinity. In 1986 Pope John Paul II made the first-ever papal visit to a Jewish synagogue here, declaring that Jews are the oldest brothers of Christians. The synagogue houses the **Jewish Museum,** a collection of ancient Torahs and Holocaust artifacts that document the community's history. *(☎68 40 06 61; www.museobraico.roma.it. Open for services only. Museum open June-Sept. M-Th and Su 10am-7pm, F 9am-4pm; Oct.-May M-Th and Su 10am-10pm, F 10am-4pm. Last entry 45min. before closing. Closed Sa, Jewish holidays from 1pm the day before, and after 1pm on Catholic holidays. €7.50, students €3, under 10 free. Groups €6.50. Reservations required. Cash only.)*

TESTACCIO AND OSTIENSE

Take Metro B to Piramide, Garbatella, or San Paolo.

South of the Aventine Hill, the working-class district of Testaccio is known for its cheap trattorie and raucous nightclubs. The neighborhood centers around the castle-like **Porta San Paolo,** a remnant of the Aurelian walls built in the AD 3rd century to protect Rome from barbarians. Another attraction is the colossal **Piramide di Gaius Cestius,** built in 330 days by Gaius Cestius's slaves under Augustus at the height of Roman Egyptophilia. Piramide also shuttles droves of sun-loving Romans to Ostia, so don't be surprised if you're sitting next to a bathing-suit-clad *signora* on the metro. Ostiense is the district south of Testaccio and is mostly residential apartments and industrial complexes.

BASILICA DI SAN PAOLO FUORI LE MURA. The massive Basilica di San Paolo Fuori le Mura is one of the four churches in Rome with extraterritorial status—only the Pope is allowed to say mass here. It's also the city largest church after St. Peter's Basilica. St. Paul's body, after his beheading at the Tre Fontane, is said to have been buried beneath the altar, while his head remained with St. Peter's at the Arcibasilica of San Giovanni. The exact point above the body's resting place is marked by a tiny red light on the front of the altar. S. Paolo is also home to many less-significant relics; they are held in the **Capella delle Reliquie,** which you can access through the cloister. In addition to an impressive cadelabrum, the basilica also displays the likenesses of every pope since the beginning of the church, with a light shining on face of the current pope, Benedict XVI. Before leaving, pick up a bottle of monk-made Benedictine liqueur (€5-15) in the gift shop. *(M: B-Basilica S. Paolo, or take bus #23 or 769 from Testaccio, at the corner of V. Ostiense and P. Ostiense. Basilica open daily in summer 7am-6:30pm; in winter 7am-6pm. Cloister open daily in summer 9am-1pm and 3-6:30pm; in winter 9am-1pm and 3-6pm. Modest dress required. Donation requested. Audio booths for short history of basilica €1. Audio tour €5. Gift shop cash only.)*

CIMITERO ACATTOLICO PER GLI STRANIERI. This peaceful Protestant cemetery, the "Non-Catholic Cemetery for Foreigners," is one of the only burial grounds in Rome for those who don't belong to the Roman Catholic Church. Keats, Shelley, von Goethe, and Antonio Gramsci rest here. Keats's grave, in his typically self-effacing style, is dedicated to "A Young Poet." *(From Piramide, go in between the pyramid and the castle. Once on V. Marmorata, immediately turn left on V. Caio Cestio. Ring bell. www.protestantcemetery.it. Cemetery open M-Sa 9am-5pm. Last entry 4:30pm. €2 donation requested. Cat sanctuary open daily 2:30-4:30pm.)*

ABBAZIA DELLE TRE FONTANE (ABBEY OF THE THREE FOUNTAINS). Legend has it that when St. Paul was beheaded here in AD 67, his head bounced on the ground three times and created a fountain at each bounce. The supposed column upon which Paul was decapitated lies in the back-right corner of the chapel. The chapels have a serenity entirely distinct from the dramatic exuberance of Rome's Baroque churches; visit the Abbey for an hour of quiet contemplation. *(M: B-Laurentina. Walk straight and take a right on V. Laurentina; proceed about 1km north, and turn right on V. delle Acque Salve. About a 15min. walk, or take bus #761 from Laurentina, get off after 2 stops, and walk the rest of the way. The abbey is at the bottom of the hill. ☎ 54 60 23 47. Open daily 8am-1pm and 3-6pm. Free.)*

SOUTHERN ROME

▨ SAN GIOVANNI IN LATERANO. The immense **Arcibasilica of San Giovanni in Laterano,** the cathedral of the diocese of Rome, was home to the Papacy until the 14th century. Founded by Constantine in AD 314, it is the city's oldest Christian basilica. The golden *baldacchino* (canopy) rests over two golden reliquaries with the skulls of St. Peter and St. Paul. Note the immense statue of Constantine, the fresco by **Giotto,** the octagonal Battistero, and the intimate **cloister.** A museum of Vatican history is on the right when facing the church. *(Enter the church at the left. Cathedral open daily 7am-6:30pm. Free. Cloister open 9am-6pm. Cloister €2, students €1. Audio tour €5, students €4. Let's Go discount €1. Battistero open 7am-12:30pm and 4-7pm. Free. Museum open M-Sa with entrances at 9, 10, 11am, noon. €4, students €2. Cash only.)*

The **Scala Santa,** outside the church and to the left facing out of the front doors, are revered as the marble steps used by Jesus outside Pontius Pilate's home in Jerusalem. Indulgences are still granted to pilgrims if they ascend the steps on their knees, reciting prayers on each step. Martin Luther experienced a break with Catholicism here when he was unable to experience true piety in the act and left without finishing. The steps lead to the chapel of the **Sancta Sanctorium,** which houses the Acheiropoieton, or "picture painted without hands," said to be the work of St. Luke assisted by an angel. *(M: A-S. Giovanni or bus #16 from Termini. Walk through the archway of the city walls to the P. S. Giovanni. Church ☎ 69 88 63 92. Open daily in summer 6:15am-noon and 3:30-6:45pm; in winter 6:15am-noon and 3-6:15pm. Modest dress required. Free. Scala Santa and Sancta Sanctorium ☎ 77 26 641. Open daily 6:30am-noon and 3-6pm; in summer 6:30am-noon and 3-6:30pm. Donation requested.)*

PORTA SAN GIOVANNI. The **Chiesa della Santa Croce in Gerusalemme** holds the fascist-era **Chapel of the Relics,** with fragments of the "true cross." For doubters, perhaps the most intriguing of the relics is St. Thomas's dismembered finger, which, when still attached, was used to probe Christ's wounds. *(P. S. Paolo della Croce in Gerusalemme M: A-S. Giovanni. From Pta. S. Giovanni north of the stop, go east on Vle. Carlo Felice; church is on the right. Or, from P. V. Emanuele II, take V. Conte Verde. ☎ 70 14 769; www.basilicasantacroce.com. Open daily 7am-12:45pm and 2-7pm. Modest dress required. Donation requested.)*

AVENTINE HILL. V. di Valle Murcia climbs past some of Rome's swankiest homes and the **Roseto Comunale,** a beautiful public rose garden. Formerly a Jewish cemetery, the rose gardens are now marked by commemorative pillars at each entrance containing the Tablets of Moses. Continuing up the hill, along the left side the gardens, the street turns into V. di Santa Sabina. On the right side of V. di S. Sabina, just before the crest of the hill, is a park with orange trees and a sweeping view of southern Rome. Nearby the **Chiesa di Santa Sabina** has wooden front doors dating to AD 450. The top, left-hand panel contains one of the earliest-known representations of the Crucifixion. V. di Santa Sabina continues along the crest of the hill to **Piazza dei Cavalieri di Malta,** home of the once-crusading order of the Knights of Malta. On the right as you approach the *piazza* is a large, cream-colored, arched gate; peer through its tiny, circular ▨**keyhole** for a hedge-framed view of the dome of St. Peter's Cathedral. *(Take V. di San Gregorio from the Colosseum. Turn right at the intersection with V. del Cerchi, and take the stairs across the Circus Maximus to P. Ugo la Malfa and V. di Valle Murcia. Rose garden open May-June 8am-7:30pm. Free.)*

■ THE APPIAN WAY

M: A-San Giovanni, you will get out in P. Appio. Follow the signs back through the brick archways to P. S. Giovanni. Then take bus #218 to V. Appia Antica; get off at the info office, just before Domine Quo Vadis; hit the button to stop after you turn left onto V. Appia Antica. Or, M: B-Circo Massimo or Piramide, then take bus #118 to the catacombs; M: A-Colli Albani, then bus #660 to Cecilia Metella. Info office of the Parco dell'Appia Antica, V. Appia Antica 60/62. ☎51 35 316; www.parcoappiaantica.org. Provides maps and pamphlets about the ancient road and its history, excavations, and recreational opportunities. Also rents bikes €3 per hr., €10 per day. Open in summer M-Sa 9:30am–1:30pm and 2-5:30pm, Su and holidays 9:30am-5:30pm; in winter M-Sa 9:30am–1:30pm and 2-4:30pm, Su and holidays 9:30am-4:30pm. Free.

About 30min. outside the city center, V. Appia Antica, also known as the Appian Way, was the most important thoroughfare of Ancient Rome. In its heyday it stretched from Campania to the Adriatic Coast and rightfully gained the nickname "The Queen of Roads." Marcus Linius Crassus, a 1st-century BC tycoon and sometime general, crucified 6000 slaves along this road as punishment for joining the rebellion of the legendary gladiator Spartacus. Today, it is a perfect oasis away from the grind of Rome's streets, vendors, and Vespas. Third-century catacombs, medieval and Baroque churches, and a wealth of ancient Roman ruins make their home on the Appian Way. On Sundays, when the street is closed to vehicles, take the opportunity to bike through the countryside. Listen to birds chirping and watch the wind ripple through the wheat fields.

■ **BASILICA OF SAN SEBASTIANO.** Perhaps second only to St. Peter's in overall quality, this basilica should not be missed. Originally dedicated to St. Peter and St. Paul, it now honors St. Sebastian. When Sebastian, a captain in the Roman army, was discovered to be a Christian, he was shot with arrows and left for dead. Miraculously, he was nursed back to health and continued to practice his faith, but was eventually executed. He is the patron saint of athletes due to his remarkable endurance, of soldiers due to his profession and perseverance, and of archers—despite his vested interest in their doing poorly. His likeness is reproduced on the gorgeous ceiling, the work of a Flemish artist. In 2000, the magnificent statue of Jesus Christ the Redeemer was attributed to Bernini as his final masterpiece, completed at age 81. However, the oldest but most recently discovered of the church's relics are the snail fossils, which are probably 120 million years old and are visible in the marble that covers the floor. The marble sports the fitting nickname *lumacella*, or "little snails," though the snails seem gigantic by today's standards. *(V. Appia Antica 136. ☎78 08 847. Open daily 8:30am-6pm. Free.)*

CHIESA DELLA SANTA MARIA IN PALMIS. On the site of this church, which is also called Domine Quo Vadis, St. Peter had a vision of Christ. He said to Jesus, *"Domine, quo vadis?"* ("Lord, where are you going?"). To this Christ replied that he was going to Rome to be crucified again because Peter had abandoned him. Peter understood his vision's significance and returned to Rome to suffer his own martyrdom: he was crucified upside down. In the middle of the aisle, just inside the door, Christ's alleged footprints are set in stone. *(At the intersection of V. Appia Antica and V. Ardeatina. Open daily in summer 8am-12:30pm and 2:30-7:45pm; in winter closes at 6:45pm. Free.)*

CATACOMBS. Since burial inside the city walls was forbidden during ancient times, fashionable Romans buried their beloved along Appian Way, while early Christians dug maze-like catacombs—an economic solution for pricey land. **San**

Callisto is the largest catacomb in Rome, with nearly 22km of subterranean paths. Its four levels once held 16 popes, seven bishops, St. Cecilia, and 500,000 other Christians. **Santa Domitilla** holds a 3rd-century portrait of Christ and the Apostles, along with other colorful frescoes. **San Sebastiano** houses the massive underground tomb of St. Sebastian himself, and was reputedly the home for the bodies of Peter and Paul before their relocation to their final resting places. San Sebastiano also contains three impressive stucco-ceilinged tombs from the pre-Christian period. Stop by the info office for maps, booklets, and advice. *(All catacombs accessible only with guided tours in English, Italian, and Spanish, which run every 20min. San Sebastiano: V. Appia Antica 136. ☎78 50 350. www.fratilazio.it. Open M-Sa 9am-noon and 2-5pm. €5, ages 6-15 €3. MC/V. San Callisto: V. Appia Antica 126, entrance on road parallel to V. Appia. ☎51 30 15 80; www.catacombe.roma.it. M-Tu and Th-Su 9am-noon and 2-5pm. €5, ages 6-15 €3. Cash only. Santa Domitilla: V. delle Sette Chiese 282. Facing V. Ardeatina from San Callisto exit, cross street, and walk right up V. Sette Chiese. ☎51 10 342; www.catacombe.domitilla.it. €5, ages 6-15 €3. Open Feb.-Dec. M and W-Su 9am-noon and 2-5pm. Cash only.)*

VILLA AND CIRCUS OF MAXENTIUS. Before Constantine took over Rome in AD 312, Maxentius held the title of emperor long enough to build along the Appian Way. The complex consists of a villa, a 10,000-spectator chariot racetrack, and the tomb of his son Romulus. *(V. Appia Antica 153. ☎78 01 324. Open 9am-1:30pm. Last entry 30min. before closing. Mausoleum of Romulus closed indefinitely for restoration. €3, students €1.50. Cash only.)*

🏛 MUSEUMS

Rome's museums are some of the world's best. Though traveling, contemporary exhibits do occasionally come through the city, permanent masterpieces have been secured through the wealth and influence of prominent families and the Vatican. Reserving or buying tickets in advance will give you more time to enjoy the art. Keep your eyes on the ceilings—in many museums they are richly decorated with frescoes. For more info on Rome's museums, visit www.beniculturali.it.

🖼 VATICAN MUSEUMS (MUSEI VATICANI)

Walk north from the right side of P. S. Pietro along the wall of the Vatican City for about 10 blocks. From M: Ottaviano, turn left on V. Ottaviano to reach the Vatican City Wall; turn right and follow the wall to the museum's entrance. ☎69 88 49 47; www.vatican.va. Major galleries open Mar.-Oct. M-F 10am-4:45pm, Sa 10am-2:45pm; Nov.-Feb. M-Sa 10am-1:45pm. Last entry 1¼hr. before closing. Closed on major religious holidays (Jan. 1 and 6, Feb. 11, Mar. 19, Easter, Easter Monday, May 1, Ascension, Corpus Domini, Aug. 15, Nov.1, Dec. 8, Dec. 25, and Dec. 26). Snack bar between the collection of modern religious art and the Sistine Chapel; full cafeteria near main entrance. Most of the museums are wheelchair-accessible, though less visited parts, such as the upper level of the Etruscan Museum, are not. Admission €13, ISIC members €8, with guided tour €21.50, children under 1m tall free. Free last Su of the month 9am-1:45pm. Info and gift shop sell a useful guidebook (€7.50) on ground level past the entrance. Audio tour €6.

The Vatican Museums hold one of the world's greatest collections of art, with ancient, Renaissance, and modern paintings, sculptures, and papal odds and ends. After a day of art-overload, be sure to admire the famous **bronze double-helix ramp** as you ramble down it towards the exit.

🖼 SISTINE CHAPEL. Since its completion in the 16th century, the Sistine Chapel, named for its founder, Pope Sixtus IV, has been the site of the College of Cardinals' election of new popes, most recently **Pope Benedict XVI** in April 2005. Michelangelo's **ceiling,** the pinnacle of artistic creation, gleams from its 20-year restoration, which ended in 1999. The simple compositions and vibrant colors

hover above, each section depicting a story from Genesis. The scenes are framed by the famous *ignudi* (young nude males). Michelangelo painted the masterpiece by standing on a platform and craning backward—he never recovered from the strain to his neck and eyes. *The Last Judgement* fills the altar wall; the figure of Christ as judge lingers in the upper center, surrounded by his saintly entourage and the supplicant Mary. Michelangelo painted himself as a flayed human skin that hangs symbolically between the realms of heaven and hell. The frescoes on the side walls predate Michelangelo's ceiling; they were completed between 1481 and 1483 by a team of artists under Perugino including Botticelli, Ghirlandaio, Roselli, Signorelli, and della Gatta. On one side, scenes from the life of Moses complement parallel scenes of Christ's life on the other. Sitting is only allowed on the benches along the side. Guards will ask you to remain silent, as the chapel is a holy place.

OTHER VATICAN GALLERIES. The **Museo Pio-Clementino** houses the world's greatest collection of antique sculpture. The world-famous statue of **Laocoön,** who was strangled by Neptune's sea serpents for being suspicious of the Greek's gift of the wooden horse, is located in the octagonal courtyard. Proceeding through the courtyard, two slobbering hounds guard the entrance to the **Stanza degli Animali,** a marble menagerie highlighting Roman brutality. The statues of ◙**Apollo Belvedere and Hercules** are both masterful works. The last room of the gallery has the red sarcophagus of Sant'Elena, Constantine's mother. From here, the Simonetti Stairway climbs to the **Museo Etrusco,** filled with artifacts from Tuscany and northern Lazio. Back on the landing of the Simonetti Staircase is the **Stanza della Biga** (room of an ancient marble chariot) and the **Galleria della Candelabra,** which contains over 500 smaller statues. The route to the Sistine Chapel begins here, passing through the dimly lit **Galleria degli Arazzi** (tapestries), the **Galleria delle Mappe** (maps), the **Apartamento di Pio V** (where there is a shortcut to the Sistine Chapel), the **Stanza Sobieski,** and the **Stanza dell'Immacolata Concezione.** From the Stanza dell'Immacolata Concezione, a door leads into the first of the four ◙**Stanze di Rafaele,** apartments built for Pope Julius II in the 1510s. A door at the back of the 2nd room, originally called the **Room of the Parrot,** depicts St. John the Baptist with parrots on either side of him. The door below leads to the Room of the Swiss Guard and is closed to the public. Another room features Raphael's *School of Athens,* painted as a trial piece for Julius, who was so impressed that he fired his other painters, destroyed their frescoes, and commissioned Raphael to decorate the entire room. From here, there are two paths: one to the Sistine Chapel and the other a staircase to the frescoed Borgia apartments and the **Museum of Modern Religious Art.**

> **☆TIP☆ ARE WE THERE YET?** Lines for the Vatican Museums begin forming around 6:30am and become increasingly unbearable as the hours pass. It's not a bad idea to drag yourself out of your rock-hard hostel bed at an ungodly hour.

PINACOTECA. This collection, one of Rome's best, includes Filippo Lippi's *Coronation of the Virgin,* Perugino's *Madonna and Child,* Titian's *Madonna of San Nicoletta dei Frari,* and Raphael's ◙**Transfiguration.** On the way out of the Sistine Chapel, take a look at the **Room of the Aldobrandini Marriage,** which contains a series of rare, ancient Roman frescoes.

PRINCIPAL COLLECTIONS

◙**GALLERIA BORGHESE.** Located in the Villa Borghese's serene grounds of the Villa Borghese, the Galleria Borghese may be Rome's most enjoyable museum. The collection—including masterpieces by Bernini, Titian, Raphael, Caravaggio, and Rubens—can be appreciated in one afternoon. The spoils of Cardinal Scipione

the agony and the ecstasy

Everyday, visitors rush through the Vatican Museum's Belvedere courtyard, eager to bask in the glory of the nearby Sistine Chapel. One by one, however, each courtyard on-looker becomes par-

"The Laocoön became the artistic standard of beauty."

alyzed at the sight of the *Laocoön* and his sons. As his marble muscles ripple, *Laocoön*'s grimace seems ever more deeply etched on his face. His anguished expression is almost the opposite of beauty, and those who stop to witness his struggle react with awe and terror. The struggle and writhing of this dying man gave rise to much beauty—and not just that of Michelangelo's Sistine Chapel—for arguably, the *Laocoön* was the most influential work of art in the Western world for some 300 years after its discovery.

On January 14, 1506, a momentous discovery was made in the city of Rome. While digging in his vineyard on the Esquiline Hill, a farmer uncovered nine fragments of an ancient marble statuary. Pope Julius II promptly dispatched the architect Giuliano da Sangallo to inspect the new discovery. Though ancient sculptures were regularly pulled from the ground in Renaissance Rome, this find proved to be of extraordinary interest. Almost immediately, the fragments were identified as being from the *Laocoön*, a sculpture that had belonged to the Roman Emperor Titus, and that was known to Renaissance humanists because it had received the highest of praise from the first-century writer Pliny the Younger.

Finding the *Laocoön* was a dream come true for well-educated Renaissance artists and patrons intent on restoring Rome to its ancient glory. At the very moment in which the idea of "Rome Reborn" was being made manifest in art and architecture projects, the *Laocoön* emerged from the earth, further fueling the Renaissance dream. In July of the same year, Julius triumphantly transported the sculpture

through Roman streets. Throngs of citizens lined the streets and showered the *Laocoön* with flower petals while the Sistine Chapel Choir heralded the sculpture's journey to the Belvedere Courtyard of the Vatican Palace. Without a doubt, the *Laocoön* was the find of the century. The *Laocoön* was revered by Renaissance artists who admired the skill required to sculpt a work of such intense pathos and anatomical precision. Michelangelo, the greatest of them all, found himself humbled by the ancient sculpture. Asked to replace the sculpture's missing arms, he declined, claiming his talents to be less than those of the Greek sculptors who had created the work 1500 years earlier.

The *Laocoön* became the artistic standard, thereby establishing a canon of beauty that influenced art for the next 400 years. Almost without a doubt, the artist most influenced by the sculpture was Michelangelo himself, whose representation of the human figure in motion was fundamentally changed by his study of the *Laocoön*. Michelangelo's work clearly demonstrates that he was intrigued by the sculpture's muscular tension and by the central figure's spiraling motion as he struggles to free himself from the strangling snakes. On the Sistine Chapel ceiling, Michelangelo created numerous figures in *serpentinata* positions reminiscent of the central figure in the *Laocoön*.

It's not just artists who found themselves stimulated by the *Laocoön*, however. The intense pain suffered by *Laocoön* and his sons, and the contrast of this pain with the beauty of the sculpture, was a topic of discussion for the 18th-century father of art history, J. J. Winckelmann. How, Winckelmann asked, can a viewer cope with the inevitable mental conflict that arises when one admires the beauty of the *Laocoön*, but is at the same time painfully aware that the sculpture portrays the final, painful moments of a man who has failed to save his own life and those of his own children? Unanswered for centuries, this question continues to enthrall mankind to this very day.

Dr. Laura Flusche teaches art history at the University of Dallas's Rome campus. She is the founder of Friends of Rome (www.friendsofrome.org), a nonprofit dedicated to the preservation of Roman monuments. She's also president of The Institute of Design & Culture in Rome (www.idcrome.org).

Borghese, the **Museo Borghese** should be part of any trip to Rome. Reservations are required, however, as tickets sometimes sell out one month in advance.

Upon entering, don't miss Mark Antonio's **ceiling**, depicting the Roman conquest of Gaul. After perusing the Roman mosaics on the floor, check out the dragon and eagle statues, symbols of the Borghese family, on opposite ends of the room. **Room I** houses Canova's sexy statue of **Paolina Borghese** portrayed as Venus triumphant, holding the golden apple given to her by Paris. The myth is also depicted on the ceiling. The next rooms display the most famous sculptures by Bernini: the breathtaking ◪**Apollo and Daphne,** in which Daphne's hands and feet appear to be taking leaf and root, and a magnificent *David* crouching with his slingshot.

While in the museum, feel free to marvel at Pluto and Prosperina's weightless bodies in *The Rape of Proserpina* statue. Don't miss the six brooding Caravaggio paintings which grace the walls of the ◪**Caravaggio Room,** including his self-portrait as **The Sick Bacchus,** which he painted during a stay in the hospital (supposedly recuperating from either depression or a horse kick to the head). *The Sick Bacchus* bears a striking resemblance to *Young Boy with Basket of Fruit*, as it is more commonly referred to, but the Galleria has it labeled as *Young Girl*. The questionable gender of the main subject and his/her pose of nonchalant suggestiveness (slightly parted lips, tenderly revealed shoulder) has led some art historians to psychoanalyze Caravaggio's sexuality. The stark ◪**David and Goliath** is another self-portrait, one that epitomizes the artist's rash, tragic reputation.

The collection continues in the *pinacoteca* upstairs, accessible from the gardens around the back by a staircase. **Room IX** holds Raphael's important ◪**Deposition,** a masterpiece showing the midpoint between the traditional moments of the Pietà and the Entombment, while Sodoma's *Pietà* graces **Room XII.** Look for self portraits by Bernini, del Conte's *Cleopatra and Lucrezia*, Rubens's *Pianto sul Cristo Morto*, and Titian's famous *Amor Sacro e Amor Profano*. (*Ple. Scipione Borghese 5. M: A-Spagna; take exit labeled "Villa Borghese," walk to the right past the Metro stop to V. Muro Torto and then to P. Pta. Pinciana; Vle. del Museo Borghese is ahead and leads to the museum. Or take bus #116 or 910 to V. Pinciana. ☎84 216 542; www.galleriaborghese.it/borghese/it/default.htm. Open Tu-Su 9am-7:30pm. Entry every 2hr.; last entry 5pm. Limited capacity; reservation required. Tickets for high season may become booked a month in advance. Reservations ☎32 810 M-F 9am-6pm, Sa 9am-1pm; www.ticketeria.it. The ticket office and a bookshop share the villa's basement. Tickets including reservation and bag charge €8.50, EU citizens ages 18-25 €5.25, EU citizens under 18, over 65 and students €2. Audio tour €5. Guided tours in English at 9:10 and 11:10am. €5. MC/V.*)

MUSEI CAPITOLINI. This collection of ancient sculptures is the world's first public museum of ancient art and one of the largest. Pope Clement XII Corsini bought the *palazzo* to exhibit Cardinal Alessandro Albani's ancient sculptures in 1733. The Palazzo dei Conservatori's courtyard contains fragments of the **Colossus of Constantine,** whose muscular, six-foot-tall right arm demonstrates that bicep curls get the girls. The original statue of **Marcus Aurelius,** Bernini's interesting **Head of Medusa,** and the famous **Capitoline Wolf,** a statue that has symbolized the city of Rome since antiquity, occupy the first floor. At the top of the stairs, the **pinacoteca** masterpieces include Bellini's *Portrait of a Young Man*, Titian's *Baptism of Christ*, Rubens's *Romulus and Remus Fed by the Wolf*, and Caravaggio's *St. John the Baptist* and *Gypsy Fortune-Teller*. The collection continues in the Palazzo Nuovo, which can be accessed through the **Tabularium,** a hall of ancient Rome built in 79 BC. The entryway patio holds **Maforio,** one of Rome's five original "talking statues," to which people would give messages for the public. This gallery also holds the **Galata,** one of the oldest specimens of Roman sculpture. (*☎82 05 91 27; info.museicapitolini@comune.roma.it. Open Tu-Su 9am-8pm. Musei Capitolini's wheelchair-accessible entrance at V. del Tempio di Giove; Tabularium's wheelchair entrance at Palazzo*

Nuovo. Reservations ☎ 82 05 91 27. Reservations necessary for groups Sa and Su. €6.50; with temporary exhibition €8; combined Musei Capitolini and Centrale Montemartini valid for 7 days €8.50, ISIC & EU students €6.50. Musei Capitolini, Centrale Montemartini, and temporary exhibition €10, ISIC and students €8; ISIC and EU students €4.50. EU citizens under 18 or over 65 free. Reservations €25. Audio tour €5. Guidebook €7.75, exact change required.)

MUSEO NAZIONALE ETRUSCO DI VILLA GIULI. The villa was built under Pope Julius III, who reigned from 1550 to 1555. Highlights include the sarcophagus of a married couple in **Room 9.** Upstairs, archaeologists have put together fragments of a facade of an Etruscan temple, complete with terra-cotta gargoyles, chips of paint, and a relief of the warrior Tydaeus biting into the brain of a wounded adversary. Perhaps more interesting than the jewelry, ceramics, and other artifacts is the villa itself. Make sure to stroll around the well-manicured grounds and check out the lilypads and goldfish in the center. *(P. Villa Giulia 9, just south of Villa Borghese, near P. Thorvaldsen. M: A-Flaminio; then tram #30 or 225, or bus #19 from P. Risorgimento or 52 from P. San Silvestro. From Galleria Borghese, follow V. dell'Uccelliera to the zoo, and then take V. del Giardino to V. delle Belle Arti. Museum is on the left after Galleria d'Arte Moderna. ☎ 32 01 951, reservations 82 45 29. Open daily 8:30am-7:30pm. €4, EU citizens ages 18-24 €2, EU citizens under 18 and over 65 free. Audio tour €4.)*

VILLA FARNESINA. The Villa was the home to Europe's one-time wealthiest man, Agostino "Il Magnifico" Chigi. For show, Chigi had his banquet guests toss his gold and silver dishes into the Tiber River after every course, but he secretly hid nets under the water to recover his treasures. To the right of the entrance lies the breathtaking **Sala di Galatea,** mostly painted by the villa's architect, Baldassare Peruzzi, in 1511. The vault displays symbols of astrological signs that added up to a symbolic plan of the stars at 9:30pm on November 29, 1466, the moment of Agostino's birth. The room's masterpiece is Raphael's *Triumph of Galatea.* The ceiling of the Loggia di Psiche depicts the marriage of Cupid and Psyche. Returning to the entrance, a stunningly detailed, stucco-ceilinged stairway ascends to the **Salone delle Prospettive.** This room, decorated by Peruzzi, incorporates five different colored marbles in the floor design and offers views of Rome between fictive columns. The adjacent bedroom, known as the **Stanza delle Nozze** (Marriage Room), is the real reason for coming here. Il Sodoma, who had previously been busy painting the pope's rooms in the Vatican, frescoed the chamber until Raphael showed up and took over. Il Sodoma bounced back, making this masterful fresco of Alexander the Great's marriage to the beautiful Roxanne. *(V. della Lungara 230. Across from Palazzo Corsini on V. della Lungara. Bus #23, 271, or 280; get off at Lungotevere della Farnesina or Ponte Sisto. ☎ 68 02 72 67; www.lincei.it. Open M-Sa 9am-1pm; 1st Su of the month 9am-1pm. Last entry 20min. before closing. €5, under 18 €4, EU citizens over 65 free.)*

MUSEO NAZIONALE D'ARTE ANTICA. This collection of 12th- to 18th-century art is split between Palazzo Barberini and Palazzo Corsini. Palazzo Barberini contains paintings from the medieval through Baroque periods. Don't miss Rafael's lover delicately cradling her exposed breast in *La Fornarina. (V. Barberini 18. M: A-Barberini. Bus #492 or 62. ☎ 48 14 591. Open Tu-Su 9am-7:30pm. €5; EU citizens ages 18-24 €2.50; EU citizens under 18, over 65, and EU students €1. Cash only.)* Galleria Corsini holds a collection of 17th- to 18th-century paintings, including works by Rubens, Caravaggio, Bernini, and Brueghel. *(V. della Lungara 10. Opposite Villa Farnesina in Trastevere. Take bus #23; get off between Ponte Mazzini and Ponte Sisto. ☎ 22 58 24 93. Open Tu-Su; entry from 9:30-9:45am, 11-11:15am, and 12:30-12:45pm. Wheelchair-accessible. €4, EU students €2, Italian art students and EU citizens over 65 free. Guidebooks in Italian €10.50. Cash only.)*

GALLERIA SPADA. Cardinal Bernardino Spada bought a large assortment of paintings and sculptures, and he commissioned an even more opulent set of great rooms to house them. Time and good luck have left the palatial 17th-century apartments nearly intact—a visit to the gallery offers a glimpse of the luxury of Baroque courtly life. Before heading into the gallery rooms upstairs, check out Borromini's fantastic example of ■**3D perspective** in the courtyard. Watch in awe as the seemingly distant, life-size statue through the corridor is revealed to be only three feet tall and less than 35 feet away. In **Room 1** of the gallery's four rooms, the modest cardinal hung portraits of himself by Guercino, Guido Reni, and Cerini. In **Room 2,** look for paintings by the Venetians Tintoretto and Titian and a frieze by Vaga, originally intended for the Sistine Chapel. In **Room 4** are three canvases by the father-daughter team of Orazio and Artemisia Gentileschi. *(P. Capo di Ferro 13, in the Palazzo Spada. From Campo dei Fiori, take any of the small streets leading to P. Farnese. Facing away from Campo dei Fiori, turn left on Capo di Ferro. Bus #64. ☎68 32 409. Open Tu-Su 8:30am-7:30pm. Last entry 7pm. Guided tour Su 10:45am from museum book shop. Pamphlet guides in English available for each room of the exhibit. €5, EU students €2.50, EU citizens under 18 or over 65 free. Guidebooks €10.50. Cash only.)*

OTHER COLLECTIONS

GALLERIA DORIA PAMPHILI. The Doria Pamphili family, whose illustrious kin include Pope Innocent X, maintain this stunning private collection in their palatial home. Its Classical art is organized by size and theme, and Renaissance and Baroque masterpieces include Caravaggio's *Rest During the Flight in Egypt*, Raphael's *Double Portrait*, and Velasquez's portrait of Pope Innocent X, generally considered to be one of the most outstanding papal portraits of all time. The pope was shocked by the depiction, exclaiming, "It's too real!" The back gallery's mirrors and windows evoke the feeling of a miniature Versailles. *(P. del Collegio Romano 2. Bus #40 Express or 64 to P. Venezia. From P. Venezia, walk up V. del Corso and take the 2nd left. ☎67 97 323; www.doriapamphilj.it. Open M-W and F-Su 10am-5pm. Last entry 4:15pm. Closed Jan. 1, Easter, May 1, Aug. 15, and Dec. 25. €8, students and seniors €5.70. Informative audio tour in English, French, or Italian included. Cash only.)*

MUSEO CENTRALE MONTEMARTINI. The building, a former turn-of-the-century electrical plant, has a striking colelction of Classical art. Highlights include *Hercules's Presentation at Mount Olympus*, a huge well-preserved floor mosaic of a hunt, and a statue of Dionysus, the god of wine and revelry, whose hair is interwoven with grapes. *(V. Ostiense 106. M: B-Piramide. From P. Ostiense take V. Ostiense, then walk or take bus #23 or 702 3 stops. ☎ 82 05 91 27; www.centralemontemartini.org. Open Tu-Su 9:30am-7pm. €4.20, with entry to the Capitoline Museums €8.50; EU citizens ages 18-24 €2.60/7.80; EU citizens under 18 or over 65 free. Reservations €1.50. Cash only.)*

MUSEO NAZIONALE D'ARTE MODERNA E CONTEMPORANEA. Nineteenth- and twentiethth-century art, ranging from nationalistic Italian paintings to abstract works, populate this gallery. In *la sala giardiniere*, Van Gogh's well known *L'Arlesiana* and Edgar Degas's *Dopo il bagno* hang among other works completed by Italians in Paris. It also houses temporary traveling exhibitions. *(Vle. delle Belle Arti 131, in Villa Borghese, near Museo Nazionale Etrusco. M: A-Flaminio; then tram #30 or 225, or bus #19 from P. Risorgimento or #52 from P. S. Silvestro. From Galleria Borghese, follow V. dell'Uccelliera to the zoo, and then take V. del Giardino to V. delle Belle Arti. ☎32 29 82 21; www.gnam.arti.beniculturali.it. Open Tu-Su 8:30am-7:30pm. Last entry 6:45pm. €9, EU citizens ages 18-24 €7, EU citizens under 18 or over 65 free. Cash only.)*

MUSEO MARIO PRAZ. This small, eccentric museum was once the home of Mario Praz (1896-1982), an equally small and eccentric professor of English literature and 18th- and 19th-century art collector. This evil-eye-wielding, club-footed man preferred books, fans, paintings, and serpent-like musical instruments to people. Superstitious neighbors spat or flipped coins when they saw him. *(V. Zanardelli 1, top fl. At the east end of Ponte Umberto, next to Museo Napoleonico. ☎68 61 089;*

www.gnam.arti.benicultural.it/prazco.htm. Mandatory 35-45min. tour in Italian, given every hour. Open M 2:30-6:30pm, Tu-Su 9am-1pm and 2:30-6:30pm. Max. 10 people on tour. Free.)

MUSEO NAZIONALE D'ARTE ORIENTALE. An array of artifacts from prehistory to the 1800s, with exhibits on art in the Near East, Islamic art, Nepalese and Tibetan art, Indian art, Southeast Asian art, and Chinese history. *(V. Merulana 248. In Palazzo Brancaccio on Esquiline Hill. ☎48 74 415. Open M, W, and F 8:30am-2pm; Tu, Th, and Su 8:30am-7:30pm. Closed 1st and 3rd M of each month. €4, reduced €2. Cash only.)*

MUSEO NAZIONALE ROMANO PALAZZO ALTEMPS. The museum displays Roman sculpture, like the famous 5th-century Ludovisi Throne. *(P. Sant'Apollinare 44, just north of P. Navona. Bus #30 Express, 492, 70, 81, 87, or 628 to C. del Rinascimento/P. Cinque Lune. Museum ☎78 33 566, ticket office 68 33 759. Open Tu-Su 9am-7:45pm. Last entry 7pm. €9, EU citizens ages 18-24 €6.50, EU citizens under 18 or over 65 free. Audio tour €4. Cash only.)*

GALLERIA COLONNA. Despite its limited hours, this gallery is worth a visit. The 18th-century *palazzo* shows off the Colonna family's collection, including Tintoretto's *Narcissus*, and works by Melozzo da Forli, Veronese, Palma il Vecchio, and Guercino. Notice how Pope Martino V's velvet chair faces away from visitors in the throne room. This strategy ensured that the pope could refuse visitors, but couldn't see those who walked out on him. *(V. della Pilotta 17. North of P. Venezia, in the centro storico. ☎66 78 43 50; www.galleriacolonna.it. Open Sa 9am-1pm; closed Aug. €7, students €5.50, under 10 or over 65 free. Tour 11am in Italian and 11:45am in English. Cash only.)*

MUSEO DEL RISORGIMENTO. Underneath the left side of the Vittoriano monument in P. Venezia, this museum contains items relating to the Risorgimento, the 19th-century "resurgence," which ultimately led to the unification of Italy in 1861. *(Entrance on V. di San Pietro in Carcere. ☎67 93 526. Open daily 9:30am-6pm. Free.)*

MUSEO DELL'ARA PACIS. Right beside Augustus's Mausoleum, this museum highlights the art of the Ara Pacis (Altar of Peace), a temple built in 13 BC to celebrate Augustus' return from Spain and Gaul. Inside, the restored temple displays an impressive floral frieze on its lower half and noteworthy Romans on top. *(From P. Popolo, walk down V. di Ripetta. The museum is the white building on the right. ☎82 05 91 27; http://en.arapacis.it. €6.50, EU citizens ages 18-25 €4.50, under 18 and over 65 free. Audio tour €3.50. AmEx/MC/V.)*

🎭 ENTERTAINMENT

The weekly *Roma C'è* (with a section in English) and *Time Out*, both available at newsstands, have comprehensive and up-to-date club, movie, and event listings.

LIVE MUSIC

Rome hosts a variety of worthwhile performances, most of them in the summer. Telecom Italia's classical music series takes place at the Teatro dell'Opera. At 9am on concert days, unsold tickets are given out for free at the box office; get in line early. Local churches often host free choral concerts. Check newspapers, tourist offices, and church bulletin boards for details. Finally, and perhaps most interestingly, the *carabinieri* give rousing (and free) concerts in P. di Sant'Ignazio and other outdoor venues on the occasional holiday or festival.

Alexanderplatz Jazz Club, V. Ostia 9 (☎39 74 21 71; www.alexanderplatz.it). M: A-Ottaviano. Head left on V. G. Cesare, take 2nd right on V. Leone IV and 1st left on V. Ostia. Night buses to P. Venezia and Termini leave from P. Clodio. Considered one of Europe's best jazz clubs. Mixed drinks €6.20. Required 1-month membership €10. Shows start at 10pm. Open daily Sept.-May 9pm-2am. Moves outside to Villa Celimontana in summer.

Teatro Ghione, V. delle Fornaci 37 (☎63 72 294; www.ghione.it), near the Vatican. This red velvet theater hosts Euromusica's classical concerts and other big-name musical guests. English-speaking staff. Box office open Oct.-Apr. daily 10am-1pm and 4-8pm. Tickets €12-22. Call for info on morning concerts and discounts. MC/V.

Accademia Nazionale di Santa Cecilia, V. Vittoria 6 (☎36 11 064 or 800 90 70 80; www.santacecilia.it), off V. del Corso. This conservatory, named for the martyred patron saint of music, is now home to Rome's symphony orchestra. It hosts over 250 concerts and events during the year. Call for more info.

Parco della Musica, Vle. Pietro de Coubertin 30 (info ☎80 24 12 81, tickets ☎19 91 09 783; www.auditorium.com), near P. del Popolo, where you can also buy tickets (€8-15). Season runs Sept.-June and includes classics and special presentations like the music of Jimi Hendrix played by a string quartet. Box office open daily 11am-6pm and from 8pm until the start of the performance on concert nights.

OPERA AND DANCE

In the summer Rome fills with arias of world-famous operas, especially those by national composer Giuseppe Verdi (p. 81). Countless flyers and posters list performances at fantastic outdoor venues. *Roma C'è* also lists the week's upcoming performances, and tourist offices can often help you book tickets at a reduced rate.

THEATER

Roman theater generates a number of diverse and quality productions. For info on English theater, check the tourist office, *Roma C'è*, or online (www.musical.it or www.comune.roma.it).

Teatro Argentina, Largo di Torre Argentina 52 (☎68 40 00 111; www.teatrodiroma.net). Bus #64 from Termini or tram #8, right off V. Arenula. Home to the Teatro di Roma company, Argentina hosts plays, concerts, and ballets. Main venue for many annual drama and music festivals. Call for specifics. Box office open M-F 10am-2pm and 3-7pm, Sa 10am-2pm. €14-26, students €12-21. AmEx/MC/V.

Teatro Colosseo, V. Capo d'Africa 5 (☎70 04 932). M: B-Colosseo. Walk down V. dei Fori Imperiali past the Colosseum, then go right through P. Colosseo; V. Capo d'Africa is 2 blocks down on the left. Plays normally in Italian; has English night. Box office open Sept.-Apr. Tu-Sa 6-9:30pm. €10-20, students €8.

CINEMA

Unfortunately, most theaters in Rome show dubbed movies. For foreign films with Italian subtitles, look for a "v.o." or "l.o." in listings (*versione originale* or *lingua originale*). In summer, huge screens spring up in *piazze* around the city for **outdoor filmfests.** Films are usually shown outdoors on Isola Tiberina's southern tip. Cinemas citywide offer discounts on Wednesdays, and most have reductions for the 5pm showing. There are usually three or four showings a day, with the earliest at 5pm and the last one at 10:30pm. Check www.ilteatrodiroma.it for theaters, showings, and locations.

Metropolitan, V. del Corso 7 (☎32 00 933). Located near P. del Popolo, this cinema releases new films in English for about 1 week. 4 screens. After the initial week, the Italian dubbing begins, so catch it if you can. €7.50.

Nuovo Olimpia, V. in Lucina 16G (☎68 61 068). Just off V. del Corso, this Olympic film haven also shows American films for 1 week before dubbing. 2 screens. €7, matinees and M and W €5.

Warner Village Moderno, P. della Repubblica 45/46 (☎47 77 92 01). One of the Warner Bros. movie theaters in Rome, it periodically shows films in English. 5 screens.

Nuovo Sacher, Largo Ascianghi 1 (☎58 18 116). Take V. Induno from V. di Trastevere. This is the famed Italian director Nanni Moretti's theater, and it shows a host of indie films. Films in original language M. Tickets €7, matinee and W €5.

Cinema Reale (☎58 10 234), at the corner of Vle. di Trastevere and V. della Lungaretta, in Trastevere. Shows 2 American films dubbed in Italian without subtitles in its 2 theaters. Matinee and W €6.

SPECTATOR SPORTS

Though May brings tennis and equestrian events, Roman games revolve around *calcio* (soccer). Rome has two teams in *Serie A*, Italy's prestigious league: **S.S. Lazio** and **A.S. Roma.** Matches are held at the **Stadio Olimpico,** in Foro Italico, almost every Sunday from September to June. If possible, check out the two Roma-Lazio games, which often prove decisive in the race for the championship. Buy tickets (from €16) at team stores like **A.S. Roma,** P. Colonna 360 (www.asroma.it.), and **Lazio Point,** V. Farini 34/36, near Termini. (☎48 26 688. Open daily 9am-7pm. AmEx/MC/V.) They are also available at **Orbis,** P. Esquilino 102 (☎48 27 403).

TIP **CALCIO CRAZIES.** Tickets to intense soccer matches can also be obtained at the stadium before a game, but beware of long lines and the possibility of tickets running out; if you're buying last minute, watch out for overpriced or fake tickets.

SHOPPING

Rome offers many kinds of clothing shops. First, there are chain stores like **Motivi, Mango, Stefanel, Intimissimi, Zara,** and the ubiquitous **United Colors of Benetton.** Second there are the heart attack-inducing prices of designer shrines like **Cavalli, Dolce & Gabbana,** and **Prada.** Third are the techno-blasting teen stores that dominate central thoroughfares. Finally, tiny boutiques in the *centro storico,* including **Ethic** and **Havana,** often have locations throughout the city. Below is a list of notable boutiques, budget stores, and fashionable streets, since no trip to Italy is complete without a bit of shopping. **Via del Corso,** the main street connecting P. del Popolo and P. Venezia offers a mix of high- and low-end, disco-pumping stores with leather goods, men's suits, and silk ties. Beware of high-priced tourist traps, however, since V. del Corso is littered with them. **Etam** (170) and **Motivi** (318) are two lower-priced Italian chains. **Calzedonia** (140, 190) and **Yammamay** (309, 139) are fabulous for cheap, colorful, and fun tights, socks, and bikinis. **La Rinascente** (191) is a magnificent major department store. Try your luck with higher-end labels like **Diesel** (186/655), **Ferrari** (402), **Lacoste** (221), and **Puma** (403). Across the river from V. del Corso, **Via Cola di Rienzo** offers a more leisurely shopping sans throngs of tourists. Meander down this thoroughfare of shops and stop by stylish chain stores. **COIN** department store, V. Cola di Rienzo 171/173, won't leave you penniless.

BOUTIQUES

Unique boutiques and hot, haute couture designer stores cluster around the Spanish Steps and V. dei Condotti. Purchases of over €155 at a single store are eligible for a tax refund for non-EU residents. Most of the fancy-schmancy stores—**Bruno Magli, Dolce & Gabbana, Armani, Gianni Versace, Gucci, Prada, Salvatore Ferragamo**—can be found on **Via dei Condotti** (near the Spanish Steps). Fendi, an Italian favorite, is the exception and holds its purse strings in Largo Goldini, right off V. del Corso. If you happen to feel unsatisfied after your trip to this chic street, make your way over to **Via del Governo Vecchio,** near P. Navona. Lined with vintage clothing, furniture, and art stores, this avenue offers ageless goodies at a price.

ROME

CHEAP YET CLASSY

Tezenis, V. del Corso 148 (☎67 93 569; M-Sa 10am-8pm, Su 10:30am-8pm), offers women's, men's, and children's intimate apparel (underwear €3, shirts €5-6, full bikini set €20). The **General Store,** V. della Scala 62a (☎58 17 675; daily 10am-1pm and 4-8pm), sells discounted overstock Diesel, Adidas, and Nike goods. Off Campo dei Fiori, **Via dei Giubbonari** is dotted with authentic European clothing stores, and will have you dressed to the nines before eight.

OUTDOOR MARKETS

Street vendors will often try to sell fake Prada bags for exorbitant prices, insisting they're from the hands of Miuccia himself. Be wary of these seemingly miraculous bargains—a 2005 Italian law stipulates that buyers of fake designer items can be fined €10,000, which might make the initial euphoric purchase quite painful in the end.

Mercato Andrea Doria, on V. Andrea Doria, northwest of the Vatican Museums. M: Ottaviano; bus #23 or 70. Caters mostly to the local population, so don't expect to find many English-speaking folks here. Fruits, vegetables, fish, groceries, clothes, and shoes sold in a huge open square. Open M-Sa 7am-1:30pm.

Mercato Via C. Balbo. From Termini, take V. Cavour and turn right on V. Torino and the market will be on the left. This bustling market features fresh produce, shoes, swimsuits, and other vital items, along with useless but interesting junk. Open M-F 7am-1pm.

Mercato Viale America. Take bus #714 or Metro B: EUR Palasport. Directly above the EUR Fermi stop. A bustling market selling everything from baby clothes to Super Soakers. Open daily 6am-6pm.

Campo dei Fiori, *centro storico.* Tram #8 or bus #64. Transformed daily by stalls of fruits and vegetables, meat, poultry, and fish. Open M-Sa 7am until the individual vendors decide their food has run out—usually around 1:30pm.

Porta Portese, in Trastevere. Tram #8 from Largo di Torre Argentina. This gigantic flea market is a surreal experience, with booths selling clothing, shoes, jewelry, bags, toilets, and millions of other items you never knew you needed. Keep your friends close and your money closer, as the place swarms with pickpockets. Open Su 5am-1:30pm.

Mercato delle Stampe, Largo della Fontanella di Borghese. Bus #81, 116, 117, or 492. A bookworms' haven specializing in old books—both used and genuine antiquarian—magazines, and other pieces of art. Open M-Sa 9:30am-6pm.

> **TIP** **HAGGLING RULES.** Name your bottom price; if the vendor refuses, walk away. If he wants to make the sale, he will call you back.

■ NIGHTLIFE

Romans find nighttime diversion at the pubs of San Lorenzo, the clubs of Testaccio, and everywhere in between. Pick up *Roma C'è* for updates on clubs' openings and closings. *Time Out* covers Rome's sparse but solid collection of gay nightlife listings, many of which require an **ARCI-GAY pass** (1yr. €10; p. 114). Also check with **Circolo di Cultura Omosessuale Mario Mieli** (☎54 13 985).

PUBS AND BARS

Though *enoteche* tend to be the primary destination for locals of all ages, bars and pubs are still a fun way to knock back a few without covers or sweaty polyester.

There are many Irish pubs in Rome; the best are around Campo dei Fiori. Crowds of people flood P. Navona after the bars close at 2am to continue the revelry.

Caffè della Scala, P. della Scala 4 (☎58 03 610), on V. della Scala before it intersects with P. San Egidio. In nice weather the tables at this casual cafe/bar line the street. The special drinks menu, invented by Frances, the friendly proprietress/bartender extraordinaire, offers astoundingly creative options with unusual ingredients. Mixed drinks include the potent "Christian Alexander" (Canadian whiskey, creme of cocoa, and cardamom pods; €7) and the "Black Velvet" (Guiness and *prosecco;* €7). Open daily 5pm-2am. Cash only.

The Proud Lion Pub, Borgo Pio 36 (☎68 32 841), Vatican. Near Castle Sant'Angelo. It may be in the Vatican, but don't expect to run into any Cardinals. Authentic Scottish pub with an impressive selection of Scottish, Irish, and Bavarian beers. Beer €4-6. Open daily noon-2am.

Artu Café, Largo Fumasoni Biondi 5 (☎58 80 398), in P. San Egidio, behind Santa Maria in Trastevere. This small bar/lounge, bathed in dark-red light has won over locals' hearts. Patrons praise the bartender's exquisite martinis (€6.50-7.50). Beer €4.50. Wine €3-5.50 per glass. Free snack buffet 7:30-9pm. Open Tu-Su 6pm-2am. AmEx/MC/V.

Jonathan's Angels, V. della Fossa 14-16 (☎68 93 426). Take V. Governo Vecchio from P. Navona, turn right on V. Parione, then left on V. della Fossa. Angel sculptures and candles create a proto-chapel to the self-proclaimed messianic figure whose pictures adorn the walls. Beer €5. Mixed drinks €9. Live band F. Open daily 8pm-2am.

Freni e Frizioni, Trastevere, V. del Politeama 4/6. (☎58 33 42 10). From Ponte Sisto, turn left on Lungotevere Raffaello Sanzio, and it is in the *piazza* on the right. The hip, energetic music that spills out the doors is drowned out by the throngs of people outside. Serves delicious wine (€4), wine spritzers (white wine with either peach, kiwi, or strawberry cream; €6), mixed drinks (€6), and frozen mixed drinks (€7). Open daily 10am-2am.

Express, Trastevere, V. del Moro, 10. (☎33 82 07 44 63). From Ponte Sisto, walk across the street to P. Trilussa and go left. Mainly college crowd. Bartenders juggle bottles while classic rock blasts in the background. Shots €2. Beer €3. Mixed drinks €4.50. Happy hour 6pm-11pm. Open daily 6pm-2am.

CLUBS

Italian discos are flashy and fun, but keep in mind that many clubs close during the summer in favor of more distant destinations like Fregene or Frascati. Testaccio is dependable through early August. Check *Roma C'è* or *Time Out* for updates.

Charro Cafe, V. di Monte Testaccio 73 (☎57 83 064). Music booms from this open-air club, rattling the ground like the nearby artillery piece, which sits in the vegetation. Women dancing on benches is the norm here. Cover €5. Open daily midnight-3:30am.

Coyote, V. di Monte Testaccio 50. (☎339 46 39 667). The line outside may seem as long as the one at the Vatican, but instead of a silent Sistine Chapel, this line leads blaring music and an energetic crowd. Open daily midnight-5am.

Alien/Gilda on the Beach. This nightclub empire caters to the glitteratti of Roman nightlife. With steep covers and exclusive guest lists, these are the places to see and be seen. In the summer, Gilda on the Beach, located near Fiumicino, 30km from Rome, dominates most of the scene, since Italians prefer to party until dawn on the sand instead of the streets.

Alien, V. Velletri 13-19 (☎84 12 212; www.aliendisco.it). One of Rome's biggest discos attracting a well-dressed crowd. Cover varies (about €15, includes 1 drink; Sa €20). Mostly house with occasional theme nights. Open Tu-Su midnight- 4:30am.

Gilda on the Beach, Lungomare di Ponente 11 (☎66 56 06 49; www.gildaonthebeach.it). From May-Sept., ultra-cool clientele make the pilgrimage to Gilda for 3 dance floors, a private beach, a pool, and a restaurant. Cover €20. Dinner served from 8:30pm. Disco open Tu-Su 11pm-4am. AmEx/MC/V.

ROME

a dead language lives

A Young Classicist Experiences Italy Yesterday and Today

Although I had heard of Father Reginald Foster as a child, it was only seven years later as a Classics major that I

> **"I wasn't studying a 'dead language' and tuning out the living city around me"**

made the pilgrimage to Rome to study with Fr. Reggie, one of the Vatican's chief Latinists. I had traveled to Italy several times before and thought I would immerse myself exclusively in the old *lingua franca*. But I soon found that the more I read and spoke Latin, the more I came to understand and appreciate the modern Italian language and culture around me.

Since class did not begin until 2pm, I spent the mornings wandering. The irresistible scents wafting from the bakery on a side street off Vle. di Trastevere, the midday street festival in the Jewish Ghetto, or the cats prowling around the Mausoleum of Augustus are the city's best attractions—and are conveniently free.

In the afternoon, I journeyed back to the basement schoolroom at the top of the Gianicolo Hill. Fr. Reggie teaches Latin as if it were a living language. He often began with musings—in Latin, naturally—on his arduous commute to work in the Vatican that morning in the face of the two-week-long taxi strike or on the intricacies of the national rail service. He devoted a portion of class every week to translating *acta diurna* (headlines) from English-language news magazines into Latin. We read everything from Thomas More to 1999 Papal marriage court decisions.

After three 1½hr. sessions, we would break for an evening of casual Latin conversation or reading *sub arboribus* (under the trees) in the garden of the Carmelite monastery.

Because of the length and pace of the course, I engaged Rome as a resident rather than as a tourist. Every day, during the break after the first class, I would wander down the street to the Star Café, where Remo, the jovial owner, would give me an espresso with an extra cookie. I spent the second recess selecting fruits from the neighborhood vendor. I got to know my neighborhood, Trastevere, through regular excursions to the nearby cheese shop and Standa supermarket and morning runs up the slopes of the Gianicolo hill and through the Doria Pamphilj Gardens. This routine helped ensure that I was not just studying a "dead language" and insulating myself from the very living city.

My Latin and Italian experiences came together while watching the final match of the World Cup with 200,000 fans in the Circus Maximus, the old Roman racetrack. The triumphant march of the *azzurri* through the tournament fostered a camaraderie that manifested itself in distinctly Italian ways. With gleeful grins, the owners of a local pizzeria not far from Fr. Reggie's class carved up watermelons and offered them *gratis* to us after the semifinal win over Germany. The victory over France even inspired T-shirts with a Latin slogan—a welcome sight despite a grammatical error.

A traveler to Rome armed with knowledge of Latin can unlock mysteries of the Eternal City that would remain otherwise indecipherable. Latin inscriptions everywhere tell stories of ceremony, betrayal, victory, and defeat. Engaging the language in Fr. Reggie's way—as a living embodiment of a humanistic tradition—gives the traveler a sense of how Italy has evolved into what it is today. It doesn't take long to realize that Rome is a city with an amazing past; Latin and its connection to Italian bridges that gap between the Rome of Caesar and chariots and the Rome of Prodi and Vespas.

A DIFFERENT PATH

Clem Wood has spent summers in both Florence and Rome. He will graduate from Harvard in the spring of 2008 with an A.B. in Classics and plans to return to Italy for further adventures and studies in the near future.

> ⬧ **BE A BEACH BUM.** When heading out to the beach for a night of ocean-side clubbing, realize the trains will likely not be running when you leave the club; however, since most of the clubs stay open until 5 or 5:30am, you can fill the gap time by relaxing on the beach until trains start running again at 6am.

❊ FESTIVALS

In a nation where "work hard, play harder" seems to be the motto, it is no wonder that the capital city celebrates everything from Latin American culture and the Backstreet Boys to labor movements.

From June to August, thousands (often over 30,000) celebrate all things Latin American at **Fiesta,** in the Ippodrome delle Capannelle. Famous artists like Ricky Martin help Romans enjoy *la vida loca.* (Reach the venue using M: A-Colli Albani or bus #664. For advance tickets, call ☎ 71 82 139, or visit www.fiesta.it.) Music lovers enjoy an auditory feast at the **Cornetto Free Music Festival Roma Live,** which showcases popular international acts. Past performers have ranged from Pink Floyd and the Cure to the Backstreet Boys. (Enter to win free tickets at www.cornettoalgida.it.) On May 1 of every year, Romans are joined by hundreds of thousands of Italians for the **Festa della Primo Maggio** (Festival of the First of May). With roots dating back to the late 1800s, this festival has transformed over the past century from an often violent celebration of labor rights to a crazy, Woodstock-like music mania. Featuring big-name Italian artists like Elisa, Carmen Consoli, Tiromancino, and Articolo 31, this day-long festival continues late into the night, with close to one million students packed into P. di S. Giovanni in Laterno. Don't be surprised to see a pot-smoking, communist flag-waving Italian youth rocking out next to you. September brings an end to Rome's summer festivals with the traditional **La Notte Bianca** (The White Night), typically held during the first week of the month. Rome's "White Night" refers to an evening when the Metro, shops, museums, and restaurants remain open all night for one last hurrah, thereby leaving the city's streets illuminated all night. Most museums offer free admission.

▣ DAYTRIPS FROM ROME

▩ SPERLONGA

Trains run daily from Rome to the Fondi-Sperlonga station (70min., hourly 4:57am-11:32pm, €6.20). Take either the COTRAL bus or the Autoservizi Piazzoli urban bus from the Fondi-Sperlonga station to Sperlonga (15-20min €1). Get off at P. Europa at the top of hill. With a decrepit church to the left and a restaurant to the right, walk 30m to the Tourist Info Center, C. San Leone 23. (☎0771 55 70 00; www.communedisperlonga.it. Open daily 8am-8pm.) In P. Repubblica, there is a tabaccheria that sells tickets for maps (€5) and tickets for COTRAL buses. Facing the tabaccheria, the street to the right of the piazza, V. Ottaviano, winds its way down to the sea and to Vle. Cristoforo Colombo. Note: Because Sperlonga's main road is so long, addresses are identified using kilometers rather than plain numbers. However, since the main attractions are fairly close together, you won't really be walking that far.

Sperlonga (spehr-LON-ga; pop. 3,102) served as Emperor Tiberius's imperial getaway until he moved to Capri in AD 26. Well worth the trip from Rome, Sperlonga's curving, whitewashed streets lead through cobblestoned *piazze* to sparkling white sands and sapphire waters. Lounging inside his seaside *speluncae* (grottoes), which gave the town its name, Tiberius would invite his wealthy Roman friends to enjoy this Tyrrhenian heaven with him. A few feet away from the grottoes is the modern and well-exhibited **Museo Archelogico,** where you can see the statuary ruins of Tiberus's villa. This impressive collection represents scenes from Homer's *Odyssey*, including the blinding of Polyphemus the cyclops and the attack of Ulysses's boat by the monstrous Scylla. (V. Flacca 16,600km. 10-15min. walk from P. Europa. ☎0771 54 80 28. Open daily 8:30am-7:30pm. €2, under 18 and over 65 free. Cash only.) Sperlonga also served as a refuge for those fleeing barbarian attacks on Rome in the 6th century—watchtowers along the coast testify to this period of unrest. In 1534, the town was destroyed by Barbarossa, and it wasn't until the 18th and 19th centuries that Sperlonga regained its popularity as a vacation spot. Today, Emperor Tiberus's famous villa and fish-filled grottoes remain popular sights for all who visit this dreamworld beach getaway.

> **TIP** **DUE, PER FAVORE.** After arriving at Fondi/Sperlonga station, make sure to buy your bus tickets both to and from Sperlonga at the *bar* next door. The *tabaccheria* in Sperlonga, the only place which sells tickets, has irregular hours that can wreak havoc on your schedule.

TIVOLI

From Metro B: Rebibbia, exit the station, turn right, and follow signs for Tivoli through an underpass to reach the other side of V. Tiburtina. Take the blue COTRAL bus to Tivoli. Tickets (€1.60) are sold in the subway station or in the bar next door. Once the bus reaches Tivoli (35-45min.), debark at Ple. delle Nazioni Unite. The return bus to Rome stops across the street from the tourist office, which offers maps, bus schedules, and info on the villas. (☎07 74 31 12 49 or 07 74 31 35 36. Open Tu-Su 10am-6pm.) An info kiosk in Ple. delle Nazioni Unite distributes free maps.

Tivoli (TEE-vo-lee; pop. 51,000) is a hilltop town perched 120m above the Aniene River where poets Horace, Catullus, and Propertius all once had homes along the rocks overhanging the river. Today, Tivoli is a beautifully preserved medieval city, with narrow, winding streets and views of surrounding valleys. Though the three main villas listed below are Tivoli's chief attractions, the tourist office provides a fantastic ▓**map** detailing less known sites like a 15th-century castle, an ancient Roman amphitheater, churches, and Gothic-style houses, all within walking distance of the bus stop.

Villa d'Este, a castle and garden, was laid out by Cardinal Ercole d'Este (the son of Lucrezia Borgia) and his architect Piero Ligorio in 1550 to recreate an ancient Roman pleasure palace. The villa is known for the ingenious and abundant **fountains,** particularly the hydraulic organ fountain. Beneath the famed fountains lie dank grottoes and three reflecting pools filled with fish. The **Fontana di Diana Efesia,** a decaying multi-breasted goddess, lies behind the sprinkler-infested gardens. Additionally, the villa itself has a fantastic collection of frescoes and some modern art. One room tells the tale of Hercules, the symbolic founder of the house of Este. In the summer, concerts are held on the villa's grounds. (Walk through the P. Trento's souvenir stands to reach Villa d'Este. ☎07 74 31 20 70; www.villadestetivoli.info. Open Tu-Su May-Aug. 8:30am-6:45pm; Sept. 8:30am-6:15pm; Oct. 8:30am-5:30pm; Nov.-Jan. 8:30am-4pm; Feb. 8:30am-4:30pm; Mar. 8:30am-5:15pm; Apr. 8:30am-6:30pm. €9, EU citizens 18-24 €5.75, EU citizens under 18 or over 65 free. Audio tour €4.)

▓ **Villa Gregoriana,** at the other end of town, is a park with hiking trails that wind over waterfalls and the alleged caves of Neptune and the Sirens. Tivoli's **Temple of Vesta,** a better preserved version of the one in the Roman Forum, can be admired from lookouts. The trail goes down to the base of the waterfalls and up across the Valley of Hell, ending at the Temple of Vesta. A perfect respite from crowded Rome, the villa has many benches and grottoes, perfect for reading, relaxing, or even a romantic outing. Give yourself at least an hour to explore. (Walk 10min. from P. Garibaldi down V. Pacifici, which becomes V. del Trevio; turn left onto V. Palatina, then left again onto V. di Ponte Gregoriano. Cross the bridge and the entrance of Villa

San Gregoriana is on the left. ☎39 96 77 61. Open daily Apr.-Oct 15 10am-6:30pm; Oct. 16-Nov. 10am-2:30pm; Dec.-Feb. by reservation only; March 10am-2:30pm. €4, ISIC holders €3.20, ages 4-12 €2, EU citizens under 18 or over 65 free. Audio tour €4.) As you travel back to P. Garibaldi, stop in at **Pizzeria Sebastiani e Sorba ❶**, V. del Trevio 29, for a quick bite to eat. This hidden *tavola calda* serves delicious daily specials like *gnocchi di patate, tonarelli con pomodoro*, and *basilico* for only €3.60. (☎07 74 31 32 82. *Secondi* €2.50-4. Open 8am-3:30pm and 4:30-9pm.)

Return to the square and catch bus #4 (€1) in front of the tourist office to reach the remains of **Villa Adriana,** the largest and most expensive villa built under the Roman Empire. Emperor Hadrian, inspired by his travels, designed its AD 2nd-century buildings with an international flair. Hadrian would often retire here to escape bad moods and pursue artistic endeavors. Look for the *pecile*, built to recall the famous *Stoa Poikile* (Painted Porch) of Athens, and the *canopus*, a statue-lined expanse of water built to replicate a canal in Alexandria, Egypt. (6km from Tivoli proper; take the orange bus #4 from P. Garibaldi's *tabaccheria*, which sells €1 bus tickets. From the parking lot, head uphill away from the villa until you reach a small COTRAL bus stop sign. ☎07 74 38 27 33. Open daily 9am-7:30pm. Last entry 1½hr. before closing. €6.50, EU citizens 18-24 €3.25, EU citizens under 18 or over 65 free. Archaeological tour €3.50. Audio tour €4.)

OSTIA ANTICA

From Rome, take Metro B to Piramide (€1). At the top of the stairs, turn left and follow signs to Ferrovia Roma-Lido. Your Metro ticket includes the train ride to Ostia Antica (30min., every 15min. daily 5:40am-11:30pm). After disembarking at Ostia Antica, exit the station and cross the road using the blue pedestrian footbridge. Walk down V. della Stazione di Ostia Antica, cross Viale dei Romagoli; entrance is on the left at the end of V. degli Scavi di Ostia Antica.

An immense archaeological park, Ostia Antica is an ideal environment to experience ancient Roman life away from the hoi polloi in the Roman Forum. According to legend, Ostia was founded in the 7th century BC by King Ancus Martius to protect the *ostium* (mouth) of the Tiber River from would-be invaders. As the years progressed, Ostia blossomed into Rome's busiest commercial port. The Tiber's sedimentary deposits have pushed this former seaside port 4km from the coast. Nevertheless, Ostia continues to awe travelers with its extensive and intimate **ruins,** offering an unparalleled glimpse into every facet of Roman life.

The **necropolis,** located on V. Ostiense outside of the city walls, greets visitors upon entering the ruins. Tombs vary in size and simplicity, depending on the economic standing of the deceased. V. Ostiense ends at the **Porta Romana,** the entrance to the ancient city, which was once guarded by two towers. From here, **Decumanus Maximus,** the city's main road, leads to the **forum.** As you walk down Decumanus Maximus, an AD 1st-century statue of Minerva graces the left side, followed by the *horrea* (warehouses), where everything from grain to perfume was stored. Further down on the right lies the **Terme di Nettuno.** Walk up the steep stairs to see the magnificent black and white ▓mosaic of Neptune riding a quadriga of hippocampi, mythical creatures with the heads of horses and bodies of fish. Continuing down the main road, an ancient *enoteca* can be found, as well as the **teatro,** built by Agrippa and enlarged by Commodus and Septimus Severus. Inside, 4000 Romans would enjoy lewd plays filled with obscene puns, performed strictly by men wearing brown masks for male roles and white masks for female roles. Two millenia later, the theater continues to entertain Romans during the summer.

The forum lies at the center of the city, with the imposing **Capitolium** dominating the *piazza*. Merchants, politicians, and travelers used to flood this bustling area of global commerce in its glory days. In addition to baths, a 20-person **foriza** (latrine) remains well preserved. Just as people today converse over golf, ancient Romans chatted over bowel movements at this once elegantly decorated communal restroom. A small **museum** contains sarcophagi, busts, and Roman copies of Greek statues found among the ruins. Besides being a great place for a game of hide and seek, Ostia Antica offers a personal, engaging look into Rome's history, away from the mobs of tourists and honking horns of the Fori Imperiale. (☎06 56 35 02 15. Ruins open daily Apr.-Oct. 8:30am-7pm; Nov.-Feb. 8:30am-5pm; Mar. 8:30am-6pm. Museum open M-F 9am-1:30pm and 4:15-6:30pm, Sa-Su 9am-1:30pm. Last entry 1hr. before closing. Ruins and museum €6.50, EU citizens 18-25 €3.25, under 18 and over 65 free. Audio tour €2.50.)

CASTEL GANDOLFO

Take Metro A: Anagnina. From Anagnina, take blue COTRAL buses to Albano (30-40min., every 20min. daily 6am-11pm, €1); tickets sold at counter or from machines. Disembark at P. Mazzini, then take COTRAL bus towards Frascati (daily every 35min.). Your COTRAL ticket from Rome to Albano should still be valid if used within 75min. If it's no longer valid, replace it at the bus stop. Get off at either of the two Castel Gandolfo stops (5min. from Albano). Take a COTRAL bus back to Albano (M-F every 15-30min. 4:20am-11pm, Sa-Su and holidays every 40min. 5:30am-11pm).

Named after the Gandolfini family who ruled the area from the 11th to the 13th centuries, Castel Gandolfo (ca-stel gan-DOL-fo; pop. 8634) was chosen by the popes as the official papal summer residence in the 17th century. Construction on the palace began in 1624. Resting 426m above Lake Albano, the area offers amazing views of the lake and nearby hills. Castel Gandolfo's main attraction is the summer **papal residence,** designed by Carlo Maderno in the 17th century. The seemingly peculiar six-hour clock recalls the Italian time system before Napoleon instituted the European system in the early 19th century. The *palazzo* also contains the *specola*, a Vatican astronomical observatory. During the Pope's stay, Swiss guards man the portal and an increased *carabinieri* presence is noticeable. Although the palace is closed to tourists, the Pope holds summer papal audiences Sunday mornings in July and August in Castel Gandolfo. Visitors who attend a papal audience typically stand inside the **Piazza della Liberta,** which abuts the residence. Designed by Bernini in the latter half of the 18th century, this *piazza* also showcases **Bernini's fountain.** The church to the right of the papal residence, **Chiesa di San Tommaso da Villanova,** was also designed by Bernini and contains works by Pietro da Cartona, Gemignani, and Cortese as well as a crypt with life-size statues of the three wise men bearing gifts. (Open daily 8am-1pm and 4:30-8pm. Modest dress required. Donation requested.) For the nature-lover in the group, there's always pristine ◼Lake Albano. Believed to have been formed when the two prehistoric craters of the Lazio Volcanio merged into one, Lake Albano continued its fiery path to glory when it housed the 1960 Olympic canoe races. The crystal clear water still tempts travelers with opportunities for swimming, kayaking, canoeing, and sun-bathing. (About a 15min. walk. Take the zig-zagging V. del Stazione down to V. Antonio Gramsci. Take a right, cross the train tracks, and take another right on V. del Emissario. Take a right on V. dei Pescatori and a *balneare* is on the left, across the street from V. dei Pescatori 10. ☎34 76 66 63 34. Open May-Sept 9am-7pm. Lounge chair €5; chair €3. Canoe €5 per hr.; paddleboat €8 per hr.)

On the last Sunday of July, take a bite of a juicy peach with the Pope at the **Peach Festival.** After mass, children offer gifts to the Pope, and a peach-dominated, folksy revelry overtakes the town. Castel Gandolfo also comes together to celebrate its patron saint at the **Feast of Saint Sebastian** in September. Enjoy music, merriment, and beautiful fireworks over Lake Albano. **September for Youths** is dedicated to young men and women, with concerts, parades, and exhibitions throughout the month. And don't miss the **antique market** on the last Sunday of each month.

Along with the many shops selling artisanal crafts and dried meats, cheeses, and wine, restaurants, trattorie, cafes, and *gelaterie* line the town's main street, C. della Repubblica. **Bucci ❸**, V. dei Zecchini 31, while pricey, is worth the extra euro for the view from the flower-bedecked terrace overlooking the lake below. (☎ 06 93 23 334. Open M-Tu and Th-Su 12:30-2:30pm and 7:30-10pm. AmEx/MC/V.) A cheaper sit-down option is **Hosteria La Fraschetta ❶**, C. della Repubblica 58. (☎ 06 93 61 312. *Primi* €5.50-9.50, *secondi* €6.50-9. Open Tu-Su 12:30-3pm and 7pm-midnight. MC/V.)

To get from the bus stop to the **info kiosk,** which offers free maps and brochures, walk up the winding V. Palazzo Pontificio to the right. At the top of the summit sits P. Liberta. The info kiosk is located through P. Liberta on V. Massimo D'Azeglio. (☎ 06 93 59 18 235. Open T-Su 10am-6pm.)

PONTINE ISLANDS

The Pontine Islands are accessible by aliscafi *(hydrofoils) or slower, cheaper* traghetti *(ferries). Take the train from Termini to Anzio (1hr., hourly 6am-11pm, €3.20). From the station head downhill on V. Paolini, then go through P. Battisti and onto V. dei Fabbri. Proceed through the next piazza to C. del Popolo or take a taxi from the station to the quay (€10). From the port, you can take the CAREMAR ferry to Ponza (1½hr.; June 16-Sept. 15 M-F 9:25am, Sa 8:30am, Su and holidays 8:30am and 3pm; return M-F 5pm, Sa 5:15pm, Su and holidays 11am and 5:15pm; €19.20. Cash only). The CAREMAR ticket office is in the white booth labeled "traghetto" on the quay in Anzio (☎06 98 60 00 83; www.caremar.it) and in Ponza (☎07 71 80 565). The Linee Vetor hydrofoils are faster. (70min.; 3-5 per day 8:15am-7pm; M-F €24, Sa-Su and Aug. €28. Bikes €6. Windsurfing equipment €25. Cash only, unless reserved ahead online.) Linee Vetor ticket office also on the quay in Anzio. Open 1hr. before departure. (☎06 98 45 083; www.vetor.it). Another office on dock in Ponza (☎07 71 80 549).*

The Pontine Islands (pop. 3000), a stunning archipelago 40km off the coast of Anzio, established themselves long ago as historical hot spots: they were once believed to be home of the sorceress Circe, who captured and seduced the Greek hero Odysseus; Nero was exiled here; and Mussolini cast enemies of the state into the 30 million-year-old volcanic residuum, only to be imprisoned here himself. The cliff-sheltered beaches, turquoise waters, coves, tunnels, and grottoes have also provided pirates a place to unwind after pillaging and plundering. You'll be hard-pressed to find an English speaker in this isolated area. Ferries run from Anzio to **Ponza,** an island with superb beaches. A 10min. walk from the port leads to **Chiaia,** a beach set at the foot of a spectacular 200m cliff (tunnel to Chiaia currently closed to the public for restoration). A beautiful, though slightly harrowing, 🚌**bus ride** (€1; buy onboard) around hairpin turns and blind drives leads to the even lovelier 🚌**Piscine Naturali.** Take the bus to Le Foma, and ask to be let off at the *piscine,* or just follow the throngs of people who get off there. Facing the water, the bus stop is to your left, along V. Carlo Pisacane, just past the San Antonio Tunnel, about 3-5min. from the quay. Look for the hordes of people around the blue buses. Cross the street, and go down the long, steep path. There are no bathrooms at hill's bottom; plan accordingly. Cliffs crumbling into the ocean create a series of deep, crystal-clear natural pools separated by smooth rock outcroppings perfect for sunbathing. Snorkeling, exploring the rocks, and jumping off the cliffs will make you feel like a modern-day Jacques Cousteau. The western-most island is **Palmarola,** with irregular volcanic rock formations and steep, white cliffs. To get to Palmarola, rent a boat (from €45 per day), or take a boat tour advertised at the port. The tiny island of **Zannone** is home to a wildlife preserve. Try **Cooperativa Barcaioli Ponzesi,** V. Carlo Piscacane, at the S. Antonio tunnel, for boat tours. (☎07 71 80 99 29. Open 9am-12:30pm and 5pm-11pm. Tours 9am; return 7pm. Must reserve day before. €20.) Tours of Zannone, which is part of the **Circeo National Park,** take visitors around the coast, with time for walks through the forests on the islands filled with wild sheep, and to the medieval, legend-filled San Spirito monastery.

PIEDMONT (PIEMONTE) AND VALLE D'AOSTA

PIEDMONT (PIEMONTE)

More than just the source of the Po River, Piedmont (In Italian, "pee-yeh-MON-tay") has long been a fountainhead of nobility and fine cuisine. The area rose to prominence in 1861 when the Savoys selected Turin as capital of their re-united Italy in 1861. The capital relocated only four years later, and Piedmont fell back into obscurity. Today, European tourists escape the whirlwind city pace on the banks of Lake Maggiore, while outdoor enthusiasts and expert skiers conquer Alpine mountains to the northeast. Sometimes called the "Prussia of Italy," Piedmont is renowned for its high standard of living and modern, well-organized infrastructure. Since Turin's turn as host of the 2006 Winter Olympics, the region's profile has only continued to rise.

HIGHLIGHTS OF PIEDMONT AND VALLE D'AOSTA

EAT at Turin's enormous **Eataly,** a combination between a restaurant, a cooking school, a museum, and a fresh food market. (p. 170)

SIP *Barbera, Barbaresco,* and *Asti Spumante* in Piedmont's **wine country.** (p. 183)

JUMP into the **icy blue waters** of the streams of the Gesso Valley. (p. 180)

CONQUER the glacial slopes beneath the great **Matterhorn** (p. 195).

TURIN (TORINO)   ☎011

A century and a half before Turin (in Italian, "toh-REE-no"; pop. 910,000) hosted the 2006 Winter Olympics, it served as the first capital of unified Italy. Turin encompasses numerous parks and contemporary art masterpieces, as well as some of the country's best nightlife offerings. Though Turin's cultural offerings rival Milan's, it manages to avoid pollution and crime problems that plague larger cities. The 2006 Olympics were only a step in Turin's ongoing evolution, and it continues to welcome visitors and enhance its appeal.

▮ TRANSPORTATION

OLYMPIC UPSET. Turin's transportation system will continue to change during these post-Olympic years. Recently, a **new metro line** was built, which so far connects the Porta Susa train station on the western side of the city to the suburbs. In the future, the metro will continue east into the center's Porta Nuova station and eventually south to Lingotto, a developing urban center. Porta Susa will become Turin's main train station within several years.

Flights: Caselle Airport (www.aeroportoditorino.it) services European destinations. From Pta. Nuova, take blue **Sadem** buses to **"Caselle Airport,"** via Pta. Susa (☎30 00 611; €5.50). Buy tickets at Bar Cervino, C. Vittorio Emanuele II 57; Bar Mille Luci, P. XVIII Dicembre 5, at newsstand on corner of Corso V. Emanuele II and P. Felice, on left when exiting station, or

164

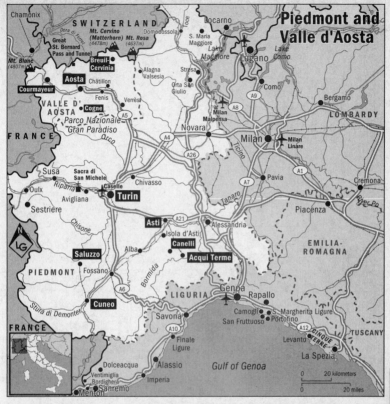

Piedmont and Valle d'Aosta

onboard (€0.50 surcharge). Airport train goes from Torino Dora to airport every 30min. To get to Torino Dora station, take **tram #10** from Torino Porta Susa, or **buses #46 or 49.**

Trains: Stazione Porta Nuova (☎66 53 098), on C. V. Emanuele II. The station has a pricey market, barber shop, post office, luggage storage, and lost and found. To: **Genoa** (2hr., every hr. 5:20am-11:05pm, €8.20); **Milan Centrale** (2hr., every hr. 4:50am-10:50pm, €8.20); **Rome Termini** (6-7hr., 26 per day 4:50am-11:05pm, from €49); **Venice Santa Lucia** (5hr., 20 per day 4:50am-10:50pm, €35). Turin's **Stazione Porta Susa** is 1 stop toward Milan and runs **TGV** trains to **Paris** via **Lyon, France** (5-6hr.; 8:10, 10:40am, 5:35, 9:18pm).

Buses: Autostazione Terminal Bus, C. V. Emanuele II 131/H in front of the Court (☎43 38 100). From Pta. Nuova, take tram #9 or 15 (5 stops). Ticket office open daily 6:30am-1:15pm and 2-8:30pm. Serves ski resorts, the Riviera, and the valleys of Susa and Pinerolo. To **Aosta** (2hr., M-F 3 per day, €7.50), **Courmayeur** via **Aosta** (4hr., €8.40), and **Milan** (2hr., every hr., €8.70).

Public Transportation: Buy tickets at *tabaccherie*, newsstands, or bars. Buses run daily 5am-1am, some stop at midnight. 70min. ticket to **city buses** and **trams** €1; 1-day ticket €3. Metro tickets 1 use only, but valid for 70min. for other modes of transport. Get public transport map with buses and trams from tourist office.

Taxis: ☎57 37, 57 30, or 33 99.

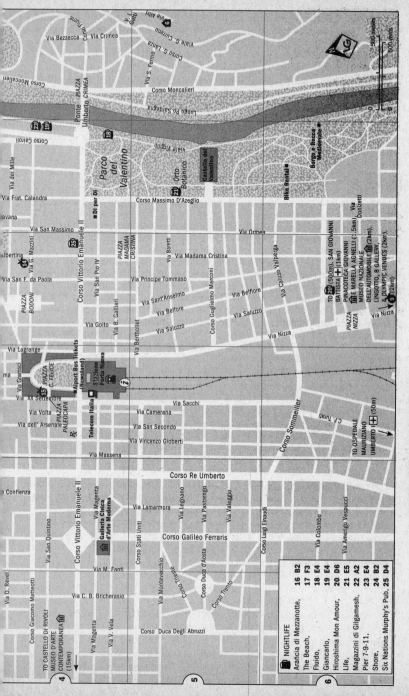

PIEDMONT AND
VALLE D'AOSTA

■ NIGHTLIFE

Arancia di Mezzanotte,	16	B2
The Beach,	17	F3
Fluido,	18	E4
Giancarlo,	19	E4
Hiroshima Mon Amour,	20	D6
Life,	21	E5
Magazzini di Gilgamesh,	22	A2
Pier 7-9-11,	23	E4
Shore,	24	B2
Six Nations Murphy's Pub,	25	D4

Car Rental: in Stazione Porta Nuova, on the right side by the platforms. **Avis,** C. Turati 37 (☎50 11 07). Open M-F 8:30am-noon and 3-6pm, Sa 8:30am-noon. **Maggiore,** C. Vittorio Emanuele II 53 (☎65 03 013). Open M-F 8am-noon and 3-6pm, Sa 8am-noon. **Europcar,** V. Nizza 346 (☎69 60 284). Open daily 7am-11pm. C. Grosetto 152 (☎22 29 802). Open daily 8:30am-1pm and 2:30-6:30pm.

Bike Rental: Parco Valentino Noleggio Biciclette, V. Ceppi (☎38 28 380), in Parco Valentino. Walk east (toward the Po River) down C. V. Emanuele; just before Ponte Umberto I, turn right. One of many city-run bike rentals in parks. Also in Parco della Pellerina, Parco della Colletta, and P. Vittorio Veneto. €2.10 per 3hr., €5 per 10hr. Open May-Sept. Tu-F 2:30-7:30pm, Sa 11am-8pm. **Club Amici della Bicicletta,** V. San Domenico 28 (☎56 13 059; clubamicidellabici@email.it) and **Bici & Dintorni,** Vle. Bistolfi 20/a (☎339 58 29 332 and 44 23 014; www.biciedintorni.org). Both €4 per 6hr., €8 per day.

■✦⓿ ORIENTATION AND PRACTICAL INFORMATION

Stazione Porta Nuova, in the heart of the city, is the usual place of arrival. The city itself is an Italian rarity: its pre-designed streets meet at right angles, making it easy to navigate by bus and on foot. **Corso Vittorio Emanuele II** runs east past the station to the **Po River,** where it intersects **Parco del Valentino** on the south and the **Murazzi** district on the north. **Via Roma,** the major north-south thoroughfare, houses many banks and the principal sights and shops. North of the station, it heads through **Piazza Carlo Felice, Piazza San Carlo,** and **Piazza Castello.** From P. Castello, **Via Pietro Micca** extends southwest to **Piazza Solferino** where the tourist office is located, while **Via Po** veers southeast to **Piazza Vittorio Veneto** and the University district, intersecting the river above the Murazzi. **Via Giuseppe Garibaldi** stretches west from P. Castello to **Piazza Statuto** and **Stazione Porta Susa,** a launching point for international trains and the metro to the suburbs. Above P. Castello, the **Palazzo Reale** and **Giardini Reali** lie below the **Corso Regina Margherita,** which connects **Piazza della Repubblica** west to the **Docks Dora** district north of the Giardini Reali. **Via Nizza** heads south from Stazione Pta. Nuova to the **Lingotto** area the former Olympic district.

Tourist Office: ⌨**Turismo Torino,** P. Solferino (☎53 51 81; www.turismotorino.org), in the Atrium 2006, the northern of the 2 glass pavilions. English, French, German, and Spanish spoken. Excellent map of Turin. Info regarding museums, cafes, hotel booking, and tour reservations. Detailed brochures include *Literary Tour of Torino, Walks to Explore the City, Contemporary Art Guide,* and the *Art of Living* brochure, focusing on the Turin pleasure triumvirate: chocolate, aperitifs, and nightlife. Open daily 9:30am-7pm. **Info booth** at Pta. Nuova, opposite platform 17. Open daily 10am-7pm. Volunteer-run info points near main attractions open during big events.

Currency Exchange: In Pta. Nuova. Offers a decent rate. Open M and W-Sa 8am-8pm, Tu and Su 10am-5:30pm. D/MC/V. Otherwise try the **banks,** most with 24hr. **ATMs** along V. Roma and V. Alfieri. Generally open M-F 8:20am-1:20pm and 2:20-4:20pm.

Beyond Tourism: Informagiovani, V. delle Orfane 20 (☎800 99 85 00 or 44 24 977; www.comune.torino.it/infogio). Youth center providing info on jobs, volunteering, and enterprises for young people. Internet access. Open Tu-Sa 9:30am-6:30pm.

English-Language Bookstore: Libreria Internazionale Luxembourg, V. Accademia delle Scienze 3 (☎56 13 896), across from P. Carignano. Staff helps navigate 3 floors of English, French, German, and Spanish books, papers, and magazines. Open M-Sa 8am-7:30pm, Su 10am-1pm and 3-7pm.

Laundromat: "Lavasciuga" Laundrettes and Internet Points (www.lavasciuga.torino.it) are located throughout the city. Check website for complete list.

First Aid: ☎57 47.

Pharmacy: Farmacia Boniscontro, C. V. Emanuele 66 (☎54 12 71). 3 blocks east of Pta. Nuova. Open 9am-12:30pm and 3pm-9am. Posts after-hours rotations. Rotational 1-day closings. MC/V.

Hospital: San Giovanni Battista, C. Bramante 88-90 (☎63 31 633), commonly known as Molinette. **Maria Adelaide,** V. Zuretti 29 (☎69 33 293). **Maurìziano Umberto I,** Largo Turati 62 (☎50 81 111).

Internet Access: 1pc4you, V. Verdi 20/G (☎83 59 08; www.1pc4you.com), in front of the Mole. 72 speedy machines with flat screens. €4 per hr.; €2 per hr. with purchased card (€5, includes €3 of use). Open M-Sa 9am-10pm, Su noon-10pm. **Telecom Italia Internet Corners,** V. Roma 18, just off P. Castello. **Branch** inside the Pta. Nuova (entrance from V. Sacchi, to the right when facing station) with **Western Union** transfer station. Both have phone-card web stations. €3 per hr. Open M and W-Su 8am-10pm.

Post Office: V. Alfieri 10 (☎50 60 260), off P. San Carlo, facing north (toward P. Reale), head left 2 blocks down on the right. Fax and telegram service. Grab ticket slip by door. Open M-F 8:30am-7pm, Sa 8:30am-1pm, last day of the month 8:30am-noon. *Fermoposta* open M-Sa 9am-noon and 3-7pm. **Postal Code:** 10100.

![] ACCOMMODATIONS

Turin's budget accommodations are not clustered together, though several can be found near Stazione Pta. Nuova. Many new hotels and residences were built to accommodate Olympic crowds. Family-run B&Bs offer some of the best deals in the city, though municipal law requires them to close for two months during the year. Many take this time in July and August, so call ahead for reservations.

> **TIP** **WEEKEND OF TOURIN'.** The embodiment of Turin's warm welcome to visitors, the **Turin Week-End offer** includes a 2-night stay (F-Sa or Sa-Su nights) with breakfast at a hotel, as well as a **Torino Card** with wide access and discounts (p. 172). Prices start at €69 per person; 4- to 5-star hotels cost about €89-150. Considering the hotels involved and the long list of benefits, this deal is a steal. All hotels bestow guests with special offers and welcoming gifts. Check www.turismotorino.org for a list of hotels and details of offers. Reserve directly through the hotel; make sure to specify that you want the Turin Week-End offer.

▨ **Open 011,** C. Venezia 11 (☎25 05 35; www.openzero11.it). To reach this brand-new hostel, take bus #52 (#64 on Su) from Pta. Nuova to V. Chiesa della Salute. 5min. walk from Stazione Dora. 34 comfortable rooms (2-4 beds with bathroom). Services include restaurant, bar, TV, terrace, Wi-Fi, and library. Check-in until 10pm. Reception 24hr. Reserve ahead. Dorms €16.50; singles €30; doubles €42. Cash only. ❶

▨ **Ostello Torino (HI),** V. Alby 1 (☎66 02 939; www.ostellotorino.it). Take bus #52 (#64 on Su) from Pta. Nuova. Cross the river and get off at the Lanza stop at V. Crimea and follow the "Ostello" signs to C. Giovanni Lanza, before turning left at V. Luigi Gatti. Young crowds pack 76 beds in basic rooms. TV room. Breakfast included; dinner €9.50. Laundry €4. Reception M-Sa 7am-12:30pm and 3-11pm, Su 7-10am and 11pm. Lockout 10am-3pm. Curfew 11pm; ask for key if staying out later. Closed Dec. 21-Jan. 14. Single-sex and co-ed 3- to 8-bed dorms €14.50; doubles €34, with bath €38; triples €51; quads €68. MC/V. ❶

La Foresteria degli Artisti, V. degli Artisti 15 (☎83 77 85 or 228 14 37 493; www.foresteriadegliartisti.it). La Foresteria is a furnished apartment with wood floors, antique furniture, DVD player, library, laundry, and kitchen. Ring bell for Coss F&G, then walk to 2nd door on left and ring again. Breakfast included. Reservations required. Closed Aug. Singles €50; doubles €80. Extra bed €20. Cash only. ❹

Albergo Azalea, V. Mercanti 16, 3rd fl. (☎53 81 15 or 333 24 67 449; albergo.azalea@virgilio.it). Exit Pta. Nuova on the right and take bus #58 or 72 (or any bus towards the *centro*, including #4, 12, 11, 52 or 63) to V. Garibaldi. Turn left on V. Garibaldi, away from P. Castello, and left on V. Mercanti. If you take bus #52, turn right from the stop. 15min. walk otherwise. 10 clean and cozy rooms with flowered wallpaper and white furniture in central location. No reception; call ahead. Singles €35, with bath €45; doubles €55/65. MC/V. ❸

Nicosia Schaya, Largo Montebello 33, top fl. (☎19 71 28 73 or 347 00 21 184; www.bedandbnicosia.it). Take bus #3, 68, 13, 16 or 18; get off near Largo Montebello. Sliding-glass door leads to the privacy of comfortable rooms with framed family pictures, phone, fridge, balcony, and bath. Breakfast included. Singles €50; doubles €70; triples €105. Cash only. A floor below, **B&B Pelù Schaya** is a simple and traditional option with laundry and kitchen facilities. Same prices as Nicosia. Discounts for extended stay. Both closed 2 months per year, but alternate so 1 fl. is always operating. Cash only. ❹

Campeggio Villa Rey, Strada Superiore Val San Martino 27 (☎/fax 81 90 117). From Pta. Nuova take the #72 or 63 bus to Pta. Palazzo, change to tram #3 on C. Regina, and ride to the end of the line (stop: Hermada). From there, walk 500m uphill or take bus #54. Quiet hillside location with views of the Basilica Superga has caravans and tent campers. Bar, small market, and restaurant. 2-course meal €15. Laundry €3. Office open daily 8am-10pm. €6 per person, €4 per child, €4-7 per tent, €10-11 per car, €11 per site. Electricity €1. Shower €0.80. MC/V. ❶

☐ FOOD

Ever since the Savoys started taking an evening cup of *cioccolato* in 1678, Turin has grown into one of the great international centers of chocolate. Ferrero Rocher and Nutella are its most famous products. Napoleonic restrictions on buying chocolate brought the hazelnut substitute *gianduiotto*, now the key ingredient in a distinctly *torinese* ice-cream flavor known as *gianduia*, available at cafes around P. Castello. On the savory side, Piemontese cuisine is a blend of northern Italian peasant staples and elegant French garnishes. Butter replaces olive oil, while cheese and mushrooms—occasionally along with white truffles—are used more than vegetables or spices. *Agnolotti*, ravioli stuffed with lamb and cabbage, is the local pasta specialty, but *polenta*, warm cornmeal often topped with *fontina* cheese, is the more common starch. The three most outstanding red wines in Italy—*Barolo, Barbaresco,* and *Barbera,* in descending price order—are available in markets and restaurants. To sample the true flavors of Piemontese cuisine, be ready to pay—restaurants that specialize in regional dishes are expensive. Self-caterers can head to **Di per Di** supermarket, all over the *centro*. (Branches: V. Maria Vittoria 11 and V. San Massimo 43. Open M-Tu and Th-Sa 8:30am-1:30pm and 3:30-7:30pm, W 8:30am-1pm. MC/V.) Find food at Porta Palazzo in P. della Repubblica, in what claims to be Europe's largest **open-air market** (M-F 7:30am-2pm, Sa until sunset). Many restaurants participate in **Torino Gourmet,** offering fixed-price *menù* for much less than they would run normally (€20-28). Updated price guides are available at the tourist office.

> **TIP** **CHOCOHOLICS UNITE.** Sample Turin's best with a **ChocoPass** (www.turismotorino.org), offering tastings of chocolate products, including *gianduiotti*, pralines, and ice cream. Buy a pass for €10 (24hr.; 10 tastings) or €15 (48hr.; 15 tastings) at any tourist office. This pass is for the truly dedicated chocoholic.

▨ **Eataly,** V. Nizza 224 (☎19 50 68 11). Take bus #1, 18 or 35 to the "Biglieri" stop, near Lingotto Expo Center. Turin's new culinary amusement park is a 10,000 sq. ft. facility that could realistically take at least a half day of sightseeing on its own. Tastings of wine and beer are just the beginning: classrooms feature scheduled cooking classes by famous guest chefs (in English by group reservation), meat and cheese lockers, and museum-quality exhibits demonstrate various foods and preparation techniques. Browse the restaurant counters, each with its own daily menu and specialty. Open daily 10am-10pm; meat and fish restaurants daily 10am-3:30pm and 5:30-10pm. ❷

▨ **Hafa Café,** V. Sant'Agostino 23/C (☎43 62 899 or 43 67 091; www.hafa.it). Sit on low Moroccan cushions and sip either the creamy *Hafa Café* (a mix of tea, spices, milk, and amaretto; €5) or the traditional Moroccan mint tea (€3). Food platters €5-6. Mixed drinks €7. Open Tu-Sa 10:30am-2:30am, Su 5pm-1am. MC/V. ❷

Stars & Roses, P. Paleocapa 2 (☎51 62 052), near P. Carlo Felicehead. Head upstairs and pick a room which matches your mood: the color scheme, lighting, and furniture change through each doorway. Photographs of celebrities in notorious poses, including a room dedicated to mug shots, decorate the walls. Takeout available. Cultural calzones (Indian, Irish, Japanese, Russian, and Scottish) €7-10. Pizza slices €3.50-8, 0.5m diameter pie €6.50-15.50. *Primi* €5-7, *secondi* €8-15. Cover €2. Open M and Su 7:30pm-12:30am, Tu-Sa noon-3pm and 7:30pm-12:30am. AmEx/MC/V. ❷

Il Punto Verde, V. San Massimo 17 (☎88 55 43), off V. Po, near P. Carlo Emanuele II. If a California juice bar and a traditional Italian trattoria had a vegetarian baby, named il Punto, and entrusted it to a kind owner, this would be it. Vegan options. Student lunch *menù* €5, 3-course *menù* €9. Giant dinner *monopiatti* (wine, dessert, and coffee) €11.50, lunch €6. *Primi* €6.50-11, *secondi* €5-8. Dinner cover €1.80. Open M-F 12:30-2:30pm and 7:30-10:30pm, Sa 7-10:30pm. Closed Aug. MC/V. ❷

Caffè Gelateria Fiorio, V. Po 8 (☎81 73 25 or 81 70 612), just off P. Castello. Famous for its buffet lunch (€14-15) and the smoothest *gelato* in the city. Founded as a hangout for the student movement, Fiorio was frequented by noblemen and artists alike, such as Mark Twain and Herman Melville. Cones from €1.50, sundaes €4.50-9. Open M-Th and Su 8am-1am, F-Sa 8am-2am. AmEx/MC/V. ❸

Le Vitel Etonné, V. San Francesco da Paola 4 (☎81 24 621; www.leviteletonne.com). A popular spot for Turin's casual professionals, Le Vitel Etonné has a wine cellar in the basement (€3-5 per glass) and an artisan cafe upstairs, with a menu that changes depending on what's fresh. *Primi* €9-11, *secondi* €13-15. Open M-F 5pm-1am, Sa 10am-3:30pm, Su 10am-3:30pm and 5pm-1am. Closed 1wk. in Aug. MC/V. ❹

Spaccanapoli, V. Mazzini 19 (☎81 26 694). Pizza by the meter (€20-30); try gorgonzola or the special *"spaccanapoli"* pizza, large enough to feed an army. Worth the trip if coming with at least 4 people. Delicious desserts. *Primi* €6-10, *secondi* €10-14.50. Dinner cover €2, lunch €1. Open daily noon-2:30pm and 7pm-midnight. AmEx/MC/V. ❸

Caffè Cioccolateria al Bicerin, P. della Consolata 5 (☎43 69 325; www.bicerin.it). The cafe has sold its namesake drink (€4), a hot mixture of coffee, chocolate, and cream since 1763 to such notables as Nietzche, Dumas, and Puccini. Open M-Tu and Th-F 8:30am-7:30pm, Sa-Su 8:30am-1pm and 3:30-7:30pm. ❶

EAT. SHOP. LEARN.

In January 2007, a new restaurant opened in Turin. Actually, 10 of them did, all under one roof. More than just a food court, Eataly (p. 170) is a culinary amusement park.

Each of Eataly's restaurants specializes in a different food group and prepares your meal in front of you. Including the €1 cover, dishes generally cost €8-15 at each station, a bargain for their high quality. Splitting meals is highly recommended in order to taste from more stations. The daily menus of meat, seafood, vegetables, deli meat, cheese, pizza, and pasta are only the beginning. A coffee shop and *gelato* stand are also on the ground floor, while the basement has meat and cheese selections. The basement also has two more restaurants, one dedicated to wine and the other to beer. The bottled wine selection is overwhelming but, if you are the mood for something simple, you can fill up your own liter of wine from the tap for €1.30-4 per L.

You can take the cooking into your own hands at the expansive organic food store or at the learning center, which offer varied and valuable cooking lessons from world-famous guest chefs (€20-100). While the calendar of classes is in Italian, many of the cooking lessons are also available in English for groups. (*V. Nizza 224. Take bus #1, 18, or 35 to the Biglieri stop. Reservations ☎011 19 50 68; www.eataly.com.*)

Ristorante da Mauro, V. Maria Vittoria 21/D (☎81 70 604). After 40 years in the same location, Signor Mauro is known for his exquisite and affordable Tuscan and *piemontese* cuisine. *Bue del Piemonte ai ferri* (roast ox; €9.30) and *castellana al prosciutto* (€7.50) are delicious. *Primi* €6, *secondi* €6-13. Open Tu-Su noon-2pm and 7:30-10pm. Cash only. ❷

🌀 SIGHTS

▨MOLE ANTONELLIANA. Once the largest structure in the world built using traditional masonry (a title sadly lost in the 1900s with the addition of some concrete), and the world's tallest museum, the Mole dominates Turin's skyline. The towering spire is gloriously reproduced today on the two-cent euro coin. Begun as a synagogue in 1863, it ended as an architectural eccentricity. The glass elevator that runs through the middle of the building goes to the observation deck. Today, the Mole houses the unique **Museo Nazionale del Cinema.** The ground floor has a mod bar with color-changing tables and movie screens. Interactive exhibits chronicle the history of cinema. At the center of the museum on the 2nd floor, **Temple Hall** holds a field of red velvet chairs for visitors to watch Italian films projected on screens high above. A variety of movies screen in wild settings, like a 60s living room, a Neolithic cave, and a giant fridge with toilets for seats. A suspended staircase nearby winds to hundreds of movie posters. Every hour, images on the dome disappear and music plays, while the Mole's walls are drawn up to reveal the building's skeleton beneath. *(V. Montebello 20, east of P. Castello. ☎81 25 658; www.museonazionaledelcinema.org. Museum and bar open Tu-F and Su 9am-8pm, Sa 9am-11pm. Last entry 1hr. before closing. Museum €5.20, students €4.20. Elevator €3.62/2.58; combined ticket €6.80/5.20.)*

> **⏣TIP** **TOURIN' CARD.** The best deal in the city wisely combines unlimited access to all public transportation as well as all sights. The **Torino Card** (48hr. €18, 72hr. €20), provides free entrance to *all* museums and monuments in Turin and throughout Piedmont. It also allows free access to the **TurismoBus Torino,** the panoramic lift in the Mole, the Sassi-Superga cable car, and the boats for river navigation on the Po, as well as discounts on guided tours, transportation, and shows. The card is available at any Turismo Torino info point and at most hotels.

PIEDMONT AND VALLE D'AOSTA

▨CATTEDRALE DI SAN GIOVANNI (DUOMO) AND CHIESA DI SAN LORENZO. The Holy Shroud of Turin, one of the most enigmatic relics in Christendom, has been housed in the Cappella della Santa Sindone of the **Cattedrale di San Giovanni Battista** since 1694. Said to be the burial cloth of Jesus, the 3 ft. by 14 ft. cloth first entered official accounts when the Crusaders brought it back from Jerusalem in the 13th century. Transferred to Turin from Chambéry, France, by the Savoys in 1578, the shroud rests today in a climate-controlled case. With rare exceptions, a photograph of the unfolded shroud to the left of the cathedral's entrance is as close as visitors will get to the real thing. A negative below the photograph of the shroud reveals more detail, including the countenance of a man with a fractured nose and bruised cheek. It was carbon-dated to 1350, though recent studies have suggested that a newer, repaired piece of the shroud from the Middle Ages had been tested, and the original may in fact be 2500 years old. In any case, the shroud continues to represent a sustained confrontation between science and faith, resulting in attempted arson in 1997; repairs to the chapel are still ongoing behind its *trompe l'oeil* painted-facade stand-in. *(Behind Palazzo Reale where V. XX Settembre crosses P. S. Giovanni. ☎43 61 540. Open daily 7am-noon and 3-7pm. Modest dress required. Free.)* Nearby, to the left of the Palazzo Reale, the 16th-century **Chiesa di San Lorenzo** served as temporary home to the shroud before completion of San Giovanni in the

15th century. Its soaring dome was designed by Guarino Guarini, and its ribs form an overlapping, eight-pointed star reminiscent of the Islamic architecture that influenced Guarini on his travels. In the sacristy to the right, an exact-size replica of the shroud hangs on the wall. *(V. Palazzo di Città 4, at the corner with P. Castello.* ☎ *43 61 527; www.sanlorenzo.torino.it. Open daily 8am-noon and 3-6pm. Free.)*

■ **CASTELLO DI RIVOLI MUSEO D'ARTE CONTEMPORANEA.** This museum houses one of Europe's most impressive contemporary art collections in a 14th-century Savoy residence. The sleek venue holds works from the 50s onward, and many exhibits, including Sol Lewitt's 1992 *Panels and Towers*, were designed specifically for the *castello*'s cavernous spaces. Other featured artists include Bruce Nauman, Claes Oldenburg, and Michelangelo Pistoletto—his controversial 1967 work, *Venus in Rags*, is on display. *(P. Mafalda di Savoia in Rivoli, 22km outside Turin. Take bus #36 or 66 from Turin, or subway from Pta. Susa to Fermi Station and then bus #36 to Rivoli. Inquire at the bus station about the direct shuttle bus.* ☎ *95 65 220; www.castellodirivoli.org. Open Tu-Th 10am-5pm, F-Su 10am-9pm. €6.50, students €3.50.)*

PALAZZO DELL'ACCADEMIA DELLE SCIENZE. The *palazzo* houses two of Turin's best museums—the **Museo Egizio** and the **Galleria Sabauda.** From 1903-37, the Italian Archaeological Mission brought thousands of artifacts home to Turin, making Museo Egizio the 2nd largest Egyptian collection outside Cairo. Museum highlights include both wrapped and unwrapped mummies, life-size wooden Nubian statues, the massive Ellesiya temple, and the well-furnished tomb of Kha, a 14th-century BC architect; Kha's tomb was one of the few Egyptian tombs spared by grave robbers. The ground floor also holds a cast of the Rosetta Stone, the artifact used to deciphered the ancient Egyptian language. *(V. Accademia delle Scienze 6. 2 blocks from P. Castello.* ☎ *56 17 776; www.museoegizio.it. Open Tu-Su 8:30am-7:30pm. €6.50, ages 18-25 €3, under 18 or over 65 free.)* On the 3rd floor, the **Galleria Sabauda** houses art collections from Palazzo Reale and Palazzo Carignano, and is renowned for its 14th- to 18th-century Flemish and Dutch paintings, including Van Eyck's *St. Francis Receiving the Stigmata* (1427), Memling's *Passion* (1470), and Rembrandt's *Old Man Sleeping* (1629), among others. *(V. Accademia delle Scienze 6.* ☎ *54 74 40; www.museoitorino.it/galleriasabauda. Open Nov.-May Tu and F-Su 8:30am-2pm, W 2-7:30pm, Th 10am-7:30pm; June-Oct. Tu and F-Su 8:30am-2pm, W 2-7:30pm, Th 2-7:30pm. €4, 18-25 €2, under 18 or over 65 free. Combined ticket for both museums €8.)*

PINACOTECA GIOVANNI E MARELLA AGNELLI. This tiny museum atop a former Fiat factory holds 26 pieces from the last 300 years. The collection features Venetian landscape works by Il Canaletto, Impressionist works by Matisse and Renoir, and pieces by Tiepolo, Picasso, and Modigliani. *(V. Nizza 230.* ☎ *00 62 713; www.pinacoteca-agnelli.it. Open Tu-Su 9am-7pm. €4, students €2.50. Special exhibits €6.)*

PALAZZO REALE. The Palazzo Reale forms part of the *"Corona di Delitie,"* a ring of Savoy royal residences that came under the protection of UNESCO as a World Heritage site in 1997. Home to the Princes of Savoy from 1645 to 1865, the ornate *palazzo* contains over 300 rooms. Thirty of the rooms, mostly unfurnished, are covered on the long Italian-language tour. André le Nôtre, famous for his work on the gardens of Versailles, designed the grounds in 1697, but the gardens have been since deeply reduced. *(In Piazzetta Reale, at the end of P. Castello.* ☎ *43 61 455; www.ambienteto.arti.beniculturali.it. Palazzo Reale open Tu-Su 8:30am-7:30pm. Visit only with mandatory guided tour. €6.50, students €3.25. Gardens open 9am-1hr. before sunset. Free.)* In the right wing of the Royal Palace lies the **Armeria Reale** (Royal Armory) with an extensive collection of medieval and Renaissance war tools. *(P. Castello 191.* ☎ *54 38 89. Open Tu-F 9am-2pm, Sa-Su 1-7pm. €4, under 18 or over 65 free.)*

GALLERIA CIVICA D'ARTE MODERNA E CONTEMPORANEA (GAM). The city's premiere modern and contemporary art museum devotes four floors to 19th- and 20th-century works made mostly by Italians, including some Modiglianis and de Chiricos. Though its collection is not the most representative of the diverse styles of these periods, it does have Andy Warhol's gruesome *Orange Car Crash* and a few works by Picasso, Chagall, Klee, and Renoir. *(V. Magenta 31. On the corner of C. Galileo Ferraris, off Largo V. Emanuele. Take tram #1, 9, or 15. ☎44 29 518; www.gamtorino.it. Open Tu-Su 9am-7pm. €7.50, under 26 or over 65 €6, Tu free.)*

BASILICA DI SUPERGA. When the French siege on Turin culminated in the attack on September 6, 1706, King Vittorio Amedeo II made a promise to the Virgin Mary to build a basilica in her honor should the city withstand the invasion. Turin stood unconquered, and famous architect Juvarra helped fulfill the vow, erecting a Neoclassical portico and high drum to support the basilica's spectacular dome. The church houses the tombs of the Savoys. In a tragic event in 1949, a plane carrying the entire Turin soccer team crashed into the basilica; a memorial stands at the accident site today, listing the names of the victims. The basilica is built on a 640m summit outside Turin, described by Le Corbusier as "the most enchanting position in the world." Indeed, it offers panoramic views of the city, the Po Valley below, and the Alps beyond. *(Take tram #15 from V. XX Settembre to Stazione Sassi. From the station, take bus #79 or board a small cable railway for a clanking 18min. ride uphill. Every hr. on the hr. Cable Car ☎57 64 733; www.gtt.to.it. Runs M and W-F 9am-noon and 2-8pm, Sa-Su 9am-8pm. Round-trip €3.10, Su and holidays €4.13. Basilica ☎89 80 083; www.basilicadisuperga.com. Open daily Apr.-Oct. 9am-noon and 3-6pm; Nov.-Mar. 9am-noon and 3-5pm. Dome of basilica and Savoy tombs each €3, students €2.)*

PARCO DEL VALENTINO. One of Italy's largest parks and the first Italian public park, the designer Valentino's lush grounds on the banks of the Po provide a safe haven for whispering lovers and frolicking children. Upon entering the park from C. V. Emanuele, **Castello del Valentino** is on the left. Its distinctly French air honors the royal lady Christina of France, who in turn made the castle her favorite residence. It now houses the University's Facoltà di Architettura and is open to the public only by appointment *(☎66 94 592)*. However, the fake *rocca* (castle) in the nearby **Borgo e Rocca Medievale,** built for the Italian Industry and Crafts Exhibition of 1884, and its attached shop-filled village are open to the public. *(Park and castle at Vle. Virgilio 107, along the Po. ☎44 31 701; www.borgomedievaletorino.it. Castle open Tu-Su 9am-7pm. €5, students €4. Village open daily 9am-7pm. Free.)*

SANTUARIO DELLA CONSOLATA. This ornate Baroque church belongs to Turin's cult of the Virgin, with gold and jeweled offerings of gratitude from the wealthy in glass boxes by the entrance. In the rooms to the right is a collection of ex-voto paintings. Reminiscent of children's drawings, they depict catastrophes averted across the decades, including scenes from WWI and WWII. *(P. della Consolata. ☎43 63 235; santuario.consolata@libero.it. Open daily 6:30am-12:30pm and 3-7:30pm. Free.)*

PALAZZO AND TEATRO CARIGNANO. This *palazzo* was designed by the Guarini family in 1679 to house the Princes of Savoy; it was later the seat of the first Italian parliament. The building contains the **Museo Nazionale del Risorgimento Italiano,** which commemorates Italy's unification between 1706 and 1946. *(V. Accademia delle Scienze 5. ☎56 21 147. Closed for restoration until 2008.)* Across from the *palazzo* is the Baroque **Teatro Carignano,** where Italian poet Vittorio Alfieri premiered his tragedies. *(☎54 70 54. Call for info on tours. Free.)*

PALAZZO MADAMA. On the site of the ancient Roman military camp, this palace was converted to a castle in the Middle Ages. It lost its defensive function in the 17th century, became a museum in 1934, and today houses an enormous Baroque collection of paintings and artifacts from churches. The religious seems awk-wardly displayed in its open, well-lit interior. Highlights include the view from the castle's tower and a small circular room on the ground floor with four medieval marble carvings. *(P. Castello. ☎44 33 501; www.palazzomadamatorino.it. Open Tu-F and Su 10am-6pm, Sa 9am-8pm. €7.50, over 65 and students under 25 €6.)*

MUSEO DELL'AUTOMOBILE. With a focus on Italian cars and racing, this museum documents the automobile's evolution through prints, drawings, more than 150 original cars, and 1st models by Ford, Benz, Peugeot, Oldsmobile, and Fiat. *(C. Unità d'Italia 40. Head south 20min. along V. Nizza from Stazione Porta Nuova. ☎67 76 66; www.museoauto.it. Closed for restoration until 2008; call ahead to see if open.)*

🎵 🎍 ENTERTAINMENT AND FESTIVALS

For the most updated calendar of Turin's yearly events, visit www.torinocultura.it (mostly in Italian) or www.turismotorino.org (translated into English). If you want the news in print, Turin's daily newspaper, *La Stampa*, publishes *Torino Sette*, a thorough Friday section on cultural events. Turin's **Teatro Regio**, in P. Castello, is home to the city's beloved **opera, ballet,** and **orchestra,** which showcase a combined 130 events a year. (☎88 15 557; www.teatroregio.torino.it. Ticket office open Tu-F 10:30am-6pm, Sa 10:30am-4pm, and 1hr. before shows.) Eclectic music, theater, and cinema events enliven Turin between June and August, when **Torino d'Estate** draws many local and international acts to the city. Included in the summer festiv-ities are **Torino Puntiverdi,** 19 July nights of dance and music from tango to orches-tra in the Giardini Reali and other venues. (☎50 69 967 or 80 00 15 457. Tickets €10-15, available from ticket office at V. San Francesco da Paola 6. Open M-Sa 10:30am-6:30pm.) The ▓**TRAFFIC Turin Free Festival,** during late June or early July, attracts international acts to the free celebration of contemporary youth culture (www.trafficfestival.com). Previous performers include Franz Ferdinand and The Strokes. Last but not least, chocoholics venture to Turin every year at the end of February for the **Chocolate Fair** (www.cioccola-to.it).

During the 20s, Turin was home to over 100 movie production companies, and its love affair with cinema still lives on today. During the academic year, Turin's university organizes screenings of **foreign films** in their original languages. Two important cinematic festivals take place annually. The **Turin Film Festival** in Novem-ber (www.torinofilmfest.org) is one of the most important and liveliest festivals of contemporary cinema in Italy, paying particular attention to up-and-coming cin-ema auteurs. The various categories explore the many diverse aspects of contem-porary cinema: feature films by famous directors, experimental cinema, and documentaries and retrospectives. In addition, **Da Sodoma ad Hollywood** is Turin's GLBTQ Film Festival held in April (www.tglff.com), one of the most important queer festivals in the world. Head to the turn-of-the-century glamour of **Cinema Romano,** Galleria Subalpina, P. Castello 9, near the beginning of V. Po. (☎56 20 145. Movies daily, usually 4-10:30pm. Tickets €4-6.50.) In the fall, the tourist office organizes guided city tours with a cinematic bent.

🛍 SHOPPING

One of Turin's unique events is the **Gran Balon flea market,** held every 2nd Sunday of the month behind Porta Palazzo. Here, junk sellers rub shoulders with treasure-hunters. A smaller-scale **Mercato del Balon** (www.balon.it) occurs every Saturday. The biggest **open-air market** in Europe takes place under Porta Palazzo in P. della Repubblica. (M-F 8:30am-1:30pm, Sa 8:30am-6:30pm.) Over 600 vendors sell food, clothing, and odds and ends. Though clothing stores line Turin's streets, the big-name designer shops on **Via Roma** are more conducive to window shopping. Turin's student population has attracted trendy and affordable clothing shops to **Via Garibaldi** and **Via Po;** the latter is also home to antique bookshops and record stores. In the **Quadrilatero Romano,** up-and-coming designers have set up shop on the renovated streets within the rectangle outlined by V. Bligny, V. G. Garibaldi, V. XX Settembre, and P. della Repubblica. **8 Gallery,** V. Nizza 262 (www.8gallery.it), is housed inside Lingotto's former Fiat factory in Turin's future cultural center, and features over 100 shops, restaurants, bars, and movie theaters.

■ NIGHTLIFE

Turin's nightlife rivals that of Milan or Rome. With something to offer every age group, Turin has a variety of options, ranging from good wine and grooving background music, to vodka and tonics in a packed, pounding club. Turin's nightlife is unlike Milan's: the clubs are less pretentious, the covers are cheaper, and the numerous choices are more conveniently concentrated—mostly along the Po River. Especially in the summer, Turin's social scene centers on ◪**I Murazzi,** two stretches of boardwalk, one between Ponte V. Emanuele I and Ponte Umberto and another smaller stretch downstream from the Ponte V. Emanuele I. Every night, Murazzi del Po attracts all types of crowds. Most show up around 7:30-9:30pm for aperitifs, while others arrive around 11pm to spend the next 4-6hr. sipping drinks, maneuvering through crowds along the waterfront, or dancing inside one of the livelier establishments. Some charge covers late at night, but free bars or clubs can be easily found (some distribute consumption cards at the door that must be stamped, paid for, and returned upon departure; lost card fee €30). ◪**Quadrilatero Romano,** the recently renovated collection of buildings between P. della Repubblica and V. Garibaldi, attracts nightgoers who would rather sit, drink, and chat until 4am than dance to techno music. Additionally, several English and Irish pubs line C. V. Emanuele II from Stazione Porta Nuova to the Po, attracting an English-speaking student crowd. Head south on the I Murazzi side of the river for a few blocks to reach the growing **Valentino Park** riverfront nightlife, near the Valentino castle.

◪**The Beach,** V. Murazzi del Po 18-22 (☎88 87 77). With strobe lights and energetic crowd, this club easily has the best dance floor in Turin. By 1am, this large, modern club is filled with the young trendsetters, electronica music, and Redbull and vodkas. During the week, it hosts occasional performance-art pieces, film openings, and book signings. Mixed drinks €5-6; after 10pm from €6. Lunch €12. Happy hour 7-10pm. Open Tu-W 10pm-2am, Th-Sa noon-4am. MC/V.

Giancarlo, V. Murazzi del Po 47 (www.arcitorino.it), closest to Ponte V. Emanuele. The 1st bar to invade I Murazzi, drawing huge after-hours crowds with €3-4 beers. Its rock and punk music draws an alternative crowd to its cavernous dance floor, and after 4am almost everyone who is not sitting by the river will be cutting a rug here. Mixed drinks €4-5. Student night Tu. Open M-Sa 10pm-6am. Cash only.

Pier 7-9-11, V. Murazzi del Po 7-11 (☎83 53 56). Groove to the latest chart-toppers at this flashy dance club with the most outdoor seating in I Murazzi. Shots €3. Beer €4. Mixed drinks €8. Cover with 1 drink included €8. Open M-Sa 10:30pm-3am.

Fluido, Vle. Umberto Cagni 7 (☎66 94 557; www.fluido.to). Riverside wine bar and restaurant, with a dance club downstairs.

Life, C. Massimo D'Azelio 3/A (☎339 69 13 111), in the center of the Parco Valentino. This outdoor club can be heard from the edge of the Murazzi. A slightly older crowd—not inclined to dancing—listens to loud dance music and buys pricey drinks from the outdoor bar. Mixed drinks €8. Cover €13 includes 1 drink. Open F-Su midnight-4am.

Shore, P. Emanuele Filiberto 10/G. Serves large mixed drinks until the wee hours. Chillout fusion music completes the mood. Open daily 6:30pm-2:30am.

Arancia di Mezzanotte, P. E. Filiberto 11/I (☎52 11 338; www.aranciadimezzanotte.it). Set in a quaint interior, this is a popular place for an aperitif. Beer €4-5. Mixed drinks €6.50. Open daily 6pm-4am. MC/V.

Six Nations Murphy's Pub, C. V. Emanuele 28 (☎88 72 55). Exit Pta. Nuova, and turn right; the pub is a few blocks down on the left. Beer taps glow in the dim interior, filled with British expats, darts, and billiards. Beer €3-4.50. Open daily 6pm-3am. MC/V.

Magazzino di Gilgamesh, P. Moncenisio 13/B (☎74 92 801; www.ilmagazzinodigilgamesh.com). A little bit off the beaten path. Packed concert program of blues, jazz, and classic rock, occasionally switching to international music. Open Tu-Sa 10pm-3am.

Hiroshima Mon Amour, V. Carlo Bossoli 83 (☎31 76 636; www.hiroshimamonamour.org). Take bus #1 or 34 to Lingotto Centro Fiere. This club is a dancer's paradise, often with live tunes ranging from reggae to rock. Open daily 9pm-3am.

◼ DAYTRIPS FROM TURIN

◼ SACRA DI SAN MICHELE

From Turin, take the train to Avigliana (30min., 15 per day, €2.20). From there, either take a taxi (☎93 02 18; around €30) or make the 14km, 3hr. hike. Alternatively, tackle the scenic 1½hr. climb from the village of Sant'Ambrogio to the monastery. Take a train to Sant'Ambrogio (30min.; 8 per day, last return 7:10pm; €2.50). Exiting the station, walk straight up V. Caduti per la Patria, and turn right on V. Umberto. Continue straight until Chiesa Parrocchiale. Behind the church on the right is a "Sacra di San Michele Mulattiera" sign. The rest of the hike is clearly marked. Do not hike alone, as the unpaved path can be difficult and slippery. Wear sturdy shoes and bring water.

On a bluff above the town of Avigliana, the Sacra di San Michele (sa-cra dee san mee-KEH-leh) grows from the very rock on which it was built. *The Name of the Rose*, a movie based on a novel by Umberto Eco, was not filmed at this megalithic stone monastery, but it probably should have been. Eco based his book's plot on the Sacra's history, and even in full summer sunshine, there is an ominous air about the place. Ugo di Montboissier, an Alevernian pilgrim, founded it in 1000, and the **Scalone dei Morti** (Stairway of the Dead), a set of steps chiseled from the mountainside, helps to buttress the structure. Monks' corpses were once draped across the staircase for the faithful to pay their last respects; currently, their skeletons are more tactfully concealed in the cavities on the side. The stairs ascend to the **Porta dello Zodiaco** (Door of the Zodiac), a door sculpted by 11th-century artist Nicolao with zodiac signs and symbols. Steps in the middle of the nave descend into the shrine of St. Michael and three tiny **chapels.** The oldest dates to the time when St. Michael was first venerated. In AD 966, St. John Vincent built the largest chapel; today, it holds the medieval members of the Savoy family. (☎93 91 30; www.sacradisanmichele.com. Open Mar. 16-Oct. 15 Tu-Sa 9:30am-12:30pm and 2:30-6pm, Su 9:30am-noon and 2:40-6:30pm; Oct. 16-Mar. 15 Tu-Sa 9:30am-12:30pm and 2:30-5pm, Su 9:30am-12:30pm and 2:40-6pm. Last entry 30min. before closing. €4, children and over 65 €3.) For a map of the arduous trek, head to Avigliana's **Informazione Turistica,** C. Torino 6/d, a 5-10min. walk straight ahead from the train station. (☎93 66 037. Open M-F 9am-noon and 3-6pm.)

PARCO DELLA MANDRIA AND VENARIA CASTLE

By car: from the by-pass in Turin, take the Venaria Reale exit. By train: take the Torino-Ceres (Airport) line from Stazione Dora to Venaria. By bus: take GTT line #11, 72, or 72b from the centro to Venaria. Alternatively, a shuttle bus conveniently runs between C. Stati Uniti, Porta Nuova, Porta Susa, and the palace. (45min.; depart 14 per day 8:05am-6:55pm, return 16 per day 9am-7:50pm; round-trip €5.)

An immense project mostly constructed by a single architect during the 17th and 18th centuries, this newly restored royal palace has an immaculate contemporary garden and over 5000 sq. m of frescoes and decorations. Parco Della Mandria is a rural, historical park characterized by alluvial terraces where woods alternate with pastures, lakes, and fields. The variable countryside landscape invites you to relax and enjoy the ancient churches and royal residences, which date back to the times of King Vittorio Emanuele II. The area's vegetation includes an ancient forest rich in oaks and ash trees that offers shelter to many animal species. Many activities, such as horseback riding, trekking, and cycling are available. The plan for the building of the Castle was begun in 1659 at the request of Duke Carlo Emanuele II. The layout by Amedeo di Castellamonte was finished in 1675, and consists of a village, a palace, and gardens. (Info: ☎800 32 93 29; www.parks.it/parco.mandria or www.lavenari-areale.it. Castle: La Venaria Reale, P. della Republica 4. ☎45 93 675; www.reggiave-nariareale.it. Open Tu, Th, and Sa-Su 9:30-11:30am and 2:30-5:30pm.)

CUNEO ☎0171

Cuneo's (COO-neh-oh; pop. 55,000) name means "wedge," and for good reason: it's wedged between the Stura di Demonte River and the Torrente Gesso. Over the years, no fewer than nine different armies have besieged strategically located Cuneo, but the town has lived up to its motto, *"ferendo"* (to bear), surviving each attack. These days, invasion comes in the form of bargain hunters, who over-whelm serene Cuneo during its open-air market every weekend. Its 14km of *portici* (arcades) provide ample space for an afternoon of window shopping and people-watching; however, most travelers visit Cuneo as a launching point for explorations of the nearby valleys and Maritime Alps National Park.

[⛶] TRANSPORTATION AND PRACTICAL INFORMATION. The **train station** (ticket office open 6am-midnight) in P. Libertà provides service to Mondovì (1hr., 13 trains per day 6:20am-7:09pm, €2.70), Saluzzo (30min., 14 trains per day 5:35am-7:38pm, €2.70-4), and Turin (1hr., 30 trains per day 4:35am-10pm, €5.30). Local **buses** also depart from the station, serving Mondovì (12 buses per day 7am-7:35pm, €2.70), Saluzzo (1hr., 21 buses per day 6:45am-7:35pm, €2.45), and Turin via Saluzzo (4:55am-8:25pm, €5.30). Schedules vary daily and seasonally; the tour-ist office provides up-to-date timetables. To explore the Cuneo Valleys, rent a **car** from Europcar, V. Torino 178 (☎41 23 63), inside the Hyundai dealership. To get there from Cuneo, take a cab or bus 4, 8, or 15 from the center (bus stops directly in front of delearship). For those above 25, try Avis, C. Francia 251 (☎49 34 86; open M-F 8:30am-12:30pm and 2:30-6:30pm, Sa 8:30am-12:30pm; AmEx/MC/V) or Hertz, V. Savona 17 (☎34 80 70), under the bridge after crossing the river. Borrow a **bike** for free from the town hall next to the tourist office and grab a copy of the brochure, *Cuneo's Bicycle Touring District.* A comprehensive English-language walking-tour guide, *Cuneo In Your Pocket*, with artistic and historical information, can be obtained from the tourist office.

Cuneo lies 80km south of Turin. **Via Roma, Piazza Galimberti,** and **Corso Nizza** are the main thoroughfares; the rest of the streets form an easily navigable grid. To reach C. Nizza from the train station, follow **Corso Giolitti** from **Piazza Libertà.** The **tourist office,** V. Roma 28, provides info and helps find lodgings. (☎69 32 58; www.comune.cuneo.it. Open M-Sa 10am-12:30pm and 3-6:30pm.) For info on the Cuneo province, contact **ATL,** V. Amedeo 82. From C. Nizza, turn onto V. Amedeo when you're one block before the *piazza.* (☎69 02 16. Open daily 8:30am-noon and 2:30-6pm.) **Banks** with **ATMs** line V. Roma and C. Nizza. In case of **emergency,** call the **police** (☎67 777) or **paramedics** (☎44 13 37). Several **pharmacies** on C. Nizza post after-hours rotations, including one at V. Roma 19b (open M-F 8:30am-2pm; Sept.-June also Sa 8:30am-1pm; closed July), and another at P. Galimberti 5 (open M, W-Th, Sa-Su 9am-12:30pm and 3:30-7:30pm, Tu and

F 8:30am-12:30pm). The **Santa Croce hospital** is at V. Coppino 26 (☎45 01 11). **Internet** is available at the **Call Center**, V. Fossano 19. (☎60 54 75. €4 per hr. Open M-Sa 9am-9pm, Su 2:30-9pm.) The **post office** is at V. Francesco Andrea Bonelli 6. (☎69 33 06. Open M-F 8:30am-7pm, Sa 8:30am-1pm.) **Postal Code:** 12100.

▌🖸 ACCOMMODATIONS AND FOOD. Luxurious, newly renovated, hotel rooms, all with A/C, Wi-Fi (€5 per day), TV, phone, and bath, can be found at **Hotel Ligure ❹**, V. Savigliano 11. Exit P. Galimberti on V. Roma and turn right; V. Savigliano runs parallel to V. Roma. Kitchens are available for those staying at least seven days. (☎63 45 45; www.ligurehotel.com. Breakfast included. Parking €7. Singles €50; doubles €70; triples €90. AmEx/MC/V.) To save money, cheap rooms without private baths are found at **Albergo Cavallo Nero ❸**, V. Seminario 8. From P. Galimberti, head one block up V. Roma and turn left. Smaller rooms have TV and phone; some also have balcony. (☎69 21 68 or 60 20 17; cavallo.nero@virgilio.it. English spoken. Breakfast and parking included. Singles €38, with bath €50; doubles €50/70; triples €85; quads €95. Half pension and full pension options available. MC/V.) At **Bisalta ❶**, V. San Maurizio 33, on the outskirts of the city, 200 campsites offer plenty of recreational activities. (☎49 13 34; campingbisalta@libero.it. €5-6 per person, €5-6 per site. Electricity €1.50. Bungalows €20-30 per person. Cash only.) Cafes line the arcades of V. Roma and C. Nizza, providing cheap spots to stop for a sandwich or *gelato*. At **🖪Ristorante Les Gourmands ❸**, V. Statuto 3/A, bright colors and modern furniture send traditional restaurant decoration out the window, while the cuisine innovatively fuses food styles from around the world. Look for the strawberry risotto with shrimp and rosemary, which costs €7. (☎60 56 64; www.lesgourmands.it. *Primi* €6.50-8, *secondi* €6-15. **🖪3-course lunch menù** €10. Cover €1.50. Open Tu-F and Su noon-3pm and 7pm-midnight, Sa 7pm-midnight. Closed last 2wk. of July. AmEx/MC/V.) For a traditional dinner experience, head to **Ristorante Zuavo ❷**, V. Roma 23, where a simple menu, wooden tables, and walls adorned with family mementos guarantee an experience emblematic of the city. (☎60 20 20. *Primi* €6, *secondi* €8-9. Open M-Tu and F-Su 12:30-2pm and 7-10pm, Th 7:30-10pm. AmEx/MC/V.) The restaurant attached to **Albergo Cavallo Nero ❷**, also run by the Carle family, serves a dinner *menù* for €15-20. (*Primi* €4-8, *secondi* €5-13. Open Tu-Su noon-2pm and 7:30-9pm. MC/V.) Nearby, the **Enoteca Club de L'Enoteca Artistica ❶**, V. Savigliano 17, is a creative wine bar with rotating art exhibits downstairs. (☎320 87 52 617. *Panini* €2-5. Wine €2-5 per glass. Open Tu-W and Su 6pm-midnight, F-Sa 6pm-2am. Cash only.) A **Maxisconto** supermarket, at the corner of V. Cesare Battisti and V. Ponza di San Martino, off P. Galimberti, sells groceries. (Open M-W 8:30am-1pm and 3-7:30pm, Th 8:30am-1pm, F-Sa 8:30am-7:30pm.)

▐🖸 SHOPPING AND SIGHTS. Cuneo's famous **open-air market** sprawls over 1km, filling P. Galimberti, most of V. Roma, and much of C. Nizza—not to mention all the side streets. Stalls full of clothes, antiques, postcards, cookware, and everything else imaginable delight shoppers, but make parking a nightmare. (Every Tu during daylight hours. Summer approximately 7am-6pm; winter 8am-4pm.) There is also an antiques market on the last Saturday of every month in P. Europa. The facade of the **duomo,** at the corner of C. Nizza and V. Bologna, may blend in with the municipal government buildings around it, but inside there is a Baroque wonderland, complete with crystal chandeliers. (Open daily 8am-noon and 3-7pm.) The **Museo Civico di Cuneo,** V. Santa Maria 10, occupies the retired convent of San Francesco, and displays archaeological artifacts showcasing the history of the Cuneo territory as well as Bronze Age cave drawings. (☎63 41 75. Open Tu and Sa 8:30am-1pm and 2:30-5:30pm, W-F 8:30am-1pm and 2:30-5pm, Su 3-7pm. Closed June 15-30. €2.60, students €1.55.)

VALLEYS OF CUNEO

The mountain villages in the sparsely inhabited valleys that surround Cuneo provide a picture of how the quaint life skirting the Italian Alps has subsisted for centuries. Shops selling local crafts and restaurants serving genuine *piemontese* cuisine abound. Infrequent bus service and long journeys, however, make it difficult to visit more than one valley in a single day.

> **TIP** **PIMP YOUR RIDE.** A car is to the Valleys of Cuneo like duck sauce is to spring rolls—necessary. After picking up your sweet set of wheels, grab the excellent map of the Cuneo province at any tourist office, and get going. Always remember to honk at the bend on blind curves. The beauty of having a car is that you can make pit stops at roadside rivers and ▧ **jump in.**

▧ VALLE GESSO

From Cuneo, go west out of the city and take SS 20 for 33km, continuing straight to Borgo San Dalmazzo; switch to SP 22 road into Valle Gesso to Valdieri, ending in Terme di Valdieri. Info office in Terme di Valdieri (☎ 0171 97 397; www.parcoalpimarittime.it).

The lush Valle Gesso (VA-leh JEH-so) is the gateway to the **Parco Naturale Alpi Marittime,** a protected area of 28,000 hectares in the Alps, along the border of France and Italy. Nature lovers can not miss this paradise. This fairy-tale land rewards hikers and mountain bikers with stunning views of the Alpine countryside.

· Originally part of the Sardinian King Vittorio Emanuele II's private hunting reserve, the park is now home to chamois, ibex, wild boar, 1500 species of plants, about 80 of which are types of orchids. Also find many of the best- and least-trafficked Italian Alpine **hiking trails,** which were born out of mule-tracks and initially made for hunting purposes. Pockets of provincial language and culture are scattered throughout the valley and its towns. Tiny **Terme di Valdieri** (1386m) lies in the heart of the park, a few hours' walk from many *rifugi* (hiker huts). The Terme also houses the **park center,** Terme di Valdieri 5, in the stone building to the left of the Albergo. (☎ 0171 97 208. Open June 15-Sept.15 9am-1pm and 2-6pm. Parking €3; pay inside.) Trails depart from the road to the right of the park info office, since you cannot drive any farther. The office provides the *Rifugi delle Provincia di Cuneo* map, which pinpoints the numerous *rifugi* throughout the park. The center also has info on many routes of varying length and difficulty, such as the **Piano del Valasco** path (2hr.), which climbs to 1780m and circles a lake. Alternatively, continue on the **Giro dei Laghi Valscura** route (4-7hr.) for stunning views: this path allows you to see the many military roads built during WWII to fortify the border against France. After a long day on the trails, nothing feels better than the 34°C **Valdieri Thermal Baths,** 500m down the main road where it splits, across the street from Hotel Royale. Soak in the pools or smear yourself with mud from the sulfur-rich thermophilic mosses in the springs—they allegedly have healing powers. (☎ 0171 26 16 66 or contact Hotel Royale 0171 97 106/7/8; www.termedivaldieri.it. Open mid-June to mid-Sept. daily 9am-6pm and 8-11pm. Thermal pool €10 per half- day; €15 per day. Mud baths €21. Thermal hydromassage €24. 45min. massage €40.) The **Valderia Botanic Gardens,** a 2min. walk up the hill, offers a 1hr., 950m nature trail that showcases a fourth of all Italian flora. (Open June 15-Sept. 15 9am-12:30pm and 2:30-6pm. €3, ages 6-14 and over 65 €2.)

If driving, the ideal way to visit Parco Marittime is to stay in a B&B. About 10min. from the beginning of the trails, in the last town before the park center, is **Ciaburna dei Ribota ❷,** 54 Frazione Santa Anna. Look for the right fork on the SS 20 for S. Anna, just after Borgo San Dalmazzo. Turn on the small road immediately after the post office. Look on left for long white sign: "W LA REGINA." The B&B has beautiful views of the mountains and access to hiking. (☎ 349 29 15 839;

www.bedandbreakfastcuneo.it/ciaburnadeiribota.asp. €25 per person.) Next door to the park center, **Albergo Turismo ❹**, Terme di Valdieri 3, offers simple rooms right by the mountains, ideal for those without vehicles, who can reach Valdieri by bus from P. Torino in Cuneo. (☎0171 97 334. Doubles €50-58, with bath €66-74. Half pension €43-53 per person; full pension €52-62. Cash only.) A restaurant downstairs offers breakfast (€4-9), lunch, and dinner (both €15-23). **Public restrooms** are past the Albergo and to the right.

VALLE CASOTTO

Take SS 28 from Cuneo for 27km or the A6 from Turin. Vicoforte is 4km east of Mondovì. For info, contact the Ufficio IAT del Comune di Mondovì, C. Statuto 16 (☎0174 40 389; www.comune.mondovi.cn.it). Open Tu-Su 10am-12:30pm and 3-6:30pm.

During a visit in 1796, Napoleon called the Valle Casotto's (VA-leh ca-ZO-toh) **Mondovì** "the most beautiful town in the world." The *centro storico*, an impossibly dense collection of buildings dating from 1198, is on P. Maggiore. Located behind the cathedral, the **Torre Civica** symbolizes Mondovì's strength and undefeatable prowess. Destroyed by fire and war, its current incarnation stands over 30m, adorned on each side with a giant clock. Climb past the exposed clock gears to the top for a view all the way to Monte Bianco. (Open June-Sept. Tu-Su 3-6:30pm. €3.) Stores throughout the *centro* sell blue-patterned pottery embossed with the town's symbol, a rooster; the town is known regionally for its fine pottery. **Skiing** is a popular recreation in Mondovì. Call ☎0174 46 893 for info on **Mondolé Ski Resort** slopes and day passes. The **Castello di Casotto** was constructed as a Carthusian monastery in the 11th century. It was destroyed by Napoleon, then rebuilt in the 19th century and used as a hunting lodge for the Savoys. Widespread efforts to restore the *castello*'s exterior are currently underway. (11km south of Pamparato. ☎0174 35 11 31. Open daily 9am-noon and 2-6pm. Last entry 30min. before closing. Admission includes tour in Italian; €3.)

Farther up the valley is the village of **Vicoforte,** home to the soaring ⛪**Santuario di Vicoforte** and the four square towers surrounding it. Originally begun in 1596 to house a revered image of the Madonna that was believed to have bled when struck, the sanctuary wasn't actually finished until 1733. Notable artifacts include the blue elliptical cupola built in 1731, which at 75m high and 38m long, is the largest in the world; the 6000 sq. m fresco of the Madonna's life on the inside is considered the world's largest single-subject painting. Skylights and the bright, heavily frescoed interior make the altar glow with reflected light. (☎0174 56 55 55. Open daily 7:30am-noon and 2-7pm. Free.) Next to the Santuario, **Casa Regina Montis Regalis ❸** mostly houses nuns in its maze of small rooms and hallways of faded frescoes but also lets rooms to travelers. (☎0174 56 53 00; www.santuariodivicoforte.com. Breakfast €5; excellent on-site restaurant. Curfew 11pm. Singles €35, half-pension €45, full pension €55; doubles €52/74/96. MC/V.)

SALUZZO ☎0175

For over four centuries, the hilltop town of Saluzzo (sa-LOOT-so; pop. 16,400) reigned as the capital of a fiercely independent marquisate before falling under the influence of the House of Savoy in 1601. The arcade-lined *centro storico* and churches of the "Siena of the North" remain well preserved and tourist-free— unless you count the crowds of farmers who come up on weekend nights for a glass of wine in the trattorie. Saluzzo is well known for its crafts and historic past, making it not just a great base to explore the Po Valley but a nice stopover itself.

▤ ☎ TRANSPORTATION AND PRACTICAL INFORMATION. Saluzzo lies 33km north of Cuneo. **Trains** depart from the P. Vittorio Veneto station off C. Roma for

Cuneo (1hr., M-Sa every 45min. 6:45am-8:17pm, €5) and Turin (1hr., M-Sa 6:10am-7:46pm, €4.50) via Savigliano. Local ATI **buses** (www.atibus.com) leave from the station at V. Circonvallazione 19, connecting Saluzzo to villages in the surrounding valleys, including Turin (1hr., 1-2 per hr. 4:25am-8:25pm, €3) and Cuneo (1hr., 1-2 per hr. 6:10am-7:25pm, €2.45). On the weekend, the train station closes, but buses still run. Purchase tickets at the machine behind the station; buses pick up passengers in front of the station. For a **taxi,** call ☎45 098.

Saluzzo's main street changes its name from **Via Spielberg** to **Corso Italia** to **Corso Piemonte** as it moves east to west. From the train station, head straight up **Via Piave;** from the bus station, turn left on **Via Circonvallazione,** then immediately right on **Via Torino.** The *centro storico* and most of the sights lie uphill on the north side of town. To reach the fantastically helpful **tourist office,** Piazzetta dei Mondagli 5, enter the old town through the arched passageway at V. Volta, near the junction of V. Spielberg and C. Italia. It provides info on detailed bike routes and sights in nearby villages and valleys. (☎46 710; www.comune.saluzzo.cn.it. Open Apr.-Sept. Tu-Sa 9am-1pm and 2:30-5:30pm, Su 9am-1pm and 2:30-6pm; Oct.-Mar. Tu-Sa 9am-12:30pm and 2-5:30pm, Su 9am-12:30pm and 2-6pm.) **Unicredit Banca,** C. Italia 28, has an **ATM.** (Open M-F 8:20am-1:20pm and 2:30-4pm.) The **public library, Biblioteca Civica,** V. Volta 39, offers free **Internet** access. (Open Tu-Th 9:30am-12:30pm and 3-7pm, F 3-7pm, Sa 9:30am-1pm and 2:30-5:30pm. Internet available Tu-F 3-7pm, Sa 9:30am-1pm and 2:30-6:30pm.) **Farmacia Chiaffredo,** C. Italia 56, posts a list of after-hours rotations with the three other nearby pharmacies. (Open daily except for rotating rest day 8:30am-12:30pm and 3:30-6pm.) The **Ospedale Civile** lies on V. Spielberg 58 (☎21 51 11), two blocks outside the *centro storico*. The **post office,** V. Peano 1, is on the other side of the river, not far from the train station. (Open Jan.-July and Sept.-Dec. 8:30am-7pm, Sa 8:30am-1pm; Aug. M-F 8:30am-2pm, Sa 8:30am-1pm.) **Postal Code:** 12037.

🎒🛏 ACCOMMODATIONS AND FOOD. Budget digs are tough to find in the town proper; visitors with cars should inquire at the tourist office about B&Bs in the countryside. Otherwise, visit Saluzzo as a daytrip from Cuneo. **Hotel Përpoin ❹,** V. Spielberg 19, through a covered passage, offers spacious modern rooms with TV, phone, and bath. The restaurant serves rich and filling *piemontese* cuisine. (☎42 552; www.hotelsaluzzo.com. Breakfast included. Wheelchair-accessible. Singles €40-50; doubles €70. Extra bed €15. Pension €15 per extra meal. AmEx/MC/V.) **Albergo Persico ❹,** Vco. Mercati 10, is near P. Cavour. (☎/fax 41 213; www.albergopersico.net. Singles with breakfast €40-42; doubles €60, with breakfast €68; triples €75/85. AmEx/MC/V.) The menu changes seasonally at **Le Quattro Stagioni ❸,** V. Volta 21. Traditional dishes like *tajarin* (homemade pasta made with egg yolks; €7.50) compete with pizza (€6-9.50) for table space in the dimly lit interior. In season, peaches stuffed with chocolate and hazelnut sauce (€5) are a knockout. (☎47 470; www.ristorantele4stagioni.it. *Primi* €7.50-10, *secondi* €10-20. 3-course *menù* €17. Open M-Tu and Th-Su noon-2:30pm and 7-11pm. AmEx/MC/V.) **Hotel Përpoin's restaurant ❷,** on the ground floor, lists their affordable local fare on a chalk board transported between tables. You can't go wrong with the €12-25 *menù*. (*Primi* €4-6, *secondi* €6-8. Cover €1.50. Open M-Th and Sa-Su noon-2:30pm and 7:30-9:30pm. AmEx/MC/V.) **Albergo Persico's restaurant ❸** specializes in *piemontese* cuisine, including the *fritto misto* farmer's plate (€12) of deep-fried everything—meat, vegetables, fruit, and bread. (☎0175 41 213. *Primi* €7-9, *secondi* €9-12. Open M-Th and Sa-Su noon-2pm and 7:30-10pm. AmEx/MC/V.) **Supermercati Maxisconto** offers cheap groceries at C. Piemonte 21. (Open Jan.-June and Aug.-Dec. M-Sa 9am-7:30pm. MC/V.)

📷 SIGHTS. The **Cattedrale di Maria Assunta** lies on C. Italia. The recently restored Lombard Gothic cathedral is decorated with bright Baroque frescoes that contrast sharply with the somber exterior. (Open daily 7-11:30am and 3:30-7pm. Free.) To reach the *centro storico*, head uphill from the tourist office along Salità Castello. At the summit in P. Castello, visit **La Castiglia**, which was the town fortress and prison until the 80s. When current renovations are completed, it will be reborn as a cultural center. As you turn right on V. San Giovanni, the 48m tall **Torre Civica**, built in 1556, commands a sweeping view of the Po Valley. (☎41 455. Open daily 9:30am-12:30pm and 2:30-6:30pm. €1.30; combined ticket with Casa Cavassa €5.) The **Museo Civico** (also called the **Casa Cavassa**), V. San Giovanni 5, one of Saluzzo's most important Renaissance buildings, was once home to the politically important Cavassa family and features pieces like Hans Clemer's *Madonna della Misericordia*. (☎41 455; cavassa@comune.saluzzo.cn.it. Open Th-Su Apr.-Sept. 10am-1pm and 2-6pm; Oct.-Mar. 10am-1pm and 2-5pm. €4.) The most important building after the *duomo* is the **Chiesa di San Giovanni**, V. San Giovanni 15, that holds a rare wooden choir in the Gothic-flamboyant style sitting behind the altar. The ceiling of the adjoining chapel, accessible through the cloisters to the church's left, is decorated with frescoes representing the night sky. (Open daily 8am-noon and 3-7pm. Free.) In Piasco, 15km from Saluzzo toward Cuneo lies the **Museo dell'Arpa Victor Salvi**, V. Rossana 7, the world's first museum dedicated only to the harp. Inaugurated in 2005, the *museo* has 100 antique harps. (☎27 05 10; www.museodellarpavictorsalvi.it. Open W-Su 10am-1pm and 2-5pm. €5, under 10 and over 65 €2.50). To reach the extensive **Giardino Botanico Villa Bricherasio**, V. Giambattista Bodoni 88, follow V. Bodoni west out of the *centro*, 800m past V. Matteo Olivero. (☎41 061 or 340 80 54 313. Open Apr.-Oct. during daylight hours. €5.)

ASTI   ☎0141

Set in the hillsides of Piedmont's wine country, the provincial seat of Asti (AHS-tee; pop. 73,000) has bustled with activity since it was founded by the Romans in the AD first century. It rose to power as a trading center during the Middle Ages, becoming one of the richest cities in Italy by 1200. Asti is best known today for its wines—limestone-rich soils on gentle south-facing slopes produce grapes destined for bottles of *Barbaresco*, dark red *Barbera*, and sparkling *Asti Spumante*.

▐ TRANSPORTATION. The **train station** is in P. Marconi, where V. Cavour meets C. Luigi Einaudi. (Ticket office open daily 6am-9:30pm, or use ticket machine.) Connections to most destinations are available through Alessandria. **Trains** run to: Acqui Terme (1hr., 19 per day 6:22am-8:35pm, €3.50); Alba (40min., 20 per day 5:49am-8:34pm, €2.70); Alessandria (30min., 55 per day 12:27am-11:40pm, €2.70); Cuneo (2½hr., 5:49am, €7); Milan Centrale (2hr., 6:43 am, €7.10); Turin Porta Nuova (1hr., 53 trains, 4:32am-11:51pm, €4). **Buses** (☎43 329 or 43 34 53), in P. Medaglie d'Oro, to the right when exiting the train station, are run by various carriers and run to: Canelli (every 2hr. 7:20am-7:10pm); Castagnole (every 2hr. 7:20am-6:40pm); Costigliole (9 per day 7:15am-6:50pm); Isola d'Asti (6 per day 10am-6:50pm). Buy tickets (€1.60-2.20) onboard or at *tabaccherie*. **Taxis** are in P. Alfieri (☎53 26 05) or at the train station (☎59 27 22).

▐▌ ORIENTATION AND PRACTICAL INFORMATION. The *centro* lies in the triangular **Piazza Alfieri**. From the station, go up **Via Cavour** through **Piazzetta San Paolo, Piazza Statuto,** and **Piazza San Secondo,** then right on **Via Garibaldi.** Most sights are along **Corso Vittorio Alfieri**, the major east-west road, connecting with the top of P. Alfieri. Between P. Alfieri and the train station sits **Piazza Campo del Palio,** now used for parking and weekly markets. The ATL **tourist office**, P. Alfieri 29, provides maps and valuable info on wine cellars. (☎53 03 57 or for tours 32 09 78; www.asti-turismo.it. Open M-Sa 9am-1pm and 2:30-6:30pm, Su 9am-1pm.) **Currency exchange**

is available at banks along C. Vittorio Alfieri and V. Dante. There are **ATMs** in the train station and on V. Dante, or at **Banca Popolare di Lodi** in P. Alfieri 15. (Open M-F 8:20am-1:20pm and 2:30-4pm.) **Libreria Mondadori,** C. Alfieri 324, has a selection of English books. (Open in summer M 3:30-7:30pm, Tu-Sa 9:30am-noon and 3:30-7:30pm; in winter hours vary.) In an **emergency,** call the **police,** C. XXV Aprile 19 (☎41 81 11). **Farmacia Alfieri** is at P. Alfieri 3. (☎59 46 05 or 35 43 05. Open daily 8:30am-12:30pm and 3:30-7:30pm. Closes 1 month in summer.) The **post office,** C. Dante 55, is at the intersection of P. Alfieri and V. Verdi. (☎35 72 51. Open M-F 8:30am-7pm, Sa 8:30am-1pm.) **Postal Code:** 14100.

** r ACCOMMODATIONS.** For a better value, those with cars should consider a B&B or *agriturismo* in the scenic wine country just outside of Asti. Ask at the tourist office for more info. Just across from the train station, **Hotel Cavour ❹,** P. Marconi 18, has clean, modern rooms with large bath, TV, Internet access, thick blinds, and phone; most also have A/C. (☎/fax 53 02 22; www.hotelcavour-asti.com. Breakfast included. Free parking. Reception 6am-1am. Singles €45-50; doubles €65-73; triples €85. AmEx/MC/V.) To get to **Hotel Genova ❸,** C. Alessandria 26. cross P. Marconi, in front of the train station, and turn right on C. L. Einaudi. Stay alongside P. Campo as it curves left. Turn right on C. Galileo Ferraris and then left on C. Pietro Chiesa. As you come to P. Maggio, make a right onto C. Alessandria. This simple, homey establishment offers rooms with TV, sink, and towels. (☎59 31 97. Reception 6:30am-11pm. Call ahead if arriving on Su. Singles €32-42; doubles €52, with bath €65. AmEx/D/MC/V.) To reach **Campeggio Umberto Cagni ❶,** Località Valmanera 152, 4km from P. Alfieri, turn on V. Aro, which becomes C. Volta; then turn left on V. Valmanera. Or, take bus #5 from P. Alfieri or the bus station. (☎27 12 38. Open Apr.-Sept. €4.50 per person, €4 per tent, €3.50 per car, €7 per RV; bungalows €30-35. Electricity €2.50. Showers free. Cash only.)

◻ FOOD. *Astigiana* cuisine is known for its reliance on a few crucial ingredients, especially gorgonzola and other pungent cheeses. *Coniglio* (rabbit), *cinghiale* (wild boar), truffles, and mountain herbs make up classic *piemontese* dishes. Restaurant cellars are stocked with Asti's local wines, including the sparkling white *Moscato*. Local vineyards also produce *grappa*, a strong grape liqueur. The dining room of **◪Ristorante Tacabanda/L'Osteria della Barbera ❸,** V. al Teatro 5, off P. San Secondo, is set in an underground brick basement. In this candlelit setting, waiters double as wine experts and serve the surprisingly savory *agnolotti di asino* (ravioli stuffed with donkey meat; €8.50) along with other delicious cuisine in heaping portions. The **◪lunch menù,** which includes is a *primo, secondo,* glass of wine, and a glass of water, is a great deal. (☎53 09 99. *Primi* €7.50-8.50, *secondi* €8.50-12.50. Lunch *menù* €11. Open Tu-Su noon-2:30pm and 8pm-midnight. AmEx/MC/V.) The family-owned **Ristorante La Vecchia Carrozza ❸,** V. Carducci 41, serves home-style food beneath arched brick ceilings in a quiet back room. (☎/fax 53 86 57. *Primi* €6-10, *secondi* €8-13. Open Tu-Su noon-3pm and 8pm-midnight. AmEx/D/MC/V.) An unadvertised entrance and quiet dining rooms create an intimate setting at **L'Angolo del Beato ❹,** V. Guttuari 12, off V. Cavour. (☎/fax 53 16 68. *Antipasto* €7.50. *Primi* €9-11, *secondi* €13-15. Cover €1.50. Open M-Sa noon-2pm and 7:30-10:30pm. AmEx/MC/V.) Chef Francese of **Pizzeria Francese ❷,** V. dei Cappellai 15, off P. San Secondo, knows his pizza—he's even written a 692-page guide to the best pizzerias in Italy. Try the special *pizza di tartufo* (€20-25) in winter. (☎59 23 21; www.pizzerie-italia.it. Pizza from €5.50. *Primi* and *secondi* €7-9. Cover €1.50. Open in summer daily noon-3pm and 6pm-1am; in winter closed W. Closed mid-Aug. AmEx/MC/V.) While other restaurants close for their midday rest, **Al Volo Food in motion ❶,** C. Vittorio Alfieri 335, has pizza, *primi,* and *secondi* all under €4. (☎13 02 71. Open M-Th 10:30am-10:30pm, F-Sa 10:30am-midnight, and Su 3-10:30pm.) An extensive fruit and vegetable **market** is at P. Campo del Palio and P. Alfieri. (Open W and Sa 7:30am-1pm. Clothing booths open until sunset.) The **Di per Di** supermarket, P. Alfieri 26, has low prices and a wide selection. A second location is on V. Bruno, off P. S. Secondo. (☎34 759. Open M-Tu, Th-F, and Su 8:30am-1pm and 3:30-7:45pm, W and Sa 8:30am-7:45pm. D/MC/V.)

🟦 **SIGHTS.** Walk down C. V. Alfieri and turn right at P. Carioli to reach the town's **cattedrale.** The 14th-century cathedral is a noteworthy example of the *piemontese* Gothic style. Its *piazza* entrance is decorated by statues of monks and priests. In the 11th century, artists blanketed the floor around the altar with mosaics, while in the 16th and 17th centuries, local artists covered every inch of the walls with frescoes. (☎59 29 24. Open daily 8:30am-noon and 3-5:30pm. Free.) On the far end of C. V. Alfieri, the 15th-century **Chiesa di San Pietro in Consavia** served as an army hospital in WWII. Beside the *chiesa* is the 12th-century octagonal baptistry. On the 1st floor of the *chiesa*, the **Museo Paleontologico** has a small collection of fossils and bones from the *astiano* area. On the 2nd floor, the **Museo Archeologico** showcases 4th-century BC Greek vases and jugs. (☎43 74 54. Museums open in summer Tu-F 9am-1pm and 4-7pm, Sa 10am-1pm and 3-6pm, Su 10am-1pm; in winter Tu-F 3-6pm, Sa 10am-1pm and 3-6pm, Su 10am-1pm.) From P. Alfieri, a short walk west on V. Garibaldi leads to **Piazza San Secondo,** home of the 18th-century **Palazzo di Città** and the Romanesque-Gothic **Chiesa Collegiata di San Secondo,** the latter built in the 14th century in honor of Asti's patron saint. The 1st chapel holds colorful banners from Palio festivals of the past. Statues of San Secondo represent him holding a sword in one hand and the city of Asti in the other. (☎53 00 66. Open M-Sa 8:30am-noon and 3:30-5:30pm, Su 3:30-5:30pm.) During the city's medieval prominence, feuding nobles constructed brick towers to flout their wealth. In the 13th century, the city was famed for its more than 100 **towers,** but now only 30 or so remain, many of them crumbling. The city symbol, the **Torre Troyana,** in P. Medici, was built in the 13th and 14th centuries. (☎39 94 60 or 43 74 54. Open Sa-Su Apr.-Oct. 10am-1pm and 4-7pm; Nov. 10am-1pm and 3-6pm. €1.50.) The 16-sided **Torre Rossa** in P. Santa Caterina, at the western end of C. V. Alfieri, is much older, with foundations dating to end of the 1st century BC. Connected to the tower is the elliptical Baroque **Chiesa di Santa Caterina.** (Open daily 7:30am-noon and 3-7pm.) The **Giardini Pubblici,** between P. Alfieri and P. Campo del Palio, are great for a picnic or stroll. On the edge of the city, the **Tapestry Museum Scassa,** V. dell'Arazzeria 60, is located in the **Antica Certosa di Valmanera** (Ancient Monastery of Valmanera) and features impressive modern tapestries and designs made using ancient looms. (☎27 13 52; ugscasa@tin.it. Guided tours with reservation.)

🟦 **ENTERTAINMENT.** In the 2nd and 3rd week of September, agricultural Asti revels in the **Douja d'Or** (www.doujador.it), a 10-day local wine fair, with competitions and tastings. Also during the 2nd weekend in September, the **Paisan,** or the **Festivale delle Sagre,** brings 45 towns from the province to the city to serve their traditional dishes around the P. Campo del Palio. This culinary exhibition unfolds with an accompaniment of 19th-century costumes, and parades. On the 3rd Sunday in September, the Douja d'Or ends with the **Palio di Asti.** Asti's *palio* starts with a procession commemorating the town's liberation in 1200, followed by Italy's oldest bareback horse race that dates back to 1275. Each jockey represents a quarter of the city, and the winner takes a banner with the city's coat of arms and patron saint. **Asti Teatro,** a series of theatrical performances, is held in **Teatro Alfieri,** V. al Teatro 2, from June through July. (☎39 90 32; www.astiteatro.it. Reserve tickets in advance. Some events are free, others cost €15.) Throughout July, the **Asti Musica** (☎39 93 99) showcases bands in P. Cattedrale for dancing crowds every (nightly starting at 10pm; tickets range from free to €25). Other than at annual festivals, the only place to hear live music in Asti is at **Diavolo Rosso**, P. San Martino 4. Ironically named considering that it is housed in a deconsecrated church, the building serves as a community center and political forum during the day before hosting concerts at night. (☎35 56 99; www.diavolorosso.it. Mixed drinks €4. Wine €2. Open Th-Su 7:30pm-2am. Closed during most of July and Aug.)

CANELLI   ☎0141

The sparkling *Asti Spumante* and super-sweet *Moscato* bubble forth from the countryside vineyards surrounding Canelli (ca-NEH-lee; pop. 11,000), providing both an economic base and a source of worldwide renown. Though wine has flowed from the verdant, vineyard-striped hills since Roman times, the first Italian sparkling wine matured in the Gancia family winery just 150 years ago. The region's long-standing wine-making tradition has created kilometers of vaulted underground tunnels used as wine cellars. The "underground cathedral," as the interconnected brick cellars are known, may soon earn designation as a UNESCO World Heritage site; the distinction would provide enough money to finish the tunnels, enabling one to walk underground from one end of the city to the other.

At **Cantine Gancia**, C. Libertà 66, tour the wine-bottling facilities, the cellar, and the museum of the Gancia family's wine-making business. The factory has come a long way since Carlo Gancia invented the classic method of creating sparkling wine from Moscato grapes through in-bottle refermentation; while in the past all was done by hand, today, a machine slowly turns the bottles for 70 days to sift the sediments against the cork. Gancia's annual production is now 30 million bottles a year, making the modern facility Italy's biggest producer of sparkling wine. (☎83 02 53; www.gancia.it. Open daily 9am-6pm, but hours vary. Free 30min. guided tour in English; reservations required. Wine tasting free. Wine from €4 per bottle.) Afterward, head to the neighboring 9th-century cellar of **Enoteca Regionale di Canelli e dell'Astesana**, C. Libertà 65/A, located under a palace, for a taste of Canelli's finest wines, most notably the *Moscato d'Asti*, *Barbera d'Asti*, and *Dolcetto d'Asti*. (☎83 21 82; enotecacanelli@inwind.it. Open Th-F 5pm-midnight, Sa-Su 11am-1pm and 5pm-midnight. Tastings after 8pm.) On the 3rd Saturday of June, over 2000 townspeople in medieval garb reenact the **Siege of Canelli**, a 1613 battle. Entrance is free, but obtain a pass from military authorities at the gate, or risk being thrown in the stocks. Inn-keepers and restaurants participate by serving 17th-century feasts (€8-21). A **market** held every Tuesday features over 100 stalls, with goods in P. Gancia, produce in P. Gioberti, and other foods in P. Zoppa. A small market is held on Fridays. On the 2nd Sunday of November, Canelli holds its annual **Fiera Regionale di Tortufo**, a truffle fair with roots back to the 14th century.

Trains run to Asti (6:45am-7:57pm, €3) via Castagnole. **Buses** run from Canelli to the bus station in Asti (30min., every 1½hr. 6:05am-6:15pm, €2.50). The **tourist office** is at V. Roma 37. (☎82 01 11; www.comune.canelli.at.it. Open M, W, F 8:30am-12:30pm, Tu and Th 8:30am-12:30pm and 3-5pm. Hours subject to change; call ahead.) **Banca Popolare di Novara**, V. Roma 1, has an **ATM**. (Open M-F 8:20am-1:20pm and 2:35-3:35pm, Sa 8:20-11:50am.) A **pharmacy, Bielli Dott. Renata Farmacia**, V. XX Settembre 1 (☎82 34 46), is in the *centro*.

ACQUI TERME   ☎0144

Steaming-hot fountains, brick archways, and aqueduct ruins have drawn luxury-seeking vacationers to Acqui Terme's (AH-kwee TEHR-meh) healing waters and mud baths since Roman times when the town was known as "Aquae Statiellae." Sulfuric springs at temperatures of 75°C (167°F) gurgle beneath the ground in P. della Bollente and across the Bormida River in the private Lago delle Sorgenti.

🖪🗷 TRANSPORTATION AND PRACTICAL INFORMATION. The **train station** (☎89 20 21) is in P. Vittorio Veneto. (Ticket booth open M-F 6am-7:30pm, Sa-Su 6am-12:35pm and 1-7:30pm.) **Trains** run to: Alessandria (43min., 23 trains per day 5:35am-8pm, €2.70); Asti (1hr., 17 trains per day 5:15am-7:50pm, €3.50); Genoa (1½hr., 51 per day 5:18am-8:55pm, €3-3.50); Savona (1½hr., 13 trains per day 6am-8:08pm, €4.80). **Buses** also run daily to Turin (€10) and Milan (€11.50). **Taxis** wait at the station (☎32 32 80 or 32 20 40). To reach town from the station, turn left on **Via Alessandria**, which becomes C. Vigano and ends in **Piazza Italia**. From here, view most sights by taking **Corso Italia**, which follows an ancient riverbed.

To reach the **IAT tourist office**, V. Manzoni 34, follow Corso Italia and make a right on V. Saracco until reaching P. della Bollente from where V. Manzoni stems. The office rents **bikes** and provides info on itineraries for the city and surrounding region. (☎32 21 42; www.comuneacqui.com. Bikes €3 per ½-day, €5 per day. Open M-Sa 9:30am-12:30pm and 3:30-6:30pm, Su 10am-1pm. Closed Su Jan.-Feb.) **Banks** line C. Dante, including **Unicredit Banca**, C. Dante 26, with a branch in P. Italia, both with **ATMs** and **currency exchange.** (Open M-F 8:20am-1:20pm and 2:30-4pm, Sa 8:20am-12:45pm.) The **public library,** located on V. Maggiorino Ferraris, off V. Crenna, offers **Internet** access. (☎77 02 67. Open in summer M and Th 8:30am-1:30pm and 4-6pm, Tu-W and F 8:30am-1pm, Sa 9am-noon; in winter M and Th 2:30-6pm, Tu-W and F 8:30am-12:30pm, Sa 9am-noon.) In an **emergency,** call the **carabinieri** (☎32 33 59). A **pharmacy** is at P. Italia 2. (Open M-F and Su 8:45am-12:30pm and 3-6:45pm. MC/V.) The **hospital, Ospedale Civile,** is located at V. Fatebenefratelli 1 (☎77 71). **Internet** is available at **Internet Cafe Balalah,** on V. Giacomo Bove off V. Garibaldi. (☎32 54 19. Open Tu-Sa 7:30am-9pm, Su 3-9pm.) Take V. XX Settembre from P. Italia through P. Matteotti to the **post office,** V. Trucco 27. (☎38 21 11. Open M-F 8am-7pm, Sa 9am-12:30pm.) **Postal Code:** 15011.

🖪 ACCOMMODATIONS. Reserve in advance during the 2nd half of August and much of September, when hotel rooms are booked by those looking to be soothed by the thermal waters. Many hotels, budget and otherwise, line Vle. Einaudi behind the station and across the Ponte Carlo Alberto. For an affordable, centrally located hotel, head to 🖫**Albergo San Marco ❸,** V. Ghione 5. From P. Italia, take C. Bagni and make the 1st right on V. Ghione. Eighteen comfortable and spacious rooms with TV are well-kept by a welcoming staff. A restaurant is downstairs. (☎32 24 56; fax 35 64 65. Half pension and full pension available. Free parking. Closed Dec. 24-Feb. 1 and mid-July. Singles €30-35; doubles €55. Cash only.) **Albergo San Marco's restaurant ❷** serves some of the best home-cooked meals and stocks some of the best wine in town. Dishes are so fresh that there is no written menu. Try the house specialty, a crepe-like flatbread that is stuffed with tasty delights such as truffles and cheese. (*Primi* €5-6.50, *secondi* €6.50-9. Open Tu-Su noon-2pm and 7:30-10pm.) **Villa Glicinia ❸,** Vle. Einaudi 11, is a quiet and enormous accommodation outside of town, near the Centro Fitness Regina. The non-English-speaking management offers a homey living room and well-maintained guest rooms with large bathrooms and antique furniture. (☎32 28 74. Breakfast €3-5. Half and full pension available. Open May-Oct. Singles €35-38; doubles €48-49. Extra bed €12.50. Cash only.)

🖪 FOOD. Acqui Terme offers a wide selection of excellent, well-priced restaurants, serving traditional Roman fare and lining the consequently fragrant V. Mazzini. At the 🖫**Enoteca Regionale Acqui "Terme e Vino" ❷,** P. Levi 7, off V. Garibaldi, choose from over 230 types of wine, including the local, sweet specialties of *Dolcetto* and *Bracchetto*, from the shelves along the cavernous brick walls. (☎77 02 73. Open Tu and Th-Sa 9:30am-1pm and 3:30-7pm, Su 10am-1pm and 4-7pm. MC/V.) For fine dining, take C. Dante from P. Italia across V. Mariscotti to reach the white awnings of **Il Nuovo Ciarlocco ❸**, V. Don Bosco 1. Courteous service accompanies a high-quality, daily-rotating fish and meat menu. (☎57 720. *Primi* €7-8, *secondi* €9-17. Cover €2.50. Open M and Th-Su noon-2pm and 7:30-10pm, Tu noon-2pm. AmEx/MC/V.) At **Antica Osteria da Bigat ❶**, V. Mazzini 30/32, a town fixture since 1885, the crisp *farinata* (chickpea-flour pancake; €3.70) tempt hungry patrons. (☎32 42 83. Pizza €3-4. *Primi* and *secondi* €6.50-8. Open M and Th-Su noon-2pm and 5-9pm, Tu noon-2pm. Closed last 2wk. of Feb. and July. MC/V.) **Il Sarto ❷**, C. Italia 47, serves food all day long and also provides the town's only significant nightlife option. The trendy leather couches and modern glass tables provide seating for drinking either beer (€6) or tea. (☎32 27 65; www.ilsarto.eu. Open M-Tu and Th 8am-2am, F-Su 8am-3am. AmEx/MC/V.) The **Di per Di** supermarket, V. Garibaldi 50, sells groceries. (Open M-Tu and Th-Sa 8:30am-12:30pm and 3:45-7:45pm, W 8:30am-12:30pm, Su 9am-12:30pm. AmEx/MC/V.) Every Tuesday and Friday morning from 8:30am-1pm, a **market** fills the *centro storico* around P. Addolorata, C. Italia, and P. Ferraris. During the same time, vendors hawk fruit, vegetables, cheese, and fish in P. Orfo San Pietro and P. San Franceso. An **antique market** is held on the 4th Sunday of each month along C. Bagni (9am-7pm).

◪ SIGHTS. Down V. Garibaldi, P. Addolorata is home to the 11th-century restored Romanesque **Basilica di SS. Pietro e Addolorata,** with its floor at the same level that the land was during its 5th-century construction (☎32 27 91. Open daily 7am-noon and 3-6pm.) From P. Bollente, take V. Bollente across town and up a short hill to P. Duomo, where the **Cattedrale di San Guido** (1067) holds the famous 15th-century triptych of *Madonna our Lady of Montserrat* by Bartolomeo Bermejo in its **sacristy.** In the late 18th century, the masterpiece was spared by Napoleon's troops because the triptych was closed at the time, hiding its intricate interior. Look closely—the Madonna is seated on a sword blade. (Cathedral open daily 7am-noon and 3:30-6pm. Sacristy open daily 4-6pm. Ask church caretaker at the sacristy to view the triptych. Free.) Up V. Barone from the *duomo*, the 11th-century **Castello dei Paleologi,** V. Morelli 2, houses the **Museo Civico Archeologico.** The museum displays a small but evocative collection of Roman tombs and mosaics. (☎57 555; www.acquimusei.it/archeo. Open W-Sa 9:30am-12:30pm and 3:30-6:30pm, Su 3:30-6:30pm. €5, ages 18-25 €3, under 18 or over 65 free.)

No trip to Acqui is complete without at least dipping a toe in the steamy sulfuric water. Beneath the marble chapel in **Piazza Bollente** (from C. Italia, enter through the Torre Civica), hot sulfuric water streams out of a fountain, sending up visible steam even in summer. To see where four arches of the **Roman Aqueduct** overlook the banks of the Bormida River, exit P. Italia, part of Pisterna's medieval *centro*, by taking C. Bagni through Borgonuova. Though the Roman public baths are gone, you can still see the ruins along C. Bagni. (Open Sa-Su 3:30-5:30pm) The **Grand Hotel Nuove Terme,** P. Italia 1, has a spa right near the town center which offers thermal baths (sulfur content is weak, but detectable) and a Turkish bath, among other services. (€13; hair net, robe, and locker €10.) The **Terme Regina,** V. Donati 2, in the *zona bagni*, offers many options for pampering, as well as serious alternative medicine. A dip in the **sulfuric pool** with hydro massage runs as little as €18 per day. (☎32 90 74; www.reginaterme.com. Open M-F 10am-9pm, Sa-Su 10am-6pm. Make an appointment.) To bathe in non-sulfuric water, head down the street to one of the largest pools, **Piscine di Acqui Terme,** equipped with trampolines, a bar, and a beach volleyball court. (☎32 20 65. Open June-Sept. daily 9am-6:30pm. €6.50-8.50, depending on day of the week.) Next door to the Museo Civico Archeologico, off P. della Conciliazione, the outdoor **Teatro Estivo Giuseppe Verdi** hosts performances in summer, including the **Acqui in Palcoscenico** international dance festival in July and early August. (Contact tourist office for info and schedules. Some events free; others €15, students €10.)

VALLE D'AOSTA

Stunning peaks, pine forests, waterfalls, and tiny villages color Italy's least-populated and most-elevated region, Valle d'Aosta (VA-leh da-OS-ta). The valley is a key transportation hub; Hannibal and his elephants once crossed Aosta's St. Bernard Pass, and today an even greater stampede of heavy-goods vehicles barrels through the Monte Bianco tunnel. Some locals fear that Aosta's new status as a trade gateway may damage the natural splendor and destabilize the tourist economy. Before the tractor trailers and even before the skiers, Aosta first welcomed elites seeking its hot springs and alpine air. Living so close to their Swiss and French neighbors, *valdostani* have taken on much of their continental cousins' cultural character, evident at intersections of a *via* with a *rue* or *strasse*. Though not the Italy of the popular imagination, Valle d'Aosta's unique setting and culture, its relative seclusion from the masses, and the stunning Alps make it a perfect destination who want to taste some Alpine glory.

◪ HIKING

The scenic trails of Valle d'Aosta are a hiker's paradise. The best times to hike are July, August, and the 1st week of September, when much of the snow has melted and the public buses run frequently. In April and May, thawing snow can cause avalanches. Monte Bianco and surrounding peaks may be classic climbs, but only pros should attempt them. Because of the snow, spring hiking should only take place below 1000m. Each area's tourist office or Alpine guide office assists hikers of all levels with suggested itineraries and info on weather and trail conditions. Offices in Aosta and in the smaller valleys also provide details on campgrounds, *pranzo al sacco* (bagged lunches), *rifugi alpini* (mountain refuges or chalets overseen by a proprietor, which offer filling meals and dorm rooms to hikers; €15-20 per night, half pension €35-40), and *bivacchi* (empty public huts)—ask for *Mountain Huts and Bivouacs in Aosta Valley*, which offers a list of accommodations and prices of hiking-friendly regions. For information, call the guide societies in the appropriate valleys or the tourist office. They offer insurance and *rifugi* discounts. For explorations on foot, most regional tourist offices also carry the booklet *Alta Vie* (High Roads), with maps, photographs, hiking recommendations, and helpful advice pertaining to the two serpentine mountain trails that wind around the valley and link the region's most dramatic peaks. These trails require no expertise, but still offer adventure and beautiful panoramas. Beginning in Cogne, **Parco Nazionale del Gran Paradiso** is also nearby. This park, replete with *rifugi*, is paradise for any outdoor enthusiast. Its endless hiking, skiing, and climbing possibilities could even serve as an entire vacation on their own.

◿ SKIING

Skiing Valle d'Aosta's mountains and glaciers is a fantastic experience; unfortunately, doing so is not a bargain. One-week **Settimane Bianche** (White Weeks) packages for skiers are one source of discounts. For info and prices, call the **Aosta Ufficio Informazioni Turistiche** (☎23 66 27; www.regione.vda.it/turismo) or go to the AIAT Aosta office, P. Chanoux 45 (☎0165 33 352; www.aiataosta.com), and request the pamphlet *White Weeks: Aosta Valley*, detailing skiing packages (from €168-210), hotels, prices, and tourist office info. Or contact the tourist offices of the ski resorts directly: **Courmayeur** (☎0165 84 20 60; www.aiat-monte-bianco.com) and **Breuil-Cervinia** (☎0166 94 91 36; www.montecervino.it) are the best-known ski resorts in the 11 valleys, though **Val d'Ayas** (☎0125 30 71 13; www.aiatmonte-

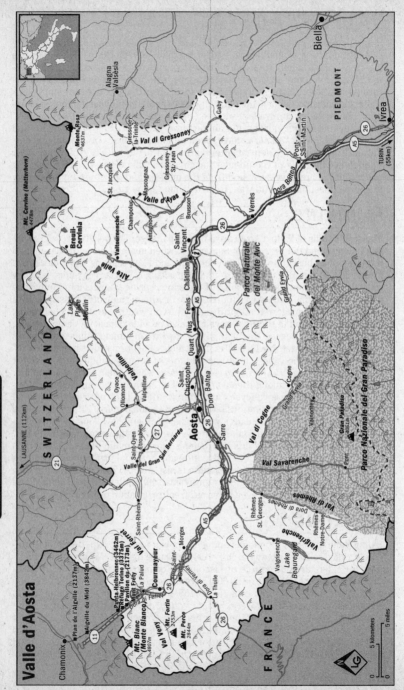

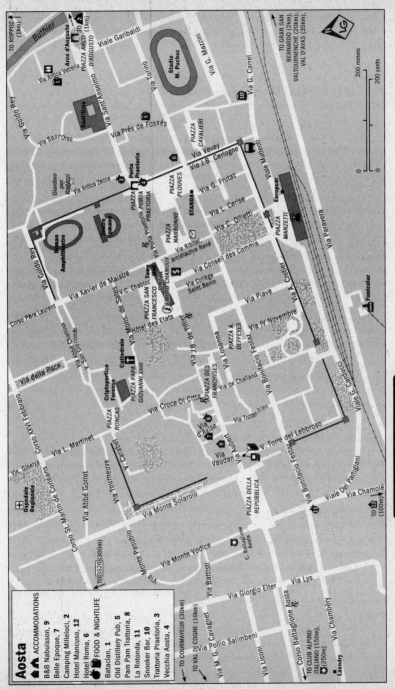

Aosta

PIEDMONT AND
VALLE D'AOSTA

rosa.com) and **Val di Gressoney** (☎0125 35 51 85; www.aiatmonterosawalser.it) offer equally challenging terrain for lower rates with a joint pass. **Cogne** (☎0165 74 040; www.cogne.org) and **Brusson** (☎0125 30 02 40), halfway down Val d'Ayas, have cross-country skiing and less demanding trails. Pick up descriptions and maps of all resorts at most tourist offices in the region.

⚠ OUTDOOR SPORTS

A host of other sports—rock climbing, biking, hang-gliding, hydrospeeding, and rafting—will keep your adrenaline pumping in the valleys. Rafting and other water expeditions are available from many companies. For a full list, contact the tourist office. One unique program put on by **Rafting: Morgex & Valsesia** (☎0165 80 00 88) offers 8km of rafting from 3-6pm, then gives access to the thermal baths until the 10pm closing. (☎1065 86 72 72; www.termedipre.it. June-Sept M-F €49-72.) Run by a band of Argentine brothers, **Rafting Adventure,** Località Perole, to the right off the A5 "Chatillon" exit, is a small, friendly business, which offers rafting, hydrospeeding, canyoning, and kayaking. (☎346 30 90 856; www.raftingadventure.com. Guides available in English, French, and Spanish upon request. Reservations recommended. Open May-Sept. M-Su 9am-7pm. Rafting packages from €40 for 2hr.; kayaking and hydrospeeding from €50; canyoning from €60. Cash only.) On the road to Cogne, **Grand Paradis Emotions,** in Aymavilles, also offers rafting, kayaking, and canyoning. (☎0165 90 06 05; www.gpemotion.com. Call ahead to reserve. Open June-Sept. daily 9am-6:30pm. Packages for rafting or hydrospeeding €40, canyoning €60. Cash only.) The **Società delle Guide** in most cities around the valley arranges ice- and rock-climbing lessons and excursions, as well as mountain biking trips. Ask a local tourist office for a complete list of recreational activities. Near the Aosta airport, **Club Aerostatique Mont Blanc** flys hot air balloons up to over the Alps. (☎339 85 26 950. 1hr. flight €180 per person. Flights to France or Switzerland €500. Call ahead to reserve.) Take the ⛰funicular (20-30min.) at the **Pila Ski Resort** for amazing mountain biking. One trail even runs from the top of Pila's lift all the way to Aosta, a descent of over 1000m! (☎0165 52 10 45 or 0165 52 10 55; www.pila.it. Chairlift pass €10.50 per half-day, €15.50 per day.)

AOSTA   ☎0165

Aosta (ah-OS-ta; pop. 37,000) walks the line between Italian and French *valdostana* cultures. For many years, Aosta was ancient Rome's launching point for military expeditions, resulting in impressive ruins throughout the town. Inside the walls that once defended Rome's Alpine outpost, boutiques and food shops now pack the *centro storico*. Even in the crowded *centro*, however, you can admire the imposing Alps. From the city, many valleys, perfect for hiking, are nearby.

▐ TRANSPORTATION

Trains: In P. Manzetti. Ticket window open M-Th 7:20am-2pm and 2:15-5:25pm, F-Sa 6:15am-7:40pm, Su 11:30am-6:10pm. MC/V.) Trains run to: **Turin** (3hr., 14 per day 5:10am-9:41pm, €7.10) via **Châtillon** (20min., €2); **Chivasso** (2hr., 5 trains per day, €4); **Ivrea** (1hr., 5 per day 6:12am-5:12pm, €4); **Milan Centrale** via **Chivasso** (4½hr., 12 per day 6:12am-8:40pm, €10.50); **Pré-Saint-Didier** (1hr., 14 per day 6:41am-7:46pm, €2.50); **Verrès** (30min., €2.70).

Buses: SAVDA (☎26 20 27; www.savda.it), on V. Carrel off P. Manzetti, to the right exiting the train station. Office open daily 6:40am-7:20pm. Tickets also available on bus. To: **Chamonix** (1¾hr., 6 per day 8:15am-4:45pm, €13); **Châtillon** (30min.; 5:30am, 1:35, 3:15, 5:40 and 8pm; €2.20); **Courmayeur** (1hr., every hr. 6:45am-9:45pm, €3);

Great St. Bernard Pass (1hr., in summer 2 per day, €3); **Turin** (2-3 per day, €7.70). Regional buses serve **Cogne** (1hr., 7 per day 8:05am-7:45pm, €2.50) and **Fenis** (1hr.; 12 per day 6:20am-8pm, reduced service Su; €2). Buses also leave from the Châtillon train station for **Breuil-Cervinia** (2hr., 7 per day 6:10am-7:25pm, €3.25) and **Valtournenche** (30min., 4 per day 9:30am-7:30pm). Local buses are orange and are operated by **SVAP** (www.svap.it). Tickets can be purchased onboard.

> **CONNECTION PERFECTION.** Aosta makes a good starting point for exploring the Italian Alps, but be aware that daytrips to surrounding valleys often require tricky train and bus connections, so plan carefully.

Taxis: P. Manzetti (☎36 36 23 or 31 831).

Car Rental: Europcar, P. Manzetti 3 (☎41 432), to the left of the train station. 18+. Limited insurance. Usually only manual cars available. Open M-F 8:30am-12:30pm and 3-7pm, Sa 8:30am-12:30am. AmEx/MC/V.

Bike and Ski Rental: Gal Sport Shop, V. Paravera 6/B, 3rd fl. (☎23 61 34; shop@gal-sport.com), past the funicular base station. Offers bike rentals and sells equipment. Mountain bikes €6 per hr., €8 per 2hr., €12 per half day, €18 per full day. Bike rentals include helmet. Ski rental available during the winter season. 1 day €20, 6 days €78, €8 per additional day. Rental prices include boots, skis, and poles.Open M-Sa 9am-12:30pm and 3-7pm. D/MC/V.

✳ 🛈 ORIENTATION AND PRACTICAL INFORMATION

Trains stop at **Piazza Manzetti**. From there, take **Avenue du Conseil des Commis** past the ruins of the Roman wall until it ends in the enormous **Piazza Chanoux,** Aosta's *centro*. The main street runs east-west through P. Chanoux and changes its name several times: Ave. du Conseil des Commis, **Via de Tillier,** (which eventually becomes **Via Aubert**) is to the left; to the right, **Via Porta Praetoria** leads to the historical gate, **Porta Praetoria** (and becomes **Via Sant'Anselmo**).

Tourist Office: P. Chanoux 2 (☎23 66 27; www.aiataosta.com), down Ave. du Conseil des Commis from train station. Provides town maps, maps of the valley, accommodations booking, and art guides. English spoken. Open July-Sept. daily 9am-1pm and 2:30-8pm; Oct.-June M-Sa 9:30am-1pm and 3-6:30pm, Su 9am-1pm. **Branch:** P. Arco d'Augusto, across from the Roman arch, offering info only on the city of Aosta itself. In winter, a tourist office opens in **Pila,** at 11020 Gressan, near the top of the funicular.

Alpine Information: Club Alpino Italiano, C. Battaglione Aosta 81, 3rd fl. (☎/fax 40 194; www.caivda.it), off P. della Repubblica. Info from Alpine climbing pros. Open Tu 7-8:30pm, F 8-10pm. **Interguide,** V. Monte Emilius 13 (☎ 40 939; www.interguide.it).

Tours: Associazione Guide Turistiche (☎338 69 51 558; www.guideturistichevaldostane.it) Guided group tours.

Currency Exchange: Monte dei Paschi di Siena, P. Chanoux 51 (☎27 68 88). **ATM** outside. Open M-F 8:30am-1:30pm and 2:40-4:10pm. Another ATM at post office.

Laundromat: Onda Blu, V. Chambéry 60. Wash €3.50 per 6.5kg, dry €3.50. Detergent €1, softener €0.50. Snack machines on premises. Open daily 8am-10pm.

Police: at C. Battaglione Aosta.

Pharmacy: Farmacia Chenal, V. Croix-de-Ville 1 (☎26 21 33), near V. Aubert. Posts after-hours rotations. Open M-F 9am-12:30pm and 3-7:30pm. MC/V. **Farmacia Comunale No. 1,** C. Battaglione Aosta 59 (☎26 23 16). Open M-Sa 9am-12:30pm and 3-7:30pm. Cash only.

Hospital: Vle. Ginevra 3 (☎54 31 or 54 32 45).

Internet Access: Snooker Bar (p. 195). Also at **Public Library,** V. Torre del Lebroso 2 (☎27 48 43) Reserve ahead. Open M 2-7pm, Tu-Sa 9am-7pm. **Aosta Web Service**

Internet Point (☎06 00 15), at the corner of C. Padre Lorenzo and C. XXVI Febbraio. Open M-Sa 9am-10pm and Su 2-10pm.

Post Office: P. Narbonne 1a (☎44 138), in the huge semi-circular building. Open M-F 8am-6:30pm, Sa 8am-1pm. **Postal Code:** 11100.

ACCOMMODATIONS

Prices vary seasonally in Aosta. Prices are lowest from January to April and from October to mid-December, and highest during the first three weeks of August and around Christmas. The Valle d'Aosta Pass, managed by the Association of Hoteliers of Aosta Valley, allows you to book hotels online or by phone for free with at least 2 days advance notice. (☎23 00 15; www.valledaostapass.com.)

Bed & Breakfast Nabuisson, V. Aubert 50 (☎36 30 06 or 339 60 90 332; www.bedbreakfastaosta.it). In a building through the iron gate under the arch between the *tabaccheria* and *libreria*. Near the *centro*. 3 large, rustic-themed rooms have wooden floors, antique furniture, TV, and bath; 1 with kitchen. Breakfast €4. Reservations recommended. Singles €45-55; doubles €50-65. Extra bed €10-15. Cash only. ❹

Hotel Mancuso, V. Voison 32 (☎34 526 or 320 757 37 75; www.albergomancuso.com). 15min. walk from P. Chanou. Affordable, clean rooms have great views, bathroom, TV, and hair dryer; some with balcony. Free parking. Singles €30-40; doubles €38-48; triple €55-60; quad €65-70. *Let's Go* discount 10%. ❷

Belle Epoque, V. d'Avise 18 (☎26 22 76; fax 26 11 56). Central location and affordable price partially compensate for small and spartan rooms. Breakfast €6.50. Singles €22-26; doubles €50-60; triples €65-85. MC/V. ❸

Hotel Roma, V. Torino 7 (☎41 000; hroma@libero.it), close to the train station and the *centro*, around the corner from Hotel Turin (enter off Rue Vevey). Recently renovated rooms; all have bath, phone, and TV. Breakfast €6. Parking €6. Singles €40-54; doubles €68-76. Extra bed 30% surcharge. AmEx/MC/V. ❹

Camping Milleluci, Località Roppoz 15 (☎23 52 78; www.campingmilleluci.com), a 1km hike from station. Reception in Hotel Milleluci. Each site has a cabin connected to a trailer. Quiet location with great views. Crowded June-Sept. Laundry €5. €6-8 per person, €4-5 per child under 10, €11 per tent, €11 per RV. Showers free. AmEx/MC/V. ❶

FOOD

Aosta's cold climate and predominantly agricultural lifestyle have generated a cuisine rich in fat. *Fonduta*, a cheese sauce made from the local *fontina*, usually served with toast, is a rich local specialty. Regional wines include *Blanc de Morgex* and *Pinot Gris*. Pick up local varieties of *fontina* at **STANDA**, on V. Festaz 10. (☎35 757. Open M-Sa 8am-8pm, Su 9am-1pm and 3:30-7:30pm. AmEx/D/MC/V.) A Tuesday **market** is in P. Cavalieri di V. Veneto.

Trattoria Praetoria, V. Sant'Anselmo 9 (☎44 356), past Pta. Praetoria. A calm trattoria with a rotating menu that frequently includes the delicious *fonduta valdostana* (cheese fondue with toast; €10) or the *crespelle valdosano* (French crepe layered with cured ham and baked cheese; €7.50). *Primi* €7-10, *secondi* €6.50-15. Cover €1.50. Open in summer daily 12:15-2:30pm and 7:15-9:30pm; in winter M-Tu and Sa-Su 12:15-2:30pm and 7:15-9:30pm, W and F 12:15-2:30pm. AmEx/MC/V. ❸

Pam Pam Trattoria, V. Maillet 5/7 (☎40 960). Romantic trattoria tucked in an ivy-lined lane. Try the *polenta grassa* (polenta with butter and *fontina*; €7.50). *Primi* €7.50-8.50, *secondi* €8-17.50. Open Tu-Sa 12:30-2pm and 7:30-10pm. AmEx/MC/V. ❸

La Rotonda, Vle. dei Partigiani 30 (☎43 927). Serves overwhelmingly large portions at very low prices that keep the large restaurant always full and lively. Beer and wine from €2. Pizza

€4.20-6.30. *Primi* €4.20-6.30, *secondi* €6.30-10. Cover €1.10. Open M-Tu and Th-Su noon-2:30pm and 6:30pm-midnight. AmEx/MC/V. Discount for guests of Hotel Mancuso. ❷

Vecchia Aosta, P. Pta. Praetoria 4 (☎36 11 86). Incredible location between the arches of the Porta. The *mocetta lardo di Arnad con castagne glassate al miele* (cured meat with lard and honey-glazed chestnuts; €7.50) is particularly good. Try the *fonduta alla valdostana* (€15). *Primi* €8-11, *secondi* €15-19. Cover €2.50. Open Tu-Su 12:15-2:30pm and 7:30-10pm. AmEx/MC/V. ❹

👁 SIGHTS

Vestiges of the Roman Empire are thoroughly integrated with modern Aosta; a partially intact, 2000-year-old wall rings the *centro* and houses modern streets that run neatly through its gaps. The **Porta Praetoria,** now on the street bearing its name, once served as a guard house. To its left lie the remains of the massive **Teatro Romano** (Open Apr.-Aug. 9am-8pm; Sept. and Mar. 9am-7pm; Oct. and Feb. 9am-6:30pm; Nov.-Jan. 9am-5pm. Free.) Through Pta. Praetoria, V. Sant'Anselmo leads to the **Arco d'Augusto,** built in 25 BC. The monument has sported its hanging Christian cross inside the arch since the Middle Ages. Between Pta. Praetoria and Arco d'Augusto, the renowned **Complex of Sant'Orso** includes the Collegiate Church of Saints Pietro and Orso, the *campanile,* and the cloister. (Open daily July-Aug. 9am-8pm.; Oct.-Feb. 10am-12:30pm and 1:30-5pm; Mar.-June 9am-7pm. Free.) **Museo Archeologico,** P. Roncas, has a reconstruction of the old town and information on its history. (☎27 59 02. Open daily 9am-7pm. Free.) The ruins of the ancient forum, **Criptoportico Forense,** are off P. Papa Giovanni XXIII. Because the forum has not been excavated, there is not actually much to tour here. (☎27 59 11. Open Apr.-Sept. 2pm-6pm; Nov.-Feb. 2-5pm upon request. Free.)

🎭 🌿 NIGHTLIFE AND FESTIVALS

Nightlife options include the Scottish **Old Distillery Pub,** V. des Prés Fossés 7, a local favorite. From Pta. Praetoria, walk down V. S. Anselmo and turn right through a small archway on the winding V. des Prés Fossés (☎23 95 11; www.olddistillery-pub.com. Beamish €5 per pint. Open daily 6pm-2am.) At **Snooker Bar,** V. Sylvian Lucat 3, relax with a game of pool, or surf the Internet (€4 per hr.) with Aosta's young crowd. (☎40 093. Sandwiches €2.70-6.50. Beer €2-7. Open daily 7am-4am. AmEx/MC/V.) **Bataclan,** P. Arco d'Augusto 40, is one of the town's newest and most popular nightlife establishments. Lounge upstairs beneath the stars, or order a bottle of wine from a candle-lit table while listening to live jazz (F-Sa 9:30-11:30pm) in a grass courtyard. (☎36 39 21; www.bataclan.it. Wine €16 per bottle. *Primi* €7-9, *secondi* €12-16. Open Tu-Su 12:30-3pm and 7:15pm-12:30am. Kitchen open 12:30-3pm and 7:15-11pm; pizza available till closing. MC/V.)

The **Fiera di Sant'Orso,** the region's 2000-year-old craft fair, takes place January 30-31 and the 2nd weekend of August in the *centro storico* from P. Arco d'Augusto all the way to P. della Repubblica (open 8am-6pm). The heart of the fair is **L'Atelier,** on P. Chanoux, which showcases the work of local craftsmen who typically offer demonstrations. The schedule changes annually, so ask at the tourist office.

🏃 DAYTRIPS FROM AOSTA

VALTOURNENCHE: THE MATTERHORN AND BREUIL-CERVINIA

SAVDA buses (☎0166 94 90 54, www.savda.it) run to Breuil-Cervinia (1hr., 7 per day 9:05am-12:35pm, €2.30) from Châtillon, on the Aosta-Turin line. Buses run daily from Milan's P. Castello (5hr.) and from Breuil-Cervina to Turin (4hr.; M-Sa 3 per day, Su 1 per day; €7.80).

The most famous mountain in Switzerland, the **Matterhorn (Il Cervino)** looms majestically over the Italian town of **Breuil-Cervinia** in Valtournenche. Despite high costs in this heavily touristed area, fresh-air fiends consider it a small price for the chance to climb up the glaciers of one of the world's most spectacular mountains. A funicular provides service to **Plateau Rosà**, where die-hard skiers tackle the slopes in bathing suits for extensive ☀**summer skiing.** (July-Sept. 7-11am. €24 per day, students and children €18; 2-day pass €40/25. Combo pass with slopes in Zermatt, Switzerland €38/19 per day, 2-day €71/36.) Most hiking trails start just beyond the funicular. Follow **Trail 12/13** for a day hike with breathtaking views between two waterfalls beneath the Matterhorn (1½-2 hr; follow trail 13 when the trails part). Hikers can also attempt the 3hr. ascent to **Colle Superiore delle Cime Bianche** on Trail 16 (2982m), with views of Val d'Ayas to the east and the Cervino glacier to the west. A shorter trek (1½hr.) on the same trail leads to **Lake Goillet.** In Breuil-Cervinia, the **tourist**

> ❗ Don't forget your passport on hiking excursions; many trails enter Switzerland.

office, V. Guido Rey 17, is the first building on the left when entering town, just after the round-about (☎0166 94 91 36). They have detailed trail maps (€1), as well as information about skiing. If you would feel more comfortable with a roadmap before even reaching the valley, stop at the Monte Cervino **tourist office,** V. Carrel 29, located right off the A5 highway next to the Total gas station by the Châtillon E0xit; follow signs on highway for the Info Exit. (Open M-F 8am-noon and 2:30-5pm, Sa 8am-noon and 2-4pm, Su 8am-1pm.) The English-speaking staff provides info on the winter *Settimana Bianca* (White Week) packages and *Settimane Estive,* the summer equivalent. (☎0166 94 91 36; www.cervinia.it. Open high season daily 9am-6pm; low season 9am-12:30pm and 2-5:30pm.) The **Società Guide** (☎0166 94 81 69), across from the tourist office, arranges group outings.

VALLE DEL GRAN SAN BERNARDO

Valle del Gran San Bernado is only accessible by car. To reach the valley, get off the A5 autostrada; or from Aosta, take the T2 or SS 27 into the valley. To reach the Great St. Bernard Pass, follow SS 27 5km past Etroubles, go right when the road forks; the hospice is 9km into the winding pass.

A spectacular valley with more medieval towers than tourists, **Valle del Gran San Bernardo** links Aosta to Switzerland via the **Great St. Bernard Pass** and the **Great St. Bernard Tunnel** (5854m); the former is only accessible from July-Sept. In summer, motor-tourists and intrepid cyclists tackle this winding mountain road. Tourists can also spend an afternoon following the footsteps of Hannibal and his elephants, who passed through in the 3rd century BC, as well as Napoleon, who trekked through the pass with 40,000 soldiers in the 19th century. Also, the valley holds **La Via Francigena,** a medieval road from France to Rome. This region boasts the **Hospice of St. Bernard,** dating from 1505, home to the patron saint of pups. The legendary life-saver was stuffed for posterity and is conveniently displayed for people driving through the pass. The hospice, just across the Swiss border on the Great St. Bernard Pass, is just a tail-wag away from the **dog museum** (☎41 27 78 71 236; www.musee-saint-bernard.ch), where St. Bernards are trained. (☎41 27 78 71 236; www.gsbernard.ch. Open June and Sept. 9am-noon and 1-6pm; July-Aug. 9am-7pm. Entrance to hospice and its museum €5, children €3.50.) Approximately 5km before the hospice, a trail takes visitors to a series of lakes. The town of **Saint-Oyen,** on SS 27 after passing **Etroubles** but before the St. Bernard Pass, is about as close to the border as you can get. The primary AIAT **tourist office** for the valley is in Etroubles on Strada Nazionale Great St. Bernard 13. If on the SS 27, you will pass right through Etroubles; the office is in the center of town, by a Tamoil station. (☎0165 78 559; www.gransanbernardo.net. Open Tu-Sa 9am-12:30pm and 2:30-6:30pm, Su 9:30am-12:30pm and 2-5pm.)

VAL D'AYAS

Trains run from Aosta to Verrès (30min.; 6:20am, 2:20, 10:15pm; €2.45). SAVDA buses run from the train station at Verrès to Champoluc (1½hr.; 6 per day 8:55am-12:25am, return 6 per day 6:50am-5:30pm; €2.10), as do VITA buses (☎0125 96 65 46; 1hr., 9 per day 7:12am-9:22pm). VITA also runs between Val d'Ayas towns (6:27am-11:04pm). When entering Champoluc, look for the tourist office, V. Varase 16, on the right side of the main road. It may be difficult to identify with signs; look for five flags flying above the wooden lodge. It has accommodations info and trail maps. (☎0125 30 71 13; infoa-yas@aiatmonterosa.com. Open daily 9am-12:30pm and 3-6pm.)

Budget-minded sports enthusiasts should consider visiting the gently sloping Val d'Ayas, which offers the cheapest **skiing** in the region at **Monterosa Ski Resort.** (☎0125 30 31 68; www.monterosa-ski.com. Open M-F 8:30am-noon and 1-5:30pm. Dec. 19-Apr. 2 €33 per day, children €24; start of season to Dec. 18 and Apr. 3-Apr. 19 €27/20.) The small town of **St. Jacques** is the last along the valley road and offers the most **hiking** trails. This should be your departure point if you plan to stay in one of the many *refugi.* The town of **Champoluc** offers the most tourist amenities; the tourist office here should be your stop to plan out any excursions from the valley. An easy hike is the 45min. **Trail #14** from Champoluc to the hamlet of **Mascognaz,** home to a farming population of 10 and an excellent restaurant. An easy to medium difficulty hike is **Trail #105,** which wanders over rocks and through pastures to the impressive ◧**Mount Zerbion** (2700m). A 360-degree panorama displays the soaring Five Giants: the **Matterhorn, Mont Blanc, Monte Rosa, Grand Combin,** and **Gran Paradiso.** Expert hikers may try the **Walser Trail,** staying overnight in tents and following the path of the Germanic migration through Champoluc, Gressoney, St. Jacques, and Valtournenche. For the best views of the valley, turn left after Champoluc and follow the road up the hill to **Antagnod.** While it has fewer restaurants than its neighbor, it does have numerous B&Bs along the steep slope and its own ski lift. **Rafting** is a great way to enjoy the scenery. **Totem Adventure,** Route Mont Blanc 4, has packages for €40-60. (☎0165 87 677; www.totemadventure.com. Reservations recommended. Open July-Aug. daily 8:30am-7:30pm. Cash only.)

VAL DI COGNE

Cogne and its rocky valley are a scenic bus ride from Aosta (1hr., 7 per day 8:05am-7:45pm, €2.10). The bus stops in front of the AIAT tourist office. From June to August, buses run from Cogne to Valnontey, and can take you another 3km into the Gran Paradiso National Park (every 30min. 7:30am-8pm, €1.10; buy tickets onboard).

When Cogne's (COHN-yeh) mines failed in the 70s, the citizens resorted to a more genteel pursuit—separating cross-country skiers from their cash. Cogne is one of the world's premier places to ice climb, but it remains little-known and largely untouched. A funicular transports Alpine addicts to the modest downhill **skiing** facilities. In summer, the valley is the gateway to Italy's largest nature reserve, **Gran Paradiso National Park.** In addition to an endless network of trails, the park has the highest glacier (4061m) fully contained by Italian borders, known as the Gran Paradiso. For spectacular views of the glaciers, try ◧**Trail 17/17A.** To get there, follow the signs in town to the *"cabinivia"* or *"funivia."* The funicular (in summer open daily 9am-12pm and 2-5:30pm; round-trip €7) will take you to the start of the "Bellevue" trail, a moderately difficult hike that leads you to Montseuc (2hr.; elev. 2328m). From the town, a huge white building is visible along the mountainside. Though it may seem like a ski lodge, it is one of the abandoned iron-mining villages. A 3hr. hike brings you there, but don't go inside because the building is not safe. The Cogne AIAT tourist office is at V. Borgeois 34. (☎0165 74 040 or 0165 74 056. Open in summer M-Sa 8:30am-1:00pm and 2-7pm, Su 8:30am-1pm and 2-6pm; in winter M-Sa 9am-12:30pm and 2:30-5:30pm, Su 9am-12:30pm.)

PIEDMONT AND VALLE D'AOSTA

COURMAYEUR ☎ 0165

Italy's oldest Alpine resort lures tourists to the spectacular shadows of Europe's highest peak. French Mt. Blanc (known in Italy as Monte Bianco), with its jagged ridges and snowy fields, is perfect for hiking and skiing. Unfortunately, attractions often cater to the elegant vacationing styles of Europe's rich. However, in May and June, when the snow has melted, quiet descends upon Courmayeur (coor-ma-YUHR; pop. 2800), and shopkeepers take their high-season prices on vacation.

☎? **TRANSPORTATION AND PRACTICAL INFORMATION.** A single large complex, the **Centro Congressi Courmayeur,** in **Piazzale Monte Bianco,** houses most travel services, including the **bus station. Buses** run to Aosta (1hr.; M-F every hr. 6:45-9:55pm; €3, round-trip €5.10), Milan (4hr.; 3-4 per day; €16, round-trip €27), and Turin (3hr.; M-F 6:45 and 9:45am, Sa-Su 6:45am; €9, round-trip €16). SAVDA and SADAEM, Ple. Monte Bianco 3, buses have frequent service to larger towns. (☎84 20 31 or 84 13 97. Office open daily July-Aug. 8am-7:30pm; Sept.-June 8:45am-1pm and 2-7pm. Tickets also sold onboard.) **Taxis** (☎84 29 60) are available 24hr. at Ple. M. Bianco. Pick up a map from the multilingual staff at the **AIAT tourist office,** Ple. M. Bianco 13 (☎84 20 60; www.aiat-monte-bianco.com. Open M-Sa 9am-12:30pm and 3-6:30pm, Su 9am-noon and 3-6pm.) An accommodations board, next to the office, can also help you find a room. The bus station ticket office has **currency exchange,** as does the **San Paolo Istituto Bancario di Torino,** P. Brocherel 1, which also has an **ATM.** (☎84 20 23. Open M-F 8:25am-1:25pm and 2:40-4:10pm.) In case of **emergency,** go to the **police,** Strada della Margherita 8. A **pharmacy,** V. Circonvallazione 69, posts after-hours rotations. (Open M-F 9am-12:30pm and 3-7:30pm, Sa 9am-12:30pm and 3:30-7:30pm. MC/V.) The **post office** is at Ple. M. Bianco 5, behind the main complex. It also offers **currency exchange.** (☎84 20 42. Open M-F 8am-1:30pm, Sa 8am-12:30pm.) **Postal Code:** 11013.

☎☎ **ACCOMMODATIONS AND FOOD.** You can't book accommodations far enough ahead, especially if you are hoping to be in Courmayeur for snow season. **Pensione Venezia ❸,** V. delle Villete 2, is by far the best deal in town. From Ple. M. Bianco, head uphill, then left on V. Circonvallazione, to this centrally located chalet with rustic rooms, shared bathroom, and TV lounge. (☎/fax 84 24 61. Breakfast included. Singles €35; doubles €46; triples €69. Cash only.) **Hotel Select ❹,** Strada Regionale 27, after V. Roma, offers more expensive and modern rooms with private bath, TV, and phone. (☎84 66 61; www.courmayeurhotel.com. Singles €35-50; doubles €63-108; triples €90-130. AmEx/MC/V.) **📖Pastificio Gabriella ❶,** Passaggio dell'Angelo 2, toward the end of V. Roma, has freshly made side dishes, breads, pastries, pasta, and sauces. It's the perfect place to pack for a picnic in the shadow of Mt. Bianco. (☎84 33 59. Open M-Tu and Th-Su 8am-1pm and 4-7:30pm. Closed 2 wk. in June. MC/V.) Off-piste skiers recharge in the center of town at the unique **Cafe des Guides ❶,** Vle. Monte Bianco 2, below the Società delle Guide. (☎84 24 35. *Panini* €4-5. Beer €5-6. Mixed drinks €6-8. Cover €1. Open daily 7:30am-2:30am. Cash only.) **Petit Bistrot ❶,** V. Marconi 6, whips up cheap crepes in a city with few cheap eateries. (☎347 50 84 158. Crepes €4 for takeout, €6.50 inside. Open 11:30am-midnight. Cash only.) In summer, many restaurants close, but **La Terraza ❺,** V. Circonvallazione 73, is open year-round. Just uphill from Ple. Monte Bianco, this restaurant specializes in *valdostano* cuisine, serving fondue and lard garnished with warm chestnuts and honey. (☎84 33 30; www.ristorantelaterrazza.com. Pizza €7-12. *Primi* €12-14, *secondi* €17-30. Cover €2.50. Open daily noon-2:15pm and 7pm-late. MC/V.)

⚠️⛷ OUTDOOR ACTIVITIES AND SKIING. Courmayeur Ski Resort is famous for its scenic downhill runs, off-piste itineraries, and cross-country offerings (info ☎84 20 60, tickets ☎84 66 58. High season is Dec. 8-11 and Dec. 19-April 2. In high season ski passes €41 per day, €224 per week; inquire at the tourist office for the most up-to-date prices.) The brochure *Settimane Bianche* lists rental prices and often offers discounts. **Buses** also run to **Pré-Saint-Didier** (15min, 8 per day 7:55am-7:15pm, €1.20), which has thermal baths. Pré-Saint-Didier then connects to **La Thuile** (20 min., 11 per day 7:55am-8:40pm, €1.20), another ski resort with 150km of intermediate and expert downhill trails and five cross-country skiing tracks.

Buses run from Courmayeur to the trailheads in **Val Veny** and **Val Ferret**, which branch in opposite directions along the base of Monte Bianco. Inquire at the tourist office for a *Valdigne Mont-Blanc: Les Sentiers* map and the brochure *Seven Itineraries around Mont Blanc, Val Veny, and Val Ferret*. The most popular hike in Val Veny is the 1hr. path past the Lac du Miage to Refuge Elisabetta (2197m). In Val Ferret, the two short hikes to the Refuge Bonatti (2150m) from Lavachey (45min.) and to the Refuge Elena (2055m) from Arp Nouva (40min.) make for a relaxing trip. An excellent place to ask questions is **Società delle Guide di Courmayeur,** Strada Villair 2, to the left behind the church. Since 1850, the office has been providing free advice to hikers and finding guides for all major treks and climbs. (☎84 20 64; guidecourmayeur@tiscali.it. Open in summer M-Tu and Th-Su 9am-noon and 4-7pm, W 4-7pm; in winter Tu-Su 9am-7pm.) A number of excellent **biking** trails traverse Monte Bianco. **Scott Center,** Ple. M. Bianco 15 (☎84 82 54), runs a ski-school and ski-rentals during the winter. During the summer, it becomes **Sirdar** (☎346 57 89 776; www.sirdar-montagne.com), and rents bikes, which are only available by phone reservation.

To explore Monte Bianco, use the **⛷Funivie Monte Bianco** (☎89 925; www.montebianco.com). *Funivie* depart from **La Palud,** which is accessible by bus from Courmayeur's Ple. Monte Bianco (10min., 8:30am-4:20pm, €1). Head first to the glacier terrace at **Punta Helbronner** (3462m), then across the border to **Aiguille du midi** (3842m), and then to **Chamonix** (1030m). You can take the funicular to La Palud and from there to Punta Helbronner, Italy's highest point (round-trip €36; €17 surcharge to continue to Chamonix in summer). In winter, Chamonix is reachable from here by skiing with a guide. Punta Helbronner affords views of Monte Bianco and the spectacular **Matterhorn, Monte Rosa,** and **Gran Paradiso National Park.**

LIGURIA

Italy's answer to the French Riviera, Liguria (lih-GOO-ree-ah) stretches across 350km of Mediterranean coastline. Along with this coast full of beaches, Liguria is also home to terraced hillsides, the Apennine Mountains, vineyards, and olive groves. Every restaurant boasts the best *frutti di mare* (seafood) and *pesto alla Genovese* (sauce made of basil, pine nuts, and garlic), and often can't be proven wrong. With trains chugging along the coast, exploring Liguria is easy and convenient. Stroll through the winding streets lined with colorful houses and elaborately painted architectural details in Portofino, hike along the coastal cliffs of *Cinque Terre*, or gaze at the masterpieces of Caravaggio in Genoa's Palazzo Bianco. No matter which part of Liguria you discover, trade those Italian leather shoes for flip flops and follow the Italians' lead to their laid-back vacation oasis.

HIGHLIGHTS OF LIGURIA

STRUT among the villas of Genoa's **Via Garibaldi,** called the Golden Street. (p. 205)

TREK the **trails** that connect the colorful towns of the Cinque Terre. (p. 213)

BEACH BUM with classy Italians on the **sandy stretches of coast** of Alassio. (p. 226)

DOUBLE YOUR MONEY in San Remo's **casino,** a turn-of-the-century gem. (p. 231)

GENOA (GENOVA)   ☎010

As any Genovese will proclaim, *"Si deve conoscerla per amarla"*—you have to know Genoa to love her. Often obscured by fog and steam from passing ships, Genoa (in Italian "JEH-no-va"; pop. 600,000) anchors the luminescent Ligurian coast between the Riviera di Levante (rising sun) to the east and the Riviera di Ponente (setting sun) to the west. A city of grit and grandeur, it has little in com-

mon with neighboring beach towns along the Riviera. Genoa's main streets are lined with *palazzi* and *piazze* from past wealthy families, but just steps away from these opulent homes lie reminders of an older city whose maze-like pathways echo with history. Recent cultural events, along with a world-famous aquarium, have revitalized Genoa. Once a city of exploration from which adventurers like Christopher Columbus set out in search of a New World, Genoa is no longer a mere point of departure for exploration, but rather a compelling destination.

▐ TRANSPORTATION

Flights: Cristoforo Colombo Internazionale (☎ 60 151), in Sesti Ponente, sends flights to European destinations. **Volabus #100** runs to the airport from Stazione Principe (every hr. 5:40am-10:40pm, €4).

Trains: Stazione Principe, in P. Acquaverde, and **Stazione Brignole,** in P. Verdi. Trains (5min., every 15min., €1) and buses #18, 19, 20, 33, and 37 (25min., €1) connect the 2 stations. Ticket validation good for 1½hr. **Luggage storage** available (see **Practical Information,** p. 201). Open daily 7am-11pm. Trains run from stations to points along the Ligurian Riviera and major Italian cities including **Rome** (5-6hr., 10 per day, €33) and **Turin** (2hr., every 20-30min., €8-12).

Ferries: At Ponte Assereto arm of the port. Take bus #20 from Stazione Principe or bus #1 from the aquarium. Purchase tickets at travel agency or Stazione Marittima. Arrive at Terminal Traghetti Ponte Assereto at least 1hr. before departure. **Tirrenia** (☎ 081 31 72 999; www.tirrenia.it) runs ferries to **Sardinia. Grandi Navi Veloci** (☎ 20 94 591; www.gnv.it) heads to **Sardinia, Sicily, Spain,** and **Tunisia. EnerRmaR** (☎ 119 76 00 03) goes to **Olbia** and **Palau. Moby lines** runs to **Olbia, Bastia,** and **Porto Torres** (☎ 199 30 30 40; www.moby.it).

Local Buses: AMT (☎ 800 08 53 11) buses leave from V. Gramsci, in front of the aquarium, or Stazione Brignole. 1-way tickets within the city €1.20. Day passes €3.50. Passport necessary for foreign visitors. Tickets and passes also valid for funicular and elevator rides.

Taxis: (☎ 59 66). From P. de Ferrari.

ORIENTATION AND PRACTICAL INFORMATION

Genoa has two train stations: **Stazione Principe,** in P. Acquaverde, and **Stazione Brignole,** in P. Verdi. From Stazione Principe take bus #18, 19, or 30, and from Stazione Brignole take bus #19 or 40 to **Piazza de Ferrari** in the center of town. To walk to P. de Ferrari from Stazione Principe, take **Via Balbi** to **Via Cairoli,** which becomes **Via Garibaldi,** and at **Piazza delle Fontane Marose** turn right on **Via XXV Aprile.** From Stazione Brignole, turn right out of the station, left on **Via Fiume,** and right onto **Via XX Settembre,** ending in P. de Ferrari. To get to the **Porto Antico** from P. de Ferrari, take V. Boetto to **Piazza Giacomo Matteoti,** then follow **Via di San Lorenzo** to the water. Genoa's streets can stump even a native, so don't head out without a map.

> **! TROUBLE IN PARADISE.** Though most of Genoa's problems with crime are a thing of the past, travelers should avoid **Via di Prè** entirely, and be especially cautious in the area around **Via della Maddalena.** Walking alone at night or in the **centro storico** on weekends when stores are closed is dangerous.

Tourist Offices: GenovaInforma, Palazzo Ducale, P. G. Matteoti (☎ 86 87 4 52). Facing the water, walk 30m left from the aquarium toward the complex of buildings. Provides decent maps. Open daily 9am-1pm and 2-6pm. Kiosks near aquarium on Porto Antico (☎ 24 87 11), in Stazione Principe (☎ 24 62 633), and airport (☎ 60 15 247). All open M-Sa 9:30am-1pm and 2:30-6pm.

LIGURIA

Budget Travel: CTS, V. San Vincenzo 117r (☎56 43 66 or 53 27 48), off V. XX Settembre, near Ponte Monumentale. Walk up the flight of stairs at the shopping complex to the left. Student fares available. Open M-F 9:30am-6:15pm. MC/V.

Consulates: UK, P. Giuseppe Verdi 6/A (☎57 40 071; fax 53 04 096). Take bus #30 (dir.: Sampierdarena) from Stazione Principe to the last stop. Open M-Th 9:30am-12:30pm. **US,** V. Dante 2, 3rd fl., #43 (☎58 44 92). Open M-Th 11am-3pm.

Beyond Tourism: Informagiovani, Palazzo Ducale, P. G. Matteotti 24r (☎55 73 952 or 55 73 965; www.informagiovani.comune.genova.it). Youth center offers info on apartment rentals, jobs, volunteer opportunities, and concerts. Free **Internet** access with 1hr. limit. Open M-F 9am-1pm and Tu-Th 2-5:30pm.

Bank: Banca Intesa, C. Buenos Aires 4. Open M-F 8:30am-1:30pm and 2:45-4:15pm, Sa-Su 8:30am-noon.

Luggage Storage: ☎27 43 4 63, in Stazione Principe. €3.80 for 1st hr., €0.60 per additional hr. up to 12hr., €0.20 per hr. thereafter. Open 7am-11pm. Cash only.

English-Language Bookstore: Mondadori, V. XX Settembre 210r (☎58 41 40). Huge, with a full wall of classics and some best-sellers. Open M-Sa 9am-8pm, Su 10:30am-1pm and 4:30-8pm. AmEx/MC/V.

Pharmacy: Pescetto, V. Balbi 185r (☎26 16 09), near Stazione Principe. After-hours rotation posted outside. Open M-F 7:30am-12:30pm and 3:30pm-midnight. Sa-Su 8pm-midnight. AmEx/MC/V. **Farmacia Ghersi,** C. Buenos Aires 18r, across town. Open M-F midnight-12:30pm and 3:30pm-midnight, Sa-Su 7:30pm-midnight. MC/V.

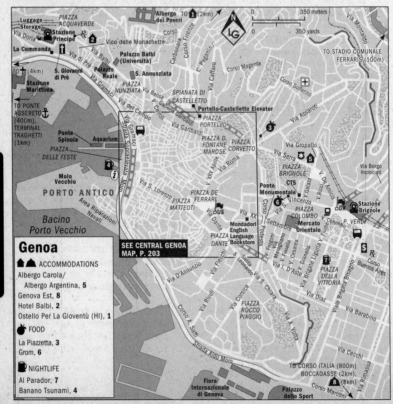

Genoa

▲▲ ACCOMMODATIONS
Albergo Carola/
 Albergo Argentina, **5**
Genova Est, **8**
Hotel Balbi, **2**
Ostello Per La Gioventù (HI) **1**

🍴 FOOD
La Piazzetta, **3**
Grom, **6**

🎵 NIGHTLIFE
Al Parador, **7**
Banano Tsunami, **4**

Hospital: Ospedale Evangelico, C. Solferino 1a (☎ 55 221).

Internet: Free at **Informagiovani** (see **Beyond Tourism** above). **Number One Bar/Cafe,** P. Verdi 21r (☎ 54 18 85), near Stazione Brignole. €4 per hr. Open M-Sa 7:30am-11:30pm. MC/V. **In-Centro.it Agenzia Viaggi,** V. Roccatagliata Ceccardi 14r, between V. Dante and V. XX Settembre. €3 per hr., students €2.50. Also a bookstore and travel agency. Open M 3-7:30pm, Tu-Sa 9:15am-7:30pm. MC/V.

Post Office: P. Dante 4/6r (☎ 25 94 687). 2 blocks from P. de Ferrari. *Fermoposta* available. Open M-F 8am-6:30pm, Sa 8am-1:30pm. **Postal Code:** 16121.

ACCOMMODATIONS

Rooms are scarce in October, when the city hosts a wave of nautical conventions. Some budget lodgings in the *centro storico* and near the port rent rooms by the hour for reasons best left uninvestigated. Establishments are more refined around Stazione Brignole and P. Corvetto. The area around Genoa is teeming with camp-grounds, but because they fill up in summer, book ahead when possible.

Ostello Per La Gioventù (HI), V. Costanzi 120 (☎/fax 24 22 457; www.geocities.com/hos-telge). From Stazione Principe, take bus #35; transfer to #40 at the first stop on V. Napoli. From Stazione Brignole, take bus #40 (evening #640) 30min. all the way up the hill. Cafeteria, free lockers, and TV. Multilingual staff. Breakfast included. Laundry €7 per 5kg. Wheelchair-accessible. Reception 7-11:30am and 3pm-12:30am. Check-out 10am. Lock-out

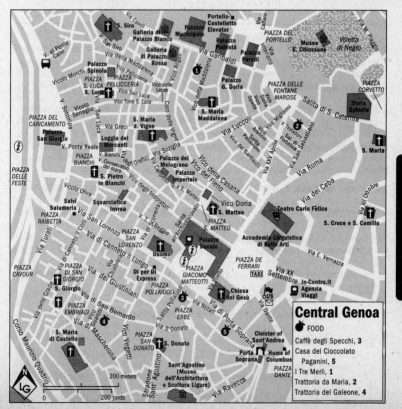

Central Genoa

🍴 FOOD

Caffè degli Specchi, **3**

Casa del Cioccolato
Paganini, **5**

I Tre Merli, **1**

Trattoria da Maria, **2**

Trattoria del Galeone, **4**

LIGURIA

10am-3pm. Curfew 2am, but last bus from Stazione Brignole departs at 12:50am. HI card required (available at hostel). Dorms €16; family rooms €16-20 per person. ❶

Albergo Carola, V. Gropallo 4/12, 3rd fl. (☎83 91 340; www.pensionecarola.com), near Stazione Brignole. Look for big doors with lion heads on the left. Ring buzzer to enter. English-speaking staff and 9 meticulously decorated rooms. Some with a garden view. Singles €30; doubles €50, with bath €60; triples €80; quads €90. Cash only. ❸

Albergo Argentina, V. Gropallo 4 (☎/fax 83 93 722), near Stazione Brignole, 2 flights down from Albergo Carola. 9 large, clean, comfortable rooms. Limited English. Singles €28-32; doubles €47-50, with bath €56-60; triples €62-70; quads €82-85. V. ❷

Hotel Balbi, V. Balbi 21/3 (☎/fax 25 23 62), close to Stazione Principe. Get beyond the unpromising exterior stairwell and you will be greeted by spacious rooms with wooden floors and painted ceilings. All rooms with bath. Breakfast included. Internet access €4 per hr. Singles €65; doubles €80; triples €105; quads €120. MC/V. ❺

Genova Est (☎34 72 053; www.camping-genova-est.it), on V. Marconi, Località Cassa. Take the train from Stazione Brignole to the suburb of Bogliasco (10min., 6 per day, €1); from here, take the free van (5min., every 2hr. 8am-8pm) to the campground. Shaded sites on a terraced hill overlook the sea, with clean, shared bathroom facilities. Laundry €3.50 per load. €6 per person, €5.60-8.60 per tent. Electricity €2.20. ❶

JESUS! THOSE PRICES ARE HIGH. For any travelers visiting Genoa during the Easter season, be aware: prices rise for most accommodations.

🗋 FOOD

A dish prepared *alla Genovese* is served with Genoa's pride and joy—*pesto*, a traditional sauce made from basil, pine nuts, olive oil, garlic, and parmesan cheese. The *genovesi* put it on just about everything, so if you love *pesto*, don't be afraid to experiment. Other delectables include *farinata* (a fried pancake of chickpea flour), focaccia filled with cheese or topped with olives or onions, and *pansotti* (ravioli stuffed with spinach and ricotta in a creamy walnut sauce). To sample a slice of Genoa's famous salami or pick up a jar of *pesto*, stop by **Salvi Salumeria,** V. di San Lorenzo 2, near Porto Antico. Also, don't forget to sample the seafood, sold fresh from vendors lining the port-side arcade. For cheap groceries, head to **Di per Di Express,** V. di Canneto Il Lungo 108-112. From P. Matteotti go down Salita Pollaioli, take an immediate right onto V. di Canneto Il Lungo; the supermarket is on the right. (Open M-Sa 8am-7:45pm, Su 9am-1pm and 4-7pm. MC/V.)

🗺 **Trattoria da Maria,** V. Testadoro 14r (☎ 58 10 80), near P. delle Fontane Marose, off V. XXV Aprile. Typical Italian restaurant with checkered tablecloths and a faithful lunch crowd. Outgoing staff serves fresh, delicious dishes of the day. *Menù,* including *primo* and *secondo* and a drink €9. Open M-Sa 11:45am-3pm. MC/V. ❷

🗺 **I Tre Merli,** V. della Maddalena 26r (☎24 74 095), on a narrow street off V. Garibaldi. A hidden gem with soft music and a mellow atmosphere. Impeccable service and delicious food make the price well worth it. Wine connoisseurs take note—the list is 16 pages long and very well compiled. *Primi* €10-12, *secondi* €14-16. Open M-F 12:30-3pm and 7:30-11pm, Sa 7:30-11pm. AmEx/MC/V. ❹

🗺 **Grom,** V. San Vincenzo 53r (☎56 54 20; www.grom.it), near Stazione Brignole. All you ever wanted *gelato* to be, made daily with fresh ingredients. Cups and cones from €2. Open M-Th and Su noon-10pm, F-Sa noon-11pm. Cash only. ❶

Trattoria del Galeone, V. di San Bernardo 55r (☎24 68 422). From P. G. Matteoti, take Salita Pollaiuoli, and turn right on V. di S. Bernardo. Galeone is 100m up on the left. Nautically decorated dining rooms are crowded with older yet lively locals. *Primi* €5-6, *secondi* €7-11. Open M-Sa 12:30-2:30pm and 7:30-10pm. Cash only. ❷

La Piazzetta, V. Calatafimi 9 (☎87 70 28), off P. Marsala. Convenient location in a quiet *piazza* offers Ligurian specials on an outdoor wooden deck. *Primi* €8-12, *secondi* €11-15. Open M-Th 12:30-2:30pm and 7:30-11pm, F-Sa 12:30-2:30pm and 7:30pm-midnight. MC/V. ❸

Casa del Cioccolato Paganini, V. di Porta Soprana 45r (☎95 13 662). Like the composer of its namesake, the chocolate here just might draw tears of passion. Indulge in unique homemade sweets, from Niccolo Paganini chocolate (boxes from €6.50) to signature *sciroppo di rosa,* a sublime liquid made from sugar, water, and rose petals (€7.30 per bottle). Open M-Sa 12:30-7:30pm. AmEx/V/MC. ❶

Caffè degli Specchi, Salita Pollaiuoli 43r (☎26 68 193), on the left, down Salita Pollaiuoli from P. G. Matteotti. *Specchio* means mirror, and narcissists will surely enjoy this sophisticated, mirror-lined cafe. The crowds enjoy *bicchierini* (glasses of wine; €3.60) or mixed drinks (€5-5.50) at pleasant outdoor seating. Mini *panini* (€1.50-3) make a tasty snack. Open M 7am-2am, Tu-F 7am-midnight, Sa 8am-midnight. AmEx/MC/V. ❶

👁 SIGHTS

FROM STAZIONE PRINCIPE TO THE CENTRO STORICO

Outside the winding alleys of the *centro storico*, Genoa boasts a multitude of *palazzi*, many of which have been converted to museums that showcase 16th- and 17th-century Flemish and Italian art. **Via Garibaldi,** which skirts the edge of the *centro storico*, and **Via Balbi,** which runs through the university quarter from Stazione Principe to P. Nunziata, offer the best views of the glamorous buildings.

> ✴**TIP** **BUS IT.** Though the *centro* is compact, many of Genoa's sights are just beyond a comfortable walking distance. City buses are a frequent and convenient alternative. A 24hr. pass with unlimited rides is just €3.50; if you're traveling with friends, pick up a 24hr. pass for three for just €7. Longer stays merit the €12 week-long pass with unlimited rides.

▓**AQUARIUM.** The aquarium is Genoa's most elaborate tourist attraction and has the largest volume of water of any in Europe. Wander through the exhibits, then climb aboard **Grande Nave Blu,** a huge barge filled with habitat recreations, from the forests of Madagascar to the reefs of the Caribbean. There's also an interactive tank where visitors can touch sea rays. Take a **"Behind the Scenes"** tour from a multilingual guide. *(On Porto Antico, across from tourist kiosk. ☎23 45 666; www.acquario-digenova.it. Open July-Aug. daily 9am-11pm; Mar.-June and Sept.-Oct. M-F 9am-7:30pm, Sa-Su 9am-8:30pm; Nov.-Feb. daily 9:30am-7:30pm. Last entry 1½hr. before closing. €15. Discounts for groups and children. Tour M-F 10am, meets inside aquarium. AmEx/MC/V.)*

▓**PALAZZO REALE.** Built between in the 15th century, this *palazzo* was originally home to the Balbi family. It became the Palazzo Reale (Royal Palace) in 1823. The *piemontese* Rococo throne room, covered in red velvet, remains untouched, along with the royal waiting room and sleeping quarters. The resplendent **Galleria degli Specchi** is modeled after the Hall of Mirrors at Versailles. In the Queen's bedroom, the **queen's clock** is really a *notturlabio,* a clock with stenciled numbers lit from behind by a candle. Don't miss the spectacular view from the *palazzo's* terrace, off Room 22. To see paintings by Tintoretto, Van Dyck, and Bassano, ascend the red-carpeted stairs on the left after purchasing a ticket. *(V. Balbi 10. 5min. walk west of V. Garibaldi. ☎27 101; www.palazzorealegenova.it. Open Tu-W 9am-1:30pm, Th-Su 9am-7pm. Entrances on the half hr. €4, ages 18-25 €2, under 18 or over 65 free. Cash only.)*

▓**VIA GARIBALDI.** The most impressive street in Genoa, V. Garibaldi deserves its nickname, *Via Aurea* ("Golden Street"). In the 17th century, wealthy families lined the way with elegant palaces. **Galleria di Palazzo Rosso,** built in the 16th century, earned its name when it was painted red in the 17th. Red carpets cover the floors of exhibit halls featuring several hundred years' worth of *genovese* ceramics. The 2nd floor now holds several Van Dyck portraits of nobility. Across the street, the **Galleria di Palazzo Bianco** exhibits a large collection of Ligurian art. The 3rd floor contains Van Dyck's *Red-Eyed Christ*, as well as works by Caravaggio, Rubens, and Vasari. Several doors down lies **Palazzo Tursi** (also known as the **Palazzo Municipale**). The former home of the Savoy monarchy built between 1565 and 1579, now serves as the city hall and showcases a courtyard and Niccolo Paganini's violin, Il Cannone, made by the legendary Giuseppe Guarneri. This instrument is still played by the winner of Premio Paganini, an international violin competition held annually on October 12. *(Galleria di Palazzo Rosso: V. Garibaldi 18. Galleria di Palazzo Bianco: V. Garibaldi 11. Palazzo Tursi: V. Garibaldi 9. All three sights ☎ 27 59 185. Open Tu-F 9am-7pm, Sa-Su 10am-7pm. Ticket office, V. Garibaldi 9, open daily 9am-8pm. 1 gallery €5, both €7, students €3, over 65 €4, under 18 free. Palazzo Tursi free. AmEx/MC/V.)*

PORTELLO-CASTELLETTO ELEVATOR. Walk down the tunnel in P. Portello to ride this elevator with locals, who take it as regularly as the bus. A plaque on the tunnel to the elevator quotes Giorgio Caproni: *"Quando mi sarò deciso d'andarci, in paradiso ci andrò con l'ascensore di Castelletto."* ("When I will have decided to go there, in paradise I will go with the elevator of Castelletto.") The 30 second ride, which connects the *centro storico* with neighborhoods in surrounding hills, leads commuters to perfect panoramas and a step closer to paradise. *(Through the tunnel entrance in P. Portello. Open daily 6:40am-midnight. Single-use tickets can be purchased for €0.50 from machines at the entrance to the elevator or from newsstands nearby.)*

VILLETTA DI NEGRO. This relaxing park offers waterfalls, grottoes, and terraced gardens. *(From P. delle Fontane Marose, take Salita di San Caterina to P. Corvetto. Entrance along V. Piaggio. Open daily 8am-dusk.)*

PORTO ANTICO. Genoa's enormous port yields a mixture of fascinating history and commercial bustle. The port is sectioned into several wharves. The oldest, 15th-century **Molo Vecchio,** on the far left facing the water, is home to Genoa's former cotton warehouses, as well as a movie theater and restaurants. The central *Quartieri Antichi* (historical districts) still hold some 16th-century bondhouses. Nearby Ponte Spinola is the site of Genoa's famed **aquarium,** and the adjacent **Piazza del Caricamento** is lined with merchants peddling fresh fish and produce.

THE CENTRO STORICO

The eerily beautiful and sometimes dangerous *centro storico* is a mass of narrow, winding streets and cobblestone alleyways bordered by **Porto Antico, Via Garibaldi,** and **Piazza de Ferrari.**

WHEN THE THUG HITS YOUR EYE, and your purse starts to fly, that's *la notte.* Due to a high crime rate, the center is not safe on weekends, when stores are closed and streets are less crowded. Also avoid the area at night, when most of the people clear out and the city's seedy underbelly emerges.

CHIESA DI SANTA MARIA DI CASTELLO. With foundations from 500 BC, this church is a labyrinth of chapels, courtyards, cloisters, and crucifixes. In the chapel to the left of the high altar looms the spooky **Crocifisso Miracoloso** (c. 1200). According to legend, the wooden Jesus moved his head to attest to the honesty of a damsel betrayed by her lover, and his beard is still said to grow every time a crisis hits the city. To see the painting of **San Pietro Martire di Verona,** complete with a halo and a large cleaver conspicuously thrust into his cranium (the handiwork of incensed adversaries), go up the stairs to the right of the high altar, turn right, and right again. The painting is above the door. After walking through the door, check out the famous **L'Annunciazione** by Jost di Favensburg (c. 1400) on the right. *(From P. G. Matteotti, head up V. di San Lorenzo toward the water and turn left on V. Chiabrera. A left on serpentine V. di Mascherona leads to the church in P. Caricamento. Open daily 9am-noon and 3:30-6:30pm. Closed to tourists for Su mass. Free.)*

DUOMO (SAN LORENZO). The *duomo* was reconstructed between the 12th and 16th centuries after religious authorities deemed it "imperfect and deformed." The result may have been an improvement, but it sure wasn't symmetrical; because only one of the two planned bell towers was completed, the church has a lopsided appearance. Climb the completed *campanile* (bell tower) for dizzying views of the city. On the left side of the church, the golden **Cappella di San Giovanni** houses a relic from St. John the Baptist. *(In P. San Lorenzo, off V. di San Lorenzo. Open daily 9am-noon and 3-6pm. Guided tour every 30min. Modest dress required. Tickets for campanile sold M-Sa in Museo del Tesoro on left side of church. Campanile €5.50, duomo free. Cash only.)*

CHIESA DEL GESÙ. Also known as **Sant'Andrea e Ambrogio,** this former Jesuit church, completed in 1606, houses two Rubens canvases: *The Circumcision* (1605) over the altar, and *The Miracle of St. Ignatius* (1620) in the 3rd alcove on the left. *(From P. de Ferrari, take V. Boetto to P. G. Matteotti. Open M-Sa 7am-4pm, Su 8am-5pm. Closed Su masses 7:15, 10, 11am, noon, and 6:30pm. Free.)*

PALAZZO DUCALE. The majestic centerpiece of the centro storico, this palazzo was constructed in 1290 as the seat of Genoa's government. The facade, completed a few years before the end of the Republic of Genoa in 1797 by architect Simone Cantoni, is an example of Neoclassical architecture, while the interior is done up in Rococo decor. Visit the **museum** on the 2nd floor for rotating exhibits of international artwork. *(P. G. Matteotti 9. ☎55 74 004; www.palazzoducale.genova.it. Museum open Tu-Su 9am-9pm. €7, students €6. AmEx/MC/V.)*

PORTA SOPRANA. Built in 1115 as a gate to the city and to intimidate enemies, the Porta is both the historical centerpiece of P. Dante and the passageway from the modern *piazza* into the *centro storico*. Would-be assailant Emperor Federico Barbarossa took one look at the arch, whose Latin inscription welcomes all coming in peace but threatens doom to enemy armies, and abandoned his attack. **Christopher Columbus's boyhood home** lies nearby alongside the remains of the Cloister of St. Andrew's Church. *(From P. G. Matteotti, head down V. di Porta Soprana. ☎25 16 714. Porta and Columbus's home open daily 10am-6pm. Porta €4, home €4; both €7. Cash only.)*

PALAZZO SPINOLA DI PELLICCERIA. Built at the end of the 16th century, this *palazzo* once hosted Peter Paul Rubens, who described it warmly in his 1622 book on pleasing palaces. It is now home to the **Galleria Nazionale,** a collection of art and furnishings, most donated by the family of Maddalena Doria Spinola. The building tells its own history, as different sections represent centuries' worth of varying architectural styles. The 18th-century kitchen simulation is particularly intriguing, with a lit stove and flour on the countertop. The 4th floor houses Antonello da Messina's 1460 masterpiece *Ecce Homo*, and Van Dyck's portraits of the evange-

LIGURIA

lists reside on the 2nd floor. *(P. di Pellicceria 1, between V. Maddalena and P. San Luca.* ☎ *27 05 300. Open Tu-Sa 8:30am-7:30pm, Su 1:30-7:30pm. €4, ages 18-25 €2.)*

🎵 🎭 ENTERTAINMENT AND NIGHTLIFE

Genoa's new **Cineplex,** V. Magazzini de' Cotone, at Molo Vecchio, shows dubbed American movies. (☎ 89 90 30 820; www.cineplex.it. Box office open M-F 4-10:30pm, Sa 2:15pm-1am, Su 2-11:30pm. Tickets €7.30, matinees €5.) A walk farther down the port, to the end of the pier, reveals **Banano Tsunami,** V. di Brera 22, a hot spot for cool wooden decks and fruity drinks. (*Panini* €4.50. Wine €5 per glass. Mixed drinks €7. Open daily noon-3am. Kitchen closes 9pm. Cash only.) **Corso Italia** is a swanky promenade, home to much of Genoa's nightlife. A 20min. ride down the long boulevard on bus #31 leads to **Boccadasse,** a fishing village and seaside playground for wealthy *genovesi*. Unfortunately, many clubs are difficult to reach on foot, so travelers in Genoa often drive to reach their nightlife destinations. Local university students flock to bars in **Piazza delle Erbe** and along **Via San Bernardo.** Closer to Stazione Bringole, **Al Parador,** P. della Vittoria 49r, is located in the northeast corner of P. Vittoria, near the intersection of V. Cadorna and V. B. Liguria. Upscale *bar* by day, by night this watering hole is frequented by both real celebrities like Uma Thurman and Claudia Schiffer and the wanna-bes who idolize them. (☎ 58 17 71. Mixed drinks €4.50. Open M-Sa 24hr. Cash only.)

RIVIERA DI LEVANTE

CAMOGLI ☎ 0185

Camogli (ca-MOL-yee; pop. 6000) is a postcard-perfect town with lively red and turquoise boats bobbing in the harbor, fishing nets draped over docks, and pebbly beaches dotted with bright umbrellas. Its colorful houses with painted-on balconies, windows, and "brick" facades fool the less observant. Less ritzy and more youth-friendly than nearby Portofino and Santa Margherita, Camogli is a gem in Liguria's aptly named *Golfo Paradiso* (Gulf of Paradise). Lounge, eat, and hike your way to happiness—you won't care that it's remote; it's heaven.

🚆 TRANSPORTATION. Camogli is on the Genoa-La Spezia train line. (Ticket office open M-Sa 6:15am-3pm, Su 10am-7pm.) Trains run to Genoa (40min., every hr., €1.60); La Spezia (1½hr., every hr., €4) via Santa Margherita (5min., every 30min., €1.10); and Sestri Levante (30min., every 30min., €3). Tigullio buses leave from P. Schiaffino near the tourist office for nearby towns. Buy tickets at the tourist office or at *tabaccherie.* Buses go to Santa Margherita (20min., 20 per day, €1.10), Rapallo, Ruta, and San Lorenzo. For Golfo Paradiso ferries, V. Scalo 2 (☎ 77 20 91; www.golfoparadiso.it), look for the *"Servizio Batelli"* sign near P. Colombo by the water. Buy tickets at dock or on the ferry (cash only). Round-trip ferries go to Monterosso (July and Aug. Su, check at office for more information and summer specials; €20), Portofino (June 10-Sept. 5 Tu-Su depart morning, return late afternoon; €13), and San Fruttuoso (June-Sept., every hr. 8am-7pm, €9).

📋 🛈 ORIENTATION AND PRACTICAL INFORMATION. Camogli extends uphill from the sea to pine and olive groves and downhill from the train station toward a stretch of beach. To get to the *centro*, turn right out of the **train station** on **Via XX Settembre,** walk 100m, and then turn left down the stairs to beachfront **Via**

Garibaldi. The English-speaking staff at the **tourist office,** V. XX Settembre 33, helps book accommodations. (☎77 10 66. **Internet** access €1.50 per 30min. Open in summer M-Sa 9am-12:30pm and 4-7pm, Su 9am-12:30pm. Cash only.) **Currency exchange** is available at **Banco di Chiavari della Riviera Ligure,** V. XX Settembre 19, which has an **ATM** outside. (☎77 51 13. Open M-Sa 8:20am-1:20pm and 2:30-4pm.) In case of emergency, call **police,** G. B. Ferrari (☎77 07 25), or the **carabinieri,** V. Cuneo 30/F (☎77 00 00). A **pharmacy,** V. Repubblica 4-6, posts after-hours rotation. (☎77 10 81. Open daily July-Aug. 8:30am-12:30pm and 4-8pm; Sept.-June 3:30-7:30pm. MC/V.) The **post office** is at V. Cuneo 4. (☎77 68 31. Open M-F 8am-1:30pm, Sa 8am-12:30pm. Cash only.) **Postal Code:** 16032.

⌂ ACCOMMODATIONS. Prices and availability vary greatly according to season and day of the week. Though the tourist office can help with last-minute rooms, reserve ahead and be prepared to pay a higher price in summer. The gorgeously renovated █Hotel Augusta ❸, V. Piero Schiaffino 100, attends to every detail. Fourteen blue and yellow rooms are handsomely furnished; all have bath, TV, and phone. Some overlook the harbor from private balconies. From the train station, turn right and keep walking until V. Repubblica turns into V. P. Schiaffino. (☎77 05 92; www.htlaugusta.com. Breakfast €10. Internet access free; limit 15min. Doubles €68-98; triples €105-150. AmEx/MC/V.) The █Albergo La Camogliese ❹, V. Garibaldi 55, is just steps from the beach. Exit train station, walk down the long stairway to the right, and look for the blue sign. Large, comfortable rooms are as convenient as the English-speaking staff is helpful. All rooms have bath, TV, safe, and phone. (☎77 14 02; www.lacamogliese.it. Breakfast included. Internet access available. Singles €50-87; doubles €67-99; triples €90-120. 10% discount with cash payment. AmEx/MC/V.) The **Pensione Faro ❹,** V. Schiaffino 116-118, above the restaurant of the same name, offers six quiet rooms with bath, TV, and tranquil sea views. (☎/fax 77 14 00. Breakfast €4. Singles €40-50; doubles €60-80. AmEx/MC/V.)

❐ FOOD. Focaccia is the specialty in Camogli, along with fresh seafood caught by local fishermen. █Focacceria Pasticceria Revello ❶, V. Garibaldi 183, is famous in the region for fresh, crispy flatbreads and delectable pastries. This shop invented the town's beloved *camogliesi* (dense and crumbly cookies; €21 per kg). Make like the locals and lunch on focaccia with onions or *formaggio*. (☎77 07 77; www.revellocamogli.com. Focaccia €8.50 per kg. Open daily 8am-2pm and 4-8pm. MC/V.) The creamy *gelato* from █Gelato e Dintorni ❶, V. Garibaldi 104/105, puts nationally ranked rivals to shame. Just as heavenly as the town itself, their specialty yogurt is topped with fresh fruit. (☎77 43 53. 2 scoops €1.40. Sicilian *granita* €1.70. Open daily 11:30am-11pm. Cash only.) Il Portico Spaghetteria ❷, V. Garibaldi 197A, offers creative pastas at excellent value that will satisfy every craving; try the *pasta alla turidu* (with anchovies, raisins, tomatoes, and fennel) for €8. (☎77 02 54. Pasta €6.50-9. Cover €1.50. Lunch 12:30pm; dinner 8pm. Cash only.) Find groceries and picnic supplies at shops on V. Repubblica (one block from the harbor) or at the **Picasso** supermarket, V. XX Settembre 35. (Open M-Sa 8:15am-12:30pm and 4:30-7:30pm, Su 8:30am-12:30pm. MC/V.) On Wednesdays, an **open-air market** fills P. del Teatro with local produce and cheap clothing. (Open 8am-noon.)

⚠█ OUTDOOR ACTIVITIES AND NIGHTLIFE. The Camogli tourist office has a useful **trail map.** Painted red shapes mark the paths, which start at the end of V. Cuneo near the *carabinieri* station. Ferry or snorkeling trips also make inter-

LIGURIA

esting (but more costly) diversions. **B&B Diving Center,** V. San Fortunato 11/13, off V. Schiaffino, sails boats for scuba diving at points along the coast. (☎/fax 77 27 51; www.bbdiving.it. Open daily June 15-Sept. 15 9am-1pm and 2:30-7:30pm; Sept. 16-June 14 9am-1pm and 3:30-7pm. 1-person canoe €17 per ½-day, 2-person €30 per ½-day. Scuba tours with guide and equipment Sa-Su 4 per day, €37. 10-person boat capacity. Cash only.) The **Sagra del Pesce,** an enormous fish fry, is held annually on the 2nd Sunday in May. The night before the big fry, the town gathers for a procession honoring the patron saint of fishermen, followed by a fireworks display and a bonfire-building contest. The next day the fryers cook in a gargantuan frying pan, which measures 4m in diameter and holds 2000 fish to feed the jolly crowd. After the sardine rush, the colossal pan hangs on a city wall along the stairs to the beach.

Spend nights in peaceful Camogli enjoying a cool drink and a sea view. Order a mojito (€5) or sangria (€4) to cap off the day at the upscale bar **Il Barcollo,** V. Garibaldi 92. (☎ 77 33 22. Open M-F 4pm-3am, Sa-Su 11am-3am. Cash only.) Just down the boulevard is the pirate-themed **Hook,** V. al Porto 4, decorated like a ship's cabin and offering over 60 types of rum (€3-18) to wash down the good food. (☎ 77 07 11. *Panini* €3-4. Happy hour 6-9pm; drinks €5. Open M, W, Su 8am-3am, Tu 6pm-3am. AmEx/MC/V.) Around the corner, the hot spot, **Bistingo Sea Bar,** P. Colombo 12, offers many mixed drinks. (☎ 77 43 26. Drinks €5-7. Happy hour 6-9pm; all mixed drinks €5.16. Open M-Tu and Th-Su 5pm-3am. AmEx/MC/V.)

▨ DAYTRIP FROM CAMOGLI: SAN FRUTTUOSO. The hikes from Camogli to tiny San Fruttuoso (san FROO-too-OH-so; pop. 8, 10 including dogs) follow two labeled trails that wind through Portofino's nature reserve. The easier 2hr. hike along **Trail #1,** marked by a red circle, climbs up and around Mt. Portofino through ancient forests and olive groves, with a descent to the harbor on a stone path. Only experts should venture the 2½hr. trek on **Trail #2,** marked by two red dots, which winds along the coast, past Nazi anti-aircraft bunkers and through forests to vistas of the sea before descending into town. Proper shoes are essential. Trail maps are available at the Camogli tourist office.

The town is named after its abbey, the Benedictine **Abbazia di San Fruttuoso di Capodimonte,** constructed from the 10th through 13th centuries. The monastery and tower rotate archaeological exhibits. (☎ 77 27 03. *Abbazia* open daily 10am-7pm. Tower open daily 10am-1pm and 2-5:30pm. Last entry 30min. before closing. €7, children €4.) Fifteen meters offshore and 17m underwater, the bronze *Christ of the Depths* stands with arms upraised in memory of the sea's casualties. The statue now protects scuba divers, and a replica stands in **Chiesa di San Fruttuoso,** enticing visitors who travel by ferry to make an offering to the *Sacrario dei Morti in Mare* (Sanctuary for the Dead at Sea). Locals with small boats offer rides to the underwater statue from the docks for €2.50. Pack a picnic lunch or head to **Da Laura ❷** for delicious *lasagne al pesto* for €8. (Open noon-3pm. Cash only.) *(San Fruttuoso is accessible by trails from Portofino Mare 1½hr., Portofino Vetta 1½hr., or Camogli 2-2½hr. Golfo Paradiso (☎ 77 20 91; www.golfoparadiso.it) runs boats from Camogli to San Fruttuoso in summer; Tu and Th-Sa every hr. 8am-5pm, last return 6-7pm; round-trip €8. Servizio Marittimo del Tigullio (☎ 28 46 70) runs ferries from Camogli to Portofino every hr. 9:30am-4:30pm, round-trip €12, and Santa Margherita every hr. 9:15am-4:15pm, €7.)*

SANTA MARGHERITA LIGURE ☎ 0185

Since its founding in the 12th century, Santa Margherita Ligure (SAN-ta Mar-ge-REE-ta LEE-goo-reh; pop. 10,244) led a calm existence as a fishing village far from the Levante limelight. In the early 20th century, however, Hollywood stars popularized it, and its fame expanded further following a 50s *National Geographic* feature. A glitzy beachfront and palm tree-lined harbor provide plenty of photo ops. Though Santa Margherita remains a bit pricey, the town sports good-value restaurants and its location is ideal for daytrips to other coastal towns.

TRANSPORTATION. The town lies on the Genoa-La Spezia line that also connects to the Cinque Terre. **Trains** run every hour to Genoa (50min., €2.10) and Monterosso (1hr., €3). Ticket office is inside the station. (Open daily 6am-7pm. MC/V.) Tigullio **buses** (☎28 88 34) depart from the small green kiosk in P. Vittorio Veneto for Camogli (30min., every 45min., €1.10) and Portofino (20min., 3 per hr., €1). The ticket office is open daily 6:55am-7:25pm. Servizio Marittimo del Tigullio, V. Palestro 8/1B (☎28 46 70; www.traghettiportofino.it), runs **ferries** from docks at P. Martiri della Libertà to: Cinque Terre (1st Su of May-last Su of Sept. 9am, round-trip €22) and Portofino (M-F hourly 10:15am-4:15pm, Sa-Su hourly 9:15am-5:15pm; €4.50). **Taxis** are in P. Stazione (☎28 65 08) and on V. Pescino (☎28 79 98).

ORIENTATION AND PRACTICAL INFORMATION. From the **train station**, turn left on **Via Roma**, and follow it towards the water to **Piazza Vittorio Veneto**. Turn right on V. Pesciano, which winds around **Piazza Martiri della Libertà**. **Piazza Caprera** is between them set back from the water. From P. V. Veneto, V. Guglielmo Marconi winds around the port and V. XXV Aprile leads to the tourist office, becoming **Corso Matteotti** near the town's main square, **Piazza Mazzini**. The staff at **Pro Loco tourist office**, V. XXV Aprile 2/B, provides maps and lodging advice. (☎28 74 85. Open M-Sa 9:30am-12:30pm and 3-7:30pm, Su 9:30am-12:30pm and 4:30-7:30pm.) In case of **emergency**, call the **police**, P. Mazzini 46 (☎20 54 50). **Farmacia Dr Machi**, V. Palestro 44, off P. Caprera, posts after-hours rotation. (☎28 70 02. Open M-W and F-Su 8:30am-12:30pm and 4-8pm. MC/V.) A **hospital** (☎68 31) is on V. Fratelli Arpe. Check email at **The Internet Point**, V. Giuncheto 39. Follow V. Dogali from P. Mazzini; it's on the left. (☎29 30 92; liguriacom@tigullio.it. €3.50 per 30min. Open M-Sa 10am-1pm and 3-7:30pm. Cash only.) The **post office**, V. Roma 36, has **currency exchange**, *fermoposta* services, and a 24hr. **ATM** outside. (☎29 47 51. Open M-F 8am-6:30pm, Sa 8am-12:30pm. Cash only.) **Postal Code:** 16038.

ACCOMMODATIONS. Ritzy waterfront accommodations are by no means the only options, and in Santa Margherita, there's no such thing as a long walk to the sea. Accommodations do tend to be pricey, though, so be prepared to spend a little more during a stay here. Immaculately clean rooms with cozy beds and private showers truly make for a heavenly stay at ■ **Hotel Conte Verde ❹**, V. Zara 1, off V. Roma. From train station turn right on V. Trieste which becomes V. Roma. Rates vary by amenities and season. (☎28 71 39; www.hotelconteverde.it. Breakfast included. Singles €40-55, with bath €65-120; doubles €65-90/70-150; triples €90-120; quads €100-230. AmEx/MC/V.) **Hotel Nuova Riviera ❺**, V. Belvedere 10, is run by an English-speaking family. Large, bright rooms in main house all have private bath as do the four rooms in neighboring annex. (☎287 403; www.nuovariviera.com. Breakfast included for hotel rooms, €5 for annex rooms. Internet access €5 per 30min. Hotel singles €65-95; doubles €75-105; triples €95-130; quads €150. Annex doubles €60-90; triples €75-110. Pay in the main house. Cash only for annex rooms; MC/V for hotel rooms.) Find **Albergo Annabella ❹**, V. Costasecca 10/1, behind P. Mazzini and across from the hospital. Kind owner Annabella aims to make guests feel at home in 10 comfortable rooms, some with bath. Shared bath is large and clean. (☎28 65 31. Breakfast €4. Singles €40-45; doubles €60; triples €80-90; quads €100-120. Cash only.)

FOOD. Markets and bakeries line C. Matteotti. Locals descend on the famous ■**Trattoria Da Pezzi ❶**, V. Cavour 21, for its home-style cuisine and jovial atmosphere. *Farinata* (€4) and *torta pasquelina* (€4.70-5.50) are great choices. (☎28 53 03. Takeout available. *Primi* €3.80-6.70, *secondi* €4.80-14.50. Cover €0.80.

Open M-F and Su 10am-2:15pm and 5-9:15pm. MC/V.) ▨**Trattoria Baicin ❸**, V. Algeria 5, is off P. Martiri della Libertà. Mama Carmela serves glorious plates like the *trofie alla Genovese* (pasta with string beans and pesto) for €6.50. (☎28 67 63. *Primi* €5.50-7.50, *secondi* €9.50-16.50. Cover €1.50. Open Tu-Su noon-3pm and 7-11:30pm. AmEx/MC/V.) It's hard to find better dishes than the *pansotti alla salsa di noci* (vegetable-filled pasta in walnut cream sauce; €7) at **La Locanda Azzura ❸**, V. San Bernardo 3. From the sea, turn right off C. Matteotti. This unpretentious spot with plastic furniture for outdoor seating is surprisingly elegant inside. (☎28 53 94. *Primi* €6-10, *secondi* €7.50-17. Cover €2. Open M-Tu and Th-Su 12:10-2pm and 7:10-10:30pm. MC/V.) **L'Approdo ❺**, V. Cairoli 26, is a bit of a splurge, but excellent food, beautiful presentation, and courteous service are worth the extra expense. Old family recipes have created succulent €26 *scampi*. (☎28 17 89. *Primi* €11-15, *secondi* €16-36. Cover €3. Open Tu 7:30pm-midnight, W-Su 12:30-2pm and 7:30pm-midnight. AmEx/MC/V.) Finish your meals at **Gelateria Centrale ❶**, Largo Giusti 14. Crowds gather for *pinguini* (€2.50), cones of *gelato* in a thick chocolate shell. (☎28 74 80. Open daily 8:30am-midnight. Cash only.) Buy essentials at the **Coop**, C. Matteotti 8, off P. Mazzini. (☎28 43 15. Open M-Sa 8:15am-1pm and 3:30-8pm, Su 8:30am-1pm. AmEx/MC/V.)

▧▨ **SIGHTS AND NIGHTLIFE.** If lapping waves at the pebbly public **beach** across from the main promenade, C. Doria, aren't sufficiently invigorating, visit the Rococo **Basilica di Santa Margherita**, in P. Caprera, dripping with gold and crystal chandeliers. The church also contains fine Flemish and Italian artwork. (☎28 65 55. Open daily 7:30am-noon and 3-6:45pm.) Off V. della Vittoria, paths wind uphill to the pink-and-white **Villa Durazzo**, which is surrounded by gardens and holds 16th-century paintings. (Basilica open daily July-Aug. 9am-8pm; Sept. and May-June 9am-7pm; Oct. and Apr. 9am-6pm; Nov.-Dec. 9am-5pm. Villa open daily 9am-1pm and 2:30-6pm. Both free.)

Come nightfall, youthful crowds claim the funky-colored tables at **Sabot American Bar**, P. Martiri della Libertà 32, for drinks, sushi platters, and the DJ. (☎28 07 47. Beer €4-6. Mixed drinks €7. Open daily 4pm-4am. MC/V.) Mingle with the fashionistas a few doors down at über-hip **Miami**, P. Martiri della Libertà 29, complete with neon lights, vinyl booths, and €7 Manhattan mixed drinks. (☎28 34 24. *Primi* €7-12, *secondi* €10-20. Open daily 5pm-3am. AmEx/MC/V.)

▧ **DAYTRIP FROM SANTA MARGHERITA**

PORTOFINO

Take bus #82 to Portofino Mare—not Portofino Vetta—from the green bus kiosk in P. Martiri della Libertà in Santa Margherita, where tickets are sold. From Portofino's P. Martiri della Libertà, Tigullio buses run to Santa Margherita (3 per hr., €1). Portofino is also accessible by ferry from Santa Margherita (hourly 10:30am-4pm, €4.50), and Camogli (2 per day, €11).

Portofino (POR-toh-FEE-no; pop. 542) is a perfect half-day outing from Santa Margherita. Yachts fill the harbor, chic designer boutiques and art galleries line the cobblestone streets, and luxury cars crowd parking lots. Nevertheless, the tiny bay of this fine port can be enjoyed by the glamorous and the budget-minded alike. A nature reserve surrounds Portofino and nearby resort village Paraggi which boasts a crowded but beautiful public beach. Treks through the hilly terrain past ruined churches and stately villas lead to Rapallo (2hr.), Santa Margherita (1½hr.), and San Fruttuoso (2hr.). Information regarding hikes is available at the tourist office. Facing the sea, head right, around the port, and climb the stairs for 10min. to reach the cool, stark interior of the **Chiesa di San Giorgio**. Don't forget your camera for the picturesque views of the port from the nearby lookout. Farther up the hill another

10min. is the 16th-century **Castello Brown,** V. alla Penisola 13/A. The castle was once a fortress, but the wealthy Brown family converted it into a summer home after Consul Montague Yeats Brown bought it in 1867 from the Kingdom of Sardinia for 7000 lire. (☎26 71 01 or 26 90 46. Open daily 10am-7pm. €4.)

TIP

A FERRY TALE. Though the hikes and train rides through Portofino's nature reserve are gorgeous, the real charm of the small coastal towns is best experienced from the sea. Hop on one of the many ferries between Camogli, San Fruttuoso, Portofino, and Santa Margherita for incomparable panoramas of colorful buildings nestled among the mountains.

Back in town, **Alimentari Repetto,** P. Martiri dell'Olivetta 30, in the main square in front of the harbor, fortifies hikers with sandwiches from €3 and regional goods such as *limoncello* for around €10. (Open daily in summer 8am-10pm; in winter 9am-6pm. Cash only.) **Trattoria Concordia ❸,** V. del Fondaco 5, behind P. della Libertà, serves authentic Ligurian cuisine in a small, nautical-themed dining room. Local favorites are cheaper here than at many other harbor haunts. (☎26 92 07. *Primi* €9-30, *secondi* €12-30. Service 10%. Open M and W-Su noon-3pm and 7:30-10pm. AmEx/MC/V.) A drink at one of the numerous bars along the harbor costs upward of €6.50, though watching town life unfold along the harbor may be worth it. The APT **tourist office,** V. Roma 35, has free maps and brochures and an English-speaking staff. (☎26 90 24. Open M-Tu 10:30am-1:30pm and 2:30-7:30pm, W-Su 10:30am-1:30pm and 2-7:30pm.)

CINQUE TERRE   ☎0187

Cinque Terre (CHEEN-kweh TEHR-reh; pop. 6000) is an outdoorsman's paradise: strong hikers can cover all five villages in about 5hr., and numerous opportunities for kayaking, cliff jumping, or horseback riding present themselves along way. For those who prefer not to break a sweat, trains connect the five villages. Rather than rushing through, take the time to wander through the villages' tiny clusters of rainbow-colored houses amid hilly stretches of olive groves and vineyards. Though Cinque Terre was formerly a hidden treasure of the Ligurian coastline, increased publicity and word of mouth have made the towns fodder for a booming tourism industry; now, conversations in English, French and German are just as common as those in Italian. So reserve ahead, put on your hiking boots, and step away from the modern world for a few days to soothe mind, body, and spirit.

▐ TRANSPORTATION

Trains: The towns lie on the Genoa-La Spezia line. Schedules are available at tourist offices. Most trains stop at **Monterosso,** making it the most accessible of the 5 towns. From the station on V. Fegina, trains run to: **Florence** (3½hr., hourly, €8) via **Pisa** (2½hr., €5); **Genoa** (1½hr., hourly 4:55am-11:35pm, €4.50); **La Spezia** (20min., every 30min., €2); **Rome** (7hr., every 2hr., €17-27). Frequent local trains connect the 5 towns (5-20min.; every 50min.; M-F €1.10, Sa-Su €1.20).

Ferries: Monterosso can be reached by ferry from **La Spezia** (2hr., 4 per day, €12). Ferries from Monterosso also connect the towns. **Navigazione Golfo dei Poeti** (☎81 84 40 or 73 29 87), in front of the IAT office at the port (in the old town; see **Practical Information,** below). To: **Manarola** (7 per day, €6.50); **Portovenere** (7 per day, €12); **Riomaggiore** (8 per day, €8); **Vernazza** (8 per day, €3).

Taxis: ☎335 61 65 842.

Boat Rental: Samba (☎339 68 12 265; open daily 9am-6pm), across from the train station and along the beaches in Monterosso, rents 2-person canoes for €25 per 3hr.

Cash only. **Il Corsaro Rosso** (☎328 69 35 355), on the harbor in Riomaggiore, rents kayaks and 3-person canoes for €18 per hr. Snorkeling €10 per day. Cash only.

ORIENTATION AND PRACTICAL INFORMATION

The five villages string along the coast between Levanto in the northwest and La Spezia in the southeast, and are connected by trains, roads (although cars are not allowed inside the towns), and footpaths that traverse the rocky shoreline. **Monterosso** is the largest and western-most town, followed from west to east by **Vernazza, Corniglia, Manarola,** and **Riomaggiore.** The following are the principal listings. Separate listings follow for individual towns.

> **TIP** **TERRE TRIPPING.** The train stations and Cinque Terre National Park offices in each of the 5 towns sell 1-day (€8), 3-day (€18.50), and 7-day (€34) **Cinque Terre Cards** with unlimited train, bus, and path access among the 5 villages, La Spezia, and Levanto.

Tourist Offices:

Cinque Terre National Park Office, P. Garibaldi 20 (☎81 70 59 or 80 20 53; www.parconazionale5terre.it), in Monterosso, has info on hiking trails and accommodations. **Cinque Terre Cards** available. Open daily 8am-8pm.

Pro Loco, V. Fegina 38 (☎/fax 81 75 06), below the Monterosso train station. Provides info on boats, hikes, and accommodations. Open daily 9:30am-6:30pm.

Tourist Office, in the train station in Riomaggiore (☎76 99 61). Has info on hotels and excursions. Open daily June-Sept. 6:30am-9pm. Tourist offices in Manarola, Riomaggiore, and Monterosso have **Internet** points.

Tours: Navigazione 5 Terre Golfo dei Poeti (☎73 29 87; fax 73 03 36) offers boat tours to **Vernazza** (€3, round-trip €5), **Manarola** (€6.50, round-trip €10.50), and **Riomaggiore** (€8, round-trip €11.50) from **Monterosso** (8 per day 10:30am-5:50pm) and **Vernazza** (8 per day 10:40am-6pm). Round-trip boats also go to **Portovenere** (€20) and **Lerici** (€20). Dates and times subject to change seasonally.

First Aid: ☎338 85 30 949 for doctor on call M-W and F-Su. **Carabinieri:** in Monterosso (☎81 75 24); in Riomaggiore (☎92 01 12).

Post Office: Main branch in **Monterosso,** V. Roma 73 (☎81 83 94). Open M-F 8am-1:15pm, Sa 8am-12:30pm. **Postal Codes:** 19016 (Monterosso); 19017 (Manarola and Riomaggiore); 19018 (Corniglia and Vernazza).

> **TIP** **TREK THE TERRE.** If pressed for time, take the train (€1.20) to Monterosso or Corniglia and hike the 2 paths connecting those 2 towns. The better of the 4 trails along the Cinque Terre, the footpaths connecting Monterosso, Vernazza, and Corniglia, while strenuous, provide great vistas of the precariously positioned Cinque Terre towns along the Ligurian coast. Passes available for footpaths and trains at each Cinque Terre tourist office.

THE TOWNS

MONTEROSSO

The largest and most developed of the five villages, Monterosso (Mohn-teh-ROS-so; pop. 1500) is the beach bum's town of choice. Three sandy shores and a spirited backpacking and hiking crew create the liveliest nightlife in the five *terre.* Monterosso's character endures in the friendly local ambience and the *centro storico*'s winding streets.

⚡☏ ORIENTATION AND PRACTICAL INFORMATION. Descend the steps from the **train station** (where there is a **tourist office**) and turn left on **Lungomare di Fegina** through a tunnel into **Piazza Garibaldi,** the heart of town. **Exchange currency** at **Cassa di Risparmio della Spezia,** V. Roma 47 (open M-F 8:10am-1:10pm and 2:30-3:30pm, Su 8:10-11:30am) and **Banca Carige,** V. Roma 69 (open daily 8:05am-1:15pm and 2:30-3:45pm); **ATM** outside. ATMs also at **Bancomat,** V. Fegina 40, under the train station. Do **laundry** at **Laundry Matic,** one on V. Molinelli 12, and one on the corner of V. Roma and V. Mazzini. (Wash, detergent, and dry €11 per 5kg. Open daily 9am-1pm and 2-7pm. Cash only.) The **pharmacy,** V. Fegina 44, posts after-hours rotations outside. (☏18 18 394. Open M-F 8:30am-12:30pm and 4-8pm, Sa-Su 9am-12:30pm and 4-7:30pm. Cash only.) **The Net,** V. Vittorio Emanuele 55, offers **Internet access.** (☏81 72 88. €1 per 10min., €0.10 per min. thereafter, or €10 per 2hr. Open daily 9:30am-12:30pm and 3:30-7:30pm. Cash only.)

☏☐ ACCOMMODATIONS AND FOOD. While most of Cinque Terre's hotels are in Monterosso, they generally fill up in early June. Inquire at the tourist office for help finding the more plentiful *affittacamere* (room rentals). The lively ▨**Hotel Souvenir ❷,** V. Gioberti 24, popular with students, has 47 beds in comfortable rooms and a private garden perfect for socializing. (☏/fax 81 75 95; hotel_souvenir@yahoo.com. Breakfast €5. Rooms with shared bath for students €25; private rooms €40. Cash only.) The friendly owners of nearby Cantina di Sciacchetrà also rent rooms at **Alle 5 Terre ❷,** V. Molinelli 87. Five rooms all have bath, TV, and fridge; some with balcony view. (☏81 78 28 or 328 55 05 623. €25 per person. MC/V.) To get to **Albergo La Pineta ❹** at V. Padre Semeria 3, turn right from the train station away from the *centro,* then right on V. Padre Semeria. Amiable owners keep a private beach and no-frills rooms with bath and TV, some with sea views. (☏82 90 29; hotel_lapineta@virgilio.it. Breakfast included. Singles from €40-50; doubles from €60. Cash only.)

Allegedly, every restaurant in Cinque Terre prepares the best pesto, the freshest fish, and the most savory *acciughe* (anchovies) or *cozze ripiene* (mussels stuffed with grains and vegetables). To avoid high prices, consider a picnic of pesto-spread focaccia and juicy local fruit; wash it all down with a glass of light, dry *Cinque Terre bianco,* or some *Sciacchetrà* dessert wine. ▨**Il Ciliegio ❸,** Località Beo

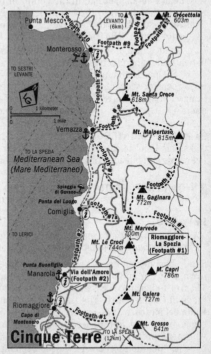

2, cooks fantastic meals with ingredients fresh from the owner's gardens. Savor the exceptional *trofie al pesto* (pasta with pesto; €7.50) and *cozze ripiene* (stuffed mussels; €9) featured in reviews worldwide, in the flowered garden overlooking the coastline. The restaurant is a 10min. drive from town; management offers free shuttle service from V. Roma on request. (☎81 78 29. *Primi* €6-10, *secondi* €7-13. Cover €2. Open Tu-Su 12:30-2:30pm and 7:30-10:30pm. AmEx/MC/V.) In a narrow alley off V. Roma, **Ristorante Al Carugio ❸**, V. San Pietro 9, serves hefty portions of traditional Ligurian dishes. Share the excellent *risotto con frutti di mare* (seafood risotto; €9.30) between at least two people. (☎/fax 81 73 67. *Primi* €6-10.50, *secondi* €7-15. Open M-W and F-Su noon-2:30pm and 6-10:30pm. AmEx/MC/V.) **Focacceria Il Frantoio ❶**, V. Gioberti 1, bakes tasty *farinata* and focaccia stuffed with olives, onions, or herbs. (☎81 83 33. Slices €1-3. Open M-W and F-Su 9am-2pm and 3:30-8pm. Cash only.) Those interested in fine wine should visit **◧Cantina di Sciacchetrà**, V. Roma 7, which has free tastings, delicious *antipasti*, and deals on gourmet souvenirs. English-speaking staff is patient with tourists. (☎81 78 28. Bottles of *Cinque Terre bianco* €4-19, *Sciacchetrà* €28. Open Feb.-Dec. daily 9am-11pm. AmEx/MC/V.) **SuperConad Margherita**, P. Matteotti 9, stocks groceries. (Open June-Sept. M-Sa 8am-1pm and 5-7:30pm, Su 8am-1pm. MC/V.)

◧◧ SIGHTS AND NIGHTLIFE. Monterosso has Cinque Terre's largest **free beach,** surrounded by a cliff-cove in front of the *centro storico*. About 200m to the right of the train station, **Il Gigante,** an enormous, craggy giant carved into the rocky cliff, watches over the sunbathers on the free beach below. The 15th-century **Chiesa dei Cappuccini,** in the center of town, yields broad vistas of the five towns. In the chapel to the left is the impressive 17th-century *Crucifixion* by Flemish master Anthony Van Dyck, who sojourned here during his most productive years. (Open daily 9am-noon and 4-7pm. Free.)

At night, chow down on hot sandwiches (from €4) and mixed drinks (€5) beneath hanging electric guitars at **FAST,** V. Roma 13. (☎81 71 64. Beer €3-4, tap €2.80-8. Open in summer daily 8am-2am; in winter M-W and F-Su 8am-noon. MC/V.) Enjoy seaside views from the patio over beer, liquor and snacks at **Il Casello,** V. Lungo Ferravia 70. (☎81 83 30 or 333 49 27 629. Drinks from €3. Mixed drinks about €6. Open daily 11am-midnight. Cash only.)

◧ HIKING: MONTEROSSO-VERNAZZA. The hardest of the four town-linking treks, this 1½hr. hike climbs steeply up a cliff-side staircase, winding past terraced vineyards and hillside cottages before the steep descent into Vernazza.

◧ DAYTRIP FROM MONTEROSSO

LEVANTO
A difficult 2½hr. hike connects Levanto with Monterosso. Trains run to Levanto from Monterosso (5min. to Monterosso, every 30min. 4:46am-11:42pm, €1.30).

Sandy beaches and seaside promenades are the main attractions at this beach town, a busier and more urban alternative to the laid-back Cinque Terre towns. The trek to Levanto (LE-van-toh) is more uncultivated and rugged than most of the hikes in Cinque Terre. The trail leaves Monterosso for a harsh 45min. climb to **Punta del Mesco,** a 19th-century lighthouse converted from the ruins of an Augustinian monastery. Before descending to Levanto, it wraps around cliffs and passes vineyards, orchards, and the remains of a 13th-century castle. Private and public beaches line the promenade. **Ostello Ospitalia del Mare ❷**, V. San Nicolo 1, is the perfect option for an overnight stay and only a 5min. walk from the beach. The rooms are spacious, sunny, and have baths. (☎80 25 62; www.ospitaliadelmare.it. Last train from Cinque Terre arrives at 12:35am. Breakfast included. Internet access €5 per hr. Reception 8am-1pm, 4-8pm, and 9:30-11pm. 8-bed dorms €20.50; 6-bed dorms €23; 4-bed dorms €26; doubles with bath €28-30. MC/V.) Load up for a beach picnic at **La Focacceria Dome ❶**, V. Dante Alghieri 18, serving fresh focaccia, *farinata*, and pizza (€1-2) in heaping portions. (Open Sept.-Apr. daily 9am-8:30pm. Closed Oct.-Mar. Tu. Cash only.) Those staying for dinner shouldn't miss **Da Rino ❸**, V. Garibaldi 10, for a family-style Ligurian feast where the fish is always fresh. (☎328 38 90 350. *Primi* €6-9, *secondi* €10-16. Cover €1.50. Open daily 7-10pm. Cash only.) To reach the **tourist office** in P. Mazzini from the station, cross the *piazza*, go down the stairs that lead to a bridge, cross the bridge, and continue on C. Roma (☎80 81 25. 10min. walk. Open M-Sa 9am-1pm and 3-6pm, Su 9am-1pm).

VERNAZZA

Graced by a large seaside *piazza* and a small but beautiful stretch of sandy beach, Vernazza (Vehr-NAT-sa; pop. 1000) is historically the wealthiest of the five Cinque Terre towns. Climb to the remains of the 11th-century Castello Doria, up a staircase on the left of P. Marconi, for great views of the other four towns.

> **✦TIP** **TUNNEL VISION.** Depending which train car you're in, stops in Cinque Terre stations, particularly Vernazza and Riomaggiore, are in tunnels! This may not appear to be the station stop, but often it is; ride in the center of the train and watch for your stop to be sure.

■🖪 **ORIENTATION AND PRACTICAL INFORMATION.** Lined with shops and restaurants, **Via E. Q. Visconti** runs from the station towards the sea and turns into **Via Roma** about halfway to the beach. **Piazza Marconi** overlooks the harbor at the end of V. Roma. There is a **tourist office** in the train station.

🖍🖸 **ACCOMMODATIONS AND FOOD.** Vernazza has some great hotels and private rooms. **Hotel Gianni Franzi ❹**, P. Marconi 1, has 23 rooms, all with antique decor, in several small rustic buildings at the top of the town. Some sport balconies with postcard views of the coast and Corniglia. (☎82 10 03; www.giannifranzi.it. Singles €42-65; doubles €60-85; triples with bath €105. AmEx/MC/V.) The friendly owners of **Albergo Barbara ❸**, P. Marconi 30, on the top floor, make their guests feel at home. The nine rooms are bright and some have views of the port. (☎81 23 98; www.albergobarbara.it. Ring bell to enter. Doubles €50, with bath €65, with bath and view €100. Extra bed €10. Closed Dec.-Feb. Cash only.)

Reputedly home to the best restaurants in Cinque Terre, P. Marconi fills with hungry tourists each evening. The oldest trattoria in Vernazza, **Trattoria Gianni Franzi ❷**, P. Marconi 1, is famed for its pesto and friendly local charm. Dine casually in the roomy stone-walled interior or outside on the *piazza*. (☎82 10 03; fax 81 22 28. *Primi* €4-12, *secondi* €6.50-20. Open M-Tu and Th-Su noon-3pm and 7:30-9:30pm. AmEx/MC/V.) For a delicious splurge, visit elegant **Gambero Rosso ❺**, P. Marconi 7. Touted by *vernazzesi*, the service is excellent and the food superb. (☎81 22 65; fax 82 12 60. *Primi* €12-16, *secondi* €15-23. Cover €3. Open Tu-Su noon-3:15pm and 7-10pm. AmEx/MC/V.) For a slice of pizza (€3), pop into to **Pizzeria Baja Saracena ❶**, P. Marconi 16, to enjoy a quick snack between rounds of hiking and sunbathing. (Open daily 10am-7pm. Cash only.) Groceries, fresh produce, and gourmet foods are available at **Salumi e Formaggi**, V. Visconti 19. (☎82 12 40. Open M-Sa 8am-2pm and 5:20-7:30pm, Su 8am-1:30pm. Cash only.)

LIGURIA

THE HIDDEN DEAL

GUVANO BEACH

n 1873, the first Italian railroad ut a tunnel through the Guvano alley surrounding Corniglia, and made a sparkling cove newly accessible. The track was abandoned in 1968, but before long, ocal youth discovered the secluded stretch and turned it nto a liberal, lawless—and clothingless—haven. In the 90s, the ocal government gave the lands over to a group of agricultural workers who cleaned the beaches, planted vineyards and omatoes, and began charging an entrance fee; they are awaiting a license from the state to hire a lifeguard and sell food. he area, though, hasn't lost its naturalist charm and remains a emnant of the wild spirit of the 60s and 70s. Open-minded travelers who find the tunnel can strut their stuff with locals along he two pristine coves and take brisk, nude dips in the sea.

To reach Guvano, take a left rom the Corniglia station, pass he stairs, and turn left down the amp on the other side of the racks. At the bottom of the ramp, urn right. When you get to the unnel, press the button; the gate will open. A 15min. walk through a dark, damp, tunnel (don't go alone—female travelers should bring a friend to the beach to avoid unwanted attention) delivers you to the cove. (Open May-Sept. M-F 9am-6:30pm, Sa-Su 9am-7pm. €5, or €4 with *Let's Go: Italy* in hand.)

HIKING: VERNAZZA-CORNIGLIA. Geographic diversity and **unparalleled views** are the rewards along this 1½hr. hike. The trail climbs harshly from Vernazza, passing through vineyards and olive groves before curving through uncultivated landscape. Scents of rosemary, thyme, lemon, and lavender perfume the air in the summer. At one point, the trail bends to reveal the secluded, clothing- optional **Guvano beach** hundreds of feet below, occupied largely by students and adventurous types willing to make the trek down the mountain. Corniglia, perched spectacularly on a cliff in the distance, is in view for the duration of the hike.

CORNIGLIA

Hundreds of steps and a 10min. climb from the station bring travelers to this colorful village clinging to a seaside cliff. Without the beachside glitter of the other towns, Corniglia (Cor-NEEL-ya; pop. 500) offers a more peaceful ambience that makes it a good resting point midway through the Cinque Terre hike. A pebbly strip of public beach beneath the tracks packs in sunbathers, while more secluded beaches beckon hikers off the trail on the way to Vernazza.

ORIENTATION. **Via Alla Stazione** begins at the top of the station steps, turning into **Via Fieschi** in the center of town. To the right of the *centro*, down **Via Serra,** is the entrance to the trail from Vernazza.

ACCOMMODATIONS AND FOOD. Due to its small size and cliffside location, Corniglia is a better daytrip than place to spend the night. If you do plan to stay, private rooms are the way to go, as there are few hotels. **Ristorante Cecio ❹**, V. Serra 58, on the road that leads from Corniglia to Vernazza, rents eight rooms above the restaurant with views of the sea and mountains, and eight rooms in the village with terraces. All rooms have bath. (☎81 20 43 or 334 350 6637; www.cecio5terre.com. Singles €55; doubles €60; triples €80. Cash only.) Pizzerias serve hungry hikers all over town, but follow your nose to **La Gata Flora ❶**, V. Fieschi 109, for delicious slices in many varieties. Crispy *farinata* (€1) is also available. (☎82 12 18. Focaccia €1.10-2. Slice €2.50. Whole pizza €4-7. Open M and W-Su 9:30am-4pm and 6-8:30pm; Aug. also open Tu. Cash only.) To get to **La Posada ❸**, V. Alla Stazione 11, climb the staircase from the train station. Turn right on the road at the top; follow for about 50m. The food is delicious, the garden gorgeous, and the sweeping seaside views priceless. (*Primi* €6-8, *secondi* €7-10. Cover €2. Open daily noon-3pm and 7-10:30pm. MC/V.) The cavernous **Cantina de Mananan ❸**, V. Fieschi 117, provides a dark, cool setting in which to enjoy hearty meals from the mix-and-match pasta and sauce menu. (**☎**82 11 66. *Primi* €8-10, *secondi* €11-15. Cover €1.55. Open M and W-Su 12:45-2:15pm and 7:45-9:15pm. Cash only.) On the outdoor terrace of **Ristorante Cecio ❸**, V. Serra 11, sip wine and twirl spaghetti. (**☎**81 20 43. *Primi* and *secondi* €7-18. Cover €2.50. Open Jan.-Oct. and Dec. M-Tu and Th-Su noon-3pm and 7:30-10pm. MC/V.)

⚑ HIKING: CORNIGLIA-MANAROLA. Take the stairs down to the station from V. Alla Stazione and turn left, following the path along the railroad tracks. The 1hr. trail begins just after the public beach. Though less picturesque than the hikes between the previous towns, the gentle trail to Manarola boasts an easier, flatter trek than the other trails and does still have some sweeping, open-sea vistas.

MANAROLA

Two large swimming coves, sheltered by rocky inlets, attract swimmers and sunbathers to Manarola (Ma-na-RO-la; pop. 900). Its laid-back pace and newly renovated hostel make this the ideal hangout for the backpacking crowd.

⊞ 🛈 ORIENTATION AND PRACTICAL INFORMATION. From the train station, walk through the tunnel and emerge onto **Via Antonio Discovolo.** Turn left and cross **Piazza Dario Capellino,** after which **Via Birolli** runs to the sea, or turn right and head uphill for the hostel and stunning views. **Farmacia del Mare,** V. A. Discovolo 238, posts a list of late-night pharmacies. (**☎**92 09 30. Open M and F-Sa 9am-1pm and 4-8pm, Tu-Th 9am-1pm. MC/V.)

🏠🍴 ACCOMMODATIONS AND FOOD. To reach the **🏠Ostello Cinque Terre ❶**, V. B. Riccobaldi 21, turn right from the train station, continue uphill 300m and turn left at sign. Here, 48 beds, a bright dining room, a rooftop terrace, and a shelf full of board games contribute to the summer-camp atmosphere. Ask about kayak, bike, and snorkeling equipment rental. (**☎**92 02 15; www.hostel5terre.com. Breakfast €4. 5min. shower and linens included. Laundry wash €4, dry €2 per 30min. Internet access €1.50 per 15min. Wheelchair-accessible. Reception daily 7am-1pm and 5pm-1am. Lockout 1-5pm. Curfew in summer 1am, in winter midnight. Reserve at least 2 weeks ahead. Dorms €18-22; double with private bath €65; quad with private bath €88. AmEx/MC/V.) The cheery **🏠Bed and Breakfast La Torretta ❸**, Vico Volto 20, is filled with flowers. All nine rooms are spacious and have balcony, TV, and A/C. Apartments with kitchen are also available. Common terrace yields some of the town's best sea views. (**☎**92 03 27; www.torrettas.com. Breakfast included. Doubles €70-100. AmEx/MC/V.) The restaurant **Il Porticciolo ❸**, V. Renato Birolli 92, rents five rooms with bath, TV, and balcony. (**☎**/fax 92 00 83; www.ilporticciolo5terre.com. Breakfast €5. Singles €30; doubles €50-60. AmEx/MC/V.)

At **Trattoria da Billy ❸**, V. Rollandi 122, get away from the town center above P. della Chiesa and eat lunch with the locals. Treat your stomach to delicious home-cooked food listed on a handwritten menu and feast your eyes on the lovely views. (**☎**92 068. *Primi* €6-8, *secondi* €7-14. Open M-W and F-Su 12:30-2:30pm and 7-10:30pm. MC/V.) **Marina Piccola ❸**, V. lo Scalo 16, just off V. Renato Birolli, is a little place with big meals. Savor *cozze ripiene* (stuffed mussels; €11) on the edge of a rocky cove. (**☎**92 09 23. *Primi* €7-15, *secondi* €7-16. Open Jan.-July and Sept.-Dec. M and W-Su noon-2:30pm and 7pm-midnight. AmEx/MC/V.) **Trattoria Il Porticciolo ❷**, V. Renato Birolli 92, serves hearty meals in a casual ambience at a good value. Il Porticcioto boasts excellent *gnocchi al pesto* (€5.50) and superb

LIGURIA

torta di noci (nut cake) for €4. (☎92 00 83. *Primi* €4-8, *secondi* €6.50-15.50. Open M-Tu and Th-Su 7am-3:30pm and 5-11pm. AmEx/MC/V.)

■ **NIGHTLIFE.** One of the quieter towns of the five, a night in Manarola is more likely to be a low-key evening than a bass-pumping rager, though a few times each summer, Manarola hosts disco parties in a *piazza* above the harbor, advertised on posters around town. **Bar Enrica,** on V. Renato Birolli in Punta Bonfiglio, serves *gelato* by day and mixed drinks by night. (☎92 02 77. *Bruschette* €2.70-4.70. Hot *panini* €3.60-4.20. Beer €2.50-4.40. Mixed drinks €4.50. Open daily 8:30-11am and 8-11pm. Cash only.)

■ **HIKING: MANAROLA-RIOMAGGIORE. Via dell'Amore,** the most famous stretch of Cinque Terre hikes (20min.), passes through a stone tunnel of love decorated by romantic graffiti scenes. With elevators at its beginning and end, the slate-paved walk is almost wheelchair-accessible except for some steps in the middle, and is a good way to ease into the hikes and views the park provides.

RIOMAGGIORE

A castle crowns a cliff above the bright houses that cascade down the valley of Riomaggiore. Here, fishermen varnishing boat hulls are as numerous as sunbathers smoothing on lotion. There are rooms for rent around the harbor; Riomaggiore (REE-yo-ma-JO-reh; pop. 2100) is the best bet to find last-minute lodging, and as a result, houses a busy population of young travelers and a lively nightlife.

■■ **ORIENTATION AND PRACTICAL INFORMATION.** Turn right from the **train station** and walk through a tunnel to the *centro*. The main street, **Via Cristoforo Colombo,** runs up the hill to the left. A **Pro Loco tourist office** in the train station provides info on trails, hotels, and excursions. (☎92 06 33. Open M-F 6:30am-8pm, Sa-Su 7am-9pm.) The **National Park Office** next to the station offers **Internet** access for €0.08 per min. and **currency exchange.** (☎76 05 15. Open daily 8am-9:30pm.) You can also find currency exchange at **Banca Carige,** V. C. Colombo 215. (Open M-F 8:20am-1:20pm and 2:30-4pm. AmEx/MC/V.) **Farmacia del Mare,** V. C. Colombo 182, posts a list of late-night pharmacies. (☎92 01 60. Open M-Sa 9am-noon and 4-8pm, Su 9am-1pm. AmEx/MC/V.) The self-service **Wash and Dry Lavarapido** is at V. C. Colombo 109. (Wash €3.50 per 30min. Open daily 8am-8pm. Cash only.) A **post office** is at V. Pecunia 7. (☎80 31 60. Open M-F 8am-1pm and Sa 8am-noon.)

■■ **ACCOMMODATIONS AND FOOD.** The clean and welcoming ■**Mar-Mar ❷,** V. Malborghetto 4, rents dorms and rooms with bath; some have TV and balcony. Apartments for two to six people are also available. (☎/fax 92 09 32; www.5terre-mar-mar.com. Dorms €20; doubles €60-90; apartments €65-120. Cash only.) **Hotel Ca Dei Duxi ❹,** V. C. Colombo 36, is pleasant and well situated, offering elegant wood furnishings and good value. Six rooms all have bath, TV, A/C, and fridge; some have a terrace. (☎92 00 36; www.duxi.it. Breakfast included. Doubles €80; triples €90-120. Let's Go discount. AmEx/MC/V.) At **5Terre Affitti ❷,** V. C. Colombo 97, Papa Bernardo rents rooms located mostly on the harbor with bath and satellite TV; some have a balcony. (☎92 03 31; www.immobiliare5terre.com. Doubles €50-60; studios with kitchen and views for 2 or 3 people €65-75; quad with kitchen and terrace €90-120. Cash only.) **La Dolce Vita ❷,** V. C. Colombo 120, has a young, friendly staff that attract similar clientele. Rent dorm-style rooms, doubles with bath and minibar, and four-person apartments. (☎76 00 44. Reception open 9:30am-7:30pm. Doubles €50-65; triples €75; quads €90-120. Cash only.) **Edi ❸,** V. C. Colombo 111, rents rooms with bath and minibar as well as apartments for up to four people. Reserve ahead. (☎/fax 92 03 25. Doubles €60, with view €70; apartments doubles €80/130, quads €120/150. AmEx/MC/V; cash only for some privately owned properties, ask ahead.)

At popular **Trattoria La Lanterna ❸**, V. San Giacomo 46, enjoy delicious fresh fish or filling pastas while watching the fishing boats roll by. (☎92 01 20. *Primi* €7-9, *secondi* €5-21. MC/V.) On a cliff above town, the upscale but unpretentious **Ripa del Sole ❹**, V. de Gasperi 282, serves some of the area's most authentic and flavorful cuisine in a dining room bathed in sunlight. The *gnocchi* with scampi and white truffles (€11) are excellent. (☎92 01 43. *Primi* €9.50, *secondi* €9.50-21. Open Tu-Su noon-2pm and 6:30-9:30pm. AmEx/MC/V.) For groceries and fresh produce, stop by **Alimentari della Franca**, V. C. Colombo 253. (☎92 09 29. Open daily 7:45am-1pm and 3-8pm. MC/V.)

⚠️🎶 OUTDOOR ACTIVITIES AND NIGHTLIFE. Coopsub Cinqueterre Diving Center, on V. San Giacomo, conducts supervised dives off the coast, where dolphins abound in June and September. Boat trips include stops to the natural waterfalls of nearby Caneto Beach. (☎92 00 11; www.5terrediving.com. Single kayak €7 per hr.; double kayak €12 per hr. Open daily Easter-Sept. 8:30am-6pm. Cash only.) Nightlife in Rio is not particularly bustling. The bar and outdoor patio at **Bar Centrale**, V. C. Colombo 144, fill up with young international backpackers. Ivo, the energetic bartender, serves a cold brew and turns up the swingin' Motown to please the rowdy crowds. (☎92 02 08. Beer €2-5. Mixed drinks €5-6. Open daily 7:30am-1am. Cash only.) **A Pie de Ma, Bar and Vini**, with sweeping views of turquoise waters below on V. dell'Amore, is a hot spot to grab pre-dinner drinks. (☎92 10 37. Focaccia €3.50. Mixed drinks €5. Live music some F and Sa nights. Open daily 10am-midnight. Cash only.)

ROCK THE BEACH. Free beaches are easy to find in Cinque Terre if you don't mind rocks. Grab a towel and picnic lunch and avoid the private beaches near the city centers. A great stretch of pebble beach lies just beyond the ferry dock in Riomaggiore. Or, pay for a 1-day trail pass and seek out one of the many cliff-side sun-bathing spots along the coast between Riomaggiore and Corniglia.

LA SPEZIA ☎0187

Though the laid-back beach ambience of Cinque Terre is only a short ride away, La Spezia's urban atmosphere seems like another world. Bombarded heavily during WWII because of its naval base and artillery, La Spezia (la SPET-see-ya; pop. 94,000) has since evolved into a commercial port that's proud of its nautical history. Though La Spezia boasts none of the majestic architecture or cobblestone passageways that grace some neighboring villages, it does make a great starting point for daytrips to the small fishing village of Porto Venere, the beach resorts of San Terenzo and Lerici, and the beautiful coves of Fiascherino; it's also an unavoidable stopover to and from Cinque Terre.

🚉 TRANSPORTATION. La Spezia lies on the Genoa-La Spezia-Pisa **train** line. The station is included in the **Cinque Terre Card**, which allows unlimited train use between destinations. **Navigazione Golfo dei Poeti**, V. Don Minzoni 13 (☎73 29 87; www.navigazionegolfodeipoeti.it), runs ferries to each of the Cinque Terre towns (€12; round-trip M-Sa €21, Su €23); Capraia (3hr., round-trip July-Aug. €40); Portovenere (€3.50, round-trip €6.50). Call ahead for schedule. For a **taxi**, call ☎52 35 23 or hail one at the train station.

📋🛈 ORIENTATION AND PRACTICAL INFORMATION. From the **train station**, turn left, and walk down **Via Fiume**, which goes through P. San Bon before turning into **Via del Prione**, the city's main drag. Continue on V. del Prione for 15min. until it

THE BEATEN PATH

Cinque Terre is doubtless a paradise for hikers, with trails connecting cliff-hugging towns along the mountainous shore of the Ligurian coast. Its beauty has even earned it inclusion on the UNESCO World Heritage List. The uniqueness of this land, however, is far from undiscovered, and the tourist stands that line the main streets of the towns offer proof of just that.

Even the picturesque trails, far into the brush, have been unable to escape tourism's impact. The shoes that have packed down the dirt trails have caused deterioration to the landscape, causing it to go (literally) downhill. In response, Cinque Terre was placed on the "World Monument Fund's List of 100 Sites at Risk," and dedicated workers at the Parco Nazionale delle Cinque Terre are committed to its restoration.

The Park's Landscape University organizes work camps to rebuild stone walls and stabilize trails. In exchange for your able hands, you will gain knowledge of the region's geography, customs, and specialized work techniques (hopefully perching on precarious cliffs doesn't faze you) and contribute to an effort that will ultimately enhance and preserve this vibrant patch of earth.

For further information, contact the Parco Nazionale delle Cinque Terre (☎0187 76 00 00; info@parconazionale5terre.it).

hits **Via Chiodo. Via Mazzini** runs parallel to V. Chiodo, closer to the water. The main **tourist office** is at V. Mazzini 45. (☎25 43 11. Open M-Sa 9:30am-1pm and 3:30-7pm, Su 9:30am-1pm.) Another branch is outside the train station. (Open daily 8am-1:30pm and 2-7:30pm.) **CTS**, V. Sapri 86, helps with ferry tickets to Greece and Sardinia and car rentals. (☎75 10 74. Open M-F 9:30am-12:30pm and 3:30-7:30pm, Sa 9:30am-12:30pm. MC/V.) **Farmacia dell'Aquila**, V. Chiodo 97, posts a list of late-night pharmacies. (☎23 162. Open daily 8:30am-12:30pm and 4-8pm. Closed in July but posts a list of other open locations. MC/V.) **Phone Center,** P. Saint Bon 1, has **Internet** and **Western Union** services. (☎76 77 24; fax 71 21 11. €4 per hr. Open M-Sa 9:15am-12:30pm and 3-10pm, Su 3-10pm. Cash only.) For **currency exchange,** try **Banca Carige,** C. Cavour 154. (☎73 43 69. Open M-F 8:20am-1:20pm and 2:30-4pm.) An **ATM** is outside. Have a cappuccino while your surf the Internet at centrally located **Map Caffe',** V. Sapri 78. (☎77 84 88. €5 per hr. Open M-Sa 8am-1am.) The **post office,** P. Verdi 1, is a few blocks from the port and offers **currency exchange.** (☎25 84 31. Open M-Sa 8am-6:30pm. Cash only.) **Postal Code:** 19100.

⌂⌂ ACCOMMODATIONS AND FOOD. Try the family-run **Albergo Il Sole ❷,** V. Cavalotti 31, close to the port. English-speaking staff keeps basic but spacious rooms decorated in shades of yellow and rose with large windows. (☎73 51 64; www.albergoilsole.com. Breakfast €4. Singles €25-35; doubles €45, with bath €55; triples €53-61; quads €80-92. MC/V.) The next street over, **Albergo Teatro ❷,** V. Carpenino 31, near the Teatro Civico, offers six comfortable rooms with TV; some have bath. (☎/fax 73 13 74. Singles €25-30; doubles €40-50, with bath €50-65. Extra bed 15% of room price.) If you're willing to splurge, try the luxurious **Hotel Firenze & Continentale ❺,** V. Paleocapa 7, across from the train station. The hotel retains a *fin-de-siècle* look, with marble floors and plush sitting areas. The rooms are decorated with rugs and wood furniture, and all have bath, A/C, TV, and phone; some have balcony. (☎71 32 00; www.hotelfirenzecontinentale.it. Breakfast included. Wi-Fi €10 per day. Wheelchair-accessible. Singles €68-94; doubles €90-154; triples €122-181. AmEx/MC/V.)

Reasonably priced trattorie line V. del Prione. The new **Osteria Duccio ❷,** V. Roselli 17, off V. del Prione, serves the eclectic creations of owner Luccio, who handpicks his ingredients daily. (☎25 86 02. *Primi* €6.50-7.50, *secondi* €7-10. 3-course lunch *menù* €10. Cover at dinner €1. Open Tu-Su noon-2:30pm and 7:45-11:45pm.) **La Pia ❶,** V. Magenta 12, also off V. del Prione, is a favorite for hot, cheesy focaccia and *farinata* and is a cheaper alternative to the posh cafes lining V. del Prione and V. Chiodo. Dine in casually, or take a heaping plate to go. (☎73 99 99. Most items €2.80-4.50. Open M-Sa 10am-3pm and 5-11pm. MC/V.) **Osteria con Cucina all'Inferno ❷**, V. Lorenzetti Costa 3, off P. Cavour, has been serving Ligurian specialities since 1905. Try *acciughe ripiene* (stuffed anchovies) for €7.50 and hearty *mesciua* (a thick soup of beans, cornmeal, olive oil, and pepper) for €4.50. (☎29 458. *Primi* €5.50-6.50, *secondi* €5-9. Open M-Sa 12:15-2:30pm and 7:30-10:30pm. Cash only.) An **open market** fills P. Cavour (Open M-Sa 7am-1pm). For the town's biggest selection of groceries and fresh produce, try **Supermercato Spesafac-Ile,** V. Colombo 101. (Open M-Sa 8:30am-1pm and 4:15-8pm. MC/V.)

◙ **SIGHTS.** La Spezia, being a port town, offers promenades peppered with palm trees and busy boutiques. Besides people-watching, the seaside city has several other sights. A three-day **museum pass** (€12) can be bought at any museum in the city. The unique collection of the **Museo Navale,** in P. Chiodo next to the entrance of the Maritime Military Arsenal, features diving suits dating from WWII and carved prows of 19th-century ships (including a huge green salamander). Check out the gargantuan iron anchors and tiny replicas of Egyptian, Roman, and European vessels. (☎78 30 16. Open M-Sa 8am-6:45pm, Su 8am-1pm. €1.55. Cash only.) **Museo Amadeo Lia,** V. del Prione 234, houses a collection of paintings from the 13th-17th centuries, including Raphael's *San Martino and the Beggar* in Room 6. Find Titian's *Portrait of a Gentleman* and Bellini's *Portrait of an Attorney* in Room 7. (☎73 11 00; www.castagna.it/mal. Open Tu-Su 10am-6pm. Last entry 30min. before closing. €6, students €4.) Next door, the **Museo del Sigillo,** V. del Prione 236, in the Palazzina delle Arti, displays a large collection of civic wax seals from all over the globe. (☎77 85 44; www.castagna.it/musei/museodelsigillo. Open Tu 4-7pm, W-Su 10am-noon and 4-7pm. €3.) **The Museo Entografico,** V. del Prione 156, has an important collection of traditional costumes, furniture, jewelry, and pottery from the surrounding region. (☎/fax 25 85 70; www.comune.sp.it/citta/guida/podenzana.htm. Open F-Su 10am-12:30pm and 4-7pm. €4.)

RIVIERA DI PONENTE

FINALE LIGURE ☎019

A plaque at the base of a statue along the promenade claims that Finale Ligure (fee-NA-leh LEE-goo-reh; pop. 12,000) is the place for *"il riposo del popolo,"* or "the people's rest." Whether *riposo* involves bodysurfing in the choppy waves, browsing chic boutiques, or sipping coffee in Finalborgo's medieval *piazze*, there are countless ways to pass the time in this sleepy town.

▐ **TRANSPORTATION**

The **train station** (☎27 58 777 or 89 20 21) is in P. Vittorio Veneto. The ticket office is open daily 5:55am-7:10pm. Trains run to Genoa (1hr., every 30min. 7:25am-11:39pm, €10-17) and Ventimiglia (30min., every 30min. 6:37am-11:46pm, €5). Most trains to Genoa stop at Savona and most trains to Ventimiglia stop at San Remo. ACTS **buses** depart from a side street left of the train station to Finalborgo (5min., every 30min., €1.20) and Savona (45min, every 30min., €2). Buy tickets at *bar* in train station. For **taxis,** call Radio Taxi ☎69 23 33, or 69 23 34.

TOP TEN LOVELY LIGURIAN SPIAGGIE

1. Follow the Italian vacationers to a sandy paradise in **Alassio** (p. 226).

2. Finale Ligure's free beach (p. 225) is well worth the 15min. walk east of town for sand and picturesque cliffs.

3. Take the train one stop north of the Cinque Terre for **Levanto's** (p. 216) sweeping coast.

4. Venture down treacherous terrain between Corniglia and Vernazza in the Cinque Terre, or head through the tunnel below the Corniglia station to reach the pebbly and liberal **Guvano beach** (p. 218) where it's okay to forget your bathing suit.

5. Though crowded in high season, **Monterosso** (p. 214) is worth the long hike for the people-watching and vibrant town life.

6. San Fruttuoso (p. 210) is a tiny haven with turquoise waters that lap calmly on the pebbly shore.

7. Arrive early for a spot among the umbrellas on the white shores of youth-oriented, friendly **Camogli** (p. 208).

8. Join the ultra rich and ultra tan under the colorful cabanas at **San Remo** (p. 228).

9. If you crave a quick dip, **Santa Margherita's free beach** (p. 212) is easily accessible from the main boulevard.

10. The sun and fun seekers carpet **Bordighera's** (p. 231) beaches with towels and chairs by day, while discos and bars heat up the town by night.

ORIENTATION AND PRACTICAL INFORMATION

The city is divided into three sections: **Finalpia** to the east, **Finalmarina** in the center, and **Finalborgo,** the old city, inland to the northwest. The train station and most of the listings below are in Finalmarina. Finalmarina's main street winds through the town between the station and **Piazza Vittorio Emanuele II,** changing its name from **Via di Raimondi** to **Via Pertica** to **Via Garibaldi.** From P. V. Emanuele II, **Via della Concezione** runs parallel to the shore. To reach Finalborgo, turn left from the station, cross under the tracks, and keep left on **Via Domenico Bruneghi** for about 10min.

The **IAT tourist office** is at V. San Pietro 14. From the station, walk straight to the water, and then take the only left; signs lead the way. (☎68 10 19; www.inforiviera.it. Open M-Sa 9am-1pm and 2:30-6:30pm, Su 9am-noon. Closed in winter Su.) **Currency exchange** and an **ATM** are available at **Banca Carige,** V. Garibaldi 4. (Service charge €5. Open M-F 8:20am-1:20pm and 2:30-4pm.) In an **emergency,** call the **police,** V. Brunenghi 67 (☎69 26 66). **Farmacia della Marina,** V. Ghiglieri 2, at the intersection where V. Raimondi becomes V. Pertica, lists after-hours rotations. (☎69 26 70. Open M-Sa 8:30am-12:30pm and 4-8pm. Ring bell for emergencies.) **Internet** access is available at **Net Village Internet Cafe,** V. di Raimondi 21, across from the train station. (☎68 16 283. €5 per hr. Open daily 8am-10pm.) For rock climbing in the area, the **Mountain Shop,** V. Nicotera 4, in Finalborgo, provides maps and the necessary gear. (☎68 16 230. Open M and W-Su 9:30am-1pm, 5-8pm, and 9:30pm-midnight. MC/V.) The **post office** is at V. della Concezione 29. (☎69 04 79. Open M-F 8am-6:30pm, Sa 8am-12:30pm.) **Postal Code:** 17024.

ACCOMMODATIONS

The youth hostel has the best prices—not to mention the best view. It may also have the only unbooked rooms, especially in July and August; it's still best to call ahead. The tourist office can help find rooms for rent in private houses.

■ **Castello Wuillerman (HI),** V. Generale Caviglia 46 (☎/fax 69 05 15). From the train station, turn left on V. Raimondo Pertica (just after the intersection), and continue straight. Turn left at the corner of V. Pertica and V. Alonzo, and climb the thigh-burning stairs to the top. The cliffside castle-turned-hostel has locking cabinets in rooms, a beautiful courtyard, and a good restaurant.

Breakfast included. Laundry €4 per load. Reception 7-10am and 5-10pm. Curfew midnight. HI members only. Dorms €13.50. Cash only. ❶

Albergo Carla, V. Colombo 44 (☎69 22 85; fax 68 19 65). Conveniently located on a cobblestoned street across from the seaside walkway. All rooms with bath and phone; some with sea view. Small restaurant downstairs. Breakfast €4. Reservations recommended. Singles €28-40; doubles €48-60. MC/V. ❸

Del Mulino (☎60 16 69; www.campingmulino.it), on V. Castelli. From the train station, take the Calvisio bus to Boncardo Hotel, then turn left at P. Oberdan. Turn right on V. Porro and follow signs uphill. Popular, with sites along a terraced hillside. A 15min. walk from the center of town. Bar, pizzeria, and mini-market. Hot showers. Laundry €5. Reception 8am-8pm. Open Apr.-Sept. €5-7 per person, €5-7 per tent. MC/V. ❶

⚫ FOOD

Reservations are often helpful for dinner, as restaurants fill up quickly. Get basics at **Di per Di Express,** V. Alonzo 10. (Open M-Sa 8:15am-1pm and 4:30-7:30pm. MC/V.)

> **TIP** **NO FOOD FOR YOU.** During the high season in towns along the Riviera, dinner reservations might be harder to come by than a hostel bed. Make reservations a few nights in advance if you're set on a restaurant, otherwise you might find yourself staring at a *completo* sign on the door instead of a menu.

Il Dattero, on the fork where V. Pertica splits into V. Rossi and V. Garibaldi. Decadent flavors and refreshing *granita* come with free toppings. *Gelato*-filled pastries €2.50. 2 scoops *gelato* €1.50. *Granita* €1.70. Open daily 11am-midnight. Cash only. ❶

Spaghetteria Il Post, V. Porro 21 (☎60 00 95). Follow V. Colombo from the beachfront past P. Cavour. Turn left onto V. Genova, which becomes V. Porro. Try *penne quattro stagioni* (with bacon, mushrooms, tomatoes, artichokes, and mozzarella; €6.50). Lots of vegetarian options. Bring a few friends, as each dish is made for 2. Cover €1. Open Tu-Su 7-10:30pm. Closed 1st 2 weeks of Mar. Cash only. ❶

Farinata Vini, V. Roma 25 (☎69 25 62). Small, popular trattoria serves fresh seafood and pasta dishes. Menu changes daily. *Primi* €7-10, *secondi* €9-15. Open M and W-Su 12:30-2pm and 7:30-9pm. MC/V. ❸

Sole Luna, V. Barrili 31 (☎681 61 60). Bikini-clad beachgoers breeze in and out for a quick, fresh meal. Try the *farinata* (€1.50), a pie made from chickpeas and filled with meat and vegetables. Pizza slices €1.50-2. Grilled focaccia *panini* €1.50-3. Savory crepes €3. Open daily 10am-8pm. Cash only. ❶

Belgisela, V. Colombo 2 (☎69 52 75), at the intersection of V. Alonzo and V. Colombo. Sleek furniture and a stone-inlaid floor give this restaurant a chic ambience. Scrumptious homemade desserts €4.50. *Primi* €10-19, *secondi* €8-19. Wine bar Th 7pm-12:30am. Open daily 7:30-10:30pm, Th-Su also open 12:30-2:30pm. MC/V. ❸

⚫ ♫ SIGHTS AND ENTERTAINMENT

Finalmarina's best asset is its unbeatable sandy **beaches.** Unfortunately, people tend to cram in like sardines on this narrow, free strip. To escape the crowds, walk 15min. east along V. Aurelia and through the first tunnel to another beach, cradled by overhanging cliffs. **Finalborgo,** the historical quarter of Finale Ligure, is a 1km walk or 2min. bus ride up V. Bruneghi from the station. Past the **Porta Reale** (its main entrance), the Chiostro di Santa Caterina houses the **Museo Archeologico del Finale,** dedicated to Ligurian history with displays ranging from Paleolithic artifacts to Roman and Byzantine finds. (☎69 00 20. Open Tu-Su Sept.-

June 9am-noon and 2:30-5pm; July-Aug. 10am-noon and 4-7pm. Free.) Enjoy the town's medieval architecture and quiet ambience while sipping a *caffè* in one of many small *piazze*. If you crave the small town charm of narrow streets and ancient churches, consider making a short trip to nearby villages of **Borgio** and **Verezzi** (bus every 15min. 5:45am-10:30pm, round-trip €1.80). Consider, in particular, visiting during July and August, when the annual **Festival Teatrale** holds live theater performances by national touring companies.

In Finalmarina, late summer nights are the norm, and bars are packed late into the night. A few blocks away from the shore is **Pilade,** V. Garibaldi 67, featuring live music ranging from blues to soul on some Friday nights and rock and Italian techno during the week. Posters of old jazz legends fill the walls and an older, calmer crowd fills the tables, ordering drinks (€5) or beer (from €3). Pizza (€1.50-1.80 per slice), burgers, salads, crepes (dinner only; €2.60-6.20), and delicious *panini* (€2.60-3) are available for a sit-down meal or takeout. (☎69 22 20. Open daily 10am-2am. Closed in winter Th.) As the sun sets, it's easy to find more nightlife—just follow the crowds to the waterfront, where bathhouses turn into dance parties and bars fill up with dehydrated sunbathers along **Via della Concezione.**

ALASSIO
☎0182

Sun-splashed Alassio (ah-LA-see-yo) has attracted high-class Italians and dedicated beachgoers to its sparkling seas for over a century. Though its residential population is only about 13,000, this number seems to triple in the summer thanks to sun-worshipping tourists. Vacationers come for the white-sand beaches, excellent cuisine and nightlife, or a case of the town's signature *Baci* chocolate pastries (p. 227). Even with these luxuries, Alassio maintains a cheery, unpretentious character that makes it distinctly youth-friendly.

▐ TRANSPORTATION

The **train station** is between V. Michelangelo and V. Giuseppe Mazzini. Call ☎89 20 21 for schedules. The ticket office is open daily 6am-7:15pm. **Trains** run to: Finale Ligure (20min., every 30min., €3); Genoa (2hr., every 2hr., €6); Milan (3½hr., every 3hr., €12); Ventimiglia (1¼hr., every 30min., €4). SAR **buses** stop every 20min. along V. Aurelia connecting nearby towns to Alassio. For **bike rental,** stop by Ricciardi, C. Dante Alighieri 144, near the train station. (☎64 05 55. Bikes €5 per hr., €13 per day. Open M-Sa 9am-7pm, Su 10am-12:30pm and 4:30-7pm. AmEx/MC/V.)

✦❷ ORIENTATION AND PRACTICAL INFORMATION

Alassio is a small, navigable town with activity centering around the pedestrian walkways along its seacoast. Head straight out of the **train station** and turn right on **Via Giuseppe Mazzini** in front of the park. V. G. Mazzini forms one part of the city's main street, collectively referred to as **Via Aurelia.** Three streets, V. Aurelia, **Corso Dante Alighieri,** and **Via Vittorio Veneto,** run parallel to the sea. To arrive at the center of the seafront, head straight from the train station. The **APT tourist office** is at V. G. Mazzini 68. From the train station, turn left. The staff offers useful maps and brochures. An agency that books accommodations is also in the same building. (☎64 70 27; alassio@inforiviera.it. Open M-Sa 9am-12:30pm and 3-6:30pm, Su 9am-noon.) You can **exchange currency** at **Unicredit Banca,** V. Gibb 14, two blocks to the left from the train station on V. Aurelia. (Open M-F 8:20am-1:20pm and 2:35-4:05pm, Sa-Su 10am-12:30pm and 4:30-7pm. AmEx/MC/V. 24hr. **ATM** available.) **Luggage storage** is available to the left of the train station's main exit (€3 per day. Open daily 7am-noon and 2-6:15pm). **Farmacia Nazionale** is at V. V. Veneto 3. (☎64

06 06. Open daily 8:30am-12:30pm and 3:30-7:30pm. MC/V.) **Internet** access is available at **Punto.it,** V. Torino 30. (☎47 01 24. Open M 4-7:30pm, Tu-Sa 9:30am-12:30pm and 4-7:30pm. MC/V.) The **post office** is at P. Airaldi Durante. (☎66 091. Open M-F 8am-6pm, Su 8am-1:15pm. Cash only.) **Postal Code:** 17021.

█ ACCOMMODATIONS AND CAMPING

Rooms disappear quickly in this lively resort town, so reserve early. Beachfront views come at hefty prices. Welcoming staff, quiet gardens, and a central location make **Hotel Fiorenza & Banksia ❸,** V. Privata Marconi 11-13, a great option. All rooms have TV, phone, and private bath. Take a left out of the train station, walk along V. Hanbury, and turn right on V. P. Marconi. (☎64 05 04; www.alassio.it/ banksia. Breakfast included. Parking €5 per day. Singles €35-48; doubles €60-90. Cash only.) To reach **Hotel Panama ❸,** V. Brennero 27, from the train station, turn right on V. G. Mazzini and left on V. Torino. Follow it to the sea, and then turn right on V. V. Veneto, which becomes V. Brennero. A private beach and cheery dining room enliven this hotel. All rooms have TV, A/C, and phone; some have shower and bath. (☎64 59 16; www.panamavacanze.com. Breakfast included. Storage lockers and Internet access available. Doubles €60-120. Full pension €50-115. AmEx/MC/V.) **Camping La Vedetta Est ❶,** V. Giancardi 11, is 1.5km from Alassio. From V. G. Mazzini, take bus toward Albenga. Bus stops just in front, but still on the highway, so be careful. Bungalows and tent sites overlook the sea. (☎64 24 07; fax 64 24 27. Open daily 8:30am-12:30pm and 3-10pm. Campsites €6-8 per person; 2-person bungalows with car and tent €24-35; bungalows €30-145. Cash only.)

◖ FOOD

More pizzerias and *gelaterie* per capita than seem possible crowd Alassio's streets. Don't leave without sampling the famed *Baci di Alassio* (fudge pastry) at **Balzola,** P. Matteotti 26 (☎64 02 09. Open daily in summer 9am-4am, in winter 9am-2am.) ■**Osteria Mezzaluna ❸,** V. Vico Berno 6, sits on the waterfront, with an intimate, Spanish-influenced atmosphere and delectable Mediterranean cuisine. Try their unique take on open-faced *panini*. (☎64 03 87; www.mezzaluna.it. Salads €6.50-8.50. *Secondi* €7.50-10. Live music nightly. Open daily 7:30pm-2am. AmEx/ MC/V.) After 25 years in business, the Sicilian wizards at **Gelateria Acuvea ❶,** P. Matteotti 3, have the whole town in their power, scooping out fresh, airy *gelato* (2 scoops €1.50). While waiting for your share, watch flavors being hand-churned. (☎66 00 60. Open daily 8am-2am. Cash only.) Friendly staff at **Pizzeria Italia ❷,** Passeggiata Toti 19, serve ultra-thin pizzas just steps from the beach. The *boscaiola* (grilled eggplant, *proscuitto*, and fresh mozzarella; €7.50) packs a flavorful punch. (☎64 40 95. *Primi* €8-10, *secondi* €10-16. Cover €1. Open daily May-Aug. noon-3:30pm and 7pm-4am. Closed Sept.-Apr. Cash only.) Attentive waiters and a waterfront patio make **Ristorante Sail Inn ❹,** V. Brennero 34-38, a classy choice for a fishy feast. (☎64 02 32. *Primi* €10-20, *secondi* €12-33. Open Tu-Su for lunch and dinner. AmEx/MC/V.) There is a **STANDA** supermarket at V. San Giovanni Bosco 36/ 66, part of V. Aurelia. (Open daily 8am-8:30pm. AmEx/MC/V.)

LIGURIA

◉ 🅿 SIGHTS AND NIGHTLIFE

Alassio has kilometers of pristine, sandy **beaches** stretching in both directions down the coast, leaving little reason to venture inland. There are a few **free** public beaches about a 15min. walk down the beach, but if central location and lively activity are a priority, then it's worth the €3-20 for a chair and umbrella. Take a short stroll down the beach to the east to join the throng of local boys and older fishermen at the **pier,** a favorite spot for loafing, line-casting, and relaxed sea-gazing. If you need a beach break, the fishing village of **Laigueglia** offers colorful houses, tiny *piazze*, and twisting stone streets. (30min. walk or 5min. bus ride toward Andorra. SAR buses leave from points on V. Aurelia every 20 min., buy tickets for €1.20 in *tabaccherie* nearby.)

Stoked by tourists and an influx of youth from nearby towns, Alassio comes to life at night. Decorated with red lanterns, **Tokai Bar,** V. V. Veneto 151, draws an international crowd for beachfront refreshments and animated conversation. (*Panini* from €3.50. Mixed drinks and sangria €5.50. Open M-W and F-Su 10:30am-3am. Cash only.) Local favorite **Bar Cabaret,** V. Hanbury 58, has live music and a raucous crowd that sings along. Grab a pint (€3-7) and one of many *panini* named after classic rock legends. (☎347 96 15 372. Open daily 9:30pm-3am; closes periodically. Cash only.) Trendy **Caffe Roma,** V. Dante 308-310, is the new place to see and be seen among the Euro-chic. All-white decor adorns the two-story lounge, and a young and hip crowd relaxes on plush couches. (☎64 03 78. *Panini* €3-5. Mixed drinks €4-7. Open Tu-Su noon-4am.)

SAN REMO   ☎0184

Once a glamorous retreat for Russian nobles, czars, literati, and artists, San Remo (san RAY-mo; pop. 66,000) is now the largest casino resort town on the Italian Riviera. San Remo upholds its glamorous profile with finely dressed couples strolling along the palm-lined promenade of C. Giacomo Matteotti or gambling in the turn-of-the-century casino. The city's many boutiques and upscale shops offer plenty of opportunities for big winners to become big spenders. Upholding the reputation of the *Riviera dei Fiori* (Riviera of Flowers), San Remo blooms with carnations year-round. Adding to the musical click of dice and chink of poker chips, the town resounds with an international jazz competition each summer.

▐ TRANSPORTATION

The **train station**, Stazione F.S., faces C. Felice Cavalotti, at V. Carlo Pisacane. The ticket office is open daily 6:30am-8pm. **Trains** run to Genoa (2½hr., every hr. 5:24am-10:24pm, €7.70), Milan (4¼hr., every 2hr. 5:07am-7:07pm, €13.80), and Ventimiglia (20min., every 30min. 7:25am-12:55am, €1.60). Allow 5min. to walk from ticket booth to train tracks. Prices listed are the minimum and vary seasonally. Forgo the train station for Stazione Autolinee, San Remo's **bus depot** located in P.Colombo (☎59 27 06). Riviera Trasporti runs **buses** along the coast, west to Ventimiglia (30min., every 15-30min. 5am-12:55am, €2) via Bordighera (20min., every 15-30min. 5am-12:55am, €1.25). For a **Radio Taxi,** call ☎54 14 54.

🌄 🔢 ORIENTATION AND PRACTICAL INFORMATION

The city is comprised of three main streets that run east-west, parallel to the beach. The train station faces the northern-most of the three, **Corso Felice Cavalotti,** which changes names moving west into the center of town to **Corso Giuseppe**

Garibaldi, and then to **Corso Giacomo Matteotti.** To the south is **Via Roma,** followed by **Via Nino Bixio** close to the water. To get to the center of town from the station, turn right on C. F. Cavalotti, cross **Rondo Giuseppe Garibaldi** (a rotary), and veer left down C. G. Garibaldi. At **Piazza Colombo,** continue straight, bearing left while crossing the *piazza* to reach swanky C. G. Matteotti, which leads to the **lungomare** and the sea. The tourist-free old town, **La Pigna,** is uphill from P. Colombo.

Tourist Office: APT, V. Nuvoloni 1 (☎59 059; www.rivieradeifiori.travel). From P. Colombo, go left onto C. G. Matteotti and follow it to the end. The office is on the corner on the right, offering maps and brochures. Open M-Sa 8am-7pm, Su 9am-1pm.

Bank: There are plenty of banks for the high rollers coming to San Remo. **Banca Intesa,** V. Roma 62 (☎59 23 11), offers **currency exchange** and **ATM.** Open M-F 8:30am-1:30pm and 2:45-4:15pm, Sa 8:30am-noon.

Bookstore: Libreria Beraldi, V. Cavour 8 (☎54 11 11). Reasonable collection of bestsellers in English, French, German, and Spanish. Considerable travel section. Open M-Sa 8:30am-12:30pm and 3:30-7:30pm. MC/V.

Laundromat: Blu Acquazzura, V. Alessandro Volta 131 (☎340 41 78 480), off Rondo Garibaldi. Self-service. Wash and dry €5 per kg; €7 per 16kg.

Pharmacy: Farmacia Centrale, C. G. Matteotti 190 (☎50 90 65). After-hours rotation posted outside. Open M-Sa 8:30am-8:30pm.

Hospital: Ospedale Civile, V. Giovanni Borea 56 (☎53 61).

Internet Access: Mailboxes, Etc., C. Cavallotti 86 (☎59 16 73). Photocopier and fax available. €2.50 per 30min., €5 per hr. Open M-F 9am-6:30pm. AmEx/MC/V.

Post Office: V. Roma 156. Open M-F 8am-6:30pm, Sa 8am-1pm. **Postal Code:** 18038.

▐ ACCOMMODATIONS

San Remo enjoys a high standard of accommodation. Although this means higher prices, it also means that even one-star hotels tend to be clean and comfortable.

▨ **Albergo Al Dom,** C. Mombello 13, 2nd fl. (☎50 14 60). From the train station, turn right onto C. F. Cavallotti and pass through Rondo G. Garibaldi. Follow C. G. Garibaldi and turn left on C. G. Matteotti to reach C. Mombello. Ring bell to enter. Rooms, all with bath and TV, are furnished by friendly owners. Comfortable sitting room has TV. Breakfast €5. Singles €25-30; doubles €50-60. ❷

Hotel Graziella, Rondo Garibaldi 2 (☎57 10 31; fax 57 00 43). 2min. from the train station. Turn right on C. F. Cavalotti, then right around Rondo G. Garibaldi. Hotel is set back from the road in a villa. Elegant rooms with high ceilings and private balconies. All with TV, fridge, and phone; most with A/C. Breakfast €5. Singles €60; doubles €80. Aug. prices €10-15 higher per person. MC/V. ❹

Hotel Sorriso, C. Raimondo 73 (☎50 03 56; www.soloalberghi.com/hotelsorriso). From the train station, turn right on C. F. Cavalotti, left on V. Fiume, and right on C. Orazio Raimondo. Larger, more mainstream hotel with basic furnishings, in-room TVs and showers. English-speaking staff is happy to point the way to nearby dining and entertainment options. Breakfast included. Singles €40-80; doubles €60-120. Prices soar in high season. AmEx/MC/V. ❸

Camping Villaggio dei Fiori, V. Tiro a Volo 3. (☎66 06 35; info@villaggiodeifiori.it) A 10min. bus ride west of town. Take bus from bus station in P. Colombo to Villa Elios (every 20min., €1) or any bus to Ventimiglia and ask the driver to stop at Villa Elios. Campground is across the street. The shaded sights and relaxed atmosphere, combined with amenities of a pool and restaurant on site make this a solid option. 2-person tent pitch €18-31; 4-person €27-51. High season 3- to 5-person bungalows €99-125, low season €62-122. Electricity €2. Cash only. ●

◖ FOOD

There are some unique and affordable dining options hidden among San Remo's pizzerias and pricey restaurants. Try *sardinara*, a local focaccia-like specialty topped with tomato sauce, herbs, and olives. Buy basics at **Casitalia** supermarket in P. Eroi 44. (Open M-F 8:15am-12:45pm and 2-7:30pm, Sa 8:15am-1pm and 4-7:45pm. Closed W afternoon. MC/V.) The huge **indoor market**, the Mercato Ortofruitticolo, in neighboring P. Mercato, sells fresh produce, meat, and bread. (Open M-Sa 6am-1:30pm, Sa 4-7:30pm.)

Vin D'Italia, C. Mombello 5 (☎59 17 47). Modern vases accent the otherwise rustic interior of this upscale restaurant with down-to-earth staff. Local food is their middle name; be sure to add *sardinara* (€0.80), hot from a grand wood-burning oven, to your meal. *Primi* and *secondi* €8-13. Open M-Sa 11am-3pm and 7-10pm. AmEx/MC/V. ❸

Trattoria A Cuvea, C. G. Garibaldi 110 (☎50 34 98). Follow C. F. Cavalotti away from the train station. Quality cuisine served in this hole-in-the-wall favored by locals. *Primi* €5.70-7.60, *secondi* €7.30-8.75. Open M-Sa noon-2pm and 7:30-10pm, Su 7:30-10pm. Cash only. ❷

Urbicia Vivas, P. dei Dolori 5/6 (☎75 55 66; www.urbiciavivas.com), in a charming *piazza* in the old city. From V. Palazzo, turn left on V. Cavour, and walk through the archway, turn left onto V. San Sebastiano and continue straight until you reach the 1st *piazza*. Join the locals for sumptuous fish dishes and delicious homemade pasta at this snug family-run trattoria. *Primi* €9-12, *secondi* €9-15. Open daily 8am-3pm and 7pm-midnight. AmEx/MC/V. ❸

RistoPizza Grill da Giovanni, V. Cesare Pesante 7 (☎50 49 54), off V. XX Settembre. Innovative pizza options in 28 varieties are this restaurant's specialty. Well located on a quiet side street away from the crowded restaurants by the water. Pizza €5-8. *Primi* €5-12, *secondi* €7-25. Open M-W and F-Su noon-3pm and 7-11:30pm. AmEx/MC/V. ❷

◉ ◖ SIGHTS AND BEACHES

San Remo has a number of historical treasures. Across the street from the tourist office stands the Byzantine-style, onion-domed Russian Orthodox **Chiesa di Cristo Salvatore** (also called **Chiesa Russa**), V. Nuvoloni 2. The intricate exterior is the highlight; the simple interior has a few gleaming icons and plain walls. (Open daily 9:30am-12:30pm and 3-6:30pm. Suggested donation €1.) Leaving the church, follow C. G. Matteotti away from the sea and turn left onto the little V. Pietro Calvi, which winds its way into P. San Siro. Here looms the 13th-century, Roman-Gothic **Basilica di San Siro**, regarded as the city's most sacred monument. (Open M-Sa 8:30am-noon and 3-6pm, Su 8:30am-12:15pm and 3:30-8pm. Free.) From here, steer through the vendors along the *gelateria*-lined V. Palazzo and turn left on V. Cavour to **La Pigna,** San Remo's historical town, which most tourists miss entirely. Narrow streets are crowded with tiny medieval churches connected by secret underground passageways. The streets can be confusing; be sure to bring along a map from the tourist office. From La Pigna, follow the tree-lined road upward to P. Assunta, to the elaborate **Il Santuario della Madonna della Costa.** This 17th-century monument features a high dome covered in frescoes and twisting rose marble columns. The *Madonna and Child* painting above the altar, attributed to Fra Nicoló of Voltri, dates to the late 14th century. (☎50 30 00. Open daily 9am-noon and 3-6pm. Modest dress required. Free.)

In the daytime, Speedo- and bikini-clad crowds pack the beach and numerous *bagni* that line the water, so get there early to snag a sand dune. Most commercial

> **SAN REMO FOR POCKET CHANGE.** Think you can't find some great deals in a city which revolves around gambling and shopping? Grab some fresh-baked *sardinara* to go at Vin d'Italia and take it down to the free public beach at the end of V. Roma. When you're ready to get out of the sun, climb through old La Pigna up to Il Santuario della Madonna della Costa and enjoy views of the city. After dark, head to Casino Municipale for free admission on weeknights—where your money goes after that is up to Lady Luck.

beaches are open from 8:30am to 7:30pm. Lounge chair and umbrella rental run around €3 each per day, but expect to pay a €1-2 entrance fee as well. Penny pinchers can head to the end of V. Roma for a **public beach.**

♪ 🎭 ENTERTAINMENT AND NIGHTLIFE

When darkness hits in San Remo, so do the gamblers who frequent the enormous **Casino Municipale,** C. Inglesi 18, at the end of C. G. Matteoti. Built in 1905, the casino is a dazzling example of *Belle Epoque* architecture. No sandals or shorts are allowed upstairs, and a coat and tie for men and formal wear for women are required in winter. Five hundred slot machines clang away on the lower floors, while the swank rooms upstairs host the Riviera's most dapper, sipping mixed drinks and hoping to win the famed "Mystery Jackpot." (☎ 59 51; www.casinosanremo.it. 18+. Passport required. Cover F-Su for upstairs rooms €7.50. Open M-F 2:30pm-2am, Sa-Su 2:30pm-4am.) After dark, couples meander along the swanky **Corso Matteotti** for *gelato* or liqueurs. Mellow **Sax Pub,** V. Roma 160, sports- and jazz-inspired decor and outdoor seating to attract an all-ages crowd. Drinks run €3-7 and come with a free plate of appetizers. (☎ 0184 50 37 43; www.saxpub.it. Open M, and W-Su 7pm-4am. AmEx/MC/V.) Ten minutes from the casino is **Pico de Gallo,** Lungomare V. Emanuele 11/13, where the liquor starts flowing long before sundown. Sip a Caribbean-inspired drink (€5) as you sit on the beach. The *bagni* (beach area) is open daily 9:30am-7:30pm. (☎ 57 43 45; www.picosanremo.com. Cash only. Bar open 24hr. Restaurant open 12:30-3pm. MC/V.) On a side street off C. G. Matteotti, **Zoo Bizarre,** V. Gaudio 10, is a small, trendy spot with electric-green tables and a ceiling plastered with movie posters. The hip, though non-pretentious, crowd kicks off its weekend evenings here around 9pm with drinks (€4-6.50) and free munchies. (☎ 50 57 74. Open M-F5:30pm-2am, Sa-Su 5:30pm-3am. Cash only.) Alternatives to dice and drinking are harder to find. At the end of January, a float parade livens up the city streets for the annual festival **San Remo in Fiore.** The **Jazz and Blues Festival,** held in late July and early August, draws international artists to soothe the sunburned crowds.

BORDIGHERA   ☎ 0184

When Italian writer Giovanni Ruffini crafted his 1855 melodrama, *Il Dottor Antonio*, he unwittingly laid the foundation for the development of both Bordighera (bor-dee-GEH-ra; pop. 16,000) and the Italian Riviera's tourism industry. English travelers were entranced by his story of an ailing English girl miraculously revived by Bordighera's Mediterranean charm. In the early 20th century, residents turned the town into a summer vacation hot spot, and it's not surprising that intellectuals and artists like Claude Monet and Louis Pasteur chose Bordighera as their special retreat. Though its outer edges are busy with traffic and vacationers, Bordighera remains a chic center of affluence: mansions and palm-lined roads stretch to the sprawling seaside promenade. The more humble *centro storico* offers compelling, quieter routes for a *passeggiata* (stroll). For those seeking sun, Bordighera also offers beaches packed with vacationing Italians.

LIGURIA

⌷ TRANSPORTATION. The **train station** is in P. Eroi Libertà. Trains run to: Genoa (3hr., 4:53am-10:23pm, €7.35); Milan (4hr., 4:53am-7:05pm, €25); San Remo (10min., every hr. 4:53am-10:23pm, €1.45); Ventimiglia (10min., every hr. 7:35am-12:57am, €1). The ticket office is open daily 6:15am-7:35pm. Riviera Transporti **buses** stop every 300m on V. Vittorio Emanuele and run to San Remo (25min., every 15min. 5:42am-1:22am, €1.15) and Ventimiglia (15min., every 15min. 5:42am-1:22am, €1.15). Buy tickets at *tabaccherie* on V. V. Emanuele or at the post office. Tourist office provides more detailed bus schedules.

◪◪ ORIENTATION AND PRACTICAL INFORMATION. The bus from Ventimiglia stops on the main street in the busy, modern city, **Via Vittorio Emanuele,** which runs parallel to the sea and the scenic **Lungomare Argentina.** To get to the *lungomare,* walk down V. Agostino Noaro or V. Generale Luigi Cadorna, and go through the tunnels under the train tracks. The **train station** is located between V. V. Emanuele and the sea, at **Piazza Eroi della Libertà.** To reach the *centro storico,* follow V. V. Emanuele to P. Ruffini. Bear left across the *piazza* and continue straight. This road changes names to V. Libertà, V. Matteotti, and V. Arziglia. Turn left and walk uphill on V. Botafogu Rossi and follow it to the top. To reach the **tourist office,** V. V. Emanuele 172, from the train station, walk along V. Roma and turn left at the first main intersection. (☎26 23 22; fax 26 44 55. Open in summer M-Sa 9am-12:30pm and 3-6:30pm.) **Currency exchange** and **ATM** are available at **Banca Intesa,** V. Roma 4. (☎26 67 77. Open M-F 8:30am-1:30pm and 2:45-4:15pm, Sa 8:30am-noon.) In case of **emergency,** call the **police,** V. Primo Maggio 49 (☎26 26 26). **Farmacia Centrale,** V. V. Emanuele 145, posts a list of after-hours service. (☎26 12 46. Open M-F 8:30am-12:30pm and 3:30-7:30pm.) The **post office** is at P. Eroi della Libertà 5/6, and has an **ATM** outside. (☎26 91 51 or 26 91 31. Open M-F 8am-6:30pm, Sa 8am-12:30pm.) **Postal Code:** 18012.

⌷⌷ ACCOMMODATIONS AND FOOD. In the high season, many hotels in Bordighera require that clients accept full or half pension. It is also standard practice to raise prices for guests staying under three days, usually by €5-10. Many large, expensive hotels built in a white *fin de siècle* style line the sea, but the town's few budget options are also pleasant. Across from the train station, on the left, is **Albergo Nagos ❷,** P. Eroi della Libertà 7, 3rd fl. Nine small rooms are neat and functional; three have private showers. (☎26 04 57. Singles €28; doubles €40. Half pension €33-35; full pension €40-45. MC/V.)

To escape the beach crowds, head to ▩ **Ristorante la Piazzetta ❷,** P. del Popolo 13, in the *centro.* Savor Ligurian fare in bountiful portions such as the specialty wood-fired pizzas for €4.50-8. (*Primi* €6.50-9, *secondi* €10-15. Cover €1.20. Open M-Tu and Th-Su noon-2:30pm and 6:30-11pm. AmEx/MC/V.) Local youths crowd the marble tables of **Creperie-Caffè Giglio ❷,** V. Vittorio Emanuele 158. A dizzying selection of creative dinner crepes with many vegetarian options complement the seven-page drink menu. Dessert crepes (€3.50-6) are all sweet and satisfying. (☎26 15 30. Open Tu-Su 5:30pm-3am. Cash only.) The lively, beach-themed **La Reserve ❹,** V. Arziglia 20, at the eastern end of the *lungomare,* is a great place to grab a seaside drink. Just follow the blaring island music. (☎26 13 22. *Primi* €10-16, *secondi* €15-30. Bar open 24hr. Kitchen open 8-10am, noon-2:30pm, and 8-10pm.) An **outdoor market** on the *lungomare* sells produce and clothing every Thursday from early morning until 1pm. There is an **IEFFE Discount** supermarket at P. Garibaldi 32/35. (Open M-Sa 8:30am-12:45pm and 4:30-8pm, Su 9am-1pm. Reduced winter hours. MC/V.) There is also a **STANDA** at V. della Libertà 32. (Open M-Sa 8am-8pm, Su 9am-8:30 pm. AmEx/MC/V.)

LIGURIA

◎ 🏖 **SIGHTS AND BEACHES.** Bordighera's **beach** is crammed with locals and tourists who arrive early to rent their own lounge chairs, umbrellas, and cabanas from one of the many *bagni* (each around €5 per day). To rent jet skis, windsurf boards, or motorboats, call ☎348 51 83 835. For sailing, kayaking, or canoes, contact the Nautical Club of Bordighera (☎26 66 46; www.clubnauticobordighera.it.). For information on windsurfing, check at the tourist office. Follow V. Arziglia for 20min. to reach the **Giardino Esotico Pallanca.** Pass the tunnel and it's on the left, or take a bus from V. V. Emanuele heading in the direction of San Remo and ask the driver to stop at the *Giardino.* The exotic garden, once open only to scientists, contains over 3000 species of cacti and flora. The hour-long walking tour leads along meandering terraces. (☎26 63 47; www.pallanca.it. Open Tu-Su 9am-12:30pm and 2:30-7pm. €6, under 13 free, groups more than 8 €5.) Returning to town, the **Giardini del Capo** offer spectacular sea views and a glimpse of a statue of Queen Margherita Di Saviolo, one of Italy's first queens. The park leads to the town's **centro storico,** established in 1471, which is often too narrow for cars. Walk through the parking lot at the top of the park and through the archway at the end of V. del Campo to explore the narrow stone streets.

🔊 🎆 **NIGHTLIFE AND FESTIVALS.** **Il Barretto** is Bordighera's most renowned spot for beachside nightlife—you'll know it when you see it. A town staple since 1960, it has a spring break vibe and no-frills attitude. Come for a cheap-eating, floor-packing, liquor-saturating good time. (☎26 25 66. Pizza €1.50. Tequila shots €3.50. Open daily 9am-4am. Cash only.) A raucous, mostly male crowd fills the dim interior and outdoor tables under international flags and an arched arcade at **Graffiti Pub/Risto House,** V. V. Emanuele 122. Along with a wide choice of liquor (€3.50-5), beer on tap (€2-4), and wine (€11-13), they also serve cheap meals, including *panini* for €3.50-4. (☎26 15 90. Open M-Sa 5pm-3am. Cash only.) A classier, more upscale *discoteca,* the **Kursaal Club,** Lungomare Argentina 7, has both live and recorded underground, house, and industrial music. A younger crowd floods the dance floor on Saturday. (☎26 46 85. 25+ on F and Su. Open Sept.-July F-Su 5pm-midnight; Aug. daily 11pm-5am. AmEx/MC/V.)

Despite its small size, Bordighera loves revelry. In April each year, the city becomes **La Città dell'Umorismo** (The City of Humor), when comedians, cartoonists, and cabaret performers descend upon the town for a celebration of laughter. For 10 days surrounding May 14, the church hosts the **Festa di Sant'Ampelio,** when the whole town gathers in celebration with fireworks, a feast of savory specialties, dancing, and music. Summer brings a host of outdoor festivities, including an international ethnic music festival at the end of July and a series of concerts and plays at the seaside gazebo **Chiosca della Musica.**

VENTIMIGLIA ☎0184

"Bonjour" is almost as common as *"buongiorno"* in this quiet commercial town. Ventimiglia (VEN-tee-MEEL-ya; pop. 25,000) is only a 10min. train ride from the French border; the coastline between the town and Monaco were part of the same state until Napoleon's 1860 invasion drew clearer boundaries. Ventimiglia lacks the spunk of its more touristy neighbors, though the 11th-century *città alta* and the pebbly beaches are notable. The town is truly a unique blend of cultures, as restaurant signs reading *"jambon di Parma," "piatti du jour,"* and the friendly, bilingual citizens will attest.

LIGURIA

TRANSPORTATION

The **train station** (☎89 20 21) is in P. Cesare Battisti. **Trains** run to Genoa (3hr., every hr. 5:22am-7:51pm, €9) and Nice (40min., 4 per day, 9:08am-7:22pm, €9). Ticket office open daily 5:15am-8:40pm. Riviera Transporti (☎0183 70 01; www.rivieratrasporti.it) runs **buses** to regional and local destinations, including San Remo (35min., 4 per hr. 5:30am-1:10am, €1.70) via Bordighera (15min., €1.15), and Dolceacqua (20min., every 30min., €1.25). Tickets are available in the *tabaccherie* lining V. Cavour and at **Turismo Monte Carlo** (see below), which also provides schedules. The bus stops every 100m along V. Cavour. If taking transportation to France, remember your passport!

ORIENTATION AND PRACTICAL INFORMATION

From the **train station**, walk straight down **Via della Stazione** to the *centro*. The second crossroad is **Via Cavour**, where V. della Stazione becomes **Corso Repubblica** as it continues toward the waterfront. A footbridge at the end of C. Repubblica leads across a small river to *Ventimiglia Alta* (or *città alta*), the medieval section of town. Turn left directly before the footbridge onto **Lungo Roia Giolamo Rossi** to stroll along a restaurant-lined promenade in the newer, commercial part of town.

Tourist Office: V. Cavour 61 (☎35 11 83; infoventimiglia@rivieradefiori.org), 5min. from the train station. English-speaking staff offers maps and information on local and nearby attractions. A stop here is particularly useful, as many interesting sights lie outside the city proper. Open M-Sa 9am-12:30pm and 3:30 -6:30pm. The travel agency 2 doors down, **Turismo Monte Carlo,** V. Cavour 57 (☎35 75 77; fax 35 26 21), has **currency exchange** and bus and hotel info. Open M-Sa 9am-12:30pm and 2:30-7pm.

Bank: Cariparma, V. Roma 18/D. 24hr. **ATM.** Other bank services inside. Open M-F 8:30am-1:30pm and 2:45-4:15pm.

Bookstore: Libreria Casella, V. della Stazione 1/D (☎35 79 00). Small English selection. Open M-Sa 9am-1pm and 3:30-7:30pm. MC/V.

Emergency: ☎800 55 44 00. **Police:** V. Aprosio 12 (☎23 821). **Red Cross:** V. Dante Alighieri 16 (☎23 20 00). **Croce Verde:** P. XX Settembre 8 (☎35 11 75).

Pharmacy: Farmacia Internazionale, V. Cavour 28/A (☎35 13 00). Open M-F 8:30am-12:30pm and 3:30-7:30pm, Sa 8:30am-12:30pm. AmEx/MC/V.

Hospital: Ospedale Bordighera, V. Aurelia 122 (☎53 61), in Bordighera.

Internet Access: Mail Boxes, Etc., V. Vittorio Veneto 4/B (☎23 84 23), just past the Giardini Pubblici from C. Repubblica. 2 computers. €3 per 30min. Also houses a **Western Union.** Open M-F 8:30am-12:30pm and 3-8:30pm.

Post Office: V. della Repubblica 8/C (☎23 63 31), on the right, after crossing V. Roma. 24hr. **ATM** outside. Open July and Aug. M-F 8am-1:15pm, Sa 8am-12:30pm; Sept.-June M-F 8am-6:30pm, Sa 8am-12:30pm. **Postal Code:** 18039.

ACCOMMODATIONS

Though Ventimiglia is often less crowded than neighboring cities, it fills up quickly in July and August; reserve ahead in the summer to benefit from the town's budget options. Large rooms with simple, modern decor and spotless baths await at ◪**Calypso Hotel ❸,** V. Matteotti 8/G. Friendly, English-speaking staff fill the hotel with charm in its calm, central location. (☎35 15 88; www.calypsohotel.it. Breakfast included. Parking €10 per day. Reception 7am-midnight. Closed Jan. 15-Feb. 10. Singles €40; doubles €75, with bath €79; triples €89/108. AmEx/MC/V.) From the station, to reach **Camping Roma ❶,** V. Freccero 9, follow V. della Repubblica, turn right on V. Roma, cross the *Ponte Doria*, and make an immediate right to C.

Francia; after 50m it becomes V. Freccero. Family-friendly spot has well-maintained, brightly painted bungalows and immaculate facilities. (☎23 90 07; informazioni@campingroma.it. Camper service 8-10am and 3-6pm. Closed Nov.-Dec. 24. €7 per person, €8-10 per tent, €5 per car. 4-person bungalows with kitchen €45-65, with private bath €60-100, with both €90. Showers free. MC/V over €50.)

█ FOOD

The **covered market** (M-Sa 6am-1pm) displays a staggering array of fruit, vegetable, and fish stands along V. della Repubblica, V. Libertà, V. Aprosio, and V. Roma. A **STANDA** supermarket is at the corner of V. Roma and V. Ruffini. (Open M-Sa 8am-8:30pm, Su 9am-8:30pm. AmEx/MC/V.) Pizzerias along the water all offer similar fare for €8-12. Head away from the beach and into the city for more variety.

> **Ristorante Cuneo,** V. Aprosio 16/D, off V. della Repubblica. Tables decorated with fresh flowers create a welcoming and comforting atmosphere. Slightly high prices are worth it. Delicious Ligurian cuisine including homemade *gnocchi* (€9.50). *Primi* €6.50-12, *secondi* €12-24. Open M-Sa 11:45am-3pm and 7-10:30pm, Su 11:45am-3pm. MC/V. ❸

> **Pasta & Basta,** Passeggiata Giacomo Marconi 20/A (☎23 08 78). Take the Passerella Squarciafichi bridge to the *città alta,* turn left onto V. Trossarelli and follow it until it becomes Passeggiata G. Marconi. Pick 1 of 20 sauces (€7-11) to pair with 1 of 6 pastas (€1-3.50) or try one of the house seafood specials (€13-16). A/C and ocean views. Open Tu-Th noon-midnight. MC/V. ❷

> **Ristorante Marco Polo,** Passeggiata Felice Cavalotti 2 (☎35 26 78). Waterfront, candlelit terrace and mind-blowing flavors make this the place to splurge or take a date in Ventimiglia. Don't miss the *tagliatelle* with lobster (€25) or any special from the dessert cart. Service is poised and professional. *Primi* €13.50-25, *secondi* €15-30. Open July-Aug. daily noon-2:30pm and 7-10:30pm; Sept.-June closed M. AmEx/MC/V. ❺

◎ SIGHTS

Though pebbly **beaches** stretch along the waterfront—the quietest ones are on the *alta* side, along Passeggiata Marconi—Ventimiglia is not known for its beaches.

▧ BOTANICAL HANBURY GARDENS. Riviera Transporti buses stop at La Mortola, home of these gardens. Begun in 1867 by English aristocrat Sir Thomas Hanbury, the gardens hold exotic flora from three continents and cascade down the summit of Cape Mortola. Hike down to the seaside cafe for *panini* (€3.50) or *gelato* (€1). The steep and challenging course mapped out in the brochure takes about 2hr. *(C. Montecarlo 43. Follow V. Guiseppe Verdi around the città alta until it becomes V. Biancheri. At P. della Costituente, bear left and walk for 15min. down V. Francia. ☎22 95 07. Open daily June 16-Sept. 15 9:30am-6pm; Sept. 16-Oct. 16 9:30am-5pm; Oct. 16-Feb. 28 9:30am-4pm; Mar.- June 15 9:30am-5pm. Last entry 1hr. before closing. €7.50. MC/V.)*

SPIAGGIA LE CALANDRE. For those set on sunbathing, a 15min. walk down a footpath from the end of Passeggiata Marconi leads onto Spiaggia Le Calandre, the town's only sandy beach. A snack bar serves drinks and *panini* and rents essential beach equipment. It's best to head home before sundown (in summer around 8pm) to avoid navigating the cliff-side path in the dark. *(☎0347 43 15 393. Open daily 8am-9pm. 2 lounge chairs with umbrella €12 per ½-day, €18 per day. Cash only.)*

CITTÀ ALTA. Follow Passeggiata Giacomo Marconi along the water as it curves to the left and until it becomes V. Trossarelli, which leads up to the historic *città alta,* Ventimiglia's cliff-side medieval area. To reach the *città alta* from the main town, cross the footbridge and turn right on V. Trossarelli. Fifty meters ahead is Discesa Porta Marina; climb to V. Galerina and then V. Falerina. From there streets lead to P. Cattedrale, where the ancient **Cattedrale dell'Assunta** stands guard over the town below. The 11th-century church of **San Michele** is on the other side of the old town, off V. Garibaldi, at P. Colleta. Its crypt was constructed using pilfered Roman columns. *(Open daily 8am-noon and 3-8pm. Free.)*

MUSEO ARCHEOLOGICO. The museum is accessible by the Blue Riviera Transporti. Roman artifacts found in the area are on display, including a dozen marble heads. The museum also holds rotating exhibits by town artists. *(V. Giuseppe Verdi 41. Buses leave from the corner of V. Cavour and V. Martiri della Libertà. Dir.: Ponte San Luigi, 15min., 10 per day from 9:05am, €1.25. ☎35 11 81; http://fortedellannunziata.it. Open Tu-Sa 9am-12:30pm and 3-5pm, Su 10am-12:30pm. €3; under 18, €2. Cash only.)*

BALZI ROSSI (RED CLIFFS). From the neighboring town of Latte, take the Riviera Transporti Bus along Corso Europa or walk 40min. through two large tunnels for about 700m to these cliffs. Prehistoric man once lived in the enormous grottoes. Enter to see a cave drawing of a horse painted thousands of years ago. The two small buildings of Museo Preistorico contain skeletons and fossils over a million years old. *(☎38 113. Open Tu-Su 8:30am-7:30pm. €2. Cash only.)*

▶ DAYTRIP FROM VENTIMIGLIA

▧ DOLCEACQUA

Riviera Trasporti frequently runs buses from Ventimiglia's V. Cavour, near C. Repubblica. (20min.; 18 per day 6am-7:05pm, last return 7:32pm; round-trip €2.50.) In Dolceacqua, the bus stops at P. Garibaldi, the new town's central square. The medieval town is located across the river.

Dolceacqua (DOL-chay-AH-kwa; pop. less than 2000) is a hidden treasure not to be missed on any Ligurian vacation. Narrow cobblestone streets, low-ceilinged shops, and a towering castle give travelers a sense of the local character. Though the city's origins are ancient—dating as far back as the 5th century BC—its landmark year came in 1270 when a Genoan captain constructed the famous Doria Castle. During the Middle Ages, Dolceaqua became the largest and strongest of a string of villages that rose up along the Roya River to accommodate traders between Ventimiglia and the rest of northern Italy.

Cross the **Roman footbridge,** whose high arch and ingenious construction prompted Monet to call it a "jewel of lightness." Turn right after the bridge and follow the walkway to a *piazza* where the 15th-century parish church of **San Antonio Abate** stands overlooking the river. Decorated with paintings and a frescoed ceiling, the church is as traditional as the sea-pebble mosaics in the *piazza* outside. (Open M-Sa 11:30am-5pm. Mass Su 8am. Free.) From the *piazza,* follow the multilingual signs that give a history of the town as they lead you through the narrow cobblestone streets of the old city. Many of the ancient stone houses have been converted into artist's studios, containing everything from Monet-knock-offs to sculptures made from bathroom tiles. Admission to most galleries is free.

Those in town for the night shouldn't miss a meal at **Pizzeria La Rampa ❷,** V. Barberis Colomba 11, on the left side of P. Garibaldi. In 2002 the National Agency of Pizza Chefs named La Rampa's pesto pizza with vegetables "Best Typically Regional Pizza" in Italy, selecting it from 900 contenders. (☎20 61 98. Open Aug. 24hr.; Sept.-July Tu-Su 7pm-midnight. Pizza €4-7; gluten-free pizza available. *Primi* €4-6.50, *secondi* €4.50-7.50. AmEx/MC/V.) Ask at the **tourist office** in P. Garibaldi, for info on August's **Ferragosto,** which fills the *piazza* with swirling regional *balletti,* traditional costumes. (Tourist office open Tu-Su 10am-12:30pm and 4-7pm.) The **Festa della Michetta,** which takes place on August 16, celebrates the town's local pastry variant on the *brioche,* the mouth-watering *michetta.* Local *alimentari* that dot the medieval stone streets sell the pastry year-round.

LOMBARDY (LOMBARDIA)

Lombardy (in Italian, "lom-bar-DEE-ah") specializes in the finer things in life. Though coveted by the Romans, Goths, French, Spaniards, Austrians, and Corsicans, the disputing European powers failed to rob Lombardy of its prosperity. Graced by masters like da Vinci and Bramante, the region is filled with ornate art and architecture. From the fashion runways of Milan to the Stradivari violin shops of Cremona, cultural sophistication permeates every aspect of the region.

HIGHLIGHTS OF LOMBARDY

GET DIZZY looking over Cremona from the Torazzo, Italy's **tallest campanile.** (p. 272)

DAYTRIP to **Certosa di Pavia,** where the monastery stands as a monument to the evolution of northern Italian art from early Gothic to Baroque (p. 256).

SPOT the *moda* of the minute as **stylish Milanesi** exhibit Europe's latest fashions. (p. 252).

WANDER the streets of Mantua, where Renaissance artists **Verdi and Mantegna** got their inspiration. (p. 267)

MILAN (MILANO)   ☎02

Milan (in Italian, "mee-LA-no"; pop. 1,200,000) is a modern metropolis and proud of it. Tire giant Pirelli, fashion master Armani, and various executive banks anchor the city as Italy's economic powerhouse. Rushed, refined, and unapologetically cosmopolitan, Milan has its share of problems, including traffic congestion and a high cost of living. But its beautifully ornate *duomo* and stunning La Scala theater, thriving symbiotically with big designer shopping and even bigger spenders, attract throngs of visitors. Overlooked as a center of commerce, this Italian urban center also hides artistic treasures: da Vinci's *Last Supper*, the Pinacoteca di Brera, and the Pinacoteca Ambrosiana. Now, the city flourishes as the country's leading producer of cutting-edge style, hearty risotto, and die-hard soccer fans. The city's pace quickens twice a year when local soccer teams AC Milan and Inter Milan face off in matches with fanfare that rivals many religious holidays. Milan's bustling lifestyle has established the city as a mini-capital of the North.

✈ INTERCITY TRANSPORTATION

Flights: 24hr. flight info for Malpensa and Linate (☎ 74 85 22 00; www.sea-aeroportimilano.it).

Malpensa Airport (MXP), 48km from the city. Intercontinental flights. **Luggage storage** and lost property services available (p. 244). Shuttle buses run to and from right side of Stazione Centrale (1hr.; every 20min. to airport 5am-9:30pm, to Stazione Centrale 6:20am-12:15am; €4.50). **Malpensa Express** train departs Cadorna Metro station and Stazione Nord (40min.; every 30min. to airport 5:50am-8:20pm, to Stazione Centrale 6:45am-9:45pm; onboard €11/13, round-trip €14.50/17).

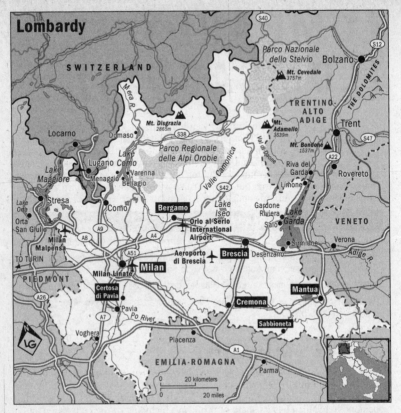

Lombardy

Linate Airport (LIN), 7km from town. Logistically more convenient. Domestic, European, and intercontinental flights with European transfers. **Starfly buses** (☎58 58 72 37) run to Stazione Centrale (20min.; every 30min. to airport 5:40am-9:35pm, to Stazione Centrale 6:05am-11:35pm; €2.50). City bus #73 runs to Milan's San Babila Metro station (€1, less convenient and secure than Starfly).

Bergamo Orio al Serio Airport (☎035 32 63 23; www.orioaeroporto.it), 58km from town, serves some budget airlines including **RyanAir.** Shuttle runs to Stazione Centrale (1hr.; to airport 4:15am-10pm, to Milan 8am-1am; €6.70).

Trains:

Stazione Centrale, (☎89 20 21), in P. Duca d'Aosta. Ticket office open daily 6am-8:40pm. To: **Bergamo** (1hr., every hr. 7:20am-11:37pm, €4.05); **Florence** (3½hr., every 1-2 hr. 5:30am-8pm, €15; Eurostar €33); **Rome** (Eurostar 5½hr., €53; TBIZ 5hr., €62; sleeper car 8hr., €73); **Turin** (2hr., every hr. 5:18am-12:30am, €8.20); **Venice** (2½ hr., every hr. 6:05am-9:05pm, €23; Eurostar 2hr., €27).

Stazione Cadorna (☎199 15 11 52). Part of **Ferrovia Nord,** the local rail system that connects to **Como** (1hr., every 30min. 6:12am-9:12pm, €3.45) and **Varese** (1hr., every 30min. 7:06am-1:03am, €4). **Malpensa Express** runs from the station to the airport (40min., every 30min. 4:20am-11:27pm, €11). **Lockers** available at the station to the left of the Express Cafe (small bag €3.50 per 2hr., medium €4.50, large €6.50.)

Stazione Porta Genova, in P. Stazione di Pta. Genova, is on the western line to **Alessandria** (1½hr., every hr. 5:10am-8:09pm) and **Mortara** (1hr., every hr. 5:57am-10:42pm).

Stazione Porta Garibaldi (☎ 65 52 078; ticket office open daily 6:30am-9:30pm), runs to: **Bergamo** (1hr., every hr. 4:50am-6:45pm); **Domodossola** (2hr., every 1½hr. 5:05am-8:47pm); **Lecco** (1hr., every hr. 5:35am-9:41pm); **Piacenza** (1½hr., every 1½hr. 8:26am-11:04pm).

Buses: At Stazione Centrale. Signs for destinations, times, and prices posted outside. Ticket office open 6:30am-8:10pm. Shuttle buses also available from the *tabaccherie* outside the station on V. Vitruvio. **Intercity** buses depart from locations on the periphery of town. **Autostradale** departs from P. Garibaldi; **SAL, SIA,** and many others depart from P. Castello (M1: Cairoli) around V. Jacini near Stazione Nord, and Porta Garibaldi for **Bergamo; Certosa di Pavia;** the **Lake Country; Rimini; Trieste; Turin.**

▟ ORIENTATION

Milan's layout is a series of concentric squares. There are four central squares: **Piazza del Duomo,** where **Via Orefici, Via Mazzini,** and **Corso Vittorio Emanuele II** meet; **Piazza Castello** and the attached **Largo Cairoli,** near Castello Sforzesco; **Piazza Cordusio,** connected to Largo Cairoli by V. Dante and P. del Duomo by V. Orefici; and **Piazza San Babila,** the entrance to the business and fashion district. The **duomo** and **Galleria Vittorio Emanuele II** are at the center of town. To the northeast and northwest sit two parks, the **Giardini Pubblici,** with several museums, and **Parco Sempione,** home to the Castello Sforzesco and its **Musei Civici. Stazione Centrale,** Milan's transportation hub, lies northeast of the *centro* in a commercial district above the Giardini Pubblici. To reach P. del Duomo, take M3 to the "Duomo" stop. By foot, walk straight from the platforms through the station's main entrance into **Piazza Duca d'Aosta.** Follow **Via Pisani** as it becomes **Via Turati** and veers into **Via Manzoni,** which leads to **Piazza della Scala,** home to Milan's opera house, and through the Galleria Vittorio Emanuele II to P. del Duomo. From V. Manzoni, turn on **Via della Spiga** to the **fashion district.** From P. San Babila take **Corso Venezia** north, becoming **Corso Buenos Aires,** leading to the *pensioni* (budget hotels) district by **Piazzale Loreto. Via Torino,** going away from P. del Duomo, runs to **Corso Porta Ticinese** and the **Navigli Canal District.**

> **!** Women should avoid walking alone after dark in the areas east of Stazione Centrale, north of Porta Garibaldi, and below the Navigli.

▐ LOCAL TRANSPORTATION

The layout of Milan's streets makes it difficult to navigate by car. Pick up a map with a street index at the tourist office or any bookstore, or a public transit map at the ATM Point (☎ 800 80 81 81; www.atm-mi.it; open M-Sa 7:45am-8:15pm) in the Metro station under Stazione Centrale or P. del Duomo.

Public Transportation: The **Metropolitana Milanese,** the city subway, operates 6am-midnight and is by far the most useful branch of Milan's transportation network. **Line #1** (red; M1) stretches east to west from the *pensioni* district east of Stazione Centrale (M1: **Sesto FS**), through the center of town, and west to the youth hostel (**Molino Dorino** northwestern end; **Bisceglie** southwestern end). **Line #2** (green; M2) links Milan's 3 train stations from **Cologno Nord** and **Gessate** in the east to **Abbiategrasso (Famagosta)** in the west and crosses M1 at **Cadorna** and **Loreto. Line #3** (yellow; M3) runs southward from the area north of Stazione Centrale at **Comasina** to **San Donato,** crossing M2 at **Stazione Centrale** and M1 at the **duomo.** Use the **bus** system for trips outside the city proper. **Trams #29** and **30** travel the city's outer road, **buses #94** and **61** traverse the inner road. **Azienda Trasporti Milanese (ATM)** tickets (€1) are good for buses, trams, and Metro for 1¼hr. Nightly tickets €1.30; 10 tickets €9.50; 24hr. pass €3, 48hr. €5.50. Metro tickets can be purchased at station machines; be sure to choose the *"urbano"* tickets.

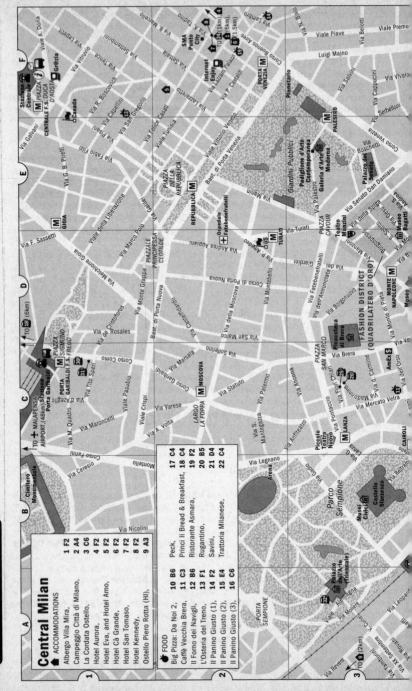

Central Milan

▲ ACCOMMODATIONS

Albergo Villa Mira,	1 F2
Campeggio Città di Milano,	2 A4
La Cordata Ostello,	3 C6
Hotel Aurora,	4 F2
Hotel Eva, and Hotel Arno,	5 F2
Hotel Cà Grande,	6 F2
Hotel San Tomaso,	7 F2
Hotel Kennedy,	8 F2
Ostello Piero Rotta (HI),	9 A3

● FOOD

Big Pizza: Da Noi 2,	10 B6
Caffè Vecchia Brera,	11 C3
Il Forno dei Navigli,	12 B6
L'Osteria del Treno,	13 F1
Il Panino Giusto (1),	14 F2
Il Panino Giusto (2),	15 E4
Il Panino Giusto (3),	16 C6
Peck,	17 C4
Princi Il Bread & Breakfast,	18 C4
Ristorante Asmara,	19 F2
Rugantino,	20 B5
Savini,	21 D4
Trattoria Milanese,	22 C4

LOMBARDY

LOMBARDY

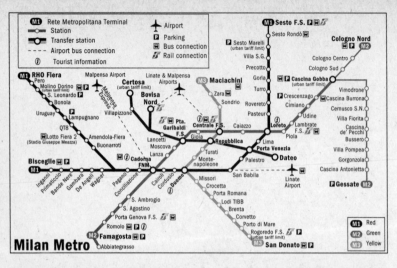

Milan Metro

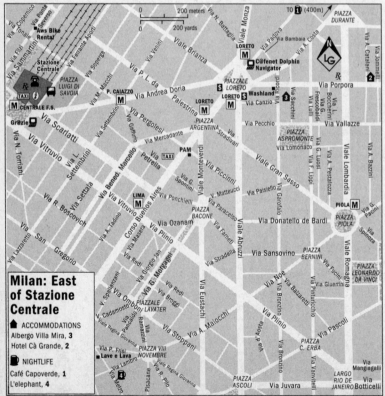

LOMBARDY

Milan: East of Stazione Centrale

▲ **ACCOMMODATIONS**
Albergo Villa Mira, **3**
Hotel Cà Grande, **2**

◗ **NIGHTLIFE**
Café Capoverde, **1**
L'elephant, **4**

Taxis: White taxis are omnipresent in the city, especially around the train stations. Call **RadioTaxi** (☎85 85 or 02 40 40). Meter starts at €3. Nighttime surcharge €3.10.

Car Rental: All have offices in Stazione Centrale facing P. Duca d'Aosta.

Avis: (☎66 90 280 or 67 01 654). Open M-F 8am-8pm, Sa 8am-2pm.

Europcar: (☎66 98 78 26). Open daily 7am-midnight. AmEx/MC/V.

Maggiore National: (☎66 90 934; www.maggiore.it). Open M-F 8am-8pm, Sa 8:30am-12:30pm and 3-6pm. D/MC/V.

Bike Rental: Companies require €100 security deposit and ID. **Rossignoli,** C. Garibaldi 65/71 (☎80 49 60). €6 per ½-day, €10 per day, €18 per weekend, €35 per week. Open M 2:30-7:30pm, Tu-Sa 9am-12:30pm and 2:30-7:30pm. **AWS,** V. Ponte Seveso 33 (☎67 07 21 45). €5.50 per ½-day. Open Th-Su 9am-1pm and 3-7pm.

🔢 PRACTICAL INFORMATION

TOURIST AND FINANCIAL SERVICES

Tourist Office: IAT (Informazioni Accoglienza Turistica), P. Duomo 19A (☎77 40 43 43; www.visitamilano.it). Local and regional info, including city maps. Accommodation booking. Pick up *Hello Milano* for info in English on events and nightlife. City walking tours depart from outside the tourist office every hr. M-Sa 10am-3pm; €10-20. Office open M-Sa 8:45am-1pm and 2-6pm, Su 9am-1pm and 2-5pm. **Branch:** Stazione Centrale (☎77 40 43 18/19), on ground fl. Smaller venue with shorter lines. Same outstanding service. Open M-Sa 9am-6pm, Su 9am-1pm and 2-5pm.

Tours: Autostradale (☎339 10 794; www.autostradale.it). Offers hop-on-hop-off sightseeing tours that make circuits of the city center. Taped commentary in 8 languages. Buy tickets by phone, at the tourist office, online, or at M2: Garibaldi. Tours (from €40) usually depart at 9:30am from P. del Duomo. Some tours (€50) include admission to all the stops, including La Scala Theater and da Vinci's *Last Supper.*

Consulates: Australia, V. Borgogna 2 (☎77 70 41). M1: S. Babila. Open M-Th 8:30am-1pm and 1:30-5pm, F 8:30am-1pm. Appointments recommended. **Canada,** V. Vittor Pisani 19 (☎67 58 34 20; www.canada.it). M2/3: Centrale FS. Open M-F 9am-noon. **New Zealand,** V. Guido d'Arezzo 6´(☎49 90 201). M1: Pagano. Open M-Sa 8:30am-noon and 1:30-5:30pm. **UK,** V. San Paolo 7 (☎72 30 00 08; emergency 03 35 81 06 857; www.britain.it). M1/3: Duomo. Open daily 9am-1pm and 2-5pm. **US,** V. Principe Amedeo 2/10 (☎29 03 51; www.milan.usconsulate.gov). M3: Turati. Open M-F 8:30am-noon.

Banks and Currency Exchange: Most banks open M-F 8:30am-1:30pm and 3-4pm. **ATMs** abound; some with automated **currency exchange. Western Union:** In Stazione Centrale. Open daily 9am-7:45pm. Also at **Money Transfer Point,** V. Porpora 12 (☎20 40 07 63). Open M-Sa 9:30am-9pm. Currency exchange offices are omnipresent, especially around P. del Duomo.

American Express: V. Larga 4 (☎72 10 41). Near the *duomo,* at the corner of V. Larga and V. San Clemente. Holds mail for up to 1 month for members for free. Moneygram international money transfer (fees vary; €500 wire €32). Also **exchanges currency.** Open M-F 9am-5:30pm, Sa 9am-12:30pm. Also at corner of V. dell'Orso and V. Brera. Open M-F 9am-5:30pm.

Beyond Tourism: InformaGiovani, Vco. Calusca 10 (☎88 46 57 60; www.comune.milano.it/giovani), enter at C. Porta Ticinese 106. Take trams #3, 15, 9, 29, 30 or bus #59 or 94. Info for young people looking to work, volunteer, study, or tutor. Also keeps resources of social events, professional associations, and apartment listings. Open M-W 10am-6pm, Th-F 2-6pm. Also at V. Laghetto 2. Open M-F 2-6pm. **Easy Milano** (www.easymilano.it), a bi-weekly publication for Milan's English-speaking community, lists work opportunities including childcare and tutoring. Available at tourist office.

LOMBARDY

LOCAL SERVICES

Luggage Storage: Malpensa Airport (☎58 58 02 98), ground fl. €3.50-4 per bag per day. Open daily 6am-10pm. **Linate Airport** (☎71 66 59), ground fl. €3.50-4 per bag per day. Open daily 7am-9:30pm.

Lost Property: Ufficio Oggetti Smarriti Comune, V. Friuli 30 (☎88 45 39 00). Open M-F 8:30am-4pm. **Malpensa Airport** (☎74 86 83 31; lostpropertymalpensa@sea-aeroportimilano.it). Open M-F 10am-noon. **Linate Airport** (☎70 12 44 51). **Stazione Centrale** (☎63 71 22 12), at luggage storage. Open daily 7am-1pm and 2-8pm.

English-Language Bookstore: The American Bookstore, V. Camperio 16 (☎87 89 20), at Largo Cairoli. Open M 1-7pm, Tu-Sa 10am-7pm. AmEx/MC/V. **English Book-shop,** V. Ariosto 12, at the corner with V. Mascheroni (☎46 94 468). Open M-Sa 10am-7pm. **Street vendors** on Largo Mattioli have cheaper options, though their English selection is limited.

GLBT Resource: ARCI-GAY "Centro D'Iniziativa Gay," V. Bezzeca 3 (☎54 12 22 25; www.arcigaymilano.org). Open M-F 3-8pm.

Handicapped/Disabled Services: AIAS Milano Onlus, V. Paolo Mantegazza 10 (☎33 02 021; www.milanopertutti.it).

Laundromat: Washland, V. Porpora 14 (☎340 08 14 477). Wash €3.50 per 7kg, dry €3.50 per 18min. Open daily 8am-10pm. **Lavanderia Self-Service ad Acqua,** V. Vigevano 20 (☎49 83 902). Wash €3.50 per 7kg, dry €3.50. Detergent €0.60. Open daily 8am-10pm. **Lava e Lava,** V. Melzo 17 (☎347 14 04 237). Wash €2, dry €3. Detergent €0.75. Open daily 8am-9:30pm.

EMERGENCY AND COMMUNICATIONS

Police: (☎77 271), in P. San Sepelcro.

Pharmacy: Farmacia Stazione Centrale (☎66 90 735). In Stazione Centrale's ground fl. galleria across from the tracks. Open 24hr. **Farmacia Carlo Erba,** P. del Duomo 21 (☎86 46 48 32), next to tourist office. Open M 2-7pm, Tu-F 9:30am-1:45pm and 3-7pm. **Farmacia Lombardia,** V. Porpora 65. Open M-F 8:30am-12:30pm and 3:30-7:30pm, Sa 8:30am-12:30pm. **Farmacia Stazione Porta Genova** (☎58 10 16 34), Ple. Stazione Porta Genova 5. Open M-F midnight-12:45pm and 3:30pm-midnight, Sa 3:30pm-8:30am, Su 8pm-midnight. AmEx/MC/V. All post after-hours rotations.

Hospital: Ospedale Maggiore di Milano, V. Francesco Sforza 35 (☎02 55 031), 5min. from *duomo* on inner ring road. **Ospedale Niguarda Ca'Granda,** in P. Ospedale Maggiore, is north of the city. **Ospedale Fatebenefratelli,** in C. Pta. Nuova.

Internet Access:

Internet Enjoy, Vle. Tunisia 11 (☎36 55 58 05). M1: Pta. Venezia. €1.80 per hr. Open M-Sa 9am-midnight, Su 2pm-midnight.

Gr@zia, P. Duca d'Aosta 14 (☎89 69 57 33; www.grazianet.com). M2/M3: Centrale FS. To the left and across the street from Stazione Centrale's main door. Wi-Fi and free webcam. €2.80 per 30min., €4 per 1hr., €8 per 3hr. Open daily 8am-midnight.

C@fenet Dolphin Navigator, V. Padova 2 (☎28 47 209). M1/M2: Loreto. Frappes, *panini,* and focaccia €3. Fast connection. €1.30 per 15min., €5 per 1hr. Open M-Sa 6:30am-7pm.

Post Office: P. Cordusio 4 (☎72 48 21 26), near P. del Duomo toward the *castello.* Offers **currency exchange** and **ATM.** Open M-F 8am-7pm, Sa 8:30am-noon. **Postal Code:** 20100

▛ ACCOMMODATIONS

Milan has a remarkably high standard of living, and its accommodations tend to be priced accordingly. Advanced booking is strongly advised two weeks to one month in advance for most hotels, especially during the summer and theater seasons. Prices vary considerably from low season (Dec. and July-Aug.) to high season (Sept.-Nov. and Mar.-May), when room prices often triple. For additional help, contact the tourist office, which assists travelers in booking accommodations.

EAST OF STAZIONE CENTRALE

Unless stated otherwise, all hotels are easily accessible from M1 or M2: Loreto, or by tram #33 from Stazione Centrale. Women should use caution when traveling alone at night in this area.

Hotel Cà Grande, V. Porpora 87 (☎26 14 40 01; www.hotelcagrande.it), 7 blocks from Ple. Loreto. Tram #33 stops 50m from the hotel. Though a bit far, it is a pleasant option with English-speaking owners and a pleasant garden. All rooms have A/C, TV, sink, and phone. Breakfast included. Singles €40-65, with bath €45-80; doubles €55-85/60-110. AmEx/D/MC/V. ❹

Albergo Villa Mira, V. Sacchini 19 (☎29 52 56 18). Small rooms in this 10-room family-run hostel are simple and impeccably clean. A few of the rooms overlook the garden patio. Singles €26-35; doubles €45-62; 1 triple €70. Cash only. ❷

NEAR GIARDINI PUBBLICI

Hotel San Tomaso, Vle. Tunisia 6, 3rd fl. (☎29 51 47 47; www.italiaabc.it/santomaso). M1: Porta Venezia. From the C. Buenos Aires Exit, turn left on Vle. Tunisia. Small rooms with TV, fan, phone, and showers; some with bath. Elevator. Singles €35-65; doubles €45-95, with bath €50-120; triples €75-135. AmEx/MC/V. ❸

Hotel Kennedy, Vle. Tunisia 6, 6th fl. (☎29 40 09 34; www.kennedyhotel.it). M1: Pta. Venezia. From the C. Buenos Aires exit, turn left on Vle. Tunisia. Simples rooms with clean bathrooms. Elevator. Singles €36-75; doubles €55-80, with bath €70-120; triples €90-120; quads €100-160. AmEx/D/MC/V. ❸

Hotel Aurora, C. Buenos Aires 18 (☎20 47 960; www.hotelaurorasrl.com). M1: Pta. Venezia. On the right side of hectic C. Buenos Aires after V. Felice Casati. Aurora offers rooms with new furniture, large beds, A/C, TV, and thick blackout curtains. Reservations recommended. Singles €50-80; doubles €80-125; triples €85-150. AmEx/MC/V. ❹

Hotel Eva and Hotel Arno, V. Lazzaretto 17, 4th fl. (☎67 06 093; www.hotelevamilano.com or www.hotelarno.com). M1: Pta. Venezia. Follow along V. Felice Casati, then right on V. Lazzaretto. Ring bell to enter. 18 large rooms with wooden floors, TV, and phone. Clean, shared bathroom. Free luggage storage. Free 30min. Internet access. Singles €30-45; doubles €50-100; triples €65-90. AmEx/MC/V. ❸

ON THE CITY PERIPHERY

La Cordata Ostello, V. Burigozzo 11 (☎58 31 46 75; www.ostellimilano.it). M3: Missori. From P. Missori, take tram #15 2 stops to Italia San Luca; then walk in the same direction for 1 block and turn right on V. Burigozzo. Entrance around the corner on V. Aurispa. Ideal for female and solo travelers. Close to the Navigli area, a lively crash pad for a young, international crowd ready to party. TV room and large, impressive kitchens. Laundry €3. Free Internet access. 7-night max. stay. Check-in 2-10pm. Check-out 11am. Closed Aug. 10-20 and Dec. 23-Jan 2. Dorms €21; doubles €70-100; triples €90-110; quad €100-120. Cash only. ❷

Ostello per la Gioventù AIG Piero Rotta (HI), V. Martino Bassi 2 (☎39 26 70 95; www.ostellomilano.it). M1: QT8. Facing Santa Maria Nascente, turn right on V. Salmoiraghi. While not near any sights and a good distance from the Metro, this enormous hostel has 400 beds. Breakfast included. Laundry €5.50. 3-night max. stay. 24hr. reception. Check-out 10am. Lockout 10am-2pm. Reserve online one day in advance;

book well ahead for Apr.-Oct. Closed Dec. 24-Jan. 12. 6-bed dorms €22; private rooms €25 per person. HI-member discount €3. MC/V. ❷

Campeggio Città di Milano, V. Gaetano Airaghi 61 (☎48 20 01 34; www.parcoaquatica.com). M1: De Angeli. From metro, take bus #72 to San Romanello Togni. Backtrack 10m and turn right on V. Tongi. Campground is 20min. walk straight ahead. Enter at Aquatica waterpark. Modern facilities, volleyball, and barbecue. Laundry €5. Reservations recommended. Closed Dec.-Jan. €7.50 per person, €11 per tent, €6.50 per car. 2-6-person cabins €37-88; bungalows with bath and A/C €80-120. Electricity free. MC/V. ❶

☐ FOOD

Choose between munching focaccia with the lunch-break crowd, clinking glasses over silver and satin, or taking your palate on a world tour through the city's ethnic neighborhoods. Old-style trattorie still follow Milanese culinary traditions with *risotto alla milanese* (rice with saffron), *cotoletta alla milanese* (breaded veal cutlet with lemon), and *osso buco* (shank of lamb, beef, or veal). Many local bars offer Happy-hour buffets of focaccia, pasta, and risotto free with drink purchase. In the city center, weary tourists near the *duomo* often succumb to P. del Duomo's pricey yet mediocre offerings, but those who dare to venture a bit off the beaten path can reap cheap and delicious rewards.

▨ **Princi II Bread & Breakfast,** V. Speronari 6 (☎87 47 97), off P. del Duomo. Take V. Torino and make 1st left. Close to the P. del Duomo. Local favorite for authentic food on-the-go. Pastries €1-4. Pizza €3.50-5. *Primi* and *secondi* €5. Open M-Sa 7am-8pm. Cash only. ❶

Trattoria Milanese, V. Santa Marta 11 (☎86 45 19 91). M1/3: Duomo. From P. del Duomo, take V. Torino; turn right on V. Maurilio and again on V. S. Marta. Serves *costolette alla milanese* (breaded veal; €17) and *mondeghili milanesi* (breaded meatballs; €12) in 2 rooms under brick arches. *Primi* €9-10, *secondi* €15-22. Cover €2. Open M-F noon-3pm and 7-11:30pm. Closed last 2wk. of July. AmEx/MC/V. ❸

Peck, V. Spadari 9 (☎80 23 161; www.peck.it). Aromas from the ground fl. spread from the wine cellar in the basement to the bar and restaurant above. Open M 3-7:30pm, Tu-Sa 8:45am-7:30pm. AmEx/MC/V. ❷

Savini, Galleria V. Emanuele II (☎72 00 34 33; www.thi.it). This world-famous restaurant has kept its decor and clientele extravagant. Pay dearly for exquisite food, like *carpaccio* (€29) and *foie gras* (€30). *Primi* €18-36, *secondi* €30-38. Cover €7. Service 12%. Open M-Sa noon-3:30pm and 7:30-10:30pm. AmEx/MC/V. ❺

Caffè Vecchia Brera, V. dell'Orso 20 (☎86 46 16 95; www.vecchiabrera.it). M1: Cairoli. Take V. Cusani, which becomes V. dell'Orso, out of P. Cairoli for 2 blocks. Sweet, meaty, or liqueur-soaked crepes (€3.50-7). *Primi* €7.50-9, *secondi* €12-14. Cover €1. Service 10%. Happy hour 5-8:30pm; drinks €5. Open daily 7am-2am. AmEx/MC/V. ❸

NAVIGLI AND ENVIRONS

An area infested with students means cheap grub. Many bars serve dinner or offer Happy-hour buffets with mixed drink purchase. The **Fiera di Sinigallia,** a bargaining extravaganza, occurs Saturdays on Darsena Banks, a canal around V. d'Annunzio. **PAM** supermarket, Vle. Olona 1/3, is by the Museo "da Vinci." (M2: Sant'Ambrogio. Open M-Sa 8am-9pm, Su 9am-7:30pm.) A **Di per Di Express** supermarket is located at Vigevano 22. (M2: Porta Genova F. S. ☎58 10 00 20. Open M-Sa 8:30am-1pm and 3:45-8:15pm. Closed late July-late Aug. M morning. MC/V over €15.)

▨ **Big Pizza: Da Noi 2,** V. Giosué Borsi 1 (☎83 96 77). Takes its name seriously. Beer and house wine flow liberally at this riverfront location, which has the feel of a restaurant but the prices of a small pizza joint. Separated smoking room removes the ubiquitous Italian tobacco from much of the restaurant interior. The *pizza della casa* is topped with pasta (€8). If not in the mood for pizza, try the crab pasta (€5). *Calzoni* €5-7. Pizza €4-8.50. Cover €1. Open M-Sa 10am-2:30pm and 7pm-midnight. MC/V. ❶

▨ **Il Forno dei Navigli,** Alzaia Naviglio Pavese 2 (☎83 23 372). At the corner of Ripa della Porta Ticinese. Out of "the oven of Navigli" come some of the most delicious pastries in the city. The *cestini* (pear tart with Nutella; €3) defines decadence. Pastries and breads €0.50-6. Open M-Sa 7am-2pm and 6pm-1am, Su 6pm-1am. Cash only. ❶

Rugantino, V. Fabbri 1 (☎89 42 14 04), between the Chiesa di San Lorenzo and the Roman pillars of C. Porta Ticinese. From M2: Sant'Ambrogio, walk down V. Edmondo De Amicis. Savor famous oven-baked dishes. Beer €4. Pizza €7-10. *Primi* and *secondi* €9-18. Open daily 12:30-3pm and 7:30pm-midnight. AmEx/MC/V. ❸

CORSO BUENOS AIRES NEAR GIARDINI PUBBLICI

Avoid the *menù turistico* at a typical trattoria in favor of foods from the neighborhood's immigrant populations. **SMA Punto City** supermarket is at C. Buenos Aires 21. (Open M-Sa 8:30am-8:30pm, Su 9am-1pm.)

Ristorante Asmara, V. Lazzaro Palazzi 5 (☎89 07 37 98; www.ristoranteasmara.it). M1: Pta. Venezia. Eat spicy Eritrean food, including a *zighini* platter with flavorful meat and vegetable pieces served on *ingera* (thin, flat bread; €10.50), with your hands. Vegetarian options available. *Antipasti* €4-5.50. Entrees €8-12.50. Cover €1.50. Open M-Tu and Th-Su 10am-4pm and 6pm-midnight. AmEx/MC/V. ❸

Il Panino Giusto, V. Malpighi 3 (☎29 40 92 97). M1: Pta. Venezia. From the *piazza*, head down Vle. Piave and turn left on V. Malpighi. If you believe sandwiches should contain goat cheese, truffled olive oil, or veal pâté for under €8, welcome home. Beer €4-5. Artisan *panini* €5-8. Open daily noon-1am. AmEx/MC/V. ❷

NEAR STAZIONE CENTRALE

A **PAM** supermarket, V. Piccinni 2, is just off C. Buenos Aires. (M1: Loreto. ☎29 51 27 15. Open M-Sa 8am-9pm.) **Punto SMA** is on V. Noe between P. Piola and P. Bernini. (Open M-F 8:30am-1:30pm and 3:30-7:45pm, Sa 8:30am-7:45pm.)

L'Osteria del Treno, V. San Gregorio 46/48 (☎67 00 479). M2/3: Centrale F. S. From P. Duca d'Aosta, take V. Pisani; turn left on V. S. Gregorio. *Primi* €8-9, *secondi* €12-13.50. Cover €2.20. Open M-F 11am-7pm and 8:30pm-12:30am, Sa 7pm-1am, Su 10am-1pm and 3pm-12:30am. AmEx/MC/V. ❹

◎ SIGHTS

NEAR THE DUOMO

▧ **DUOMO.** As Milan's geographical and spiritual center, the *duomo* is a good starting point for any walking tour of the city. Built over the remains of three other basilicas, it is the second-largest church in Italy. The structure is home to more than 3400 statues, 135 spires, and 96 gargoyles. The newly renovated facade, juxtaposes the original Italian Gothic with the newer Baroque elements that Archbishop Borromeo commissioned to show allegiance to Rome during the Protestant Revolution. The imposing 16th-century marble tomb of **Giacomo dei Medici** in the southern transept was inspired by the work of Michelangelo. Climb (or ride) to the top of the cathedral from outside the northern transept to the ▧**roof walkway** for prime views of the city below. The rooftop statue of the *Madonnina* has become the symbol of Milan. *(M1/3: Duomo. ☎86 03 58; www.duomomilano.com. Cathedral open daily 7am-7pm. Modest dress strictly enforced. Roof open daily Feb. 16-Nov. 14 9am-5:45pm; Nov. 15-Feb. 14 9am-4:15pm. Stairs €4, elevator €6.)* The **Museo del Duomo** is currently closed for restoration, but normally displays paintings, tapestries, jewels, and stained glass relating to the *duomo*'s construction. *(P. del Duomo 14, to the right of the duomo next to the Palazzo Reale.)*

■**PINACOTECA AMBROSIANA.** The 23 palatial rooms of the Ambrosiana display exquisite works from the 14th-19th centuries, including Botticelli's *Madonna of the Canopy*, da Vinci's *Portrait of a Musician*, Caravaggio's *Basket of Fruit* (the 1st Italian still-life), Titian's *Adoration of the Magi*, and works by Flemish landscapists Brueghel and Bril. Raphael's immense **School of Athens** sketch is dramatically displayed in a darkened room and deserves the praise it gets for the life-like nuances of its professors and students engaged in lively discussion. The courtyard's statues, fountains, and staircase are also enchanting, as is Bertini's 1867 two-story *Vetrata Dantesca*, a stained-glass window with allusions to Dante's *Inferno*. *(M1/3: Duomo. P. Pio XI 2. Follow V. Spadari off V. Torino, and turn left on V. Cantù. ☎80 69 21; www.ambrosiana.it. Open Tu-Su 10am-5:30pm. Last entry 1hr. before closing. €7.50, under 18 or over 65 €4.50.)*

TEATRO ALLA SCALA. Founded in 1778, La Scala has established Milan as the opera capital of the world. Its understated Neoclassical facade and lavish interior set the stage for works by Rossini, Puccini, Mascagni, and Verdi, performed by virtuosos like Maria Callas and Enrico Caruso. Visitors can peek into the theater's interior and soak up La Scala's history at the **Museo Teatrale alla Scala.** From poster art to a plaster cast of Toscanini's hand, the museum offers a glimpse into the operatic past. *(M1/3: Duomo. Largo Ghiringhelli 1 or P. della Scala. From P. del Duomo walk through the Galleria Vittorio Emanuele II. Museum on left side of building. ☎88 79 24 73; www.teatroallascala.org. Open daily 9am-12:30pm and 1:30-5:30pm. Last entry 30min. before closing. See Entertainment, p. 251, for info about performances. €5, students €4.)*

MUSEO POLDI PEZZOLI. Poldi Pezzoli, an 18th-century nobleman and art collector, bequeathed his house and art to the city "for the enjoyment of the people" in 1879. Wind past the 19th-century indoor fountain with bronze cherubs to famous paintings including Mantegna's *Virgin and Child*, Botticelli's *Madonna and Child of Mary Teaching an Infantile Christ to Read*, and the signature piece, Pollaiuolo's *Portrait of a Young Woman*. Smaller collections of china, marble busts, furniture, ancient Roman jewelry, Tiepolo oil sketches, and 18th-century clocks fill Pezzoli's unique museum. *(M3: Montenapoleone. V. Manzoni 12, near La Scala. ☎79 48 89; www.museopoldipezzoli.it. Open Tu-Su 10am-6pm. €7, students €5, under 12 or over 60 free. English-language audio tour free.)*

GALLERIA VITTORIO EMANUELE II. A 48m glass-and-iron cupola, ground breaking at the time of construction both in its concept and in the combination of materials, towers over a five-story arcade of offices, overpriced shops, and cafes. Intricate mosaics representing the continents sieged by the Romans adorn the floors and walls. In the years before electricity, a miniature train circulated the top of the arcade, keeping the candles lit along the glass. Once known as "Milan's Living Room," this 1870s gallery is now a center of tourist activity, connecting P. del Duomo to P. della Scala. Spin on the mosaic bull clockwise three times for good luck. *(To the right of the duomo. Free.)*

PALAZZO REALE. This *palazzo* served as the town hall in 1138 before serving as the residence of Milanese royalty until the 19th century. Giuseppe Piermarini, architect of La Scala, designed its facade. *(To the left of the duomo. P. del Duomo 12. ☎88 451. Only open during exhibitions. Wheelchair-accessible. Prices vary; usually €8, students €6.)*

NEAR CASTELLO SFORZESCO

■**CASTELLO SFORZESCO.** Restored after WWII damage in 1943, the Castello Sforzesco is one of Milan's best-known monuments. Its towers and courtyard were constructed in 1368 by the Visconti to defend against the Venetians. Da Vinci also had his studio here before invaders used the grounds as army barracks and horse stalls. Inside are the 10 **Musei Civici** (Civic Museums), with something for everyone. Highlights include the **Museum of Ancient Art,** which contains Michelangelo's unfinished *Pietà Rondanini* (1564), and da Vinci's frescoes on the ceiling of the **Sala delle Asse;** his design was once considered so insignificant it was whitewashed over, actually protecting the original colors. The **Museum of Decorative Art** showcases furnishings, Murano glass, and a giant porcelain crab; at the superb **Museum of Musical Instruments,** don't miss the African harps made from rattlesnake heads. *(M1: Cairoli or M2: Lanza. ☎88 46 37 03; www.milanocastello.it. Castello grounds open daily Nov.-Mar. 7am-6pm; Apr.-Oct. 7am-7pm. Free. Museums open Tu-Su 9am-5:30pm. Combined admission €3, students and over 65 €1.50. 3-day pass for Castello, Museo Archeologico, Museo di Storia Naturale e Museo del Risorgimento €7/3.50. F 2-5:30pm free.)*

CHIESA DI SANTA MARIA DELLE GRAZIE. The church's Gothic nave is elaborately patterned with frescoes, contrasting the airy Renaissance tribune added by Bramante in 1497. Look up to observe the intricate blue and red geometric drawings on the white walls and the gold sunbursts in the middle of each arch on the ceiling. *(P. S. Maria delle Grazie 2. M1: Conciliazione or M2: Cadorna. From P. Conciliazione, take V. Boccaccio and then right onto V. Ruffini for 2 blocks. Open M-Sa 7am-noon and 3-7pm, Su 7:30am-12:15pm and 3:30-9pm. Modest dress required. Free.)* To the left of the church entrance is the *Cenacolo Vinciano* (Vinciano Refectory, the convent dining hall), home to one of the best-known pieces of art in the world: Leonardo da Vinci's ▨**Last Supper.** Following a 20-year restoration effort, the painting was re-opened to the public in 1999; pieces have been flaking off almost since the day Leonardo finished it in 1498. As a result, only groups of 25 or fewer are allowed in the refractory for max. 15min. Advance booking is absolutely mandatory—reserve at least a month in the summer. *(Reservations ☎89 42 11 46; www.cenacolovinciano.org. Refectory open Tu-Su 8:15am-6:45pm. Wheelchair-accessible. €6.50, EU residents 18-25 €3.25, EU residents under 18 or over 65 free. Reservation fee €1.50. Tours €3.25. Audio tour €2.50.)*

PINACOTECA DI BRERA. The Brera Art Gallery presents a superb collection of 14th- to 20th-century paintings, with an emphasis on those from the Lombard School. Works include Bellini's *Madonna col Bambino* and *Pietà*, Mantegna's innovative *Dead Christ*, Raphael's *Marriage of the Virgin*, Caravaggio's *Supper at Emmaus*, and Francesco Hayez's *The Kiss*. A small collection of works by modern masters includes works by Modigliani and Picasso. A glass-enclosed restoration chamber in Gallery 14 allows visitors to watch conservationists at work on the aged canvases. *(V. Brera 28. M2: Lanza or M3: Montenapoleone. Walk down V. Pontaccio, and turn right on V. Brera. Or from La Scala, walk up V. Verdi until it becomes V. Brera. ☎72 26 31; www.brera.beniculturali.it. Open Tu-Su 8:30am-7:15pm. Last entry 45min. before closing. Wheelchair-accessible. €5, EU citizens 18-25 €2.50, under 18 or over 65 free. Audio tour €3.50.)*

MUSEO NAZIONALE DELLA SCIENZA E DELLA TECNOLOGIA "DA VINCI". This family-friendly, hands-on museum traces the development of science and technology from the age of Leonardo to the present. The hall of computer technology features a piano converted into a typewriter. Don't miss the da Vinci room, which contains wooden mock-ups of his flying machines, cranes, and bridges. *(V. San Vittore 21, off V. Carducci. M2: Sant'Ambrogio. ☎48 55 51; www.museoscienza.org. Open Tu-F 9:30am-5pm, Sa-Su 9:30am-6:30pm. Last entry 30min. before closing. €8, students €6.)*

BASILICA DI SANT'AMBROGIO. A prototype for Lombard-Romanesque churches throughout Italy, Sant'Ambrogio is the most influential medieval building in Milan. The 4th-century **Cappella di San Vittore in Ciel d'Oro** is through the chapel on the right. The asymmetrical **campanili** are the result of an 8th-century feud between Benedictine monks and priests, each of whom owned one tower. *(P. Sant'Ambrogio*

After only a day or two in Italy, it's apparent that just a few big names run Italy's streets.

1. In 1849 **Vittorio Emanuele II** became unified Italy's 1st king.

2. Giuseppe Garibaldi, a 19th-century military hero, is credited with making the unification of Italy possible.

3. Count Camillo Benso di Cavour designed the constitutional structure of the "Kingdom of Italy" in the 19th century.

4. Guglielmo Marconi sent three short beeps to Canada in 1901—the 1st transatlantic telegraph signals.

5. XX Settembre (1870) is the date of Italy's final unification.

6. Giacomo Matteoti, a socialist born in 1885, wrote a book critical of fascism in 1924, but was murdered in response.

7. Cesare Battisti, a native of Trent, was a WWI martyr.

8. Giuseppe Mazzini tried to instigate popular uprisings to unify Italy, but failed time and again.

9. Solferino was a battle fought on June 24, 1859 for the the unification of Italy in the region between Milan and Verona. Italy, along with French ally Napolean III, defeated Austria.

10. Umberto I reigned as King of Italy from 1878 until 1900 when he became and remains the only modern Italian head of state to be assasinated.

15. M2: Sant'Ambrogio. Walk up V. Giosuè Carducci; the church bulwark rises up to the right. ☎ *86 45 08 95. Open M-Sa 7:15am-noon and 2:30-7pm, Su 7:15am-1pm and 3-8pm. Free. Mosaics* ☎ *86 45 08 95. Open Tu-Su 9:30am-11:45pm and 2:30-6pm. €2, students €1.)*

FROM NAVIGLI TO THE CORSO DI PORTA TICINESE

BASILICA DI SANT'EUSTORGIO. Founded in the 4th century to house the bones of the Magi, it lost its function when the dead sages were spirited off to Cologne in 1164. The 1278 building hosts a Lombard-Gothic interior of low vaults and thick columns. A great masterpiece of early Renaissance art is the 1468 **☒Portinari Chapel** to the left of the entrance. The frescoes in the chapel below the rainbow dome illustrate the life of St. Peter. The elevated sarcophagus in the center is supported by eight statues representing the five cardinal virtues and the three theological virtues; Prudence has the faces of a young, middle-aged, and old woman. *(P. S. Eustorgio 1. M2: Sant'Ambrogio. From V. E. de Amicis, turn right on C. Porta Ticinese, and follow it toward the Navigli. Basilica: open daily 7:30am-noon and 3:30-6:30pm; closed 2wk. mid-Aug. Free. Cappella:* ☎ */fax 89 40 26 71. Open Tu-Su 10am-6pm. €6, students and seniors €3.)*

NAVIGLI DISTRICT. As the Venice of Lombardy, Milan's Navigli district boasts canals, elevated footbridges, open-air markets, and trolleys. The Navigli are sections of a larger medieval canal system that transported thousands of tons of marble to build the *duomo* and linked Milan to northern cities and lakes. Da Vinci designed the original canal locks. *(From the M2: Pta. Genova station take V. Vigevano.)*

CHIESA DI SAN LORENZO MAGGIORE. The oldest church in Milan, San Lorenzo Maggiore testifies to the city's 4th-century greatness. Begun as an early Christian church according to an octagonal plan, it was later rebuilt to include a 12th-century *campanile* and a 16th-century dome. To the right of the church sits the 14th-century **Cappella di Sant'Aquilino.** Inside, a 5th-century mosaic of a beardless Christ with his apostles looks over St. Aquilino's remains. *(M2: Sant'Ambrogio to V. E. de Amicis, which leads to P. Vetra and the church. V. Porta Ticinese 39.* ☎ *02 89 40 41 29. Open M-Sa 7:30am-12:30pm and 2:30-6:45pm, Su 9am-6:45pm. Cappella €2, students and seniors €1.)*

PARCO DELL'ANFITEATRO ROMANO. This archaeological park is home to the remains of Milan's Roman **amphitheater,** which stretched from V. E. de Amicis to V. Arena and south to V. Conca del Naviglia. Known as Mediolaum, it served as the capital of the western

Roman Empire and included a gladiatorial stadium, which was destroyed in the 6th century so that the Lombards couldn't use it as a stronghold. Pieces of the stadium now make up the town walls and Chiesa San Lorenzo. A better testament to Milan's Roman past might be found in the portals and columns lying along C. Porta Tininese. *(In the courtyard of V. E. de Amicis 17. M2: Sant'Ambrogio.* ☎*89 40 05 55. Park open in summer M-F 9am-7pm, Sa 9am-2pm; in winter Tu-F 9am-4:30pm. Free. Museum open in summer W and F-Sa 9am-7pm; in winter 9am-2pm. Free.)*

IN THE GIARDINI PUBBLICI

GALLERIA D'ARTE MODERNA (MUSEO DELL'OTTOCENTO VILLA BELGIOJOSO BONAPARTE). Napoleon and Josephine lived here when Milan was the capital of Napoleonic Italy (1805-1814). The gallery displays modern Lombard art as well as works from Impressionism onward. Of special note are Modigliani's *Beatrice Hastings*, Picasso's *Testa*, Klee's *Wald Bau*, and Morandi's *Natura Morta con Bottiglia*, as well as pieces by Matisse, Mondrian, and Dufy. *(V. Palestro 16. M1/M2: Palestro.* ☎*76 34 08 09; www.villabelgiojosobonaparte.it. Open Tu-Su 9am-1pm and 2-5:30pm. Free.)* The adjacent **Padiglione D'Arte Contemporanea (PAC)** is a rotating extravaganza of contemporary photographs, paintings, and visiting exhibits. *(V. Palestro 14. Tu-F* ☎*76 00 90 825, Sa-Su 76 02 04 00; www.comune.milano.it/pac. Open Tu-W and F 9:30am-5:30pm, Th 9:30am-9pm, Sa-Su 9:30am-7pm. Free.)*

❚ ENTERTAINMENT

The city sponsors many free events, all of which are detailed in the free, monthly ■Milano Mese, distributed at the tourist office. *Hello Milano* (www.hellomilano.it), an English monthly publication, can also be found at the tourist office.

OPERA, BALLET, AND LA SCALA

Milan's operatic tradition and unparalleled audience enthusiasm make ■La Scala one of the best places in the world to see an opera. The theater's acoustics are phenomenal; even those in the cheap seats appreciate a glorious sensory experience. Opera season runs from December to July and September to November, overlapping the **ballet** season. In December and March, La Scala hosts **symphonic concerts.** (Infotel Scala ☎72 00 37 44; www.teatroallascala.org. Open daily noon-6pm. Closed Aug. Ticket office at theater, V. Filodrammatici 2. Opens 3hr. before performances and closes 15min. after performance begins. Remaining tickets sold at a discount 2hr. before a show. Tickets €10-105; ask for student discounts.) **Teatro degli Arcimboldi,** Vle. dell'Innovazione 1, has modern concert performances. (☎800 121 121; www.teatroarcimboldi.org. Open M-Sa 8am-6:45pm, Su 1-6:30pm.)

THEATER, MUSIC, AND FILM

Founded after WWII as a socialist theater, the **Piccolo Teatro,** V. Rovello 2, near V. Dante, specializes in small-scale classics and off-beat productions. (☎72 33 32 22. Performances Tu-Sa 8:30pm, Su 4pm. €23-26, student rush tickets €13.) **Teatro delle Erbe,** V. Mercato 3, hosts lyrical opera from October to April. (M1: Cairoli or M2: Lanza. www.felixcompany.it.) Teatri d'Italia sponsors **Milano Oltre,** a drama, dance, and music festival (June-July). Call the **Ufficio Informazione del Comune** for the latest updates (☎86 46 40 94; www.comune.milano.it). In July the **Brianza Open Jazz Festival** (☎23 72 236; www.brianzaopen.com) draws jazz fans. Brianza is accessible by car from Milan. The **Milan Symphony Orchestra** season runs from September to May. Concerts are primarily at **Auditorium di Milano** at Largo Gustav Mahler. (☎83 38 92 01, reservations 89 40 89 16; www.orchestrasinfonica.milano.it. Ticket office open daily 10am-7pm. Tickets are also on sale at the tourist office. Tickets

€13-50, students €10-25.) Concerts also held at the **Conservatorio,** V. Conservatorio 12 (☎ 76 21 20), and **Dal Verme,** V. San Giovanni sul Muro 2 (☎ 87 90 52 01). For concert listings look under "Spettacoli" in the 'Tempo Libero" section of the daily papers. Movie listings are also in every major paper (check Th editions). Many cinemas screen English-language films, listed on the back cover of *Hello Milano*.

SPORTS

In a country where *calcio* is taken as seriously as Catholicism, nothing compares to the rivalry between Milan's soccer clubs, **Inter Milan** and **AC Milan.** The sport's feverish competition has political overtones: Inter fans are often left-wing, while AC fans tend toward the right. The face-off takes place in their shared three-tiered stadium, packing in 87,000 fans. For Inter tickets, check out www.inter.it or head to the team's offices at V. Durini 24. (☎ 77 151; www.acmilan.com. M1: S. Babila.) AC tickets are available at the team offices at V. Turati 3. (☎ 62 281 or 622 85 660. M3: Turati.) **Milan Point** has tickets, C. San Gottardo 2, or on V. Marino by P. della Scala (☎ 89 42 27 111; www.bestticket.it), also has tickets. **Ticket One,** located in FNAC department stores, one on V. Torino off P. del Duomo, sells tickets for games, concerts, and other events. (☎ 39 22 61; www.ticketone.it) Tours (M-Sa on non-game days 10am-6pm) of the **San Siro stadium,** V. Piccolomini 5, with its unique exterior spiraling ramps, include a visit to the soccer museum. (M1: Lotto. Take Vle. Federico Caprilli or tram #16. ☎ 40 42 432; fax 40 42 251. Enter at south Gate 21. €12.50, under 18 or over 65 €10.)

☐ SHOPPING

Milan is a city where clothes really do make the man (or woman): fashion pilgrims arrive in spring and summer to watch the newest styles take their first sashaying steps down the runway. Shows are generally by invitation only, but once designers take their bows, window displays and world-renowned biannual *saldi* (sales) in July and January usher new collections into the real world at more reasonable prices. With so many fashion disciples in the city, the fashion district known as the **Quadrilatero d'Oro** has become a sanctuary in its own right. This posh land, where denim jackets can sell for €2000 and Bentley limos transport poodles dressed-to-impress, is the block formed by V. Monte Napoleone, Borgospresso, V. della Spiga, and V. Gesu. On these streets, Giorgio and Donatella not only sell their styles, they live in the suites above their stores and nightclubs. Although most stores close at 7:30pm, have no fear. You can shop 24/7 at the touchscreens outside the Ralph Lauren store, so long as you don't mind waiting for delivery until the next morning.

Designer creations are available to mere mortals at the trendy boutiques along **Corso di Porta Ticinese,** which extends from **Piazza XXIV Maggio** in the **Navigli** district toward the *duomo,* and its offshoot **Via Molino delle Armi.** Trendsetters and savvy shoppers flock to the affordable mix of shops along **Via Torino** near the *duomo* and the stores along **Corso Buenos Aires.** Another option is the department store **La Rinascente,** V. Santa Radegonda 3, where Giorgio Armani began his career. (☎ 88 52; www.rinascenteshopping.com. Open M-Sa 10am-10pm, Su 10am-8pm.)

Fashionistas who can tolerate being a season behind can buy discounted top names from *blochisti* (wholesale clothing outlets). The well-known **Il Salvagente,** V. Fratelli Bronzetti 16, is located off C. XXII Marzo. (☎ 76 11 03 28. M1: San Babila. Walk up C. Monforte across P. Tricolore to C. Concordia, which becomes C. Indipendenza. Turn right on V. F. Bronzetti. Open M-Tu 3-7pm, W-Sa 10am-7pm.) **Gruppo Italia Grandi Firme,** V. Montegani #7/A, stocks brand names at 70% off regular price. (☎89 51 39 51; www.gruppoitaliagrandifirme.it. M2: Famagosta. Head 300m along Vle. Famagosta, then Cavalcavia Schiavoni, under the overpasses and across the river to V. Montegani; turn right. Open M 3:30-7:30pm, Tu-F 10am-1pm and 3:30-7:30pm, Sa 10:30am-7:30pm.) For those who want to stay in the fashion center, **DMAGAZINE Outlet,** V. Monte Napoleone 26 sells big names for more reasonable prices. Don't be surprised, however, when you see 90% discounts that still leave €300 price tags. (☎76 00 60 27. Open daily 9:30am-7:45pm.)

There are also markets and second-hand stores located around C. Porta Ticinese, the Navigli district, and C. Garibaldi. True bargain hunters attack the bazaars on Tuesday mornings and all day Saturday on **Via Fauché** (M2: Garibaldi). Also on Saturday, **Viale Papinian** (M2: Agostino) and the 400-year-old **Fiera di Sinigallia,** on V. Valencia (M2: Porto Genova), has a mix of junk and great deals.

NIGHTLIFE

Milan is known internationally for its too-cool nightlife. Each of the town's neighborhoods has its own personality. To make the most of a night out, don't seek out a single bar or club; instead, choose a district and then wander the streets. Outstanding bars, cafes, and other hot spots fill every street corner, and a true *milanese* night out isn't complete by staying seated at one table all night. The **Brera district** calls to those with creative flair, inviting tourists and *milanesi* alike to test their vocal skills at one of its piano bars. In the nearby **Porta Ticinese,** the young and beautiful meet after a long workday to sip fancy concoctions in the shadow of ancient ruins. Students descend upon the **■Navigli canal district's** endless stream of cafes, pizzerias, pubs, bars, barges, and bars on barges. A single block of **Corso Como** near Stazione Garibaldi is home to Milan's most exclusive clubs, where bouncers reject the underdressed. Bars and clubs dot the rest of the city, especially around **Largo Cairoli,** home to Milan's hottest outdoor dance venue, as well the areas southeast of **Stazione Centrale** and east of **Corso Buenos Aires,** which features a mix of bars along with much of Milan's gay and lesbian scene. The best jazz clubs are on the periphery of town.

> **TIP** **GET BUZZED IN BARS, NOT BY BUGS.** Before heading out, don't underestimate Milan's sizable mosquito population, especially around the Navigli, where insect repellent is the cologne of choice.

Check any paper on Wednesday or Thursday for info on clubs and events. *Corriere Della Sera* publishes an insert called **Vivi Milano** on Wednesday, and *La Repubblica* produces **Tutto Milano** every Thursday. The best guide to nightlife is **Pass Milano,** published in Italian every two months and available in bookstores (€12.50). **Easy Milano** (www.easymilano.it), published bi-weekly by the city's English-speaking community, contains the latest on hot night spots and is free in many bars and restaurants. **Hello Milano** also has nightlife listings and can be obtained at the tourist office. Free booklets listing bars and club venues, as well as calendars of performances, can be picked up at almost any club or bar: look through **2night** (www.2night.it), a guide to the city's top bars, and **Zero2,** the Milanese edition of an Italian bi-weekly guide to music, disco, and bar acts.

> **!** **IN DA CLUB.** The Metro closes around midnight, so if you plan to party, find a hostel near the clubs. While Milan is mostly safe at night, the areas near Stazione Centrale, Stazione Garibaldi, and C. Buenos Aires deserve caution.

BRERA DISTRICT

You won't find any clubbing here; instead, mostly older couples stroll the pedestrian thoroughfares between V. Brera and V. Mercado Vetero. The highlight of an evening in Brera is usually belting out some karaoke. To reach the heart of the district from M2: Lanza, head to V. Pontaccio, turn right on V. Mercato and then left on V. Fiori Chiari.

> **Club 2,** V. Formentini 2 (☎86 46 48 07), down V. Madonnina from V. Fiori Chiari. This bar sets the mood with red lights on the ground fl. and a maze of cushions in its dark downstairs "discopub." Loud bass downstairs. F-Sa DJ and karaoke. Basement open daily in winter. Beer €8. Mixed drinks €10. Open M-F 8:30pm-3am, Sa-Su 8pm-3am.

> **Cave Montmartre,** V. Madonnina 27 (☎86 46 11 86). With dozens of outdoor tables set at a perfect people-watching corner, Cave Montmartre serves *gelato* and mixed drinks to help the weary party-goer enjoy the catwalk of Milan locals. *Gelato* cones and cups €1.50-2.60, sundaes €3.70-7.80. Beer €3.50-5. Mixed drinks €6.50-7. Open M-Sa 7am-2am, Su 5pm-2am. Closed Oct.-Mar. Su.

CORSO DI PORTA TICINESE AND PIAZZA VETRA

Welcome to the land of the all-night Happy-hour buffet—one mixed drink buys you dinner. Chill, well-dressed crowds of locals come to drink and socialize at bars with no cover. This area is best accessible by M2 stop Sant'Ambrogio.

> ■ **Yguana Café Restaurant,** V. Papa Gregorio XIV 16 (☎89 40 41 95), just off P. Vetra, a short walk down V. E. de Amicis and V. Molino delle Armi. Beautiful people sipping fruity mixed drinks (€8). Lounge on a couch outside, or groove to the nightly DJs spinning house and hip hop downstairs. Mixed drinks €8-10. Su brunch noon-4pm. Happy-hour buffet with 50 rotating dishes M-Sa 5:30-9:30pm, Su 5:30-10pm. Open daily 5:30pm-2am, F-Sa 5:30pm-3am. Kitchen open M-F 12:30-3pm.

> **Flying Circus,** P. Vetra 21 (☎58 31 35 77; www.flyingcircusmilano.com). Walk down V. E. de Amicis and V. M. delle Armi to P. Vetra. A pair of cactus trees welcomes you to this airplane-themed, red-walled, glass-encased lounge room. Mixed drinks and wine €7-8. W "Kill Beer" night (€3 small beers 9pm-2am). Happy-hour buffet daily 6-9:30pm with €6 mixed drink. Open M-Sa 6pm-2am.

> **Exploit,** V. Pioppette 3 (☎89 40 86 75; www.exploitmilano.com), on C. Porta Ticinese near Chiesa di San Lorenzo Maggiore down V. E. de Amicis. Where the old meets the new: a chic bar-restaurant next to Roman ruins. Enjoy an extensive drink menu, organized by ingredient. Free Wi-Fi. Mixed drinks €7-9. Wine €6 per glass, €18-20 per bottle. *Primi* €10, *secondi* €18-25. Diverse Happy-hour buffet daily 6-9:30pm. Open daily noon-3pm and 6pm-2am.

■ THE NAVIGLI

On summer nights Navigli's sidewalks fill with outdoor vendors, and students flock to its bars for their friendly prices. From M2: Pta. Genova, walk along V. Vigevano until it ends, and turn right on V. Naviglio Pavese. After you see the canals, look for ■**Via Sforza,** which has countless bars and cafes, most with outdoor seating. Less refined and younger than the other neighborhoods, a night out in the Navigli is a perfect way to experience Milan and still afford a plane ticket home.

> ■ **Le Trottoir,** P. XXIV Maggio 1 (☎/fax 83 78 166; www.letrottoir.it). This self-proclaimed *"Ritrovo d'Arte, Cultura, e Divertimento"* (House of Art, Culture, and Diversions) may be the Navigli's loudest, most crowded bar and club. A young, slightly alternative crowd comes nightly to get down to live underground music 10:30pm-3am on ground fl., while upstairs features a DJ or jazz (M and W). Check schedule for weekly roster and other music nights. Mixed drinks €6-9. Pizza and sandwiches €8. Cover depends on act; usually €8, includes 1 drink. Happy hour daily 6-8pm with beer €4, mixed drinks €6. Open daily 3pm-3am. AmEx/MC/V.

Scimmie, V. Sforza 49 (☎89 40 28 74; www.scimmie.it). Near the end of a street filled with nightlife choices is a night club in 3-part harmony: pub on a river barge, polished *ristorante,* and cool bar with nightly performances. Talented underground musicians play fusion, jazz, blues, Italian swing, and reggae. Concert schedule online. 1st drink €8, €4-9 thereafter. *Primi* €8-14, *secondi* €18-24. Open daily 7pm-2am.

Spazio Movida Cocktail Bar, V. Sforza 41 (☎58 10 20 43; www.spaziomovida.it). Like its namesake Spanish cultural movement, Movida changes the tone of the social scene, spilling Latin music out onto the street. Free Wi-Fi. Mixed drinks €7. Happy hour 6-9pm; €6. Open daily 6pm-2am.

AROUND CORSO COMO

While models mingle with movie stars over €15 mojitos inside the clubs, crowds of people are served curbside drinks and share a smoke along C. Como and C. Garibaldi. Many clubs close in August. Take the M2 metro line to Garibaldi FS, and go one block south on C. Como.

Loolapaloosa, C. Como 15 (☎65 55 693). Guests are invited to dance on the bar while the bartenders entertain by swinging lamps and ringing bells. Mixed drinks €6-8. Cover from €6. Buffet 6:30-10:30pm. Open M-Sa noon-4am, Su 2pm-4am.

Hollywood, C. Como 15 (☎65 98 996; www.discotecahollywood.com). Slip into something stunning and pout for the bouncer: this club selects revelers with discretion. Mixed drinks from €10. Tu hip hop. W house. Th-Sa mixed music by resident DJs. Su tends to be invite-only party for sports stars and celebs. Cover €12-30. Open Tu-Su 11pm-5am.

AROUND LARGO CAIROLI

Take the Metro to M2: Cairoli. While the bars don't exactly cluster into one scene, it's one of the few places west of the Castello Sforzesco that is worth the trip.

Old Fashion Café, Vle. Emilio Alemagna 6 (☎80 56 231; www.oldfashion.it). M1/2: Cadorna F. N. Walk up V. Paleocapa next to the station, and turn right on Vle. Alemagna before the bridge. Club is to left of Palazzo dell'Arte along a dirt path. Summer brings stylish clubgoers to couches encircling an outdoor dance floor and stage, with live music and DJ. Elites sip Dom Perignon and converse at VIP tables. Tu is the most popular night, with mixed music. F R&B. Cover M-Tu and Th-Sa €20; W €10, students free. *Menù* €42. Su brunch noon-6pm; €20. Appetizer buffet 7:30-10pm; €13. Open M-Tu and Th-Sa 10:30pm-4:30am, W 10:30pm-4am, Su 11am-4pm and 7:30pm-midnight.

Bar Magenta, V. Carducci 13 (☎80 53 808; www.barmagenta.it). M1/M2: Cardona. A short walk down V. G. Carducci at the intersection with C. Magenta. More than a Guiness bar, this popular institution dates back to 1807. Free Wi-Fi. Pints €5.50. Happy-hour buffet 6-9pm €6 with 1 drink. Open daily 2pm-3am.

EAST OF CORSO BUENOS AIRES

The establishments southeast of Stazione Centrale are mostly frequented by locals. Most are accessible from M1/2: Loreto or M1: Pta. Venezia.

🏴 **L'elephant,** V. Melzo 22 (☎29 51 87 68; www.lelephant.it). M2: Pta. Venezia. From C. Buenos Aires turn right on V. Melzo and walk 5 blocks. An almost entirely male crowd sits at tables under chandeliers and socializes along the street corner. Gay and lesbian friendly. Mixed drinks €7-8. Happy-hour food 6:30-9:30pm; €6. Open Tu-Su 6:30pm-2am.

Café Capoverde, V. Leoncavallo 16 (☎26 82 04 30). M1/M2: Loreto. Walk 30min. along V. Costa, which becomes V. Leoncavallo. Greenhouse/bar/restaurant. Pick a cactus for mom; grab a strawberry daiquiri for yourself. Mixed drinks €8. Organic Happy-hour buffet 6:30-9:30pm with a drink. Open daily 6:30pm-2am.

❇ FESTIVALS

Rival to Venice's famed festivities, Milan's increasingly popular **Carnevale** is the oldest in Italy. The masked mystique and medieval revelry radiates from the *duomo* and spreads through the city. Carnevale occurs annually during the days preceding Ash Wednesday in February. The **Mercatone dell'Antiquariato sul Naviglio Grande** (☎89 40 99 71; www.navigliogrande.mi.it), a giant antiques extravaganza, takes place the last Sunday of each month, except July. Experience true flower power during the **Fiori sul Naviglio,** the 1st Sunday of April, when flowers fill the district. **Festa di Naviglio** is usually the 1st Sunday of June, holding another special market. The 2nd week of May, don't miss **Arte sul Naviglio Grande,** when the Naviglio plays host to the creativity of over 300 young Italian artists whose work takes over a 10,000m long area. **La Notte Bianca** (White Night) occurs annually one night in June when the Metro, theater, shops, and restaurants stay open all night from 3pm-6am. The *Assessorato alla Cultura* publishes a special summer edition (in Italian) of **Milano Cultura,** found at the tourist office, highlighting all summer events. The **Feast of Sant'Ambrogio,** the patron saint of Milan, is the 7th of December. During the first weeks of December, a special market named **Oh Bej** sets up around the basilica. The **Serate al Museo** celebration with free concerts (both classical and contemporary) spreads throughout Milan's museum courtyards and great halls; check the schedule at the tourist office.

▷ DAYTRIP FROM MILAN

▩ CERTOSA DI PAVIA

SILA buses F5 or F6 from M2: Milan-Famagosta serve Certosa (30min.; €2.40). From there, continue to Pavia by bus (30min.; M-F 61 per day 7am-10pm, Sa 50 per day 7am-10pm, Su 8 per day 8:50am-9pm). In Certosa, return tickets to Milan are sold at Il Giornale stand in the bus lot. Bus to Milan stops next to the stand; bus to Pavia stops opposite the stand. Exiting the bus in Certosa, go to the traffic light, and turn right; continue straight for a few blocks on the road, which becomes the long, tree-lined V. Certosa. The monastery is at the end. Trains also run from Milan to Certosa (20min., hourly 5:44am-10:37pm, €2.65), but arrive quite a lengthy walk from behind the walled city. From the train station, head through the parking lot and turn left in front of the wall, right at the cross street at the end, then right at the 1st street after the wall (500m). Continue 400m, and go through the portal on the right.

Seven kilometers north of Pavia stands the ▩**Monastero della Certosa di Pavia** (chehr-TOH-zah dee pa-VEE-ya). Gian Galeazzo Visconti founded it in 1396 as a mausoleum for the Visconti clan, who ruled the area from the 12th-15th centuries. Consecrated as a monastery in 1497, the building testifies to the evolution of Italian art. Inlaid marble, bas-reliefs, and sculptures embellish every available surface. The work required over 250 craftsmen during the 15th-century Lombard Renaissance. Statues of biblical figures, carvings of narratives, and 61 medallions adorn the base, while the upper half relies more on geometric patterns formed by the contrasting colors of marble for embellishment. Today, the Cistercians oversee the monastery in place of the Carthusian monks. Past the gate in the left apse, note the figures of Ludovico il More and Beatrice d'Este. On Beatrice's feet may be the oldest artistic rendition of platform shoes, which she wore to match her husband's height. The old **sacristy** houses a Florentine triptych carved in ivory; 99 sculptures and 66 bas-reliefs depict the lives of Mary and Jesus. Encircling the **choir** are 42 intricate wood inlay representations of saints, prophets, and apostles. Beyond Gian Galeazzo's mausoleum, walk through an unoccupied monk's quarters and its peaceful courtyard. (☎92 56 13; www.comune.pv.it/certosadipavia. Open Tu-Su Apr. 9-11:30am and 2:30-5:30pm; May-Sept. 9-11:30am and 2:30-6pm; Oct. and Mar. 9-11:30am and 2:30-5pm; Nov.-Feb. 9-11:30am and 2:30-4:30pm. Modest dress required. Free.)

BERGAMO ☎035

A trip to Bergamo (BEHR-ga-mo; pop. 115,000) is a visit to two different worlds. The *città bassa* (low city) is a modern, commercial town. On the bluff above, however, lies the historical *città alta* (high city), with palaces, churches, and huge stone fortifications. Through its narrow cobblestone streets, the modern world disappears. On V. Gombito, brochure-clutching tour groups share *pasticcerie*, *piazze*, and museums with a smattering of locals. Visitors will appreciate photographs and memories of panoramic views seen from the picturesque *città alta*.

▐ TRANSPORTATION

Bergamo Orio al Serio Airport (☎32 63 23; www.orioaeroporto.it) serves some budget airlines, including **RyanAir.** Bergamo's **train station** is in Ple. Marconi. (☎24 79 50 or 98 20 21. Ticket office open 5:50am-8:45pm. AmEx/MC/V.) Trains run to: Brescia (1hr., hourly 5:27am-11:11pm, €3.50); Cremona (1½hr., every 3hr. 6:16am-8:34pm, €6.70); Milan (1hr., hourly 4:41am-11:11pm, €3.50); Venice (3hr., 5:27am-11:11pm, €13). From Milan, there are connections to all major cities. **Buses** from the neighboring SAB station serve suburbs and nearby towns. Buses to Lake Como run more frequently in the summer beginning in mid-June. Check www.sptlinea.it for schedule. The **airport bus** runs between Colle Aperto, the train station, and Bergamo's airport (30min., 5:30am-10:05pm, €1.60). **ATB** runs buses in Bergamo, as well as between *città alta* and *città bassa;* for a complete route map, inquire at the ATB Point in Largo Porta Nuova or at the tourist office in *città bassa*. (☎23 60 26; www.atb.bergamo.it. Tickets for both buses and *funicolare* €1 per 1¼hr., from €2.55 per day.) For a **taxi,** call ☎45 19 090, 24 45 05, or 24 20 00. **Car rental** is available at Avis, V. Pietro Paleocapa 3, inside the central parking lot (☎27 12 90 or 31 60 41), or V. Aeroporto 13 (☎31 60 41 or 31 01 92).

✦ 🛈 ORIENTATION AND PRACTICAL INFORMATION

The train and bus stations, as well as a few budget hotels, are found in the *città bassa*, the industrial part of the city. To get to the *città alta* from the bus and train stations in **Piazza Marconi,** use line 1A (8 per hr., 7:08am-midnight). **Viale Papa Giovanni XXIII** becomes **Viale Vittorio Emanuele II** and ends as **Viale della Mura.** If you dare to walk to the *città alta,* climb the stairs on **Via Salita della Scaletta,** which starts to the left of the funicular on Vle. V. Emanuele II. Both sets of stairs go to **Porta San Giacomo** along **Via Tre Armi.** Continue through the stone Pta. San Giacomo for another 15min. to reach the tourist office on V. Gombito.

BERGAMO ON A BUDGET. A great, cheap way to see the city is to purchase an all-day ATB ticket (€3) from a vending machine or *tabaccheria*. Tickets are good on both ATB city buses and the funiculars that climb to the *città alta* and the Castello San Vigilio.

The walled *città alta* is a well-preserved medieval town, which contains most of Bergamo's major sights and churches. Enter through Pta. S. Giacomo, following V. San Giacomo to the Mercato delle Scarpe and then up **Via Gombito,** which passes through **Piazza Vecchia,** where V. Gombito turns into **Via Bartolomeo Colleoni** before reaching the **Cittadella.** Just beyond the *Cittadella,* through **Colle Aperto** and **Porta Sant'Alessandro,** the San Vigilio funicular takes riders to Bergamo's highest point.

Tourist Offices: *Città alta:* V. Gombito 13, on the ground fl. of the tower (☎24 22 26; www.commune.bergamo.it). *Città bassa:* building in center of P. Marconi in front of train station (☎21 02 04 or 21 31 85). English spoken. Both open M-F 9am-12:30pm and 2-5:30pm.

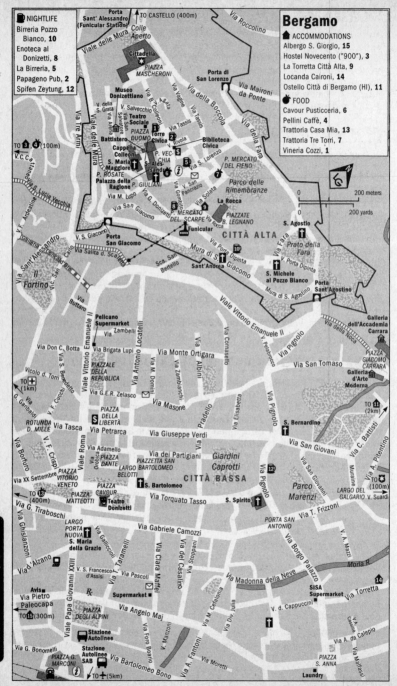

NIGHTLIFE
Birreria Pozzo Bianco, **10**
Enoteca al Donizetti, **8**
La Birreria, **5**
Papageno Pub, **2**
Spifen Zeytung, **12**

Bergamo

ACCOMMODATIONS
Albergo S. Giorgio, **15**
Hostel Novecento ("900"), **3**
La Torretta Città Alta, **9**
Locanda Caironi, **14**
Ostello Città di Bergamo (HI), **11**

FOOD
Cavour Pusticceria, **6**
Pellini Caffè, **4**
Trattoria Casa Mia, **13**
Trattoria Tre Torri, **7**
Vineria Cozzi, **1**

Tours: Gruppo Guide Città di Bergamo (☎34 42 05; www.bergamoguide.it). 2hr. tours in English Su, French F, German Sa, and Italian F-Su. €10, children free. **Associazione Guide Interpreti e Accompagnatori Turistici** (☎26 25 65; www.agiatguidebergamo.it) also offers informative walking tours of the city. Seasonal schedule; check with the tourist office.

Currency Exchange: Banca Nazionale del Lavoro, V. Petrarca 12 (☎23 80 16), off Vle. Roma/Vle. V. Emanuele II, near P. della Libertà. Open M-F 8:20am-1:20pm and 2:35-4:05pm, Sa 8:20-11:50am. Also at the **post office** and other banks.

ATMs: Throughout the *città bassa* and at the train station, especially along Vle. Roma straight up from the train station.

Western Union: Many locations throughout the *città bassa*, especially lining V. Giacomo Quarenghi, including **Multi Link Business Center,** V. G. Quarenghi 39/C, right off V. Pietro Paleocapa. Offers cheap long-distance calls. English spoken. Open M-Sa 9:30am-9pm.

Police: V. Noli in the *città bassa*, or P. della Citadella 2 (☎39 95 59).

Pharmacy: *Città alta:* **Farmacia Guidetti,** V. S. Giacomo 2 (☎23 72 20), in Mercato delle Scarpe. Open M-F 9am-12:30pm and 3-7:30pm. Posts after-hours rotations. *Città bassa:* **Farmacia Internazionale,** V. Maj 2/A. Head up V. Giovanni from the station and turn right. Open M-F 9am-12:30pm and 3-7:30pm. AmEx/MC/V.

Hospital: Ospedale Maggiore, Largo Barozzi 1 (☎26 91 11).

Internet Access: In many phone centers within *città bassa*, especially along V. G. Quarenghi. **Chiocciola,** V. D'Alzano 2d (☎24 52 36). €1 per 10min., €2.70 per 30min., €4.80 per hr. Open M-F 9:30am-7:30pm.

Post Office: *Città alta:* Mercato di Fieno 13 (☎23 95 23; fax 21 17 96). From V. Gombito, turn on V. San Pancrazio. Open M-F 8:30am-2pm, Sa 8:30am-12:30pm. *Città bassa:* V. Locatelli 11 (☎53 22 11). Take V. Zelasco from Vle. V. Emanuele. Open M-F 8:30am-7pm, Sa 8:30am-12:30pm. **Postal Codes:** 24121, 24124, 24129.

▚ ACCOMMODATIONS

Prices usually rise with altitude; the most affordable hotels are in the *città bassa*, but many have easy access to bus routes that go to the *città alta*.

Ostello Città di Bergamo (HI), V. G. Ferraris 1 (☎36 17 24; www.ostellodibergamo.it), located 2.5km from train station. Walk up Vle. Papa Giovanni to Largo Porta Nuova and take bus #6 to Montesorro (every 15min.; M-Sa 5am-11pm, Su 5am–8:30pm). Walk up road or steps to top of the hill. Hostel also accessible by line #3 from *città alta*. Modern rooms with bath, shower, and balcony. Terrace on roof with amazing view of *città alta*. Common room has TV, microwave, and fridge. Breakfast included. Wi-Fi cards for those with laptop €3. Internet access €5.16 per hr. Reserve at least a week in advance during summer. Dorms €18; singles €27; doubles €40; 4- to 8- bed family rooms €66-132. HI-member discount €3. MC/V. ❶

La Torretta Città Alta, V. Rocca 2 (☎ 23 177 or 349 57 52 596). Bed and breakfast within a historic tower. Unbelievable view from balcony onto the *piazza*. Large common area with dining room table and couch. Breakfast included. Reservation required. Singles €50-70; doubles €70-90; triples €90-110. Cash only. ❹

Hostel Novecento ("900"), V. Statuto 23 (☎25 46 96 or 337 42 32 71). From train station, take bus #2 to Ospedale stop, directly in front of hostel. Offers large, spotless rooms with phone and private bath. Affordable restaurant downstairs is filled with locals. No reception; call ahead and check in at pizzeria. Singles €30; doubles €40. Extra bed €10. AmEx/MC/V. ❸

Locanda Caironi, V. Torretta 6E (☎24 30 83; hotelcaironi@virgilio.it). From train station, take Vle. Papa Giovanni XXIII to V. Maj, turn right, and walk for 1.5km to P. Sant'Anna. Turn left on V. Borgo Palazzo, then right at 2nd block. Or take bus #5 or 7 from V. Maj.

Clean rooms share a single bath. Reception inside Caironi Trattoria. Reservations recommended. Singles €20. MC/V. ❷

Albergo San Giorgio, V. San Giorgio 10 (☎21 20 43; www.sangiorgioalbergo.it). Take bus #7 or walk from the train station down Vle. P. Giovanni XXIII. Turn left on V. P. Paleocapa, which becomes V. San Giorgio. Spacious rooms with fan, fridge, TV, phone, and sink. English spoken. Wheelchair-accessible. Reception 7:30am-midnight. Singles €33, with bath €53; doubles €53/70; triples €85; quads €105. AmEx/MC/V. ❸

◖ FOOD

Polenta, a yellow cornmeal paste, is a staple of the *bergamasco* plate, often found accompanying meals of *cavallo* (horse) or *asino* (donkey). Polenta is also used in pastries called *polentine* that are filled with rum and chocolate and coated in sugar. Traditional meals in Bergamo conclude with a *formaggio*—try sharp *branzi* or *taleggio* cheese accompanied by local red and white *Valcalepio* wines. Many of Bergamo's best restaurants and cozy bakeries are on the main tourist drag, V. Bartolomeo, and its continuations, V. Colleoni and V. Gombito. In comparison to their *città alta* counterparts, restaurants in the *città bassa* have fewer tourists, but without the *città alta*'s vacation-oriented atmosphere. Pick up staples at **Pellicano** supermarket, Vle. V. Emanuele II 17, a straight walk from the train station past P. Repubblica. (Open M 8:30am-1:30pm, Tu-F 8:30am-1:30pm and 3:30-8pm, Sa 8:30am-8pm. MC/V.)

▨ Trattoria Casa Mia, V. San Bernardino 20 (☎22 06 76). From Pta. Nuova, go down V. Gerolamo Tiraboschi, which becomes V. Zambonate. Turn left at the last intersection to V. San Bernadino. 15 tables in an intimate setting with a welcoming staff and a strong local flavor. Lunch (€9) and dinner (€15) includes a *primo*, a *secondo*, dessert, 0.25L of wine or 0.5L of water, and coffee. Open M-Sa noon-2pm and 7-10pm. Cash only. ❷

Trattoria Tre Torri, P. Mercato del Fieno 7/A (☎24 44 74). Heading downhill from P. Vecchia, turn left off V. Gombito on V. S. Pancrazio. Small home-style menu. Larger covered patio and 5 tables in the stony interior. *Antipasto* €7. *Primi* €7, *secondi* €10-14. Cover €1.50. Open M-Tu and Th-Su noon-1:30 pm and 7-10:30pm. MC/V. ❸

Cavour Pasticceria, V. Gombito 7 (☎24 34 18). Assorted €1 pastries and croissants make a perfect and inexpensive breakfast or snack. Narrow coffee bar with picturesque setting. Cash only. ❶

Trattoria da Ornella, V. Gombito 15 (☎23 27 36; www.paginegialle.it/trattoriadaornella). After exiting the funicular, walk up V. Gombito. This tourist hot spot with a *piazza* view specializes in rich polenta *taragna*, made with butter, local cheeses, and rabbit (€15). *Primi* €8-10, *secondi* €11-15. Cover €2. Open M-W and F-Su 12:30-3pm and 7:30-11pm. Reservations recommended. AmEx/MC/V. ❸

"900" Ristorante (Pellini Caffè), V. Statuto 23. With plastic tables set underneath a canopied garden, Pellini serves as the meeting place of many friendly locals. Pizza €5-8. *Primi* €6-8, *secondi* €9-14. Open M-Tu and Th-Su noon-3pm and 5:30pm-1am. AmEx/MC/V. ❷

Vineria Cozzi, V. Bartolomeo Colleoni 22 (☎23 88 36). This classy hidden gem has a small front room with wine and liquor bottles lining the walls. Romantic back dining room. Wine €3-7. *Antipasto, primi* and *secondi* €9-12. Lunch M-F 20% discount. Open M-Tu and Th-F 10:30am-3pm and 6:30pm-2am, Sa-Su 11am-2am. MC/V. ❷

◎ SIGHTS

CITTÀ ALTA

▨ BASILICA DI SANTA MARIA MAGGIORE. This 12th-century basilica, attached to the Cappella Colleoni, is Bergamo's most famous church. Tapestries and paintings depicting biblical stories adorn the walls surrounding the tomb of Bergamo's famous son, composer Gaetano Donizetti, who earned world renown through more than 70 compositions. *(Head through archway flanking P. Vecchia to reach P. del Duomo. ☎22 33 27. Open Apr.-Oct. M-Sa 9am-12:30pm and 2:30-6pm, Su 9am-1pm and 3-6pm; Nov.-Mar. M-F 9am-12:30pm and 2:30-5pm, Sa 9am-12:30pm and 2:30-6pm, Su 9am-noon and 3-6pm. Free.)*

CAPPELLA COLLEONI. Marble braids weave through the colorful Renaissance facade, and an 18th-century Tiepolo ceiling frescoes illuminate the interior of this chapel. G. A. Amadeo designed the *cappella* in 1476 as a funerary chapel for the celebrated *bergamasco* mercenary Bartolomeo Colleoni. Elaborate exterior carvings combine biblical and classical allusions—the saints wear togas and Julius Caesar and Augustus are granted divine status. *(To the right of the basilica. ☎21 00 61. Open Tu-Su Nov.-Feb. 9am-12:30pm and 2-4:30pm; Mar.-Oct. 9am-12:30pm and 2-6:30pm. Free. Audio tour €1.)*

PIAZZA VECCHIA. This *piazza* is filled with medieval and Renaissance buildings set among restaurants and cafes in the heart of the *città alta*. Locals lounge on the steps of the 400-year-old **Biblioteca Civica,** which houses Bergamo's 16th-century manuscripts. On summer weekends, artists sell paintings on the library steps. Across the *piazza* is the 12th-century Venetian Gothic **Palazzo della Ragione** (Court of Justice), featuring a lion, St. Mark's symbol. Behind it is the **Cattedrale di San Alessandro,** a cathedral for Bergamo's patron saint. To the right, connected to the *palazzo* by a walkway, stands the 12th-century **Torre Civica** (Civic Tower). The 230 steps to the top of the 54m tower lead to a 360-degree view of Bergamo. Commemorating the town's medieval curfew, the 15th-century bell rings 180 times at 10pm each night. *(Check tower opening schedule at the tourist office. Wheelchair-accessible.)*

PARCO DELLE RIMEMBRANZE. Views from this former Roman military camp make the hike up to the *città alta* worthwhile. Inscriptions immortalize Italian battle casualties. Above the park, **La Rocca** houses the **Museo Storico,** featuring weaponry, uniforms, and historical city plans. *(P. Brigata Legnano 12. At the end of V. Rocca. ☎24 71 16 or 22 63 32; www.bergamoestoria.org. Open June-Sept. Tu-F 9:30am-1pm and 2-5:30pm, Sa 9:30am-7pm; Oct.-May Tu-Su 9:30am-1pm and 2-5:30pm. La Rocca €2, with admission to all Bergamo museums €3. Ask about group discounts.)*

MUSEI DI CITTADELLA. Housed within the Citadella near the top of the *città alta,* the Civic Museums of Bergamo include the **Museo di Scienze Naturali,** features a collection of fossils and taxidermy specimens native to Bergamo, as well as an exhibit on Bergamo's silk industry that includes live silk worms. *(P. Cittadella 10. ☎28 60 11; www.museoscienzebergamo.it.)* The **Museo Archeologico** presents cultural memorabilia from Africa. *(P. Cittadella 9. ☎24 28 39; www.museoarcheologicobergamo.it. Both open Apr.-Sept. Tu-F 9am-12:30pm and 2:30-6pm, Sa-Su 9am-7pm; Oct.-Mar. Tu-Su 9am-12:30pm and 2:30-5:30pm. Free)*

ABOVE THE CITTÀ ALTA. The **San Vigilio funicular** runs from just past Pta. Sant'Alessandro and Colle Aperto in the *città alta* to **Castello San Vigilio,** Bergamo's castle in the clouds. (3min.; every 15min. M-Th 10:14am-11:51pm, F-Sa 10:15am-1:24am; €1 ticket good for 75min. on *funicolare* and city buses.) While few halls and staircases are open for exploration, the fortification's isolation and the 360-degree views of Bergamo make it worth the ride. Hiking trails run down to the historical center, including one just to the left of the funicular station, Salita dello Scorlassone. *(Head right up V. San Vigilio after exiting the funicular; castle on left. Castle open daily Apr.-Sept. 9am-8pm; Mar. and Oct. 10am-6pm; Nov.-Feb. 10am-4pm. Free.)*

CITTÀ BASSA

GALLERIA DELL'ACCADEMIA CARRARA. The cornerstone of the gallery's collection resides on the villa's top floor, where 13th- to 15th-century canvases showcase the work of Titian, Rubens, Brueghel, Bellini, Van Dyck, and El Greco. Works on display include Botticelli's *Ritratto di Giuliano dei Medici*, Lotto's *Ritratto di Giovinetto*, and Rizzi's *Maddalena in Meditazione*, in which Mary Magdalene looks down on a crucified Christ. *(P. Giacomo Carrara 82/A. From Largo Pta. Nuova, take V. Camozzi to V. Pignolo, then turn right onto V. San Tomaso. ☎39 96 77; www.accademiacarrara.bergamo.it. Open Tu-Su 10am-1pm and 2:30-5:30pm. €3.)*

GALLERIA D'ARTE MODERNA E CONTEMPORANEO. This art museum hosts a modest collection of works primarily from the 50s to the 70s, including many bronze sculptures completed by local artist Manzu as well as a few notable works by painters such as Kandinsky. View Raphael's *San Sebastiano* and Antonio Pisano's *Ritratto di Lionello d'Este*. A separate building hosts temporary exhibitions. *(V. San Tomaso 53. ☎39 96 77; www.gamec.it. Temporary exhibitions open Tu-W and F-Su 10am-9pm, Th 10am-10pm. Currently undergoing renovation; contact tourist office for info on open exhibitions. Permanent collection open Apr.-Sept. daily 10am-1pm and 3-6:45pm; Oct.-Mar. Tu-Su 9:30am-1pm and 2:30-5:45pm. Free.)*

OTHER SIGHTS. In the heart of *città bassa* is P. Matteotti, where the first glimpse of the *città alta* stops you in your tracks. Continuing away form the *piazza*, V. Torquato Tasso leads to the Chiesa del Santo Spirito, marked by its stone and brick facade and Modernist iron sculpture over the door. The stark gray Renaissance interior contrasts strongly with decorative paintings by Lotto, Borgognone, and Previtali. Check out the life-size sculptures of saints. *(V. Torquato Tasso. ☎22 05 18. Open July-Aug. M-Sa 7-11:45am and 4-6:30pm, Su 5-7pm; Sept.-June M-Sa 7-11:30am and 4-6:30pm, Su 8am-noon and 4-7pm. Free.)* On the left, V. Pignolo connects the upper and lower cities, winding past 16th- to 18th-century villas whose large doors open into elaborate inner courtyards. At the intersection with V. San Giovanni is tiny Chiesa di San Bernardino, whose bright interior features icons celebrating the town's agricultural and industrial heritage. *(V. Pignolo 59. ☎23 00 37. Open M-F 8-11am and 4-6pm, Sa and holidays 8-11:30am, Su 9am-noon. Free.)* If you are interested in finding out more about native composer Gaetano Donizetti, Museo Donizetti can be found in the *città alta* housed in the palace of Misericordia Maggiore, an ancient religious foundation. *(V. Arena 9. ☎39 92 69. Open June-Sept. daily 9:30am-1pm and 2-5:30pm; Oct.-May M-F 9:30am-1pm, Sa-Su 9:30am-1pm and 2-5:30pm. Same prices and package tickets as Museo Storico.)*

🎵🎭 ENTERTAINMENT AND NIGHTLIFE

Even outside its museums, the arts thrive in Bergamo. The opera season lasts from September to November and includes a celebration of native composer Gaetano Donizetti's works. The drama season follows, from November to April, at **Teatro Donizetti**, P. Cavour 15 (☎41 60 602 or 41 60 603), off P. Matteotti in the *città bassa*. (Box office open daily 1-9pm.) Between May and June, the spotlight falls on the highly acclaimed **Festival Pianistico Internazionale Arturo Benedetti Michelangeli** (☎24 01 40; www.festivalmichelangeli.it.), a celebration of classical works cohosted by the city of Brescia. (Tickets €8-35.) Complementing these traditional offerings is **Andar per Musica** (☎41 75 453; www.bgavvenimenti.it), a contemporary folk extravaganza in June, July, and August, featuring cultural dance and music offerings in the city and surrounding area. During the summer, the tourist office provides a program of free monthly events, *Estate Viva la Tua Città.*

The *città alta* comes alive at night as people pack the eateries, pubs, and *enoteche* along V. Colleoni and V. Gombito. The 200 different types of Belgian beers at **Papageno Pub**, V. Colleoni 1/B, make for a good time even on weekdays. (☎23 66 24. Open daily 11am-3pm and 7pm-2am. MC/V.) Continuing along the central street of *la città alta*, **La Birreria** at 1/B V. Gombita, has a young clientele and offers a special menu available only to university students upon demand. (Open daily 9am-2pm and 7pm-2am.) A bit off the beaten path, **Birreria Pozzo Bianco,** V. Porta Dipinta 30/B, offers a late-night kitchen. (☎24 76 94. Beer €2.50-8. Wine €12-19 per bottle. *Primi* and *secondi* €6.50-16.50. Open daily 11:30am-3pm and 7pm-2am. MC/V.) **Enoteca al Donizetti,** V. Gombito 17/A, has platters of local *bergamaschi* cheeses and salami as well as wine tastings. There is limited indoor seating and an often-crowded stone patio. (☎24 26 61. Cover €2. Specialty plate €9-16. Open M and W-Su 10:30am-midnight. AmEx/MC/V.) One sure bet in the *città bassa* is **Speifen Zeytung,** V. Pignolo 37, which can be found about 30 yd. off the cobblestone street, through a courtyard. German beer and waitresses in lederhosen set a Bavarian tone. (☎23 89 64. Open daily noon-2:30pm and 7pm-midnight. MC/V.)

BRESCIA   ☎030

Upon arriving in Brescia (BREH-shee-ya; pop. 200,000), try not to become dismayed at the industrial city which lies before you. In an attempt to shed its dangerous and dirty reputation, the city has recently begun new tourism initiatives; its new self-guided tourist walk narrates the impressive Roman history of the *centro storico*, the castle, the museums, and piazze. Although the charming stone buildings and history have their appeal, Brescia should perhaps be considered more as a daytrip from Milan than a destination in its own right.

▟ TRANSPORTATION

Brescia is on the Turin-Trieste line. Check the machines in the train station for your particular route. **Trains** run to: Bergamo (1hr., 10 per day 5am-10:16pm, €3.50); Cremona (45min., 15 per day 6:21am-9:25pm, €4.05); Milan (1½hr., hourly 4:15am-10:37pm, €5.35); Venice (2hr., every hr. 6:05am-9:57pm, €9.40); Verona (45min., 11 per day 5:45am-11:23pm, €3.50). When exiting the station, SIA **buses,** Vle. Stazione 14, run to many cities along the western shore of Lake Garda. (☎37 74 237. Ticket office open 7am-7pm; use machine in front of station for after hours purchases.) On the other side of the station, SAIA buses run hourly, except on Sunday, from V. Solferino 6 to Cremona, Verona, and Sirmione. (☎840 62 00 01 or 44 915; www.saiatrasporti.it. Ticket office open M-F 7am-7pm, Sa 7am-3:10pm.) The tourist office in P. della Loggia lends bikes at no cost. (€20 deposit and ID required. Must be returned before 5:30pm.) Servizio di Noleggio Biciclette also rents **bikes** from a small stand to the right of the train station. (€1 per morning ½-day, €2 per day; €5 deposit and ID required. Open June 5-Sept. 30 M-F 7:30am-7:30pm, Sa 7:30am-6:30pm.) **Taxis** (☎35 111) are available 24hr. **Rental cars** are just beyond the bike rentals at National Rental Car, V. Stazione 88. (Open M-F 8:30am-12:30pm and 2:30-6:20pm, Sa 8:30am-noon. AmEx/MC/V.)

▟ ▟ ORIENTATION AND PRACTICAL INFORMATION

After getting off the train, walk straight ahead on V. Foppa. Turn right two blocks later onto V. XX Settembre, and then left onto V. Gramsci. The first major square you will come to is **Piazza della Vittoria.** Continue on either side of the post office to P. della Loggia, the location of the tourist office.

> **Tourist Offices: Città di Brescia Tourist Office,** P. della Loggia 6 (☎24 00 357; www.comune.brescia.it). English-speaking staff provides maps of the city and other info. Ask for information about the self-guided walking tour of the city. Open in summer M-Sa 9am-6:30pm, Su 9am-1pm; in winter M-F 9:30am-12:30pm and 2-5:30pm, Sa 9:30am-1pm. **Informazioni Accogliente Turismo (IAT),** V. Musei 32 (☎37 49 916 or 37 49 438). Info about guided city tours. Open M-F 9am-12:30pm and 2:30-5:30pm.

Bank: Banca di Brescia, C. Zanardelli 54. Open M-F 8:25am-1:25pm and 2:40-4:10pm.

Laundromat: Acquazzurra Lavanderia Self-Service, V. delle Battaglie 32 (☎37 57 611), at the corner of V. Elia Capriolo. Wash and dry each €3.50-6. Detergent available. Open daily 8am-8pm. **Lavanderia Acqua,** R. Confettora 5a, at corner with V. San Faustino. Wash and dry each €2.50-6. Detergent €0.50. Cash only.

Police: V. Volta 6 (☎45 001), north of P. della Vittoria.

Pharmacy: Farmacia Croce Bianca, C. Martiri della Libertà 70. Open Tu-W and F-Su 9am-12:30pm and 3-7:30pm, Th 3-7:30pm. **Farmacia Dr. Caponati,** V. Cairoli 19/D (☎800 23 10 61). Open Tu-Su 9am-12:30pm and 3-7:30pm. After-hours rotation posted outside. Many other pharmacies throughout *centro storico*.

Hospitals: Ospedale Sant'Orsola is nearest to the city center, on V. Vittorio Emanuele II 27 (☎29 711). **Spedali Civili,** Ple. Spedali Civili 1, is the largest hospital.

Internet Access: Biblioteca di Largo Torrelunga, in P. Arnaldo. Free. Open Tu-Sa 1:30-6:30pm, Sa 9:30am-noon and 1:30-6:30pm. **Swift Cyber & Telecom Center,** Vle. Stazione 12/B (☎/fax 29 43 514). €1.50 per hr. Open M-Tu and Th-Su 9am-10pm.

Post Office: P. della Vittoria 1 (☎44 421). Open M-F 8:30am-7pm, Sa 8:30am-12:30pm. **Postal Code:** 25100.

> **❗ BRESCIA'S BAD SIDE.** At night, be careful near the train station and west of Piazza di Loggia.

⌂ ACCOMMODATIONS. Hostels near the bus and train station are the least expensive but are mostly inferior in terms of location and quality. The tourist office has complete information about hotel pricing and can book rooms throughout the city. **Hotel Sirio ❸,** V. Elia Capriolo 24, is one of most affordable hotels near city center. (☎37 50 706; www.albergosirio.com. Curfew 1am. Singles €35, with bath €45; doubles €60/65; 3- to 5-person room €20/25 per person. AmEx/MC/V.) To get to **Hotel Solferino ❷,** V. Solferino 1/A, turn left in front of the train station onto Vle. Stazione. Then take the first right, just before P. Repubblica. Ring bell to enter; reception is on the 2nd floor. The hotel is a 5min. walk from the train station and has a small shared bath. (☎46 300. Singles €26; doubles €42. Cash only.) To arrive at **Albergo Stazione ❷,** Vco. Stazione 15/17, 5min. from the train station, head left when exiting the train station and veer left onto the small street. Be sure to check changing daily lockout time. (☎37 74 614; www.italiaabc.it/az/albergostazione. Singles €30, with bath €40; doubles €60. AmEx/MC/V.)

◻ FOOD. Brescia's specialty dishes include *manzo all'olio* (beef prepared in olive oil) and *tortelli di zucca* (pumpkin-stuffed pasta). Food here, however, plays second fiddle to wine. *Tocai di San Martino della Battaglia* (a dry white), *Groppello* (a medium red), and *Botticino* (a dry red) are all local favorites. While pre-made pizza and *panini* abound near the bus and train stations, fancy restaurants fill V. Beccaria, a street winding between P. della Loggia and the *duomi*, as well as V. San Faustino. **◪Martha ❷,** P. Tito Speri 10, has an outdoor patio in the midst of the *piazza*'s greenery. Their luscious *tortellini di zucca* will make a lasting impression. (Delicious house wine €3.50 per 0.5L. *Primi* €7, *secondi* €7. Open Tu-Sa 6pm-2am, Su 6pm-midnight.) To get to **Ristorante e Pizzeria Cavour ❷,** C. Cavour 56, take V. V. Emanuele II to C. Cavour. Try the *cavour*, topped with tomatoes, mozzarella, and bacon. A steady stream of locals comes for takeout, and men frequently play cards on tables in front. (☎24 00 900. Pizza €4-9. *Primi* €5-9. Open M and W-Su noon-3pm and 6:30pm-midnight. Cash only.) For food items as well as inexpensive clothing, try the **open-air market** in P. del Mercato and along V. Francesco d'Assisi. (Open M and Sa 8:30-11am, Tu-F 8:30am-6pm.) Saturday morn-

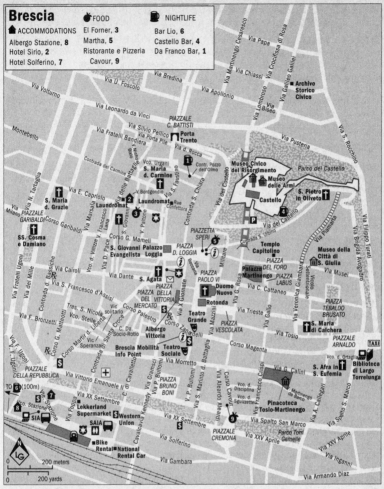

Brescia

🏠 ACCOMMODATIONS
Albergo Stazione, **8**
Hotel Sirio, **2**
Hotel Solferino, **7**

🍴 FOOD
El Forner, **3**
Martha, **5**
Ristorante e Pizzeria
Cavour, **9**

🍺 NIGHTLIFE
Bar Lio, **6**
Castello Bar, **4**
Da Franco Bar, **1**

ing brings a produce **market** to P. della Loggia. A **Pam** supermarket is on V. Porcellaga 26, one block from P. del Mercato. (Open M-Sa 8am-8pm.)

👁 SIGHTS

Brescia's *centro storico* is a tangled mix of paved and cobblestone streets and walkways. Around every corner lies another historical *piazza* or medieval church. The tourist office and many of the museums can provide a combined history and map guide of the *piazze*.

🖼 PINACOTECA TOSIO-MARTINENGO. This 22-room *palazzo* displays a fine collection of paintings and frescoes by local masters Moretto, Ferramola, Romanino, Foppa, and Lotto. Lotto's *Adorazione dei Pastori* is notable, as is the unattributed yet stunning 15th-century *San Giorgio e Il Drago*. (P. Moretto 1. From V. V. Emanuele II, take V.

Francesco Crispi, and turn right on V. Martinengo da Barco. ☎37 74 999. Open June-Sept. Tu-Su 10am-1pm and 2:30-6pm; Oct.-Mar. 9:30am-1pm and 2:30-5pm. €5, students and over 65 €4.)

▨**MUSEO DELLA CITTÀ DI SANTA GIULIA.** The chapels of the three churches in this former Benedictine nunnery are covered with well-preserved and breathtaking frescoes. Santa Giulia served as the final retreat for Charlemagne's ex-wife, Ermengarda, before it was converted into a convent in AD 753. The halls of the cloister contain over 11,000 archaeological and artistic items and often hold special exhibitions. Until May 2008, paintings by notable American artists, including John Singer Sargent and Mary Cassatt, are on display. *(V. dei Musei 81/B. Leaving P. della Loggia, take V. Cesare. In front of La Provincia, turn left and take first right on to V. dei Musei. ☎800 76 28 11 or 29 77 834; www.museiarte.brescia.it. Open June-Sept. Tu-Su 10am-6pm; Oct.-May Tu-Su 9:30am-5:30pm. €8, groups €6, ages 14-18 or over 65 €4.)*

DUOMO NUOVO AND ROTONDA. Not content with just one cathedral, Brescia built the **Duomo Nuovo** in 1825, adjacent to the smaller ▨**Rotonda,** or **Duomo Vecchio.** The 3rd-highest dome in Italy tops the courthouse-like Rococo structure and Corinthian columns of the newer church. The round, dark-stone Rotonda was built in the 11th and 12th centuries on the remains of the 6th-century Basilica of Santa Maria di Maggiore; mosaic remnants of the original church can be seen through glass-covered holes in the floor of the apse. The building also rests on top of the 8th-century crypt of St. Filastrio. *(P. Paolo VI. Take V. San Martino della Battaglia, which becomes V. Mazzini and runs into P. Paolo VI. Rotonda open Apr.-Oct. Tu-Su 9am-noon and 3-7pm; Nov.-Mar. Sa-Su 9am-noon and 3-6pm. Duomo open M-F 7:30am-noon and 4-7pm, Sa-Su 8am-12:45pm and 4-7:15pm. Modest dress required. Free.)*

TEMPIO CAPITOLINO. Traces of Brescia's classical past lie in the P. del Foro, the center of commercial, religious, and political life in Roman times. The most notable ruins are those of Emperor Vespasian's vast Tempio Capitolino, built in AD 73 and dedicated to Jupiter, Juno, and Minerva. The white sections of its columns are from a 30s restoration; the red terra-cotta brick is original. *(V. dei Musei 55, off V. Gabriele Rosa. Open daily 10am-1pm and 2-5pm. Free.)*

CASTELLO. Like every proper fairy-tale castle, the *castello* on Cidneo Hill is fitted with a drawbridge, underground tunnels, and ramparts. Though rebuilt continually from the 13th to the 16th centuries, the most striking features, notably the fortified keep (1343), date from the late middle ages. The castle also contains the **Museo Civico del Risorgimento,** which details the town's history in a variety of temporary exhibitions, and the **Musei delle Armi,** a weapons museum displaying over 500 items of armor and weaponry. *(V. del Castello. 20min. climb up Cidneo Hill. Approaching the castle, keep to residential streets and the main road until you cross through the archway, and then climb the steps on the right. ☎29 77 833. Open in summer 10am-1pm and 2-6pm; in winter 9:30am-1pm and 2:30-5pm. Both museums €3, with guide €4.50; ages 14-18 or over 65 €1.)*

🎵▨ **FESTIVALS AND NIGHTLIFE**

The **Mille Miglia** (Thousand Miles; ☎28 00 36; www.millemiglia.it), a round-trip car race between Brescia and Rome, complements Brescia's gamut of high-brow cultural events. Although a fatal accident in 1957 brought the cutthroat version of the race to a crashing end, a leisurely running in late-May brings in a fine showing of Ferraris, Maseratis, Alfa Romeos, Porsches, and Astin Martins. The annual **Stagione di Prosa,** a series of dramatic performances, runs from October to April at the **Teatro Grande,** C. Zanardelli 9 (☎29 79 333), and the **Teatro Sociale,** V. Felice Cavallotti 20 (☎28 08 600). From April to June, the focus shifts to the **Festivale Pianistico Internazionale Arturo Benedetti Michelangeli** (☎29 30 22; www.festivalmichelangeli.it), is co-hosted by nearby Bergamo. **Festival del Circo**

Contemporaneo (www.festadelcirco.com) brings a Cirque du Soleil-style circus to town in July. From late-June to September, the city hosts an **open-air cinema** (€3) at the castle, in addition to concerts, dance recitals, and operas. On February 15, celebrate the feast of Brescia's patron saint, **San Faustino,** with over 600 vendor stalls stretching across the city center. Inquire at the tourist office for further info on these events, as dates and prices can change.

Most bars are open daily from dinner until 1am. Closer to the hostels, numerous bar-restaurants with outdoor seating line P. Paolo VI and P. della Loggia, but tend to draw crowds only on weekends. During the week, one of the only hopping places for the late-night crowd is **Bar Lido,** V. Zara 66 (☎22 38 10), which has a rotating schedule of live music performances. A younger crowd heads toward the university near the end of V. San Faustino, in the northern part of the historic center. You will most likely be the only tourist at **Da Franco Bar,** Contrada Pozzo dell'Olmo 14. (Open M-Sa 6pm-2am, Su 5:30pm-2am. MC/V.)

MANTUA (MANTOVA)   ☎0376

Although Mantua (in Italian, "MAHN-toh-vah"; pop. 46,372) did not become a bustling cultural haven until the Renaissance, art and culture have shaped the city's history since the birth of the poet Virgil in 70 BC. Having provided inspiration for native and foreign artists alike including Verdi (1813-1901), the Renaissance writer Castiglioni (1478-1529), and artist Pisanello (1380-1456), the town is brimming with art. While there is much to see within the city, country towns outside the city proper like Castellaro, Cavriana, and Solferino house scenic vineyards with Lombardy's greatest gem, sparkling red wine.

▟ TRANSPORTATION. The **train station** is in P. Don Leoni, at the end of V. Solferino. (☎32 16 47. Ticket office open M-Sa 5:40am-7:45pm, Su 6am-7:45pm.) **Trains** run to Cremona (1hr., 8 per day 5:51am-8:50pm, €4.40); Milan (2¼hr., 9 per day 5:25am-7:43pm, €8.35); Modena (1hr., 6:33am-8:49pm, €3.50); Verona (40min., 20 per day 6:01am-11:52pm, €2.25). APAM **buses** (☎23 01; www.apam.it) run locally and to nearby towns, including the village of Sabbioneta (see **Daytrip from Mantua,** p. 271). Check the *biglietteria* to the left of the train station for small schedule booklets of urban and interurban buses. There are two stations: one directly in front of the train station and the other at Stazione Risorgimento, in front of Palazzo Te. **Taxis** (☎32 53 51, 36 88 44, or 32 44 08) are available 5am-1am. For **bike rentals** try La Rigola, on V. Trieste, next to Antica Osteria ai Ranari (☎36 66 77 or 335 60 54 958. €2.50 per hr., €10 per day. Open daily 9:30am-8pm. Cash only.)

▟▟ ORIENTATION AND PRACTICAL INFORMATION. Getting to most of the city's sights and shops from the train station takes 10-15min. From **Piazza Don Leoni,** turn left on **Via Solferino,** then right on **Via Bonomi** to the main street, **Corso Vittorio Emanuele II.** Follow it to **Piazza Cavallotti,** crossing the **Sottoriva River,** to get to **Corso Umberto I.** This leads to **Piazza Marconi, Piazza Mantegna,** and the main **Piazzas d'Erbe** and **Sordello.** The helpful, English-speaking staff at the **tourist office,** P. Mantegna 6, offers free brochures, maps, and lists of accommodations and restaurants. (☎43 24 32; www.aptmantova.it. Open daily 9:30am-6:30pm.) Check out the **museum tourist office,** P. Sordello 23, located in the *Casa di Rigoletto.* (☎36 89 17. Open Tu-Su 9am-noon and 3-6pm.) C. V. Emanuele II is lined with **banks,** most with **ATMs,** including **UniCredit Banca,** C. V. Emanuele II 26. (Open M-F 8:20am-1:20pm and 2:35-4:05pm.) In an **emergency,** call the **carabinieri** (☎32 88 88) or the **police,** P. Sordello 46 (☎20 51). Call the **Ospedale Carlo** (☎28 61 11 or 28 60 11), V. Albertoni, for **medical assistance. Farmacia Silvestri** (☎32 13 56), V. Roma 24 (open Tu-Sa 8:30am-12:30pm and 4-8pm; MC/V), is one of many **pharma-**

cies. Bit and Phone, V. Bertinelli 21, across from the train station, offers **Internet** access and **Western Union.** (☎22 05 94; www.bitandphone.it. Open M-Tu and Th-Sa 10am-10pm, Su noon-10pm. €2 per hr.) The **post office,** P. Martiri Belfiore 15, up V. Roma from the tourist office, offers **currency exchange.** (☎31 77 11; fax 32 53 04. Open M-F 8:30am-7pm, Sa 8:30am-12:30pm.) **Postal Code:** 46100.

ACCOMMODATIONS. Accommodations in neighboring towns like Castellaro and Monzambano are less expensive than Mantua itself. In Mantua, accommodations near the train station and main *piazze* are pricey and hard to find. B&Bs as well as *affittacamere* are the least expensive options. If the smaller establishments listed below are unavailable, check with the tourist office for more information about others. Ring the bell to enter **B&B La Zucca ❷,** V. Giovanni Battista Spagnoli 10. You won't have to sacrifice location for price if you can snag a room here. (☎339 61 89 870. Call ahead. Double €20-60, with bath €30-120.) **Hotel ABC ❹,** P. Don Eugenio Leoni 25, across from train station, is a modern hotel with comfortable rooms and an outdoor patio. All rooms have TV, A/C, and new bathrooms. Ring bell to enter after 11pm. (☎/fax 32 23 29; www.hotelabcmantova.it. Breakfast included. Luggage storage €5. Parking €8. Singles €44-88; doubles €66-121; triples €77-160; quads €88-180. Prices skyrocket early September during *Festivaletteratura*. Discount when paying with cash.) **Ostello del Mincio ❶,** V. Porto 23/25, is 15km away from Mantua. On the sidewalk to the left of the train station, buy a ticket for bus #1; take it to Stazione Risorgimento. At the station, find bus #13 (last departure at 7:40pm) to Rivalta. Though far, it is the only youth hostel in the area. (☎65 39 24; www.ostellodelmincio.org. Free Wi-Fi. Dorm €14.)

FOOD. Mantuan cuisine is known for its *tortelli di zucca* (pumpkin-filled ravioli) and its reliance on local produce and livestock. Specialties include parmesan cheese, risotto, Mantuan salami (identifiable by its light color due to the proportion of quality meat) and *sbrisolona*, a crumbly almond cake. Outdoor restaurants along **Piazza delle Erbe** and **Piazza Sordello** are packed well into the night. To get to **Trattoria con Pizza da Chiara ❸,** V. Corridoni 44/A, from P. Cavallotti, follow C. Libertà and turn left on V. Roma, then right on the narrow V. Corridoni. Young professionals dine in this chic but unpretentious restaurant. Brick ceilings, black-clad waiters, and prints on the walls create a modern twist. Venture beyond pizza to try the delicious *risotto con zucca* for €6.50. (☎22 35 68. Pizza and *primi* €4.50-9, *secondi* €9-14.50. Cover €2. Open M and W-Su noon-2:30pm and 7-10:30pm. MC/V.) **Panificio Pasticceria Pavesi ❶,** V. Broletto 19 (☎32 24 60), is on the right just before P. Sordello. The best pastry shop in Mantua serves local specialties, including *sbrisolona, torta tagliatelle,* and *mantovana.* (Pastries and cookies €1-6. Open M 7am-1:30pm, Tu-Sa 7am-7:30pm. Cash only.) A **market** is held every Thursday morning in P. delle Erbe. **Supermarket Sma,** V. Giustiziati 11, is located directly behind the Rotonda di San Lorenzo on P. d'Erbe. (Open M-Sa 8:30am-7:30pm. AmEx/MC/V.) **GS Supermarket** can be found in P. Cavallotti. (Open M-Sa 8am-8pm, Su 9am-7pm. AmEx/MC/V.)

SIGHTS

PALAZZO DUCALE. The behemoth Palazzo Ducale, home of the Gonzaga family since the start of the 14th century, dominates the Mantuan skyline. In medieval times, this was the largest palace in Europe, with 500 rooms and 15 courtyards constructed by the best architects and artists of the 14th-17th centuries. Originally many separate buildings, the *palazzo* expanded as the Gonzagas annexed surrounding structures, the most prominent being the **Castello di San Giorgio.** This

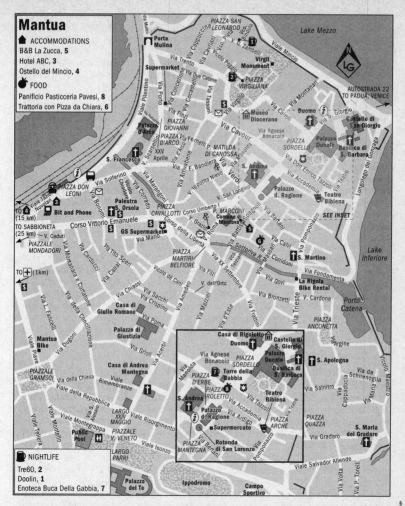

Mantua

♠ ACCOMMODATIONS
B&B La Zucca, **5**
Hotel ABC, **3**
Ostello del Mincio, **4**

● FOOD
Panificio Pasticceria Pavesi, **8**
Trattoria con Pizza da Chiara, **6**

▣ NIGHTLIFE
Tre60, **2**
Doolin, **1**
Enoteca Buca Della Gabbia, **7**

four-towered castle once served as a fortress and boasts an elaborate 17th century ceiling in its **Hall of Mirrors,** modified to suit Neoclassical tastes by Giocondo Albertoli a century later. In the **Pisanello Room,** the recent removal of a painted plaster frieze revealed a heroic cycle of frescoes depicting the knights of King Arthur. The **New Gallery** houses dozens of locally produced altarpieces from the 16th-18th centuries, removed from monasteries during the Habsburg and Napoleonic eras. *(P. Sordello 40. ☎ 22 48 32; www.mantovaducale.it. Open Tu-Su 8:45am-7:15pm. Last entry 45min. before closing. Ticket office under porticos facing the piazza. €6.50, EU students €3.25, EU citizens under 18 or over 65 free. Audio tour €4.)*

TEATRO BIBIENA. Originally commissioned by Maria Theresa of the Habsburgs to serve as a venue for cultural events and scientific expositions, this theater resembles a miniature fairy-tale castle and is one of the only ones in

LOMBARDY

northern Italy not modeled after Milan's La Scala. Four tiers of rose- and gray-stone balconies with intricately painted wood rise to the ceiling, illuminated by soft lantern light. Music lovers first filled the small, velvet couches when a 14-year-old Mozart inaugurated the building in 1769. Patrons continue to pour in today to attend music, dance, and drama performances. *(V. Accademia 47, at the corner with V. Pomponazzo. ☎32 76 53; fax 31 08 57. Open Tu-Su 9:30am-12:30pm and 3-6pm. Last entry 30min. before closing. €2.50, under 18 and over 60 €1.20.)*

PALAZZO TE. Built by Giulio Romano in 1534 as a hideaway for Federico II Gonzaga and his mistress Isabella, this opulent *palazzo* combines the layout of a Roman villa with the flamboyant ceiling frescoes that range in theme from the mythological to the Biblical. Pause in the **Sala dei Cavalli** (Room of Horses) to ponder the Gonzaga family's passion for animals, then continue past racy murals of **Cupid and Psyche.** The ⊠**Room of Giants** is adorned with a fresco that depicts the demise of the Titans at the hands of Jupiter. In summer, concerts are often held in the courtyard. Lastly, the oft-overlooked **hidden garden** of the *palazzo* and **grotto** at the far end are not to be missed. *(At southern end of the city through P. Veneto and down Largo Parri. ☎32 32 66. Open M 1-6pm, Tu-Su 9am-6pm. Last entry 30min. before closing. €8, over 60 €5.50, ages 12-18 and students €2.50.)*

PALAZZO D'ARCO. The former residence of the prominent D'Arco family, this *palazzo* is still furnished as it was during the 18th century. A separate wing houses a library and a kitchen, complete with pots, pans, and a dilapidated staircase. Navigate through the Neoclassical statues that dot the rose gardens to reach the *palazzo*'s highlight: the extraordinary Giovan Maria Falconetto-designed **zodiac chamber.** The room is divided into 12 sections, each decorated with frescoes dedicated to an astrological sign. The **murals** along the top of the walls are drawn from Ovid's *Metamorphoses. (P. d'Arco 4. ☎32 22 42; www.museodarco.it. Open Mar.-Oct. Tu-Su 10am-12:30pm and 2:30-6pm; Nov.-Feb. Sa-Su 10am-12:30pm and 2-4:30pm. Visit only by guided tour in Italian with English supplemental brochure. €3.)*

CHIESA DI SANT'ANDREA. Bequeathed to the Pope by Matilde di Canossa, a powerful and devout countess of Mantua, the oldest church in Mantua (built in the 11th century) is dwarfed by the surrounding buildings, including the **Palazzo della Ragione** (Palace of Justice) next door. *(☎22 38 10 or 22 00 97. Open only during exhibitions Tu-Su 10am-1pm and 4-7pm. €3.)* Opposite the **Rotunda di San Lorenzo** rises Mantua's most important Renaissance creation, Leon Battista Alberti's **Chiesa di Sant'Andrea** (1472-1594). The gargantuan interior was the first monumental space constructed in the Classical style since the days of imperial Rome, and the plan served as a prototype for ecclesiastical architecture for the next 200 years. Giorgio Anselmi painted the dome's frescoes in muted colors. Mantegna's (1431-1506) tomb rests in the first chapel on the left after the entrance. The church's **sacri vasi del preziosissimo sangue** (sacred vases of the precious blood), a piece of earth believed to be in Christ's blood, parades through the streets in two intricate gold vessels during the annual Good Friday procession. The rest of the year, this relic is kept in a crypt under the nave. To view the relic, ask a *chiesa* volunteer, to the right of the entrance. *(Open daily 7:30am-noon and 3-7pm. Free.)*

🎵 🎎 **ENTERTAINMENT AND FESTIVALS.** Located in the park near the monument to Virgil, the popular outdoor bar ⊠**Tre60,** P. Virgiliana 17, has raised outdoor patios scattered with lounge-style furniture. *(☎22 36 05. Open spring and summer daily 5:30pm-1am. MC/V.)* Irish pub **Doolin,** V. Zambelli 8, near P. Virgiliana, is a hidden bar popular with the locals. *(☎36 25 63. Open Tu-Sa 6:30pm-2am, Su 6pm-1am. Cash only.)* New pubs in P. Mantegna that have recently grown in popularity are **La Cantina** and **Cafe degli Artisti.** Both are small and their central location make them easily accessible at night form all over the city. A more traditional night spot is **Enoteca Buca Della Gabbia**, V. Cavour 98, a semi-underground restaurant in a wine cellar with over 650 vintages. (☎36 69 01. Open M-F 10:30am-3pm and 6:30pm-1am, Sa 10:30am-3pm and 5:30pm-2am, Su 10:30am-1pm. Cash only.) If running with the locals is really what you want, C. Umberto I, especially where it runs into P. Cavallotti, commonly hosts large groups of young locals on the weekends between 11pm and 2am. The **Teatro Bibiena** (☎32 76 53), V. Accademia 4, hosts countless musical and dramatic events, including the **Concerti di Fine Settimana,** a series of operettas and recitals every Sunday, and the similar **Concerti della Domenica** series from November to February. Between October and April, enjoy the first classical concert season, while April to June hosts round two of classical concerts as well as the jazz season. In early September, Italian scholars pack Mantua for the five-day **Festivaletteratura,** which attracts hordes of literary buffs from around the world to attend discussions, lectures, book signings, and writers' workshops with Nobel Prize winners and international best-selling authors. (Office at V. Accademia 47. ☎36 70 47; www.festivaletteratura.it.)

▶ DAYTRIP FROM MANTUA

SABBIONETA

Sabbioneta is 30km southwest of Mantua and is accessible by APAM bus #13 from Mantua. (45min., 6:35am-7:15pm, €3.30. Return buses 6:45am-6:45pm, €3.30. Buy return tickets at tabaccheria on V. Gonzaga 67.) Get off in front of the Pta. Imperiale.

Built to rival his family's success in transforming Mantua into an artistic and cultural center, Sabbioneta (SA-bee-yo-NEH-ta; pop. 4000) founder Vespasiano Gonzaga (1532-1591) developed this bustling town. Three centuries later, the town earned the title "Little Athens of the Gonzagas" for its importance as an artistic center in the late Renaissance. Today, town residents are just as proud of their nature reserves and their slow, simple way of life.

A self-guided tour of the *centro storico* is possible with historical printouts from the tourist office. Begin at the **Palazzo Giardino**, with its frescoes of mythical figures and intricately decorated alcoves. Look up to see one on the ceiling that shows the head of Medusa surrounded by rosettes in stucco relief. The **Palazzo Ducale** has fewer surviving frescoes but is nevertheless noteworthy for its **Room of Eagles,** which, in addition to painted eagles, houses a collection of eerie, life-size wooden statues of Gonzaga family members on horseback. Today, the *palazzo* is used for temporary exhibits of many different art exhibitions. The small **Teatro all'Antica,** down V. Gonzaga from the tourist office, stands out as reportedly the first theater in Europe to house a permanent theater company. It boasts a colorful mural along the back wall of the balcony and a stage surrounded by columns in imitation of a Roman amphitheater. While meandering around western Sabbioneta, note the oldest gate in the town, the **Porta Vittoria,** built in 1565. The tourist office offers guided tours in English and Italian of the aforementioned attractions upon request, included with the ticket to enter all monuments. The **Sinagoga** (Synagogue), V. Bernadino Campi 1, is an 1824 construction in Sabbioneta's Jewish quarter. **La Chiesa dell'Incoronata** has the mausoleum of the city's founder, Vespasiano Gonzaga. (☎0375 52 035. Open Su 3-6pm; other days by reservation.) On the 1st Sunday of the month (except in Jan. and Aug.), antique aficionados arrive for the exhaustive **Mercato dell'Antiquariato.** In September and October, traveling music, theater, and ballet groups also stop here.

To reach the tourist office, P. D'Armi 1, follow signs for the office along V. Gonzaga after entering city. (☎0375 22 10 44; www.comune.sabbioneta.mn.it. Tourist office and monuments open M-F 9:30am-1pm and 2:30-6pm, Sa 9:30am-1pm and 2:30-6:30pm. Buy tickets at tourist office. 1 monument €3; all monuments €10, students €5.)

CREMONA   ☎ 0372

Viewed from the top of the Torazzo, the tallest bell tower in Italy, Cremona (cre-MO-na; pop. 71,313) is a sea of terra-cotta rooftops and warm red brickwork. Above all, Cremona is awash in music, proud to be the home of violin genius Antonio Stradivari and the birthplace of the father of modern opera, Claudio Monteverdi. The city thus draws tourists looking to admire its violin-makers, who often welcome those wishing to watch them in their craft. This city of music is home to the University of Music Palaeography and Philology and the International School of Violin Making. Whether you're looking for scenery or serenading, Cremona is worth at least a day of your travels.

🖥🚋 TRANSPORTATION AND PRACTICAL INFORMATION. The **train station** is at V. Dante 68 (☎89 20 21). The ticket office is open daily 6am-7:30pm. **Trains** run to: Bergamo (1hr., 6 per day 5:02am-9:34pm, €6.70); Brescia (45min., 15 per day 5:24am-9:34pm, €4.05); Mantua (1hr., 19 per day 5:15am-9:20pm, €4.45); Milan (1¼hr., 15 per day 5:02am-9:34pm, €5.80); Parma (1hr., 5:52am-9:37pm, €3.35); Pavia (2¼hr., 5:15am-9:05pm, €6.70); Piacenza (1hr., 11 per day 5:32am-9:37pm, €2.60). The **bus station,** V. Dante 90 (☎29 212), is one block to the left of the train station. (Open M-F 7:40am-12:15pm and 2:30-6pm, Sa 7:40am-12:15pm.) **Buses** run to small surrounding towns and also to Brescia (2hr.; M-Sa hourly 6:05am-8pm, Su 4 per day). The new service Prenotabus offers buses on demand. (☎800 19 05 20. Available M-F 7am-7pm, Sa 7am-noon. Tickets available at *tabaccheria*. Check with tourist office for more info.) Orange **local buses** run from the train station throughout the city. **Taxi** stands are in P. Roma (☎21 300) and at the train station (☎26 740). Mata Store, on V. Eridano (☎45 74 83 or 333 62 26 061), rents city and mountain **bikes.** (Prices vary, call for rates.) Astrocar, V. Brescia 77 (☎45 24 67), provides **car rental.**

From the train station, walk straight ahead until reaching **Via Palestro,** which becomes the shop-lined **Corso Campi,** then **Via Verdi,** ending in **Piazza Stradivari** on the left. Cross P. Stradivari and follow **Via Baldesio** to reach the **tourist office,** P. del Comune 5, which provides maps and sells a "City Card" for discounts around town. (☎23 233; www.provincia.cremona.it. Open daily 9am-12:30pm and 3-6pm.) Those seeking info about alternatives to tourism should visit **Informagiovani di Cremona,** V. Palestro 11/A, for job listings, course offerings, and various other opportunities for long-term residents. **Internet** access is also available. (☎40 79 50; informagiovani@comune.cremona.it. Open M-Tu and Th-F 10am-1:30pm, W 10am-6pm, or call for an appointment.) **Banco Nazionale del Lavoro,** C. Campi 4-10, has **currency exchange** and a 24hr. **ATM.** (☎40 01. Open M-F 8:20am-1:20pm and 2:30-4pm, Sa 8:20-11:50am.) **Fast Call Phone Center** in P. Roma 28 has photocopying, fax, Western Union, and phone booths (calls to US €0.10 per min.). A self-service **laundromat, S. Agata a Gettone,** is located at C. Garibaldi 132 (☎30 314). In case of **emergency,** call the **police,** V. Tribunali 6 (☎40 74 27). The **hospital** (☎40 51 11) is in Largo Priori. **Farmacia (Centrale) Communale #2** is at V. del Gesù 2. (☎27 581. Open M 3:30-7:30pm, Tu-F 9am-1pm and 3:30-7:30pm, Sa 9am-1pm, and 3-8pm. After-hours rotation posted outside. MC/V.) **Libreria Giramondo,** V. Palestro 44, straight from the train station, offers **Internet** access. (☎22 414. €1 per 15min., €1.50 per 30min., €3 per hr. Open M 3:30-7pm, Tu-Sa 9:30am-12:30pm and 3:30-7pm.) The **post office,** V. Palestro 53, **exchanges currency.** (☎20 42 50. Open M-F 8:30am-2pm, Sa 8:30am-12:30pm.) **Postal Code:** 26100.

🛏 ACCOMMODATIONS. Albergo Duomo ❹, V. Gonfalonieri 13, is in the center of everything. Well-kept rooms have bath, shower, large TV, phone, and A/C. The hotel restaurant is always crowded. (☎35 242 or 35 255. Breakfast €5. Parking free. Singles

€45; doubles €65; triples €80. AmEx/MC/V.) Owned by an English-speaking violin-maker, **B&B La Mansarda ❸**, V. Larga 8, a 5min. walk from the *centro*, has three rooms with new furniture. (☎30 374; www.heyligerscremona.com/beb.html. Singles €30-40; doubles €50-80.) **Camping Parco al Po ❶**, Lungo Po Europa 12, on the banks of the Po River, is a 30-40min. walk outside the *centro* along V. del Sale through some fairly abandoned areas. Camper hookups, tent spaces, and cabins are available. (☎27 137; www.campingcremonapo.it. €10 key deposit. Open Apr.-Sept. €9 per tent, €10 per car. Cabins for 2-4 people €30-50 per person. Showers €0.50.)

⬒ FOOD. *Mostarda di Cremona*, first concocted in the 16th century, consists of cherries, figs, apricots, and melons. It has a honey-like consistency, is a bit spicy, and is traditionally eaten with meat. Delicious *grana padano*, a sophisticated cousin of parmesan cheese, is available in any *salumeria* (deli). In addition, every sweet shop sells bars of *torrone* (egg, honey, and nut nougat). The oldest sweets store in town ◼**Sperlari ❶**, V. Solferino 25, has been selling sweets like homemade *torrone* and other local favorites since 1836. (☎22 346; sperlari.negozio@tin.it. Candy €0.40-15. Open daily 8:30am-12:30pm and 3:30-7:30pm. AmEx/MC/V.) At **Pierrot ❷**, Largo Boccaccino 2, sit at one of the wicker tables, gaze out onto the lively P. del Comune, and agonize over picking one of the tantalizing *gelato* sundaes pictured in the menu. (☎29 318. *Gelato* and coffee €1.50-3. *Granita* €2-3. *Panini* €2.50-3.50. Fruit and sundaes €4-8. Open daily 7:30am-1am. AmEx/MC/V.) To sample local specialties while admiring the *duomo*, head to **Ristorante-Pizzeria Albergo Duomo ❸**, V. Gonfalonieri 13. Choose between outdoor tables stretching to P. del Comune and stare at the piles of homemade pasta in the open air kitchen. (☎35 22 96 or 35 242. Pizza €4-7.50. *Antipasto* €7-10. *Secondi* €10. Open daily 11:30am-3:30pm and 7pm-12:30am. AmEx/MC/V.) Near the center, **Bolero ❶**, V. Bordigallo Domenico 12, is the best budget option—nothing on the menu costs more than €8. (☎37 223. Crepes €5.) Packed with locals, an open-air **market** in P. Stradivari sells fresh produce, meats, and cheeses. Vendors also sell clothing. (☎40 74 50. Open W and Sa 8am-1pm.) A **GS** supermarket, V. San Tomaso 13, is close to P. del Comune. (Open M 9am-8:15pm, Tu-Sa 8am-8:15pm, Su 9am-1pm.) **Supermarket Quice** is just beyond Teatro Ponchielli on C. V. Emanuele. (Open M-Sa 8am-1pm and 3:30-10pm.) On weekends, bars and cafes fill **Piazza della Pace**, off P. Stradivari and down V. Lombardini, with live music.

◙ SIGHTS. The **Piazza del Comune** has historically been the center of Cremonese life, housing the *duomo*, Torrazzo, the baptistry, Palazzo Comunale, and Loggia dei Militi. With an excellent collection of Amati, Ceruti, and Stradivari violins, the ◼**Civica Collezione di Violini** at the **Palazzo Comunale** draws in musically minded tourists. Reserve ahead for brief performances on Stradivari and Amati instruments. (Reservations ☎20 502, questions 22 138; www.comune.cremona.it. Open Tu-Sa 9am-6pm, Su 10am-6pm; also Apr.-Oct. M. Wheelchair-accessible. €6, students €3.50. Concerts €1.50. Buy tickets at the bookshop to the right inside the courtyard.) Directly across from the Palazzo Comunale, **Santa Maria Assunta**, a pink-marble, 12th-century *duomo*, towers above the Gothic lions that guard its entrance. The interior displays 16th-century frescoes, and an ornate Grand Cross. (Open daily 7:30am-noon and 3:30-7pm. Free.) To the left of the *duomo* rises the late 13th-century **Torrazzo**. Standing at 111m, it is Italy's tallest *campanile*. Climb the 487 steps to the top where you and the pigeons can enjoy the view of the city and surrounding countryside. (☎49 50 29. Open Tu-Su 10am-1pm and 2:30-6pm. €4, students €3.) The dome of the **battistero** (baptistry), built in 1167, ascends in an octagonal pattern. The **Museo delle Pietre Romaniche** shelters treasures that include a wooden crucifixion piece and the disturbing 17th-century *Altare dell'Addolorata*, complete with a dagger piercing the heart of a golden Virgin. (☎49 50 29; beniculturali@diocesidicremona.it. Open Tu-Su 10am-1pm and 2:30-

LOMBARDY

6pm. €2, students €1. Combined ticket for Torazzo and baptistry €5/4.) At the **Palazzo Affaitati,** V. Ugolani Dati 4, off V. Palestro, a grand marble staircase leads to the Museo Civico and the Museo Stradivariano within. The **Museo Civico** exhibits a diverse collection of paintings from the 15th to 19th centuries including works by Boccaccio, the Campi family, Caravaggio, and Il Genovesino. In the same building, famous Stradivari violins are suspended within glass cases. Soft violin music plays as visitors enter the **Museo Stradivariano,** which boasts a room of the artisan's tools, molds, models, and drawings donated after his death in 1737. There is also a collection of violins from other famous makers. An English video tour and interactive exhibit explain the violins' production. (Museo Civico and Stradivariano ☎31 222. Open Tu-Sa 9am-6pm, Su 10am-6pm. €7, students and groups of more than 15 €4.) The 250-year-old, lavishly decorated Baroque **Teatro Ponchielli,** C. V. Emanuele 52, once provided the testing ground for the Stradivari and Amati violins, but today is only home to Cremona's artistic and cultural events. One of the largest stages in Italy, it is also one of the world's most beautiful opera houses. Unless for a performance, visits are by reservation only. (☎02 20 01; www.teatroponchielli.it. Ticket office open M-Sa June-Sept. 4:30-7:30pm; Oct.-May 4-7pm. €1.)

■ **FESTIVALS.** In Cremona, music and festivity are in the air year-round; tickets and info can be found at the Teatro Ponchielli ticket booth. (☎02 20 01; www.teatroponchielli.it. Open June-Sept. M-Sa 4:30-7:30pm; Oct.-May daily 4-7pm.) October 2009 will bring the biggest music festival of all, the **Triennale Internazionale degli Strumenti ad Arco,** in which 550 contestants from 34 countries exhibit newly crafted instruments, followed by performances. The actual contest takes place every three years, but every October there are related performances. (☎/fax 21 454; www.cremonamondomusica.it or www.entetriennale.com.) The **Monteverdi Festival** from May to June honors the great Cremonese composer's music. (Info and tickets ☎02 20 10/01, info www.teatroponchielli.it, tickets www.vivaticket.it. Tickets €10-22.) From June to August, Cremona sponsors theatrical performances, musicals, culinary *degustazioni*, and fireworks displays in the surrounding towns on the Po River as part of the annual **Il Grande Fiume** (☎0521 37 40 77; www.ilgrandefiume.it). Complementing these fine-art offerings is Arena Giardino's **Festival di Mezza Estate,** in Parco Tognazzi, along Vle. Po to the southeast of the city, a summer festival from May to September, mainly celebrates Italian cinema, but also features drama, concerts, and ballet. (☎333 39 55 235; www.cinemacremona.it. Tickets about €5.) Lastly, the **Strada del Gusto Cremonese** (www.stradadelgustocremonese.it) aims to boost ecological production and encourage culinary tourism by having local restaurants feature special menus; contact the tourist office for the schedule.

THE LAKE COUNTRY

Travelers who need the kind of rejuvenation that is only proffered by nature should follow the example of artistic visionaries like List, Longfellow, and Wordsworth: retreat to the serene shores of the northern lakes, where clear waters lap at the foot of snowcapped mountains. Summer attracts droves of tourists, foreign and native alike, who spread out among the many towns bordering these Italian lakes. A young, mostly-German crowd descends upon the more affordable Lake Garda, enjoying aquatic sports by day and bars by night. The mansion-spotted coast of Lake Como fills its abundant hotels year-round with visitors seeking Kodak moments and a picture-perfect resort getaway. A playground for the rich and famous, Lake Como's shoreline harbors a couple well-run and inexpensive hostels in addition to its famous villas. In the neighboring province of Piedmont, palatial hotels dot Lake Maggiore's sleepy shores (p. 299). Tourism is least obtrusive and scenery most tranquil in tiny Lake Orta (p. 299).

HIGHLIGHTS OF THE LAKE COUNTRY

BASK in the sun along the **grass "beaches"** in Riva del Garda (p. 282).

CATCH A WAVE while **windsurfing** in breezy, relaxed Domaso (p. 293).

DE-STRESS in Stresa, a **resort town** that draws visitors from all over (p. 299).

LAKE GARDA (LAGO DI GARDA)

Lake Garda, the largest lake in Northern Italy, draws tourists by the busload to enjoy its surrounding mountains and resort-style living. Stretching 52km into the regions of the Veneto, Lombardy, and Trent, Lake Garda's shores are the destination of choice for Europeans seeking beaches, food and wine. In the north, beachgoers enjoy aquatic sports and relax on the breezy beaches. Their trips are framed by the gorgeous Dolomite mountains, which also provide fantastic hiking opportunities. In the south, the more crowded cities emphasize the good life that comes from quality food and wine.

SIRMIONE ☎030

Isolated on a peninsula from the surrounding lakeside towns, tiny Sirmione (seer-mee-OH-neh; pop. 7000) retains some of the old-world charm that once moved the poet Catullus to praise the beauty of his home here. Among the town's chief attractions are the healing powers of its spa waters, which have been renowned since ancient times. Local authorities maintain the town's peace and tranquility by transforming the *centro storico* into a pedestrian-only zone; nonetheless, the heavy tourist traffic gives Sirmione the feel of a bustling resort. Trendy boutiques, lively restaurants, and sophisticated hotels line the cobblestone sidewalks, sharing the space with traces of Sirmione's Roman history and medieval architecture.

TRANSPORTATION AND PRACTICAL INFORMATION. SAIA **buses** run from the station, V. Marconi 26, to all stops along the Brescia-Verona line, includ-

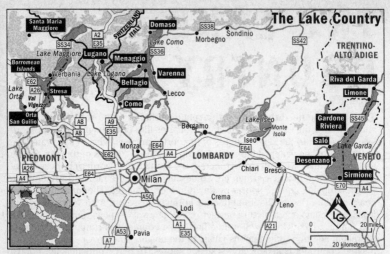

ing Desenzano, the nearest train station. (Ticket office open M-Tu 9am-1pm and 2-6pm, W-Su 7am-1pm and 2-8pm. After hours, purchase bus tickets from the *tabaccheria* on Vle. Marconi located about 200m from the ticket counter, or in S. Cantro.) Navigazione Lago di Garda (☎91 49 511; www.navigazionelaghi.it) at the end of P. Carducci runs **ferries** to Desenzano (15min.; 17 per day 10am-8pm; €3.30, express €5.10), Gardone via Salò (1¼-2hr.; 11 per day 8:27am-5:41pm; €6.50, express €9.50), and Riva del Garda via Limone (2-3hr.; 9:46, 10:20, 10:28am, 2:15, 3:00, 4:55pm; €9.60, express €13). Pick up a schedule in the tourist office or at the ferry ticket offices. For a **taxi**, call ☎91 60 82. Rent **bikes, scooters,** and **motorbikes** at Adventure Sprint, P. Virgilio 31 (☎91 90 00). (Bikes €12 per day; scooters €50-75; motorbikes €110-140. Insurance included. Open daily 9am-6:30pm. MC/V)

The **tourist office**, V. Guglielmo Marconi 8 (☎91 61 14; www.comune.sirmione.bs.it), is in the circular building in front of the SAIA station toward the *centro storico.* (Open Apr.-Oct. daily 9am-8pm; Nov.-Mar. M-F 9am-12:30pm and 3-6pm, Sa 9am-12:30pm.) **Banca Popolare di Verona** is at P. Castello 3/4. (Open M-F 9am-1:20pm and 2:35-3:35pm, Sa-Su 9-11:20am). In case of emergency, call the **police** (☎99 05 772), or the **Tourist Medical Clinic,** P. Virgilio 35 (☎347 97 16 620). **Farmacia di Turno** is on V. Santa Maria Maggiore in the old city. (Open M-W and F-Su 9:45am-12:15pm and 4:30-7pm, Th 9:45am-12:15pm.) The **post office,** V. G. Marconi 28, is behind the SAIA station, on the left. (Open M-F 8:30am-2pm, Sa 8:30am-12:30pm.) **Postal Code:** 25019.

■ ■ **ACCOMMODATIONS AND FOOD.** A thorough exploration of Sirmione takes only an afternoon, but those looking for prolonged relaxation can choose from among a number of fairly pricey hotels or slightly cheaper accommodations in Colombare. Reserve early for summer sojourns; rates are steeper during the summer. The tourist office can help with accommodations, even offering free accommodations reservations. Closer to the end of the island by Grotte di Catullo, lovely host Sordelli's ❚**Villa Paradiso ❸**, V. Arici 7, offers accommodations inside a privately-owned, almost regal house. Rooms provide nearly 360-degree views of the lake from atop Sirmione. (☎91 61 49. Doubles €66. Cash only.) Closer to the *centro storico,* ❚**Hotel Speranza ❹**, V. Casello 2, feels brand-new and has a breakfast room that would make Martha Stewart jealous. Though still expensive, it is one of the more reasonable options in the older part of the town. (☎91 61 16;

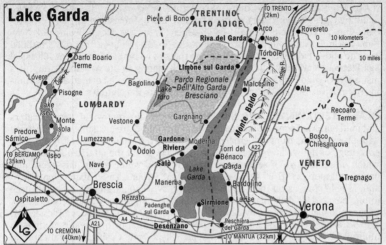

Lake Garda

www.hotelsperanzasirmione.it. Breakfast included. Open late-Feb. to mid-Nov. Singles €55; doubles €75; triples €90; quads €105. AmEx/MC/V.) **Albergo Grifone** ❸, V. Bocchio 4, off V. Dante to the right of V. Vittorio Emanuele II past the *castello*, has country-style rooms all with small bathrooms and lake views. (☎91 60 14; fax 91 65 48. Doubles €60. Extra bed €20. Cash only.) **Campeggio Sirmione** ❶, V. Sirmioncino 9, in Colombare, offers some of the least expensive accommodations on the peninsula for two or more people. It also boasts a swimming pool and beach access as well as a small market and cafe. (☎99 05 089; www.camping-sirmione.com. Open late Mar.-Oct. €6-9 per person, €6-16 per tent. 2-person cabins €45-75; 3-person cabins €52-86; 4-person cabins €65-110. MC/V.)

Sirmione's restaurants are numerous, but there are few that fit well in a budget. **Ristorante Pizzeria Valentino** ❷, P. Porto Valentino 10, off V. V. Emanuele II, however, is one of the more affordable establishments. It offers delicious fare including homemade *gnocchi* and the local specialty, trout with Garda sauce and polenta, for €10. (☎61 13 14. Pizza €4.50-9.50. *Primi* €7-9.50, *secondi* €7.50-17. Cover €1.50. Open daily 11:15am-4pm and 6:30-10:30pm. AmEx/MC/V.) The *gelato* piles high at **Master del Gelato Artigianale** ❶, near P. Castello. (Open daily 9:30am-midnight. Cash only.) The **Ristorante-Pizzeria Roberto** ❷, on V. Garibaldi, specializes in shrimp pizza (€8.70), *tagliolini* in cream sauce, and mushroom ravioli (both €7). After getting off the Colombare bus stop, walk 5min down V. Colombare. House specialties include. (*Bruschetta* €2. Pizza €3.50-8.70. *Antipasto* €4-8.90. Service 10%. Open Tu-Su 11:45am-2:30pm and 5:30-11pm.)

◗ SIGHTS. At the far end of the peninsula, along V. Catullo, is the **Grotte di Catullo,** perhaps the best-preserved aristocratic Roman villa in northern Italy, spread over five acres of olive groves and offering some of the most spectacular panoramas of Lake Garda. Although named for the poet Catullus, the ruins appear to date from the late first century BC, after the poet's death. Artifacts in the **archaeological museum** inside the grotto have English explanations. (☎91 61 57. Ruins and museum open Tu-Su Mar.-Oct. 8:30am-7pm; Nov.-Feb. 8:30am-5pm. €4, EU students 18-25 €2.) A small train runs between Sirmione center and the grotto (€1, 8:30am-6:30pm). The 13th-century **Castello Scaligero** sits in the center of town as a testament to the power of the della Scala family who controlled the Veronese region from 1260 to 1387. Completely surrounded by water, the *castello*'s commanding turret views are its main attraction. Except for some dirt and cannonballs, the interior is empty. (☎91 64 68. Open Tu-Su Mar.-Oct. 8:30am-7pm; Nov.-Feb. Tu-Su 8:30am-7pm. €4, EU students 18-25 €2.) Ruins of the city's **fortified walls** lie above Lido delle Bionde, near the ruins of a Lombardian church. **Chiesa di San Pietro in Mavino,** Sirmione's oldest church, dating to the AD 8th century, lies just off V. Catullo but is temporarily closed, due to newly discovered artifacts during excavation. Sixteenth-century frescoes decorate the church's interior.

🎭🎵 ENTERTAINMENT AND NIGHTLIFE. Sirmione's renowned thermal waters and mud baths at **Terme di Sirmione,** V. Punto Staffalo 1, are available only for those with prescriptions from a doctor. However, even the young and healthy can take advantage of the wellness packages (starting at €28) at the attached **Aquaria Spa,** which offers a range of services including thermal water soaks, massages, mud baths, and more. (☎91 60 44. Open Mar.-Oct. M 1-10pm, Tu-Su 10am-10pm; Nov.-Mar. M-F 4-10pm, Sa-Su 10am-10pm. AmEx/MC/V.) Though slightly rocky, the free public beach, **Lido delle Bionde,** on Sirmione's east shore may be a better choice. **Canoes** and **paddleboats** are available for rent just below the Lido delle Bionde bar, off V. Catullo. (☎333 54 05 622. €6 per 30min., €8 per hr.; beach chair with umbrella €7 per day. Open daily Apr.-Sept. 8:30am-7pm. Cash only.) Walk around the tip of the peninsula to reach the ✦**Punta Grotte,** a striking line of jagged cliffs slicing through the water. The town also has summer events, which generally include musical and dance performances, art exhibits, and fish tastings. Ask at the tourist office or look for Sirmione d'Estate flyers (www.commune.sirmione.bs.it).

A few bars and *enoteche* can be found on V. Santa Maria Maggiore, off V. V. Emanuele II, the most scenic place to have a drink at night may be the beachside **Bar La Torre,** off V. Antiche Mura, just behind the *castello*. (Drinks €3-8. Food €3-4. Open daily 10am-8pm, Sa until 2am. MC/V.) There is live jazz in P. Carducci on Friday evenings during the summer.

DESENZANO ☎030

As the only town with train access and home to the largest port, Desenzano (dehsen-ZA-no; pop. 23,000) is the gateway to Lake Garda, but it also offers extensive shopping and nightlife that is unavailable in most of its quieter neighboring towns. Whether walking along its pedestrian-friendly streets, eating in one of numerous restaurants, or shopping along the lake during the weekly visit from the open air market, this town never lets a traveler down.

> **CHOO-CHOO.** Desenzano is the only town on Lake Garda with train access.

📍 TRANSPORTATION AND PRACTICAL INFORMATION. Trains, on the corner of V. da Vinci and Vle. Cavour, serve Milan (24 per day 6:33am-10:16pm; €6.70), Venice (22 per day 6:30am-10:13pm; €8.20), and Verona (14 per day 6:09am-11:39pm; €3). **Buses** leave across the street from the train station and stop by the port (tickets sold in a yellow newsstand there), serving Gardone (45min.; 6 per day 6am-6pm; €2.80); Limone (1½hr., 6 per day 6am-6:30pm, €4.80); Riva (2hr., 6 per day 6am-6:30pm, €5.30); Salò (30min., 6 per day 6am-6:30pm, €2.80); Sirmione (19 per day 5:40am-7:05pm; €1.55-4). The tourist office provides bus schedules. From the port in P. Matteotti on V. Anelli, Navigazione sul Lago di Garda runs **ferries** to Garda (8 per day 10:15am-5:40pm; €6.70, express €9.50) and Riva del Garda (4 per day 10am-4:55pm; €10.80, express €14.40). Both ferries pass through several other towns. (☎91 49 511 or 800 55 18 01; www.navigazionelaghi.it. Ticket office open 20min. before departure time.) For **taxis,** call ☎91 41 527.

The **tourist office** is at V. Porto Vecchio 34. (☎91 41 510. Open M-Tu and Th 9am-12:30pm and 3-6pm.) Other services include: **Banco di Brescia,** V. Guglielmo Marconi 18, with **ATM** (open M-F 8:25am-1:25pm and 2:40-4:10pm); **police** (☎91 43 572); **medical emergency** (☎91 20 393); **pharmacy**, V. Santa Maria 1, off P. Matteotti (open 9am-12:30pm and 3:30-7:30pm; MC/V); **Internet and Western Union**, V. Mazzini 3. (€1 per 15min., €3 per hr.; open daily 9am-10pm); **post office**, V. Crocefisso 27-29, near Villa Romana (open M-F 8:30am-7pm, Sa 8:30am-12:30pm). **Postal Code:** 25015.

⚙🏠 ACCOMMODATIONS AND FOOD. Accommodations are plentiful in Desenzano, though they can be quite expensive, especially compared to those in nearby towns. **Hotel Marino ❸**, V. Angelo Anelli 20, offers small rooms with TV and A/C on the waterfront. (☎91 41 910. Singles €32, with bath €38; doubles €58/60. AmEx/MC/V.) Family-run **Hotel Flora ❸**, V. Guglielmo Marconi 22, on the main road entering the city, and walking distance from the water, has 11 spacious rooms in addition to free parking, Internet access, and fax. Rooms include TV, telephone, A/C, and a small safe. From the train station, take V. Cavour until V. G. Marconi; make a right. (☎99 12 547; www.hotelflora.org. Breakfast included. Singles €40-55; doubles €55-78; triples €80-98. AmEx/MC/V.) **Hotel Trattoria Alessi ❸**, V. Castello 5, is two blocks inland, right beneath the *castello* and next door to its trattoria. (☎91 41 980; www.hotelalessidesenzano.com. Breakfast included. Singles €40-50; doubles €60-70. AmEx/MC/V.)

Back-to-back restaurants line P. Giacomo Matteotti as well as the pedestrian streets parallel to the waterfront, V. Santa Maria, V. Papa, and V. Roma. Get your breakfast croissant with pizza cut to order at **Panificio Artigianale**, V. Roma 29. (Open 8:30am-1pm and 4:30-7:50pm. Cash only.) Walk a while west on V. Roma until it becomes V. Cesare Battisti to get to Spiaggia Desenzanino, the home of **Ristorante-Pizzeria Desenzanino ❷**, C. Battisti. (☎91 28 096. Pizza €3-10. Open Tu-Su noon-2:15pm and 7-10:30pm. MC/V.) On the east end of town, **La Briciola ❶**, V. Tommaso dal Molin 5, offers inexpensive self-service food. Menu changes daily; most items under €7. (Open M-Sa noon-4:20pm. AmEx/MC/V.) To escape the heavy tourist feel of the center, make the short uphill trip to P. Garibaldi and try **La Frasca Osteria ❸**, which combines high-end cuisine with a homey atmosphere. (*Primi* €7-9, *secondi* €12-15. Open daily 12:15-2:30pm and 7-10:30pm. Cash only.) Supermarkets do not get cheaper than the 🅼**Supermercato**, V. G. Marconi 17. (Open M-Sa 8:30am-12:30pm and 3:15-7:15pm, Su 9am-1pm.)

🅶 SIGHTS. Beaches, Desenzano's chief appeal, are on the far west end of town (Desenzanino), as well as some cultural attractions. 🅼**Pedal-boats** run €6 per

TOP TEN LIST

TOP TEN SIGHTS TO TAKE YOUR BREATH AWAY ON LAKE GARDA

Any view of Lake Garda is guaranteed to be gorgeous, but here are a few unique spots:

1. The heart-stopping view from the tiny **Chiesetta Santa Barbara** (p. 282), in Riva's mountainside, will literally leave you breathless after the steep 1hr. hike.

2. Vews of Sirmione's luxurious architecture and cypress groves are best seen by **ferry** (p. 276).

3. On a cliffside road overlooking the water, the **drive from Limone** to Riva offers jaw-dropping views.

4. Hop between the flat rocks in **Punta Grotte's** (p. 278) waters.

5. Wandering through the expansive **citrus orchards** (p. 283) in Limone will overwhelm your senses.

6. Witness Riva's beautiful scenery from a **pedalboat** (p. 279) in the middle of Lake Garda.

7. Unique hostel-on-a-hill **Villa Paradiso** (p. 276) offers gorgeous views of Lake Garda right from your room, overlooking the Grotte di Catullo.

8. The waterfall **Cascata Varone** (p. 282) and its impressive gorge can't be missed.

9. Pick a balmy night, grab a *gelato*, and take the beautiful walk through Desenzano's **piazze** (p. 278).

10. The best way to see Lake Garda may very well be to slice across it while **windsurfing** (p. 284).

30min. and €15 per 2hr., and kayaks cost €6-10 per hr. Views from the **Castello,** in the center of town, are striking. Inquire at the tourist office about free performances inside the castle. (Open Tu-Su 10:30am-12:30pm and 4-7pm. €1, free on Th.) The **Villa Romana,** constructed before the AD first century, offers some of the most important remnants of Roman villas in northern Italy built during the demise of the Empire. (☎91 43 547. Open daily Mar.-Oct. 8:30am-6:30pm; Oct.-Feb. 8:30am-5pm. €2.) The **Galleria Civica di Palazzo Todescini,** around the corner from the tourist office, has rotating art exhibits. (Open Tu-Su 3:30-7:30pm; Tu, Su and holidays also 10:30am-12:30pm. Hours depend on exhibition. Free.)

🖼🎭 FESTIVALS AND NIGHTLIFE.

From the end of June to the first days of July, Desenzano celebrates its revered saint, **San Luigi.** Check www.commune.desenzano.brescia.it for more festivals. Many of the restaurants along P. Matteotti and P. Capelletti double as bars; check out the (relatively) hip offerings along P. Matteoti. The tourist office has a listing of bars. The area on V. Castello is less mainstream, but is home to unique establishments such as the Irish pub **Fiddler of Dooney,** V. Castello 36. (☎91 42 262. Pints €3.50. Pizza €2.50. F an Sa live music. Open M-F 6pm-2am, Sa 5:30pm-2am, Su 4pm-2am.) As you might notice from its hours, **Internet Caffè,** V. Castello 17, is more of a bar than an Internet point. (Internet access €6 per hr. Open Tu-Su 6pm-4am.)

RIVA DEL GARDA   ☎0464

With its aquamarine lake waters lapping at the foot of the Brenta Dolomites, Riva del Garda (REE-va del GAR-da; pop. 14,500) is a spot for budget travelers looking to experience the Lake Country's beautiful views. Gentle mountain winds make Riva del Garda ideal for windsurfing, and its aquatic sports schools are world-renowned. The area is also a prime location for hiking, canoeing, whitewater rafting, kayaking, bicycling, swimming, and, above all else, relaxing on its extensive beaches—all made accessible and affordable by the attractive youth hostel.

◩ TRANSPORTATION

Buses: Vle. Trento 5 (☎55 23 23). Ticket office open M-Sa 6:30am-7:15pm, Su 9:05am-noon and 3:35-7:05pm. Local tickets available at dispenser in station. Buses run to: **Brescia** (2hr., 4 per day 7:45am-7:35pm, €5.30); **Desenzano** (6 per day 5:40am-5:10pm); **Limone** (20min., 6 per day 5:40am-5:10pm, €1.55); **Milan** (3hr.; 7:45am, 3:45pm; €8.50); **Rovereto** (1hr., 15 per day 5:50am-7:05pm, €2.45); **Salò** (6 per day 5:40am-5:10pm, €3.35); **Verona** (hourly 5am-8pm).

Ferries: Navigazione Lago di Garda (☎91 49 511; www.navigazionelaghi.it) in P. Catena, next to an information booth. Pick up a schedule in the tourist office or at the ferry ticket offices. To Limone (30min.; 17 per day 8am-6:05pm; €3.30, express €5.10), Sirmione (2-4hr.; 5 per day 8:35am-5pm; €9.60, express €13) via Gardone Riviera (1-3hr.; 5 per day 8:35am-5pm; €8.50, express €11.60), and Salò (€8.50, express €11.60). Ticket office open 20min. before each departure.

Taxi: ☎848 800 779.

Bike Rental: Cicli Pederzolli, Vle. dei Tigli 24 (☎/fax 55 18 30). Bikes €8-13 per day. **Bike Shop Girelli,** Vle. Damiano Chiesa 15/17 (☎55 66 02). €13 per day. Both open M-Sa 9am-noon and 3-7pm. MC/V.

Scooter Rental: Sembenini Moto, Vle. Dante 3 (☎55 45 48). €19 per 2hr., €49 per day. Open Tu-Su 9:30am-12:30pm and 4-7pm. MC/V.

✦❷ ORIENTATION AND PRACTICAL INFORMATION

To reach the *centro* from the **bus station,** walk straight on **Viale Trento,** then cross the traffic circle and go behind the church, taking **Via Roma** to reach **Piazza Cavour.**

Tourist Office "Ingarda Trentino": Largo Medaglie d'Oro 5 (☎55 44 44; www.gardatrentino.it), at the old bus station at the end of V. della Liberazione. Lists hotel vacancies and offers a variety of cheap regional tours. Ask for a city map and hiking routes. City tour Sa 9:30am (3hr., €3); book 1 day in advance. English spoken. Wheelchair-accessible. Open M-Sa 9am-noon and 3-6:30pm, Su 9am-noon and 3:30-6:30pm.

Laundry: Vle. Rovereto 74. Head down V. Dante Alighieri which changes to V. Giosuè Carducci and then Vle. Rovereto.

Internet: Internet Point, V. Dante Alighieri 70/B, has 10 computers and Wi-Fi. €3 per 30 min., €5 per hr. Open M-Sa 10am-12:30pm and 3:30-10pm, Su 3:30-10pm. **Café San Marco,** V. Roma 18 (☎55 16 09; www.sanmarcocafe.it), has 1 computer. €3.50 per 30min., €5.50 per hr. Open daily 8am-8pm.

Police: V. Brione 5 (☎57 80 11).

Pharmacy: V. D. Alighieri 12/B (☎55 25 08). Open M-F 8:45am-12:30pm and 3:30-7:30pm. Also at V. Maffei 8 (☎55 23 02). Open M-Sa 8:45am-12:30pm and 3:30-7:30pm, Su 9am-12:30pm and 3:30-7:30pm.

Post Office: V. San Francesco 26 (☎57 87 00). Open M-F 8am-6:30pm, Sa 8am-12:30pm. Also has **ATM. Postal Code:** 38066.

⚑ ACCOMMODATIONS AND CAMPING

▨ **Ostello Benacus (HI),** P. Cavour 10 (☎55 49 11). From bus station, head right down V. Trento; cross through the traffic circle to V. Roma, turn left after the arch, and cross left through P. Cavour. Central location and clean facilities. Breakfast included; dinner €9. Laundry €4. Internet €2 per hr. Reception 7-9am and 3-11pm. Check-out 9am. Bathrooms closed 11am-3pm. Curfew 11pm; ask for key if returning after 11pm. Reservations recommended. Dorms €19. HI-member discount €3. MC/V. ❶

Albergo Garni Rita, V. Brione 19 (☎55 17 98; www.garnirita.com). B&B in a quiet area 25min. outside the city center. Breakfast included. Reservations recommended. Open Mar. 10-Nov. 3. €38 per person. Cash only. ❸

Bavaria, V. Rovereto 100 (☎55 25 24), on the road toward Torbole. Pizzeria and *gelateria* in front of campground. Take lessons in windsurfing and sailing right behind the campground at Surfsegnana. Hot shower €1. Reception 9am-1pm and 3-6pm. Quiet hours 3-5pm and 11pm-8am. No entry by car 11pm-7am. Open Apr.-Oct. €7.50 per person, €6 per child. Site €10. AmEx/MC/V for €60 or more. ❶

Camping Monte Brione, V. Brione 32 (☎52 08 85; www.campingbrione.com). Offers a pool, bar, laundry services, and minimarket situated 800m from the lake, next to biking trails. Free hot showers. Reception 8am-1pm and 3-7pm. Reservations recommended. €6.50-8.50 per person. Small site without electricity €7.50-8.70; large site with electricity and parking €9-11.50. MC/V. ❶

🍴 FOOD

An **open-air market** sells produce in P. delle Erbe. (Open M-Sa mornings.) A **Despar** supermarket sells groceries just outside the *centro* at V. Roma 19. (Open M-Sa 8:30am-1pm and 3:30-7:30pm, Su 9am-12:30pm. Cash only.)

Leon d'Oro, V. Fiume 28 (☎55 23 41). Windows provide views of the bustling street. Try the *risotto mantecato alle code di gambero* (with lemon-marinated prawns; €10). *Primi* €6.50-10, *secondi* €8.50-16. Cover €1.30. Open daily mid-March to mid-Nov. 11am-3pm and 5pm-midnight. AmEx/MC/V. ❸

Ristorante Ancora, V. Montanara 2 (☎52 21 31). Maritime decor and sun-kissed rooftop terrace. Pizza €3-8. Salads €4-6. *Primi* €8-13, *secondi* €12-18. Open daily noon-2:30pm and 7-11:30pm. AmEx/MC/V. ❸

THE LAKE COUNTRY

Ristorante-Pizzeria Commercio, P. Garibaldi 4 (☎52 17 62; www.ristorantecommercio.com), patio seating looks out at La Rocca castle. Try the special Lake Garda pizza (*carpaccio, rucola,* parmesan, and tomato). *Primi* €6-10, *secondi* €8-11. Open Tu-Su noon-3pm and 6:30pm-midnight. AmEx/MC/V. ❸

🗊 🏃 SIGHTS AND OUTDOOR ACTIVITIES

Take local bus #1, 2, or 6 from V. Martiri to reach **Cascata Varone,** which has a waterfall, stunning views, swimming, and pebbly sunbathing on amazing ▨**grass beaches.** follow the lakeside path behind the tourist office and head away from the mountains to **Lungolago dei Sabbioni** and **Lungolago dei Pini.** Three kilometers outside town, the 20,000-year-old waterfall **Cascata Varone** has chiseled a huge 110m gorge in the mountain. Foliage arches over surrounding mountain paths, making them ideal for easy strolls. (☎52 14 21; www.cascata-varone.com. Open May-Aug. daily 9am-7pm; Sept. daily 9am-6pm; Oct. daily 9am-5pm; Nov.-Feb. Su 10am-5pm; Mar. daily 9am-5pm; Apr. daily 9am-6pm. €5. Cash only.) The **Ponale,** a road previously used by the military to connect Riva del Garda with Valle di Ledro during WWI, begins south of the city, a few hundred meters down the western shore, just before tunnel leading to Limone. The road boasts impressive views, walkable tunnels, and mountain bike paths. For fun in the water, **Noleggio Rudderboat Rental,** in front of P. Battisti, by the castle, rents paddleboats by the hour. (☎55 44 75. Rental for 2 people €7 per hr., €8 per 4hr., €9 per 5hr. Pay 2hr., get 1 free. Open daily 8:30am-7pm. Cash only.) **Surfsegnana,** behind campground Bavaria, offers windsurfing, sailing, and canoeing lessons. (☎50 59 63; www.surfsegnana.it. Open daily 8am-6pm.) In the cliffs above the lake, historical hot spots draw hikers out of the city *centro.* Follow V. D. Alighieri to the mountains as it changes to V. Bastione; then, take a left up the ramp and follow the winding cobblestone path for 20min. to the 15th-century **Bastione** (the white building seen from below), a circular fortress that survived Napoleon's onslaught in 1796 but lost its upper half in the process. Today, hikers can explore the edges of the historical treasure or admire the aerial view of the vibrantly blue Lake Garda, speckled with tiny boats. Farther up, a steep 1hr. ▨hike leads to **Chiesetta Santa Barbara,** a tiny chapel poised over misty mountains and the valley below. Just look far up into the mountains for the white speck to locate it. There are numerous well-regarded **mountain biking** paths; for details, go to the tourist office.

🗊 NIGHTLIFE

The *centro* is peppered with English-style pubs that cater to a large German tourist contingent. The tourist office keeps a schedule of free beach parties during the summer that offer lakeside fireworks.

Pub All'Oca, V. Santa Maria 9 (☎55 34 57; www.puballoca.com). Listen to jazz upstairs in an old leather booth or around the horseshoe bar. The downstairs is more fashionable, with black modern furniture. Young, international clientele and English-speaking staff. Open daily 6pm-2am. Cash only.

Pub Barracuda, P. Catena 7a (☎55 31 73; pubbarracuda@yahoo.it), has plenty of seats looking out onto the lake. Owners change the wall decorations every month, showcasing different local artists. Offers fresh fruity concoctions as well as a wide selection of rum and whiskey (€3.50-7 per glass). Open daily in summer 10:30am-2pm and 6pm-2am; in winter 8pm-2am. MC/V.

Covent Garden, V. dei Fabbri 11/13 (☎335 16 08 471). From P. Cavour, take V. Disciplini onto V. Diaz; V. dei Fabbri is at the intersection with V. Fiume. 2 rooms spread out the guests in this Irish-themed pub. Old signs on buildings still give directions to bar's old name, "Papagaio." Happy hour daily 6-8pm. Open daily 6pm-2am. Cash only.

LIMONE ☎ 0365

On the northwestern coast of Lake Garda, jagged mountainsides dive deeply into the clear blue waters of Limone's (lee-MO-neh; pop. less than 1000) shores. The steep cobblestone streets of the small town draw some tourists looking to windsurf or kayak, and Limone's small center caters to tourism and provides a wonderful starting point for hikes to the surrounding mountaintops. Above all, Limone is best recognized as the lemon capital of Europe. Limone recently garnered the curiosity of scientific researchers who found a protein, Apolipoproteina A-1, unique to Limone locals. The wonder protein seems to naturally combat heart plaque in these lucky residents—or maybe it's just the beautiful views.

🖪 PRACTICAL INFORMATION. Ferries are run by Navigazione Lago di Garda (☎ 91 49 511; www.navigazionelaghi.it) in P. Catena, next to an information booth. Pick up a schedule in the tourist office or at the ferry ticket offices. Ferries run to Desenzano (4 per day 10:25am-4:27pm; €9.60, express €13), Riva (17 per day 9:20am-7:36pm; €3.30, express €5.10), and Sirmione (8 per day 8:56am-5:21pm; €9.60, express €13).

Located across from the bus stop, the **tourist office,** V. IV Novembre 29 (☎ 95 44), offers maps of the town and info on sights and accommodations. To get to the tourist office from the ferry stop, immediately turn left and follow V. Roma through Pta. Vecchio. After P. Garibaldi, the road will become V. Camboni. Then turn right on the steep Cottili. Keep following the road uphill when it dead ends, then make a left on V. Capitelli. Take the next right and the tourist office is across the street. (Open daily 8:30am-9pm.) In case of **emergency,** contact the **police** (☎ 95 47 44), Ufficio Piazzetta Erminia 3. Call ☎ 95 40 27 for the **carabinieri,** V. Tamas 6. Services include: **Banco di Brescia,** V. Comboni 24 (☎ 95 40 24; open June-Sept. M-F 8:25am-1:25pm and 2:40-4:10pm, Sa 8:30am-12:30pm; Oct.-May M-F 8:25am-1:25pm and 2:40-4:10pm); **pharmacy,** V. IV Novembre 29 (☎ 95 40 45; open June 15-Sept. 15 8:30am-12:30pm and 3:30-7:30pm; Sept. 16-June 14 M-W and F-Sa 8:3am0-12:30pm and 4:30-7:30pm); **Internet** at **Caffè Milennio,** V. IV Septembre 29d, near the pharmacy and post office (☎ 95 42 37, open 8am-9:30pm); and the **post office,** V. IV Novembre, uphill from the tourist office, behind the parking garage (☎ 95 47 46; open M-F 8:30am-2pm, Sa 8:30am-12:30pm). **Postal Code:** 25087.

🝑🝑 ACCOMMODATIONS AND FOOD. As with lower Lake Garda towns, affordable accommodations are scarce. Your best bet is the B&B ◪**Pensione Silvana ❷,** V. Nanzello 6. From the tourist office, walk south down V. IV Novembre for about 10min. After a bridge, make a right onto V. Luigi Einaudi and then a quick left by the "Silvana" sign. Enjoy the spacious rooms. (☎ 95 40 58. Breakfast included. €22 per person, with bath €30. Cash only.) More convenient rooms can be found directly by the bus stop at **Hotel Susy ❸,** V. IV Novembre 46. (☎ 95 41 49. Breakfast included. Dinner €6. Single €36; double €62. Reserve ahead. AmEx/ MC/V.) **Hotel Alla Noce ❸,** V. Monsignor Daniele Comboni 33, three blocks from the bus stop, lies perched on the hill with stunning views of the town below. (☎ 95 40 22; www.allanoce.it. Breakfast included. Singles €35-42; doubles €60-74. Rooms without lake view €4 discount. AmEx/MC/V.) Overpriced restaurants filled with German tourists line the waterfront; venture inland to find more interesting (and wallet-friendly) fare. Don't expect pastries at **Pasticceria Piva ❶,** V. Tovo, downhill from the bus stop. They do, however, offer a variety of sizable *panini* for less than €3. (☎ 95 41 96. Open daily 9am-11pm. Cash only.)

◧ 🝑 SIGHTS AND ENTERTAINMENT. Perched uphill from the quaint *centro* near the water, **La Limonaia del Castèl,** V. IV Novembre 25, transports tourists into the world of a functioning 18th-century citrus farm spread over 1633 sq. yd. of terraces. This impressive structure, with many of its original pillars and walls, grows a variety of citrus fruits. (☎95 40 08; www.limone-sulgarda.it. €1.) Another source of pride for Limone is the **Tesöl,** the homestead of Monsignor Daniele Comboni, a Limone native and missionary whose dream to "save Africa through Africa" led him far from home in the late 1800s. The house, church, and surrounding park invite tourists to contemplate Saint Comboni's perseverance embodied in his motto *"O Nigrizia o Morte"* ("Africa or Death"). His relationship with Africa is captured in letters he wrote. Comboni was canonized by Pope John Paul II in 2003. (Religious services Su 10am and 4pm; contact tourist office for seasonal opening hours and ask about free tours Th July 6-Aug. 31). **Chiesa San Benedeto** is one of the Lake Country's hidden treasures, overflowing with realistic and emotive artwork. Much of the moving artwork is by Andrea Celesti, a late 17th-century painter. The building itself was built in the 17th century. (Mass Su 8am and 10:30am.) Maps given at the tourist office note the locations of **public beaches** as well as **windsurfing schools.** Any significant visit to Limone wouldn't be complete without a lesson in windsurfing, but it does come at a steep price. A less expensive but excellent option is personal instruction at **Windsurfing Lino.** This small company is run by a German ex-pat who was once a windsurfing World Cup participant. About a 10min. walk down the beach to Foce San Giovanni. (€40 per hr.; multiple day packages available. 3hr. lessons 10am and 1pm. Open daily 9:30am-5:30pm.)

The town's one nightclub is **Pub Alì,** V. Einaudi 4; walk down V. IV Novembre for about 10min. until V. Einaudi. Regular live music performances, posh white seats, a large dance floor, and a game room provide many entertainment options. Expect a crowd in July and August. (☎91 41 42. Large beers €3. Mixed drinks €6. Open F-Su 10pm-3am.) Don't be dismayed by the somewhat unappealing name of **Bar Turista,** IV Novembre 48; in fact, it is frequented by a fairly equal mixture of tourists and locals, all drawn to its live music. (Large beers €3.50. Mixed drinks €6. Open daily 8pm-2am. MC/V.)

GARDONE RIVIERA   ☎0365

For tranquility far removed from its heavily touristed neighbors, Gardone will work wonders. A trip here was once commonly prescribed by doctors for European elites. The collection of villages that comprise the Gardone Riviera (gar-DOH-neh REE-vee-yeh-ra; pop. 2500) now serve as laid-back lake vacation destinations for many British visitors. Gracefully aging villas of colored stucco and lush gardens of Mediterranean citrus and olive trees surround the calm town. **≥Il Vittoriale** is the sprawling estate of Gabriele D'Annunzio, a poet, novelist, WWI soldier, and latter-day Casanova. Inside, there are ornate rooms and artifacts, and the Museo della Guerra (Museum of the War). The Fondazione al Vittoriale sponsors the **Festival d'Estate** in music: dance, theater, and lyrical opera in the 1500-seat open-air **Teatro del Vittoriale,** V. Vittoriale 12. (Festival d'Estate ☎0522 45 51 93; fax 0522 45 43 19. Ticket office ☎29 65 06; www.teatrodelvittoriale.it. Performances July-Aug. Tickets €20-40.) Gardone's brand-new museum **Il Divino Infante,** V. dei Colli 34, features over 200 sculptures of the baby Jesus in every scene and costume imaginable. (☎29 31 05; www.il-bambino-gesu.com. Open June-Aug. Tu-Su 6-10pm; Oct.-Feb. F-Su 10am-6pm; Nov.-Jan. Tu-Su 10am-6pm. €5, children and over 65 €4.) Climbing stairs from Zanardelli past the Bank from P. Marconi leads to the **Giardino Botanico** (Botanical Gardens), an oasis of criss-crossing brooks and bridges built from 1910 to 1970, at the corner of V. Roma and V. Disciplina. Admire 2000 varieties of plants and modern sculptures by Haring and Lichtenstein, but beware getting in a spitting contest between two sculpted heads. (☎336 41 08 77. Open daily 9:30am-6:30pm. €8.)

Southbound **buses** stop in front of Grand Hotel (off P. Wimmer), northbound in front of the newsstand. Speedier, more frequent service to major cities is available on the Milan-Verona **train** line; take the bus to Desenzano, then board at the train station next to the bus stop.

Take V. Repubblica on the left from the ferry dock for about 250m to reach the English-speaking **tourist office,** V. Repubblica 8, which lists area establishments and events, as well as maps. (☎/fax 20 347. Open daily June-Sept. 9am-12:30pm and 3-6:30pm; Oct.-May 9am-12:30pm and 2:30-6pm.) For **currency exchange** and **ATM,** head to the **Banco di Brescia,** V. Roma 6, across the street and upstairs from the Grand Hotel on C. Zanardelli. (☎ 20 081. Open M-F 8:25am-1:25pm and 2:40-3:40pm.) In case of **emergency,** dial the **police** (☎ 20 179), located in Gardone Sopra (high village), where V. Carere leads away from V. Disciplina. A **pharmacy** is located just past the travel agency at P. Wimmer 4. (☎ 20 117. Open M-Sa 8:30am-12:30pm and 3:30-7:30pm.) The **post office,** V. Roma 8, is next door to the bank. (☎ 20 862. Open M-F 8:30am-2pm, Sa 8:30am-12:30pm.) **Postal Code:** 25083.

SALÒ   ☎ 0365

During the peak of WWII (Sept. 1943-Apr. 1945), Salò (sa-LO; pop. 10,000) was the "Capital of a Divided Italy" and was declared the Republic of Salò as a last attempt by Mussolini and Hitler to reorganize fascism in Italy. Hotel Laurin was once Mussolini's headquarters. The town, which is typically filled with yachters coming ashore, totally lacks affordable accommodations. If you seek stately allure and refined charm, try Salò as a daytrip from Sirmione or Desenzano. Head right toward the lake on Lungolago Zanardelli from the ferry stop to reach Salò's beautiful Gothic Venetian **duomo,** built by Filippo della Vacche and measuring 36 ft. in height and 144 ft. in circumference. Stand underneath the intensely realistic wooden crucifix, which hangs in the center, and look into Jesus's eyes. It seems almost as if you can see him exhale. (Open daily 8:30am-noon and 3:30-7pm. Free.) Two of the town's three museums, **Museo Archeologico** and **Museo Storico,** V. Fantoni 49, are in the same location, and both offer an overarching historical account of the region. (☎ 29 68 34. Museo Storico open Su 10am-noon and 3-5pm. €4. Museo Archeologico M-F 10am-noon. €2.) Lastly, the cafe by the tourist office has a small off-beat **Museo di Mussolini** exploring fascism. Adding to its mystique, the museum has no official hours. (Free.)

Transporti Brescia Nord Buses (☎ 840 62 00 01) stop at the bus stop on V. Calsone, the farthest street inland in the town, where it meets Vco. Oratorio. Buses serve Desenzano (30min., 6 per day 6:57am-6:27pm, €2.40), and Gardone (5min., 6 per day 6:33am-7:03pm, €1), continuing on to Limone (1hr., €3) and Riva (1½hr., €3.35). Tickets can be purchased at the *tabaccheria* in front of the stop; if it is closed, purchase tickets on the bus with €1 surcharge. **Navigazione Lago di Garda** (☎ 91 49 511; www.navigazionelaghi.it) runs ferries to Desenzano (4 per day 10:25am-4:27pm; €9.60, express €13), Riva (17 per day 9:20am-7:36pm; €3.30, express €5.10), and Sirmione (8 per day 8:56am-5:21pm; €9.60, express €13). From the ferry station, head inland and left through P. della Vittoria to reach the **tourist office,** P. Sant'Antonio 4, which offers a great map of the town. (☎/fax 21 423. Open daily 9:30am-1pm and 3-6:30pm.) **Postal Code:** 25087.

LAKE COMO (LAGO DI COMO)

As indicated by the luxurious villas lining its shores, Lake Como has been a refuge for the well-to-do since before the Roman Empire. But you don't need a *palazzo* to appreciate the stately beauty that surrounds one of Europe's deepest lakes (410m)—many artists, including Rossini, Bellini, and Shelley, relied on this lake for inspiration. The three central lake towns—Bellagio, Menaggio, and Varenna—make for a more relaxing stay than Como, the largest city on the lake, by offering pristine and peaceful villages quietly tucked into the dense, green slopes.

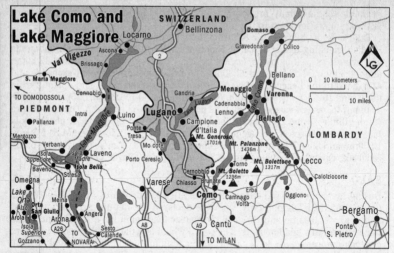

COMO ☎031

Situated on the southwestern tip of Lake Como, closest to Milan, Como (COmo; pop. 86,000) is the lake region's token semi-industrial town, where physicist Alessandro Volta (who brought us the battery) was born and where Giuseppe Terragni immortalized his fascist architectural designs. Industry is vastly overshadowed by the quaintness of a typical lake town that attracts tourists from all over the world seeking a launching point for exploring the lake. While it lacks the resort lifestyle of the central lake, Como's nearby, spectacular hiking is more than enough to entertain those passing through.

⌐ TRANSPORTATION

Trains: Stazione San Giovanni (☎89 20 21). Open daily 6:40am-8:25pm. Ticket office open daily 6:40am-8:25pm. To: **Chiasso** (10min., every hr. 6:29am-1:29am, €1); **Milan Centrale** (1hr., 15 per day 6:25am-11:08pm, €3.50); **Milan Porta Garibaldi** (1hr., 21 per day 5:08am-10:20pm, €3.50); **Basel, Switzerland** (5hr., 5 per day 10:07am-7:17pm, €56); **Zurich, Switzerland** (4hr., 5 per day 7:43am-8pm, €43). **Ferrovia Nord** runs trains from **Stazione Ferrovia Nord** (☎30 48 00), near P. Matteotti, to **Cadorna Stazione Nord** and **Milan** (1hr., 32 per day 5:46am-9:16pm, €3.45).

Buses: SPT (☎24 73 11; www.sptlinea.it) in P. Matteotti runs buses to nearby lake towns. Ticket office open M-Sa 6:15am-8:15pm, Su 8:10am-12:25pm and 1:25-7:40pm. Info booth open M-F 8am-noon and 2-6pm, Sa 8am-noon. **C30** to **Bellagio** departs from Station San Giovanni. (1hr.; M-Sa 16 per day 6:25am-8:14pm, Su 8 per day 8:45am-8:14pm; €2.60). **C46** to **Bergamo** departs from P. Matteotti (2hr.; M-Sa 6:45, 9:30am, 12:10, 3:45, 6:30pm; Su 9:10am, 1:10, 4, 6:20pm; €4.40). **C10** to **Domaso** departs from P. Matteotti (dir.: Colico), but some end in **Menaggio** (2hr.; M-Sa 12 buses 7:10am-8:35pm, Su 9 buses 8:20am-8:15pm; €4).

Ferries: Navigazione Lago di Como (☎57 92 11; www.navigazionelaghi.it). Ticket office open 8:10am-6:50pm. Departs daily to all lake towns from piers along Lungo Lario Trieste in front of P. Cavour. Ferries run to: **Bellagio** (1-2hr.; 21 per day 7:33am-7:10pm; €6.30, express €9.40); **Domaso** (1½-4hr.; 11 per day 8:45am- 7:10pm; €8, express

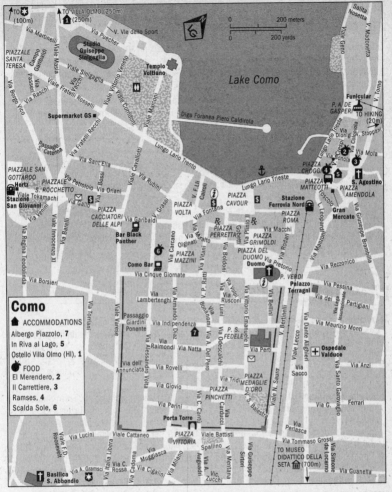

€11.50); **Menaggio** (1-2½hr.; 20 per day 7:33am-7:10pm; €6.30, express €9.40); **Varenna** (1-2hr.; 13 per day 8:45am-7:10pm; €7.20, express €10.50). Day-passes €20. Pick up the booklet *Orario* for a schedule, including summer night service.

Public Transportation: Buy bus tickets (€1) at *tabaccherie*, bus station, or hostel.

Taxis: RadioTaxi (☎26 15 15) in front of both train stations.

Car Rental: Europcar, Vle. Innocenzo XI 14. (☎24 16 43).

✈ 🛈 ORIENTATION AND PRACTICAL INFORMATION

From Como's **Stazione San Giovanni,** head down the stairs, and then straight ahead through the park. At **Piazzale San Rocchetto,** take V. Fratelli Recchi on the left, and

THE LAKE COUNTRY

then turn right on Vle. Fratelli Rosselli, which becomes **Lungo Lario Trento** and leads to **Piazza Cavour.** The **bus station** and **Stazione Ferrovia Nord** are in **Piazza Matteotti,** 2min. farther down the lake along **Lungo Lario Trieste.**

Tourist Office: ATC, P. Cavour 17 (☎26 97 12; www.lakecomo.it), on the right when facing the *piazza* from the lake. Offers maps and extensive info. Ask about hiking and hotels. Open M-Sa 9am-1pm and 2:30-6pm, Su 9:30am-1pm. **Como Viva,** a small booth on V. Comacini next to the *duomo,* also has maps and general info about events in the city. Open Su 10am-6pm.

Currency Exchange: Banca Nazionale del Lavoro, P. Cavour 32 (☎31 31), near tourist office, has good rates and a 24hr. **ATM.** Open M-F 8:20am-1:20pm and 2:35-4pm. Currency exchange also available at tourist office, train station, and post office.

Carabinieri: V. Borgo Vico 171.

Pharmacy: Farmacia Centrale, V. Caio Plinio Secondo 1, off P. Cavour. Posts after-hours rotations. Open M 3:30-7:30pm, Tu-Su 8:30am-12:30pm and 3:30-7:30pm.

Hospitals: Ospedale Valduce, V. Dante 11 (☎32 41 11). **Ospedale Sant'Anna,** V. Napoleana 60 (☎58 51 11).

Internet Access: Bar Black Panther, V. Garibaldi 59 (☎24 30 05). €3 per hr. Open Tu-Su 7am-midnight. **Como Bar,** V. Alessandro Volta 51 (☎26 20 52). 1 free drink with 2hr. of Internet use. €1.40 per 30min., €2.80 per hr. Open M-Sa 8am-9pm. Cash only.

Post Office: V. V. Emanuele II 99 (☎26 02 10), in the *centro.* Open M-F 8:30am-7pm, Sa 8:10am-12:30pm. Branch on V. Gallio. **Postal Code:** 22100.

⚑ ACCOMMODATIONS

▨ **In Riva al Lago,** P. Matteotti 4 (☎30 23 33; www.inriva.info), near the bus station. Newly renovated rooms and apartments with bath, TV, A/C; some have minifridge. July-Aug. prices jump but breakfast is included, otherwise €2-4. Internet access €1.50 per 20min. Reception 8am-11:30pm. Reservations recommended. Singles €35-45, with bath €40-53; doubles €40-63; triples €58-80; quads €68-98; 4- to 6-person apartments €95-115. AmEx/MC/V over €105. ❸

Ostello Villa Olmo (HI), V. Bellinzona 2 (☎57 38 00; ostellocomo@tin.it). From Stazione San Giovanni, turn left and walk 20min. down V. Borgo Vico to V. Bellinzona. Or take bus #1, 6, or 11 to Villa Olmo (€1). Summer-camp feel. Single-sex rooms. Ask about discounts for local attractions. Bike rental €12.50 per day. Breakfast included; dinner €6.50-11.50. Laundry €4, dry €3; ironing €1. Parking available. Open Mar. 1-Nov.15. Reception 7-10am and 4pm-midnight. Checkout 10am. Lockout 10am-4pm. Curfew midnight. Reservations recommended. Dorms €17.50; family room €19 per person (only for families with children). HI-member discount €3. Cash only. ❶

Albergo Piazzolo, V. Indipendenza 65 (☎/fax 27 21 86). From P. Cavour, take V. Bonta, which becomes V. Boldini, and then V. Luni. V. Indipendenza is on the right. Tastefully decorated rooms above restaurant, all with bath, TV, and phone. Closed Nov. Breakfast €7. Singles €45; doubles €60; triples €80; quad €100. AmEx/MC/V. ❹

▣ FOOD

Resta (sweet bread with dried fruit) is a Como specialty sold at **Beretta Il Fornaio,** Vle. Fratelli Rosselli 26/A. (Open M 7:30am-1:30pm, Tu-Sa 7:30am-1:30pm and 4-7pm. July-Aug. M-Sa 7:30am-1:30pm.) Local cheeses, like the pungent *semuda* and *robiola,* are available at supermarkets. Try **GS,** on the corner of V. Fratelli Recchi and V. Fratelli Roselli. (☎57 08 95. Open M 9am-8pm, Tu-Sa 8am-8pm, Su 9am-1pm.

AmEx/D/MC/V.) **Gran Mercato** is by the bus station in P. Matteotti. (Open M and Su 8:30am-1pm, Tu-F 8:30am-1:30pm and 3:30-7:30pm, Sa 8am-7:30pm.) An **open-air market** is held in P. Vittoria (Tu and Th mornings, all day Sa).

Il Carrettiere, V. Coloniola 18 (☎30 34 78), off P. Alcide de Gasperi, near P. Matteotti. A Sicilian outpost in the middle of Lombardy, the restaurant draws crowds with *risotto con filote di pesce persico.* Pizza €4.50-8. *Primi* €8-9, *secondi* €8-16.50. Cover €1.30. Open Tu-F 7pm-1am, Sa-Su noon-2:30pm and 7pm-2am. Reservations recommended. AmEx/MC/V. ❸

Ramses (☎30 19 54), located on V. Crespi behind P. Croggi. Serves traditional *pizza napolitana,* as well as more daring dishes such as *gnocchi a la bava* (layered with *fontina;* €7.50). Pizza €5-8. *Primi* €7-10, *secondi* €8-14.50. Cover €1.80. Open Tu-Su noon-2:15pm and 7-11:15pm. AmEx/MC/V. ❸

Scalda Sole, V. Alessandro Volta 41 (☎26 38 89). Sift through the sea of collared shirts for a table at this lunch spot for professionals who know their fish. *Primi* €5-10, *secondi* €6-18. Open M-Sa 10am-midnight. AmEx/MC/V. ❸

El Merendero, V. Crespi 4 (☎30 44 77). Has served as a lively hangout for 28 years, offering 75 different types of beer to all types of locals. Beer €3.50-6. Mixed drinks €4. *Panini* €4. *Secondi* €6-8. Open daily noon-3pm and 7:30pm-2am. Closed May-Sept. all day W and Su afternoon. Cash only. ❷

🔘 SIGHTS

DUOMO. Dating from 1396, Como's recently restored octagonal *duomo* harmoniously combines Romanesque, Gothic, Renaissance, and Baroque elements. The Rodari brothers' life-like sculptures of the Exodus from Egypt animate the exterior, while a collection of 16th-century tapestries brighten the cavernous interior. Statues of Pliny the Elder and Pliny the Younger, long-past Como residents, flank the main door; inside, each massive column hosts its own illuminated statue. *(From P. Cavour, take V. Caio Plinio II to P. Duomo. Open daily 7am-noon and 3-7pm.)*

TEMPIO VOLTIANO. The Neoclassical structure was dedicated to native son Alessandro Volta, inventor of the battery. Items on display include early attempts at wet-cell batteries the size of a kitchen table, and various apparatuses for experimenting on frog muscles. *(From P. Cavour, walk left along the waterfront, and turn onto Lungolago Mafalda di Savoia; look for the small building with a dome. ☎57 47 05 and 27 13 43. Open Tu-Su Apr.-Sept. 10am-noon and 3-6pm; Oct.-Mar. 10am-noon and 2-4pm. €3.)*

VILLA OLMO. Around the western edge of the lake right next to the youth hostel, the light yellow ambassadorial Villa Olmo, built in Lombard style, sits in a spacious, statue-lined waterfront park of the same name. It hosts notable exhibits throughout the year. *(On V. Cantoni. ☎25 24 43 and 27 13 34. Gardens open daily Apr.-Sept. 8am-11pm; Oct.-Mar. 9am-7pm. Exhibit prices vary.)*

MUSEO DIDATTICO DELLA SETA. The worms and silk looms that put Como on the textile map now sit on display. *(V. Vallegio 3. Entrance at V. Castelnuovo 1. ☎30 31 80; www.museosetacomo.com. Open Tu-F 9am-noon and 3-6pm. Wheelchair-accessible. €8.)*

🏔 HIKING

For some of the best hiking in the lakes region, start by taking the **funicular** from P. dei Gasperi 4, at the far end of Lungo Lario Trieste, to **Brunate** (8min.) for an excellent hike back down to Como. (☎30 36 08; info@funicolarecomo.it. Daily every 15-30min. June-Sept. 6am-midnight; Oct.-May 6am-11:30pm. €2.45, under 12 €1.55; round-trip €4.10/2.60, 8:30pm-midnight €1.50. AmEx/MC/V.) The tourist office provides excellent trail descriptions of the lands above Brunate and the Lecco district east of Como. Adventures of all levels start in Brunate, where you can launch a two-day hike all the way to Bellagio. For more effortless panoramas, take the red-brick *passeggiata pedonale* to the left of the pink church and hike toward **Faro Voltiano** (906m), a lighthouse dedicated to Volta (30min.). On a clear day, views from the Faro stretch from Milan to the Matterhorn. A bus runs from Brunate to near the Faro (every 30min. 8:15am-6:45pm, €1). From Faro Voltiano, another 15min. of hiking leads to **San Maurizio,** and another hour will take you to **Monte Boletto** (1236m). If the hike to Monte Boletto isn't too exhausting, keep strolling to reach **Monte Bolettone** (1317m).

Another option is to head northwest past San Maurizio after the restaurant Baita Carla before reaching Monte Boletto, on a path to lakeside **Torno,** 8 km north of Como (1hr.); this is a good place to catch a ferry back to Como (every hr. 6:58am-8:14pm, €2). In Torno, check out the **Chiesa di San Giovanni** (open daily 8am-6pm) or the **Villa Pliniana,** 15min. north of the dock, closed to visitors but worth a look from afar. For more extensive exploration of the mountains near Como, take bus C40 to **Erba** (30min.; every hr. 5:25am-10:20pm, last return 10:56pm; €2.55). From Erba, make the beautiful hike to **Caslino D'Erba,** which leads to **Monte Palanzone** (1436m). It is also possible to reach Erba by hiking south from Monte Bolettone (2hr.). Head to the cool recesses of **Buco del Piombo** for an encounter with prehistory—caves formed during the Jurassic Period over 150 million years ago.

▶ DAYTRIP FROM COMO

DOMASO

Domaso lies 50km away from Como and can be reached by hydrofoil (1½hr.; €11.50) or bus (2hr.; €4). Contact the tourist office in Como for more information.

The breezes in Domaso (doh-MA-zoh; pop. 1500), located at the top of the lake, create perfect **windsurfing** conditions. **Windsurfcenter,** V. Case Sparse 24, at Camping Paradiso, outfits sailors and windsurfers and offers classes from May 1 to October 14. (☎0386 70 00 010; info@windsurfcenter-domaso.com. Board and sail rental €37 per half-day, €45 per day. Private lessons €70 per hr. Bikes €10 for 1st hr., €3 per hr. thereafter, €15 per half-day. Cash only.) If the wind isn't cooperating, travel 30min. farther along the main road to **Canottieri Domaso,** V. Antica Regina 36, where waves take out **wakeboarders.** (☎97 462; www.canottieridomaso.it. Wakeboarding €98 per hr., water skiing €105 per hr. Open daily 9am-noon and 1-6pm; best time due to wind 9-9:30am. AmEx/MC/V.) The **tourist office,** in Ple. Madonnina, has maps and info on aquatic sports. (☎96 322; www.comunedomaso.it. Open June-Sept. daily 10am-noon and 4-8pm.)

BELLAGIO ☎031

Once favored by the upper-crust of *milanese* society, Bellagio (beh-LA-zhee-yo; pop. 3000, in summer 6000) is one of the loveliest—and certainly the most heavily visited—of the central lake towns. It is so small that everything seems lake-front. Its name is a compound of *bello* (beautiful) and *agio* (comfort); fittingly, the town is filled with restful lakeside promenades, sidewalk cafes, and shaded streets.

▣▶ TRANSPORTATION AND PRACTICAL INFORMATION. The best way to reach Bellagio is by **ferry.** The ferry next to the *biglietteria* in P. Mazzini only serves people, while the one across the port also serves cars. Ferries depart to most lake

towns every 30min. to 1hr., including Menaggio (10-15min., 8:36am-7:53pm, €3.40), Varenna (10-15min., 9:08am-10:20pm, €3.40), and Como (45min.-2hr., 6:47am-8:34pm, €7.80). SPT C30 **buses** run to Como (1hr., 19 per day 5:55am-6:55pm, €2.65). Lecco Trasporti runs buses to Lecco (1hr., 6 per day 6:30am-7:05pm, €2.05). Ferries dock at **Piazza Mazzini,** which becomes **Via Roma** to the left and **Lungo Lario Manzoni** to the right. The English-speaking staff at the **tourist office,** in P. Mazzini, gives detailed daytrip info. (☎95 02 04; www.bellagiolakecomo.com. Open M-Sa 9am-12:30pm and 3-6:30pm, Su 9am-2:30pm.) A **pharmacy** is just uphill at V. Roma 8. (☎95 01 86. Open June-Sept. M-Sa 8:30am-12:30pm and 3:30-7:30pm, Su 9am-12:30pm; Sept.-June M-Tu and Th-Sa 8:30am-12:30pm and 3:30-7:30pm.) **Banks** with **ATMs** are on Lungo Lario Manzoni, including **Banco San Paolo,** Lungo L. Manzoni 24. (Open M-F 8:20am-1:20pm and 2:35-4pm.) Use the **Internet** or taste wine at **bellagiopoint.com,** Salita Plinio 8/10/12, off V. Garibaldi. (☎95 04 37. €2 per 15min., €6 per hr. Open daily 10am-10pm. AmEx/MC/V.) The **post office,** Lungo L. Manzoni 4, offers **currency exchange.** (☎95 19 42. Open M-F 8:30am-2pm, Sa 8:30am-12:30pm.) **Postal Code:** 22021.

⌐⌐ ACCOMMODATIONS AND FOOD. Expect higher rates in Bellagio than in other lake towns. ▨**Albergo Giardinetto ❹,** V. Roncati 12, off P. della Chiesa, is by far the best deal in town, with 13 simple rooms overlooking beautiful terraces with quiet gardens and grape arbors. (☎95 01 68; tczgne@tiscali.it. Breakfast €6. Open Easter-Nov., weather permitting. Singles €42; doubles with bath €55, with balcony €60; triples with bath €75. Cash or traveler's checks.) **Hotel Suisse ❹,** P. Mazzini 8/10, is the only other choice for less expensive accommodations in the city, even though it is a bit pricey. (☎95 03 35; www.bellagio.co.nz/suisse. Breakfast €10. Doubles €85, with lake view €100; triples €125. AmEx/MC.)

Walk down a winding street away from the *centro,* starting from P. della Chiesa, to reach **Ristorante La Punta ❹,** V. Vitali 19. The cheese and walnut ravioli in a cream sauce (€12) is a dream. (☎95 18 88. *Primi* €9-13, *secondi* €12-14. Cover €2.50. Open daily noon-2:30pm and 7-10pm. AmEx/MC/V over €50.) **Ristorante Barchetta ❺,** Salita Mella 15, is on a shaded 2nd-floor terrace in the heart of the old town and has featured Lombard cuisine since 1887. Try the *gnocchi* with shrimp and asparagus tips for €14.50. (☎95 13 89. *Primi* €14.50-15.50, *secondi* €15-24. Open M and W-Su noon-2:15pm and 7-10pm. AmEx/MC/V.) **Baba Yaga ❶,** V. Eugenio Vitali 8, has huge pizzas served on long wooden boards and serves food later than anywhere else. (☎95 19 15. Takeout available. *Primi* and *secondi* until 10:30pm, pizza until 11pm.) **Far Out ❸,** Salita Mella 4, has live jazz every night at 9pm. Well-dressed couples in their forties come here for their mixed drink fix. (☎95 17 43; www.farout.it. *Primi* €6-12, *secondi* €10-17.50. Cover €2. Open noon-3pm and 7pm-midnight. Kitchen open noon-3pm and 7-10pm.)

⊙ SIGHTS. The 17th-century **Villa Serbelloni** (not to be confused with the stately, five-star Grand Hotel Villa Serbelloni down the hill) offers spectacular views from the fortifications on the promontory and a lovely, cyprus-lined garden with artificial grottoes. Today, it is home to the Rockefeller Foundation and can be toured (except for the inside) twice daily in a guided group. (☎/fax 95 15 55. 1½hr. tours Apr.-Oct. Tu-Su 11am and 3:30pm. Purchase tickets 15min.-1hr. beforehand at P. Chiesa 14. Small tourist info office only open 1hr. before tours. €7, children €3.50.) From the ferry dock, 800m along Lungo Largo Europa, down Lungo Largo Manzoni to reach **Villa Melzi.** The lakeside gardens here, constructed by famous architect Albertolli at the beginning of the 19th century, blossom at the other end of town. The villa is still a private residence, but the grounds are open to the public. (Open daily Mar.-Oct. 9am-6pm. €6.) The **Basilica of Saint James,** namesake of the P. della Chiesa, is an excellent example of 10th- to 12th-century Lombard Romanesque architecture—worth a stop for the glittering mosaic scenes in the cupolas of the chapels on either side of the main altar and the life-like wooden carving of Jesus, encased in glass along the left wall. While many simply stroll Bellagio's streets daintily, most aquatic sports and other organized recreation activities are based in this lake-side town. **Sports and Adventures-Cavalcalario Club,** Località Gallasco 1, offers sailing, motorboats, lake fishing, rock climbing, kayaking, canyoning, horseback riding, mountain biking, and paragliding. (☎339 53 08 138 or 96 48 14; www.bellagio-mountains.it.)

▚ DAYTRIP FROM BELLAGIO: VILLA DEL BALBIANELLO. Central Lake Como is known for its grandiose villas, a testament of the luxurious Como of days past. Reputed to be the lake's most gorgeous, **Villa del Balbianello** in Lenno, originally a Franciscan convent, was rebuilt in 1787 by Cardinal Durini as a "splendid palace of delights." The motto "Do what you would like" welcomes visitors at the entrance. More recently, it was featured as the otherworldly site of the wedding in *Star Wars II: Attack of the Clones* (2002). The highlight of the villa's peninsula is a panoramic, terraced garden dominated by an elegant loggia. *(Lenno is accessible by ferry. 20-40min., 18 per day 6:37am-6:28pm, €3-4.60. From ferry, go left on the Lungolago Lomazzi all the way to the end. From there, villa is accessible by 1km walk, or by taxi boat Th-F only. ☎333 41 03 854. 10min. ride every 30min., round-trip €5. Villa ☎56 110. Open Mar. 17-Oct. 31 Tu and Th-Su 10am-6pm. Last entry 5:30pm. Garden €5, ages 4-12 €2.50. Guided tour of villa €11/6, with reservation €8/4.)*

VARENNA   ☎0341

A short ferry ride from Bellagio or Menaggio, Varenna (va-REHN-na; pop. 900) is a narrow version of its more famous neighbors. Varenna distinguishes itself from other lake towns with its pedestrian feel and small *piazze,* making it the true getaway destination for those seeking a slower pace. The 14th-century **Chiesa di San Giorgio** looms above the main *piazza* overlooking the city. The ornate, Baroque-style confessional, built in 1690 by Giovanni Albiolo, offers a strong contrast against the exceedingly simple interior, which features frescoes painted by locals. (☎83 02 28. Open daily 7am-noon and 2-7pm. Free.) Varenna's most famous sights are the two lakeside gardens of **Villa Monastero,** 150m to the right of the church, in a former Cistercian monastery. The grounds contain 2km of paths past dark cyprus groves and giant, otherwordly aloe plants, and are also home to a museum. (☎29 54 50; www.villamonastero.it. Gardens open daily Mar. 28-Nov. 1 9am-7pm. Museum open Sa 1-5pm, Su 10am-1pm and 2-6pm. Museum €2; gardens €2. Combined ticket with Villa Cipressi €4.) Smaller, terraced gardens of 16th-century **Villa Cipressi,** once strolling grounds of aristocrats, now serve patrons of the villa's luxury hotel. Enter through the Hotel Villa Cipressi, past Villa Monastero. (Gardens open daily Mar.-Oct. 9am-7pm. €2, with Villa Monastero €4.) From the tourist office, a 30min. hike up V. IV Novembre, then on V. Roma, leads to **La Sorgente del Fiumelatte,** so named for the *latte*-like foam on the river. Fiumelatte, the shortest river in Italy (250m), disappears in mid-October only to reappear in March.

One of the few affordable accommodations is **Albergo Beretta ❷,** V. per Esino 1, on the corner on the way to the train station. All 10 rooms have TV, telephone, and view. The ground-floor bar offers a home-style €12 *menù* available throughout the day upon request. (☎/fax 83 01 32. Breakfast €6. Doubles €58, with bath €68, with balcony and sofa for 3rd person €80. Extra bed €12. MC/V.) **B&B Orange House di Mara Angeloni ❸,** V. Venini 156, is the only other affordable accommodation in town. (☎347 91 87 940; www.orangehouse.org. Reservations recommended. Singles €39; doubles €58. MC/V.) **Ristorante Montecodeno ❸,** V. Croce 2, uphill from the ferry station, is a local favorite for lake fish. (☎83 01 23; www.hotelmontecodeno.com. *Primi* €9, *secondi* €12-18. *Menù* €25-35. Open M and W-Su noon-2pm and 7-9pm. AmEx/MC/V.) Huge crepes (€5-8.50) at water-front **Nilus Bar ❶**, Riva Garibaldi 4, burst with fillings. (☎81 52 28. *Panini* €4-4.50. Pizza €4.50-7. Mixed drinks €4-6. Open April-Sept. daily 10am-1am.) The superb **Vecchia Varenna ❹**, V. Scoscesa 10, lets guests dine in a terrace over the water. Serves fine cuisine such as Grand Marnier duck breast with citrus sauce (€16), and pumpkin ravioli. (☎83 07 93. *Primi* €11-12, *secondi* €15-16. Cover €3. Open Tu-Su 12:30-2pm and 7:30-9:30pm. Closed Nov.-Jan. MC/V.)

Varenna is one of few towns with a **train station,** directly uphill from the ferry dock, linking the eastern side of the lake to Milan. Buy tickets from the machine in the waiting room or at the travel agency next door to Albergo Beretta. (Open M-F 8:30am-12:30pm and 3-7pm, Sa 8:30am-12:30pm.) **Trains** run to Lecco (30min., 5:25am-10:29pm, €3) and Milan (5:25am-9:23pm, €5). From other parts of the lake, the best way to access Varenna is by **ferry,** arriving at the northern point of town. Pick up a ferry schedule from the tourist office. Part of the central lake route, ferries serve Bellagio (15-20min., every 1-2hr. 6:33am-7:52pm, €3-4.60), Como (1-2½hr., 6:33am-6:36pm, €7.20-10.50), and Menaggio (10-15min., every 30min.-1hr. 6:33am-6:36pm, €3-4.60). For a **taxi,** call ☎81 50 61. The **tourist office** is in the train station. (Open daily 10am-1:30pm and 3-7pm.) If arriving by ferry, see ticket office for location of closest tourist office. Off P. San Giorgio, **Banca Popolare di Lecco,** V. IX Novembre 4, has an **ATM.** (☎81 50 15. Open M-F 8:20am-1:20pm and 2:45-3:45pm.) **Pharmacy Pedrani** is at V. Venini 2. (☎83 02 03. Open M-Tu and Th-Sa 9am-12:30pm and 3:30-7:30pm, W 9am-12:30pm. AmEx/MC/V.) **Internet** access is available at **Barilott,** V. IX Novembre 6, which is also a wine bar. (€2.50 per 15min., €5 per hr. Open M-Sa 7am-8pm.) In case of **emergency,** call the **carabinieri** (☎82 11 21) or an **ambulance** (☎81 02 50). The **post office** is at V. del Prato 13. (☎83 02 31. Open M-F 8:30am-2pm, Sa 8:30am-12:30pm.) **Postal Code:** 23829.

MENAGGIO   ☎0344

Menaggio (meh-NA-jee-yo; pop. 3200) is home to terra-cotta rooftops and stunning scenery. In the last few years, tourists have caught on, and Menaggio has become one of the lake's most popular towns. Despite these crowds, Menaggio's beauty, central location, cheap accommodations, and excellent ferry connections make it the perfect base for exploring any part of Lake Como or the nearby mountains.

◧ ⊅ TRANSPORTATION AND PRACTICAL INFORMATION. SPT buses (☎32 118) leave from the waterfront stop in front of P. Garibaldi. The C12 serves Lugano (1hr., 11 per day 6:02am-5:34pm, €4.30) and the C10 serves Como (1¼hr., 17 per day 5:20am-7:04pm). Navigazione Lago di Como (☎32 255), in P. Traghetto, 6 blocks south of the *centro*, runs **ferries** to Bellagio (15min., 31 per day 6:37am-8:24pm, €3-4.60); Como (2hr, 22 per day 6:37am-8:24pm, €7.80); Domaso (1½hr., 12 per day 9:39am-8pm, €4.10-6.10); Varenna (15min., 16 per day 8:13am-8:52pm, €3-4.60). There are three **taxi** drivers in Menaggio: Pozzi (☎335 80 36 670), Ezio (☎338 20 47 279) and Diego (☎333 86 01 035). There is a yellow callbox in front of P. Garibaldi if you can't get to a phone.

In the *centro* the **tourist office,** P. Garibaldi 4, has info and maps to plan lake excursions. The helpful, multilingual staff can suggest hiking itineraries for any level of difficulty. (☎32 924; www.menaggio.com. Open Apr.-Sept. daily 9am-12:30pm and 2:30-6pm; Oct.-Mar. M-Tu and Th-Sa 9am-12:30pm and 2:30-6pm, Su 9:30am-12:30pm.) **Ostello la Primula** (☎32 356; www.menaggiohostel.com; p. 293) has been known to offer short-term **work opportunities** (3hr. daily shift in return for room and board), but they require a face-to-face interview. In case of **emergency,** call the **carabinieri,** V. Regina, in the neighboring town of Nobiallo (☎32 025). **Antica Farmacia Kluzer** is at V. IV Novembre 30. (Open M-W and F-Su 8:30am-12:30pm and

3-7:15pm.) The **hospital** (☎33 111) is on V. Cazertelli, off V. Cadorna above the *centro*. **Internet** access is available at the **library,** V. Camozzi 21, two blocks north of the tourist office (available Tu 9:30am-1pm, W-Th 9:30am-noon and F 9am-12:30pm; €1.50 per 30min.) and at **Video Mix,** V. IV Novembre 52, across from the Grand Hotel Menaggio. (☎34 110. €1.50 per 15min. Open Tu-Sa 9:30am-12:30pm and 4-7pm. AmEx/MC/V.) The **post office,** V. Lusardi 50, has **currency exchange** and **ATM.** (☎32 106. Open M-F 8:30am-2pm, Sa 8:30am-12:30pm.) **Postal Code:** 22017.

▌▐ ACCOMMODATIONS AND FOOD. ▨**Ostello La Primula (HI) ❶,** V. IV Novembre 106, offers the best budget value on Lake Como. From the ferry dock, walk straight to V. IV Novembre, then turn left and ascend the tiny path that clings to the right side of the road. Perks include public beach access behind the big orange house across the street, bike and kayak rental (€13 per day), and a social porch with stunning lake views. (☎32 356; www.menaggiohostel.com. Breakfast included 8-10am; 3-course dinner *menù* €12; picnic lunch by request €7. Towel €2. Laundry €3.50. Internet access €2 per 15min. Reception 8-10am and 4pm-midnight. Lockout 10am-4pm. Strict midnight curfew and quiet hours. Open Mar.-Nov. Reservations recommended. Dorms €16; 4- to 6-bed family suites with bath €72-108. HI-member discount €3. Cash only.) **Vecchia Menaggio ❶,** V. al Lago 13, offers hotel rooms at hostel prices, in an unbelievable location right next to the *centro*. Traditional, affordable Italian dining downstairs. (☎32 082. Doubles €33, with bath €40, with queen bed and bath €50.) **Albergo Il Vapore ❸,** P. T. Grossi 3, just off P. Garibaldi, has rooms with bath, phone; some have TV and balcony facing the lake. (☎32 229; il.vapore@email.it. Reception open 8am-midnight. Breakfast €6.50. Restaurant downstairs. Reservations only for stays over 3 days; fax confirmation required. Singles €35; doubles €55; triples €75. Cash only.) Lakeside **Camping Europa ❶,** V. Cipressi 12, a 15min. walk from the ferry docks down V. Lusardi, then V. Roma, comes complete with a rocky beach. (☎31 187. Open daily 8am-11pm. €5.70 per person, €9.10 per tent. 1-person bungalow €30; 4- to 6-person €60. Cash only.) Enjoy a waterfront dinner at the classy though touristy, **Il Ristorante di Paolo ❹,** Largo Cavour 5, off P. Garibaldi, where you can listen to arias and watch as dusk falls across the lake. Try the *risotto con mele e brie* (risotto with apple and brie) for €10. (☎32 133. *Primi* €8-10, *secondi* €14-19. Cover €2.50. Open daily noon-3pm and 7-10pm. AmEx/MC/V.) Head uphill at the junction near Banca San Paolo for **Pizzeria Lugano ❶,** V. Como 26. Try peppers and eggplant, along with a mess of other flavors, on the *pizza della casa* for €6.50. (☎31 664. Pasta €5.50-6. Open Tu-Su 11:30am-2:45pm and 6:30-11pm. MC/V.) Near the ferry dock, **Super Cappa Market,** V. IV Novembre 107, stocks groceries. (☎32 161. Open M 8am-12:30pm, Tu-Sa 8am-12:30pm and 3:30-7pm. MC/V.)

◙▟ SIGHTS AND HIKING. The only sandy **beach** in Menaggio is toward the campground, near the end of V. Benedetto Castelli and past the miniature golf course. This large beach club has sand-side soccer, a pool, a bar, and lots of chairs. (M-F €9, under 14 and over 65 €6; after 2:30pm €4. Sa-Su €12/8, and after 2:30pm €9/7.) The tourist office and hostels stock three main informative printouts: suggested scenic **boat trips,** recommended **driving excursions** by car or bus, and a collection of **hiking itineraries,** which allow you to tour the mountains flanking the lake. Explore the romantic park, breathtaking waterfall, local rural settlements, or archaeological sites. The Rifugio Menaggio mountain station is the starting point for a 2½hr. round-trip hike to **Monte Grona** (1736m) that offers views of the pre-Alps and the three lakes or a 2¼hr. hike to **Chiesa di San Amate** (1623m) that takes you over a mountain ridge to sneak a peak at alpine pastures and Val Menaggio. A number of shorter hikes start in Menaggio. A 2hr. hike (1-

way) winds through outlying villages and farms to the picturesque **Sass Corbee Gorge,** overlooking a waterfall. Another option is the 2hr. hike toward **Lake Lugano** and **Lake Piano,** which intersects a small nature reserve in **Val Menaggio,** (bus C12 heads back). For a less strenuous adventure, take the 30min. walk through an old mule track up to **La Crocetta** (450m), a small cross located above Menaggio. On your way to the cross, you'll pass by *linea cadorna*—trenches built in 1915 and used during WWI as a defense against German invasion.

ACROSS THE BORDER FROM LAKE COMO

LUGANO, SWITZERLAND   ☎091

Lugano (loo-GAH-no; pop. 53,000), Switzerland's 3rd-largest banking center, rests on Lake Lugano in a valley between the San Salvatore and Monte Brè peaks. Though it officially joined the Swiss Confederation in 1803, Lugano still feels like part of the Italian *famiglia* due to its shop-filled cobblestone streets and arcade-lined *piazze*. With Italian influence dating back to the Roman era, Lugano continues to be a popular spot for Swiss retirees and young travelers alike.

> **!** Remember to bring your **passport** for excursions into Switzerland. If you are planning to stay for a while, exchange your currency for **Swiss Francs** (SFr or CHF), since euros are not accepted in many shops and bus ticket offices. As of Aug. 2007, exchange rates for the **Swiss Franc (SFr)** are as follows: 1SFr=€0.61; €1=1.65SFr.

⬛⁊ TRANSPORTATION AND PRACTICAL INFORMATION. To reach Lugano from Menaggio, take a direct train, or, for a cheaper route, take the #1 bus (€4) from V. Borgo Vico into Chiasso, on the border with Switzerland. Walk uphill to the left to reach the **train station,** on V. Motta (☎058 12 279 233; www.fts.ch), to take the direct route to Lugano (1-3 per hr. 4:55am-1:41am, 9SFr). **Trains** in Lugano (☎92 35 120; station open M-Sa 6:30am-8pm, Su 7:30am-8pm) run from P. della Stazione to Chiasso (30min., every hr. 6:10am-1:14am, 9.20SFr), Bellinzona (30min., every 30min.-1hr. 5:26am-12:12am, 11.40SFr), and Milan (45min., every hr. 6:10am-9:48pm, 25SFr).

> **⁕TIP⁕** **YOU GOT TOLLED.** All cars entering Switzerland are charged 40SFr to use the A9. This charge is a yearly toll applying to any car coming through, whether for a one-time visit or a regular commute. If you aren't in a hurry, get off the road in Chiasso and take side streets to Lugano. Or, coming from Malpensa, take the 233 to Lugano. The extra 20min. will buy your bed for the night.

SPT **buses** (www.sptlinea.it) run to and from neighboring towns, including Menaggio (C12; 1hr., every hr. 7:19am-6:46pm, €4.30). Schedules and ticket machines are at each stop. (Tickets 1.60-3.20SFr, Carta Giorno day-pass 5SFr.) For **taxis,** call ☎92 28 833, 97 12 121, or 92 20 222, or find one in front of the train station. The 15min. downhill walk from the train station to the classically Italian **Piazza della Riforma,** the *centro,* winds through Lugano's large pedestrian zone. For those who would rather avoid the walk, a **funicular** runs between the train station and the waterfront **Piazza Cioccaro.** (Open 5:20am-1150pm. 1.10SFr.)

THE LAKE COUNTRY

> ⓘ **DIALING ACROSS THE BORDER.** To dial out of Italy, start with its **international dialing prefix,** 00. Switzerland's **country code** is 41, and Lugano's **city code** is 091. Drop the 0 if calling from within Switzerland.

The **tourist office** is found in the Palazzo Civico; its entrance faces the waterfront on Riva Albertolli. The office offers free maps. Ask about free, guided city walks in English, such as the **Classic Tour** (M), which focuses on the architectural monuments from the past; the **Testimony of History Tour** (Th), which tours the whole city to find the evidence of past events still seen in its *piazze;* and the **Garden Tour** (Su), which allows you to peer at the thriving oak and olive trees. (☎91 33 232; www.lugano-tourism.ch. Open Apr.-Oct. M-F 9am-7pm, Sa 9am-6pm, Su 10am-6pm; Nov.-Mar. M-F 9am-noon and 2-5:30pm, Sa 10am-noon and 1:30-5pm.) A tourist office representative also has a desk in the travel agency to the right when exiting the train station, and offers maps and hotel booking. Lockers for **luggage storage** (5-7SFr per locker) are at the train station. There are **pharmacies** in all major *piazze* and along the waterfront. In case of **emergency,** call the **police,** in P. Riforma, (☎80 08 111 or 117), **ambulance** (☎144) or **medical information** (☎18 11). The **hospital** is located on V. Terserele 46 (☎091 81 16 002). **MondialPay,** V. Canova 9, has **Internet** access, **Western Union,** and international calling. (☎92 22 569. 3SFr per 15min., 8SFr per hr. Open M-F 9am-6pm, Sa 10am-5pm.) Cash travelers checks at the **post office,** on V. della Posta 7, two blocks up from the lake near V. al Forte. (Open M-F 7:30am-6:15pm, Sa 8am-4pm.) **Postal Code:** CH-6900.

ⓘ◗ ACCOMMODATIONS AND FOOD. Inexpensive accommodations are nearly impossible to find right near the lake, where hotels with a view of the water tend to charge 250SFr and up for double rooms. View-touting budget accommodations should be reserved well in advance in summer. Converted from an 19th-century villa, the palm-tree enveloped ◪**Hotel & Hostel Montarina ❶**, V. Montarina 1, has a large swimming pool amidst grape vines, TV room, kitchen, reception stocked with maps and travel guides, and a terrace overlooking the city. From the station, walk right 200m, cross the train tracks, then walk uphill and up the stairs to the left. (☎96 67 272; www.montarina.ch. Breakfast 12SFr. Linen 4SFr. Laundry 4SFr; detergent 2SFr. Internet access 10SFr per hr. Common area with fridge open 7:30am-9:30pm. Pool open 9am-7pm. Reception 7:30am-11pm; after 11pm, ring buzzer. Reservations recommended. Dorms 25SFr; singles 70SFr, with bath 80SFr; doubles 100/120SFr. AmEx/MC/V.) **Hotel Pestalozzi ❸**, P. Indipendenza 9, is just outside the city center and only two blocks from Casino Lugano along C. Elezia. Its location makes this hotel a steal for the price. (☎91 921 46 46. Breakfast included. Internet access available. Singles 64SFr, with bath 84-106SFr; doubles 108/168-178SFr. Extra bed 20SFr.) Family-run **Ostello della Gioventù (HI) ❶**, V. Cantonale 13, is in Lugano-Savosa. Walk 350m left from the station, pass the parking lot, and cross the street to the bus stop; take bus #5 to "Crocifisso." Backtrack and turn left up V. Cantonale. Gardens and pool complement comfortable rooms that are popular with families. (☎96 62 728; www.luganoyouth-hostel.ch. Breakfast 9SFr. Kitchen access 1SFr after 7pm. Towels 2SFr. Laundry 5SFr. Internet access available. Reception 6:30am-noon and 3-10pm. Curfew 10pm. Reservations recommended. Open mid-Mar. to Oct.; re-opening May 2008 due to renovations. Dorms 31SFr; singles 51SFr; doubles 70SFr, with bath 90SFr; family rooms 35SFr per person. HI-member discount 6SFr. AmEx/MC/V.) There are several campgrounds near Lugano in Agno. To reach the lakeside **La Palma ❶**, V. Molinazzo 21 (☎60 52 561; fax 60 45 438), located at the mouth of the Vedeggio River, or the convenient **Eurocampo ❶** (☎60 52 114;

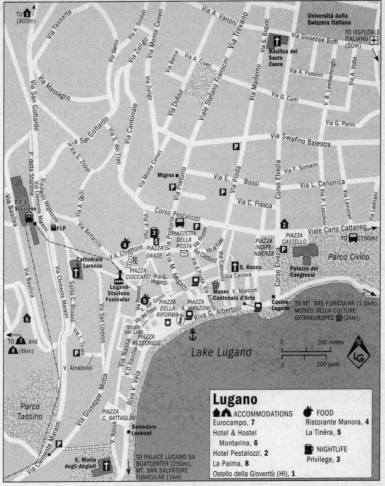

Lugano

▲▲ ACCOMMODATIONS
Eurocampo, **7**
Hotel & Hostel
  Montarina, **6**
Hotel Pestalozzi, **2**
La Palma, **8**
Ostello della Gioventù (HI), **1**

🍴 FOOD
Ristorante Manora, **4**
La Tinèra, **5**

📀 NIGHTLIFE
Privilege, **3**

www.eurocampo.ch), take the 20min. Ferrovia-Lugano-Ponte-Tresa (FLP; ☎60 51 305; www.flpsa.ch) tram from V. Stazione 8, to Agno (departs every 20min., 4.60SFr) via Ponte Tresa. From the station, turn left, then left again on V. Molinazzo. (La Palma: 9SFr per person, 10-12SFr per tent. Eurocampo: 9SFr per person, 8SFr per tent. Both include showers. Both cash only.)

Satisfying fare is easy to find at the outdoor restaurants and cafes that pay homage to Lugano's Italian heritage by serving delicious *penne*, *gnocchi*, and freshly spun pizzas. Avoid restaurants in the square; they're overpriced and of low quality. The scrumptious grab-as-you-please food at ▧**Ristorante Manora ❷**, in the Manor Department Store in P. Dante, 3rd fl., will make your mouth water as you walk past aisles of pasta, fresh fruit juice, and self-drafted beer. Hungry budget travelers will love this gourmet spot's salad bar (5-10.70SFr), pizza (4.60-13SFr), pasta (8-11SFr), hot daily specials (10-15SFr), and beer (2.50-5SFr). Outdoor seating is available by the 2nd entrance to the restaurant, located off Salita Mario e Antonio Chiattone. (Wheelchair-accessible. Open M-Sa 7:30am-10pm, Su 10am-10pm. AmEx/MC/V.) The romantic **La Tinèra ❷**, V. dei Gorini 2, is a dimly lit, underground restaurant specializing in Lombard cuisine, thus the most "Italian" restaurant you'll find near the water. Try the *risotto a la gorgonzola* for 14SFr. (☎92 35 219. Daily *menù* 12-26SFr. Open Tu-Sa 8:30am-3pm and 5:30-11pm. AmEx/MC/V.) For some quick eats, the **outdoor market** in P. della Riforma sells seafood, produce, flowers, and veggie sandwiches for 4SFr. (Open Tu and F 8amnoon.) Also try the **outdoor stands** on V. Pessina, off P. della Riforma.

◪ SIGHTS. A lakeside villa houses the **Museo delle Culture,** V. Cortivo 24-28, showcasing cultural artifacts from beyond Europe. Carved masks and statues from Africa, Oceania, and Indonesia adorn the staircases. From the tourist office, take bus #1, dir.: Castagnola, to San Domenica and walk to the street below; the villa is on the right. Or, take the ferry to Museo Helenum. (☎058 86 66 960; www.mcl.lugano.ch. Open Mar. 23-Nov. 6 Tu-Su 2-7pm, 1st Sa each month also 7pm-10pm. 8SFr, students 5SFr.) Ornate frescoes filling the 16th-century **Cattedrale San Lorenzo,** located downhill from the train station and overlooking the whole city, still gleam with vivid colors. (☎92 28 842. Open daily 9:30am-6pm. Free.) The small 14th-century **Chiesa San Rocco,** in P. Maghetti, two blocks left of P. della Riforma, houses an ornate altarpiece and a series of frescoes depicting the life of its patron saint. (Open daily 10:30am-12:30pm and 3:30-6:30pm. Free.) Diagonal to Chiesa San Rocco, the **Museo Cantonale d'Arte,** V. Canova 10, exhibits a rotating collection of 5000 pieces of 19th- and 20th-century art from regional artists, as well as works by Degas, Renoir, and Pisarro. The collection is frequently complemented by contemporary art exhibits. (☎91 04 780; www.museo-cantonalearte.ch. Open Tu 2-5pm, W-Su 10am-5pm. Wheelchair-accessible. Permanent collection 7SFr, students 5SFr. Special exhibits 10/7SFr. MC/V.)

◪◪ ENTERTAINMENT AND NIGHTLIFE. Music fills Lugano's *piazze* yearround. Summer heat ushers in **Lungolago ai Pedoni** every Friday and Saturday evening, featuring classical and Latin music concerts as well as cabaret shows by the lake (July-Aug. 8:30pm-midnight). During the 1st two weekends of July, Lugano's **Estival Jazz** (www.estivaljazz.ch) fills P. della Riforma with free nightime jazz concerts by contemporary artists. Past performers include Miles Davis and Bobby McFerrin. In June and August, the young and old trek down to the beach for **Cinema Lago,** where movies are screened lakeside for 15SFr. On August 1, Swiss-flag-studded parades, fireworks, and a choreographed airshow over Lake Lugano ring in the **Swiss National Day** celebration. During the beginning of September, the looser **Blues to Bop Festival** (www.bluestobop.ch) celebrates R&B and blues with free performances by well-recognized international singers alongside local amateurs throughout the city. At the end of September, Lugano reaffirms its Italian associations and celebrates the end of summer by honoring the country's *aqua vitae* at the **Festa D'Autunno,** where food- and wine-tastings are accompanied by traditional music.

Lugano's discos, nightclubs, and piano bars cater to partying night owls. Sit and relax with a drink, or opt to join others at the crowded dance floor playing house, 70s, and 80s music at the basement club **Privilege,** P. Dante 8. (☎92 29 438 or 079 62 01 235; www.privilegelugano.ch. Open W-Sa 10pm-2am.) Another nighttime attraction is the hulking **Casino Lugano,** V. Stauffacher 1, sitting by the water at Riva G. Albertolli and C. Elvezia. Equipped with roulette tables, a poker room, and slot machines, this maze will keep you occupied. (☎97 37 111; www.casinolugano.ch. Open Su-Th noon-4am, F-Sa noon-5am.)

⚑ OUTDOOR ACTIVITIES. The dock for the **Società Navigazione del Lago di Lugano** (☎97 15 223; www.lakelugano.ch) is across the street from the tourist office. Tours of Lake Lugano pass tiny, lakeside towns, many with attractions like chocolate museums or miniature Swiss houses.

Reach the peaks of **Monte Brè** (933m) and **Monte San Salvatore** (912m) by funicular. The ◪**Monte Brè funicolare** (☎97 13 171; www.montebre.ch) is a 20min. ride down the river along Riva Albertolli from the *centro*. (Every 20min. Open 9:10am-6:45pm.) An easier way is to take bus #1 (dir.: Castagnola) to the Cassarate-Monte Brè stop, or to catch the tourist train at the tourist office. (☎079 68 57 070. Tourist train runs every 40min. daily 10am-8pm. 8SFr, children 5SFr.) At the top of the funicular are a number of bike and hiking paths. Rent bikes at the top and return them at then bottom; tell employee that you would like to rent a bike when purchasing lift ticket (one-way ticket and half-day bike rental 23SFr; bring passport). A map of routes is available in tourist and funicular offices; difficulty ranges from easy (30min.) to difficult (5hr.). The **San Salvatore funicolare** is 20min. from the tourist office at the intersection of V. delle Scuole and V. San Salvatore in Paradiso; from the lakefront, follow V. E. Bosio inland and turn right on V. delle Scuole. (☎98 52 828; www.montesansalvatore.ch. Open June 17-Sept. 17. 10min., every 30min. 8:30am-11pm. 17SFr, round-trip 24SFr; ages 6-16 7-8.50/10-15.80SFr.)

Bike rental is available at the Stazione Trenitalia, next to ticket office #1. (☎0512 21 56 42; www.rentabike.ch. Open 8:30am-6pm. 23SFr per half-day, 31SFr per day; 38SFr to return the bike at a different location; lock and helmet included.) **Balmelli's Sport Shop,** V. Pioda 12 (☎92 35 867), also rents bikes. **Boatcenter Saladin** (☎92 35 733; www.boatcentersaladin.ch) in P. Luini rents *motoscafi* (speedboats) for 30min. (from 25SFr) or an hour (from 40SFr). **Club Nautico** (☎64 96 139) rents windsurfing boards (10SFr per hr.) as well as waterskis and wakeboards. For a more relaxing lake trip, rent paddleboats from the hut to the left of the Navigazione del Lago office. (☎079 62 13 530. 3-person boat 8SFr per 30min., 4-person boat 9SFr per 30min. Open daily 10am-7pm.)

LAKE MAGGIORE (VERBANO) AND LAKE ORTA

"If it should befall that you possess a heart and shirt, then sell the shirt and visit the shores of Lago Maggiore."
—Stendhal

Steep green hills punctuate the dark blue shoreline, and to the west, the glaciated outline of Monte Rosa (4634m) peers across the temperate mountain waters of Lake Maggiore, also known as Lake Verbano. Though many writers and artists have been seduced by the lake's beauty—Byron, Stendhal, Flaubert, Dickens, Hemingway, and da Vinci have all spent time here—today, Lake Maggiore is more family-friendly than the getaway cities along Lake Como. Stresa or Verbania serve as convenient bases for exploring the Borromean Islands and nearby Lake Orta, while secluded Santa Maria Maggiore in Valle Vigezzo offers hiking trails, inexpensive skiing, and a breathtaking elevated train journey through the valley.

STRESA   ☎0323

Stresa (STREH-zah; pop. 5000) retains much of the manicured charm that lured visitors, like Queen Victoria, in the 19th and early 20th centuries. Hydrangeas and Art Nouveau hotels line the waterfront, giving the small town a romantic, old-fashioned feel. Stresa is very much a resort town, albeit a peaceful and low-key one;

tourists from all over the world, many of them elderly or families, swell the population to three times its usual size in the summer. Many visitors come here for a trip to the Borromean Islands or for a ride up the funicular with options to bike or hike back down. The real draw, however, is in an evening walk along the lake.

🖪🖬 TRANSPORTATION AND PRACTICAL INFORMATION. Stresa lies 1hr. from Milan on the Milan-Domodossola train line. (Ticket office in lobby open M-Sa 6:10-10:45am, 11am-4:15pm, and 4:30-7:20pm; Su 7-10:45am, 11am-4:15pm, and 4:30-8:10pm.) **Trains** run to Milan (1¼hr., every 30min. 5:20am-10:32pm, €4.23) and Domodossola (40min., 14 per day 6:37am-11:01pm, €2.65). **Buses** going to Orta (1hr.; 10am, 2, 5pm; €2.45) and Verbania-Pallanza depart from the front of the lakeside church. The best way to see the region's scenery is to make the complete circuit through Lake Maggiore to Switzerland by ferry and return through Valle Vigezzo on rail, connecting from Locarno-Domodossola-Stresa. This loop can be easily done by **Lago Maggiore Express** (☎23 32 00 or 091 75 18 731. Ferries run April-May Th-Su; June 1-Sept. 23 daily. Departures from Stresa 10:50am and 11:30am. Last connection between Locarno to Domodossola 7:25pm, connection from Domodossola to Stresa 9:55pm. 1-day round-trip €28, children €14; 2-day round-trip €34/17. Bring passport.) **Bikes** can be rented from Sapori d'Italia, V. de Lartini 35.(☎93 46 42. €10 per half-day, €18 per day, €45 per 3 days. Insurance €4.) Or try Bici Co, at the base of the funicular. (☎30 399; www.stresa-mottarone.it or www.bicico.it. €21 per half day, €26 per day. Includes helmet and lock. Ask for detailed trail map. Open daily Apr.-Sept. 9:30am-5:30pm; funicular stops 12:30-1:30pm. Cash only.) Most services line the water on **Corso Umberto, Piazza Marconi, Corso Italia** or the major north-south thoroughfares, **Via Principe Tomaso** and **Via Roma**, which run uphill from the water. To reach the *centro* and the **IAT tourist office,** P. Marconi 16, on the ferry dock, exit the train station, turn right on V. Principe di Piemonte, take a left on V. Duchessa di Genova, walk downhill toward the waterfront, and turn right. (☎30 150. Open Mar.-Oct. daily 10am-12:30pm and 3-6:30pm; Nov.-Feb. M-F 10am-12:30pm and 3-6:30pm, Sa 10am-12:30pm.) For **currency exchange** and **ATM,** try **Banca Popolare di Intra,** C. Umberto 1, just off P. Marconi. (☎30 330. Open M-F 8:20am-1:20pm and 2:35-4pm, Sa 8:20am-12:15pm.) In case of **emergency,** call the **carabinieri,** on Vle. D. di Genova, at ☎30 118, **first aid** (☎31 844), or an **ambulance** (☎33 360). **Farmacia Dott. Polisseni,** V. Cavour 16, posts after-hours rotations. (Open M-W and F-Sa 8:30am-1pm and 3:30-8pm, Th 8:30am-1pm.) **New Data,** V. De Vit 15/A, off P. Cadorna, provides **Internet** access, including connections for personal laptops. (☎30 323. €3 per 30min. Open daily 9:30am-12:30pm and 3:30-10pm.) **Lidrovolante Internet Cafe,** Ple. Lido 6 (☎31 384; www.lidrovolante.com), offers Internet access near the funicular. The **post office** is at V. Anna Maria Bolongaro 44. (☎30 065. Open M-F 8:30am-7pm, Sa 8:30am-1pm.) **Postal Code:** 28838.

🖪🖸 ACCOMMODATIONS AND FOOD. To truly get your money's worth, head to **🖪Gigi Meuble ❹,** P. San Michele 1, which has seven clean, modern rooms with bath and some with balconies. Don't miss the fantastic panoramic view of the lake from the breakfast room. (☎30 225; gigihotel@email.it. With *Let's Go* discount, singles €40; doubles €50. AmEx/MC/V.) The pristine **🖪Albergo Luina ❸,** V. Garibaldi 21, centrally located and on the water, has very well-kept rooms with TV, bath, and phone. From the train station, walk to the waterfront and head right until you pass the ferry dock. Fantastic, multilingual proprietress Renata makes you feel at home and offers extensive advice on travel options. (☎30 285; luinastresa@yahoo.it. Breakfast €3.50. Reservations recommended in summer. Singles €35-52; doubles €55-80; triples €56-80. *Let's Go* discount. MC/V.) With numerous 4-person rooms, **Hotel Meeting ❺,** V. Bonghi 9, is the best choice for groups and families. Make sure to lie out and enjoy the panoramic view of the city, lake, and islands from the large rooftop sundeck. (☎32 741; hotelmeeting@stresa.it. Singles €60-80; doubles €75-100; quads €85-110. AmEx/MC/V.) Popular **Taverna del Pappagallo ❷**, V. Principessa Margherita 46, serves great brick-oven pizza (€4.50-8) and various pastas in a lively indoor seating or in the grapevine covered courtyard. Greet the embalmed parrot on your way in. (☎30 411. *Primi* €5-8, *secondi* €7-12. Cover €1.30. Open M-Tu and Th-Su noon-2:30pm and 6:30-11pm. AmEx/MC/V.) Lounge bar **El Gato Negro Café ❷**, V. Principessa Margherita 52, has a charming garden, young staff, and soothing music. (☎33 621. Mixed drinks €5. *Panini* €3.50. Salads €6. *Primi* €5, *secondi* €6-9. Cover €0.50. Open daily 8am-10pm. AmEx/MC/V.) For refuge from the more expensive restaurants, **Il Capriccio ❶**, V. de Vit 15, offers creative pizza slices for only €2-2.20. (☎31 687. Open Tu-Su 10:30am-2:30pm and 5-9pm. Cash only.) **Lago Maggiore ❷**, V. Cavour 34-36, is tucked behind the lakeside church. (☎32 746. *Primi* €5-8, *secondi* €7-15. Lake fish €9-19. Open daily 11:30am-3pm and 6:30pm-11:30pm. AmEx/MC/V.) Food in Stresa can be overpriced and often unsatisfying; a great option is to stock up on groceries at **GS**, V. Roma 11, and eat by the water or on the mountain. (Open M-Sa 8:30am-1pm and 3-8pm, Su 8:30am-12:30pm. AmEx/MC/V.)

🖲🎭 SIGHTS AND ENTERTAINMENT. Turn right out of the tourist office and follow the waterfront all the way to Vle. Lido to reach the **Stresa-Alpino-Mottarone Funivia,** P. Lido 8, which allows visitors to explore Mottarone's (1491m) extensive hiking and mountain biking trails. (☎30 295; www.stresa-mottarone.it. Open daily 9:30am-12:30pm and 1:50-5:30pm; usually closed Nov. for repairs. 20min.; every 20min., last return 5:40pm; €5-7.50.) Close to the water, **Villa Pallavicino,** down C. Italia, boasts 50 acres of gardens filled with over 40 species of exotic animals such as flamingoes and zebras. (☎31 533; www.parcozoopallavicino.it. Open Mar.-Oct. daily 9am-6pm. €9, children €5.) From the last week in July to the 2nd week in September, classical musicians and fans gather for the **Settimane Musicali di Stresa e del Lago Maggiore,** a celebration of the full canon of classical music. Performances crowd Stresa's Palazzo dei Congressi or on Isola Bella. Contact the ticket office at V. Carducci 38. (☎31 095 or 30 459; www.settimanemusicali.net. Open daily 9:30am-12:30pm and 3-6pm. Tickets €20-100, under 26 half-price, limited number of tickets €10. Package tickets available.) Stresa's new and only nightclub, **Loco Beach Club,** P. Lido, is next to the funicular. The rooftop bar, swanky beachside patio, and modern dining room draws a crowd of older tourists after 9pm. (☎93 47 40. Mixed drinks €6.50. *Primi* €11, *secondi* €13-20. Open daily 9am-3pm.) For a more low-key scene, the great *enoteca* (wine bar) **Da Giannino,** V. Garibaldi 32, offers a multitude of reasonably priced wines, served indoors at a few wooden kegs-turned-tables or outside where large groups sit and chat over glasses of wine. (☎30 781. Wine from €2. Open daily 9am-midnight. Kitchen open noon-2pm and 7pm-midnight. AmEx/MC/V.)

THE BORROMEAN ISLANDS (ISOLE BORROMEE)　☎0323

Beckoning visitors with dense greenery and stately villas, the lush beauty of the Borromean Islands (in Italian "EE-so-leh bo-ro-MEY") is one of the lake's major attractions. Situated between Stresa and Pallanza, the islands are easily accessed by ferry. The opulent **▨Palazzo e Giardini Borromeo** is set on the pearl of Maggiore, **Isola Bella.** This Baroque palace, built in 1670 by Count Vitaliano Borromeo, features meticulously designed rooms constructed over 300 years, with priceless tapestries and Van Dyck paintings. Napoleon and Josephine slept in the alcove of the grand **Napoleon Room** during his 1st Italian campaign in 1797. The **Sala della Musica** hosted Mussolini, Laval, and MacDonald at the 1935 **Conference of Stresa,** the last attempt to stave off WWII. Six underground man-made **grottoes** are covered in mosaics; for years, peasants collected black stones to complete the masterpieces. Ten terraced gardens rise up like a wedding cake, punctuated by statues of gods and topped with a unicorn, the symbol of the Borromeo family, whose motto, *Humilitas* (humility), is not so apparent here. (☎30 556; www.borromeoturismo.it. Open daily Mar. 21-Oct. 21 9am-5:30pm, garden until 6:15pm. Last entry 30min. before closing. Guided tours for 2-50 people can be arranged at least one day in advance by phone or at info@borromeoturismo.it. €11, ages 6-15 €4.50. Combined ticket for the *palazzo* and the Villa Taranto on Isola Madre €16, children €7. Audio tour €2.50. Tours €30 per group, separate from admission.)

From Isola Bella, a short ferry ride leads to **Isola Superiore dei Pescatori,** a quaint fishing village full of souvenir vendors and their cats who come for the daily catch. There's a little-used rocky swimming beach on the west end of the island, but keep in mind this is an alpine lake; the water may be more chilling than refreshing. On top of the hill in the village, the only other attraction is the **Chiesa di San Vitore,** dedicated to a *borromese* nobleman who later became a saint. (Open daily 9am-6pm. Free.) There is no such thing as a non-touristy restaurant on these popular islands, but head left when exiting ferry to reach **Ristorante Italia ❸,** V. Ugo Ara 58, which specializes in local fish and serves it in a charming blue and white house overlooking the lake. (☎30 456; www.stresaonline.com/italia. *Primi* €6-9, *secondi* €9-13. Cover €1.50. Open daily noon-2:30pm and 7-10pm. AmEx/MC/V.)

Isola Madre, almost entirely covered by its garden, is not only the longest and most tranquil of the islands, but also the local favorite—perhaps because it feels like a step back in time. Its elegant, 16th-century **Villa Taranto** was started in 1502 by Lancelotto Borromeo and finished by Count Renato 100 years later, after Lancelotto reputedly met his unfortunate end in the mouth of a ◪**dragon.** It contains several room-sized puppet theaters and Princess Borromeo's extensive marionette collection. The villa's gardens have exotic flora and fauna—a white peacock guards the 200-year-old Cashmere Cyprus. Visit in July to see the rare lotus blossoms in bloom. (☎/fax 31 261. Open daily Mar.-Sept. 9am-noon and 1:30-8:30pm; Oct.-Feb. 9:30am-12:30pm and 1:30-5pm. €9, ages 6-15 €4.50. Combined ticket with the Palazzo e Giardini Borromeo €16, children €7. Audio tour €2.50.)

If you have budgeted a day for island hopping, stop across the lake from Stresa at the small monastery ◪**Santa Caterina del Sasso.** Tucked along the coast, a few miles away from Laveno, the monastery is difficult to reach other than by boat; the complete isolation is worth exploring for the amount of late-Renaissance artwork inside, the highlight being an early 17th-century fresco of God the Father. (www.provincia.va.it/preziosita/ukvarese/itin/maggiore/gemonio.htm. Open daily Apr.-Oct. 8:30am-noon and 2:30-6pm. Nov.-Mar. 9am-noon and 2-5pm. Free.)

Ferries (☎800 55 18 01; www.navigazionelaghi.it) run from Stresa to Carciano, Isola Bella, Isola Superiore, Baveno, Isola Madre, then Pallanza, and ending in Intra. Ferries leave Stresa every 15-30min. from 7:10am to 7:10pm and return from Intra until 6:15pm. A one-day ticket for unlimited travel between Stresa, Pallanza, and the three islands costs €11.50 (including Intra €14). Individual tickets from Stresa to Isola Bella or Superiore cost €6.40, and to Isola Madre €8.20. All tickets are valid until returning to departure point. A single day combined entrance to Isola Bella, Isola Superiore, and Isola Madre with ferry ride costs €28.

SANTA MARIA MAGGIORE ☎0324

Carved out by the same glaciers that melted to become Lake Maggiore and Lake Orta, Valle Vigezzo (VAL-lay vee-JET-soh) is a gorgeous valley with few tourists. The area has served as artistic inspiration so often that it is now known as "Painter's Valley." Santa Maria Maggiore (SAN-ta ma-REE-ah ma-JO-reh; pop.

1280), the lake's largest town, is bordered by the smaller towns of Arvogno, Craveggia, Re, and Toceno. Perhaps the biggest highlight, however, is journeying through the valley to witness its stunning landscape resplendent with enormous mountains, fields, villages, waterfalls, and streams.

⊏ TRANSPORTATION. From Stresa, take the **train** to Domodossola (☎24 20 55; 40min., 14 per day 6:37am-11:01pm, €2.65), then transfer to the SSIF (or Centovalli) line by exiting the station, going left, and then underground; take the train toward Locarno, getting off at Santa Maria Maggiore (40min.; 17 per day 5:30am-7:58pm, last return 8:28pm; €2.53.) The ticket office (☎24 20 55) is open 20min. before train departures. For a **taxi**, call ☎92 405 or 98 045.

⟁ PRACTICAL INFORMATION. From the train station on **Piazzale Diaz**, cross **Via Luigi Cadorna** to **Via Dante**, which ends at **Via Antonio Rosmini**, where you turn right to reach **Piazza Risorgimento**, the *centro*. The **Ufficio Turistico Pro Loco**, P. Risorgimento 4, offers free maps of the town and valley, and **Internet** access. (☎94 565. Internet access €3 per 30min. Open in summer M-Sa 10am-noon and 4-7pm, Su 10am-noon; in winter Sa 10am-noon and 4-7pm, Su 10am-noon.) Follow V. Cavalli from P. Risorgimento until it becomes V. Rossetti Valentini to reach **Banca Popolare di Novara**. (☎95 002. Open M-F 8:20am-1:20pm and 2:35-3:35pm.) In case of **emergency**, call the **carabinieri** (☎95 007) or the **guardia medica turistica**, V. Guglielmo Marconi 4. (☎94 360. Open July-Aug. daily 2-6pm.) A **pharmacy** is on V. Matteotti 5. (☎95 018. Open M-Sa 9am-12:30pm and 3:30-7:30pm, Su 9am-12:30pm.) The **post office** is at V. R. Vaneltini 26. (☎90 53 87. Open M-F 8:30am-2pm, Sa 8:30am-1pm.) **Postal Code:** 28857.

⌂⌂ ACCOMMODATIONS AND FOOD. There are few budget accommodations in Santa Maria Maggiore. **B&B Ül Ruska ❷**, V. Matteotti 84, offers quaint rooms with friendly service. (☎94 717. Breakfast included. Call ahead. €35 per person. Cash only.) For local food, head to **Osteria Bar Al Cortiletto ❸**, V. Cavalli 20, in a charming, hidden location. (☎90 56 78. Pizza €4-7.50. *Primi* €6.50-7.50, *secondi* €8.50-13. Cover €1.80. Open daily 9am-midnight. Closed in winter Th. AmEx/MC/V.)

◉⛰ SIGHTS AND OUTDOOR ACTIVITIES. There are a variety of attractions in the Valle Vigezzo, in and around Santa Maria Maggiore. One of the main attractions in Santa Maria Maggiore is the **Museo dello Spazzacamino (Chimney Sweep Museum)** in the Parco

LOCAL LEGEND

IT'S A BLOODY MIRACLE!

The small town of Re, near Santa Maria Maggiore, has been a center for pilgrims since 1494. In that year a man named Zuccone and his friend were gambling over the Italian game *piodella*. Zuccone, unfortunately for him, was the loser. Furious and defeated, Zuccone trudged through the streets until he came upon a painting of the Virgin and Child beneath the arcade of the church. He became enraged at the expression of the Madonna, which seemed calm and unconcerned with his misfortune. In his rage, he hurled the rock from the game at the Virgin, striking her on the forehead. Immediately after realizing what he had done, he fell to his knees, but his remorse quickly turned into fear and he ran away.

Around dawn, an old man came by to open up the church only to discover that the Virgin was bleeding from her forehead! For the next day and night, people came from far and wide to see the miracle; the painting continued to pour out thick blood intermittently for 20 days.

Today, the sanctuary (p. 304) holds the tablecloth covered in blood and lights up a slightly blood-speckled wall behind the altar. Pilgrims still come to venerate the Madonna del Sangue, and it is said that the Virgin bestows health and safety upon them for their piety.

Villa Antonia, which holds a small collection of clothing and equipment, and sends visitors through a tunnel of pictures, sounds, and smells. Young Vigezzo inhabitants, due to the poor quality of the soil in the region, were forced to emigrate as chimney sweeps to cities throughout Europe. The museum is a dedication to those who returned and used their earnings to boost the valley's economy. (☎90 56 75; www.museospazzacamino.it. Open June-Sept. daily 10am-noon and 3-6pm; Oct.-May Sa-Su only. €2.) The **Santuario della Madonna del Sangue** houses the painting of the *Madonna del Sangue* (Madonna of the Blood), which is said to have bled for 20 days in 1494 after being hit with a stone. To get to the sanctuary, take the Piana di Vigezzo Funivia (see below) to the stop in the town of Re. (☎97 016. Open daily 8am-9pm. Free.) The best outdoor excursions in the area are to the **Parco Nazionale Val Grande,** created in 1992. The 15,000 hectare park is less than 100km from Milan; it can be accessed only by car from the A8 motorway from Milan or the A26 from Genoa/Turin, exiting at "Gravellona Toce" and then taking Ossola highway toward the Simplon Pass. The park is not only known for its wilderness but also its relics of a once-major alpine civilization. Ask the tourist office for park info, and acquire hiking itineraries and maps at the office inside the park entrance. (☎0323 55 79 60; www.parcovalgrande.it.) **Arvogno** (1260m), starts hiking paths toward higher peaks, and the **La Cima chair lift** takes visitors ever higher on summer weekends (8:30, 11:30am, 2:30, and 5pm). In winter, it becomes part of the Valle Vigezzo ski ticket, which also includes the **Piana di Vigezzo Funivia** (cable car) that mounts to **Colma Trubbio** (2064m) from **Prestinone.** (Ascents daily 8am-5:30pm. 1-way €7, children €4; round-trip €10/6. Full-day ski pass M-F €19, Sa-Su €22; children 4-12 €14.50/17.50. Half-day pass €13/15, children €10/13. Equipment rental available at top of *funivia*. AmEx/MC/V.)

ORTA SAN GIULIO
☎0322

Orta San Giulio (OR-ta san JOO-lee-oh; pop. 1120) is the gateway to Lake Orta—by far the smallest and least touristed of the lakes—though just as striking as any of them. The 19th-century villas that line the narrow, cobblestone streets evoke the very best of old Italy. Difficult to reach without a car, the town has drawn many to its secluded location. In fact, the privacy is precisely what drew Friedrich Nietzsche here in 1882 with his young love, Lou Salome, in order to escape the watchful eye of her mother. Nietzsche claimed he couldn't remember whether or not the two had kissed, because the views had sent him into a state of grace.

■ TRANSPORTATION. The Orta-Miasino **train** station is 1.5-2km from old Orta, which is on a peninsula; many simply walk (downhill from the station; ask for a map in the *bar*/ticket office). Down the hill from the train station, a small red train, Il Trenino di Orta, shuttles passengers between the intersection of V. Panoramica and V. Giuseppe Fava (in front of the tourist office that is halfway on the walk) and the *centro;* train also stops in front of Sacro Monte. (☎347 48 83 509. 5min.; Apr. 15-Oct. 15 M-Tu and Th-Su every 15-30min. 9am-8pm, Oct. 16-Apr. 14 Su; €2, children €1; round-trip €3/2.) If coming by train from Stresa, switch lines at Premosello (1½hr.; 4 per day 6:37am-6:47pm, return 6:28am-8:17pm; €3), getting off at Orta-Miasino. In Orta, buy train tickets at the nearby *bar.* (Open M-F 6:30am-midnight, Sa 7:30pm-midnight.) You can also access Orta-Miasino from Domodossola, north of Stresa on the Milan-Domodossola line. If coming or going to Milano Centrale, switch trains at Novara to the line ending in Domodossola (9 per day 6:39am-7:20pm, €4.70). **Bus 30** (or Nerini Mini-Bus; ☎0323 55 21 72; €2.70) runs to Orta from Stresa. In Stresa the bus departs from in front of the church near the ferry station (5 per day 7:40am-5pm, 1hr.). In Orta the bus departs from the bus lane in Ple. Prarondo (1hr., 3 per day 11am-6pm). Small **motoscafi** (motorboats) in P.

Motta weave back and forth from Isola di San Giulio to the mainland during the summer upon request. (☎333 60 50 288; www.motoscafipubbliciorta.it. 10min.; Apr.-Oct. every 15min. daily 9am-6:30pm; Nov.-Mar. every 40min. 9am-5pm; €3.50). Navigazione Lago d'Orta runs larger boats between the island and the mainland. (☎84 48 62. 5min.; Apr.-Sept. daily every 30min. 9:55am-7:10pm, Oct. Sa-Su, Nov. Su; €2.50-4.) On the mainland call a **taxi** (☎328 39 11 670 or 335 65 56 340).

◪ PRACTICAL INFORMATION. The *centro* is **Piazza Motta.** Amble along **Via Olina,** which becomes **Via Bossi,** then **Via Gippini** to reach **Via Motta** and the footpath, Strada del Movero, and ultimately **Lungo Lario 11 Settembre,** where you can sunbathe on the docks or jump off them into the clear blue water. There are two **tourist offices** in Orta. The primary one is on V. Panoramica, across the street and downhill from Villa Crespi. To reach the office from the train station, exit left from the station, make the 1st left downhill, and continue through the rotunda straight ahead. (☎90 56 14 or 90 51 63; inforta@distrettolaghi.it. Open W-Su 9am-1pm and 2-6pm.) The 2nd office is in the Palazzo Comunale, V. Bossi 11, straight past P. Motta. (☎90 155; www.ortainfo.com. Open Apr.-Oct. M and W-F 11am-1pm and 2-6pm, Sa-Su 10am-1pm and 2-6pm.) **Banca Popolare di Novara** is at P. Ragazzoni 16. (☎90 57 01. Open M-F 8:20am-1:30pm and 2:35-3:35pm, Sa 8:20-11:20am.) A **pharmacy,** V. Albertolletti 10, is off P. Motta. (☎90 117. Open M-W and F-Sa 9am-12:30pm and 3:30-7:30pm. D/MC/V.) In case of **emergency,** call the **carabinieri,** V. Comoli 142 (☎90 114), in nearby Omegna or an **ambulance** (☎81 500). The only **Internet** point is at the hotel booking center on V. Poli 13. (☎90 55 32. €4 per 5min., €10 per 30min. Open daily 9am-7pm. Cash only.) They also rent bikes. (☎90 51 88. €7 per half-day, €10 per day.) The **post office,** P. Ragazzoni 9, offers **currency exchange.** (☎90 157. Open M-F 8:30am-2pm, Sa 8:30am-1pm.) **Postal Code:** 28016.

▐▐ ACCOMMODATIONS AND FOOD. Orta's relative seclusion means high accommodation prices. Just down the street from Villa Crespi, **B&B Villa Pinin ❸,** on V. Fava, is the best deal in town. Admire a gorgeous view of the lake from any spot in the spacious yard. (☎90 55 05 or 340 00 69 323. Reservations required. High-season doubles €80, low-season €60. Cash only.) The enormous **Villa Franceso ❸,** V. Prisciola 6, has clean rooms, a breakfast room, restaurant, bar, garden, and good views from the large upstairs patio. Facing the train station, go left and continue 300m down the road. (☎90 258; www.hotelsanfrancesco.it. Breakfast included. Singles €34; doubles €56. MC/V.) **Piccolo Hotel Olina ❹,** V. Olina 40, houses guests in spacious, modern rooms with wood floors, private baths, and TV. (☎90 56 56 or from the US 800-220-6201; www.ortainfo.com. Breakfast included. Free parking. Reception 8am-10pm. Singles €50-65; doubles €65-80; triples €95-110. Discounts for longer stays. AmEx/MC/V.) The restaurant downstairs offers *pesce di lago* plates (*Primi* €10-13, *secondi* €13-20. Discount for hotel patrons.) The lakeside **◪Camping Orta ❶,** V. Domodossola 28, welcomes campers with a private beach, bikes (€4 per hr., €8 per half-day), kayaks, and windsurfing boards (€8 per half-day) for rent. (☎90 26; www.campingorta.it. Wash €3, dry €3. €5-6.50 per person, €3.50-4.50 per child under 12, €8-15 per tent, €4.5.50 per car. Bungalows €65-90. Electricity €2. Hot showers free. Cash only.)

Local cuisine is known for *tapulon* (spiced, minced donkey and horse meat cooked in red wine) eaten with cornmeal polenta, typically only served in winter. There isn't a better place to try the locally produced wine, *Ghemme,* or the native cheese, *Tomo di Motarone,* than at **◪Al Boeuc ❷,** V. Bersani 28, a tiny wine bar one street inland from P. Motta. Large *bruschette* (€10) or mixed *salame* plates go well with wine. (☎339 58 40 039. Open M and W-Su 11am-3pm and 6:30pm-1am. Cash only.) In season, *Ghemme* is available with other local recipes at **Taberna Antico Agnello ❸,** V. Olina 18, where second-story windows overlook the *piazza* below. (☎90 259. *Primi* €6.50-9, *secondi* €12-13.50. Cover €2.50. Open M and W-Su 12:30-2pm and 7:30-9:30pm, also Tu evenings in Aug. AmEx/MC/V.) At night, the mature crowd heads to classy **Caffè and Jazz ❷,** V. Olina 13, where Thursday (July-Sept.) means live jazz at 10pm. (☎91 17 00. Wine €3-5 per glass. *Panini* and *bruschetta* €3-6. Salads €8-9. Open Tu-Su 11am-3pm and 6pm-1am. Cash only.) Since 1228, P. Motta has had a weekly Wednesday market, selling produce, clothes, and household necessities. Also, the food market **La Dispensa,** V. Bersani 38, off P. Motta, and the fruit market next door offer *panini* (€2.30-2.80) and picnic basics. (Open M-Tu and Th-Sa 9am-6:30pm, W 9am-2pm, Su 10am-6:30pm.)

◪ **SIGHTS.** At the intersection of V. Panoramica and V. G. Fava, the ornate **Villa Crespi,** which now houses a hotel, was built in 1873 in an Arabian style to satisfy cotton pioneer Cristoforo B. Crespi's nostalgia for his trips to the Orient. The large stone columns of the ground floor portico of the beautiful city hall, also known as the **"Palazzoto,"** dominate P. Motta. Right up V. Albertoletti is the **Chiesa Santa Maria Assunta,** a church built to celebrate the end of the 1485 plague. (Open daily 9am-6pm.) On the lake across from Orta lies the **Isola di San Giulio.** According to legend, the island was inhabited by ◪**dragons** and serpents until they were destroyed by Julius, a traveler from Greece, in the AD 4th century. Today it is inhabited by three families as well as a convent of 72 nuns who have taken a vow of silence. While the convent is not open to the public, the island can be visited by ferry or motorboat ride. Pedestrians can cover the tiny island on a cobblestone path (10min.), known as **Meditation Way,** where periodic multilingual markers comment on the beauty of silence. The 12th-century **Romanesque Basilica di San Giulio,** built on 4th-century foundations, is filled with Baroque ornamentation and adorned with pink cloud frescoes. The true masterpiece is the **pulpit,** carved from black *oira* stone. Downstairs, the skeleton of San Giulio, dressed in brocade robes and a golden mask, rests in a gold and glass sarcophagus. (Open daily 9:30am-12:15pm and 2-6:30pm. Modest dress required. Free.) A short 15min. hike off V. Panoramica onto V. della Cappelletta leads to the **Sacro Monte** monastic complex, a UNESCO World Heritage site. The complex holds 20 chapels filled with life-size, terra-cotta statues and frescoes that chart the life of St. Francis of Assisi. (☎91 19 60; monteorta@tin.it. Open daily in summer 9am-5pm; in winter and 9am-7pm. Free guided tours with reservations. Park open 24hr. Free.)

THE VENETO

From the rocky Dolomite foothills to the fertile Po valleys, the Veneto's (VEH-neh-toh) geography is as diverse as its history. Once loosely united under the Venetian Empire, the towns of the Veneto have retained their cultural independence; today, visitors are more likely to hear regional dialects than standard Italian. The region's marine supremacy, enviable location near the peninsula's mid-section, and heavy international and inter-provincial traffic have brought a variety of cuisines and cultural traditions. The influx of Austrian and Slovenian cultures has created a pleasant surprise for people who come expecting only mandolins and gondolas.

HIGHLIGHTS OF THE VENETO

BEHOLD St. Mark's remains at Venice's **Basilica di San Marco.** (p. 322)

SERENADE your loved one during a **gondola ride** down Venice's Grand Canal. (p. 324)

FLIRT with your star-crossed lover in **fair Verona,** where Shakespeare set the scene for *Romeo and Juliet.* (p. 342)

WANDER the hallowed halls of the Università di Padova, where **luminaries** such as Dante, Galileo, and Copernicus set the academic world on fire. (p. 338)

VENICE (VENEZIA)   ☎041

From its hedonistic, devil-may-care Carnevale, to the repentant God-may-care-too services of its soaring marble cathedrals, Venice (in Italian, "ve-NET-see-ah"; pop. 60,000) is a mystical, waterlogged city. Founded by Roman fishermen in the 11th century, the city soon became a world-class trading post between East and West. Global commerce depended on Venetian merchants to supply silks, spices, and coffee for over a century before its trade dominance diminished. Since then, seabound ships have been replaced with gondolas as Venice has traded its naval prowess for a booming tourism industry. Today, the romantic arched bridges and waterways that lap at ancient doorways are its everyday sidewalks. People flock year-round to float down labyrinthine canals, peer into delicate blown-glass, and gaze awestruck at the master works of Titian, Tintoretto, and Giorgione. While dodging hoards of tourists and pigeons and getting lost in Venice's maze of alleys and canals will prove inevitable, the city is nonetheless a worthwhile wonder.

✈ INTERCITY TRANSPORTATION

Flights: Aeroporto Marco Polo (☎26 09 260; www.veniceairport.it), 10km north of the city. **ATVO shuttle bus** (☎042 13 83 671) links the airport to P. Roma on the main island (30min., hourly 8am-midnight, €3). ATVO ticket office open daily 5am-8:40pm.

Trains: Stazione Santa Lucia (☎89 20 21), the main station, is in the northwestern corner. When coming into the city, disembark at S. Lucia, not Mestre on the mainland. Info office open daily 7am-9pm. Ticket windows open M-F 8:30am-7:30pm, Sa-Su 9am-1:30pm and 2-5:30pm. AmEx/MC/V. To: **Bologna** (2hr., 30 per day 12:04am-7:57pm, €8.20); **Florence** (3hr., 8 per day 6:32am-6:58pm, €30); **Milan** (3hr., 19 per day 5:17am-9:07pm, €13); **Padua** (45min., 75 per day 12:04am-11:40pm, €2.70); **Rome** (4½hr., 7 per day 12:04am-6:32pm, €57); **Trieste** (2hr., 26 per day 12:10am-

10:47pm, €8.20). Reservations may be required; check info booth. **Lost and found** (*oggetti rinvenuti;* ☎78 55 31; open daily 6am-midnight) and **luggage storage** by track #14 (**Practical Information,** p. 315).

Buses: ACTV (☎24 24; www.hellovenezia.it), in Ple. Roma. Open daily 7:30am-8pm. Office open daily 7am-8pm. Ticket window open daily 6am-11:30pm. **ACTV long-distance carrier** runs buses to **Padua** (1hr., every 30min. 6:45am-11pm, €4.20) and **Treviso** (1hr., every 30min. 4:55am-8:55pm, €3). Cash only.

✠ ORIENTATION

Venice comprises 118 islands in a lagoon, connected to the mainland city of Mestre by a thin causeway. With the **Canale Grande** snaking throughout, the city is divided into seven *sestieri* (sections): **San Marco** in the center, encircled by **Cannaregio** to the north, **San Polo** and **Santa Croce** to the west, **Dorsoduro** along the southwestern shore, **Castello** along the eastern shore, and **Giudecca** to the south, separated from Venice proper by the large Giudecca canal. *Sestieri* boundaries are vague but should be of some use for navigating the city's narrow alleys.

Venice's layout consists of a labyrinth of *calli* (narrow streets), *campi* (squares), *liste* (large streets), and *ponti* (bridges). It's practically impossible to avoid getting lost in Venice—maps are of little use, as many streets are either too narrow to be plotted, do not display street signs, or have erratic street numbers. To get by, simply learn to navigate like a true Venetian. Locate the following sights on the map: **Ponte di Rialto** (in the center), **Piazza San Marco** (central south), **Ponte Accademia** (southwest), **Ferrovia** (or Stazione Santa Lucia, the train station; northwest), and **Piazzale Roma** (southwest of the station). These are Venice's main orientation points. A plethora of yellow signs posted throughout the city point the way to all the major landmarks and bridges.

When trying to find a place, locate the *sestiere*, then find a nearby landmark, and follow signs in that general direction. As you get closer, use the address numbers and busier streets to work your way toward the destination. As a general rule, follow the arrows on the yellow signs as precisely as possible. If a street suddenly leads into a *campo* and branches in five different directions, pick the street that follows the original direction of the arrow as closely as possible until reaching the next sign. Note that in Venice, addresses are not specific to a particular street, and every building in a *sestiere* is given a number ("San Marco 3434" is a typical address). Buildings are generally numbered consecutively, but there are also often large jumps, so the next number could be one block away or down an alleyway.

To get to **Piazza San Marco** or the **Rialto Bridge** from the train station, take V #82 (30min., every 20min.) or V #1 (40min., every 10min.). On foot, follow signs to P. San Marco, starting left of the station on Lista de Spagna.

◖ **V MARKS THE SPOT.** Vaporetti stops appear in the text as V.

⊟ LOCAL TRANSPORTATION

The cheapest—and often the fastest—way to see the city is to walk through it. Pedestrians can cross the Grand Canal at the *ponti* Scalzi, Rialto, and Accademia. ◖**Traghetti** (gondola ferry boats) traverse the canal at seven locations, including Ferrovia, San Marcuola, Cà d'Oro, and Rialto (€0.50). *Vaporetti* (water buses) provide 24hr. service around the city, with reduced service after midnight. Tickets cost €5 for the Grand Canal. An extended pass is more economical for longer visits (24hr. pass €12, 3-day €25). Schedules, route maps, and tickets are available at tourist offices (**Practical Information,** p. 315). Tickets are also sold in front of stops. Stock

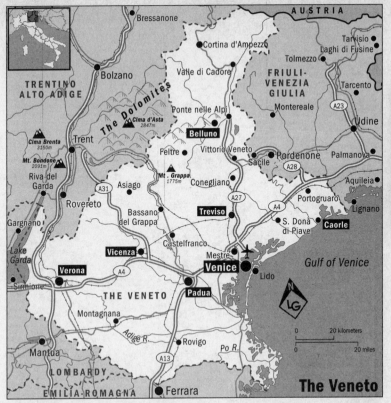

The Veneto

up on tickets by asking for an unvalidated pass *(non timbrato)*, then validate it before boarding by inserting the ticket into one of the yellow boxes located at each stop. Unvalidated tickets risk a fine; the "confused foreigner" act won't work in a town where tourists often outnumber residents two to one.

MAIN VAPORETTO LINES

V #82, 4: Run from P. San Marco, up the Giudecca Canal, to the station, down the Grand Canal, back to P. San Marco, and then to Lido. Always crowded, with long lines.

V #1: Has a similar route to #82, but can be less crowded; offers a nice view of the canalside palaces. 10min. slower than #82, and with more stops.

V #41, 42, 51, 52: Circumnavigate Venice. #41 and 51 run from the station, through the Giudecca Canal to Lido, along the northern edge of the city, and back to the station; #42 and 52 follow the same route in the opposite direction.

V #LN: Runs from F. Nuove to Murano, Burano, and Lido with connections to Torcello.

Car Rental: Expressway, P. Roma 496/N (☎52 23 000; www.expresswayautoleggio.com). From €65 per day, €255 per week. Free car delivery to and from airport. 18+. Open M-F 8am-noon and 1:30-6pm, Sa-Su 8am-noon and 1:30-4:30pm. *Let's Go* discount 10%. AmEx/MC/V. **Hertz,** P. Roma 496/F (☎52 84 091; fax 52 00 614). From €87 per day in summer; €58 per day in winter. Credit card required. 25+. Open M-F 8am-6pm, Sa-Su 8am-1pm. AmEx/MC/V.

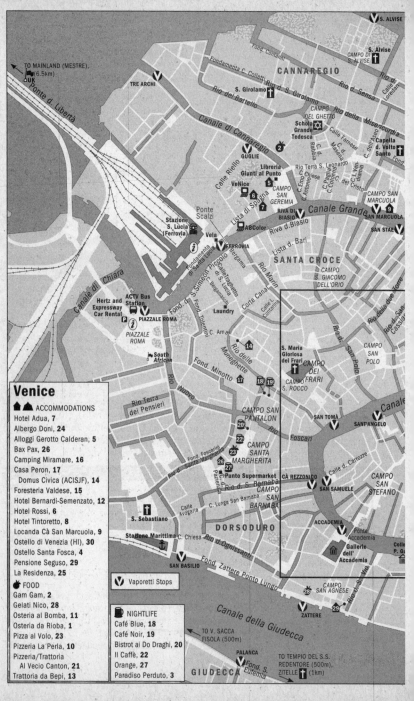

Venice

🏠🏠🏠 ACCOMMODATIONS
Hotel Adua, **7**
Albergo Doni, **24**
Alloggi Gerotto Calderan, **5**
Bax Pax, **26**
Camping Miramare, **16**
Casa Peron, **17**
  Domus Civica (ACISJF), **14**
Foresteria Valdese, **15**
Hotel Bernardi-Semenzato, **12**
Hotel Rossi, **6**
Hotel Tintoretto, **8**
Locanda Cà San Marcuola, **9**
Ostello di Venezia (HI), **30**
Ostello Santa Fosca, **4**
Pensione Seguso, **29**
La Residenza, **25**

🍴 FOOD
Gam Gam, **2**
Gelati Nico, **28**
Osteria al Bomba, **11**
Osteria da Rioba, **1**
Pizza al Volo, **23**
Pizzeria La Perla, **10**
Pizzeria/Trattoria
  Al Vecio Canton, **21**
Trattoria da Bepi, **13**

Ⓥ Vaporetti Stops

🍷 NIGHTLIFE
Café Blue, **18**
Café Noir, **19**
Bistrot ai Do Draghi, **20**
Il Caffè, **22**
Orange, **27**
Paradiso Perduto, **3**

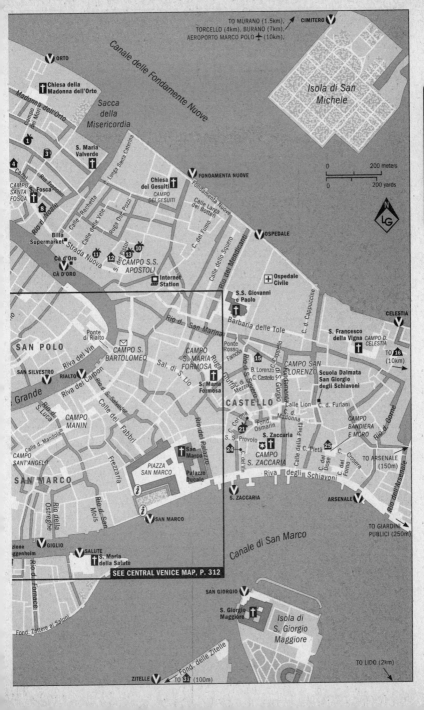

TO MURANO (1.5km),
TORCELLO (4km), BURANO (7km),
AEROPORTO MARCO POLO (10km),

CIMITERO

Isola di San
Michele

ORTO

Chiesa della
Madonna dell'Orto

Madonna dell'Orto

Sacca
della
Misericordia

Canale delle Fondamente Nuove

S. Maria
Valverde

Chiesa
del Gesuiti

FONDAMENTA NUOVE

CAMPO
DEL GESUITI

Calle Lunga Santa Caterina

Calle Larga
del Botteri

Fondamenta Nuove

OSPEDALE

CAMPO
SANTA
FOSCA

S. Fosca

Calle Racchetta

Calle delle Vele

Ruga Dei Oro

C. dei Fumi

C. del Forno

Calle dello Squero

Rio dei Mendicanti

Ospedale
Civile

Billa
Supermarket

Strada Nuova

Cà d'Oro

CÀ D'ORO

Cal de Pistor

CAMPO S.S.
APOSTOLI

Internet
Station

S.S. Giovanni
e Paolo

Barbaria delle Tole

C. d. Cappuccine

CELESTIA

S. Francesco
della Vigna

CAMPO D.
CELESTIA

TO 16
(10km)

SAN POLO

Ponte
di Rialto

Rio d. San Marina

CAMPO S.
BARTOLOMEO

CAMPO
S. MARIA
FORMOSA

Ponte
Rosso

B. Lorenzo

C. Castello

CAMPO SAN
LORENZO

Scuola Dalmata
San Giorgio
degli Schiavoni

Riva del Vin

SAN SILVESTRO

RIALTO

Riva del Carbon

Sal. di S. Lio

S. Maria
Formosa

Calle Lion

C. d. Furlani

Grande

Calle del Fabbri

CASTELLO

CAMPO
BANDIERA
E MORO

TO ARSENALE
(150km)

S. Luca

CAMPO
MANIN

Calle dei Fabbri

Corona

S.S.
Provolo

Calle d.
Madonna

Fond.
Osmarin

S. Zaccaria

C. Pietà

C. Crosera

Rio dela Gorna

Rio dell'Arsenale

CAMPO
SANT'ANGELO

Frezzaria

PIAZZA
SAN MARCO

San
Marco

Palazzo
Ducale

CAMPO
S. ZACCARIA

Riva degli Schiavoni

C. del
Dose

C. del
Forno

TO GIARDINI
PUBLICI (250km)

SAN MARCO

Rio di San Moisè

Calle de Mandola

Rio della Ostreghe

SAN MARCO

S. ZACCARIA

ARSENALE

GIGLIO

SALUTE

S. Maria
della Salute

Canale di San Marco

zione
ggenheim

Fond. Zattere ai Saloni

SEE CENTRAL VENICE MAP, P. 312

SAN GIORGIO

S. Giorgio
Maggiore

Isola di
S. Giorgio
Maggiore

TO LIDO (2km)

ZITELLE

TO 31 (100km)

Fond. delle Zitelle

0   200 meters

0   200 yards

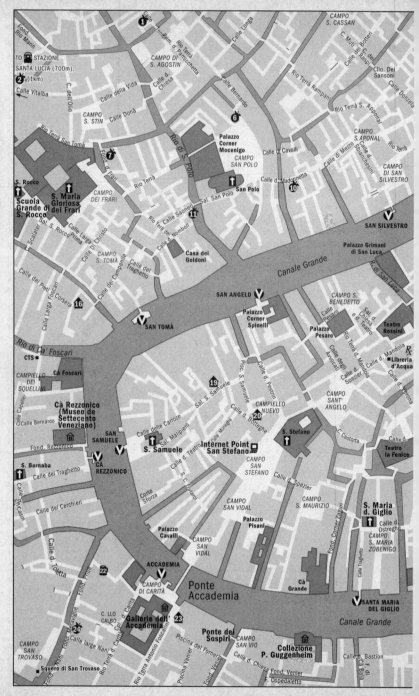

THE VENETO

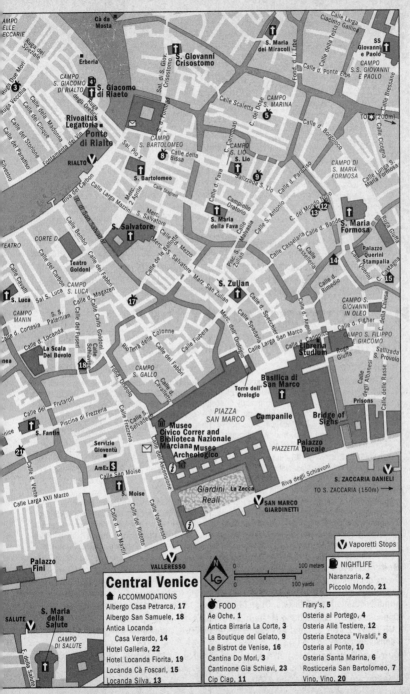

Central Venice

⬛ ACCOMMODATIONS
Albergo Casa Petrarca, 17
Albergo San Samuele, 18
Antica Locanda
  Casa Verardo, 14
Hotel Galleria, 22
Hotel Locanda Fiorita, 19
Locanda Cà Foscari, 15
Locanda Silva, 13

🍴 FOOD
Ae Oche, 1
Antica Birraria La Corte, 3
La Boutique del Gelato, 9
Le Bistrot de Venise, 16
Cantina Do Mori, 3
Cantinone Gia Schiavi, 23
Cip Ciap, 11

Frary's, 5
Osteria al Portego, 4
Osteria Alle Testiere, 12
Osteria Enoteca "Vivaldi," 8
Osteria al Ponte, 10
Osteria Santa Marina, 6
Rosticceria San Bartolomeo, 7
Vino, Vino, 20

🍷 NIGHTLIFE
Naranzaria, 2
Piccolo Mondo, 21

Ⓥ Vaporetti Stops

0 100 meters
0 100 yards

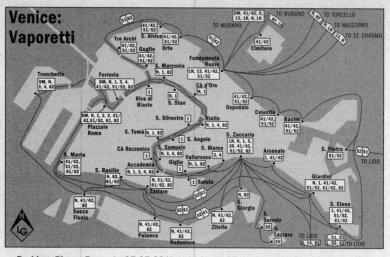

Venice: Vaporetti

Parking: Piazza Roma (☎27 27 301) and island of **Tronchetto** (☎52 07 555). Around €20 per day. 24hr. Parking is considerably cheaper on the mainland. Consider parking in **Mestre** (1st train stop out of Venice).

🄯 PRACTICAL INFORMATION

TOURIST AND FINANCIAL SERVICES

Tourist Offices:

APT Tourist Offices are located all over the city. Avoid the train station office, as it is always packed with people. **Branches:** P. Roma (☎24 11 499; open daily 9:30am-1pm and 1:30-4:30pm; AmEx/MC/V); P. S. Marco 71/F, directly opposite the Basilica (☎/fax 52 98 740; open daily 9am-3:30pm; AmEx/MC/V); Lido, Gran Viale 6/A (☎52 65 721; open June-Sept. daily 9am-noon and 3-6pm). Every location offers pricey city tours, *vaporetto* tickets, schedules (€0.60), the **Rolling Venice Card,** and theater and concert tickets. Ask for the magazine *Leo* or visit www.turismovenezia.com for info about history, sights, and activities.

VeneziaSi (☎800 84 30 06), in train station, to right of tourist office. Finds available hotel rooms and makes same-day reservations in Venice and Rome (€2). Open daily 8am-9pm. **Branches** at P. Roma (☎52 28 640) and airport (☎54 15 133) also book rooms (€2). If you call (instead of going in person), there is no charge for booking reservations.

Rolling Venice Card: Provides discounts at over 200 restaurants, cafes, hotels, museums, and shops for people ages 14-29. Tourist offices provide lists of participating vendors. Card costs €4 and is valid for 1 year from date of purchase. A 3-day *vaporetto* pass with card discount costs €18 instead of the undiscounted €25. Purchase it at the **ACTV VeLa** office (☎27 47 650), in P. Roma, at all APT tourist offices, and at ACTV VeLa kiosks next to the **Ferrovia, Rialto, S. Marco,** and **Vallaresso** *vaporetto* stops. Open daily 7am-8pm.

Budget Travel: CTS, Fondamenta Tagliapietra, Dorsoduro 3252 (☎52 05 660; www.cts.it). From Campo S. Barnaba, cross bridge closest to the church and follow the road through the small *piazza*, then turn left at the foot of the large bridge. Sells ISICs and discounted plane tickets. Open M-F 9:30am-1:30pm and 2:30-6pm. MC/V.

Consulates: UK consulate in Mestre, Ple. Donatori di Sangue 2 (☎50 55 990). Closest **US** (☎02 29 03 51) and **Australian** (☎02 77 70 41) consulates in Milan; **Canadian** consulate (☎049 87 64 33) in Padua.

Currency Exchange: Use banks whenever possible for best rates, and inquire about additional fees beforehand. The streets around San Marco, San Polo, and the train station are full of banks and **ATMs.**

American Express: Calle San Moisè, San Marco 1471 (☎52 00 844 for lost or stolen checks). Exit P. S. Marco facing away from the basilica and walk 2min. **Currency exchange,** but no commission for members or Rolling Venice cardholders. **Western Union** also available. M-F 9am-5:30pm, Sa 9am-12:30pm. Closed in winter Sa.

LOCAL SERVICES

Luggage Storage: At the train station. €3.80 for 1st 5hr., €0.60 per hr. up to 12hr., €0.20 thereafter. Open daily 6am-midnight. Cash only. **Deposito Pullman Bar,** P. Roma 497/M (☎52 31 107). €3.50 per day. Open daily 6am-9pm. Cash only.

English-Language Bookstores:

Libreria Studium, San Marco 337/C (☎/fax 52 22 382). From P. S. Marco, turn left on Calle delle Canonico between the basilica and the clock tower; it's the last shop on the right. Largest selection in town, with novels and guidebooks. Rolling Venice discount 10%. Open M-Sa 9am-7:30pm, Su 9:30am-1:30pm. AmEx/MC/V.

Libreria Linea D'Acqua, Calle della Mandola, San Marco 3717/D (☎52 24 030). Follow Calle Cortesia out of Campo Manin. Open M-F 10:30am-12:30pm and 4-7pm, Sa 11:30am-12:30pm and 4-5pm. AmEx/MC/V.

Giunti Al Punto, Campo S. Geremia, Cannaregio 283/A (☎27 50 152). Open M and W-Sa 9am-midnight, Tu 9am-8pm, Su 10am-midnight. MC/V.

Laundromat: Lavanderie Self-Service, Calle della Chioverette, Santa Croce 665/B (☎348 30 17 457). From Ponte Scalzi, turn right on Fondamenta San Simeon Piccolo, and take first left on Calle del Traghetto de S. Lucia. Laundromat is on the right. Wash €3.50 per 30min., dry €3 per 20min. Detergent €1. Open daily 7:30am-10:30pm.

Public Toilets: AMAV W.C. Under white and blue signs. €0.50. Open daily 9am-6pm.

Disabled visitors: Informa Handicap (☎27 48 144) offers assistance to physically disabled and deaf travelers in Italy. Free braille maps. Open Th 9am-1pm and 3-5pm. **APT tourist office** provides a list of wheelchair-accessible lodgings in Venice. Pick up a free **map** of the city outlining wheelchair-friendly routes in each *sestiere*, keys for wheelchair lifts at the bridges. V #1 and 82 are wheelchair-accessible.

EMERGENCY AND COMMUNICATIONS

Carabinieri: Campo San Zaccaria, Castello 4693/A. **Questura,** Fondamenta S. Lorenzo, Castello 5056 (☎27 05 511).

Pharmacy: Farmacia Italo-Inglese, Calle della Mandola, San Marco 3717 (☎52 24 837). Follow Calle Cortesia out of Campo Manin. There are no 24hr. pharmacies in Venice, but late-night and weekend pharmacies rotate. After-hours rotations posted outside. Open Apr.-Nov. M-F 9am-1:30pm and 2:30-7:30pm, Sa 3-7:30pm; Dec.-Mar. M-F 9am-12:30pm and 3:45-7:30pm, Sa 9am-12:45pm. MC/V.

Hospital: Ospedale Civile, Campo Giovanni e Paolo Santissimi, Castello (☎52 94 111).

Internet Access:

ABColor, Lista di Spagna, Cannaregio 220 (☎52 44 380; www.abcolor.it). Look for the "@" symbol on yellow sign, left off the main street heading from train station. Regular rate €6 per hr.; students €4 per hr. Printing €0.15 per page. Open M-Sa 10am-8pm. Cash only.

Internet Station, Cannaregio 5640. Just over the bridge heading towards S. Marco from C. Apostoli. €4 per 30min., €7 per hr. 20% discount for students with ID. Open M-Sa 10am-1pm and 3-11pm. Cash only.

VeNice, Lista di Spagna, Cannaregio 149 (☎27 58 217) has fax, webcams, and CD burning. Student discounts and international calling cards are available. €4.50 per 30min., €8 per hr. Printing €0.35 per page. Open daily 9am-11pm. MC/V over €10.

Internet Point San Stefano, Campo San Stefano, San Marco 2967 and 2958 (☎89 46 122). Also has laptop connections. €9 per hr., with ISIC or Rolling Venice €6. Open Tu-Sa 10:15am-11pm, Su 12:15-11pm. MC/V.

Post Office: Poste Venezia Centrale, Salizzada Fontego dei Tedeschi, San Marco 5554 (☎27 17 111), off Campo San Bartolomeo. *Fermoposta* at window #16. Open M-Sa 8:30am-

6:30pm. Cash only. **Branch:** (☎52 85 949), through the arcades at the end of P. S. Marco and opposite the basilica. ATM, pay phones, and a phone for the hearing-impaired. Open M-F 8:30am-2pm, Sa 8:30am-1pm. Cash only. **Postal Codes:** 30121 (Cannaregio), 30122 (Castello), 30123 (Dorsoduro), 30124 (San Marco), 30125 (San Polo), 30135 (Santa Croce).

ACCOMMODATIONS

Venetian hotels are often more expensive than those in other areas of Italy, but savvy travelers can find cheap alternatives if they explore their options early. Agree on a price before booking, and reserve at least one month ahead, especially in summer. Dorm-style rooms are sometimes available without reservations.

SAN MARCO

Surrounded by designer boutiques, souvenir stands, scores of restaurants, quasi-domesticated pigeons, and many of Venice's most popular sights, these accommodations are pricey options for those in search of Venice's showy side.

Albergo Casa Petrarca, Calle Schiavine, San Marco 4386 (☎52 00 430; fax 09 94 320). From Campo San Luca, follow Calle Fuseri; take 2nd left, and then turn right. Cheerful owners keep 7 bright rooms, most with bath and A/C. Breakfast included. Singles €80-90; doubles €125, with canal view €155. Extra bed €35. Cash only. ❹

Albergo San Samuele, Salizzada San Samuele, San Marco 3358 (☎52 28 045; www.albergosansamuele.it). Follow Calle delle Botteghe from Campo Santo Stefano; turn left on Salizzada San Samuele. 2min. from V: San Samuele, 10min. from P. S. Marco. Small but well-kept rooms with friendly staff and great location. Breakfast €5, served 5min. away at sister hotel Locanda Art Deco. Wi-Fi €5 per 5hr. Reception until midnight. Reserve 1-2 months ahead. Singles €55; doubles €75-90, with bath €100-120; triples €110-130. Check website for special deals. Cash only. ❸

Hotel Locanda Fiorita, Campiello Nuovo, San Marco 3457/A (☎52 34 754; www.locandafiorita.com). From Campo S. Stefano, take Calle del Pestrin, then climb onto the raised *campiello*. Three buildings with a courtyard and deep-red facade have rooms with TV and A/C. Annex nearby has satellite TV and Internet access. Breakfast included. Reception 24hr. Singles €110-140; doubles €98-230, depending on location and whether shower is private. 30% surcharge for extra bed. AmEx/MC/V. ❺

CANNAREGIO

The area around the Lista de Spagna has excellent budget options. Although it might require a 20min. *vaporetto* ride or a 15-25min. walk to most sights, the area bustles at night and offers *vaporetto* access from Fondamenta Nuove.

⧉Alloggi Gerotto Calderan, Campo San Geremia, Cannaregio 283 (☎71 55 62; www.casagerottocalderan.com). Half hostel, half hotel. Location makes it a great deal. Internet access €4 per hr. Check-in 2pm. Check-out 10am. Curfew 1am. Reservations recommended. Dorms €25; singles €40-50; doubles €50-90; triples €75-105. Rolling Venice discount 10%; lower prices with extended stay. Cash only. ❷

Hotel Bernardi-Semenzato, Calle dell'Oca, Cannaregio 4366 (☎52 27 257; www.hotel-bernardi.com). From V: Cà d'Oro, go right on Strada Nuova, left on Calle del Duca, and right on Calle dell'Oca. Squeaky clean, elegantly furnished rooms all with A/C and TV, some with private bath. Breakfast included. Internet access €5 per hr. Check-out 11am. Singles €30-40; doubles €70-75, with bath €95; quads €120-130. Rolling Venice discount 10% on larger rooms. AmEx/MC/V. ❸

Hotel Rossi, Lista de Spagna, Cannaregio 262 (☎71 61 84; www.hotelrossi.ve.it). Friendly owner keeps spacious rooms down a charming alley. A/C in summer. Breakfast included. Reception 24hr. Singles €44-53, with bath €54-69; doubles €77-92; triples €92-112; quads €107-132. Rolling Venice discount 10%. MC/V. ❹

Hotel Adua, Lista di Spagna, Cannaregio 233/A (☎71 61 84; www.aduahotel.com). Relatively well-sized rooms with serene decor, A/C, and TV. Singles €70, with bath €90; doubles €110/140; triples €170. Breakfast €7. Cheaper rooms at a different location in Castello; inquire at reception, or call for more info. AmEx/MC/V. ❺

Locanda Cà San Marcuola, Campo San Marcuola, Cannaregio 1763 (☎71 60 48; www.casanmarcuola.com). From the Lista di Spagna, follow signs for S. Marcuola. Large rooms have bath, A/C, refrigerator, and TV. Wheelchair-accessible. Breakfast included. Free Internet access. Reception 24hr. Singles €70-90; doubles €120-140; triples €140-170; quads €170-200. Discount with cash payment. AmEx/MC/V. ❹

Hotel Tintoretto, Santa Fosca, Cannaregio 2316 (☎72 15 22; www.hoteltintoretto.com). Head down Lista di Spagna from the station and follow the signs. Caring owners let cheery, wide rooms with bath, A/C, and TV. Many rooms have canal view. Amenities vary from hotel to annex. Breakfast included. Reception 24hr. Singles €41-140; doubles €74-195. Extra bed €37. Prices vary seasonally. AmEx/MC/V. ❹

Ostello Santa Fosca, Fondamenta Canal, Cannaregio 2372 (☎/fax 71 57 33). From Lista di Spagna, turn into Campo S. Fosca. Cross 1st bridge, and turn left on Fondamenta Canal. A brick walkway leads to this social hostel nestled in romantic courtyards. Student-operated and church-affiliated. Kitchen available July-Aug. Lockout 9:30-11:30am. Curfew July-Sept. 12:30am. Dorms €19; doubles €44. Discount €2 with ISIC or Rolling Venice, or for those under 26. MC/V. ❷

SAN POLO AND SANTA CROCE

In the western heart of Venice, these neighborhoods are hugged by the city's winding river, providing easy *vaporetto* access to any sight in the city.

Domus Civica (ACISJF), Campiello Chiovere Frari, San Polo 3082 (☎72 11 03; www.domuscivica.com). From station, cross Ponte Scalzi, and turn right. Turn left on Fondamenta dei Tolentini and left through the courtyard on Corte Amai; hostel is to the right after the bridge. Shared bath and TV room. Free Internet access. Reception 7am-12:30am. Strict curfew 12:30am. Open June-Sept. 25. Singles €31; doubles €54; triples €81. Rolling Venice discount 15%; ISIC discount 20%. AmEx/MC/V. ❸

Casa Peron, Salizzada S. Pantalon, Santa Croce 84 (☎71 00 21; www.casaperon.com). From station, cross Ponte Scalzi, turn right, and then left before the bridge; continue down Fondamenta Minotto. Casa Peron is on the left. Lace-accented lobby and white rooms with bath, some with A/C. Breakfast included. Reception until 1am. Singles €50; doubles €80, with bath €95; triples €100/120. V. ❸

DORSODURO

Situated near the Grand Canal between Chiesa dei Frari and Ponte Accademia, this *sestiere* is home to many pricey hotels. Spartan facades line the canals that trace the quiet streets of Dorsoduro. Art museums here draw visitors to canal-front real estate, while the interior remains a little-visited residential quarter surrounding Campo Santa Margherita, the city's most vibrant student social hub.

Bax Pax, C. Santa Margherita, Dorsoduro 2931 (☎09 94 554; baxpaxvenice@yahoo.it). As its name suggests, this spot is a backpacker's dream. At an unbelievable location in the heart of the student bar scene, large single-sex or co-ed dorm rooms are situated in a romantic *palazzo*. Free kitchen, laundry, and Internet. Breakfast included. Dorms €20-32. Cash only. ❸

Locanda Cà Foscari, Calle della Frescada, Dorsoduro 3887/B (☎71 04 01; www.locandacafoscari.com), in a quiet neighborhood. From V: San Tomà, turn left at the dead end, cross the bridge, turn right, then turn left at the alley. *Carnevale* masks embellish this tidy hotel, which offers basic rooms, some with private bath. Breakfast included. Reception 24hr. Reserve 2-3 months ahead. Closed July 28-1st wk. in Aug. Singles €68; doubles €78, with bath 98; triples €110/130; quads €130. MC/V. ❺

Hotel Galleria, Rio Terrà Antonio Foscarini, Dorsoduro 878/A (☎52 32 489; www.hotelgalleria.it), on the left facing the Accademia museum. Hardwood floors and fantastic proximity to the Grand Canal lend an aura of elegance. Breakfast included. Reception 24hr. Singles €110; doubles €110, with bath €130; triples €140/160. Extra bed 30% surcharge. AmEx/MC/V. ❺

Pensione Seguso, Fondamenta Zattere ai Saloni, Dorsoduro 779 (☎52 86 858; www.pensioneseguso.it). From V: Zattere, walk right. Views of the Giudecca Canal and antique decor. Breakfast included; half- and full-pension options available. Singles €80-110, with bath €100-120; doubles €120-150/180-190; triples €180-230. Prices vary seasonally. AmEx/MC/V. ❺

CASTELLO

Castello, the *sestiere* where most Venetians live, is arguably the prettiest part of Venice. A 2nd- or 3rd-floor room with a view of the sculpted skyline is worth the confusion of navigating some of the narrowest and most tightly clustered streets in the city.

Foresteria Valdese, Castello 5170 (☎52 86 797; www.diaconiavaldese.org/venezia). From Campo Santa Maria Formosa, take Calle Lunga Santa Maria Formosa; it's over the 1st bridge. An 18th-century house with 64 beds run by a Protestant church. Excellent location. Breakfast included. Internet access €5 per hr. Lockout 10am-1pm. Reception 9am-1pm and 6-8pm. Reservations required. Dorms €21-23; doubles with TV €60-64, with bath and TV €76-80; quads with bath and TV €110-118; quints with bath €127-137. Apartments (no breakfast) €104. Rolling Venice discount €1. MC/V. ❷

Albergo Doni, Calle del Vin, Castello 4656 (☎52 24 267; www.albergodoni.it). From P. San Marco, turn left immediately after the 2nd bridge on Calle del Vin and take the left fork when the street splits. Cheery staff, headed by proprietress Annabella, and proximity to P. San Marco make this hotel an amazing deal. Rooms with phone, TV, and either a fan or A/C; some have private bath. Breakfast included. Reception 24hr. Singles €40-65; doubles €60-95, with bath €80-120; triples €80-125/120-160; quads €140-200. Discount €5 with cash payment. MC/V. ❸

Antica Locanda Casa Verardo, Castello 4765 (☎52 86 138; www.casaverardo.it). From the basilica, take Calle Canonica, turn right before bridge and left over the bridge on Ruga Giuffa into Campo Santi Filippo e Giacomo. Follow Calle della Chiesa left out of the *campo* until the bridge. Housed in a national monument, this 16th-century hotel's mosaic floors and heavy drapes makes travelers feel like Venetian royalty. Rooms with A/C, safe, minibar, and TV. Breakfast and Internet access included. Singles €60-150; doubles €90-298. Discount for web reservations or cash payment. AmEx/MC/V. ❺

La Residenza, Campo Bandiera e Moro, Castello 3608 (☎52 85 315; www.venicelaresidenza.com). From V: Arsenal, turn left on Riva degli Schiavoni and right on Calle del Dose into the *campo*. Great location 5min. from P. S. Marco. Lavishly decorated 15th-century *palazzo* overlooking courtyard. All rooms are recently renovated, with bath, safe, A/C, TV, and minibar. Breakfast included. Reception 24hr. Singles €50-100; doubles €80-180. Extra bed €35. MC/V. ❹

Locanda Silva, Fondamenta del Rimedio, Castello 4423 (☎52 27 643 or 52 37 892; www.locandasilva.it). From P. S. Marco, walk under clock tower, turn right on Calle Larga S. Marco, and left on Calle de l'Anzolo before the bridge. Head right on Calle del Rimedio before next bridge; follow to the end. Rustic rooms with exposed beams and a sunny 18th-century breakfast room near P. San Marco overlooking the canal. Reception 24hr. Open Feb.-Nov. Singles €35-50, with bath €50-70; doubles €60-80, with bath €70-90, with shower €80-110; triples €110-140; quads €130-160. MC/V. ❹

GIUDECCA

Separated from the center of Venice by the 400m-wide Giudecca canal, this 7th neighborhood is often forgotten by tourists. It will take about a 5-10min. *vaporetto* ride from San Marco to reach Venice proper from the island of Giudecca, and travelers looking for peace and quiet will be rewarded by the untouristed streets.

Ostello di Venezia (HI), Fondamenta Zitelle, Giudecca 87 (☎52 38 211; www.hostel-booking.com). Take V: #41, 42, or 82 to Zitelle. Turn right along canal; the hostel is 3min. down on the left. This efficiently managed hostel has sparkling baths and sweeping views of the city. 250 beds on single-sex floors. Breakfast included; dinner €9.50. Reception 7-9:30am and 1:30pm-midnight. Lock-out 9:30am-1:30pm. Curfew 11:30pm. Reserve through website. Dorms €20. HI members only. MC/V. ❷

CAMPING

While the cheaper prices of campgrounds seem appealing, take into account that you'll be paying for pricey transportation to and from Venice, which may cost more than just staying in the city. Plan on at least a 40min. boat ride from Venice. In addition to this campground, the Litorale del Cavallino, on the Lido's Adriatic side, has multiple beach campsites.

Camping Miramare, Lungomare Dante Alighieri 29 (☎96 61 50; www.camping-miramare.it). A 50min. ride on V: #LN from P. S. Marco to Punta Sabbioni. Campground is 700m along the beach on the right. Min. 2-night stay in high season. Open Apr.-Oct. €4.70-7 per person, €9.60-15 per tent. Bungalows €29-67 plus normal per person camping charge. Rolling Venice discount 15% with cash payment. MC/V. ❶

◪ FOOD

In Venice, authentic dining may require some exploration since many of the best restaurants lie in less-traveled areas. Naturally, Venetian cuisine is dominated by fish. *Şarde in saor* (sardines in vinegar and onions) is available only in Venice and can be sampled at most bars with *cicchetti* (Venetian appetizers similar to tapas). The Veneto and Friuli regions produce an abundance of wines. Local whites include *prosecco della marca*, the dry *tocai*, and *bianco di custoza*. For reds, try a *valpolicella*. The least expensive option is by no means inferior: a simple *vino della casa* (house wine) is usually a fine local merlot or chardonnay. For informal alternatives to traditional dining, visit an *osteria* or *bacaro* for pastries, seafood, or *tramezzini* (white bread with any imaginable filling).

Venice's Rialto **markets**, once the center of trade for the Venetian Republic, spread between the Grand Canal and the San Polo foot of the Rialto every morning from Monday to Saturday. Smaller produce markets are set up in Cannaregio, on Rio Terà San Leonardo by Ponte delle Guglie, and in many of the city's *campi*. The **BILLA** supermarket, Strada Nuova, Cannaregio 5660, has groceries and a small bakery and deli near Campo San Fosca. (Open M-Sa 8:30am-8:30pm, Su 9am-8:30pm. AmEx/MC/V.) A **Punto** supermarket is at Campo Santa Margherita 3017 (☎52 26 780. Open M-Sa 8:30am-8pm. MC/V.)

SAN MARCO

▨ **Le Bistrot de Venise,** Calle dei Fabbri, San Marco 4685 (☎52 36 651; www.bistrotde-venise.com). From P. S. Marco, head through 2nd Sottoportego dei Dai under the awning. Follow road around and over bridge; turn right. Scrumptious Venetian dishes, true to medieval and Renaissance recipes reconstructed by the owner and a Venetian historian. Heavy wine menu and a relaxed atmosphere. *Enoteca: cicchetti* €3-4, meat/

cheese plates €12-24. Restaurant: *primi* €12-22, *secondi* €29-32. Wine from €5 per glass. Service 12%. Open daily 10am-1am. Rolling Venice discount 10%. MC/V. ❺

Vino, Vino, Ponte delle Veste, San Marco 2007/A (☎24 17 688). From Calle Larga XXII Marzo, turn on Calle delle Veste. Jazz plays quietly in this bar, which serves over 350 wines and the traditional *sarde in saor* (€8). *Primi* €7.50-9.50, *secondi* €9.50-16.50. Cover €1. Open daily 11:30am-11:30pm. Rolling Venice discount 10%. Cash only. ❸

Rosticceria San Bartolomeo, Calle della Bissa, San Marco 5424/A (☎/fax 52 23 569). From Campo S. Bartolomeo, follow the Calle de la Bissa to the neon sign. A haven for weary tourists, the *rosticceria* serves food upstairs in its full-service restaurant and downstairs in its laid-back cafe. Pizza €5.80-11. *Panini* from €1.10. *Primi* and *secondi* from €7. Cover €2. Open Tu-Su 9am-9:30pm. AmEx/MC/V. ❷

CANNAREGIO

Gam Gam, Canale di Cannaregio, Cannaregio 1122 (☎041 71 52 84). From Campo S. Geremia, cross the bridge and turn left. Fresh ingredients and canal-side tables make this kosher neighborhood favorite a great choice. Try the specialty Israeli appetizer plates (€9.50). Main courses €9-15. Open Su-Th noon-10pm, F noon-4pm. *Let's Go* discount 10%. Cash only. ❷

Pizzeria La Perla, Rio Terrà dei Franceschi, Cannaregio 4615 (☎/fax 52 85 175). From Strada Nuova, turn left on Salizzada del Pistor in Campo dei Santissimi Apostoli. Continue to the end, then follow signs for the Fondamente Nuove. American movie posters and heaping portions of hearty, fresh pizza in over 40 varieties (€4.65-9). Pasta €6.10-8.20. Cover €1.10. Service 10%. Open M-Tu and Th-Su noon-3pm and 6:30-10:30pm; daily in Aug. AmEx/MC/V. ❷

Osteria al Bomba, Cannaregio 4297/98 (☎52 05 175; www.osteriaalbomba.it). From Hotel Bernardi-Semenzato, exit right on Strada Nuova, then turn right into the next alleyway. Enjoy a glass of *prosecco* (€1) or *cicchetti* (skewer €1, large mixture €15) inside at the long communal table or outside on the tiny patio. *Primi* €10-15, *secondi* €12-20. Cover €2. Open daily 11am-3pm and 6-11pm. MC/V. ❸

Osteria da Rioba, Fondamenta della Misericordia, Cannaregio 2553 (☎52 44 379). This sleepy canal-side eatery serves fish dishes like *talioni con scampi e asparagi* (€9). Romantic outdoor seating on summer evenings. *Primi* €8-12, *secondi* €15-22. Cover €1.50. Open Tu-Su 12:30-2:30pm and 7:30-10:30pm. Call ahead on summer weekends to reserve outdoor seating. MC. ❸

Trattoria da Bepi, Cannaregio 4550 (☎/fax 52 85 031). From Campo SS. Apostoli, turn left on Salizzada del Pistor. Traditional Venetian trattoria with a warm atmosphere. *Primi* €7-12, *secondi* €12.50-19. Cover €1.50. Open M-W and F-Su noon-3pm and 7-10pm. Reservations recommended for outdoor seating. MC/V. ❸

SAN POLO AND SANTA CROCE

Antica Birraria La Corte, Campo S. Polo, San Polo 2168 (☎27 50 570; www.anticabirrarialacorte.com). The expansive interior of this former brewery houses a large restaurant and bar as well as outside tables on the peaceful *campo*. Pizza €5-9. *Primi* €9-11, *secondi* €10.50-19. Cover €2. Open mid-Aug. to mid-July daily 12:30-3pm and 7-10:30pm; mid-July to mid-Aug. M-F 12:30-3pm and 7-10:30pm, Sa-Su 12:30-3pm. AmEx/MC/V. ❸

Frary's, Fondamenta dei Frari, San Polo 2559 (☎72 00 50). Across from entrance to S. Maria Gloriosa dei Frari. Tasty Greek and Arab cuisine served in a colorful, air-conditioned dining room. Lunch *menù* (€10) of *antipasto* plus main course is a deal, or sample a little bit of everything with the selection of small plates (€4-6). Main course €8-13. Open M and W-Su noon-3:15pm and 6-10:30pm. ❸

Osteria al Ponte, Calle Saoneri, San Polo 2741/A (☎52 37 238). From Campo S. Polo, follow signs to Accademia; it's immediately across the 1st bridge. Enjoy seafood dishes at this quaint restaurant. Try the black *spaghetti al nero di seppia* (cooked in squid ink). *Primi* €7-12, *secondi* from €9-16. Cover €2. Open Tu-Su 8:30am-2:30pm and 6-10pm. AmEx/MC/V. ❸

Osteria Enoteca "Vivaldi," San Polo 1457 (☎52 38 185). From the Campo S. Polo, opposite the church, cross the bridge to Calle della Madonnetta. Tiny neighborhood restaurant celebrates food and music with hearty cuisine and violins hung on the walls. *Primi* €8-13, *secondi* €12-22. Cover €1.50. Service 10%. Open M-Tu and Th-Su 11am-3pm and 6pm-midnight. AmEx/MC/V. ❸

Cantina Do Mori, Calle dei Do Mori, San Polo 401 (☎52 25 401). From the Rialto, take left onto Ruga Vecchio, then the 1st right, and then left. Watch your head on dangling brass pots in the dark interior of Venice's oldest wine bar. A great spot to try *sarde in saor* (€1.40 per piece) or another of the diverse small plates (€.80-1.40). Very limited seating. Open M-Sa 8:30am-8pm. Cash only. ❶

Ae Oche, Santa Croce 1552A/B (☎52 41 161). Walls lined with American relics like typewriters and Pepsi ads. Over 100 different types of pizza (€4.50-9) served to a bustling crowd at canal-side tables. *Primi* €5.50-7, *secondi* €8-14.50. Cover €1.50. Service 12%. Open daily noon-3:30pm and 7-11:30pm. MC/V. ❷

DORSODURO

🏮 **Cantinone Gia Schiavi,** Fondamenta Meraviglie, Dorsoduro 992 (☎52 30 034). From the Frari, follow signs for the Accademia bridge. Just before Ponte Meraviglie, turn right toward the Chiesa di San Trovaso. Cross the 1st bridge. In this quirky restaurant, take your pick from hundreds of bottles (from €3.50), or enjoy a glass canal-side with some tasty *cichetti* (€1-4). Open M-Sa 8:30am-2:30pm and 3:15-8:30pm. Cash only. ❶

🏮 **Geltati Nico,** Fondamenta Zattere, Dorsoduro 922 (☎52 25 293). Near V: Zattere, with a great view of the Giudecca Canal from outdoor seating. For a guilty Venetian pleasure, try the *gianduiotto da passeggio* (chocolate-hazelnut *gelato* dropped into a cup of dense whipped cream; €2.50). 1 scoop €1, 2 scoops €1.70, 3 scoops €2.10. Open M-W and F-Su 6:45am-10pm. Cash only. ❶

Pizza al Volo, Campo S. Margherita, Dorsoduro 2944 (☎52 25 430). Students and locals come for delicious, cheap pizza, ready-made by a young, friendly staff. Enormous thin-crust slices from €1.50. Pizza from €3.50. Oversized pizza for 2 from €5. Open daily 11:30am-4pm and 5pm-1:30am. Cash only. ❶

CASTELLO

🏮 **Cip Ciap,** Calle del Mondo Novo, Castello 5799/A (☎52 36 621). From Campo S. Maria Formosa, follow Calle del Mondo Novo. Pizzeria uses fresh ingredients on Sicilian pizza sold by weight (€1-2.50 per kg) or in filling calzones (€2.50). No seating, but you can nab a bench in the nearby *campo*. Open M and W-Su 9am-9pm. Cash only. ❶

Osteria al Portego, Calle Malvasia, Castello 6015 (☎52 29 038). Heading south on Salizzada S. Lio, turn left onto Calle Malvasia, and left towards Cte. Perina. Hidden *osteria* filled with wine barrels and photos of Venice. Dizzying array of *cicchetti* and wine—try the *malvasia* wine (€2). Glasses €1.80-3. Open in summer M-Sa 10:30am-3pm and 5:30-10pm, Su 6-10pm; in winter M-Sa 10:30am-3pm. Cash only. ❶

La Boutique del Gelato, Salizzada S. Lio, Castello 5727 (☎52 23 283). From Campo Bartolomeo, walk under Sottoportego de la Bissa, then go straight, crossing the bridge into Campo S. Lio. Follow Salizzada S. Lio; *gelateria* is on the left. Though it could be easily missed, many swear it's the best *gelato* in town. 1 scoop €1, 2 scoops €1.70. Open daily July-Aug. 10:30am-10:30pm; Sept.-June 10:30am-8:30pm. Cash only. ❶

Pizzeria/Trattoria Al Vecio Canton, Castello 4738/A (☎52 85 176). From Campo S. Maria Formosa, with church on right, cross the bridge, and follow Ruga Giuffa. Turn right at the end. A 2-floor neighborhood favorite. Try any of the 50+ pizza varieties, or the *menù veneziano*—a plate overflowing with spaghetti, clams and calamari for €14. Pizza €4.50-10. *Primi* €6-18, *secondi* €12-20. Cover €2. Open M and W-Su 9am-3pm and 6pm-midnight. Cash only. ❸

Osteria Alle Testiere, Calle del Mondo Novo, Castello 5801 (☎/fax 52 27 220), off Campo S. Maria Formosa. Small restaurant serving light, healthy cuisine loaded with fruits and vegetables. *Primi* €16, *secondi* €24-28. Open Tu-Sa noon-3pm and 7pm-midnight. Closed Aug. Reservations recommended. MC/V. ❹

Osteria Santa Marina, Campo Santa Marina, Castello 5911 (☎/fax 52 85 239; www.osteriadisantamarina.it). From Calle Lio, take Calle Carminati to the end, turn right, follow to the end, and turn left. Delicate dishes, a fresh, seasonal menu, and an intimate, upscale setting. *Primi* €14-18, *secondi* €24-30. Cover €3. Open M 7:30-10pm, Tu-Sa 12:30-2:30pm and 7:30-10pm. MC/V. ❺

◉ SIGHTS

AROUND PIAZZA SAN MARCO

> **TIP** **ALL FOR ONE AND ONE FOR ALL.** Those planning to visit several museums in Venice should consider investing in a museum pass. Valid for 3 months, the pass grants one-time admission to 10 museums, including those on P. S. Marco, as well as those on the islands of Murano and Burano. It is available at all participating museums and costs €18 or €12 for students and Rolling Venice cardholders.

▨**BASILICA DI SAN MARCO.** Venice's crown jewel, San Marco is a spectacular fusion of gold mosaics, marble walls, and rooftop balconies, gracing P. San Marco with symmetrical arches and incomparable mosaic portals. As the city's largest tourist attraction, the **Basilica di San Marco** also has the longest lines. However, the line moves surprisingly quickly, which makes for crowded walkways inside. Visit in the early morning for the shortest wait or in late afternoon for the best natural illumination. Construction of the basilica began in the 9th century, when two Venetian merchants stole St. Mark's remains from Alexandria and packed them in pork meat to smuggle them past Arab officials. After the first church dedicated to St. Mark burned down in the 11th century, Venice designed a new basilica, choosing a Greek-cross plan with four arms and five domes instead of the Roman Catholic Church's standard cross-shaped layout. A cavernous interior sparkles with massive Byzantine and Renaissance mosaics and elaborate gold ornaments. The blue-robed **Christ Pantocrator** (Ruler of All) sits above the high altar. Twelfth-century stone mosaics cover the floor in geometric designs, though the church's floor, which has been sinking for 900 years, has wavy patches throughout. Behind the altar screen, the rectangular **Pala d'Oro** relief frames a parade of saints in gem-encrusted gold. Behind this masterpiece, the cement tomb of St. Mark himself rests within the altar, adorned with a single gold-stemmed rose. Steep stairs in the atrium lead to the **Galleria della Basilica,** with an eye-level view of the tiny golden tiles that compose the basilica's vast ceiling mosaics, a balcony overlooking the *piazza* below, and an intimate view of the bronze **Cavalli di San Marco** (Horses of St. Mark). Nearby, the **Cassine** displays mosaic heads (the most valuable and artistically challenging section of a masterpiece) removed during 1881 renovations. (*Basilica open M-Sa 9:45am-5pm, Su 2-4pm; illuminated 11:30am-12:30pm. Modest dress required. Baggage prohibited; follow signs to free baggage storage at nearby Ateno San Basso on Calle San Basso; open daily 9:30am-*

5:30pm. Free. Pala d'Oro open M-Sa 9:45am-5:30pm, Su 2-4:30pm. €1.50. Treasury open M-Sa 9:45am-7pm, Su 2-4:30pm. €2. Galleria open M-F 9:45am-4:15pm, Sa-Su 9:45am-4:45pm. €3.)

 IT'S A MIRACLE! The foundation for the Churches of Venice sells the **Chorus Pass** that covers admission to all of Venice's churches. A yearly pass (€8, students €5) includes S. Maria dei Miracoli, S. Maria Gloriosa dei Frari, S. Polo, Madonna dell'Orto, Il Redentore, and S. Sebastiano, and is available at participating churches. (For info, ☎27 50 462; www.chorusvenezia.org.)

PALAZZO DUCALE (DOGE'S PALACE). Once the home of the Doge, Venice's mayor, the Palazzo Ducale displays spectacular artwork, including Veronese's *Rape of Europa*. In the courtyard, Sansovino's enormous sculptures, *Mars* and *Neptune*, flank the **Scala dei Giganti** (Stairs of the Giants), upon which new Doges were crowned. On the balcony stands the **Bocca di Leone** (Lion's Mouth), into which the Council of Ten, the Doge's assistants, who also acted as judges and administrators, would drop the names of criminal suspects. Admire the sculptures of Hercules slaying the Hydra and Atlas bearing a brilliant blue, starry world on either side of the elaborate **Scala D'Oro.** From there, climb up to the **Sala delle Quattro Porte** (Room of the Four Doors), whose ceiling is covered in biblical judgments and representations of mythological tales related to events in Venetian history. More doors lead through the courtrooms of the much-feared Council of Ten, the even-more-feared Council of Three, and the **Sala del Maggior Consiglio** (Great Council Room), dominated by Tintoretto's *Paradise*, the largest oil painting in the world. Near the end, thick stone lattices line the covered **Ponte dei Sospiri** (Bridge of Sighs) and continue into the prisons. The bridge gets its name from 19th-century Romantic writers' references to the mournful groans of prisoners descending into the small, damp cells. The rest of the palace is best enjoyed by allowing yourself to get lost in the endless maze of tunnels. *(☎52 09 070. Open Nov.-Mar. daily 9am-5pm; Apr.-Oct. 9am-7pm. Last entry 1hr. before closing. Wheelchair-accessible. €12, students €6.50, ages 6-14 €3. Includes entrance to P. San Marco museums. Audio tour €5.50. MC/V.)*

CHIESA DI SAN ZACCARIA. Dedicated to the father of John the Baptist and designed in the late 1400s by Coducci, the Gothic-Renaissance church holds S. Zaccaria's corpse in an elevated, glass-windowed sarcophagus along the right wall of the nave. Nearby, watch for Bellini's *Virgin and Child Enthroned with Four Saints*, one of the masterpieces of Venetian Renaissance painting. Ask the custodian for entrance into the 10th-century crypt, which features paintings by Tintoretto and others. *(V: S. Zaccaria. From P. S. Marco, turn left along the water, cross two bridges, and turn left through the tunnel marked "San Zaccaria." ☎52 21 257. Open daily 10am-noon and 4-6pm. Church free. Crypt entrance €1.)*

PIAZZA SAN MARCO. Unlike the labyrinthine streets that tangle through most of Venice, P. S. Marco, Venice's only official *piazza*, is a magnificent expanse of light, space, architectural harmony, and pigeons. Although hoards of photo-snapping tourists jostling each other may be annoying, the *piazza* is certainly worth it: the sights are some of the best the city has to offer. Enclosing the *piazza* are rows of cafes and expensive glass and jewelry shops along the ground floors of the Renaissance **Procuratie Vecchie** (Old Treasury Offices), the Baroque **Procuratie Nuove** (New Treasury Offices), and the Neoclassical **Ala Napoleonica** (more Treasury Offices). At the end of the *piazza* near the shoreline of the lagoon sits the **Basilica di San Marco**, where mosaics and marble horses overlook the chaos below. Between the basilica and the Procuratie Vecchie perches the **Torre dell'Orologio** (Clock Tower), constructed between 1496 and 1499, according to Coducci's design. The 24hr. clock indicates the hour, lunar phase, and ascending constellation. A 96m brick **campanile** provides one of the best elevated views of the city. Though it originally served as a watchtower and lighthouse, cruel and unusual Venice took advantage of its location to create medieval entertainment by dangling state prisoners in cages from its top. The practice ceased in the 18th century, but public fascination with the tower did not. The *campanile* collapsed during a 1902 restoration project, but was reconstructed in 1912 with the enlightened addition of an elevator. (☎ 52 25 205. Campanile *open daily May-Oct. 9am-9pm; Nov.-Apr. 9:30am-4:15pm. €6. Audio tour €3.)*

MUSEUMS OF PIAZZA SAN MARCO. Beneath the arcade at the short end of P. S. Marco lies the entrance to a trio of museums. The **Museo Civico Correr**, a Venetian history museum, fills most of the two-story complex with curiosities from the city's imperial past, including naval maps and models, ornate Neoclassical artwork, and weapons, like a 16th-century key that fires poison darts. Highlights of the collection include Antonio Canova's sculptures *Winged Cupid* and *Daedalus and Icarus* in the first room. Near the end of the 1st floor, the **Museo Archeologico** houses a sizable collection of ancient pieces, from first-century Egyptian funeral parchment to Greek and Roman sculptures. A series of ceiling paintings by seven artists, including some from Verona, adorn the dark gilded reading room of the **Biblioteca Nazionale Marciana**, built between 1537 and 1560. (☎ 52 24 951. Museums open daily Apr.-Oct. 9am-7pm; Nov.-Mar. 9am-5pm. Last entry 1hr. before closing. No single tickets, must buy museum pass. €18, students €12. Includes entrance to Palazzo. Free guided tours in English for Museo Archeologico Sa-Su 11am; for Biblioteca Nazionale Marciana Sa-Su 10am, noon, 2, and 3pm. Cash only.)

LA SCALA DEL BOVOLO. This marble "staircase of the snails," as it translates into English, takes guests up five stories of tightly spiraling marble loggia to a circular portico at the top. Legend has it that the staircase was designed by Leonardo da Vinci. Once leading to a now-destroyed palace, today, the top affords views of the green courtyard below as well as an eye-level view of red rooftops and the distant domes of S. Marco. (From the Campo Manin, facing the bridge, turn left down the alley, and look for the signs. ☎ 53 22 920. Closed for renovations until 2009.)

AROUND THE RIALTO BRIDGE

▧ **THE GRAND CANAL.** Over 3km long, the Grand Canal loops through the city and passes under three bridges: **Ponte Scalzi**, **Ponte Rialto**, and **Ponte Accademia.** (There are discussions of building a 4th bridge, but local politics have stalled the plan.) Coursing past the facades of cheek-to-cheek palaces that crown their banks, the blue-green waters are a constant reminder of Venice's history and immense wealth. Although each *palazzo* displays its own unique architectural blend of loggia, canal-side balconies, and marble sculptures, most share the same basic structural design. The most decorated floors, called *piani nobili* (noble floors, or 2nd and 3rd stories), housed luxurious salons and bedrooms. Rich merchant families stored their goods in the ground-floor rooms, and servants slept in tiny chambers below the roof. At night the facades are illuminated, producing a dazzling display of reflections. The candy-cane—called *bricole*—posts used for mooring boats on the canalare painted with the family colors of the adjoining *palazzo*. (For great facade views, ride V #82, #4, or the slower #1 from the train station to P. S. Marco. For the best canal views open to the public, visit Collezione Peggy Guggenheim or Ca Rezzonico.)

▧ **RIVOALTUS LEGATORIA.** Step into the book-lined Rivoaltus on any given day and hear Wanda Scarpa shouting greetings from the attic, where she has been sewing leather-bound journals for three decades. The tiny shop, run by arguably the nicest couple in Italy, overflows with Wanda's deep red portfolios, leather journals, and photo albums. As the Scarpas are eager to tell you, each one is a hand-crafted copy of 13th-century work and is made with all-natural vegetable dye leather and cotton paper from the Amalfi Coast. Though Venice is now littered with shops advertising handmade journals, Rivoaltus was the first and sells products of such renowned quality that even movie stars have been known to send their agents specifically to this shop to buy portfolios—but unchanging prices mean that anyone can enjoy the books' love-laced quality craftsmanship. *(Ponte di Rialto 11, just over the hump of the bridge. ☎52 36 195. Open daily 10am-7:30pm. Basic notebooks €18-31. Photo albums €31-78. Murano glass fountain pens with ink €5. MC/V.)*

RIALTO BRIDGE. This architectural structure was named after Rivo Alto, the first colony in Venice. Originally built of wood, the bridge collapsed in the 1500s. Antonio da Ponte designed the present-day stone structure, where strips of boutiques separate a wide central lane from two side passages with picture-perfect views. Expensive stores and tourists dominate the bridge, but unauthorized vendors selling overpriced, cheaply made goods manage to find their way onto the thoroughfare as well. Cross over the bridge from S. Marco to grab some fresh fruit or *gelato* at the market's dozens of stands.

CANNAREGIO

JEWISH GHETTO. In 1516, the Doge forced Venice's Jewish population into the old cannon-foundry area, creating the first Jewish ghetto in Europe. (*Ghetto* is the Venetian word for foundry.) At its height, the ghetto housed 5000 people in buildings up to seven stories high, making them among the tallest tenements in Europe at the time. Now, locals gather in this sequestered spot for the tranquility of the **Campo del Ghetto Nuovo,** where delicious smells from the nearby local bakeries inevitably waft. In the *campo,* the **Schola Grande Tedesca** (German Synagogue), the oldest synagogue in the area, now houses the **Museo Ebraica di Venezia** (Hebrew Museum of Venice). In the adjacent Campiello delle Scuole stand the opulent **Schola Levantina** (Levantine Synagogue) and **Schola Spagnola** (Spanish Synagogue), both designed at least in part by Longhena. The Canton and Italian synagogues also occupy the area. *(Cannaregio 2899/B. V: S. Marcuola. Follow signs straight, then turn left into Campo del Ghetto Nuovo. ☎71 53 59. Hebrew Museum open M-F and Su June-Sept. 10am-7pm; Oct.-May 10am-4:30pm. 40min. English tours leave from the museum hourly June-Sept. 10:30am-5:30pm; Oct.-May 10:30am-4:30pm. €3, students €2. Museum and tour €8.50, students €7. MC/V.)*

THE LOCAL STORY

THE ART OF SELF-PROMOTION

In addition to being one of the last great Italian Renaissance painters, Tintoretto also acted as his own Hollywood agent of sorts. Born in Venice in 1518 by the name of Jacopo Robusti, Tintoretto extracted his one-word, celebrity name from real life—with a *tintore* (dyer) father, Jacopo quickly earned the nickname *tintoretto,* or dyer's boy. Like any good stage father, Signor Robusti immediately saw talent in his son's doodling and brought the boy to the great Titian's workshop for an apprenticeship. Unfortunately, catty celebrity behavior surfaced, and Titian kicked Tintoretto out after growing jealous of the talented novice's "spirited drawings."

Given the cold shoulder by the Venetian art world, Tintoretto still made a name for himself with his devotion to painting and ingenious self-promotion. Perhaps the best example of these talents was the Scuola di San Rocco's competition for altar space. Five famous artists were invited to send sketches of their painting ideas, but before judging commenced, Tintoretto offered his entry as a gift to the Scuola, well aware that the Scuola's rules forbade it from rejecting presents. The morning of the competition, judges arrived to find Tintoretto's piece already placed in the altar, and there it remained. Who needs an agent when you can promote yourself?

CHIESA DELLA MADONNA DELL'ORTO. Tintoretto's brick 14th-century parish church on the city's northern tip, the final resting place of the painter and his children, contains 10 of his largest paintings, as well as some works by **Titian**. Look for **Tintoretto's** *Last Judgment*, a spatially intense mass of souls, and *The Sacrifice of the Golden Calf* near the high altar. On the right apse is the brilliantly shaded *Presentation of the Virgin at the Temple.* There is a light switch for illuminating the works at each of the far corners. *(V: Madonna dell'Orto. ☎ 27 50 462; www.chorusvenezia.org. Open M-Sa 10am-5pm. Last entry 4:45pm. Included in the Chorus Pass. €2.50. Audio tour €0.50. Cash only.)*

CHIESA DEI GESUITI. Founded in the 12th century and reconstructed in the 18th, Dei Gesuiti features a gilt-rimmed stucco ceiling with painted portals to heaven. Exterior columns open onto a sea of marble that stretches from the floor to the realistic stone curtain in the pulpit. **Titian's** *Martyrdom of Saint Lawrence* hangs in the altar to the left of the entrance, while **Tintoretto's** lighter *Assumption of the Virgin* shows Mary on her way to Heaven. *(V: Fondamenta Nuove 4885; turn right, then left on Sala dei Specchieri. Open daily 10am-noon and 4-6pm. Free.)*

CÀ D'ORO. Built between 1425 and 1440, this "Golden House" houses the **Galleria Giorgio Franchetti.** Highlights include Andrea Mantegna's *Saint Sebastian* (temporarily out for restoration) in the small chapel on the first floor, Bonaccio's *Apollo Belvedere* (one of the most important bronzes of the 15th century), several frescoes by **Titian** (on the second floor), and two balconies above the Grand Canal. For the best view of the balconies and Cà d'Oro's tiered "wedding cake" facade, take a *traghetto* across the canal to the Rialto Markets. *(V: Cà d'Oro. ☎ 52 03 652; www.cadoro.org. Open M 8:15am-2pm, Tu-Su 8:15am-7:15pm. Last entry 30min. before closing. €5, EU students and under 25 €2.50, art students free. Audio tour €4. Cash only.)*

SAN POLO

▨ BASILICA DI SANTA MARIA GLORIOSA DEI FRARI. Even if you're not interested in seeing all of Venice's churches, this one is worth it. Its legendary paintings, looming sculptures, and dangling chandeliers will awe any visitor. Franciscans began construction on the Gothic church, also known simply as *I Frari*, in 1340. Today, the cavernous gray interior boasts two paintings by **Titian** as well as the corpse of the Renaissance master himself, who is entombed within the cathedral's cavernous terra-cotta walls. His ▨**Assumption** (1516-18), on the high altar, marks the height of the Venetian Renaissance. Titian's other work, *The Madonna and Child with Saints and Members of the Pesaro Family* (1547), is on the left from the entrance. Titian's elaborate tomb, a lion-topped triumphal arch with bas-relief scenes of Paradise, lies directly across from the enormous pyramid in which the sculptor Canova (1757-1822) rests. Donatello's gaunt wooden sculpture, ▨**St. John the Baptist** (1438), stands framed in gold in the Florentine chapel to the right of the high altar. *(V: S. Tomà. Follow signs back to Campo dei Frari. ☎ 27 28 611; www.basilicadeifrari.it. Open M-Sa 9am-6pm, Su 1-6pm. Last entry 30min. before closing. Included in the Chorus Pass. €2.50. Cash only.)*

CHIESA DI SAN GIACOMO DI RIALTO (SAN POLO). Smack in the middle of the chaos between the Rialto and the surrounding markets, Venice's first church, diminutively called "San Giacometto," is remarkably peaceful. An ornate clockface adorns its *campanile*. Across the *piazza*, a statue called *Il Gobbo* (The Hunchback) supports the steps, once used for public announcements. It was at the foot of this sculpture that convicted thieves could finally collapse after being forced to run naked from P. S. Marco and lashed all the way by spectators. *(V: Rialto. Cross bridge and turn right. Church open daily 9:30am-noon and 4-6pm. Free.)*

SCUOLA GRANDE DI SAN ROCCO. The most illustrious of Venice's *scuole*, or guild halls, is a monument to **Jacopo Tintoretto**, who left Venice only once in his 76 years, and who sought to combine the techniques of Titian and Michelangelo. Tintoretto's works are scattered all over the city, but most are concentrated here. The school commissioned Tintoretto to complete all the paintings in the building, a task that took 23 years. The large room on the 2nd floor provides hand mirrors to admire the delicate paintings mounted on the ceiling, but the wall-to-wall *Crucifixion* in the last room upstairs is the collection's crowning glory. Lined with intricately carved columns and colored marble, the *scuola* is a masterpiece in itself; step outside to admire it while listening to the strains of classical music performed by street musicians. *(Behind Basilica dei Frari in Campo S. Rocco. ☎52 34 864; www.scuolagrandesanrocco.it. Open daily Apr.-Oct. 9am-5:30pm; Nov.-Mar. 10am-4pm. Last entry 30min. before closing. €7; students, under 26, and Rolling Venice cardholders €5; under 18 free with parents. Audio tour free. AmEx/MC/V.)*

CAMPO SAN POLO. The second largest *campo* in Venice, **Campo San Polo** once hosted bull-baiting matches during the *Carnevale*, when authorities would release a wild bull into the crowds and set dogs on its tail. After the dogs began to tear the bull's flesh, the defeated animal would be decapitated before a cheering mob. A painting depicting the chaos hangs in the Museo Correr in P. S. Marco. Fortunately, modern visits generally involve less bloodshed; more often, visitors enjoy a drink or a bite to eat at one of the several surrounding establishments with outside seating. *(Between the Frari and Rialto Bridges. V: S. Silvestro. Straight back from the vaporetto. Or from in front of the Frari, cross bridge, then turn right, left on Rio Terà, right on Seconda Calle dei Saoneri, and left at the end.)*

DORSODURO

▧ COLLEZIONE PEGGY GUGGENHEIM. Guggenheim's elegant waterfront **Palazzo Venier dei Leoni,** once her home and a social haven for the world's artistic elite, now displays a private modern art collection maintained by the Solomon Guggenheim Foundation. The museum includes works by Duchamp, Klee, Kandinsky, Picasso, Magritte, Pollock, Dalí, and Guggenheim's confidante, Max Ernst. Guggenheim and her beloved pet shih tzus are buried in the peaceful garden. The Marini sculpture *Angel in the City*, which sits (apparently aroused) on horseback on the terrace, was designed with a detachable penis so Ms. Guggenheim could make emergency alterations depending on the church groups that were riding by on the Canal. The ivy-lined marble terrace offers a rare unobstructed-view of the Grand Canal. See Beyond Tourism (p. 95) for internship opportunities. *(Fondamenta Venier dei Leoni, Dorsoduro 701. V: Accademia. Turn left, and follow the yellow signs. ☎24 05 411; www.guggenheim-venice.it. Open M and W-Su 10am-6pm. Last entry 15min. before closing. €10; seniors €8; students, ISIC, and Rolling Venice cardholders €5; under 12 free. Audio tour €7. AmEx/MC/V.)*

▧ GALLERIE DELL'ACCADEMIA. This colossal gallery boasts the most extensive collection of Venetian art in the world. Start at the top of the stairs in Room I, then continue behind Veneziano's ornate *Lion Polyptych with the Annunciation.* Among the enormous altarpieces in Room II, Giovanni Bellini's *Madonna Enthroned with Child, Saints, and Angels* stands out with its soothing serenity. Rooms IV and V display more works by Bellini, including the magnificent *Madonna and Child with Magdalene and Saint Catherine*, and two works by Giorgione, who defied contemporary convention by creating works that apparently told no story. Attempts to find plot or moral in *The Tempest* have been fruitless. An x-ray of the pictures reveals that Giorgione originally painted a bathing woman where the young man now stands. In Room VI, three paintings by Tintoretto—*The Creation of the Animals, The Temptation of Adam and Eve,* and

Cain and Abel—become progressively darker. Venetian Renaissance works line the rooms leading to Room X, home to Veronese's colossal *Supper in the House of Levi*. Originally painted as a Last Supper, the infuriated Inquisition council tried to force Veronese to modify his unorthodox interpretation of the memorable event, which depicts a Protestant German, a midget, dogs, and fat men. Instead, Veronese cleverly changed the title, saving his artistic license and his life. On the opposite wall is Titian's last painting, a *Pietà* intended for his tomb, a request that was apparently ignored. Art historians speculate that this final painting was an autobiographical statement, and that the luminous figure is Titian suffering in the raging plague. In Room XX, works by Bellini and Carpaccio display Venetian city-scapes so accurately that scholars use them as "photos" of Venice's past. *(V: Accademia. ☎52 22 247. To pre-order tickets, call Teleart M-F ☎52 00 345. Open M 8:15am-2pm, Tu-Su 8:15am-7:15pm. Last entry 45min. before closing. Guided tours in English Tu-Su 11am-noon. €6.50, EU citizens under 18 or over 65 free. Tours €7. Audio tour €4. Combined ticket to with Ca' d'Oro and Museo Oriental €11. Cash only.)*

CHIESA DI SANTA MARIA DELLA SALUTE. The *salute* (Italian for "health") is a hallmark of the Venetian skyline; perched on Dorsoduro's peninsula just south-west of San Marco, the church and its domes are visible from everywhere in the city. Inside, the central area is marked off with ropes, so stroll around its circum-ference for a look at its paintings, including one by Titian by the sacristy entrance. In 1631, the city commissioned Longhena to build the church for the Virgin, whom they believed would then give them a break and end the plague. These days, Ven-ice celebrates the end of the plague on the 3rd Sunday of November by building a pontoon bridge across the Canal and lighting candles in the church (**Festivals,** p. 333). Next to the *salute* stands the *dogana*, the old customs house, where ships sailing into Venice were required to stop and pay appropriate duties. *(V: Salute. ☎52 25 558. Open daily 9am-noon and 2:30-5:30pm. The inside of the dogana is closed to the public. Church free. Entrance to sacristy €2, students €1.)*

CÀ REZZONICO. Longhena's great *palazzo* houses the newly restored **Museo del Settecento Veneziano** (Museum of 18th-Century Venice), which holds 18th-century art collected from all over the city. Known as the "Temple of Venetian Settecento," this grand palace features a regal ballroom, complete with flowing curtains and Crosato's frescoed ceiling. To reach the ballroom on the first floor, ascend the elaborate staircase near the courtyard entrance. Other rooms contain elaborate Venetian Rococo decor. Upstairs, two extensive portrait galleries display works by Tiepolo, Tintoretto, Guardi, and Longhi. *(V: Cà Rezzonico. ☎24 10 100. Open M and W-Su Apr.-Oct. 10am-6pm; Nov.-Mar. 10am-5pm. Last entry 1hr. before closing. €6.50, students and Rolling Venice cardholders €4.50. Audio tour €4. MC/V.)*

CHIESA DI SAN SEBASTIANO. This church is completely devoted to the work of Renaissance painter Veronese, who took refuge in this white-marble and brow-stucco 16th-century church when he fled Verona in 1555 after allegedly killing a man. By 1565 he had filled the church with an amazing cycle of paintings and fres-coes. His *Stories of Queen Esther* covers the ceiling, while the artist himself rests under the gravestone by the organ. Several works by Titian are also displayed. *(V: S. Basilio. Continue straight ahead. Open M-Sa 10am-5pm, Su 1-5pm. Last entry 15min. before closing. Included in the Chorus Pass. €2.50. Cash only.)*

CASTELLO

CHIESA DI SANTISSIMI GIOVANNI E PAOLO. Also called San Zanipolo, this imposing structure is primarily built in the Gothic style, but has a Renaissance por-tal and an arch supported by columns of Greek marble. Inside, monumental ceilings enclose tombs and monuments of the Doges. One fresco depicts the gory death of Marcantonio Bragadin, who valiantly defended Cyprus from the Turks in 1571, only to be skinned alive after surrendering. His remains rest in the urn above the monument. Next to Bragadin is an altarpiece by **Bellini** depicting St. Christopher, St. Sebastian, and St. Vincent Ferrer. The bronze equestrian statue of local mercenary Bartolomeo Colleoni stands outside. Colleoni left his inheritance to the city on the condition that a monument in his honor be erected in front of San Marco; the city, unwilling to honor anyone in such a grand space, decided to place the statue in front of the Scuola di San Marco to loosely satisfy the conditions of the will and claim his fortune. The statue was designed in 1479 by da Vinci's teacher Verrochio. *(V: Fondamenta Nuove. Turn left, then right on Fondamenta dei Mendicanti. ☎ 52 35 913. Open M-Sa 9:30am-6pm, Su 1-6pm. €2.50, students €1.25. Cash only.)*

CHIESA DI SANTA MARIA DEI MIRACOLI. The Lombardi family designed this small Renaissance jewel in the late 1400s. Inside the tiny pink-, white-, and blue-marble exterior sits a fully functional church with a dark golden ceiling and pastel walls interrupted only by the vibrant blue-and-yellow window above the apse; the window and pastel marble wall panels make the church's interior glow blue. *(From SS. Giovanni e Paolo, cross the bridge directly in front of the church, and continue down Calle Larga Gallina over 2 bridges. Open July-Aug. M-Sa 10am-5pm; Sept.-June M-Sa 10am-5pm, Su 1-5pm. Included in the Chorus Pass. €2.50. Cash only.)*

GIARDINI PUBBLICI AND SANT'ELENA. For a short respite from urban crowds, walk through the shady lanes of Napoleon's bench-lined public gardens where children swarm over playgrounds and the local geriatric elite gossip on benches. Throughout the year, the Giardini plays host to the Biennale, Venice's international art festival. For a larger lounging area, continue past the gardens, and bring a picnic lunch to the lawns of Sant'Elena. *(V: Giardini or S. Elena. Free.)*

SCUOLA DALMATA SAN GIORGIO DEGLI SCHIAVONI. Carpaccio's finest paintings, rendering episodes from the lives of St. George, Jerome, and Tryfon, are on the ground floor of this early 16th-century building. *(Castello 3259/A. V: S. Zaccaria. From the Riva Schiavoni, take Calle Dose to Campo Bandiera e Moro. Follow S. Antonin to Fondamenta Furlani. ☎ 52 28 828. Open M and Su 9:15am-1pm, Tu-Sa 9:15am-1pm and 2:45-6pm. Last entry 20min. before closing. Modest dress required. €3, Rolling Venice cardholders €2.)*

GIUDECCA

BASILICA DI SAN GIORGIO MAGGIORE. Standing on its own monastic island, S. Giorgio Maggiore contrasts sharply with most other Venetian churches and is a gorgeous sight from the southern edge of San Marco. Palladio, the architect, ignored the Venetian fondness for color and opted for an austere design. Light fills the enormous interior, although unfortunately it does not hit Tintoretto's *Last Supper* by the altar. Don't miss the 16th-century carved wood chorus hiding behind the main altar. Take the elevator to the top of the **campanile** for an amazing city view. *(V: S. Giorgio. ☎ 52 27 827. Church open M-Sa 7:30am-12:30pm and 2:30-6:30pm. Free. Campanile open 9:30am-12:30pm and 2:30-6pm. €3. Purchase ticket in the elevator.)*

TEMPIO DEL SS. REDENTORE. Palladio's religious masterpiece, this church is small, but striking from across the Giudecca Canal. Like the Salute (p. 328), it commemorates a deal that Venice struck with God to end a plague. Every year the city celebrates with fireworks at the **Festa del Redentore** (see **Festivals,** p. 333). Paintings by Veronese and Bassano hang in the sacristy. *(V: Redentore. Ask to enter the sacristy. Open M-Sa 10am-5pm. Included in the Chorus Pass. €2.50.)*

ISLANDS OF THE LAGOON

> **TIP**
>
> **ISLAND HOPPING.** *Vaporetto* ticket prices border on extortionate. To save money, the best way to visit all the islands is the 24hr. *vaporetto* pass for €13—hop between islands as often as you'd like for a full day!

■ **LIDO.** The breezy resort island of Lido provided the tragic setting for *Death in Venice*, Thomas Mann's haunting novella of love and lust. Visonti's film version was also shot here at the famous **Hotel des Bains**, Lungomare Marconi 17. Tree-lined streets, crashing blue waves, and the popular public beach seem miles away from Venice's mobbed urban seafront. An impressive shipwreck looms at one end. The island also offers a casino, horseback riding, and one of Italy's finest golf courses. *(V #1 and 82: Lido. From the vaporetto stop, cross the street, and continue until you reach Gran Viale, which traverses the island to the beach. Beach open daily 9am-8pm. Free. Lockable changing rooms €16 per day, €8 after 2:30pm. Beach umbrella and chair €21; long deck chair €9; small safe free. AmEx/MC/V.)*

■ **MURANO.** Famous since 1292 when glass artisans were forced off Venice proper because their kilns started fires, the six-island cluster of Murano affords visitors the opportunity to witness resident artisans blowing and spinning crystalline creations free of charge. Quiet streets are lined with tiny shops and glass boutiques with jewelry, vases, and delicate figurines for a variety of prices; for demonstrations, look for signs directing to the *fornace*, concentrated around the Colona, Faro, and Navagero *vaporetto* stops. The speed and grace of these artisans are stunning, and some studios let visitors blow their own glass creations. The **Museo Vetrario** (Glass Museum) houses a collection that begins with funeral urns from the 1st century and ends with pieces like an ornate model garden made entirely of glass and a cartoonish, sea-green octopus presumably designed by Carlo Scarpa in 1930. *(Fondamenta Giustian 8. V #DM, LN, 5, 13, 41, 42: Faro from either S. Zaccaria or Fondamenta Nuove.* ☎/fax *73 95 86. Open Apr.-Oct. M-Tu and Th-Su 10am-5pm; Nov.-Mar. M-Tu and Th-Su 10am-4pm. €4, students and Rolling Venice cardholders €2.50. Combined ticket with Burano Lace Museum €6/4.)* Farther down the street, a marble loggia lines the 2nd story of the light brick, 12th-century **Basilica di Santa Maria e San Donato**, which features hundreds of mosaics forming the church's floor, blue chandeliers in the side apses, and a holy waterfront with fused pieces of bright yellow, red, green, and blue glass. A huge crucifix, all blown from one piece of glass, hangs to the right of the altar. *(*☎*73 90 56. Open daily 8am-7pm. Modest dress required. Free.)*

■ **BURANO.** As you approach Burano, the lagoon's most postcard-worthy island, you'll immediately notice the brightly colored house that distinguished this destination. Carefully handmade lace has become the art form of choice for this traditional fishing village. The small and somewhat dull **Scuola di Merletti di Burano** (Lace Museum), once the home of the island's professional lace-making school, features 16th-century lace strips and yellowing lace-maker diplomas. **Chiesa di San Martino** sits across from the museum, and its altar features gorgeous blue stained-glass windows as bright as Burano's pastel buildings. *(40min. by boat from Venice. V #LN: Burano from Fondamenta Nuove. Museum in P. Galuppi.* ☎*041 73 00 34. Open M and W-Su Apr.-Sept. 10am-5pm; Oct.-Mar. 10am-4:30pm. Watch the lace makers in action Oct.-June 10am-1pm and 2-5pm. Combined ticket with Murano Glass Museum €4. Included in full museum pass. Church open daily 8am-noon and 3-7pm. Free.)*

TORCELLO. Torcello, originally a safe haven for fishermen fleeing barbarians on the mainland, was the most powerful island in the lagoon before Venice usurped its glory in the 14th century. The cathedral **Santa Maria Assunta** contains a resplendent wall, which has tiers of 11th- and 12th-century mosaics depicting the Last

Judgment and the Virgin Mary. The soaring **campanile** affords splendid views of Torcello, a distant Burano, and the outer lagoon, but the rambling walk to the church along an undisturbed canal is a pleasure in itself. *(45min. by boat from Venice. V #T: Torcello from Burano. Cathedral ☎ 73 01 19. Open daily 10:30am-6pm. Last entry 30min. before closing. Modest dress required. €3. Combined church, campanile, museum admission, and audio tour €8; groups €5.50. Combined ticket sales end 4:30pm. Cash only.)*

ISOLA DI SAN MICHELE. You'll find much smaller crowds on Venice's cemetery island, San Michele. The island closest to Venice proper, San Michele is home to Coducci's tiny **Chiesa di San Michele in Isola** (1469), the first Renaissance church in Venice. Enter the cyprus-lined grounds through the church's right-hand portal, ornamented by a relief depicting St. Michael slaying a dragon. Quiet grounds offer the opportunity for peaceful reflection away from the hustle and bustle of Venice. Poet, fascist sympathizer, and enemy of the state **Ezra Pound** is buried in the Protestant cemetery, while Russian composer **Igor Stravinsky** and choreographer **Sergei Diaghilev** are entombed in the Orthodox graveyard. *(V: Cimitero, from Fondamenta Nuove. Church and cemetery open daily Apr.-Sept. 7:30am-6pm; Oct.-Mar. 7:30am-4pm. Free.)*

▢ SHOPPING

Venice offers a variety of shops, ranging from international designer chains to scores of authentic, family-operated establishments. Be wary of shopping in the heavily touristed P. S. Marco or around the Rialto (excluding Rivoaltus). Shops outside these areas often have better selection and quality for about half the price. Boutiques selling clothing, glass, and masks line the streets leading from the Rialto to Campo S. Polo and Strada Nuova and from the Rialto toward the station, but even these are still mobbed with visitors in summer and on weekends. The map accompanying the Rolling Venice Card lists many shops that offer discounts for cardholders. The most concentrated and varied selections of Venetian glass and lace require trips to the nearby islands of Murano and Burano, respectively.

♫ ENTERTAINMENT

The weekly guide *A Guest in Venice*, free in hotels, tourist offices, and online at www.unospitedivenezia.it, lists current festivals, concerts, and gallery exhibits.

GONDOLAS

Gondolas were once displays of multicolored brilliance. Winding slowly through the city's tiny canals, gondolas have become an emblem of Venetian beauty and culture. Legend has it that their lavish reds and purples turned to black when the Plague struck: wooden boats were supposedly coated with tar and pitch to stop further contamination from spreading throughout the disease-infested canal waters. The morbid color was also a sign of respect for Venice's dead and dying. A more likely story, however, is that a 17th-century city ordinance ordered that all boats be painted black to prevent noble families from waging gondola-decorating wars. Certain dignitaries, of course, were exempt. Now, the boats are mainly filled with tourists seeking the most gorgeous views of Venetian houses and palaces from the original canal pathways. Rides are most romantic about 50min. before sunset and most affordable if shared by six people. Gondolas are a private service; the rate that a gondolier quotes is negotiable, but expect to pay €80-100 for 40min. (and don't pay more). The most bargain-friendly gondoliers are those standing by themselves, rather than those in the groups at "taxi stands" throughout the city.

ORCHESTRAL MUSIC

Venice swoons for **orchestral music,** from the outdoor chamber orchestras in P. S. Marco to costumed concerts. **Vivaldi** (p. 81), the priest and choirmaster of the Chiesa di S. Maria della Pietà (a few blocks along the waterfront from P. S. Marco), was forgotten for centuries after his death. Today, his compositions, particularly *The Four Seasons*, can be heard regularly in the summer and during the winter. The **Chiesa di San Vidal**, next to Campo S. Samuele in San Marco, hosts performances using period instruments. (Open daily 9am-5pm. Concerts M-Sa 9pm. €23, students €18. Tourist office has information. Purchase tickets at the church or visit www.interpretiveneziani.com.)

THEATER, CINEMA, AND ART EXHIBITIONS

Teatro Goldoni, Calle del Teatro, San Marco 4650/B, showcases varying types of live productions, often with a seasonal theme. Check with the theater for upcoming listings. (☎24 02 011; teatrogoldini@libero.it. Rolling Venice discount 10%. AmEx/MC/V.) The **Mostra Internazionale di Cinema** (Venice International Film Festival), held annually from late August to early September, is a worldwide affair, drawing both rising talents and more established names like Steven Spielberg. Movies are shown in their original languages. (☎52 18 878. Tickets €20, sold throughout city. Some late-night outdoor showings free.) Venice's main cinemas include: the **Giorgione,** Campo S. Apostoli, Cannaregio (☎52 26 298); and the **Rossini,** San Marco 3988 (☎52 30 322), off Campo Manin, which generally shows films in Italian. The famed **Biennale di Venezia,** an international contemporary art exhibition with musical and dance performances, takes over the Giardini Pubblici and the Arsenal with provocative art in odd-numbered years, while even-numbered years feature contemporary architects. Check the website for the exact dates. (Info ☎52 11 898; for tickets, HelloVenezia ☎24 24; www.labiennale.org. Open daily 7:30am-8pm.)

▓ NIGHTLIFE

Though pubs and bars are not uncommon, most residents agree that a truly vibrant nightlife in Venice is virtually nonexistent. Most residents would rather spend an evening sipping wine or beer in a *piazza* than bumping and grinding in a disco, but the island's fluctuating population means that new establishments spring up (and wither and die) with some regularity. Student nightlife is concentrated around **Campo Santa Margherita,** in Dorsoduro, while tourists swarm **Lista di Spagna,** in Cannaregio.

▓ **Café Blue,** Campo S. Pantalon, Dorsoduro 3778 (☎71 02 27). Grab a glass of wine (from €1.50) to watch the daytime coffee crowd turn into the nighttime trendy crowd. Free Wi-Fi and one computer for Internet. W night DJ. F evening live music in winter. Open daily 8am-2am. MC/V.

Piccolo Mondo, Accademia, Dorsoduro 1056/A (☎52 00 371). Facing away from the canal toward the Accademia, turn right and follow the street around. Heavy, locked doors open up late at this self-advertised "disco club." Disco, hip hop, and vodka with Red Bull (€10) keep a full house at this small but popular spot—but don't expect anything to heat up before 1am. Framed collages of the wide-ranging clientele include notables like Michael Jordan, Boy George, Shaquille O'Neal, Mick Jagger, and Prince Albert of Monaco. Ring bell to enter. Drinks from €7. Cover varies, usually €10 with free drink. Open nightly 11pm-4am. AmEx/MC/V.

Naranzaria, Sottoportego del Banco, S. Polo 130 (☎72 41 035; www.naranzaria.it). At the canal-side corner of C. S. Giacomo. Up-close views of the Grand Canal and Rialto are secondary to the wine, arrays of *cicchetti* (including sushi), and trendy atmosphere at this tiny bistro. Open Tu-Su noon-2am. MC/V.

Bistrot ai Do Draghi, Campo S. Margherita 3665 (☎52 89 731). While not as fierce as the name implies, tiny bistro is more artsy than that at its C. S. Margherita counterparts. Its wide selection of wine (from €1.20 per glass) has won it many accolades. Open daily 7am-1am.

Paradiso Perduto, Fondamente della Misericordia, Cannaregio 2540 (☎09 94 540). From Strada Nuova, cross Campo S. Fosca, cross bridge, and continue in same direction, crossing 2 more bridges. Students flood this bar, where waitstaff doles out large portions of *cicchetti* (small plates €2-5, large €11-15). F night live jazz. €2 cover for meals. Open daily 11am-3pm and 6pm-1am.

Orange, Campo S. Margherita, Dorsoduro 3054/A (☎52 34 740; www.orangebar.it). The painted bar seems to be on fire at this modern spot, where everything except the lush aquamarine garden is consistently and totally orange. Beer from €2. Wine from €1.50. Mixed drinks €3.50-7. Open daily 9am-2am. AmEx/MC/V.

Café Noir, Dorsoduro 3805 (☎71 09 25). Faded images of Marilyn Monroe and a saxophone player cover the walls of Café Noir, where no-nonsense decor gives off a sophisticated vibe. Black leather booths and street-side windows in front are great for coffee-drinking or people-watching. Open M-Sa 7am-2am, Su 9am-2am. Cash only.

Il Caffè, Campo S. Margherita, Dorsoduro 2963 (☎52 87 998). Lying in between the loud student bars of Campo S. Margherita, Il Caffè is a low-key, high-quality bar with a tiny red facade that caters to an older set of patrons. Great outdoor seating in the summer. Wine from €1 per glass. Open M-Sa 7am-1am. Cash only.

❀ FESTIVALS

Banned by the church for several centuries, Venice's famous Carnevale was successfully reinstated in the early 70s. During the 10 days preceding Ash Wednesday, masked figures jam the streets and street performances spring up throughout the city. On Mardi Gras, the city's population doubles. Contact the tourist office in December or January for details and make lodging arrangements far ahead. Venice's 2nd most colorful festival is the Festa del Redentore (3rd Sunday in July), originally held to celebrate the end of a 16th-century plague. It kicks off on Saturday night with a fireworks display at 11:30pm. On Sunday, craftsmen build a pontoon bridge across the Giudecca Canal, connecting Il Redentore to the Zattere. On the first Sunday in September, Venice stages its classic regata storica, a gondola race down the Grand Canal. During the religious Festa della Salute (Nov. 21), which originated to celebrate the end of a plague, the city celebrates with the construction of another pontoon bridge, this time over the Grand Canal.

PADUA (PADOVA)   ☎049

Padua's (in Italian, "PA-do-va"; pop. 215,000) oldest institutions are the ones that still draw visitors: pilgrims flock to San Antonio's tomb, athletes skate around peaceful picnickers along the looping Prato della Valle, and lecturers and academics frequent the hallowed university halls. Dante, Petrarch, Galileo, Copernicus, Donatello, and other luminaries once fostered the city's long-standing reputation as a center of learning. The Università di Padova, founded in 1222 and second in seniority only to Bologna's university, brings scores of students into the city's cluster of busy *piazze*, where crowds of twentysomethings stay to roam the brightly lit streets late into the night.

▐ TRANSPORTATION

Trains: In P. Stazione, at the northern end of C. del Popolo, the continuation of C. Garibaldi. Station open daily 5am-midnight. Ticket office open daily 6am-9pm. Info booth open daily 7am-9pm. To: **Bologna** (1½hr., 34 per day 12:41am-8:33pm, €6); **Milan** (2½hr., 25 per day 5:50am-8:24pm, €11.70); **Venice** (30min., 82 per day 4:21am-11:08pm, €2.70); **Verona** (1hr., 44 per day 5:51am-11:28pm, €4.30).

Buses: SITA (☎82 06 834), in P. Boschetti. From the train station, walk down C. del Popolo, turn left on V. Trieste, and bear right at V. Vecchio. Ticket office open M-Sa 5:30am-8:30pm, Su 6:20am-8:40pm. To **Venice** (45min., 31 per day 5:25am-10:25pm, €3.05) and **Vicenza** (1hr., 50 per day 5:50am-8:15pm, €3.20). Reduced service Sa-Su. Cash only.

Public Transportation: ACAP (☎82 41 111), at the train station, runs local buses. Ticket office open daily 6am-midnight. To go downtown, take buses #8, 12, or 18 M-F and #8 and 32 Sa-Su. 1hr. pass €1.

Taxis: RadioTaxi (☎65 13 33). 24hr.

Car Rental: Europcar, P. Stazione 6 (☎65 78 77), across parking lot from train station. 19+. Open M-F 8:30am-noon and 3-7pm, Sa 8:30am-12:30pm. AmEx/MC/V. **Maggiore National**, P. Stazione 15 (☎87 58 605; fax 87 56 223). Turn right after exiting station. Open M-Sa 8:30am-12:30pm and 2:30-7pm, Su 9am-12:30pm. MC/V.

✈ 🛈 ORIENTATION AND PRACTICAL INFORMATION

The **train station** is on the northern edge of town, outside the 16th-century walls. A 10min. walk down **Corso del Popolo**, which becomes **Corso Garibaldi**, leads to the heart of town and main area of the **Università degli Studi di Padova**.

Tourist Office: Main office, Vco. Cappellato Pedrocchi 7 (☎87 67 927; infopedrocchi@turismopadova.it), off P. Cavour. Offers maps and information on local events. Free Internet with 15min. limit. Open M-Sa 9am-1:30pm and 3-6:40pm. **Branches:** in P. del Santo (☎87 53 087), across from the basilica. Open Apr.-Oct. M-Sa 9am-1:30pm and 3-6pm, Su 10am-1pm and 3-6pm. In the train station (☎87 52 077). Open M-Sa 9am-7pm, Su 9am-12:30pm.

Budget Travel: CTS, V. Santa Sofia 96. (☎87 51 719). Sells ISICs and train tickets. Open M-F 9am-12:30pm and 3-6:30pm, Sa 9am-noon. Cash only.

English-Language Bookstore: Feltrinelli International, V. San Francesco 14 (☎87 50 792). From the train station, turn left off V. Cavour. Wide selection of foreign magazines, novels, and travel guides. Open M-Sa 9am-1pm and 3:30-7:30pm. AmEx/MC/V.

Hospital: Ospedale Civile, V. Giustiniani 2 (☎82 11 111), off V. Ospedale.

Internet Access: Free at the **main tourist office** (see above). **Internet Point Padova**, V. Altinate 145 (☎65 92 92). Printing, fax, and photocopy. €1 per 20min., €3 per hr. Open M-Sa 10am-midnight, Su 4pm-midnight. MC/V.

Post Office: C. Garibaldi 25 (☎87 72 111). Open M-Sa 8:30am-6:30pm. **Postal Code:** 35100.

🏠 ACCOMMODATIONS

Padua's size and major attractions mean high hotel prices, but the hostel is a good choice to save some euros.

Ostello Città di Padova (HI), V. Aleardi 30 (☎87 52 219; www.ostellopadova.it). From station, take bus #12 or 18 to Prato della Valle, or walk 25min. Large, efficiently run hostel rents mostly 6-bed dorms. TV room and good location 10min. from *centro*. Breakfast included. Laundry €3. Internet €5 per hr. €3 key deposit for locker in room. Wheelchair-accessible. Reception 7-9:30am and 4-11pm. Lockout 9:30am-4pm. Curfew 11:30pm. Call ahead. 6-bed dorms €16.50; 4-person family rooms €66, with private bath €72. MC/V. ❶

Hotel Al Santo, V. del Santo 147 (☎87 52 131; fax 87 88 076), near the basilica. Stone artwork graces the lobby of this very professional hotel; modern paintings adorn the walls of its spacious rooms. All have TV, A/C, wood floors, and new bathrooms; some have impressive views. Breakfast included; lunch or dinner *menù* €15.50. Res-

Otel.com

Are you aiming for a budget vacation?

DO NOT DISTURB

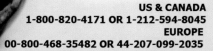

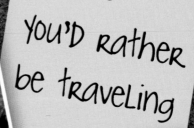

www.letsgo.com

YOU'D rather be traveling

LET'S GO
NEW ZEALAND

LET'S GO
FRANCE
2008

LET'S GO
MEXICO

READY.
SET. **LET'S GO**

Padua

🏠 **ACCOMMODATIONS**

Casa del Pellegrino, **12**
Hotel Al Santo, **11**
Hotel Corso, **1**
Hotel Sant'Antonio, **2**
Locanda la Perla, **10**
Ostello Città di
  Padova (HI), **13**

🍴 **FOOD**

Alexander Birreria
  Paninoteca, **5**
Antica Trattoria
  Paccagnella, **9**
Lunanuova, **7**
Patagonia Ice Cream, **3**
Piadineria Italiana, **6**
Trattoria Pizzeria
  Marechiaro, **4**

🎵 **NIGHTLIFE**

Fly, **8**

taurant downstairs. Reception 24hr. Singles €65; doubles €80-100; triples €120. Prices may drop with longer stays. AmEx/MC/V. ❺

Casa del Pellegrino, V. Cesarotti 21 (☎82 39 711; www.casadelpellegrino.com). Sleep in the shadow of the Basilica di San Antonio at this large hotel, which once hosted Emperor Joseph II of Austria and the Spanish Bourbon royal family. All rooms with TV and telephone; the *dipendenza* rooms also have A/C. Breakfast €6. Parking €5 per day, bike parking €1 per day. Singles €40-45, with bath €55-60; double €51-57/67-75; triples €75-83. MC/V. ❹

Locanda la Perla, V. Cesarotti 67 (☎87 58 939), a 5min. walk from the Basilica di San Antonio. Friendly owner Paolo rents 8 clean, reasonably sized rooms with stone floors, phone, and 1 shared bath on each floor. Fan and TV provided upon request. Closed last 2wk. of Aug. Singles €34; doubles €44. Cash only. ❸

THE VENETO

Hotel Sant'Antonio, V. San Fermo 118 (☎87 51 393; www.hotelsantantonio.it), halfway between train station and town center. Pleasant rooms with wooden furniture and green decor overlook the river. Rooms have TV, A/C, and phone. Breakfast €7. Singles €42, with bath €66; doubles €90; triples €114; quads €136. MC/V. ❸

Hotel Corso, C. del Popolo 2 (☎87 50 822; htlcrs@virgilio.it), at V. Trieste. Simple rooms with bath, phone, A/C, and TV on a busy street. Breakfast included. Reception 24hr. Singles €60-80; doubles €80-110, triples €100-120. Discounts with longer stays. AmEx/MC/V. ❺

🍴 FOOD

Morning **markets** are held in P. delle Erbe and P. della Frutta from M-F 7am-1:30pm, Sa 7a-8pm; sidewalk vendors also sell fresh produce, meats, and cheeses. A **PAM** supermarket is downtown in Piazzetta della Garzeria 3, past Palazzo Bo to the right of Caffè Pedrocchi. (Open M-Tu and Th-Sa 8am-8:30pm, W 8am-2pm. MC/V.) For an inexpensive taste of the gourmet, visit **Franchin,** V. del Santo 95, which sells fresh meats, cheeses, breads, and wines. (☎87 50 532. Open M-Tu and Th-Su 8:30am-1:30pm and 4:30-8pm, W 8:30am-1:30pm. MC/V.) Wine lovers should sample a glass from the nearby Colli Euganei wine district. Visitors to the Basilica di Sant'Antonio can nibble on *dolci del santo* (saint's sweets), a flaky, powdered cake with creamy nut and fig filling, in nearby *pasticcerie.*

🍽 **Antica Trattoria Paccagnella,** V. del Santo 113 (☎/fax 87 50 549). The place to go for authentic Paduan cuisine. Regional favorites like *ventaglio di petto d'anatra alle ciliegie e rosso dei colli* (duck in red wine and cherry sauce; €14) in an elegant yet relaxed atmosphere. *Primi* €7-11, *secondi* €7-15. Cover €2.50. Open M-Sa 8am-4pm and 6:30pm-midnight. Closed in winter M afternoon. AmEx/MC/V. ❷

🍽 **Patagonia Ice Cream,** P. dei Signori 27 (☎87 51 045), on the side by to V. Dante. Fruit adorns the heaping piles of *gelato*. Try the surprisingly uplifting *fin del mundo* (swirls of chocolate and caramel in white chocolate *gelato*). 1 scoop €1, 2 scoops €2. Open M-Sa 11am-midnight, Su 11am-1pm and 3pm-midnight. Cash only. ❶

Piadineria Italiana, V. del Santo 7 (☎328 46 61 021), serves *piadine* (pitas) with a variety of fillings to students at the nearby university. With grilled vegetables and mozzarella €3.40, with Nutella €2.20. Half-sized with 2 ingredients €2.40, 3 ingredients €3. Open in summer M-F 11am-3pm and 7-10pm; in winter M-F 10am-6pm. Cash only. ❶

Lunanuova, V. San Gregorio Barbarigo 12 (☎87 58 907), heading off P. Duomo. Ring bell at stained glass doors for entrance. Change up the same ol' pizza and pasta routine by mixing and matching vegetarian and Middle Eastern dishes. Indoor and outdoor seating. Individual plates €4.30, 2 plates €8.30, 3 plates €9.30, 5 plates €10.30. Open Tu-Sa 12:30-2:15pm and 7:30pm-midnight. Cash only. ❷

Alexander Birreria Paninoteca, V. San Francesco 38 (☎65 28 84). From the basilica, take V. del Santo to V. S. Francesco, and turn left. Wide range of sandwiches (€3-4) served at small round tables; beer ads and sports on multiple TVs give a casual, bar-like vibe. Open daily 9am-2am. ❶

Trattoria Pizzeria Marechiaro, V. Manin 37 (☎87 58 489). The friendly Mandara brothers draw crowds of locals to their pizzeria for *marechiaro* (pizza covered with seafood and oregano; €6.50) and other specialties. Pizza €4.50-7.50. *Primi* €4.50-7. Cover €1.50. Open Sept.-July Tu-Su noon-2:30pm and 6:30-10:30pm. AmEx/MC/V. ❶

👁 SIGHTS

🍽 **CAPPELLA DEGLI SCROVEGNI (ARENA CHAPEL).** Enrico Scrovegni dedicated this tall brick chapel to the Virgin Mary in an attempt to save the soul of his father Reginald, a usurer famously lambasted in the 17th *canto* of Dante's *Inferno*. Pisano carved the statues for the chapel, and Giotto covered the walls with frescoed scenes from the lives of Jesus, Mary, and her parents, Saints Joachim and Anne. Completed between 1305 and 1306, this 38-panel cycle is one of the first examples of depth and realism in Italian Renaissance painting. A brilliant blue ceiling is adorned with bright golden stars and images of Jesus and Mary, each surrounded by the prophets. Above the door, the *Last Judgment* depicts the blessed wearing halos to the left of the cross; to the right, a less fortunate crowd is eaten by hairy blue demons. Along the bottom, allegorical figures depicting the seven deadly sins face their opposites—the four cardinal and theological virtues—across the nave. Down a short gravel path from the museum, there is a multimedia room, featuring a short multilingual video on the chapel's history (narrated amusingly from Scrovegni's perspective) and an in-depth explanation of the fresco-painting technique. Additionally, the **Musei Civici Erimitani** has assembled an art collection including ancient Roman inscriptions and a beautiful crucifix by Giotto that once adorned the Scrovegni Chapel. (*P. Eremitani 8. ☎20 10 020; www.cappelladegliscrovegni.it. Entrance to the chapel only through the museum. Open Feb.-Oct. 9am-7pm; Nov.-Jan. 9am-6pm. Tickets may be purchased at the Musei Civici ticket office or online. Reserve ahead. Museum €10; combined ticket €12, students €8, disabled €1. AmEx/MC/V.*)

> **GIOTTO'S JUDGMENT.** In the *Last Judgment*, Giotto painted himself among the blessed as a sort of signature and perhaps self-assessment. Check him out—4th person from the left, with the pink robe and yellow hat.

BASILICA DI SANT'ANTONIO (IL SANTO). An array of rounded gray domes and conic spires caps Padua's enormous brick basilica. Bronze sculptures by Donatello grace the high altar, which is surrounded by the artist's *Crucifixion* and several Gothic frescoes. Upon entering, walk along the left side to reach the **Tomba di Sant'Antonio,** which sits on a platform underneath a huge marble arch. Each year, thousands of pilgrims crowd the marble bas-reliefs to cover the black stone of the sepulcher with framed photographs and prayers. Behind the main altar in the apse sits the **Cappella delle Reliquie,** where ornately carved sculptures look down on shrines containing everything from St. Anthony's tunic to his jawbone and tongue. A **multimedia show** in the courtyard (follow *"Mostra"* signs) details St. Anthony's life. Exit the basilica and turn right to reach the tiny **Oratorio di San Giorgio,** which displays Giotto-school frescoes and briefly served as a prison under Napoleon's rule, and the **Scuola del Santo,** which includes three of Titian's frescoes. (*P. del Santo. ☎82 42 811; www.basilicadelsanto.org. Basilica open daily Apr.-Sept. 6:15am-7:45pm; Nov.-Mar. 6:15am-7pm. Modest dress strictly enforced. Free. Mostra open daily 9am-12:30pm and 2:30-6pm. Free English audio tour available at front desk. Oratorio and Scuola ☎/fax 87 55 235. Oratorio open daily Apr.-Oct. 9am-12:30pm and 2:30-7pm; Nov.-Mar. 9am-12:30pm and 2:30-5pm. Scuola open daily 10-11am and 3-4pm. Wheelchair-accessible. €2.50, students and Padova Card €2. Cash only.*)

ORTO BOTANICO (BOTANICAL GARDEN). Leafy trees and high stone walls ring a circular grid of iron fences, gravel walkways, and low fountains in Europe's oldest university botanical garden, recognized as a UNESCO World Heritage site. Take your time wandering through the quiet oasis of water lilies, cacti, and medicinal herbs, or inhale the fresh scents from one of the many benches. "Goethe's palm," planted in 1585, was named after the poet visited and developed his (incorrect) pre-Darwinian theory of evolution based on the garden's leaves. (*V. Orto Botanico 15. Follow signs from basilica. ☎82 72 119. Open Apr.-Oct. daily 9am-1pm and 3-7pm; Nov.-Mar. M-F 9am-1pm. €4, over 65 €3, students €1. Cash only.*)

THE VENETO

PALAZZO BÒ AND ENVIRONS. The university campus is spread throughout the city but centers around the two bustling interior stone courtyards of Palazzo Bò, adorned with students' coats of arms and a war memorial. In the **Teatro Anatomico** (1594), a medical lecture hall that was the first of its kind, students peered in on a small anatomical table from above. Nearly all Venetian noblemen received their mandatory law and public policy instruction in the **Great Hall,** which is decorated with the coat-of-arms of university directors and administrators. The chair of Galileo is preserved in the **Sala dei Quaranta,** where the great physicist once lectured. *(V. VIII Febbraio. ☎82 73 047. Entrance with 45min. guided tour only. Tours M, W, F 3:15, 4:15, 5:15pm; Tu, Th, Sa 9:15, 10:15, 11:15am. Buy tickets 15min. before tour. €5, students €2.)* Across the street, ⬛**Caffè Pedrocchi,** founded in 1831, once served as the headquarters for 19th-century liberals who supported Risorgimento leader Giuseppe Mazzini. A turning point in the revolution occurred here in 1848, when a battle exploded between students and Austrian police. While considerably less revolutionary these days, it is still a cafe. *(V. VIII Febbraio 15. ☎87 81 231; www.caffepedrocchi.it. Open daily July to mid-Sept. 9am-1am; mid-Sept. to June 9am-9pm. AmEx/MC/V.)* The **Museo Risorgimento e dell'Eta Contemporanea** carefully follows the city's development within the larger political cycles of Italy up through the middle of the 20th century. The later galleries display from the human aspects of war, like propaganda posters and a powerful, shakily written WWII note. *(☎87 81 231. Open Tu-Su 9:30am-12:30pm and 3:30-6pm. €4, students €2.50. Cash only.)*

PALAZZO DELLA RAGIONE (LAW COURTS). A long balcony that overlooks the busy P. delle Erbe marks the entrance to this giant *palazzo*. The building's vast interior awes visitors under a barrel vault roof. Admire the giant wooden horse at the western end of the hall, then trace the frescoes depicting the astrological cycle all the way around. To the right of the entrance is the **Stone of Shame.** Inspired by the exhortations of St. Anthony in 1231 to abolish debtors' prisons, Padua adopted the practice of forcing half-clothed debtors onto the stone, surrounded by hundreds of heartless hecklers. *(At P. delle Erbe. ☎82 05 006. Open Tu-Su Feb.-Oct. 9am-7pm; Nov.-Jan. 9am-6pm. €4, students and Padova Card holders €5.)*

⬛TIP **GIMME TEN.** Padua's sights are best visited with the **Padova Card** (€14), which covers entrance to 10 museums: Scrovegni Chapel, Musei Civici Erimitani, Palazzo Zuckerman Museum, Palazzo della Ragione, Caffè Pedrocchi's Piano Nobile, Oratorio di San Michele, Oratorio di San Giorgio, Museo Risorgimento, Petrarch's House, the baptistry, and Botanical Gardens (of the major sights, only the *duomo* isn't included). The card also provides free transport on local buses and discounts from participating merchants. Visit the tourist office for more info.

PRATO DELLA VALLE. Originally a Roman theater, this ellipse is one of Europe's largest *piazze*. On the paved outermost track, joggers and bikers orbit the dog walkers, teenagers, and families who cross the moat to walk the pebbly paths, sit by the large fountain, or relax on the grass among statues of 78 famous *padovani*.

DUOMO. Michelangelo supposedly participated in the design of this hulking church, erected between the 16th and 18th centuries. The *duomo*'s white-walled simplicity makes the steps of the apse especially unusual—chunky, half-carved, marble statues of Saints Prosdocimo, Gregorio, and Giustina accompany a golden, praying figure whose flowing hair melds with a marble tree to create the church's lectern. *(P. Duomo. ☎66 28 14. Open M-Sa 7:20am-noon and 4-7:30pm, Su 8am-1pm and 4-8:30pm. Free.)* Next door, the striking 12th-century ⬛**battistero** (baptistry) is dedicated to St. John the Baptist. The interior walls are covered in colorful frescoes of New Testament scenes, while a massive, wide-eyed Christ and rings of painted saints look down from the hollow dome above. *(☎65 69 14. Open daily 10am-6pm. €2.50, students €1.50. Cash only.)*

🎵 ENTERTAINMENT

As the sun goes down on summer evenings in Padova, *piazza* seating fills and customers spill from bars and cafes into the squares. Nightlife rages in Padua during the school year, but most clubs close in summer and there is no full listing of clubs. Look for specific *discoteche* like **Villa Barbieri** and **Banale. Fly,** Galleria Tito Livio 4/6, between V. Roma and Riviera Tito Livio, is a pedestrian cafe by day and a swinging hot spot by night. The nearby V. Roma and bustling student population make this bar a great choice anytime. (☎87 52 892. Wine €2-3.50. Mixed drinks €3.50-4.50. Open M-Sa 9am-midnight.) For a different kind of celebration, pilgrims pack the city on June 13, as Padua commemorates the death of its patron saint, with a procession bearing Saint Anthony's statue and jawbone. An **antique market** assembles in the Prato della Valle on the 3rd Sunday of the month. Every Saturday the area holds a **clothing market**.

VICENZA ☎0444

Bustling Vicenza (vee-CHEN-za; pop. 106,000) found its hero in Renaissance architect Palladio. He designed the magnificent Teatro Olimpico in the town center, and his stately villas outside the city are the present-day legacies of a 15th-century real estate boom that moved nobles from Venice to the mainland. While Vicenza is characterized by its glamorous inhabitants and works of art, its easily navigable streets and friendly residents welcome visitors.

▉ TRANSPORTATION

The **train station** is at P. Stazione, at the end of V. Roma, across from Campo Marzo. (Info office open daily 7am-9pm. Ticket office open daily 6am-8:30pm. AmEx/MC/V.) **Trains** run to: Milan (2½hr., 27 per day 6:10am-8:42pm, €9.40); Padua (30min., 52 per day 6:08am-11:19pm, €2.70); Venice (1¼hr., 42 per day 6am-10:48pm, €6); Verona (40min., 48 per day 6:10am-11:47pm, €3.60). FTV, Vle. Milano 7 (☎22 31 15; ticket office open M-F 6am-7:40pm, Sa-Su 6:15am-7:40pm; cash only), left after exiting the train station, runs **buses** to Padua (30min.; 30 per day 5:50am-8:20pm, reduced service Sa-Su; €3.50). **RadioTaxi** (☎92 06 00) is available 24hr. at either end of C. Palladio. **Hertz** rents cars from the train station. (☎19 91 13 311 or 19 91 12 211. Open M-F 8:30am-12:30pm and 2:30-6:30pm, Sa 8:30am-12:30pm. MC/V.)

✳ 🔢 ORIENTATION AND PRACTICAL INFORMATION

The train station and adjacent intercity bus station occupy the southern part of the city. **Viale Roma** leads from the station into town. At the **Giardino Salvi**, turn right under the Roman archway on **Corso Palladio**. Walk straight several blocks to the old Roman wall that serves as a gate to the **Teatro Olimpico.** The tourist office is the door just to the right. **Piazza Matteotti** lies in front, at the end of C. Palladio.

Tourist Office: P. Matteotti 12 (☎32 08 54; www.vicenzae.org). Free maps of city and villa locations. Open daily 9am-1pm and 2-6pm. Branch at P. dei Signori 8 (☎54 41 22; iatvicenza2@provincia.vicenza.it). Open 10am-2pm and 2:30-6:30pm.

Budget Travel: AVIT, Vle. Roma 17 (☎54 56 77; www.avit.it). Open M-F 9am-12:30pm and 3-7pm, Sa 9:30am-12:30pm. AmEx/MC/V for plane tickets only.

Currency Exchange: At train station and post office. **ATMs** in the train station, on Contrà del Monte, and throughout the downtown area.

Pharmacy: P. dei Signori 49 (☎32 12 41). Posts after-hours rotation. Open June-Aug. M-F 8:45am-12:30pm and 4-7:30pm, Sa 8:45am-12:30pm; Sept.-May M-F 8:45am-12:30pm and 3:30-7pm, Sa 8:45am-12:30pm. Closed 2wk. in Aug. MC/V.

Internet Access: Galla 2000, Vle. Roma 14 (☎22 52 25). Bookstore with two Internet computers. €1.50 per 30min., €2.50 per hr. Open M 3:30-7:30pm, Tu-Sa 9am-7:30pm. AmEx/MC/V. **Vicenza.com,** P. dei Signori 6, to the left of the tourist office. €2.50 per 30min., €4 per hr.; students €1.60 per 30min, €3 per hr. Open M 4-7:30pm, Tu-Su 10am-1:30pm, 4-7:30pm. Cash only.

Post Office: Contrà Garibaldi 1 (☎33 20 77), between *duomo* and P. Signori. **Currency exchange** until 6pm. Open M-F 8:30am-6:30pm, Sa 8:30am-1:30pm. Cash only. **Postal Code:** 36100.

ACCOMMODATIONS AND CAMPING

Accommodations in Vicenza are conveniently located right in the heart of town, but are fairly pricey with the notable exception of the hostel.

Ostello Olimpico Vicenza (HI), V. Giuriolo 9 (☎54 02 22; fax 54 77 62). From the tourist office, walk up the street with the Museo Civico on the right. Buses #1, 2, 4, 5, and 7 also run from the station, ask bus driver for hostel stop. The *ostello* is the yellow building on the left. Small dorm rooms within sight of the Teatro Olimpico. Lockers free. Wheelchair-accessible. Reception 7:30-9:30am and 3:30-11:30pm. Dorms €17.50; singles €21, with bath €23; doubles €40/46. MC/V. ●

Hotel Castello, Contrà P. del Castello 24 (☎32 35 85/83; www.hotelcastelloitaly.com), just off P. del Castello. Centrally located hotel offers well-decorated rooms with A/C, satellite TV, telephone, and minibar, some with views and terraces. The lobby features a bar and funky modern art. Breakfast and parking included. Singles €70-90; doubles €100-120; triples €120-150. MC/V. ●

Hotel Giardini, V. Giuriolo 10 (☎/fax 32 64 58; www.hotelgiardini.com), across the street from Ostello Olimpico Vicenza. Modern, clean rooms and large beds steps from city sights. Rooms have satellite TV, A/C, bath, and minibar. Breakfast included. Reception 7am-1am. Singles €83; doubles €114; triples €119. AmEx/MC/V. ●

Campeggio Vicenza, Strada Pelosa 239 (☎58 23 11; www.ascom.vi.it/camping). Take bus #1 (€1) from the train station and ask for camping; the *campeggio* is a 10min. walk from the bus stop. Small mini-golf course on-site. Restaurant, TV, and free Internet access available at adjacent hotel. Laundry €6. Open Apr.-Sept. €5.70-7.40 per person, €8.20-10.60 per tent. Showers free. AmEx/MC/V. ●

FOOD

Vicenza's specialties include dried cod with polenta, asparagus with eggs, and *torresani* (pigeon). An enormous **market** sprawling across P. delle Erbe, P. Signori, and Vle. Roma sells cheese, fish, produce, and clothing (open Tu-Th 7:30am-2pm). Buy essentials at **PAM** supermarket, Vle. Roma 1, which has a huge wine selection. (Open M-Tu and Th-Sa 8am-8pm, W 8am-2pm. AmEx/MC/V.)

Righetti, P. del Duomo 3 (☎54 31 35), with another entrance at Contrà Fontana 6. A cool, traditional interior and *piazza*-side seating suggests high prices, but locals know better: this self-service trattoria is all budget. *Primi* from €3.80, *secondi* from €4.65. Cover €1. Open M-F noon-3pm and 6:30pm-1am; closed 1st 3wk. of Aug. Cash only. ●

Ristorante Agli Schioppi, Contrà P. del Castello 26 (☎54 37 01), right off P. del Castello. Traditional restaurant serves local specialties like codfish with polenta (€13) and *bigoli* pasta with meat, mushrooms and chili peppers (€7). *Primi* €6.50-8.50, *secondi* €10-12.50. Cover €2.50. Open M-F noon-2pm and 7-10pm, Sa noon-2pm. MC/V. ●

Zi' Teresa, Contrà S. Antonio 1 (☎32 14 11), at the end of the street, just left of the post office. Marble arches lead to this relaxing trattoria, where pizza like the *zi' teresa* (with mushrooms and grilled peppers; €8) or the 3-course *menù* (€20 with meat, €26 with fish) are served among plants and paintings. *Primi* €7-12, *secondi* €12-18. Cover €2. Open M-Tu and Th-Su noon-2:30pm and 6pm-midnight. AmEx/MC/V. ➍

Soraru Virgilio, Pta. Palladio 17 (☎32 09 15), to the right of the basilica. Shelves of liqueurs and candy jars tempt at this *pasticcerie* and cafe (allegedly the city's oldest), but the real draws are the pastries and creamy *gelato*, like the deliciously smooth *nocciola* (hazelnut), made fresh on-site. Enjoy your cone or pastry at *piazza* seating or sit on the steps of the Palladio statue in front. 2 scoops €1.60. Open M-Tu and Th-Su 8:30am-1pm and 3:30-8pm. Cash only. ➊

Nirvana Caffè Degli Artisti, P. Matteotti 8 (☎54 31 11). From C. Palladio, enter the *piazza* and turn left. Incense, Buddha statues, and a generally hippie vibe. Offers everything from *bruschetta* topped with tofu or mushrooms (€3.40-4) to a large selection of coffee and teas. *Primi* from €4, *secondi* €3.50-7.50. Open M and W 7:30am-8pm, Th-Sa 7:30am-midnight. ➋

◉ SIGHTS

The ▨**Teatro Olimpico,** in P. Matteotti, is the last structure planned by Palladio; he died before its completion. A beautiful sculpture garden leads to the ticket office and portrait gallery, but the *teatro* itself is the main attraction. The Accademia Olimpica, the city's organization for promotion of culture and the sciences, commissioned the project to introduce theater to the local public; the architect insisted that the Greek and Roman amphitheater style was the only one appropriate for the dramas the Accademia hoped to stage. Inside the *teatro*, carved statues (one for each of the Academy's members) fill the walls under a ceiling fresco of cloudy skies. Three main doors on stage and two side doors reveal the main streets of Thebes, crafted in perspective with excruciating attention to detail for the theater's 1st performance, *Oedipus Rex*, in 1585. Excellent English explanations leading to the theater provide insight into the details of that 1st performance. (☎22 28 00; www.olimpico.vicenza.it. Open Tu-Su 9am-5pm. Last entry 4:45pm. €8, students €5; includes entrance to Museo Civico. Cash only. English audio tour €3.) Each summer the city showcases local and imported talent in the Teatro Olimpico; check www.comune.vicenza.it for a list of productions. (☎22 28 01. MC/V.) The **Piazza dei Signori** was Vicenza's showpiece when the town was under Venetian control. Andrea Palladio's revamping of the **Basilica Palladiana** brought the architect his first taste of fame. (Basilica closed indefinitely for renovations.) The **Torre di Piazza,** a brown brick clock tower on the left of the building, reveals a glimpse of the basilica's pre-Palladio architecture. The **Loggia del Capitano,** a city hall building across from the Torre di Piazza, shows the results of the reconstruction, with two stories of marble arches and pillars masking the crumbling brick beneath. Housed in Palladio's stately **Palazzo Chiericati,** the collection in the **Museo Civico,** across from the tourist office, includes Renaissance art from Veneto powerhouses Tintoretto, Veronese, and sculptor Alessandro Vittoria. Giovanni Battista's first signed and dated work, *The Madonna of the Pergola* is in the last room, after Montagna's *Madonna Enthroned* and Tintoretto's *Miracle of St. Augustine*. (☎32 13 48. Open Tu-Su 9am-5pm. Last entry 15min. before closing. Entrance included with Teatro Olimpico ticket.) For a view of Vicenza and Palladio's architecture, exit the train station and turn right on Vle. Venezia for about 10min., then turn left and go uphill at V. X Giugno. A long loggia to the left contains a staircase and ramp leading up **Monte Berico** to the plateau of **Piazzale Vittoria,** where balconies jut out over the hillside and provide a view of the city.

▨ DAYTRIP FROM VICENZA: THE PALLADIAN VILLAS

Venetian expansion to the mainland began in the 15th century as Venice's maritime supremacy faded and nobles turned their attention to the acquisition of real estate on the mainland. The Venetian senate ordered nobles to build villas rather than castles to preclude the possibility of fiefdoms. The rush to build these residential estates provided scores of opportunities for the renowned architect Palladio to use his talents. Consequently, the Veneto region now contains hundreds of Europe's most splendid villas. Some offer classical music concerts during summer; others can be rented for exorbitant rates—just remember that Neoclassical luxury doesn't come cheap. Check with local and regional tourist offices for details and contact info on regional villas. Many of the Palladian villas scattered throughout the Veneto are difficult to reach, but fortunately, some of the most famous lie within a scenic 30min. walk of Vicenza. Stop for a moment at the **Villa Valmarana** (open mid-Mar. to Oct. Tu-Su 10am-noon and 3-6pm; €5) to admire its perfectly manicured rose gardens before moving on to the ■**Villa Rotonda**, one of the 16th century's most harmonious architectural achievements. Begun in 1550, the villa's precision and alignment with the cardinal points produced a majestic configuration. It became a model for buildings in England, France, and the US, most notably Thomas Jefferson's Monticello. Don't feel badly if you miss a look at the villa's interior (entrance is only offered W only); the majesty of Villa Rotonda can be just as easily appreciated from the outdoors. (☎32 17 93. Open mid-Mar. to mid-Oct. Interior open W 10am-noon and 3-6pm. Grounds open Tu-Su 10am-noon and 3-6pm. Grounds €5, with interior €10.) For those devoted to Palladio's architectural vision, the "Palladio by the Hand" Tour Company (☎32 08 54; www.vicenzae.org), run through the tourist office, offers Saturday and Sunday half- and full-day tours (€15/20) of Vicenza and some of the villas, with bus transportation to the villas provided. *(From Mt. Berico's P. Vittoria, head straight, keeping the mountains on the right. Bear left, and continue down Stradella Valmarana. Or from Vle. Roma, just to the right of the train station, take bus #8 (€1) and ask for "La Rotonda.")*

VERONA
☎045

Though *Romeo and Juliet* may bring tourists to Verona (ve-RO-na; pop. 4000), it is the city's rich history, architecture, and culture that truly makes it Italy's fourth most visited city. From the winding river Adige to the city's dizzying towers, Verona offers the perks of a large city while maintaining a reputation for authentic local cuisine, rich wines, and an internationally renowned opera.

▐ TRANSPORTATION

Flights: Aeroporto Valerio Catullo (☎80 95 666; www.aeroportoverona.it), 16km from *centro*. For shuttles from train station (☎805 7922; www.aptv.it; 5:40am, then every 20min. 6:10am-11:10pm; €4.50), buy tickets on bus. Cash only.

Trains: In P. XXV Aprile (☎89 20 21). Ticket office open daily 5:50am-9:30pm. Info office open daily 7am-9pm. To: **Bologna** (2hr., 22 per day 5:05am-10:30pm, €6); **Milan** (2hr., 34 per day 5:30am-10:42pm, €7); **Rome** (7hr., 4 per day 5:30am-11pm, €45); **Trent** (1hr., 25 per day 12:46am-10:48pm, €4.65); **Venice** (1½hr., 41 per day 5:52am-10:43pm, €8); **Vicenza** (45min., 55 per day 5:52am-10:42pm, €3.40).

Buses: APTV, (www.aptv.it) in P. XXV Aprile, in the gray building in front of the train station. Station open M-Sa 6am-8pm, Su 6:30am-8pm. Buses run to **Brescia** (2hr., hourly 6:40am-6:10pm, €5.30), **Riva del Garda** (2hr., 15 per day 6:40am-6:45pm, €5.20), and **Sirmione** (1hr., 17 per day 6:40am-8pm, €2.80). Reduced service Sa-Su.

Taxis: RadioTaxi (☎53 26 66; www.radiotaxiverona.it). 24hr.

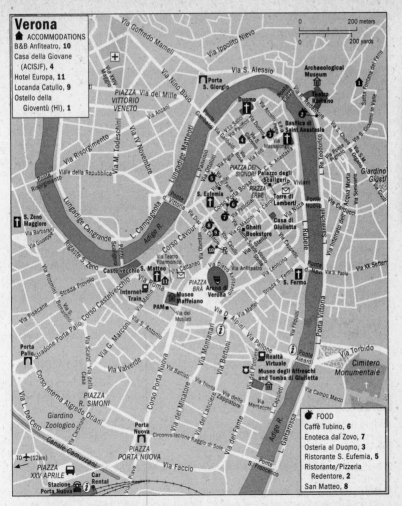

Verona

ACCOMMODATIONS
B&B Anfiteatro, **10**
Casa della Giovane
  (ACISJF), **4**
Hotel Europa, **11**
Locanda Catullo, **9**
Ostello della
  Gioventù (HI), **1**

FOOD
Caffè Tubino, **6**
Enoteca dal Zovo, **7**
Osteria al Duomo, **3**
Ristorante S. Eufemia, **5**
Ristorante/Pizzeria
  Redentore, **2**
San Matteo, **8**

Car Rental: Avis (☎80 06 636). Open M-F 8am-noon and 3-7pm, Sa 8am-noon. **Europcar** (☎92 73 161). Open M-F 8:30am-noon and 2:30-7pm, Sa 8:30am-noon. **Hertz** (☎80 00 832) and **Maggiore** (☎80 04 808). 21+. Both open M-F 8am-noon and 2:30-7pm, Sa 8am-noon. All 4 have offices at the train station. AmEx/MC/V.

✈🛈 ORIENTATION AND PRACTICAL INFORMATION

From the **train station** in P. XXV Aprile, walk 20min. up **Corso Porta Nuova,** or take bus #11, 12, 13, 51, 72, or 73 (weekends take #91, 92, or 93; tickets €1, full day €3.50) to Verona's *centro,* the **Arena di Verona,** in **Piazza Brà.** Most sights lie between P. Brà and the **Adige River. Via Mazzini** connects the Arena to the monuments of **Piazza delle Erbe** and **Piazza dei Signori**. The **Teatro Romano** and the **Giardino Giusti** lie across the bridges **Pietra, Navi,** and **Nuovo** on the Adige.

Tourist Office: At V. degli Alpini 9 (☎80 68 680; iatverona@provincia.vr.it). From C. Pta. Nuova, enter P. Brà; stay right until you reach the office. Open M-Sa 9am-7pm, Su 9am-3pm. Branches at the airport (☎ 86 19 163; iataeroporto@provincia.vr.it; open M-Sa 9am-6pm) and the train station (☎ 80 00 861; iatferrovia@provincia.vr.it; open M-Sa 9am-6pm, Su 9am-3pm).

Luggage Storage: (☎80 23 827; info@grandistazioni.it), at the train station. €3.80 for 1st 5hr., €0.60 per hr. for 6-12hr., €0.20 per hr. thereafter; 5-day max. 20kg max. per bag. Open daily 7am-11pm. Cash only.

English-Language Bookstore: Ghelfi & Barbato, V. Mazzini 34 (☎01 23 456), at the intersection with V. Quattro Spade. Small, yet balanced English section. Open M 10am-1pm, Tu-Sa 9am-1pm and 2-8pm. MC/V.

Beyond Tourism: Informagiovani, V. Ponte Aleardi 15. (☎80 10 796; www.informagiovani.comune.verona.it), helps find work or study opportunities in Verona. Additional tourist info and bike rental available. Open M, W, F 9am-1pm; Tu and Th 3-5pm.

Police: V. del Pontiere 32/a (☎80 78 411).

Pharmacy: Farmacia Due Campane, V. Mazzini 52 (☎80 06 660). Open M-F 9:10am-12:30pm and 3:30-7:30pm, Sa 9:10am-12:30pm. Check *L'Arena* newspaper for 24hr. pharmacy listings. MC/V.

Hospital: Ospedale Civile Maggiore (☎80 71 111), on Borgo Trento in P. Stefani in the north part of town.

Internet Access: Internet Train, V. Roma 17/A (☎80 13 394). From P. Brà, turn right on V. Roma; 2 blocks down on left. High-speed computers. €2.50 per 30min. 1st-time users get a bonus hr. after 1st hr. Open M-F 10am-10pm, Sa-Su 2-8pm. MC/V.

Post Office: V. Cattaneo 23 (☎80 59 911). Open M-Sa 8:30am-6:30pm. **Postal Code:** 37100.

ACCOMMODATIONS

Budget hotels are sparse in Verona, and those that do exist fill up quickly. Make reservations ahead of time, especially during the opera season (June-Sept.). Prices rise when there are opera performances, and drop precipitously in the low season.

Bed and Breakfast Anfiteatro, V. Alberto Mario 5 (☎347 24 88 462; www.anfiteatrobedandbreakfast.com). Walking toward P. Brà, V. Alberto Mario branches off from V. Mazzini to the right. Romantic rooms with TV and central location make this brand-new B&B one of the town's best options. Breakfast included. Doubles €90-110. ❹

Ostello della Gioventù Villa Francescatti (HI), Salita Fontana del Ferro 15 (☎59 03 60; fax 80 09 127). Take bus #73 or night bus #90 to P. Isolo. By foot from the Arena, turn on V. Anfiteatro, cross Ponte Nuovo on V. Carducci, turn left on V. Giusti, then right on V. San Giovanni in Valle, and follow yellow signs uphill. A communal dining and hangout area creates a social atmosphere, as do the close quarters in the 8- and 10-person single-sex dorms. Breakfast included; dinner €8. Laundry €2.50. 5-night max. stay. Check-in 5pm. Lockout 9am-5pm. Curfew 11:30pm, for opera-goers 1:30am. Lights out at midnight. Reservations accepted for family rooms. HI members only. Dorms €16. Cash only. ❶

Locanda Catullo, Vco. Catullo 1, 2nd fl. (☎800 27 86; fax 59 69 87). Follow V. Mazzini to V. Catullo, then turn left on Vco. Catullo. Elegant hallway leads to simple, spacious rooms. No fans or A/C. Advance payment required. Reception 9am-11pm. Singles €40; doubles €55, with bath €65; triples €80/96. Cash only. ❸

Casa della Giovane (ACISJF), V. Pigna 7 (☎59 68 80; info@casadellagiovane.com). From P. delle Erbe, turn right on C. Sant'Anastasia and take 1st left on V. Rosa; V. Pigna is 3rd street on the right. Bedrooms and baths aren't fancy, but are comfortable for the price. Peaceful atmosphere. Showers until 10pm. Laundry wash only €1.55. Lockout 9am-1pm. Curfew 11pm, except for opera-goers (present ticket upon return). Reserve ahead by email. Women only. Dorms €20.50; singles €20.50; doubles €33, with bath €39; triples €46.50/49.50. Cash only. ❶

Hotel Europa, V. Roma 8 (☎59 47 44; www.veronahoteleuropa.com), close to P. Brà. Small but comfortable rooms. A/C, TV, minibar, phone and brightly colored bathrooms. Breakfast included. Singles €90; doubles €130; triples €155. AmEx/MC/V. ❺

🗒 FOOD

Verona is famous for its wines, among them the dry white *Soave* and the red *Valpolicella, Bardolino, Recioto,* and *Amarone.* Local specialties include *gnocchi, pasta e fagioli* (pasta and beans soup), and locally grown asparagus. **PAM,** V. dei Mutilati 3, sells essentials. From P. Brà, pass through the arch to C. Pta. Nuova, and turn right on V. Mutilati. (Open M-Sa 8am-8:30pm. AmEx/MC/V.)

🖾 **Enoteca dal Zovo,** Vco. San Marco in Foro 7/5 (☎80 34 369; www.enotecadalzovo.it), off C. Pta. Borsari. Though the cluttered shelves of bottles make this small winery seem more like an apothecary shop, this *enoteca* occupies a converted chapel with original frescoes still adorning the ceiling. Owners Oreste and Beverly dal Zovo serve impressive wines (glasses from €0.75) and the potent Elixir of Love (an herbal, after-dinner liqueur) while welcoming visitors like old friends. Open daily 8am-8pm. Closed M in winter. Cash only. ❶

🖾 **Osteria al Duomo,** V. Duomo 7/a (☎80 04 505), on the way to the *duomo*. Small restaurant with dark wood interior contains a few cozy tables, a bar and a small menu, but serves excellent, simple cuisine like *tagliatelle* with shrimp and zucchini. *Primi* €6-6.30, *secondi* €8-12. Cover €1. Open Tu-Sa noon-2:30pm and 7-10pm. Cash only. ❶

San Matteo, Vco. del Guasto 4 (☎80 04 538; fax 59 39 38), from P. delle Erbe on C. Pta. Borsari, walk 5min., and turn left. Housed in a deconsecrated church. Beautiful exterior with a simply and elegantly decorated interior. *Primi* €7.50-11, *secondi* €9-17. Cover €1.50. Open daily noon-2:30pm and 6pm-12:30am. AmEx/MC/V. ❸

Ristorante/Pizzeria Redentore, V. Regaste Redentore 15 (☎80 05 932), right across Ponte Pietra. Offers indoor and outdoor seating, though this casual restaurant's best feature is its patio seating with views of the Adige River, *duomo,* and Torre dei Lamberti. Pizza €3.50-7.50. *Primi* (with good vegetarian options) €6-8.50, *secondi* €7-9.50. Cover €1.30. Open Tu-Su noon-2pm and 7pm-midnight. AmEx/MC/V. ❸

Ristorante San Eufemia, V. Emilei 21/B (☎80 06 865; www.s.eufemia.it). Perfect for a romantic pre-opera meal. Serves dishes like the *tagliatelle S. Eufemia* (with mushrooms, asparagus, and tomatoes; €9) in a Roman *palazzo. Primi* €7-16, *secondi* €8-16. Cover €2. Open June-Aug. daily noon-2:30pm and 6-10:30pm; Sept.-May M-Sa noon-2:30pm and 7:30-10:30pm. AmEx/MC/V. ❹

Caffè Tubino, C. Pta. Borsari 15/D (☎80 31 313), near the intersection of C. Pta. Borsari and V. Fama. Housed in a 17th-century *palazzo.* Serves up healthy doses of coffee and kitsch with rich brews and floor-to-ceiling wall of teacups. Seating is scarce, but come for the popular ground coffee (€18-25 per kg). Espresso €0.90. Cappuccino €1.40. Open daily 7:15am-8:30 pm. Cash only. ❶

👁 SIGHTS

■ **SHAKESPEAREAN HUBRIS.** People still flock to Verona for its role as the setting of *Romeo and Juliet,* hoping to absorb some love from the Bard's ill-fated couple. In the **Casa di Giulietta,** tourists pose on the stone balcony, but the house is best admired from the outside, where the vastly more entertaining lovers' graffiti builds up. The Veronese authorities have protected the building from further poetic injury by slyly installing plastic sheets where people write graffiti. They are replaced every two months, and no young Romeo is the wiser. Contrary to popular belief, the Capulet family never lived here, so save your money and don't go inside. *(V. Cappello 23. ☎80 34 303. Open M 1:30-7:30pm, Tu-Su 8:30am-7:30pm. Ticket office closes 6:45pm. €4, students and seniors €3. Cash only.)* A canopy shades the walkway into the **Museo Degli Affreschi,** which displays Veronese artwork, including an excellent collection of Italian frescoes from the 10th to 16th centuries. In the museum's garden is the faux **Tomba di Giulietta,** a cave with a single window illuminating the sepulcher. It only takes a moment to mourn at the *tomba,* but the atrium courtyard provides a quiet place to rest your feet after touring the art inside. *(V. del Pontiere 5. ☎80 00 361. Open M 1:30-7:30pm, Tu-Su 8:30am-7:30pm. Ticket office closes 6:45pm. €3, students and seniors €2.)* The **Casa di Romeo,** reportedly once the home of the Montecchi (Montague) family, sits around the corner from P. dei Signori at V. Arche Scaligeri 2. The villa is privately owned and closed to the public.

> **TIP** **ROMEO, ROMEO, WHEREFORE ART THOU ROMEO?** Juliet & Co. provides excellent 2hr. walking tours of Verona, from Apr. 1 to Nov. 5 daily at 5:30pm. The tour departs from the statue of Vittorio Emanuele in P. Brà. (☎045 81 03 173; www.julietandco.com. €10.)

■ **PIAZZA ERBE AND PIAZZA DEI SIGNORI.** Tourists and school groups swarm P. Erbe, which features a market selling fruit and tacky souvenirs. Shops and restaurants line the *piazza;* in its center, pigeons hop around tiers of the **Madonna Verona's Fountain.** Ironically, fruit vendors' awnings nearly hide the **Berlina,** a platform on which medieval convicts were punished by being pelted with produce. The eerie chains still dangle from the platform today. P. delle Erbe lies near **Via Mazzini,** where pink marble leads local *glitterati* to Gucci and Louis Vuitton along the city's fashion row. The **Arco della Costa** (Arch of the Rib) connects P. delle Erbe to **Piazza dei Signori.** A whale rib, prophesied to fall on the first passing person who has never told a lie, still dangles from the arch, and a statue of Dante stands in the center of the *piazza.* The 15th-century **Loggia del Consiglio** sits behind the *piazza* just behind Dante's back. The views from the first terrace alone (either elevator or stairs) are worth the money, but climb the extra steps for the best views of the Adige, Verona's brick rooftops. and the mountains beyond. *(Turn right after Arco della Costa when P. dei Signori begins. ☎80 32 726. Open M 1:30-7:30pm, Tu-Su 8:30am-7:30pm. Last entry 45min. before closing. Elevator €4, students €3; stairs €3. Cash only.)* The della Scala family lived in the **Palazzo degli Scaligeri,** and the medieval **Tombs of the Scaligeri,** on V. Arche Scaligeri, are through the arch in P. dei Signori.

THE ARENA. This first-century Roman amphitheater, which was rocked by an earthquake in the 12th century, is an odd mix of old and new. An eroded stone slab still towers over the replacement metal seats. Each summer, loud construction accentuates the anachronism as the stadium gears up with sets and concession stands to become Verona's **opera house,** where the city stages the famed **Verona Opera Festival.** *(In P. Brà. ☎80 03 204. Open M 1:30-7:30pm, Tu-Su 8:30am-*

7:30pm. Closes 4:30pm on opera nights. Last entry 1hr. before closing. Wheelchair-accessible. €4, students and seniors €3, children 8-13 with accompanying adult €1.)

BASILICA DI SANT'ANASTASIA. This Gothic church, Verona's largest, hides artistic treasures behind crumbling brick doors. To the left of the main altar, the Lavagnoli Chapel features three 15th-century frescoes, including a crucifixion scene. To the right, the Cappella Pellegrini depicts the life of Christ with Michele da Firenze's series of 24 terra-cotta reliefs. *(At the end of C. Sant'Anastasia. For info, call the Associazione "Chiese Vive" at ☎ 59 28 13. Open Mar.-Oct. M-Sa 9am-6pm, Su 1-6pm; Nov.-Feb. Tu-Su 10am-1pm and 1:30-4pm. €2.50, students €1. Cash only.)*

DUOMO AND ENVIRONS. History lives beneath the floorboards of this 12th-century *duomo*, including ancient Roman thermal baths and two previous basilicas. The excavation of one of the older basilicas, the Church of St. Elena, is accessible through the *duomo*, just to the left of the apse. Titian's *Assumption of the Virgin*, which is a less potent version of his later *Assumption* that now hangs in Venice is in the 1st chapel on the left. *(At the end of V. Duomo. From the basilica, turn on V. Massalongo, which becomes V. Duomo. ☎ 59 28 13. Open Mar.-Oct. M-Sa 10am-5:30pm, Su 1-6 pm; Nov.-Feb. Tu-Sa 10am-1pm and 1:30-4pm, Su 1:30-5pm. €2.50, students €2. Cash only.)*

> **⚡TIP** **MY FAIR VERONA.** The **Verona Card** (day pass €8, 3 days €12) is an excellent money-saving option, covering entry to all museums, churches, and sights, excluding only the Giardino Giusti and the Scavi Scaligeri. Purchase it at any participating museum or church. Churches also offer their own pass (€5, students and seniors €4), permitting entrance to the basilica, *duomo*, S. Fermo, S. Zeno, and S. Lorenzo.

TEATRO ROMANO AND ENVIRONS. A crumbling **Roman theater** comes alive with productions of Shakespeare's works translated into Italian (**Entertainment,** p. 331). Behind the theater's seats, precarious Roman stairs weave up a small hillside to the city's **archaeological museum.** Built in 1480, this former Jesuit monastery now houses a museum displaying Roman and Greek artifacts excavated from the area. In the center sits the **Grande Terrazza,** a quiet, leafy garden lined with Roman bas-reliefs and pedestals. *(V. R. Redentore 2. Cross Ponte Pietra from the centro, and turn right. ☎ 80 00 360; fax 80 10 587. Open M 1:15-7:30pm, Tu-Su 8:30am-7:30pm. Ticket office closes 6:45pm. €3, students €2. Cash only.)* Behind a brown facade, the gates of the 16th-century **🔲Giardino Giusti** open onto a spacious hillside dotted with trickling, moss-covered fountains and rows of meticulously trimmed hedges—including **Il Labirinto,** a thigh-high hedge maze, which children and adults alike can explore. The cypress-lined avenue gradually winds upward to a series of picturesque porticoes and curving balconies with breathtaking views of Verona at each of the many stopping points. *(Down V. S. Chiara from Teatro Romano at V. Giusti 2. ☎ 80 34 029. Open daily Apr.-Sept. 9am-8pm; Oct.-Mar. 9am-7pm. €5, students €2.50, under 18 free. Cash only.)*

CASTELVECCHIO AND ENVIRONS. The 14th-century *castello* was built by the della Scala family, whose coat of arms and frescoes still line the interior walls. These days, the castle is a **museum** of sculptures and paintings, among them Pisanello's celebration of natural paradise in *Madonna della Quaglia*, but the castle is most interesting when admired from the outside. **Ponte Castelvecchio,** to the left of the castle, provides a lovely view of Verona along the swirling **Fiume Adige.** *(From P. Brà, take V. Roma to C. Castelvecchio 2. ☎ 80 62 611; www.comune.verona.it/castelvecchio/cvsito. Open M 1:30-7:30pm, Tu-Su 8:30am-7:30pm. Last entry 45min. before closing. €4, students €3. Audio tour in English, German,*

OUT, OUT, BRIEF CANDLE

On August 10, 1913, Giuseppe Verdi's *Aïda* opened the Verona Opera Festival. Performed before thousands of spectators in the Arena di Verona, it echoed through the theater on the ceremonial evening, Verdi's 100th birthday. Still several years before the installation of electric lights, the theater was dark, the stage dim, and the programs impossible to read. Despite the less-than-ideal conditions, the crowd remained eager, since Verdi had long been a favorite of the Italians, and the lighting created a superbly dramatic effect, as each opera-goer had brought a candle to keep the arena aglow throughout the night.

Soon after, the advent of electricity meant that the Arena di Verona traded candlelight for the spotlight, and the tradition quickly fell out of favor. But in the mid-30s, a wealthy patron of the arts decided to revive the enlightened ritual by making candles available to modern operagoers. Now boxes of candles greet spectators as they enter the theater for every summer performance. Just before the first act, as if on silent cue, everyone in the theater lights a candle, setting the entire arena ablaze with twinkling lights. Over the course of the performance, the candles are left to burn out on their own. As the acts unfold, one by one, individual candles wink out, allowing only the actors to shine.

and Italian €4. Cash only.) Scipione Maffei's devotion to preserving stone inscriptions is enshrined in the nearby **Museo Maffeiano,** where much of the sizable array of Greek, Roman, and Etruscan art is over 2000 years old. *(At the corner of V. Roma and C. Pta. Nuova. ☎59 00 87. Open M 1:30-7:30 pm, Tu-Sun 8:30am-2pm. €3, students €2. Cash only.)*

SAN ZENO MAGGIORE. Named for Verona's patron saint, who converted the city to Christianity in the 4th century, this massive brick church 15-20min. outside the city is one of Verona's finest examples of Italian Romanesque architecture. An urn in the subterranean crypt holds Zeno's remains, and one particularly beautiful balcony among the church's multiple levels features statues of Christ and the 12 Apostles. *(From Castelvecchio, walk up Rigaste San Zeno and turn left at the piazza on V. Barbarani, then right on V. San Procolo to the church on the right. For info, call the Associazione "Chiese Vive" at ☎59 28 13. Open Mar.-Oct. M-Sa 8:30am-6pm, Su 1:30-6pm; Nov.-Feb. M 8:30am-noon and 3-5pm, Tu-Sa 8:30am-1pm and 1:30-4pm, Su 1:30-5pm. €2.50. Cash only.)*

🎵 ENTERTAINMENT

The Arena di Verona is the venue for the world-famous 🎭**Verona Opera Festival,** which attracts opera buffs in droves every year from June to September. Past productions have included Verdi's *Nabucco, Aida,* and *La Traviata;* Puccini's *La Bohème;* and Rossini's *The Barber of Seville.* The 2008 opera season runs from June 20 to Aug. 31.(Tickets and info at V. Dietro Anfiteatro 6/B, along the side of the Arena. ☎80 05 151; www.arena.it. Open M-F 9am-noon and 3:15-5:45pm, Sa 9am-noon. Open on performance days 10am-9pm. Admission €21-198 weekends, €19-183 weekdays; seats range from stone steps to reserved "gold" membership seating; purchased online. AmEx/MC/V.) Also in summer, the **Teatro Romano,** V. R. Redentore 2, close to the Ponte Pietà, stages dance performances and Shakespearean plays performed in Italian. June brings the Verona jazz festival. (Info ☎80 77 201 or 80 77 500; www.estateteatraleveronese.it. Ticket office at Palazzo Barbieri, V. Leoncino 61. Open M-Sa 10:30am-1pm and 4-7pm. Tickets for both €11-21.)

CAORLE ☎0421

The small fishing town of Caorle (kah-OR-leh, pop. 10,000) has been nicknamed "Little Venice," and with its winding *calli* (narrow pedestrian streets) and brightly-colored buildings, it's easy to see why. Although it may remind visitors of its colossal cousin, which is just a

2hr. train ride away, Caorle has a charm all its own. Stroll through the quiet stone streets of the Old City, sample the seafood fresh from local docks, and sunbathe on miles of pristine shoreline. What it lacks in cultural attractions, Caorle makes up in relatively affordable accommodations, beautiful beaches, and an unpretentious attitude.

TRANSPORTATION. Caorle is accessible by a 45min. bus ride from the nearest train station in Portogruaro. The **bus** station is located at the intersection of Strada Traghete and C. So Chiggiato, a 5min. walk from the town center. (☎38 36 75. Ticket office open daily 6am-7pm and 8:45-10:30pm.) Buses run between Portogruaro and Caorle (17 per day 5:45am-10:30pm, €3.10). Buses also run directly from Carole to Venice (1½hr., 19 per day 5am-8pm, €4.70). From Portogruaro, **trains** run to Trieste (1¼hr., 14 per day 1am-midnight, €6.60) and Venice (1½ hr., 38 per day 4:24am-10:38pm, €4). The ticket office is open daily 6:05am-5:25pm and 5:40-7:40pm. Local bus lines connect the central bus station with Porto Falconeraon the western end of town and Traghetto on the eastern end. (Tickets €1, on sale at tourist office and *tabaccherie*.) Rent **bikes** at Liliano, V. Santa Margherita 17. (☎338 887 440. €3 per hr., €10 per day. Open daily 9am-7pm. Cash only.) Or try Da Fiammetta, V. Istria 3. (☎338 86 01 794. €3.50 per hr., €10 per day. Open daily 8:30am-midnight.)

ORIENTATION AND PRACTICAL INFORMATION. From the bus station, take V. San Giuseppe, then turn right on V. Altinates and left on Strada Nuova to reach P. Papa Giovanni, which marks the northeastern border of Caorle's Old City. The **tourist office,** Calle Dele Liburniche 26, just off the *piazza*, offers great **maps** and info on local and regional attractions. (☎81 401. Open daily 8am-2pm and 4-10pm.) In an **emergency,** call the **police** (☎27 82 11). The nearest **hospital** is in Portogruaro, but the **clinic** on Vle. Buonarroti has 24hr. first aid and an on-call doctor. A **pharmacy** is located at Rio Terra 30 (☎81 044; open daily 8:45am-12:30pm and 4:30-10:30pm). For **Internet** access, head next door to Central Photo at Rio Terra 38. (☎81 039. Open May-Sept. daily 9am-noon and 4:30-11pm; Oct.-Apr. Tu-Su 9am-noon and 3:30-7pm. €2 per 30min., €3 per hr.) The post office is at Calle Lunga 1. (☎21 99 11. Open M-F 8:30am-2pm, Sa 8:30am-1pm.) **Postal Code:** 30021.

ACCOMMODATIONS. Caorle offers scores of hotels on or near the beach. Expect that a beach chair, umbrella, and some pension package will be included in your nightly rate. From the bus station, turn left on C. So Chiggiato, then turn right on V. Falconera to reach **Albergo Villa Venezia ❷,** V. Falconera 13, which welcomes guests to simple, comfortable rooms and a bustling dining room. The real draws, however, are the friendly staff and winning location—less than 5min. from both the bus station and the beach. (☎21 23 13; www.villavenezia.caorle.it. Free bike rental. €23-31 per person; varies seasonally. MC/V.) Just a few blocks from the center and Spiaggia di Ponente, **Hotel Palladio ❷,** V. dello Storione 11, is a reasonably-priced option with funky lobby decor. Take V. Santa Andrea out of the *centro;* V. dello Storione is on the left. Rooms have bath, TV, and phone. Some rooms have balcony and A/C. (☎81 205; www.caorlepalladio.com. Breakfast €5. Meals served 50m away at Hotel Marco Polo. €6 for beach equipment if not on half/full pension option. €22-27 per person. €7 surcharge for singles. MC/V.) To get to **Hotel Meduna ❸,** V. Nicesolo 11, from the bus station, turn left on C. So Chiggiato, then turn right on V. Nicesolo; the hotel is on the corner. English-speaking owner Roberto offers clean, quiet rooms with bath, phone, A/C, balcony, and satellite TV. (☎21 29 96; www.hotelmeduna.com. Breakfast €5. Beach equipment included. Min. 3-night stay. €30-40 per person; prices vary seasonally. MC/V.) **Camping Santa Margherita ❶,** V. Duca degli Abruzzi, is a hike from the bus station and Old City, but only steps away from the shoreline of Spiaggia di Ponente. From the bus station, take local bus #98-99 toward Traghetto (hourly 7:30am-10:30pm, €1) and ask for Camping S. Margherita, or walk 20-25min. down

STONED

Along the boardwalk that begins at the historic Santuario della Madonna and stretches along the town's beautiful coastline to the east, Caorle is developing an art tradition to match its beach scene. Every other year in late June, five sculptors from around the world arrive in the small fishing town to work one of the hundreds of shoreline stones into a personal creation. The project, called Viva Scogliera (Long Live the Stones), allows locals and visitors an unobstructed view of the creative process: during selected hours, the five sculptors allow the public to look on as they continue to transform the boardwalk.

Initiated in 1993, Viva Scogliera began as an annual event; in 2003, town officials decided to alternate years, worrying that they might run out of stones! Now, the competition takes place only during even-numbered years.

Jin Hee Lee, a South Korean sculptor, takes credit for the stone that has come to symbolize the project: an exaggerated nose and pair of lips, entitled "Self-Portrait." The dramatic 1994 sculpture "Umanità," by Italian artist Franco Maschio, features a man reaching off a cliff for the outstretched hand of a falling comrade. To browse the sculptures, start at the Madonna and meander down the boardwalk, stopping briefly to take in each of the labeled stones against the blue-green Adriatic Sea.

Lungomare Venezia from the center of town. A supermarket and restaurant/bar are located on the premises of this quiet, shaded spot. (☎81 276; www.campingcaorle.it. Open Apr.-Oct. €3.60-7.45 per person, €6.60-17.50 per tent site.)

◻ **FOOD.** True to its reputation as a fishing town, Caorle specializes in fresh seafood straight from the Adriatic. Sit in one of the colorful booths at **Ristorante Pizzeria de Mauri ❷**, P. San Pio X. The simple menu offers grilled fish and delicious seafood pasta, like *spaghetti pescatore* (€8), at slightly lower prices than its nearby competitors. (☎81 279. Open daily 10am-3pm and 5:30-10pm. *Primi* €6-7.50, *secondi* €7-15.50. MC/V.) Despite the illuminated Coca-Cola sign, **Taverna Caorlina ❷**, V. Francesconi 19, is no tourist trap. Locals consistently recommend the piping-hot pizza served either at either the shaded outdoor tables or inside among the colorful tablecloths and photographs. (☎81 115. Open daily 11:40am-midnight. Pizza €4.45-9.45. *Primi* €7.45-11.45. MC/V.) To enjoy ocean views along with your fresh daily catch, make the 20min. trip down Lungomare Venezia to **Picnic**, V. Timavo 6, on the western shore. Eat in your bathing suit at the cafe's plastic outdoor tables, or cover up for the classier ambience at the restaurant indoors, which has the same menu and views. (☎21 15 75. Open daily 7am-midnight. *Primi* €6-9.50, *secondi* €9-15. MC/V.) Small markets can be found in and around the *centro*, but the closest supermarket is **Super M**, V. delle Orate 47, entrance is around the corner on V. Calamri. (☎81 167. Open M-F 8am-1pm and 3:30-8:30pm, Sa-Su 8am-8:30pm. MC/V). On Saturdays from 8:30am-1pm, the stands of the **outdoor market** behind the bus station sell fresh fruit, vegetables, and cheese.

◪◙ **BEACHES AND SIGHTS.** Vacationers from Italy, Austria and Slovenia converge in Carole during the summer months, sharing adjacent beach umbrellas and waiting at one of the town's many *gelaterie*. The town's two main **beaches**, Spiaggia di Levante and Spiaggia di Ponente, extend to the left and right, respectively, from the *centro* as you face the water. Access to both beaches is free, but you must either pay for a chair and umbrella, or stay at one of the many hotels that provide them. **Spiaggia di Levante** has shallower water and fewer crowds, but it's all relative on summer weekends—expect squealing children wherever you spread your towel. For a less chaotic seaside experience, check out the **lagoon** on the western shore of town. Undisturbed by hordes of beachgoers, the lagoon, which once inspired Ernest Hemingway, harbors the abandoned thatched-roof fisherman's huts. A walking and biking path runs along the lagoon, then turns back eastward to join the main road heading into town. This route offers particularly striking views, but well-marked bike paths run all over town. Just be aware in the areas immediately surrounding the *centro;* you'll have to swerve around crowds of pedestrians. If you have more than a passing interest in the lagoon, consider a boat tour given by **Motonave Arcobaleno** explaining the port history of Caorle and the lagoon. (☎21 04 28. Boats run Apr.-Sept. and depart from Caorle's fishing port. 2½hr., 9am and 2:30pm. €14, ages 2-10 €8. Ask at the tourist office for more details.) Between trips to the beach, spend some time exploring the small, twisting streets of Carole's **Old City.** While *gelaterie* and souvenir shops have taken over the main pedestrian thoroughfares, the stunningly bright pastels of the buildings remain. The **Santuario della Madonna dell'Angello,** a striking sight at the tip of the *centro* against the blue-green Adriatic, contains a beloved statue of the Madonna that watches over Carole and its fishermen at sea. (Open daily 7am-10pm. Free.) Slightly inland from the sanctuary, **Cathedral St. Stefano** provides an example of Romanesque-Byzantine architecture and holds the skull of the martyr St. Stephen. Adjacent to the cathedral is its bell tower, which historically served as a watchtower over the ocean. (Cathedral open daily 7am-10pm. No admittance to bell tower. Free.)

TREVISO ☎0422

Treviso (treh-VEE-zoh; pop. 80,000), provincial capital of the Veneto and a low-cost flight hub, is known by two other names: *Città d'Acqua* (City of Water) and *Città Dipinta* (Painted City). Treviso's predominant feature, however, is its wealth. While fashion aficionados peer at the glitzy storefront arcades in the birthplace of Benetton, anyone can enjoy the local specialty—tiramisu—at outdoor tables and explore the wide, cobblestone lanes that weave through the old city.

▤ TRANSPORTATION. RyanAir **flies** from the **Treviso (TSF) airport** (www.trevisoairport.it) to Barcelona, Spain; Dublin, Ireland; London, UK; Paris, France; and Rome. The ACTT Line 6 bus runs from the airport to the Treviso train station (15-20min.; every half hr. 6:10am-10:15pm; €1, €2 on board). Treviso is the main stop on the busy Venice-Udine train line. The **train station** is in P. Duca d'Aosta, south of the *centro.* (☎89 20 21. Ticket counter open daily 6am-8pm. AmEx/MC/V.) **Trains** depart to Trieste (2½hr., 12 per day 6am-10:27pm, €9.40), Udine (1½hr., 40 per day 12:27am-11:30pm, €6), and Venice (30min., 69 per day 5:06am-11:46pm, €2.20). Trains to Milan or Padua connect in Venice. A variety of carriers operate from the **bus station** at Lungosile A. Mattei 21 (☎57 73 11), off C. del Popolo where it crosses the river. From the train station, turn left on V. Roma. La Marca (☎57 73 11; www.lamarcabus.it; ticket window open daily 6:25am-7:45pm) services the Veneto region and the Palladian Villas, sending **buses** to Padua (1½hr., 20 per day 5:50am-8:15pm, €4) and Vicenza (1½-2hr., 9 per day 6:15am-4:10pm, €4.20). ACTV (☎0415 28 78 86; informazioni@actv.it) runs buses to Venice (1hr., 40 per day 4:10am-10:45pm, €2.60). All buses run reduced service on the weekend.

▤▤ ORIENTATION AND PRACTICAL INFORMATION. Treviso lies 30km inland from Venice. Surrounded by the Sile River, the old city walls encompass Treviso's *centro storico* and most points of interest. From the **train station,** the ACTV (intra-city) bus hub is across from **Piazza Duca d'Aosta.** Left of the buses, **Via Roma** leads to the river; it then becomes **Corso del Popolo,** crosses the river, and enters **Piazza della Borsa.** From there, a walk up **Via XX Settembre** leads to **Piazza dei Signori,** Treviso's main square. Pedestrian-dominated **Via Calmaggiore** leads to the *duomo.* The **tourist office**, P. Monte di Pietà 8, on the side of Palazzo dei Trecento from P. dei Signori, has city maps, accommodations listings, and Sile River walking tour itineraries. (☎54 76 32; www.provincia.treviso.it. Open M 9am-noon, Tu-F 9am-12:30pm and 4-6pm, Sa-Su 9am-12:30pm and 3-6pm.) **Luggage storage** is available at the train station. (€3 for 1st 12hr., €2 per each additional 12hr. Open M-F 7am-8pm, Sa-Su 8:30am-6pm. Cash only.) In case of **emergency**, call the **police**, V. Carlo Alberto 37 (☎57 71 11). **Ospedale Civile Ca' Foncello** is at P. Ospedale 1 (☎32 21 11). Find employment and study opportunities at **Centro Giovani**, P. Duomo 23. (☎65 85 40; www.informagiovani.tv.it. Open Tu 10am-12:30pm and 3:30-6pm, W 10am-12:30pm, Th 3:30-6pm, F 3:30-6pm and 8:30-10:30pm). Find **Internet** access at **Atta and Sons**, Vle. D'Alviano Bartolomeo 52, on the northern edge of the town. (☎54 54 77. €1 per hr. Open M-Th and Sa-Su 7:30am-8:30pm. Cash only.) The **post office**, P. Vittoria 1, is at the end of V. Cadorna, off C. del Popolo. (☎65 32 11. Open M-F 8:30am-6:30pm, Sa 8:30am-1pm.) **Postal Code:** 31100.

⌂ ACCOMMODATIONS. 💥**Albergo Il Focolare ❺**, P. Ancilotto 4, is situated behind Palazzo dei Trecento. This gorgeous hotel rents large, bright rooms with TV, phone, and AC. Cheery, well-lit rooms are decorated with flowers. (☎/fax 56 601; www.albergoilfocolare.net. Breakfast included. Reception 24hr. Reservations recommended. Singles €65; doubles €95; triples €110. AmEx/MC/V.) A 2min. walk heading left on Borgo Cavour from the *duomo*, 🏠 **19 Borgo Cavour ❺**, at (surprise) 19 Borgo Cavour, is a B&B of incomparable style in the *centro*. Rooms are decked out in modern, minimalist decor, and owner Luca welcomes guests with his vast knowledge of the area. (☎380 25 89 743 or 41 91 45; www.cre-attivi.it. Breakfast included. Singles €70; doubles €100; triples €140. MC/V.) To reach **Locanda Da Renzo ❹**, V. Terraglio 108, exit the train station, turn right, climb the stairs to the overpass, and head right down Strada Terraglio for 10-15min.; or, take bus #7, 8, or 11 (€0.80). Ask the driver for Da Renzo or the Borgo Savoia stop. The charming rooms of this villa share a breakfast nook. All rooms have bath, A/C, and phone. (☎40 20 68; www.locandadarenzo.it. Breakfast included. Reception 7am-12:30am. Singles €48; doubles €68; triples €88. AmEx/MC/V.) The **Hotel Carlton ❺**, Largo Porta Altinia 15, right off V. Roma, 2min. from the train station, has rooms with A/C, satellite TV, phone, and minibar. Professional service complements marble pillars, a garden terrace, and a sitting room with international magazines. (☎41 16 61; www.hotelcarlton.it. Breakfast and Internet access included. Reception 24hr. Singles €100-120; doubles €160-190; suites €220. AmEx/MC/V.)

⌂ FOOD. Treviso is famous for its cherries, which ripen in June; *radicchio*, a bitter and spicy vegetable that peaks in December; and tiramisu, a heavenly combination of espresso-and-rum-soaked cake, layered with mild *mascarpone* cheese. In summer, try a cool scoop of tiramisu *gelato*. 💥**La Vera Terra ❷**, V. Girolamo di Treviso 5, near Hotel Carlton, cooks hearty macrobiotic and vegetarian dishes in an elegant setting in a relaxed atmosphere. (☎41 02 03. *Primi* from €7-14, *secondi* from €12.50-16.50. Cover €2. Open M-F 8:30am-4pm and 8-11pm, Sa 9am-3:30pm and 8-11:30pm. Market open M-Sa 9am-9pm. MC/V.) **All'Oca Bianca ❸**, V. della Torre 7, is on a side street off V. Calmaggiore. This casual trattoria serves excellent fish dishes from a fresh, seasonal menu. (☎54 18 50; www.allocabianca.com. *Primi* €6-7, *secondi* €7-16. Cover €2; includes mineral water. Open M and Th-Su 12:15-2:15pm and 7:30-11pm. AmEx/MC/V.) To taste local delights, head to the Saturday and Tuesday morning produce **market** in Borgo Mazzini, near the northeastern walls of the center. (Open Tu-Sa 7:30am-12:30pm.) For basics, head to the **PAM** supermarket, V. Zorzetto 12, off C. del Popolo. (☎58 39 13. Open M-Sa 8am-8pm, Su 9am-1pm. AmEx/MC/V.)

◉ SIGHTS. The busy and boutique-laden V. Calmaggiore stretches from beneath the arcades of the P. dei Signori to the unusual pillars marking the entrance to the seven-domed Neoclassical **duomo.** Its Renaissance chapels were restored in 1947 after World War II damage. Check out the Annunciation Chapel, featuring Titian's masterpiece of the same name; it's to the right and slightly behind the main altar. (Open M-Sa 7:30am-noon and 3:30-7pm, Su 7:30am-1pm and 3:30-8pm. *Duomo* free. Cappella illumination €0.30.) From V. XX Settembre, skirt the right side of the busy, cafe-lined loggias of **Piazza dei Signori** to find the marble staircase of the **Palazzo dei Trecento.** Originally the town's municipal and judicial buildings, it is now a memorial to the 1944 Good Friday air raid that devastated the small town. A marble plaque under the stairs commemorates local citizens killed in German concentration camps. (☎65 82 35. Closed to the public. Call to make a reservation or contact the tourist office about group tours.)

BELLUNO ☎0437

On the southeastern border of the Dolomites, Belluno (beh-LOO-no; pop. 37,000) is a great choice for outdoorsmen on a budget. You won't find any obnoxious tourists or souvenir stands here, just quiet *piazze* and locals who all seem to know each other. Easy train access combined with inexpensive dining and lodging make Belluno a great base for exploring the beautiful snow-covered peaks.

🚆🛈 TRANSPORTATION AND PRACTICAL INFORMATION. Belluno runs trains to a number of cities, but plan ahead because some lines run much less frequently than others. The **train** station is in Ple. della Stazione and offers service to Padua (1½hr., 12 per day 5am-7:13pm, €6.10) via Conegliano (1hr., 9 per day 6:08am-9:37pm, €3), on the Venice-Udine line. Some scheduled trains run directly to Conegliano, but many require a change in nearby Ponte nelle Alpi. (☎89 20 21. Ticket office open daily 5:50am-7:50pm.) Belluno's **bus station,** across Ple. della Stazione from the train station, serves the pre-Alps to the west and the eastern Dolomites. **Buses** (www.dolomitibus.it) run to Calalzo (1hr., 10 per day 6:15am-6:05pm, €3), Cortina (2hr., 13 per day 6:10am-8:05pm, €4), and Feltre via Tai di Cadore (40min., 16 per day 6:35am-8:35pm, €2.50). Service is greatly reduced on Sunday; check station for schedules. (Ticket office ☎94 11 67. Open M-F 7am-12:15pm and 3-7:15pm, Sa 7am-12:15pm. When closed, buy ticket from tourist office.) Orange **local buses** (€0.90) stop in P. Stazione. For a **taxi,** call ☎94 33 12.

The city center, **Piazza dei Martiri,** is a 5min. walk from the train and bus stations in **Piazzale della Stazione.** From the train terminal, cross the parking lot and follow **Via Dante** through **Piazzale Battisti** and across **Via Caffi** to **Via Loreto.** Turn left on **Via Matteotti** so that P. dei Martiri is in sight. The **tourist office** in P. del Duomo offers maps, a list of Internet points, and hiking info. Cross the garden in P. dei Martiri and pass through **Porta Dante** onto **Via XXX Aprile.** (☎94 00 83; www.infodolomiti.it. Open M-Sa 9am-12:30pm and 3:30-6:30pm, Su 9am-12:30pm.) The **Club Alpino Italiano office,** P. San Giovanni Bosco 11, offers additional hiking info. (☎93 16 55; www.caibelluno.it. Open F 8-10pm; also Jan.-Mar. Tu 6-8pm.) **Banks** with similar exchange rates and 24hr. **ATMs** line P. dei Martiri. In case of **emergency,** call the **police** (☎94 55 11). **Pharmacies** post a list of after-hours rotation; **Farmacia Dott. Perale,** P. Vittorio Emanuele 12, is centrally located and open late. (☎ 25 271. Open M-F and Su 8:45am-12:30pm and 4-7:30pm, Sa 8:45am-12:30pm. AmEx/MC/V.) The **hospital** is at Vle. Europa 32 (☎16 111). Find **Internet** access at **Ki-Point,** V. Feltre 192, a 5min. walk down V. Feltre from the train station. (☎94 05 33. €1.30 per 15min., €3 per hr. Open M-F 8:45am-12:45pm and 3:30-7:15pm, Sa 8:45am-12:45pm. Cash only.) The **post office,** P. Castello 14/A, is just off P. Duomo. (☎95 32 11. Open M-F 8:30am-6:30pm, Sa 8:30am-1pm; reduced hours in Aug.) **Postal Code:** 32100.

🛏🍴 ACCOMMODATIONS AND FOOD. Central locations and cliff-side balconies come at low nightly rates. Inquire at the tourist office about accommodations and *affittacamere.* At ■**La Cerva B&B ❷,** V. Paoletti 7/B, comfortable rooms, a home-cooked breakfast, and free Internet access are just a few of the perks. Exit the train station heading to the left and following Vle. Volantari Libertà, then turn left on V. Fantuzzi. After crossing the rotary at V. Col di Lana, look for V. Paoletti on the right. (☎338 82 53 608; www.lacerva.it. Singles €23; doubles €35. Extra bed €8.50. Cash only.) The rooms at **Casa per Ferie Al Centro ❷**, P. Piloni 11, may not have the frills of local B&B options, but the price is right, considering the central location. Turn right on V. Fantuzzi and follow it as it becomes V. Jacopo Tasso. Look for Casa al Ferie on the left at P. Piloni. All rooms have bath and phone, and the self-service restaurant in front offers cheap meals in a cafeteria atmosphere. (☎338 82 53 608; casaferie@diocesi.it. Breakfast €3.60. Call ahead to reserve a double room. Singles €29; doubles €42. Prices drop with weeklong stays. AmEx/MC/V.) At the **Albergo Cappello e Cadore ❸**, V. Ricci 8, a friendly English-speaking staff welcomes guests into cheerful, carpeted rooms. Turn left on Vle. Volantari Libertà from the station, and then turn right on V. Fantuzzi, which changes to V. Jacopo Tasso; V. Ricci branches off to the left. Rooms in the recently restored building come with minifridge, TV, Internet access, and phone; some have a jacuzzi and balcony. (☎94 02 46; www.albergocappello.com. Breakfast included. Singles €40; doubles €75-85; triples €115. AmEx/MC/V.) At the end of a little side street, **B&B Centro Storico ❸**, V. Torricelle 6, offers three small, comfortable rooms and an open-air terrace overlooking the mountains. Take V. Rialto south from P. Emanuele, follow as it becomes V. Mezzaterra and turn left on V. S. Croce and right on V. Torricelle. The friendly owner, who speaks little English, cooks breakfast for his guests. (☎94 20 92; giocard13@virgilio.it. Breakfast included. Singles €35; doubles €60. Prices drop with longer stays. Cash only.)

Dining options in the *centro* are plentiful and inexpensive. ◪**La Trappola Birreria e Spaghetteria ❷**, Ple. Cesare Battisti 6, serves massive portions of excellent pasta in steaming pots brought right to your table. Sit outside at picnic tables or in the trattoria, whose walls are adorned with whimsical pictures of boozing monks. (☎27 417. *Primi* €6-8. Open M-Th 11:30am-3:30pm and 5:30pm-2am, F 11am-3:30pm and 5:30pm-3am, Sa 4pm-3am. AmEx/MC/V.) **Al Mirapiave ❶**, V. Matteotti 29, satisfies big appetites with more than 60 types of pizza, a balcony, and dramatic views of the Dolomites. (☎94 18 13. Pizza €3.50-9. Pasta €5-10. Cover €1. Open M, W-Su 11:30am-3:30pm and 6pm-1am. MC/V.) Descend through the red-walled bar into **Ristorante Taverna ❸**, V. Cipro 7, where a variety of pastas and local specialties like *galletti alla diavola* (€7) are served in the traditional dining room. (☎25 192. Wine from €1.80 per glass. *Primi* €7-8, *secondi* €7.50-16. Cover €2. Open M-Sa noon-2pm and 8-10pm. AmEx/MC/V.) While the small shop might not look like much, locals swear **Il Gelato ❶**, Ple. Cesare Battistie 3, is the best in town. (☎94 33 32. Cones €0.80-€1.60. Open daily 10am-10pm. Cash only.) **Super A & O**, P. dei Martiri 9/10, has a hot deli as well as groceries. (☎94 20 00. Open M-Tu and Th-Su 8am-1pm and 4-7:30pm, W 8am-1pm. V.)

◪ SIGHTS. Changes in the city's government can be traced through the architecture of the **Piazza del Duomo.** In the mid-17th century, academics gathered in the nearby **Palazzo dei Giuristi,** whose benefactors' busts line its facade. Since 1876, the building has housed the **Museo Civico,** which exhibits local artifacts ranging from prehistory to the 20th century. Metal flowers, Caffi's Venetian scenes, and sprawling paintings by Belluno native Sebastino Ricci are the real highlights. (☎94 48 36. Open Apr.-Sept. Tu-Su 10am-1pm and 4-7pm; Oct.-Apr. M-Sa 9am-1pm and Th-Su 3-6pm. Last entry 20min. before closing. €3; students, over 60, or groups of 10 or more €1.50; under 5 free.) Since 1838, the town government has rested next to the tourist info office in the **Palazzo Rettori,** P. del Duomo 38. The vast **Parco Nazionale Dolomiti Bellunesi** (Bellunese Dolomites National Park) starts at the city's northern edge. (☎0439 33 28; www.dolomiti-park.it.) For a more high-flying travel package, the **Botanical Garden of the Eastern Alps** rests at the top of a chairlift on the western slope of nearby **Monte Favergh-**

era. In July and August buses from Belluno service the chairlift, which zooms 1500m up the mountain, at Ple. Nevegal. Both bus and chairlift schedules are unpredictable, so consult the tourist office for the latest information. (☎94 48 30. Open June-Sept. Tu-Su 9:30am-noon and 1-5:30pm. €1.50, 14 and under €0.80.)

TIP **YOU DRIVE ME CRAZY.** Due to unpredictable bus and chairlift schedules, both the Parco Nazionale Dolomiti Belunesi and the Botanical Garden of the Eastern Alps are nearly impossible to reach without a car. Consult the tourist office for the schedules, but consider renting a car to take in all the views!

 HIKING. Belluno offers excellent, well-marked hiking trails; one of the best is along the *altavia*, stretching north to south from Belluno to Braies. Hiking the entire *altavia* would take eight to 15 days, but the hike along the first stretch, from Belluno to **Rifugio #7**, can be done in a day. From Belluno's P. dei Martiri, take V. Jacopo Tasso, which changes to V. Fantuzzi, and then V. Col di Lana. Follow this for about 1km until a sign points right, toward Bolzano; walk uphill about 9km. The paved road is easily cycled or walked in about 3hr., ending at **Casa Bortot** (707m). Get a bit to eat at the restaurant here—it's the last stop before Rifugio #7. Follow the small gravel path to the left, leading to the Parco Nazionale Dolomiti Bellunesi, or the start of **Altavia #1.** The route is well-marked and sticks close to the river gorge, with views of waterfalls and deep pools etched out of the boulders. A 3-4hr. hike leads to a small meadow and Rifugio #7 at **Pils Pilon.** (☎94 16 31; www.rifiugiosettimoalpini.it. Call ahead to confirm availability. Serves hot meals. Inquire about more difficult hikes. Open June-Sept. Rooms €16, CAI members €8. Cash only.) For info on the *altevie*, visit www.dolomiti-altevie.it. For more info on hiking, visit the tourist office or the **CAI office** (**Practical Information**, p. 353). If you want to see Belluno's surroundings in all their majesty but would rather leave the hiking boots behind, just take the leisurely walk down V. Dino Buzzati on the western edge of the *centro storico*. Don't forget your camera: gorgeous views of the Dolomites, Piava River, and the bell tower of the *duomo* await.

TIP **CLUB ALPINO ITALIANO (CAI).** Those intending to do a serious amount of hiking in Italy should consider purchasing a **Club Alpino Italiano membership.** CAI runs many mountain *rifugi,* and members pay half-price for lodgings. *Rifugi,* which generally operate late June-early Oct., may also rent out *vie ferrate* hiking equipment essentials. Membership is €39, under 18 €11, with a €6 supplement for new members and €18 surcharge for non-Italians. It can be purchased at a CAI office (except during Aug.); bring a passport photo.

TRENTINO-ALTO ADIGE

The Mediterranean feel of Italy's southern and eastern regions fades under Germanic influences in the jagged peaks of the Dolomites in Trentino-Alto Adige (tren-TEE-noh AL-toh ah-DEE-jay). One glance at the lush conifers and snow-covered peaks of Le Dolomiti (leh doh-loh-MEE-tee) explains why backpackers and skiers still flock to the area. At the onset of the 19th century, Napoleon conquered this part of the Holy Roman Empire, but eventually relinquished it to the Austro-Hungarian Empire. Trentino and the Südtirol (South Tyrol) came under Italian control at the end of WWI, a transition that left behind diverse linguistic patterns and cultural traditions. Though Germany thwarted Mussolini's brutal efforts to Italianize the region, Benito did manage to give every German name an Italian equivalent, which explains the dual street and town names used today. From *wurst* stands in Bolzano's *piazze* to the Deutsch-speaking locals in Bressanone, Trentino-Alto Adige's Germanic aura bears witness to a deep-rooted Austrian culture, which still thrives today.

HIGHLIGHTS OF TRENTINO-ALTO ADIGE

DISCOVER Il Mart, **Italy's largest modern art museum,** in Rovereto, housing over 7000 pieces by masters such as Warhol, Lichtenstein, and Rosenquist. (p. 360)

CHILL OUT with Bolzano's Ötzi the Iceman from the 4th millennium BC. (p. 361)

CHANGE IT UP with **Germanic flair** in Bressanone, a northern city that rubs shoulders with Austria. **(P. 365)**

TRENT (TRENTO, TRIENT)　　☎ 0461

Pedestrian-friendly streets and an idyllic mountain location give Trent (TREN-toh; pop. 111,000) a small-town feel. The city represents a historical convergence of Italian and Nordic cultures. While the delicious strudel in Trent's many bakeries attests to the town's proximity to Austria, the colorfully-painted buildings and many *piazze* are quintessentially Italian. Named Alpine City of the Year in 2004 for its local pride and carefully preserved culture, Trent is growing in prominence in contemporary culture and hosts annual festivals and events. It is easily explorable and combines a vibrant student life with excellent nearby hiking options.

▛ TRANSPORTATION

Trains: V. Dogana (☎89 20 21). Ticket office open daily 5:40am-8:30pm. Info office open M-F 8:30am-12:15pm and 1:15-4:30pm. To: **Bologna** (3hr., 12 per day 1:00am-9:27pm, €15); **Bolzano** (45min., 33 per day 1:55am-10:59pm, €2.89); **Venice** (3-4hr., 12 per day 7:05am-5:00pm, €10); **Verona** (1hr., 2 per hr. 4am-9:48pm, €4.65).

Buses: **Atesina** and **Trentino Transporti** (☎82 10 00; www.ttspa.it), on V. Pozzo next to the train station. Info office open M-Sa 7am-7:30pm. Check bulletin board at the back of the station for line suspension alerts. Buses run to **Riva del Garda** (1¾hr., every 2hr. 5:57am-7:50pm, €3.20) and **Rovereto** (50min., hourly 5:57am-7:50pm, €2.70).

Public Transportation: Atesina operates an extensive local bus network. Tickets (valid for 70min., €0.90) on sale at the bus station, train station, or *tabaccherie.*

Cableways: Funivia Trento-Sardagna (☎23 21 54), on Lung'Adige Monte Grappa. From bus station, turn right on V. Pozzo; take 1st right on Cavalcavia San Lorenzo. Cross bridge over train tracks, and head across the intersection to the building to the left of the river bridge on the near bank. To the tiny village ■**Sardagna** on Mt. Bondone (4min.; every 15-30min.; €0.90 70min. ticket, €1.20 2hr. ticket). Open daily 7am-10:30pm. Cash only.

Taxi: RadioTaxi (☎93 00 02). 24hr.

Bike Rental: Uffizio di Relazione Publico, V. Manci 2, next to the tourist office (☎88 44 53). Bikes are kept at the intersection of V. Torre Vanga and V. Pozzo. Stop at the office to make the €5 key deposit. Free with key deposit. Late drop fee €5, each additional day €2. Open M-F 9am-6pm, Sa 9am-noon. Bikes available daily 6am-8pm.

Moser Cicli, V. Calepina 63 (☎23 03 27). Mountain bikes €15 per day. Open M 3-7pm, Tu-Sa 9am-noon and 3-7pm. MC/V.

⚡🛈 ORIENTATION AND PRACTICAL INFORMATION

The **bus** and **train** stations are on the same street, between the gardens next to the Adige River and the circle-of-hell statue of **Piazza Dante.** The town center lies east of the Adige. From the stations, walk right to the intersection of Via Pozzo with **Via Torre Vanga.** Continue straight as **Via Pozzo** becomes **Via Orfane** and then the curving **Via Cavour** before reaching **Piazza del Duomo** in the town's center. **ATMs** are nearby.

Tourist Office: APT, V. Manci 2 (☎21 60 00; www.apt.trento.it). Turn right from the train station and left on V. Roma, which becomes V. Manci. Offers info on biking, theater, and frequent festivals. Offers guided tours of the city and the castle; the castle tour includes a wine tasting. Tours leave from the office. No reservation required. Limited to groups of 10 or less. City tours July-Aug. Th and Sa 3pm, Sept.-June Sa 3pm; €3. Castle tours July-Aug. Th and Sa 10am; Sept.-June Sa 10am; €3. Open daily 9am-7pm.

Bookstore: Libreria Disertori, V. Diaz 11 (☎98 14 55), near V. Battisti. A slim selection of English books. Open M 3-7pm, Tu-Su 9am-noon and 3-7pm. AmEx/MC/V.

Police: Vle. Verona, outside the *centro* to the south.

Pharmacy: Farmacia dall'Armi, P. Duomo 10 (☎23 61 39). Serving the city since 1490. After-hours rotation posted in window. Open July-Aug. M-Sa 8:30am-12:30pm and 3-7pm; Sept.-June M-Sa 8:30am-12:30pm and 5-7pm. Cash only.

Hospital: Ospedale Santa Chiara, Largo Medaglie d'Oro 9 (☎90 31 11 or 91 43 09), up V. Orsi past the swimming complex. From the bus stand directly in front of train station, take bus #2.

Internet Access: Call Me, V. Belenzani 58 (☎98 33 02), off P. del Duomo. Internet access €3 per hr. Fax available. **Western Union,** phone booths, and international phone cards available. Open daily 9am-9pm.

Post Office: V. Calepina 16 (☎98 47 15), offers fax services and money exchange just off P. Vittoria. Open M-F 8am-6:30pm, Sa 8am-12:30pm. **Postal Code:** 38100.

ACCOMMODATIONS

Ostello Giovane Europa (HI), V. Torre Vanga 11 (☎26 34 84; www.gayaproject.org). Exit train station and turn right; hostel is the white building on the corner of V. Pozzo and V. Torre Vanga. Spotless dorms offer private bathrooms, desks, and phones. Sunny terraces, foosball table, TV, reading area and restaurant downstairs. Breakfast and linens included. 3-course dinner *menù* €9. Lockers €3 per day. Laundry €4.50; dry €2.50. Reception 7:30am-11pm. Check-out 10am. Curfew 11:30pm; ask for door code to return later. Reservations recommended. Dorms €14-16; singles €25; doubles €42. AmEx/MC/V. ❶

Hotel Venezia, P. Duomo 45 (☎23 45 59/fax 23 41 14; www.hotelveneziatn.it). Parquet floors and wrought-iron beds give this hotel a dated feel, but big bathrooms and a winning location make for a pleasant stay. Breakfast included. Singles €38, with bath €49; doubles €55-69. MC/V. ❹

Hotel America, V. Torre Verde 52 (☎98 30 10; www.hotelamerica.it). Located 5-10min. from both the train station and the town center. All rooms have TV, bath, and minibar, and some have balconies with views of Castello del Buonconsiglio. Breakfast included. Wi-Fi €2 per 30min., €3.50 per hr. Singles €68; doubles €102; triples €120. AmEx/MC/V. ❺

FOOD

Trentino cuisine owes much to the local production of sterling cheeses like *nostrano*, *tosela*, and the highly prized *vezzena*. *Piatti del malgaro* (herdsman's plates) include cheeses, polenta, mushrooms, and sausage. Another favorite is the chewy *minestrone trippe* (tripe soup). A Germanic undercurrent shows itself in the exceptional local version of *apfelstrudel;* small shops selling this and other delicious baked goods abound. **Supermercati Trentini** lies across P. Pasi from the *duomo* at P. Lodron 28. (☎22 01 96. Open daily 9am-8pm, closed M morning. MC/V.) The **Superpoli** supermarket, V. Orfane 2, sits where V. Orfane meets V. Roma. (☎98 50 63. Open M-Tu 8:30am-7:15pm, W 8:30am-1pm, Th-Sa 8:30am-7:15pm. AmEx/MC/V.)

Osteria Il Cappello, P. Lunelli 5 (☎23 58 50). From the station, turn right, then left on V. Roma. After 4 blocks, turn right on V. San Pietro, then take the tunnel near #27 through to its opening into P. Lunelli. This classy restaurant overlooking a private courtyard serves traditional Trentino cuisine like *canederli* (bread and cheese dumplings with a simple tomato and basil sauce; €9). Delicious assortment of breads. *Primi* €8-9.50, *secondi* €9-19. Cover €2. Open Tu-Sa noon-2pm and 7:30-10pm, Su noon-2pm. AmEx/MC/V. ❸

Alla Grotta, Vco. San Marco 6. (☎98 71 97). A casual atmosphere and huge pizzas heaped with toppings make this noisy spot perfect for students looking for a cheap bite or a late-night drink. Pizza €4.10-7.20. *Primi* €5.60-7.20. Open Tu-Su noon-3pm and 6:30-11:30pm. MC/V. ❷

Graziano's, V. Esterle 9 (☎26 05 44). Near the *duomo*. Budget travelers and busy locals fill up on gargantuan slices of pizza in more than 20 varieties (€1.60-2). Open M-F 11am-2:30pm and 5:30-9pm, Sa 5:30-9pm. AmEx/MC/V. ❶

Ristorante Al Vò, Vco. del Vò 11 (☎98 53 74; www.ristorantealvo.it). From the stations, turn right, and walk to V. Torre Vanga. Turn left; 200m down on the right. A friendly staff and a brightly lit interior complete a casual dining experience. Try the *spaghettini* with mushrooms for a taste of traditional Trentino cuisine. Menu changes daily. Lunch with *primo, secondo,* and side dish costs €13. *Primi* €6, *secondi* €8. Cover €1.20. Open M-Sa 11:30am-2:30pm and 7pm-9:30pm. AmEx/MC/V. ❸

La Cantinota, V. San Marco 22/24 (☎23 85 27). From the station, turn right and then left on V. Roma, which becomes V. San Marco. Sip sparkling wine in the elegant piano bar upstairs or indulge in traditional Italian cuisine like gnocchi with pesto, arugula and green beans in the trattoria downstairs. *Primi* €7.50-9, *secondi* €13-17. Restaurant open M-W and F-Su noon-3pm and 7:30-10pm. Piano bar open M-W and F-Su noon-3pm, 7pm-3am. Closed Aug. MC/V. ❸

La Gelateria, V. Belanzani 50, near P. del Duomo. This colorful *gelateria* serves up intimidatingly large scoops of rich *gelato*—exotic flavors include violet and 2 different types of pistachio. 3 huge scoops €2.30. Open daily 11:30am-11:30pm. Cash only. ❶

👁 SIGHTS

PIAZZA DEL DUOMO. Trent's P. del Duomo offers everything from religious history to modern shops and services. At the **Fontana del Nettuno** in the center of the *piazza*, a majestic Neptune waves his trident as merpeople spit incessantly around his feet. Nearby stands the **Cattedrale di San Vigilio.** Its majestic interior housed the historical Council of Trent (1545-1563), which standardized Catholic traditions during the Counter-Reformation. Dark, rich art adorns the massive incense-filled building, illuminated only by sunlight and clusters of red and white votive candles. *(Open daily 7am-noon and 2:30-6pm. Open to tourists 10am-noon and 2:30-5pm. Free.)* Underneath, the **Basilica Sotterranea di San Vigilio,** entered from the left of the altar, displays religious artifacts and statues uncovered in excavations around the *duomo. (Open M-Sa 10am-noon and 2:30-5pm. €1.50, ages 12-18 €1. Free admission with ticket to Museo Diocesano.)*

MUSEO DIOCESANO TRIDENTINO. Nearby, the **Museo Diocesano** was officially reopened by Pope John Paul II in 1995 after renovations for elaborate tapestries, paintings, and illuminated manuscripts from various regional churches. The museum offers insight into the importance of the diocese, local history, and politics. The eight expansive Flemish tapestries depicting the Passion of Christ, located on the museum's 2nd floor, once decorated the hall where sessions of the Council of Trent were held. *(P. del Duomo 18. ☎23 44 19; www.museodiocesanotridentino.it. Open M and W-Su 9:30am-12:30pm and 2:30-6pm. Hours extended during exhibitions. Ticket counter closes 15min. before museum. €4, students €2.50. Entrance includes access to Basilica Sotterranea di San Vigilio. Free audio tours in English, Italian, German and French.)*

CASTELLO DEL BUONCONSIGLIO. Made up of buildings from different eras of Trentino history, the Castello del Buonconsiglio looms over the city from its dominant position east of the *centro.* In the **loggia** at the end of the *castello*'s rooftop garden, the ceiling features Diana depicted as the moon and Apollo as the sun with scenes from Greek, Roman, and Hebrew history and mythology in the lunettes. Stairs lead down from the loggia to the **Fossa dei Martiri,** the *castello*'s old moat and the execution site of famed martyrs Cesare Battisti, Damiano Chiesa, and Fabio Filzi in 1916. Tours of the **Torre dell'Aquila,** which depart from the loggia, offer a glimpse into the court life of the Trentino Middle Ages. *(From V. Belenzani, turn right on V. Roma and continue as it becomes V. San Marco; the castello is in front of you as the road ends. ☎23 37 70; www.buonconsiglio.it. Castello open Tu-Su 9:30am-5pm. Tours 10 per day 10:30am-5:15pm. €6, students and under 18 or over 60 €3. Torre d'Aquila additional €1. Ticket price includes admission to museum and Tridentum, an excavation of Roman ruins under P. Battisti. Free audio tours in multiple languages. Tours €1.)*

ROVERETO   ☎0464

An easy daytrip from Trent, the town of Rovereto (ro-veh-REH-toh; pop. 34,000) offers picturesque views at every turn, but without crowds of camera-toting tourists. Cobblestone alleys weave around frescoed buildings, decorative stone fountains dot the *piazze*, and mountain breezes waft delicately through the streets.

This small mountain town combines the best of both worlds. While the surrounding countryside offers opportunities for biking, hiking, walking, and horseback-riding, the Museo d'Arte Moderna e Contemporanea, or Il Mart, houses the largest collection of modern art in Italy and is the *centro*'s star attraction.

🖪 🖬 TRANSPORTATION AND PRACTICAL INFORMATION. The **train station** is at P. Orsi 11. **Trains** run to: Bologna (3hr., 11 per day 6:03am-9:44pm, €10); Bolzano (1hr., 29 per day 6:14am-11:36pm, €7); Trent (15min., 34 per day 6:14am-11:36pm, €2.40); Verona (1hr., 31 per day 6:03am-10:20pm, €3.36). Check schedules at ticket office. (☎89 20 21. Open M-F 5:50am-7:30pm, Sa 9am-6:30pm. AmEx/MC/V.) The **bus station,** C. Rosmini 45, runs **buses** frequently to Riva del Garda (1hr., 24 per day 6:55am-10:50pm, €2.40) and Trent (50min., 29 per day 5:07am-6:56pm, €4.15). Check station for schedules. (☎43 37 77. Open M-Sa 6:30am-7:15pm. MC/V.) For a **taxi,** call ☎42 13 65. The **APT tourist office,** C. Rosmini 6/A, has maps and info on lodging and nearby activities. Ask about the **Rovereto In-Card** (€2), which provides discounts at museums, hotels, and restaurants. (☎43 55 28; www.aptrovereto.it. Open M-F 9am-12:15pm and 2:30-6:30pm, Sa 9am-12:45pm.) **Branch** located at C. Angelo Bettini 43, in Il Mart. (☎42 52 06. Open Tu-Su 10am-1pm and 2-5:30pm.) In case of **emergency,** call the **police,** V. Sighele 1 (☎48 46 11). **Farmacia Thaler** is at V. Dante 3. (☎42 10 30. Open M-F 8:30am-12:15pm and 3-7pm, Sa 8:30am-12:15pm.) The **post office,** V. Largo Posta 7, is just up C. Rosmini from the bus station. (☎40 22 18. Open M-F 8am-6:30pm, Sa 8am-12:30pm. MC/V.) **Postal Code:** 38068.

🖪 🖸 ACCOMMODATIONS AND FOOD. Low tourist traffic means that budget hotels are scarce in Rovereto, but ▧ **Ostello di Rovereto ❷,** V. delle Scuole 18, can serve those in search of cheap accommodations. To reach the hostel, turn right from the station onto V. Stoppani off C. Rosmini and follow until the road becomes V. delle Scuole. The hostel is close to the *centro* and has bright rooms and a big garden. (☎48 67 57; www.ostellorovereto.it. Breakfast, lockers, Internet access, parking, bike rental included. Reception closes at 10pm. Singles €22; doubles €40; triples €60; quads €72; quints €90. MC/V.) On the more upscale end of housing options, **Hotel Rovereto ❺,** 82/D C. Rosmini, offers clean, spacious rooms with bath, TV, and breakfast in the elegant restaurant downstairs. Conveniently located between the train station and town center. (☎43 52 22; www.hotelrovereto.it. Singles €85; doubles €115.) Up a narrow staircase from P. delle Erbe, **Vecchia Trattoria Birrara Scala della Torre ❷** serves both Italian and Austrian specialities in a half-covered courtyard. Potted plants, candles and rustic furniture complement the cuisine. (☎43 71 00. *Primi* €6-7, *secondi* €9-13. Bread and cover €1. Open daily noon-2:30pm and 7:30-9:30pm. AmEx/MC/V.) **Trentini** supermarket, V. Mazzini 65, stocks basics. (☎42 11 97. Open M 8:30am-1:30pm, Tu-Sa 8:30am-12:30pm and 3:15-7:15pm. V.)

🖸 🖫 SIGHTS AND NIGHTLIFE. An unlikely sight in a small town, the enormous ▧**Museo d'Arte Moderna e Contemporanea** (commonly known as "Il Mart"), C. A. Bettini 43, is the largest modern art museum in Italy. Dozens of waving international flags welcome visitors. Inside, 5600 sq. m of sleek rooms house over 7000 pieces. While Fortunato Depero's *La Rissa* anchors the Futurist wing, 20th-century Italian pieces and American works such as Warhol's *Four Marilyns*, Lichtenstein's *Hot Dog*, and Rosenquist's *Sliced Bologna* complete the collection. (☎43 88 87; www.mart.trento.it. Open Tu-Th 10am-6pm, F 10am-9pm, Sa-Su 10am-6pm. €8, under 18 €5. Audio tours in English, German or Italian €5. AmEx/MC/V.)

Looming from its perch high above the city, the gray **Castello di Rovereto,** V. Castelbarco 7, has served mostly military purposes since its construction in the 4th century. From P. Podestà, follow V. Della Terra (near the cannon), turn right on V. Castelbarco, and head up the stairs. The **Museo della Guerra** (Museum of War) now fills the *castello* with war materials ranging from medieval spears to bombshells from WWII. The collection also includes a set of Samurai armor. Above the museum, an observation deck affords a stunning 360° view of Rovereto and the Dolomites. (☎43 81 00; www.museodellaguerra.it. Open July-Sept. Tu-F 10am-6pm, Sa-Su 10am-6:30pm; Oct.-June Tu-Su 10am-6pm. €6, ages 6-18 €2. MC/V.) About an hour walk uphill from the *centro*, the **Campana della Pace** (Bell of Peace), on V. Miravalle, tolls 100 times each night at 9pm in memory of war victims and in a call for global tolerance and peace. The bell was cast in 1924 from 226 tons of bronze recycled from the cannons of the 19 nations involved in WWI, and was later blessed by Pope Paul VI. (☎43 44 12. Open daily Nov.-Feb. 9am-4:30pm; Mar. and Oct. 9am-6pm; Apr.-Sept. 9am-7pm. €2, children 6-14 €0.50. Cash only.) The **Museo Civico,** Borgo Santa Caterina 41, provides tours of the astronomical observatory on Monte Zugna and of the dinosaur tracks in southern Rovereto. From various places along the mountain trail, these ancient prints are still visible in the gray hillside. (☎43 90 55. Open June-Oct. Tu-Su 9am-noon, 3-6pm, and 8-10pm; Nov.-May Tu-Su 9am-noon and 3-6pm. Planetarium show Sa and Su 4:45pm. Adults €3.50, students €2.50, kids €1.55. Call to arrange a tour.)

Nightlife in Rovereto is fairly tame, but **Bacchus,** V. G. Garibaldi 29, manages to keep its patrons out late with drinks like the *Shakerati* (€4). The interior, filled with barrel-shaped tables, is deceptively small, but patrons always manage to find a place at the bar or just outside in the street. (Open M, Th, Su 10:30am-1:30pm and 4:30-9pm, W 4:30-9pm, F-Sa 11am-1:30pm and 4:30pm-midnight. Cash only.) By day, **Caffè de Min,** V. Dante 6, is just another place to grab a pastry or some *gelato*, but a long, hardwood bar and plush booths bring local patrons in for drinks starting around 7pm. (☎43 77 76. Open Tu-Su 7:30am-midnight.)

BOLZANO (BOZEN)   ☎0471

Bolzano (bohl-ZAH-no; pop. 100,000) is most famous for 5000-year-old Ötzi the Iceman, a partially decayed body found frozen in 1991, held in the South Tyrol Museum of Archaeology. The best sights in the city, however, don't charge admission. In winter hikers climb to the snowy peaks. Summer visitors bike along the crystal-green Talvera River, wander up the stone pathway to Castel Roncolo, or gaze at the steep hills, resplendent with rows of grape vines. Whether it is the *duomo*'s mixed architecture or the city's two languages, Italian and German, Bolzano seems to rise above national borders.

▐ TRANSPORTATION

Trains: in P. Stazione (☎48 89 93). Ticket office open daily 5am-9pm. Information office open M-Sa 8am-7pm, Su 9am-1pm and 2-5pm. Luggage storage available. To: **Bologna** (3hr., 16 per day 5:11am-3:36am, €20); **Bressanone** (30min., 33 per day 4:32am-10:40pm, €3.25); **Munich, Germany** (4hr., 8 per day 2:25am-6:32pm); **Trent** (45min., 36 per day 1:00am-10:49pm, €3); **Venice** (3hr., 1 per day, €16); **Verona** (1¾hr., 31 per day 3:36am-9:31pm, €10).

Buses: SAD, V. Perathoner 4 (☎45 01 11), between train station and P. Walther. Bus station and tourist office distribute bus schedules for travel to the western Dolomites. Reduced service Su. Office open M-Sa 7am-7:25pm, Su 7am-1:15pm. MC/V.

Funiculars: 3 cableways, located at the edges of Bolzano, regularly carry visitors to nearby mountain towns. Tourist office has schedules. For info, call ☎80 08 46 047 or visit either the tourist office or the alpine information office.

Funivia del Colle, V. Campiglio 7 (☎97 85 45), the world's oldest cableway, leads from V. Campiglio to **Colle** or **Kohlern** (9min.; every 30min. daily June-Sept. 7am-7:30pm, Oct.-May 7am-7pm, no service 11am-12pm year-round; €3; round-trip €4; bikes €2).

Funivia del Renon, V. Renon 12 (☎97 84 79), a 5min. walk from the train station, heads from V. Renon to **Renon** or **Ritten** atop **Monte Soprabolzano** (12min.; 3 per hr. 7:10am-7:25pm; €2.50, round-trip €3.50; bikes €2, luggage €1-2).

Funivia San Genesio, V. Rafenstein 15 (☎97 84 36), off V. Sarentino, across the Talvera River, near Ponte Sant'Antonio. Connects Bolzano to **Salto's** high plateaus (9min.; daily 2-3 per hr. Mid-June to mid-Sept. 10am-12:30pm and 2:30-7pm, mid-Sept. to mid-June 9am-6pm; round-trip €3.50; bikes €2).

Public Transportation: SASA (☎45 01 11 or 800 84 60 47). All lines stop in P. Walther or the station at V. Perathoner 4. Buy tickets (€1) at *tabaccherie* or from machines near some stops.

Taxi: RadioTaxi, V. Perathoner 4 (☎98 11 11). 24hr.

Bike Rental: Run by the **Cooperativa Sociale** (☎97 55 92), on Vle. Stazione, right off P. Walther. Main office at V. Carduci 9. 1st 6hr. €1, over 7hr. €2. Open daily Apr.-Oct. 7:30am-7pm; Nov.-Mar. 7:30am-8pm. Cash only.

▟ ❓ ORIENTATION AND PRACTICAL INFORMATION

The *centro storico* lies between the **train station** and the **Talvera River** *(Talfer Fluss)*. All major *piazze* are within walking distance. Street and *piazze* names appear in Italian and German, and most maps mark both. From the bus stop, follow **Via Alto Adige** *(Südtirolerstrasse)* to **Piazza Walther** *(Waltherplatz)* and the *duomo*. Farther along, **Piazza del Grano** leads right to **Via Portici** *(Laubenstrasse)*. Here, German and Italian merchants set up shop on opposite sides of the arcade. To reach **Ponte Talvera,** take V. Portici past **Piazza delle Erbe.**

Tourist Office: AST, P. Walther 8 (☎30 70 00; www.bolzano-bozen.it). Has maps, the funicular schedule, and a list of lodgings, activities, and upcoming events throughout the city and region. Organizes horseback-riding expeditions and publishes *Bolzano a Passeggio* (a guide to 14 walks in the surrounding hills). Open M-F 9am-1pm and 2-7pm, Sa 9am-2pm.

Alpine Information: Club Alpino Italiano (CAI), P. delle Erbe 46, 2nd fl. (☎97 81 72). Ring bell. Info on hiking, climbing, and tours. Open Tu-F, Sa 1-5pm.

Currency Exchange: Banca Nazionale del Lavoro, P. Walther 10, next to tourist office. Good rates. Open M-F 8:20am-1:20pm and 2:30-4pm. An **ATM** is around the right corner of the bank and down the stairs, but plenty of others exist throughout the *centro.*

Laundromat: Lava e Asciuga, V. Rosmini 81, near Ponte Talvera. Wash €3, dry €3. Detergent €1. Open daily 7:30am-10:30pm.

Pharmacy: Farmacia all'Aquila Nera, V. Portici 46/B. Open M-F 8:30am-12:30pm and 3-7pm, Sa 8:30am-12:30pm. After-hours rotation posted outside.

Hospital: Ospedale Regionale San Maurizio (☎90 81 11), on V. Lorenz Böhler. Take bus #10 to last stop.

Internet Access: MultiKulti, V. Dott Streiter 9 (☎05 60 56; www.multikulti.info), 1 street past V. Portici. Internet €1 per 15min., €3 per hr. Offers international calling and fax. Open M-Sa 10am-10pm, Su noon-10pm. Cash only. **Caffè Brennpunkt,** V. Brennero 7 (☎98 29 53), is a slick bar with two even slicker flat-screen computers. 1st 30min. free, €1 per 15min. thereafter. Open M-W and Su 7:30am-8pm, Th-F 7:30am-1 am, Sa 7:30am-2am.

Post Office: V. della Posta 1 (☎32 22 81), by the *duomo*. Open M-F 8am-6:30pm, Sa 8am-12:30pm. **Postal Code:** 39100.

▐ ACCOMMODATIONS AND CAMPING

The tourist office lists affordable *agriturismi* options, but most require private transportation—rent a bicycle and enjoy the countryside or reserve ahead for the inexpensive accommodations in the *centro*.

Youth Hostel Bolzano, V. Renon 23 (☎30 08 65; www.ostello.bz). From train station, turn right onto V. Renon. Squeaky clean rooms, friendly staff, and bountiful amenities make this new hostel a great deal. Linens, breakfast, showers, and lockers free. Laundry €4. Internet access €2 per hr. Reception daily 8am-9pm with key available for late arrivals. Dorms €19.50; singles €22. €2 surcharge for 1-night stay. AmEx/MC/V. ❷

Garni Eisenhut-Cappello di Ferro, V. Bottai 21 (☎97 83 97; www.cappellodiferro.com). 1 block north of P. Walther, follow V. Bottai out of P. Municipio. English-speaking owner keeps small but comfortable rooms with TV and bath. Breakfast included; half- and full-board pension options available. Singles €50; doubles €80. Extra bed €25. MC/V. ❸

Hotel Regina, V. Renon 1 (☎97 21 95; www.hotel-reginabz.it). From the train station, take a right and the hotel is across the street. Steps from the train station and a 5min. walk from P. Walther. Accommodating staff and snug rooms. All rooms have private bath, TV and phone. Some have views of the green mountains looming over Bolzano. Breakfast included. Internet access €1.50 per 30 min. Singles €55-65; doubles €83-100; triples €108-120. MC/V. ❺

Schwarze Katz, Stazione Maddalena di Sotto 2 (☎97 54 17; schwarze.katz@virgilio.it), near V. Brennero, 15min. from the city center. From the train station, turn right at V. Renon; keep left along V. Renon as you pass the cable car station, and look for signs. All rooms with sinks and TV; one with bath. Breakfast included. Reception open in summer M-Sa 7am-10pm; in winter M-F 7am-midnight, Sa 7am-9pm. Reservations recommended. Singles €25-30; doubles €45-50. MC/V. ❷

Moosbauer, V. San Maurizio 83 (☎91 84 92; www.moosbauer.com). Take SAD bus (15 per day, 7am-10:20pm) toward Merano; ask driver to stop at Moosbauer. Though slightly off the beaten path, beautifully tended campground has pool, bar, Internet cafe (€0.10 per min.), market, and playground. Friendly English-speaking staff has brochures on local activities. Reception open 8am-noon and 4-9pm. Wash €3, dry €3. €7-8 per person, €4.50-5.50 per child, €3-4 per dog, €5.50 per tent, €5.50 per car. Showers free. MC/V. ❶

🍴 FOOD

No trip to Bolzano would be complete without a sampling of the city's unique convergence of Italian and Austrian cuisines. For a full smorgasbord, start with a bowl of *rindgulasch* (a tasty beef stew); then munch on *wurst* (thick, spicy sausage) or *speck* (smoked bacon that tops pizzas and breads across mainland Italy). Hearty *knödel*

THE LOCAL STORY

THE ICEMAN OF BOLZANO

In September 1991, Erica and Helmut Simon were hiking through the Tyrolean region of northeastern Italy, enjoying the scenery and getting some exercise. In between their photo ops and trail mix stops, they discovered something a little out of the ordinary: a fully-clothed but completely frozen human being.

As it turned out, the body belonged to a man from the late Neolithic Age (3300-3100 BCE) whom *bolzanini* have nicknamed Ötzi and taken under their wing in Bolzano's South Tyrol Museum of Archaeology. Though some too-cool locals insist that only tourists are interested in this human artifact, most take a sense of pride in the fact that Ötzi has made his way to their town.

In his real form, Ötzi isn't much to look at: he's a skeleton in a refrigerator. Plus, he's a little guy—at the time of his death he stood only 5 feet, 2 inches tall and weighed only 132 pounds. His shoe size was 5½ (It turns out that this was about normal size in those days.)

But the museum has taken special care to portray him in a more flattering light, creating a replica on which a soft spotlight shines. Ötzi's no Prince Charming, but he's armed with a heavy coat, trusty tools, and a look of determination.

To see Ötzi, head to Bolzano's South Tyrol Museum of Archaeology (p. 364).

(dumplings) come in dozens of rib-sticking varieties. For dessert, try three types of flaky *strudel: apfel* (apple), *topfen* (soft cheese), and *mohn* (poppy-seed). An all-day **market** in P. delle Erbe and along V. della Roggia has been selling fine produce, cheese, baked goods, and cold meats since 1295. (Open M-F 7am-7pm, Sa 7am-1pm.) For a quick regional staple, try the market's **wurst stand** at the intersection of V. Museo and P. delle Erbe. (*wurst*, bread, and sauces €3. Beer €1.55. Open M-Sa 8am-7pm. Cash only.) A **Despar** supermarket, V. della Rena 20, is downstairs in the indoor shopping center. (☎97 45 37. Open M-F 8:30am-7:30pm, Sa 8:30am-7pm.)

Hopfen & Co., P. delle Erbe 17 (☎30 07 88, www.boznerbier.it). Perfect for carnivores and beer-lovers, this 3-story, no-frills pub with 3 types of beer—dark, light, and double malt—offers a hearty Bavarian menu with a variety of specialties cooked in (what else?) beer. Beer from €1.90-3.50. Plates "for the very hungry" €6.30-7. Cover €1. Open M-Sa 9:30am-1am. MC/V. ❷

Exil Lounge, P. del Grano 2 (☎97 18 14). Dishes like "Fit 4 Fun" (a bowl of yogurt, granola, and seasonal fruits; €3.70), or the Summer Salad, piled high with *finocchio* (fennel), tomatoes, arugula, carrots, and mozzarella (€5) will delight wurst-intolerant travelers. Extensive tea, wine, and drinks list. Open M-W 10am-midnight, Th-Su 10am-1am. Cash only. ❷

Lowengrube, P. Dogana 3 (☎97 68 48). The name of this Bolzano favorite, which opened in 1543, translates from German to "the place of the lion." Cheerful Austrian decor and crowds of locals attest to its popularity as a great lunch spot. *Panini* from €3.20, beer €1.60. Open daily 8am-1am. MC/V. ❸

Hostaria Argentieri, V. Argentieri 14 (☎98 17 18). Upscale restaurant specializes in fish and classy dining. Flower-lined patio and quiet, candlelit interior under soft blue and yellow arches. *Primi* €8, *secondi* €9.50-19.30. Cover €1.50. Open M-Sa noon-2:30pm and 7-10:30pm. AmEx/MC/V. ❹

Trattoria Bar Nadamas, P. delle Erbe 44. What little nightlife Bolzano has to offer is centered around P. delle Erbe, mostly due to its cheap drinks. Locals and tourists alike fill the spacious, wood-furnished interior and spill out into the *piazza*. Lunch buffet offers vegetables, pasta, and bread (small plate €6, large €8). Glasses of wine and beer from €1. Open M-Sa noon-1am. Kitchen open noon-2:30pm and 7-10:30pm. ❶

TIP **RIDOTTO!** Bolzano offers a **Museum Card** (€2.50), which grants holders the "ridotto" price of entry to five of the city's museums and Castel Roncolo. The card pays for itself with just two museum visits and provides holders with a free guided city tour. Purchase the card at the tourist office or any museum.

👁 🥾 SIGHTS AND HIKING

The **duomo,** in P. Walther, demonstrates Bolzano's transition from Romanesque to Gothic religious architecture. Gothic influences added the bell tower's spined hollow spire and the ornate masonry around the eaves. Paintings, frescoes and statues line the walkways inside. (Open M-F 9:45am-noon and 2-5pm, Sa 9:45am-noon. Free.) Steps from P. delle Erbe, the **Chiesa dei Francescani,** V. dei Francesca 1, seems miles away from the crowded market square. From the main doors, the crucifix in the expansive apse seems to float in front of the three tall, stained-glass windows that fill the white-walled church with vibrant color. (Open M-Sa 10am-noon and 2:30-6pm, Su 3-6pm. Free.) The **South Tyrol Museum of Archaeology,** V. Museo 43, near Ponte Talvera, traces the region's history from the Stone Age to the time of early Christianity. Most tourists, however, come to file by the giant refrigerator, which houses **Ötzi**. This famous 5000-year-old Neanderthal was found by hikers in the Alps. The results of the extensive investigations into his life and times are on display with excellent English explanations on Ötzi's very own floor of the museum. (☎32 01 00; www.iceman.it. Open Tu-Su 10am-5:30 pm; July-Aug. and Dec. also open M. Wheelchair-accessible. €8, students and seniors €6, under 6 free. Audio tours €2.) Perched on the vine-covered hills above town, **Castel Roncolo** is the most accessible of Bolzano's medieval fortresses and looks like it came out of a Disney wonderland. Lavish frescoes, which narrate the legend of Tristan and Isolde, bring the walls to life. The winding stone path to the castle and the connector between the museum's two wings offer spectacular views of the mountains and Bolzano below. Take city bus #12 from P. Walther to the Funivia stop (every 30min. M-Sa 7:05am-7:15pm, €1), then go up V. Weggerstein to V. San Antonio. Ask at the ticket desk about the free bus for tourists back to P. Walther. (☎32 98 08; www.comune.bolzano.it/roncolo. Open Tu-Su 10am-6pm. Gates for frescoes close 5:30pm. €8; groups of 10 or more, students, and seniors €5.50.)

Bolzano is technically located at the beginning of the Alps, despite local allegiance to the Dolomites. The hiking here pales in comparison to that in the Alps to the west or the Dolomites to the east. In addition to the tourist office, the CAI office (p. 362) has helpful info on outdoor activities. The best hikes can be accessed by the three *funivie* that surround the town and run straight to vista level. While **Funivia del Renon** and **Funivia del Colle** have limited marked trails, **Funivia San Genesio** services extensive marked trails of moderate difficulty. On Funivia del Renon, the ride itself is an attraction, as it gives a bird's-eye view of curving grape arbors. All three *funivie* offer free maps that should suffice for the easier hikes. Drop by the San Genesio **tourist office**, Schrann 7 (☎35 41 96; www.jenesien.net) before starting out. The gentle walk from the San Genesio Funivia to the Edelweiss rest house, to the Tachaufenhaus, and then back to the *funivie* via the Locher rest house, makes for a pleasant 4½hr. hike. Even on the easiest hikes, take precautions against dehydration and sun exposure.

BRESSANONE (BRIXEN) ☎ 0472

Northwest of the Dolomites and south of Austria, Bressanone's (breh-sa-NO-neh; pop. 20,000) Alpine valley dazzles visitors with unobstructed views of green mountains, crystalline rivers, and rows of pastel houses. Its layout blends patches of urbanity with vast expanses of green space, where cobblestone roads wind around swirling rivers and cool shade trees. Pedestrians can stroll through the town center's quiet walkways, exploring the towering *duomo* and small shops nearby, but the real appeal for travelers is the hiking, biking, and skiing opportunities.

TIP **CULTURE SHOCK.** The people of the northern Dolomites have been ethnically and linguistically German and Austrian for centuries. This means that most natives' 1st language is German, then Italian, and English a distant 3rd.

■ ☎ **ORIENTATION AND PRACTICAL INFORMATION.** Bressanone is an easy daytrip by train or bus from Bolzano or Trent. **Trains** run to: Bolzano (30min., hourly 12:36am-10:12pm, €3.25); Brennero (45min., every hr. 5am-11:11pm, €4.65); Munich, Germany (4hr., 7 per day 5am-7pm, €50); Trent (1-1½hr., 14 per day 12:30am- 10pm, €4.65); Verona (2½ hr., 15 per day 6:30am-9pm, €10). Train info is available at ☎89 20 21 or www.trenitalia.com. (Ticket office open M-F 6:10am-8pm, Sa-Su 6:40am-8pm.) **Luggage storage** is available at the *edicola* in the *biglietteria*. Price will depend on the number and size of the bags, as well as the mood of the man behind the counter. (Open M-Sa 6:15am-11am and 12:45-7pm.)

To reach the *centro* in **Piazza del Duomo,** turn left from the bus and train stations onto **Viale Stazione,** walk 500m past the tourist office, and when Vle. Stazione becomes **Via Bastioni Minore,** turn immediately right through the arch to enter the courtyard of the **Palazzo Vescovile.** P. del Duomo is to the left. The **tourist office,** Vle. Stazione 9, distributes town maps and info on suggested hikes; hotel listings outside list up-to-date vacancies throughout town. (☎83 64 01; www.brixen.org. Open M-F 8:30am-12:30pm and 2-8pm, Sa 9am-12:30pm.) **ATMs** line V. Bastioni Maggiore at the end of Vle. Stazione. Find **Internet** access at the **Biblioteca Civica,** P. Seminario 4, which charges €1 per 30 min. to use of one of its three computers. (☎26 21 90. Open M-Sa 9am-7pm.) A sign in the window of **Farmacia di Corte Principevescovile,** V. Portici Minori 2/A, posts a list of after-hours rotations outside. (Open M-Tu and Th-Su 8am-12:30pm and 3-7pm, W 8am-12:30pm.) The **hospital** (☎81 21 11) is on V. Dante, toward Brenner. The **police station** is located on V. Vittorio Veneto 13 (☎83 61 31). **Currency exchange** is available at Bressanone's **post office,** behind the tourist office at V. Cassiano 4/B. (☎27 20 01; fax 27 20 40. Open M-F 8am-6:30pm, Sa 8am-12:30pm.) **Postal Code:** 39042.

⌂ ACCOMMODATIONS. Many of the more expensive hotels are near the river; the *centro* has three-star rooms in convenient locations for €40-50. Head from P. del Duomo into P. Palazzo, then turn left on V. Bruno to find **◪Ostello della Gioventù Kassianeum ②,** V. Bruno 2. Friendly staff, remarkably clean rooms, and buffet breakfast make this hostel a bargain. Take advantage of its great views and proximity to the *duomo.* (☎27 99 99; www.ostello.bz. Breakfast and linens included. Towels €1. Laundry €2.50. Reception M-Sa 8am-8pm, Su 8am-6pm. Dorms €19. €2 surcharge for 1-night stay. MC/V.) From the tourist office, take a right onto V. Roma from V. Bastioni, left onto V. Fienili, and right onto V. Tratten for **Pensione Mayrhofer ③,** V. Tratten 17. Friendly, English-speaking owner Colette offers a secluded garden and comfortable rooms with TV and safe. (☎83 63 27; www.mayrhofer.bz. Half pension €52 per person; B&B €40 per person. €5 surcharge for singles. MC/V.) **Academia Cusano ③,** P. Seminario 2, is located behind the *duomo.* In the *piazza,* walk past the church to the right. Brick walls in the rooms may be austere, but spacious bedrooms and baths and a convenient location make this accommodation a steal. (☎83 48 83. Breakfast and linens included. Summer rooms fill up more than six months in advance. Singles €30; doubles €54. Cash only.) Located near P. del Duomo, **Cityhotel Tallero ④,** V. Mercato Vecchio 35, offers a classier alternative to the town's cheaper, no-frills options. Friendly, English-speaking owner Alex welcomes you to comfortable rooms with TV, safe, and Internet jack. (☎83 05 77; www.tallero.it. Singles €58; doubles €88-92. MC/V.)

❑ FOOD. At the 100-year-old **Fink ②,** Portici Minor 4, waitresses in traditional garb serve house specials like *rösti,* a pizza-sized mat of fried potatoes and veggies (€8.20), and Alto Adige wines from €15 per bottle. (☎83 48 83. *Primi* €7-8, *secondi* €12-19. Open M and Th-Su 11am-10pm. AmEx/MC/V.) At **Tapas Bistro & Paninoteca ❶,** V. Croce 2, lively locals crowd booths and tables on the street. *Panini,* salads, and small plates, including enormous *bruschetta* arrays in several varieties (€3.70-3.90), are served all day. (Beer from €1.50. Wine from €2.50 per glass. Open daily 7am-8pm. Cash only.) Bressanone's oldest restaurant, **Finsterwirt ③,** specializes in elegant dining on the tiny Vco. del Duomo off the main *piazza.* The 2nd floor's dark wood interior provides the perfect compliment to chef Hermann Mayr's carefully designed menu. (*Primi* €9-10, *secondi* €10-19. Open daily 10:30am-3pm and 5:30pm-midnight. AmEx/MC/V.) Sit indoors or under the canopy at **Torre Bianca ②,** V. Torre Bianca 6, which serves a wide variety of pizzas (€5.50-9) and traditional Tyrolean food on a quiet street in the *centro.* Walk past the left side of the cloister's *campanile,* and pass through the arch. (☎83 29 72. Cover €1.

Open M and W-Su 9am-11pm. MC/V.) A **Despar** supermarket, V. Bastioni Minori 4, is near the *centro*. (☎83 70 32. Open M-Sa 8am-7pm. MC/V.)

⬛⬛ **SIGHTS AND HIKING.** To kick off your sightseeing, head to **Piazza del Duomo.** A few meters south of the *piazza*, look for a golden lamb-topped monument in P. Palazzo, where the pale yellow **Palazzo Vescovile,** completed in 1595, houses the **Museo Diocesano.** Its predominantly ecclesiastical collection traces the development of Western Christianity. The majestic interior courtyard features over two dozen terra-cotta sculptures constructed around 1600 and depicting various members of the royal Habsburg family. Ask for the info brochure in English. (☎83 05 05. Open Mar. 15-Oct. 31 Tu-Su 10am-5pm; Dec. 1-Jan. 31 daily 2-5pm. €5.) The candy-colored **duomo** is as colorful inside as out; huge chandeliers illuminate the golden altar and the Baroque and Neoclassical frescoes. To the right of the *duomo*, the peaceful **cloister** displays traditional Stations of the Cross, which contrast with the stunningly ornamented organ in the back. The garden holds a WWI and WWII monument dedicated to local soldiers. (Both open daily 8am-noon and 3-6pm. Guided *duomo* tours Easter-Nov. 1 M-Sa 10:30am and 3pm; meet just left of the main doors. Free.) For a break from central Bressanone's boutiques and pedestrians, follow Ponte Aquila behind the *duomo* and cross the bridge to the winding footpaths east of the **Altstadt** (old town), where shops and pastel houses huddle along quiet streets. The **Plose Plateau,** towering over Bressanone at heights of over 2000m, is a popular skiing area made accessible by the **Sant'Andrea Cable Car** (10min.; 2 per hr. July 7-Oct. 3 M-F 9am-6pm, Sa-Su 9am-6pm; round-trip €7; bikes €3), which operates from the nearby hillside town of Sant'Andrea. **SAD bus #126** makes round-trips between the Bressanone train station and Sant'Andrea (20min., 7 per day 7:15am-7:20pm) and Bressanone *centro* (7:15am-7:25pm, round-trip €2). Buy tickets on the bus. From the upper cable-car station in Valcroce, **trail #30** leads along the smooth terrain of the Plose's western slope, and **trail #17** follows the meadows on the Plose's southern slope. For a longer, more strenuous hike, traverse **trail #7** along the summits of Monte Telegrafo and Monte Fana, reaching altitudes of 2600m. Before tackling this hike, check the weather and plan for possible overnights in *rifugi* (hiker huts), such as the **Plose** and **Rossalm,** which also offer hot meals. Be prepared to face rough terrain and high altitudes. A multilingual tourist office brochure details three 3-6hr. hikes on the Plose.

For a more leisurely and lower altitude option, the hike to the strikingly beautiful **Abbey Novacella,** V. Abbazia 1, in Varna runs along River Isarco. Cross Ponte Aqueila and walk north along the river, then follow **trail #16,** which brings you through the tiny town of **Varna** and to the Abbey (1½-2hrs. round-trip). The abbey, founded in 1147, contains examples of Gothic, Romanesque, Baroque, and Rococco art and decor. (☎83 61 89. Museum visits for groups of 10 or more at 10, 11am, 2, 3, and 4pm. €2.50.)

FRIULI-VENEZIA GIULIA

Bounded by the Veneto to the west and Slovenia to the east, Friuli-Venezia Giulia (free-OO-lee veh-NETS-ya gee-OOL-ya) was once several distinct provinces that were unified by clergy between the 6th and 15th centuries. The Habsburgs claimed the area in the early 1700s as an important economic center for Austria and Hungary. Since then, the region has changed hands multiple times, resulting in an assortment of cuisines, cultures, and architecture. Its natural beauty also draws from a variety of sources; serene lakes and jagged peaks characterize the northern towns, while dramatic views of the Adriatic Sea shape the coastal regions. James Joyce wrote the bulk of *Ulysses* in coffeehouses that still dot Trieste, Ernest Hemingway found inspiration for the plot of *A Farewell to Arms* in the region's Carso cliffs, and Sigmund Freud was inspired by Friuli's natural beauty. Although smaller towns retain their idyllic charm, Friuli-Venezia Giulia's cultural quilt and growing metropolises make it one of Italy's most international provinces.

HIGHLIGHTS OF FRIULI-VENEZIA GIULIA

INDULGE in the cuisine of **Trieste,** Italy's gateway to central Europe (p. 371).

SNAP a photo against the stunning backdrop of the **Laghi di Fusine** (p. 381).

RUMMAGE through the ruins at **Aquileia,** the former Roman city and gateway to the Adriatic sea (p. 374).

SUNBATHE on the beautiful beaches of **Lignano** (p. 376).

TRIESTE ☎ 040

After volleying between Italian, Austrian, and Slavic allegiances for hundreds of years, Trieste (tree-YE-steh; pop. 241,000) has finally settled down, celebrating its 50th anniversary as an Italian city in 2004. Nevertheless, subtle reminders of Trieste's Central European past are manifest in its architecture, cuisine, and artwork. Locals strut along bustling waterfront *piazze*, while the natural beauty of the Carso cliffs and seemingly omnipresent Adriatic Sea complement Trieste's constant excitement.

▆ TRANSPORTATION

Flights: Aeroporto Friuli-Venezia Giulia/Ronchi dei Legionari, V. Aquileia 46 (☎ 04 81 77 32 24 or 04 81 77 32 25), 20km from the *centro*. To get to the airport, take bus #51 from the bus station next to the train station (1hr., M-Sa hourly, €2.85). Ticket counter open daily 7am-noon and 1-7pm.

Trains: P. della Libertà 8 (☎ 89 20 21), down C. Cavour from the quay. Ticket counter open daily 6:05am-7:50pm. Info office open daily 7am-9pm. Trains run to **Udine** (1½hr., 28 per day 5am-9:19pm, €6.60) and **Venice** (2hr., 31 per day 4:30am-9:25pm, €8.20).

Buses: P. della Libertà 11 (☎ 42 50 20), next to train station. Ticket office open M-Sa 6:20am-7:40pm, Su 6:30am-1pm and 5-6pm. Buses depart for **Udine** as well as destinations in **Croatia, Serbia,** and **Slovenia.**

Ferries: Depart on a number of lines for **Albania.** Schedules and tickets can be found at **Agemar Viaggi,** P. Duca degli Abruzzi 1/A (☎ 36 37 37; fax 63 81 72), off C. Cavour. Open M-F 8:30am-1pm and 3-6:30pm.

Friuli-Venezia Giulia

Public Transportation: ACT buses travel city and provincial routes to **Carso, Miramare,** and **Opicina.** Tickets (€1 per hr., €3.30 per 24hr.) for sale at *tabaccherie.*

Taxis: RadioTaxi (☎30 77 30). 24hr.

■✴🛈 ORIENTATION AND PRACTICAL INFORMATION

The center of Trieste is a grid, bounded on the east by **Via Carducci,** which stretches south from **Piazza Oberdan** toward the historical **Capitoline Hill.** To the west, **Corso Italia** runs from the spectacular **Piazza dell'Unità d'Italia,** a vast square beside the harbor. The two streets intersect at busy **Piazza Goldoni.** Along C. Italia, just steps from P. dell'Unità d'Italia, lies **Piazza della Borsa,** where *triestini* come to see and be seen.

Tourist Office: APT, P. dell'Unità d'Italia 4/B (☎34 78 312; fax 34 78 320), has great info and lists of *manifestazioni* (artistic events). Open daily 9:30am-7pm.

Luggage storage: At the train station. 1st 12hr. €3, each 12hr. thereafter. €2. Pay up front. Open 7am-9pm.

Consular Services: UK, V. Roma 15 (☎34 78 303). Open Tu 10am-noon, F 2:30-4:30pm.

Currency Exchange: Deutsche Bank, V. Roma 7 (☎63 19 25). Open M-F 8:20am-1:20pm and 2:35-3:35pm.

Pharmacy: Farmacia alla Borsa, P. della Borsa 12/A (☎36 79 67). Open M-F 8:30am-1pm and 4-7:30pm, Sa 8:30am-1pm. Posts after-hours rotations.

Internet Access: Bar Unità, Capo di P. Monsignor Anotonio Santin 1/B (☎36 80 33). €4 per hr. Open daily 8am-midnight. **Maranzina Service,** V. Milano 22/C (☎34 78 246), off V. Carducci. Internet access €2 per hr. Also offers fax, photocopy, and money transfer services. Open daily 10am-1:30pm and 3:30-8pm. Cash only.

Post Office: P. Vittorio Veneto 1 (☎67 64 282), along V. Roma. From the train station, take 3rd right off V. Ghega. Open M-Sa 8:30am-7pm. **Postal Code:** 34100.

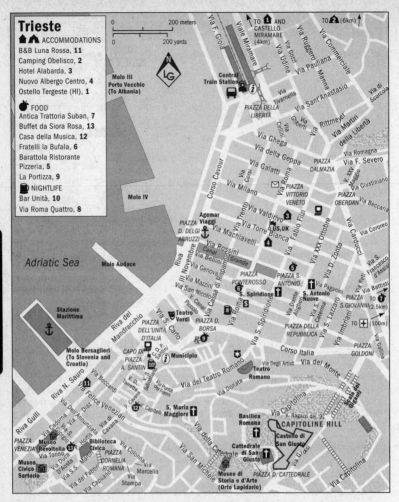

Trieste

ACCOMMODATIONS
B&B Luna Rossa, **11**
Camping Obelisco, **2**
Hotel Alabarda, **3**
Nuovo Albergo Centro, **4**
Ostello Tergeste (HI), **1**

FOOD
Antica Trattoria Suban, **7**
Buffet da Siora Rosa, **13**
Casa della Musica, **12**
Fratelli la Bufala, **6**
Barattola Ristorante
Pizzeria, **5**
La Portizza, **9**

NIGHTLIFE
Bar Unità, **10**
Via Roma Quattro, **8**

ACCOMMODATIONS AND CAMPING

Nuovo Albergo Centro, V. Roma 13 (☎34 78 790; www.hotelcentrotrieste.it). Centrally located hotel with spacious rooms that have wooden floors, minibar, phone, fan or A/C, and satellite TV. Breakfast included. Internet access €4 per hr. Call ahead for summer and weekend stays. Singles €37, with bath €52; doubles €54/72. *Let's Go* discount 10%. AmEx/MC/V. ❸

Bed and Breakfast Luna Rossa, V. Felice Venezian 2 (☎348 525 3009; www.bed-trieste.com). Take bus #8 or 30 from train station and exit at Stazione Marittima, or walk 20min. along the water down C. Cavour and turn left. Friendly owner Patrizia hosts guests in bright, colorful rooms, all with TV, A/C, and shared bath. Access to refrigerator and washing machine. Very close to port. Breakfast included. Singles €30; doubles €50. Prices drop with longer stays and in winter. Cash only. ❸

Hotel Alabarda, V. Valdirivo 22, 3rd fl. (☎63 02 69; www.hotelalabarda.it). From the station, head down C. Cavour and turn left on V. Valdirivo. Cheerful staff offers clean, simple rooms with satellite TV. Breakfast included. Internet access €2.50 per hr. Wheelchair-accessible. Singles €35, with bath €55; doubles €50-72. *Let's Go* discount 10%. AmEx/MC/V. ❸

Ostello Tergeste (HI), V. Miramare 331 (☎22 41 02; ostellotrieste@hotmail.com), 4km from the *centro*. Cross V. Miramare from the station to take bus #36 (last bus at 9pm, €1); ask for the Ostello stop. Rooms are small, but staff is friendly. Amazing views of the Gulf of Trieste beckon from the balcony. Breakfast included; dinner €9.50. Reception 8-10am and 3:30pm-midnight. HI members only. Lockout 10am-3:30pm. Midnight curfew. Dorms €14-18. Cash only. ❶

Camping Obelisco, Strada Nuova per Opicina 37 (☎21 16 55; fax 21 27 44), in Opicina. Take tram from P. Oberdan to Obelisco stop and follow the signs up the hill. Showers, bar, and activities organized for guests. No tents provided. Reception Tu-Sa 9am-1pm, 2-6pm. €3.70-4.50 per person, €2.50-3 per tent. MC/V. ❶

🍴 FOOD

Trieste's cuisine has distinct Central European overtones, evident in the region's sauerkraut, strudel, and *iota* (sauerkraut, bean, and sausage stew). There's no shortage of quality seafood restaurants along Riva Nazario Sauro and Riva Gulli. The *alimentari* on V. Carducci provide an ideal place to eat on the cheap, while the city's hundreds of cafes offer a chance to people-watch. A giant **PAM supermarket,** V. Miramare 1, is across from the train station (☎42 61 004. Open M-Sa 8am-8pm, Su 9am-7pm. MC/V). At Trieste's **covered market,** V. Carducci 36/D, on the corner of Vle. della Majolica, dishware booths and magazine vendors can be found amidst vendors hawking fruits and cheeses. (Open M 8am-2pm, Tu-Sa 8am-5pm.)

🏅 **Buffet da Siora Rosa,** P. Hortis 3 (☎30 14 60). This family-run joint serves *triestini* favorites like bread *gnocchi* (€6.20) and prosciutto *panini* (€1.20-4) doused in *senape e kren* (mustard and horseradish). Reservations recommended. *Primi* €6.60, *secondi* €6.50-12.80. Cover €1. *Piazza* seating service charge 10%. Open M-F 8am-4pm and 6:30-9:30pm. MC/V. ❷

🏅 **Antica Trattoria Suban,** V. Comici 2 (☎54 368). Take bus #35 from P. Oberdan. Austro-Hungarian and Italian dishes so heavenly that even Pope John Paul II indulged. Try the house specialty of crepes with basil (€7). *Primi* €6-8, *secondi* €11-16. Cover €2.50. Open M and W-F 4pm-midnight, Sa-Su 10am-3pm and 6pm-midnight. Closed Aug. Reservations recommended. AmEx/MC/V. ❸

Barattolo Ristorante Pizzeria, P. Sant'Antonio 2 (☎63 14 80; www.albarattolo.it). People-watch by a dribbling fountain at this casual restaurant. A large menu in Italian, English, and German describes favorites like *schiacciata* (a pizza with vegetables, cheese, basil, and garlic; €7). Pizza €4.30-8.80. *Primi* €5.20-13, *secondi* €6-9.80. Service 15%. Open daily 8:30am-midnight. AmEx/MC/V. ❷

Fratelli la Bufala, V. Roma 12 (☎34 81 31 61). Colorful decor and food inspired by (what else?) buffaloes. The *mozzarella di bufala* is the best there is, and worth the extra money. Lunch *menù* (*primo, secondo,* and bread) €10. Pizza €5-10.50. *Primi* €8.50, *secondi* €8-18. Open daily noon-3:30pm and 7-11:30pm. AmEx/MC/V. ❸

La Portizza, P. della Borsa 5 (☎36 58 54). Enjoy wine (€2.50-4), mixed drinks (€4-5.50), sandwiches (€1.80), or homemade *gelato* (€1.10) at this cafe. Open in summer M-Sa 6:30am-late; in winter M-Sa 6:30am-9pm, Su 8am-1pm and 4-9pm. AmEx/MC/V. ❶

Casa della Musica, V. Capitelli 3 (☎39 24 08), on the ground fl. of the Scuola di Musica 55. Turn right off Largo Riccardo Pitteri onto V. Sebastiano and then onto V. Capitelli. Enjoy *panini* (€1.50-2) among hardworking music students at the red backlit bar. Wine €1.50-1.80. Open daily 8am-8pm. ❶

👁 SIGHTS

THE CENTRO

 MUSEO REVOLTELLA. Also known as the **Galleria d'Arte Moderna,** this museum displays temporary modern art exhibits and an extensive permanent collection. The Revoltella Palace is an ornately decorated building containing older collections, while the more stark Brunner Palace holds modern works. Don't miss Magni's **Fontana della Ninfa Aurisiana,** a marble fountain of a woman representing Trieste. *(V. Diaz 21. ☎ 67 54 350; www.museorevoltella.it. Open Jul-Aug. M 9am-1:30pm and 4-7pm, W-Sa 9am-1:30pm and 4pm-midnight, Su 10am-7pm; Sept.-June M and W-Su 9am-1:30pm and 4-7pm, Su 10am-7pm. Guided tours Su 11am. €6, students €4.)*

> **⚡TIP** **TRIESTE FOR VIPS.** A great way to experience Trieste is the **T For You Card.** Available at the tourist office for €8 (24hr.) or €10 (48hr.), the card grants entrance to civic museums, travel on local buses, a Grotta Gigante tour, and more. Modest discounts at hotels and restaurants are another perk.

CITTÀ NUOVA. The oldest areas in the southern half of Trieste (the *Castelvecchia,* or "Old City") sport a tangle of roads in no discernible pattern. In the 1700s, Empress Maria Theresa of Austria commissioned a *città nuova* plan, which 19th-century Viennese urban planners implemented between the waterfront and the **Castello di San Giusto.** The resulting grid, lined with Neoclassical palaces, centers around the **Canale Grande,** where colorful rowboats bob past the pedestrian-only paths. Facing the canal from the south is the majestic Serbian Orthodox **Chiesa di San Spiridione,** an AD 9th-century church with blue domes and frescoes of biblical characters. *(Open Tu-Sa 9am-noon and 5-8pm, Su 9am-noon. Modest dress required.)* The vast **Piazza dell'Unità d'Italia,** Italy's largest waterfront square, provides a full view of the Adriatic coastline. On the eastern side of the *piazza,* the Municipio (Town Hall) faces the **Mazzoleni Fountain of the Four Continents,** which represents the world as it was known at the time of the fountain's completion in 1750.

PIAZZA DELLA CATTEDRALE. This hilltop *piazza,* on the site of an ancient Roman basilica, overlooks the Adriatic and downtown Trieste. The remains of the old Roman city center lie directly below, and the restored **Cattedrale di San Giusto** is across the street. The cathedral assumed a square shape rather than the traditional cross design after a 14th-century renovation that combined the original church with the basilica of Santa Maria Assunta. Sparkling in the sunlight that streams in from the windows below, ▪**mosaics** grace the ceiling of the main altar. Climb the *campanile* next door for a nice breeze and views of the city and Gulf. *(☎ 30 93 62. Open Tu-Sa 8am-noon and 2:30-6:30pm, Su 8am-1pm and 3:30-8pm; closed to tourists Su mornings for mass. Cathedral free. Campanile €1.50. Printed guides €1.)*

TEATRO ROMANO. In the AD 1st century the Emperor Trajan supervised this amphitheater's building, which staged both gladiatorial games and dramatic performances. Although weeds have overtaken the structure and the nearby supermarket reduces its majesty, the theater when illuminated after dusk still manages to impress. *(On V. del Teatro Romano, off C. Italia. From Capitoline Hill, descend toward P. Ponterosso. Free.)*

CITY ENVIRONS

▪**CASTELLO MIRAMARE.** Archduke Maximilian of Austria commissioned this luxurious castle in the mid-19th century. This was, of course, before he was assassinated in Mexico and his wife Carlotta went crazy with grief. Each of the castle's carefully preserved rooms contain explanatory panels in English. Miramare's towers are easily visible from the Capitoline Hill in Trieste and most points along the **Barcola**, a boardwalk extending 7km between the Castello and Trieste. *(Take bus #36 (15min., €0.90) to Ostello Tergeste and walk along the water for 15min. ☎22 47 013. Open M-Sa 9am-7pm, Su 8:30am-7pm. Ticket office open daily 9am-6:30pm. €4, EU citizens ages 18-25 €2, EU citizens under 18 or over 65 free. Guided tours in English €3.50; audio tours €3.50, 2 for €5. Gardens open daily 8am-6pm. Free.)*

MARINE PARK. Up the gentle slope from the Castello, in the gardens of **Castelletto Miramare**, this small World Wildlife Federation aquatic museum has an aquarium and, for more adventurous travelers, scuba tours just off the Mediterranean shore. *(☎22 41 47; www.riservamarinamiramare.it. Museum open daily 9am-7pm. Scuba diving Sa-Su. Land dive €20, night dive or boat dive €28. Equipment and tank €5 each. Scuba certification and reservation required. Must be in groups of 6-10; ask to be grouped with others if your group is fewer than 6. Call ahead to inquire about guided tours. Museum €4, students and seniors €3.)*

NAPOLEONICA AND GROTTA GIGANTE. The tram to Opicina from P. Oberdan, which started running in 1902, is one of Europe's oldest. It clatters up a steep climb from Trieste, past vineyards and breathtaking views of the Adriatic coastline. Hop off at the Obelisk stop to meet up with the Napoleonica, a popular trail that cuts along the sides of the Carso cliffs. At the end of the tram route, local bus #42 takes you close to Grotta Gigante, where guided tours in Italian descend into the base of the world's largest touristed cave. Its 500 stairs wind in and around the 107m interior, which could fit St. Peter's Basilica comfortably inside. *(V. Donota 2. Bus #42 arrives in the small parking lot across V. Nazionale from the tram stop. Buy tickets in town for return journey. ☎32 73 12; www.grottegigante.it. Open Tu-Su 10am-6pm. Entrance by guided tour only, every 30min. €8, groups of 25 or more €6.50.)*

RISIERA DI SAN SABBA. Italy's only WWII concentration camp occupied this abandoned factory outside Trieste, where an estimated 3000-5000 prisoners were put to death. The *risiera* now houses a museum detailing Trieste's role in the Slovenian-born resistance movement fighting Nazi occupation. *(V. Giovanni Palatucci 5. Take bus #10 from P. Goldoni and ask for the "Risiera" stop. ☎82 62 02. Open daily 9am-7pm. Free. Brochure in English €1.)*

FARO DELLA VITTORIA. Towering over the Gulf, this lighthouse is a tribute to those who gave their lives at sea in WWI. Inaugurated in 1927 in the presence of Vittorio Emanuele III, the 70m tower incorporates the anchor of the first Italian ship to

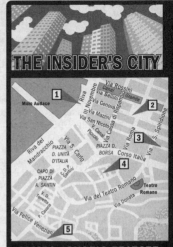

THE INSIDER'S CITY

JAMES JOYCE'S TRIESTE

During his self-imposed exile from Ireland between 1904 and 1920, James Joyce, author of *Ulysses* and *Finnegan's Wake*, lived off and on in Trieste, leaving behind a wake of monuments to his life.

1 At the **Greek Orthodox Church of San Nicolò**, Joyce attended services simply to observe the rituals. (Open daily 9am-12:30pm, 3:30-7:30pm.)

2 In 1905 Joyce lived at P. Ponterosso 3. Continue a few steps and say hello the man himself—a statue of him sits on the bridge of the Canal Grande.

3 V. Roma 32 was the site of the Berlitz School, where Joyce taught English for two years. On the 2nd floor of V. Roma 30 lies one of Joyce's many flats.

4 Take a meal at the dimly lit Osteria da Marino, V. del Ponte 5, where Joyce met friends. (Open M-F 11:30am-3pm and 6:30pm-4am, Sa-Su 6:30pm-4am.)

5 End your odyssey at the Joyce Museum, which opened in 2007 at V. Madonna del Mare 6.

enter the harbor during the 1918 liberation. *(Strada del Friuli 141. Bus #42, 44, 45.* ☎ *41 04 61. Open Apr.-Sept. Tu-Th 3-7pm; Oct.-Mar. M-Sa 10am-3pm. Free.)*

🎵🎭 ENTERTAINMENT AND NIGHTLIFE

On the 2nd Sunday in October, Trieste stages the annual **Barcolana,** a regatta that blankets the harbor with thousands of billowing sails. The acclaimed **Teatro Verdi** hosts operas, ballets, and a six-week operetta season from July to mid-August. Buy tickets or make reservations at the **box office,** Riva III Novembre 1. Enter on the P. Giuseppe Verdi side of the building. (☎ 67 22 298; www.teatroverdi-trieste.com. Open Tu-Sa 9am-noon and 4-7pm, Su 9am-noon. Tickets €8-40.)

The night heats up early at ▧ **Via Roma Quattro,** whose name is also its address. Funky orange decor and a flat-screen TV distinguish this central spot, where young trendsetters come for drinks. (☎ 63 46 33. Beer €2-4.10. Mixed drinks €2.50-6. Open M-Sa 7:30am-11:30pm. AmEx/MC/V.) Trieste's *glitterati* are out in full force along the bars of **Capo di Piazza Monsignor Antonio Santin,** part of the pedestrian district that connects P. della Borsa and P. dell'Unità d'Italia. On summer evenings, the crowd gravitates toward fresh mixed drinks and *piazza* seating at **Bar Unità,** Capo di P. M. A. Santin 1/B, on the southwestern corner of P. dell'Unità d'Italia, which also has Internet access. (☎ 36 80 33. Open M-Sa 8pm-midnight.)

GRADO AND AQUILEIA ☎ 0431

Grado (GRA-doh; pop. 8700), an island beach resort renowned for its *terme* spas, and Aquileia (ah-kwee-LAY-ah; pop. 3300), named a UNESCO world heritage sight for its extensive Roman ruins, lie at opposite ends of the Italian vacation spectrum. However, because the towns are only 15km from each other and are linked by frequent buses, visitors can take a dip in the Adriatic on Grado's gently sloping beaches and then explore the ruins of Aquileia's ancient port in the same day.

🚍🚆 TRANSPORTATION. For both Grado and Aquileia, Cervignano is the nearest city with a train station, on the Trieste-Venice line. From the Cervignano **train station,** frequent **buses** depart for Aquileia's *centro* (15min., every 30min. 6am-8:30pm, €1.40). From Grado, buses run to Aquileia (15min., 35 per day 5:35am-11:15pm, €1.15) and Trieste (1½hr., 6 per day 6:15am-7:05pm, €4.10). In Grado, **City buses** 37A and 37B (every 30min.; €1) stop at major points across the island as well as at the wide array of spas and hotels along its south side.

🏠🚆 ORIENTATION AND PRACTICAL INFORMATION. From the bus station in Grado, take **Via Roma;** continue on **Via Venezia,** then turn left on **Via Dante Alighieri** to reach the **tourist office,** V. D. Alighieri 72, which provides maps of the Grado and listings of spa treatments and prices. (☎ 87 71 11; www.gradoturismo.info. Open daily 9am-7pm.) The Aquileia **APT Tourist Office** is at the bus terminal on V. Giulia Augusta in the center of town. (☎ 91 491. Open M-F Apr.-Oct. 9am-1pm; Nov.-Mar. 9am-noon.) Find the Grado **police** at V. Goldoni 8 (☎ 80 781). A **pharmacy** is at V. Orseolo 1. (☎ 80 058. Open Tu-Su 8:30am-12:30pm and 4-8pm.) Find **Internet** access at **Nova Internet Café,** P. Carpaccio 26. (☎ 87 70 22. €5 per hr. Open daily 6am-8pm. Cash only.) A **post office** at V. Caprin 34, has an **ATM** as well. (☎ 88 357. Open M-F 8:30am-2pm, Sa 8:30am-1pm.) **Postal Codes:** 34073 (Grado); 33051 (Aquileia).

🎒 ACCOMMODATIONS. A variety of lodgings can be found in Grado; however, the hostel in Aquileia is the best budget option. In sleepy Aquileia, **Domus Augusta (HI) ❶,** V. Roma 25, has free bike rentals, clean dorms, a small kitchen, and a spacious common area just minutes from the bus station. (☎ 91 024; www.ostelloaqui-

> **TIP** **TRUST THE PROFESSIONALS.** Be sure to visit the Aquileia tourist
> office for the option of an audio or walking tour. Audio tours are offered in
> English, Italian and German (€4, €7 for 2; includes reduced-rate for basilica
> entrance). Walking tours are offered in English, French and German and cover
> excavations at the forum, some ancient homes, the river harbor, and the basil-
> ica. Walking tours (€7.50, including basilica entrance) run May-Oct. and leave
> at 10:30am and 3:30pm from the tourist office at V. Giulia Augusta.

leia.it. Breakfast included. Laundry €4, dry €4. Reception 2-11:30pm. Check-out
10am. Lockout 10am-2pm. Curfew 11:30pm. Dorms €15.50; singles with bath €25.
MC/V.) **Hotel Capri ❸,** Vle. Vespucci 1, on the lagoon in Grado and 5-10min. from
the beach, offers spacious rooms with A/C, phone, TV, and bath; some have hot
tubs and balconies. (☎80 091; www.hotelcaprigrado.it. Breakfast €5. Reception
7am-midnight. June and Sept. €33-51 per person; Jul.-Aug. €40-60. AmEx/MC/V.)
Seconds from the ruins of Porto Fluviale, **Camping Aquileia ❶,** V. Gemina 10, features a pool and a restaurant. Bulletin boards suggest local activities. (May 15-
Sept. 15 ☎91 042; Sept. 16-May 14 ☎91 958. Reception 8am-8:30pm. €5-7 per person, €8-10 per tent. 3-person bungalow €42-52; 4-person bungalow €58-73. MC/V.)

❐ FOOD. In Grado, you'll smell the wonderful fish specialties at **Ristorante Taverna
Al Canevon ❹,** Calle Corbatto 11, before you can taste them. (☎/fax 81 662. *Primi*
€7.50-15, *secondi* €12-16. Cover €2.10. Open in summer daily noon-2pm and 7-
10pm; in winter M-Tu and Th-Su noon-2pm and 7-10pm. AmEx/MC/V.) If you're trying to save your euro for that new bathing suit, grab a huge slice before heading to
the beach at the tiny **Pizza Number One ❶,** V. Morosini 21, across from the post office.
(☎80 477. Open W-Su 11am-3pm and 6pm-midnight.) Wind through the twisting side
streets of the Old City to reach **Agli Artisti ❹,** Campiello Pta. Grande 2, where round
stones form the shape of Grado on the wall inside. Seating in the small *campiello*
offers views of P. Duca d'Aosta as well as a maze of medieval streets. (☎/fax 83 081.
Primi €5-12, *secondi* €5-15. Cover €2.50. Open M and W-Su noon-2:30pm and 7:30-
10pm. AmEx/MC/V.) If hunger strikes while you're checking out the ruins in Aquileia, stop by **Pizzeria alla Basilica ❷,** V. della Stazione, behind the tourist office off V.
Giulia Augusta. A wood-burning stove churns out crispy pizzas with generous toppings. (☎91 74 49. Pizzas €3.50-7.50. *Menù* with *antipasto*, pizza, dessert, and drink
€20. Open M-Sa noon-3pm and 6:30-10:30pm. MC/V.) For all your grocery needs, the
Coop supermarket in Grado, Vle. Europa Unità 35, has the essentials. (☎81 237. Open
M-F 8am-1pm and 5-8pm, Sa 8am-8pm, Su 8am-1pm. AmEx/MC/V.)

◧ ⚠ SIGHTS AND OUTDOOR ACTIVITIES. Visitors willing to pay top dollar
come to **Grado** for spa treatments at the **terme,** a set of spas along the lagoon on
Grado's south side. For those reluctant to splurge on eternal youth, fees for the
beach along the *terme* vary based on time of day and season, but tickets are usually available along V. Regina Elena for €5-10, depending on the extra beach services you want. Don't miss the **free beach** located at the western end of the island
15min. beyond the *centro storico.* **Santa Eufemia,** an AD 7th-century basilica along
P. Duca d'Aosta, hosts visitors under its soaring ceiling; nearby, an unearthed
mosaic is on display from a raised walkway. The angel sitting atop the church's
spire has come to represent the city. (☎/fax 80 146.)

Tourists in **Aquileia** may want to begin their visit with a **walking tour** of the center
and its archaeological sites, offered by the tourist office. The floor of the ▥**basilica,**
a remnant of the original building, is a giant mosaic of over 700 sq. m of geometric
patterns and images of animals, cherubs, and field workers; don't miss the
unique—but tiny—depiction of a rooster (Christ) battling a turtle (Satan) just to

the right of the entrance. Beneath the altar, 12th-century frescoes illustrate the trials of Aquileia's early Christians in addition to scenes from the life of Christ. Damp catwalks guide visitors through the **Cripta degli Scavi** and its half-uncovered mosaics and other artifacts buried in this 1st-century Roman house. (☎91 067. Basilica open daily 9am-7pm. Free. Crypt entrance €3, under 10 free.) The nearby **campanile** was constructed in 1031 using the remains of a Roman amphitheater. Visitors sweat their way up 127 steep, sharply turning steps before enjoying unobstructed views of the countryside and shoreline. (Open daily 9:30am-1pm and 2:30-6pm. €1.20.) **Porto Fluviale,** a cypress-lined alley behind the basilica that spans the former dockyard of Aquileia's river harbor, is listed as one of UNESCO's most valuable World Heritage Sites. It conveniently leads to Roman ruins at the forum. Frequent placards in Italian and English explain the ruins along the tranquil path. The **Museo Archeologico,** at the corner of V. Augusta and V. Roma, features the preserved remains of a boat used by Roman citizens as well as an ancient bronze chandelier, which now hangs in a display case. (☎91 016. Open M 8:30am-2pm, Tu-Su 8:30am-7:30pm. €4, ages 18 to 25 €2, under 18 or over 65 free.) From there, walk down V. G. Augusta, take a right on V. Gemina, and follow signs to the **Museo Paleocristiano** in P. Pirano to see mosaics that document the region's transition from paganism to Christianity. (☎91 131. Open Tu-Su 8:30am-1:45pm. Free.)

LIGNANO
☎0431

There isn't a *duomo* in sight nor a medieval *centro storico* to wander around—just miles and miles of sandy beaches packed with bronzed Italians and pale German tourists. As one of Italy's best resort towns, Lignano (leen-YA-no; pop. 6000) is packed with fun-seeking beachgoers. The energetic atmosphere of Lignano can make even the most scholarly visitor forget about the lack of museums and churches and do nothing but relax on the beach.

⌶ TRANSPORTATION. Lignano is best accessed by a 40min. bus ride from the nearest **train station** in Latisana. **Buses** run from Latisana to Lignano (every 30min. 6:30am-11:30pm; €2.50) and from Lignano to Latisana (hourly 5:50am-10:30pm). Lignano's **bus station,** Vle. Gorizia 26, is around the corner from the AIAT Tourist Office in the center of town. (☎ 71 373. Open daily 6:20am-1pm and 3-9:30pm.)

▣ ORIENTATION AND PRACTICAL INFORMATION. The island of Lignano is actually divided into three areas: **Riviera** in the west, **Pineta** in the middle, and **Sabbiadoro,** where all the action is, at the eastern-most point. In Sabbiadoro, **Viale Centrale, Via Latizana,** and **Viale Europa** run parallel along the island until ending in the center of town. **Lungomare Trieste** begins just after Camping Sabbiadoro and runs along the coast. In the center of town, Vle. Centrale turns into **Viale Venezia, Via Tolmezzo,** and finally, **Via Udine.**

The **AIAT tourist office,** V. Latisana 42, distributes detailed maps and bus schedules. (☎71 821; www.infolignano.it. Open daily 9am-7pm.) Find the **police** at Vle. Europa 98 (☎72 14 14). Pick up designer sunscreen at **Farmacia De Roia,** V. Tolmesso 3 (☎71 263. Open daily 8:30am-12:30pm and 4-10pm. MC/V.) A **medical clinic** is located at Parco S. Giovanni Bosco 20/A, just off V. Tolmezzo (☎71 001). For **Internet** access, head to **Alexander Cocktail Bar,** V. Udine 12, where a few computers are hidden in the back. (☎71 611. €3 for 30min., €5 per hr. Open in summer daily 7pm-midnight. Cash only.) The **post office,** Vle. Gorizia 39, is also near the tourist office. (☎40 93 11. Open M-F 8:30am-7pm, Sa 8:30am-1pm.) **Postal code:** 33054.

⌐ ACCOMMODATIONS. Faced with deciding among the hundreds of indistinguishable resorts that line the beach, look out for special services—like free daily passes for a chair and umbrella at the beach—that not every hotel offers. Most hotels also offer good pension options (approx. €5-10 per meal), which definitely beat the bills at Lignano's touristy and overpriced restaurants. ◪**Hotel Castiglione** ❸, Lungomare Trieste 126, offers free beach chair and umbrella passes, cheap *pensione* plans, and bikes at no cost. Only 30m from the beach, Castiglione welcomes guests to comfortable rooms with A/C, TV, phone, and safe. (☎71 551; www.castiglionehotel.it. Breakfast included. €37-59 per person. 10% discount for week stay. MC/V.) **Pensione Zen** ❷, Ple. San Giovanni Bosco 15, is a cheaper, family-run option in the center of the action, offering basic rooms, some with terraces. Parking and a free beach umbrella pass are included in the daily rate. (☎71 237. Breakfast €5. Open May-Oct. Singles €25-33; doubles €33-70. Cash only.) At the family-oriented **Camping Sabbiadoro** ❶, V. Sabbiadoro 8, a pool, supermarket, restaurant, and beach access are all on-site. Walk 15min. from center of town, or ask the driver for Camping Sabbiadoro on the bus from Latisana. (☎71 455; www.campingsabbiadoro.it. €4.60-9 per person, €7-14 per tent. AmEx/MC/V.)

◩ **FOOD.** The ratio of *gelaterie* to vacationer is high in Lignano. Try out Lignano's best *gelateria*, **Tropicana Gelateria** ❶, V. Tolmezzo 37, for frappes (€2.50), *macedonia* (fruit salad; €4), and *gelato* topped with fresh fruit (1 scoop €1). (Open daily 10:30am-late. Cash only.) Those not on a hotel's *pensione* plan can try out **O Sole Mio** ❸, V. Udine 62, for great wood-oven pizza. Run by the same family for three generations, the atmosphere is laid-back and social. (☎71 364. Pizza €4-10. Pasta €4-12. Cover €1.10. Open Feb.-Nov. daily 10:30am-1am. AmEx/MC/V.) To replace all the energy spent sunbathing, the **alimentari**, at V. Udine 20, supplies fresh picnic items like *panini* for €3-4. (Open in summer daily 8am-1pm and 4-10pm. MC/V.)

◪◩ **BEACHES AND NIGHTLIFE.** The **free beach** on the southern side of Lignano Sabbiadoro stretches the full length of Lungomare Trieste, but be prepared to shell out a little extra for a beach chair or umbrella if it's not included with your hotel's rates. In summer, the young children and the elderly fade with the setting sun as Lignano's night scene gets going along **Via Tolmezzo** and **Via Udine.** A number of popular cafes and wine bars line this street, but those looking for a quicker beat head to **Disco Italia,** on the corner of V. Udine and V. Italia. The town's most popular club keeps the top 40 hits playing until the wee hours. (Mixed drinks €5. Cover men €7, women free. Open daily 11pm-5am.) Before hitting the dance floor, sip a tall drink at **Tango,** V. Gorizia 5. Neon lights, fruity mixed drinks (€5-7), and buff bartenders keep customers feeling hip and happy. (Open daily 5pm-4am.)

CIVIDALE DEL FRIULI ☎ 0432

On the banks of the Natisone River, tiny Cividale (chee-vee-DA-leh; pop. 11,000) is perhaps the most enchanting town in the Friuli region. Founded by Julius Caesar as Forum Iulii, Cividale eventually became the capital of the first Lombard duchy in AD 568 and later flourished as a meeting point for artists and nobility in the Middle Ages. Cividale, just a 15min. train ride from Udine, draws visitors with its well-preserved medieval monuments and natural beauty.

◪◪ **TRANSPORTATION AND PRACTICAL INFORMATION.** Cividale is best reached by **train** from Udine (15min., 25 per day 6am-8pm, €2.10). Buy tickets in the *tabaccherie* in the Udine train station. The **train station,** Vle. Libertà 43, is close to the center of town. (☎73 10 32. Open M-Sa 5:45am-8pm, Su 7am-8pm.) From the train station, take **Via Guglielmo Marconi.** Turn left through the stone gate, **Porta Arsenale Veneto,** when V. G. Marconi ends. Cross **Piazza Dante** and turn right on **Via San Pellico,** then left on **Largo Boiani;** the **duomo** is straight ahead. To reach the **tourist office,** P. Diacono 10, take C. Mazzini from P. Duomo to its end. The office also serves as an **Informagiovani** to help youths find work opportunities in the area and offers free **Internet** access. (☎71 04 60; www.cividale.net. Open daily 9:30am-noon and 3:30-6pm.) In case of **emergency**, contact the **police**, P. Armando Diaz 1 (☎70 61 11). Services include: **Banca Antoniana Popolare Veneto**, Largo Boiani 20 (open M-Sa 8:20am-1:20pm and 2:35-3:35pm, Su 8:20am-11:20pm); **Farmacia Minisini**, Largo Boiani 11 (open M 3:30-7:30pm, Tu-F and Su 8:30am-12:30pm and 3:30-7:30pm, Sa 8:30am-12:30pm; MC/V); **Ospedale Cividale**, P. dell'Ospedale, south of the Natisone river (☎70 81); and the **post office**, Largo Boiani 37-39 (☎70 57 11; open M-F 8:30am-7pm, Sa 8:30am-1pm). **Postal Code:** 33043.

⌂◻ ACCOMMODATIONS AND FOOD. Quiet Cividale lacks a wide variety of budget accommodations, but the tourist office lists all available *affittacamere* (rooms for rent). **Casa Franca ❷**, V. Alto Adige 15, is a 5min. walk from the train station. Turn left from the station, then left on V. Bottego and follow it until it becomes V. San Moro; V. Alto Adige is the first street on the left. This large accommodation has three spacious rooms with shared bath. (☎73 40 55. Breakfast €5. Singles €25; doubles €60. Cash only.) Find friendly service at the centrally located **Locanda Al Pomo d'Oro ❹**, P. San Giovanni 20, a restored medieval inn. All rooms have TV and bath. (☎73 14 89; www.alpomodoro.com. Breakfast included. Wheelchair-accessible. Rooms held until 6pm. Singles €55; doubles €75. AmEx/MC/V.) The few rooms at **B&B La Casa Dai Toscans ❸**, V. Mazzini 15, are spacious and elegantly furnished; the central location and cozy breakfast nook add extra perks. (☎349 32 48 997. Breakfast included. Singles €40; doubles €70. Cash only.)

Regional culinary specialties include *stakanje* (a puree of potatoes and seasonal vegetables) and *gubana* (a large fig- and prune-filled pastry laced with *grappa*). Try the flaky *gubana* (€0.75) at ▨ **Gubane Cividalese ❶**, C. Paolino d'Aquileia 10. (☎73 21 52. Open M-Sa 7:30am-1:30pm and 3:30-7:30pm, Su 8:30am-1pm and 2:30-8pm. Cash only.) At **Antica Trattoria Dominissini ❷**, Strada Matteotti 11, in the stone courtyard of Casa il Gelsomino, try the *gnocchi alla carniga* (stuffed with meat; €7) under a canopy of vines. (☎73 37 63. *Primi* €6-7.50, *secondi* €6-11. Cover €1. Open Tu-Sa 10:30am-3pm and 6-11pm, Su 10:30am-3pm. AmEx/MC/V.) **Antica Osteria alla Speranza ❷**, Foro Giulio Cesare 15, across from the post office, offers a rotating menu and Friulian wine under frescoed ceilings or among hanging plants in its back courtyard. (☎73 11 31. *Primi* €6.20, *secondi* €7-12. Cover €1.20. Open M noon-2pm, Tu-Su noon-2pm and 7:30-9:30pm. MC/V.) **Mandi Mandi ❶**, C. P. d'Aquileia 8, has great pizza at even better prices. (Pizza €1.70-2. Open Tu-Su 8am-1:30pm and 4pm-8pm. Cash only.) For more upscale dining, **Alla Frasca ❸**, V. Stretta de Rubeis 11, serves traditional pastas in the elegant booths. (☎73 12 70; www.allafrasca.it. *Primi* €7-8, *secondi* €12-19. Cover €1.90. Open Tu-Su in summer 12:30-2:30pm and 6:30-midnight; in winter 12:30-2:30pm and 7-9:30pm. AmEx/MC/V.) **Coopca**, V. Adelaide Ristori 15, sells groceries. (☎73 11 05. Open M and W 8:30am-12:45pm, Tu and Th-Su 8:30am-12:45pm and 4-7:30pm. Cash only.)

◧ SIGHTS. The dark, gray stone interior of the *centro*'s 16th-century **duomo** houses the Renaissance sarcophagus of Patriarch Nicolò Donato, left of the entrance. Annexed to the *duomo* is the **Museo Cristiano**, displaying the *Battistero di Callisto*, commissioned by the first Aquileian patriarch in Cividale, and the *Altar of Ratchis*, a Lombard sculpture from AD 740. (☎73 11 44. *Duomo* and museum open M-Sa 9:30am-noon and 3-6pm, Su 3-6pm. Free.) Circle around the right side to the back of the *duomo* and follow Riva Pozzo di Callisto to the bottom of the stairs where signs point to the **Tempietto Longobardo**, an AD 8th-century sanctuary built on the remains of a Benedictine convent. Inside, a sextet of stucco figures, called *The Procession of Virgins and Martyrs*, stare down from their high perch; these icons are rumored to have been painted by a Muslim who had fled westward to avoid persecution for his religious art. (☎70 08 67. Open Apr.-Sept. M-F 9:30am-12:30pm and 3-6:30pm, Sa-Su 9:30am-1pm; Oct.-Mar. M-F 9:30am-12:30pm and 3-5pm, Sa-Su 9:30am-12:30pm and 2:30-6pm. €3, students €2.) Finds from recent excavations of pre-Roman settlements at the **Museo Archaelogico Nazionale**, P. Duomo 13, include an extensive display of jewelry found at Longobard funerary sites. English explanations trace the Longobard rule in Cividale. (☎70 07 00. Open M-Sa 8:30am-7:30pm. Last entry 1hr. before closing. Tickets €2, 18-25 €1.) From the *duomo*, follow C. Paolino d'Aquileia to **Ponte del Diavolo,** a 15th-century stone bridge set between verdant cliffs 22m above the emerald green **Natisone River.** The bridge, which has come to symbolize Cividale, is named for the Devil, who allowed the bridge to stand in exchange for the soul of the first to cross. The townspeople got the better of the Devil by sending a cat across first. Head behind the Chiesa San Martino to reach another lookout point on the river from the quiet balcony that lines the steep banks. From there, turn off C. P. d'Aquileia on Vle. Monastero Maggiore right before the bridge to explore the dim, steep stone tunnels of **Ipogeo Celtico**, Monastero Maggiore 10, an ancient Roman prison with open-jawed skulls engraved in the walls, remnants from its former use as a graveyard. Don't forget to the turn on the light! (☎70 12 11. Open Tu-Su 7am-10pm; call tourist office for M visits. 10 people max. For the key, visit Bar all'Ipogeo at Monastero Maggiore 2. Free.)

TARVISIO   ☎0428

Pristine wilderness and an amalgam of Italian, Austrian, and Slovenian cultures set Tarvisio (tar-VEE-see-oh; pop. 5000) apart from other ski resort towns in Italy. In the winter, Tarvisio bustles with nordic enthusiasts from nearby Austria and Slovenia. The mountains of Carnia and the majestic Fusine Lakes are the centerpieces for summer tourism as well. Hiking and biking paths abound as do picture-perfect views. In the *centro*, a large, daily market brings shoppers over the border to stalls hawking Italian clothing and accessories.

▐ TRANSPORTATION. Trains run from Stazione Tarvisio Boscoverde, a 10min. bus ride from town to Trieste (3hr., 7 per day 4:57am-8:11pm, €8) and Udine (1½hr., 7 per day 4:57am-8:11pm, €6.90). Frequent **buses** from Udine stop in Tarvisio's center, listed on schedules as "Tarvisio Città." Buses run from Tarvisio Città to Udine (10 per day 5:30am-6:25pm, €6.90), typically with a transfer in Carnia or Gemona. Both train and bus services are greatly reduced on Sundays. For timetables, call the Boscoverde's ticket office (☎64 46 94) or grab schedules from the tourist office. The area around Tarvisio has little public transportation—to truly explore the area, renting a car is recommended. For **car rental,** call Mauro Collini at **Maggiore** (☎347 26 02 636). For a **taxi,** call Luciana Zossi (☎348 71 47 493).

▐▐ ORIENTATION AND PRACTICAL INFORMATION. Tarvisio is essentially three long, parallel streets that come together at each end of the *centro*. Approaching Tarvisio from the east, V. Diaz splits into **Via Romana**, **Via Roma,** and **Via Vittorio Veneto.** The large covered market extends down V. V. Veneto after V. Roma ends. The **tourist office,** V. Roma 10, across the street from the bus stop, offers bus and train schedules and a stash of other glossy brochures. (☎23 92; www.tarvisiano.org. Open M-Sa 9am-1pm and 2-7pm, Su 9am-1:30pm and 4-7pm.) For **emergencies,** call the **police,** V. Romana 50 (☎41 69 00); or an **ambulance** (☎29 31). A **pharmacy,** V. Roma 18, is across the street from Hotel Adriatico. (☎20 46. Open M-Sa 9am-12:30pm and 3-7pm. MC/V.) A **clinic** is located on V. Veneto, and the nearest **hospital** is in Gemona. **Internet** access in town can be found at the computer in the lobby of **Hotel Nevada,** V. Kugy 4, right next to the tourist office. (☎23 32. €3 per 30min., €5 per hr. Open daily

9am-9:30pm.) The **post office,** V. V. Veneto 18, is near Tarvisio's school building. (☎21 59. Open M-F 8am-1:30pm, Sa 8am-12:30pm.) **Postal code:** 33018.

◨◧ ACCOMMODATIONS AND FOOD. Many accommodations in Tarvisio shut down during June, the lowest point of ski season; however, you can also use this opportunity to take advantage of amazing bargains. A great budget choice is **Hotel Adriatico ❷,** V. Roma 51. All rooms have TV, bathroom, and mountain views. (☎26 37; fax 63 246. Breakfast included M-Sa. Singles €25; doubles €50. MC/V.) A slightly more upscale option is the quaint **Hotel Haberl ❸,** V. Kugy 1, which features free Internet access and sunny rooms with bath, TV, phone, and a breezy patio. (☎23 12; www.hotelhaberl.com. Breakfast included. Singles €40; doubles €70. MC/V.) Plenty of restaurants can be found on V. V. Veneto around the covered market, but better meals are often closer to the *centro.* Unfortunately, these restaurants either close or reduce their opening hours during low season as well. At **Raibl ❷,** V. IV Novembre 12, the menu includes traditional Italian pastas and *secondi,* but the more than 40 varieties of pizza are the obvious draw. Walk on V. Roma toward the *duomo;* V. IV Novembre goes up the hill to the left after the tourist office. (☎22 47; www.albergoraibl.com. Open Tu-Su 11am-10pm. Pizza or *primi* €5-9.50, *secondi* €6-13. MC/V.) Reward yourself after a long day of hiking (or shopping) with one of the seafood specialties, like the *linguine al scoglio* (€9), at **Ristorante Adriatico ❸,** V. Roma 51. The dining room's tall windows reveal green hills and snow-capped peaks beyond. (☎26 37. Open M-Sa 11:30am-10pm. *Primi* €5.50-8.50, *secondi* €9-12.50. MC/V.) The town's most-crowded *gelateria* is **Bar Commercio ❶,** P. Unità 1. One-scoop cones (€0.80) and sundaes (€3-4) are great buys. (☎21 33. Open daily 6:30am-midnight; in winter daily 6:30am-9pm. Cash only.) Find basics at the **Pellicano Supermarket,** V. V. Veneto 192, just past the town market. (☎40 083. Open M-Sa 9am-7pm. MC/V.)

◪ SIGHTS AND OUTDOOR ACTIVITIES. The main sights in the center of Tarvisio are the market and the *duomo.* The **market,** run primarily by Neopolitans who have migrated north, draws crowds from Austria and Slovenia with its reasonably priced leather goods and discounted clothing. While local artisans sport their wares, more upscale boutiques also compete for business across the street. (Open daily from 9am-6:30pm, although some stalls may have different hours.) The **Tarvis Card** offers discounts at the market and the boutiques and allows holders to accumulate points toward prizes like a free, week-long vacation in Tarvisio (www.tarviscard.it; €10). The *duomo,* **Chiesa di San Pietro e Paolo,** in P. Unità, constructed in 1445, is a striking sight against the mountains beyond. It remains a rare example of a fortified church, protected by a high stone wall meant to defend against Turkish invasions in 1474. The hushed and soothing interior features wall frescoes of King Charles V and the Last Judgement. Fragments of Roman monuments are scattered behind the church. (Open daily 9am-noon and 2-6pm. Free.)

Tarvisio's main draw is undoubtedly the abundance of **hiking** and **skiing** possible in the Julian Alps. The largest ski resort near Tarvisio is actually in Austria, **Pramollo-Nassfield,** and has 101km of trails and 30 lifts. Before hitting the slopes, don't forget your passport! (☎43 0428 58 242; www.nassfield.at/it. Lift ticket 9am €35; prices decrease later in the day.) Also near Tarvisio is the famous **Monte Lussari,** sometimes called "Di Prampero," the highest peak in the area (3400m); enjoy night skiing until 11pm in the winter. (☎65 39 15; www.tarvisiano.org gives updated snow and weather reports.) The tourist office is the best resource for info about ski resorts and discounted outdoor activities. **Hiking** excursions generally take visitors into the western half of the Julian Alps. For package tours of the area and detailed trail maps, contact **Consorzio Servizi Turistici del Tarvisiano,** above the tourist office at V. Roma 12 (☎23 92; consorzio@tarvisiano.org).

▓ **DAYTRIP FROM TARVISIO: LAGHI DI FUSINE.** Worth every effort to explore, the ▓**Fusine Lakes** (in Italian, "LA-gee dee Foo-SEE-neh") are stunning natural creations. Hedged on the south by the glacier-covered **Mangart Mountains** (2677m) and surrounded by forest in all other directions, the lakes reflect the scenery perfectly on clear days. The best vistas can be seen from the leisurely hike around **Lake Superiore,** while **Lake Inferiore,** though less dramatically set, is surrounded by an easily walkable path through the thick woods that closely encircle its shore. The region has been protected since 1971 by Friuli-Venezia Giulia's regional park. Be sure to pack a snack for the hike; benches and picnic tables on the trails of both lakes provide the perfect setting for a picnic lunch. Descend the bus from Tarvisio at the second of the two stops, which will leave you in the parking lot next to Lake Superiore. From here, **Trail #1** (2hr.) circles around and connects both lakes, while **Trail #2** (4hr.) leads to the feet of the Mangart Mountains and runs roughly parallel with the Slovenian border. Trail #1 is not too difficult but still requires proper footwear. Pay close attention to the tourist office map to avoid missing the section that links the two lakes, as it is not clearly marked. Trail #2, a more difficult hike, requires prior preparation; consult the tourist office before setting out.

For lodging, **Capana Edelweiss ❸,** V. dei Laghi 8, offers isolation amidst the forest of the Fusine Lakes. The charming brown cottage and restaurant sits on the shore of Lake Inferiore, but there is not much else in the area. A car would be a good idea if you choose to stay, since bus service is infrequent. (☎61 050. Breakfast included. Call ahead. Singles €40; doubles €70. Cash only. Row boat rental €4.50 per 30min.) After trekking all day, take a break to snack and enjoy the view from the porch of **Osteria Belvedere ❷,** at Lake Inferiore. (☎349 812 10 52. *Primi* €4.50-8. Cover €1. Open late June-Sept. daily 9:30am-8pm.) The *osteria* also rents row boats for €4.50 per 30min. *(Buses depart from V. V. Veneto 54, in front of the school, by the sign for Pellicano Supermarket. M-Sa 5 per day 6:40am-5:25pm, last bus back to Tarvisio 6pm; round-trip €2.30. Consult tourist office for most up-to-date schedules. Buy tickets from Bar Commercio; open M-Sa 7am-7pm. Cash only.)*

FRIULI-VENEZIA GIULIA

EMILIA-ROMAGNA

Italy's wealthiest wheat- and dairy-producing region, Emilia-Romagna (eh-MEE-lya ro-MAN-ya) spans the Po River Valley's fertile plains and fosters some of the finest culinary traditions on the Italian peninsula. Gorge on Parma's famous *parmigiano-reggiano* and prosciutto, Bologna's fresh *pasta alla bolognese* and *mortadella*, and Ferrara's *salama* and *grana* cheese; complement the local specialties with regional wines like the sparkling red *Lambrusco*. Although the Romans originally settled this region, most of the visible ruins are remnants of medieval structures, and travelers today find bustling urban scenes that have escaped the oppressive tourism of other major Italian cities. Visitors will enjoy authentic cuisine, well-preserved sights with low admission fees, and enough quiet to contemplate both the art and the natural beauty.

HIGHLIGHTS OF EMILIA-ROMAGNA

SAVOR Modena's renowned **balsamic vinegar.** (p. 398)

BIKE along Ferrara's 9km **medieval wall.** (p. 390)

ABSORB the Byzantine influence through Ravenna's world-famous **mosaics.** (p. 409)

PARTY with students and backpackers at the **superb clubs** in Rimini. (p. 415)

ESCAPE Italy for majestic views off San Marino's **Castello della Guaita.** (p. 420)

BOLOGNA
☎051

Affectionately referred to as the *grassa* (fat) and *dotta* (learned) city, Bologna (bo-LOHN-ya; pop. 370,000) has a legacy of excellent food, education, and art. While the Po Valley provides tables with hearty egg pasta and savory local wines, Bologna's museums and churches house priceless artistic treasures. The city is also home to Europe's oldest university—a law school founded in 1088 to settle disputes between the Holy Roman Empire and the Papacy. After taking in the city's many free sights, unbelievable food, and lively student-based nightlife, travelers leave Bologna more than satisfied with their taste of *la dolce vita*.

▐ TRANSPORTATION

Flights: Aeroporto Guglielmo Marconi (☎64 79 615; www.bologna-airport.it), at Borgo Panigale, northwest of the *centro.* The **Aerobus** (☎29 02 90) runs to the airport from Track D outside the train station and makes stops at several locations in the city center (every 15min. 5:30am-11:10pm, €5).

Trains: Info office open daily 7am-9pm (☎89 20 21). West platform **disability assistance** (☎199 30 30 60) open daily 7am-9pm. To: **Florence** (1½hr., 53 per day 5:13am-10:20pm, €4.80); **Milan** (3hr., 46 per day 3:44am-10:15pm, €19); **Rome** (3hr., 36 per day 5:15am-8:46pm, €32); **Venice** (2hr., 29 per day 3:18am-9:42pm, €8.20).

Buses: Terminal Bus (☎24 21 50), next to ATC ticket counter, provides **Eurolines** bus service. Open M-F 9am-6:30pm, Sa 8:30am-6pm, Su 3-6:30pm. Cash only.

Public Transportation: ATC (☎29 02 90) runs efficient buses that get crowded in the early afternoon and evening. Intra-city tickets (€1) are good 1hr. after onboard validation. Purchase at newsstands, self-service machines, or *tabaccherie.* Buses **#25** and **30** run from the train station up V. Marconi and across V. Ugo Bassi and V. Rizzoli.

EMILIA-ROMAGNA

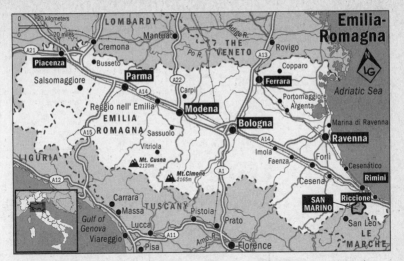

Car Rental: Hertz, V. Amendola 16/A (☎25 48 30). Turn right from the train station, and left on V. Amendola. 25+. Open M-F 8am-8pm, Sa 8am-1pm. AmEx/MC/V.

Taxis: C.A.T. ☎53 41 41. **RadioTaxi** ☎37 27 27. 24hr.

✷ 🛈 ORIENTATION AND PRACTICAL INFORMATION

From the **train station**, turn left on **Viale Pietro Pietramellara**, and head to **Piazza XX Settembre**. From there, take **Via dell'Indipendenza**, which leads to **Piazza del Nettuno**; behind it is **Piazza Maggiore**, the *centro*. At P. del Nettuno, V. dell'Indipendenza intersects **Via Ugo Bassi**, which runs west, and **Via Rizzoli**, which runs east to **Piazza Porta Ravegnana**. **Via Zamboni** and **Strada Maggiore** lead out of this *piazza*.

> **❗ NO BOLOGNA.** Treat Bologna like a big city—use caution, and hold onto your wallet. At night, solo travelers should avoid the train station, the northern part of V. dell'Indipendenza, and the areas surrounding the university.

Tourist Office: P. Maggiore 1 (☎24 65 41), in Palazzo del Podestà. Offers maps, guided city tours, and info on events and lodgings. Open daily 9:30am-7:30pm. Branch in train station. Open M-Sa 9am-7pm, Su 9am-3pm. **Call Center** (☎24 65 41) open M-Sa 9am-7pm. **CST:** P. Maggiore 1, (☎800 85 60 65 or 23 47 35; www.cst.bo.it). In the tourist office. Books accommodations at no charge. Open M-Sa 10am-2pm and 3-7pm, Su and holidays 10am-2pm.

Budget Travel: CTS, Largo Respighi 2/F (☎26 18 02 or 23 75 01), across Largo Respighi from the Teatro Communale. Resources include ISICs (€10), train tickets, tour packages, and discounts on air and sea travel. Posters concerning accommodation rentals are outside. Open M-F 9am-12:30pm and 2:30-6pm. MC/V.

Luggage Storage: At the train station. Max. bag weight 20kg. €3.80 for 1st 5hr., €0.60 per hr. up to 11hr., €0.20 per hr. thereafter. Open daily 6am-midnight. Cash only.

English-Language Bookstore: Feltrinelli International, V. Zamboni 7/B (☎26 80 70). Wide selection of classics, new novels, and travel guides. Open M-Sa 9am-8pm, Su 10am-1:30pm and 3-7:30pm. AmEx/MC/V.

EMILIA-ROMAGNA

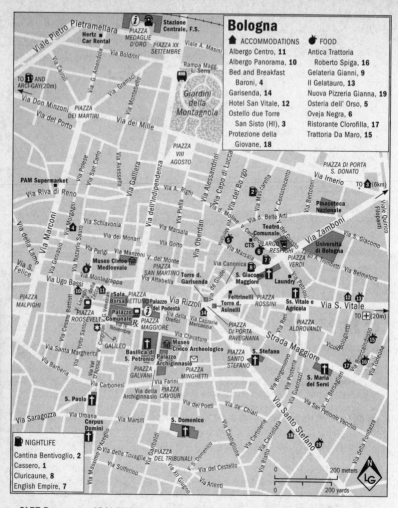

Bologna

⌂ ACCOMMODATIONS

Albergo Centro, 11
Albergo Panorama, 10
Bed and Breakfast
Baroni, 4
Garisenda, 14
Hotel San Vitale, 12
Ostello due Torre
San Sisto (HI), 3
Protezione della
Giovane, 18

● FOOD

Antica Trattoria
Roberto Spiga, 16
Gelateria Gianni, 9
Il Gelatauro, 13
Nuova Pizzeria Gianna, 19
Osteria dell' Orso, 5
Oveja Negra, 6
Ristorante Clorofilla, 17
Trattoria Da Maro, 15

◗ NIGHTLIFE

Cantina Bentivoglio, 2
Cassero, 1
Cluricaune, 8
English Empire, 7

GLBT Resources: ARCI-GAY, V. Don Minzoni 18 (☎64 94 416; www.cassero.it). Sociopolitical organization with a library and reference and counseling center. Cassero nightclub downstairs (p. 390). Open daily 9am-10pm.

Laundromat: Lavarapido, V. Petroni 38/B, off P. Verdi, near V. Zamboni. Wash €3.40 per 8kg. Detergent €0.60. Open M-Sa 9am-9pm, Su 10:30am-9pm. Cash only.

Police: P. Galileo 7 (☎16 40 11 11).

Pharmacy: Farmacia Comunali AFM Bologna, P. Maggiore 6 (☎23 85 09). Open 24hr.

Internet Access: Sportello Iperbole, P. Maggiore 6 (☎20 31 84). Wi-Fi available. Free Internet. Reserve a few days ahead. Limit 2hr. per week. Also provides lists of other Internet locations (some free). Open M-F 9:30am-6:30pm; last use at 5:30pm. **Everest**

Works, V. della Zecca 3/B (☎29 60 464). €1.50 per hr, min. €0.40. Fax, photocopy and print services. Open daily 8am-10:30pm. Cash only.

Post Office: P. Minghetti 4 (☎80 31 60), southeast of P. Maggiore, off V. Farini. **Exchanges currency.** Open M-F 8am-6:30pm, Sa 8am-12:30pm. **Postal Code:** 40100.

ACCOMMODATIONS

Bologna's hotels are pricey and fill up quickly; reservations are recommended. The most affordable establishments are located near V. Ugo Bassi and V. Marconi.

Albergo Panorama, V. Livraghi 1, 4th fl. (☎22 18 02; www.hotelpanoramabologna.it). Take V. Ugo Bassi from P. del Nettuno, then take the 3rd left. Spacious rooms off a small hallway have charming decorations and good views. All rooms have sink and TV. Reception 7am-3am. Curfew 3am. Singles €50; doubles €60-70; triples €75-85; quads €85-95; quints €100. ❹

Ostello due Torre San Sisto (HI), V. Viadagola 5 (☎/fax 50 18 10), off V. S. Donato, in Località di S. Sisto. Take bus #93 from V. Marconi 69 (15min., M-Sa every 30min. 6:16am-8:06pm) or #301 (on Su) from bus station. Exit at S. Sisto. Social, but out-of-the-way hostel with basketball court, satellite TV, and DVDs. Laundry €2.60 per load. Internet access €5 per hr. Wheelchair-accessible. Reception 7:30-10am and 3:30-11:30pm. Lockout 9:30am-1pm. Dorms €18.50; doubles €36; family rooms €17 per person. HI-member discount €3. AmEx/MC/V. ❶

Bed and Breakfast Baroni, V. Morgani 9 (☎340 29 41 752). From V. Marconi, take a left onto V. Riva di Reno and right onto V. Morgani. Centrally located B&B sports simple rooms in quiet area near the *centro*. Breakfast included. Singles €45-65; doubles €65, with bath €80. MC/V. ❹

Garisenda, Galleria Leone 1, 3rd fl. (☎22 43 69; www.albergogarisenda.com). Take V. Rizzoli and turn right into the gallery. A hallway lined with antiques leads to 7 spacious rooms with basic furnishings. Breakfast included. Singles €45; doubles €65, with bath 85; triples €95/115. MC/V. ❹

Protezione della Giovane, V. Santo Stefano 45 (☎22 55 73). Past the church, on the right. Ring buzzer and climb the large staircase at the end of the long hallway. Gorgeous building with frescoed ceilings and French windows overlooks a garden of potted trees. Curfew 10:30pm. Dorm €15. Women only. Cash only. ❶

Hotel San Vitale, V. San Vitale 94 (☎22 59 66; fax 23 93 96). Follow V. Rizzoli past towers to V. S. Vitale; ring bell to enter. Rooms of varying sizes all have fan, bath and TV. Sunny courtyard. Close to nightlife. Wheelchair-accessible. Reception until 2am. Singles €52-66; doubles €72-96; triples €90-114; quads €110-136. AmEx/MC/V. ❹

Albergo Centrale, V. della Zecca 2, 3rd fl. (☎22 51 14; www.albergocentralebologna.it). Take V. Ugo Bassi from P. del Nettuno, then 2nd left on V. della Zecca. A snazzy hotel with blue furnishings, professional staff, and bright halls. All rooms with A/C and TV. Breakfast €7. Singles €50, with bath €60; doubles €80; triples €95; quads €110. Extra bed €20. AmEx/MC/V. ❹

FOOD

Bologna is known for its stuffed pastas, such as *tortellini* with ground meat or with ricotta and spinach. Bologna is also famous for its variety of salamis and hams, including *mortadella*, a sausage-like creation that bears little resemblance to America's processed bologna. Restaurants cluster on side streets near the *centro;* try the areas around V. Augusto Righi, V. Piella, and V. Saragozza. Indoor **Mer-**

IF YOU CAN'T TAKE THE HEAT, GET OUT OF THE KITCHEN

To take a little of the "fat" city home with you, try a class at any of Bologna's short-term culinary schools. Consult the tourist office for a complete listing.

La Vecchia Scuola Bolognese (☎051 64 93 627; www.lavecchiascuola.com) is the mother of local cooking schools, offering a 4hr. course topped off by a fabulous meal. Learn to make fresh pasta from a professional, English-speaking staff. When all is said and done, you'll get to eat your own pasta creations; if your attempts don't quite succeed, you'll still be served the school's own menu of typical Bolognese specialties.

La Cucina di Petronilla, V. San Vitale 53 (☎051 22 40 11), offers 8 classes or single one-on-one lessons upon request. The courses focus on pairing wine with food, table preparation, and making regional dishes. The chef believes in healthy organic cuisine, but fear not: it's still typical, hearty Bolognese fare.

La Cantina Bentivoglio (☎051 26 54 16; www.affari.com/bentivoglio), a classy restaurant offering delicious local cuisine and live jazz, also has demonstrations (though not lessons) of the pasta-making process. The price and length of demonstrations vary, so call to create a custom demo with the restaurant.

cato delle Erbe, V. Ugo Bassi 27, sells produce, cheese, meat, and bread. (Open in summer M-W 7am-1:15pm and 5-7:30pm, Th and Sa 7am-1:15pm, F 7am-1:15pm and 4:30-7:30pm; in winter M-W and F 4:30-7:30pm. Cash only.) Buy essentials at **PAM** supermarket, V. Marconi 26. (Open M-Sa 7:45am-8pm. AmEx/MC/V.)

🕎 **Osteria dell'Orsa,** V. Mentana 1/F (☎23 15 76; www.osteriadellorsa.com). Popular casual joint caters to students with fresh, simple local dishes like *piadinas* (a flat round bread; €3.50-4.50) and big salads (€6.50). Communal seating makes for social dining, perfect for a meal before hitting the nearby nightlife. Wine €4 per 0.5L. Open daily noon-4pm and 7pm-midnight. Cash only. ❶

🕎 **Gelateria Gianni,** V. Montegrappa 11 (☎23 30 08), at the corner of V. degli Usberti. In the spirit of *grassa* Bologna, sample as many of the 99 flavors of *gelato* as you can at this madly popular chain of *gelaterie* throughout the city. Flavors named after movies are unthinkably decadent, as are fruit flavors. 1 scoop €2, 3 scoops €3. Open M-Tu and Th-Sa noon-1am, Su 11am-1am. Cash only. ❶

Il Gelatauro, V. San Vitale 98/B (☎23 00 49). This *gelateria* flanks flavors like ginger and *aurora* (pine nut) with classics like *stracciatella* (vanilla with a chocolate swirl). Any sweet tooth will gravitate toward the gourmet chocolates and decadent pastries. Open M 8am-7pm, Tu-Su 8am-11pm; closed Aug. Cash only. ❶

Nuova Pizzeria Gianna, V. Santo Stefano 76/A (☎22 25 16). Locals know this hidden gem as "Mamma's." Watch owner Gianna roll dough for fresh pizzas (€3.20-7) behind a busy bar. Seating is limited, so devour the special *gianna* (with fontina cheese and arugula; €7) from a stool, or get a slice (€2) to go. Open M-Sa 8:30am-11:30pm. Closed 2wk. in Aug. 10% student discount. Cash only. ❶

Trattoria Da Maro, V. Broccaindosso 71/B (☎22 73 04; trattoriamaro@libero.it), between Str. Maggiore and V. S. Vitale. At this popular neighborhood trattoria, try the favorite *pasta con le sarde* (with sardines) amid cluttered bottles and colorful paintings of unicorns and crabs in starry skies. *Primi* €10-11, *secondi* €11-15. Cover €1.50 for lunch, €2 for dinner. Open M and Su 8-11pm, Tu-Sa noon-2:30pm; in summer hours reduced. AmEx/MC/V. ❸

Oveja Negra, Largo Respighi 4 (☎22 46 79), near the *Teatro Communale* and the student scene. Funky furniture and modern art come together at this popular cafe adorned with its signature sheep logo. Espresso €1. *Panini* €1.50-3. Open M-F 8am-midnight. Cash only. ❶

Ristorante Clorofilla, Strada Maggiore 64/C (☎23 53 43). Get fruits and veggies at this wholesome organic eatery with the motto "eat your way to good health."

Try the fabulous couscous with tofu, vegetables, and tomato sauce (€6) complemented by organic wine (from €2.80 per carafe). Check the blackboard for daily specials. Hot entrees from €6. Salads from €4.50. Fresh juices €2.30. Cover €1. Open
M-Sa noon-3pm and 7:30-11pm. Closed Aug. AmEx/MC/V. ❷

Antica Trattoria Roberto Spiga, V. Broccaindosso 21/A (☎23 00 63), between
Strada Maggiore and V. S. Vitale. Black-and-white photos of old Bologna line the
walls of this traditional, family-run restaurant. Menu changes daily. W *bolognese* specialty €14. *Primi* €7.50-12, *secondi* €9-10. Cover €1.50. Open M 8-10:30pm, Tu-Sa
noon-3pm and 7-11pm. Closed Aug. MC/V. ❸

◔ SIGHTS

▨ PIAZZA MAGGIORE. Aristotle Fioravanti, designer of Moscow's Kremlin,
remodeled the Romanesque **Palazzo del Podestà,** now the boxy, brick home of various cafes, shops, and info centers lining its loggia. The 15th-century building is a
feat of engineering: the weight of the palace rests on columns, not on the ground
itself. Directly across the *piazza* sits the **Basilica di San Petronio,** designed by Antonio da Vincenzo in 1390. The *bolognesi* originally plotted to make their basilica
larger than St. Peter's in Rome, but the Vatican ordered that the funds be used to
build the nearby Palazzo Archiginnasio. The cavernous Gothic interior hosted
both the Council of Trent and the 1530 ceremony in which Pope Clement VII gave
Italy to German Kaiser Karl V. Golden panels and cherubs fill the **Cappella di San
Petronio,** left of the entrance, where opulence contrasts the basilica's predominantly bare walls. From the base of the nave nearby, a marble track dotted with
constellation symbols and a single golden line extends across the church's floor to
create the largest **zodiac sundial** in the world. Don't neglect the gorgeous main
altar, which elevates ornate stone statues toward the arches above. The tiny
museum contains models of the basilica, beautiful chalices, and illuminated books.
*(P. Maggiore 3. ☎22 54 42. Basilica open M-Sa 7:15am-1:30pm and 2:30-6:30pm, Su 7:30am-
1pm and 2:30-6:30pm. Museum open daily 9:30am-12:30pm and 2:30-5:30pm. Both free.)*

PALAZZO ARCHIGINNASIO. This *palazzo*, the first seat of the city's university,
features thousands of names and coats of arms of professors and students who
worked here. The building, constructed to consolidate the once-scattered schools
of the university, now houses the **Biblioteca dell'Archiginnasio,** the university's main
reading room and a city library with over 800,000 texts. Above the central courtyard's 30 arches sits the **Teatro Anatomico,** a lecture hall where bronze statues of
famous ancient and Bolognese doctors blend into the wood walls. A marble table
marks where dissections were performed beneath the starry ceiling decorations.
*(V. Archiginnasio 1, next to the Museo Archeologico. Follow signs from P. Maggiore. ☎27 68 11.
Palazzo open M-F 9am-1pm. Closed 1st 2wk. of Aug. Free.)*

PIAZZA DEL NETTUNO. This *piazza* contains Giambologna's 16th-century stone
and bronze fountain *Neptune and Attendants.* Affectionately called "The Giant,"
a nude Neptune reigns over a collection of water-babies and sirens spraying water
from every bodily orifice. According to local legend, Pope Pious IV, who commissioned the statue, was disturbed by the large original size of Neptune's manhood
and ordered Giambologna to change it. Giambologna, who agreed to alter the
actual member, had the last laugh: standing near the steps of Sala Borsa, it appears
as if Neptune is at his original—ahem—grandeur, thanks to an outstretched hand.
Nearby, a wall of portrait tiles commemorates the Bolognese resistance to Nazi
occupation, while a Plexiglas plaque lists the names and ages of more recent victims of terrorism from the 1974, 1980, and 1984 Bologna train bombings.

PINACOTECA NAZIONALE. The Pinacoteca displays religious artwork spanning from the Roman era to Mannerism, with pieces by Giotto, Titian, and Giovanni Battista. In the museum's east wing, **Gallery 15** contains works by Raphael and his Florentine followers. For impressive works by Bologna's own Guido Reni, try **Gallery 24's** triumphant *Sampson Victorious* and the *Pietà detta dei Mendicanti*, a floor-to-ceiling canvas. **Gallery 26** displays Francesco Albani's beautiful *Madonna e Bambino*, and **Gallery 22** holds several large canvases, including Vasari's *Christ in Casa di Marta*. *(V. delle Belle Arti 56, off V. Zamboni. ☎42 09 411; www.pinacotecabologna.it. Open Tu-Su 9am-7pm. Last entry 30min. before closing. €4, EU students €2, under 18 and over 65 free. Cash only.)*

PALAZZO COMUNALE. Nicolò dell'Arca's terra-cotta *Madonna* and Alessandro Menganti's bronze statue of Pope Gregory XIV adorn the outside this *palazzo*. The **Collezioni Comunali d'Arte** houses regional art from the 13th to the 20th century. Walk through the Rusconi wing, which displays furnishings from ornate Bolognan homes, to the gorgeous Sala Boschereccia, where walls painted with serene landscapes and playful winged angels surround Baruzzi's 19th-century statue of Apollo. *(P. Maggiore 6. Office ☎20 36 31; tickets 20 35 26. Open Tu-F 9am-3pm, Sa-Su 10am-6:30pm. Free.)* If you're looking for slightly more secular art, don't miss the adjoining **Museo Morandi,** which displays luminous oil paintings and watercolors and the reconstructed V. Fondazza studio of early 20th-century painter, Giorgio Morandi. His landscapes and muted oil still-lifes of jugs, cups, and bottles are a welcome alternative. *(P. Maggiore 6. ☎20 36 46; www.museomorandi.it. Wheelchair-accessible. Open Tu-F 9am-3pm, Sa-Su 10am-6:30pm. Free.)*

MUSEO CIVICO MEDIOEVALE. Anything remotely associated with Bologna is featured here, including a collection of Bologna's patron saints, wax seals of local nobility, an impressive collection of sepulcher lids, and weaponry. Watch for a 17th-century dagger that shatters after stabbing its victim and the 17th-century Roman *Sileno con Otre,* a rare example of an obese marble statue. In the basement, funerary slabs depicting classroom scenes immortalize celebrated Bolognese professors. *(V. Manzoni 4. Off V. dell'Indipendenza, near P. Maggiore. ☎20 39 30; www.comune.bologna.it/iperbole/MuseiCivici. Open Tu-F 9am-3pm, Sa-Su 10am-6:30pm. Free. Audio tour €4.)*

THE TWO TOWERS. After seismic shifts left Bologna with an unexpectedly tilted **Torre degli Garisenda,** the determined city strove for new heights with the 97.2m **Torre degli Asinelli.** Visible from all over the city, the adjacent towers have evolved into architectural symbols of the town. Breathless climbers mount 498 narrow wooden steps past four landings to a breezy perch where a sea of red rooftops, Gothic church spires, yellow villages, and miles of uninterrupted horizon sit stories below. *(P. Porta Ravegana, at the end of V. Rizzoli. Open daily 9am-6pm. €3. Cash only.)*

MUSEO CIVICO ARCHEOLOGICO. This museum of artifacts unearthed near Bologna features long glass cases and shelves brimming with Roman inscriptions, red and black Greek pottery, and two dirt-covered, mummified Etruscans. The enormous Etruscan section packs display cases full of tiny ornaments and pieces of jewelry. An impressive Egyptian collection in the basement displays items from 2640 BC, including stone reliefs from the tomb of Pharaoh Horemheb. *(V. Archiginnasio 2. Follow signs from P. Maggiore. ☎27 57 211; www.comune.bologna.it/Musei/Archeologico. Open Tu-F 9am-3pm, Sa-Su 10am-6:30pm. Free. Audio tour €4.)*

CHURCHES

◪CHIESA SANTO STEFANO. This cluster of buildings and courtyards was shaped from remains of Egyptian temples honoring the goddess Isis. Four of the seven churches of the original **Romanesque basilica,** known collectively as

"Holy Jerusalem," remain. Built to hold the relics of Saints Vitalis and Agricola, the **Cripta** now contains the tomb of Martin the Abbot. In the small **Chiesa di San Sepolcro,** another of Bologna's patron saints, St. Petronio, is entombed in the towering **Edicola del Santo Sepolcro,** supposedly modeled from Christ's sepulcher in Jerusalem. In the rear courtyard is the **Cortile di Pilato** (Basin of Pilate), where the governor reportedly absolved himself of responsibility for Christ's death. *(In P. Santo Stefano. Follow V. S. Stefano from V. Rizzoli. ☎ 22 32 56. Open M-Sa 9am-noon and 3:30-6:45pm, Su 9am-12:45pm and 3:30-7pm. Modest dress required. Free.)*

CHIESA DI SANTA MARI DEI SERVI. A long walkway marked by glittering red votives and faded patches of fresco hides the bottom half of this soaring basilica from street-level view. Inside the well-preserved Gothic structure, octagonal columns support an unusual blend of arches and ribbed vaulting that cover shallow altars. Cimabue's *Maestà* hangs in a dimly lit chapel behind an exquisite altar that was sculpted by Giovanni Antonio Montorsoli, a pupil of Michelangelo. *(Take Strada Maggiore to P. Aldrovandi. ☎ 22 68 07. Open daily 7:30am-12:30pm and 3:30-7:45pm. Free.)*

CHIESA DI SAN DOMENICO. Tall marble columns line San Domenico's clean interior, but its signature minimalism stops at the two transept chapels. In the **Cappella di San Domenico,** the St. Dominic's body lies in a marble tomb sculpted with religious themes by Nicolò Pisano and Michelangelo. Across the nave in the **Cappella del Rosario,** 15 small paintings by Fontana, Carracci, and others depict the mysteries of the rosary and frame a statue of the Virgin beneath a painted ceiling of playful angels. Because St. Dominic is largely credited with institutionalizing the rosary as a conventional form of prayer, this chapel is especially notable. *(From P. Maggiore, follow V. Archiginnasio to V. Farini and turn right on V. Garibaldi. ☎ 64 00 411. Open M-Sa 9:30am-12:30pm and 3-6:30pm. Free. English tours daily at 3pm; ask for Tarcisio.)*

CHIESA DELLE SANTISSIME VITALE E AGRICOLA. With its polygonal brick spire jutting over the walls of local homes, this small church incorporates shards of capitals and columns from Roman temples into its facade. A lavish gold altar illuminates the otherwise dimly-lit interior, and underneath the building, an 11th-century crypt holds paintings by Francia and Sano di Pietro. Look for a sculpture of Christ based on the Shroud of Turin's (p. 172) anatomical clues. *(V. S. Vitale 48. ☎ 22 05 70. Open daily 8am-noon and 3:30-7:30pm. Chapel free. Crypt €1.)*

CHIESA DI SAN GIACOMO MAGGIORE. The exterior of this church is a blend of Romanesque and Gothic styles, but it is the artwork inside that makes it worth a visit. The aging church is next to the **Oratorio di Santa Cecilia,** which contains a colorful fresco cycle depicting S. Cecilia's marriage and martyrdom. *(Follow V. Zamboni to P. Rossini. ☎ 22 59 70. Church open daily 7am-noon and 3:30-6pm. Enter Oratorio from V. Zamboni 15. Oratorio open daily in summer 10am-1pm and 3-7pm; in winter 10am-1pm and 2-6pm. Both free.)*

🎵 📺 ENTERTAINMENT AND NIGHTLIFE

Every year from June to September, Bologna sponsors an ▨**entertainment festival** of dance, music, cinema, and art. Many events are free, but some cost €5. Summer visitors should contact the tourist office for a program. The **Teatro Comunale,** Largo Respighi 1, hosts world-class operas, symphonies, and ballets. To order tickets ahead, call or sign up outside the ticket office two days before performances. In summer, the theater hosts free concerts that begin at 9pm. Pick up a schedule at the tourist office. (☎ 52 99 99; www.comunalebologna.it. Box office open Tu-Sa 11am-6:30pm. 10% surcharge for pre-order. AmEx/MC/V.)

Bologna's student population accounts for the city's large number of bars, pubs, and nightclubs. A mass of them are on **Via Zamboni,** near the university.

EMILIA-ROMAGNA

Call ahead for hours and cover, as info changes frequently. In June and July, clubs close and the party scene moves outdoors. The tourist office has a list of outdoor music venues. But don't expect much activity in August—even the outdoor *discoteche* shut down, and locals head to the beach.

Cluricaune, V. Zamboni 18/B (☎26 34 19). This huge, multi-leveled Irish pub attracts local students with its extensive beer selection. Pints €3.10-4.20. Happy hour W 7:30-10:30pm; pints €2.50. Open daily noon-3am. AmEx/MC/V.

Cassero, V. Don Minzoni 18 (☎051 64 94 416). Take V. Marconi to P. dei Martiri and turn left on V. Don Minzoni. This popular club, housed in a former 17th-century salt warehouse, draws chatty crowds of students and locals, but is especially popular with the gay community. Dance inside under the high arched ceiling, or enjoy a drink outside on summer nights. ARCI-GAY card required for entrance; can be acquired during the day at its office upstairs (p. 384). Drinks €3-6. Special *discoteca* nights W, F, Sa-Su. Cover F and Sa €6-8. Open M-F 10pm-3am, Sa-Su 10pm-5am. Cash only.

English Empire, V. Zamboni 24, near the University. Drawing crowds of loyal patrons, this bar mixes old-world pub with the pumping music and flashing lights of a new-world club. Under the pub motto of "one day of pleasure is worth two of sorrow," enjoy a variety of beers (€3-4.50) and light meals (burger, drink, and coffee €5). Open M-F noon-3am, Sa-Su 2pm-3am. Cash only.

Cantina Bentivoglio, V. Mascarella 4/B (☎26 54 16), near Largo Respighi and the Teatro Comunale. Serving pricey food and cheap drinks by night, this bar caters to a classier crowd with an umbrella-covered patio and a relaxed atmosphere. Wine from €4.50 per glass. Jazz outdoors Th and F nights in July-Aug., indoors every night Sept.-May. Cover €1.20. Open in summer M-Sa 8pm-2am; in winter daily 8pm-2am.

FERRARA   ☎0532

Rome has its mopeds, Venice its boats, and Ferrara (feh-RA-ra; pop. 130,000) its *biciclette*. In a city with more bicycles than people, girls in stilettos, businessmen with cell phones, and elderly ladies cycle through low arches and narrow streets of the area outside the *centro*. On the city's outskirts, biking aficionados can spend an afternoon cycling a gorgeous 9km bike path atop the crumbling medieval walls, while rambling medieval streets, art museums, and an ominous *castello* offer eye-candy and adventure to the exertion-phobic crowd.

▐ TRANSPORTATION

Trains from Ferrara run to: Bologna (30min., 60 per day 1:41am-10:45pm, €3); Padua (1hr., 41 per day 3:52am-11:07pm, €4.40); Ravenna (1hr., 22 per day 6:11am-8:15pm, €4.40); Rome (3-4hr., 12 per day 4:40am-7:50pm, €22.50); Venice (1½hr., 34 per day 3.48am-10:10pm, €6.10). The ticket office is open daily 6:15am-8:30pm. (☎89 20 21. AmEx/MC/V.) ACFT (☎59 94 92), GGFP, and most other **buses** leave from the train station; the bus station is on the southeast side of town, at Rampari S. Paolo and Corso Isonzo (ticket office open daily 6:40am-6:50pm). Buses run to local beaches (1½hr., 12 per day 7:30am-6:50pm, €4.23), Bologna (1½hr., 21 per day 5:20am-7:50pm, €3.31), and Modena (2hr., 13 per day 5am-7:32pm, €4.65). **RadioTaxi** (☎ 90 09 00) is available 24hr. Head to Pirani e Bagni, P. Stazione 2, for **bike rental.** (☎77 21 90. €2 per hr., €7 per day. Open M-F 7am-8pm, Sa 6am-2pm. Cash only.)

◀▶ ▐ ORIENTATION AND PRACTICAL INFORMATION

To get to the *centro storico*, turn left from the **train station** on **Viale Costituzione,** which becomes **Viale Cavour** and runs to the **Castello Estense.** Alternatively, take

Ferrara

⌂🏠 ACCOMMODATIONS
Albergo San Romano, **9**
Casa degli Artisti, **6**
Estense Campground, **1**
Hotel de Prati, **2**

● FOOD
Il Ciclone, **5**

Il Cucco, **10**
Osteria al Brindisi, **4**
Osteria degli Angeli, **7**
Ristorante Italia Big Night
da Giovanni, **3**
Ristorantino
Viaragnotrentino, **8**

EMILIA-ROMAGNA

bus #2 to the Castello stop or #1 or 9 to the post office (every 15-20min. 5:42am-8:30pm, €1). Turn right after the *castello* onto **Corso Martiri della Libertà**. The **tourist office** is in Castello Estense, near P. Castello, and offers maps and information and local events. (☎20 93 70; www.ferrarainfo.com. Open M-Sa 9am-1pm and 2-6pm, Su 9:30am-1pm and 2-5pm.) **Currency exchange** is available at **Banca Nazionale de Lavoro,** C. Pta. Reno 19. (☎78 16 11. Open M-F 8:20am-1:20pm and 2:35-4:05pm, Su 8:20-11:50am.) In case of **emergency,** call the **police,** C. Ercole I d'Este 26 (☎41 86 00), off Largo Castello. **Fides Pharmacy,** C. Giovecca 125, is open M-Sa 7am-11pm. (☎20 25 24. AmEx/MC/V.) **Ferrara Internet Point,** V. Aleardi 17, alongside the *duomo*, has Internet, printing, photocopy, and fax services. (☎20 70 05. €6 per hr., students €3. Open M-Tu and Th 9am-1pm and 3:30-8:30pm, W and F-Sa 9am-1pm and 3:30-10pm. Cash only.) The **post office**, Vle. Cavour 29, which offers *fermo-posta* and **currency exchange,** is a block toward the train station from the *castello*. (☎29 72 11. Open M-F 8am-6:30pm, Sa 8am-12:30pm.) **Postal Code:** 44100.

> **BIRD'S-EYE VIEW.** For a different perspective, rent a bike and survey Ferrara from atop the medieval walls that surround the city. A paved road runs below and alongside this gravel path, but both are flat, making for a stress-free ride around town.

ACCOMMODATIONS AND CAMPING

Pensione Artisti, V. Vittoria 66 (☎76 10 38). From C. Martiri della Libertà, turn left at the cathedral, right on V. San Romano, left on V. Ragno, and then immediately left. Spacious rooms have stone floors and sink. Guests share access to an ivy-covered garden, bikes, minibar, and a small cooking area. Curfew 12:30am. Singles €28; doubles €48, with bath €60. Cash only. ❷

Albergo San Romano, V. San Romano 120 (☎ 76 94 59; www.albergosanromano.com). A friendly staff keeps cavernous rooms with bath, TV, and phone; some with A/C and view of Ferrara. Fans provided upon request. Breakfast included. Wi-Fi free. Singles €50; doubles €70; triples €85; quints €105. ❹

Hotel de Prati, V. Padiglioni 5 (☎24 19 05; www.hoteldeprati.com). Central location, friendly staff, and tasteful rooms with TV, fridge, and A/C make it worth the splurge. Breakfast included. Wi-Fi free. Wheelchair-accessible. Singles €50-75; doubles €85-110; suites €100-140. Extra bed €16. AmEx/MC/V. ❹

Estense Campground, V. Gramicia 76 (☎/fax 75 23 96). Take bus #1 to P. San Giovanni (€1), then V. Gramicia for 15min. through the traffic circle to campsite 1km from the *centro* (a 30min. walk or a €7-8 taxi drive). From the *castello,* take C. Ercole I d'Este, turn right on C. Pta. Mare, and left on V. Gramicia. Surrounded by cornfields in a quiet spot northeast of the *centro,* this campground is near some of Ferrara's best bike paths. Bike rental €4 per ½-day. Office open daily 8am-10pm. Closed mid-Jan. to late Feb. €7 per day. €5 per person, under 8 free; €7.50 per car and tent site; RV rental €26 per day. Electricity €2.50. Hot showers free. MC/V over €50. ❶

FOOD

Aside from the seafood-heavy regional diet of eel, clams, scallops, mullet, and sea bass, Ferrara's specialties also include *cappellacci di zucca* (pasta stuffed with pumpkin and parmesan), *salama da sugo* (pork, spices, and wine) and *pasticcio alla ferrarese* (sweet bread stuffed with macaroni and meat sauce). Corpus Domini nuns invented Ferrara's *pampepato* (chocolate cake with almonds, candied fruit, and icing). For wine, try the sparkling *Uva d'Oro* (Golden Grape). A **Conad** supermarket is at V. Garibaldi 53. (Open M-Sa 8:30am-8pm, Su 9:15am-1:15pm. MC/V.) **Ferrara Frutta,** a local produce market, is in P. Castello 24-26. (☎20 31 36. Open M-W, F, Su 8am-1pm and 5-7:30pm; Th and Sa 8am-1pm. Cash only.)

Osteria al Brindisi, V. Guglielmo degli Adelardi 11 (☎20 91 42), near the *duomo*. Reputedly the oldest *osteria* (alehouse) in the world, al Brindisi has welcomed luminaries like Titian, Cellini, and Pope John Paul II into its intimate interior since 1435. Waiters ascend ladders to choose from the countless rows of dusty wine bottles. *Primi* €7-10. Cover €2. Open Tu-Su 11am-1am. AmEx/MC/V. ❸

Osteria degli Angeli, V. delle Volte 4 (☎76 43 76). Hearty regional fare inside a 16th-century dining room. From the *duomo,* take C. Pta. Reno, and turn left under the arch. *Primi* €7-8, *secondi* €7-15. Open daily 6pm-11pm. Kitchen open 7-10pm. MC/V. ❸

Ristorantino Viaragnotrentino, V. Ragno 31/A (☎76 90 70). For a splurge, try any of the seafood specialties at this elegant side-street spot. Offers a special fish tasting *menù* Th nights (€28, including water and wine; call ahead to reserve). *Primi* €9-15, *secondi* €12-25. Cover €2. Open M and W-Su 12:30-2:30pm and 7:30-10:30pm. AmEx/MC/V. ❹

Il Ciclone, V. Vignatagliata 11, 2nd fl. (☎21 02 62; fax 21 23 22), on a quiet side alley. Try the specialty *pizza ciclone* (€7), a whirlwind of pepperoni, onions and arugula. Pizza €4-8. *Primi* €7-15, *secondi* €8-16. *Menù* €12. Cover €1.50. Open Tu-Su noon-3pm and 7pm-1am. AmEx/MC/V. ❷

Ristorante Italia Big Night da Giovanni, V. Largo Castello 38 (☎24 23 67). Inspired by the Italian brothers in the film *Big Night,* this *ristorante* presents elegant dishes like asparagus and truffle pudding (€15). *Primi* €11-19, *secondi* €18-32. Cover €3. Open daily 12:30-2:15pm and 8:15-10pm. AmEx/MC/V. ❺

Il Cucco, V. Voltacasotto 3 (☎76 00 26; www.trattoriailcucco.it). Nestled in a residential neighborhood in the medieval part of town, Il Cucco serves traditional *ferrarese* cuisine, like *cappellacci di zucca al burro e salvia* (€7), at cozy indoor tables or outside on the ivy-shaded terrace. *Primi* €6-7.50, *secondi* €6-11.50. Open M-Tu and Th-Su 12:30-2pm and 7:30-10pm. AmEx/MC/V. ❷

◉ SIGHTS

Leonello d'Este, ruler and patron of the arts, molded Ferrara into an important artistic center with its own school of painting, the *Officina Ferrarese.* Works by Pisanello, Piero della Francesca, and Titian grace the city's palaces and monuments. Those yearning for natural beauty can ride or walk down the 9km concourse that runs atop the medieval wall, providing impressive panoramic views.

> ▥ **MUSEUM MANIA.** The **Cumulativo Arte Antica** (€8) offers entrance to Museo della Cattedrale, Museo Laidario, Palazzina Marfisa d'Este, and Palazzo Schifanoia. The **Cumulativo Arte Moderna** (€6) offers entrance to Museo Boldini, Museo dell'Ottocento, Museo Filippo de Pisis, and Padiglione d'Arte Contemporanea. Finally, the **Museum Card** (€14), allows entrance to all communal museums (essentially, the *Arte Antica* and the *Arte Moderna* cards combined) and is valid for the entire year. Purchase cards at participating museums.

▧ **CASTELLO ESTENSE.** This castle debuted as a small fortress in the 14th century and has been carefully preserved, complete with drawbridges over a murky green moat. Today, excellent English panels guide visitors through the castle and its many rooms, remnants of the distinguished *ferrarese* court life. The tour tracks the city's development to military and cultural prominence in the region. The red-tiled **Garden and Loggia of the Oranges,** where Eleanor of Aragon filled her terrace with orange trees, was added later. Less heartwarming are the tunnels of the dank **prigione** (prisons). After King Nicolo III got wind of the illicit affair between his son Ugo and his 2nd wife, Parisina, the king commanded that the risqué couple be imprisoned here, to await their beheadings. (☎29 92 33. Open Tu-Su 9:30am-5:30pm. €6, under 18 and over 65 €5. Supplement for Estense tower €1. Audio tour €3, children €2.50. Cash only.)

▧ **DUOMO SAN ROMANO.** Dedicated to the city's patron saints, the 12th-century cathedral is a stunning masterpiece of loggia, rose windows, and bas-reliefs. Biagio Rosetti designed the arches and terra-cotta apse, and Leon Battista Alberti fashioned the pink *campanile.* A dim interior houses the beautiful Santuario Beata Vergine delle Grazie, a gleaming side altar illuminated by red votives and soft white bulbs on candlesticks. The fresco above the altar was inspired by Michelangelo's *Last Judgment* in the Sistine Chapel. Across the street, the **Museo della Cattedrale** displays the church's precious works, including Jacopo Quercia's amazing statue *Madonna of the Pomegranate*. *(Museum across the street from the duomo, through the courtyard on V. S. Romano. Museum ☎ 24 49 49. Duomo open M-Sa 7:30am-noon and 3-6:30pm, Su 7:30am-12:30pm and 3:30-7:30pm. Free. Museum open Tu-Su 9am-1pm and 3-6pm. Last entry 30min. before closing. €5, students €3. AmEx/MC/V.)*

PALAZZO DEI DIAMANTI. Built in 1493 by Rossetti, the *palazzo* is easily recognizable by the many white, pyramid-shaped studs that cover its facade. Inside is the **Pinacoteca Nazionale,** a collection of art including a series of tablets by El Greco depicting scenes from Christ's life. Other standouts include Bastianino's **La Resurrezione di Cristo** and Scarsellino's two versions of **Ultima Cena** (The Last Supper), huge 16th-century paintings in the collection's later rooms. *(C. Ercole I d'Este 1. Just before intersection with C. Rossetti. ☎ 20 58 44. Open Tu-W and F-Sa 9am-2pm, Th 9am-7pm, Su 9am-1pm. Last entry 30min. before closing. €4, over 65 and students €2. Cash only.)*

PALAZZO MASSARI. Once a 16th-century residence, the *palazzo* now houses three separate museums. The **Padiglione d'Arte Contemporanea** has temporary modern art exhibitions. The **Museo d'Arte Moderna e Contemporanea Filippo de Pisis** displays a collection of paintings and sculptures, all by *ferrarese* artists. Upstairs, the **Museo Ferrarese dell'Ottocento/Museo Giovanni Boldini** displays a range of 18th- through 20th- century works, but Boldini's intimate paintings are the highlights. *(C. Porta Mare 9. Turn right off C. Ercole I d'Este. ☎ 24 49 49. Museums open Tu-Su 9am-1pm and 3-6pm. Last entry 30min. before closing. Filippo de Pisis €3, students €2. Ottocento/Boldini €5/3. Combined ticket €8/3. Cash only.)*

SINAGOGHE E MUSEO EBRAICO. The city's Jewish museum displays art and documents the history of Ferrara's Jewish community, including the keys that once locked the gates closing the ghetto off from the rest of the city. The synagogue is still used for Shabbat and high holiday services. *(V. Mazzini 95. From the duomo, the museum is on the left side of the street. ☎ 21 02 28. Open Tu-Sa 10am-1pm and 3-6pm, Su 10am-1pm. Guided tours M-Th and Su 10, 11am, and noon. Admission with guided tour. €4, students €3.)* Inquire at the synagogue for directions to the **Cimitero Ebraico** (Jewish Cemetery), where most of Ferrara's 19th- and 20th-century Jewish community is buried. The tourist office also provides a map of Jewish sights throughout the city. *(From the castello, head down C. Giovecca, turn left on V. Montebello, and continue to end.)*

PALAZZO SCHIFANOIA. The word Schifanoia translates to "shunning boredom." and in its day this palace was entirely dedicated to court entertainment. The 15th-century **Hall of the Months,** a Renaissance fresco series representing each month, its astrological sign, and its corresponding Greek deity, is the *palazzo*'s main attraction. *(V. Scandiana 23. ☎ 64 178. Open Tu-Su 9am-6pm. €2.50, students €1.50. With Palazzina Marfisa €8/5. Cash only.)*

CASA ROMEI. After a legal tug-of-war, this 15th-century Renaissance showpiece, halfway house, and one-time candidate for demolition opened as a museum in 1952. Giovanni Romei, an ambitious merchant, administrator to the *ferraresi* lords, and husband of princess Polisenna d'Este, constructed the brick *palazzo* to bolster his reputation in 1440. It now stands as the prototype of the 15th-century aristocratic house, and its rooms, which wind around a sunny interior courtyard, are filled with ceiling frescoes, artwork from destroyed churches, and the remains of one of Ferrara's oldest thermal baths. *(V. Savonarola 30. Follow V. Adelardi left of the duomo until it becomes V. Savonarola. ☎ 24 03 41. Open Tu-Su 8:30am-7:30pm. Last entry 30min. before closing. €2, EU students €1, under 18 free. Cash only.)*

MUSEO ARCHEOLOGICO NAZIONALE. Two walls of a neighboring brick build-ing and two stories of marble loggia compose the courtyard of the Palazzo di Ludovico il Moro, built in 1495 for an official of the d'Este court. Glass cases display artifacts from Ferrara's own mysterious Atlantis, called **Spina**—the Greek-Etruscan city that disappeared into the Adriatic Sea 2000 years ago. Non-Italian speakers should be aware that there is no information in English to guide you through the museum's many galleries. *(V. XX Settembre 122. A short walk down V. Porta d'Amore from Palazzo Schifanoia. From P. Trento Trieste, follow V. Mazzini, which becomes V. Saraceno, to the end; turn left on V. Mayr, then right on V. Borgovado. ☎66 299; mnafe@tiscalinet.it. Open Tu-Su 9am-2pm. €4, 18-25 €2. Cash only.)*

PALAZZINA MARFISA D'ESTE. The furniture in this brick dwelling is positioned as if the *palazzina* were still in use. Note the walnut benches supported by Ionic columns, which have been called one of the most perfect creations of 16th-century Tuscan furniture. *(C. Giovecca 170. Follow C. Giovecca from Largo Castello, or take bus #9. ☎20 74 50. Open Tu-Su 9am-1pm and 3-6pm. €3, students €2. Combined ticket with Palazzo Schifanoia and Museo della Cattedrale €6.50/€4.50. Cash only.)*

▓ NIGHTLIFE

As in Padova and Bologna, its college town neighbors to the north and south, nightlife in Ferrara peaks during the school year when university students fill the city's cobblestone side streets, especially on Wednesday nights when students flood P. della Cattedrale. Still, summer brings outdoor tables with groups lingering late into the evening over drinks. Close to the university and the center of town is **Tsunami,** V. Savonarola 2, at the corner of V. Terranuova. Flat-screen TVs and zebra-striped cushions on the bar stools draw a young crowd to this bar, which offers small plates and a long list of mixed drinks. (☎21 11 03. Beers €2.50-5. Mixed drinks €2.50-7. Happy hour Sept.-June Tu 10-11pm. Open M-Tu and Th 7:30am-1am, W and F-Sa 7:30am-2am. Cash only.) **La Cantina del Duca,** V. della Luna 30, on P. Repubblica is a cafe by day and bar by night. This spot, freshly opened in 2007, has tables and chairs in its spacious, minimalist back room. Look around for promotions for upcoming concerts. (☎24 57 58. Beers €2.50-4. Mixed drinks €3-7.50. Open M-F 8:30am-1:30am, Sa 9:30am-1:30am.)

▓ FESTIVALS

On the last Sunday of May, Ferrara revives the ancient **Palio di San Giorgio** (☎75 12 63; www.paliodiferrara.it.). Dating from the 13th century, this event begins with a lively procession of delegates from the city's eight *contrade* (districts), followed by a series of four races held in P. Ariostea: the boys' race, the girls' race, the don-key race, and the great horse race. During the last full week of August, street per-formers display their talents at the **Busker's Festival** (☎24 93 37; www.ferrarabuskers.com). Even the finicky will appreciate the countless methods of eel preparation at the annual **Eel Festival,** celebrated at the beginning of October in the province of Comacchio. (Info ☎33 10 161; www.comune.comacchio.fe.it.)

MODENA   ☎059

On Sunday evenings, the colorful, narrow side streets of Modena (MO-deh-na; pop. 170,000) are quiet, but UNESCO-protected Piazza Grande never stops bustling. While the rhythm of life here appears to follow a simple beat, don't be fooled; Modena is a small town that packs a big punch, boasting Luciano Pavarotti, the

Ferrari and Maserati factories, and internationally renowned *aceto balsamico di Modena* (balsamic vinegar). While enjoying Modena to the fullest may require advance planning and reservations for entrance into more famous attractions, its ornate structures, tantalizing flavors, and cultural history make it worth a stop.

⌐ TRANSPORTATION

Trains: (☎89 20 21), in P. Dante Alighieri. Info office open daily 8am-7pm; ticket office open daily 5:30am-11:10pm. Trains run to: **Bologna** (30min., every 30min. 12:27am-11:18pm, €2.60); **Milan** (2hr., every hr. 4:37am-10:04pm, €9.40); **Parma** (30min., 2 per hr. 4:37am-10:53pm, €3.35); **Verona** (4hr., 8 per day 5:58am-8:22pm, €4.40).

Buses: ATCM (☎199 11 11 01 or 800 11 11 01; www.atcm.mo.it) in V. Fabriani, off V. Monte Kosica to the right of the train station. Open M-F 7am-7:30pm, Sa 7am-2pm, Su 8:30am-12:30pm and 2:30-6:30pm. Buses go to **Maranello** (every 1-2hr., €2.18; €1 extra on bus) and also run throughout the city.

Taxis: (☎37 42 42). 24hr.

Bike rental: Locations are scattered throughout the city.

✦ ❷ ORIENTATION AND PRACTICAL INFORMATION

From the **train station,** take bus #7 (dir: Policlinico) or 11 (dir.: Zodiaco) to **Piazza Grande** and the *centro*. On foot, take **Via Galvani** from the station and turn right on **Viale Monte Kosica.** A left on **Via Ganaceto** leads to **Via Emilia,** Modena's main thoroughfare. Continue through **Piazza Matteotti** to **Piazza della Torre,** which opens into P. Grande. V. Emilia changes names from **Via Emilia Ovest** on the west side to **Via Emilia Centro** in the center to **Via Emilia Est** in the east.

Tourist Office: P. Grande 14 (☎20 32 660; www.comune.modena.it), located in the Palazzo Comunale building close to V. Emilia Centro. Open M 3-6pm, Tu-Sa 9am-1pm and 3-6pm, Su 9:30am-12:30pm. **Modenatur,** V. Scudari 10 (☎22 00 22; www.modenatur.it), located on the other side of the building from the tourist office. Organizes guided tours inside the province of Modena, offers tourist info, and arranges themed tours of the city's automobile factories, culinary specialties, and castles. Open M 2:30-6:30pm, Tu-F 9am-1pm and 2:30-6:30pm. MC/V.

Beyond Tourism: Informagiovani, P. Grande 17 (☎20 65 83). Geared toward younger travelers. Provides travel info, job listings, alternatives to tourism, and Internet (one-time €1.50 registration fee; €2 per hr.). Open M-F 9am-1pm and 3-6:30pm, Sa 9:30am-12:30pm. Closed W afternoon.

Currency Exchange: Credito Italiano, V. Emilia Centro 102 (☎21 80 86). Open M-F 8:20am-1:20pm and 2:45-4:45pm, Sa 8:20am-12:45pm. **ATMs** at **Unicredit Banca,** P. Grande 40. Open M-F 8:20am-1:20pm and 3-4pm, Sa 8:20am-12:45pm.

Laundry: Washing Point, 31 V. Piave. Open daily 8am-9:30pm.

Ambulance: ☎34 31 56.

Pharmacy: Farmacia del Collegio, corner of V. Emilia Est and V. San Carlo, near P. Grande. Open M-F 8:30am-1pm and 3:30-7:30pm, Sa 8:30am-1pm. AmEx/MC/V. Another pharmacy on Rua Muro. Open daily 8:30am-12:30pm and 3:30-7:30pm.

Internet Access: Informagiovani (see **Beyond Tourism**). **Internet Point,** P. Grande 34 (☎/fax 21 20 96). €1 per 15min. Open M-Sa 10am-8pm. **Internet and Phone Center,** V. Cervetta. Open daily 10am-8pm.

Post Office: V. Emilia Centro 86 (☎20 53 211). Open M-F 8am-6:30pm, Sa 8am-12:30pm. **Postal Code:** 41100.

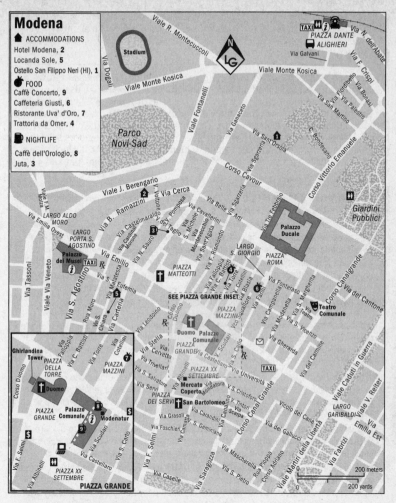

Modena

⌂ ACCOMMODATIONS
Hotel Modena, 2
Locanda Sole, 5
Ostello San Filippo Neri (HI), 1

🍴 FOOD
Caffè Concerto, 9
Caffeteria Giusti, 6
Ristorante Uva' d'Oro, 7
Trattoria da Omer, 4

🌙 NIGHTLIFE
Caffè dell'Orologio, 8
Juta, 3

EMILIA-ROMAGNA

ACCOMMODATIONS AND CAMPING

Ostello San Filippo Neri (HI) ❶, V. Sant'Orsola 48-52, is Modena's best budget option in Modena. Walk down V. Galvani from the station, turn right along Vle. Monte Kosica, left on V. Ganaceto, and another left on V. Sant'Orsola. (☎/fax 23 45 98; hostelmodena@hotmail.com. Wheelchair-accessible. Check-out 9:45am. Lockout 10am-2pm. Dorms €18.50; doubles €40. AmEx/MC/V.) To find **Hotel Modena ❹**, V. Ramazzini 59, from the station, turn left on V. Ganaceto, right on V. Cerca, and then keep straight. The hotel rents clean, spacious rooms with TV, sink, phone, large windows, and shared bath. (☎/fax 22 36 34. Reception 7am-1am. Reservations recommended. Singles €40; doubles €60; triples €85. Discounts for longer stays. AmEx/MC/V.) **Locanda Sole ❸**, V. Malatesta 45, has rooms with sink, TV, desk, and closet. From V. Ganaceto, turn right on V. Emilia, then left to reach this hotel and its quiet yet central location. (☎21 42 45; fax 43 99 016. Closed in Aug. for 3 weeks. Singles €35; doubles €60. Cash only.)

FOOD

Modena specializes in *prosciutto crudo* and sparkling *Lambrusco* red wine, but its most prominent product is fragrant *aceto balsamico* (balsamic vinegar), a thick condiment worlds away from the stuff at home. While in town, be sure to taste the difference between the traditional and non-traditional styles. ⬛**Mercato Coperto di Via Albinelli,** down V. Albinelli, was built by the city in 1931 to house a food market that's been around since medieval times. Vendors sell fresh produce, flowers, wines, and even squid. (Open June-Sept. M-F 6:30am-2pm and 4:30-7pm, Sa 6:30am-2pm; Oct.-May M-F 6:30am-2pm, Sa 6:30am-2pm and 4:30-7:30pm. Cash only.)

> **BRAVO, BALSAMICO!** Traditional Italian *aceto balsamico* (balsamic vinegar) is not what you're used to finding on the shelves of your local supermarket. Balsamic vinegar originated in Modena nearly 1000 years ago. Made from *trebbiane* grapes of the hills of Modena, authentic *aceto balsamico di Modena* is made from a top-secret recipe; the complex process, which can take years, likely contributes to the skyrocketing costs of the true product—a good bottle can run hundreds of euro. At restaurants, you might find it drizzled over a fresh salad, but don't be surprised to see it in less-expected places on the menu, adding zing to your strawberries or flavoring creamy *gelato*.

Caffeteria Giusti, V. Farini 83 (☎21 91 32). This shop is famous as a supplier of *aceto balsamico* and sparkling wine. Free tasting of both traditional and non-traditional balsamic vinegars (bottles €22-82) to aid in this difficult decision. Also serves coffee and snacks. Open M-Sa 7:30am-midnight. AmEx/MC/V. ❶

Ristorante Uva' d'Oro, P. Mazzini 38 (☎23 91 71). Common dining choice for local families. Regional specialty *fileto al balsamico* (€15) prepared to perfection and artistically presented. House wine €4 per ½L. *Primi* €7.50, *secondi* €5-18. Cover €2. Open M-Sa noon-2:30pm and 7:30-10:30pm. AmEx/MC/V. ❷

Trattoria da Omer, V. Torre 33 (☎21 80 50), off V. Emilia, across from P. Torre. Grandma's kitchen goes gourmet. All dishes, including *scaloppe* and *salmone*, are €8. Open M-Sa 1-2pm and 7:30-10pm. Reservations recommended. AmEx/MC/V. ❷

Caffè Concerto, P. Grande 26 (☎22 22 32; www.caffeconcertomodena.it). Relax at wooden tables that overlook the *duomo* and *piazza*. All-you-can-eat lunch buffet noon-3pm €14-16. *Primi* €10-14, *secondi* €10-16. Open daily 8am-3am. Amex/MC/V.) ❸

👁 SIGHTS

DUOMO. Modena's towering Romanesque *duomo* is built over the grave of its patron saint, San Geminiano. Guards used to signal the opening of the city gates from the *duomo*'s 87m tower. The church houses San Geminiano's encased arm, which is paraded around in a religious procession in January. Legend holds that he prevented Attila the Hun from destroying the city by shrouding it in mist. Sculptor Wiligelmo and his students decorated most of the *duomo*'s red Veronese marble with carvings of local, Roman, biblical, and Celtic themes. Scenes from the Old Testament and San Geminiano's travels frame the door. Visit the 3D clay nativity scene in a cave on the right wall. (*P. Grande.* ☎21 60 78; *www.duomodimodena.it. Open daily 7am-12:30pm and 3:30-7pm. Free.*) The **Museo del Duomo** allows visitors to see gold chalices, crosses, and embroidered ecclesiastical robes that in centuries past were paraded only on holy feast days. *(V. Lanfranco 6. ☎ 43 96 969. Open Tu-Su Apr.-Sept. 9:30am-12:30pm and 3:30-7pm; Oct.-Mar. 9:30am-12:30pm and 3:30-6:30pm. €3.)*

 MO' MODENA. To save on museums, buy a combined ticket. A 2-day ticket costs €6 and allows admission to civic museums, Este Gallery, and the Cathedral museums.

PALAZZO DEI MUSEI. Inside the *palazzo*, the **Biblioteca Estense** holds a collection of exquisitely illuminated 14th- to 16th-century books, including a 1501 Portuguese world map. The library's **Sala Campori,** accessible by appointment only, houses the **Biblia di Borso d'Este,** a 15th-century, 1200-page Bible partially illustrated by Emiliano and painter Taddeo Crivelli. *(On Largo Sant'Agostino at the western side of V. Emilia. ☎ 22 22 48; www.cedoc.mo.it/estense. Exhibits open M-Sa 9am-1pm. Call the library in advance to see the Sala Campori and Biblia di Borso d'Este. €2.60, under 19 or over 65 free.)* Above the library, the **Galleria Estense** displays huge canvases like Velázquez's *Portrait of Francesco d'Este* and Bernini's bust of the same subject, a triptych by El Greco, and a crucifix by Guido Reni. *(☎ 43 95 711; www.galleriaestense.it. Open Tu-Su 8:30am-7:30pm. €4.)* In the **Archaeological Ethnological Civic Museum** and the **Civic Art Museum,** large glass cases contain musical instruments, 19th-century scientific instruments, and artifacts from the Americas, Asia, and Africa. *(Civic museums ☎ 20 01 00. Open Tu-Sa 9am-noon and 3-6pm, Su 10am-1pm and 3-7pm. €4, students €2.)*

GHIRLANDINA TOWER. This 95m tower, built in the 13th century, incorporates Gothic and Romanesque elements. Climb to the top for a view of Modena's stucco rooftops. A photo collection at the base commemorates those who died fighting the Nazis and Fascists during WWII. *(P. Torre, off P. Grande. Open Apr.-July and Sept.-Oct. Su 9:30am-12:30pm and 3-7pm or by reservation through the tourist office. €2.)*

FERRARI FACTORY. Modena's flashiest claim to fame is the Ferrari, created in 1940 by Enzo Ferrari, which makes its home southwest of Modena in **Maranello,** a 40min. bus ride from Modena (round-trip €4). View antique and modern Ferraris, Formula One race cars, trophies, and exhibits on founder Enzo Ferrari at the **Ferrari Galleria.** On small TV screens, watch a live feed of the complex's recreated Grand Prix, where owners race by invitation only. *(Galleria at V. Dino Ferrari 43. From Ferrari factory bus stop, continue along road in same direction as bus for 200m; turn right at Galleria Ferrari sign. ☎ 0536 94 32 04; galleria@ferrari.it. Open daily June-Sept. 9:30am-7pm; Oct.-May 9:30am-6pm. €12, seniors and students under 18 €10.)* The **Maserati Factory** is closed to the public, but the **museum** can be visited with a reservation at least 10 days in advance. *(V. Corletto 320. ☎ 51 06 60.)* **Modenatur** organizes tours for car enthusiasts to these sites. *(☎ 21 82 64; www.motorsite.it. Tours from €35.)*

❄️ 🎭 FESTIVALS AND NIGHTLIFE

In May, Modena demonstrates its love of all things fast with the **Land of Motors** festival, featuring parades of both vintage and ultra-modern cars and other spectacles in P. Grande. (Info ☎ 20 66 60.) The **Millemiglia** vintage car race that finishes in Brescia also passes through Modena in May. In June and July, Modena stages the **Serate Estensi** *(☎ 20 32 707; www.comune.modena.it/seratestensi),* a week-long festival recreating the city's history of Estense rule with jousting, art shows, street theater, dances, fireworks, and a Renaissance costume show. Lastly, the **Fiera Antiquaria,** Emilia-Romagna's largest antique market, with over 300 exhibitions, is held the fourth Saturday of each month and the following Sunday. **Juta,** V. del Taglio 91, has the most twentysomethings in one place after 10pm. It's hip and modern appeal has customers filling the outdoor patio area and spilling onto the street. (☎21 94 49. *Primi* €5, *secondi* €6-8. Sa-Su DJ-spun music from 8pm. Cover €1.50. Open Tu-Th noon-1am, F-Sa noon-2am, Su 5pm-1am. AmEx/MC/V.) **Caffè dell'Orologio,** Piazzetta delle Ova 4, next to the tourist office, has an upscale atmosphere. Relax with espresso or indulge in an evening drink. (☎338 92 56 608. Mixed drinks from €6. Open M and W-Su 8am-midnight. Cash only.)

PARMA ☎0521

Although a trip to Parma (PAR-ma; pop. 180,000), where platters overflow with aged parmesan cheese and rosy-pink prosciutto, will certainly never leave the taste buds unsatisfied, Parma's artistic excellence is not confined to the kitchen. In the 16th century, Mannerist painting flourished under native artists Parmigianino and Correggio. The city was also the birthplace of composer Giuseppe Verdi, who resided in Parma while writing some of his greatest works. Pervasive French influences inspired Stendhal to choose the picturesque town as the setting of his 1839 novel *The Charterhouse of Parma.* Parma combines the mannered elegance of its heritage with the youthful energy of the nearby Università degli Studi di Parma, which keeps its *piazze* and side streets packed at night.

◪ TRANSPORTATION

Flights depart from **Giuseppe Verdi Airport,** V. dell'Aeroporto 44/A (☎98 26 26; fax 99 20 28), to both national and international destinations. Parma lies northwest of Bologna on the Bologna-Milan line. **Trains** leave the station in Ple. Carlo Alberto della Chiesa (☎89 20 21 or 77 14 26; ticket office open daily 5:55am-12:05am) to: Bologna (1hr., 3 per hr. 5:46am-11:51pm, €5); Florence (2hr., 5:46am-9:24pm, €9.20); Milan (1½hr., 3-5 per hr. 5:14am-10:36pm, €7.10); Modena (30min., 4 per hr. 5:46am-11:51pm, €3.35); Rome (4hr., 6:46am-11:51pm); Turin (3hr., 5 per day 5:53am-10:36pm, €11.70). **Buses** to nearby towns including Bardi, Busseto, and Colorno stop at P. Carlo Alberto della Chiesa 7/B, at the InfoBus booth, to the right of the train station. (☎27 32 51. Ticket office open M-Sa 6am-7:15pm, Su 7am-1pm.) **Intra-city buses** run throughout Parma from the front of the train station. For bus rides between 8pm and 1am, reserve a ride with ProntoBus (☎800 977 900; www.tep.pr.it; around €3). Call a **taxi** (☎25 25 62) for 24hr. service. **Car rental** is available at the airport from Avis (☎29 12 38). For **bike rental,** Parma PuntoBici, Vle. P. Toschi 2, offers both regular and electric bikes. (☎28 19 79; www.parmapuntobici.it. Bikes €0.70 per hr., €10 for 1st day, €5 each day thereafter. Electric bikes €1/20/10. Open M-Sa 9am-1pm and 3-7pm, Su 10am-1pm and 3-7pm.)

◪ ◪ ORIENTATION AND PRACTICAL INFORMATION

To get to the city, exit the station, keeping the fountain on your right. Turn left on **Viale Bottego,** right on **Strada Garibaldi,** and follow it 1km into town. Turn left on **Strada Mazzini** to reach **Piazza Garibaldi,** the *centro.* **Strada della Repubblica, Strada Cavour,** and **Strada Farini,** Parma's main streets, all branch out from this central *piazza.*

Tourist Office: Strada Melloni 11/A (☎21 88 89; www.turismo.comune.parma.it). From train station, walk left on Vle. Bottego, turn right on Strada Garibaldi, then left on Strada Melloni. Open M 9am-1pm and 3-7pm, Tu-Sa 9am-7pm, Su 9am-1pm.

Beyond Tourism: Informagiovani, Strada Melloni 1 (☎21 87 49; http://informagiovani.comune.parma.it), next to the tourist office. Posts jobs, volunteer work, and apartment listings. Info on cultural events and activities. English spoken. Free **Internet** and study room. Open M-Tu and F-Sa 9am-1pm and 3-7pm, W 9am-1pm, Th 9am-7pm.

Bank: Banca Antonveneta, Strada dell'Università 2, just off P. Garibaldi. Open M-F 8:20am-1:20pm and 3-4pm, Sa 8:20-11:50am. Also has 24hr. **ATM.**

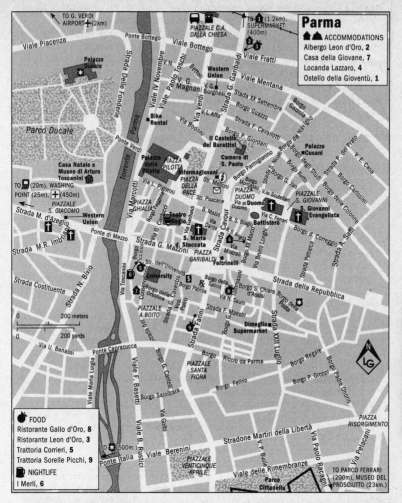

Parma

▲ ▲ ACCOMMODATIONS
Albergo Leon d'Oro, **2**
Casa della Giovane, **7**
Locanda Lazzaro, **4**
Ostello della Gioventù, **1**

🍎 FOOD
Ristorante Gallo d'Oro, **8**
Ristorante Leon d'Oro, **3**
Trattoria Corrieri, **5**
Trattoria Sorelle Picchi, **9**

🅝 NIGHTLIFE
I Merlí, **6**

Western Union: Infinitho, Strada M. D'Azeglio 23/A (☎23 45 55; www.hopera.net), just across the river over Ponte di Mezzo from V. Mazzini. Internet access €1.10 per 15min., students €0.90; €4/3 per hr. Skype and webcam access also available. Open M-W and F-Sa 8:30am-9pm, Th 8:30am-2pm. AmEx/MC/V. **Branch:** V. Borghesi 11/a (☎23 56 19). Open M and W-Sa 9am-10pm, Tu 2-10pm.

English-Language Bookstore: Feltrinelli, Strada della Repubblica 2 (☎23 74 92), on the corner of P. Garibaldi. 2nd fl. has collection of British and American authors. Open M-Sa 9am-8pm, Su 10am-1:30pm and 4:30-8pm. AmEx/MC/V.

Laundromat: WashingPoint, Strada Massimo D'Azeglio 108a. Wash and dry €2. Detergent €1. Open daily 8-10pm.

Police: Vle. Villetta 12/A, (☎21 87 30).

Pharmacy: Farmacia Guareschi, Strada Farini 5/C (☎28 22 40). Open M-F 8:30am-12:30pm and 3:30-7:30pm. After-hours rotation posted outside all pharmacies.

Hospital: Ospedale Maggiore, V. Gramsci 14 (☎70 21 11 or 70 31 11), over the river past the Parco Ducale. For emergencies go to entrance on V. Abbeveratoria.

Internet Access: Free at **Informagiovani** (see **Beyond Tourism**). **Web'n'Wine,** Strada M. D'Azeglio 72/D (☎03 08 93; www.webnwine.it), across the river. €2.50 per 30min. Wine €1.50-4 per glass. English spoken. Open M-Th 9am-8pm, F 9am-9pm, Sa 10am-8pm.

Post Office: Main office on Strada Melloni across from the tourist office. Open M-F 8:30am-5pm, Sa 8:30am-12:30pm. **Currency exchange** also available. **Postal Code:** 43100.

🏠🏕 ACCOMMODATIONS AND CAMPING

🛏 **Ostello della Gioventu (HI),** V. San Leonardo 86 (☎19 17 547; www.ostelloparma.it). From the train station, turn left onto V. Bottego. Make a right onto Strada G. Garibaldi. The bus stops on the other side of the street, in front of the fountains. Take bus 2, 2N, or 13 (until 8pm—if later, use ProntoBus). Or, to walk, turn left onto Strada G. Garibaldi, which becomes V. S. Leonardo. Hostel on left immediately after highway overpass. Beautiful, brand-new, and easily accessible hostel. Young, English-speaking staff, large common spaces, laundry (€7), and Internet access. Dorms €18; singles €20. ❶

Albergo Leon d'Oro, Vle. Fratti 4a (☎77 31 82; www.leondoroparma.com), 1 block from the train station, just after the intersection with Strada Garibaldi. Required advance payment may seem unorthodox, but guests will find clean rooms with large windows and big beds. Shared large, modern bath. Restaurant downstairs. Singles €35-55; doubles €60, with private bath €80; triples €105. AmEx/MC/V. ❸

Casa della Giovane, Strada del Conservatorio 11 (☎28 32 29; www.casadellagiovane.it). From Strada Mazzini, turn left on V. Oberdan; hotel is on the right. Religious community. 2 beds per room and shared bath. Breakfast and choice of lunch or dinner included. Free laundry. Fridge access. Check-out 10am. Curfew M-Tu, Th-F, and Su 10pm; W and Sa 11pm. Women only. €26 per person, under 22 €21. Cash only. ❷

Locanda Lazzaro, Borgo XX Marzo 14 (☎20 89 44; fax 38 56 00), between Strada della Repubblica and P. Duomo. Upstairs from the popular, wicker-decorated restaurant. 8 well decorated rooms with sinks and showers, some with large bathrooms and toilets. Reception daily 12:30-2:30pm and 7:30-10:30pm; otherwise call before arrival. Closed Aug. 1st 2 weeks. Reservations recommended. Singles €35, with bath €45; doubles €50/65; triples €80. AmEx/MC/V. ❸

🍴 FOOD

Parma's cuisine is rich, delicious, affordable, and renowned throughout Italy. Aged parmesan cheese and *prosciutto crudo* fill the windows of the *salumerie* (delicatessens) along V. Garibaldi. The local *Malvasia* is the wine of choice. When exported, this sparkling white loses its natural fizz, so carbon dioxide is usually added to compensate—sip a glass here to sample the real thing. An **open-air market** displays its goods at P. Ghiaia every Wednesday and Saturday morning, and Wednesday and Friday nights during summer. It offers local varieties of cheese, meats, and vinegar. **Dimeglio** supermarket is located at Strada XXII Luglio 27/C. (☎28 13 82. Open daily 8:30am-1:30pm and 4:30-8pm.) **ECU Convenience** market is on V. San Leonardo 17. (Open 8:30am-1pm and 4pm-7:30pm. Closed Th afternoon. AmEx/MC/V.)

Trattoria Sorelle Picchi, Strada Farini 27 (☎23 35 28), several blocks from P. Garibaldi. Food served out of a *salumeria* of the same name. This local secret cooks traditional dishes including roast pheasant, homemade lasagna, and sweet-and-sour onions. Let the waitstaff advise on specialties and starters, like the *parmiggiano reggiano* plate (€4.50), or mixed prosciutto plate (€9). *Primi* €8-9, *secondi* €10-15. Cover €2. *Salumeria* open 8:30am-7pm. Open for lunch M-Sa noon-3pm. AmEx/MC/V. ❸

Ristorante Gallo d'Oro, Borgo della Salina 3 (☎20 88 46). From P. Garibaldi, take Strada Farini and turn left. Resist the urge to dine outside on the patios and eat downstairs in this 14th-century stone building. Wines €3 per ¼ bottle, €4 per ½-bottle, €7-11 per bottle. *Primi* €6.50-9, *secondi* €6.50-9.50. Cover €2. Open M-Sa noon-2:30pm and 7:30-11pm. AmEx/MC/V. ❷

Ristorante Leon d'Oro, V. Fratti 4a (☎77 31 82; www.leondoroparma.com), off Strada Garibaldi. Huge platters of colorful *antipasto*, typical *parmigiano* meals, and desserts. *Primi* €6.50-8, *secondi* €11-15. Cover €2. Open daily 12:30-2pm and 8-10pm. Reservations recommended Sa-Su. AmEx/MC/V. ❸

Trattoria Corrieri, Strada del Conservatorio 1 (☎23 44 26; www.trattoriacorrieri.it). Rustic decorations surround a narrow ivy-draped courtyard. Vibrant atmosphere draws attention from the street. Modest prices keep tables full. Staff admits that primi (€7-8.50) take the backseat to the chef's savory secondi (€7.50-8.50). AmEx/MC/V. ❸

👁 SIGHTS

PALAZZO DELLA PILOTTA. Built in 1602, the *palazzo*'s grandeur suggests the ambitions of the Farnese dukes. Today, the *palazzo* houses several museums, accessible through the courtyard. Though there have been no actual performances in the theater since the curtain last fell in 1732, the elegant, wooden **Teatro Farnese,** completed in 1618, underwent restorations in the 50s to repair damage inflicted by WWII bombs. Beyond the theater, the **Galleria Nazionale** contains numerous medieval polyptychs and portraits, including Leonardo da Vinci's *Testa d'una Fanciulla* (Head of a Young Girl), as well as a gallery devoted to Parmigianino and Correggio. **Museo Archeologico Nazionale** displays bronzes, and sculptures of ancient origin. *(From Strada Cavour, turn left on Strada Pisacane and cut across P. della Pace to P. Pilotta. ☎23 37 18. Open June-Sept. Su 9:30am-12:30pm and 4-7pm. Closed in afternoon Aug. €2.)*

DUOMO, BATTISTERO, AND MUSEO DIOCESANO. Parma's 11th-century Romanesque *duomo* balances vibrant paintings of clouds with more austere masterpieces like the Episcopal throne and Benedetto Antelami's bas-relief *Descent from the Cross* (1178). The stunning *duomo* features Correggio's *Virgin* ascending to heaven. *(In P. Duomo. From P. Garibaldi, follow Strada Cavour, and turn right on Strada al Duomo. ☎23 58 8. Open daily 9am-12:30pm and 3-7pm. Free.)* The pink- and white-marble *battistero* (baptistry) displays early medieval frescoes of enthroned saints and apostles that rise to the top of each of the dome's 16 sides. *(☎23 58 86. Open daily 9am-12:30pm and 3-6:30pm. €4, with Museo Diocesano €5.)* Diagonally across the *piazza* from the baptistry, the **Museo Diocesano** holds examples of 12th- and 13th-century sculpture while preserving Roman ruins in the basement. *(In P. Duomo. ☎20 86 99; www.fabbriceriacattedraleparma.it. Open daily 9am-12:30pm and 3-6:30pm. €3.)*

IL MONASTERIO DI SAN PAOLO. This aged monastery holds an impressive fresco above the **Camera di San Paolo,** depicting the coat of arms of the Abbess, under whose direction the monastery prospered. *(V. Melloni 3. From P. Garibaldi, head up Strada Cavour, turn left on Strada Melloni, and follow the signs. ☎53 32 21. Open Tu-Su 8:30am-1:30pm. Last entry 1pm. €2, ages 18-25 €1, under 18 or over 65 free.)* The complex of St. Paul also houses **Il Castello dei Burattini** (Puppet Castle), showcasing a collection of over 1500 puppets. (☎ 23 98 10; fax 22 15 91. Open Tu-Su Apr.-Oct. 9am-7pm; Nov.-Mar. 9am-5pm. €2.50, students €1.50.) Just around the corner, the **Pinacoteca Stuard** holds 270 paintings from the 14th-19th centuries. Two of its most prized works are near the entrance: *Madonna in trono con Bambino* by Maestro della Misericordia (c. 1350-75) and *Virgin Mary with Child. (Borgo Parmigianino 2. ☎ 50 81 84. Open M and W-Sa 9am-6:30pm, Su 9am-6pm. €4, under 25 and over 65 €2.)*

CHIESA DI SAN GIOVANNI EVANGELISTA. This 10th-century church is a long-standing Italian classic. The dome was famously frescoed by Correggio, while frescoes by Parmigianino run along the left nave and over the 1st, 2nd, and 4th chapels. The belltower was constructed in 1613. *(In P. San Giovanni, behind the duomo. ☎ 23 53 11. Open daily 8am-noon and 3-7:45pm. Monastery closes 6pm. Reservations recommended for guided tours. Free.)*

CHIESA MAGISTRALE DI SANTA MARIA DELLA STECCATA. Built in 1521 to house a miraculous picture of the Virgin Mary, the church now frames the icon with red marble columns. This Renaissance church also features impressive frescoes by Parmigianino. Call ahead to see the **Crypt of the Farnese Dukes** and pay respect to the famous Alexander, whose helmet and sword still sit above his tomb, and Antonio Farnese, the last Duke of Parma. *(P. Steccata 9, up V. Garibaldi. ☎ 23 49 37. Open daily 9am-noon and 3-6pm. Free.)*

TEATRO REGIO. Commissioned by Marie Louise in 1821, the Teatro Regio is known worldwide. Its Neoclassical facade is complemented by Borghesi's decorations inside. The four-tiered Baroque balconies feature red velvet seats interrupted only by the large crowned ducal box that faces the stage. *(V. Garibaldi 16, next to P. della Pace. ☎ 03 93 93; www.teatroregioparma.org. Open M-Sa 10:30am-noon. Guided tours in Italian every 30min. Advance booking recommended. €2, students €1.)*

PARMIGIANO AND PROSCIUTTO FACTORIES. Cheese enthusiasts interested in seeing the origin of 38kg blocks of *Parmigiano* should contact the **Consorzio del Parmigiano-Reggiano** to arrange a 2hr. tour of factories around Parma. Tours are difficult to obtain. They are offered infrequently, occur only during the week, are not accessible by public transportation, and must be booked in advance. *(Strada dei Mercati 9. ☎ 29 27 00; sezionepr@parmigiano-reggiano.it.)* Visits to a prosciutto factory are usually available only during the Proscuitto Festival in the 1st week of September. *(For more info call the Consorzio del Prosciutto di Parma. ☎ 24 39 87; fax 24 39 83.)* A somewhat more feasible and satisfying option is the **Museo del Prosciutto di Parma.** *(V. Bocchialini 7. 23km outside Parma in Langhirano, accessible by bus #12. ☎ 85 83 47 and ☎ 33 56 66 4220. Open Sa-Su 10am-6pm. €3; Parma ham tasting €3, "typical products tasting" €9.)* The **Parmigiano-Reggiano Museum** is in Soragna. *(☎ 22 81 52. Open Mar.-Oct. M-F only by reservation, Sa-Su 9:30am-12:30pm and 3-6pm; Nov.-Feb. only by reservation. €5, includes tasting.)*

OTHER SIGHTS. Although many French palaces were destroyed during WWII, Marie Louise's gardens remain by the Baroque **Palazzo Ducale** in **Parco Ducale.** *(West of Palazzo della Pilotta, across Ponte Verdi. Park open daily in winter 7am-8pm; in summer 6am-midnight. Free. Palazzo: ☎ 53 76 78; call in morning. Open M-Sa 9:30am-noon. €3, students and under 25 €2.)* Across the river, the **Palazzo Cusani,** or **Casa della Musica,** first served as the seat of the University of Parma and later as the Mint of the Duchy of Parma. Today, it houses a museum. *(Ple. San Francesco 1. Follow Borgo del Parmigianino from the tourist office, then turn right on V. Daimazia. ☎ 03 11 70. Open July to mid-Aug. M-Sa 9am-1pm and 3-7pm; Sept.-June Tu-Sa 9am-6pm, Su 9am-1pm.)*

🎭🎶 **NIGHTLIFE AND ENTERTAINMENT.** At night, *parmigiani* stroll along Strada Farini, or the intersection of Strada Maestri and V. Nazario Sauro, and sit to enjoy the balmy nights and cool green grass in front of P. Pilotta. The area is safe, with stadium lights and *carabinieri* close by. Italians of all ages can be seen lolling about late into the night. Bars nearby ensure presence of a young, energetic crowd. Tucked away but full of character is the bar **I Merli,** Borgo Piccinini 7a. (☎38 68 46. Wine €2-3 per glass. Beer €2.50-4. Lunch *primi* €7-8, *secondi* €9-14. Open daily noon-3pm and 7:30pm-1am.AmEx/MC/V.)

The **Teatro Regio** is one of Italy's premier opera houses, hosting operatic, cultural, and theatrical extravaganzas throughout the year. (Strada Garibaldi 16/A, next to P. della Pace. ☎03 93 93; www.teatroregioparma.org.) The opera season runs from November to April, while the popular **Verdi Festival,** honoring the native composer with local concerts and operas, takes place each year usually in October at the *teatro*. The **Parma Poesia Festival,** debuted in 2005, organizes a week of poetry readings, lectures, and slams throughout the city in June. In May, the city hosts **Parma Danza,** an international festival of ballet and modern dance. **Grande Estate** brings classical music, opera, jazz, and tango concerts to Ple. della Pilotta in July. (☎21 86 78. Tickets €10-35.) Info for all events may be obtained at the *teatro*'s ticket office. The **Cinema Astra,** V. Rondizzoni 1 (☎96 05 54; www.cinema-astra.it), also hosts the summer movie festival **Estive Astra** in June and July. (All movies begin at 9:30pm. €5.50, students €4.) Last but not least, the annual **Prosciutto Festival** takes over the city and the surrounding area during the first two weekends in September; contact the *Consorzio del Prosciutto di Parma* for annual scheduled events. (☎24 39 87; www.festivaldelprosciutto.it or www.finestreaperte.it.)

PIACENZA
☎0523

One of the first Roman colonies in northern Italy and the long-time headquarters of Julius Caesar, Piacenza (PEE-ah-CHEN-za; pop. 95,132) has historical treats for every taste. Shoppers seeking the latest fashions wander down C. Vittorio Emanuele II and V. XX Settembre. Those looking for respite relax in P. Duomo or pack P. dei Cavalli during concerts. Finally, those in search of modern Italian art find a great exhibit at the Galleria Ricci Oddi. Reluctant to encourage a tourist economy, Piacenza was nevertheless recently voted one of Italy's most hospitable cities. It is an ideal stopover on the way to Parma, Bologna, or Milan.

┌─┐ TRANSPORTATION AND PRACTICAL INFORMATION

Trains from P. Marconi to: Bologna (2hr., 7 per day 5:31am-11:46pm, €7.70); Milan (1½hr., 66 per day 4:15am-11:12pm, €5); Parma (45min., 3 per hr. 5:31am-11:46pm, €3.35); Turin (2½hr., 10 per day 4:46am-11:12pm, €9.40). The ticket office (☎89 20 21) is open daily 5:25am-11:40pm. **City buses** (☎39 06 11; www.tempi.piacenza.it; €1) leave from the front of the station on Borgo Sant'Ambrogio; a map of routes is posted inside the station. For a **taxi,** call ☎59 19 19. **Car rental** is available from Europcar, close to the station at V. Alberoni 93. (☎33 22 76. Open M-F 8:30am-1pm and 3-7pm, Sa 8:30am-1pm. AmEx/MC/V.)

From the **train station,** cross the *piazza* to **Viale dei Mille,** and turn right on **Via Giulio Alberoni.** Make a right at **Via Roma** and then turn left on **Via Daveri,** which leads to **Piazza Duomo.** From there, a right on shop-lined **Via XX Settembre** leads straight to **Piazza dei Cavalli.** The **IAT tourist office,** P. dei Cavalli 7, is on the left side of **Palazzo Gotico** behind the horse statues. (☎32 93 24; www.comune.piacenza.it. Open Tu-Sa 9am-1pm and 3-6pm, Su 9am-noon.) **Banca Agricola Mantovana,** P. Marconi 41, is at the intersection with Vle. dei Mille. (Open M-F 8:20am-1:20pm and 2:50-3:50pm, Sa

8:20am-11:20am.) For those seeking alternatives to tourism, the **Centro Informagio-vani**, P. dei Cavalli 2, has info on volunteer work, study abroad, professional associations, and travel. They also have free **Internet** access and Wi-Fi after registration. (☎49 22 24. Open M-F 8:30am-1pm and 3-6pm, Th 8:30am-6pm, Sa 9am-noon.) **Farmacia Dr. Parmigiani**, P. Duomo 41, posts after-hours rotations. (Open daily 8:30am-12:30pm and 3:30-7:30pm. AmEx/MC/V.) In case of **emergency**, call the **police**, V. Rogerio 3 (☎49 21 08). A **hospital**, Ospedale G. da Saliceto, is on V. Taverna 49 (☎30 11 11). **Internet** access is available at **Internet Train**, located at V. Cittadella 32, off P. dei Cavalli. (☎0523 31 27 72. €1.80 per 15min., students €1.50; €4.50/3.70 per hr. Open M-W 9:30am-10pm, Th 9:30am-2:30pm, F-Sa 9:30am-7:30pm.) The **post office**, V. Sant'Antonino 38-40, **exchanges currency**. (☎31 64 68. Open M-F 8am-6:30pm, Sa 8am-12:30pm.) **Postal Code:** 29100.

⌂ ☐ ACCOMMODATIONS AND FOOD

There are few affordable accommodations in Piacenza, though the tourist office can help in booking lodging. From C. Vittorio Emanuele, turn right on V. del Tempio to reach **Protezione della Giovane ❸**, V. Tempio 26. Nun-run establishment welcomes women only. (☎32 38 12. Breakfast included. Reception 6:30am-10:30pm. Curfew M-Th and Su 10:30pm, F-Sa midnight. Reservations strictly required. Singles €25. 1-person apartments €425 per month; 2-person €790. Cost per week estimated based on monthly rate. Cash only.) Enjoy dinner either outdoors or inside the charming dining room at **Osteria del Trentino ❸**, V. del Castello 71, off P. Borgo, past the police station. Options include seasonal meat and fish menus. (☎32 42 60. *Primi* €7-11, *secondi* €9-16. Cover €2. Open M-Sa noon-3pm and 7:30pm-10:30pm. MC/V.) At the feet of the lavish *duomo* is the surprisingly affordable **L'Orologio da Pasquale ❸**, P. Duomo 36. With its simple white patio furniture, this restaurant is a relaxing place to have a cheese platter or dessert with a quarter-liter of house wine (€4). For full meals, the large menu of *primi* (€6.50-10) and *secondi* (€8-14) are priced comparably to surrounding restaurants. (☎32 46 69. Open M-W and F-Su 12:30-2:30pm and 7:30-11pm. AmEx/MC/V.) A popular Spanish restaurant, **Taberna Movida ❷**, V. Daveri 8, offers tapas in a modern indoor setting. (☎31 81 31; www.tabernamovida.it. Tapas and entrees €4.50-14.50. Open M-F 12:30-2:30pm and 7:30pm-1am, Sa 7:30pm-2am, Su 5pm-1am.) A very convenient **Sigma** supermarket is located on the 2nd floor of the mall to the left of the train station. (Open M 5am-9pm, Tu-Sa 9am-9pm, Su 9:30am-8pm. MC/V.) In the center, **Punto Supermercato** is on XX Septembre, across from the Basilica di San Francesco. (Open M-Sa 8am-7:45pm. AmEx/MC/V.) An **open-air market** is held every Wednesday and Saturday morning in P. Duomo and P. dei Cavalli.

◔ ♫ SIGHTS AND ENTERTAINMENT

Piazza dei Cavalli, the central square, is named for the two 17th-century equestrian statues that grace the *piazza* in tribute to Duke Rannucio I and his father, Duke Alessandro Farnese. The true jewel is the Gothic **Palazzo del Comune**, or **Il Gotico**. The impressive *palazzo* was constructed in 1280 when Piacenza led the Lombard League, one of Italy's most powerful trade groups. A monument to war veterans sits under the *palazzo*, directly across from the **Palazzo del Governatore**. Completing the trio of impressive buildings is the **Basilica di San Francesco**, whose *Capella della Concezione di Maria* (1594) and vibrant altarpiece (1663) stand out against the rest of the basilica's modest decoration. (Open daily 6:30am-noon and 2:30-6:30pm. Free.) In P. Duomo, the town's *duomo*, constructed between 1122 and 1233, contains a wealth of frescoes dating to the 12th century. A side chapel has the embalmed body of San Giovanni Battista Scalabrini. The **crypt**, a spooky maze of thin columns, holds to the bones of Santa Giustina d'Antiocha at its center and two dark tombs at the rear. (Open daily 7:30am-12:30pm and 4-7:30pm. Modest dress required. Free.) A great collection of obscure modern Italian art can be found in **Galleria Ricci Oddi**, V. San Siro 13, which displays art from the early 1800s to the present. Works are divided among 19 rooms by the region of the artist's hometown. The collection includes **Bruzzi's** scenes of the countryside and **Michetti's** episodes of villagers in landscapes. (☎32 07 42; www.riccioddi.it. Open Tu-Su 10am-noon and 3-6pm. €4, students €3. Free last Th of every month.) The commanding **Palazzo Farnese**, P. Cittadella 29, houses the **Museo Civico**, the **Pinacoteca**, the **Museo del Risorgimento**, and the **Museo delle Carrozze**. The Museo Civico's Etruscan and Roman collection from the AD 2nd and 3rd centuries is a highlight, while the most notable work in the Pinacoteca is a Botticelli fresco depicting Christ's birth. (*☎49 26 62. Visit by Italian guided tour only: Tu-Th 9:30am, F 9:30am and 3:30pm, Sa-Su 9, 11am, 3, and 4:30pm; July-Aug. all 9:30am tours begin at 10am. Museo Civico and Pinacoteca €4.80, students €4; Museo delle Carrozze €2.50/2. All museums €6/4.80.)*

RAVENNA   ☎0544

Ravenna's (ra-VEH-na; pop. 150,000) mosaics are everywhere; they appear under your drink at the bar, behind the glass windows of tourist shops, and in almost every major site. The streets paved with colored stones are almost entirely car-free, and travelers walk past monuments like Dante's tomb (to the chagrin of Florentines, who maintain an empty sepulcher for their exiled son). After the decline of the Roman empire, Ravenna rose from the ashes as a bejeweled pillar of strength. Justinian and Theodora, rulers of the Byzantine Empire in the AD 6th century, chose the city as the central administrative point for restoring order in the anarchic West, creating a thriving artistic culture still seen in its churches, which hold some of the world's finest and most awe-inspiring mosaics.

E TRANSPORTATION. The **train station** is in P. Farini. The ticket counter is open daily 6:05am-8:35pm and accepts AmEx/MC/V. The station is open daily 3:50am-12:35am. **Trains** run to: Bologna (1hr., 23 per day 6:35am-8:35pm, €5), Ferrara (1hr., 22 per day 4:13am-9:33pm, €4.50) with connections to Florence and Venice, and Rimini (1hr., 36 per day 12:05am-9:35pm, €3). ATR (regional) and ATM (municipal) **buses** leave outside the train station for Lido Adriano (20min.; in summer every 15min., in winter every 30min. 5:40am-8:10pm; €1) and Marina di Ravenna (20-30min., every 30min. 5:40am-7:55pm, €1). Tickets (3-day pass €3) are sold at the booth marked "PUNTO" to the right when you exit the station. Return tickets are hard to get outside Ravenna but can be bought on board with a surcharge. (☎68 99 00. Office open in summer M-Sa 6:30am-8:30pm, Su 7am-8:30pm; during school year M-Sa 6:30am-7:30pm, Su 7:30am-7:30pm. AmEx/MC/V.) **RadioTaxi** (☎33 888), in P. Farini, is available 24hr.

◼◪ ORIENTATION AND PRACTICAL INFORMATION. The **train station** is in **Piazza Farini** at the eastern end of town. **Viale Farini** leads from the station to **Via Diaz**, which runs to **Piazza del Popolo**, the *centro*. Ask about city maps and accommodation listings at the **tourist office**, V. Salara 8. Walk to the end of P. del Popolo, turn right on V. Matteotti, and follow the signs. (☎35 404; www.turismo.ravenna.it. Open Apr.-Sept. M-Sa 8:30am-7pm, Su 10am-6pm; Oct.-Mar. M-Sa 8:30am-6pm.) **Informagiovani**, V. Guida da Polenta 4, offers work, volunteer, and travel information for students. (☎48 24 56; www.racine.ra.it/informagiovani/ravenna. Free Internet for students. Limit 30min. Open Tu and F 9am-1pm, W-Th 2:30-7pm, Sa 10am-1pm.) **Luggage storage** is available to the left of the train station exit. (Lockers €2.50-5. 24hr. max. Open M-Sa 7am-7:30pm.) In case of **emergency**, call the **police**, V. Rocca Brancaleone 1 (☎48 29 99). The **hospital**,

Santa Maria delle Croci, is on Vle. de Gasperi (☎28 51 11). **Internet access** is available at the **Internet and Phone Center,** V. Rocca Brancaleone 4/6, off P. Mameli. (☎33 744. €2 per hr. Open daily 9am-11pm.) The **post office,** P. Garibaldi 1, is off V. Diaz before P. del Popolo and offers **currency exchange.** (☎24 33 04; fax 38 485. Open M-F 8am-6:30pm, Sa 8am-12:30pm. Cash only.) **Postal Code:** 48100.

▐▐ ACCOMMODATIONS AND FOOD. A former orphanage has aged gracefully into the luxurious ▨**Ostello Galletti Abbiosi ❹,** V. Roma 140, which now offers A/C, TV, minibar, and bath in cavernous rooms. Luxurious facilities include exercise machines and a beautiful breakfast room. (☎31 313; www.galletti.ra.it. Breakfast included. Free Wi-Fi. Reception M-F 8am-6:30pm, Sa-Su 8am-6pm. Singles €55-60; doubles €80-100; triples €100-110; quads €120-130. AmEx/MC/V.) Take V. Farini, and turn right across P. Mameli to reach **Albergo Al Giaciglio ❸,** V. Rocca Brancaleone 42, just outside the *centro.* The cheery staff runs simple rooms with TV, fan, and sink. (☎/fax 39 403; www.albergoalgiaciglio.com. Breakfast €5. Restaurant downstairs. Singles €30; doubles €45, with bath €55. Extra bed €10. MC/V.) To reach **Ostello Dante (HI) ❶,** V. Nicolodi 12, take bus #70, 80, or red or yellow line (every 10-20min. 5:40am-8:10pm, every 30-40min. 8:30-11:30pm) from V. Pallavicini, across from the station. An industrial-style building houses foosball tables, couches, and board games and offers free bike rental. Each room is named for a different section of Dante's *Inferno.* (☎42 11 64; hostelravenna@hotmail.com. Breakfast included. Safes available. Wash €2.50, dry €2.50. Wheelchair-accessible. Reception 7-10am and 3:30-11:30pm. Lockout 10am-3:30pm. Curfew 11:30pm, €1 key card to enter past curfew. Dorms €17; singles €21; family rooms €16 per person. HI-member discount €3. MC/V.) Bus #80 departs across the street from the train station (every 30min. 6:30am-8pm, every hr. 8:30-11:30pm) and stops at camping **Adriano ❶,** V. del Campeggio 7, in Punta Marina Terme, 8km from the *centro.* Near a public beach, these four-star, family-friendly facilities have a pool, *bocce* courts, and a soccer field. (☎43 72 30; www.campingadriano.com. Reception daily 8:30am-1pm and 3-9pm. Reservation required for bungalows. Open mid-Apr. to mid-Sept. €5-10 per person, €8-11 per tent. MC/V.)

The distinctive flavors of Ravennese salt, extra-virgin olive oil, and chestnuts characterize Ravenna's cuisine. Accompany a filling meal with a full-bodied *Albana* or *Trebbiano* wine. For dessert, try *zuppa inglese,* a combination of biscuits and custard with a splash of cordial. For a blast of local color, try ▨**Verderame ❶,** V. Cavour 82, where dried flowers, hand-painted menus, and mosaic tabletops complement the famous hot chocolate. (☎/fax 32 248. Open in summer M-Sa 8:30am-8pm; in winter M-Th and Su 8:30am-8pm, F-Sa 8:30am-midnight. Cash only.) Feast on thin-crust pizzas and local specialties like *cappelletti con ragù* (stuffed tortellini; €6.50) at the outdoor tables at **Babaleus ❷,** Vco. Gabbani 7, on a quiet side street behind the Mercato Coperto. (☎21 64 64. Pizza €2-7.50. *Primi* €6.50, *secondi* €7-13. Open M-Tu and Th-Su noon-2:30pm and 7pm-midnight. AmEx/MC/V.) Grab lunch at the self-service **Ristoro Sant'Apollinare Nuovo ❷,** V. di Roma 53, for a cheap meal. Turn right by the basilica entrance. (☎35 679. *Primi* and *secondi* €3.50-5.50. Four-course lunch *menù* €8. Open M-F and Su noon-3pm. AmEx/MC/V.) A creative variation on the Ravennese dessert *zuppa inglese* is the creamy *zuppa inglese gelato* at **Gelateria Nuovo Mondo ❶,** V. Farini 60, where a double cone goes for €1.80 and low-fat options are also available. (☎35 538. Open M-Sa 10:30am-11:30pm, Su 11am-11:30pm. Cash only.) Hostel guests benefit from the **Coop,** conveniently across the street at V. Aquileia 110. (Open M and W-Sa 8am-8pm, Tu 8am-1pm. AmEx/MC/V.) Fruit, meat, and cheese stands fill

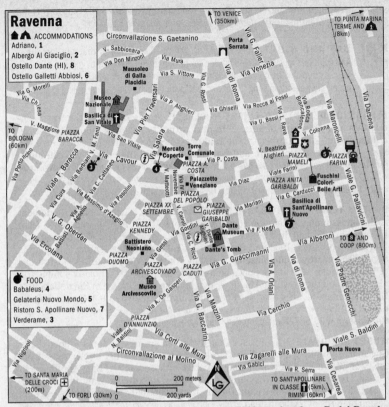

Ravenna

▲ ♠ ACCOMMODATIONS
Adriano, **1**
Albergo Al Giaciglio, **2**
Ostello Dante (HI), **8**
Ostello Galletti Abbiosi, **6**

🍎 FOOD
Babaleus, **4**
Gelateria Nuovo Mondo, **5**
Ristoro S. Apollinare Nuovo, **7**
Verderame, **3**

the **covered market** at P. Andrea Costa 2, up V. IV Novembre from P. del Popolo. (Open M-Th and Sa 7am-2pm, F 7am-2pm and 4:30-7:30pm. Most stands cash only.)

👁 SIGHTS

■**BASILICA DI SAN VITALE.** The glimmering jewel in mosaic-crazy Ravenna, Basilica di San Vitale leaves visitors with wide eyes and sore necks after long periods of admiring its ornate designs. The church's octagonal shape (as opposed to the typical cross) reflects eastern influences, while the interior sparkles as gold sets off the brilliant blues and greens of the mosaic scenes. Above the apse, a Christ Pantocrator sits on a blue globe with the Book of Seven Seals. Walk around to either side of the roped-off section for the best view of the Byzantine mosaics that depict Empress Theodora offering a golden chalice and Emperor Justinian's presentation of a gilded plate. (*V. S. Vitale 17. From tourist office, turn right on V. Cavour, then again on V. Argentario. ☎21 62 92. Open daily Apr.-Sept. 9am-7pm; Mar. and Oct. 9:30am-5:30pm; Nov.-Feb. 10am-5pm. Free.*) Mosaics cover the interior of the tiny brick ■**Mausoleo di Galla Placidia,** where a single lamp illuminates 570 gold stars situated against a brilliant night sky and arranged in concentric circles around a cross. Around the sides, three stone sarcophagi are said to contain the remains of Costanzo III, Empress Galla Placida, and Valentiniano III. *(Behind S. Vitale. Same hours as basilica.)*

> ♪ **DAY AND NIGHT, NIGHT AND DAY.** It is rumored that the famous American jazz musician Cole Porter, after having toured Ravenna by night in 1920, was so struck by the beauty and light in the Mausoleo di Galla Placida that he composed the well-known song "Night and Day" with the structure's starry ceiling in mind.

■ **BASILICA DI SANT'APOLLINARE IN CLASSE.** A bus ride from the town center, this church seems simple, with dark wood beams and unlabeled marble columns. But keep exploring: the real draw is the massive mosaic above the apse, where Sant'Apollinare and flocks of sheep fill the enormous half-dome. *(In Classe, south of the city. Take bus #4 or 44; both stop across from the train station. ☎ 34 424. Open M-Sa 8:30am-7:30pm, Su 9am-7pm. Last entry 30min. before closing. €3, EU students 18-25 €2, under 18 and over 65 free. Cash only.)*

DANTE'S TOMB AND THE DANTE MUSEUM. Ravenna's most popular monument is the unassuming, green-domed tomb of Dante Alighieri, who was exiled from Florence in 1301 and died in Ravenna in 1321. A suspended lamp has burned with Florentine oil since 1908 and illuminates a relief of Dante leafing through his books. The nearby Dante Museum normally contains Wostry Carlo's illustrations of Dante's works, the poet's bones held in a fir chest, 18,000 scholarly volumes on his works, and the trowel and hammer that laid the cornerstone of Rio de Janeiro's Dante Monument. However, it is currently under renovations for an indefinite period of time. *(V. D. Alighieri. From P. del Popolo, cut through P. Garibaldi to V. D. Alighieri. Museum ☎ 33 667. Tomb open daily 9am-7pm. Free.)*

MUSEO NAZIONALE. This former Benedictine monastery features Roman, early Christian, Byzantine, and medieval works, like the 6th-century bronze cross from the roof of San Vitale's cupola and the original apse vault of Sant'Apollinare in Classe. Discovered in the 70s during excavations, the original vault featured peacocks, doves and fruit trees, but the creators eventually went with the existing design of herds of lambs instead. *(On V. Fiandrini. Ticket booth to the right of Basilica di San Vitale's entrance. Museum is through courtyard. ☎ 34 424. Open Tu-Su 8:30am-7:30pm. Last entry 30min. before closing. €4, EU students €2, under 18 and over 65 free. Cash only.)*

> ✍ **RAVENOUS FOR ART.** Individual tickets to five of Ravenna's must-see monuments are not available, but the Ravenna Card (€7.50, students €6.50) provides admission to five museums and monuments: the Basilica di San Vitale, Basilica di Sant'Apollinare Nuovo, the Battistero Neoniano, the Mausoleo di Galla Placidia, and the Museo Arcivescovile. From Mar. 1 to June 15, the Mausoleo di Galla Placidia costs an extra €2. For info on any of the churches, contact the Ufficio Informazioni e Prenotaxioni dell'Opera di Religione della Diocesi di Ravenna, V. Canneti 3. (☎ 54 16 88; fax 54 16 80. Open M-F 9am-12:30pm and 3:30-6pm.)

BASILICA DI SANT'APOLLINARE NUOVO. The 6th-century basilica features arched windows, white tile floors, and mortar made from crushed seashells. Long mosaics of martyrs line the central aisle and frescoes in the central apse recount miracles performed by Jesus. Outside, a tall, circular brick *campanile* spirals up six stories over the church's sloping, red-tiled roof. *(On V. di Roma. ☎ 21 95 18. Open daily Apr.-Sept. 9am-7pm; Mar. and Oct. 9:30am-5:30pm; Nov.-Feb. 10am-5pm.)*

BATTISTERO NEONIANO. The central dome of this pint-sized baptistry features a mosaic of Jesus and John the Baptist in the Jordan River, with a representation of the river as a nude old man. The mosaic is one of the many that Bishop Neon—after whom the baptistry is named—ordered in AD 452. Tossed coins litter the bottom of the baptismal font in the center of the room. *(From P. del Popolo, follow V. Cairoli, turn right on V. Gessi, then head toward P. Arcivescovado. Duomo open daily 7:30am-noon and 3:30-6:30pm. Baptistry open daily Apr.-Sept. 9am-7pm; Mar. and Oct. 9:30am-5:30pm; Nov.-Feb. 10am-5pm.)*

MUSEO ARCIVESCOVILE. This one-room museum offers an up-close look at the city's most celebrated art form, displaying detailed religious mosaics that were rescued from the now-destroyed Ursian Basilica. It also exhibits tattered vestments, a marble Easter calendar from AD 532-626, and the centerpiece, the *See of Maximilian*, an ivory throne trimmed with ornate vines and relief panels of the life of Christ. *(To the right of the Battistero Neoniano. ☎ 21 52 01. Open daily Apr.-Sept. 9am-7pm; Mar. and Oct. 9:30am-5:30pm; Nov.-Feb. 10am-5pm.)*

🎵 🌿 ENTERTAINMENT AND FESTIVALS

A host of bars and cafes stays open late around P. del Popolo. If the mosaics of the basilica leave you breathless, channel your slack-jawed awe at **Fuschini Colori-Belle Arti**, P. Mameli 16, off Vle. Farini, which sells *tesserae* (cut glass or stone) for do-it-yourself personalized mosaics. (☎ 37 387. Glass pieces €3-8.50 per 100g. Open M-W 9:15am-12:30pm and 4:30-7:30pm, Th and Sa 9:15am-12:30pm, F 9:15am-12:30pm and 5-10:30pm. AmEx/MC/V.) Watch for the **Organ Music Festival,** held annually in late July, in the basilica, and the **Ravenna Festival,** which brings together some of the world's most famous classical performers each June and July. (Info office at V. D. Alighieri 1. ☎ 24 92 44; www.ravennafestival.org. Ticket office at V. Mariani 2. Open M-W and F-Sa 10am-1pm, Th 4-6pm. During festival, open M-Sa 10am-1pm and 4-6pm, Su 10am-1pm. Reserve ahead for popular events. Tickets from €10.) In the 2nd week of September, Dante's legacy comes to life with the exhibits and theatrical performances of the **Dante Festival** (☎ 30 252).

RIMINI ☎ 0541

Given the lack of surprise on doormen's faces when they let in mojito-stained lodgers at 3am, Rimini (REE-mee-nee; pop. 136,000) is clearly a city that's used to playing fast and loose. Inland, the *centro storico* preserves its Roman heritage with more picturesque streets and *piazze* overshadowed by immense monuments. But the town shows its true colors on buses crammed with teens singing drinking songs and during colorful midnight explosions of impromptu fireworks. Beaches, pastel-colored hotels, and wide boardwalks filled with clothing vendors and fortune tellers all contribute to an atmosphere in which it's perfectly acceptable—and even admirable—to collapse into bed and wish the rising sun "good night."

▐ TRANSPORTATION

Flights: Miramare Civil Airport (☎ 71 57 11), on V. Flaminia. Mostly charter flights. Serves many European cities. Bus #9, across from the train station, goes to the airport (every 20min. 5:37am-10:52pm and 1:02am, €1).

Trains: in P. Cesare Battisti and on V. Dante Alighieri (☎ 89 20 21). Open daily 5am-12:30am. Info office open daily 7am-8:30pm. Ticket office open daily 5:15am-10:15pm. To: **Ancona** (1¼hr.; 41 per day 12:30am-10:40pm, €4.80); **Bologna**

(1½hr., 48 per day 2:30am-10pm, €6.65); **Milan** (3hr., 25 per day 2:36am-10:22pm, €28); **Ravenna** (1hr., 21 per day 3:33am-10:53pm, €3); **Riccione** (10min., 36 per day 12:30am-10:07pm, €1). MC/V.

Buses: Buy both intercity and municipal tickets at ticket booth across from train station. Open daily 5:50am-12:20am. Municipal bus tickets available (1½hr. pass €1, purchased onboard €1.50; 24hr. pass €3; 7-day pass €11). 24hr. service to many inland towns (€1.03-3.36). Local bus #11 travels to **Riccione**. TRAM intercity bus station (☎30 05 33; www.tram.rimini.it), at V. Roma in P. Clementini, near the station. From the train station, follow V. D. Alighieri, and take 1st left.

Taxis: RadioTaxi (☎50 020). Available 24hr.

Car Rental: Avis, Vle. Trieste 16/D (☎51 256; fax 56 176), off V. Amerigo Vespucci. Bus #11: stop 12. 25+. Open M-F 8:30am-1pm and 3-7:30pm, Sa 8:30am-1pm and 4:30-7:30pm. AmEx/MC/V.

Bike/Scooter Rental: P. Kennedy 6 (☎27 016). Bikes €3 per hr.; pedal-powered cars €7-12 per hr.; scooters from €13 per hr. Open Apr.-Oct. daily 9am-midnight. AmEx/MC/V.

✦ 🔃 ORIENTATION AND PRACTICAL INFORMATION

To reach the beach from the **train station** in **Piazzale Cesare Battisti,** turn right from the station, take another right into the tunnel at the yellow arrow indicating *"al mare,"* and follow **Viale Principe Amedeo.** To the right, **Viale Amerigo Vespucci,** the hub of Rimini activity, runs one block inland along the beach. Bus #11 runs from the train station to the beach and continues along Vle. Vespucci and V. Regina Elena (every 15min. 5:30am-2am). Buy tickets at the kiosk in front of the station or at *tabaccherie.* To reach the *centro storico,* follow **Via Dante Alighieri** from the station to **Piazza Tre Martiri.** The center of Rimini is **Marina Centro. Rimini Sud** (south) branches out from the main city along the coast and comprises the neighborhoods of Bellariva, Marebello, Rivazzurra, and Miramare. **Rimini Nord** (north) goes toward the less-visited Rivabella, Viserba, and Viserbella.

Tourist Offices: IAT, P. Fellini 3 (☎56 902; www.riminiturismo.it), at the beginning of V. Vespucci. Bus #11: stop 10. Open in summer M-Sa 8:30am-7:30pm, Su 8:30am-2:30pm; in winter M-Sa 9am-12:30pm and 3:30-6pm. **Branch:** Ple. Cesare Battisti 1 (☎51 331), on the left after the train station. Open in summer M-Sa 8:30am-7:30pm, Su 8:30am-2pm; in winter M-Sa 10am-4pm. **Hotel reservations office,** also at train station. (☎24 760. Open June-Aug. M-Sa 8:15am-8pm; Sept.-June M-Sa 9:30am-12:30pm and 3:30-6:30pm.)

Budget Travel: CTS/Grantour Viaggi, V. Matteucci 2/4 (☎51 001 or 55 525), off V. Principe Amedeo. Sells tickets and ISICs (€11). Open M-W and F 9am-noon and 3:30-6:30pm, Th 9am-4pm, Sa 9:30am-noon. Cash only.

Luggage Storage: In train station. €3-5 for 1st 6hr., €1 per hr. thereafter.

Laundromat: Lavanderia Trieste Express, Vle. Trieste 16 (☎26 764). Wash €10, dry €10. No self-service. Open M-F 8:30am-12:30pm and 3-7:30pm, Sa 2-6pm.

Police: C. d'Augusto 192.

Pharmacy: Farmacia del Kursaal, V. Vespucci 12/E (☎21 711). Open daily 8:30am-1pm and 4-10pm. Cash only.

Hospital: Ospedale Infermi, V. Settembrini 2 (☎70 51 11 or 78 74 61).

Internet Access: Central Park, Vle. Vespucci 21 (☎37 44 50). €1 per 10min., €2 per 30min., €5 per 80min. Open daily in summer 9am-2am; in winter 10am-2am. Cash only. Many **call centers** on C. Giovanni XXIII offer Internet access.

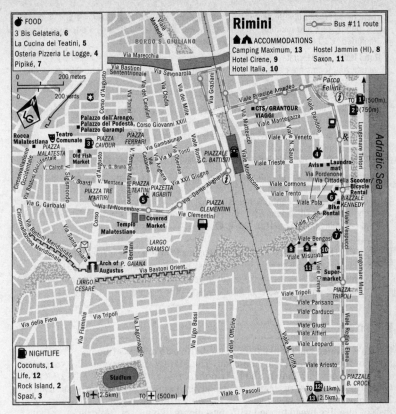

Rimini

⊙—⊙ Bus #11 route

🍴 FOOD
3 Bis Gelateria, 6
La Cucina dei Teatini, 5
Osteria Pizzeria Le Logge, 4
Pipiké, 7

🏠🏠 ACCOMMODATIONS
Camping Maximum, 13   Hostel Jammin (HI), 8
Hotel Cirene, 9   Saxon, 11
Hotel Italia, 10

🎵 NIGHTLIFE
Coconuts, 1
Life, 12
Rock Island, 2
Spazi, 3

Post Office: C. d'Augusto 8 (☎78 16 73), off P. Tre Martiri, near the Arch of Augustus. **Currency exchange** available. Open M-F 8am-6:30pm, Sa 8am-12:30pm. **Branch** at P. Marvelli 3, open M-F 8am-1:30pm, Sa 8am-12:30pm. **Postal Code:** 47900.

🏨 ACCOMMODATIONS AND CAMPING

With 1146 hotels and 62,000 beds, Rimini overwhelms visitors with its array of cookie-cutter accommodations. The smaller streets off Vle. Vespucci and Vle. Regina Elena between stops 12 and 20 of bus #11 are filled with more hotels than homes. Prices peak in August, and reservations are necessary far in advance. If plans fall through, the tourist office provides booking services.

Hostel Jammin (HI), Vle. Derna 22 (☎39 08 00; www.hosteljammin.it). Bus #11: stop 13. Brand new hostel just seconds from the beach boasts enthusiastic owners and excellent amenities. Free bike rental. Breakfast included. Lockers €1 per 24hr. Internet access 1st 15min. free, €2 per hr. thereafter. Open 24hr. Closed Jan. Dorms €19, with bath €21. AmEx/MC/V. ●

Saxon, Vle. Cirene 36 (☎/fax 39 14 00). Bus #11: stop 13. Exit bus to the left, turn right on Vle. Misurata, then left on V. Cirene. This 30-room hotel in close proximity to the beach has small but sufficient rooms with sea-green decor. All rooms have private bath, TV, phone, fan, and minibar. Umbrella and chair €6 per day. Breakfast and beach safe included. €30 per person. AmEx/MC/V. ❸

Hotel Italia, Vle. Misurata 13 (☎39 09 94; www.hotelitaliarimini.it). Bus #11: stop 13. Newly refurbished rooms are clean and bright; all with TV, bath, balcony, and fan. Bike rental and breakfast included. Reception 24hr. Rooms €20-40 per person. Surcharge for single room €6; stays of less than 3 days require surcharge of 10% of stay. AmEx/MC/V. ❷

Hotel Cirene, Vle. Cirene 50 (☎39 09 04; www.hotelcirene.com). Bus #11: stop 13. Lodgers enjoy nautical-themed linens, porcelain bathrooms, and a large, bright dining room. All rooms have bath, fan, phone, and TV; some have balcony. Some rooms have A/C; otherwise, fans available. Breakfast included. Half and full pension available. Open May-Sept. Singles €25-38; doubles €44-70; triples €66-105; quads €90-120. AmEx/MC/V. ❷

Camping Maximum, Vle. Principe di Piemonte 57 (☎37 26 02; www.campingmaximum.com). Bus #11: stop 33. Right across from the beach on the way from Rimini to Riccione, this lively campground is sandwiched between seaside hotels. Reception daily 7am-9pm. Open June-Sept. €7-10 per person, €4-5 per child; €8.50-12 per tent and car; bungalows €60-100. MC/V. ❶

CLUB HOPPING. Nightlife in Rimini changes so frequently that it is difficult to keep up with what is popular. Ask around (especially on bus #11), follow the crowds, and, if a venue is not to your liking upon arrival, just hop back on the bus—there is a world of Rimini ragers left to discover.

◘ FOOD

Rimini's **covered market** between V. Castelfidardo and the Tempio provides an array of foods. (Open M-Sa 7am-7pm.) The **STANDA** supermarket, Vle. Vespucci 133, is between P. Kennedy and P. Tripoli. (Open daily 8am-9pm. AmEx/MC/V.) On Saturday nights, reservations are advisable at nicer, popular restaurants. For a quick lunch or late-night snack, grab a *piada*, a typical Emilia-Romagna dish of pita-like bread topped with ingredients like *prosciutto crudo*, arugula, and *squacerone* (a soft, regional cheese).

La Cucina dei Teatini, P. Teatini 3 (info ☎28 008, reservations 339 23 87 695), just off V. IV Novembre, close to the temple. A young staff serves creative takes on typical Italian fare. Dine in the brightly-colored interior or on the shaded deck, which looks out onto a romantic brick grotto. *Primi* €8.50-9.50, *secondi* €9.50-17. Open M-F 12:30-2:30pm and 7:30-11pm, Sa 7:30-10:30pm. AmEx/MC/V. ❸

PIPIKe', V. Bengasi 1 (☎39 21 52), off Vle. Vespucci, close to P. Kennedy. Friendly proprietors cater to the masses of hungry beachgoers, serving big *piade*, heaping kebabs, and slices of pizza topped with fresh ingredients. Takeout available. Drink and pizza, *piada*, or kebab €3.80-6.50. Open M-F noon-3pm and 5pm-4am, Sa-Su noon-4am. MC/V. ❶

Osteria Pizzeria Le Logge, Vle. Trieste 5 (☎55 978), a few blocks from the crowded beachfront. Clusters of grapes and palm awnings surround crowds of happy eaters. Look out for the specialty *Nino*, a huge pizza with mozzarella, gorgonzola, spicy salami, and crisp red onions (€7.20). Pizza €2-10. Cover €1.50. Open M-Tu and Th-Su 7pm-2am. AmEx/MC/V. ❶

3 Bis Gelateria, Vle. Vespucci 73 (☎328 26 18 979). This hip *gelateria/*creperie, with flat-screen TVs and large crowds, tempts sweet tooths with rich, gourmet *gelato* heaped high with cookies and fresh fruit. Try the hot crepes (€2.70-3.70) stuffed with *gelato,* fresh fruit, Nutella, or cream. *Gelato* €1.70-2.50. Open daily Mar.-Sept. noon-1am. Cash only. ❶

👁 🌊 SIGHTS AND BEACHES

TEMPIO MALATESTIANO. Rimini's cultural life once relied largely on Sigismondo Malatesta, a 15th-century lord who refurbished the *tempio* with funereal chapels for himself and his 4th wife. To the right of the apse, Piero della Francesca's *Sigismondo Pandolfo Malatesta in preghiera davanti a San Sigismondo* shows Malatesta kneeling in front of his Rimini castle, complete with the family dog lying dutifully behind. In the first chapel, a statue of the ruler sits atop two elephants—the family emblem. The apse holds a painted crucifix by Giotto, the only work by the artist in Rimini today. On the exterior, the small brick protrusion was added by Leon Battista Alberti to resemble the Arch of Augustus (below) as per Malatesta's orders. *(On V. IV Novembre. Follow V. D. Alighieri from the train station. ☎ 51 130. Open daily 8:30am-1pm and 3:30-7pm. Free.)*

ARCH OF AUGUSTUS. This impressive arch (built 27 BC) triumphantly marks the entrance to the city's *centro storico*. The arch was designed as a peace offering after decades of civil war. The top of the structure, probably destroyed by an earthquake, was refinished with brick ramparts from the Middle Ages, while the arch features original marble pillars, depictions of the gods, and an inscription honoring Augustus. *(Follow V. IV Novembre to P. Tre Martiri, and turn left on C. d'Augusto.)*

PIAZZE. Shops and bars surround the 18th-century **pescheria** (fish market) under the brick arches in **Piazza Cavour**. The four stone fish in the corners of the interior arcade once spouted water for cleaning fish on the market tables. Perpendicular to the municipal building lies the modern **Teatro Comunale**, which lost its auditorium in WWII. In the center of the *piazza*, **Fontana della Pigna** is a 1543 marble fountain adorned with an inscription by Leonardo da Vinci. In the center of the square, a militant Pope Paul V sits on a throne, his fierce gaze little protection against the cape of pigeons he usually wears. Farther south on the Corso D'Augusto lies **Piazza Tre Martiri**. Once a venue for jousting tournament in the Middle Ages, it's now home to outdoor cafes, the city's 18th-century brick bell tower, and the mint-green domes of the **Chiesa di Sant'Antonio di Padova**.

BEACHES. Hotels own most of the shoreline, and offer guests a strip of beach for a minimum charge of about €3.50 for a lounge chair, use of whirlpools, volleyball courts, lockers, Internet access, and other facilities. The fun continues at night with bars and live music. Vendors by the beach offer watersports equipment. A **free beach,** located at the top of the shore, is less picturesque and offers no storage or lounge amenities, but the price is right and the waves are huge.

🔊 NIGHTLIFE

Rimini is notorious for its nonstop partying, with clubs near the *lungomare* in Rimini Sud. A bustling nightlife scene lights up the *centro storico* by the old fish market. From P. Cavour, follow **Via Pescheria,** where pubs and bars stay open until 3am—but the real action in Rimini is outside the *centro storico*, near the port. Many clubs offer free bus services (check the travel agency in P. Tripoli at stop 14 for schedules; ☎ 39 11 72; open M-Sa 8:30am-7pm, Su 9am-noon), but there is also a **Blue Line bus** (www.riminilive.com; July to Aug. every 20-30min. after bus #11 stops running around 2am; 1-night pass €3.50, 1wk. pass €14 for 7 nights) for disco-goers. It has color-coded lines depending on the *discoteca* destination. Buy tickets onboard. The last bus leaves around 5:30am, after which bus #11 resumes service. During the high season, 🚌bus #11 is an institution—by midnight, expect a crowd of strangers singing drinking songs, comparing outfits, and cheering (on the rare occasion that a group waiting at the stop can successfully fit inside). The route runs from Rimini to the bus station in Riccione, where Blue Line buses allow easy access to seven more nightclubs grouped together in a valley. Clubs change their hours and prices frequently, and many close in winter.

Coconuts, Lungomare Tintorin 5 (☎52 35; www.coconuts.it). Crowds pack the two dance floors, but the place to be is out on the street, where cushioned seating, a huge bar, and male platform dancers draw scores of young fun-seekers. The party doesn't slow until the wee hours. Drinks €4-8. Open daily 6pm-5am.

Rock Island by Black Jack (☎50 178; www.rockislandrimini.com), at the pier's farthest point. In the evening, the restaurant offers seafood specialties and classy seaside ambience; later on, the outdoor bar and dance floor ignite. Dancing until late. Kitchen open Tu-Su 7:30pm-midnight. Reserve dinner ahead of time, especially on weekends.

Life, Vle. Regina Margherita 11 (☎37 34 73), in Bellariva. Take bus #11 to stop 22; the club also offers a free bus service. Hosts either karaoke or theme parties nightly for two floors of partygoers, from teenagers to a more mixed crowd later in the night. The top level has a laid-back bar and a collage of movie and music posters, while the bottom kicks it up a notch with a fog machine and an elevated stage. Free drink at 2:30am. Cover varies, but usually €8-12 with discount pass, available near the door. Open daily 11pm-4am. Cash only.

Spazi (☎23 439), in P. Cavour. A good spot for a relaxed drink before hitting the *discoteche*. Attracts a slightly older clientele with an extensive wine list and their trendy bar and patio. Wine from €3 per glass. Open M-Sa 5pm-7am. AmEx/MC/V.)

▶ DAYTRIP FROM RIMINI

SAN LEO

San Leo is accessible from Rimini by buses operated by Ferrovie Emilia-Romagna. Buses depart across from the Rimini train station at 8:40am, 12:10, 1:10, 5:30pm; all but the 12:10pm departure require a brief connection via van at Piestrascuta. Vans leave San Leo at 8am, 1, and 6pm. Direct trips €2.53. Connecting trips €2 for the 1st leg, €1.40 for the 2nd. Buy Ferrovie Emilia-Romagna tickets at the kiosk outside the Rimini train station. Buy tickets for the connection on the van. Ask the Rimini tourist office about schedule changes.

Perched atop the Apennines and surrounded by craggy cliffs, San Leo (SAN LEH-oh) has a fascinating history. Once a Kingdom of Italy under King Berngard II and later the Papacy's maximum-security prison, La Fortezza (The Fortress) at San Leo is most famous as the place of detention of Count Cogliostro, a prisoner held here for causing innumerable scandals in the European court. No longer a prison, today the tiny hamlet offers a quiet, untouristed alternative to the swarming streets of nearby Rimini and San Marino. It takes only a few hours to explore the entire area, but plan to linger and indulge in San Leo's timeless charm. Just before P. Dante Alighieri, signs point up a rocky path that zig-zags steeply to ◪**La Fortezza**. Inside, glass cases contain 14th- to 19th-century military artifacts, but the history of the famous prisoners held there is more interesting. More than the history, however, the views of the surrounding countryside alone are worth the trip. (☎91 63 02. €8, students and over 65 €5, ages 6-14 €3. Cash only.) Across from the tourist office sits **La Pieve**, a tiny church made of sandstone blocks that contains one row of pews and a simple brick apse; in the basement's **crypt,** a softly illuminated statue honors Santa Maria Assunta, to whom the church is dedicated. (Open daily 9:20am-12:30pm and 2:30-7:30pm. Free.) If you're not tired out by the trip up to La Fortezza, work those legs a little more with a climb up **Torre Campanaria**, past La Pieve to the right. A cool breeze and views of the valley and the fortress reward those who make the climb. (Open Mar.-Sept. daily 9am-noon and 3:30-6:30pm. €3.) Though an ideal daytrip from Rimini, San Leo has a few good lodging options. **Albergo Rocca's ❹** welcoming owner Ivo lets seven small and charming rooms with bath, but the real draw is the outdoor terrace that looks out on the rooftops of San Leo. (☎91 62 41. Reception 8am-10:30pm. Call ahead for Aug. stays. Singles €45-55; doubles €50-60; triples €70-85; quads €90-110.) **Albergo Castello ❹**, in the main *piazza*, has 16 rooms with TV, phone, and bath. Call ahead to reserve one of the rooms with great valley views. (☎91 62 14; albergo-castello@libero.it. Singles €45-50, doubles €60-65. AmEx/MC/V.) **Il Bettolino ❸**, V. Montefeltro 4, serves piles of pasta in the quiet interior or at canopied tables along the street. Ask to sit by the window; you won't regret it. (☎91 62 65. Pizza €3-7.50. *Primi* €6-9.50, *secondi* €7-12. Cover €1.50. Open M-Tu and Th-Su 10am-3:30pm and 7-11pm. AmEx/MC/V.) After exiting the tourist office, turn left for **La Corte ❷**, V. Michele Rosa 74, which offers traditional dishes, like the specialty *ravioli al formaggio di fossa* (€8), on a wooden deck or booths inside. The attached *gelateria* has *gelato* from €1.70 a scoop and crepes for €3. For lighter eaters, the *conini* (tiny cones of *gelato* dipped in chocolate) are just €0.50. (☎91 62 14; osterialacorte@liberto.it. *Primi* €6.50-8, *secondi* €6.50-9.50. Cover €1.50. *Gelateria* open daily Mar.-Oct. 9am-midnight. Restaurant open M and W-F 12:15-2pm and 7:15-9pm, Sa-Su 12:15-2:30pm and 7:15-9:20pm. MC/V.) The **tourist office**, at the far end of P. D. Aligheri, provides maps and brochures. (☎91 63 06 or 800 55 38 00; fax 92 69 73. Open daily July-Aug. 9:30am-10:30pm; Sept.-June 9am-7pm.)

RICCIONE   ☎0541

In Riccione (ree-CHYO-neh; pop. 33,000), a tangible rift exists between the shaded lanes where residents make their homes and the steamy beachfront streets, where wide-eyed vacationers wander through boardwalks lined with brightly lit video arcades, risqué sex shops, and a constant stream of busy disco-bars and hotels. The city itself is humming with electricity and neon until early in the morning, but the true partygoers make the trek to the hillside of world-renowned *discoteche* just a bus ride away.

TRANSPORTATION AND PRACTICAL INFORMATION. The **train station** is between Ple. della Stazione and Ple. Vittorio Veneto. (☎89 20 21. Station open daily 5:40am-8:30pm. Ticket booth open daily 5:45am-8:17pm. Binario #1 open 24hr.) The station has **no luggage storage**. Trains run to Bologna (1¾hr., 25 per day 5:23am-9:47pm, €10), Pesaro (20min., 45 per day 12:42am-10:18pm, €2), and Rimini (10 min., 47 per day 5:08am-11:30pm, €1). **Local bus #11** (€1, purchased onboard €1.50) runs northward along the waterfront from Riccione to Rimini.

To get to the beach, exit the train station toward Ple. V. Veneto, walk down **Viale Martinelli,** and turn left on **Via Gramsci;** then head right on V. Ceccarini for 2 blocks to **Piazzale Roma.** The **public beach** is on the other side of the *piazzale*. An **IAT tourist office,** Ple. Ceccarini 10, offers accommodations booking and a free map. (☎69 33 02; iat@comune.riccione.rn.it. Open daily June-Aug. 8am-10pm; Sept. 8am-8pm; Oct.-May 8am-7pm.) In case of **emergency,** call the **police,** Vle. Sirtori 2 (☎42 61 00). The hospital, **Ospedale G. Ceccarini,** is at V. Cervi 48 (☎60 85 11). **Internet** access, printing, fax, and photocopy sevices are available at **Phone Center and Internet Point,** V. Amendola 17/D. (☎69 38 11. €1 per 15min. Open M-Tu and Th-Su 11am-10pm. Cash only.) The **post office,** V. Corrodoni 13, offers **currency exchange.** (☎47 39 11. Open M-F 8am-6:30pm, Sa 8am-12:30pm.) **Postal Code:** 47838.

ACCOMMODATIONS AND FOOD. Hotel reservations are essential for the high season; for the rest of the year, bargains abound. **Hotel Garden ❸,** V. Bixio 24, a short walk from the beach, offers its guests free bike rental along with comfortable rooms that have TV, bath, and balcony. Most rooms have AC; fans are available upon request. (☎60 15 00; www.hotelgardenonline.com. Reception 24hr. Breakfast included. Half and full pension available. €28-45 per person, depending on season. AmEx/MC/V.) Close to Hotel Garden, **Hotel La Nidiola ❸**, V. Bixio 30, is also on the beach. Exit the train station and turn right on V. Trento e Trieste. Walk straight for 10min.; the hotel is on the left and offers bright rooms with TV, bath, A/C, and balcony. (☎60 15 58; www.lanidiola.com. Free bike rental. Breakfast included. Reception 24hr. Singles €35-65, with full pension €41-70; doubles €60-120/76-120. AmEx/MC/V.) In a town with so many tourists, conformity reigns in countless cafes and pizzerias. On one of the main pedestrian malls, the self-service **Hot Café ❶**, Vle. Dante 170/A, offers a well-priced pasta *menù* and a flat-screen TV near its street-side seating. (☎64 63 28. *Piade* €3-5. Pasta €6. Open daily 6:30am-3am. AmEx/MC/V.) A reprieve from the Riccione's *gelaterie* as well as the stifling summer humidity is **Campi di Fragole ❶**, V. Dante 180, a *gelateria* named for The Beatles' "Strawberry Fields Forever." After sampling the freshly made *gelato*, add your tag to the graffiti-covered mirrors with neon gel pens from the counter. (1 scoop €1.60, 2 scoops €2. Open daily July-Aug. 10am-4am; Sept.-June 10am-2am. Cash only.) **Supermarket Angelini**, Vle. Dante 18, has groceries. (Open M-Sa 7:45am-1:15pm and 4-11pm, Su 7:45am-1:15pm. AmEx/MC/V.)

■ **NIGHTLIFE.** Riccione's real action is in the clubs, conveniently nestled together in a valley accessible by bus. From the bus station near the waterfront, take bus #46 to the "Discoteche" stop—from there, signs point to a half-dozen bumping joints. Even easier to reach, though, is ◼**Hakuna Matata**, Vle. d'Annunzio 138, a dance club and bar right on the beach that offers the carefree attitude of the Disney tune from which it takes its name. Take the #11 bus to stop 37. (☎64 12 03. Drinks €4-7. Open daily 8am-5am. AmEx/MC/V.) It's pricey and it's far, but ◼**Baia Imperiale**, in Cattolica on V. Panoramica 41, is a must-see for the incredible—almost surreal—scale of its party. Take the Blue Line's *"linea gialla."* In a gigantic faux-Roman complex, complete with imitation baths and temples, world-famous DJs spin records for countless hundreds of young and sweaty clubgoers, who keep alive the memory of the bacchanalian ancient Romans. Hang out on the balconies or stairs outside or one of the several bars or dance floors on the club's multiple floors. (☎95 03 12; www.baiaimperiale.net. Cover depends on nightly events; typically from €10, usually including at least one free drink. Women enter free W before 1am.) In Miramare, **L'Altro Mondo Studio's**, V. Flaminia 388, is well off the beaten path. Lights illuminate a huge floor lined with portals, sliding doors, and steel platforms. A young and international crowd grooves to house and techno, pausing only for the laser show around 2am. Avoid heading to this club alone; the 15-20min. walk to and from the bus route is mostly unlit. (☎37 31 51; www.altromondo.com. Cover approx. €15; discount for groups. Open daily 11pm-4am. Cash only.)

TIP **BARS ON A BUDGET.** Bars in Riccione have a tendency to be pretty expensive. Plan ahead by hanging onto the **discount passes** that promoters distribute along V. Vespucci and V. R. Elena.

SAN MARINO ☎ 0549

San Marino (san ma-REE-no; pop. 30,000) is one of two independent states inside Italy—the other is the Vatican. Officially titled the *Serenissima Repubblica di San Marino* ("The Most Serene Republic of San Marino"), it was founded in AD 301 by Marinus, a pious stone cutter who fled to Mt. Titano to escape the caresses of an overly affectionate girl. San Marino's residents remain proud of their history and enjoy welcoming the busloads of tourists that stream across its borders each year. In fact, in proportion to its population, the 26 sq. km country is the most visited in the world. Tax-free shopping, the Republic's modern Parliament, and three towering castles may reel in the tourists, but the steep stone streets and panoramic views form visitors' most lasting memories of their time in this Most Serene Republic.

 STAYING IN TOUCH WITH SAN MARINO. San Marino's country code is ☎328. It is only necessary to dial it when calling from outside Italy. Within Italy and San Marino, just dial the city code ☎0549.

TRANSPORTATION. The closest **train station** is in Rimini. Fratelli Benedettini (☎90 38 54) and Bonelli (☎0541 66 20 69) **bus** companies run from San Marino's *centro* to Rimini's train station (50min., 12 per day 6:30am-7pm, €3.40). In town, a **funicular** connects Borgo Maggiore to the *centro storico*. (☎88 35 90. Every 15min. in summer 7:50am-1am; in winter 7:50am-6:30pm. Round-trip €4.) **Taxis** (☎99 14 41) are in P. Lo Stradone.

ORIENTATION AND PRACTICAL INFORMATION. To get from one monument to another, follow signs; the city is difficult to navigate, and you'll probably get lost. San Marino's streets wind around **Monte Titano.** From the bus, exit to the left, climb the staircase, and pass through the **Porta San Francesco** to begin the ascent. **Via Basilicus** leads to **Piazza Titano.** From there, turn right to **Piazza Garibaldi,** then follow **Contrada del Collegio** to **Piazza della Libertà.** The **tourist office,** Contrada del Collegio 40, stamps passports for €2.50 and provides a free map. (☎88 29 14; www.visitsanmarino.com. Open daily in summer 8:30am-6:30pm; in winter 10am-1pm and 2-5pm. Cash only.) San Marino mints coins interchangeable with the euro, though they're more collector's items than anything else. Pick them up at the **Coin and Stamp Office,** P. Garibaldi 5. (☎88 23 70. Open M-F 8:15am-5:50pm and Sa-Su 1-6pm. MC/V.) In case of **emergency,** call the **police** (☎88 77 77). **Internet** is available at **Caffè del Titano,** Piazzetta del Titano 4. (☎99 24 73. €1 per 15min. Open daily Apr.-July 7am-7pm, Aug. and Nov.-Mar. 7am-5pm. Cash only.) The **post office** is at Vle. Onofri 87. (☎88 29 09. Open M-F 8:15am-4:45pm, Sa 8:15-11:45am. Cash only.) **Postal Code:** 47838.

ACCOMMODATIONS AND FOOD. Most of San Marino's affordable hotels are family-run affairs above adjoining restaurants. The kind staff at **Hotel La Rocca ❹,** Salita alla Rocca 33, down the street from the castle, offers spacious rooms with TVs and fantastic views. (☎99 11 66; fax 99 24 30. Breakfast included; restaurant downstairs. Singles €45-55; doubles €47-76; triples €75-98; quads €100-120. AmEx/MC/V.) With frescoed staircases and wrought-iron railings, the **Diamond Hotel ❸,** Contrada del Collegio 48, across from the basilica, offers five simple yet large rooms with bath. (☎/fax 99 10 03. Breakfast included; restaurant downstairs. Reception open daily 8:30am-10pm. Open Mar.-Oct. Doubles €60; triples €83; quads €93. AmEx/MC/V.)

For a sizable sampler of regional pastas, try **Buca San Francesco ❷,** Piazzetta Placido Feretrano 3, past Porta San Francesco, where the specialty is *Tris della Buca* (a plate of ravioli, *tagliatelle*, and cheesy lasagna in a light *ragù*) for €7. (☎99 14 62. *Primi* €4.50-7, *secondi* €6-7.50. *Piatto unico* with drinks and side dish €12. Bar open daily 10am-6:30pm. Restaurant open daily 11:30am-3pm. MC/V.) **Hotel Ristorante Rosa ❸,** V. Lapicidi Marini 23, serves scrumptious local dishes like *tagliatelle* with *ragù* or mushrooms (€8), but the real specialty is the view of the valley from the outdoor terrace. From Salsita alla Rocca, follow signs for the Museo delle Cere. (☎99 19 61. Primi €6.30-10.50, secondi €8-16. *Menù* €16. Open M and W-Su noon-2:30pm and 7-9:30pm. AmEx/MC/V.) To escape the packed streets, slip into the serene **Caffè del Titano ❶,** Piazzetta del Titano 4, where a wall-

an Marino, a tiny country in
Emilia-Romagna proud of its sta-
us as a quiet nation on a hill
and as an independent country,
has always done things a little
differently. Perhaps that's why
their soccer team's nickname, *La
Serenissima* (The Most Serene
One), isn't intended to terrify
anyone. Its nickname may not
inspire much fear in opponents,
but—truth be told—the team itself
really doesn't either. Since
1990, when San Marino's soccer
team busted into world of international play, the team has
recorded only one victory. In San
Marino's debut, she fell flat in a
0-4 loss to Switzerland, a coun-
ry with 250 times more people.

Still, it's astounding that the
country even manages to put a
team on the international stage.
The country itself is the size of
most Italian small towns and has
ess than 30,000 residents.

Despite its weak record, San
Marino does hold the bragging
rights for a wacky record: the fastest goal ever scored in World Cup
history. Just 8.3 seconds after the
opening whistle, La Serenissima's
Davide Gualtieri scored a goal
that put his country up briefly over
England. But after that, the Brits
tightened things bit, going on to
take the match 7-1. San Marino's
greatest moment came in 2004,
when she beat that perennial
powerhouse (ahem) Liechtenstein
1-0 in a friendly match.

length mural depicts a colorful cafe scene. The gooey *brioche cioccolato* (€1.30) and rich cappuccino (€1.70) can't be beat. (☎99 24 73. Open daily Apr.-July 7am-7pm; Aug. 7am-10pm; Nov.-Mar. 7am-5pm. Cash only.) Find basics at **Alimentari Chiaruzzi**, Contra del Collegio 13, between P. Titano and P. Garibaldi. (☎99 12 22. Open daily Aug. 7am-midnight; Sept.-July 7:30am-7:30pm. AmEx/MC/V.)

◙ ♫ **SIGHTS AND ENTERTAINMENT.** The late 19th-century **Palazzo Pubblico** serves as the seat of San Marino's parliament. The marble interior features the **Sala del Consiglio** (Hall of the Council), where the city is still run, amid a depiction of Justice (holding a broadsword) and Peace (at a slight disadvantage holding an olive branch). The changing of the guard takes place in front of the *palazzo* from April to September at half past the hour from 8:30am to 6:30pm. Arrive 10min. early to secure a spot. (P. della Libertà. ☎88 31 52. Open daily June-Sept. 8am-8pm; Oct.-May. 9am-5:12pm. Last entry 30min. before closing. €3. Cash only.) Two of the three points along San Marino's defensive network are open to the public, but just traveling between them offers many of the same views for free. The 1st tower is the **Castello della Guaita**, an 11th-century structure carved out of the mountain. Climb to the top of the tower for great views, but be careful descending the narrow ladder. (Follow signs from P. della Libertà. ☎99 13 69. Open daily Apr.-Sept. 8am-8pm; Oct.-Mar. 9am-5pm. Last entry 30min. before closing. €3, combined with Castello della Cesta €4.50. MC/V.) Follow signs along the trail to the highest peak of Mt. Titano, where the **Castello della Cesta** offers the best views of the distant Adriatic and the Castello della Guaita. Inside, the **Museo delle Armi Antiche,** an arms museum, displays a selection of fierce weapons ranging from 15th-century tridents to medieval helmets. (☎99 12 95. Open daily Apr.-Sept. 8am-8pm; Oct.-Mar. 9am-5pm. Last entry 30min. before closing. €3, with Castello della Guaita €4.50. MC/V.) Die-hard castle lovers can follow the trail to the 3rd tower, **Torre del Montale,** a squat, mossy turret closed to the public. Nearby, stone outcroppings offer quiet views of the hills and ocean. In late summer, a **medieval festival** brings parades, food, musicians, and jugglers to San Marino. September 3rd is San Marino's day of independence; the **Palio delle Balestre,** or crossbowman's show, also in early September, commemorates this event; increased bus service makes daytripping easy. (For dates and info, call ☎88 29 98 or the tourist office, p. 419.)

TUSCANY (TOSCANA)

Recently, popular culture has glorified Tuscany (in Italian, "tos-CAH-nah") as a sun-soaked sanctuary of frescoes, cypress trees, and bottles of *vino*. For once, popular culture has gotten it right. In Tuscany, every town was home to a Renaissance master, every highway provides vistas of ancient hills, and every year, the *Chianti Classico* flows at local celebrations of their illustrious history with costumed parades and festivals. This concentration of art, coupled with some of Italy's best cuisine, including famous meaty dishes like *bistecca alla fiorentina* from Florence and *cinta senese* from Siena, rightfully lures millions of visitors each year. Go ahead and wander through medieval sidestreets of hill towns, marvel at the genius of Brunelleschi's dome in Florence, and linger over *gelato* and conversation in Siena's P. del Campo. While it's tempting to blindly shuffle from *duomo* to museum, remember that patience, good timing, and a bit of wanderlust can ensure an even richer experience.

HIGHLIGHTS OF TUSCANY

EXILE yourself to Elba and enjoy **gorgeous beaches** fit for an emperor (p. 493).

SIP the unique *Brunello* wine at a **local vineyard** in Montalcino (p. 463).

CHEER on your favorite horse and jockey during Siena's famed **Palio** (p. 492).

BIKE along the intact **medieval baluardi** (battlements) that surround Lucca (p. 484).

SIGH as the sun sets gloriously over the **Ponte Vecchio** in Florence (p. 441).

FLORENCE (FIRENZE)   ☎ 055

Sopping-wet, war-weary, emaciated, and plagued, Florence (in Italian, "Fee-REN-zeh"; pop. 400,000) did not escape the floods, wars, famine, and Black Death that haunted Europe during the 13th-14th centuries. However, by the late 14th century, Florence was able to pick itself up and etch itself into the Renaissance history books. Florentines Boccaccio, Dante, and Giotto created trend-setting masterpieces and, in the 15th century, Florence gained distinction for artistic excellence as the Medici family amassed a peerless collection, supporting masters like Botticelli, Brunelleschi, Donatello, and Michelangelo. This incredible input of creative spirit generated the beauty many tourists flock to experience today. Beyond its abundance of museums and churches, Florence's vitality prevails. Leather bags are still handcrafted and *gelato* is still homemade. The view of the Ponte Vecchio at sunset has not changed much over the centuries, and, ultimately, the beauty and aesthetic-awareness that inspired such masters is timeless and unflagging, and deserves every ounce of energy you can give it.

✈ INTERCITY TRANSPORTATION

Flights: Aeroporto Amerigo Vespucci (FLR; main line ☎30 615, 24hr. automated flight info line 30 61 700; www.aeroporto.firenze.it) in the suburb of Peretola. Mostly domestic and charter flights. **SITA,** V. Santa Caterina da Siena 157 (☎800 37 37 60), runs buses (20min., 5:30am-11pm, €4.50) between the station and the Florence airport.

Trains: Stazione Santa Maria Novella, just north of Chiesa di Santa Maria Novella. Info office open daily 7am-9pm (after-hours ☎89 20 21). **Luggage storage** and lost property services available. Trains hourly to: **Bologna** (1hr., 5:48am-1:47am, €4.65-6.80); **Milan** (3½hr., 6am-1:47am, €29); **Rome** (3½hr., 5:55am-10:55pm, €30); **Siena** (1½hr., 5:31am-11:07pm, €5.70); **Venice** (3hr., 5:18am-1:47am, €16).

Buses: 3 major bus companies run out of Florence. Offices near P. della Stazione.

SITA, V. Santa Caterina da Siena 17 (☎800 37 37 60; www.sita-on-line.it). Office open M-Sa 5:50am-8:30pm, Su 6:15am-7:55pm. MC/V. To: **Arezzo** (2½hr., 3 per day, €4.13); **Poggibonsi** (1hr., 11 per day, €4.13); **San Gimignano** (1½hr., 14 per day, €6); **Siena** (1½hr., 2 per day, €6.50); **Volterra** (2hr., 6 per day, €7.50) via **Colle Val D'Elsa.**

> **NOT SO DIRETTA.** When busing it with SITA's frequent, convenient buses, be sure to check the schedule to see if the bus is a *"rapida"* or *"diretta."* As counter-intuitive as it is, the *diretta* is **not** direct and makes many stops in smaller towns along the way. The *rapida* is faster and nearly as panoramic.

LAZZI, P. Stazione 4/6r, (☎35 10 61; www.lazzi.it). Departures from P. Adua. Office open M-Sa 6:10am-8:15pm, Su 7am-7:20pm. MC/V. To: **Lucca** (1hr., hourly 7am-8:15pm, €4.70); **Pisa** (1hr., hourly 6am-8:15pm, €6.10); **Pistola** (1hr., hourly 7am-6pm, €2.70); **Prato** (1hr., hourly 6am-11pm, €2.20).

CAP, Largo Alinari 10 (☎21 46 37; www.capautolinee.it). Office open M-F 9am-12:30pm and 2:30-7pm, Sa 9am-12:30pm. To **Prato** (1hr., 6:40am-8pm, €2.20).

⬛ ORIENTATION

From the front steps of **Stazione Santa Maria Novella,** a short walk down **Via de' Panzani** and a left on **Via dei Cerrentari** leads to the **duomo,** in the heart of the city. Most streets in Florence lead to this instantly recognizable dome, which soars high above every other city structure and makes being lost a little easier to remedy. **Via dei Calzaiuoli,** dominated by throngs of pedestrians, leads south from the *duomo* to the statue-filled **Piazza della Signoria,** in front of the **Palazzo Vecchio** and the **Uffizi Gallery.** The other major *piazza* is the **Piazza della Repubblica,** down **Via Roma** from the *duomo.* Major streets run north from this *piazza* toward the *duomo* and south toward the shop-lined **Ponte Vecchio** (literally, "Old Bridge"). The Ponte Vecchio is one of five bridges that cross from central Florence to the **Oltrarno,** the district south of the **Arno River.** When navigating Florence, note that most streets change names unpredictably, often every few blocks. For guidance, grab a free map with a street index from the tourist office across from the train station.

> **WHAT'S BLACK AND WHITE AND RED ALL OVER?** Florence's streets are numbered in red and black sequences. Red numbers indicate commercial establishments, and black (or blue) numbers denote residences (including most sights and hotels). Black addresses appear here as a numeral only, while red addresses are indicated by a number followed by an "r." If you reach an address and it's not what you expected, you probably have the wrong color.

⬛ LOCAL TRANSPORTATION

Public Transportation: Orange **ATAF buses** cover most of the city from 6am to 1am. Buy tickets at any newsstand, *tabaccheria,* or coin-operated ticket dispenser. €1.20 for 70min., €4.50 for 4 tickets, €5 for 1 day, €12 for 3 days. Validate ticket onboard using the orange machine or risk a €50 fine. Once validated, the ticket allows unlimited bus travel for the allotted time. Tickets sold on buses 9am-6pm (€2). From the train station, ATAF info office (☎800 42 45 00; www.ataf.net) is on the left. Free map. Open M-F 7:15am-1:15pm and 1:45-7:45pm, Sa 7:15am-1:15pm. Bus #7 to Fiesole, #13 to Ple. Michelangelo.

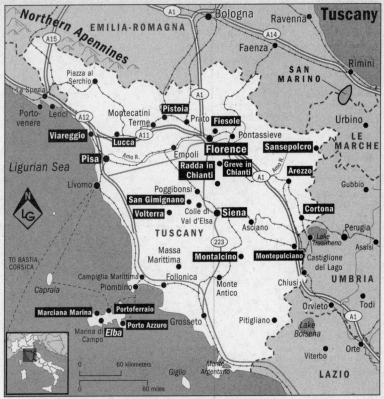

Taxis: (☎43 90, 47 98, 44 99 or 42 42). Outside the train station.

Car Rental: Avis (☎31 55 88; www.avisautonoleggio.it), at airport. 25+. Open daily 8am-11pm. **Branch:** Borgo Ognissanti 128r (☎21 36 29). Open M-Sa 8am-7pm, Su 8am-1pm. **Hertz,** V. Finiguerra 33r (☎23 98 205; www.hertz.it). 25+. Open M-F 8am-8pm, Sa 8am-7pm, Su 8am-1pm. **Maggiore** (☎31 12 56; www.maggiore.it), at airport. 23+. Open daily 8:30am-10:30pm. **Branch:** V. Finiguerra 13r (☎29 45 78). Open M-Sa 8am-7pm, Su 8am-12:30pm.

Bike and Scooter Rental: Alinari Noleggi, V. San Zanobi 38r (☎28 05 00; www.alinari-rental.com). Bikes €12-16 per day; scooters €30 per day. Open M-Sa 9:30am-1:30pm and 2:45-7:30pm, Su and holidays 10am-1pm and 3-6pm. MC/V. **Florence by Bike,** V. San Zanobi 120/122r (☎48 89 92; www.florencebybike.it). Bike rental includes helmet, locks, spare tubes, pump, insurance, maps, and suggested itineraries. Bikes €3.70 per hr., €14-35 per day; scooters €65-95 per day. Reserve ahead. Open Apr.-Oct. daily 9am-7:30pm; Nov.-Mar. M-Sa 9am-1pm, 3:30-7:30pm. AmEx/MC/V.

⁊ PRACTICAL INFORMATION

TOURIST AND FINANCIAL SERVICES

Tourist Offices: Informazione Turistica, P. della Stazione 4 (☎21 22 45; turismo3@comune.fi.it), directly across *piazza* from the station's main exit. Info on cul-

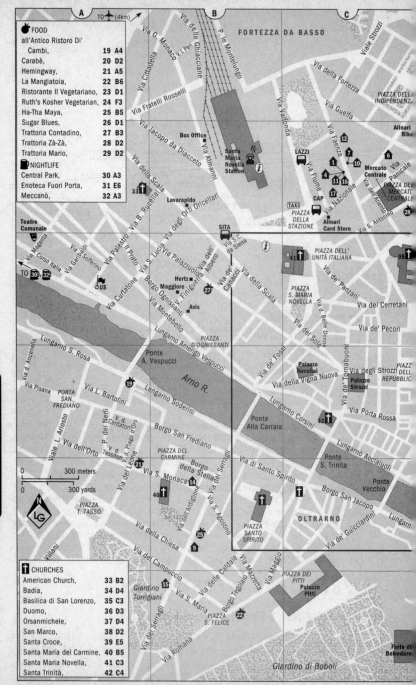

FOOD

all'Antico Ristoro Di'	
Cambi,	**19 A4**
Carabè,	**20 D2**
Hemingway,	**21 A5**
La Mangiatoia,	**22 B6**
Ristorante II Vegetariano,	**23 D1**
Ruth's Kosher Vegetarian,	**24 F3**
Ha-Tha Maya,	**25 B5**
Sugar Blues,	**26 D1**
Trattoria Contadino,	**27 B3**
Trattoria Zà-Zà,	**28 D2**
Trattoria Mario,	**29 D2**

NIGHTLIFE

Central Park,	**30 A3**
Enoteca Fuori Porta,	**31 E6**
Meccanò,	**32 A3**

CHURCHES

American Church,	**33 B2**
Badia,	**34 D4**
Basilica di San Lorenzo,	**35 C3**
Duomo,	**36 D3**
Orsanmichele,	**37 D4**
San Marco,	**38 D2**
Santa Croce,	**39 E5**
Santa Maria del Carmine,	**40 B5**
Santa Maria Novella,	**41 C3**
Santa Trinità,	**42 C4**

TUSCANY

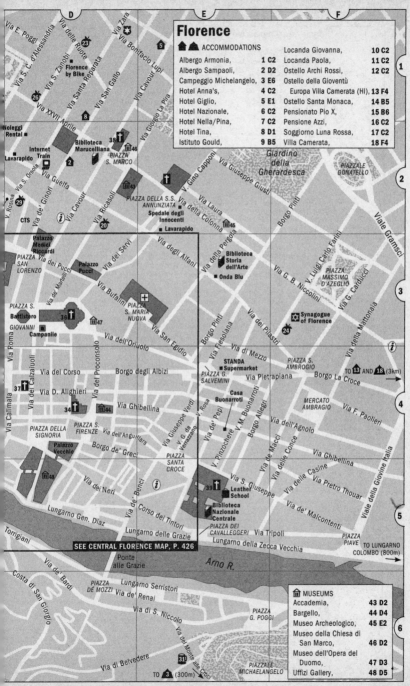

Florence

🏠🏠 ACCOMMODATIONS

Albergo Armonia,	1 C2
Albergo Sampaoli,	2 D2
Campeggio Michelangelo,	3 E6
Hotel Anna's,	4 C2
Hotel Giglio,	5 E1
Hotel Nazionale,	6 C2
Hotel Nella/Pina,	7 C2
Hotel Tina,	8 D1
Istituto Gould,	9 B5
Locanda Giovanna,	10 C2
Locanda Paola,	11 C2
Ostello Archi Rossi,	12 C2
Ostello della Gioventù	
Europa Villa Camerata (HI),	13 F4
Ostello Santa Monaca,	14 B5
Pensionato Pio X,	15 B6
Pensione Azzi,	16 C2
Soggiorno Luna Rossa,	17 C2
Villa Camerata,	18 F4

🏛 MUSEUMS

Accademia,	43 D2
Bargello,	44 D4
Museo Archeologico,	45 E2
Museo della Chiesa di	
San Marco,	46 D2
Museo dell'Opera del	
Duomo,	47 D3
Uffizi Gallery,	48 D5

TUSCANY

PIAZZA DELLA STAZIONE

PIAZZA DELL'UNITÀ ITALIANA

Capelle dei Medici

Basilica di San Lorenzo

S. Maria Novella

Via S. Antonino

Via Faenza

Via del Canto de' Nelli

PIAZZA MADONNA ALDOBRANDINI

Via del Melarancio

Via della Scala

Via Benedetta

Via de' Panzani

Via del Giglio

Via dell'Alloro

Via de' Conti

Via F. Zannetti

Via Palazzuolo

PIAZZA S. MARIA NOVELLA

Via dei Banchi

Via dei Cerretani

Piazza dell'Olio

Via del Porcellana

Via delle Belle Donne

Via del Trebbio

Via dei Rondinelli

Via Teatina

Via Antinori

Via degli Agli

Via de' Vecchietti

Via de' Pecori

PIAZZA ANTINORI

PIAZZA OTTAVIANI

Via del Sole

Lavarapido

Via dei Corsi

Via Campidoglio

Via de'

100 meters

100 yards

Via de' Pescioni

Via Brunelleschi

Via della Spada

N
LG

Via de' Fossi

Via del Moro

Via dei Federighi

Via del Purgatorio

Palazzo Rucellai

Via di Tornabuoni

Via degli Strozzi

PIAZZA DELLA REPUBBLIC

Borgo Ognissanti

BM Bookstore

Via de' Palchetti

Via della Vigna Nuova

Via del Inferno

Palazzo Strozzi

PIAZZA STROZZI

Via Sassetti

Lungarno Amerigo Vespucci

PIAZZA CARLO GOLDONI

Via del Parione

Via de' Tornabuoni

Via degli Anselmi

Via d.

Via Pellicceria

Via de

Ponte Alla Carraia

Via del Parioncino

Via Monalda

PIAZZA DAVANZATI

Merca Nuo

Lungarno Corsini

S. Trinità

PIAZZA SANTA TRINITA

Via Porta Rossa

Palazzo Davanzati

UK

Via delle Terme

Borgo S. S. Apostoli

Chiassa Cornino

Lungarno Acciaiuoli

Via Por Santa Mar

FOOD

Acqua al 2,	10 E4	La Loggia degli Albizi,	16 F3
Il Borgo Antico,	11 A6	Osteria de' Benci,	17 E6
Danny Rock,	12 F4	Perche No!,	18 D4
Gelateria dei Neri,	13 E5	Trattoria Anita,	19 E5
Grom,	14 D3	Tre Merli,	20 A3
Il Latini,	15 B3	Vivoli,	21 F4

PIAZZA FRESCOBARDI

Via di San Spirito

Via Maffia

Via di Coverelli

Borgo San Jacopo

Arno R.

PIAZZA ANGOLIERI

Ponte Vecchio

Voltad

St. Mark's Church of England

OLTRARNO

Via Ramaglianti

Via Barbadori

Via de' Bardi

Santo Spirito

Via del Presto di San Martino

Via del Vellutini

Via Toscanella

Via dello Sprone

Via Guicciardini

PIAZZA D. FELICITA

Costa di San Giorgio

PIAZZA SANTO SPIRITO

Via Maggio

Via dei Vellutti

Via Squazza

Via Michelozzi

TO PALAZZO PITTI (200m)

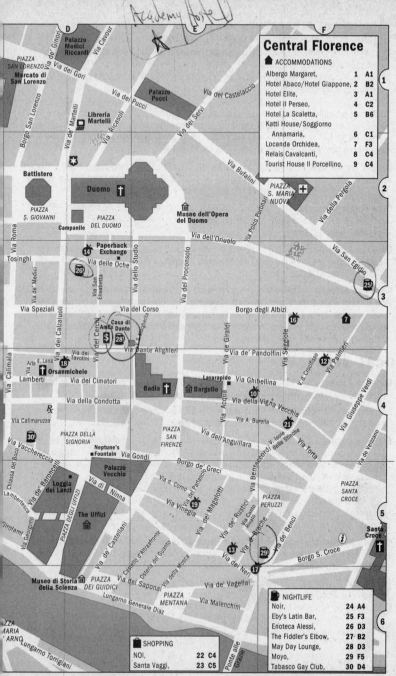

Academy Hotel

Central Florence

ACCOMMODATIONS

Albergo Margaret,	1	A1
Hotel Abaco/Hotel Giappone,	2	B2
Hotel Elite,	3	A1
Hotel Il Perseo,	4	C2
Hotel La Scaletta,	5	B6
Katti House/Soggiorno Annamaria,	6	C1
Locanda Orchidea,	7	F3
Relais Cavalcanti,	8	C4
Tourist House Il Porcellino,	9	C4

SHOPPING

NOI,	22	C4
Santa Vaggi,	23	C5

NIGHTLIFE

Noir,	24	A4
Eby's Latin Bar,	25	F3
Enoteca Alessi,	26	D3
The Fiddler's Elbow,	27	B2
May Day Lounge,	28	D3
Moyo,	29	F5
Tabasco Gay Club,	30	D4

TUSCANY

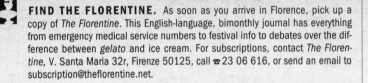

FIND THE FLORENTINE. As soon as you arrive in Florence, pick up a copy of *The Florentine*. This English-language, bimonthly journal has everything from emergency medical service numbers to festival info to debates over the difference between *gelato* and ice cream. For subscriptions, contact *The Florentine*, V. Santa Maria 32r, Firenze 50125, call ☎23 06 616, or send an email to subscription@theflorentine.net.

tural events, walking-tour brochures, listings of hours for all city sights, and free maps with street index. Open M-Sa 8:30am-7pm, Su and holidays 8:30am-2pm. Branches: at airport (☎31 58 74); V. Cavour 1r (☎29 08 32 or 29 08 33); Borgo Santa Croce 29r (☎23 40 444); V. Alessandro Manzoni 16 (☎23 320).

Budget Travel: CTS, V. de'Ginori 25r (☎28 95 70). Provides Transalpino tickets, discount airfares, car rentals, organized trips, and ISICs. Get there early and take a number. Open M-F 9:30am-1:30pm and 2:30-6pm, Sa 9:30am-12:30pm. MC/V.

Consulates: UK, Lungarno Corsini 2 (☎28 41 33). Open M-F 9am-1pm and 2-5pm. **US,** Lungarno Amerigo Vespucci 38 (☎26 69 51), at V. Palestro near the station. Open M-F 9am-12:30pm.

Currency Exchange: Local banks offer the best rates—beware of independent exchange services with high commissions. Most banks open M-F 8:20am-1:20pm and 2:45-3:45pm. 24hr. **ATMs** all over the city.

American Express, V. Dante Alighieri 22r (☎50 98; www.americanexpress.com). From the *duomo*, walk down V. dei Calzaiuoli, turn left on V. dei Tavolini, and continue to the small *piazza*. Cashes personal checks for cardholders. Mail and Travelers Cheques for members at no cost. For lost Treavelers Cheques, call ☎800 87 20 00, lost cards 067 22 80 371. Open M-F 9am-5:30pm.

LOCAL SERVICES

Luggage Storage: In train station at track #16. €3.80 for 1st 5hr., €0.60 per hr. 6-12hr., €0.20 per hr. thereafter; 5-day max. Open daily 6am-midnight. Cash only.

Lost Property: Ufficio Oggetti Rinvenuti (☎23 52 190), next to the baggage deposit in train station. **Lost and Found,** V. Circondaria 19 (☎32 839 42/43).

English-Language Bookstores: ▨**Paperback Exchange,** V. delle Oche 4r (☎24 78 154; www.papex.it). Friendly, English-speaking staff. Offers store credit for used books. Special Italianistica section features novels about Brits and Americans in Italy. Free Wi-Fi for customers. Open M-F 9am-7:30pm, Sa 10am-7:30pm. Closed 2 wk. in mid-Aug. AmEx/MC/V. **BM Bookstore,** Borgo Ognissanti 4r (☎29 45 75; bmbookshop@dada.it). English-language books on every subject imaginable. Stocks English-language travel guides and textbooks for American study-abroad programs. Open Mar.-Oct. M-Sa 9:30am-7:30pm, Su afternoons; Nov.-Feb. M-Sa 9:30am-7:30pm. AmEx/MC/V.

Bulletin Boards: The American Church, V. Bernardo Rucellai 9 (☎29 14 77), lists ads for roommates, English teachers, and baby-sitters, as well as religious and cultural activities in English. Open Tu-F 9am-1pm.

Box Office: V. Alamanni 39r (☎21 08 04; www.boxol.it). Sells tickets for performances in Florence and Fiesole, including rock concerts. Online and phone reservations only with credit cards. Open Mar.-Nov. M-F 10am-7:30pm, Sa 10am-1pm; Nov.-Feb. M 3:30-7:30pm, Tu-Sa 10am-7:30pm. Pick up a listing of events in any tourist office or buy the city's entertainment monthly, *Firenze Spettacolo* (€2).

Laundromats: Wash and Dry Lavarapido, V. dei Servi 105r, 2 blocks from the *duomo.* **Branches:** V. della Scala 52-54r, V. del Sole 29r, V. Nazionale 129r, and V. Ghibellina 143r. Self-service wash and dry €6. Detergent €0.80. Open daily 8am-10pm. **Onda Blu,** V. degli Alfani 24r. Self-service wash and dry €6. Open daily 8am-10pm.

EMERGENCY AND COMMUNICATIONS

Police: Central Office (Questura), V. Zara 2 (☎49 771 or 49 77 602). **Branch:** P. del Duomo 5. Open M-Sa 8:30am-7:30pm, Su 8:30am-1:30pm. **Tourist Police: Ufficio Stranieri,** V. Zara 2 (☎49 771). For visa or work-permit problems. Open M-F 9:30am-1pm. To report lost or stolen items, go around the corner to **Ufficio Denunce,** V. Duca d'Aosta 3 (☎49 771). Open M-Sa 8am-8pm. Also, check out the **Lost and Found,** V. Circondaria 19 (☎32 839 42/43).

Pharmacies: Farmacia Comunale (☎28 94 35), by track #16 at the train station. **Molteni,** V. dei Calzaiuoli 7r (☎28 94 90). Both open 24hr. AmEx/MC/V. **Tourist Medical Service,** V. Lorenzo il Magnifico 59 (☎47 54 11). General practitioners and specialists. English-speaking doctors on call 24hr. Office visits €45; daytime house calls €65, night €80. For **dental** emergencies call ☎24 12 08. AmEx/MC/V.

Internet Access:

    Internet Train, V. Guelfa 54/56r (www.internettrain.it). 15 locations in the city. €4.30 per hr., students €3.20 per hr. Hours vary slightly depending on location. Most open M-F 9am-midnight, Sa 10am-8pm, Su noon-9pm. AmEx/MC/V.

    Libreria Martelli, V. Martelli 22r, just north of the *duomo.* Relaxed atmosphere amid books and coffee upstairs. Wi-Fi available. €3.25 per hr., students €2 per hr. Open M-Sa 9am-8pm, Su 10am-8pm.

Post Office: (☎27 36 480), on V. Pellicceria, off P. della Repubblica. Open M-Sa 8:15am-7pm. **Postal Code:** 50100.

ACCOMMODATIONS

Because of the constant stream of tourists, it is best to reserve a room at least 10 days ahead, especially for visits in the summer or during Easter. Most *pensioni* prefer reservations in writing with at least one night's deposit; others simply ask for a phone confirmation. Florence has so many budget accommodations that it's possible to find a room without a reservation, but last-minute options are often of a lower quality. Hotel owners are typically willing to suggest alternatives if their establishments are full, so don't hesitate to ask. Complaints should be lodged with the **Tourist Rights Protection Desk,** V. Cavour 1r (☎29 08 32/33; open M-Sa 8:30am-6:30pm, Su 8:30am-1:30pm.) or the **Servizio Turismo,** V. Alessandro Manzoni 16 (☎23 320; uff.turismo@provincia.fi.it. Open M-F 9am-1pm). The municipal government strictly regulates hotel prices, so proprietors must charge within the approved range for their category and must also post these rates in a place visible to guests. Rates uniformly increase approximately 10% every year, and new rates take effect in March or April. For **long-term housing** in Florence, check bulletin boards; classified ads in *La Pulce,* published three times weekly (€2), or *Grillo Fiorentino,* a free monthly paper. Reasonable prices range €200-600 per month.

> **TIP** **DON'T LET THE BED BUGS BITE.** Each day at Stazione Santa Maria Novella, boosters assail unwitting travelers with offers for rooms at ridiculously cheap prices. As these fly-by-night operations are illegal and unregulated, they are dangerous and unsanitary. Hotels, hostels, campsites, and *affitta-camere* in Tuscany are subject to government inspection and must post their official rating from the *comune* outside their establishment (1-5 stars).

HOSTELS

■ **Ostello Archi Rossi,** V. Faenza 94r (☎29 08 04; www.hostelarchirossi.com), 2 blocks from the train station. A legacy of a hostel where the walls aren't covered in floor-to-ceiling frescoes but with the signatures and wise words of past visitors. Convenient location. Ceramic tiles and brick archways complement a welcoming courtyard and dining/TV room. Wheelchair-accessible. Breakfast included; dinner €5-6. Laundry €6. Free Internet access. Luggage storage available. Room lockout 11am-2:30pm; no hostel lockout. Curfew 2am. Reserve online a week ahead, especially during summer. 9-bed dorms €22; 6-bed dorms €24; 4-bed dorms €26; singles €35. MC/V. ❷

■ **Istituto Gould,** V. dei Serragli 49 (☎21 25 76; www.istitutogould.it), in Oltrarno. Take bus #36 or 37 from the station to the 2nd stop across the river. The building is not well marked; look for the signs of the larger Istituto Gould complex, then buzz yourself into the courtyard. 97 beds, great common spaces, and a large colonnaded courtyard create a truly comfortable atmosphere. Reception M-F 8:45am-1pm and 3-7:30pm, Sa 9am-1:30pm and 2:30-6pm. 3- or 4-bed dorms €21, with bath €24; singles €36/43; doubles €52/62. MC/V. ❷

Ostello Santa Monaca, V. Santa Monaca 6 (☎26 83 38; fax 28 01 85). Follow directions to Istituto Gould, but turn right on V. S. Monaca. 114 beds stacked in high-ceilinged rooms. Friendly management. Kitchen facilities. Breakfast €2.70-3.80; lunch or dinner €10.50. Hot water for showers 7-9am and 2-11pm. Laundry €6.50 per 5kg. Internet access €3 per hr. Max.7-night stay. Reception daily 6am-1pm and 2pm-1am; June-Sept. arrive before 9am. Lockout 10am-2pm. Curfew 2am. Reserve by fax 3 days ahead. 16- to 22-bed dorms €17; 10-bed dorms €17.50; 8-bed dorms €18; 6-bed dorms €18.50; 4-bed dorms €19. AmEx/MC/V. ❶

Ostello della Gioventù Europa Villa Camerata (HI), V. Augusto Righi 2-4 (☎60 14 51; fax 61 03 00). Take bus #17 outside train station (near track #5), or from P. dell'Unità; ask for Salviatino stop. Walk 10min. up driveway. Tidy and crowded, this beautiful but remote villa has an arcade, bar, and TV with English-language movies nightly at 9pm. 4, 6, 8, or 12 beds per room. Breakfast included; dinner €9. Laundry €5.20. Max. 3-night stay. Reception 7am-12:30pm and 1pm-midnight. Lockout 10am-2pm. Strict midnight curfew. Dorms €21.50. HI-members discount €3.50. MC/V. ❷

Pensionato Pio X, V. dei Serragli 106 (☎22 50 44; www.hostelpiox.it), just beyond Istituto Gould, in the courtyard on the right. Clean rooms in a quiet area, with 3-6 beds per room. Co-ed shared bath. Check-out 9am. Curfew 1am. Dorms €17. Cash only. ❶

HOTELS

PIAZZA SANTA MARIA NOVELLA AND ENVIRONS

The budget accommodations around this *piazza* in front of the train station offer convenient access to the *duomo* and *centro storico*.

■ **Hotel Abaco,** V. dei Banchi 1 (☎23 81 919; www.abaco-hotel.it). The convenient location and 7 beautiful, extravagant rooms make this a popular choice. Named after Renaissance greats, rooms are graced with reproduction 17th-century headboards, and noise-proof windows. All rooms have phone and TV. Breakfast and A/C €5 each or free when bill is paid in cash. Laundry €7. Internet access. Valet parking €24 per day. Doubles €65-75, with bath €75-90; triples €110; quads €135. *Let's Go* discount 10% Nov.-Mar. excluding holidays. Accepts traveler's checks. MC/V. ❺

■ **Soggiorno Luna Rossa,** V. Nazionale 7, 3rd fl. (☎23 02 185). Airy rooms popular with students have trim furnishings, TV, fan, and colorful stained-glass windows. Small shared baths. Breakfast included. Internet access. Single bed €22; singles €35; doubles €85; triples €100; quads €140. Cash only. ❷

Hotel Elite, V. della Scala 12 (☎21 53 95; fax 21 38 32). Exit train station right on V. degli Orti Oricellari, which leads to V. della Scala; turn left. Friendly family owners make reservations for guests at Uffizi and other sights. Wooden stair leads to 10 well-maintained rooms, all with TV, phone, and A/C. Quieter rooms in the back have enormous bathrooms. Singles with shower €50, with bath €70; doubles €75/90; triples €110; quads €130. MC/V. ❶

Hotel Giappone, V. dei Banchi 1 (☎21 00 90; www.hotelgiappone.com). 10 refined rooms sport large beds, phone, TV, A/C, and Internet connections. Immaculate shared bath. Singles €50, with bath €55; doubles €65; triples €85. MC/V. ❶

Albergo Margaret, V. della Scala 25 (☎21 01 38; www.dormireintoscana.it/margaret). An English-speaking staff runs 7 rooms with TV and A/C. Curfew midnight. June-Aug. singles €60; doubles with shower €80, with full bath €90. Discounts Sept.-May and for longer stays. Cash only. ❶

OLD CITY (NEAR THE DUOMO)

Closest to Florence's most famous monuments, this area is full of high-quality accommodations that are also extremely expensive. Follow V. de' Panzani from the train station, and turn left on V. dei Cerretani to reach the *duomo*.

▨ **Locanda Orchidea,** Borgo degli Albizi 11 (☎24 80 346; www.hotelorchideaflorence.it). Turn left off V. Proconsolo from the *duomo*. Dante's wife was born in this 12th-century *palazzo*, built around a still-intact tower. Rooms with marble floors and famous Renaissance prints; some with garden view. Friendly, helpful, native English-speaking management. Clean shared baths; some rooms with shower. Singles €55; doubles €75; triples with shower €100; quads €120. Prices drop €10 in low season. Cash only. ❶

▨ **Hotel Il Perseo,** V. dei Cerretani 1 (☎21 25 04; www.hotelperseo.com). Exit the train station and take V. de' Panzani, which becomes V. dei Cerretani. Aussie-Italian couple and English-speaking staff welcome travelers to 20 sophisticated rooms and large, gleaming baths. All have fans, satellite TV, and free Internet access; some have views of the *duomo*. Intimate bar and TV lounge decorated with proprietor's art. Breakfast included. Valet parking €24 per day. Singles €85-95; doubles €110-125; triples €135-155; quads €160-180. AmEx/MC/V for min. 2-night stay. ❺

Relais Cavalcanti, V. Pellicceria 2 (☎21 09 62; www.relaiscavalcanti.com), steps from P. della Repubblica. Mother-daughter owners Anna and Francesca welcome guests to gold-trimmed rooms with antique wardrobes and double-paned windows to keep your evening peaceful. Look for the cookie jar and English-language magazines in the shared kitchen. All rooms have bath, A/C, phone, TV, and fridge. Free luggage storage. Singles €70-100; doubles €90-125; triples €120-155. *Let's Go* discount 10%. MC/V. ❶

Tourist House Il Porcellino, P. del Mercato Nuovo 4 (☎28 26 86; www.hotelporcellino.com). In one of Florence's oldest buildings. Brick arches poke out from white walls in rooms with wrought-iron beds, handpainted furniture, bath, TV, and phone. Rooms can be noisy; request one at the back. 3 rooms with A/C. Pay for portion of stay in advance. Singles €65-70; doubles €96-115. AmEx/MC/V. ❶

VIA NAZIONALE AND ENVIRONS

From P. della Stazione, V. Nazionale leads to budget hotels that are a short walk from both the *duomo* and the train station. The buildings on V. Nazionale, V. Faenza, V. Fiume, and V. Guelfa are filled with inexpensive establishments, but rooms facing the street may be noisy due to throngs of pedestrians. Women should use caution when walking alone in this area at night.

▨ **Katti House/Soggiorno Annamaria,** V. Faenza 21 (☎21 34 10; www.kattihouse.com). From the train station, take V. Nazionale for 1 block, and turn right on V. Faenza. Katti's well-kept lodgings feature handmade drapes and 400-year-old antiques. Attentive staff. 5 large rooms have TV, A/C, and bath. Friendly owners rent an additional 4 rooms and a newly furnished apartment with TV, A/C, and bath, down the street at **Soggiorno Annamaria,** V. Faenza 24. 6th-century building features artfully tiled floors, frescoed ceilings, and immaculate bathrooms. Singles €60-75; doubles €75-120; triples €100; quads €120; 2-bedroom apartment €150. Prices drop significantly Nov.-Mar. MC/V. ❺

Hotel Nazionale, V. Nazionale 22 (☎23 82 203; www.nazionalehotel.it). From train station, turn left on V. Nazionale. 9 sunny and spacious rooms overlooking a busy street. All with comfy bed and A/C. Breakfast €6. Singles €60, with bath €70; doubles €85/115; triples €115/145; quads €160/175. Extra bed €25. MC/V. ❺

Via Faenza 56. These 4 *pensioni* under the same roof, all with the same amenities, are among the best deals in the area. From V. Nazionale, turn left on V. Faenza.

Pensione Azzi (☎21 38 06; www.hotelazzi.com), enter on ground fl. next door to main building. Presents itself as an artists' inn with stylish prints on the walls, but all travelers will appreciate the friendly management, relaxing terrace, fluffy towels, and 21 large rooms with bath and Internet access. Splurge on the huge suite with a whirlpool. Wheelchair-accessible. Breakfast included. Singles €55-70; doubles €80-110. Extra bed €25. AmEx/MC/V. ❹

Hotel Anna's (☎23 02 714; www.hotelannas.com), 2nd fl. The only 2-star option in the main building features 7 large, bright rooms with TV, minibar, phone, and A/C. Breakfast €5. Singles €61, with bath €80; doubles €80/100; triples €75-130. AmEx/MC/V. ❹

Locanda Paola (☎21 36 82), 3rd fl. 28 beds in 7 bright, minimalist rooms with plush armchairs. Breakfast and Internet access included. Curfew 2am. Dorms €33. MC/V. ❸

Albergo Armonia (☎21 11 46), 1st fl. American film posters and antique, black and white photos adorn 7 basic rooms with high ceilings and wooden beds. Shared baths. Internet access available. Min. 2-night stay. Singles €42; doubles €50-60; triples €75; quads €100. Extra bed €25. Prices drop in winter. Cash only. ❹

Via Faenza 69. 2 comfortable, no-frills accommodations under the same roof:

Locanda Giovanna (☎/fax 23 81 353; www.albergogiovanna.it), top floor. 7 fair-sized, well-kept rooms, some with garden views. Cheerful staff. Singles €35, with bath €40; doubles €60/70; triples €60/85. Prices drop about €5 in winter. Cash only. ❸

Hotel Nella/Pina (☎26 54 346), 1st and 2nd fl. 14 basic but functional rooms with wood paneling and clean shared bath. Nella rooms have A/C, phone, and satellite TV. Pina: singles €47; doubles €65. Nella: singles €55, with bath €60; doubles €85. Extra bed €20. *Let's Go* discount 10%. AmEx/MC/V. ❹

NEAR PIAZZA SAN MARCO AND THE UNIVERSITY

This area is calmer and quieter than its proximity to the *centro* and university would suggest. All accommodations listed are within a few blocks of the beautiful, untouristed Chiesa di San Marco. To reach this neighborhood, exit the train station and turn left on V. Nazionale. Then turn right on V. Guelfa, which intersects V. San Gallo and V. Cavour.

▨**Albergo Sampaoli,** V. S. Gallo 14 (☎28 48 34; www.hotelsampaoli.it). Clean, comfortable rooms with fans; some have balcony. Large common room. Fridge available. Free Internet access with 30min. limit. Singles €25-48, with bath €30-60; doubles €35-65/45-84; triples €75-114; quads €90-140. Extra bed €25. MC/V; cash preferred. ❷

Hotel Tina, V. San Gallo 31 (☎48 35 19; www.hoteltina.it). Small *pensione* with blue carpets and bright bedspreads. Cozy sitting room stocks international magazines. Carpeted rooms with A/C and phone. Larger shared baths upstairs. Doubles with shower €46-65; triples €63-88; quads €80-120. Extra bed €25. MC/V. ❹

Hotel Giglio, V. Cavour 85 (☎48 66 21; www.hotelgiglio.fi.it). Fantastic, professional staff and an overflow of luxuries—hardwood floors, embroidered drapes, ornate furnishings, fluffy towels, and a price tag to match the extra perks. All rooms have bath, A/C, TV, safe, and phone. Breakfast included. Internet access €2.50 per 30min. Singles €85-115; doubles €105-155; triples €145-180; quads €150-160. *Let's Go* discount. AmEx/MC/V. ❺

IN THE OLTRARNO

Across the Arno and only 10min. from the *duomo*, this area offers a respite from the busy *centro*. From Chiesa di San Spirito to Palazzo Pitti and the Boboli gardens, there are enough sights nearby to make this an attractive location, and a significant population of bohemian students keep the atmosphere lively.

▨ **Hotel La Scaletta,** V. Guicciardini 13 (☎28 30 28; www.hotellascaletta.it). Cross the Ponte Vecchio and continue on V. Guicciardini. 14 gorgeous rooms filled with antiques. All rooms have A/C. Rooftop terrace with spectacular view of Boboli Gardens. Breakfast included. Singles €55-100; doubles €70-140; triples €85-160; quads €100-180. *Let's Go* discount €10 with cash payment. MC/V. ❹

CAMPING

Campeggio Michelangelo, V. Michelangelo 80 (☎68 11 977; www.ecvacanze.it), beyond Ple. Michelangelo. Take bus #13 from the station (15min., last bus 11:25pm). Very crowded, but offers a distant vista of the city and a shaded olive grove. Market and bar available for use. Internet access €7.50 per hr. Linen €2. Towels €1. Laundry €7. Reception daily 7am-11pm. Apr.-Nov. tent rental €15.50. €10.50 per person, €12 per tent, €6 per car, €4.60 per motorcycle. MC/V over €100. ❶

Villa Camerata, V. A. Righi 2-4 (☎60 14 51; fax 61 03 00). Take bus #17 outside train station (near track #5), or from P. dell'Unità across from station; ask driver for Salviatino stop. Same reception and same entrance as HI hostel, with basic but comfortable, shaded sites. Breakfast at hostel €2. 6-night max. stay. Reception 7am-12:30pm and 1pm-midnight. Check-out 7-10am. €8 per person, €5.50 with camping card; €7 per tent; bungalows €50. MC/V. ❶

▣ FOOD

Florentine cuisine developed from the peasant fare of the surrounding countryside. Characterized by saltless bread and rustic dishes prepared with fresh ingredients and simple recipes, Tuscan food ranks among Italy's best. White beans and olive oil are two staple ingredients. A famous specialty is *bruschetta*, toasted bread doused with olive oil and garlic, usually topped with tomatoes, and basil. For *primi*, Florentines favor the Tuscan classics *minestra di fagioli* (a white bean and garlic soup) and *ribollita* (hearty bean, bread, and black cabbage stew). Florence's classic *secondo* is *bistecca alla Fiorentina* (thick sirloin steak); locals order it *al sangue* (very rare; literally "bloody"), though it's also available *al punto* (medium) or *ben cotto* (well-done). The best local cheese is *pecorino*, made from sheep's milk. A liter of house wine usually costs €3.50-6 in a trattoria, but stores sell bottles cheaply (€2.50). Avoid ordering soda at restaurants; it often costs over €3 per can, though prices are often not marked on menus. The local dessert is *cantuccini di prato* (hard almond cookies with egg yolk) dipped in *vinsanto* (a rich dessert wine made from raisins).

Buy fresh produce at the **Mercato Centrale,** between V. Nazionale and S. Lorenzo. (Open June-Sept. M-Sa 7:30am-2pm; Oct.-May Sa 7am-2pm and 4-8pm.) For basics, head to the **STANDA,** V. Pietrapiana 1r. Turn right on V. del Proconsolo and the first left on Borgo degli Albizi. Continue straight through P. G. Salvemini; the supermarket is on the left. (Open M-Sa 8am-9pm, Su 9am-9pm. MC/V.) **Ruth's Kosher Vegetarian,** V. Luigi Carlo Farini 2/A, serves kosher fare on the second floor of the building to the right of the synagogue. (☎ 24 80 888; kosherruth@katamail.com. *Primi* €7, *secondi* €9-18. Open M-F and Su 12:30-2:30pm and 7:30-10:30pm. AmEx/MC/V.) Several health-food markets cater to vegetarians. The two best draw inspiration from the American book **Sugar Blues**. One is at V. XXVII Aprile 46r/48r, 5min. from the *duomo*. (☎ 48 36 66. Open M-Sa 9am-1:30pm and 5-7:30pm, Su 9am-1:30pm. Closed Aug. 1wk. V.) The other, renamed **Ha-Tha Maya**, is next to the Istituto Gould, in the Oltrarno at V. dei Serragli 57r. (☎ 26 83 78. Open daily 8am-1:30pm and 4:30-8pm. Closed Aug. Sa afternoon. MC/V.)

OLD CITY (NEAR THE DUOMO)

▨ **Osteria de' Benci,** V. de' Benci 13r (☎ 234 49 23), on the corner of V. dei Neri. Friendly owners serve Tuscan classics like *carpaccio* (thinly sliced beef; €14) at this locally known hot spot. *Primi* €9, *secondi* €9-14. Cover €3.30. Open M-Sa 1-2:45pm and 7:30-11:45pm. Reservations recommended. AmEx/MC/V. ❹

▨ **Acqua al 2,** V. della Vigna Vecchia 40r (☎ 28 41 70), behind the Bargello. A snug, air-conditioned restaurant popular with young Italians and foreigners. The *assaggio* (a selection of pastas; €8) and *filetto al mirtillo* (steak in a blueberry sauce; €14.50) demand a taste. Salads from €7. *Primi* around €7, *secondi* €8-19. Cover €1. Service 10%. Open daily 7pm-1am. Reservations strongly recommended. AmEx/MC/V. ❸

▨ **Trattoria Anita,** V. del Parlascio 2r (☎ 21 86 98), behind Palazzo Vecchio. Traditionally Tuscan in design and cuisine. Fare includes filling pastas and an array of meat dishes from roast chicken to *bistecca alla Fiorentina*. Outgoing staff engages in friendly banter. Clientele is frequently young and American, so you can puzzle out the menu together. *Primi* €5, *secondi* from €6. Fantastic lunch *menù* €6. Cover €1. Open M-Sa noon-2:30pm and 7-10pm. AmEx/MC/V. ❷

Danny Rock, V. de' Pandolfini 13r (☎ 23 40 307), 3 blocks northwest of the Bargello. Casual pizzeria with outdoor patio and large dining room favored by locals; turns into a hot night spot after hours. Check the specials, as they often feature toppings from different Italian regions. Pizza from €5. Cover €2. Open M-Th 12:15-3pm and 7:30pm-1am, F 12:15-3pm and 7:30pm-1:30am, Sa 7:30pm-2am, Su noon-3pm and 7:15pm-1am. Closed July-Aug. Su mornings. MC/V. ❷

SANTA MARIA NOVELLA AND ENVIRONS

▨ **Il Latini,** V. dei Palchetti 6r (☎ 21 09 16; www.illatini.com). You'll see the crowd outside before you see the restaurant. Convivial spirit pervades this old favorite with solid Tuscan classics. *Bistecca alla Fiorentina* (€16) is a crowd-pleaser. Waiters keep house wine flowing. *Primi* €6-8, *secondi* €10-18. Open Tu-Su 12:30-2:30pm and 7:30-10:30pm. Reservations recommended. AmEx/MC/V. ❸

▨ **Trattoria Contadino,** V. Palazzuolo 71r (☎ 23 82 673). Casual, home-style meals. Dining room has black-and-white decor and a relaxed atmosphere. Only offers a *menù* (€10-11), including *primo, secondo*, bread, and 0.25L of house wine. Open M-Sa 11am-3pm and 6-9:30pm. AmEx/MC/V. ❷

Tre Merli, V. del Moro 11r (☎ 28 70 62). Another entrance on V. de' Fossi 12r. Sumptuous meals served in a dining room close to the river with cushioned banquettes, matching ceramic tableware, and soft, red light. Talented chef prepares tender, delicious dishes like *spaghettino all'Imperiale* (with mussels, clams, and shrimp; €13.50). Delightful owner Massimo welcomes *Let's Go* readers with a free glass of wine and 10% discount. *Primi* €6.50-12, *secondi* €12-18.50. Lunch *menù* €12. Cover €2. Open daily 11am-10:30pm. AmEx/MC/V. ❸

THE STATION AND UNIVERSITY QUARTER

Trattoria Zà-Zà, P. del Mercato Centrale 26r (☎21 54 11). Wooden ceilings, brick arches, and wine racks greet diners. Outdoor patio is perfect for a summer dinner. Try the *tris* (bean and vegetable soup; €7) or the *tagliata di manzo* (beef; €14-18). Cover €2. Open daily 11am-11pm. Reservations recommended. AmEx/MC/V. ❹

Trattoria Mario, V. Rosina 2r, around the corner from P. del Mercato Centrale. Tightly packed tables and outgoing staff help you to get acquainted with fellow diners immediately. Incredible pasta, cheap eats, and enthusiastic following of Florentines and foreigners in the know. *Primi* €3.10-6, *secondi* €3.10-10.50. Cover €0.50. Open M-Sa noon-3:30pm. Closed most of Aug. Cash only. ❶

Ristorante Il Vegetariano, V. delle Ruote 30r (☎47 50 30), off V. San Gallo. True to its name, this self-service restaurant is popular with students and locals and fills the vegetarian niche, offering fresh, filling dishes in a peaceful bamboo garden or indoor dining rooms. Salads €4-5. *Primi* from €5, *secondi* from €6. Open Sept.-July Tu-F 12:30-3pm and 7:30pm-midnight, Sa-Su 7:30pm-midnight. Cash only. ❷

THE OLTRARNO

all'Antico Ristoro Di' Cambi, V. San Onofrio 1r (☎21 71 34; www.anticoristorodi-cambi.it). Prosciutto hangs from the beautifully restored 5th-century ceilings. 3rd-generation owner Stefano serves up Florentine specialities like *bistecca alla fiorentina* (€4 per 100g). Choose among over 100 types of wine (€10-300 per bottle). Lemon sorbet (€4) is the perfect ending. *Primi* €6-8, *secondi* €7-16. Cover €1. Open M-Sa noon-3pm and 7:30pm-midnight. Closed 2wk. in mid-Aug. AmEx/MC/V. ❷

Il Borgo Antico, P. Santo Spirito 6r (☎21 04 37). Trendy spot with many student customers. Pastas and fantastic salads (€7) with fresh ingredients such as shrimp, avocado, or fresh mozzarella. Pizza €7. *Primi* €7, *secondi* €13-18. Cover €2. Open daily noon-midnight. Reservations recommended. AmEx/MC/V. ❹

La Mangiatoia, P. San Felice 8r (☎22 40 60). Cross Ponte Vecchio, continue on V. Guicciardini, and pass Palazzo Pitti. Grab a table in the back dining room, or sit at the stone counter to watch the cooks baking pizza in a brick oven. Satisfying pasta and quality local fare. Extensive takeout menu. Pizza €4.50-8. *Primi* €4-5.50, *secondi* €5-9. Cover €1.50. Open Tu-Su 11am-3pm and 6:30-10pm. AmEx/MC/V. ❷

GELATERIE AND PASTICCERIE

Grom, V. del Campanile (☎21 61 58), off P. del Duomo. The kind of *gelato* you'll be talking about in 50 years. As fresh as it gets; sublimely balanced texture. Cups from €2. Open daily Apr.-Sept. 10:30am-midnight, Oct.-Mar. 10:30am-11pm. ❶

Hemingway, P. Piatellina 9 (☎28 47 87; www.hemingway.fi.it). An extensive selection of chocolate drinks and sweets make Hemingway a delight. Black-and-white photos keep it classy. Free Wi-Fi weekdays until 9pm. Coffee €3.50-6.50. Mixed drinks €7. Chocolate tasting €8. Open M-Th 4:30pm-1am, F-Sa 4:30pm-2am, Su 2pm-1am. ❶

Gelateria dei Neri, V. dei Neri 20-22r (☎21 00 34). Watch as dozens of delicious flavors are mixed before your eyes. *Crema Giotto* (a blend of coconut, almond, and hazelnut) is incredible. *Gelato* from €1.40. *Granita* from €1.50. Cash only. ❶

Vivoli, V. Isole delle Stinche 7r (☎29 23 34), behind the Bargello. A household name of Florentine *gelaterie*. Pint-sized interior and even smaller portions, but specialties like *crema caffè* (a shot of espresso in a creamy *gelato*-lined mug; €3.50) is like nothing you've ever tasted before. Pay first and order with receipt. Cups from €1.60. Open Tu-Sa 7:30am-1am, Su 9:30am-1am. AmEx/MC/V. ❶

TUSCANY

Perche No! V. dei Tavolini 19r (☎23 98 969). In refreshing flavors like green tea and mango, this *gelato* is so light and tasty you'll never want it to end. Cups from €1.80. Open M and W-Su in summer 10am-1am; in winter 10am-8pm. Cash only. ❶

Carabè, V. Ricasoli 60r (☎28 94 76; www.gelatocarabe.com). Enjoy pistachio, *nocciola*, and the unusual *susine* (plum). Owners Antonio and Loredana get the lemons for their *gelato di limone* from Sicily every week. The *granita* (from €2.50) is outstanding, particularly *mandorle* (almond) and *more* (blackberry). Cups from €2. Open daily May-Sept. 9am-midnight; Oct. and Mar.-Apr. noon-midnight. Cash only. ❶

La Loggia degli Albizi, Borgo degli Albizi 39r, (☎24 79 574). A hidden treasure, this bakery offers an escape from the tourist masses. Pastries from €0.80. Coffee from €0.80, at table €1.50. Open M-Sa 7am-8pm. ❶

ARTIFICIAL AVOIDANCE. *Gelato* is said to have been invented in Florence centuries ago by the Buontalenti family; you'll want to make sure you get the most authentic kind. Before shelling out €1.50 for a *piccolo cono* (small cone), assess the establishment's quality by looking at the banana flavor: if it's bright yellow, it's from a mix—keep walking. If it's slightly gray, real bananas were used. Likewise, steer clear of bright yellow lemon *gelato;* fresh lemons make white-colored *gelato*. Metal bins also signify homemade *gelato*, whereas plastic tubs indicate mass production.

ENOTECHE (WINE BARS)

Check out an *enoteca* to sample some of Italy's finest wines. A meal can often be made out of free side-dishes (cheeses, olives, toast and spreads, and salami).

Enoteca Alessi, V. delle Oche 27/29r (☎21 49 66; fax 23 96 987), 1 block from the *duomo*. Among Florence's finest, stocking over 1000 wines in the cavernous interior. Doubling as a chocolate and candy store, it offers nibbles between sips. Open M-F 9am-1pm and 3:30-7:30pm. AmEx/MC/V. ❷

Enoteca Fuori Porta, V. del Monte alle Croci 10r (☎23 42 483; www.fuoriporta.it), in the shadows of San Miniato. This more casual *enoteca* is free of tourists but crowded with young Italians. Reasonable meals of traditional Tuscan pasta, with an extensive *bruschette* (€1-2.50) and *crostoni* (€4.50-7.50) menu. On the way down from Ple. Michelangelo, it's a great alternative to the expensive hilltop cafes. Cover €1.50. Open daily noon-4pm and 7-10pm. Closed Aug. Su. MC/V. ❷

⦿ SIGHTS

Considering the *duomo* views, the perfection of San Spirito's nave, and the overwhelming array of art in the Uffizi Gallery, it's hard to take a wrong turn in Florence. For comprehensive listings on museum openings, check out www.firenzeturismo.it. To make phone reservations, call **Firenze Musei.** (☎29 48 83; www.firenzemusei.it. Open M-F 8:30am-6:30pm, Sa 8:30am-12:30pm.)

PIAZZA DEL DUOMO AND ENVIRONS

▨**THE DUOMO (CATTEDRALE DI SANTA MARIA DEL FIORE).** In 1296 the city fathers commissioned Arnolfo di Cambio to erect a cathedral so magnificent that it would be "impossible to make it either better or more beautiful with the industry and power of man." Arnolfo succeeded, designing a massive nave with the confidence that by the time it was completed (1418), technology would have advanced enough to provide a solution to erect a dome. It was Filippo Brunelleschi, after studying Classical methods of sculpture, who devised the ingenious techniques needed to construct a dome large enough for the nave. For the *duomo*'s sublime crown, now known simply as **Brunelleschi's Dome,** the architect designed a revolutionary, double-shelled structure that incorporated self-supporting, interlocking bricks. During construction, Brunelleschi built kitchens, sleeping rooms, and lavatories between the two walls of the cupola so the masons would never have to descend. The **Museo dell'Opera del Duomo** (p. 438) chronicles Brunelleschi's engineering feats in an in-depth exhibit. A 16th-century Medici rebuilding campaign removed the *duomo*'s incomplete Gothic-Renaissance facade. The walls remained naked until 1871, when Florentine architect Emilio de Fabris won the commission to create a facade in the Neo-Gothic style. Especially when viewed from the southern side, the patterned green-white-and-red marble walls are impressively grand.

Today, the *duomo* claims the world's third-longest nave, after St. Peter's in Rome and St. Paul's in London. It rises 100m into the air, making it as high as the hills surrounding Florence and visible from nearly every corner of the city. Though ornately decorated on the outside, the church's interior is rather chilly and stark; unadorned dark stone was believed to encourage devotion through modesty. One notable exception to this sober style is the extravagant frescoes on the dome's ceiling, where visions of the apocalypse glare down at visitors in a stunning display of color and light. Notice, too, Paolo Uccello's celebrated monument to the mercenary captain Sir John Hawkwood on the cathedral's left wall and his *trompe l'oeil* clock on the back wall. This 24hr. timepiece runs backward, starting its cycle at sunset, when the *Ave Maria* is traditionally sung. (Duomo open M-W and F 10am-5pm, Th 10am-4:30pm, Sa 10am-4:45pm, Su 1:30-4:45pm; 1st Sa of the month 10am-3:30pm. Shortest wait at 10am and just before opening. Mass daily 7am, 12:30pm, and 5-7pm. Free. Ask inside the entrance to the left about free guided tours in English.) Climb the 463 steps inside the dome to Michelangelo's lantern for an expansive view of the city from the external gallery. Halfway up, visitors can enjoy a great view of the dome's frescoed interior just inches from their faces. (Entrance on southern side of the duomo. ☎23 02 885. Open M-F 8:30am-7pm, Sa 8:30am-5:40pm. €6.)

BATTISTERO. Though built between the 5th and 9th centuries, the octagonal *battistero* was believed in Dante's time to have originally been a Roman temple. The building's exterior has the same green- and white-marble patterning as the *duomo*, and the interior contains magnificent 13th-century, Byzantine-style mosaics. Dante was christened here, and he later drew upon the murals of damnation as inspiration for his *Inferno.* Florentine artists competed fiercely for the commission to execute the famous **bronze doors,** which depict scenes from the Bible in exquisite detail. In 1330 the winner, Andrea Pisano, left Pisa to cast the first set of doors, which now guard the southern entrance (facing the river). In 1401 the cloth guild announced a competition to choose an artist for the remaining two sets. Two young artists, Brunelleschi and Ghiberti, were asked to work in partnership to enter the competition, but the uncompromising Brunelleschi left in an arrogant huff, allowing Ghiberti to complete the project alone. Their separate entries into the competition are displayed side by side in the Bargello (p. 442). Ghiberti's project, completed in 1425, was so admired that he immediately received the commission to forge the final set of doors. The ⬛**Gates of Paradise**, as Michelangelo reportedly called them, are nothing like Pisano's earlier portals. Originally intended for the northern side, they so impressed the Florentines that they were moved to their current eastern position facing the *duomo*. Best admired in the morning or late evening after the tourist crowds have thinned, the doors are truly a masterpiece, each individual panel a work of art itself. *(Opposite the duomo. ☎23 02 885. Open M-Sa noon-7pm, Su 8:30am-2pm. Mass M-F 10:30 and 11:30am. €3. Audio tour €2.)*

CAMPANILE. Also called "Giotto's Tower," the 82m bell tower next to the *duomo* has a marble exterior that matches its neighboring monuments. Three great Renaissance minds contributed to its construction: Giotto drew the design and laid the foundation in 1334, but died soon thereafter; Andrea Pisano took over the project and added two stories to the tower; and Francesco Talenti completed construction in 1359. The 414 steps to the top offer stunning views of the *duomo*, baptistry, and city skyline. The best time to make the trek is in the early morning, when skies are smog-free. *(☎23 02 885. Open daily 8:30am-7:30pm. €6.)*

⬛**ORSANMICHELE.** Built in 1337 as a granary, the Orsanmichele was converted into a church after a great fire convinced city officials to move grain operations outside the city. The loggia structure and ancient grain chutes are still visible from the outside. Secular and spiritual concerns mingle in the statues that are situated within the small niches along the facade. Works include Ghiberti's *St. Matthew* (1419-20) and a copy of *St. John the Baptist* (1414-16), Donatello's *St. George* (1416) and *St. Mark* (1411), and Giambologna's *St. Luke* (1405-10). Inside, a Gothic tabernacle designed by Andrea Orcagna encases Bernardo Daddi's miraculous *Madonna* (1347). The top floor occasionally hosts special exhibits. *(V. Arte della Lana, between the duomo and P. della Signoria. ☎28 49 44. Open Tu-Su 10am-5pm. Free.)*

MUSEO DELL'OPERA DEL DUOMO. Most of the *duomo*'s art resides in this modern and less-crowded museum, including a late *Pietà* by Michelangelo, up the first flight of stairs. He started working on it in his early 70s, and the soft curves and flowing lines of the marble and the limpness of Christ's body are said to reflect the artist's conception of his own mortality. Allegedly, Michelangelo severed the statue's left arm with a hammer in a fit of frustration. An over-eager apprentice touched up the work soon after, leaving lines visible on Mary Magdalene's head. Also in the collection are Donatello's wooden *St. Mary Magdalene* (1455), Donatello and Luca della Robbia's *cantorie* (choir balconies with bas-reliefs of cavorting children), and four frames from the baptistry's original Gates of Paradise. A huge wall displays all of the paintings submitted by architects in the 1870 competition for the *duomo*'s facade. *(P. del Duomo 9, behind the duomo. ☎ 23 02 885. Open M-Sa 9am-7:30pm, Su 9am-1:40pm. €6. Audio tour €4.)*

PIAZZA DELLA SIGNORIA AND ENVIRONS

From P. del Duomo, V. dei Calzaiuoli, one of the city's oldest streets, leads to P. della Signoria. Built by the Romans, V. dei Calzaiuoli now bustles with crowds, chic shops, street vendors, and *gelaterie*.

■ **UFFIZI GALLERY.** Giorgio Vasari designed this palace for Duke Cosimo in 1554 and called it the Uffizi because it housed the offices *(uffizi)* of the Medici administration. An impressive walkway between the two main branches of the building, full of street performers, human statues, and vendors hawking trinkets and prints, leads from P. della Signoria to the Arno River; the street is surrounded every morning by a line of art-hungry tourists waiting to enter the museum. Beautiful statues overlook the walkway from niches in the columns; play spot-the-Renaissance-man and try to find da Vinci, Machiavelli, Petrarch, and Vespucci.

> **TIP** **NO ART FOR YOU.** To avoid disappointment inside the museum, keep in mind that a few rooms are usually closed each day and famous pieces often go on temporary loan, so not all works are always available for viewing. A sign outside the ticket office lists the rooms that are closed for the day; ask when they will be open again.

Before visiting the main gallery on the second floor, stop to see the **Cabinet of Drawings and Prints** on the first floor. This exhibit includes rare sketches by Botticelli, Leonardo, Raphael, and Michelangelo. Upstairs, in a U-shaped corridor, is a collection of Hellenistic and Roman marble statues. Arranged chronologically in rooms off the corridor, the collection promises a thorough education on the Florentine Renaissance, as well as a sampling of German and Venetian art. Framing the entrance to **Room 2** are three magnificent Madonnas by Renaissance forefathers Cimabue, Duccio di Buoninsegna, and Giotto. **Room 3** features art from 14th-century Siena, including works by the Lorenzetti brothers and Simone Martini's *Annunciation*. **Rooms 5** and **6** hold examples of International Gothic art, popular in European royal courts. Check out the rounded war-horses in the *The Battle of San Romano*, Paolo Uccello's noble but slightly jumbled effort to conquer the problem of artistic perspective. **Room 7** houses two paintings by Fra Angelico (also called Beato Angelico) and a *Madonna and Child* (1426) by Masaccio. Domenico Veneziano's *Sacra Conversazione* (1445) is one of the first paintings of Mary surrounded by the saints. Piero della Francesca's double portrait of Duke Federico and his wife, Battista Sforza, stands out for its translucent color and honest detail. (A jousting accident gave the Duke's nose its unusual hooked shape.) **Room 8** has Filippo Lippi's *Madonna and Child with Two Angels* (1440).

Rooms 10-14 are a shrine to Botticelli—the resplendent *Primavera* (1478), *Pallas and the Centaur* (1482), *Birth of Venus* (1485), and *Madonna della Melagrana* (1487) glow from recent restorations. **Room 15** moves into the High Renaissance with Leonardo da Vinci's *Annunciation* (1480) and the remarkable, unfinished *Adoration of the Magi* (1481). **Room 18**, the tribune designed

TUSCANY

by Buontalenti to hold the Medici treasures, has a mother-of-pearl dome and a collection of portraits, most notably Bronzino's *Bia dei Medici* (1542), Vasari's *Lorenzo il Magnifico* (1485), and del Sarto's *Woman with the Petrarchino* (1528). Also note Rosso Fiorentino's oft-duplicated *Musician Angel* (1515). **Room 19** features Piero della Francesca's pupils, Perugino and Signorelli. **Rooms 20** and **22** detour into Northern European art. Note the contrast between Albrecht Dürer's lifelike *Adam and Eve* (1504) and Lucas Cranach's haunting, more surreal treatment of the same subject. Bellini's *Sacred Allegory* (1490) and Mantegna's *Adoration of the Magi* (1495) highlight **Room 23.**

Room 25 showcases Florentine works, including Michelangelo's only oil painting in Florence, *Doni Tondo* (1503). Raphael's *Madonna of the Goldfinch* (1505) and Andrea del Sarto's *Madonna of the Harpies* (1517) rest in **Room 26. Room 28** displays Titian's sensual *Venus of Urbino* (1538). Parmigianino's Mannerist, eerily lovely and regal *Madonna of the Long Neck* (1534), now in **Room 29,** was discovered unfinished in the artist's studio following his death. Works by Paolo Veronese and Tintoretto dominate **Rooms 31** and **32. Room 33,** in fact a corridor, holds Vasari's *Vulcan's Forge* (1545). The staircase vestibule, **Rooms 36-40,** contains an ancient Roman marble boar, inspiration for the brass Porcellino in Florence's Mercato Nuovo. **Rooms 41** and **43-45** house works by Rembrandt, Goya, Rubens, and Caravaggio, currently on display after lengthy restorations. The Uffizi architect, Vasari, designed a secret corridor running between the Palazzo Vecchio and the Medici's Palazzo Pitti. The corridor runs through the Uffizi and over the Ponte Vecchio, housing more art, including a special collection of artists' self-portraits. The corridor is opened sporadically and requires both a separate entrance fee and advance booking. (*Off P. della Signoria.* ☎ *23 88 651. Open Tu-Su 8:15am-6:50pm. €6.50. Save hours of waiting by reserving tickets in advance for €3 extra. Pick up reserved tickets at Door 1 before entering at Door 3 on the other side of the walkway. Audio tour €4.65.*)

⬥TIP⬦ **MAKE FRIENDS WITH THE UFFIZI.** If you plan on visiting 3 or more museums in Florence, consider obtaining an **Amici degli Uffizi card.** Students under 26 pay €25 for the card (regularly €60) and receive free admission to the Uffizi and all state museums in Florence (including the Accademia and Bargello). It includes just one visit to each of the museums and gets you straight to the front of the line. For more information, call Amici degli Uffizi, V. Lorenzo il Magnifico 1, ☎ 47 94 422, or email amicidegliuffizi@waf.it.

▨**PALAZZO VECCHIO.** Arnolfo del Cambio designed this fortress-like *palazzo*, built between 1299 and 1304, as the seat of the *comune*'s government. The massive brown stone facade has a thin, square tower rising from its center and turrets along the top. Its apartments once served as living quarters for members of the *signoria* (city council) during their two-month terms, when they prayed, ate, and lived together in complete isolation from the outside world. The building later became the Medici family home. In 1470, Michelozzo decorated the **courtyard,** now open to the public. He filled it with religious frescoes and placed ornate stone pediments over every door and window. The courtyard also has stone lions and a replica of Verrocchio's 15th-century *Putto* fountain. Once inside the palace, visitors can take advantage of numerous tour opportunities. The worthwhile **Activities Tour ticket** includes both the "Secret Routes" and "Invitation to Court" tours. "Secret Routes" fulfills Clue® fans' fantasies of hidden passages with visits to stairwells tucked in walls behind beautiful oil paintings, an area between the ornate ceiling and the roof of the Salone del Cinquecento, and the private chambers of Duke

Cosimo I dei Medici. "Invitation to Court" includes reenactments of Medici court life, complete with a tour guide playing Cosimo's wife, Eleonora di Toledo, decked out in Renaissance finery. "The Encounter with Giorgio Vasari" tours through the **Monumental Apartments** with a guide playing the part of Vasari, Duke Cosimo's court painter and architect and a biographer of Renaissance artists. The Apartments house the *palazzo*'s extensive art collections. The rooms contain 12 interactive terminals with virtual tours of the building's history and detailed computer animations. (☎ *27 68 224 or 27 68 558. Office open M-W and F-Su 9am-6pm, Th 9am-2pm. Tours daily in English and French. 20-person group max. Reservations required. "Monumental Apartments" tour €6, ages 18-25 €4.50; Activities Tour €8/5.50.*)

The city commissioned Michelangelo and Leonardo da Vinci to paint opposite walls of the **Salone dei Cinquecento,** the meeting room of the Grand Council of the Republic. Although they never completed the frescoes, their preliminary sketches for the *Battle of Cascina* and the *Battle of Anghiari* were studied by Florentine artists for years. The Salone's ceiling is so elaborately decorated with moldings and frescoes that an intricate network of beams between the ceiling and roof suspend each wall painting. The tiny **Studio di Francesco I,** designed by Vasari, has a plethora of Mannerist art, with paintings by Bronzino and Vasari as well as bronze statuettes by Giambologna and Ammannati. The mezzanine houses Bronzino's portrait of the poet Laura Battiferi and Giambologna's *Hercules and the Hydra.* (☎ *27 68 465. Open M-W and F-Su 9am-6pm, Th 9am-2pm. Palazzo Vecchio €6, ages 18-25 €4.50; courtyard free. Combined ticket with Cappella Brancacci €8/6.*)

PIAZZA DELLA SIGNORIA. With the turreted Palazzo Vecchio to the west and a corner of the Uffizi Gallery to the south, this 13th-century *piazza* is now one of the city's most touristed areas. The space fills daily with photo-snapping onlookers who return after the sun goes down for drinks and dessert at one of the many overpriced, but great people-watching cafes that line the sides of the square. With the construction of the Palazzo Vecchio, the square blossomed into Florence's civic and political center. In 1497, religious zealot Girolamo Savonarola convinced Florentines to light the Bonfire of the Vanities in the *piazza*, barbecuing some of Florence's best art, including (according to legend) all of Botticelli's secular works held in public collections. A year later, disillusioned citizens sent Savonarola up in smoke on the same spot, marked today by a comparatively discreet commemorative disc near the **Fountain of Neptune.** Monumental sculptures cluster around the Palazzo Vecchio, including Donatello's *Judith and Holofernes* (1460), a copy of Michelangelo's *David* (1504), Bandinelli's *Hercules* (1534), and Giambologna's equestrian *Cosimo I* (1567). The awkward *Neptune* (1560), to the left of the Palazzo Vecchio, so revolted Michelangelo that he decried the artist: "Oh, Ammannato, Ammannato, what lovely marble you have ruined!" Apparently, most *fiorentini* share his opinion. Called *Il Biancone* (The Big White One) in derision, *Neptune* is regularly subject to attacks of vandalism by angry aesthetes. The 14th-century stone **Loggia dei Lanzi,** adjacent to the Palazzo, originally built as a stage for civic orators, is now one of the best places in Florence to see world-class sculpture for free, including Giambologna's spiraling composition of *The Rape of the Sabines*. Indeed, as a sign near the entrance proclaims, the towering works of marble are "on par with the gallery in the Uffizi."

THE PONTE VECCHIO. Built in 1345, this is indeed Florence's oldest bridge. In the 1500s, butchers and tanners lined the bridge and dumped pig's blood and intestines in the river, creating an odor that, not surprisingly, offended the powerful bankers as they crossed the Arno on their way to their offices. In an effort to improve the area, the Medici clan kicked out the lower-class shopkeepers, and the goldsmiths and diamond-cutters moved in. Today, their descendants line the street in medieval-looking boutiques, and the bridge glitters with rows of necklaces, brooches, and charms. While technically open to vehicles, it is chiefly tourists and street musicians who swamp the roadway. The Ponte Vecchio was the only Florentine bridge to escape German bombs during WWII. A German commander who led his retreating army across the river in 1944 couldn't bear to destroy it, choosing instead to make it impassable by toppling nearby buildings. From the neighboring **Ponte alle Grazie,** the heart-melting ◪**sunset view** of the Ponte Vecchio showcases its glowing buildings and the shimmering Arno River running beneath. *(Toward P. Santa Croce. From the Uffizi, turn left on V. Georgofili and right at the river.)*

THE BARGELLO AND ENVIRONS

◪**THE BARGELLO.** In the heart of medieval Florence, this 13th-century brick fortress was once the residence of Florence's chief magistrate. Later it became a brutal prison with public executions held in its courtyard. In the 19th century, the Bargello's former elegance was restored, and it now gracefully hosts the spectacular, yet largely untouristed **Museo Nazionale,** a treasury of Florentine sculpture. On the second floor and to the right is the spacious, high-ceilinged **Salone di Donatello,** which contains Donatello's bronze *David* (c. 1430), the first free-standing nude since antiquity. This "nude" David chose to discard his clothes but is still posing in a hat and boots. David's playful expression and youthful posture provide quite the contrast to Michelangelo's determined figure of chiseled perfection in the Accademia. Donatello's earlier marble *David*, fully clothed and somewhat generic, stands near the left wall. On the right are two beautiful bronze panels of the *Sacrifice of Isaac* submitted by Ghiberti and Brunelleschi to the baptistry door competition. The next floor contains some dramatic works by Andrea del Verrochio, teacher of Leonardo da Vinci, as well as a vast collection of small bronzes and coins. Dominating the ground floor are some of Michelangelo's early works, including a debauched *Bacchus* (1496), an intense bust of *Brutus* (1540), and an unfinished *Apollo* (1530). Baccio Bandinelli's *Adam and Eve* (1504), in the same room, seem to have been captured by a snapshot in a moment of relaxed conversation. The spacious courtyard is filled with plaques of dozens of noble Florentine families' coats of arms. *(V. del Proconsolo 4, between the duomo and P. della Signoria. ☎23 88 606. Open daily 8:15am-6pm. Closed 2nd and 4th M of each month. €4. Audio tour €4.)*

BADIA. This was the site of medieval Florence's richest monastery. Buried in the interior of a residential block, a quiet respite from the busy streets, the church's simple facade belies the treasures within. Filippino Lippi's stunning *Apparition of the Virgin to St. Bernard,* one of the most appreciated paintings of the late 15th century, hangs in eerie gloom to the left of the church. Note the beautiful frescoes and Corinthian pilasters, and be sure to glance up at the intricately carved dark wood ceiling. Visitors are asked to walk silently among the white-robed monks. *(Entrance on V. Dante Alighieri, off V. Proconsolo. ☎26 44 02. Officially open to tourists M 3-6pm, but respectful visitors can walk through the church at any time.)*

MUSEO DI STORIA DELLA SCIENZA. This impressive and unique collection is well worth a visit to offset the Renaissance art overload. It boasts scientific instruments from the Renaissance, including telescopes, astrological models, clock workings, and wax models of anatomy and childbirth. The stellar **Room 4** displays a number of Galileo's tools, including his embalmed middle finger and the objective lens through which he first observed the satellites of Jupiter in 1610. Detailed English guides are available at the ticket office. *(P. dei Giudici 1,* *behind Palazzo Vecchio and the Uffizi. ☎ 26 53 11. Open M and W-F 9:30am-5pm, Tu and Sa 9:30am-1pm; Oct.-May also 2nd Su of each month 10am-1pm. €6.50, under 18 €4.)*

CASA DI DANTE. This residence is reputedly identical to the house Dante inhabited. Anyone who can read Italian and has a fascination with Dante will enjoy the displays, otherwise it's not worth the money. Displays trace the poet's life from youth to exile and pay homage to the artistic creation that immortalized him; check out Giotto's early but representative portrait of Dante on the third floor. Nearby is a facsimile of the abandoned and melancholy little church where Beatrice, Dante's unrequited love and spiritual guide in *Paradiso*, attended mass. *(Corner of V. Dante Alighieri and V. Santa Margherita, 1 block of the Bargello. Ring bell to enter. ☎ 21 94 16. Open Tu-Sa 10am-6pm, Su 10am-1pm; 1st Su of each month 10am-4pm. Closed last M and Su of each month. €4, groups over 15 €2 per person.)*

PIAZZA DELLA REPUBBLICA AND FARTHER WEST

After hours of contemplating great Florentine art, visit the area that financed it all. In the early 1420s, 72 banks operated in Florence, most in the area around the Mercato Nuovo and V. Tornabuoni. With a lower concentration of famous sights, this area is more residential and commercial, though still crowded with visitors. Surrounding cafes and stores are often overpriced.

■ **CHIESA DI SANTA MARIA NOVELLA.** The wealthiest merchants built their chapels in this church. Constructed between 1279 and 1360, the Dominican *chiesa* boasts a Romanesque-Gothic facade, considered one of the greatest masterpieces of early Renaissance architecture. The facade, made of Florentine marble, is geometrically pure and balanced, a precursor to the Classical revival of the high Renaissance. The church was originally home to Dominican friars, or *Domini canes* (Hounds of the Lord), who took a bite out of sin and corruption. Thirteenth-century frescoes covered the interior until the Medici family commissioned Vasari to paint new ones. Fortunately, Vasari spared Masaccio's powerful ■**Trinity,** the first painting to use geometric perspective. This fresco, on the left side of the nave, creates the illusion of a three-dimensional tabernacle. The **Cappella di Filippo Strozzi,** to the right of the high altar, contains frescoes by Filippo Lippi, including a cartoon-like green Adam, a woolly Abraham, and an excruciating *Torture of St. John the Evangelist* (1502). Brunelleschi's *Crucifix* stands in the **Gondi Chapel** as a response to Donatello's *Crucifix* in Santa Croce (p. 446), which Brunelleschi found to be too full of "vigorous naturalism." A cycle of Ghirlandaio frescoes covers the **Tournabuoni Chapel** behind the main altar. *(☎ 26 45 184. Open M-Th and Sa 9am-5pm. €2.70, ages 13-18 €1.50.)*

PIAZZA DELLA REPUBBLICA. The largest open space in Florence, this *piazza* teems with crowds and street performers in the evenings. An enormous arch filling in the gap over V. Strozzi marks the square's western edge. Overpriced cafes, restaurants, and *gelaterie* line the rest of the *piazza*. In 1890 the *piazza* replaced the Mercato Vecchio as the site of the city market, but has since traded market stalls for the more fashionable Guess and Pucci. The inscription *"Antico centro della città, da secolare squalore, a vita nuova restituito"* (the "ancient center of the city, squalid for centuries, restored to new life") makes a derogatory reference to the fact that the *piazza* is the site of the old Jewish ghetto. When the "liberation of the Jews" of Italy in the 1860s allowed Jews to live elsewhere, the ghetto slowly diminished. An ill-advised plan to demolish the city center's historical buildings and remodel Florence destroyed the Old Market, but an international campaign successfully thwarted the razing of the entire ghetto, leaving the present-day gathering space as a vibrant center for city life.

CHIESA DI SANTA TRINITÀ. Hoping to spend eternity as they had lived—in elite company—the most fashionable *palazzo* owners commissioned family chapels in this church. The facade, designed by Bernardo Buontalenti in the 16th century, is almost Baroque in its elaborate ornamentation, and is an exquisite example of late-Renaissance architecture. Scenes from Ghirlandaio's *Life of St. Francis* (1486) decorate the **Sassetti chapel** in the right arm of the transept. The famous altarpiece, Ghirlandaio's *Adoration of the Shepherds* (1485), is in the Uffizi. The one here is a convincing copy. *(In P. di Santa Trinità. ☎ 21 69 12. Open M-Sa 7am-noon and 4-7pm, Su 7am-noon. Free.)*

MERCATO NUOVO. Under their Corinthian-columned splendor, the loggias of the New Market have housed gold and silk traders since 1547. Today, gold falsely glints amongst the wares of the more prominent vendors selling imitation designer purses, belts, and clothes. Pietro Tacca's pleasantly plump statue, *Il Porcellino* (The Little Pig; actually a wild boar; 1612) appeared some 50 years after the market opened. Rub its snout and put a coin in the pig's mouth; if the coin drops neatly into the grate below your luck will be golden, but it still won't turn your newly purchased "Fendi" purse into real leather. *(Off V. Calimala, between P. della Repubblica and the Ponte Vecchio. Vendors hawk wares from dawn to dusk.)*

PALAZZO DAVANZATI. As Florence's 15th-century economy expanded, its bankers and merchants flaunted their new wealth by erecting grand edifices. The great boom began with construction of the Palazzo Davanzati. Today, the cavernous *palazzo* houses the **Museo della Casa Fiorentina Antica.** In 2005, the building's interior was reopened after extensive renovations. The courtyard is adorned with antique furniture, restored frescoes, and wooden doors and ornaments, giving visitors a small glimpse of the 15th-century merchants' luxury. The second floor sports wood furniture from Florentine workshops and intricately painted walls and ceilings. Check out the trap doors on the floor in the Sala dei Pappagalli. The courtyard below was open to the public, and the holes in the floor look down over the very spots of entrance below, so the rich families could monitor visitors and drop heavy stone balls (kept in wall niches nearby) if need be. *(V. Porta Rossa 13. ☎ 23 88 610. Open daily 8:50am-1:50pm. Closed 1st, 3rd, and 5th M, and 2nd and 4th Su of each month. Video screenings about the palazzo 10, 11am, and noon on 4th fl. Free.)*

SAN LORENZO AND FARTHER NORTH

ACCADEMIA. No matter how many pictures of Michelangelo's triumphant sculpture you've seen, seeing ▨**David** in his marble flesh will blow you away. From 5ft. away, Michelangelo's painstaking attention to detail—like the veins in David's hands and at the back of his knees—bring the statue to life. The sheer size of the work, and the fact that Michelangelo used a piece of stone abandoned by another artist, gives new appreciation to Michelangelo's genius. In a series of unfortunate events, the statue's base was struck by lightning in 1512, damaged by anti-Medici riots in 1527, and was finally moved here from P. della Signoria in 1873 after a stone hurled during a riot broke David's left wrist in two places. If this real *David* seems a bit different from the copy in front of the Palazzo Vecchio, there's a reason: Michelangelo intended the David to be positioned on a high pedestal and therefore exaggerated his head and torso to correct for distortion from viewing far below; in the Accademia, the statue stands on a relatively high pedestal and appears a bit less top-heavy. In the hallway leading up to the *David* are Michelangelo's four ▨**Slaves** (1520) and a *Pietà* (1499). Even today, it is hotly debated whether the statues were meant to appear unfinished. Chipping away only enough to show the figures emerging from the marble, Michelangelo remained true to his theories about "releasing" his figures from the living stone. Also worth a look are Botticelli's paintings of the Madonna as well as works by Uccello. Two panel paintings, Lippi's *Deposition* (1504) and Perugino's *Assumption* (1504), sit in the room just in front of the rotunda. The Serviti family, who commissioned the two-sided panel, disliked Perugino's depiction so much that they only displayed Lippi's portion in their church. *(V. Ricasoli 60, between the churches of San Marco and SS. Annunziata. Line for entrance without a reservation begins at V. Ricasoli 58. ☎ 23 88 609. Open Sept.-May Tu-Su 8:15am-6:50pm; June-Aug. also F until 10pm. Last entry 45min. before closing. Most areas wheelchair-accessible. May-Sept. €10; Oct.-Apr. €7.)*

■ **MUSEO DELLA CHIESA DI SAN MARCO.** Remarkable works by Fra Angelico adorn the Museo della Chiesa di San Marco, one of the most peaceful and spiritual places in Florence. A large room to the right of the courtyard contains some of the painter's major works. The 2nd floor houses Angelico's most famous *Annunciation*, across from the top of the stairwell, as well as the monks' quarters. Every cell in the convent contains its own Fra Angelico fresco, each painted in flat colors and sparse detail to facilitate the monks' somber meditation. To the right of the stairwell, **Michelozzo's library,** based on Michelangelo's work in San Lorenzo, is a simple space for reflection. In **Cells 17** and **22,** underground artwork peeks through a glass floor, excavated in the medieval period. Look also for Savonarola's cells, at the end of the northwest corridor, which display some of his relics. On the way out, the **Museo di Firenze Antica** of Florence's ancient roots is worth a quick visit. These two rooms showcase numerous archaeological fragments, mostly pieces of stone work from Etruscan and Roman buildings in the area. Be sure to peek into the church itself, next door to the museum, to admire the elaborate altar and vaulted ceiling. *(Enter at P. di San Marco 3. ☎ 23 88 608. Open M-F 8:15am-1:50pm, Sa 8:15am-6:50pm, Su 8:15am-7pm. Closed 2nd and 4th M and 1st, 3rd, and 5th Su of each month. English guides available near the entrance. €4, EU citizens 18-25 €2, over 65 or under 18 free.)*

BASILICA DI SAN LORENZO. In 1419 Brunelleschi designed this spacious basilica, another Florentine example of simple, early-Renaissance lines and proportion. Because the Medicis lent the funds to build the church, they retained artistic control over its construction. Their coat of arms, featuring five red balls, appears all over the nave, and their tombs occupy the two sacristies and the Cappella dei Principi (see below) behind the altar. The family cleverly placed Cosimo dei Medici's grave in front of the high altar, making the entire church his personal mausoleum. Donatello created two **pulpits,** one for each aisle; his *Martelli Sarcophagus* in the left transept takes the form of a wicker basket woven in marble. Michelangelo designed the church's exterior, but, disgusted by the murkiness of Florentine politics, he abandoned the project to study architecture in Rome, which accounts for the basilica's still unadorned brown-stone facade. *(☎ 26 45 184. Open M-Sa 10am-5pm; Mar.-Oct. also Su 1:30-5pm. €2.50, includes entrance to Laurentian Library.)*

The **Cappelle dei Medici** (Medici Chapels) consist of dual design contributions by Matteo Nigetti and Michelangelo. Michelangelo created and sculpted the entire **New Sacristy**—architecture, tombs, and statues—in a mature, careful style that reflects his study of Brunelleschi. Designed to house the bodies of four of the Medici family, the room contains two impressive tombs for Medici Dukes Lorenzo and Giuliano. Lounging on the tomb of the military-minded Lorenzo are the smooth, minutely rendered female Night and the muscle-bound male Day, both left provocatively "unfinished." Michelangelo rendered the hazier Dawn and Dusk with more androgynous figures for the milder-mannered Giuliano's tomb, which is closer to the entrance. Some of the artist's sketches are in the basement. *(Walk around to the back entrance in P. Madonna degli Aldobrandini. ☎ 23 88 602. Open daily 8:15am-5pm. Closed 1st, 3rd, and 5th M and 2nd and 4th Su of each month. €6.)* The adjacent **Laurentian Library** houses one of the world's most valuable manuscript collections. Michelangelo's famous entrance **portico** confirms his virtuosity; the *pietra serena* sandstone staircase is one of his most innovative architectural designs. *(☎ 21 07 60. Open daily 8:30am-1:30pm. Free with entrance to San Lorenzo.)*

MUSEO ARCHEOLOGICO. Unassuming behind its bland plaster facade, the archaeological museum has a surprisingly diverse collection. Its rooms teem with collections of statues and other monuments of the ancient Greeks, Etruscans, and Egyptians. A long, two-story gallery devoted to Etruscan jewelry runs the length of the plant-filled courtyard. In almost any other city in the world, this museum would be a major cultural highlight, but in Florence, it's possible to enjoy it without large crowds. Don't miss the *Chimera d'Arezzo*, a bronze sculpture from the late 5th century BC in **Room 14.** *(V. della Colonna 38. ☎ 23 57 50. Open M 2-7pm, Tu and Th 8:30am-7pm, W and F-Su 8:30am-2pm. €4.)*

PIAZZA SANTA CROCE AND ENVIRONS

■**CHIESA DI SANTA CROCE.** The Franciscans built this church as far away as possible from their Dominican rivals at Santa Maria Novella. Started in 1210 as a small oratory, the ascetic Franciscans ironically produced what is arguably the city's most splendid church, with a unique Egyptian cross layout. Breathtaking marble sculptures adorn the grand tombs of Florentine luminaries on both sides of the main aisle, frozen in expressions of grief and mourning. The Renaissance greats buried here include Michelangelo, who rests near the beginning of the right aisle (his tomb is by Vasari, but his body is actually buried in the floor slightly to the left); Galileo, directly opposite in the left aisle; and Machiavelli, farther down and on the right. Donatello's *Crucifix* (1412-13), which left Brunelleschi awestruck, is in the Vernio Chapel of the left transept under heavy scaffolding; the artist's gilded *Annunciation* (1435) is to the right of humanist Leonardo Bruni's tomb. The Florentines who banished Dante in 1302 eventually prepared a tomb for him here. Dante died in Ravenna in 1321, however, and, due to his exile, the literary necrophiles there never sent him back. To the right of the altar, the frescoes of the **Cappella Peruzzi** vie with those of the **Cappella Bardi.** Giotto and his school painted both, but unfortunately, the works are badly faded. While wandering through the church, note the water mark 8ft. up the walls and pillars, an enduring reminder of the 1966 flood. *(☎ 24 66 105 or 23 02 885. Open Mar. 15-Nov. 15 M-Sa 9:30am-5:30pm, Su and holidays 1-5:30pm. €5, under 18 €3.)*

The **Museo dell'Opera di Santa Croce,** which forms three sides of a peaceful courtyard, is accessible through a door from the right aisle of the church. At the end of the cloister next to the church is Brunelleschi's ■**Cappella Pazzi,** a humble marvel of perfect proportions. Its decorations include Luca della Robbia's *tondi* (circular paintings) of the apostles and Brunelleschi's moldings of the evangelists. Across the courtyard down a gravel path, a former dining hall contains Taddeo Gaddi's fresco *The Tree of the Cross* and his rendition of the *Last Supper* (1360). Also in the room is Cimabue's *Crucifixion* (1287), left in a tragic state by the 1966 flood, when the water actually carried it out into the *piazza. (Enter through the loggia in front of Cappella Pazzi. Hours same as church. Free with entrance to church.)*

SYNAGOGUE OF FLORENCE. This synagogue, also known as the **Museo del Tempio Israelitico,** sits behind a hefty iron gate and is resplendent with Sephardic domes and horseshoe arches. David Levi, a wealthy Florentine Jewish businessman, donated his fortune in 1870 for the construction of "a monumental temple worthy of Florence," in recognition of the fact that Jews were newly allowed to live and worship outside the old Jewish ghetto. Architects Micheli, Falchi, and Treves created one of Europe's most beautiful synagogues. *(V. Luigi Carlo Farini 4, at V. Pilastri. ☎24 52 52 or 24 52 53. Open M-Th and Su 10am-6pm, F 10am-2pm. €4, students €3. Includes free, informative hourly tours; book in advance.)*

CASA BUONARROTI. This small museum houses Michelangelo memorabilia and two of his most important early works, *The Madonna of the Steps* and *The Battle of the Centaurs*. Both pieces sit on the second floor and were completed by a 16-year-old Michelangelo. The panels illustrate his growth from bas-relief to sculpture. Some of his rare sketches are on rotating display. *(V. Ghibellina 70. From P. Santa Croce, follow V. dei Pepi and turn right on V. Ghibellina. ☎25 17 52. Open M and W-Su 9:30am-2pm. €6.50, students €4.)*

IN THE OLTRARNO

The far side of the Arno River is a lively, unpretentious quarter filled with young people that grants a small reprieve from the tourist throngs. Though you'll likely cross over the Ponte Vecchio on the way to the Oltrarno, consider coming back over the Ponte di Santa Trinità, which affords excellent views of the Ponte Vecchio, or dally a bit in P. di Santo Spirito, which thrives with markets in the day and street artists at night.

⬛PALAZZO PITTI. Luca Pitti, a 15th-century banker, built his *palazzo* east of Santo Spirito against the Boboli hill. The Medici family acquired the *palazzo* and the hill in 1550 and enlarged everything they could. During Italy's brief experiment with monarchy, the structure served as a royal residence. Today, the **Palazzo Pitti** is fronted with a vast, uninhabited *piazza* and houses a gallery and four museums, providing enough diversions for a lengthy and unhurried visit. *(Ticket office is on the right before the palazzo. ☎29 48 83. 3-day ticket €12.50.)*

The ⬛**Galleria Palatina** was one of only a few public galleries when it opened in 1833. Today, it houses Florence's second-most important collection (after the Uffizi). Its artistic smorgasbord includes works by Botticelli, Canova, Caravaggio, del Sarto, Perugino, Raphael, Rubens, Tintoretto, Titian, Vasari, Velasquez, and Veronese. The **Appartamenti Reali** (Royal Apartments), at the end of the *galleria*, are lavish reminders of the time when the *palazzo* served as the Royal House of Savoy's living quarters. The apartments hold a few Renaissance and Baroque greats. For a change of pace, check out the early 19th-century proto-Impressionist works of the Macchiaioli group in the **Galleria d'Arte Moderna.** *(☎23 88 616. Open Tu-Su 8:15am-6:50pm. Combined ticket for Palatine Gallery, Royal Apartments and Modern Art Gallery €8.50, EU students €4.25.)*

Find out if the clothes make the Medici in the **Galleria del Costume,** a decadent display of the family's finery. The **Museo degli Argenti** on the ground floor exhibits the Medici family treasures, including cases of precious gems, ivories, silver pieces, and Lorenzo the Magnificent's famous collection of vases. The *salone* depicts a floor-to-ceiling fresco of blind Homer and the nine Muses leaving Mount Parnassus, alluding to scholars who fled to Tuscany from Greece after the Turkish invasion of 1453. An elaborately landscaped park, the ⬛**Boboli Gardens** is an exquisite example of a stylized Renaissance garden and provides seemingly endless paths that meander past beautifully groomed lawns. A large oval lawn sits just up the hill behind the palace, marked by an Egyptian obelisk and lined with a hedge dotted by marble statues. Labyrinthine avenues of cypress trees lead eager wanderers to bubbling fountains with graceful nudes. Be sure to see the fountain of a portly Bacchus, sitting astride a very strained turtle. While the gardens seem like the perfect picnic spot, visitors are unfortunately prohibited from bringing in outside food. The **Museo della Porcellana,** hidden in back of the gardens, exhibits fine porcelain ceramics from the Medici collection. (☎ *23 88 709. Gardens open June-Aug. 8:15am-7:30pm; Sept.-Oct. and Apr.-May 8:15am-6:30pm; Nov.-Feb. 8:15am-4:30pm; Mar. 8:15am-5:30pm. Museo degli Argenti and Museo della Porcellana open daily 8:15am-7:30pm. Closed 2nd and 4th M and 1st, 3rd, and 5th Su of each month. Combined ticket for all 4 sights €6, EU students €4. Cash only.)*

CHIESA DI SANTA MARIA DEL CARMINE. Inside this church, the ■**Brancacci Chapel** holds Masaccio's stunning 15th-century frescoes, declared masterpieces in their own time. Fifty years later, a respectful Filippino Lippi completed the cycle. Masolino's *Adam and Eve* and Masaccio's pain-filled *Expulsion from Eden* stand face to face, demonstrating the latter's innovative depiction of human forms. With such monumental works as the *Tribute Money*, this chapel became a school for many later Renaissance artists, including Michelangelo himself. *(P. del Carmine 14. ☎ 27 68 224. Church open daily 9am-noon. Chapel open M and W-Sa 10am-5pm, Su 1-5pm. Reservation required for Chapel. Church free. Chapel €4, 18-25 €3, under 18 €1.50. Combined ticket with Palazzo Vecchio €8/6/3.)*

SAN MINIATO AL MONTE AND ENVIRONS

■**PIAZZALE MICHELANGELO.** This hilltop *piazza*'s romantic view demands a visit. At sunset, waning light casts a warm glow over the city; views from here are even better than those from the top of the *duomo*. Make the challenging uphill trek at around 8:30pm during the summer to arrive at the *piazza* in time for sunset. The large *piazza* doubles as a parking lot, home to hordes of tour buses on summer days, and occasionally hosts concerts as well. *(Cross Ponte Vecchio, and turn left. Walk through the piazza, and turn right on V. dei Bardi. Follow it uphill as it becomes V. del Monte alle Croci, where a staircase to the left heads to the piazzale. Or take bus #13 from P. Santa Maria Novella, or any other point on route.)*

■**SAN MINIATO AL MONTE.** One of Florence's oldest churches, San Miniato gloriously surveys all of Florence. Its inlaid marble facade and 13th-century mosaics provide a prelude to the incredible floor inside, patterned with lions, doves, and astrological signs. Inside, the **Chapel of the Cardinal of Portugal** holds a collection of superb della Robbia terra-cottas. The cemetery is an overwhelming profusion of tombs and mausoleums. For a special treat, visit at 5:40pm, when monks perform chants inside the church. *(Take bus #13 from the station or climb stairs from Ple. Michelangelo. ☎ 23 42 731. Open daily Mar.-Oct. 8am-7pm; Nov.-Feb. 8am-1pm and 2:30-6pm. Free.)*

◩ SHOPPING

Florentines design their window displays (and their goods) with flair. For both the budget shopper seeking a special gift and the big spender looking to splurge, Florence offers ample options and many temptations to drop some cash. Watch for store windows to flood with *saldi* (sales) signs in January and July. In July and August, Florentine families rush to the beach for the weekend and nearly all stores close early on Saturday, and some close for the entire month of August.

V. Tornabuoni's swanky **boutiques** and the well-stocked goldsmiths on the Ponte Vecchio serve a sophisticated clientele. To join this crowd, try **Santa Vaggi,** Ponte Vecchio 2/6r and 20r. Charms start at €25 and 18k gold earrings cost €40 or more. (☎ 21 55 02. Open daily 9am-7:30pm. Closed Aug. and Nov. Su. AmEx/ MC/V.) Florence makes its contribution to *alta moda* with a number of fashion shows, including the biannual **Pitti Uomo** (info ☎ 23 580), one of Europe's most important exhibition of menswear in January and June.

The city's artisan traditions thrive at the **open-air markets. San Lorenzo,** the largest, cheapest, and most touristed, sprawls for several blocks around P. S. Lorenzo. In front of the leather shops, stands stock all kinds of goods—bags, clothes, food, toys, and flags. High prices are rare, but so are quality and honesty. (Open daily 9am-dusk.) For everything from pot-holders to parakeets, shop at the market in **Parco delle Cascine** on Tuesday morning, which begins four bridges west of the Ponte Vecchio at P. Vittorio Veneto and stretches along the Arno River. For a flea market specializing in old furniture and postcards, visit **Piazza Ciompi,** off V. Pietrapiana from Borgo degli Albizi. (Open Tu-Sa.)

Alinari, Largo Alinari 15, stocks the world's largest selection of art prints and high-quality photographs from €25, as well as a selection of journals and *carta fiorentina,* paper covered in intricate floral designs typical of Florence. (☎23 951; www.alinari.it. Open M 2:30-6:30pm, Tu-F 9am-1pm and 2:30-6:30pm, Sa 9am-1pm and 3-7pm. Closed 2wk. in Aug. AmEx/MC/V.)

Florentine **leatherwork** is affordable and internationally known for its high quality. Some of the city's best leather artisans work around P. Santa Croce and V. Porta Santa Maria. The **Santa Croce Leather School,** in Chiesa di Santa Croce, offers first-rate products at reasonable prices, as well as the chance to observe craftsmen making fine leather bags and jackets. (Enter through the church or V. San Giuseppe 5r. ☎24 45 34 and 24 79 913; www.leatherschool.it. Open Mar. 15-Nov. 15 daily 9:30am-6pm; Nov. 16-Mar. 14 M-Sa 10am-12:30pm and 3-6pm. AmEx/MC/V.) **NOI,** at V. delle Terme 8, produces leather apparel of superb quality for hotshot clientele, but also carries more affordable goods. (Wallets from €25. Bags €60-200. Jackets from €250. *Let's Go* discount 10%. Open M-Sa 9am-7pm. AmEx/MC/V.)

BARGAIN IT BABY! Even when prices are marked, don't hesitate to bargain. As a general guideline, start with half the price offered or at least show disinterest to get the price lowered. Only propose a price you are willing to pay. Brush up on your Italian shopping phrases, as vendors are more likely to lower the price for shoppers who can "talk the talk." Bargain only if paying with cash.

🎵 🌸 ENTERTAINMENT AND FESTIVALS

Florence disagrees with England over who invented modern soccer, but every June, the various *quartieri* turn out in costume to play their own medieval version of the sport, known as **calcio storico.** Two teams chase a wooden ball in *piazze* around the city; unsurprisingly, matches often blur the boundary between athletic contest and riot. A makeshift stadium in P. Santa Croce hosts three nights of matches in June. Check newspapers or the tourist office for the exact dates and locations of historical or modern *calcio,* and always book tickets ahead. In 2007, the event was suspended due to rowdiness in previous years; check with the tourist office for the most updated information. The **stadio,** north of the *centro,* hosts modern soccer matches. Tickets (from €10 in the bleachers, from €40 in the smaller, less crowded stands along the sidelines) are sold at the Box Office and at Marisa, across the street from the stadium. Take bus #25 from the station to the **Giardini del Drago** for a pick-up game of soccer.

The most important of Florence's traditional festivals celebrates the city's patron saint, **San Giovanni Battista** on June 24. A tremendous fireworks display in Ple. Michelangelo starts around 10pm—grab a spot anywhere along the Arno and watch for the specially coordinated combinations of red, purple, and white fireworks in honor of Florence's Series-A soccer team. The summer is also packed with music festivals, starting in May with the classical **Maggio Musicale.** Take in an evening of opera or ballet with locals in the **Teatro Comunale.** (Box office: C. Italia 16. ☎21 35 35. Open Tu-

F 10am-4:30pm and Sa 10am-1pm. Tickets €15-150.) To avoid an obstructed view, always ask to see a seating chart before simply springing for the cheapest seats.

In summer, the **Europa dei Sensi** program hosts **Rime Rampanti** (☎348 58 04 812), a series of nightly cultural shows featuring music, poetry, and food from a chosen European country. Call the info office for reservations. The same company also hosts **Le Pavoniere** (☎30 81 60), a pseudo beach party with live music, pool, bar, and pizzeria, in the Ippodromo delle Cascine (along the river and past the train station). The **Festa del Grillo** (Festival of the Cricket) is held the first Sunday after Ascension Day, which is 40 days after Easter. Crickets in wooden cages are sold in the Cascine Park to be released into the grass—Florentines believe a cricket's song brings good luck.

🎵 NIGHTLIFE

For reliable info, consult the city's entertainment monthly, *Firenze Spettacolo* (€2), found at newsstands or the entertainment website (www.informacittafirenze.it). *Firenze Notte* is also a reliable source (www.firenzenotte.it). **Piazza Santo Spirito** in Oltrarno has live music in the summer. For clubs or bars that run late and are far from the *centro*, keep in mind that the last bus may leave before the fun train comes to a halt. Taxis are also rare in the area of the most popular discos, so plan ahead and make sure you have the number of a taxi company.

> **DISCO FEVER.** Rather than paying an entrance fee, many *discoteche* in Italy give you a ticket upon entrance and you pay when you leave. Do not lose this! The slip of paper is your first drink ticket (usually €8), and it also serves as your exit fee. Lost tickets can result in fines of up to €40.

BARS

🍸 **Moyo,** V. de' Benci 23r (☎24 79 738; www.moyo.it), near P. Santa Croce. New and modern, this hip spot is crowded with young Italians lunching on fresh salads and tasty burgers. Try the *insalata Moyo* (lettuce, strawberries, nuts, and feta cheese; €7). Lunch from €7. Evening mixed drinks come with free, self-serve snacks. Wi-Fi available. Open daily 8am-3am. AmEx/MC/V.

🍸 **Noir,** Lungarno Corsini 12r (☎21 07 51). Buzzing with locals, this bar serves refreshing mixed drinks like mojitos (€7). Pay for your drink at the bar and take it outside to enjoy by the Arno. Beer from €3.50. Mixed drinks €5-6.50. Open daily 11am-1am. Closed Aug. 2wk. AmEx/MC/V.

May Day Lounge, V. Dante Alighieri 16r (www.maydayclub.it). This eclectic lounge is lit by all manner of lamps and light installations and filled with quirky Italians. Play pong on the 80s gaming system or sip mixed drinks (€4.50-6.50) to a funk beat. Try the "banana cow" shot (rum, creme of banana, *panna*, and *granatina;* €3). Draft beer €4.50. M sangria night (€3 per glass). Th watermelon night. Happy hour 8-10pm. Open daily 8pm-2am. Closed most of Aug. AmEx/MC/V.

The Fiddler's Elbow, P. Santa Maria Novella 7r (☎21 50 56). Ex-pat bartenders serve cider and beer (€4.50 per pint) to crowds of convivial foreigners. Don't be surprised if impromptu rounds of karaoke arise in the wee hours. Open daily 11am-1am. MC/V.

Eby's Latin Bar, V. dell'Oriuolo 5r (☎338 65 08 959). Shake your booty to the Latin music on the palm-covered patio while waiting in line for fresh-fruit mixed drinks blended with seasonal ingredients. Fantastic nachos, burritos, and sangria. Beer €1.40-4.50. Mixed drinks €5.50-7. Lunch special: burrito and drink €4.50. Happy hour M-F 6-10pm, drinks €3.50. Open M-Sa 11am-3am. Closed 1st 2wk. of Aug.

DISCOS

Central Park, in Parco delle Cascine (☎35 35 05). 3 open-air dance floors pulsate with hip-hop, reggae, and Italian "dance rock." Favored by Florentine and foreign teens and college students. Mixed drinks €8. Cover €20; no cover for foreign students before 12:30am. Open F-Su 8pm-3am. AmEx/MC/V.

Meccanò, V. degli Olmi 1 (☎33 13 71), near Parco delle Cascine. Meccanò and Central Park are the most popular of Florence's discos, with Meccanò catering to a slightly older crowd. Open-air dance floors make for wild summer nights. Special nights include soul, hip-hop, house, and reggae; call for schedule. Cover €16 includes 1 drink; each subsequent drink €7. Open Tu-Sa 11pm-4am. AmEx/MC/V.

Tabasco Gay Club, P. di Santa Cecilia 3r (☎21 30 00), in tiny alley across P. della Signoria from Palazzo Vecchio. This dark basement club features smoke machines, strobe lights, and low-vaulted ceilings. Caters to gay men. 18+. Cover €10, after 1am €13; includes 1st drink. Open Tu-Su 10pm-4am. AmEx/MC/V.

⊠ DAYTRIPS FROM FLORENCE

FIESOLE

A 30min. bus ride from Florence. Catch the ATAF city bus #7 (€1) from the train station; it stops at P. Mino da Fiesole in the centro. The tourist office, V. Portigiani 3 (☎59 87 20; www.comune.fiesole.fi.it), is next to the Teatro Romano, half a block off P. Mino da Fiesole, directly across the piazza from the bus stop. Office provides a free map with museum and sights listings. Open Mar.-Oct. M-Sa 9am-6pm, Su 10am-1pm and 2-6pm; Nov.-Feb. M-Sa 9am-5pm, Su 10am-4pm.

Fiesole (FEE-yeh-SOH-leh; pop. 14,200) is the site of the ancient Etruscan settlement that later extended down the hill to become Florence. Fiesole and its clean, cool breezes have long been a welcome escape from the sweltering summer heat of the Arno Valley as well as a source of inspiration for famous figures: Alexander Dumas, Anatole France, Paul Klee, Marcel Proust, Gertrude Stein, and Frank Lloyd Wright all had productive sojourns here. Leonardo da Vinci even used the town as a testing ground for his famed flying machine.

Facing away from the bus stop, walk across P. Mino da Fiesole and down V. Dupre half a block to the entrance of the **Museo Civico,** V. Portigiani 1 (☎59 477). One ticket provides admission to three associated museums—the Teatro Romano, Museo Civico Archeologico, and Museo Bandini. The **Teatro Romano** includes the perfectly rectangular foundations of Etruscan thermal baths and the toppled columns and sturdy archways of temple ruins. The well-preserved amphitheater is gussied up with modern sound equipment and spotlights for summer concerts. The amphitheater grounds lead into the **Museo Civico Archeologico,** housing an extensive collection of Etruscan artifacts, well-preserved Grecian urns, a reconstructed tomb with skeleton, and vases from *Magna Graecia* (southern Italy, once the Greek Empire). Hop across the street to breeze through the **Museo Bandini,** V. Dupre 1, which holds a collection of 15th-century Italian paintings, including works by Cortona's Signorelli, and from the studios of Giotto and the della Robbias. (☎59 477. Ruins and museums open Apr.-Oct. daily 9:30am-7pm. Closed Nov.-Mar. Tu. Last entry 30min. before closing. €13, students and over 65 €10. MC/V.) A short yet steep walk uphill from the bus stop and to the left leads to the **Convento Francesco** and **public gardens.** The panorama of the valley below is perhaps the only context in which Florence's massive *duomo* appears small. The monastery contains a frescoed chapel and a tiny museum of artifacts, including items brought back by Franciscan missionaries, precious Chinese pottery and jade figurines, and an Egyptian mummy. (☎59 175. Open June-Sept. Tu-F 10am-noon and 3-6pm, Sa-Su 3-6pm; Oct.-May Tu-F 10am-noon and 3-5pm, Sa-Su 3-5pm. Free.) The **Estate Fiesolana** (☎800 41 42 40; www.estatefiesolana.it), from June through September, fills the Roman theater with concerts, opera, theater, and film.

Accommodations in Fiesole are expensive, so a daytrip is more budget-friendly. However, the town is a great place for lunch. Take in the fantastic view of the Arno Valley over coffee (from €0.80) or *gelato* (from €1.60) at **Blu Bar ②**, P. Mino 39. The table charge can be expensive, so enjoy your snack at the bar. (☎59 72 35. Pizza €5-6. Crepes €6. Mixed drinks €10. Min. charge for table service €3.10. Open Apr.-Oct. daily 8am-1am; Nov.-Mar. Sa-Su 8am-midnight. AmEx/MC/V.)

GREVE IN CHIANTI

Greve is most easily accessed by SITA bus from Florence (1hr., hourly 7am-8pm, €3.10; reduced serivce Su and holidays). There are 2 stops in Greve; get off at the first at P. Trento. From P. Trento, either continue to walk in the direction of the bus on Vle. Vittorio Veneto, turning right at the first stop light onto V. Battisti, leading to the main piazza, P. Matteotti, or walk in the opposite direction, to reach the tourist office (☎85 46 287), a hut at Vle. Giovanni da Verazzano 59. Find maps and general info on area wineries. Open Tu-F 9:30am-1pm and 2:30-7pm.

Welcome to Chianti country, where the cheese and olive oil are exquisite and the wine is even better. The tiny town of Greve (GREV-ay; pop. 5,000), is the hub of it all. To find out what that *Chianti Classico* (key-AN-tee CLAS-see-ko) is all about, get your taste buds ready and sip with the best. Just down Vle. Vittorio Veneto and on the right in P. delle Cantine, a wine lover's paradise awaits at ☒ **Le Cantine di Greve in Chianti**, P. delle Cantine 2, which is part wine museum, part *enoteca*. Recently opened in 2000, the Cantine uses a new technology for wine tasting where the bottles rest in vacuum-valves that enable over 150 bottles to be available for tasting at one time, including a wide range of local *Chianti Classico* and *Supertuscans*. They also stock *Nobile*, *Brunello*, and *Bolgheri*, wines from other Tuscan towns. Grab a tasting card in denominations of €10, 15, 20, or 25, and insert the card above the wine you wish to taste; tastes start around €0.80, depending on the type of wine. Helpful staff will help you navigate the stands that pack the brick-arched, stone-walled basement. (☎85 46 404; fax 85 44 521. Open daily 10am-7pm. Free. AmEx/MC/V.) Many other *enoteche* in town offer free wine tastings of 3-5 wines in the hopes that you'll love that bottle of red enough to whip out the wallet. The selection at **Enoteca del Chianti Classico**, P. Santa Croce 8, is especially impressive. (☎85 32 97. Open daily in summer 9:30am-7:30pm, in winter 9:30am-12:30pm and 3:30-7:30pm. AmEx/MC/V.)

For a list of local vineyards and help booking accommodations, head to **Chianti Slow Travel Agency**, P. Matteotti 11 (☎85 46 299. Open daily 9am-1pm and 2:30-6:30pm). **Officina Marco Ramuzzi**, V. Italo Stecchi 23 (☎85 30 37), offers scooter and mountain bike rentals. Accommodations in the *centro* are scarce and many nearby villas are not easily accessible by public transportation. However, **Albergo del Chianti ⑤**, P. Matteotti 86, belies this generalization. Located in the main *piazza*, the hotel offers 16 clean, comfortable rooms with bath, minibar, telephone, A/C, and TV. The rustic lobby and adjoining bar open onto an outdoor oasis: a lovely patio, garden, and swimming pool. (☎85 37 63; www.albergodel-chianti.it. Breakfast included. Singles €70; doubles €95.) For a truly Tuscan meal, the well-known **Mangiando, Mangiando ❸**, P. Matteotti 80, will please, serving traditional plates such as *cinta senese* (boar) under a wood-beamed ceiling or under outdoor umbrellas. (☎85 46 372. *Primi* €7-9.50, *secondi* €14-16. Open Tu-Su in summer 11am-11pm, in winter noon-3pm and 7-10:30pm. MC/V.) For fresh, local goods, **Macelleria**, P. Matteotti 69-71, is as authentic as it gets. Choose from the wide array of meats and cheeses or pop into the back room to taste several varieties free of charge. Private tastings, including 8 wines, 3 salamis, 2 cheeses and 1 oil, are offered for €7.70. Wine tastings start at €10. (Open M-Sa 8am-1pm and 3:30-7:30pm, Su 10am-1pm and 3:30-7pm. AmEx/MC/V.) Dirt cheap picnic eats can be found at **Coop,** Vle. Vittorio Veneto 76 (☎ 85 30 53. Open M-Sa 8am-1pm and 4-8pm. MC/V.) Pick up fresh bread and sweets from €1.50 at **Forno,** P. Matteotti 89. (Open daily in summer 7am-1pm and 4:30-7:30pm; in winter 5-8pm. Cash only.)

SIENA   ☎ 0577

Siena's (see-EH-na; pop. 50,000) vibrant character and local energy make it a distinctly Tuscan city. Locals are fiercely proud of their town's history, which dates back to the 13th century when the first Sienese crafted a sophisticated metropolis rich in wealth and culture. The city's vehement (and still palpable) rivalry with Florence resulted in grandiose Gothic architecture and soaring towers, though the arrival of the Black Death stunted much potential for innovation. These days, the Sienese celebrate their heritage with festivals like the semi-annual Palio, a riotous display of pageantry in which jockeys race bareback horses around the central square. Situated in the heart of the Tuscan wine country, Siena also makes an ideal base for exploring the surrounding countryside.

▐ TRANSPORTATION

Trains: In P. Rosselli. 15min. by bus (#3, 4, 7, 8, 9, 10, 17, 77; buy local bus tickets from vending machines by the station entrance or at the ticket office, €1) from the *centro*. Ticket office open daily 6:30am-1:10pm and 1:40-8:10pm. Trains to **Florence** (1¾hr., 16 per day 5:44am-9:22pm, €5.70) and **Rome** (3hr., 20 per day 5:40am-8:21pm, €12.30) via **Chiusi.**

> **▐ DON'T LET YOUR BUS PASS YOU BY.** Though infrequent, the buses that connect the neighboring wine towns of Tuscany run on time. However, the bus stops are usually only marked by a pole, so don't be afraid to ask one of the locals where the nearest stop is. Furthermore, the buses only stop on request, so (cautiously) step into the road, make yourself visible, and furiously flag one down. Otherwise, the bus will fly by without a second glance, and you'll be stuck waiting another 3hr. for the next ride to your destination.

Buses: TRA-IN/SITA (☎20 42 46; www.trainspa.it). Some intercity buses leave from P. Gramsci and others from the train station. Ticket offices are in the underground terminal in P. Gramsci and at the train station. Open daily 6:15am-8:15pm. To: **Arezzo** (7 per day, €5); **Florence** (hourly, €6.50); **Montalcino** (7 per day, €3.20); **Montepulciano** via **Buonconvento** or **Torrenieri** (4 per day, €4.50); **San Gimignano** via **Poggibonsi** (31 per day, €5.20); **Volterra** (M-F 4 per day, €2.50; get off at Colle Val d'Elsa and **CPT** bus ticket at newsstand). **TRA-IN** also runs buses within Siena. Buy tickets (€1, valid 1hr.) at the office in P. Gramsci or from any vendor that displays a TRA-IN sign. All buses have reduced service Su.

Taxis: RadioTaxi (☎49 222), in P. Indipendenza.

Car, Bike, and Scooter Rental: Perozzi Noleggi, V. dei Gazzani 16 (☎28 83 87). Bikes €10 per day; scooters €26-52; cars €72; vans €115. Insurance included. Open M-Sa 9am-2pm and 3-7pm, Su 9am-1pm and 7-8pm. AmEx/MC/V.

✦▐ ORIENTATION AND PRACTICAL INFORMATION

From **Piazza Gramsci,** the main bus drop-off point, follow **Via Malavolti** into **Piazza Matteotti.** Cross the *piazza* and continue straight on **Via Banchi di Sopra,** heading through the heart of town. Continuing downhill, pass through one of the several archways that lead to **Piazza del Campo,** Siena's *centro storico,* also known as **Il Campo.** The Palazzo Pubblico, the tourist office, and the best people-watching in the town are located here. To get to the *centro* from the **train station,** cross the street and take one of the buses listed above. These buses stop in **Piazza del Sale** or P. Gramsci. Some buses stop just before P. Gramsci, which makes it difficult to know when to get off; ask the bus driver. From either *piazza,* follow the signs to Il Campo. Buy local bus tickets from vending machines by the station entrance or at the ticket office. From the **bus station** in **Piazza San Domenico,** follow the signs to P. del Campo. **Piazza del Duomo** lies 100m west of Il Campo.

FUN FOR FOREIGNERS. For an inexpensive, untouristed part of Siena, veer into the university area along V. Pantaneto. The University per Stranieri (University for Foreigners) has a gorgeous terrace with great views, not to mention V. Pantaneto is lined with cheap Internet spots, *alimentari,* and lively cafes.

Tourist Office: APT, P. del Campo 56 (☎28 05 51; www.terresiena.it). Knowledgeable, busy staff provides brochures. Open Mar. 16-Nov. 14 daily 9:30am-1pm and 2:30-6pm; Nov. 15-Mar. 15 M-Sa 8:30am-1pm and 3-7pm, Su 9am-1pm. **Prenotazioni Alberghi e Ristoranti** (☎28 80 84/84 80; fax 28 02 90), in P. San Domenico, reserves accommodations (€2). Also books reservations for 2hr. walking tours of Siena (M-F 3pm; reserve by 1pm; €20) and San Gimignano. Open M-Sa 9am-7pm, Su 9am-noon. AmEx/MC/V.

Budget Travel: CTS, V. Sallustio Bandini 21 (☎28 50 08). Student travel services. Open M-F and Su 9am-12:30pm and 3:30-7pm. MC/V.

Laundromat: Lavorapido, V. di Pantaneto 38. Wash €3 per 8kg, dry €3. Detergent €0.80. Open daily 8am-10pm. **Onda Blu,** V. Casato di Sotto 17. Wash €3 per 7kg, dry €3. Open daily 8am-10pm.

English-Language Bookstore: Libreria Ticci, V. delle Terme 5/7 (☎28 00 10). Extensive selection. Open M-Sa 9am-7:30pm. AmEx/MC/V. **Feltrinelli,** V. Banchi di Sopra 64 (☎44 009). Classic and popular fiction, as well as English-language magazines. Open M-Sa 9am-7:30pm, Su 11am-1:30pm and 3:30-7:30pm. AmEx/MC/V.

Luggage Storage: At TRA-IN ticket office beneath P. Gramsci. €3 per ½-day, €5.50 per day. No overnight storage. Open daily 7am-7:15pm. Cash only.

Police: on V. del Castoro near the *duomo.*

Pharmacy: Farmacia del Campo, P. del Campo 26. Open M-F 9am-1pm and 4-8pm. Posts after-hours rotations. MC/V.

Hospital: V. Le Scotte 14 (☎58 51 11). Take bus #3 or 77 from P. Gramsci.

Internet Access: Cafe Internet/International Call Center, V. Cecco Angiolieri 16 (☎41 521). €1.80 per hr. Open M-Sa 8:30am-11pm, Su 9am-11pm. Cash only. **Internet Train,** V. di Città 121 (☎22 63 66). Wi-Fi available. €5 per hr. Open M-F 10am-8pm, Sa-Su noon-8pm. MC/V. **Branch** at V. Pantaneto 54 (☎24 74 60). €5 per hr. Open M-F 10am-10pm, Su 2-8pm. MC/V.

Post Office: P. Matteotti 36. Offers **currency exchange.** Open M-Sa 8:15am-7pm. **Postal Code:** 53100.

ACCOMMODATIONS

Finding a room in Siena can be difficult and expensive in the summer. Book months in advance for the Palio (p. 492). For visits over a week, *affittacamere* (room rental) are an popular option. Tourist offices can provide a list of these private rooms and help with booking.

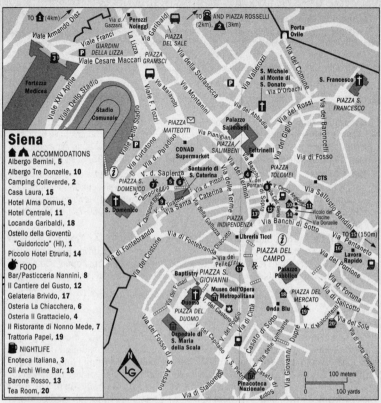

Siena

♠ � ⋀ ACCOMMODATIONS
Albergo Bernini, **5**
Albergo Tre Donzelle, **10**
Camping Colleverde, **2**
Casa Laura, **15**
Hotel Alma Domus, **9**
Hotel Centrale, **11**
Locanda Garibaldi, **18**
Ostello della Gioventù
 "Guidoriccio" (HI), **1**
Piccolo Hotel Etruria, **14**

⬤ FOOD
Bar/Pasticceria Nannini, **8**
Il Cantiere del Gusto, **12**
Gelateria Brivido, **17**
Osteria La Chiacchera, **6**
Osteria Il Grattacielo, **4**
Il Ristorante di Nonno Mede, **7**
Trattoria Papei, **19**

⬤ NIGHTLIFE
Enoteca Italiana, **3**
Gli Archi Wine Bar, **16**
Barone Rosso, **13**
Tea Room, **20**

⊠ Casa Laura, V. Roma 3 (☎22 60 61; fax 22 52 40), 10min. from Il Campo, in the university area. Ring 3rd doorbell down labeled *"Bencini Valentini."* Hospitable and generous owner Laura rents 10 spacious and homey *affittacamere* at stellar prices. Some with private bath. Kitchen access available. Singles €35-40; doubles €65-67; triples €70; quads €75. MC/V. ❸

Piccolo Hotel Etruria, V. Donzelle 3 (☎28 80 88; www.hoteletruria.com). A stone's throw from Il Campo. Family-run establishment maintains 20 immaculate, modern rooms with phone, TV, and hair dryer. Breakfast €5. Curfew 1am. Singles €48, with bath €53; doubles €86; triples €114. Extra bed €28. AmEx/MC/V. ❹

Ostello della Gioventù "Guidoriccio" (HI), V. Fiorentina 89 (☎52 212), in Località Lo Stellino, a 20min. bus ride from town. Take bus #10 or 15 from P. Gramsci. Bus #15 stops at front door. For bus #10, continue from stop in bus's direction and take 1st right. Continue past McDonald's and gas station, hostel is on the right about 50m down. With mostly 2- to 4-person rooms, excellent-value hostel has a friendly atmosphere. Breakfast €1.70; dinner €9.75. Key deposit €1. Lockout 9:30am-3pm. Curfew midnight. Reservation recommended. Dorms €14. Cash only. ❶

Albergo Tre Donzelle, V. Donzelle 5 (☎28 03 58; fax 22 39 33). Basic rooms have tasteful wood furnishings and lots of space. Close to Il Campo, but often noisy as a result. Friendly, English-speaking staff. Curfew 1am. Singles €38; doubles €46, with bath €66; triples €65/85; quads €84/104. AmEx/MC/V. ❸

Albergo Bernini, V. della Sapienza 15 (☎28 90 47; www.albergobernini.com). 9 antique-laden rooms have picture-perfect views of the *duomo*. Outdoor patio is lined with plants, which makes for the perfect setting for a serenade by the accordion-playing owner. Breakfast €7. Curfew midnight. July-Sept. singles with bath €78; doubles €65, with bath €85. Extra bed € 15. Oct.-June prices drop 20%. Cash only. ❺

Locanda Garibaldi, V. Giovanni Dupré 18 (☎28 42 04). Sleek and classy decor. Most rooms with bath. Reception in restaurant. Curfew midnight. Reservation recommended. Doubles €75. Extra bed €10. Cash only. ❸

Hotel Alma Domus, V. Camporeggio 37 (☎44 177; fax 47 601), next to Santuario di Santa Caterina in a quieter part of town. Nun-run. 22 comfortable rooms have bath, polished stone floors, and A/C. Ask ahead of time for a *duomo* view at no extra cost. Curfew 11:30pm. Singles €42; doubles €65; triples €80; quads €95. Cash only. ❹

Hotel Centrale, V. Cecco Angiolieri 26 (☎28 03 79; hotelcentrale.siena@libero.it). Don't be deceived by the dimly lit staircase—this hotel is well-kept and comfortable. 7 rooms with fridge, phone, satellite TV, fan, hair dryer, and views of the *duomo*. Breakfast €5. Singles €40-50, with bath €50-60; doubles €60-70/70-80; triples €90/100; quads €110/120. AmEx/MC/V. ❹

Camping Colleverde, Strada di Scacciapensieri 47 (☎28 00 44). Take bus #3 from train station or bus #8 from P. del Sale; confirm destination with driver. Buses run every 30min. Grocery store, restaurant, and access to nearby bar. Pool open 10am-6pm; €1.55. Reception 7:20am-11pm. Open late Mar. to mid-Nov. €7.75 per person, ages 3-11 €4.13; €3.50 per tent. MC/V. ❶

🍴 FOOD

Siena specializes in rich pastries. The most famous is *panforte*, a concoction of honey, almonds, and citron, first baked as trail mix for the Crusaders. For a lighter snack, try *ricciarelli*, soft almond cookies with powdered vanilla on top. Sample either (€2.20 per 100g) at the **Bar/Pasticceria Nannini,** Siena's oldest *pasticceria*, with branch at V. Banchi di Sopra 22-24 and others throughout town. The local meat specialty, *cinta senese*, spots menus as well. Siena's **open-air market** fills P. La Lizza each Wednesday (8am-1pm). For groceries, head to **Conad,** in P. Matteoti (open M-Sa 8:30am-8:30pm, Su 9am-1pm and 4-8pm; MC/V), or the **Coop** a few blocks from the train station. Turn left from the station, then left again one block down at the overpass; it's in the shopping complex immediately to the right. (Open M-F 8am-9pm, Sa 8am-8:30pm. Cash only.)

🔲 Trattoria Papei, P. del Mercato 6 (☎28 08 94), on the far side of Palazzo Pubblico from Il Campo. Shaded, outdoor tables and a large, stone-arched dining room can get crowded and noisy. Vast range of homemade pasta dishes, including scrumptious *pici alla cardinale* (spaghetti with tomato-pepper sauce and *pancetta;* €7), and traditional *secondi* like savory *coniglio all'arrabbiata* (rabbit with hot spices; €9). Wines are served by the bottle (€10), but you're only charged for what you drink. Cover €2. Open Tu-Su noon-3pm and 7-10:30pm. AmEx/MC/V. ❸

🔲 Il Cantiere del Gusto, V. Calzoleria 12 (☎28 90 10), off V. Banchi di Sotto. Delicious aromas waft up from the intimate and elegant dining area downstairs. Friendly waitstaff serves hearty Tuscan classics and great veggie options (large salads €5-7.50). *Primi* €5-6, *secondi* €8-20. Cover €1. Service 10%. Open M 12:30-2:30pm, Tu-Sa 12:30-2:30pm and 7-10pm. MC/V. ❷

🔲 Osteria La Chiacchera, Costa di San Antonio 4 (☎28 06 31), next to Santuario di Santa Caterina. Frequented by young Italians and savvy tourists, the restaurant offers delicious food at extremely low prices in a casual and lively atmosphere. *Primi* €5-6, *secondi* €8-12. Open M and W-Su noon-3:30pm and 7pm-midnight. AmEx/MC/V. ❷

Il Ristorante di Nonno Mede, V. Camporeggio 21 (☎24 79 66), down the hill to the left of Chiesa San Domenico. Although indoor seating is cramped, choose from an extensive menu of pizzas and enjoy in the expansive outdoor seating area that has great views of the *duomo*. Delicious *antipasto di bosco* (mixed vegetables; €7.80). Pizza €5-7.80. Open M and W-Su 12:30-3pm and 7pm-midnight. MC/V. ❶

Osteria Il Grattacielo, V. dei Pontani 8 (☎334 63 11 460), between V. dei Termini and V. Banchi di Sopra. Culinary delights, including baby artichokes, olives, sun-dried tomatoes in oil, and hunks of salami and *pecorino*, abound here. Half the fun here is ordering—point at jars and create your dream lunch. A full meal with wine runs under €10. Open M-F 8am-2:45pm and 5:30-7pm, Sa 8am-2:45pm and 5:30-6pm. Cash only. ❷

Gelateria Brivido, V. dei Pellegrini 1-3 (☎28 00 58). *Gelato* in flavors like kiwi and watermelon served standing-room only. Don't miss the *biscotto gelato* packed with chocolate cookie crumbs. Cones from €1.50. Open daily 10am-midnight. Cash only. ❶

SIGHTS

IL CAMPO. Siena radiates from the **Piazza del Campo,** the shell-shaped square designed for civic events and affectionately referred to as "Il Campo." The *piazza*'s brick paving is divided into nine sections, representing the city's medieval Council of Nine. Dante's *Inferno* referred to the square in his account of the real-life drama of Provenzan Salvani, the heroic Sienese merchant who panhandled in Il Campo to pay a friend's ransom. Later Sienese mystics used the *piazza* as a public auditorium. For €2.50, claim a table and an espresso at one of the many cafes lining the curved walkway, or better yet, grab a bottle of wine and stake out a seat on the cobblestone *piazza* itself. Twice each summer, the **Palio** (p. 492) morphs the mellow Campo into a chaotic arena as horses race around its edge. At the top of the slope is the **Fonte Gaia,** a rectangular marble fountain nestled into the slanted *piazza*. The water here emerges from the same 25km aqueduct that has refreshed Siena since the 14th century. Standing at the bottom of the *piazza* is the imposing **Palazzo Pubblico,** with its looming *campanile*, the **Torre del Mangia.** In front of the *palazzo* is the **Cappella di Piazza,** which was started in 1348, but took 100 years to complete due to the Black Death's untimely arrival.

> **TIP**
> **THIRSTY? WHY WAIT?** While you should be cautious about drinking from some of Italy's public fountains, the constantly churning aqueduct in Siena's Il Campo is clean and refreshing. Rather than paying €1.50 for a tiny bottle of water, drink deep from the fountain's cold, clear waters.

PALAZZO PUBBLICO. This impressive medieval building was home to Siena's Council of Nine in the Middle Ages. It still houses city government offices, but the main tourist draw is the **Museo Civico.** Although the Sienese art pieces here range from medieval triptychs to 18th-century landscapes, the greatest treasure is the collection of late medieval to early Renaissance painting in the distinctive Sienese style. The large and airy **Sala del Mappamondo,** named for a lost series of astronomical frescoes, displays Simone Martini's *Maestà*, which combines religious overtones with civic and literary awareness. The Christ Child is depicted holding a parchment inscribed with the city motto of upholding justice, *"Expertus fidelem,"* and the steps of the canopied throne are engraved with two stanzas from Dante's *Divine Comedy*. In the next room, the **Sala dei Nove** holds Ambrogio Lorenzetti's famous frescoes, the *Allegories of Good and Bad Government and their Effects on Town and Country*, with opposing visions of damnation and utopia on the right and left walls. *(Open daily Mar.- Oct. 10am-6:15pm; Nov.-Feb. 10am-5:30pm. €7, students €4.50, under 11 free. Cash only.)* The Palazzo Pubblico's other star attraction is the **Torre del Mangia,** named for the gluttonous bell-ringer, Giovanni di Duccio, also called *"Mangiaguadagni"* (Eat the profits). At 102m, the tower is Italy's tallest secular medieval monument. After 500 dizzying and narrow steps, persistence pays off underneath the tower's highest bell: from the top, Siena's tile rooftops, farmlands, and vineyard hills form an enchanting mosaic. Arrive early as it gets crowded in the afternoon. *(Open daily Mar. 16-Oct. 10am-6:15pm; Nov.-Mar. 15 10am-4pm. €6, combined ticket with Museo Civico €10. Cash only.)*

> **TIP** **MORE BANG FOR YOUR BUCK.** Siena offers 2 combined tickets. The first allows 2 days of entry to the Museo Civico, Palazzo Papesse, and Ospedale di Santa Maria della Scala (€10). The second, valid for 1 week (€16), covers those 3 plus the *battistero*, Museo dell'Opera Metropolitana, and the Oratorio di San Bernardino. Purchase both tickets at participating museums.

■ **DUOMO.** Atop one of the city's seven hills, the *duomo* is one of few completely Gothic cathedrals south of the Alps. A huge arch, part of a striped wall facing the front of the cathedral, is the sole remnant of Siena's 1339 plan to construct a new nave, which would have made this *duomo* the largest church in all Christendom. The grandiose effort ended when the Black Plague decimated the working populace, beginning in 1348. One of the *duomo*'s side aisles has been enclosed and turned into the **Museo dell'Opera Metropolitana.** Statues of philosophers, sibyls, and prophets, all by Giovanni Pisano, hold sway beneath impressive spires.

The bronze sun symbol on the *duomo*'s recently renovated facade was the creation of San Bernadino of Siena, who wanted the feuding Sienese to relinquish their emblems of nobility and unite under this symbol of the risen Christ. Alas, his efforts were in vain—the Sienese continue to identify with the animal symbols of their *contrade* (districts). The marble floor, like the rest of the *duomo*, is richly ornate, depicting such widely varying and often violent themes as alchemy and the "Slaughter of the Innocents." A series on the left showing multi-ethnic sibyls represents the spread of Christianity. Most of the pieces are covered for preservation, except in September when visitors can look for the works by Machese d'Adamo, perhaps the most spectacular in the entire building. Halfway up the left aisle is the Piccolomini Altar, designed by Andrea Bregno in 1503. The statue was honorably built to host a very special holy relic—St. John's right arm. The lavish Libreria Piccolomini, commissioned by Pope Pius III in 1492, houses elaborately illustrated books of his uncle, Pius II. On the right, the Papal Chapel of Madonna del Voto houses two Bernini statues. *(Open June-Aug. M-Sa 10:30am-8pm, Su 1:30-6pm; Mar.-May and Sept.-Oct. M-Sa 10:30am-7:30pm, Su 1:30-6pm; Nov.-Feb. M-Sa 10:30am-6:30pm, Su 1:30-5:30pm. Modest dress required. €4-5.50. Cash only.)*

Outside and downhill lies the 15th-century **baptistry.** Lavish and intricate frescoes depict the lives of Christ and St. Anthony inside. The central part of the ceiling, known as the *"Vecchietta,"* depicts scenes from the Apostles Creed. The baptistry's centerpiece is the hexagonal Renaissance baptismal font (1417-31). Panels include Ghiberti's Baptism of Christ and Prediction of John the Baptist, as well as Herod's Feast by Donatello. *(Open daily Mar. 15-Sept. 9:30am-8pm; Oct. 9am-6pm; Nov.-Mar. 14 10am-1pm and 2:30-5pm. Modest dress required. €3. Cash only.)*

CRIPTA. Recently rediscovered in 1999, these 700-year-old underground rooms were not tombs but a preparation for pilgrims entering the *duomo*. These 13th-

X MARKS THE SPOT: If you look closely, you'll notice a small cross two-thirds of the way up the stairs that lead from Piazza San Giovanni to the front entrance of the *duomo*. This mark is not a trick of the pavement nor is it graffiti. Legend has it that this step is where St. Catherine of Siena tripped and fell down the stairs in the 14th century, supposedly pushed by the devil. Yet despite the steepness and severity of the marble steps, she walked away without a scratch: *un miracolo* only worthy of a saint, as any Sienese will tell you.

century depictions of the Old and New Testament are attributed to the pre-Duccio Sienese painters, including Diotisalvi di Speme, Guido da Siena, and Guido di Graziano. Due to the absence of light, climatic instability, and human intervention, the colors remain vibrant and detailed. *(In P. del Duomo, entrance halfway down stairs, to the right of the baptistry. Open June-Aug. 9:30am-8pm; Mar.-May and Sept.-Oct. 9:30am-7pm; Nov.-Feb. 10am-5pm. €6, students €5. Ticket includes informative audio guide. Cash only.)*

MUSEO DELL'OPERA METROPOLITANA. The cathedral museum holds all the art that won't fit in the *duomo*. The first floor contains some of the foremost Gothic statuary in Italy, all by Giovanni Pisano. Upstairs the 700-year-old *Maestà*, by Duccio di Buoninsegna, originally served as a screen for the cathedral's altar. Other noteworthy works are the Byzantine *Madonna dagli Occhi Grossi*, paintings by Lorenzetti, and two altarpieces by Matteo di Giovanni. Follow signs for the **Panorama dal Facciatone,** in Room 4 on the upper floor, to a balcony over the nave. A very narrow spiral staircase leads to a tiny tower for an unadvertised but beautiful view of the entire city. *(Museum entrance outside of duomo. Exit portals, and turn left. Open daily Mar. 15-Sept. 9am-7:30pm; Oct. 9am-6pm; Nov.-Mar. 14 9am-1:30pm. €6. Cash only.)*

OSPEDALE DI SANTA MARIA DELLA SCALA. Built as a hospital in the 13th century, the *ospedale* is now a museum displaying its original frescoes, chapels, and vaults. The **Sala del Pellegrinaio,** or the Pilgrims' Hall, used as a ward until the late 20th century, contains an expressive fresco cycle by Vecchietta, which tells the narrative history of the hospital building. The **Sagrestia Vecchia,** or Cappello del Sacro Chiodo, houses masterful 15th-century Sienese frescoes. On the way downstairs, duck into the dim underground chapels and vaults, sites of rituals and "acts of piety for the dead" performed by various *contrade*. One level down is the entrance to the **Museo Archeologico,** included in admission to the *ospedale*. Established in 1933 to collect and preserve Etruscan artifacts from the Siena area, the museum is now almost entirely in the eerie, medieval, underground water works of the city. Signs point the way through dank, labyrinthine passageways before emerging into rooms containing well-lit glass cases of Etruscan pottery and coins. *(Opposite the duomo. Open daily Mar.-Nov. 10:30am-6:30pm; Dec.-Feb. 10:30am-4:30pm. Last entry 30min. before closing. €6, students €3.50. Cash only.)*

PINACOTECA NAZIONALE. Siena's superb art gallery displays works by every major artist of the highly stylized Sienese school. Masters represented include seven followers of Duccio—Simone Martini, the Lorenzetti brothers, Bartolo di Fredi, Bartolomeo Bulgarini, Sano di Pietro, and Il Sodoma. The museum is refreshingly free of tourist hordes, although the collection is best geared toward art-lovers. *(V. San Pietro 29, in the Palazzo Buonsignori down V. del Capitano from the duomo. Open M 8:30am-1:30pm, Tu-Sa 8:15am-7:15pm, Su 8:15am-1:15pm. €4, EU citizens and students 18-26 €2, EU citizens under 18 or over 65 free. Cash only.)*

SANTUARIO DI SANTA CATERINA. This sanctuary honors the Sienese St. Catherine, who had a miraculous vision in which Christ came to her with a ring and proposed marriage. Known for her outspoken manner, her eloquence persuaded Pope

Gregory XI to return to Rome from Avignon in 1377; in 1939 she was proclaimed one of Italy's patron saints. The brick buildings and airy courtyards, converted into a Renaissance loggia, branches into many Baroque chapels. The **Chiesa del Crocefisso,** on the right, is impressive, but don't overlook the beautiful, smaller **Oratorio della Cucina** on the left. *(Entrance at the intersection of Costa di San Antonio and V. dei Pittori, down from P. San Domenico on V. della Sapienza. Open daily 9am-12:30pm and 3-6pm. Free.)*

OTHER SIGHTS. As in many Italian towns, Siena's Franciscan and Dominican basilicas rival each other from opposite ends of town. The **Chiesa di San Domenico** contains Andrea Vanni's portrait of Saint Catherine and several other dramatic frescoes illustrating her miraculous acts. The exquisite chapel inside, dedicated to Santa Caterina, was built in 1460 to store her preserved head and half of one of her fingers, still on display today for the curious and non-squeamish. *(In P. San Domenico. Open daily Nov.-Apr. 9am-1pm and 3-5:30pm; May-Oct. 7am-1pm and 3-7pm. Modest dress required. Free.)* Those interested in the Palio may enjoy one of Siena's 17 **contrada museums.** Each neighborhood organization maintains its own collection of costumes, banners, and icons. *(Most require an appointment at least 1wk. in advance; inquire at the tourist office for information.)* Take time out from sightseeing for a stroll within the brick walls of the **Fortezza Medicea,** filled with fountains and towers. *(Just north of P. Gramsci on Vle. Cesare Maccari. Open dawn until dusk. Free.)*

🎵 📷 ENTERTAINMENT AND NIGHTLIFE

Siena's ■**Palio,** hands-down the highlight of the town's entertainment, overtakes the city twice each year, on July 2 and August 16, transforming Siena into an exciting frenzy as people pack Il Campo to watch the bareback horse race. Even when it doesn't involve barbaric races, Siena's nightlife is kept booming by the large, local and foreign student population. At the new and popular **Gli Archi Wine Bar,** V. Pantaneto 22, try an assortment of vintage wines paired with deliciously cheap *antipasti.* (☎24 75 79; www.gliarchi.it. *Antipasti* €6-8, 1 portion €3.50. Pasta €4.50-6. Open M-Sa noon-3pm and 7-11:30pm. AmEx/MC/V.) Another great place to sample wines is **Enoteca Italiana,** in the Fortezza Medicea near the entrance off Vle. Cesare Maccari, where they sell fine wines by the bottle or by the glass, from €3. (☎22 88 13. Open Apr.-Sept. M noon-8pm, Tu-Sa noon-1am; Oct.-Mar. M-W noon-8pm, Th-Sa noon-1am. AmEx/MC/V.) The study-abroad crowd, sprinkled with locals, gets down at **Barone Rosso,** V. dei Termini 9, where themed parties, music, and alcohol are all in abundance. (☎28 66 86; www.barone-rosso.com. Open daily 9pm-3am. AmEx/MC/V.) For a slightly calmer evening out, head to ■**Tea Room,** V. di Porta Giustizia 9, down a small staircase to the left behind P. Mercato. Friendly owner, Illario, bakes an array of desserts daily that complement a vast menu of loose teas and mixed drinks. Melt into the cushions of a comfy couch near the fireplace or grab a tiny, candle-lit table for two. (☎22 27 53. Tea and other drinks from €4. Open Tu-Su 9pm-3am. Closed for 2 months in summer.) **Accademia Musicale Chigiana,** V. di Città 89 (☎22 091; www.chigiana.it) organizes classical music concerts throughout the year.

> **GETAWAY CAR.** Bus service in and out of Siena is less than reliable. Enjoy daytrips from Siena by renting a car, which will spare you the agony of waiting for, flagging down, and chasing after buses.

📷 DAYTRIPS FROM SIENA

RADDA IN CHIANTI

Buses connect Siena to Radda in Chianti (1hr., 4 per day, round-trip €5.80). Buses leave from Siena's train station. Buses also connect Radda to Florence, though sched-

ules are sporadic; call 800 37 37 60 for info. (1½hr.; 3 per day; last bus to Florence 6:10pm, last bus to Siena 6:40pm.) In the morning, buses arrive at and depart from V. XX Settembre. In the afternoon, return buses to Florence and Siena leave from a stop across the street about 100m down. This stop is not well marked, so flag down the bus as it approaches.

Siena lies within easy reach of the Chianti region, a harmonious landscape of green hills, ancient castles, tiny villages, and of course, uninterrupted vineyard expanses. In the Middle Ages, the small countryside towns of Castellina, Radda, and Gaiole formed a military alliance against French and Spanish invaders, adopting the black rooster as their symbol. Today, the rooster adorns the bottles of Chianti wines, which are famous throughout the world. Peaceful **Radda in Chianti** (RAD-da; pop. 4000) is just 30km from Siena, and it makes a great base for exploring the surrounding countryside. Every year on the 2nd of June, the town comes together for **Radda in the Glass.** On this one-day event the *enoteche* provide ample bottles of Chianti on outdoor tables along V. Roma as rosy-cheeked citizens and lucky visitors make frequent stops with wine glasses in hand. For more info on touring the nearby wineries, vacation rentals, and excursions to the countryside, inquire at **A Bit of Tuscany,** V. Roma 39, next to Camere di Giovannino. (☎73 89 48. Open M-F 10am-1pm and 2:30-6pm.) If you can get out of town, most wineries in the area give free tastings, though a stroll down V. Roma will also reveal numerous *enoteche* willing to let you sample for free. Cellar tours often require reservations—tourist offices provide booking services.

Located in the center of town, the out-going staff at **La Bottega di Giovannino** ❷, V. Roma 37, serve filling plates on a breezy outdoor patio or in a wine-bottle laden dining room. Pair pasta with a glass of *Chianti Classico* (from €3). Owners also offer transportation and tours for groups up to seven to local wineries with reservations. (☎73 80 56; www.labottegadigiovannino.it. *Primi* €5.50-6, *secondi* €6-9. Open M and W-Su 8:30am-10:30pm. MC/V.) After a rigorous day of wine-tasting, relax in the shaded **public gardens** outside the city walls, near P. IV Novembre. Inside the reputable **⬛Porciatti Alimentari** ❷, P. IV Novembre 1-3, master butchers sell aged, handmade salami, pork sausages, and cheese that are also available for tasting. Across the street and down **Camminamento Medievale,** a medieval passageway from the 14th century, is **Casa Porciatti,** run by the same owners. Savor the free samples of wine, *grappa,* and olive oil or schedule a tasting with a larger group (6-8 people) for €7-10. (☎73 80 55; www.casaporci-

THE HIDDEN DEAL

FINE WINE FINDS

Whether connoisseur or amateur, to taste wine in Tuscany is the real deal. Armed with your best wine glass swirl, take a sip of a local *vino rosso,* and let the flavors coat your tongue. While some prices may make your head spin, there are ways to skirt high charges and delight the palate.

From Florence, **Greve in Chianti** (p. 452) is an easy day trip into the heart of the Chianti region. Stop in at **Le Cantine,** browse the bottles in their museum, and then grab a tasting card for €10 that allows you to choose from over 150 bottles.

Siena makes the best base for exploring the rest of the wine country. **Radda in Chianti** (p. 460) is packed with wine bars. Pepper the knowledgeable staff at **Casa Porciatti** with questions about the blends of *Chianti Classico* and enjoy their free tasting samples. Bus it down to **Montalcino** (p.470) to try the local *Brunello,* and allow time in your day trip to visit **Fattoria dei Barbi,** a winery offering free 30min. tours. **Montepulciano** (p. 462) is home to the *Nobile.* Look for signs that read *degustazione gratis* for free tastings. You'll find the region's only traditional white wine, *Vernaccia,* in **San Gimignano** (p. 463) and visit the local Museo del Vino and attached wine bar.

Tuscany's wine country is a wealth of scents, though perhaps the sweetest taste of all is to end a trip to the Chianti with purple teeth and money in your wallet.

atti.it. Wine from €6 per bottle. *Alimentari* open May-Oct. M-Sa 8am-1pm and 4-8pm, Su 8am-1pm; Nov.-Apr. M-Sa 8am-1pm and 4:30-7:30pm. *Casa* open M-Sa 10:30am-7pm, Su 10:30am-12:30pm and 3-7pm. MC/V.) The casual **Pizzeria da Michele ❸**, P. IV Novembre 4, down a flight of stairs from the main bus stop, has valley views and a seasonally-based daily menu. (☎73 84 91. Pizza served only at dinner. *Primi* €6-12, *secondi* €12-18. Cover €2. Open Tu-Su noon-2:30pm and 7pm-midnight. AmEx/MC/V.) The cheapest place to pick up wine is the **Coop** supermarket, V. Roma 26, which stocks bottles from €2.50. (Open M-Tu and Th-Sa 8:30am-1pm and 4-8pm, W 8:30am-1pm. MC/V.)

 HIGH TIMES. Many hotels in the wine country of Tuscany consider Sept. and Oct. to be their high season (instead of the typical July and Aug. tourist peak in Italy) because of the wine harvest season. Prices can jump €10-30 per night.

MONTEPULCIANO

A bus is the easiest way to reach Montepulciano; the train station is 10km out of town, with no reliable bus linking it with the city. A TRA-IN bus connects Siena to Montepulciano (1½hr., M-Sa 5 per day, €4.50), some via Buonconvento. The Ufficio delle Strade del Vino, P. Grande 7, provides maps and bus schedules, makes free arrangements for hotels and nearby affittacamere, and sells tickets for wine and olive-oil tours. (☎0578 71 74 84; www.stradavinonobile.it. Open M-Sa 10am-1pm and 3-6pm.) The tourist office in P. Don Minzoni, off V. Sangallo, also supplies maps and brochures. (☎0578 75 73 41. Open daily 9:30am-12:30pm, M-Sa 3-7:30pm.)

Situated atop a limestone ridge, this small, medieval hamlet is Tuscany's highest hill town. Sixteenth-century *palazzi*, *piazze*, and churches grace Montepulciano's ("Mohn-teh-pool-CHYA-no"; pop. 10,000) narrow streets and walkways. After being neglected for centuries after the Renaissance, this walled town is now wealthy and heavily touristed, largely as a result of its traditional *Vino Nobile* and its famous red wine industry. Visitors keep themselves plenty busy browsing the wine stores and tasting free samples. Enjoy a few sips at the shop at **Porta di Bacco**, on the left immediately inside the city gates. (Open daily 9am-8pm.) **Alimentari** selling local Tuscan products line V. Gracciano nel Corso. For a delicious selection of typical Tuscan food, visit ▨**Osteria Acquacheta ❷**, V. del Teatro 22, off V. di Voltaia nel Corso, where you savor a platter of *pecorino fresco al tartufo* (soft *pecorino* cheese with truffles; €5.20) while chatting up fellow diners. (*Primi* €5.20-7.50, *secondi* €3 per 100g. Open M and W-Su 12:30-3pm and 7:30-10:30pm. MC/V.) Try the *pollo e coniglio all'Etrusca* (Etruscan-style chicken and rabbit; €10.40) at **Il Cantuccio ❸**, V. delle Cantine 1-2, where tuxedo-clad waiters and dim lighting create a romantic atmosphere. (☎0578 75 78 70. *Primi* €7.30-9.40, *secondi* €8.60-15.50. Service 12%. Open Tu-Su 12:30-2:30pm and 7:30-11pm. MC/V.) The **open-air market** is every Thursday in P. del Mercato, in parking lot #5 off V. delle Lettere. For cheap groceries head to **Conad,** V. Bernabei 4/A, 50m downhill from Chiesa Sant'Agnese. (☎0578 71 67 31. Open M-Sa 8:30am-8pm. MC/V.)

■ **A PLAN A DAY KEEPS THE HIKING AWAY.** On its way to Siena, the southbound bus stops twice in Montepulciano. The 1st stop is at V. dell'Oriolo, in a parking lot at the higher end of the city. From the bus stop, climb the stairs along V. delle Mura to arrive at V. dell'Opio nel Corso. The 2nd stop is at the bus station at the bottom of the hill. Before entering Montepulciano, know which stop you want: the 1st on top of the hill, or the 2nd at the bottom. While the trek offers great views, hiking is never fun with a gargantuan backpack.

From P. Grande, follow V. Ricci to V. della Mercezia. Turn left down staircase before Piazzetta di S. Francesco. Follow signs, through the city walls, and along V. di San Biagio. The **Chiesa di San Biagio,** built on a wide, grass-covered plateau, is a stunning example of high-Renaissance symmetry. The cavernous interior was redone in the 17th century in overwrought Baroque, but the simplicity of the original still shines through. The surrounding area has stunning views of the rolling Tuscan hills and the houses perched in between. (Open daily 9am-1pm and 3:30-7pm. Free.) Montepulciano's main square, **Piazza Grande,** is surrounded by the **Palazzo Tarugi** to the north, an unfinished **duomo** to the south, the **Palazzo Contucci** to the east, and the 14th-century **Palazzo Comunale** to the west. The interior of the *duomo* is somber, its simple, bare walls contrasting with several great oil paintings. Note the Sienese master Taddeo di Bartolo's poignant *Assumption of the Virgin* above the altar. (Open daily 9am-12:30pm and 2:30-6:30pm. Free.) Since most lodgings in Montepulciano are pricey three- or four-star hotels, *affittacamere* (rooms for rent) are the best option if you absolutely must spend the night.

SAN GIMIGNANO ☎0577

The hilltop village of San Gimignano (san jee-meen-YA-no; pop. 7000) looks like an illustration from a medieval manuscript. Prototypical towers, churches, and the town's 14 famous towers, all that remain of the original 72, loom above the city's walls. The impressive towers date back to a period when prosperous families battled each other, using their towers to store grain for sieges. They were also conveniently used for dumping boiling oil on attacking enemies. After WWII, the skyline began to lure tourists, whose tastes and wallets resuscitated production of the golden *Vernaccia* wine. Despite hordes of daytrippers and an infestation of souvenir shops, the fortress-top sunsets, nighttime *gelato* strolls, and ample spots for lounging on *piazza* steps make an overnight stay worthwhile.

▐ TRANSPORTATION

The nearest **train station** is in Poggibonsi. Buses go from the station to town (20min.; M-F every 30min. 6:05am-8:35pm, Sa-Su hourly 7:35am-8:20pm; €1.70). TRA-IN **buses** (☎800 57 05 30 or 20 42 46; www.sienamobilita.it) leave from Ple. Martiri Montemaggio, outside Pta. San Giovanni. Schedules and tickets are at Caffè Combattente, V. San Giovanni 124, on the left after entering the city gates. Tickets are also available at *tabaccherie* or the tourist office. Change at Poggibonsi for Florence (1½hr., hourly, €6). Buses also run to Siena (1½hr., every 1-2hr., €5.20). For **bike** and **car rental** try **Bruno Bellini,** V. Roma 41, 200m down the hill from Pta. San Giovanni. (☎94 02 01; www.bellinibruno.com. Bikes €7-11 per hr., €15-21 per day. Scooters from €31 per day. Cars from €57 per day. Open daily 9am-1pm and 3-7:30pm. AmEx/MC/V.)

◢◤ ▐ ORIENTATION AND PRACTICAL INFORMATION

Buses to San Gimignano stop in **Piazzale Martiri Montemaggio,** just outside the city walls. To reach the *centro*, pass through **Porta San Matteo** and climb the hill, following **Via San Giovanni** to **Piazza della Cisterna,** which merges with **Piazza del Duomo** on the left. The other main street in town, **Via San Matteo,** extends down from the opposite side of P. del Duomo. Addresses in San Gimignano are marked in both faded black stencil and etched clay tiles; since most establishments go by the black, these are listed.

Tourist Office: Pro Loco, P. del Duomo 1 (☎94 00 08; www.sangimignano.com), has lists of hotels and rooms for rent, bus and train schedules, and bus tickets. Self-guided audio tours of the town €5. Excellent free maps. 2hr. tours of wineries Tu and Th 5pm; includes multiple tastings and transportation by bus (€20) or with own transportation (€18); reserve by noon the day before. Also makes private room reservations in person. Open daily Mar.-Oct. 9am-1pm and 3-7pm; Nov.-Feb. 9am-1pm and 2-6pm.

Accommodations Services: Siena Hotels Promotion, V. S. Giovanni 125 (☎94 08 09; fax 94 01 13), on the right entering the city gates. Look for the *"Cooperativa Alberghi e Ristoranti"* sign. Reserves hotel rooms in San Gimignano and Siena for 10% commission. Open M-W 9:30am-12:45pm and 2:30-7pm, Th-Sa 9:30am-7pm. AmEx/MC/V. **Associazione Strutture Extralberghiere,** P. della Cisterna 6 (☎/fax 94 31 90). Patient staff makes free reservations for private rooms. Call a week ahead to stay in the countryside; the *centro* is easier to book. Open Mar.-Nov. daily 10am-1pm and 3-6pm. MC/V.

Currency Exchange: Pro Loco tourist office and post office offer best rates. **ATMs** scattered along V. San Giovanni, V. degli Innocenti, and P. della Cisterna.

Carabinieri: (☎94 03 13), on P. Martiri.

Pharmacy: P. della Cisterna 8 (☎94 03 69; at night ☎348 00 21 710). Open M-Sa 9am-1pm and 4:30-8pm. AmEx/MC/V.

Internet Access: Edicola La Tuscia, V. Garibaldi 2, outside the gates to the right of Pta. San Matteo. €4.50 per hr. Open daily 7:30am-1pm and 2:30-7:30pm. Cash only.

Post Office: P. delle Erbe 8, behind the *duomo*. Open M-F 8:15am-4pm, Sa 8:15am-12:30pm. **Postal Code:** 53037.

ACCOMMODATIONS

San Gimignano caters to wealthy tourists, and most accommodations are well beyond budget range. *Affittacamere* provide an alternative to overpriced hotels, with most doubles with bath from €70. Look for the signs for "Camere/Rooms/Zimmer" that hang in souvenir shops, restaurants, and other storefront windows along main streets. The tourist office and the Associazione Strutture Extralberghiere have lists of budget rooms

Camere Gianni Cennini, V. San Giovanni 21 (☎347 07 48 188; www.sangiapartments.com). Enter through Pta. San Giovanni. Reception is at the *pasticceria* at V. San Giovanni 88. Each room is homey and luxurious, with large bath and scenic views of the surrounding vineyards. Kitchen use €15. Reservations recommended. Singles €45; doubles €55-60; triples €70; quads €85. MC/V. ❶

Albergo Il Pino, V. Cellolese 4 (☎/fax 94 04 15), just off V. San Matteo before exiting Pta. S. Matteo. 7 rustic and spacious rooms owned by the restaurant downstairs have quilted comforters, comfy sofa chairs, and TV. Reservations recommended. Singles €45; doubles €55. AmEx/MC/V. ❹

Hotel La Cisterna, P. della Cisterna 23 (☎94 03 28; www.hotelcisterna.it). Centrally located. Large rooms with flowing curtains complement the pastoral panorama. All 49 rooms have bath, A/C, and satellite TV. Breakfast included. Singles €60-78; doubles €85-98, with view €105-116, with balcony €105-132. Extra bed €30. AmEx/MC/V. ❺

Camping Boschetto di Piemma (☎94 03 52; www.boschettodipiemma.it), at Località Santa Lucia 38/C, 2km downhill from Pta. San Giovanni. Buses (€0.50) run from Ple. Martiri Montemaggio; confirm destination with driver before boarding. Small, wooded sites close together, but near community pool. Bar and market on premises. Reception daily 8am-1pm and 3-11pm. €9.25 per person, €5 per child, €7.30 per small tent. Apartment for 2 people €65. Hot showers free. AmEx/MC/V. ●

◳ FOOD

San Gimignano specializes in boar and other wild game, though it also caters to less daring palates with mainstream Tuscan dishes at higher prices. A weekly **open-air market** is in P. del Duomo and P. della Cisterna. (Open Th 8am-1pm.) Purchase the famous *Vernaccia di San Gimignano*, a light, sweet white wine, from **La Buca**, V. San Giovanni 16, for around €4.50 per bottle. This cooperative also offers tastes of terrific sausages and meats produced on its own farm. The boar sausage *al pignoli* (with pine nuts; €2.07 per 100g) and the oddly satisfying *salame con mirto* (salami with blueberry) are delicious. (☎94 04 07. Open daily Apr.-Oct. 9am-8pm; Nov.-Mar. 10am-6pm. AmEx/MC/V.)

▨ **Trattoria Chiribiri**, P. della Madonna 1 (☎94 19 48). From the bus stop, take 1st left off V. San Giovanni and climb a short staircase or follow your nose down the sidestreet. Amazing local fare at unusually affordable prices. *Primi* €5-7.50, *secondi* €7-14. Open M-Tu and Th-Su Mar.-Oct.11am-11pm; Nov.-Feb. noon-2pm and 7-10pm. Cash only. ❷

▨ **Pluripremiata Gelateria**, P. della Cisterna 4 (☎94 22 44). 3 counters hold *gelato* flavors never seen before. Try the *champelmo*, a mix of champagne and grapefruit, or the *Vernaccia*, a *gelato* version of the region's famous wine. Cups from €1.50. 3 flavors in a chocolate-lined cone €2.50. Open daily 11:30am-9pm. Cash only. ❶

Ristorante Perucà, V. Capassi 16 (☎94 31 36). Behind V. San Matteo. Charming benches, lanterns, and cheery staff welcome diners to a quieter spot hidden away from the tourist bustle. Adventurous types will love the *semifreddo ai zafferano*, an ice cream dessert made with saffron (€5). *Primi* €5-9, *secondi* €9-16. Cover €2. Open daily noon-2:30pm and 7-10:30pm. MC/V. ❸

La Stella, V. San Matteo 77 (☎94 04 44). Food made with produce from the restaurant's own farm and served in the long, narrow dining room. Sample wild boar and herbs (€13.50). Extensive wine list includes *Vernaccia*. *Primi* €6-8.55, *secondi* €8-13.20. *Menù turistico* €15. Cover €2. Open M-Tu and Th-Su Apr.-Oct. noon-3pm and 7-10pm; Nov.-Mar. noon-2pm and 7-9pm. AmEx/MC/V. ❸

◉ SIGHTS

Famous as the *Città delle Belle Torri* (City of the Beautiful Towers), San Gimignano has always appealed to artists. During the Renaissance, they came in droves, and the collection of their works complements San Gimignano's cityscape. Indeed, it's hard not to be impressed by the proud towers and the humble, winding streets caught in their shadows.

TIP **TICKET FOR *TUTTO*.** Combined tickets for the town's museums are available at varying rates. *Biglietti interi* (€7.50) are full-priced, adult tickets; *biglietti ridotti* (€5.50) are discounted tickets available to children between the ages of 8 and 18. Children under 7 are allowed *ingresso gratuito* (free entrance). 1 ticket allows entry into nearly all of San Gimignano's sights. Tickets are available at participating tourist sights or at the tourist office.

▨ **PIAZZA DELLA CISTERNA AND PIAZZA DEL DUOMO.** P. della Cisterna (1237) is surrounded by towers and palaces and is the bustling center of life in San Gimignano. It neighbors P. del Duomo, site of the impressive tower of the **Palazzo del Podestà.** To its left, tunnels and intricate loggias fill the Palazzo del Popolo. To the right of the *palazzo* rises its Torre Grossa, the town's highest tower and the only one people can climb. Also in the *piazza* stand the twin towers of the Ardinghelli, truncated due to a medieval zoning ordinance that regulated tower envy by prohibiting structures higher than the Torre Grossa. A perch on one of the steps in either *piazza* offers opportunities to watch scenery and people.

PALAZZO COMUNALE. A frescoed medieval courtyard leads to the entrance to the **Museo Civico** on the 2nd floor. The first room of the museum is the **Sala di Dante,** where the bard spoke on May 8, 1300, in an attempt to convince San Gimignano to side with the Florentines in their ongoing wars with Siena. On the walls, Lippo Memmi's sparkling *Maestà* overwhelms the accompanying 14th-century scenes of hunting and tournament pageantry. Up the stairs, Taddeo di Bartolo's altarpiece, *The Story of San Gimignano*, tells the tale of the city's namesake saint, originally a bishop of Modena. Within the museum lies the entrance to the 218-step climb up ▧ **Torre Grossa.** While the final steps are precarious (watch your head on the low ceiling at the top), they are well worth the climb, as the tower offers views of half a dozen of San Gimignano's towers, the ancient fortress, several *piazze*, and the Tuscan landscape stretching to the horizon in all directions. *(Palazzo del Popolo, Museo Civico, and Tower open daily Mar.-Oct. 9:30am-7pm; Nov.-Feb. 10am-5:30pm. €5, students €4.)*

BASILICA DI SANTA MARIA ASSUNTA. The bare facade of this 12th-century church seems unfit to shelter such an exceptionally frescoed interior. Off the right aisle, the **Cappella di Santa Fina** is covered in Ghirlandaio's frescoes of the life of Santa Fina, the town's ascetic saint who was stricken with a fatal disease at the age of 10. *(In P. del Duomo. Open Apr.-Oct. M-F 9:30am-7:30pm, Sa 9:30am-5pm, Su 12:30-5pm; Nov.-Jan. and Mar. M-Sa 9:30am-5pm, Su 12:30-5pm. €3.50, under 18 €1.50. Cash only.)*

FORTEZZA AND MUSEO DEL VINO. Follow the signs past the Basilica di Collegiata from P. del Duomo to this tiny, crumbling fortress. The courtyard is often full of street artists and musicians, and the turret offers a beautiful view of the countryside. Park benches protected by trees make for a great picnic or lounge spot when visitors clear out in the evening. There are weekly screenings of movies in the courtyard at night from June to August. Pop into the modest wine museum to brush up on your knowledge of *Chianti Classico* and *Vernaccia. (Fortezza open dawn until dusk. Museo del Vino ☎ 94 03 59. Open daily Mar.-Oct. 11:30am-7:30pm; closed W afternoon. Movie schedule and info at the tourist office. €6, children €4.)*

VOLTERRA ☎ 0588

Atop a huge bluff known as *Le Balze*, Volterra (Vol-TER-ra; pop. 12,000) is surrounded by a patchwork of green and yellow farmland. Once an important Etruscan settlement, the town shrunk to its current size during the Middle Ages, when outlying parts fell from the eroding hillside. Volterra's Roman amphitheater and famous alabaster work blend centuries of Tuscan tradition with a friendly and much-touristed atmosphere. If you've ever wondered why the Tuscan countryside is so popular with visitors, take a short walk to Volterra's perimeter and admire the sprawling vista—you'll understand what all the fuss is about.

▣ TRANSPORTATION

The **train station** that services Volterra is in the nearby town of Cecina. To get there, take the CPT **bus** to Saline (6 per day, Aug. and Su 2 per day; €1.65) and transfer to another CPT bus to Cecina (5 per day, Aug. and Su 2 per day; €1.50) for trains to Pisa (€3.90) and the coast. For other schedules and info, consult the tourist office. **Buses** (☎86 150) are more convenient and centrally located in P. Martiri della Libertà, with daily departures to Florence and Siena (1½hr., 4 per day, €7.05) via Colle Val d'Elsa (50min., 4 per day, €2.20). Be sure to anticipate plenty of time for connections. Buses also run to Pisa (2hr., 10 per day, €4.70) via Pontederra. Buy tickets at Associazione Pro Volterra, at *tabaccherie*, or at vending machines near the bus stop. For **taxis**, call ☎87 257.

> **TIP** **ALL ABOARD!** Buses from Volterra are infrequent, often departing just a few times each day. Know when buses leave the night before, or you might find yourself spending an unexpected night inside these historic Etruscan walls.

ORIENTATION AND PRACTICAL INFORMATION

To get from the bus stop in **Piazza Martiri della Libertà** to the town center, turn right from the bus stop crossing the *piazza*, and turn left on **Via dei Marchesi** which becomes **Via Ricciarelli** and leads to **Piazza dei Priori**, the central *piazza*.

Tourist Office: Consorzio Turistico, P. dei Priori 19 (☎87 257; www.volterratur.it). Provides maps, brochures, and audio walking tours (€5). Also makes hotel and taxi reservations for free. Open daily 10am-1pm and 2-6pm. **Associazione Pro Volterra**, V. Turazza 2 (☎86 150; www.provolterra.it), just off P. dei Priori, sells CPT bus tickets and provides schedule and fare info on trains to Pisa and buses to Florence, Pisa, Saline, San Gimignano, and Siena. Open M-F 9am-noon and 3-6:30pm.

Currency Exchange: Cassa di Risparmio di Volterra, V. Matteotti 1, has a 24hr. exchange machine and an **ATM** outside. Also in P. Martiri della Libertà. Open M-F 8:20am-1:20pm and 2:35-3:35pm, Sa 8:20-11:20am.

Pharmacy: Farmacia Amidei, V. Ricciarelli 2 (emergencies ☎86 060). Open M-Tu and Th-Sa 9am-1pm and 4-8pm, Su for emergencies.

Hospital: (☎91 911), on Borgo San Lazzaro.

Internet Access: ■**Web and Wine**, V. Porte all'Arco 11/13 (☎81 531; www.webandwine.com). After surfing the web, kick back with a glass of *Chianti* or one of 32 different kinds of hot chocolate, and cast an eye over Etruscan ruins visible through the glass floor. €4 per hr. Open daily 8:30am-1am. MC/V.

Post Office: P. dei Priori 14 (☎86 969). Open M-F 8:15am-7pm, Sa 8:15am-12:30pm. **Postal Code:** 56048.

ACCOMMODATIONS

Hotels can get expensive, so ask the tourist office for a list of *affittacamere*. Singles generally start at €35, doubles at €50.

■ **La Torre,** V. Guarnacci 47 (☎80 036 or 348 72 47 693). From bus stop, turn right into town, then left and immediately right on V. Matteoti, which becomes V. Guarnacci right after it crosses V. Gramsci. Either arrange arrival time or call upon arrival (no doorbell). Great *affittacamere* in the *centro storico*. Rooms sport comfy beds, large bath, and TV. Owner supplies maps and free drinks. Kitchen access. Call ahead or book through tourist office. Singles €35; doubles €45. Cash only. ❸

■ **Affittacamere Renzi,** P. Martiri della Libertà 8 (☎86 106 or 86 133; www.camere-renzi.com). Friendly locals rent 1 double and a large apartment, with private bath and thoughtful furnishings. Quietly situated along city walls with views of countryside. Minutes away from P. dei Priori. Doubles €50; apartments with kitchen and terrace €60. AmEx/MC/V. ❷

Seminario Vescovile, Vle. Vittorio Veneto, 2 (☎86 028; fax 90 791), in Ple. Sant'Andrea, next to the church. Follow directions to La Torre, but turn right on V. Gramsci. Walk through P. XX Settembre, then turn left. Exit city through Pta. Marcoli, and follow the road. Turn left on Vle. V. Veneto until Ple. Sant'Andrea. High arched ceilings, frescoed doorways, and views of the walled city and Tuscan countryside. 1- to 4-person rooms. No unmarried couples. Breakfast €3. Reception 8am-midnight. Curfew midnight. Reservation required. €14 per person, with bath €18. AmEx/MC/V. ❶

Albergo Etruria, V. Matteotti 32 (☎87 377). Walk into town, turn left, then make the 1st right on V. Matteotti. Fresh white furnishings with TV and phone, private garden, and a classy lounge make this a congenial hotel. Breakfast included. Singles €60-70; doubles €80-90; triples €100-110. AmEx/MC/V. ❹

Hotel La Locanda, V. Guarnacci 24/28 (☎81 547; www.hotel-lalocanda.com). A former convent turned 4-star hotel. Rooms are adorned with artwork from a local gallery. All have bath, satellite TV, fridge, Internet access, and safe. Breakfast included. Singles €68-96; doubles €85-120, wheelchair-accessible €80-105; suite with massaging shower and sauna €250. AmEx/MC/V. ❺

Le Balze, V. Mandringa 15 (☎87 880). Exit through Pta. San Francesco and bear right on Strada Provincial Pisana. Turn left on V. Mandringa after 20min. Campground has pool and bar. Store sells tickets for bus into town (hourly 7:11am-8:21pm). Showers included. Reception 8am-10pm. July-Aug. €7-8 per person, €8-9 per tent; Sept.-Oct. and Apr.-June €6/7. AmEx/MC/V. ❶

◘ FOOD

Sample *salsiccia di cinghiale* (wild boar sausage) and *pecorino* (sheep's milk cheese) at any of the *alimentari* along V. Gaurnacci and V. Gramsci. For a sweet snack, try *ossi di morto* (bones of the dead man), a rock-hard local candy made of egg whites, sugar, hazelnuts, and a hint of lemon; or *pane di pescatore* (fisherman's bread), a dense and delicious sweet bread full of nuts and raisins. **Despar,** V. Gramsci 12, is good for groceries. (Open M-F 7:30am-1pm and 5-8pm, Sa 7:30am-1pm. MC/V.)

Pizzeria/Birreria Ombra della Sera, V. Guarnacci 16 (☎85 274). Cooks toss pizzas to the perfect diameter while diners relax under cross-vaulted ceilings and the warm glow of red lanterns. Takeout available. Pizza €5-7.50. Salad €6.50. Pasta €6-8. Cover €1. Service 10%. Open Tu-Su noon-3pm and 7-10pm. MC/V. ❷

L'Ombra della Sera, V. Gramsci 70 (☎86 663), off P. XX Settembre. A local favorite. Candlelit, outdoor patio on busy V. Gramsci makes for great people-watching on a summer evening. Rich Volterran classics, like *tagliolini al tartufo* (pasta with truffle sauce; €9) are stellar choices. *Primi* €7-9, *secondi* €10-15. Cover €1.30. Service 10%. Open June-Aug. daily noon-3pm and 7-10pm; Sept.-Oct. and Mar.-May Tu-Su noon-3pm and 7-10pm. AmEx/MC/V. ❸

La Pizzicheria da Pina, V. Gramsci 64 (☎87 394). Serves regional wines and savory spreads at tables in an underground Roman cave. In the upstairs store bottles of wine from €6 per bottle, olive oil €6.20, balsamic vinegar €16.70. *Panini* €6-8. *Piatti* €6-15. Open daily Mar.-Nov. 9am-9pm; Oct.-Feb. 9am-1pm and 4-8pm. AmEx/MC/V. ❶

Trattoria Il Poggio, V. Porte all'Arco 7 (☎85 257). Pasta dishes with meat sauces and a "medieval" *menù* (€13) featuring local cheeses are the highlights at this casual restaurant. Interesting medieval paraphernalia on the walls includes giant crossed axes and metal shields. Pizza €5-8. *Primi* €6-8, *secondi* €7.50-14. Open M and W-Su noon-3pm and 6:30-10pm. AmEx/MC/V. ❷

◎ SIGHTS

PINACOTECA COMUNALE. This graceful building contains Volterra's best art, displayed in dimly lit rooms with few labels. The first floor showcases two dramatic works: Rosso Fiorentino's spectacular *Deposizione della Croce*, in which Christ's body has a greenish tinge and spills from the canvas onto the frame, creating the mesmerizing illusion that his subjects are not confined to the flat surface. Luca Signorelli's even richer *Annunciazione* is filled with finely realized details of architecture and cloth. *(V. dei Sarti 1, up V. Buonparenti from P. dei Priori. ☎87 580. Open daily 9am-7pm. €8, students €5, under 6 free. Combined ticket includes Pinacoteca, Museo Etrusco, and Museo dell' Opera del Duomo di Arte Sacra sold at each of the 3. Cash only.)*

PIAZZA DEI PRIORI. Life in Volterra revolves around P. dei Priori, which is surrounded by sober, dignified *palazzi*. The **Palazzo dei Priori,** the oldest government palace in Tuscany, presides over the square. Regal coats of arms line the walls of the first floor. Inside, the council hall and antechamber are open to the public. Jacopo di Cione Orcagna's damaged *Annunciation with Four Saints* occupies the right wall. *(Open Mar.-Nov. daily 10:30am-5:30pm; Nov.-Mar. Sa-Su 10am-5pm. €1.)*

CATTEDRALE DI SANTA MARIA ASSUNTA. Construction began on Volterra's preRomanesque cathedral in the 12th century and continued for 300 years. By the time the choir at the end of the nave was completed, architects had already switched to a Gothic design, indicated by the transition from rounded arches to pointed ones. The chapel off the left transept holds frescoes by Rosselli, including the luminous *Missione per Damasco*. *(In P. San Giovanni, down V. Turazza from P. dei Priori. Open daily 8am-12:30pm and 3-7pm. Free.)*

MUSEO ETRUSCO GUARNACCI. The Etruscan museum displays over 600 finely carved funeral urns from the 4th to the first centuries BC. The pieces are not well displayed and lack explanatory signs, but an audio tour (€3) covers a few rooms. The 1st floor (Room XV) holds the museum's most famous piece, the elongated bronze figure dubbed *L'Ombra della Sera* (Shadow of the Evening). The farmer who unearthed it used it for years as a fireplace poker until a visitor recognized it as an Etruscan votive figure. In Room XIX, the famous *Urna degli Sposi* depicts an obviously embittered married couple. *(V. Minzoni 15. From P. dei Priori, head down to V. Matteotti, turn right on V. Gramsci, and follow it to V. Minzoni. ☎86 347. Open daily mid-Mar. to Oct. 9am-7pm; Nov. to mid-Mar. 8:30am-1:45pm. €8, students €5. Cash only.)*

ROMAN AMPHITHEATER. These impressive ruins include partly grass-covered stone seating and Corinthian columns salvaged from the stage. The admission fee allows you to walk along the edge of the ruins behind metal rails, but the vantage point from V. Lungo le Mura is free and just as gratifying. *(Just outside the city walls next to Pta. Fiorentina. From P. dei Priori, follow V. delle Prigioni, turn right at the T-junction and left on V. Guarnacci. Proceed out the arch and through the parking lot to the left. Open Mar. 16-Oct. daily 10:30am-5:30pm; Nov.-Mar. 15 Sa-Su 10am-4pm. €2. Cash only.)*

PALAZZO VITI. This private residence is still home to heirs of the wealthy Viti family, but 12 rooms are open to the public. The furnishings and alabaster collections date from the 15th century to the present, and the beautiful interior was used as a backdrop by Italian director Luchino Visconti for his 1964 film *Vaghe stelle dell'Orsa* (Sandra). A visit to the downstairs cantine and a small tasting of wine, cheese, and salami is included. *(V. dei Sarti 41, down the street from the Pinacoteca. Open daily 10am-1pm and 2:30-6:30pm. €5, students €2.50. Cash only.)*

MONTALCINO ☎ 0577

Perched atop a hill overlooking vineyards and stately clusters of cypress trees, Montalcino (mohn-tal-CHEE-no; pop. 6000) is yet another Tuscan wine town with a view. But unlike some of its neighbors, Montalcino has a relatively low tourist influx, allowing visitors a leisurely stroll along narrow alleys and steep stairways that have changed little since medieval times. A former Sienese stronghold, its heavy walls are enduring evidence of prior belligerence, but the tiny town has long since traded war-mongering for wine-making. Its foremost industry today is the production of the heavenly, albeit pricey *Brunello di Montalcino*, a red wine acknowledged as Italy's finest. Sample the *Brunello* in the numerous wine shops, or leave Montalcino's city walls to tour a winery.

📧 🚊 TRANSPORTATION AND PRACTICAL INFORMATION. To reach Montalcino, take one of the TRA-IN **buses** from Siena's train station (1¼hr., 7 per day, €3.20). The last bus to Montalcino departs at 10:20pm, and the last bus back to Siena departs at 8:30pm from Montalcino's P. Cavour. Coming from Montepulciano (1¼hr., €3.20), change buses at Torrenieri. There is no actual bus stop, so flag the bus down as it approaches. Contact the Pro Loco **tourist office,** Costa del Municipio 8, for info on local vineyard tours, free maps, hotel booking, and **currency exchange.** From P. Cavour, where the bus stops, walk up V. Mazzini to P. del Popolo. The tourist office is under the clock tower. (☎84 93 31; www.prolocomontalcino.it. Open Apr.-Oct. daily 10am-1pm and 2-5:50pm; Nov.-Mar. Tu-Su 10am-1pm and 2-5:40pm.)

📕 🍴 ACCOMMODATIONS AND FOOD. Hotel rooms are expensive and scarce in Montalcino. *Affittacamere* are generally well-kept and run €42-52 for a double with bath. The tourist office provides a list of all hotels and *affittacamere* in the area. **⬛Anna Affittacamera ❹,** V. San Saloni, provides elegance at a luxurious price. Rooms have ceiling frescoes, comfortable beds, TV, and bath. Check in at Hotel Giglio, V. San Saloni 5. (☎84 86 66; fax 84 81 67. Singles €50; doubles €70; apartment with kitchen and courtyard €75-90. AmEx/MC/V.) Closest to the bus stop is **Albergo Il Giardino ❸,** P. Cavour 4, where the friendly owner is more than willing to share his extensive knowledge and collection of local wines. The large, tasteful rooms all have spacious baths. (☎84 82 57; www.albergogiardino.it. Singles €40; doubles €53; triples €72. Cash only.) **Il Barlanzone Affittacamere ❸,** V. Ricasoli 33, rents four color-coordinated rooms and an apartment with TV, large bath, and an unobstructed view of the fortress. Enter through *enoteca* on the corner. (☎84 61 20. Doubles €55; apartment €75. Weekly rental discount 10%. MC/V.)

Montalcino's wine menus are generally twice as thick as the food menus. *Enoteche* line V. Mazzini, the town's main street, all offering huge selections of *Brunello* and tasty snacks like *bruschette* or cheese and meat plates (€3-7). In the rustic and brightly painted **Taverna Il Grappolo Blu ❸,** Scale di V. Moglio 1, a memorable ravioli with *pecorino* cheese and *ragù* (€8) is just one of many superior options. (☎84 71 50. *Primi* €6-8, *secondi* €8-15. Cover €2. Open daily noon-3pm and 7-10pm. AmEx/MC/V.) At Maria Pia's **Re di Macchia ❹,** V. Soccorso Saloni 21, complement a typical Tuscan dish such as *pinci* (large spaghetti) with wild boar *ragù* (€8) and a bottle of Il Consiglio di Antonio (€15), one of four of Montalcino's premier wines. (☎84 61 16. *Primi* €8, *secondi* €13-16. Cover €2. Open M-W and F-Su noon-2pm and 7-9pm. AmEx/MC/V.) The best deals on *Brunello* (€18-28) are at the **Coop,** on the corner of V. Sant'Agostino and V. della Libertà. (Open M-Sa 8am-1pm and 4-8pm. MC/V.)

📷 SIGHTS. The ⬛**Abbazia di Sant'Antimo,** is in Castelnuovo, a town 10km from Montalcino on the same La Peschiera route as the Fattoria dei Barbi (€1.10; return

7:45am, 2:25, 4:55pm). The walk from Castelnuovo to the abbey takes about 8min. and passes the sloping hills and cypress trees characteristic of the Tuscan countryside. Lore holds that Charlemagne founded the abbey in AD 780 in thanks for the miraculous curing of the plague that scourged his army. The 12th-century structure was built with a rounded apse and carved alabaster capitals and is one of Tuscany's most beautiful Romanesque structures. Inside, monks celebrate mass in **Gregorian chant** seven times per day (during which the church is closed to the public). Chants float through speakers throughout the rest of the day. (☎83 56 59; www.antimo.it. Open M-Sa 10:15am-12:30pm and 3-6:30pm, Su 9:15-10:45am and 3-6pm. Visitors are asked not to take photos during prayer. Free.)

Back in town stands Montalcino's 14th-century **fortezza,** which sheltered a band of republicans escaping the Florentine siege of Siena in 1555. The fortress is almost perfectly preserved, with five towers and part of the town walls incorporated into the structure. Two interior courtyards, one shaded by foliage, the other sunny and cheered by geraniums, make nice picnic spots. Many visitors bypass the fortress itself in favor of the sophisticated **Enoteca La Fortezza,** which offers wine tastings (€9-19), cheese plates (€9), and local wines (€3-12 per glass; *Brunello* €6.50-12). A climb up the stairs, through the turret, and onto the panoramic walls is €3.50, but you can enjoy great views from the ground for free. (Fort and *enoteca* open daily Apr.-Oct. 9am-8pm; Nov.-Mar. 10am-6pm.)

To appreciate the vineyards, use the local **shuttle service,** La Peschiera (☎0564 95 31 34), to visit **Fattoria dei Barbi.** Shuttles depart daily from P. Cavour at 1:45 and 2:45pm; return 2:25 and 5pm. Ask the driver to stop at the Fattoria. Shuttle stops at the bottom of a driveway. Tours of the cellars are followed by a tasting of three different kinds of *Brunello.* Tastings (€9-18) are available any time during open hours; ring the bell for service. The winery also includes a restaurant which is open for lunch and dinner. (☎84 11 11; www.fattoriadeibarbi.it. Open July-Aug. M-F 10am-1pm and 2:30-7pm, Sa-Su 2:30-7pm; Sept.-June M-F 10am-1pm and 2:30-6pm, Sa-Su 2:30-6pm. Free 30min. tours given M-F hourly 11am-noon and 3-5pm.)

🎭🎪 **ENTERTAINMENT AND FESTIVALS.** Every year since 1957, on the last Sunday in October, Montalcino celebrates the **Sagra del Tordo.** Each of the city's four *quartieri* (districts; Borghetto, Pianello, Ruga and Travaglio) participates in the event. This festival evolved from a medieval tradition where the men returned to their houses after a day of hawk hunting, followed by archery competitions.

CORTONA ☎ 0575

Though its tranquil streets may betray it, the ancient town of Cortona (cor-TOHna; pop. 23,600) once rivaled Perugia, Arezzo, and even Florence in power and belligerence. After appropriation in 1411 by Naples, Cortona was sold to the rival Florentines, and citizens of Cortona enjoyed peace and prosperity. Impressive art collections and architecture from this period of grandeur linger within the small city's walls, including two altarpieces by Fra Angelico and the paintings of Luca Signorelli. Today, Cortona has become a tourist hot spot, known best as the setting for *Under the Tuscan Sun*. Indeed, the view from P. Garibaldi as the sun sets over the valley below would make anyone want to look up real estate listings.

📮 **TRANSPORTATION**

Trains depart **Camucia-Cortona station** to Florence (hourly, €6.70) and Rome (2½hr., every 2hr., €9.40). **LFI buses** (☎30 07 48) run to Cortona's P. Garibaldi from this station (15min., €1; check schedule ahead of time) and from **Terontola train station**

(30min., hourly, €1.65; buy ticket from train station *bar*). Buses also arrive in P. Garibaldi from Arezzo (1hr., 12 per day, €2.70). Buy LFI bus tickets from the tourist office, *bars*, or *tabaccherie*. For **taxis**, call ☎335 81 96 313.

 THE REAL DEAL: UNDER THE TREACHEROUS SUN. With the recent popularity of *Under the Tuscan Sun*, visitors to Cortona may find themselves approached by taxi drivers offering cheap rides out to the farmhouse featured in the book and film. Before embarking on this mini-pilgrimage, remember that it's a residence, not a tourist attraction. Ask yourself if it's really worth the money—or the potential for being ripped off by a less-than-honest driver.

ORIENTATION AND PRACTICAL INFORMATION

Buses stop at **Piazza Garibaldi** just outside the city walls. Enter the city by following **Via Nazionale**, which leads to **Piazza della Repubblica**. Diagonally across the *piazza* is **Piazza Signorelli**, Cortona's main square. The **tourist office,** V. Nazionale 42, provides maps, bus schedules, and tickets for buses, trains, and tours. (☎63 03 52; www.apt.arezzo.it. Open June-Sept. M-Sa 9am-1pm and 3-7pm, Su 9am-1pm; Oct.-May M-F 9am-1pm and 3-6pm, Sa 9am-1pm. No tickets sold Sa-Su.) **Currency exchange** and a 24hr. **ATM** are available at **Banca Etruria,** V. Santa Margherita 5. (Open M-F 8:20am-1:20pm and 2:35-3:35pm, Sa 8:20-11:50am.) In case of **emergency,** call the **police** at V. Dardano 9 (☎63 72 25). **Farmacia Centrale** is at V. Nazionale 38. (☎60 32 06. Open M-Sa 9am-1pm and 4:30-8pm. MC/V.) Reach the **hospital** at ☎63 91. Use the **Internet** at **Telenet,** V. Guelfa 25, which also offers a **Western Union,** phone center, cell phone rental, and shipping services. English spoken. (☎60 10 96. €1 for 1st 15min., €3.50 per hr. with subscription bought on-site. Open M-Sa 9am-8:30pm. MC/V.) The **post office** is uphill from P. della Repubblica at V. Benedetti 2. (☎60 30 21. Open M-F 8:15am-1:30pm, Sa 8:15am-12:30pm.) **Postal Code:** 52044.

ACCOMMODATIONS

Ostello San Marco (HI), V. Maffei 57 (☎60 13 92; www.cortonahostel.com). From the bus stop, walk 5min. uphill on V. Santa Margherita and follow signs curving left to the hostel. A stone, wood beamed, medieval lobby combines with amiable cheer in this clean, well-kept hostel. Breakfast included. Dinner €9.50. Reception 7-10am and 3:30pm-midnight. Open to individuals mid-Mar. to Nov., to groups year-round. Dorms €13; singles €17. Cash only. ●

Casa Betanìa, V. Gino Severini 50 (☎62 829; fax 60 42 99), downhill from P. Garibaldi. Cross Vle. Cesare Battisti and take an immediate right through the gates. 30 simply furnished rooms all have small sinks and large, sunny windows looking out over the chapel next door. Breakfast €4. Singles €32; doubles €45; triples €60. MC/V. ❸

Istituto Santa Margherita, V. Cesare Battisti 15 (☎63 03 36; fax 63 05 49). Downhill on V. G. Severini from P. Garibaldi; on the corner of V. C. Battisti on the left. Get thee to this nunnery (actually a former college), complete with antique furniture, wide hallways, and large baths. Breakfast €3. Singles €32; doubles (no unmarried couples) €46; triples €56; quads €66. Cash only. ❸

Hotel San Luca, P. Garibaldi 1 (☎63 04 60; albergosanluca@technet.it). Rooms offer comfortable amenities, including bath, TV, A/C, phone, safe, and minibar. Though the interior lacks Italian charm, vistas from the terrace sweep the Chiana valley and Lake Trasimeno. Singles €80; doubles €110; triples €145; quads €180. AmEx/MC/V. ❺

🏠 FOOD

You won't have to search long for a bustling, home-style Tuscan trattoria in Cortona; the tables spill onto the streets surrounding the town's main *piazze*. The best beef in Tuscany is raised in the surrounding valleys, so consider making a modest splurge on *bistecca alla Fiorentina* (Florentine beef steak). Complement dinner with the fine, local white wine, *Bianco Vergine di Valdichiana*. Pennypinchers can pick up a €2.50 bottle at **Despar,** P. della Repubblica 23, which also stocks basic groceries and makes *panini* (€3) with fresh ingredients. (☎63 06 66. Open Apr.-Oct. M-Sa 7am-1:30pm and 4:30-8pm, Su 9am-1pm; Nov.-Mar. M-Tu and Th-Sa 7am-1:30pm and 4:30-7:30pm, W 7am-1:30pm. AmEx/MC/V.) On Saturday P. Signorelli hosts an **open-air market.** (Open 8am-1pm.)

■ **Trattoria La Grotta,** P. Baldelli 3 (☎63 02 71). Turn left into courtyard at the end of V. Nazionale. Start with a regional *bresaola con parmigiano e rucola* (thin-sliced meat topped with parmesan and arugula; €7), followed by the *gnocchi di ricotta e spinaci al tartufo* (with spinach, ricotta cheese, and truffles; €7). If that doesn't send you through the wood-timbered roof, we don't know what will. Seating in converted wine cellar or outside in a private courtyard. *Primi* €6-11, *secondi* €7-16. Cover €1. Open M and W-Su noon-2:30pm and 7-9:30pm. MC/V. ❷

Trattoria Dardano, V. Dardano 24 (☎60 19 44; www.trattoriadardano.com). Follow your nose and your ears to the succulent smells and lively conversation that carry down the street. Simple, filling dishes with notably ample *secondi* portions. Meat dishes include a very affordable steak (€2.50 per 100g). *Primi* €5-7, *secondi* €5-8. Cover €1. Open M-Tu and Th-Su noon-2:45pm and 7:15-9:45pm. Cash only. ❷

Ristorante Preludio, V. Guelfa 11 (☎63 01 04; www.ilpreudio.net). Treat yourself to Tuscan wares with a twist, like *gnocchi di prugne* (plum pasta *gnocchi;* €9). Respectfully attentive service. High ceilings and candles add a classy touch. *Primi* €7-10, *secondi* €11-18. Cover €2. Open daily 12:30-3pm and 7:30-10:30pm. AmEx/MC/V. ❸

Gelateria Snoopy, P. Signorelli 29. Charlie Brown and Snoopy adorn the walls as patrons young and old line up at the counter for homemade waffle cones filled with ■ 4 **scoops** for €2 and other delicious treats. Open daily 10am-11pm. Cash only. ❶

🟢 SIGHTS

■ **MUSEO DELL'ACCADEMIA ETRUSCA.** Perfectly preserved Egyptian sarcophagi and mummies, Roman coins, and golden altarpieces mingle to fantastic effect in this extravagant collection. Also check out oil paintings by old masters and native sons Luca Signorelli and Pietro Berrettini (known as Pietro da Cortona), as well as by the Futurist Gino Severini. In the main hall on the first floor is an unusual 4th-century BC Etruscan chandelier decorated with intricate allegorical carvings. In the **Medici Room,** lined with coats of arms, are two 1714 globes by Silvestro Moroncelli; one depicts the "Isola di California" floating in the Pacific, the other sports vivid illustrations of all the constellations. *(P. Signorelli, inside the courtyard of Palazzo Casali, to the right of P. della Repubblica. ☎63 72 35. Open Apr.-Oct. daily 10am-7pm; Nov.-Mar. Tu-Su 10am-5pm. Guided tours available by reservations only. €7, groups of more than 15 €4 per person, students €2. Cash only.)*

■ **MUSEO DIOCESANO.** This humble museum packs some of the Italian Renaissance's greats. Admire the grace of the gold wings and the fine details in Fra Angelico's stunning *Annunciation* (c. 1436) in **Room 3** of the upstairs gallery.

TUSCANY

Luca Signorelli's masterpiece *The Deposition* (1502), a vivid portrayal of the removal of Christ's body from the cross that combines Classical Roman and medieval detailing, hangs in **Room 1.** Works by the Sienese Pietro Lorenzetti, like his fresco *The Way to Calvary* in **Room 2** and his meticulously rendered *Crucifix* in **Room 3,** also impress. Severini's modern interpretations of traditional biblical scenes line the stairwell. *(From P. della Repubblica, pass through P. Signorelli and follow the signs. ☎62 830. Open daily 10am-7pm. €5, groups of more than 15 people and children under age 15 €3. Audio tour €3. Cash only.)*

FORTEZZA MEDICEA. Views of the Val di Chiana and Lake Trasimeno are incomparable from any other points in town. The courtyard and bastions contain temporary art installations, and shrines decorated with mosaics based on Severini's series in the Museo Diocesano line the uphill path. On the way, the unassuming white marble facade of the **Basilica di Santa Margherita** bursts into bold combinations of primary colors within—blue ceilings are fancifully dotted with gold stars. The body of Santa Margherita (1247-1297) rests in a glass coffin at the center of the altarpiece. *(A thigh-burning 15min. walk up V. S. Margherita from P. Garibaldi. To reach the fortress, take a right out of the church and climb the small uphill road. ☎60 37 93. Fortress open daily July-Aug. 10am-1:30pm and 2:30-7pm; Apr.-June and Sept. 10am-1:30pm and 2:30-6pm. Closed during bad weather. Modest dress required. €3, under 12 €1.50. Basilica free.)*

PALAZZI AND PIAZZE. In P. della Repubblica, the 13th-century **Palazzo Comunale** serves as a bold backdrop for the surrounding shops and cafes. At night, people gather on the steps to enjoy their *gelato* and people-watch. **Palazzo Casali,** to the right and behind the Palazzo del Comune, dominates P. Signorelli. Only the courtyard walls lined with coats of arms remain from the original structure; the facade and interlocking staircase are 17th-century additions. **Piazza del Duomo** lies to the right and downhill from the Palazzo Casali. Inside the simple 16th-century **Cattedrale di Santa Maria** are paintings by Signorelli and del Sarto, as well as an impressive Baroque-canopied high altar and rich, dark-wood pulpit built in 1524. *(Open Mar.-Nov. 7:30am-1pm and 3-6:30pm; Nov.-Mar. 8am-12:30pm and 3-5:30pm. Free.)*

❄ FESTIVALS

When August 14-15 rolls around, Italian cows start trembling. Yes, it's time for the **Sagra della Bistecca** (Steakfest), the most important town festival, when the populace shares superb steak in the public gardens behind the church of San Domenico. The next culinary extravaganza follows during the third weekend of August with the **Festa dei Porcini,** which fills the gardens with mushroom-lovers. Tickets are sold at the garden entrance. In early June, neighborhoods commemorate a nobleman's 1397 marriage with religious ceremonies, period dress, and the **Giostra Dell'Archidado,** a crossbow challenge in which participants compete for the *verretta d'oro* (golden dart). Musical and theatrical events come in July, when Cortona absorbs the spillover from the Umbria Jazz Festival. Relax in the gardens or join in the *passeggiata* in the park, which screens **movies** in the original language (usually English) weekly from mid-June through early September. (Visit www.teatrosignorelli.com for lists of films and info. Films start 9:45pm. In bad weather screenings in Teatro Signorelli. €5.)

AREZZO ☎0575

It was Michelangelo himself who said "Any talent I have is a result of the fine air of your town, Arezzo." Indeed, for a town of its size, Arezzo (ah-RET-so; pop. 92,000) has seen a veritable bonanza of artists and thinkers. Besides Michelangelo, the Tuscan town was also home to Renaissance titans Piero della Francesca, the poet

Petrarch, the humanist Bruni, and the artist and historian Giorgio Vasari. It's also the hometown of Roberto Benigni, director and star of the Oscar-winning *La Vita è Bella* ("Life is Beautiful"), who shot many of the film's scenes in the surrounding countryside. Though largely urban and commercial, the more subdued historical district preserves many vestiges of past genius, from Vasari's stunning architecture in P. Grande to della Francesca's unparalleled *Legend of the True Cross* in the Basilica di San Francesco. Escape the busy *centro* by strolling outside the eastern portion of the medieval city walls; catch striking views of the countryside and glimpses of backyard olive trees, flowerbeds, and vegetable gardens.

▉ TRANSPORTATION

Arezzo lies on the Florence-Rome train line. From P. della Repubblica, **trains** run to Florence (1½hr., 2 per hr. 4:30am-9:50pm, €5.20) and Rome (2hr., every 1-2hr. 6:30am-10:11pm, €11.20-25). The ticket booth is open M-Sa 5:50am-8:50pm. To the left of the train station, **TRA-IN, SITA,** and **LFI buses** run to Sansepolcro (1hr., hourly, €3.30) and Siena (1½hr., 4 per day, €5). Call ☎38 26 51 for more info. Buy tickets at ATAM ticket office, in front and to the left of train station exit. (☎800 38 17 30. Open daily 5:50am-8:50pm.) For **taxis**, contact 24hr. **RadioTaxi** (☎38 26 26). **Car rental** is available at **Autonoleggi Royal,** V. Marco Perrenio 21. (☎35 35 70. 21+. Open M-F 8:30am-12:30pm and 3:30-7:30pm, Sa 8:30am-12:30pm.)

▉▉ ORIENTATION AND PRACTICAL INFORMATION

Via Guido Monaco, which begins directly across from the **train station** at **Piazza della Repubblica,** parallels **Corso Italia;** together they form the backbone of the commercial district. To get to the *centro storico,* follow V. G. Monaco from the station to the traffic circle at **Piazza Guido Monaco.** Turn right on **Via Roma** and then left on the pedestrian walkway C. Italia, which leads to the old city. **Piazza Grande** lies to the right, 250m up C. Italia. **Via Vittorio Veneto** begins a block to the right of the train station, going under the train tracks and continuing to the back of the station.

Tourist Office: APT, P. della Repubblica 28 (☎20 839; www.apt.arezzo.it). Turn right after exiting station. English spoken. Free maps and brochures of the town and nearby valleys. Open Apr.-Sept. M-Sa 9am-1pm and 3-7pm, Su 9am-1pm; Oct.-Mar. M-Sa 10am-1pm and 3-6:30pm. On the opposite side of town, just off P. del Duomo, is the **Centro Servizi Turistici,** located at P. Emiciclo Giovanni Paolo II (☎18 22 770; www.arezzoturismo.it). Facing the entrance to the *duomo,* turn left and enter the adjacent building though the door at the far left corner. Walk through the short hallway to the right, down the escalator, and the office is on the right. Services include tourist information, hotel, airline and tour bookings, luggage storage, and Internet access. Open daily 9:30am-7pm.

Budget Travel: CTS, V. V. Veneto 25 (☎90 78 08), sells Eurail passes and plane tickets. Open M-F 9am-1pm and 3-7:30pm, Sa 9am-1pm.

Currency Exchange: Banks line V. G. Monaco between the train station and P. G. Monaco. **Banca Nazionale del Lavoro,** V. G. Monaco 74, has a 24hr. **ATM.** Open M-F 8:20am-1:35pm and 2:50-4:05pm, Sa 8:20-11:50am.

Police: V. Leone Leoni 16 (☎35 931).

Pharmacy: Farmacia Comunale, Campo di Marte 1 (☎90 24 66), next to Conad supermarket on V. V. Veneto. Open 24hr.

Hospital: Ospedale Civico, V. Pietronenni (☎ 30 51).

Internet Access: InformaGiovani, P. G. Monaco 2 (☎37 78 68; informagiovani@comune.arezzo.it). Free. 30min. limit. Open M-Sa 9:30am-7:30pm and 1st Su of month 3:30-7:30pm.

Post Office: V. G. Monaco 34 (☎33 24 11). **Currency exchange** (€0.50 commission). Open M-Sa 8:15am-7pm. **Postal Code:** 52100.

ACCOMMODATIONS

Hotels fill to capacity the first weekend of every month during the **Fiera Antiquaria** (Antique Fair). Otherwise, finding a cheap room should be a cinch. Its stellar location in a 14th-century Benedictine convent in the midst of the town's main sights make **Foresteria San Pier Piccolo ②**, V. Bicchieraia 32, a wise choice for the informed tourist. Many rooms have frescoed ceilings and all surround an arcaded central courtyard. (☎32 42 19; fax 37 04 74. Breakfast €3. Reception daily 7am-11pm. Singles €23; doubles with bath €75; triples €95.) To get to **Albergo Cecco ❸**, C. Italia 215, follow V. G. Monaco from the train station, turn right on V. Roma and another right on C. Italia. Do not follow misleading signs for Hotel Cecco. The 42 no-frills rooms are basic and only suitable for the budget-minded in search of a decent location. (☎20 986; fax 35 67 30. Breakfast €3. Singles €30, with bath €42; doubles €64-70; triples €80; quads €95. AmEx/MC/V.)

FOOD

An open-air market takes place in P. Sant'Agostino on weekdays until 1pm. Head to **La Mozzarella,** V. Spinello 25, across from the train station, for a great variety of cheeses. (Open M-F 8am-1pm and 4-8pm, Sa 8am-1pm. Cash only.) **Eurospar,** V. G. Monaco 82, carries basic groceries. (Open daily 8am-8pm, closed W afternoon.)

> **◄TIP►** **PUZZLING PANE.** No, that bread is not stale, just unsalted. Traditional Tuscan bread is made without salt because, historically, salt was so valuable it was used as money for trading. Before you dig into that breadbasket, remember that Tuscan bread is best enjoyed with other dishes and sauces that *do* include salt. If you're in a grocery store buying bread for a picnic lunch and want the salted kind, ask for *pane salato.*

Antica Osteria L'Agania, V. Mazzini 10 (☎29 53 81; www.agania.com). Due to its authentic Italian eats and lively atmosphere, L'Angania has earned a solid following. *Primi* and *secondi* €5-7. Open Tu-Su noon-3pm and 7-11pm. **②**

Trattoria Il Saraceno, V. Mazzini 6/a (☎27 644), off C. Italia. This quaint local spot is unique for its *arezzese* specialties like duck and *pecorino* cheese in honey. Sardine-like seating. Pizza €6-8. *Primi* €6.50-7.50, *secondi* €6.50-10.50. Cover €2. Open M-Tu and Th-Su noon-3pm and 7:30-10:30pm. AmEx/MC/V. **❸**

Blusol, P. San Gemignano 1 (☎30 24 20). From C. Italia, turn right on V. Garibaldi, then left uphill to the *piazza*. Fish plates, lots of veggies, and all-organic meals like brown rice risotto. No-frills ambience. Veggie special includes soup and entree sampler (€7.50). Open M-Sa 12:30-3pm and 7:30-10:30pm. MC/V. **②**

Paradiso di Stelle, V. G. Monaco 58 (☎27 448). Great homemade *gelato,* especially the *nocciola* and tiramisu (from €1.60). Nutella-filled crepe €2.30. Open May-Sept. daily 11am-midnight; Oct.-Apr. M-F 11am-8:30pm, Sa-Su 11am-11pm. Cash only. **❶**

SIGHTS

BASILICA DI SAN FRANCESCO. This extraordinary 13th-century basilica houses gorgeous 15th-century frescoes, among them Piero della Francesca's **⬛Leggenda della Vera Croce** (Legend of the True Cross), in the *Bacci* chapel behind the main altar, which portrays the story of the crucifix and its role in early Christianity. The narrative begins with the death of Adam and proceeds to major events such as Emperor Constantine's conversion in the AD 4th century. St. Francis is the figure kneeling at the foot of the cross. *(Walk up V. G. Monaco from train station and turn right into P. San Francesco. Basilica open daily 8:30am-noon and 2-7pm. Free. Chapel containing della Francesca's frescoes open Apr.-Oct. M-F 9am-6:30pm, Sa 9am-5:30pm, Su 1-5:30pm; Nov.-Mar. M-F 9am-5:30pm, Sa 9am-5pm, Su 1-5pm. Closed Jan. 1, June 13, Oct. 4, and Dec. 25. Groups of 25 admitted every 30min. Last entry 30min. before closing. Reservation required. Call ☎ 20 630 or 35 27 27, or visit the office to the right of the church. €6, EU students 18-25 €4, art students or EU citizens under 18 €2. Cash only.)*

∎ **CASA VASARI.** Colors swirl on the elaborate ceilings of the Casa Vasari, which the historian and artist built for himself and decorated without restraint. Impressive portrait-frescoes by Michelangelo and del Sarto vibrantly cover the walls. In one room, Vasari's depictions of the muses crown the ceiling; one is in the likeness of his fiancée, Niccolosa. He even painted himself contemplating the lovely view from one of the windows. *(V. XX Settembre 55. Just off V. San Domenico. Ring bell to enter. ☎ 40 90 40. Open M and W-Sa 8:30am-7:30pm, Su 8:30am-1:30pm. Last entry 30min. before closing. €2, EU students €1. Cash only.)*

PIAZZA GRANDE. This square contains the **Chiesa di Santa Maria della Pieve,** a spectacular Romanesque church that dates from the 12th century and one of Arezzo's most impressive monuments. Elegant columns and rounded arches frame the 13th-century portico signed by 'Marchio.' On the elevated presbytery sits Pietro Lorenzetti's brilliantly restored *Annunciation* and *Madonna and Child.* Below lies the 11th-century church upon which the Pieve was built. The adjoining pock-marked tower is known appropriately as the "Tower of a Hundred Holes." *(Open M-Sa 8am-noon and 3-7pm, Su 8:30am-noon and 4-7pm. Free.)* The surrounding *palazzi* enclose P. Grande in a pleasingly proportional way. The 14th-century Romanesque **Palazzo della Fraternità** and the 16th-century Baroque **Palazzo delle Logge Vasariane** recall past eras. For a livelier version of history, attend the monthly **antique fair** or the semi-annual **Giostra del Saracino** each summer.

DUOMO. The massive 13th-century *duomo* sits high on the hill of Arezzo. Built in Tuscan Gothic style, the cathedral houses Arezzo native Piero della Francesca's *Maddalena* and Bishop Guido Tarlati's tomb on the left side of the nave near the altar. Carved reliefs relate stories about the iconoclastic bishop's unconventional life. The seven circular and elaborate stained-glass windows were designed by French artist Guillaume de Marcillat. The *Capella della Madonna del Conforto,* off the austere nave, holds a notable terra-cotta *Crucifixion* by Andrea della Robbia. *(Up V. Andrea Cesalpino from P. S. Francesco. ☎ 23 991. Open daily 7am-12:30pm and 3-6:30pm. Modest dress required. Free.)*

CHIESA DI SAN DOMENICO. The church's true gem is the ∎ **Cimabue crucifix** (1265-70) that hangs over the main altar. It is Cimabue's oldest and best preserved work. Other significant art in the simple, wood-timbered interior include Spinello Aretino's *Annunciation,* and a Marcillat rose window depicting St. Augustine. *(Take V. A. Celaspino from P. S. Francesco, turn left at P. Libertà on V. Ricasorli, then right on V. di Sassoverde, leading to the church. Open daily 8:30am-1pm and 3:30-7pm. Hours may vary. Closed to public during mass. Free.)*

� **FESTIVALS**

Whether your style is browsing or haggling, Arezzo's **antique fairs,** which take place in and around P. Grande on the first weekend of every month, paint a living portrait of the town's history and variety. Beautiful antique furniture and religious

TUSCANY

paraphernalia would be tough to lug home through customs, though sundry bric-a-brac can make unique souvenirs. The **Giostra del Saracino** (☎37 74 62; giostradelsaracino@comune.arezzo.it), a medieval joust, happens on the third Saturday of June and the first Sunday of September, though flags begin to plaster uncovered surfaces and celebrations engulf the town for the entire week before the event. In a ritual that recalls the Crusades, knights representing the four quarters of the town charge a wooden effigy of a Turk with lances drawn. Every July, crowds of dreadlocked and tattooed teens descend upon Arezzo for the **ArezzoWave Love Festival.** Stop at the outdoor stages to hear local and international alternative bands, watch a poetry reading, or dance to the spins of a local techno DJ.

◪ DAYTRIP FROM AREZZO

SANSEPOLCRO

Sansepolcro is most easily accessible by the hourly SITA bus from Arezzo (1hr., 15 per day, €3.30). Some routes require a change in Le Ville; ask the driver. The bus arrives just outside the walls of the old city. From the bus stop, enter the old city on V. Nord Aggiunti. Follow the street 5 blocks, until passing the Museo Civico on the right. Turn right under an arch on V. Matteotti. Sansepolcro's tourist office, V. Matteotti 8, is ahead on the right. (☎/fax 74 05 36. Open Apr.-Sept. daily 9:30am-1pm and 3-6pm.)

Retreat into this sleepy, one stoplight town that embraces its art on a level worthy of Florence or Rome. Nestled in the valley of the Tiber River at the foot of the Apennines, Sansepolcro's (sahn-seh-POHL-croh; pop. 16,000) claim to fame is its native early Renaissance painter, Piero della Francesca. The **Museo Civico,** V. Nord Aggiunti 65, displays some of della Francesca's finest works. *The Resurrection* (1450-1463) features a triumphant Jesus towering above sleeping guards, resting one foot on his coffin and staring intently out at the viewer. Look closely at the guard in the red on the lower right—it's actually a self-portrait of della Francesca himself. (☎73 22 18. Open daily June 15-Sept. 15 9:30am-1:30pm and 2:30-7pm; Sept. 16-June 14 9:30am-1pm and 2:30-6pm. €6, over 65 €4.50, 10-16 €3. Groups €4.50 per person. Audio tour €2. AmEx/MC/V.) The left chapel of the Romanesque **duomo,** V. Matteotti, just off P. Torre di Berta, shelters the town's other cherished sight, the mysterious **Volto Santo** (Holy Face), a large wooden crucifix depicting a blue-robed Jesus. Believed by some to be much older than its 12th-century attribution, the Holy Face's Assyrian features suggest Oriental origins. Scholars speculate that the same artist produced the much-celebrated Volto Santo in Lucca. (Open daily 8:30am-noon and 3:30-6:30pm. Free.)

Trattorie and pizzerias spot V. XX Settembre and parallel streets. One of the more upscale cafes with reasonable prices is **K Cafe ❷,** V. XX Settembre 73. It's partly a coffee bar, so come at any time for a cappucino and admire the modern art on the walls. (☎74 29 39. Salads €4-5. *Primi* and *secondi* €5-7. Open Tu-Su 7:30am-10pm.) Customers pack the more intimate **Enoteca Guidi ❸,** V. Luca Pacioli 44, for high-quality dishes. (☎73 65 87. *Primi* €8-15, secondi €8-9. Cover €1. Open M-Tu and Th-Su 12:30-2:30pm and 7:30-10:30pm. AmEx/MC/V.)

PISTOIA   ☎0573

Many travelers regard Pistoia (pee-STOY-yah; pop. 84,000) only as a stop on the train between Florence and Lucca. It's a small, but surprisingly urban Tuscan city that is worth a day's visit. In the perfectly flat P. del Duomo, the black-and-white checkered cathedral, *battistero,* and *campanile* dominate the scenery. In 1177 the town joined several other Italian city-states in declaring its independence, but was soon surpassed by its neighbors in military, political, and economic strength.

Thereafter, Pistoia became a murderous backwater, whose inhabitants Michelangelo maligned as "enemies of heaven." Lending its name to the pistol and pistole dagger, the town's bloody reputation spawned an enduring mythology. Today's more peaceful residents prefer to pick their battles, haggling over produce prices in the open-air markets of P. della Sala or rooting for their favorite soccer team.

▐ TRANSPORTATION

Pistoia is accessible by train or bus. The **train station** is in P. Dante Alighieri. **Trains** run to: Florence (40min., hourly 4:40am-11pm, €2.70); Pisa (1hr., every 2hr. 6:50am-11:30pm, €4.30); Rome (4hr., hourly, €30-40) via Florence; Siena (2-2½hr., 16 per day 5:51am-9:12pm, €7.50-13); Viareggio (1hr., every 2hr. 5:55am-10:47pm, €4.30). COPIT **buses** run from the train station to Empoli (1¼hr., 6:30am-6:50pm, €2.60) and Florence (1hr., 5:22am-9:05pm, €2.60). Buy tickets at COPIT vendors or across from the train station at V. XX Settembre 71. Call RadioTaxi (☎53 44 44) for a **taxi**. Panconi Andrea, V. Cesare Battisti 21, rents mountain **bikes** for €15 per day. (☎22 395. Open M-F 8am-1pm and 3:30-8pm, Sa 8am-1pm. AmEx/MC/V.)

▐▌ ORIENTATION AND PRACTICAL INFORMATION

To reach the *centro* from the **train station**, walk up **Via XX Settembre,** and continue straight as it changes names to **Via Vanucci** and then to **Via Cino.** Turn right on **Via Cavour,** then left on **Via Roma,** which leads to **Piazza del Duomo,** the heart of town. Local **buses #1** and **3** (€1, taken from the station) stop at the corner of V. Curtatone e Montanara and V. degli Orafi. From there, follow V. degli Orafi straight to P. del Duomo. An **APT Tourist Office,** P. del Duomo 4, is in Palazzo dei Vescovi. The English-speaking staff distributes free maps and brochures and helps find accommodations. (☎21 622; fax 34 327. Open daily 9am-1pm and 3-6pm.) **Currency exchange** is available at **Cassa di Risparmio di Pistoia e Pescia,** V. San Matteo 3. (☎36 91. Open M-F 8:20am-1:20pm and 2:50-3:50pm.) A **pharmacy** is at V. Cino 33. (☎36 81 80. Open M-Sa 8:30am-1pm and 3:30-8pm. MC/V.) For the **hospital,** call ☎35 21. **Internet** access is available at **Telnet Internet Point,** V. Carducci 25. (☎99 35 71. €3 per hr. Open M-F 9:30am-1pm and 3:30pm-midnight, Sa 9:30am-1pm and 3:30-8pm; 2nd and 4th Su of the month 3:30-8pm. Cash only.) The **post office,** V. Roma 5 (☎99 52 11), near the bank, provides **currency exchange.** (Open Sept.-July M-Sa 8:15am-7pm; Aug. M-F 8:15am-7pm, Sa 8:15am-12:30pm.) **Postal Code:** 51100.

▐▌ ACCOMMODATIONS AND FOOD

Most accommodations are centrally located and somewhat expensive. *Affitta-camere* listings are available from the tourist office, but most of the cheaper rooms are in localities far from town. As one happy patron wrote in the guest book, staying at ▨ **Bed & Breakfast Canto alla Porta Vecchia ❸,** V. Curtatone e Montanara 2, is living like a real Pistoian. Take V. XX Settembre from the train station; the road changes names several times before becoming V. Curtatone e Montanara. There is no sign, so watch for the address in front. Walk up the steps to buzz in. Friendly owners Anna and Giovanni serve complimentary drinks and guests gather on the terrace to chat. Carved wooden beds, red satin couches, antique furniture, and original sketches furnish the four frescoed rooms. (☎/fax 27 692. Singles €35; doubles €60, with bath €70. Cash only.) Up the street to the left, **Albergo Firenze ❹,** V. Curtatone e Montanara 42, offers basic rooms at a decent value. All 20 rooms have A/C, satellite TV, minibar, high ceilings, and lace curtains. (☎23 141; www.hotel-firenze.it. Breakfast included. Internet access free. Singles €45, with bath €62; doubles €65-84. Extra bed €25. AmEx/MC/V.)

TUSCANY

Trattoria dell'Abbondanza ❸, V. dell'Abbondanza 10, serves an excellent *insalate di Farro* (€6), a summer salad of oil-soaked lentils, basil, tomatoes, parsley, and garlic in a fresh, white-walled dining room or to outdoor tables in a quiet alley. (☎36 80 37. *Primi* €6-8, *secondi* €9-14. Open M-Tu and F-Su 12:15-2:15pm and 7-10:30pm, Th 7-10:30pm. MC/V.) **Il Duomo** ❶, V. Bracciolini 5, is low key and casual, and offers plates of pasta from €4. It's self service; order at the counter and take your tray to one of the long tables in the rear dining room. Catch up on news with locals or with the small TV in the corner. (☎31 948. Open daily 11am-3pm. MC/V.) Sample from a lengthy wine list at **La Botte Gaia** ❸, V. del Lastrone 17/19, or try gourmet cheeses, salads, and other delectable *antipasti* at outdoor tables. (☎36 56 02. *Antipasti* from €3. *Primi* and *secondi* €6.50-13. Cover €1.50. Open Tu-Sa 10:30am-3pm and 6:30pm-1am, Su 6:30pm-1am. Reservations recommended. AmEx/MC/V.) Multilingual menus present the ample choices at **Ristorante San Jacopo** ❸, V. Crispi 15. The emphasis is on meaty Tuscan dishes, and the dining room is airy. (☎27 786. *Primi* €6-11, *secondi* €9-15. Open Tu-Sa 12:15-2:30pm and 7-10pm, Su 12:15-2:30pm. AmEx/MC/V.)

Grocery stores and specialty shops line the side streets. Bargain hunters browse the **open-air market** in and around P. del Duomo for deals on items from shower curtains to silver jewelry. (Open W and Sa 8am-1pm.) P. della Sala has hosted a fruit and vegetable **market** since medieval times. (Open daily 8am-7pm.) A **Supermercato Stazione** supermarket is at V. Veneto 5, across from the train station and to the right. (Open M-F 8am-8pm, Sa 8am-1:30pm. MC/V.)

👁 SIGHTS

PIAZZA DEL DUOMO. Activity in Pistoia converges on the flat cobblestones of P. del Duomo. The green and white marble **Cattedrale di San Zeno** houses early Renaissance art tucked into pocket-sized niches on multiple floors, as well as San Zeno's greatest treasure, the ▨**Dossale di San Jacopo.** Between 1287 and 1456, nearly every significant Tuscan silversmith (including the young Brunelleschi) lent a hand to this altarpiece, a tremendously ornate affair off the right aisle, with relief work detailing biblical scenes and a procession of saints in a plain chapel. Visitors can enter the chapel for a small fee (€2), or observe the work from afar for free. (*☎25 095. Open M-Sa 7am-12:30pm and 3:30-7pm, Su 9am-1pm and 3:30-7pm. Altar open M-Sa 10am-12:30pm and 3-5:30pm; Su 8-9:30am, 11-11:30am, and 4-5:30pm. Modest dress required.*) Across from the *duomo* is the octagonal **baptistry,** designed by Andrea Pisano in the 14th century. Nino and Tommaso Pisano's sculpture *Virgin and Child* (1308) graces the facade above the entrance. (*Open Tu-Su 10am-1pm and 3-6:30pm.*) The **campanile,** adjacent to the *duomo*, has sounded the hour since the 12th century. From its 66m pyramid-shaped spire, vistas span to Florence on clear days. (*☎334 93 17 710. Open for visits Sa 11am and 4pm, Su noon and 5pm. Subject to cancellation if group is smaller than 5. €5.*)

PALAZZO COMUNALE. A 13th-century structure next to the *duomo* facing the *piazza*. Left of the central balcony (about halfway up), an arm reaches out of the wall, brandishing a club above the black marble head below—a tribute to the 1115 Pistoian victory over the Moorish King Musetto. Inside, the **Museo Civico** houses artwork dating to the 13th century. With its Gothic windows and archways, the courtyard is also well worth a peek. (*☎37 12 96. Open Tu-Sa 10am-6pm, Su 9:30am-12:30pm. Museum €3.50, students €2. Combined ticket for museo, the Centro Marini, and other museums €6.50/5.20. Cash only.*)

CENTRO MARINO MARINI. Escape an overdose of Renaissance paintings with a visit to this modern collection celebrating one of Italy's most renowned 20th-century artists, native Marino Marini. The collection's pieces include his tactile sculptures (many of the sensuous Pomona, ancient Roman fertility goddess), studies, and vibrant paintings. *(C. Silvano Fedi 30, in the Palazzo del Tau. ☎ 30 285; www.museomarinomarini.it. Open M-Sa May-Sept. 10am-6pm; Oct.-Apr. 10am-5pm. €3.50. Cash only.)*

CHIESA DI GIOVANNI FUORCIVITAS. Originally built outside the city walls, the single-naved interior of the 12th-century construction is a vast space with vibrant, stained-glass windows punctuating stark stone walls. The exterior's dark green and white stone stripes are characteristic of the Pisan school of architecture. The church contains della Robbia's terra-cotta *Visitation* (1445) on the left and a Romanesque relief of *The Last Supper* on the lintel. Giovanni Pisano's baptismal font and Guglielmo de Pisa's pulpit are among the finest 13th-century carvings. *(At the intersection of V. Cavour and V. Crispi. ☎ 24 784. Open daily 7:30am-6:30pm. Free.)*

CHIESA DI SANT'ANDREA. This typically Pisan-Romanesque church was built in the 8th century. In 1298 Giovanni Pisano carved the pulpit, now considered his masterpiece. Supported by seven red-marble columns, the pulpit's five white-marble panels have delicately carved figures illustrating the Nativity, Adoration of the Magi, Massacre of the Innocents, Crucifixion, and Last Judgment. *(Exit P. del Duomo by V. del Duca, from the corner opposite the duomo, and continue on it as it changes to V. dei Rossi and then V. Sant'Andrea. ☎ 21 912. Open daily 7:30am-6pm. Free.)*

🌺 🎭 FESTIVALS AND NIGHTLIFE

Europeans seeking to wash away their troubles converge the second weekend in July, in P. del Duomo, for the **Pistoia Blues** concert series. Past performers have included Ben Harper, Santana, Jethro Tull, Jeff Beck, Gregg Allman, and Joe Cocker. (☎ 99 46 59; www.pistoiablues.com.) During the festival, the city allows free camping in designated sites near the stadium. On July 25, Pistoia holds the **Giostra dell'Orso** (Joust of the Bear). In accordance with 13th-century custom, 12 contemporary knights from four competing districts joust a defenseless, bear-shaped target, earning points for the accuracy of their lunges. Pistoians and visitors fill the stands in the P. del Duomo, cheering on their favorite knight and recording wins and losses on the free scorecards given out by the city (☎ 37 16 90; cultura@comune.pistoia.it). With Staropramen, Hopf Weizen, and Bass on tap, **Vecchia Praga**, P. della Sala 6, at the end of V. del Lastrone, is a beer-lover's haven. Mixed drinks, liquor, wine, and light food are also available to the mostly Italian crowd. (☎31 155. Pint of beer €3. Open daily noon-1am.)

LUCCA   ☎ 0583

Lucca (LOO-ka; pop. 9000) dabbles successfully in every area of tourist pleasure. Bikers rattle through the town and on the tree-lined promenade that runs atop its medieval walls. Trendy boutiques dot the main streets, opening to picturesque *piazze* every few blocks. Notice boards are consistently plastered with signs for concerts, many of them in celebration of the operatic works of Lucca's own Giacomo Puccini. The art lover can enjoy the numerous Romanesque churches, or simply admire the elegant architecture of the *centro*. Ultimately, Lucca is a tranquil, yet compelling, gem of a Tuscan town.

⊏ TRANSPORTATION

Trains: ☎89 20 21, in Ple. Ricasoli, just outside the city walls. Most convenient transport to Lucca. Info kiosk open daily 5:30am-8:10pm. To **Florence** (1½hr., hourly 5:07am-12:34am, €4.80); **Pisa** (30min., hourly 7:40-9:40pm, €2.20); and **Viareggio** (20min., hourly 6:19am-11:31pm, €2.20).

Buses: Lazzi (☎46 49 63), in Ple. Verdi, next to tourist office. To **Florence** (1½hr., hourly 6:25am-7:45pm, €4.70) and **Pisa** (50min., hourly 5:48am-8:10pm, €2.50).

Taxis: in P. Santa Maria (☎49 41 90); in P. Napoleone (☎49 16 46); in Ple. Ricasoli (☎49 49 89); in Ple. Verdi (☎58 13 05).

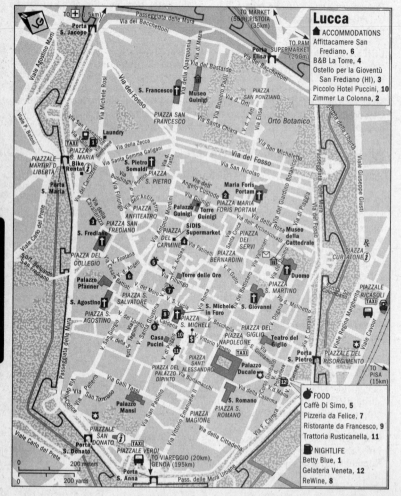

Lucca

🛏 ACCOMMODATIONS
Affittacamere San Frediano, **6**
B&B La Torre, **4**
Ostello per la Gioventù San Frediano (HI), **3**
Piccolo Hotel Puccini, **10**
Zimmer La Colonna, **2**

🍴 FOOD
Caffè Di Simo, **5**
Pizzeria da Felice, **7**
Ristorante da Francesco, **9**
Trattoria Rusticanella, **11**

🍸 NIGHTLIFE
Betty Blue, **1**
Gelateria Veneta, **12**
ReWine, **8**

Bike Rental: Cicli Bizzari, P. Santa Maria 32 (☎49 60 31), 2 doors down from the regional tourist office. Large selection of bikes. Basic bikes €2.50 per hr., €12.50 per day; mountain and racing bikes €3.50/17.50; tandem bikes €5.50 per hr. Open daily 9am-7:30pm. Cash only. **Antonio Poli,** P. Santa Maria 42 (☎49 37 87; www.biciclette-poli.com), on the other side of the regional tourist office, offers virtually identical services and prices. Open daily 8:30am-8pm. AmEx/MC/V.

■ ■ ORIENTATION AND PRACTICAL INFORMATION

To reach the *centro storico* from the **train station**, cross the road and turn left on Vle. Regina Margherita. Enter the city to the right of **Porta San Pietro,** then head left on **Corso Garibaldi.** Turn right on **Via Vittorio Veneto,** and follow it one block to **Piazza Napoleone** (also called **Piazza Grande**). Continue walking on V. V. Veneto, to reach **Piazza San Michele,** in the center of town. If arriving by bus, walk to the right through **Piazza Verdi,** follow **Via San Paolino** toward the center of town, and turn right on V. V. Veneto to reach P. Napoleone.

Tourist Office: Centro di Accoglienza Turistica (☎58 31 50; www.turislucca.com), in Ple. San Donato. English-speaking staff provides free maps, as well as train and bus info. Schedules guided tours (M, Th, Sa 3pm; €10). Self-guided audio tours (1 unit €9, 2 units €12) and bike rental (€2.50 per hr.). Open daily 9am-7pm. Branch: (☎49 57 30) in P. Curtatone, right of the train station. Provides maps, brochures, and luggage storage. Open daily 10am-6pm. **Agenzia per il Turismo,** P. Santa Maria 35 (☎91 99 31), between the bike shops. Detailed brochures and free hotel and *affittacamere* reservation service. Open daily 9am-8pm.

Currency Exchange: UniCredit Banca, P. San Michele 47 (☎47 546). Open M-F 8:20am-1:20pm and 2:35-4:05pm, Sa 8:20am-12:45pm. 24hr. **ATM** available on corner of V. San Paolino and P. San Michele, 50m away from bank.

Luggage Storage: At tourist office branch in P. Curtatone. €1.50 per bag per hr.

Laundry: Lavanderia Niagara, V. Michele Rosi 26 (☎335 62 92 055). €4 per 7kg. Open daily 8am-10pm.

Pharmacy: Farmacia Comunale, in P. Curtatone. Open 24hr.

Hospital: Campo di Marte (☎97 01).

Internet Access: Mondo Chiocciola Internet Point, V. del Gonfalone 12 (☎44 05 10). €5 per hr. Wi-Fi available. Open M-Sa 9am-1pm and 3:30-8pm. Cash only.

Post Office: ☎43 351. On V. Vallisneri. Open M-Sa 8:15am-7pm. **Postal Code:** 55100.

■ ACCOMMODATIONS

▨ **Bed and Breakfast La Torre,** V. del Carmine 11 (☎/fax 95 70 44; www.roomsla-torre.com). Hospitality is the middle name of the family that runs La Torre; call when you arrive for free pickup. 3 locations in the heart of the *centro* with large, bright rooms and well-kept bathrooms. Delicious, homemade breakfast included. Free Internet access. Singles €35, with bath €50; doubles €50/80. MC/V. ❸

▨ **Ostello per la Gioventù San Frediano (HI),** V. della Cavallerizza 12 (☎46 99 57; www.ostellolucca.it), 15min. from P. Napoleone. Walk 2 blocks on V. Beccheria, then turn right on V. Roma and left on V. Fillungo. After 6 blocks, turn left into P. San Frediano and right on V. della Cavallerizza. Good-sized rooms and great common spaces with high ceilings and plenty of couches. Breakfast €2.50; dinner €9. Towels €1.50. Linens included. Laundry facilities available. Reception daily 7:30-10am and 3:30pm-midnight. Check-out 9:45am. Lockout 10am-3:30pm. Dorms €17.50; 2- to 6-person rooms with bath €48-138. HI-member discount €3. Cash only. ❶

Affittacamere San Frediano, V. degli Angeli 19 (☎46 96 30; www.sanfrediano.com). Follow signs to hostel, but turn left on V. degli Angeli. English-speaking staff. Light spills into well-kept rooms from big windows. Rooms have TV, antique furniture; some have A/ C. Large, clean community baths. Breakfast included. Singles €48, with bath €70; doubles €68/90. AmEx/MC/V. ❹

Zimmer La Colonna, V. dell'Angelo Custode 16 (☎/fax 44 01 70), off P. Maria Foris Portam. Column-lined hallways lead to 5 spacious rooms with TV and antique decor; windows open onto a courtyard. Clean shared baths. Doubles €45, with bath €65. Extra bed €16. AmEx/MC/V. ❹

Piccolo Hotel Puccini, V. di Poggio 9 (☎55 421; www.hotelpuccini.com). Catch the operatic spirit of Puccini's birthplace; each room is decorated with framed playbills from his operas. 14 cozy, comfortable rooms have bath, TV, phone, and safe. Singles €65; doubles €90. AmEx/MC/V. ❺

◗ FOOD

An **open-air market,** located outside and to the left of Pta. Elisa, overruns V. dello Stadio. (Open W and Sa 8am-1pm.) **SIDIS,** in P. del Carmine, stocks basic groceries. (Open daily 8am-1pm and 4:30-8pm. MC/V.) For a better selection, head outside of the city walls to **Pam,** V. Diaz 124. Turn right from Pta. Elisa, and turn left on V. Diaz; it's at the end of the block. (☎49 05 96. Open M-Sa 8am-8pm. AmEx/MC/V.)

Ristorante da Francesco, Corte Portici 13 (☎41 80 49), off V. Calderia between P. San Salvatore and P. San Michele. Ample patio seating in this quiet square and well-prepared dishes make this a haven. Despite sometimes skimpy *secondi* portions, the quality is solid. The delicious *tortelli lucchesi* (meat *tortelli* with *ragù;* €5.70) could be a meal on its own. *Primi* €5-5.70, *secondi* €8-12. Wine €7.20 per L. Cover €1.50. Open Tu-Su noon-2:30pm and 8-10:30pm. MC/V. ❷

Trattoria Rusticanella, V. S. Paolino 32 (☎55 383). While the fare is a bit standard, the value is good at this tavern setting. Caters to regulars returning home from work as well as foreigners returning from a day on the road. Dishes complemented by jovial atmosphere and warm bread. 3-course lunch *menù* €15. Pizza from €5. *Primi* €4-5, *secondi* €7-13. Cover €1. Open M-Sa 11am-3pm and 6-10:30pm. AmEx/MC/V. ❷

Pizzeria da Felice, V. Buia 12 (☎49 49 86). Pizza al taglio (by the slice) flies over the countertop into the hungry hands of locals and travelers alike. Take a seat at one of the stools and watch the action. Slices from €1.40. Open daily 10am-8:30pm. ❶

Caffè Di Simo, V. Fillungo 58 (☎49 62 34). This chic *bar* gleams with chandeliers and a zinc counter. Classy, bow-tied waiters serve delicious coffee and bite-size cakes (€1.50), while mellow jazz plays in the background. Coffee €1, at table €2.40. *Primi* €5-7, *secondi* €8. Open Tu-Sa 9am-8pm. Lunch served noon-2:30pm. MC/V. ❶

◉ SIGHTS

BALUARDI. No tour of Lucca is complete without seeing the perfectly intact medieval city walls, or *baluardi* (battlements). The shaded 4km path along the walls, closed to cars, passes grassy parks and cool fountains. Rent a bike and try your hand at mastering the Luccan sport of simultaneously biking and chatting on your cell phone, or simply stroll and admire the layout of the city. The path is perfect for a breezy, afternoon picnic or a sunset viewing.

TIP **LOOK AT LUCCA.** While some tours of Tuscan towns can be didactic or wallet-draining or both, Lucca offers something a bit more reasonable and lively. Guided walking tours (2-3hr.) cover the main tourist sights and are given on Monday, Thursday and Saturday at an easy €10 per person. If you prefer to tour at your leisure, grab an audio tour for €9 from the main tourist office. For more information on **Look at Lucca,** call ☎34 24 04, or visit www.turislucca.com.

DUOMO DI SAN MARTINO. Though the building was supposedly begun in the 6th century and rebuilt in AD 1070 by Pope Alexander II, the majority of the building that stands today is the result of another rebuilding, which took place between the 12th and 15th centuries. The multi-layered, arched facade of this ornate and asymmetrical *duomo* is the oldest aspect of the present structure. The 13th-century reliefs that decorate the *duomo*'s exterior include Nicola Pisano's *Journey of the Magi* and *Deposition*. Matteo Civitali, Lucca's famous sculptor, designed the floor and contributed the S. Martino statue to the right of the door. His prized *Colobium*, halfway up the left aisle, houses the 11th-century **Volto Santo** (Holy Face). Reputedly carved by Nicodemus at Calvary, this wooden crucifix is said to depict the true image of Christ. Other highlights include Tintoretto's *Last Supper* (1590), the 3rd painting on the right, and *Holy Conversation* by Ghirlandaio, in the sacristy off the right aisle. The **Museo della Cattedrale,** left of the *duomo*, houses religious objects from the *duomo*. *(P. San Martino. From P. Napoleone, take V. del Duomo. Duomo and sacristy open M-F 9:30am-5:45pm; Sa 9:30am-6:45pm; Su between masses 9-9:50am, 11:30-11:50am, and 1-5:45pm. Duomo free. Sacristy €2. Museum open Apr.-Oct. daily 10am-6pm; Nov.-Mar. M-F 10am-2pm, Sa-Su 10am-5pm. €4. Combined ticket for Sacristy, Museo della Cattedrale, and Chiesa di S. Giovanni €6. Audio tour €1. Cash only.)*

CHIESA DI SAN MICHELE IN FORO. Looking at its current setting in a busy *piazza*, it's hard to tell that construction on this church actually began in the 8th century on the site of a Roman forum. The church's large, stone interior holds beautiful and dramatic oil paintings, such as Lippi's bold *Saints Helen, Roch, Sebastian, and Jerome* toward the end of the right aisle, and Luca della Robbia's *Madonna and Child* near the front. Original religious statues were replaced in the 19th century with likenesses of prominent political figures: Cavour, Garibaldi, and Napoleon III. *(Open daily 9am-noon and 3-6pm. Modest dress required. Free.)*

CHIESA DI SAN GIOVANNI. Under the simple plaster dome of this unassuming church is a recently excavated AD 2nd-century Roman complex. Pass through the entrance to see the complex's mosaic pavement, the ruins of a private house and bath (the church's foundations), a Longobard burial site, and a Paleochristian chapel, as well as a 10th- to 11th-century crypt. *(From P. San Martino, walk past San Giovanni, and around the corner to the right. Open Mar.-Nov. daily 10am-6pm; Dec.-Feb. Sa-Su 10am-5pm. Nave viewing free. Museum €6. Combined ticket for church and baptistry €2.50.)*

TORRE GUINIGI AND TORRE DELL'ORE. These towers are two of the 15 remaining from medieval Lucca's original 250. The narrow **Torre Guinigi** rises above Lucca from the stone mass of Palazzo Guinigi, which is not open to the public. At the top of 227 stairs, seven little oak trees, called *"lecci,"* provide a shaded view of the city and the hills beyond. *(V. Sant'Andrea 41. From P. San Michele, follow V. Roma for 1 block, turn left on V. Fillungo and right on V. Sant'Andrea. ☎31 68 46. Open daily June-Sept. 9am-11pm; Oct.-Jan. 9am-7pm; Feb.-May 9am-5pm. €5, students €3. Cash only.)* For some more exercise, climb the 207 steps of the **Torre delle Ore** (Hour Towers/Clock Towers), where you can stop to watch the inner workings of the city's tallest timepiece. *(V. Fillungo 24. Open daily in sum-*

TUSCANY

LUCCAN LORE

The Luccan tale of Lucida Mansi breathes serious morals into Italian primping practices. Lucida was a drop-dead gorgeous woman who knew exactly how to seduce men and get what she wanted. A very active lover, she even killed her husband in order to indulge in such revelry. In vanity, she covered the rooms of her *palazzo* (Palazzo Mansi, still in Lucca today) with mirrors.

Eventually Lucida began to age—wrinkles won out on her flawless skin. To thwart these unsightly signs of age, Lucida did the only thing she could think of: she contacted the Devil. The Devil gave her 30 years of youth in exchange for her soul.

Lucida continued her hedonistic life of fashion, passion and great wine. At the end of her 30 years, the punctual Devil returned, and the two fell into an abyss; in the *palazzo*'s Camera degli Sposi, there is a ring believed to have been their entrance to Hell.

Though there is no evidence of her existence, Lucida is one of Tuscany's most famous ghosts. Luccans say that along the town's walls, and over the pond in the Botanical Gardens, her seductive ghost appears at night, riding wild and nude on a blazing chariot. Some even say you can see the reflection of her face in the pond's water.

Though in life Lucida could not conquer mortality, she has defied logic and time in her story itself.

mer 10:30am-7pm; in winter 10:30am-5pm. €4, students €2.50. Combined ticket for both towers €6/4. Cash only.)

PIAZZA NAPOLEONE. Also called "Piazza Grande" by locals, this *piazza* is the town's administrative center. The 16th-century **Palazzo Ducale** now houses government offices. In the evening, prime time for a *passeggiata* (stroll), *lucchese* young and old pack the *piazza*.

PIAZZA ANFITEATRO. The closely packed buildings that ring this *piazza* create a nearly seamless, oval wall. It was originally created an AD 1st-2nd century Roman amphitheater. Though the ruins are now nearly 3m below the ground, some of the original arches can be seen on the outer walls of the buildings. Come enjoy an atmosphere where locals and tourists mingle over coffee and conversation.

BASILICA DI SAN FREDIANO. Multiple building additions have led to San Frediano's proud, Romanesque structure. Originally built in the 6th century with the facade facing west, it was rebuilt in the first half of the 12th century with an eastward orientation. The gleaming Byzantine mosaic at the top of the facade is striking. (Open daily in summer 9am-noon and 3-6pm; in winter 9am-noon and 3-5pm. Free.)

PALAZZO PFANNER. You might catch a glimpse of Palazzo Pfanner's garden from the city walls. The sumptuous oasis complete with flowers, trees, benches, an octagonal fountain and statuary of mythical figures was designed by Filippo Juvarra in the 18th century. While the view from the wall is free, sitting in the garden makes you feel like royalty. The *palazzo* now serves as a museum showcasing 18th- and 19th-century costumes and old medical instruments belonging to Dr. Pietro Pfanner, the surgeon who owned the *palazzo* and gave it his name. (V. degli Asili 33. From the Basilica di San Frediano, take V. S. Frediano to V. Cesare Battisti and turn left. Take a right onto V. degli Angeli to reach V. degli Asili. ☎95 40 29. Open daily Mar.-Oct. 10am-6pm. Palazzo €2.50, students €2; garden €2.50/2; both €4/3.)

ORTO BOTANICO. Retreat to the calming paths of Lucca's botanical gardens for a change of pace. Created in 1820 by duchess Maria Luisa of Bourbon, the garden was originally connected to the Royal University of Lucca for scientific study. A broad main avenue leads to a pond and marshy plants. (☎44 21 60. Open daily Apr. 10am-1pm and 3-5:30pm; May-June 10am-1pm and 5-7pm; July-Aug. 10am-1:30pm and 2:30-7pm; Sept. 10am-1pm and 3-6pm; Oct. 10am-1pm and 3-5pm; Nov.-Mar. by reservation only 9:30am-12:30pm. €3, ages 6-14, over 65 and groups larger than 15 €2.)

◼ ❀ NIGHTLIFE AND FESTIVALS

For evidence that Lucca is a sleepy Tuscan town at heart, look no further than **Gelateria Veneta,** V. V. Veneto 74, the epicenter of activity in the area. The place to see and be seen on Saturday nights, Veneta offers interesting flavors and swanky seating. (☎46 70 37. Cones €1.80-3.50. *Granita* €2.30-2.60. Open M-F and Su 10am-1am, Sa 10am-2am.) For liquid refreshment, trendy **ReWine,** V. Calderia 6, has an expansive selection of wines (approx. €15 per bottle) on display inside. Head to the small patio across the street for a quieter setting. (☎48 427. *Antipasti* and *primi* €7.50. Open 8am for breakfast, noon for lunch, and 6-10pm for drinks. AmEx/MC/V.) Located slightly away from the *centro*'s action but still buzzing with life is **Betty Blue,** V. del Gonfalone 16, an Internet cafe by day and bar by night. (www.betty-blue.eu. Wine from €3. Mixed drinks €6. Open daily 10am-1am.)

Lucca's calendar is jam-packed with artistic and musical performances, especially in the summer. The **Summer Festival** (☎0584 46 477; www.summer-festival.com) takes place throughout July and has featured performances by pop stars like John Legend, Elton John, Norah Jones, Steely Dan, Joss Stone, and Lauryn Hill. Sample **Teatro Comunale del Giglio's** opera season in late September or their ballet season in January. The king of Lucca's festivals is the **Settembre Lucchese** (Sept. 13-22), a lively jumble of artistic, athletic, and folkloric presentations. On July 12 and September 14, Lucca also holds an annual **Palio della Balestra,** a crossbow competition dating from 1443 and revived for tourists in the early 1970s.

PISA   ☎050

Millions of tourists arrive in Pisa (PEE-zah; pop. 95,000) each year to marvel at the famous "Leaning Tower," forming a *gelato*-slurping, photo-snapping mire. Though a little worn around the edges, the heart of Pisa is as alive as ever. Home to one of Italy's most prestigious universities, Pisa has also thrived as a haven for opinionated and exuberant students. After that hackneyed leaning-tower Kodak moment, take some time to wander the sprawling university neighborhood through P. dei Cavalieri and P. Dante, along alleys lined with elegant buildings and impassioned political graffiti.

▐ TRANSPORTATION

Flights: Galileo Galilei Airport (**PSA;** ☎50 07 07; www.pisa-airport.com). Trains that make the 5min. trip (€1.10) between train station and airport coincide with flight departures and arrivals. Bus LAM ROSSA (red line) runs between the airport, train station, and other points in Pisa and environs (every 20min., €1). Charter, domestic, and international flights. Daily flights to **Barcelona** (2hr., 2 per day), **London** (1½hr., 11 per day), and **Paris** (2hr., 3 per day).

Trains (☎89 20 21). In P. della Stazione, at southern end of town. Info office open daily 7am-9pm. Ticket booth open 6am-9:30pm; self-service ticket machines available 24hr. MC/V. To: **Florence** (1hr., hourly 4:12am-10:30pm, €5.20); **Genoa** (2½hr., hourly 6am-3:09am, €8); **Livorno** (20min., hourly, €1.70); **Rome** (3hr., 12 per day 5:45am-2:19am, €22-28). Regional trains to **Lucca** (20min., every 30min. 6:24am-9:40pm, €2) also stop at Pisa's **San Rossore** (€1.10), close to the *duomo* and the youth hostel. If leaving Pisa from S. Rossore, buy tickets at *tabaccherie.*

Buses: Lazzi (☎055 35 10 61; www.lazzi.it) and **CPT** (☎800 01 27 73; www.cpt.pisa.it) in P. Sant'Antonio are located near train station. Ticket office open M-Sa 7am-8:20pm. To: **Florence**

(2½hr., hourly, €7.40) via **Lucca** (40min., hourly, €2.20); **La Spezia** (3hr., 4 per day, €7.40); **Livorno** (1hr., 5am-8:30pm, €2.37); **Volterra** (1½hr., 7 per day, €5.11) via **Pontedera.**

Taxis: RadioTaxi (☎54 16 00).

Car Rental: Avis (☎42 028), **Hertz** (☎43 220), and **Maggiore** (☎42 574) have offices at the airport.

 ## ORIENTATION AND PRACTICAL INFORMATION

Pisa lies near the mouth of the **Arno River,** which splits the town. Most sights lie to the north of the Arno; the main **train station** is to the south. To reach the **Campo dei Miracoli (Piazza del Duomo)** from the station, take the bus marked LAM ROSSA (red line; €1). Alternatively, opt for a 30min. walk by starting straight up **Viale Gramsci,** through **Piazza Vittorio Emanuele II,** and stroll along the busy **Corso Italia.** Cross **Ponte di Mezzo,** and follow the river left, then turn right on **Via Santa Maria.**

> **TIP** **GET YOUR MASTER'S IN BUDGETING.** Il Campo dei Miracoli is not all Pisa has to offer. Head over to the university area to find cheaper, better quality food, a lively intellectual atmosphere, and the most breathtaking architecture scrawled with passionate student musings.

Tourist Office: P. V. Emanuele II 16 (☎42 291; www.turismo.toscana.it). English-speaking, knowledgeable staff provides detailed maps. List of local hotels and campgrounds available. Open M-F 9am-7pm, Sa 9am-1:30pm. Branch (☎56 04 64) behind the Leaning Tower. Open M-Sa 9am-6:30pm.

Budget Travel: New Taurus Viaggi, V. Francesco Crispi 25/27 (☎50 20 90), sells international tickets. English spoken. Open M-F 9am-12:30pm and 3:30-7:30pm, Sa 9am-12:30pm. AmEx/MC/V.

Luggage Storage: At the train station, located on the left at the end of Platform #1. €3 per bag per day. Open 6am-9pm. Cash only.

English-Language Bookstore: La Feltrinelli, C. Italia 50. Decent selection of novels in English. Open M-Sa 9am-8pm, Su 10am-1pm and 4-8pm.

Laundromat: Bucato Point, V. Filippo Corridoni (☎800 08 04 03), 50m from train station. Wash €3.50, dry €3.50 per 7kg. Detergent €1. Open daily 8am-10pm. Cash only.

Police: ☎58 35 11.

Pharmacy: Farmacia, Lugarno Mediceo 51 (☎54 40 02). Open 24hr.

Hospital: Santa Chiara (☎99 21 11), on V. Bonanno near P. del Duomo.

Internet Access: Internet Point 77, V. Filippo Corridoni 77, 2 blocks from the train station. €3 per hr. Open daily noon-10pm. **Koine,** V. dei Mille 3/5 (☎83 07 01). Students €3 per hr. Every night after 9pm €2 per hr. Open M-F 10am-midnight, Sa-Su 1pm-midnight. MC/V.

Post Office: P. V. Emanuele II 8 (☎51 94 11), near the station, on the right side of the *piazza.* Open M-Sa 8:15am-7pm. **Postal Code:** 56100.

ACCOMMODATIONS

In Pisa, hotel and *albergo* signs flash on every street to cater to the tourist hordes. You'll pay for location though; places closer to the sights are sure to be pricier.

Albergo Helvetia, V. Don Gaetano Boschi 31 (☎55 30 84), off P. Arcivescovado. Convenient location for hitting the major sights and navigating the nearby university area. Bright, well-kept rooms have TV, ceiling fan, and phone. Small shared baths. English-

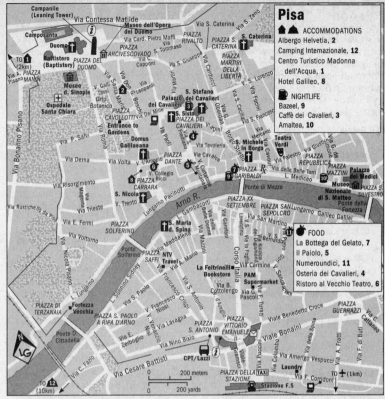

Pisa

▲▲ ACCOMMODATIONS
Albergo Helvetia, **2**
Camping Internazionale, **12**
Centro Turistico Madonna
  dell'Acqua, **1**
Hotel Galileo, **8**

■ NIGHTLIFE
Bazeel, **9**
Caffè dei Cavalieri, **3**
Amaltea, **10**

🍅 FOOD
La Bottega del Gelato, **7**
Il Paiolo, **5**
Numeroundici, **11**
Osteria dei Cavalieri, **4**
Ristoro al Vecchio Teatro, **6**

speaking staff. Breakfast €5, order night before. Reception 8am-midnight. Singles €35, with bath €50; doubles €45/62. Extra bed €15. Cash only. ❸

Hotel Galileo, V. Santa Maria 12, 1st fl. (☎40 621; hotelgalileo@pisaonline.it). A set of stellar rooms in the university district, all with frescoed ceiling, TV, antique tiling and furniture, and bath. Singles €40, with bath €45; doubles €48/60; triples €63/75. Extra bed €15. Cash only. ❸

Centro Turistico Madonna dell'Acqua, V. Pietrasantina 15 (☎89 06 22), behind old Catholic sanctuary 2km from the Tower. Bus labeled LAM ROSSA (red line) from station (4 per hr., last at 9:45pm; €0.85); ask to stop at *ostello.* Board bus across the street from 1st departure point in *piazza,* outside Hotel Cavalieri. Located by an old church and a creek with marshy banks, the hostel offers basic rooms at budget prices. Kitchen available. Linens €1. Reception daily 6-9pm. Check-out 9am. Dorms €15; doubles €28; triples €54; quads €64. MC/V. ❶

Camping Internazionale (☎35 211), 10km away on V. Litoranea in Marina di Pisa, across from its private beach. Take CPT intercity bus from P. San Antonio to Marina di Pisa (buy ticket in CPT office entering P. Sant'Antonio from P. V. Emanuele II; €1.50). Sites are small but partially shaded, with clean shared bath. Bar and market on premises. Open May-Sept. €6.50 per person, €5 per child, €7 per tent. July-Aug. prices increase by €1-2. AmEx/MC/V. ❶

⬛ FOOD

Steer clear of the countless touristy pizzerias near the Tower and head for the river or the university area, where the restaurants offer a more authentic ambience and consistently high quality. For those on the go, visit P. Vettovaglie, where an open-air market spills into nearby streets. Meanwhile, bakeries and *salumerie* fill Pisa's residential quarter. And for those in need of budget buys, try out the wide selection of groceries at **Pam**, V. Pascoli 8, just off C. Italia. (Open M-Sa 7:30am-8:30pm, Su 9am-1pm. Cash only.)

⬛ **Il Paiolo**, V. Curtatone e Montanara 9 (☎42 528), near the university. Low lighting from yellow lamps, bench seating and great music make for a fun atmosphere. Try some heavenly risotto with mussels, calamari, and salmon (€5.50) with the light, sweet, house white wine (0.25L for €3). *Primi* and *secondi* €5-8. Cover €1. Open M-F 12:30-3pm and 8pm-2am, Sa-Su 8pm-2am. MC/V. ❷

⬛ **Numeroundici**, V. San Martino 47 (☎27 282; www.numeroundici.it). Choose from the handwritten, chalkboard menu and serve yourself at this casual, popular establishment. Munch on sandwiches (€2.50) and superb vegetable torte (€2.30) on wooden benches in the high-ceilinged dining room filled with Tibetan lanterns. Self-service. *Primi* €4, *secondi* €6. Dinner specials €10. Open M-F noon-11pm, Sa 6-10pm. Cash only. ❶

Ristoro al Vecchio Teatro, P. Dante 2 (☎20 210). Dine *al fresco* (outdoors) or in the dining room over plates of delicious, traditional Pisan cuisine based on fresh vegetables and seafood. Try the *risotto mare* (with seafood; €7) or the buttery *sfogliata di zucchine* (zucchini torte; €7). *Primi* and *secondi* €6-7. Dessert €3. Cover €1.50. Open M-Sa noon-3pm and 8-10pm. Closed Aug. AmEx/MC/V. ❷

Osteria dei Cavalieri, V. San Frediano 16 (☎58 08 58). Caters to the intelligent diner with its classy setting. Slow down after a busy day at this Slow Food spot and sample traditional dishes like *cinghiale* (wild boar), *coniglio* (rabbit), or *trippa* (tripe). *Primi* €7-9, *secondi* €10-15. Open M-F 12:30-2pm and 7:45-10pm, Sa 7:45-10pm. MC/V. ❸

La Bottega del Gelato, P. Garibaldi 11, right off Ponte di Mezzo. Wide range of flavors (*limoncello*, Nutella, yogurt), plus specials of the day. Decide before reaching the counter, or you'll end up swallowed in the crowd, which is busiest after sundown. 2 generous scoops €1.30. Open daily 11am-1am. Cash only. ❶

◉ SIGHTS

⬛ **LEANING TOWER.** The white stone buildings of the Campo dei Miracoli (Field of Miracles) stretch across the grassy, well-maintained greens of the *piazza* that houses the Leaning Tower, *duomo*, baptistry, and the *Camposanto* (cemetery). Look closely—*all* of the buildings are leaning at different angles, thanks to the mischievous, shifty soil. No matter how many miniatures or postcards you see of the Tower, nothing quite compares to leaning legend in living color with its 5.5° tilt to the south. Bonanno Pisano began building it in 1173, and construction on the tower was repeatedly delayed as the soil shifted and the building began to lean. The tilt intensified after WWII, and thanks to those tourists who climb its 294 steps, it continues to slip 1-2mm every year. In June of 2001, the steel safety cables and iron girdles that had imprisoned the Tower during a several-year stabilization effort were finally removed. One year later, the Tower reopened, albeit on a tightly regulated schedule: once every 30min., guided groups of 30 visitors are permitted to ascend. *(Make reservations at the ticket offices in the Museo del Duomo, on the Internet, or* *next to the tourist info office. Tours depart daily June-Aug. 8:30am-11pm; Sept.-May 8:30am-7:30pm. Assemble next to info office 10min. before scheduled time. Free baggage storage. Children under 8 not permitted, under 18 must be accompanied by an adult. €15. Cash only.)*

 LUNAR LEANER. The wait to climb the Leaning Tower can sometimes take hours out of your day. To escape the crowds, save the ascent until after sundown; the tower is open during the summer until 11pm. You'll get a unique view of the city illuminated by moonlight.

BATTISTERO. The baptistry, an enormous barrel of a building, was begun in 1152 by a man known as Diotisalvi ("God save you") and was inspired in design by the church of the Holy Sepulchre in Jerusalem. Blending architectural styles, it incorporates Tuscan-Romanesque stripes with a multi-tiered Gothic ensemble of gables, pinnacles, and statues. Guido Bigarelli's fountain (1246) dominates the center of the ground floor. Nicola Pisano's pulpit (1260) recaptures the dignity of classical antiquity and is one of the harbingers of Renaissance art in Italy. Each of the building's four portals face one of the cardinal directions. The dome's acoustics are astounding: a choir singing in the baptistry can be heard 2km away. A staircase embedded in the wall leads to a balcony just below the dome; farther up, a space between the interior and exterior of the dome yields views of the surrounding *piazza*. *(Open daily Apr.-Sept. 8am-8pm; Oct. 9am-7pm; Nov.-Feb. 10am-5pm; Mar. 9am-6pm. €6; includes entrance to 1 other museum or monument on the combined ticket list.)*

CAMPOSANTO. This cloistered courtyard cemetery, covered with earth that Crusaders brought back from Golgotha, holds Roman sarcophagi that date from the AD 3rd century. The sarcophagi reliefs inspired Pisano's pulpit in the baptistry. Fragments of enormous frescoes shattered by WWII Allied bombs line the galleries. The **Cappella Ammannati** contains haunting frescoes of Florence succumbing to the plague; its unidentified, 14th-century creator is known as the "Master of the Triumph of Death." *(Next to the duomo. Open daily Apr.-Sept. 8am-8pm; Oct. 9am-7pm; Nov.-Feb. 10am-5pm; Mar. 9am-6pm. €6; includes entrance to 1 other museum or monument on the combined ticket list. MC/V.)*

DUOMO. The *duomo*'s dark green and white facade is the archetype of the Pisan-Romanesque style. Begun in 1064 by Buscheto (who is now entombed in the wall), the cathedral is the *campo*'s oldest structure. Enter the five-aisled nave through Bonanno Pisano's richly decorated bronze doors. Although a 1595 fire destroyed most of the interior, the cathedral was masterfully restored, and original paintings by Ghirlandaio still hang along the right wall, **Cimabue's spectacular gilded mosaic** *Christ Pantocrator* graces the apse, and bits of the intricately patterned marble Cosmati pavement remain. Giovanni Pisano's last and greatest pulpit, designed to outdo his father's in the baptistry, sits regally in the center. *(Open daily Apr.-Sept. 10am-8pm; Oct. 10am-7pm; Nov.-Feb. 10am-1pm and 3-5pm; Mar. 10am-7pm. €2. Free during Su Mass, but the roped-off area at the end of the nave provides only a partial view. Cash only.)*

TAKE A TICKET. Choose among the 3 combination options to see the *duomo*, baptistry, Camposanto, the Museo Sinopie and the Museo dell'Opera del Duomo. Go to 1 of the above (excluding the *duomo*) for €5, 2 of the above for €6, or all of the above for €10. The tower stands alone at €15.

PIAZZA DEI CAVALIERI. Designed by Vasari and built on the site of the Roman forum, this *piazza* is the seat of the **Scuola Normale Superiore**, one of Italy's premier universities. The wrought-iron baskets on either end of the **Palazzo dell'Orolo-**

TUSCANY

gio (Palace of the Clock) were once receptacles for the heads of delinquent Pisans. In the *palazzo*'s **tower,** Ugolino della Gherardesca was starved to death in 1208 along with his sons and grandsons, as punishment for treachery. This murky episode in Tuscan politics is commemorated in Shelley's *Tower of Famine*, as well as in Dante's *Inferno* with gruesome, cannibalistic innuendos.

MUSEO NAZIONALE DI SAN MATTEO. Thirty rooms hold panels by Masaccio, Fra Angelico, and Simone Martini. Sculptures by the Pisanos and a bust by Donatello also grace this converted convent. *(Off P. Mazzini on Lugarno Mediceo. Open Tu-Sa 8:30am-7:30pm, Su 8:30am-1:30pm. Last entry 30min. before closing. €5. Cash only.)*

MUSEO DELL'OPERA DEL DUOMO. For more background on the monuments of the *Campo dei Miracoli*, the Museo dell'Opera del Duomo displays artwork from the three buildings of P. del Duomo and gives excellent historical info about the art and construction of the famous buildings. Work by the Pisano clan abounds, including the 13th-century sculpture *Madonna del Colloquio* (Madonna of the Conversation) by Giovanni Pisano, which was named for the expressive gazes exchanged between mother and child. The display also includes Egyptian, Roman, and Etruscan art. *(Behind the Leaning Tower. Open daily Apr.-Sept. 8am-8pm; Oct. 9am-7pm; Nov.-Feb. 10am-5pm; Mar. 9am-6pm. €6, includes entrance to 1 other museum or monument on the combined ticket list. MC/V.)*

CHIESA DI SANTA MARIA DELLA SPINA. Pop into this tiny Gothic church perched on the south side of the Arno to glimpse at masterpiece statues by Andrea and Nino Pisano. Originally built in 1230, the Church of Saint Mary of the Thorn eventually housed a thorn taken from Christ's Crown of Thorns in 1333. *(From the Campo dei Miracoli, walk down V. Santa Maria and over the bridge. Open Mar.-Oct. Tu-F 10am-1:15pm and 2:30-5:45pm, Sa-Su 10am-6:45pm. Free.)*

🎵 🎭 ENTERTAINMENT AND NIGHTLIFE

Occasional concerts take place in the *duomo*. For info, call the **Opera della Primaziale Pisana,** P. del Duomo 17 (☎38 72 229; www.opapisa.it). On the last Sunday in June, the **Gioco del Ponte** (☎92 91 11) revives the city's tradition of medieval pageantry. Pisans divide into multiple teams, pledging their allegiance to their respective neighborhoods. Pairs of teams converge on the Ponte di Mezzo and joust until one side conquers the bridge. The night before the holiday for the city's patron saint (Nicholas) on June 16th, the **Luminara di San Ranieri** brings the illumination of Pisa (including the tower) with 70,000 lights. Watch students take back their tourist-packed *centro* after the sun goes down. Bars and cafes line the north side of the Arno, and students turn virtually every horizontal surface into seating. Bass lines blare into the street from **Bazeel,** Lungarno Pacinotti 1. (Beer €3.50-4. Mixed drinks €3-5. Open daily 7pm-1am.) Farther down the Arno, in P. Cairoli, **Amaltea,** offers outdoor, candle-lit seating and wine for about €5 a glass. Deeper into the university area on P. dei Cavalieri is another hot spot, **Caffe' dei Cavalieri,** V. Corsica 8A. Arrive during *aperitivo* hour (approx. 6-7pm) for drinks from €3, or relax after dinner with beers from €3. (☎55 39 25. Open daily 7am-1pm.)

🎿 DAYTRIP FROM PISA

VIAREGGIO
Trains connect Pisa to Viareggio frequently (20min., 6am-11pm, €2.20). Lazzi buses (☎46 233) connect Viareggio to Lucca (45min., hourly, €2.50) and Pisa (20min., 20 per day,

€2.50). *All buses stop in P. Mazzini, the town's main square near the waterfront. A tourist office at the train station has good maps, local bus schedules, and information on hotels. Ask for directions to main tourist office. (Open Tu 9:30am-1pm, W-Sa 9:30am-1pm and 4-6pm.) The personable staff at the main tourist office, V. Carducci 10, supplies decent maps, brochures, and information on hikes and car tours. Train schedules are posted outside. (☎96 22 33; www.aptversilia.it. Open M-Sa 9am-2pm and 3-7pm, Su 9am-1pm.)*

The resort town of Viareggio (vee-ah-REJ-yo; pop. 58,180) sits at the foot of the Riviera. Young Italians arrive each morning to slather on oil and soak up the sun, but usually return to the inland cities by evening to avoid the often costly accommodations. Most of Viareggio's shoreline has been roped off by the owners of private beaches. Walking to the left facing the water across the canal along Vle. Europa, 30min. from P. Mazzini, leads to the **free beach,** at the southern edge of town. Or, take city bus #10 (1-2 per hr.; tickets €0.80, €1.50 if bought on board) from the train station and save some precious tanning time. Bus #10 also returns from the beach to the station. The crowd here is younger, hipper, and noticeably less pretentious than the private beach set. Farther down the shore is **La Lecciona,** which has a reputation as an unofficial gay beach. Every year, revelers from all over Italy flock to Viareggio to celebrate **Carnevale.** The town is famous for its colorful parades, hilarious performances, and riotous parties.

Few budget accommodations exist amid Viareggio's splendor and pretense; travelers are better off finding a bed in nearby Pisa or Lucca. Accustomed to catering to a wealthy clientele, Viareggio's restaurants are none too cheap and its supermarkets few. Pack your picnic before you leave for the beach. With lower cover charges and higher quality, the best bet for a bite is to head away from the waterfront to **Ristorante da Giorgio ❺,** V. Zanardelli 71, to savor fresh seafood in a dining room filled with photos of the port. (☎44 493. *Primi* €9, *secondi* €25. Open M-Tu and Th-F noon-2:30pm and 7:30-10pm. AmEx/MC/V.)

ELBA ☎0565

According to legend, the enchanting island of Elba (EL-ba; pop. 27,000) grew from a precious stone that slipped from Venus's neck into the Tyrrhenian Sea. Since then, Elba's extensive 150km of coastline have seen their share of visitors. Renowned since Hellenic times for its mineral wealth, the island also derived considerable fame from its association with Napoleon. The Little Emperor was sent into his first exile here in 1814, creating both a temporarily war-free Europe and the famous palindrome: "Able was I ere I saw Elba." Surely, the island's turquoise waters, dramatic peaks, and velvety beaches can take the breath away of Emperor and commoner alike. Elba draws tourists to Portoferraio, the island's largest city, the glitzy and glamorous Porto Azzurro, and the clear waters of Marciana Marina. Make like the Italians and trade city dirt for Elba's sweet, salty air—a bit of Tuscany, untamed.

PORTOFERRAIO ☎0565

As the island's main port, Portoferraio (por-TOH-feh-RYE-oh; pop. 11,000) is probably Elba's liveliest city and contains most of its essential services. Visitors and locals alike spill from the pink, peach and yellow buildings of the *centro* that seem to carpet the steep hillsides. Though frequent boats make Portoferraio a main stop from the mainland, the imposing sealiners keep a comfortable distance from the centuries-old sights and gorgeous stretches of white, pebbly beaches.

TRANSPORTATION TO ELBA. Elba's **airport** (☎97 60 11; fax 97 60 08) in Marina di Campo, sends flights to Milan, Munich, Parma, Rome, Vienna, and Zurich. The best way to reach Elba is to take a **ferry** from Piombino Marittima (also called Piombino Porto), on the mainland, to Portoferraio. Ferries also dock at Porto Azzuro, on the opposite side of the island. **Trains** on the Genoa-Rome line travel to Piombino Marittima but usually stop at Campiglia Marittima (from Florence, possible change at Pisa/Livorno). From Campiglia Marittima, a connecting **intercity bus** (30min., €1.70), timed to meet incoming trains, connects to Piombino Marittima. Tickets to Piombino purchased at a **train station** include the bus ticket. Meet the bus when exiting the station. Both **Toremar** (ferry 1hr., €6-8; hydrofoil in summer 30min., €8-10) and **Moby Lines** (1hr., 5am-10pm, €9-11) run about 20 trips to Elba per day. The ticket offices of Toremar (☎31 100; www.toremar.it) and Moby Lines (☎22 12 12; www.moby.it) are in the Stazione Marittima at the ferry docks in Piombino; buy tickets for the next departing ferry at these offices or at the Trenitalia booth in the Campiglia Marittima train station. Remember to allow 10min. to descend from the ticket office to the dock.

▐ TRANSPORTATION

Ferry service is at Toremar, Calata Italia 42 (☎96 01 31; portoferraio@toremar.it), and Moby Lines, V. Elba 12 (☎91 41 33; moby.portoferraio@moby.it). Portoferraio can be accessed by bus from Elba's other towns. ATL, V. Elba 22, across from the Toremar landing, runs hourly **buses** to Marciana Marina (hourly, 7:15am-8pm) and Porto Azzuro (hourly, 5:10am-8pm). For other schedules, consult office. (☎91 43 92. Open June-Sept. daily 8am-8pm; Oct.-May M-Sa 8am-1:20pm and 4-6:30pm, Su 9am-12:30pm and 2-6:30pm. Tickets €1.20-3.10. Day pass €7, 6-day pass €19.) For **taxis**, call ☎91 51 12. Rent Chiappi, Calata Italia 38, rents **cars** (€45-65 per day), and **mopeds** (€40 per day) for exploring the island. (☎91 43 66; www.rentchiappi.it. Open daily 9am-7:30pm. MC/V.)

▐ ▐ ORIENTATION AND PRACTICAL INFORMATION

Though it's Elba's largest city, Portoferraio has a tiny *centro*. From the center of the harbor, a left leads to **Calata Italia** and a right to **Via Vittorio Emanuele II; Via Manzoni** cuts between them. From Calata Italia, a right turn on **Viale Elba** goes further inland toward services like banks and grocery stores. V. V. Emanuele II turns into **Calata Mazzini,** which curves with the borders of the harbor; follow street signs and turn left through a brick arch, **Porta Medicea,** to **Piazza Cavour.** Cut through the *piazza* to reach **Piazza della Repubblica,** the center of town.

Tourist Offices: APT, Calata Italia 43 (☎91 46 71; www.aptelba.it). From the Toremar docks facing away from the water, proceed left. Walk past a series of tourist companies and cafes and cross Vle. Elba. Office is ahead on the right. Accommodations info, bus schedules, and restaurant listings for all of Elba. Open in summer M-Sa 8am-6:50pm, Su 9:30am-12:30pm and 3:30-6:30pm; in winter daily 8am-1pm and 4-6:30pm.

Boat Excursions: Visione Sottomarina (☎328 70 95 470) runs trips along the coast (€15) in glass-bottomed boats for prime ocean views. Arrive 20min. early for decent seats. Tickets sold onboard. Morning tours depart from Portoferraio, afternoon tours from Marciana Marina.

Parks and Nature: Parco Nazionale Arcipelago Toscano, Vle. Elba 8 (☎91 94 94), provides information and maps on hikes and island wildlife. Office open daily 9:30am-1:30pm and 3:30-7:30pm.

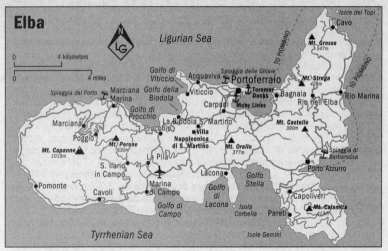

Elba

Ligurian Sea

0 — 4 kilometers
0 — 4 miles

Isole dei Topi
Cavo

Mt. Grosso
347m

TO PIOMBINO

TO PIOMBINO

Golfo di
Viticcio
Acquaviva
Spiaggia delle Ghiaie
Portoferraio
Mt. Strega
428m

Spiaggia del Porto
Marciana
Marina
Golfo della
Biodola
Viticcio
Toremar
Docks
Bagnaia
Rio nell'Elba
Rio Marina

Golfo di
Procchio
Carpani
Moby Lines

Marciana
La Biodola
Procchio
S. Martino
Mt. Castello
390m

Poggio
Mt. Perone
630m
Villa
Napoleonica
di S. Martino
Mt. Orello
377m

Mt. Capanne
1019m
La Pila
Spiaggia di
Barbarossa

S. Ilario
in Campo
Porto Azzurro

Pomonte
Cavoli
Marina
di Campo
Lacona
Golfo
Stella
Capoliveri

Golfo di
Campo
Golfo
di
Lacona
Isola
Corbella
Pareti
Mt. Calamita
413m

Tyrrhenian Sea
Isole Gemini

Currency Exchange: The waterfront is full of rip-offs, even by private agencies. Walk to V. Manganaro, near Hotel Nobel, for a **Banca di Roma** (☎91 90 07), which also has an **ATM.** Open M-F 8:25am-1:35pm and 2:50-3:40pm.

Internet Access: Da Ciro Bar, V. V. Emanuele II 14 (☎91 90 00), across from the Toremar dock. €3 per 30min., €5 per hr. Open daily 9am-10pm. AmEx/MC/V.

Post Office: V. Manganaro 7M (☎93 47 31), around the left side of the building. Open M-F 8:15am-7pm, Sa 8:15am-12:30pm. **Postal Code:** 57037.

ACCOMMODATIONS

Just uphill from a heavenly beach, ▨**Albergo Le Ghiaie** ❹, Località Le Ghiaie, has comfortable rooms with bath. Great common areas foster a sense of community. Mornings start with coffee on the wooden terrace. From the harbor, take V. Manzoni and bear left on V. Cairoli for 5min. (☎91 51 78. Breakfast included. Private parking. Singles €40-45; doubles €80-85; triples €110; quads €125. AmEx/MC/V.) Family owners welcome visitors to the cheery **Ape Elbana** ❹, Salita Cosimo dei Medici 2, in a great location overlooking P. della Repubblica. It's closer to the *centro*, but farther from the beach. Welcoming, clean white rooms come with bath, and some have TV and A/C. (☎91 42 45; fax 94 59 85. Breakfast included. Singles €50-70; doubles €80-120. Half pension €45-60; full pension €55-70. In winter €15 less. AmEx/MC/V.) The no-frills rooms at **Hotel Nobel** ❷, V. Manganaro 72, are a decent option for a tight budget in high season, though hot water is inconsistent and furnishings are a bit rundown. Follow V. Elba from the port for 10min. until it merges with V. Manganaro; the hotel is on the right. (☎91 52 17; fax 91 54 15. Singles €20-34, with bath €42; doubles €44/62; triples with bath €78. AmEx/MC/V.) **Acquaviva** ❶, Località Acquaviva, has good camping about 4km west of the *centro*. Take the bus toward Viticcio (8am, 12:30, 3, 6pm; €1) from Portoferraio and ask the driver to stop at the campground *(campeggio)*. Located right on the beach, the site features its own bar, restaurant, grocery store, and playground. (☎91 91 03; fax 91 55 92; www.campingacquaviva.it. Reserve via fax. €7-13 per person, €8-14 per tent, €2-3.50 per car. MC/V.)

TUSCANY

⬛ FOOD

Two Elban specialties of note are *schiaccia*, a flat sandwich bread cooked in olive oil and studded with onions or black olives, and *aleatico*, a sweet liqueur. Elba as a whole suffers from an infestation of overpriced, tourist-snaring restaurants, but Portoferraio has options for value-conscious diners. Dwarfed by ships, **Ristorante Stella Marina ❸**, on Banchina Alto Fondale, across from the Toremar dock, offers courteous service and fabulous seafood dishes in a busy but classy atmosphere. Try some *tagliolini ai frutti di mare* (with mussels, clams, shrimp, and octopus; €10), or splurge on Elban lobster for €13.50. (☎91 59 83. *Primi* €8.80-12, *secondi* by weight. Open May to mid-Nov. Tu-Su noon-2:30pm and 7:20-10:30pm. AmEx/MC/V.) **Il Garibaldino ❷**, Calata Mazzini 1, is well-frequented because of its stellar location on the waterfront and its plentiful menu options. (☎91 47 51. Pizza €3.50-5. *Primi* €5.50-8.50, *secondi* €6.50-18. Open daily 12:30-2:30pm and 7-10pm. AmEx/MC/V.) **Trattoria-Pizzeria Napoletana da Zucchetta ❸**, P. della Repubblica 40, is a casual spot in the *centro storico* with outdoor seating and many pizza options at reasonable prices. (☎91 53 31. Pizza €3-8. *Primi* €7-11, *secondi* €9-25. Open M-Tu and Th-Su 11:30am-3pm and 6-11:30pm, W 6-11:30pm. MC/V.) For groceries, head to the centrally located **Conad**, P. Pietri 2/4, off Vle. Elba, next to the Banca di Roma. (Open M-Sa 7:30am-9pm, Su 8am-1:30pm and 4:30-8:30pm. AmEx/MC/V.)

👁 ⬛ SIGHTS AND BEACHES

Inside Emperor Napoleon's one-time residence, the **Villa dei Mulini,** rest his personal library, a number of letters, some silk chairs once graced by his imperial derriere, and the sovereign Elban flag that he designed. (☎91 58 46. Ticket office open July-Aug. M-Sa 9am-7pm, Su 9am-1pm; Sept.-June closed Tu. €5; 3-day combined ticket with Villa Napoleonica €9. Cash only.) Monogrammatic Ns emblazon the **Villa Napoleonica di San Martino,** placed there after Napoleon's death. Note especially the Sala Egizia, with friezes depicting his Egyptian campaign. (Take bus #1 5km out of Portoferraio. ☎91 46 88. Ticket office open July-Aug. M-Sa 9am-7pm, Su 9am-1pm; Sept.-June closed M.) The **Museo Archeologico della Linguella** glorifies Elba's seafaring history, displaying finds from ancient trading boat wrecks dating back to the AD 5th century. (In the Fortezza del Lingrella, up the hill from the Villa dei Mulini in the *centro storico*. ☎91 73 38. Open daily Sept.-June 9am-1:30pm and 3-7pm; July-Aug. 9am-2:25pm and 6pm-midnight. €3, children and individuals in large groups €2. Cash only.) The **Medici Fortress,** looming over the port, is worth a quick peek. Cosimo dei Medici, Grand Duke of Tuscany, founded the complex in 1548. The structure was so imposing that the dreaded Turkish pirate Dracut declared the building impenetrable and called off his planned attack on Portoferraio in 1553. (Open daily 9am-10pm. €3, children €2. Cash only.)

Many large signs from the harbor point to **Spiaggia delle Ghiaie,** so, unsurprisingly, its shores are quickly covered with the chairs and towels of the masses grabbing their piece of the precious rocky, white beach. Bring a towel and claim a spot to avoid the roped-off areas and their corresponding fees. Farther east and down a long flight of stairs from the Villa dei Mulini is the sandy and more secluded ⬛**Spiaggia delle Viste.** Appropriately named for its views, this beach is framed with cliffs and is the perfect spot to take a dip in the crystal-blue water.

PORTO AZZURRO   ☎0565

The gleaming waters of Porto Azzurro (POR-toh Ad-ZUR-ro; pop. 3000) surround a beautiful, low-key beach town. While the postcard racks and tourist shops abound, so do stellar restaurants and dramatic coastline views. Brave the crowds at the tiny, crowded beach off the main drag, or hop over to Barbarossa beach for better sand and a bit more towel space. To reach the beach, skirt the port and take the narrow steps leading to a dirt trail (25min.) that climbs the hill and overlooks the water, taking time to look back and admire the glittering port behind you. Get tanning faster by taking the bus headed toward Marina di Campo (be sure to ask the driver if it stops at Barbarossa).

If staying overnight, camping is by far the cheapest option; prices vary depending on the month. Campgrounds are in Località Barbarossa, near the beach of the same name. Follow the directions above to Barbarossa or take the less scenic, faster route by following Vle. Italia out of town on a busy road and turn right at the sign for the campground. Near the beach the tightly packed **Arrighi ❶**, offers amenities like Wi-Fi, safe boxes, a supermarket and an air-conditioned common area. (☎95 568; www.campingarrighi.it. Open Easter-Oct. €5.80-13 per person, €5.30-17.70 per tent, €2-2.60 per car. MC/V.) From the beach, a 5min. walk down a dirt path inland and to the west of Camping Arrighi will bring you to **Il Gabbiano ❶**, with shaded grounds near the road. (☎95 087. €6-9.50 per person, €6-8.50 per tent. No cars July-Aug.; off-season €9.50 per car. Cash only.) Run by the same owners and situated directly next to Il Gabbiano, **Albergo Barbarossa ❸** offers tidy rooms and a beautiful garden. (☎95 087. Singles Sept.-June €40; doubles €55, with bath €58; triples with bath €65. Cash only.)

Porto Azzurro has an abundance of restaurants; choosing one will be more difficult than finding one. Picnickers beware: grocery stores are few and far away. **La Creperia ❶**, V. Marconi 2, is just right for a quick bite. The Nutella and *mascarpone* crepe (€3.10) is a sweet sensation. (Open Apr.-Oct. daily 11am-2am. Cash only.) **Ristorante Bella M'Briana ❸**, V. D'Alarcon 29, serves more elegant meals in a waterfront setting. (*Primi* €6.50-8, *secondi* €8-18. Cover €2. Open daily noon-3pm and 7-11pm. AmEx/MC/V.) Wind down the evening with the mellow, late-night crowd at **Bar Tamata**, V. Cesare Battisti 3. (☎348 305 88 63. Open daily 6pm-2am; reduced winter hours. Cash only.) **Morumbi**, 2km down the road to Capoliveri, is one of the island's hottest and largest discos, with indoor and outdoor dance floors, a pizzeria, and a pagoda. (☎92 01 91. Weekend cover €8-10. Open June 30-Sept. 15.)

MARCIANA MARINA ☎0565

The pebbly border of Marciana Marina's (mar-CHEE-ya-na ma-REE-na; pop. 1700) waterfront is just one of countless beaches hiding in isolated coves along the island. Explore the lopsided rocks, stake out a sunny niche, and bring along goggles to watch schools of fish swim in the still waters. Numerous stretches of shoreline are accessible only by boat: the nicest ones lie between Sant'Andrea and Fetovaia, along the western border of Elba, an area reputed to contain the island's clearest waters. The town itself, though tiny, accommodates hordes of sunbathing tourists and daytripping families who savor *gelato* when the sun shines and browse the jewelry stands when the moon glows.

🖥📶 TRANSPORTATION AND PRACTICAL INFORMATION. Reach Marciana Marina from Portoferraio by car, boat, or stomach-churning bus ride (45min., €2). The **tourist office** stands near the shore in P. Vittoria. (Open July-Aug. M-W and F-Su 10am-1pm and 8-11pm.) For information about boat excursions, pop into **Agenzia Brauntour Viaggi**, V. Felice Cavallotti 10. (☎99 68 73; abviaggi@abviaggi.it. Open high season M-Sa 9am-1pm and 4-8pm, Su 9am-1pm; low season M-F 9am-12:30pm and 3:30-7pm, Sa-Su 9am-12:30pm.) The **post office** is at Vle. Lloyd 37. (Open M-F 8:15am-1:30pm, Sa 8:15am-12:30pm.) **Postal Code:** 57033.

▐▐ ACCOMMODATIONS AND FOOD. The tourist office offers info on cheap *affittacamere* during July and August, though these fill up quickly and other options are pricey. ▓**Hotel Imperia ❸**, V. Amedeo 12, is steps from the sea. Bright rooms, an upbeat staff and an extensive breakfast buffet can't be beat. Book ahead for a room with a balcony at no extra cost. (☎99 082; www.hotelimperia.it. Breakfast included. July-Aug. €35-50 per person; half pension €45-80. Prices drop significantly Sept.-June. AmEx/MC/V.) Follow V. Amedeo away from the harbor on a slight incline for 15min., and turn right on Località Ontanelli to reach **Casa Lupi ❹**, Località Ontanelli 15. The 10 immaculate rooms all have bath, and the carefully tended rose garden looks out toward the mountains and the sea. (☎/fax 99 143. Breakfast €6. Singles €42; doubles €70. Cash only.) Located on the harborfront directly across from the sea, **Hotel Marinella ❹**, V. Margherita 38, provides large rooms, all with bath, TV, and great views. The high price reflects quality of the amenities, which include a pool and tennis courts. (☎99 018; www.elbahotel-marinella.it. Rooms June €57, July €59, Aug. €74-87. AmEx/MC/V.)

Placate a growling stomach in P. Vittoria where a slew of good restaurants serve cheap and filling seafood dishes. With a limited but very tasty selection of fish and pasta dishes, diners should fall for **First Love ❷**, V. G. Dussol 9/13, at first bite. (☎99 355. *Primi* €7-8, *secondi* €7.50-17. Open daily 7pm-2am. MC/V.) For a filling snack, head to **dall'Elba al Tramonto ❶**, V. Aurelio Saffi 9. This perfect alternative to a formal restaurant serves crepes for breakfast, lunch, and dinner. Every confection has a suggested beer and wine to complement its rich flavor. Simple crepes start at €2.50. For takeout, ring the bell at the window on V. Amadeo. (Open daily 7am-11pm. MC/V.) Fifty meters up V. Amedeo from Hotel Imperia, **Conad**, V. Cerboni 4, supplies basics. (Open M-Sa 8am-1pm and 5-7:30pm, Su 8am-1pm. MC/V.)

◙ SIGHTS. If sun and sand is what you crave, stake out a spot on Marciana Marina's **Spiaggia del Porto**, a sandy beach that runs the length of the harbor, along Vle. Regina Margherita. For a different perspective, head inland to **Monte Capanne**, Elba's highest peak at 1019m, a literally uplifting excursion. The mountaintop offers views of the entire island, with sea and sky blending in a periwinkle haze. On clear days, the view extends all the way to Corsica; otherwise, the far-off island appears to float in a mist of passing clouds. The strenuous uphill trek is poorly marked and takes 2hr. (maps available at the parks office in Portoferraio), but a ride in the small open cage of a **cable car** can shorten the trip—those afraid of heights should opt for the hike. (☎90 10 20. Cable car open for ascent Apr. 14-Oct. 10am-12:15pm and 2:45-5:30pm, for descent 10am-12:45pm and 2:45-6pm. €10, round-trip €15. Cash only.) To reach Monte Capanne, take the bus (15min., €1) from Marciana Marina toward Marciana. Ask the driver to stop at Monte Capanne; look for a parking lot and the *"Cabinovia"* signs that point to the lifts. Be sure to buy a round-trip bus ticket, as there are no *tabaccherie* near the mountain.

UMBRIA

Because of its wild woods and fertile plains, craggy gorges and gentle hills, Umbria (OOM-bree-ah) is known as the "green heart of Italy." Cobblestoned villages and lively international universities are peppered throughout the region, bringing a distinct vitality to a land tied to its past. Three thousand years ago, Etruscans settled this regional crossroads between the Adriatic and Tyrrhenian coasts. One thousand years after the Etruscan invasion, Christianity transformed Umbria's architecture and regional identity. St. Francis shamed the increasingly extravagant Church with his legacy of humility, pacifism, and charity that persists in Assisi to this day. The region also produced medieval masters Perugino and Pinturicchio and holds Giotto's greatest masterpieces. Umbria's artistic spirit gives life today to the internationally acclaimed Umbria Jazz Festival and Spoleto Festival.

HIGHLIGHTS OF UMBRIA

JOURNEY to one of Italy's most revered **pilgrimage sites,** the Basilica di San Francesco in Assisi, an elaborate monument to the ascetic St. Francis (p. 515).

EXPLORE the **underground city** of the Etruscans in Orvieto (p. 526).

TASTE locally treasured **truffles** in all their various forms in medieval Gubbio (p. 508).

PERUGIA   ☎075

The citizens of Perugia (peh-ROO-jya; pop. 160,000) rose to political prominence after chasing the *Umbri* tribe into surrounding valleys. Wars with neighboring cities dominate Perugia's history, but periods of peacetime prosperity gave rise to the stunning artistic achievements for which the city is known today. The city's own Pietro Vannucci, a painter and mentor to Raphael, is known as "Perugino" because of his association with the town. While not as pristine as neighboring cities, well-worn Perugia is loved by visitors and locals for its convenient big-city amenities and easily navigable small-town layout. Whether it's the renowned jazz festival, the decadent chocolate, the art, or the student-driven university atmosphere, Perugia displays its character with pride.

▐ TRANSPORTATION

Trains:

Stazione Fontiveggio, in P. Vittorio Veneto. Lies on the Foligno-Terontola line. Info office open daily 7am-8pm. Ticket window open daily 6:10am-8pm. To: **Arezzo** (1hr., hourly, €4); **Assisi** (25min., hourly, €1.80); **Florence** (2hr., 6 per day, from €8); **Foligno** (40min., hourly, €3); **Orvieto** (1¾hr., 11 per day, €7) via **Terontola** (40min., €5.85); **Passignano sul Trasimeno** (30min., hourly, €2.05); **Rome** (2½hr., 7 per day 6am-6pm, €11); **Spoleto** (1hr., hourly, €4); **Terni** (1½hr., 19 per day 7:31am-12:30am, €4.85).

Perugia Sant'Anna, in Ple. Bellucci. The commuter rail runs to **Sansepolcro** (1½hr., 15 per day 6:18am-7:40pm, €4) and **Terni** (1½hr., 14 per day 6:06am-6:58pm, €4.40) via **Todi** (1hr., 5 per day 6:53am-7:41pm, €2.70).

Buses: APM (☎57 31 707; www.apmperugia.it), in P. dei Partigiani. To: **Assisi** (1hr., 8 per day 6:40am-8:05pm, €3); **Chiusi** (1½hr., 5 per day 6:20am-6:35pm, €5.20) some via **Tavernelle; Gubbio** (1¼hr., 11 per day 6:40am-7:45pm, €4.30); **Siena** (1½hr.; M-

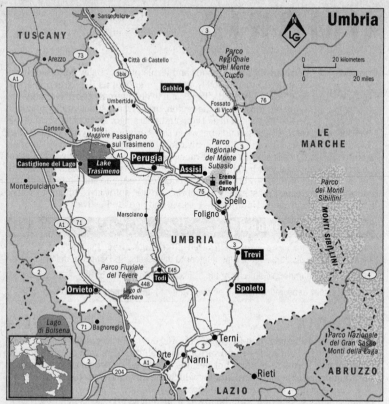

F 8:30am, 5:30pm; €11); **Todi** (1½hr., 9 per day 6:30am-6:25pm, €5.20). Reduced service Su. Additional buses leave from the train station. Tickets at RadioTaxi Perugia (☎50 04 888), to the right of the train station. **City buses** in P. dei Partigiani, down the escalator from P. Italia. Bus #6 (€1) runs to the train station.

Taxis: In P. Italia and P. Vittorio Veneto or call **Radio Taxi** (☎50 04 888).

Car Rental: Hertz, P. Vittorio Veneto 2 (☎50 02 439; hertzperugia@tiscali.it), near the train station. Open M-F 8:30am-12:30pm and 3-7pm, Sa 8:30am-1pm. AmEx/MC/V.

ORIENTATION AND PRACTICAL INFORMATION

From Fontiveggio train station, buses #6, 7, 9, 11, 13d, and 15 run to **Piazza Italia** (€1). Otherwise, it's a 2km trek uphill to the *centro*. To get to P. Italia from the **bus station** in **Piazza dei Partigiani** or from the nearby **Perugia Sant'Anna train station** at **Piazzale Belucci**, follow the signs to the **escalator** that runs beneath the old city and through the *Rocca Paolina* (open 6:15am-1:45am; free). From P. Italia, **Corso Vannucci,** the main shopping thoroughfare, leads to **Piazza IV Novembre** and the *duomo*. Behind the *duomo*, **Via Rocchi** winds downhill to **Piazza Braccio Fortebraccio** and the university district. One block off C. Vannucci is **Via Baglioni,** which leads to **Piazza Matteotti,** the municipal center.

Tourist Office: P. Matteotti 18 (☎57 36 458; fax 57 20 988). The knowledgeable staff provides maps and info on accommodations, restaurants, and cultural events. Ask for a free

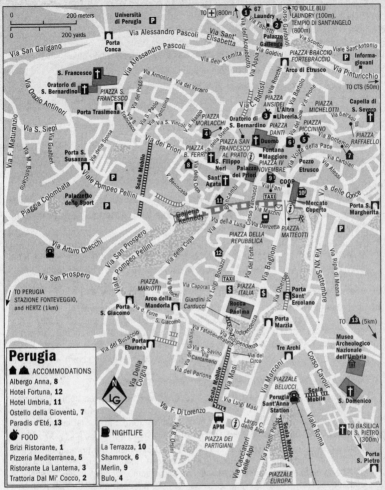

Perugia Little Blue guide in English, which is especially helpful for long-term stays in Perugia. Open M-Sa 8:30am-1:30pm and 3:30-6:30pm, Su 9am-1pm. **Info Umbria,** Largo Cacciatori delle Alpi 3/B (☎57 57; www.infoumbria.com), next to the bus station, provides maps and free booking for many hotels. Open M-F 9am-1pm and 2:30-6:30pm, Sa 9am-1pm. Check www.umbriabest.com for information on the town and events.

Budget Travel: CTS, V. del Roscetto 21 (☎57 20 284; www.cts.it), off V. Pinturicchio toward the bottom of the street, offers vacation deals to ISIC cardholders. Open M-F 9:30am-1pm and 3-6:30pm. MC.

Currency Exchange: Banks have the best rates; those in P. Italia also have 24hr. **ATMs.** The Stazione Fontiveggio charges no commission for exchanges of less than €40.

Luggage Storage: In **Stazione Fontiveggio.** €3 for 1st 12hr., €2 for each additional 12hr. Open daily 8am-7:30pm. Cash only.

UMBRIA

English-Language Bookstore: L'Altra Libreria, V. Rocchi 3 (☎57 36 104). Small selection of classics, travel guides, and, in the summer months, trendy titles. Open M-Sa 9am-1pm and 3:30-8:30pm, Su 10:30am-1pm. AmEx/MC/V.

Laundromat: 67 Laundry, V. Fabretti 7/A. Wash €3 per 8kg, dry €1 per 20kg. Open daily 8am-9pm. **Bolle Blu,** C. Garibaldi 43. Wash €3 per 8kg, dry €3. Open daily 8am-10pm.

Police: V. Cortonese 157 (☎50 621)

Pharmacy: Farmacia San Martino, P. Matteotti 26 (☎57 22 335). 24hr.

Hospital: Central line (☎57 81) directs your call for specific concerns. **Ospedale Silvestrini** (☎57 86 400) for emergencies.

Internet Access: Coffee Break, V. Danzetta 22, off V. Baglioni near P. Matteotti. Free Wi-Fi. Internet access €1 per hr. Open M-Sa 8am-11:30pm, Su 11am-11pm.

Post Office: P. Matteotti 1. Open M-Sa 8am-6:30pm. Offers **currency exchange** M-F 8am-6pm. **Postal Code:** 06100.

🏛 ACCOMMODATIONS

Reserve ahead when crowds descend on Perugia for the Umbria Jazz Festival in July and the Eurochocolate Festival in late October.

▨ **Ostello della Gioventù/Centro Internazionale di Accoglienza per la Gioventù,** V. Bontempi 13 (☎57 22 880; www.ostello.perugia.it). 300-year-old frescoes and helpful staff. A budget traveler's gem. Kitchen, library, lockers, spacious showers, lobby phone, and TV room. Linens €2. Lockout 9:30am-4pm. Curfew midnight, in summer 1am. 2-week max. stay. Open Jan. 16-Dec. 14. Dorms €15. AmEx/MC/V. ❶

▨ **Albergo Anna,** V. dei Priori 48 (☎/fax 57 36 304; www.albergoanna.it), on the corner of P. Ferri off C. Vannucci. Climb 3 floors to chandeliered hallways and 15 homey 17th-century rooms, some with ceramic fireplaces and great views of city rooftops. Breakfast €2. Singles €45; doubles €70; triples €80; quads €90. MC/V. ❹

Hotel Umbria, V. Boncambi 37 (☎ 57 21 203; www.hotel-umbria.com), off P. della Repubblica. 17 rooms with TV and clean bath. Breakfast included. Singles €38-48; doubles €55-70; triples €90; quads €120. AmEx/MC/V. ❸

Hotel Fortuna, V. Luigi Bonazzi 19 (☎57 22 845; www.umbriahotels.com). Converted 13th-century *palazzo* has 51 rooms with bath, A/C, phone, TV, minibar, and hair dryer. Rooftop terrace and frescoed reading room. Splurge-worthy. Breakfast included. Free Internet access 8pm-8am. Singles €69-88; doubles €99-128. AmEx/MC/V. ❺

Paradis d'Eté, Strada Fontana 29H (☎/fax 51 73 121), 8km from town, in Colle della Trinità. Take a city bus from P. Italia (dir.: Colle della Trinità; 30min.; every 2hr.), and ask the driver to stop at the campgrounds. Attractive campground with free hot showers and pool access. €7 per person, €5.50 per tent, €3 per car. AmEx/MC/V. ❶

🍴 FOOD

No visit to Perugia is complete without a taste of the world-famous chocolate at **Perugina,** C. Vannucci 101. (Open M 2:30-8pm, Tu-Sa 9:30am-7:45pm, Su 10:30am-1:30pm and 3-8pm.) Beyond the classic *baci* (chocolate-hazelnut kisses), try *torta di formaggio* (cheese torte) and the *mele al cartoccio* (apple pie) at **Ceccarani,** P. Matteotti 16. (☎57 21 960. Open M-Sa 7:30am-8pm, Su 9am-1:30pm.) For confections like *torciglione* (sweet almond bread), follow aromas to **Pasticceria Sandri,** C. Vannucci 32. (☎57 24 112. Open Tu-Su 8am-10pm. MC/V.) Check out the **covered market** in P. Matteotti. Entrance is below street level. (Open M-Sa 7am-7:30pm.) The **Coop,** P. Matteotti 15, stocks essentials. (Open M-Sa 9am-8pm. MC/V.) Complement meals with one of the region's native wines: *Sagrantino Secco*, a dry red, or *Grechetto*, a light white.

■ **Trattoria Dal Mi' Cocco,** C. Garibaldi 12 (☎57 32 511). This unpretentious local favorite leaves diners happily stuffed. Friendly staff serves the generous *menù* (€13) which includes *antipasti, primi* and *secondi,* daily specials, bread, dessert, and a glass of liqueur. Open Tu-Su 1-2pm and 8:15-10pm. Reservations recommended. MC/V. ❷

Pizzeria Mediterranea, P. Piccinino 11/12 (☎57 21 322). From P. IV Novembre, walk to the right of the *duomo,* and turn right. A college crowd descends by night for upscale pizza at downscale prices (€3.70-12). Cover €1.10. Open daily 12:30-2:30pm and 7:30-11pm. MC/V. ❶

Brizi Ristorante, V. Fabretti 75 (☎57 21 386). From P. IV Novembre, walk to right of the *duomo,* go left through P. Danti, and right down V. Rocchi to P. Braccio Fortebraccio. On far side of *piazza,* turn left on V. Fabretti. Follow locals to Brizi for plates of pasta or the mixed grill with lamb, sausage, and chicken (€7). *Primi* and *secondi* €5-7. *Menù* €10. Cover €1.30. Open M and W-Su noon-3pm and 7:30-10pm. MC/V. ❷

Ristorante La Lanterna, V. Rocchi 6 (☎57 26 397), near the *duomo.* Enjoy *gnocchi lanterna* (ricotta and spinach *gnocchi* with mushrooms and cheese; €9) in brick-vaulted rooms with ornate decor. Waiters in formal dress hover attentively. *Primi* €7-10, *secondi* €9-15. Cover €2. Open M-W and F-Su noon-3pm and 7-10pm. AmEx/MC/V. ❸

👁 SIGHTS

PIAZZA IV NOVEMBRE AND ENVIRONS

■ **PIAZZA IV NOVEMBRE.** The social center of Perugian life, P. IV Novembre presents a pageant of young, lively locals and internationals against a backdrop of beautiful monuments. Perugia's most-visited sights frame the *piazza* on the northern end of the city, and most other monuments lie no more than a 15min. walk away. The **Fontana Maggiore** (1278-80), designed by Fra' Bevignate and decorated by Nicola and Giovanni Pisano, sits in the center of the *piazza.* Bas-reliefs depicting both religious and Roman history cover the double-basin fountain.

> **TIP**
>
> **PERUGIA PASS.** The **Perugia Città Museo** card grants admission to up to 12 of the city's fine artistic and historical sites, including the Galleria Nazionale dell'Umbria, the Museo Archeologico, and the Pozzo Etrusco. A one-day pass for four attractions is €7, a 3-day pass for all 12 sights is €12.

PALAZZO DEI PRIORI AND GALLERIA NAZIONALE DELL'UMBRIA. The 13th-century windows and turrets of this *palazzo,* on the left when facing the Fontana Maggiore, are remnants of an embattled era. This building, one of the finest examples of Gothic communal architecture, shelters the impressive **Galleria Nazionale dell'Umbria.** The collection contains magnificent 13th- and 14th-century religious works by Duccio, Fra Angelico, Taddeo di Bartolo, Guido da Siena, and Piero della Francesca. Among these early masterpieces, Duccio's skillful rendering of delicately translucent garments in his *Virgin and Child and Six Angels* in **Room 2** is worth a closer look. Another highlight is della Francesca's detailed *Polyptych of Saint Anthony* in **Room 11.** Native sons Pinturicchio and Perugino share **Room 15.** The two right panels of *Miracles of San Bernardino of Siena* are Pinturicchio's. Note his rich tones that contrast with Perugino's characteristic soft pastels of the two panels on the right. Downstairs, three rooms display Baroque and Neoclassical works as well as a collection of jewelry and textiles. *(In P. IV Novembre at C. Vannucci 19. ☎57 21 009; www.gallerianazionaleumbria.it. Open Tu-Su 8:30am-7:30pm. Last entry 1hr. before closing. Closed Jan. 1 and Dec. 25. €6.50; reduced €3.25. Cash only.)* To the right of the Galleria sits the **Sala dei Notari,** once the citizens' assembly chamber. Thir-

UMBRIA

teenth-century frescoes adorn the eight Romanesque arches, which support the vault. Note the scene on the fourth arch on the left of the crow and the fox from Aesop's fables. *(Up the steps across from the fountain, and across from the duomo. Sometimes closed for public performances. Open June-Sept. Tu-Su 9am-1pm and 3-7pm. Free.)*

DUOMO (CATTEDRALE DI SAN LORENZO). The rugged facade of Perugia's imposing Gothic *duomo* was begun in the 14th century, but builders never completed it. Though not as ornate as other cathedrals in Tuscany and Umbria, the groin-vaulted interior and 15th- to 18th-century embellishments, lit by small chandeliers, are quite elegant. There is occasionally nighttime organ music. The church also holds the Virgin Mary's wedding ring, snagged from Chiusi in the Middle Ages, though it is kept hidden under lock and key. *(P. IV Novembre. Open M-Sa 8am-12:45pm and 4-5:15pm, Su 4-5:45pm. Modest dress required. Free.)*

COLLEGIO DELLA MERCANZIA AND COLLEGIO DEL CAMBIO. The walls of the audience chambers on either side of Palazzo dei Priori are covered in magnificent wood paneling and elaborate frescoes. The elegant, carved bench in the Collegio della Mercanzia (Merchants' Guild) is a tribute to the Republic of Perugia, marking an advancement from the previous feudal system. In the Collegio del Cambio (Exchange Guild), the **Sala dell'Udienza** (audience chamber) holds Perugino's frescoes, which portray heroes, prophets, and even the artist himself. The members of Perugia's merchant guild have met in this wood-paneled structure since the 14th century. *(Collegio della Mercanzia: C. Vannucci 15. ☎57 30 366. Open daily Mar.-Oct. and Dec. 20-Jan. 6 Tu-Sa 9am-1pm and 2:30-5:30pm, Su and holidays 9am-1pm; Nov.-Dec. 19 and Jan. 7-Feb. Tu and Th-F 8am-2pm, W and Sa 8am-4:30pm, Su 9am-1pm. €1. Collegio del Cambio: C. Vannucci 25. ☎57 28 599. Open M-Sa 9am-12:30pm and 2:30-5:30pm, Su 9am-1pm. €4.50, combined ticket including Collegio della Mercanzia €5.50. Cash only.)*

VIA DEI PRIORI. Don't be fooled by the street's present-day calm and stone-like serenity. V. dei Priori, which begins under the arch at Palazzo dei Priori, was once one of medieval Perugia's goriest streets: the spikes on the lower walls of the street were once used to impale the rotting heads of executed criminals. The Neoclassical **Chiesa di San Filippo Neri**, begun in 1627 and built in the form of a Latin cross, resides solemnly in P. Ferri; Santa Maria di Vallicella's heart is kept to the right of the altar. *(Open daily in summer 7am-noon and 4:30-7:30pm; in winter 8am-noon and 4-6pm.)* **Piazza San Francesco al Prato** is a grassy square used for lounging and strolling. At its edge the 15th-century **Oratorio di San Bernardino** serves as a retreat from urban commotion. *(Next to Chiesa di San Francesco, down V. San Francesco. Open daily 8am-12:30pm and 3:30-6pm. Free.)*

THE NORTHEAST

VIA ROCCHI. From behind the *duomo*, medieval V. Rocchi, the city's oldest street, winds through the northern city and straight underneath the **Arco di Etrusco**, a perfectly preserved Roman arch built on Etruscan pedestals. Walk straight through P. Braccio Fortebraccio, where V. Rocchi turns to C. Guiseppe Garibaldi, and follow it for 10min. toward the jewel-like **Tempio di Sant'Angelo** (also known as **Chiesa di San Michele Arcangelo**), a 5th-century circular church constructed with stone and wood taken from ancient pagan buildings. The **Porta Sant'Angelo,** an arch and tower that welcomes visitors to the city, stands next door. *(Past Palazzo Gallenga, to the right near the end of C. Garibaldi. ☎57 22 624. Open daily 10am-noon and 4-6pm.)*

CAPPELLA DI SAN SEVERO. This chapel is home to *The Holy Trinity and Saints*, one of many collaborations by Perugia's favorite mentor-student tag team, Perugino and Raphael, who painted the lower and upper sections, respectively. Raphael's natural talent shone even at a young age. Check out the *piazza* wall opposite the chapel where a plaque engraved with a quote from Dante's *Paradiso* praises the city. *(In P. Rafaello. ☎57 33 864. Open Apr.-Oct. M and W-Su 10am-1:30pm and 2:30-6pm; Nov.-Mar. 10:30am-1:30pm and 2:30-5pm. €2.50, including Pozzo Etrusco.)*

POZZO ETRUSCO. With a depth of 36m, the Pozzo Etrusco (Etruscan Well) dates to the 3rd century BC and was once Perugia's main water source. Perugians were forced to use the well again during WWII, when bombs destroyed outside water lines to the city. Descend damp stairs to the footbridge spanning the well just meters above the water. *(P. Danti 18, across from the* duomo. *Look for the "Pozzo Etrusco" sign above a small alleyway and follow the alley down to the left. ☎57 33 669. Open Apr.-Oct. Tu-Su 10am-1:30pm and 2:30-6:30pm; Nov.-Mar. Tu-Su 11am-1:30pm and 2:30-5pm. Free.)*

THE EAST SIDE

BASILICA DI SAN PIETRO. This 10th-century church consists of a double arcade of closely spaced columns that lead to a choir. Its art-filled interior contains solemn, majestic paintings and frescoes depicting saints and soldiers, all in brilliant color on a dramatic scale. Look for Perugino's *Pietà* along the northern aisle. At the far end through the arch is a garden; its lower section offers a must-see view of the surrounding countryside. *(At the end of town on V. Borgo XX Giugno, past Pta. San Pietro. Entrance to church is on the far left side of the courtyard; garden is through courtyard on right. Open daily 7:30am-12:30pm and 3-6pm. Free.)*

CHIESA DI SAN DOMENICO. This cathedral is Umbria's largest. The Gothic rose window brightens the otherwise simple, cream-colored interior, rebuilt in 1632. The magnificently carved **Tomb of Pope Benedict XI** (1325), by a follower of Taddeo di Bartolo, rests in the Capella del Santissimo Sacramento to the right of the high altar. *(In P. Giordano Bruno, on C. Cavour. Open daily 7am-noon and 4-7:30pm. Free.)*

GIARDINI CARDUCCI. These well-maintained public gardens are named after the 19th-century poet Giosuè Carducci. From the garden wall, enjoy the splendid panorama of the Umbrian countryside; a castle or an ancient church crowns every hill. *(Behind P. Italia at the far end of C. Vannucci, the main street leading from P. IV Novembre. Free.)*

ROCCA PAOLINA. The *Rocca* is the underground remains of a grandiose fortress built by the architect Antonio Sangallo il Giovane on the order of Pope Paolo III Farnese. An escalator goes through the brick structure and connects the upper and lower parts of the city—peek into old passageways as you ride up to P. Italia. *(Entrances beneath P. Italia and across from bus station in P. dei Partigiani. Open daily 6:15am-1:45am. Free.)*

▨ ▨ NIGHTLIFE AND FESTIVALS

Perugia has more nightlife options than any other city in Umbria, and its large student population keeps clubs packed nearly every night of the week from September to May. During the academic year, join the nightly bandwagon at **Piazza Braccio Fortebraccio,** known as **Piazza Grimana** to locals, where free buses depart for several nearby clubs (starting at midnight). Once there, cover charges (€8-20) put patrons in the thick of deafening electronic music and scantily clad clubbers. In the city, students congregate at all hours on the steps of **Piazza IV Novembre** to people-watch or chat over pizza and wine. Bottles aren't allowed on the steps after 8pm, but never fear—neighboring cafes happily dole out drinks in plastic cups.

For a blend of pub and club, head to local hot spot **Bulo,** ("cool" in Perugian) on V. della Stella. From P. Cavalotti, walk down the alley on the left and follow the red lights to the door on the right. **Merlin,** on V. del Forno off of V. Fani, is relaxed and the drinks flow plentifully as patrons hop in and out. (☎57 22 708. Beers from €3.50. Mixed drinks from €5.50. Happy hour 10:30-11:30pm). **Shamrock,** P. Danti

18, is down a small side street on the way to the Pozzo Etrusco. Munch on juicy bacon burgers (€3.50) at this Irish pub. (☎57 36 625. Drinks €3.50. Happy hour 6-9pm. Open daily 6pm-2am). Serving fair-trade drinks on a terrace in P. Matteotti behind the covered market, **La Terrazza** gains favor with locals. (Beer from €2.50. Mixed drinks €5. Open daily 6pm-2am, depending on weather). Late-night cafes along **Via Mazzini** and **Piazza Matteotti** are a popular alternative to bar-hopping.

Every July, the 10-day ▓**Umbria Jazz Festival** draws world-class performers like B.B. King and Alicia Keys. Grab a *panino* and a bottle of wine and head to one of the free outdoor concerts, or dance all night by the stage in P. IV Novembre. (Info ☎800 46 23 11; www.umbriajazz.com. Ticket office, P. IV Novembre 28. Open M-Sa 10am-1pm and 3:30-7:30pm, Su 10am-7pm. Tickets €15-60, some events free.) In September, the **Sagra Musicale Umbra** occurs in many Umbrian cities and fills Perugia's churches with religious and classical music. Check Palazzo Gallenga or www.sagramusicaleumbra.com for event listings. During the 10-day **Eurochocolate Festival** (www.eurochocolate.perugia.it) at the end of October, chocolate becomes the focus of fanciful creations, and throngs of chocolate devotees wait for their free samples. On the first Sunday of the festival, throughout the city, sculptors hack away at huge blocks of chocolate to make a chocolate *Pietà*, the face of Berlusconi, or animals of every kind—stand close and grab the shavings. If those aren't filling enough, buy bags of *baci*, boxes of Ferrero-Rocher, or some local homemade treats.

▶ DAYTRIPS FROM PERUGIA

LAKE TRASIMENO AND CASTIGLIONE DEL LAGO

The easiest way to Castiglione del Lago from Perugia is by bus (1hr., 6 per day, €4.70) from P. dei Partigiani. Buses stop in P. Guglielmo Marconi. From there, walk up the stairs into P. Dante Alighieri, which leads up to the city entrance. The tourist office, P. Mazzini 10, the only square in town, provides boat schedules and maps. (☎96 52 484. Open M-F 8:30am-1pm and 3:30-7pm, Sa 9am-1pm and 3:30-7pm, Su 9am-1pm and 4-7pm.) To exchange currency or for an ATM, head to bank Monte dei Paschi di Siena, V. Vittorio Emanuele 57-61. (Open daily 8:20am-1:40pm and 2:20-3:30pm.)

Thirty kilometers west of Perugia, Lake Trasimeno (trah-see-MEH-no) is a refreshing oasis. After advancing down the Alps in 217 BC during the Second Punic War, Hannibal's elephant-riding army routed the Romans just north of the lake, killing 16,000 soldiers. Today, neither elephants nor bloodshed can be found in Castiglione del Lago, the main town. A system of ferries connects Castiglione del Lago with Passignano sul Trasimeno, Tuero, San Feliciano, and Lake Trasimeno's two largest islands—Isola Maggiore and Isola Polvese.

> ✦TIP✦ **LOVE THE LAKE?** If you plan to spend a long time exploring Lake Trasimeno, consider participating in the **Museo Aperto** museum tour, sponsored by the region's tourist offices. One ticket costs €5 and includes admission to attractions in Castiglione del Lago, Città della Pieve, Pacicino and Panicale. A €3 supplement includes a tour on Isola Maggiore. Inquire at the tourist office in any of the four towns to buy tickets or book tours.

Castiglione del Lago (ca-steel-YON-ay del LA-go; pop. 14,500) is now a much quieter town than in past centuries, when it was conquered by Arezzo, Cortona, and finally Perugia in 1184. Clinging to a limestone promontory covered in olive groves, its medieval walls enclose two main streets and a single *piazza*. At the end of V. Vittorio Emanuele, next to the hospital, stand the **Palazzo della Corgna** and the medieval **Rocca del Leone**. The 16th-century *palazzo* is notable for its frescoes, particularly those in **Sala delle Gesta d'Ascanio** by Niccolò Circignani, the Italian painter known as Pomarancio. Follow a dark passageway to view the Lake from the *Rocca*. The courtyard of the crumbling *Rocca* is free and open to the public, and its grass lawn sometimes serves as a venue for open-air concerts. (☎96 58 210. Open daily Mar 21.-Apr. 9:30am-1pm and 3:30-7pm; May-June 10am-1:30pm and 4-7:30pm; July-Aug. 10am-1:30pm and 4:30-7pm; Sept.-Oct. 10am-1:30pm and 3:30-7pm; Nov.-Mar. 20 9:30am-4:30pm. Combined ticket €3.) Visitors can also catch a ferry to nearby **Isola Maggiore**, one of Lake Trasimeno's only inhabited islands. From V. Belvedere, take V. Giovanni Pascoli to Vle. Garibaldi. Ferries depart from the shoreline area and tickets can be purchased on board.

Budget lodgings are scarce in Castiglione del Lago's immediate vicinity, but **Il Torrione ❹**, V. delle Mura 2/4, right on V. Battisti just inside the gates, is a worthy option. The lush garden overlooking the lake leads to four rooms and two apartments with bath and fridge. (☎95 32 36; www.trasinet.com/iltorrione. Singles €60; doubles €70. Cash only.) **La Torre ❹**, V. Vittorio Emanuele 50, offers nine simply furnished rooms with bath, TV, A/C, and fridge in the heart of the old town. (☎95 16 66; www.trasinet.com/latorre. Breakfast €5. Singles €50; doubles €65-75; triples €80. AmEx/MC/V.) Gourmet food shops line the busier streets, while cheap pizzerias, where prices average €3-6 per person, crowd V. Vittorio Emanuele. With beautiful views and an attentive waitstaff, **La Cantina ❷**, V. V. Emanuele 93, offers a fancier dining experience full of Umbrian cuisine and sea-food specialities from the Lake. (Pizza €3-7. *Primi* €5-7.50, *secondi* €9.50-17. *Menù* €12.50. Cover €1.80. Open June-Sept. W-Su 12:30-3pm and 7pm-1am; Oct.-May W-Su 12:30-3pm and 7-10:30pm. AmEx/MC/V.) **Ristorante L'Acquario ❸**, V. V. Emanuele 69, offers a variety of lunch *menù* for €26. Or try a Trasimeno original: pasta with black truffles or *tagliatelle* with lake fish eggs and perch fil-lets. (☎96 52 432. *Primi* €7.30-10, *secondi* €8.50-14.50. Open Mar.-Oct. M-Tu and Th-Su noon-2:30pm and 7-10:30pm; Nov.-Feb. closed M. MC/V.)

TODI

APM (☎89 42 939 or 800 51 21 41) runs buses to and from Perugia (1¼hr.; M-Sa 8 per day; last bus from Todi 5pm, last bus from Perugia 7:30pm; €5.20). The bus sta-tion is in P. della Consolazione, near Tempio di Santa Maria della Consolazione. Todi is also accessible by train on the Perugia-Terni line from Ponte Rio (45min., 7 per day 6:30am-1pm and 3:30-8pm, €2.70). The last train leaves from Terni at 8:10pm and from Perugia 8:50pm; city bus C runs to the station at P. Jacopone until 7:45pm. (Buy tickets for €1.50 on board or for €1 in a nearby tabaccherie.) The IAT Tourist Office, P. del Popolo 38, has free maps, schedules, and info on restaurants and lodgings. (☎89 42 526. Open M-Sa 9:30am-1pm and 3:30-6pm, Su 10-1:30pm.)

At the foot of Todi's (TO-dee) lush hills sits the Renaissance **Tempio di Santa Maria della Consolazione,** whose elegant domes are thought to have been based on archi-tectural genius Bramante's early draft for St. Peter's in Rome. The orderly geomet-ric shapes of the central dome are pleasing when seen alongside the Baroque altarpiece and the 12 surrounding statues. (Open daily Apr.-Oct. 9am-12:30pm and 2:30-6:30pm; Nov.-Mar. 9:30am-12:30pm and 2:30-5pm. Free.) From P. della Conso-lazione, follow a sinuous, cypress-lined dirt path (Vle. della Serpentina) or the less curvy V. della Consolazione to reach **La Rocca**, a ruined 14th-century castle that fronts a public **park** with picnic tables and a basketball court. (Open daily Apr.-Oct. 6:30am-10pm; Nov.-Mar. 7am-7pm.) From the park follow V. della Rocca to the towering **Tempio di San Fortunato.** Built by the Franciscans between the 13th and 15th centuries, the church features a high vaulted ceiling with decorative medal-lions and aged frescoes like *The Madonna* and *Jesus With Angels* by Masolino da Panciale in the fourth chapel on right. Peek into the sixth chapel on the right and the fifth chapel on the left to see of vestiges of magnificent frescoes from the 14th century. (Open Tu-Su 9am-1pm and 3-7pm. Free.) From San Fortunato, head through P. Jacopone to the **Piazza del Popolo,** encircled by three palaces-turned-municipal-centers, half a dozen souvenir shops, two *gelaterie,* and a 900-year-old church. The 12th-century **duomo** is at the far end of P. del Popolo atop a flight of broad stone steps. The individually designed capitals that top the columns of the central arcade are notable and quirky. The 16th-century rose window at the rear brightens up the interior. (Open daily 8:30am-12:30pm and 2:30-6:30pm. Free.)

While high-priced luxury hotels are located inside the city walls, less expensive options are about a 20min. walk downhill from the *centro.* The best budget option is **⊠Crispolti Holiday House ❸,** V. Santa Prassede 36, near P. del Popolo. Walking down V. del Duomo, turn right on V. S. Prassede, and wind to the right until you reach V. Cesia; the Holiday House is ahead on the left. This hostel-style accommodation provides private and dormitory rooms in an old monastery. In addition to being centrally located, spacious, and friendly, Crispolti offers a bar, inexpensive restaurant, meeting room, terrace overlooking the Umbrian countryside, TV room, and Internet access. (☎89 44 827; www.crispoltiholidayhouse.com. Breakfast included. Dorms €30; doubles €80; triples €105; quads €120. Group discounts available. MC/V.) **Antica Hosteria de la Valle ❷,** V. Ciuffelli 17-21, serves meals in a stately room of brick and wood. Gaze out the windows to the street scene or grab a seat on the outdoor patio. The menu, as well as the local art displayed on the walls, changes bi-weekly. (☎89 44 848. *Primi* €7-12, *secondi* €9-17. Full-course meal €20-22. Cover €1. Open Tu-Su 12:30-2:30pm and 7:30-10pm. MC/V.)

GUBBIO ☎075

Roman remains, a thriving ceramics trade, historical festivals and the artistic feats of a local painting school are framed by medieval alleyways and packed into Gubbio's (GOO-bee-yo; pop. 33,000) picturesque setting. The town's famous 300-100BC Eugubine Tablets, one of the only existing records of the ancient Umbrian language, offer a glimpse into Umbria's history and provide important evidence of an Umbrian and Roman alliance against invading Etruscans. The town's rugged mountain backdrop offer matchless views. Although a convenient daytrip from Perugia, Gubbio itself is worthy of a night's stay.

▐▘ ▐▟ TRANSPORTATION AND PRACTICAL INFORMATION

The nearest **train station** is in **Fossato di Vico,** 15km away and on the Rome-Ancona line. Trains run to Ancona (1½hr., 14 per day, from €4.23), Rome (2½hr., 12 per day, €10.12), and Spoleto (1¼hr., 10 per day, €3.36). **APM buses** (☎50 67 81) run to and from Perugia (1hr.; M-F 11 per day, Sa-Su 4 per day; €4.30) and are much more convenient than the train, though the twisting, hilly road can be stomach-churning. The bus is the easiest way to reach Gubbio from Fossato (M-Sa 11 per day, Su 5 per day; €2). Tickets are sold at the newsstand in P. Quaranta Martiri, at the Perugia bus stop, and at the newsstand in Fossato's train station. If stranded in Fossato without bus service, call a **taxi** (☎91 92 02 or 033 53 37 48 71; €25 per 20min.). In Gubbio, **taxis** (☎92 73 800) are available in P. Quaranta Martiri.

Gubbio's medieval streets are easily navigable. Buses stop in **Piazza Quaranta Martiri.** The 24hr. **ATM** is located here. A short walk up **Via della Repubblica** is the **ITA Tourist Office,** V. della Repubblica 15, which offers bus schedules and maps. (☎92 20 693; www.gubbio-altochiascio.umbria2000.it. Open Mar.-Oct. M-F 8:30am-1:45pm and 3:30-6:30pm, Sa 9am-1pm and 3:30-6:30pm, Su 9:30am-12:30pm and 3:30-6:30pm; Oct.-Mar. M-F 8:30am-1:45pm and 3-6pm, Sa 9am-1pm and 3-6pm, Su 9:30am-12:30pm and 3-6pm.) V. della Repubblica crosses **Corso**

Garibaldi, the second major street on the right. **Farmacia Luconi** is at C. Garibaldi 12. (☎92 73 783. Open M-Sa Apr.-Sept. 9am-1pm and 4:30-8pm; Oct.-Mar. 9am-1pm and 4-7:30pm.) Signs point uphill to **Piazza Grande,** the civic headquarters on the hilltop. The **hospital** can be reached at ☎92 391. The **post office** is at V. Cairoli 11. (☎92 73 925. Open M-F 8am-1:30pm, Sa 8am-12:30pm.) **Postal Code:** 06024.

ACCOMMODATIONS AND FOOD

A private garden and enthusiastic staff make ⬚**Residenza di Via Piccardi ❸,** V. Piccardi 12, an ideal place to relax. Six comfortable rooms all have bath and TV. (☎92 76 108; e.biagiotti@tiscali.it. Breakfast included. Check-in before 8pm. Singles €35; doubles €50; triples €60. Extra bed €10. Cash only.) **Residenza Le Logge ❹,** V. Piccardi 7/9, is to the right off P. Quaranta Martiri. Open the shutters to views of Palazzo dei Consoli or the Church of San Giovanni. The *pensione* run by a friendly owner has six large, clean rooms. For a splurge, ask for the massive double suite with a whirlpool tub. (☎92 77 574; www.paginegialle.it/residenzalelogge. Breakfast included. Singles €42-50; doubles €52-80, with bath €65-100. AmEx/MC/V.) Walk up from P. Quaranta Martiri on V. della Repubblica, and turn right on V. Gioia to reach **Hotel Grotta dell'Angelo ❸,** V. Gioia 47. Simple yet large and cheery rooms contrast with Gubbio's winding alleyways. (☎92 71 747; www.grottadellangelo.it. Breakfast €5. Singles €35-38; doubles €50-55; triples €65. AmEx/MC/V.)

Sample local delicacies at **Prodotti Tipici e Tartufati Eugubini ❶,** V. Piccardi 17, including *salumi di cinghiale o cervo* (boar or deer sausage) and the region's white-truffle oil. (☎92 71 751. Open Apr.-Jan. 7 daily 10am-1:30pm and 3:30-8pm. Cash only.) Enjoy regional truffles and other specialties amidst 14th-century decor at **La Cantina Ristorante/Pizzeria ❸,** V. Francesco Piccotti 3, off V. della Repubblica. They've got pizza, too, for the not-so-fungi inclined. (☎92 20 583. Pizza €4.50-7. *Primi* €6.50-12, *secondi* €7-14. Cover €1. Restaurant open Tu-Su noon-2:30pm and 7-10pm. Pizzeria open noon-3pm. AmEx/MC/V.) The stone dining room of **San Francesco e il Lupo ❹,** V. Cairoli 24, serves homemade pizza and has a wine cellar with over 200 labels. (☎92 72 344. Pizza €4-7.50. *Primi* €7.50-12, *secondi* €8-24. Cover €2. Open M and W-Su noon-2pm and 7-10pm. AmEx/MC/V.) Dine under elegant stone vaulted ceilings in the dining rooms of **Ristorante La Lanterna ❸,** V. Gioia 2. The menu selections offer staples of Eugubine fare such as mushrooms and truffles. (☎92 76 694. *Primi* €7.50-12, *secondi* €8-11. Open M-W and F-Su noon-3pm and 7:30-10:30pm. MC/V.) Every Tuesday brings a bustling **market** under P. Quaranta Martiri's loggias. Get groceries at **Coop,** on V. Beniamino Ubaldi. Follow V. Perugina away from P. Quaranta Martiri and turn right.

SIGHTS

PIAZZA QUARANTA MARTIRI. In the middle of the *piazza* stretches the **Giardino dei Quaranta Martiri** (Garden of the 40 Martyrs), a memorial to those slain by the Nazis in reprisal for the assassination of two German officials. Across the *piazza* from the bus stop stands the **Chiesa di San Francesco,** which was completed in 1256 and is one of the many places rumored to be the site where St. Francis experienced his conversion. The left-hand apse holds the *Vita della Madonna,* a partially destroyed, 15th-century fresco series by Ottaviano Nelli, Gubbio's most famous painter. The frescoes are skillfully rendered and the 15th-century *campanile* rises gracefully outside. *(Church open daily 7:15am-noon and 3:30-7:30pm. Free.)* Via Matteotti runs from P. Quaranta Martiri, outside the city walls, to the **Teatro**

Romano, Vle. del Teatro Romano, built at the end of the first century BC. While restorations are a modern addition, a sense of power and stability still seem to emanate from the semi-circular stone tiers. Productions are staged in July and August (tickets €13). The nearby **Antiquarium** displays impressive Roman mosaics found in the city and preserved foundations beneath your feet.

PALAZZO DEI CONSOLI. In P. Grande, this white stone palace (1321-1330) was built for Gubbio's high magistrate. Inside, the **Museo Civico** displays a collection of Eugubinian and Roman artifacts. In a room upstairs, the **Tavole Eugubine** (Eugubine Tablets), are comparable to the Rosetta Stone for their linguistic significance. Five of these seven bronze tablets, dating from 300 to 100 BC, are showcased as rare proof of the ancient Umbrian language, as well as an Umbrian and Roman alliance against the encroaching Etruscans. The last two tablets are in Latin. An illiterate farmer discovered them in 1444 in an underground chamber of the Roman theater just outside the city walls; he was subsequently tricked into swapping them for a worthless piece of land. The texts spell out the social, religious, and political organization of early Umbria, and they describe how to read religious omens from animal livers. *(☎92 74 298. Open daily Apr.-Oct. 10am-1pm and 3-6pm; Nov. to mid-Mar. 10am-1pm and 2-5pm. €5, ages 7-25 €2.50, under 7 free.)*

DUOMO. The unassuming pink Gothic *duomo*, sitting up on a hill from P. Grande, was built in the 13th and 14th centuries on the site of a Romanesque church. The interior is simple, with a single pitched-roof nave. Notable are the 12th-century stained-glass windows, art by Perugino's student Dono Doni, and Antonio Tatoti's *Adoration of the Magi. (Open daily Apr.-Sept. 9am-6pm; Oct.-Mar. 10am-5pm. Free.)*

MONTE INGINO. Hop into the rather shaky cages of the **funivia,** a standing chairlift, which, in six short minutes, climbs to an unparalleled view of Gubbio's medieval rooftops and the Umbrian hills. Climb the hill behind the *funivia*'s drop off point to reach the **Basilica and Monastery of Sant'Ubaldo,** which houses the saint's pickled body in a glass case above the altar. The stained glass at the entrance tells the story of his life; the three *ceri*, large wooden candles carried in the **Corsa dei Ceri** procession each May, are also on display. Each December, lights transform the entire hill into the world's largest Christmas tree (they're in the Guinness Book of World Records). Follow the dirt trail behind the basilica up to the scaffolding where the star is placed atop the "tree," and then continue up to an ancient but well-preserved tower for spectacular 360-degree vistas of the Umbrian mountains and valleys. *(To reach the funivia, exit Pta. Romana to the left. From the uphill entrance to the basilica, bear left and continue upward on a dirt path to the top of the mountain. Chairlift open June M-Sa 9:30am-1:15pm and 2:30-7pm; Su 9am-7:30pm; July-Aug. daily 9am-8pm; Sept. M-Sa 9:30am-1:15pm and 2:30-7pm, Su 9:30am-1:15pm and 2:30-7:30pm; Mar. M-Sa 10am-1:15pm and 2:30-5:30pm, Su 9:30am-1:15pm and 2:30-6pm; Apr.-May M-Sa 10am-1:15pm and 2:30-6:30pm, Su 9:30am-1:15pm and 2:30-7pm; Oct. daily 10am-1:15pm and 2:30-6pm; Nov.-Feb. M-Tu and Th-Su 10am-1:15pm and 2:30-5pm. €4, round-trip €5.)*

❋ FESTIVALS

The annual **Corsa dei Ceri,** 900 years old and still going strong, takes place every May 15, the day of patron Saint Ubaldo's death. Three *ceri* (candles) are carved like hourglasses and topped with little statues of saints. Each one corresponds to a distinct section of the populace: the masons (Sant'Ubaldo), the farmers (Sant'Antonio Abate), and the artisans (San Giorgio). After 12hr. of furious preparation and frenetic flag-twirling, squads of *ceraioli* (candle runners) clad in Renaissance-style tights lift the heavy objects onto their shoulders and run a wild relay race up Monte Ingino. This raucous festival turns Gubbio's quiet streets into a chaotic stomping ground bristling with intense ritual fervor. Visitors will be entranced; locals will almost certainly be drunk. During the **Pallo della Balestra**, held in P. Grande on the last Sunday in May, archers from Gubbio and nearby Sansepolcro have gathered for a fierce crossbow contest since 1139. The contest provides an excellent excuse for Gubbio to throw a huge party every year and maintain an industry in medieval-weaponry toys.

ASSISI   ☎075

Assisi's (ah-SEE-zee; pop. 25,000) serene atmosphere and renowned spirituality stem from the legacy of its favorite son and Italy's patron saint, St. Francis. The 12th-century monk founded the Franciscan order and sparked an ascetic revolution within the Catholic Church. Franciscan monks and nuns, dressed in brown *cappucci* robes, still inhabit Assisi. Fervent religiosity, however, is hardly a prerequisite for a visit. Many people come simply for the city's intricate architecture. The Basilica di San Francesco is the most-frequented sight in Umbria, housing the saint's relics and Giotto's renowned fresco series of St. Francis. While local ruins attest to Assisi's Etruscan and Roman roots, grand palaces and majestic castles from a later era tower above tile roofs. A peek through almost any of Assisi's stone archways reveals patchwork panoramas of the Umbrian countryside, and the sounds of birds and the ringing bells add to the town's tranquility.

▐ TRANSPORTATION

Trains: Station near Basilica di Santa Maria degli Angeli. Assisi is on the Foligno-Terontola line. Ticket office open daily 6am-7:35pm. (☎80 40 272. AmEx/MC/V.) **Luggage storage** available. Trains to **Florence** (2½hr., 7 per day 5:48am-7:19pm, €9), **Perugia** (30min., 1-2 per hr. 5:54am-10:45pm, €1.80), and **Rome** (2½hr., 7 per day 6:18am-5:47pm, €9).

Buses: Buses leave from P. Unità d'Italia. Buy **SULGA** (☎50 09 641; www.sulga.it) tickets on board. To: **Florence** (2½hr.; 7am, 6pm; €11) and **Rome** (3¼hr.; 1:45, 4:30pm; €17). Buy **APM** (☎800 51 21 41) tickets at newsstands. To: **Foligno** (1hr., M-Sa 10 per day 6:55am-7:10pm, €4) via **Spello** and **Perugia** (1½hr., 12 per day 6:30am-6:25pm, €3). Buy **SENA** (☎72 83 203) tickets onboard. Bus to **Siena** (2hr., 2 per day, €9) leaves from Basilica di S. Maria degli Angeli. Schedules available at tourist office.

Public Transportation: Local buses (2 per hr., €0.90) run along **Linea A** from the train station to bus stops at P. Unità d'Italia, Largo Properzio, and P. Matteotti. Buy tickets on board or at *tabaccherie* in the train station. Minibuses (€0.90) run around the inner city to select points on the outside along 2 lines, A and B.

Taxis: In P. del Comune (☎81 31 93), P. Santa Chiara (☎81 26 00), P. Unità d'Italia (☎81 23 78), and the train station (☎80 40 275). **RadioTaxi** (☎81 31 00).

▐▐ ORIENTATION AND PRACTICAL INFORMATION

Towering above the city to the north, the **Rocca Maggiore** can help orient those lost among Assisi's winding streets. The bus from the train station stops first at **Piazza Unità d'Italia;** get off here for direct access to the Basilica di San Francesco. Stay on the bus until **Piazza Matteotti** to access the *centro* from above. To reach **Piazza del Comune**, take **Via del Torrione** from P. Matteotti to **Piazza San Rufino;** take the downhill left in the *piazza*, and then walk down **Via San Rufino.** From P. del Comune **Via Portica** becomes V. Fortini, V. del Seminario, and, finally, V. San Francesco and connects P. del Comune to the Basilica di San Francesco. Heading in the opposite direction from P. del Comune, **Corso Mazzini** leads to the Basilica di Santa Chiara.

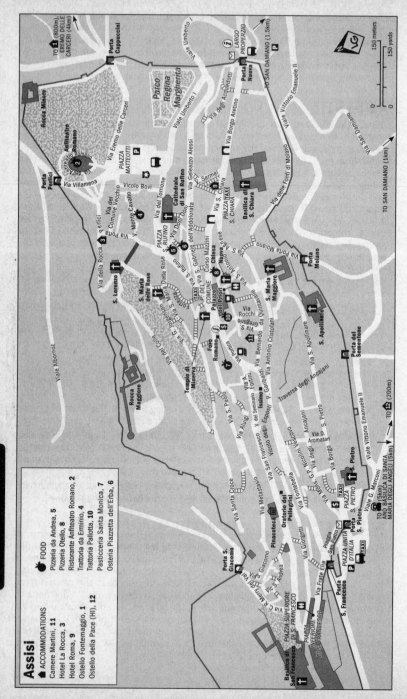

Assisi

▲ ACCOMMODATIONS

Camere Martini, **11**
Hotel La Rocca, **3**
Hotel Roma, **9**
Ostello Fontemaggio, **1**
Ostello della Pace (HI), **12**

🍴 FOOD

Pizzeria da Andrea, **5**
Pizzeria Otello, **8**
Ristorante Anfiteatro Romano, **2**
Trattoria da Erminio, **4**
Trattoria Pallotta, **10**
Pasticceria Santa Monica, **7**
Osteria Piazzetta dell'Erba, **6**

Tourist Office: P. del Comune (☎81 25 34; www.umbria2000.it). Walking into P. del Comune on V. S. Rufino, office is at far end of the *piazza*. Provides brochures, bus info, train schedules, and a decent map. Open M-Sa 8am-2pm and 3-6pm, Su and holidays 10am-1pm.

Currency Exchange: For traveler's checks, try **Banca Toscana,** in P. San Pietro. Open M-F 8:20am-1:30pm and 2:15-3:35pm, Su 8:20-11:50am. **Unicredit Banca,** in P. del Comune. Open M-F 8:20am-1:20pm and 2:35-4:05pm. **ATMs** outside.

Luggage Storage: In train station. €2.60 per 12hr. Open daily 7am-7:30pm. MC/V.

Carabinieri: P. Matteotti 3 (☎81 22 39).

Hospital: Ospedale d'Assisi (☎81 391), on the outskirts of town. Take the Linea A bus from P. del Comune and get off at stop 7 (Ospedale).

Internet Access: Bar, V. Portica 29B (☎81 62 46). €2 for 1st 15min, €1 per each additional 15min. thereafter. Open daily 9:30am-10pm. Cash only. **Caffe Minerva,** P. del Comune 15/16 (☎81 24 75). €3 per 30min., €5 per hr. Cash only.

Post Office: Largo Properzio 4, upstairs to the left, outside Pta. Nuova. Branch at P. San Pietro 41. Open M-F 8am-1:30pm, Sa 8am-12:30pm. Cash only. **Postal Code:** 06081.

■ ACCOMMODATIONS AND CAMPING

Reservations are crucial around Easter and Christmas and strongly recommended for the Festa di Calendimaggio. If you don't mind an 11pm curfew, ask the tourist office for a list of **religious institutions** that provide cheap rooms. The tourist office also provides a list of *affittacamere*, rooms for rent in private residences.

Camere Martini, V. San Gregorio 6 (☎/fax 81 35 36; cameremartini@libero.it). 6 bright rooms, some with balconies, surround a brick courtyard. Central location, soft beds, and friendly atmosphere. Laundry €5. Singles €25, with bath €27; doubles €40; triples €55; quads €65. Cash only. ❷

Ostello della Pace (HI), V. di Valecchie 177 (☎81 67 67; www.assisihostel.com). From the train station, take the bus to P. Unità d'Italia. From P. Unità d'Italia, walk downhill on V. Marconi. Turn left at sign and walk for 500m down a curving paved road bordered by olive groves. Bright rooms with 2-3 bunk beds and shared baths. Common dining room and outdoor seating make this hostel feel like a country getaway. Breakfast included. Dinner €9.50. Laundry €3.50. Reception 7-9:30am and 3:30-11:30pm. Lockout 9:30am-3:30pm. Curfew 11pm. Reservations recommended. HI card required; can purchase at hostel. Dorms €15, with bath €17. MC/V. ❶

Ostello/Hotel/Camping Fontemaggio, V. Eremo delle Carceri 24 (☎81 36 36; fax 81 37 49). V. Eremo delle Carceri begins in P. Matteotti and leads through Pta. Cappuccini; follow it 1km up the road, and then bear right at the sign. Trekkers are rewarded with well-kept hotel, hostel, campground and bungalows. On-site restaurant. Breakfast €5. Check-out 10am. Curfew 11pm. Reservations recommended. Hostel: dorms €20. Hotel: singles €35; doubles €52; triples €72.50; quads €96. Campground: camping €5.50 per person, €4.50 per tent, €2.50 per car. 4- to 8-person bungalows €50-140. MC/V. Hostel ❷/ Hotel ❸/Campground ❶

Hotel La Rocca, V. Pta. Perlici 27 (☎81 22 84). From P. del Comune, follow V. S. Rufino uphill. Cross the *piazza*, heading up V. Pta. Perlici until you reach the old arches. Tucked into the northern part of town, all 27 generically furnished rooms have bath, TV, and telephone; some have view of the *Rocca*. Restaurant downstairs. Open Feb. 5-Jan. 15. Singles €45; doubles €50; triples €70. AmEx/MC/V. ❹

Hotel Roma, P. Santa Chiara 13-15 (☎81 23 90). Tidy rooms offer spectacular views of the S. Chiara's pink and white facade and the surrounding countryside. All 28 rooms have bath, TV, and phone. Breakfast included. Singles €45; doubles €70. MC/V. ❹

UMBRIA

ON THE MENU

SLOW FOOD
SPREADS FAST

The Slow Food movement sprung in 1986 when Carlo Petrini of Bra, Italy decided enough was enough with grab-n-go fast food chains. In a mere 22 years, his movement has grown to 80,000 members from all points of the globe who are attempting to counteract consumers' dwindling interest in the food they eat. Where is it from? What does it taste like? Sometimes we eat too fast even to remember.

Slow Food's requirements are 3-fold: the food must be good, clean, and fair. In other words, it must taste good, not harm the environment, and food producers must receive fair compensation for their work. Ultimately, their view is that when you lift your fork to swirl that first bite of *linguine*, you are not a consumer, but an informed co-producer.

Keep an eye out for Slow Food's snail symbol on the doors of many restaurants in Italy for assured quality. They even opened a University of Gastronomical Sciences in 2004, offering Bachelor's and Master's degrees, along with many cultural seminars.

So before you grab that *panini "da portare via"* ("to go"), take a moment to step back and remember where your food is coming from. Even a little acknowledgement is a start.

For more information, visit www.slowfood.com.

🟥 FOOD

Pasticceria Santa Monica, V. Portica 4, right off P. del Comune, sells delectables native to Assisi. Mouthwatering *torrone* (a sweet nougat of almonds and egg whites; €3.80 per 100g) and the divine *brustengolo* (a cake packed with raisins, apples, and pine nuts; €3.20 per 100g) are among the city's alluring sweets and nut breads. (Open daily 10:30am-11pm. Cash only.) For fresh produce on weekdays, head to the market on V. San Gabriele dell'Addolorata. The only grocery stores in town are small *alimentari*, which are scattered throughout the city's center. The nearest supermarket, **Issimo**, is located in P. Garibaldi, near the Basilica di Santa Maria degli Angeli. (Open daily 7:30am-1pm and 4:30-8pm. MC/V.)

📷 Pizzeria Otello, V. Sant'Antonio 1 (☎81 51 25). On the far left of the Palazzo dei Priori. Be sure to arrive early for your spot at one of Otello's long wooden tables to taste one of their popular, diverse pizzas (€5-7). Or try the deliciously creamy *strangozzi al tartufo* (pasta with truffles; €6.80). Open daily noon-3pm and 7-10:30pm. AmEx/MC/V. ❶

Osteria Piazzetta dell'Erba, V. San Gabriele dell'Addolorata 15A. Although this Slow Food restaurant asks patrons to savor every morsel, the service is snappy. Artfully prepared plates include refreshing salads, hearty pasta, and meat plates. Try the salad with pears, *pecorino* cheese, walnuts, and honey (€8). *Primi* €9-10, *secondi* €14-18. Cover €1.50. Open Tu-Su 12:30-2:30pm and 7:30-10pm. AmEx/MC/V. ❹

Pizzeria da Andrea, P. San Rufino 26 (☎81 53 25). From P. del Comune, walk up V. S. Rufino. Look for the *pizza al taglio* sign on the right side of the *piazza*. Pleasant seats near the fountain outside make this a great rest from sightseeing. Pizza €0.90-3.50. *Panini* €3. Open Tu-Su 8:30am-8:30pm. Cash only. ❶

Trattoria da Erminio, V. Monte Cavallo 19 (☎81 25 06). A wood fire sends the savory aroma of crackling, roasting meat into the street. *Antipasti* €8. *Primi* €5-10, *secondi* €5-11. Cover €1.80. Open M-W and F-Su noon-2:30pm and 7-9pm. AmEx/MC/V. ❷

Trattoria Pallotta, Vco. della Volta Pinta 13 (☎81 26 49), off P. del Comune, enter through the arch opposite Tempio di Minerva. Succulent Umbrian classics served beneath stone arcades. Excellent veggie options, including a €24 vegetarian *menù*. *Primi* €5-18, *secondi* €7-15. *Piatti stagionali* (seasonal dishes) €4-18. Cover €2.50. Open M and W-Su noon-2:30pm and 7:15-9:30pm. AmEx/MC/V. ❸

Ristorante Anfiteatro Romano, V. Anfiteatro Romano 4 (☎81 30 25), off P. Matteotti. Hearty portions of Umbrian fare served on the refreshing, vine-rimmed patio or in the dining room adorned with a Roman-style fresco. *Primi* €4.20-8, *secondi* €5.20-8.30. Cover €1.60. Open Tu-Su noon-2:30pm and 7-9pm. MC/V. ❷

◉ SIGHTS

At age 19, St. Francis (1182-1226) abandoned his military and social ambitions, rejected his father's wealth, and embraced asceticism. His love of nature, devoted humility, and rejection of the Church's worldliness earned him a huge European following and posed an unprecedented threat to the decadent papacy and corrupt monastic orders. St. Francis continued to preach chastity and poverty until his death. Since his death, the Church has glorified the modest saint in countless cathedrals, many of which can be found in Assisi.

▨**BASILICA DI SAN FRANCESCO.** A major pilgrimage site, Basilica di San Francesco is one of Italy's greatest spiritual and artistic attractions. When its construction began in the mid-13th century, the Franciscan order protested, complaining that the elaborate church was an impious monument to the conspicuous consumption that St. Francis had scorned. Brother Elia, the vicar of the order, insisted that a double church be erected, the lower level built around the saint's crypt, the upper level used for services. The walls of the upper basilica are covered with Giotto's renowned *Life of St. Francis* fresco cycle. The dimension and volume the painter brings to his figures was not depicted by previous artists of this age. Cimabue's magnificent *Maestà* (displaying the Virgin and child surrounded by four angels and St. Francis) graces the right transept. Some of Cimabue's frescoes in the transepts and apse have so deteriorated that they now look like photographic negatives. Pietro Lorenzetti decorated the left transept with his outstanding *Crucifixion, Last Supper*, and *Madonna and Saints*. **St. Francis's tomb,** the inspiration for the entire edifice, lies below the lower basilica; the coffin itself was hidden in the 15th century for fear of the war-mongering *Perugini*, and it wasn't rediscovered until 1818. The stone coffin rests on the altar of the lower basilica, surrounded by the sarcophagi of four of the saint's dearest friends. *(☎81 90 084; www.sanfrancescoassisi.org. Info window open M-Sa 9am-noon and 2-5:30pm. Lower basilica and tomb open daily 6am-6:45pm. Upper basilica open daily 8:30am-6:45pm. Modest dress required. Free. Tours given by monks arranged in advance for groups of 20 or more, €2.50 per person; call or visit info window across from entrance to lower basilica. Audio tour €4.)*

BASILICA DI SANTA CHIARA. St. Claire (1194-1253) was one of the first followers of St. Francis. Since the Franciscan Order already took care of the pious men, St. Claire opened the door to women bent on poverty and celibacy by establishing the Order of Poor Ladies. The Basilica di Santa Chiara's pink and white stone flying buttresses seen on the left side of the basilica are notable, but it is the surrounding **courtyard** with fountains and views that make it dazzling. Standing on the site where St. Francis attended school, the church shelters the tomb and relics of St. Claire, as well as the crucifix that supposedly spoke to St. Francis, instigating his conversion. Nuns in the convent are sworn to seclusion. *(☎81 22 82. Open daily 6:30am-noon and 2-7pm. Modest dress required. Free.)*

ROCCA MAGGIORE. The craggy Rocca Maggiore looms uphill from the *duomo*. The hike up is well worth the view of the town and the Basilica di San Francesco from the gravel lot outside the fortress, or pay a nominal fee to step into the shade of the fortress and the eerie 50m tunnel to Torre Poligonale. The ▨**view** is breathtaking—miles of countryside stretch in all directions. *(From P. del Comune, follow V. S. Rufino to P. S. Rufino. Continue up V. Pta. Perlici and take 1st left up a narrow staircase. Open daily 9am-8pm. Last entry 30 min. before closing. Closed in bad weather. €3.50, students €2.50; combined ticket for Pinacoteca, Foro Romano, and Rocca €4.50/3.50. Cash only.)*

CATTEDRALE DI SAN RUFINO. Via S. Rufino climbs steeply from P. del Comune between closely packed houses, opening onto P. S. Rufino to reveal the cathedral and its massive bell tower. Inside, peach-colored pillasters frame a bright white central dome. Peer through glass tiles on the floor into the Roman ruins below. *(☎ 81 22 83; www.assisimuseocattedrale.com. Open daily 7am-12:30pm and 2-6pm. Free.)*

OTHER SIGHTS. From Basilica di San Francesco, V. S. Francesco snakes between medieval buildings and their 16th-century additions towards the center of town. Not far from the Basilica di S. Francesco, the pink facade of the **Palazzo Vallemani** houses the **Pinacoteca,** a museum containing works by important Umbrian artists like Dono Doni, and a collection of Renaissance frescoes retrieved from city gates and various shrines. *(Pinacoteca ☎ 81 20 33. Open daily Mar.-May and Sept.-Oct. 10am-1pm and 2:30-6pm; July-Aug. 10am-1pm and 2:30-7pm; Nov.-Feb. 10:30am-1pm and 2-5pm. Admission to each €3.50, students €3. Cash only.)* Up the street, the one-room colorfully frescoed **Oratorio dei Pellegrini** (Pilgrim's Oratory) is worth a peek. Built in 1457, this oratory was used to care for the health of poor pilgrims who came to visit the tomb of St. Francis. At the end of the street, P. del Comune sits on the **Foro Romano.** Enter from the crypt of St. Nicholas on V. Portica, and walk among the columns and statues of the old Roman forum. The area that stretches the length of the *piazza* above was the original ground level of the town, and in Roman times, stairs led from this area to the Tempio di Minerva in P. del Comune. *(Forum ☎ 81 30 53. Open daily Mar.-May and Sept.-Oct. 10am-1pm and 2:30-6pm; July-Aug. 10am-1pm and 2:30-7pm; Nov.-Feb. 10:30am-1pm and 2-5pm. €3.50 each, students €3. Cash only.)* Above Foro Romano's ground sits the **Tempio di Minerva,** a majestic Roman temple turned Christian church. Six crumbling Roman columns frame the interior, with a gold altarpiece and a glorious painted ceiling. The temple sits snugly between the city's *campanile* and a cafe. *(Open daily 7am-7pm. Free.)*

> **▶TIP◀** **KILL THREE BIRDS WITH ONE STONE.** Invest in a **combination ticket** (€4.50, students €3.50) which grants visitors entrance to the Foro Romano, Pinacoteca, and Rocca Maggiore; purchase at any participating site.

▓ FESTIVALS

All of Assisi's religious festivals are steeped in tradition. **Holy Week** commences on Palm Sunday with elaborate services, ushering in a week's worth of prayer and piety in the town. A play reenacts the Deposition from the Cross on Holy Thursday, and traditional torch-lit processions, virtually unchanged since medieval times (except for the camera flashes), trail through town on Good Friday. Vigils are held on Holy Saturday and grand masses of celebration take place in churches throughout town on Easter Sunday. Assisi welcomes spring with the **Festa di Calendimaggio** (1st Th-Sa of May). A queen is chosen and dubbed *Primavera* (Spring), while the upper and lower quarters of the city compete in a musical tournament. Ladies and knights overtake the streets in celebration of the young St. Francis, who wandered the streets of Assisi singing serenades at night. According to legend it was on one such night that he encountered a vision of the *Madonna della Povertà* (Lady of Poverty). October 4 marks the **Festa di San Francesco,** which kicks off in Chiesa di Santa Maria degli Angeli, the site of St. Francis's death. Aside from various religious ceremonies, the highlight of this celebration is the offering of oil for the cathedral's votive lamp. Each year a different region of Italy, whose traditional dances and songs are performed during the festival, offers the oil. In addition to these festivals, classical music concerts and organ recitals occur once or twice each week from April to October in various churches.

▶ DAYTRIPS FROM ASSISI

EREMO DELLE CARCERI AND MONTE SUBASIO

From P. Matteotti, exit Assisi through Pta. Cappuccini, and walk straight on V. Eremo delle Carceri, following signs for "Campeggio Fontemaggio." Once you reach the road for the campsite, don't turn off; continue to walk uphill along V. Fontemaggio. Follow the dirt trail next to the paved road uphill. Eremo is about 4km away. Open daily in summer 6:30am-7pm; in winter 6:30am-5pm. Taxis make the climb for €8-12 from the centro.

An intense 1hr. hike up Monte Subasio reveals the serene sanctuary and forested area of Eremo delle Carceri (EH-re-mo DE-leh CAR-che-ree), where St. Francis often retired in prayer. Though cars crowd the front gates, once inside, visitors can follow quiet paths that lead through the building and among the trees. The central courtyard gives access to the Grotta di San Francesco, a series of tiny cells and chapels where St. Francis slept and prayed. Modest dress is required, so bring a scarf or other appropriate attire in addition to hiking clothes. The trails continue past the building and run through the natural beauty of St. Francis's preferred retreat, Monte Subasio (MON-tay soo-BA-zee-yo). Navigate with a Kompass map (€7.50), available from any bookshop or newsstand in Assisi.

OTHER RELIGIOUS SITES AROUND ASSISI

Several churches associated with St. Francis and St. Claire stand near Assisi. A 15min. stroll down the steep road outside Pta. Nuova leads to the **Convent of San Damiano,** where St. Francis supposedly heard his calling and later wrote the *Canticle of the Creatures.* The entrance to the convent is inside, by the church's altar. Duck inside to see the modest sanctuary and its frescoes and take a moment of reflection. (☎81 22 73. Open daily 10am-noon and 2-6pm. Free.) The train to Assisi passes **Basilica di Santa Maria degli Angeli.** From Assisi, take the frequent bus line C to the Santa Maria degli Angeli stop. St. Francis built the small stone **Cappella Porziuncola,** which stands in the middle of the giant nave of the basilica, and died in the tiny **Cappella del Transito.** According to legend, St. Francis flung himself on the thorny rosebushes in the garden outside to overcome the temptation to break his ascetic ways, permanently staining the leaves red. Through the rose garden is the **Museo di Santa Maria degli Angeli,** which houses relics from the Porziuncola chapel. (☎80 51 430. Basilica open M-Sa 6:15am-1pm and 2:30-7:30pm, Su 6:45am-1pm and 2:30-7:30pm. Museum open daily 9am-12:30pm and 3-6pm. Free.)

SPOLETO ☎0743

The magnificent gorge and medieval walls surrounding Spoleto (spo-LEH-toh; pop. 38,000) shelter a town full of Roman ruins and friendly locals. Travelers have always admired Spoleto's dramatic gorge, spanned by the 14th-century Ponte delle Torri, but it wasn't until 1958 that Spoleto's tourist industry took off. In that year, the Italian composer Giancarlo Menotti selected the city as the trial site for a summer arts festival, and his *Festival dei Due Mondi* (Festival of Two Worlds) has attracted summer visitors there ever since.

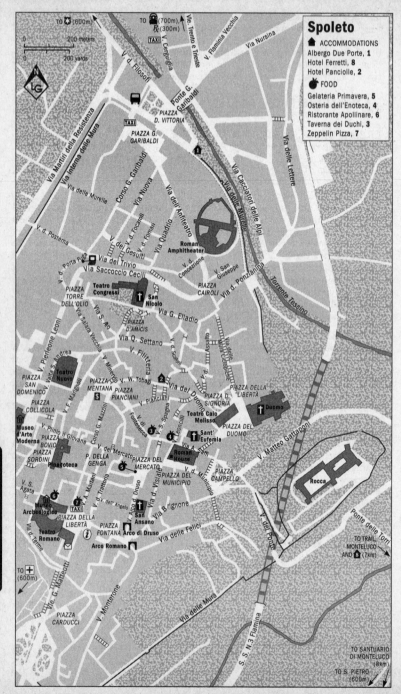

Spoleto

♠ ACCOMMODATIONS
Albergo Due Porte, **1**
Hotel Ferretti, **8**
Hotel Panciolle, **2**

🍴 FOOD
Gelateria Primavera, **5**
Osteria dell'Enoteca, **4**
Ristorante Apollinare, **6**
Taverna dei Duchi, **3**
Zeppelin Pizza, **7**

⚑ TRANSPORTATION AND PRACTICAL INFORMATION

The **train station** (☎48 516) is in P. Polvani. (Ticket window open daily 6am-8pm.) Trains run to: Ancona (2hr., 11 per day, €8.20); Assisi (40-60min., 18 per day, €2.80); Orte (1hr., 19 per day, €3); Perugia (2hr., 17 per day, €3.70); Rome (1½hr., every 1-2hr., €6-11). Trains to Assisi and Perugia sometimes run via Foligno. SSIT **buses** (☎21 22 09; www.spoletina.com) depart from P. della Vittoria for Foligno (45min., M-F 6 per day, €2.60), Monteluco (6 per day 8:45am-6:20pm mid-June to early-Sept.), and Perugia (2hr., 2 per day, €5.40). Schedule and tickets are available at Tabaccheria Scocchetti, P. della Vittoria 24. (Open daily 7:30am-2pm and 3-8:30pm.) **Taxis** are in P. della Libertà (☎44 548), in P. Garibaldi (☎49 990), and at the train station (☎22 04 89).

Piazza della Libertà is most easily accessible from the train station. Take an orange SITA bus (direct to *centro*, €0.80). Buy tickets in the station at the newsstand, marked with a yellow "Lotto" sign. From **Corso Mazzini,** turn left up Via del Mercato to **Piazza del Mercato,** a cafe-laden marketplace. Via del Municipio runs from P. del Mercato to **Piazza del Municipio** and **Piazza Campello,** and Via Saffi leads to **Piazza del Duomo.** Most of the city sights are in these *piazze*.

The **tourist office,** P. della Libertà 7, offers detailed info about tours and lodgings as well as multilingual maps of the city and nearby trails. (☎23 89 20/21; www.comune.spoleto.pg.it. Open Apr.-Oct. M-F 9am-1pm and 4-7pm, Sa-Su 10am-1pm and 4-7pm; Nov.-Mar. M-F 9am-1pm and 3:30-6:30pm, Sa 10am-1pm and 3:30-6:30pm, Su 10am-1pm; during Spoleto Festival daily 9am-1pm and 4-8pm.) The **bank, Cassa di Risparmio di Spoleto,** P. Mentana 3, just off C. Mazzini, has a 24hr. **ATM.** (Open M-F 8:20am-1:20pm and 2:50-3:50pm, Sa 8:20-11:50am.) In case of emergency, call the **police,** V. dei Filosofi 57 (☎23 22 00). **Farmacia Betti,** V. Trento e Trieste 63, is on the way to town from the train station. (☎22 31 74. Open M-F 9am-1pm and 4-8pm.) A **hospital** is on V. Madonna di Loreto, outside the southwestern walls of the *centro*. **Internet** is available at **Spider Service,** V. Porta Fuga 11, which also serves as a phone center and **Western Union** point. (☎22 51 65. €0.75 per 10min. Open daily 9am-10pm.) There is a **post office** at Vle. Giacomo Matteotti 2. (☎40 373. Open M-F 8am-6:30pm, Sa 8am-12:30pm.) **Postal Code:** 06049.

⚐ ACCOMMODATIONS

Finding accommodations is almost impossible during the summer music festival, when prices are much higher. Contact **Conspoleto,** P. della Libertà 7, next to the tourist office, for help finding a room. (☎/fax 22 07 73; www.conspoleto.com. Charges commission. Open M-Sa 9am-1pm and 3-7pm.)

Hotel Panciolle, V. del Duomo 3 (☎45 677). Central location near all major sights. 7 well-furnished rooms with phone, mini-fridge, TV, and bath. Breakfast €5. Singles €40; doubles €55-60; triples €70. Cash only. ❹

Albergo Due Porte, P. della Vittoria 5 (☎22 36 66), just outside the city walls. A convenient 10min. walk from the train station toward the *centro*. Go straight down Vle. Trento e Trieste, and bear right into P. della Vittoria. Friendly staff offers a garden and large rooms with bath, TV, A/C, and phone. Breakfast included. Wheelchair-accessible. Free parking. Singles €35-50; doubles €60-70; triples €75-85; quads €100. MC/V. ❸

Hotel Ferretti, Località Monteluco 20 (☎49 849; fax 22 23 44). A 15min. bus ride from the station or P. della Libertà. High above Spoleto in Monteluco. It's more likely to have vacancies than places downtown and has excellent proximity to hiking trails; however, its distance from Spoleto's sights can be a drawback. Friendly, family-style atmosphere accompanies rustic rooms with bath, TV, and phone. Breakfast included. Singles €42; doubles €59; triples €78; quads €85. MC/V. ❹

🔳 FOOD

Rare is the Spoleto restaurant that doesn't boast a rendition of the town's signature dish: *Strengozzi alla Spoletina,* a zesty take on homemade pasta with tomato sauce. Other specialties include the same pasta garnished with a generous portion of flavorful, shaved truffles. A large outdoor **market** runs along V. Cacciatori delle Alpi, which stretches south from Ponte G. Garibaldi (F morning).

■ **Ristorante Apollinare,** V. Sant'Agata 14 (☎22 32 56; www.ristoranteapollinare.it). Housed in a former 10th-century convent, this restaurant serves fresh local cuisine to travelers and celebrities like Sophia Loren. Its variety of multi-course *menùs* (from €25) are some of the best in Umbria. Creative a la carte menu showcases superb house specialties. To top it all off, their desserts (€5-7) are heavenly. *Primi* €7-18, *secondi* €10-24. Open daily noon-3pm and 7pm-midnight. Closed Tu in winter. AmEx/MC/V. ❸

Osteria dell'Enoteca, V. Saffi 7 (☎22 04 84). At this stylish *osteria,* torch lamps burn outside as diners enjoy traditional *Strengozzi* (€9) and truffles on wooden benches. *Primi* €6.50-12, *secondi* €6.50-14. Cover €1. Open M and W-Su 11am-3pm and 7-11pm. AmEx/MC/V. ❷

Taverna dei Duchi, V. Saffi 1 (☎44 088). All manner of Umbrian specialities, most often including truffles. Don't fill up on the focaccia before trying the *Strengozzi al rancetto* (with onion, bacon and *pecorino* cheese; €6), a tomato-less take on the local favorite. Three-course *menù* (€15) is a good deal. The restaurant is unmarked, so look for green walls with stone arches. Pizza from €5.50; dinner only. *Primi* €5-11, *secondi* from €5.50. Open July-Aug. daily noon-3pm and 7-10:30pm; Sept.-June M-Th and Sa-Su noon-3pm and 7-10:30pm, F noon-3pm. MC/V. ❷

Zeppelin Pizza, in P. della Libertà (☎47 767). For a good deal on thin-crust pizza (from €1) and *panini* (€2.50-3), locals frequent Zeppelin. Open daily 7:30am-midnight; closes in winter 9:30pm. Cash only. ❶

Gelateria Primavera, in P. Mercato (☎22 05 44). Fun flavors include chocolate-orange and white chocolate with green apple swirl. For traditionalists, the creamy hazelnut is divine. 1 scoop €1.40, 3 scoops €2. Open daily Apr.-Aug. 10am-midnight; Sept.-Oct. 10am-8pm. Cash only. ❶

🔳 SIGHTS

ROCCA ALBORNOZIANA AND PONTE DELLE TORRI. The Rocca, a **papal fortress** up V. Saffi from P. del Duomo, served as a high-security prison until 1982. During WWII, 94 Italian and Slovenian prisoners staged an escape to join the partisans in the Umbrian hills. The complex's only drama now is in the restored 15th-century frescoes of the **Camera Pinta.** (☎46 434. *Entrance only with 45min. guided tours M-F on the hr. 10am-6:45pm, Sa-Su on the half-hr. Usually one English tour at varying times; call ahead. €6.50, ages 15-25 €5, ages 7-14 and over 60 €2.50.*) On the far side of the Rocca is the massive **Ponte delle Torri,** a stunning achievement of 14th-century engineering built on an ancient Roman aqueduct. Ten 80m arches support the bridge, and the view across the Tessino Gorge is riveting. A path off V. Matteo Gattaponi offers great views of the bridge, and the trailheads of several hikes start at the end of the bridge. *(Free.)*

MONTELUCO. The 800m trail along Spoleto's steep "mountain of the sacred grove" begins across Ponte delle Torri and winds through a canopied forest, passing abandoned mountain shrines and the churches of **San Giuliano** and **San Pietro.** At the peak of Monteluco, there are hotel-restaurants, a flat grass clearing perfect for picnics, and the tiny, 13th-century **Santuario di San Francesco di Monteluco**, once the refuge of St. Francis of Assisi and St. Bernadine of Siena. (*Open 9am-noon and 3-6pm. Free.*) Rain can turn the path into a rocky stream; to avoid slippery terrain, it's best to hike there on a sunny day or take a bus. Wear proper footwear and get a trail map from the tourist office before leaving.

DUOMO. Spoleto's Romanesque cathedral was built in the 12th century and was later expanded by a 1491 portico and 17th-century interior redecoration. Inside, brilliantly colored scenes by Fra Filippo Lippi fill the domed apse, such as **The Coronation** in the half-dome of the main apse and a nativity scene on the lower right side. Check out the 15th-century **Cappella dell'Assunta** covered in eroding frescoes, as well as the more lavish 17th-century **Cappella della Santa Icone** to the right of the main apse. Lorenzo dei Medici commissioned Lippi's tomb, which was decorated by the artist's son, Filippino, and is now in the right transept. The soaring **campanile** is a mixture of styles and materials: stone blocks, fragments of inscriptions, friezes, and other remnants of the Roman era combine to form this structure. (*Down the steps from Casa Romana. Open daily 8:30am-12:30pm and 3:30-7pm. No visits during mass M-Sa 9am and 6pm; Su 8:30, 11:30am, 6pm.*)

CASA ROMANA. Duck into this small first-century Roman house, which features well-preserved mosaic floors and a few household artifacts and was used by Vespasia Polla, Emperor Vespasian's mother. (*V. di Visiale 9. Beneath city hall. From P. del Duomo, take stairs opposite duomo entrance, then take a right and follow the yellow sign. ☎ 23 42 50. Open daily Mar. 16-Oct. 14 10am-8pm; Oct. 15-Mar. 15 10:30am-7:30pm. €2.50, ages 15-25 and over 65 €2, 7-14 €1; with Museum of Modern Art and Pinacoteca €6/4/1.50.*)

CHIESA DI SANT'ANSANO AND CRIPTA DI SAN ISAACO. Built on the ruins of a Roman temple dating to the first century BC, Sant'Ansano has a Renaissance facade and interior. The stairs to the left of the main altar descend to the foundations of the 11th-century church. Haunting, well-preserved frescoes detail scenes from the life of St. Isaac, who lies in a sixth-century sarcophagus at the center of the room. (*Heading away from P. Mercato on V. dell'Arco di Druso, the Chiesa di San Ansano is at the corner on the left. ☎ 40 305. Open daily Apr.-Oct. 8:30am-noon and 3:30-6:30pm; Nov.-Mar. 8:30am-noon and 3:30-6pm.*)

THE MUSEUM OF MODERN ART. A refreshing alternative to ancient ruins and holy frescoes, this permanent art collection includes early works by Moore, Consagra, Pomodoro, and Leoncillo. The museum's first room is dedicated to American artist Alexander Calder, whose sculpture *Teodelapio* now stands in Spoleto's P. della Stazione. (*Follow V. Mercato as it turns into V. Giovane, and go down stairs; the museum lies straight ahead. ☎ 46 434. Open daily Mar. 16-Oct. 14 10:30am-1pm and 3:30-7pm; Oct. 15-Mar. 15 M and W-Su 10:30am-1pm and 3-5:30pm. €4, ages 15-25 and over 65 €3, ages 7-14 €1.50; with admission to Pinacoteca and Casa Romana €6/4/1.50.*)

OTHER ROMAN RUINS. Spoleto's ruins, a testament to the city's prominence in Roman times, are found mainly near P. della Libertà. Take V. S. Agata from the *piazza* to reach the entrance of the **Museo Archeologico Statale,** which houses a small collection of Roman artifacts found in the area. Admission includes the opportunity to explore the **Roman Theater,** which hosts concerts and plays during the summer festival. (*☎ 22 32 77. Open daily 8:30am-7:30pm. €4, EU citizens ages 18-25 €2, EU citizens under 18 or over 65 free.*) The **Arco Romano,** at the top of V. Monterone, once marked the town's entrance. Off P. Fontana, the **Arco di Druso** commemorates Emperor Druscu's military triumphs. Though closed to the public, the **amphitheater** stands just beyond the Roman walls.

UMBRIA

🎵 🌺 ENTERTAINMENT AND FESTIVALS

The 🎭**Spoleto Festival** (known as the **Festival dei Due Mondi**) has become one of the world's most prestigious international arts events. For about two weeks in late June and early July, Spoleto comes alive with concerts, operas, ballets, films, modern art shows, and craft fairs. Purchase tickets beginning in late April either online or from the ticket office at P. della Libertà 12 (open daily from April until festival's end 9am-1pm and 3-7pm). During the festival, additional box offices at **Piazza del Duomo, Teatro Nuovo,** and **Rocca Albornoziana** open 1hr. before the start of most performances in addition to regular hours. (☎ 800 56 56 00; www.spoletofestival.it. Additional box offices open Tu-Su 10:30am-1pm and 4-7pm. 15% discount if you buy tickets to more than 3 events on the same day. Book ahead. For more details write to Associazione Festival dei Due Mondi, Biglietteria Festival dei Due Mondi, 06049 Spoleto, Italia.) When the Spoleto Festival ends, **Spoleto Estate** picks up with cultural events throughout August and September; pick up a schedule at the tourist office. The renowned **Stagione del Teatro Lirico Sperimentale A. Belli di Spoleto,** an experimental opera season, runs from late August to September. The Istituzione Teatro Lirico Sperimentale di Spoleto, P. Bovio 1 (☎ 22 16 45), provides info. During the 1st weekend of June, revel in the annual **Vini nel Mondo,** a festival that includes citywide wine tastings and musical and theatrical performance.

🗺 DAYTRIP FROM SPOLETO: TREVI.
Removed and unhurried in comparison to other more trafficked Umbrian towns, Trevi (TREH-vee; pop. 7800) sits dramatically atop a hill among sloping olive groves and green and yellow hills. Most sights are easily reached from P. Mazzini, the town center. The **Pinacoteca Raccolta d'Arte di San Francesco** houses a collection of religious Renaissance art, including some dramatic, large-scale works. The unique **Museo della Civiltà Dell'Ulivo** offers a history of the city's staple industry as well as free olive oil samples and Italian recipes. Follow V. San Francesco from P. Mazzini to reach the museums, housed together in the same building on Lungo Don Bosco 5. (☎ 0742 38 16 28; www.sistemamuseo.it. Open June-July Tu-Su 10:30am-1pm and 3:30-7pm; Aug. daily 10:30am-1pm and 3-7:30pm; Sept. and Apr.-May Tu-Su 10:30am-1pm and 2:30-6pm; Oct.-Mar. F-Su 10:30am-1pm and 2:30-5pm. €4, students €2.50.) The **Flash Art Museum,** V. Placido Riccardi 4, showcases avant-garde art in a 15th-century *palazzo*. The small museum is associated with the trendy contemporary Italian art magazine, *Flash*, and hosts rotating exhibits of modern art. (☎ 0742 38 10 21; www.treviflashartmuseum.org. Open Tu-Su 4-7pm.) The **Illumination Procession,** one of Umbria's oldest religious festivals, takes place January 28. **Ristorante Maggiolini ❷**, V. San Francesco 20, near the museums off P. Mazzini, has an intimate interior and a bar for sampling Trevi's olive oil. (☎ 0742 38 15 34. *Primi* €5.46-8.26, *secondi* €6-11.65. Open M and W-Su 12:30-3pm and 7-10:30pm. MC/V.) The **Pro Loco tourist office,** P. Mazzini 5, offers great free maps and assistance in renting one of the abundant *affitacamere*, a better deal than one of Trevi's expensive hotels. (☎ 0742 78 11 50; www.protrevi.it. Open daily 9am-1pm and 4-8pm.) To reach the office from P. Garibaldi, take V. Roma to P. Mazzini. *(From Spoleto, take a train to Trevi. Dir: Perugia or Ancona, 10min., 16 per day 12:05am-9:52pm, €1.40. From there, take an orange municipal bus to town. Buses run from the station to P. Mazzini, the main piazza at the top of the hill. M-Sa 6 per day 7:30am-6:15pm, return buses M-Sa 5 per day 6:55am-5:40pm; €0.70.)*

ORVIETO   ☎ 0763

A city upon a city, Orvieto (or-vee-YEH-toh; pop. 20,000) was built in layers: medieval structures rest on ancient subterranean remains. In the 7th century BC, Etrus-

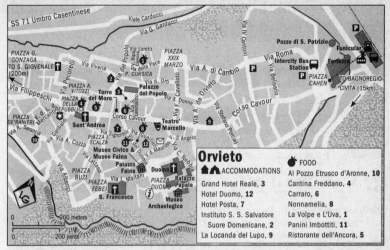

Orvieto

🏠🏔 ACCOMMODATIONS

Grand Hotel Reale, 3
Hotel Duomo, 12
Hotel Posta, 7
Instituto S. S. Salvatore
 Suore Domenicane, 2
La Locanda del Lupo, 9

🍎 FOOD

Al Pozzo Etrusco d'Aronne, 10
Cantina Freddano, 4
Carraro, 6
Nonnamelia, 8
La Volpe e L'Uva, 1
Panini Imbottiti, 11
Ristorante dell'Ancora, 5

cans burrowed for tufa (a volcanic stone out of which most of the medieval quarter is built), creating a companion city beneath Orvieto's ground surface which archeologists and tourists alike explore to learn about the area's Etruscan heritage. Five centuries later, Romans sacked and reoccupied the plateau, calling their "new" city, strangely enough, *urbus ventus* (old city), from which the name Orvieto is derived. Today, the town is a tourist destination made popular by its spectacular, mystical underground chambers, and refreshing *Orvieto Classico* wine. To escape the crowds, skip the cliché ceramic shops on C. Cavour and head to the side streets, which are full of local artisans' shops.

TRANSPORTATION

Orvieto is between Rome and Florence. **Trains** run to Arezzo (1hr., hourly 7:30am-11:22pm, €6.10), Florence (2½hr., hourly 7:30am-8:33pm, €10.40) via Cortona (45min.), and Rome (1½hr., hourly 4:29am-11:26pm, €7.10). **Buses** leave from P. Cahen and the train station. **COTRAL** (☎ 73 48 14) runs buses to Viterbo (8 per day 6:20am-5:45pm, €2.80). Purchase tickets at *tabaccherie*. **ATC** buses (☎30 12 24) stop in P. Cahen and go to Perugia (1½hr., 5:55am, €6.40) and Via Todi (1hr., 1:45pm, €5.60). Purchase tickets at the funicular ticket office, at *tabaccherie* on C. Cavour, or on the bus with a surcharge. The ✉**funicular** ascends Orvieto's hill, connecting the train station with the city's historical center at P. Cahen (every 10min.; €0.90, with shuttle to P. del Duomo €1). The tickets for the funicular are valid for 1hr., which allows for multiple journeys between the hilltop and the *centro storico*. For a **taxi**, call ☎30 19 03.

ORIENTATION AND PRACTICAL INFORMATION

Across from the **train station,** the funicular travels up the hill to **Piazza Cahen.** There, **Corso Cavour** begins running slightly uphill from P. Cahen to **Piazza della Repubblica.** About 10min. from P. Cahen, C. Cavour crosses **Via del Duomo.** At this intersection, turn left down V. del Duomo to reach the *duomo*. If you instead continue two blocks down C. Cavour, a right turn on **Via della Piazza del Popolo** will bring you to **Piazza del Popolo.** Most of the city's restaurants, hotels, and shops are found between V. Duomo and the P. della Repubblica along C. Cavour. The **tourist office,** P. del Duomo 24, supplies great free maps and info on hotels, restaurants, and sights. The office also offers deals on underground tours of Orvieto and sells the **Orvieto Unica card** (€18, students €15), which includes an underground tour, round-trip ticket for funicular-minibus or 5hr. of parking, and entrance to Museo Faina, the Torre del Moro, the Cappella della Madonna di San Brizio, the Museo Archeologico Nazionale, and the Museo dell'Opera del Duomo, as well as discounts at participating businesses. (☎34 17 72; fax 34 44 33. Open M-F 8:15am-1:50pm and 4-7pm, Sa-Su and holidays 10am-1pm and 3-6pm.) **Luggage storage** is available at the train station. In an **emergency,** call the **police** (☎34 00 88), in P. della Repubblica. The **hospital** (☎30 71) is across the tracks from the train station in Località Ciconia. A **post office** (☎39 83 49) is on V. Ravelli, off C. Cavour. (Open M-Sa 8:10am-4:45pm; last day of the month 8:10am-noon.) **Postal Code:** 05018.

ACCOMMODATIONS

■ **Grand Hotel Reale,** P. del Popolo 25 (☎34 12 47; hotelreale@orvietohotels.it). An unparalleled deal in an opulent 13th-century *palazzo* that once housed King Umberto. Fine artwork and stunning views of the Palazzo del Popolo show off the hotel's class. Rooms have TV and phone; more expensive rooms are decorated with magnificent frescoes and luxurious Murano glass light fixtures. Breakfast €8. Singles €35, with bath €66; doubles €55/88; triples €72/114; quads €88/140. V. ❸

La Locanda del Lupo, C. Cavour 231 (☎34 13 88 or 34 41 03; www.lalocandadellupo.it), halfway between the intersection of P. Cahen and V. del Duomo. Welcoming hotel above a traditional restaurant. Singles €35-50; doubles €60-80; triples €90-100; quads €120. Ask for student discount. AmEx/MC/V. ❸

Hotel Posta, V. Luca Signorelli 18 (☎34 19 09; www.orvietohotels.it). Quirky and clean hotel is undergoing renovations yet still maintains its quaint appeal. Outdoor patio. Breakfast €6. Reservations recommended. Singles €31, with bath €37; doubles €43/56; triples €60/75. Cash only. ❸

Instituto S. S. Salvatore Suore Domenicane, V. del Popolo 1 (☎34 29 10). Nun-run hotel is packed with religious icons. Simple and ultra-clean rooms. Curfew 10:30pm. Reservations recommended. Closed July. Singles €35; doubles €55. Cash only. ❹

Hotel Duomo, Vco. Maurizio 7 (☎34 18 87; www.orvietohotelduomo.com), facing the *duomo.* Rooms are named after the *duomo*'s architects and painters and are decorated with artwork from the Orvietan artist Valentini. Lovely outdoor garden. A/C, satellite TV, and minibar. Breakfast included. Internet access €2 per 15min. Parking €10. Singles €70-85; doubles €90-120; triples €120-150; quad €130-160. AmEx/MC/V. ❺

FOOD

Orvieto was once known as *Oinarea,* or the "city where wine flows." The stream is still rocking steady. Pair a light bottle of *Classico* with local treats like baked *lumachelle* (snail-shaped buns with ham and cheese), *tortucce* (fried bread dough), or *mazzafegate* (sweet or salty sausages). Also prevalent are *tartufi* (truffles) served frequently and cheaply in many dishes—sometimes even grated at your table. The sociable **Panini Imbottiti,** V. del Duomo 36, sells bottles of *Classico* from €3.50. (Open daily 8:30am-9pm. Cash only.) To sample before investing in a whole bottle, stop by **Cantina Freddano,** C. Cavour

5, which offers free winetasting. Bottles start at €3.50. (☎30 82 48. Open M-F 9:30am-1pm and 3-8pm, Sa-Su 10am-8pm. Cash only.)

▨ **Carraro,** C. Cavour 101 (☎34 28 70; carraro@orvieto.tin.it), before the intersection with V. del Duomo, as you walk toward Torre del Moro. Stop in to see Angelo, the *"paganini del prosciutto"* (violinist of prosciutto) whose masterful meat-carving technique is a thing of beauty. This shop sells homemade truffle spread (small jar €5) as well as a variety of fresh cured meats, cheeses, and baked goods. Indulge in wild boar and truffle sausage (€24 per kg) and award-winning *cenerino* cheese (€22 per kg). Picnic lunch for under €5. Open M-Tu and Th-Su 7:15am-1:30pm and 4:30-8:30pm. MC/V. ❶

Nonnamelia, V. del Duomo 25 (☎34 24 02). Take V. del Duomo towards C. Cavour, on the right. Creative recipes and intricate wooden decorations that never fail to please. Try the *maialino da latte agliaromi* (suckling pig and herbs). Pizza €3.50-9. *Primi* €5.50-10, *secondi* €7.50-13. Open daily noon-3pm and 7-10:30pm. AmEx/MC/V. ❷

Al Pozzo Etrusco d'Aronne, P. dei Ranieri 1/A (☎34 44 56). Basic hearty food beloved by locals served in an intimate dining space, complete with an actual Etruscan well and outdoor *piazza* seating. Menu changes daily; try the house specialties *nidi di rondine pecorino e miele caldo* (€7.50) or *tartufo fresco* (€8.50). *Primi* €5.50-8.50, *secondi* €7-12. Free Wi-Fi. Open M and W-Su noon-3pm and 7:15-10:15pm. AmEx/D/MC/V. ❸

Ristorante dell'Ancora, V. della P. del Popolo 7/11 (☎34 27 66; www.argoweb.it/ristorante_ancora). Somewhat upscale restaurant serves up traditional spaghetti dishes in a quiet oasis. *Primi* €7-11, *secondi* €8-14. Cover €3. Open daily 12:30pm-3:30pm and 7-11pm; closed Th during winter. Students ½-price. AmEx/MC/V. ❸

◔ SIGHTS

▨ **DUOMO.** Orvieto's architectural claim to fame, the striped *duomo* is nothing short of dazzling. Designed in the late 13th century by Sienese architect Lorenzo Maitani, the facade of Orvieto's pride and joy is an example of the transitional Romanesque-Gothic style. Its carved, marble pillars, spires, sculptures, and mosaics miraculously avoided bombings during the World Wars and today continue to awe admirers with elaborate details and brilliant colors. The bottom level features carved bas-reliefs of the Genesis and Old Testament prophecies as well as the final panel of Maitani's *Last Judgment.* Surrounding the rose window by Andrea Orcagna (1325-1364), bronze and marble sculptures illustrate the Christian canon. Thirty-three architects, 90 mosaic artisans, 152 sculptors, and 68 painters worked for over 600 years to improve the *duomo,* and the work continues—the bronze doors were installed in 1970. *(☎34 11 67. Duomo open in summer M-Sa 7:30am-12:45pm and 2:30-7:15pm, Su and holidays 2:30-6:45pm; closes in winter 1-2hr. earlier. Crypt open M-F 10am-noon. Modest dress required. Free.)* The **Cappella della Madonna di San Brizio,** also called the *Cappella Nuova,* off the right transept, includes Luca Signorelli's floor-to-ceiling frescoes of the Apocalypse. His vigorous craftsmanship, mastery of human anatomy, and dramatic compositions inspired Michelangelo in his work on the Sistine Chapel. Also note da Fabriano's *Madonna and Child* and the marble *Pietà* by di Scalza. Opposite the San Brizio chapel is the **Cappella Corporale,** which features stunning frescoes by Ugolino di Prete Ilario and holds the gold-encrusted *Reliquario del Corporale* (chalice-cloth), said to have been soaked with the blood of Christ, from the miracle of Bolsena in 1263. *(€5, under 18 and over 65 €4, under 10 free. The ticket gains you admittance to the Museo Archeologico Nazionale and the Museo dell'Opera del Duomo. Audio tour €1.)*

PALAZZO PAPALE. From this austere, 13th-century "Palace of the Popes," Pope Clement VII rejected King Henry VIII's petition to annul his marriage with Catherine of Aragon. Set back in the *palazzo* is the **Museo Archeologico Nazionale,** where visitors can examine Etruscan art from the area and walk into a restored tomb decorated with faded AD 4th-century frescoes. *(To the right facing the duomo. www.archeopg.arti.beniculturali.it. Open daily 8:30am-7:30pm. €3, with entrance to Etruscan Necropolis €5; students 18-25 €1.50; EU citizens under 18 or over 65 free.)* Above the archaeological museum is the **Museo dell'Opera del Duomo,** which displays art and cultural artifacts from the 13th to 17th centuries. Featured pieces include Simone Martini's *Politico di San Domenico,* Andrea Pisano's *Madonna and Child,* and Francesco Mochi's marble *Annunciation.* *(☎34 35 92; www.opsm.it. Open Apr.-Sept daily 9:30am-7pm; Nov.-Feb. M and W-Su 9:30am-1pm and 3-5pm; Mar. and Oct. M and W-Su 9:30am-1pm and 3pm-6pm. €5; €4 reduced.)*

UNDERGROUND CITY. The ancient Etruscan town Velzna occupied the soft *tufa* of the cliff below modern Orvieto. Although Velzna was sacked by the Romans, its cisterns, mills, pottery workshops, quarries, pigeon coops, wine cellars, and burial sites lie preserved beneath the earth. **Underground City Excursions** runs the most complete and accessible tours of the city's dark, twisted bowels. *(☎34 48 91; www.orvietounderground.it. 1hr. tours leave from the tourist office daily 11am, 12:15, 4, and 5:15pm. English guided tours 11:15am and 4:15pm. €5.50, students €3.50, under 5 free.)*

CHIESA DI SAN GIOVENALE. Built in AD 1000, the city's oldest church was dedicated to its first bishop, who is represented in a fresco near the entry. Directly next to the doors on the left is a 14th-century "Tree of Life"—a family tree of the church's founders. The courtyard outside the church offers spectacular ■**views** of the countryside below. Graves of victims of the Black Death of 1348 fill the slope below P. San Giovanni. *(From P. della Repubblica, walk downhill along V. Filippeschi, which turns into V. Malabranca. The church is at the end of the street on the right.)*

MUSEO CIVICO AND MUSEO FAINA. Directly opposite the *duomo,* these museums hold an extensive collection of Etruscan artifacts. Exhibits include collections of over 3000 coins, bronze urns, Roman ornaments, and figure vases attributed to Athenian artists from the 6th century BC. *(P. del Duomo 29. ☎34 15 11 www.museofaina.it. Open Apr.-Sept. daily 9:30am-6pm; Oct.-Mar. Tu-Su 10am-5pm. €4.50; students and over 65, families of 4, or groups of at least 15 €3.)*

❋ FESTIVALS

Though nightclubs are virtually nonexistent in Orvieto, the city has no shortage of festivals. No matter when you come, locals are always celebrating; look for craft fairs, food and wine tasting events, antique car shows, and theater and music festivals. Spring brings the **Palio dell'Oca,** which has tested equestrian skills since medieval times. On Pentecost, 50 days after Easter, Orvieto celebrates the **Festa della Palombella.** At noon, Campo della Fiera lights up with fireworks when a white dove descends across a wire to ignite the explosives. The dove, symbolizing the Holy Spirit, is entrusted to the last woman married in the church. First Communions and confirmations, sacraments in the Catholic Church, are also celebrated on this day. In June the **Procession of Corpus Domini** celebrates the Miracle of Bolsena when a communion wafer was transformed into flesh and blood. A week of medieval banquets and dancing precedes the 700-year-old procession. From December 28 to January 1, **Umbria Jazz Winter** swings in theaters, churches, and palaces, with the grand finale in the *duomo.* For details and pamphlets concerning festivals, contact **Servizio Turistico Territoriale IAT dell'Orvietano,** P. Duomo 24 (☎34 19 11 or 34 36 58), or **Informazioni Turistiche** (☎34 17 72; fax 34 44 33), at the same address.

LE MARCHE

Green foothills separate the umbrella-laden beaches along the Adriatic Sea from the inland craggy Apennines in Le Marche (LAY MARkay), one of Italy's most under appreciated regions. In its rural towns, remains of the Gauls, Picenes and Romans hint at a fascinating local history, but the present is alive and well in the friendly locals and the picturesque side streets. The legacy of Raphael and Donato Bramante in Urbino, the palm-lined boardwalk of San Benedetto del Tronto, the windy streets of Ascoli Piceno, and the hidden beauty of Ancona are all highlights of this geographically and historically diverse region.

HIGHLIGHTS OF LE MARCHE

BAKE on the untouristed **beaches** of the sleepy town of Fano (p. 530).

CLIMB up to the grand hilltop **Palazzo Ducale** in Urbino (p. 533).

STROLL along Pesaro's promenade for some of Italy's best **Adriatic views** (p. 527).

PESARO ☎0721

Pesaro (PEZ-ah-ro; pop. 92,000) strikes a balance between its neighbors—hip Rimini and laid-back Fano—offering a blend of culture, couture, and seaside serenity. While the perfectly blue Adriatic delights beachgoers, the *centro* charms visitors with its street concerts and back-alley shops.

◪ **TRANSPORTATION.** The **train station** sits at the end of V. Risorgimento and Vle. della Liberazione. (Ticket counter open daily 6:10am-8:30pm. AmEx/MC/V.) **Trains** depart to: Ancona (1hr., 38 per day 1am-11:05pm, €3.25); Bologna (2hr., 32 per day 5am-9:26pm, €7.70); Fano (10min., 32 per day 5am-11:05pm, €1.35); Rimini (30min., 46 per day 4:48am-11:19pm, €2.60). The **bus depot** (☎32 401; cash only) is 50 ft. to the right of the train station when facing the town. Buses #10, 11, 14, 20, 30, 40, 50, 60, 70, 130, and C/S stop at Ple. Giacomo Matteotti and run to Fano (15min., every 30min.

6:30am-9pm, €0.80) and Gradara (50min., hourly 6am-7pm, €1.25). SOGET (☎54 96 20) runs buses to Urbino from the train station (55min.; M-Sa 20 per day 6:15am-8:15pm, Su 9 per day 8:15am-8:15pm; €2.75). Bucci runs a bus to Rome's Tiburtina station from Ple. G. Matteotti (4½hr., 6am and 2pm, €22). Buy tickets on the bus. **Taxis** are available 24hr. at the train station (☎31 111 or 45 44 25), P. del Popolo (☎31 430), and Ple. G. Matteotti (☎34 053). **Rent bikes** in Ple. d'Annunzio, at the intersection of Vle. Trieste and V. Verdi. (☎347 75 29 634. €3 per hr., €9 per day. Open May to Sept. 8:30am-midnight. Cash only.)

LE MARCHE

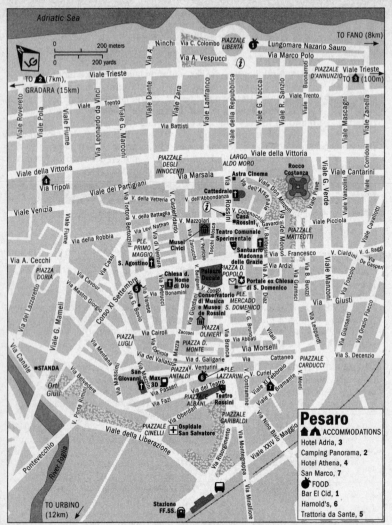

Pesaro

♦ ACCOMMODATIONS
Hotel Adria, **3**
Camping Panorama, **2**
Hotel Athena, **4**
San Marco, **7**
● FOOD
Bar El Cid, **1**
Harnold's, **6**
Trattoria da Sante, **5**

ORIENTATION AND PRACTICAL INFORMATION. From the **train station,** take **Via Risorgimento** and walk straight through P. Garibaldi and up V. Branca to reach **Piazza del Popolo,** the old *centro.* **Corso XI Settembre** runs west toward Chiesa di Sant'Agostino, while **Via San Francesco** runs east to **Piazzale Giacomo Matteotti** and the bus station. **Via Rossini** runs straight toward **Largo Aldo Moro,** which leads to **Viale Repubblica, Piazzale della Libertà,** and the sea. **Viale Trieste** runs along the beach. The **IAT tourist office,** in P. della Libertà, to the right of the bronze globe, provides maps and brochures and organizes guided tours of town sights. (☎69 341; iat.pesaro@regione.marche.it. Open in summer M-Sa 8:30am-1pm and 3-7pm, Su 9am-1pm; in winter M-Sa 9am-1pm and 3-6pm.) The **Provincial tourist office,** V.

Rossini 41, off Largo Aldo Moro, has info on tours and regional sights. (☎800 56 38 00 or 35 95 01; www.comune.pesaro.it. Open M-Sa 9am-12:30pm and 4-7pm, Su 4-7pm.) **Luggage storage** is near the "Taxis" sign outside the train station. (1st 12hr. €3, each additional 12hr. €2. Open daily 6am-11pm. Cash only.) In case of **emergency,** call the **police** (☎42 551). The **Ospedale San Salvatore** (☎36 11), is located at Ple. Cinelli 4. Speedy **Internet** is available at **Max3D,** V. Passeri 54/56. (☎35 122. €3 per hr. Open M 3:30-9pm, Tu-F 9:30am-1:30pm and 3:30-9pm, Sa 9:30am-1:30pm and 3:30-8pm. Cash only.) The **post office** is at P. del Popolo 28. (☎43 22 85. Open M-F 8am-6:30pm, Sa 8am-12:30pm.) **Postal Code:** 61100.

⌂⌂ ACCOMMODATIONS AND FOOD. Though the availability of reasonably priced lodgings makes Pesaro a real low-season deal, bargains are harder to find in the summer. To get to **San Marco ❹,** Vle. XI Febbraio 32, follow V. Risorgimento from the train station, and bear right into Ple. Garibaldi; then, turn right on the busy Vle. XI Febbraio. A friendly staff runs 40 spacious rooms with bath, phone, and TV in a busy neighborhood near the train station and the *centro.* (☎31 396; www.hotelsan-marcopu.it. Breakfast included. Wheelchair-accessible. Reception 24hr. Singles €42; doubles €68-76; triples €84-92. AmEx/MC/V.) **Hotel Athena ❸,** Vle. Pola 18, is a 20min. walk from the train station. Follow Vle. della Liberazione to Vle. Mameli, then turn right; after the street changes to V. Fiume, turn left on V. Tripoli, and walk one block. A 5min. walk from the beach, the hotel has a sunny lobby and gracious staff. The rooms are simple with bath, phone, TV, and balcony. (☎30 114; fax 33 878. Free beach umbrella. Breakfast included. 3-night min. stay. Singles €40; doubles €60. AmEx/MC/V.) Guests at **Hotel Adria ❸,** Vle. Trieste 15, benefit from beach access, free bikes, and well-kept rooms with bath, phone and satellite TV. From Ple. della Libertà, take Vle. Trieste through P.le D'Annuzio; the hotel is on the right. (☎37 21 43; www.adriahotelpesaro.it. Breakfast included; full and half pension options available. Singles €35-75; doubles €45-85; triples €60-100. Prices vary seasonally. AmEx/MC/V.) **Camping Panorama ❶** is only steps from a national park and a secluded beach, 7km north of Pesaro on Strada Panoramica toward Gabicce Mare. Take bus #14 (M-Sa 5 per day, Su 2 per day) from the train station or Ple. Matteotti and ask for Camping Panorama. (☎20 81 45; www.panoramavillage.it. Open May-Sept. €6-9 per person, €7-10.50 per tent. Electricity €2.50. Hot showers free. AmEx/MC/V.)

Celebrate the fruits of the Adriatic at **Trattoria da Sante ❸,** V. Bovio 27, with heaping portions of delicious seafood pasta. Follow C. XI Settembre north from P. del Popolo, and turn left on V. Bovio. (☎33 676. *Primi* €6-8, *secondi* €8-10. Cover €1. Open Tu-Su noon-2:30pm and 6:30-10:30pm. Reservations recommended Sa-Su. Cash only.) The perfect spot for a light lunch during a day of beaching, **Bar El Cid ❶,** Ple. della Libertà, offers a great summer salad buffet and breezy beachside outdoor seating. (☎31 891. Salad buffet and bread €5. Open Apr.-Oct. daily 7am-2am. Cash only.) Three doors down from Teatro Rossini, **Harnold's ❶,** Ple. Lazzarini 34, offers affordable fare ranging from fresh *panini* and salads to the "Big Ben," a double-decker cheeseburger (€4.80). You may have to wait for service at the busy outdoor tables on summer nights, but the food, prices, and feel-good atmosphere are worth it. From P. del Popolo, follow V. Branca away from the sea. (☎65 155. *Panini* €2-4.80. Open daily 8am-2am. Closed Su Oct.-Mar. AmEx/MC/V.) For essentials, visit the **Standa** supermarket, V. Canale 41. (Open M-Sa 7:30am-8:30pm, Su 8am-1pm and 4-8pm. AmEx/MC/V.)

◉ SIGHTS. Pesaro's main square, **Piazza del Popolo,** holds the massive **Palazzo Ducale,** commissioned in the 15th century by Alessandro Sforza. (Open to visitors during exhibitions only. Ask the tourist office about scheduled events.) Rich clay deposits from the nearby Folgia River have made the crafting of ceramics a long-standing tradition in Pesaro. One half of the Musei Civici, the **Museo delle Ceramiche,** showcases several centuries worth of local ceramics, ranging from prehistoric artifacts to colorful contemporary works. In the same building, Pesaro's **Pinacoteca** holds the fiery *Fall of the Giants* by Guido Reni and four still-life paintings by Benedetto Sartori. Don't miss Bellini's remarkable *Incoronazione della Vergine,* an image surrounded by 15 panels depicting scenes ranging from Christ's Nativity to St. George somewhat unimpressively slaying an iguana-sized ▲**dragon.** (V. Toschi Mosca 29. From P. del Popolo, head down C. XI Settembre, and turn right on V. Toschi Mosca. ☎ 38 75 41; www.museicivicipesaro.it. Open July-Aug. Tu and Th 9:30am-12:30pm and 4-10:30pm, W and F-Su 9:30am-12:30pm and 4-7pm; Sept.-June Tu-W 9:30am-12:30pm, Th-Su 9:30am-12:30pm and 4-7pm. €4, ages 15-26 and over 65 €2, under 15 free. Combined ticket with Casa Rossini €7/€4. Cash only.) Opera enthusiasts can spend hours in the **Casa Rossini,** V. Rossini 34, where composer Gioachino Rossini was born in 1792. It now houses a museum displaying photographs, theatrical memorabilia, signed opera scores, opera screenings, and even Rossini's piano. (☎ 38 73 57. Open July-Aug. Tu and Th 9:30am-12:30pm and 4-10:30pm, W and F-Su 9:30am-12:30pm and 4-7pm; Sept.-June Tu-W 9:30am-12:30pm, Th-Su 9:30am-12:30pm and 4-7pm. €4, under 26 or over 65 €2, under 15 free. Cash only.)

⚏ ▦ ENTERTAINMENT AND FESTIVALS. Pesaro hosts the **Mostra Internazionale del Nuovo Cinema** (The International Festival of New Films) from June to July (☎ 38 75 110). Live theater and movie screenings are held in buildings along V. Rossini and at the **Teatro Comunale Sperimentale** (☎ 38 75 48), an experimental theater on V. Rossini. Native composer Rossini founded the **Conservatorio di Musica G. Rossini,** P. Olivieri 5, which sponsors artistic events year-round. Contact **Teatro Rossini,** Ple. Lazzarini 29 (☎ 38 76 20), off V. Branca, for show times and prices. The annual **Rossini Opera Festival** runs from early August through September. Reserve tickets at Teatro Rossini's box office starting April 18. (☎ 38 001; www.rossiniopera-festival.it. Info line open M-F 10am-1pm and 3-6pm. Box office open Aug. daily 10am-noon and 4-6:30pm and 1hr. before performances.)

▧ DAYTRIPS FROM PESARO

FANO

Fano is accessible from Pesaro by train (10min., 33 per day 5am-11:02pm, €1.30) and by bus (every hour, €2). To go to the beach, exit the train station right on V. Cavallotti and turn right on V. Cesare Battisti. To reach P. XX Settembre, the centro, turn left on V. Garibaldi from V. Cavallotti and then right on C. Giacomo Matteotti.

Fano (FA-no; pop. 62,000) is a sleepy town stretching 20km along the coast from Pesaro to some of Italy's quietest seaside retreats. Even in summer, vacationers are scarce on the beaches to the north; farther inland, a quiet *centro* offers relatively untouristed churches and many restaurants serving regional seafood specialties. Marking the western entrance to these quiet streets is the **Arco d'Augusto,** named for the city's founder, Augustus. Nearby stands a larger-than-life bronze statue of the man himself and the crumbling brick walls he built to protect his small city. Hotels reserve most of the private shoreline for their guests, but there is a rocky public **beach;** the first entrance sits across from Vle. Adriatico 150. Though this beach is convenient, you'll need some padding in order to sunbathe comfortably. (Open daily 5am-11pm. Free.) If you schedule your trip correctly, you might just find yourself amid the July **Jazz by the Sea,** which has featured artists like Wynton Marsalis in the past. At **Al Pesce Azzuro ❷,** Vle. Adriatico 48, a brightly painted ship's hull welcomes visitors—who sometimes create lines out the door—to this funky, self-service restaurant on the beach's northern end. (☎80 31 65. *Menù* €10. Open Apr.-Oct. Tu-Su noon-2pm and 7:30-10pm.) Inland, **La Vecchia Fano ❸**, V. Vecchia 8, serves authentic *fanese* plates like *tagliolini al farro* (€6.50). From V. Garibaldi, turn left through P. Costanzi on V. Cavour, then turn right on V. Vecchia. (☎/fax 80 34 93. *Primi* €6-11, *secondi* €6.50-20. Cover €2. Open Tu-Su noon-2:30pm and 7:30-10:30pm. AmEx/MC/V.) A **PuntoSMA** supermarket is at V. Garibaldi 53. (Open M-Sa 8am-8pm. MC/V.) The **tourist office,** Vle. Battisti 10, provides a map and a list of local events. (☎80 35 34; www.turismofano.com. Open M, W, F-Sa 9am-1pm, Tu and Th 3-6pm.)

GRADARA

Gradara is accessible from Pesaro by bus (50min., hourly 6:08am-7:08pm, €1.25). To reach the walled city, walk uphill from the bus stop on V. Mancini. At the city gates, the main road becomes V. Umberto Primo and reaches P. V Novembre. For a complete investigation of the city walls, follow V. Circonvallazione around the castello.

The picturesque walled city of Gradara (gra-DA-ra; pop. 3400), 13km inland from Pesaro, sits atop a hill that surveys the surrounding landscape for miles—a beautiful patchwork of olive trees, vineyards, and millions of sunflowers. Gradara's history is less sunny—instead, it is rich with stories of war and conquest. The impeccably restored **castello** at the heart of the city was built by Pietro and Ridolfo de Grido in the beginning of the 12th century, but construction was finished by the Malatestas after their conquest of the city in the first half of the 13th century. In 1289 lovers Paolo and Francesca were murdered here; their tragic story was famously immortalized in the fifth canto of Dante's *Inferno* and less famously in the name of a restaurant on the way to the castle. In 1494, Lucrezia Borgia came to Gradara to marry Giovanni Sforza, the Sforzas having conquered Gradara in the 16th century. In 1920, the castle was restored to appear as it had under the Sforza domination 400 years ago, complete with dark-wood furniture and heavy drapes around four-post beds. At night, the ◙**views** from the castle are spectacular. One can see the entire seaside, ranging from the crystal coastline of Rimini to the sparkling lights of San Marino. In summer, these vistas are often paired with music and dance performances in the *castello*'s courtyard, next to the moat and drawbridge. (☎0541 96 41 15. Open M 8:30am-2pm, Tu-Su 8:30am-7:15pm; ticket office closes 45min. before *castello*. Night visits by guided tour only July-Aug. W-Sa 9-11:30pm. *Castello* tickets €4, EU citizens 18-25 €2, night visits €8/5.) For in-depth tours or info on upcoming performances, visit the tourist office, **Pro Loco Gradara,** in P. V Novembre. (☎0541 96 41 15; www.gradara.org. Open M-Sa 9am-1pm.) Next to the tourist office, the **Museo Storico** displays a decent collection of medieval arms and an exhibit about the daily life of a farmer in the Middle Ages. (☎0541 96 41 54. Open daily 9:30am-12:30pm, 2-7pm, and 8:30-11:30pm. €2.) **Osteria della Luna ❸**, V. Umberto Primo 6, on the way up to the castle, offers traditional dishes like *crostini al tartufo e porcini* and meat specialties for serious carnivores. Be sure to sample some of the famous regional *San Giovese* wines. (☎0541 96 98 38. *Primi* €6-9, *secondi* €12-17. Open daily 11:30am-3pm and 5pm-midnight. Closed M Nov.-Mar. MC/V.)

URBINO   ☎0722

With picturesque stone dwellings scattered along steep city streets and a turreted palace ornamenting its skyline, Urbino (oor-BEE-no; pop. 15,500) encompasses all that is classically Italian. The cobblestone streets and *piazze* lead to many artistic treasures and Renaissance monuments, including Piero della Francesca's *Ideal City* and Raphael's childhood home. The cultural beauty within the city walls is rivaled only by the magnificence of the surrounding mountains and valleys. A huge university population and stream of international visitors continually bolster Urbino's youthful vitality: When classes are in session, the town's population swells from 9,000 to nearly 30,000.

▐ TRANSPORTATION

Buses stop in Borgo Mercatale. ADRIABUS (☎37 67 11) buses run to P. Matteotti and the depot outside the train station in Pesaro (45min.-1hr.; M-Sa 20 per day 6:20am-8:35pm, Su 9 per day 7:35am-8:35pm; €2.75). Buy a ticket onboard. Bucci (☎32 401; www.autolineebucci.it) runs buses to Rome (4½hr., 6:15am and 3pm, €25). **Taxis** are in P. della Repubblica (☎25 50) and near the bus stop (☎32 79 49).

▚ ▐ ORIENTATION AND PRACTICAL INFORMATION

A short walk up **Via Mazzini** from **Borgo Mercatale** leads to **Piazza della Repubblica**, the city's hub, from which Via Raffaello, Via Cesare Battisti, Via Vittorio Veneto, and Corso Garibaldi radiate. Another walk uphill on V. V. Veneto leads to **Piazza Rinascimento** and the **Palazzo Ducale.**

Tourist Office: V. Puccinotti 35 (☎26 13; www.marcheturismo.it), across from Palazzo Ducale. Open M and Sa 9am-1pm, Tu-F 9am-1pm and 3-6pm. **Info booth** (☎26 31) in Borgo Mercatale. Open M-Sa 9am-6pm, Su 9am-1pm.

Laundromat: Powders, V. Battisti 35 (☎21 96). Wash €3.75 per kg., dry €2. Open M-Sa 9am-8pm. Cash only.

Police: ☎37 89 00.

Hospital: (☎35 05 21), on V. Bonconte da Montefeltro, off V. Comandino. Bus #1 and 3 from Borgo Mercatale stop.

Internet Access: Due Mila Net, V. Mazzini 17 (☎/fax 24 62). Over 20 computers. €4 per hr., students €2.50 per hr.; min. 3hr. Also offers printing and **Western Union** services. Open M-Sa 10am-2pm, 3pm-midnight. Cash only.

Post Office: V. Bramante 28 (☎37 791), off V. Raffaello. **Currency exchange** and **ATM** available. Open M-F 8am-6:30pm, Sa 8am-12:30pm. **Postal Code:** 61029.

▐ ACCOMMODATIONS

Cheap lodgings are relatively rare in Urbino, and reservations are a good idea.

Pensione Fosca, V. Raffaello 67 (☎32 96 22 or 32 25 42), on the top floor. Central location, sweet proprietress, and unbeatable value. Shared bath. Call ahead to arrange check-in time. Singles €21; doubles €35; triples €45. Cash only. ❷

Albergo Italia, C. Garibaldi 32 (☎27 01; www.albergo-italia-urbino.it), just off P. della Repubblica. Spotless modern rooms have views of the countryside, and the professional staff and sunny terrace create a welcoming atmosphere. Breakfast included. Wi-Fi free; computer with Internet €1 per 15min. Reception 24hr. Singles €45-65; doubles €65-115; triples €115; quads €140. AmEx/MC/V. ❹

Hotel San Giovanni, V. Barocci 13 (☎28 27). From P. della Repubblica, head toward V. Mazzini, and turn right, following the signs. Restaurant downstairs. Closed last 3wk. of July. Singles €26, with bath €38; doubles €40/58. Cash only. ❸

Piero della Francesca, V. Comandino 53 (☎32 84 28; fax 32 84 27), in front of the hospital. Bus #1 from Borgo Mercatale or a 15min. walk from P. della Repubblica. Modern rooms have bath, TV, phone, and balconies with views of the misty hills. Request a room on the top floor with A/C. Reception 24hr. Singles €31; doubles €52; triples €68. AmEx/MC/V. ❸

Camping Pineta (☎47 10), in Località San Donato, 2km from Urbino. Take bus #4 or 7 from Borgo Mercatale; ask to be let off at camping. Secluded sites have city views. Open from 1wk. before Easter-Sept. Office open daily 9am-10pm. €7-8 per person, €14-16 per car. Electricity €2. Showers free. Cash only. ❶

▣ FOOD

Urbino's *caciotta* is a delicate cheese that pairs well with a glass of *Bianchello del Metauro*. **Supermarket Margherita,** V. Raffaello 37, has meats and cheeses. (☎32 97 71. Open M-Sa 7:30am-1:55pm and 4:30-8pm. MC/V.)

▣ **Pizzeria Le Tre Piante,** V. Voltaccia della Vecchia 1 (☎48 63). From P. della Repubblica, take V. Veneto, turn left on V. Nazario Sauro, right on V. Budassi, and left down the stairs onto V. Foro Posterula. Join locals for pizza (€3-6) while watching the sun set over the Apennines from the terrace. Reservations recommended F-Sa. *Primi* €6.30-6.50, *secondi* €8-13. Cover €1.50. Open Tu-Su noon-3pm and 7-11:30pm. Cash only. ❸

La Trattoria del Leone, V. Battisti 5 (☎32 98 94). Fine dining at affordable prices, just off the *centro*. Try regional specialties like the *galletto al coccio* (a whole rooster served in a crockpot; €8). *Primi* €6.50-8, *secondi* €6-11. Cover €1.80. Open Nov.-July daily 6:30-11:30pm; Aug.-Oct. M-F 6:30-11:30pm, Sa-Su 12:30-2:30pm. AmEx/MC/V. ❷

Ristorante Ragno d'Oro, Vle. Don Minzoni 2/4 (☎32 77 05). Follow Vle. Raffaello to the statue at the top of the hill. Turn right on Vle. Don Minzoni. Students and locals make the hike to the top of the hill, where some of the town's best pizza and *piadine* awaits. Try the signature pizza, the *Ragno d'Oro*, topped with mozzarella, spinach, ricotta, and speck ham (€6.50), and wash it down with German beer on tap. Pizza €2.50-7.50. *Primi* €5.50-7.50, *secondi* €6.50-15.50. Cover €1.50. Open Apr.-Sept. daily noon-2:30pm and 7-10:30pm. AmEx/MC/V. ❸

Un Punto Macrobiotico, V. Pozzo Nuovo 4 (☎32 97 90). From P. della Repubblica, take C. Battisti and then 1st right. Long benches promote a community feel in this small market and cafeteria-type eatery that serves delicious organic food. Prices vary with the daily menu; most meals around €6. Open M-Sa 12:30-2:30pm and 7:30-9pm. Students eat ½-price. Cash only. ❶

Caffè del Sole, V. Mazzini 34 (☎26 19). Popular student hangout serves *panini*, drinks, and hearty helpings of local personality. Look around at the countless suns in various forms on the walls, and at the mural of clinking wine glasses and a giant mouth on the back wall. Sept.-May W nights jazz concerts. Open M-Sa 7am-2am. AmEx/MC/V. ❶

Bar del Teatro, C. Garibaldi 88 (☎29 11). Enjoy the best view in town: the Palazzo Ducale on one side and the valley on the other. Espresso €1.50; cappuccino €2. Open July-Aug. daily 7:30am-midnight; Sept.-June M-Sa. Cash only. ❸

▣ SIGHTS

The turreted silhouette of the Renaissance ▣**Palazzo Ducale,** in P. Rinascimento, dominates the Urbino skyline. A stairway inside leads to the **Galleria Nazionale delle Marche,** in the former residence of Duke Frederico da Montefeltro. The gallery contains an extensive collection of Italian art, including works like the *Ideal City* by Piero della Francesca. In the last rooms, Berruguete's *Portrait of Duke Federico with a Young Guidubaldo*, Raphael's *Portrait of a Lady*, and Paolo Uccello's narrative panel *The Profanation of the Host* are also on display. The building also contains the **Museo Archeologico's** varied collection of Roman art and artifacts. Free art exhibits are on display in the **Sale del Castellare;** the entrance is next to the *duomo*. (☎32 26 25. Open M 8:30am-2pm, Tu-Su 8:30am-7:15pm. Last entry 1hr. before closing. €4, students 18-25 €2.) The site of Raphael's birth in 1483, **Casa Natale di Raffaello,** V. Raffaello 57, is now filled with period furnishings and paintings. The only piece in the museum attributed to Raphael himself is a fresco of the Virgin and Child in the room where the artist was born. Within these walls, Raphael began learning the trade from his father, Giovanni Santi, a celebrated painter in his own right; his *Annunciation* hangs in the next room. (☎32 01 05. Open Mar.-Oct. M-Sa 9am-1pm and 3-7pm, Su 10am-1pm; Nov.-Feb. M-Sa 9am-2pm, Su 10am-1pm. Last entry 20min. before closing. €3. Cash only.) Next to Palazzo Ducale sits the stark facade of the **duomo.** White- and mint-green walls and notable paintings like Veronese's fantastic *Translazione della Santa Casa e Sant'Andrea* decorate the *duomo*'s interior. (Open daily 9:30am-1pm and 2:30-6:30pm. Free.) From P. della Repubblica, take V. Mazzini and turn right up the small path on the right, following the sign. The 1416 Gothic frescoes that decorate the **Oratorio di San Giovanni Battista,** on V. Barocci, include a gorgeous floor-to-ceiling Crucifixion and panels depicting events from the life of St. John. Its painters, the Salimbeni brothers Giacomo and Lorenzo, are said to have drawn their sketches with lamb's blood. (☎347 67 11 181. Open M-Sa 10am-12:30pm and 3-5:30pm, Su 10am-12:30pm. €2. Cash only.)

🔲 🌸 NIGHTLIFE AND FESTIVALS

The main *piazze* stay lit well into the night, when people head to cafes for one last shot of espresso (or tequila, as the case may be). Students keep the party scene going strong until well after 3am during the school year, but come summer, Urbino slows down as its median age rises drastically. Bars are well stocked with German beers, hard liquor, and even the occasional bottle of absinthe. Check out **The Bosom Pub,** V. Budassi 24, with its dark wood paneling and beer paraphernalia. Happy hours yield great deals, and be sure to check out the themed nights, most often on Thursdays. (☎47 83. Wine €5 per bottle. Beer from €2.50. Mixed drinks €2-6. Open daily June-July 8pm-2am; Aug.-May 6pm-2am. Cash only.) In July the town resounds with Renaissance music during the **Antique Music Festival.** Saturdays are amateur nights—bring your ancient lute and rock out. The 3rd Sunday of August brings the **Ceremony of the Revocation** of the Duke's Court. Jousting matches erupt on the eve of the festival. The **Festa dell'Aquilone,** held on the 1st Sunday in September, is a fierce kite-flying competition between different cities. (The rain date is the 2nd Su of Sept.)

ANCONA
☎ 071

Midway down the boot, Ancona (an-CO-na; pop. 102,000) is still kickin' as Northern Italy's major transportation hub for boats to Croatia, Greece, and Slovenia. As a result, most travelers only pass through Ancona on their way to more exotic locales. Those who choose to linger will enjoy the centuries-old *duomo*, a lively *centro storico*, and the sparkling water along its concrete beach.

📰 **TRANSPORTATION. Trains** run from P. Rosselli to: Bologna (2½hr., 33 per day 1:26am-8:40pm, €10.50); Milan (3-5hr., 16 per day 1:59am-7:13pm, €34); Pesaro (45min., 41 per day 4:40am-10:35pm, €3.25); Rimini (1½hr., 41 per day 1:32am-10:35pm, €4.80); Rome (3-4hr., 11 per day 3:37am-6:56pm, €14); Venice (5hr., 22 per day 2:34am-8:40pm, €27.50). The ticket office is open daily 5:55am-8:10pm and accepts AmEx/MC/V. **Ferries** go to Croatia, Greece, and northern Italy. Schedules are available at Stazione Marittima (☎20 78 91) on the waterfront. Call the day before departure to confirm, as cancellations can occur. Reserve ahead during July and Aug. The following companies all accept American Express, Master Card, and Visa. **Adria** (☎50 21 16 21; www.adriaferries.com) runs to Durazzo, Albania (18 hr.; €65, July-Aug. €85). **ANEK** (☎20 72 346; www.anekitalia.com) go to Igoumenitsa, Greece (16hr.) and Patras, Greece (21½hr.; €50, July-Aug. €70) and has a 20% discount for those under 26, a 10% discount for families and those over 60, and a 30% round-trip discount. **Jadrolinija** (☎20 43 05; www.jadrolinija.it) runs to Split, Croatia (10hr.; €40, late June-Aug. €47) and has a 20% round-trip discount 20%. **SEM Maritime Co** (**SMC;** ☎20 40 41; www.marittimamauro.it) goes to Split, Croatia (9hr.; €44; July-Aug. €52) and Hvar Island. **SNAV** (☎20 76 116; www.snav.it) goes to Spalato, Croatia (4½hr.; €63, mid-Jul. to Aug. €81).

TIP **THE FERRY FAIRY.** To find all of the most up-to-date info on ferries from all companies operating in Ancona, check out www.doricaportservices.it.

ORIENTATION AND PRACTICAL INFORMATION. The **train station** is a 25min. walk from **Stazione Marittima.** Buses #1, 1/3, and 1/4 head along the port toward Stazione Marittima and up **Corso Stamira** to **Piazza Cavour,** the *centro.* Buy tickets (€1) at *tabaccherie.* For Stazione Marittima, disembark at **Piazza della Repubblica,** walk back toward the water, and turn right on the waterfront. The **tourist office,** across the street in the Largo Dogane, offers a good map of the town and advice on lodgings. (☎20 79 29. Open daily Apr.-Aug. 9:30am-2pm and 3-7:30pm; Oct.-Dec. daily 10am-1:30pm and 2:30-6pm.) Info on long-term housing, employment, and cultural opportunities is at **InformaGiovani,** C. Stamira 55, which also offers 30min. free **Internet.** (☎54 958, ext. 8; www.anconagiovane.it. No Internet within 30min. of closing. Open M and Sa 10am-12:30pm, Tu and Th-F 10am-12:30pm and 4:30-6:30pm.) **Luggage storage** is available in Stazione Marittima. (Open daily 8am-8:30pm. €1 per bag per day for 1st 2 days, €2 per bag each day thereafter. Cash only.) In case of emergency, call the **police** (☎22 881). The hospital, **Ospedale Regionale Umberto I** (☎59 61), is on V. Conca-Torrette. **Internet** is available at **New International Service,** C. Stamira 81. Facing the port, go to the far left of P. Cavour and turn the corner. There is also a branch across from the train station with identical hours and prices. (☎20 76 981. €1 per 30min. Open daily 9am-midnight.) The **post office** is at P. XXIV Maggio 2, off P. Cavour (☎50 12 280. Open M-F 8am-6:30pm and Sa 8am-12:30pm.) **Postal Code:** 60100.

ACCOMMODATIONS AND FOOD. Ostello della Gioventù (HI) ❶, V. Lamaticci 7, provides clean rooms with wooden bunk beds and spotless bathrooms. From the train station, cross the *piazza* and turn left. Take the 1st right and make a sharp right behind the newsstand. This is a good choice for those coming and going by train. (☎/fax 42 257. Reception 6:30-11am and 4:30pm-midnight. Check-out 9:30am. Lockout 11am-4:30pm. Curfew midnight. Dorms €16. AmEx/MC/V.) Decent hotels surround the train station, such as **Hotel Italia ❸,** P. Rosselli 9, which has a convenient location and simple rooms with TV and bath. (☎42 607; fax 44 221. Singles €27, with bath €38; doubles €65. MC/V.) The clean rooms at **Hotel City ❹,** V. Matteotti 112/114, all have bath, A/C, TV, and minibar. From P. Cavour, facing away from the port, turn left on the street just before Largo XXIV Maggio, then left again at the end onto V. Matteotti. (☎20 70 949; www.hotelcityancona.it. Breakfast included. Wi-Fi €2 per hr. Singles M-Th €60, F-Su €55; doubles €92/90; triples €100. AmEx/MC/V.) Facing away from the port, walk to the far end of P. Cavour, turn right on V. Vecchini, walk straight and go up the staircase to **Pensione Milano** ❷, V. Montebello 1/A. Fourteen clean, nondescript rooms off a simple hallway come with basic furnishings and shared baths. (☎20 11 47. Reception 7am-11:30pm. Singles €26; doubles €41. Cash only.)

🏠**La Cantineta** ❷, V. Gramsci 1, teems with locals at tightly packed tables. Don't be deceived by the average exterior—a genial, welcoming staff offers large portions of regional cuisine like *stoccafisso* (cod; €14) at reasonable prices. At least among locals, this secret is out—come early or be prepared to wait. (☎20 11 07. Open Tu-Su noon-2:45pm and 7:30-10:45pm. Pizza €4.50-8. *Primi* €4-12, *secondi* €5-15. Meat *menù* €11, fish *menù* €15. Cover €1.50. AmEx/MC/V.) From P. Roma, head toward the horse fountain and turn left to find **Bontà delle Marche** ❷, C. Mazzini 96, a lunch restaurant and specialty deli. Trays of regional gourmet meats and cheeses tempt from the display cases, while white tables dot the pedestrian thoroughfare outside. (☎53 985; www.bontadellemarche.it. Market open M-Sa 8am-8pm. Restaurant open M-Sa 12:30-3:30pm. AmEx/MC/V.) For low-key dining, head to **Osteria Brillo** ❷, C. Mazzini 109. This small, pub-style eatery right off the *centro* serves hearty Italian fare at reasonable prices. From P. Roma, head toward the horse fountain and turn right on C. Mazzini. *Primi* specials change daily. (☎20 72 629. Pizza €5.50-7. *Secondi* €5.50-18. Open M-Sa 12:30-3pm and 7:30-11pm. AmEx/MC/V over €20.) The best grocery deals are at **Di per Di,** V. Matteotti 115. (Open M-W and F 8:15am-1:30pm and 5-7:35pm, Th 8:15am-1:30pm, Sa 8:15am-1pm and 5-7:40pm. Cash only.) To get to **Mercato Publico,** P. delle Erbe 130, from P. Roma, head toward the horse fountain, turn right on V. Mazzini, then turn left into P. delle Erbe. Pack a meal for the ferry ride at this old-fashioned indoor market. (Open in summer M-Sa 7:30am-12:45pm and 5-8pm; in winter M-Sa 7:30am-12:45pm and 4:30-7:30pm. Most vendors cash only.)

🔲🔳 **SIGHTS AND BEACHES.** Above the city in **Piazzale del Duomo** stands the 🏛**Cattedrale di San Ciriaco,** a Romanesque church built above the remains of an early Christian basilica and an even earlier Roman temple to Venus. From P. Cavour, follow C. Mazzini to the port and turn right on V. Gramsci at P. Repubblica. Continue to P. del Senato and climb 247 steps to the cathedral. Look in the basement on the left for the tomb of S. Ciriaco and a rather gruesome view of the body; don't miss the fantastic views of Ancona and the Adriatic. (☎52 688. Open M-Sa in summer 8am-noon and 3-7pm; in winter 8am-noon and 3-6pm. Free.) The 16th-century **Palazzo Ferretti** houses Le Marche's foremost archaeological museum, the **Museo Archeologico Nazionale delle Marche,** V. Ferretti 6, an impressive collection including the Ionian Dinos of Amandola, Greek pottery, and jewelry unearthed in the 1900s. From Palazzo Bosdari, continue toward the *duomo*. (☎20 26 02. Open Tu-Su 8:30am-7:30pm. €4, ages 18-25 €2, under 18 and over 65 free. Cash only.) From P. Roma, head down C. Garibaldi toward the port. Turn right at P. Repubblica onto V. Gramsci and go straight until you reach Ancona's art gallery, the **Pinacoteca Comunale Francesco Podesti,** in the **Palazzo Bosdari,** V. Pizzecolli 17. The gallery features works by the Camerte school including Crivelli's *Madonna con Bambino* and Titian's *Apparition of the Virgin.* The top floor features both contemporary and 18th- and 19th-century paintings. (☎22 25 045. Open M 9am-1pm, Tu-F 9am-7pm, Sa 8:30am-6:30pm, Su 3-7pm. €4.50, ages 16-25 €3.40, under 16 free. Cash only.) Far from the port's industrial clutter, **Passetto Beach** offers a chance to cool off in an unorthodox "beach." Sunbathers relax on the wide concrete sidewalk near ladders that drop directly into the sapphire waters. Above the beach, hundreds of stairs lead to the **Monumento ai Caduti,** a tribute to WWII soldiers. (In P. IV Novembre. Take bus #1/4 from the station or from P. Cavour along Vle. della Vittoria to the shoreline. Free.)

 FIND PASSETTO PASSÉ? If Passetto Beach doesn't satisfy your cravings for sand, the towns north and south of Ancona have some excellent beaches. Inquire at the tourist office. Keep in mind that the beaches to the north of Ancona are sandy but have murkier water (still clean; just the effect of sand mixing with the water), while beaches to the south are rocky with clear water.

ASCOLI PICENO ☎ 0736

According to legend, Ascoli Piceno (AS-co-lee pee-CHE-no; pop. 55,000) was founded by Sabines as they were guided westward out of central Italy by a *picchio* (woodpecker). The bird supposedly gave the city its name and the region its feathered mascot. By other accounts, Ascoli was the metropolis of the Piceno, a Latin tribe that controlled much of the coastal marshes and had the woodpecker as its totem. Whatever the origins of its name, Ascoli offers charming stone streets and *piazze* that overflow with ancient towers and stately *palazzi*. As you savor the city's signature anise-flavored liqueur, *anisetta meletti*, you won't be able to help yourself from drinking in some of the city's proud pre-Roman culture.

◗ TRANSPORTATION

The **train station** is in Ple. della Stazione, at the end of V. Marconi. (Ticket counter open M-Sa 8am-noon and 3-6pm.) **Trains** run to San Benedetto (30min., M-Sa 16 per day 6:24am-9:05pm, €2.40), but require a transfer at the Porto d'Ascoli station from July to early September. **Buses** leave from Vle. Gasperi, behind the *duomo*. Start (☎34 24 67 or 800 44 30 40; www.startspa.it) sells bus tickets at Agenzia Cameli, V. Dino Angelini 129, off P. Roma, and runs buses to San Benedetto (1hr.; M-Sa 34 per day 5:10am-11:35pm, Su 15 per day 7am-10:40pm; €2.50) and Acquasanta

Terme (1¼hr., 13 per day 5am-7:15pm, €4). Buses to Rome (3hr.; M-Sa 4 per day 3:20am-4:30pm, Su 4 per day 3:20am-5:30pm; €12) depart from P. Orlini. (☎25 90 91. Ticket office open M-Sa 9am-12:45pm and 4-7pm, Su 9-9:30am and 4-4:30pm.)

ORIENTATION AND PRACTICAL INFORMATION

From the **train station,** walk one block to Vle. Indipendenza, turn right, and continue straight to P. Giacomo Matteotti. Turn right on **Corso Giuseppe Mazzini;** follow it into **Piazza del Popolo.** To reach the main bus stop from P. Matteotti, turn left onto Vle. de Gasperi; the stop is behind the *duomo.* Next to the *duomo* lies **Piazza Arringo,** which leads into **Via XX Settembre** and **Piazza Roma.** From there, **Via del Trivio** leads back to C. G. Mazzini and P. del Popolo. The **tourist office,** or **Centro Visitatori,** P. Arringo 7 (☎29 82 04/12, www.comune.ascolipiceno.it; open daily 9:30am-1pm and 3-6:30pm), offers maps, comprehensive guides (€5, in English, French, German, and Spanish), and info about festivals and transportation. Head to **Banca Nazionale del Lavoro,** C. G. Mazzini 160, on the corner with C. Trento e Trieste, for **currency exchange.** (☎29 61. Open M-F 8:20am-1:20pm and 2:30-4pm, Sa 8:20am-11:50pm.) The **police** are at V. della Repubblica 8 (☎35 691). **Farmacia Dott. Sebastiani** is at P. Roma 1. (☎25 91 83. Open daily 9am-1pm and 4:30-8pm.) The **hospital** is on V. Monticelli (☎35 81). **Interage,** V. Pietro Marucci 10, offers **Internet.** (☎24 04 79. €3 per hr. Open M-Sa 9am-12:30pm and 3:30-7:45pm. Closed in summer Sa afternoon.) Ascoli's **post office,** V. Crispi 2, provides **currency exchange.** (☎24 22 83. Open M-F 8am-6:30pm, Sa 8am-12:30pm.) **Postal Code:** 63100.

ACCOMMODATIONS AND FOOD

The best deal in town is the pleasant ▧**Ostello dei Longobardi (HI) ❶,** V. Soderini 26. In an 11th-century building, this quiet hostel offers 16 beds separated into two single-sex dorms. If you dare, ask friendly staffer Luigi for a tour of the haunted tower—one of the city's 100 towers. Feel free to borrow a bike, and be sure to sign the latest of a stack of guestbooks, with signatures dating back to 1949. From P. del Popolo, take C. Mazzini to P. Sant'Agostino, and turn right on V. delle Torri, then left on V. Soderini. (☎26 18 62. Dorms €16. Cash only.) In the heart of town, **Cantina dell'Arte ❸,** V. della Lupa 8, is a picturesque hotel decorated with family photos. Rooms have marble floors, bath, TV, and phone. Follow C. Trento e Trieste to P. Santa Maria Inter Vineas; turn right on V. delle Canterine, then right on V. della Lupa. (☎25 57 44; www.cantinadellarte.it. Breakfast €2; meal discounts at restaurant by the same name across the street. Reservations recommended. Singles €30; doubles €40; quads €65; quint with kitchen €100. AmEx/MC/V.)

Ascoli's cuisine relies on local produce—wild mushrooms, onions, capers, garlic, fennel, and anise—while still maintaining low prices. *Olive all'ascolana* (olives stuffed with meat) is a true delight, not to be missed as an *antipasto.* Savory, anise-flavored cakes topped with powdered sugar are a holiday favorite, and the region's wines include *Rosso Piceno* and *Falerio dei Colli Ascolani.* ▧**Leopoldus ❷,** V. Vidacilio 18, a gorgeous, clean establishment, both looks and smells authentic. Their *olives all'ascolana* (€5) and lamb chops (€6) are equally delicious. (Pizza €4-7. Open Tu-Sa noon-2:30pm and 7:30-11pm.) There's no better place to try local *anisetta meletti* (€3.50 per glass, €12.40 per bottle) than ▧**Caffè Meletti ❶,** P. del Popolo 20, the old-fashioned, 100-year-old cafe where Silvio Meletti introduced his now-famous liqueur. A variety of other anise-flavored sweets are also available, including bags of biscuits from €3. (☎25 96 26; caffemeletti@virgilio.it. Open in summer daily 7:30am-midnight. AmEx/MC/V.) Take C. Mazzini from P. del Popolo and turn left, following signs for **Ristorante dal Vagabondo ❷**, V. D'Argillano 29, where a friendly owner serves heaping plates of tasty Ascoli-Picenian fare. (☎26 21 68. *Primi* €5-7, *secondi* €10. Lunch *menù* €10. Open daily noon-2:30pm and 7-10pm. MC/V.) Quell a ravenous appetite at **Cantina dell'Arte ❷**, V. della Lupa 5, across from the hotel by the same name. The medieval stone interior is a nice touch. (☎25 11 35; www.cantinadellarte.it. *Primi* €4-5, *secondi* €5-6. Lunch *menù* €12, dinner €15. Open M-Sa noon-3pm and 7-10:30pm, Su noon-3pm. AmEx/MC/V.) An **open-air market** is in P. San Francesco, behind P. del Popolo. (Open M-Sa 8am-1pm.) **Tigre** supermarket is at P. Santa Maria Inter Vineas 1, at the end of C. Trento e Trieste. (Open M-W and F 8:30am-1:30pm and 5-8pm, Th 8:30am-1:30pm, Sa 8:30am-1:30pm and 4:30-8pm. MC/V.)

👁 SIGHTS

▓PINACOTECA CIVICA. Medieval and Renaissance works by Crivelli, Titian, Van Dyck, and Reni line the walls, while frescoes cover the ceilings in the massive **Palazzo Arringo,** a sight in itself. Check out the lifelike *Il Pastorello*, a statue of a small boy from 19th-century Italy used to critique child labor. Also peruse Pietro Brenda's *I Rifuti dei Mari;* as you change perspective, the dead man's feet in the painting's seaside landscape always face you, and the waves appear to change size. *(To the left after exiting duomo in P. Arringo. Enter the garden courtyard, turn right immediately, then go left up the staircase. ☎29 82 13. Open daily 9am-1pm and 3-7pm. €5. Cash only.)*

DUOMO. Flanking one end of Oration Square in P. Arringo, Ascoli's travertine *duomo* combines Classical, Romanesque, and Baroque styles and holds work from the 5th to 18th centuries. A Roman basilica serves as the transept, topped by an 8th-century octagonal dome. Inside, freshly restored frescoes decorate the ceiling, while stairs on the left descend into the dim **Cripta di Sant'Emidio,** where shimmering mosaics and gorgeous sculptures adorn the tomb of Ascoli's 1st bishop and patron saint. According to legend, the head of the decapitated martyr is housed in Chiesa di Sant'Emidio alle Grotte (p. 539), and the tomb only holds his body. *(Open daily 7am-2pm and 3:30-7:45pm. Free.)* Next to the *duomo*, **St. Jonh's Baptristy** is an exquisite standing example of how baptistries used to be built in early Christianity: outside the church.

MUSEO ARCHEOLOGICO STATALE. Inside the 15th-century **Palazzo Panichi** is a three-floor museum with a collection of Greek and Roman artifacts, some excavated from the nearby city of San Benedetto del Tronto. The most impressive piece is a mosaic floor that depicts the face of a boy in the center; when viewed from the opposite side, it becomes the face of an old man. It also shows written examples of Piceno, the language of the area adapted from ancient Greek that predates Latin. *(P. Arringo 28. ☎25 35 62. Open Tu-Su 8:30am-7:30pm. €2, students €1.)*

PIAZZA DEL POPOLO. This vast *piazza* was once a Roman forum, and—as evidenced by its cafes, boutiques, and city offices—it still buzzes with political and consumer activity. The gleaming pavement is made of travertine, an off-white mineral that's also been used to construct the city's major buildings and squares for over two millennia. The eastern end of the Romanesque-Gothic **Templo di San Francesco** contains a wood crucifix, the only art saved from a 1535 fire. The church's "singing columns," low columns that flank the outer door on the V. del Trivio side, make a dull popping sound if you draw your hand quickly across them. *(Open daily 8am-noon and 3:30-7:30pm. Free.)*

OTHER SIGHTS. From P. del Popolo, turn left onto C. Mazzini and right on V. del Trivio. Bear left on V. Cairoli, which becomes V. delle Donne, then pass the church on the left and follow tiny pedestrian way, V. Solestà, as it curves to the right. V. Solestà leads to the single-arched **Ponte di Solestà,** one of Europe's tallest Roman bridges. Cross the bridge and take V. Rigante to the right. Then turn right on Vle. M. Federici, left on V. Carso, and follow it under the roadway to reach **Chiesa di Sant'Emidio alle Grotte** (a 15min. walk from the bridge), whose Baroque facade is crafted from the natural rock wall. Though closed to the public, the **catacombs** hold the remains of the first Ascoli Christians and (allegedly) Sant'Emidio's head (visit his body in the *duomo*).

FESTIVALS

Insanity reigns during Ascoli's **Carnevale** on the days preceding Ash Wednesday. On the 1st Sunday in August, the colorful medieval **Tournament of Quintana** honors the city's patron Saint Emidio; 1500 local enthusiasts don medieval garb and onlookers watch man-on-dummy jousting and a torch-lit procession. The tournament culminates in a fierce competition in which the town's six neighborhoods battle for the coveted winner's banner, the *palio*. Ascoli is also renowned for its fireworks displays, especially those on August 4 and 5, the eve and celebration of Sant'Emidio. On the 3rd Sunday of each month except July, an **Antique Market** unfolds in the *centro* from 8am-10pm. Stop by any tourist office or *tabaccherie* to pick up the free magazine, *What's Ap,* for an extensive list of summer events.

SAN BENEDETTO DEL TRONTO ☎0735

With over 7000 palm trees and nearly as many children playing under their waving fronds, San Benedetto (san beh-neh-DEH-toh; pop. 53,000) draws summering Italian families and over 200,000 tourists. Don't come expecting to split beach time with cultural enrichment—the only *castelli* you'll find are made of sand.

■ TRANSPORTATION. The **train station** is at Vle. Gramsci 20/A. The ticket counter is open daily 6:40am-8:35pm (AmEx/MC/V). **Trains** run to Ancona (1hr., 28 per hr. 12:28am-9:13pm, €4.30), Bologna (3hr., 12 per day 12:28am-8:31pm, €24), and Milan (5-6hr., 6 per day 12:38am-4:14pm, €35). Start (☎0736 34 24 67 or 800 44 30 40; www.startspa.it) runs **buses** from the train station or Porto d'Ascoli to Ascoli Piceno (1hr.; 34 per day M-Sa 6am-12:10am, 15 per day Su 7am-midnight; €2.50). Buy tickets at the train station or at Caffè Blue Express across the street. **Local buses** stop in front of the train station. Bus #2 departs across the street from the station (every 15-20min. 5:57am-12:45am, €0.80). Buy tickets from the newsstand in the train station. **Taxis** (☎58 41 27) run from the train station.

■ ☷ ORIENTATION AND PRACTICAL INFORMATION. Buses #4 and #5 follow Vle. dello Sport, which traverses the heart of the city. **Viale Trieste,** the *lungomare* (promenade), runs along the shore while it undergoes various name changes (see **Beaches**). **Via Trento,** which becomes **Via Volta,** runs parallel to the *lungomare*. To reach the **tourist office,** V. del Mare 203, take bus #2 to the rotunda and turn right. The office is housed in a brown building, facing the main shore. (☎75 17 98; www.rivieradellepalme.it. Open June-Sept. M-Sa 9:30am-1:30pm and 4:30pm-midnight, Su 4:30pm-midnight.) **Iris Lavanderie,** V. dei Laureati 52, offers self-service laundry with free detergent. (Wash and dry €5. Open M-F 8:30am-1pm and 3:30-7:30pm, Sa 8:30am-1pm.) The **police** are at P. Battisti 1 (☎89 22 11). **Farmacia Mercuri,** Vle. de Gasperi 61/63, posts a 24hr. rotation outside. (☎78 01 51. Open M-Sa 9am-1pm and 4-7pm.) The **hospital, Ospedale Civile** (☎79 31) is on V. Manara. Access the **Internet** across from the train station at **Easy Connect,** V. Roma 120 (€1.30 per hr.; open daily 10am-11pm), or at **ConoCafe,** V. dei Laureati 9 (☎75 78 55;

€1 per hr.; open daily 9am-midnight). The **post office,** V. Roma 125, in the parking lot outside the train station, offers **currency exchange** and an **ATM.** (☎59 58 41. Open M-F 8am-1:30pm, Sa 8am-12:30pm.) **Postal Code:** 63039.

⌗ ACCOMMODATIONS AND CAMPING. Most hotels include private beach access in their fee. To reach **La Playa ❸,** V. Cola di Rienzo 25/A, go to the end of V. dei Laureati, and turn right on V. Francesco Ferrucci. Walk one block and turn left onto V. Cola di Rienzo. The friendly owners and neat rooms with polished tile baths, TV, minibar, and balcony make travelers return year after year. A/C is available on the 2nd and 3rd floors. (☎/fax 65 99 57. Open May-Oct. No singles in Aug. Singles €30-38; doubles €40-64. Breakfast €2. AmEx/MC/V.) A 10min. walk from the beach, the newly inaugurated **Ostello IPSIA ❷,** Vle. dello Sport 60 offers a decent budget option. This huge building is a school dorm during the year but becomes a hostel from the beginning of July until the end of August. Take bus #4 or 5 to reach it from the train station. Each room has three beds and a bath. (☎78 12 63. Breakfast included. 3-night min. stay. €20 per person.) In a spacious grove, **Camping Seaside ❶,** V. dei Mille 125, offers a pool, market, and restaurant. Take bus #2, or walk from Vle. Rinascimento, turning right onto V. A. Negri and bearing left on V. dei Mille. (☎65 95 05; www.seaside.it. Open June-Aug. €7-10 per adult, €3-5 per child ages 3-7, €6.50-12 per ½-site, €12-18 per site, €2.50-5 per car. Hot showers free. MC/V.)

◖◗◙ FOOD AND NIGHTLIFE. When hunger strikes, head to one of the ubiquitous beachside foot spots then stay all night as it becomes a *discoteca.* You'll feel miles from the beach in the train wagon-inspired **Verbena ❷,** at the end of V. dei Laureati. Specialties include risotto *alle fragole* (with strawberries; €7). The restaurant becomes a *discoteca* by night, playing Latin music (W and Su) and disco on Thursday. (☎65 61 61; www.verbenadivertimentosano.it. Pizza €4-8. Open daily 7-11pm. *Discoteca* until 1am.) Surrounded by hundreds of other beachside restaurants, **Alex ❸,** Vle. Rinascimento 18, offers comfortable, beachside seating and seafood *menù,* including an *antipasto, primo, secondo,* salad, wine, water, and coffee for €20. The restaurant's *discoteca* is open nightly until 1am. (☎75 80 21. Mixed drinks €5-8. Open Easter-Nov. 24hr. AmEx/MC/V.) In a restaurant-packed part of town between beaches #8 and 9, the chic **Bagni Andrea ❹,** Vle. Trieste 17, offers romantic candlelight dining and specializes in seafood. (☎83 834; www.bagniandrea.com. *Antipasti* from €15. *Primi* €10, *secondi* €10-18. Reservations recommended Sa-Su night. Th-Su piano bar 10pm. Open daily 1-3pm and 8:30-11pm; late-night Latin and swing disco closes at 4am. AmEx/MC/V.) On Tuesday and Friday morning, head to the **open-air market** on V. Montebello. **Tigre** supermarkets abound; find one at V. dei Laureati 41a. (Open in summer M-Sa 8am-1:30pm and 4:30-8:30pm, Su 8:30am-1pm. AmEx/MC/V.)

◪ BEACHES. San Benedetto's palm-lined beaches and *lungomare* cover a lot of distance, starting with beach #1 near the train station and continuing through beach #114, which is actually in Porta d'Ascoli. The free beaches, or *"spiaggie libere,"* in San Benedetto are superb, so don't waste money paying for private ones. The best free beach (with the fewest people) is all the way at the end of the promenade. Numerous cabanas rent storage cabins (from €5.20) and umbrellas (from €6.20). From San Benedetto's train station, cross the street and take bus #2 to the seaside, or turn left on V. Gramsci and left again on V. Monfalcone toward the beach. Vle. Trieste, the *lungomare,* intersects V. Monfalcone and runs along the shore, changing from Vle. Marconi to Vle. Europa/Scipioni, and then to Vle. Rinascimento. From start to finish the *lungomare* is about an hour's walk.

ABRUZZO AND MOLISE

The foothills of the Apennine mountains are home to medieval castles, Roman ruins, and a sprawling, varied wilderness. The people of this region have been shepherds since the Bronze Age, and only in the last half-century has their way of life changed. Millennia-old shepherds' paths weave through the rugged countryside, and quiet rural villages sustain a sleepy lifestyle largely similar to that of their ancestors. About two hours. from Rome and still predominantly untouched by tourism, these highlands offer natural beauty and a unique retreat from bustling city life. A single region until they split in 1963, Abruzzo (ah-BROOTS-oh) and Molise (mo-LEEZ-eh) lie at the juncture of Northern and Southern Italy. Abruzzo offers picturesque towns, lakes, lush pines, and stunning wildlife, especially in its national park. The smaller Molise, inhabited long ago by Samnite highlanders, is home to phenomenal ruins, medieval festivals, and flavorful food. These regions may not fit in with the stereotypical image of Italy, but if you come seeking *la dolce vita*, look no farther.

HIGHLIGHTS OF ABRUZZO AND MOLISE

GLIMPSE herds of **wild horses** on the Gran Sasso d'Italia (p. 545).

DISCOVER Ovid's homeland of **Sulmona** (p. 545).

SET UP CAMP in **Abruzzo National Park** after an arduous day of hiking (p. 548).

ESCAPE to Puglia to bathe in the **azure waves** of the Tremiti Islands (p. 554).

L'AQUILA
☎ 0862

The story goes that in 1254, 99 lords from 99 castles banded together to build L'Aquila (meaning "The Eagle"; LA-kwee-la; pop. 65,000), Abruzzo's capital. Some historians claim the city plan mimics that of Jerusalem; this is best explained by Frederick II's desire to create a new seat for Catholic Christianity following the political decline of Rome and the schism that brought about the Avignon papacy in the 13th century. Called the "Salzburg of the South," this city is rediscovering its charm and recalling its glory days now that over 40,000 students crowd its streets and hikers ascend its nearby mountains.

█ TRANSPORTATION. The **train station** (☎ 41 92 90) is on the outskirts of town. (Ticket office ☎ 41 28 08. Open M-Sa 5:30am-8:30pm, Su 7:30am-1:15pm and 2:30-8pm.) **Trains** go to Sulmona (1hr., 8 per day 6:27am-8:25pm, €4.62) and Terni (2hr., 10 per day 6:27am-7:57pm, €6). L'Aquila has two **bus** systems: blue ARPA regional buses and yellow municipal buses. ARPA **buses** (☎ 41 28 08) stop at the station near P. Duomo and go to: Avezzano (50min., M-Sa 26 per day 5:55am-8:30pm, €4.50); Pescara (1½hr., M-Sa 7 per day 6am-9:10pm, €7); Rome (1¾hr., M-Sa 17 per day 4:40am-8pm, €8.50); Sulmona (40min., M-Sa 7 per day 6:20am-7:20pm, €4.50). The yellow **municipal buses** stop at AMA markers and serve surrounding towns and sights. (☎ 31 98 57; www.amaaq.191.it. One-way €0.85, 1½hr. €1, 1-day pass €1.90.) Tickets are available at *tabaccherie*, newsstands, *bars*, and at the city bus station, past P. del Collemaggio on V. Giacomo Caldora. A subterranean tramway connects the station with P. del Duomo. **Taxis** (☎ 22 115 or 27 372) are available at the bus station.

█▊ ORIENTATION AND PRACTICAL INFORMATION. Take bus #M11, 5, or 8 from the train station to **Via XX Settembre** to reach the *centro*, taking a left on **Corso Federico II**. On foot, follow signs to "Fontana delle 99 Cannelle" to the

LE MARCHE

Abruzzo and Molise

Ascoli
Piceno

San Benedetto
del Tronto

TO CROATIA
(HVAR, BRAC,
KORCULA, SPALATO)

A14

ADRIATIC SEA

0 _____ 30 kilometers
0 _____ 30 miles

Teramo

A24

Corno
Grande
2912m

Gran Sasso
National Park

Pescara

A25

Chieti

TO TREMITI
ISLANDS

TO TREMITI
ISLANDS

L'Aquila

Majella
National Park

A14

Sulmona

ABRUZZO

Termoli

Avezzano

ABRUZZO
NATIONAL PARK

Pescocostanzo

MOLISE

Subiaco

Pescasseroli
Opi

Villeta Barrea
Barrea
Lago di
Barrea

Castel di Sangro
Alfedena

PUGLIA

Civetella
Alfedena

San Vicenzo
al Volturno

Campobasso

Isernia

Saepinum

LAZIO

CAMPANIA

TRANSPORTATION TROUBLES. Since bus service can be inconvenient and inconsistent (especially on Sundays), traveling by car in Abruzzo and Molise is advisable. Before setting out, always double check the destination with both the bus station's APT office and the driver before boarding. Also confirm the return routes. Schedules and info are available by phone or Internet.

---

right and hike 2km uphill. C. Federico II becomes **Corso Vittorio Emanuele II,** the main street which stretches between **Piazza del Duomo,** the heart of L'Aquila's *centro storico,* in the south, and the **Castello Cinquecentesco** in the north. Beyond P. del Duomo, the street continues as **Corso Federico II** until reaching the gardens of the **Villa Comunale** and **Via XX Settembre.** Pick up a map at the tourist office; L'Aquila's often unlabeled streets are difficult to navigate.

The most accessible **tourist office** is the welcome point in the front of P. del Duomo, which dispenses free maps and transportation info. (☎23 021; www.centrostorico.laquila.it. Open daily 10am-10pm.) The main **APT tourist office,** V. XX Settembre 8, also stocks free maps. (☎22 306. Open M-Sa 9am-1pm and 3-6pm, Su 9am-1pm.) **Club Alpino Italiano,** V. Sassa 34, offers hiking info, maps, and guide references. (☎24 342. Open M-Sa 7am-8:15pm.) The **Centro Turistico Gran Sasso,** C. V. Emanuele II 49, has bus and train schedules and info on the Gran Sasso park. (☎22 146. Open M-F 9:30am-1:30pm and 3:30-6:30pm, Sa 9:30am-1:30pm.)

ABRUZZO AND MOLISE

The **police** are at V. del Beato Cesidio. A **pharmacy** can be found right next to the *duomo*. To reach **Internet Point @**, C. Principe Umberto 20, take C. V. Emanuele II from the *duomo* and turn left on C. P. Umberto. (☎27 364. €4 per hr. Open M-Sa daily 9am-9pm.) The **post office,** in P. del Duomo, **exchanges currency.** (☎63 71. Open M-F 8am-6:30pm, Sa 8am-12:30pm.) **Postal Code:** 67100.

■▐▌ ACCOMMODATIONS AND FOOD. While there are plenty of B&Bs right outside the city, L'Aquila itself offers no true budget accommodations. A 10min. ride on bus #79 or 81 from La Fontana Luminosa to "Cianfrano" will take you to **Bed and Breakfast "da Charlie" ❷**, V. Monte Brancastello 22. Named after the owner's dog, this B&B offers clean rooms and cheap food with a great city view. (☎347 85 97 938. Breakfast included. Singles €25; doubles €40-45.) If you're willing to pay for a central location, the intimate rooms in the central **Hotel Duomo ❺**, V. Dragonetti 6, across from the *duomo* and to the left, all have bath, TV, and phone; some also boast *duomo* views. (☎41 07 69; www.hotel-duomo.it. Breakfast €5. Singles €60-70; doubles €80; triples €100. AmEx/MC/V.) **Hotel San Michele ❺**, V. dei Giardini 6, is luxurious: all rooms are impeccably clean and equipped with free Internet, satellite TV, A/C, and minifridge. On the 3rd and 4th floors, windows overlook the mountains. (☎42 02 60; www.stmichelehotel.it. Breakfast included. Singles €65; doubles €80-90. MC/V.)

For great cheap food and good ambience, **▐La Stella Alpina ❶**, V. Crispomonti 19, is 2nd to none. The €7 lunch special buys you any pizza and a drink. (☎41 31 90. *Primi* €5-7. Open daily noon-3pm and 7-11pm.) Get a break from all the pizza and pasta with one of the many meat dishes at **Darkover ❷**, V. dell'Arcivescovado 17. Though the cool interior is decorated with mythical characters and Chinese paintings, the restaurant still maintains an Italian flavor. Try their specialty, *arros-ticini* (lamb kebab; €5). If you're really stuck on pizza, you can get it here for €4-8. (☎40 60 20. Open daily noon-2:30pm and 7:30-11:30pm) *Torrone*, a honey and almond nougat, is L'Aquila's specialty. Some of the more popular kinds are available at **Caffè Europa ❶**, C. V. Emanuele II 38, for €8 per box. The *caffè*'s delicious, chocolate-drizzled *caffè macchiato* are worth a try. (☎333 41 47 377. Open daily 7am-11pm. Cash only.) Find everything from fresh fruit and cured meats to clothes at the busy **market** in P. del Duomo. (Open M-Sa 8am-noon.) A **STANDA** supermarket, C. Federico II 1, is two blocks from V. XX Settembre. Enter at the corner of V. Monteguelfi and V. Sant'Agostino. (☎26 482. Open M-Sa 8am-8pm. AmEx/MC/V.)

◨ SIGHTS. To find the **▐Basilica di Santa Maria di Collemaggio,** take C. Federico I past V. XX Settembre, or the tramway to the bus station from P. del Duomo, and turn left onto V. di Collemaggio after Villa Comunale. At the request of Pietro da Marrone (later Pope and Saint Celestine V), L'Aquila's citizens began this church in 1287. The pink-and-white checkered facade is the symbol of the Knights Templar, associated in medieval times with a group of prestigious fighters, but now linked to the Freemasons. Notice the number eight and the serpent made by circles on the floor design, both Templar symbols. Despite its controversial cross, the basilica's claim to fame is its Holy Door—the first of only seven in the world. Opened only once a year on August 28th, it is said that all those who walk through it have all their sins washed away. (Open in summer daily 8am-12:30pm and 3-8pm; in winter hours vary. Modest dress required. Free.) **Chiesa di San Bernardino,** built in 1454 and restored after an earthquake in 1703, peers over the mountains south of L'Aquila. The interior boasts four beautiful paintings on its ceiling and the tomb of San Bernardino, complete with a Templar cross. Years ago, schoolchildren from the saint's hometown of Siena would make a pilgrimage to L'Aquila on May 22 to bring oil to light the lamp in front of the church's mausoleum for the rest of the year. Across from the church, a stairway frames a scenic mountain view; to reach both the stairway and the church, walk down V. S. Bernardino from C. V. Emanuele II. (Open daily 7:30-10am and 6-7:45pm. Modest dress required. Free.) In the 16th century, Spanish viceroy Don Pedro da Toledo built the **Castello Cinque-centesco,** V. Colecchi 1, at the end of C. V. Emanuele II, to defend himself against the rebelling *aquilesi.* Naturally, they were forced to pay for its construction. Never attacked, the *castello* is more active today in its role as the **Museo Nazionale di Abruzzo,** showcasing Roman sarcophagi, Renaissance tapestries, and a million-year-old mammoth skeleton, discovered locally in 1954. (☎ 63 34 00; www.psaelaq-uila.it. Open Tu-Su 9am-7pm. €4; ages 18-25 €2; EU university students, under 18, and over 65 free.) Commissioned in 1272, the **Fontana delle 99 Cannelle** (Fountain of 99 Spouts) is L'Aquila's oldest monument. To see the water streaming from the mouths of 99 unique heads, take V. Sallustio from C. V. Emanuele and bear left onto V. XX Settembre. Follow the small V. Borgo Rivera down the hill.

🔁 DAYTRIP FROM L'AQUILA: GRAN SASSO D'ITALIA. The snow-capped Gran Sasso d'Italia ("The Rock of Italy"), the highest mountain ridge within Italy's borders, looms 12km north of L'Aquila. Take a funicular midway up the Sasso (and above the tree line) to a flat plain, **Campo Imperatore,** home to herds of wild horses, shepherds, never-ending landscapes, and a hotel built by Mussolini. On a clear day, you can see both of Italy's coasts from the **Corno Grande,** the highest peak in the range at 2912m. The trail map (€8), available at the Club Alpino Italiano, newsstands in town, or at the base of the mountain, is useful for planning hikes. *Sentieri* (paths) are marked by difficulty, and only the more taxing routes reach the top. The peaks are snowy from September to June, when only experienced mountaineers should venture all the way up. In winter, Gran Sasso teems with **skiers.** The trails around the funicular are among the most difficult, offering one 4000m and several 1000m drops. Ten trails descend from the funicular and the two lifts. Purchase a weekly pass at the *biglietteria* at the base of the funicular. **Campo Felice,** at nearby Monte Rotondo, has 16 lifts, numerous trails of varying difficulty, and a ski school. (*In the summer a funicu-lar ascends the 1008m to Campo Imperatore, making the Sasso an easy afternoon excursion from L'Aquila. The funicular is closed during parts of June and Oct. ☎ 60 61 43. Every hr. 8:30am-5pm; €7. Trails start at the upper funicular station. Contact Club Alpino Italiano at ☎ 24 342 or www.cai.it for current conditions. For info on mountain guides, inquire at the tourist office or Club Alpino Italiano. To reach Campo Felice from L'Aquila, take yellow bus #76 or blue shuttle M6 from the bus station. 30min., 12 per day, €1. Buy tickets at tabaccherie or the station. For ski info, con-tact Campo Felice at ☎ 60 61 43. Lift tickets €14-25. Ski rentals around €10.*)

SULMONA ☎ 0864

Hidden deep in Abruzzo's Peligna Valley, medieval Sulmona (sool-MO-na; pop. 26,000) is enveloped by the hulking Apennines. The charming inhabitants of this small town churn out *confetti* (Sulmona's signature candy), and harbor great pride in their famous poet Ovid (43 BC-AD 17). The letters "SMPE," adorning Sulmona's streets and inscribed on buildings, are shorthand for the poet's famous proclamation, *"Sulmo mihi patria est"* ("Sulmona is my homeland"). A stroll around the pleasant public gar-dens, a hike in the surrounding mountains, or an amble through charming nearby towns offers an afternoon diversion when much of the town shuts down for *siesta.*

🚍 TRANSPORTATION. Two kilometers outside the city, the **train station** (☎ 34 293) joins the Rome-Pescara and Carpione-L'Aquila-Terni lines. The uphill walk to the *centro* takes around 30min.; instead you can take bus A (5:30am-8pm, €0.70) and ask to stop at P. XX Settembre. Catch the bus back to the train station from the stop near the public gardens. **Trains** run to: Avezzano (1½hr., 11 per day 4:47am-7:49pm, €3.50); L'Aquila (1hr., 9 per day 6:34am-8:30pm, €3.40); Naples

(4hr., 4 per day 6:29am-3:26pm, €14-16); Pescara (1-1¼hr., 21 per day 5:10am-9:18pm, €3.40); Rome (1½-2½hr., 5 per day 5:47am-5:23pm, €7-12). ARPA (☎20 91 33) runs a **bus** from its main stop by Porta Napoli to Castel di Sangro in Abruzzo National Park (1hr.; 10 per day 6:40am-6:10pm, reduced service Su; €4, buy ticket on bus). For a **taxi**, call ☎31 747 in the *centro* or ☎31 446 at the train station.

🖪 🛈 ORIENTATION AND PRACTICAL INFORMATION. **Viale Stazione** runs from the train station to Sulmona proper (2km). In town, it becomes **Viale Roosevelt** and continues past the public gardens where it becomes **Corso Ovidio**, the main street. C. Ovidio runs past **Piazza XX Settembre** (with the statue of Ovid), and **Piazza Garibaldi** (with the medieval aqueduct), and then exits the *centro storico* through **Porta Napoli**. The multilingual staff at the **IAT tourist office**, C. Ovidio 208, provides free city maps, as well as hotel, B&B, and restaurant listings. It also offers guided tours of the countryside, and sells Club Italiano Alpino maps for €5-7. (☎/fax 53 276. Open M-Sa 9am-1pm and 4-7pm, Su 9am-1pm.) A helpful English-speaking staff runs the **UST tourist office**, across the street in Palazzo dell'Annunziata, providing detailed hiking info, train and bus schedules, Club Alpino Italiano maps, free city maps, and references for local mountain guides. (☎21 02 16; www.comune.sulmona.aq.it. Open daily 9am-1:30pm and 4-8pm.) In case of an **emergency**, call the **carabinieri** (☎52 747). Access the **Internet** at **3D Sistemi**, V. Manlio D'Eramo 9, off P. Garibaldi. (☎/fax 21 20 47. €4 per hr. Open M-W and F-Sa 9am-1pm and 4-7:30pm, Th 9am-1pm.) The **post office,** in P. Brigata Maiella, has an **ATM**. (☎62 47 292. Open M-F 8am-6:30pm, Sa 8am-12:30pm.) **Postal Code:** 67039.

🛏🍴 ACCOMMODATIONS AND FOOD. Make reservations in summer, since this region is popular with mountain bikers and hikers. The tourist office provides a list of B&Bs outside town. In a vine-covered former *palazzo*, the family-run 🖪**Hotel Italia ❷**, P. Salvatore Tommasi 3, to the right off P. XX Settembre, maintains a medieval-inspired ambience with 27 rustic, antique-filled rooms. Some rooms have balconies and mountain views. (☎52 308. Singles €25, with bath €33; doubles €43/54. Cash only.) **Albergo Stella ❹**, V. Panfilo Mazara 16/18, off C. Ovidio, features a service-oriented staff and spacious, pleasantly decorated rooms all with bath, phone, and TV. Guests hang out around the *enoteca* connected to the hotel's restaurant. (☎52 653; www.hasr.it. Breakfast included. Singles €50-60; doubles €70-80. AmEx/MC/V.) Close to P. Plebiscito and Ovid's tomb, **Bed and Breakfast "Il Giullare" ❷**, Vco. Spezzato 32 (not to be confused with V. Spezzato), offers intimate rooms at a reasonable price. (☎347 79 16 188; www.ilguillare.net. Breakfast included. Seasonal closures; call ahead. €25 per person. Cash only.)

For a relaxed, intimate experience, head to 🖪**Hostaria dell'Arco ❷**, V. D'Eramo, 60, perhaps the cheapest restaurant in town that still offers quality, traditional dishes. Expect the lamb (€7) to be delicious and follow it with any dessert for €2-3. (☎21 05 53. Open Tu-Sa noon-2:30pm and 8-11pm, Su noon-2:30pm.) **Ristorante Gino ❸**, P. Plebiscito 12, beloved by chic locals, only opens for lunch. Dynamic waiters juggle the crowd gracefully, serving simple dishes made with fresh-off-the-farm ingredients. Try risotto (€7), made with delectable *pecorino* cheese. (☎52 289. *Primi* €7, *secondi* €9-12. Open M-Sa 12:15-2:45pm. MC/V.) **Ristorante Cesidio ❷**, V. Solimo 25, has been preparing local fare at reasonable prices for 50 years. (☎52 724. *Menù* €15. Open Tu-Su noon-3:30pm and 7-10:30pm. AmEx/MC/V.) The colorful **Osteria Del Tempo Perso ❷**, Vco. del Vecchio 7, offers an impressive selection of vegetarian toppings for their splendid pizzas (€4-7). Heaping plates of *antipasti* (from €6.50) are accompanied by fresh focaccia. (☎52 545. *Primi* from €6, *secondi* from €8. Open M and W-Su 12:30-3pm and 7:30pm-2am. AmEx/MC/V.) With real Neapolitan cooks and a perfect people-watching position, **Pizzeria Ernano ❶**, C. Ovidio, 263, is hailed by locals as the best pizza in town. (☎50 593.

Pizza €3-10. Open daily noon-2:30pm and 7-11:30pm.) A morning **market** occurs in P. Garibaldi (W and Sa). Buy basics at the **CRAI** supermarket on V. Stazione Introdaqua, 10min. outside town on the way to the Pelino factory. (Open M-Tu, Th-F, Su 8:30am-3pm and 4:30-8pm; W and Sa 8:30am-1:30pm. MC/V.)

◎ ⍰ SIGHTS AND ENTERTAINMENT. Sulmona is overflowing with interesting museums, panoramas, hikes, and medieval churches. The Romanesque-Gothic **Cattedrale di San Panfilo** is at the end of the Villa Communale. The cathedral's center was built 1000 years ago on the ruins of a temple dedicated to Apollo and Vesta, and its crypt contains 14th-century frescoes. From the public gardens, follow C. Ovidio to the cherub-decorated **Chiesa della Santissima Annunziata.** Adjacent to the church, a 15th-century Gothic *palazzo* houses the UST tourist office and a very small **museum** presenting rare local Renaissance goldwork. There is also a collection of wooden statues from local churches. (☎21 27 11. Open July-Aug. Tu-F 9am-1pm, Sa-Su 6-8:30pm and 9:30-11pm; Sept.-June Tu-Sa 9am-1pm. €1.) In same building, the **Museo Civico** features intact ruins of an ancient Roman house. (Open Tu-Su 9am-1pm and 3-7pm. Free.) The colossal **Piazza Garibaldi** surrounds the Renaissance **Fontana del Vecchio,** which flows with mountain water channeled from the nearby intact medieval aqueduct. With towering Apennines as its backdrop, P. Garibaldi is a lovely sight and a favorite hangout spot, particularly in the evening. When you feel the *confetti*-induced sugar high start to wear off, replenish your supply of these colored, sugarcoated almonds right from the source: the **Pelino factory,** V. Stazione Introdaqua 55. Turn right after Porta Napoli onto V. Trieste, continue 1km down the hill as it becomes V. Stazione Introdaqua, and enter the Pelino building on the left. The Pelino family has been making *confetti* since 1783 with traditional machinery, some of which is displayed in the free **museum.** The candy's universal appeal is evident in pictures of St. Pio and prior popes munching on religious-themed *confetti*. (☎21 00 47. Open M-Sa 9am-12:15pm and 3-6:30pm.)

The city itself dons medieval garb during the last week of July for the **Giostra Cavalleresca di Sulmona,** a festival in which beacon-bearing knights ride figure-eights around P. Garibaldi. Each knight's crest represents one of the seven *borghi* (neighborhoods) of medieval Sulmona. Purchase a seated ticket (€5-10) from the ticket office (☎340 51 846 26; open daily 10am-12:30pm and 5-8pm) in the Rotunda San Francesco, off P. Garibaldi, or stand on tip-toe in the crowd to watch for free. In preparation for the big event, the *borghi* host public festivals on June weekends. The 1st weekend of August brings another joust, the **Giostra Cavalleresca di Europa,** this time featuring international knights (€3-8).

◪ HIKING. The mountains of **Majella National Park** (also spelled "Maiella") tower over Sulmona. The park's headquarters (☎0871 40 851) are in **Guardiagrele.** From the *centro,* several trails are easily accessible by ARPA bus or on foot. If you decide to take the bus, the Sulmona tourist offices have info on the capricious schedule; keep mid-afternoon service gaps in mind. High on the cliffs, visit the cave retreat of the saintly hermit who became Pope Celestine V, the only pope to renounce his post. It's a fairly easy hike (round-trip 1½hr.) from the town of Badia, which is accessible by bus from Sulmona's public gardens (20min.; 11 per day 7:35am-7:40pm, reduced service Sa-Sun; €1, purchase at *tabaccherie*). Several longer routes can be reached from **Campo di Giove,** accessible by bus from Sulmona (25min.; 4 per day 6:30am-6pm, reduced service Sa-Su; €2.20). For hiking info, consult the UST tourist office and the Club Alpino Italiano (☎0842 10 635) for maps (€5-7). The difficulty levels in the Club Alpino Italiano guide refer to mountaineering experience, not hiking experience—so hikes of "moderate difficulty" may be challenging for those not used to mountain climbing. Take advantage of the buses since the trailheads are difficult to find on foot; ask the driver to let you off directly at the trailhead.

ABRUZZO NATIONAL PARK

As you arrive in Parco Nazionale d'Abruzzo, Lazio, e Molise, it is nearly impossible to tear your eyes away from the beautiful landscape. The highest peaks in the Apennines provide spectacular views of lush woodlands and crystal-clear lakes as frigid as they are pristine. The park's 44,000 hectares of wilderness bristle with wildlife. Grazing wild horses, white *abruzzese* sheep-dog packs, herds of chamois (hooved, goat-like animals with horns), and aloof *marsicano* brown bears are the current proprietors of abandoned castles and pre-Roman ruins. This immaculate refuge is interrupted only by five main towns scattered throughout: Barrea, Civitella Alfedena, Opi, Pescasseroli, and Villetta Barrea. Enter the park from Castel di Sangro in the south, or from Avezzano in the northeast. Pescasseroli, the park's administrative center and largest town, provides the best base for exploration. The other four towns are tiny and uneventful, but beautiful and relaxing, especially Civitella Alfedena. And while the wild creatures and landscapes are diverse, the park's human inhabitants are unified in their unfailing warmth and generosity.

> **BABY, YOU CAN DRIVE MY CAR.** Because ARPA buses falls short of many of the park's sights and quaint villages, and some trailheads are only reachable from the highway, renting a car is certainly worth it. Be extra-sure to pick up the free *Guide to Abruzzo's Hidden Wonders* at the park's tourist office.

TRANSPORTATION AND PRACTICAL INFORMATION

Trains run from Avezzano to Pescara (2-3hr., 7 per day 6:13am-8:10pm, €7), Rome (2hr., 13 per day 4am-8:50pm, €6), and Sulmona (1hr., 10 per day 6:13am-8:10pm, €3.60). An ARPA **bus** (☎0863 26 561 or 0863 22 921) runs from Avezzano through the park to Castel di Sangro on the other side (2¾hr., M-Sa 5 per day 6:40am-4:15pm, €5.20), making five stops en route: Pescasseroli (1½hr., €3.90); Opi (1¾hr., €4.20); Villetta Barrea (2hr., €4.20); Civitella Alfedena (2hr., €4.20); Barrea (2¼hr., €4.40). Buses also run to Pescasseroli from Rome (3hr., 7:45am, one-way €14). All services are reduced or nonexistent on Sunday.

Avezzano mainly functions as a convenient transportation hub to enter the park, due to its proximity to train stations connecting to elsewhere in Italy and to bus stations with service to the park (although the town isn't in the park proper). In Avezzano, a **post office** is to the right of the train station exit. (Open M-F 8am-1:30pm, Sa 8:30am-12:30pm.) **Rt.com Services,** V. Montello 2, offers **Internet** (€3.60 per hr.) and a **Western Union.** (☎0863 93 10 97. Open daily 10am-11pm.)

In Pescasseroli, stop by the **Centro Accoglienza Turistici,** Vico Consultore 1, the park's tourist office, and pick up the essential park map (€6). From the bus stop in P. Antonio, take the first left on V. della Piazza toward town. (☎0863 91 13 242; www.parcoabruzzo.it. Open daily 10am-1pm and 3-7pm.) The **IAT information office,** V. Piave 1, off P. Antonio, provides info on lodgings and restaurants. (☎0863 91 04 61; www.pescasseroli.net. Open daily 9am-1pm and 4-7pm.) In case of **emergency,** call the **police** (☎0863 91 07 16), or **guardia medica** (☎0863 91 06 75). There are free **public toilets** on V. Sorgenti, near the IAT. The **Farmacia del Parco,** P. V. Emanuele 12, stocks everything from aloe to moleskin. (☎0863 91 07 53. Open daily 9am-1pm and 4:30-8pm.) **Punto Internet** is at I Traversa di Fiume Sangro 6. (☎086 391 1064. €2.50 per 30min. Open daily 9:30am-1pm and 4-8pm.) The **post office** is at V. Piave 1/A. (☎086 39 10 731. Open M-F 8am-1:30pm, Sa 8am-noon.) **Postal Code:** 67032.

ACCOMMODATIONS AND FOOD

PESCASSEROLI. Abruzzo National Park's largest and most popular town, tranquil Pescasseroli (PES-ca-SE-ro-lee; pop. 2212) is a friendly and convenient base for

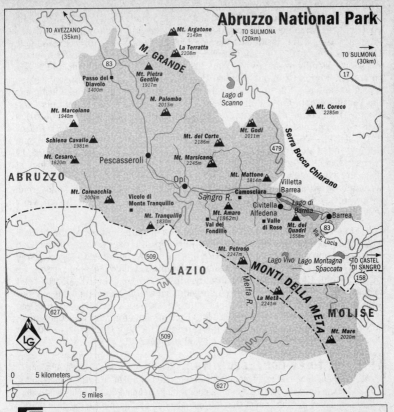

BUS-TED! Not all ARPA buses passing through Abruzzo National Park stop at all 5 towns in the park. All buses stop at Pescasseroli, but if you are trying to reach Opi or Civitella Alfedena, get a schedule from the tourist office in Pescasseroli, and confirm the destination with your driver before boarding the bus.

exploring the rest of the park. Solo travelers may have a hard time finding a single room, since establishments generally only offer doubles, especially in August; bring friends or come ready to camp. Inquire at the IAT office about *affittacamere* (rooms for rent). Run by the welcoming Elena, **▨Di Clemente Elena ❷**, V. Isonzo 2, offers cheerful, blonde-wood rooms with bath, TV, and hand-stitched quilts. (☎0863 91 05 06. Singles €25; doubles €40. Cash only.) A more centrally-located option is **Hotel Pratto Rosso ❷**, V. della Chiesa 12. Recently renovated, this hotel offers 20 elegant, clean rooms with TV, bath, and delightful decorations. (☎0863 91 05 42. €25 per person.) **Hotel Raffaello ❸**, V. Carmelo Sipari 3, offers comfort and elegance. Pink rooms have bath, TV, and minibar. (☎0863 91 28 57. Breakfast included. Singles €40-50; doubles €60-90. AmEx/MC/V.) A fun camping option is **Campeggio dell'Orso ❶**, 1km. from Pescasseroli on the road to Opi. Owned by the friendly, English speaking Geraldo, these quiet, family-oriented grounds—including a house with hostel beds—are a good base for hikes. (☎0863 91 95 or 339 76 43 656. Kitchen included. Bring linen. €8.50 per person, €4 per child ages 5-10. Hostel bed €12. Cash only.) If that is full, walk about 100m to **Camping San Andrea ❶**, a bigger and more crowded site. (☎0863 912 725 or 335 595 6029. €6 per person. 3-person bungalows €55; 4-person €70.)

The town may be small, but it still manages to pack a culinary punch. Don't leave without sampling the assorted sweets produced by the town's many excellent pastry shops. Step inside ☒**La Dolceria dell'Orso ❶**, V. Valle Cicala 5c, to sample a boundless supply of free almond-, chocolate-, and honey-laden morsels from the tiny shop's friendly owner. (☎340 14 34 303. Open M, W, F-Su 9am-1pm and 3-8pm; Tu and Th 3-8pm. Cash only.) Rural Pescasseroli's restaurants close early, so expect to eat early. For traditional fare, head to authentically cave-like **Ristorante Alle Vecchie Arcate ❸**, V. della Chiesa 57 (look for the sign saying only "*ristorante*"). Chefs prepare *abruzzese* specialties like creamy *carrati* (€6.50), a hearty *gnocchi* dish smothered in spinach and cheese. (☎0863 91 07 81. *Primi* €6.50, *secondi* €6-10. Cover €2. Open June-Sept. and Dec.-Apr. Tu-Su noon-3pm and 7:30-10pm. MC/V.) If you can get a table, eat at the delicious **da Giuseppe ❷**, IX Traversa Sangro 6 (☎0863 91 22 05. *Primi* €5-7. Open M-W and F-Su for lunch at 12:30 and 2:30pm; dinner at 7:30 and 9:30pm.) For hiking sustenance, head to the many **alimentari** and produce shops in the *centro*, most of which make fresh *panini* for €3.50. A **supermarket** is at the start of Vle. San Lucia, to the left when walking into the city. (Open daily noon-2pm and 4-8pm.)

CIVITELLA ALFEDENA. Nestled in the ridge of a small mountain, medieval Civitella Alfedena (chee-vee-TEL-la al-feh-DEH-na; pop. 310) overlooks the green Lago di Barrea. Approaching town, the ARPA bus passes the entrance to **Camping Wolf ❶**, with terraced sites and free hot showers. (☎0864 89 03 60. €6 per person, €6 per large tent. Electricity €2. Cash only.) In the *centro storico*, **Albergo "ai 4 camosci" ❷**, V. Nazionale 25, offers gorgeous views of the neighboring ravines from its rooms, which all have spotless bath, TV, and phone. (☎0864 89 02 62. Doubles €46-70; triples €57-84; quads €65-96.) For authentic food, try **Lupo Cerviero ❷**, V. Nazionale 58. *Agnello* (lamb) is the specialty, for only €8. (☎0864 89 01 71. *Primi* €7. Open daily 12:30-2:30pm and 7:30-10:30pm.)

▐ NOT TO BE CONFUSED WITH... Keep in mind that Civitella Alfedena and Alfedena are 2 different locations separated by 10km; likewise, Barrea and Villetta Barrea are also different. Before setting out from Pescasseroli, verify with the bus driver the correct stop for your intended destination. On the drive from Avezzano, Civitella comes before Alfedena, just 10min. after Villetta Barrea.

🕭 HIKING

The ascent from Avezzano to Pescasseroli is breathtaking; this trail, which marks the beginning of the park, passes by fields of poppies, dazzling valleys, and rocky outcrops. The indispensable trail map (€6) from the **Centro Accoglienza Turistici** in Pescasseroli (see **Practical Information**) indicates prime viewing spots for brown bears, deer, wolves, and eagles. This huge park is teeming with wonderful trails, so it's important to bear in mind that even a map can't always save you from getting lost—and certainly don't treat this overview of hikes as a substitute for a map. Be sure to consult professionals who know the area before setting off. Clever coordination of hikes with the ARPA bus schedule can enable hikers to embark from any of the park's major towns. From Pescasseroli, the short trail **BN1** passes castle ruins at **Monte Ceraso** (50min.; moderate difficulty), or the 5hr. round-trip **C3** takes you on a hike of medium-difficulty to the beautiful **Vicolo di Monte Tranquillo** (1673m). From Opi, the 50min. **FN1** trail takes you through the highly-praised **Val del Fon-**

dillo. True adventurers starting from Opi can take on one of the park's highest peaks, **Monte Marsicano** (2245m), with the steep and arduous **E6** trail (7-8hr. round-trip). From Civitella Alfedena, explore the **G** trails, which pass by **Camosciara** (about 1hr.; varying difficulties), or take the **I1** (3hr.; difficult) to **K6** (3hr.; difficult) through the beautiful **Valle di Rose** to see the park's largest herd of *chamois*. K6 is one of the more difficult trails. From June to early September, this area can only be explored with a guide (€7 per person). Go to an *ufficio di zona* the day before a planned excursion for more info about the trails or to obtain a permit and reserve a guide. From Barrea, the **K5** trail runs to the **Lago Vivo** (4hr. round-trip), which dries up between June and October.

If the park's creatures prove elusive, check out Pescasseroli's family-friendly **Centro di Visita,** Vle. Colle dell'Orso 2, off V. S. Lucia, heading toward Opi, which has a museum and a small zoo. (☎0863 91 131. Open daily 10am-1pm and 3-7pm. €6, children €4.) **Ecotur,** V. Piave 7, 2nd fl., in Pescasseroli, offers organized excursions throughout the park, many of which include wildlife viewing. (☎0863 91 27 60; www.ecotur.org. Hikes €10, wolf-watching €20, bear-watching €50. Open daily 9am-1pm and 4-7:30pm. Closed in winter Su.) During winter, this area offers excellent downhill skiing and snowboarding, with challenging slopes and heavy snowfall. Package deals called *Settimane Bianche* (White Weeks) provide accommodations, lift tickets, and half pension. For ticket info, call **Gestione Impianti Sportivi Pescasseroli** (☎0863 91 11 18). For the snow bulletin, call ☎0862 66 510. Pescasseroli's website (www.pescasseroli.net) also has info on winter sports.

PESCARA ☎085

The central transportation hub for Abruzzo and Molise, Pescara (pes-CAH-rah; pop. 122,000) holds little in the way of aesthetic appeal around the city. The beach, however, is a different world, with relaxed sunbathing, clean waters, and fun nightlife. Italian vacationers swarm to this 20km shoreline in July and August but leave its lackluster buildings deserted during the rest of the year. Even so, travelers waiting for a train to an Italian destination or a boat to Croatia can manage to find something worthwhile besides the beach. Museums, restaurants, and a celebrated jazz festival in mid-July offer a high-brow alternative to sunbathing.

TRANSPORTATION AND PRACTICAL INFORMATION. Domestic and international **flights** leave from **Aeroporto d'Abruzzo** (☎43 11 962) on V. Tiburtiria. Bus #38 (€0.70) runs between the train station and the airport. **Trains** run from Stazione Centrale on C. V. Emanuele to: Bari (3½-4hr., 17 per day 1am-8:08pm, €13-28); Lecce (6hr., 12 per day 3am-8:08pm, €19-34); Milan (6½hr., 11 per day 12:44am-11:59pm, €37-43); Naples (5-7hr., 11 per day 3:32am-8:08pm, €16-36); Rome (4hr., 11 per day 6:15am-10:12pm, €11.20); Sulmona (1hr., 18 per day 5:13am-10:12pm, €3.60); Termoli (1½hr., 23 per day 3am-9pm, €4.40). ARPA **buses** run from the train station to L'Aquila, Avezzano, Rome, and Naples via Sulmona on varying schedules. Consult the info booth in front of the train station for departure times. **Ferries** depart from just beyond the harbor in the old city. From June to September, SNAV (☎45 49 089; www.snavoli.it) runs ferries to the Croatian islands of Brac, Hvar, Korcula, and Spalato (one-way €64-84). Jetline (☎45 16 241) runs ferries to the Tremiti Islands (2½hr., 8am, €21).

Buses and trains stop at **Stazione Centrale** on **Corso Vittorio Emanuele,** the main street of the new city *centro.* To the right, C. V. Emanuele extends toward the **River Pescara.** Across the bridge to the right is the tiny old city, and a short walk to the left leads to the harbor. Straight across the bridge is an extensive public park. **Viale**

della Riviera, the main stretch of beach parallel to C. V. Emanuele, is especially lively at night, with of restaurants, bars, and live music. From the train station, take C. Umberto I, which extends from the train station to the main square, **Piazza della Rinascita.** The staff at the **APT tourist office,** C. V. Emanuele 301 provides maps and advice on accommodations, museums, hiking, and restaurants. (☎42 90 01; www.abruzzoturismo.it. Open M-Sa 8:30am-1:30pm and 4-8pm, Su 8:30am-1:30pm.) Find the **police** at P. Duca d'Aosta. The **hospital** is at V. Fonte Romana 8 (☎42 51). The **post office** is at C. V. Emanuele 106, between the station and the river. (☎27 541. Open M-Sa 8am-6:30pm.) **Postal Code:** 65100.

⌂▯ ACCOMMODATIONS AND FOOD. There's no cheap lodging in Pescara, and most hotels have similar prices and amenities. Staying around the beach will give you easy access to restaurants and nightlife. A good option is **Hotel Lido ❸,** Lungomare Matteoti 83, a clean hotel with a helpful owner and quick access to the beach. (☎27 084. Singles €35-45; doubles €70-80.) **Hotel Alba ❹,** V. Michelangelo Forti 14, near the station, has lavish rooms, all with bath, A/C, satellite TV, and phone. (☎38 91 45; www.hotelalba.pescara.it. Breakfast, Internet, and laundry included. June-Aug. singles €60-65; doubles €85-100; triples €105-120; quads €120-145. Oct.-May €55/80/100/115. AmEx/MC/V.) **Hotel Adria ❸,** V. Firenze 141, is a pleasant option; turn right on the street parallel to C. V. Emanuele, one block toward the waterfront. Twenty-four modestly sized rooms come with fridge, bath, and TV. (☎42 24 246. Singles €40; doubles €70. MC/V.)

Pescara's food is generally either from the sea or from a traditional *abruzzese* recipe. Local wines, including the white *Trebbiano* and red *Montepulciano,* satisfy broad tastes. On summer weekends, reservations for beach-side restaurants are essential. Excellent seafood is typically featured on the daily selections at ▮Wine and Wine ❷, V. Chieti 14, off C. V. Emanuele just before the river. This very welcoming family-run *enoteca* invites guests to dine surrounded by racks of wine bottles. There is never a menu, only what is freshest from the market. (☎42 23 180. Open daily 10am-10pm. AmEx/MC/V.) For cheap grub, grab a delicious *pizzetta* (small pizza) for €1.20 at **Zara's ❶,** on Lungomare Matteotti. Pass by late at night to enjoy free live music. (Open daily 9am-midnight.) For good seafood, try the elegant **La Sirenetta ❸,** Lungomare Matteotti 114, but be prepared to pay about €15-20 for your dish of fish. (☎42 16 490. Open daily noon-2:30pm and 7:30pm-12:30am.) **Jambo ❸,** Vle. Rivera 38, features elegant patio dining, a colorful bar, and an excellent waitstaff. The *gnocchi agli scampi* (€9) has seafood fans rejoicing. (☎42 12 79 49. Open daily noon-3am. AmEx/MC/V.) For picnic supplies, head to **Tigre** supermarket at V. Nicola Fabrizi 59. From the train station, follow C. Umberto and turn right at the *piazza.* (☎42 16 896. Open M-Sa 8:15am-8:30pm, Su 9am-1pm. MC/V.)

◪▯ SIGHTS AND ENTERTAINMENT. All the attractions of a seaside resort and shoreline town crowd Pescara's vibrant **beach:** basketball, soccer, volleyball, music, windsurfing, and sunbathing. Bikers and joggers make use of miles of boardwalk next to the beach. Laziness, meanwhile, comes at a cost: about €5-7 to sunbathe, depending on the location. A paltry public stretch is 5min. left of P. Primo Maggio when facing the sea. Pescara's cultural area, with its pleasant harbor and a few decent museums, sits across the bridge; take the 1st right to reach **Museo delle Genti d'Abruzzo,** V. delle Caserme 24, which celebrates 4000 years of Abruzzo history. Chronological galleries show the development of local crafts from the Paleolithic era to the present. (☎45 10 026. Open July-Aug. M-F 9am-1pm, Tu-Su 7-11pm. Sept.-June M-Sa 9am-1pm; Tu, Th, Su 4-7pm. €5, EU students and citizens under 18 or over 65 €2.) Straight across the bridge, the **Museo Civico "Cascella,"** Vle. Marconi 53, showcases artwork by six members of the influential Cascella family. (☎42 83 515. Open Tu and Th-Su 9am-1pm, Tu and Th also 4-6pm. €2.50, EU citizens ages 18-24 €1.50, EU citizens under 18 or over 65 free.)

To get the latest scoop on the always-pumping nightlife scene, pick up the monthly brochure *Giorno e Notte* at restaurants and stores around the city. To party beach-side, join the hordes of people packed into **Hai Bin,** Vle. della Riviera 44, for the cheap beer. (☎421 3042. Open daily 8pm-midnight.) If you're willing to spend €15 for an amazing night with good-looking people and a live DJ, try **Nettuno,** Vle. della Riviera 30. (☎42 21 542; www.nettunobeach.com. Open Th-Sa 8pm-3am.) Pescara hosts a world-renowned **jazz festival** (☎02 92 20; www.pescarajazz.com) every year in mid-July, attracting Italian and international acts. (Tickets from €10.) The popular annual **film festival,** also in July, screens both Italian and international films in several of Pescara's cinemas. Contact the APT tourist office for more info. (Tickets from €10.)

TERMOLI   ☎0875

Despite its pristine coastline and attractive old city jutting out over turquoise waters, Termoli (TER-mo-lee; pop. 30,000) is less visited than other coastal towns. Though some come for a holiday at one of the many beachside resorts, most travelers—likely deterred by the high cost of spending a night—stop over only briefly before an early ferry to the Tremiti Islands. If you choose to stay, leave the beach long enough to see the **duomo** and the **Castello Svevo,** built in 1247 by Frederico II.

Travelers who do decide to stay the night will find a simple, modern option right by the beach at **Modena ❸,** V. Vespucci. Enjoy great sunsets away from the city's hustle and bustle. (☎70 64 24. Singles €30-40; doubles €50-70.) Also by the beach, but closer to the center of town, **Villa Ida ❸,** V. Mario Milano 27, offers spacious, well-lit, comfortable rooms with A/C, phone, TV, and bath. (☎70 66 66. Breakfast included. Single €37-42; doubles €52-62; triples €70-83.) Dining options in Termoli are varied and spread out. Restaurants and shops dot **Corso Umberto I** from the station to the old town. The city center offers a variety of options. From the train station, follow C. Umberto I, turn left on C. Nazionale, right on V. Alfano, then left on V. Ruffini to find **Anema e Cuore ❶,** V. Ruffini 56/60. The restaurant offers a wide selection of pizzas (€3-7) to be eaten under canopied outdoor seating. (☎71 47 72. Cover €1.50. *Primi* €5-7, *secondi* from €7. Open M-W and F-Su noon-2:30pm and 7:30-11pm. MC/V.) Next door, **La Sacrestia ❶,** V. Ruffini 48, offers similar fare at a similar cost (☎70 56 03). For groceries, go to **Sisa Supermercato Limongi,** V. Adriatica 5, just off V. M. Milano. (☎70 72 53. Open M-Sa 7:30am-1:45pm and 5-9pm, Su 8:30am-1:30pm. MC/V.)

The **train station** lies at the western end of town. **Trains** run to: Bari (14 per day 4:01am-9:04pm, €13-21); Milan (11 per day 2:27am-12:06am, €40); Naples (11:24am, €12.34); Pescara (22 per day 12:06am-11:55pm, €4.40-10); Rome (2 per day 6:52am-5:46pm, €18-35). Across the street, **Via Mario Milano** extends to **Lungomare Colombo,** a waterfront strip lined with hotels. A right onto this street leads to the **port;** ferry docks and ticket offices are on the breakwater past the fishing boats. Larivera Lines (☎82 248) leave from the port to the Croatian islands. For a **taxi,** call (☎77 03 296). The **AAST tourist office,** at the back of P. Bega, offers maps, directories, and brochures about Termoli's lesser-known attractions. From the station, turn right on C. Umberto I. At the galleria, walk through the underpass and to the right to the back of the building. Buzz the office, then take stairway A to the 2nd floor. Ring again to enter office. (☎70 39 13; aasttermoli@virgilio.it. Open M and W 8am-2pm and 3-6:30pm; Tu, and Th-F 8am-2pm and 4:50-6:30pm; Sa 8am-1:10pm.) In case of **emergency,** dial ☎71 591, the **carabinieri** (☎70 63 40), or **police** (☎57 15 51). For a nearby **pharmacy** contact (☎70 32 33). For **Internet** access, try **Digipl@net,** V. M. Milano 24. (☎71 44 36. €3 per hr.

Open M-F and Su 10am-1pm and 4:30-9pm.) The **post office** at V. M. Milano 7 has an **ATM.** (Open M-F 9am-6:30pm, Su 9am-1:30pm.) **Postal Code:** 86039.

◪ DAYTRIP FROM TERMOLI

THE TREMITI ISLANDS

Ferry service from Termoli, operating June-Sept., is slower but cheaper than hydrofoils. Navigazione Libera (☎70 48 59; www.navlib.it.) runs ferries (1½hr.; departs 9:15am, returns 5pm; €11) and hydrofoils (50min.; departs 8:40, 10:45am, 5:30pm, returns 9:45am, 4:20, 6:45pm; €17). Ferries dock on San Nicola, forcing passengers to take small motorboats across the water to the dock at San Domino (2min., €2.50). Only the hydrofoils dock directly at San Domino.

Covered with lush vegetation, rich in natural resources, and surrounded by crystalline azure waters, the four Isole Tremiti (EE-so-leh TRE-mee-tee; pop. 370) are a relatively well-kept secret. Just 35km from the Gargano Peninsula on the mainland, Puglia's Isole Tremiti make for a relaxing daytrip. **San Domino,** the largest island in the archipelago, is dubbed the "Green Pearl of the Adriatic" because of its rich flora. Its neighbor, **San Nicola,** the only island populated year-round, was most famously home to Emperor Augustus's daughter, Julia, who was exiled there in the AD first century for her adulterous behavior. Though its monastery makes it the most historical island, San Nicola has little else to offer. The last two, **Caprara** and **Cretaccio,** are small and desolate, hospitable only to seagulls. Scuba divers (see below) around Caprara will encounter a massive underwater statue of St. Pio.

San Domino has a small but excellent ◪**free beach** with azure waters and white sand immediately to the left of the port. Entrance is free, so don't feel forced to give in to **Il Pirata,** a beachside restaurant and bar, which offers umbrellas (€5) and beach chairs (€5). Hiking paths snake through the thick **pine forest;** the main trail (#1) circles the entire island in approximately 45min. Many lead down to the small, rocky coves along the coast, where vacationers sometimes swim in sapphire waters sans suits. If you join them, be mindful of sea urchins, slippery rocks, and jellyfish. The **Marlin Club,** up the hill and to the left in San Domino Villagio (☎0882 46 37 65; www.marlintremiti.it), in the back of the Hotel Eden complex, offers **scuba diving instruction** at all experience levels. (1 dive with equipment and guide €70. 1 wk. of lessons €300. Open daily 8:30am-8:30pm.) **M.G.M.** (☎368 70 00 341), in a kiosk in San Domino's port, offers glass-bottom boat tours of the archipelago's natural caves, one including all the islands for €15, and another covering only San Nicola and San Domino for €10.

Food on the island is expensive, so consider getting an excellent *panino* (€3) or pizza slice (€1.50) at **Rossana ❶,** right by the port. (☎088 246 3298. Open daily 8am-3pm.) Otherwise, try **Ristorante Al Faro ❸,** V. Aldo Moro 22, in San Domino, which serves a short but excellent menu of local seafood dishes. (☎339 22 11 771. *Primi* €6-8, *secondi* €10-14. Open daily 8-10:30pm. MC/V.) If not, try the always-busy **Ristorante Bel Mare ❷,** San Domino Marina 1, on San Domino's beach to the left of the port, where customers choose their favorite seafood and pasta dishes from a large self-service counter. (☎339 68 74 457. *Primi* €7, *secondi* €7-8. Open daily June-Sept. 12:30-4pm. Cash only.) The cheapest food option, though, is the **Mini-Market** by San Domino's town center. Choose some picnic food and sit down by any of the various wooded areas around the island. (☎088 246 3220. Open daily 9am-1:30pm and 4-9pm.)

For tourist info, visit the Termoli **AAST office** (p. 554). There's an **ATM** right behind the pharmacy. A **first aid station,** V. Federico II, can be found at the San Domino port—it's the 2nd building on the left when heading uphill on the main road. (☎0882 46 32 34. Open in summer daily 8am-8pm.) A **pharmacy,** V. Garibaldi 23, is in San Domino. (☎0882 46 33 27. Open daily June-Sept. 9am-1pm and 5-8pm; Oct.-May 9:30am-12:30pm and 5-7:30pm.)

CAMPANIA

Campania (cam-PAH-nee-ah) is a land of contrasts. A chaotic, modern city, a wealth of remarkably preserved Roman ruins, and a coastline of peaceful villages all call the region home. The beautiful *centro storico* in Naples draws visitors to the area, and the nearby islands' emerald waters embrace them when the city's frenetic disorder gets overwhelming. Nearby, the preserved ancient cities of Pompeii and Herculaneum attest to the destructive power of Mt. Vesuvius, which remains a constant threat. The region—one of Italy's poorest—has survived natural disasters and years of foreign invasions, but the people of Campania have somehow cultivated and sustained a unique, carefree attitude—the region's true treasure.

HIGHLIGHTS OF CAMPANIA

DESCEND underneath the city of Naples to tour **catacombs** and **aqueducts** (p. 567).

PEER into the crater of **Mt. Vesuvius**, mainland Europe's only active volcano (p. 577).

RECOVER from all your ailments at Ischia's therapeutic **hot springs** (p. 588).

SIP a *granita* or *limoncello* in the shade of Amalfi's **lemon groves** (p. 603).

NAPLES (NAPOLI)   ☎081

From zipping Vespas to bustling crowds, Naples (in Italian, "NA-po-lee"; pop. 1,000,000) lives life in the fast lane. Neapolitans spend every waking moment out on the town, eating, drinking, shouting, and laughing. Surrounded by the ancient ruins of Pompeii and the gorgeous Amalfi Coast, Naples—Italy's 3rd largest city—is the anchor of Campania. Though the city has a reputation for crime and grime, UNESCO recently declared its historical center the most architecturally varied in the world. As the birthplace of pizza and the modern-day home of tantalizing seafood and pasta, Naples is also home to world-renowned culinary delights. Whereas Milan flaunts sophistication and Venice emanates mystique, Naples wallows in cheerful chaos. It is a city that demands constant activity, doesn't tolerate ambivalence, and has its own personality—you either can't stand it or can't get enough.

✈ INTERCITY TRANSPORTATION

Flights: Aeroporto Capodichino (NAP), V. Umberto Maddalena (☎848 88 87 77, info line 78 96 259; www.gesac.it), northeast of the city. The convenient white **Alibus** travels between the port near P. Municipio, Stazione Centrale, and the airport (15-20min., 6:30am-11:30pm, €3). The **3S** city bus runs from P. Garibaldi to the airport (€1). Buy tickets at any newsstand or *tabaccheria*. Although cheaper than the Alibus, the city bus makes many more stops and is a target for pickpockets. **Taxis** run to and from the airport for €19 (see p. 561). **Alitalia** (☎848 865 643), **British Airways** (☎199 71 22 66), **Lufthansa** (☎199 40 00 44), and **Easy Jet** (☎848 88 77 66) all fly from Naples.

Trains: Naples is served by 3 train companies from **Stazione Centrale** (www.napolipiazzagaribaldi.it) in P. Garibaldi. Unsafe luggage storage available.

Circumvesuviana: (☎800 05 39 39; www.vesuviana.it.) To **Herculaneum** (€1.70), **Pompeii** (€2.30), and **Sorrento** (€3.20). Trains depart every 30min. 5:09am-10:42pm.

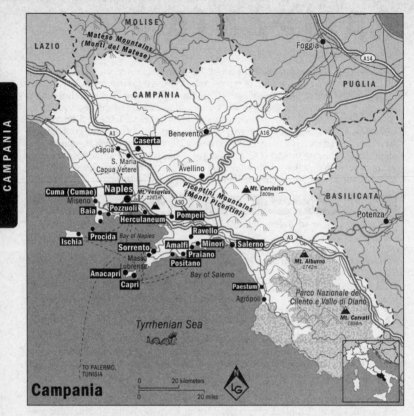

Campania

Ferrovia Cumana and **Ferrovia Circumflegrea:** (☎800 00 16 16; www.sepsa.it.) Luggage storage available. Trains from Montesanto station to **Cumae** and **Puzzuoli.** Trains depart every 20min. Info booth in Stazione Centrale open daily 7am-9pm.

Trenitalia: (☎56 72 430; www.trenitalia.it.) Ticket office open daily 6:10am-9:40pm. To: **Milan** (9hr., 13 per day 4:30am-10:30pm, €50); **Rome** (2hr., 40 per day 4:30am-10pm, €11); **Salerno** (45min., 37per day 4:50am-10:30pm, €3); **Syracuse** (10hr., 6 per day 8am-10pm, €57).

Ferries: The daily newspaper *Il Mattino* (€0.90) carries up-to-date ferry schedules, which change slightly every few months. Port taxes may apply. Hydrofoils depart from **Mergellina, Molo Beverello,** and **Pozzuoli,** and ferries from **Stazione Marittima** (on **Molo Angioino**) and **Molo Beverello.** Molo Angioino is for longer trips to **Sicily** and **Sardinia.** Molo Beverello is at the base of P. Municipio. Take the R2, 152, 3S, or Alibus from P. Garibaldi to P. Municipio.

Alilauro: (☎76 11 004 or 49 72 222.) Ticket office at Molo Angioino. Depart from Molo Beverello. Open daily 9am-7pm. Ferries to **Ischia** (8 per day 7:35am-8pm, €10-20).

Caremar: (☎19 91 23 199.) Ticket office on Molo Beverello. Open daily 6am-10pm. Ferries and hydrofoils to **Capri** (ferry 1½hr., 3 per day 7:35am-6:40pm, €4.80; hydrofoil 1hr., 4 per day 5:40am-9:10pm, €9.60), **Ischia** (ferry 1½hr., 8 per day 6:25am-9:55pm, €4.80; hydrofoil 1hr., 5 per day 7:50am-6:55pm, €9.60), and **Procida** (ferry 1hr., 5 per day 6:25am-7:20pm, €4.80; hydrofoil 40min., 5 per day 7:40am-5:55pm, €7.90).

Metro del Mare: (☎19 96 007 00; www.metrodelmare.com.) Ticket office at Molo Beverello and Mergellina. 3 Lines run between Bacoli and Salerno (€11.50), Bacoli and Sorrento (€6), and Monte di Procida and Salerno (€11.50). Lines stop at Pozzuoli, Napoli Mergellina, Napoli Bever-

CAMPANIA

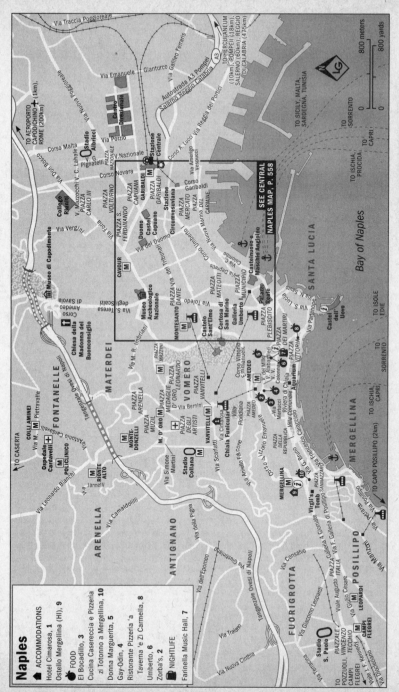

Naples

▲ ACCOMMODATIONS
Hotel Cimarosa, **1**
Ostello Mergellina (HI), **9**

🍴 FOOD
El Bocadillo, **3**
Cucina Casereccia e Pizzeria
zi Totonno a Mergellina, **10**
Donna Marguerita, **5**
Gay-Odin, **4**
Ristorante Pizzeria 'a
Taverna 'e Zi Carmella, **8**
Umberto, **6**
Zorba's, **2**

🎵 NIGHTLIFE
Farinella Music Hall, **7**

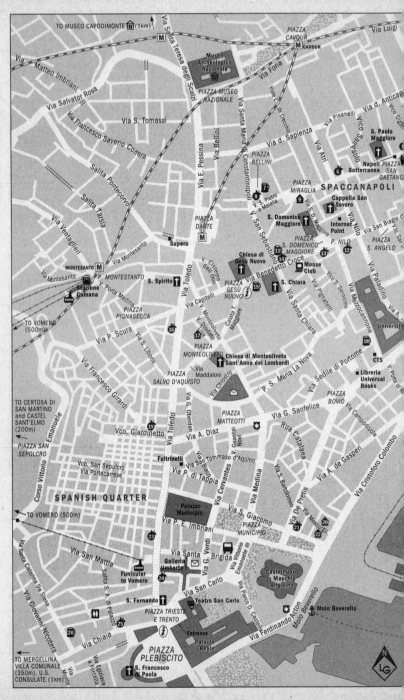

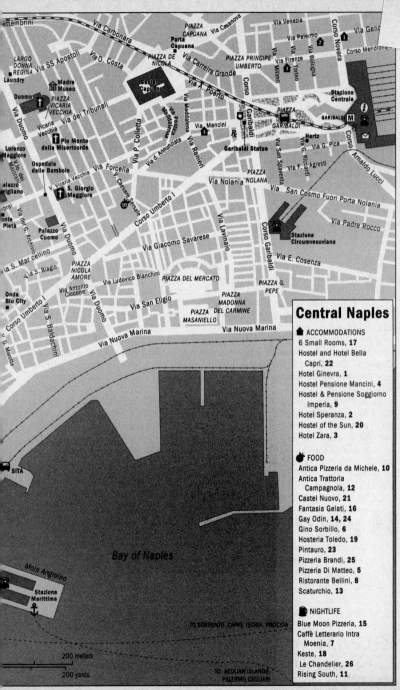

Central Naples

🏠 ACCOMMODATIONS

6 Small Rooms, **17**
Hostel and Hotel Bella
  Capri, **22**
Hotel Ginevra, **1**
Hostel Pensione Mancini, **4**
Hostel & Pensione Soggiorno
  Imperia, **9**
Hotel Speranza, **2**
Hostel of the Sun, **20**
Hotel Zara, **3**

🍅 FOOD

Antica Pizzeria da Michele, **10**
Antica Trattoria
  Campagnola, **12**
Castel Nuovo, **21**
Fantasia Gelati, **16**
Gay Odin, **14, 24**
Gino Sorbillo, **6**
Hosteria Toledo, **19**
Pintauro, **23**
Pizzeria Brandi, **25**
Pizzeria Di Matteo, **5**
Ristorante Bellini, **8**
Scaturchio, **13**

🎵 NIGHTLIFE

Blue Moon Pizzeria, **15**
Caffè Letterario Intra
  Moenia, **7**
Keste, **18**
Le Chandelier, **26**
Rising South, **11**

ello, Portici, Ercolano, Torre del Greco, Torre A. Pompeii, Castellammare di Stabia, Seiano, Sorrento, Capri, Positano, and Amalfi in between.

SNAV: (☎76 12 348.) Open daily 9am-7pm. Hydrofoils Apr.-Oct. go to **Capri** (1hr., 6 per day 7:10am-6:10pm, €10), **Ischia-Casamicciola Terme** (1hr., 4 per day 8:20am-6:45pm, €10), and **Procida** (40min., 4 per day 8:20am-6:40pm, €10). Ferries go to **Palermo** (10hr., 8pm, €27) from Stazione Marittima.

Siremar: (☎58 00 340.) Ticket office at Molo Angioino. Open daily 9am-7pm. Depart from Stazione Marittima. 2 ferries per week in summer, 3 in winter. To: **Lipari** (12hr.); **Stromboli** (8hr.); **Vulcano** (13hr.). Prices vary.

Tirrenia: (☎19 91 23 199.) Ticket office at Molo Angioino. Open daily 8:30am-1:15pm and 2:30-5:30pm. Ferries to **Cagliari** (16hr.; depart weekly, bi-weekly in summer) and **Palermo** (11hr., depart daily). Required supplemental port tax. Schedules and prices vary.

> ❗ **STREET SMARTS.** When crossing busy streets in Naples, keep in mind that if you make eye contact with the driver of an oncoming vehicle, it is assumed that you will stop and wait for the car to pass.

◧ ORIENTATION

Naples is a varied city, where chaotic modern grime rubs shoulders with historical architectural gems. To the east, the area around **Stazione Centrale** is dangerous; beware of pickpockets and exercise extra caution at night. From **Piazza Garibaldi** (right outside the station), take a left on C. Garibaldi and walk until it ends at the water in P. Guglielmo Pepe. With the water on your left, V. Nuova Marina turns into V. Cristoforo Colombo and later V. Ferdinando Acton, which leads to **Piazza Plebiscito,** the historical and social center of Naples. From here, turn away from the water onto **Via Toledo,** the town's main shop- and restaurant-lined drag. This street passes through the chaotic **Spanish Quarter** on its way to **Piazza Dante** and **Piazza Salvo D'Aquisto** (also known as **Piazza Carità**), which lie on the western extreme of the historic district, **centro storico (Spaccanapoli).** A right off V. Toledo on V. Maddaloni (which later becomes V. Capitelli, V. Benedetto Croce, and V. San Biagio dei Librai) leads through the central *piazze* of the historical district, **Piazza Gesù Nuovo** and **Piazza San Domenico Maggiore.** Lots of cool, unique places to eat and hang out are found around the university in **Piazza Ruggero Bonghi.** A short funicular ride from V. Toledo will take you to the **Vomero** district, away from the chaos of central Naples. Returning back down V. Toledo to P. Plebiscito, turn right at the water to reach little upscale restaurants and shops tucked away on tiny side streets off **Riviera di Chiaia** in the **Chiaia** district. The nearby **Piazza dei Martiri** offers a good nightlife area. The beautiful and relaxed waterfront **Mergellina** district is accessible by foot along V. Caracciolo or by Metro line #2. Even farther west, the area of Posillipo is also pleasant.

> ❗ **NAPLES'S NOTORIETY.** Although violent crime is rare in Naples, theft is not. For the love of San Gennaro, be smart: don't carry money in wallets or purses, don't wear flashy jewelry or flaunt a camera, and hold onto your bags, especially on buses. Be wary of "scooter robberies," where Vespas speed up behind you and grab your goods before you even realize what hit you. When choosing accommodations, always ask to see a room before paying; never stay anywhere that feels unsafe. At night, avoid the areas around Stazione Centrale and the Spanish Quarter. Women should not make eye contact with strangers and should avoid traveling alone.

▤ LOCAL TRANSPORTATION

One "UnicoNapoli" (☎55 13 109; www.napolipass.it) ticket is valid for all modes of transportation in Naples: **bus, metro, train,** and **funicular.** Tickets are available at *tabac-*

cherie in three types: 1½hr. (€1), full day (€3), and weekend (€2.50). The buses and metro stop running around midnight, and the *notturno* (nighttime) buses are unreliable and unsafe. Transportation around the environs of Naples includes the **Metro del Mare** (**Intercity Transportation,** p. 555), the **Circumvesuviana** train to the areas around Mt. Vesuvius and the **metro** to Pozzuoli. All buses and trains in Campania are on the **Unico-Campania** system (www.unicocampania.it). Ticket costs depend upon the *fascia* (zone) of your destination (€1-5). Purchase them at any *tabaccheria*. The daily newspaper, *Il Mattino*, is the best source for constantly changing schedules.

Public Transportation:

Buses: The public buses are orange. All stops have signs indicating routes and destinations. **R1** travels from P. Bovio to Vomero (P. Medaglie d'Oro), and **R2** runs from P. Garibaldi to P. Municipio. **3S** connects the 3 stations: the airport, Stazione Centrale in P. Garibaldi, and Molo Beverello, where boats leave for the islands in the Bay of Naples and more distant destinations.

Metro: (Info ☎800 56 89 866; www.metro.na.it.) To cover long distances (e.g., from the train station to P. Cavour, Montesanto, P. Amedeo, or Mergellina), use the efficient metro that runs west to Pozzuoli from P. Garibaldi. Go to platform #4, 1 fl. underground at Stazione Centrale. Line #1 stops at **Piazza Cavour** (Museo Nazionale), **Montesanto** (Cumana, Circumflegrea, funicular to Vomero), **Piazza Amedeo** (funicular to Vomero), **Mergellina,** and **Pozzuoli.** Transfer at P. Cavour for line #2. For Procida or Ischia, take the Metro to Pozzuoli.

Funiculars: (Info: ☎800 56 89 866; www.metro.na.it.) 3 connect the lower city to Vomero: **Centrale,** most frequently used, runs from V. Toledo to P. Fuga; **Montesanto** from P. Montesanto to V. Morghen; **Chiaia** from V. del Parco Margherita to C. Cimarosa. Centrale and Chiaia make intermittent stops at C. V. Emanuele. A 4th, **Mergellina,** connects Posillipo to Mergellina. M-Sa 4 per hr. 7am-10pm, Su reduced service 8am-7pm.

Taxis: Consortaxi: ☎55 25 252. **Radio:** ☎55 15 151. **Napoli:** ☎55 64 444. **Partenope:** ☎55 60 202. Only take official taxis with meters, and inquire about prices up front; even well-known companies have been known to charge suspiciously high rates. For all taxis, the meter starts at €2.60; each additional 70m costs €0.05. There is also a €0.50-1 surcharge for luggage. Service to and from the airport is set at €19.

Car Rental: Additional 12% tax on cars rented at the airport. **Avis** (☎75 16 052; www.avisautonoleggio.it), in the airport. Open M-F 8am-7:30pm, Sa 8:30am-1pm and 4-6pm, Su 9am-1pm. AmEx/MC/V. **Hertz,** V. Ricciardi 5 (☎20 62 28 or 199 91 12 211). Another office by the airport at V. Scarfoglio 1 (☎78 02 971). Open M-F 8am-1pm and 2-7pm, Sa 8am-noon. AmEx/MC/V. **Maggiore** (☎84 88 67 067; www.maggiore.it), in Stazione Centrale. Open M-F 8am-1pm and 3-7pm, Sa 8:30am-1:30pm. AmEx/MC/V.

⁊ PRACTICAL INFORMATION

TOURIST AND FINANCIAL SERVICES

Tourist Office: EPT, P. dei Martiri 58 (☎41 07 211; www.eptnapoli.info). Offers booking services, free maps, and the indispensable ✉**Qui Napoli,** a bimonthly tourist publication full of schedules, events, and listings. Make sure to ask for *Zero 81,* which lists all cultural, musical, and artistic events happening every night in the city. English spoken. Open M-F 9am-2pm. **Branches:** Stazione Centrale (☎26 87 79). This office is very busy; go elsewhere for better service. Open M-Sa 9am-7pm, Su 9am-1pm. Stazione Mergellina (☎76 12 102). Open M-Sa 9am-7pm. **AASCT** (☎25 25 711; www.inaples.it) at Palazzo Reale in P. Plebiscito, offers friendly info on accommodations and sights. English spoken. Open M-F 9am-3pm. **Branch:** P. Gesù Nuovo (☎551 27 01). Open M-Sa 9:30am-1:30pm and 2:30-6:30pm.

Budget Travel: CTS, V. Mezzocannone 25 (☎55 27 960; www.cts.it), off C. Umberto on the R2 line. Student travel info, ISIC and FIYTO cards, and booking services. Open M-F 9:30am-1:30pm and 2:30-6pm, Sa 9:30am-12:30pm. **Branch:** V. Cinthia 36 (☎76 77 877.) Open M-F 9:30am-1pm and 4-7pm, Sa 9:30am-1pm. Closed Oct.-Apr. Sa. **Italian Youth Hostel Organization** (☎76 12 346) supplies HI cards (€15). Open M-F 9am-1pm and 3-6pm.

Consulates: Canada, V. Carducci 29 (☎40 13 38). Open M-F 9am-1pm. **UK,** V. dei Mille 40 (☎42 38 911). Open in summer M-F 9am-12:30pm and 2-4pm. **US,** P. della Repubblica 2 (☎58 38 111, 24hr. emergency 033 79 45 083), at the western end of Villa Comunale. Open M-F 8am-1pm and 2-5pm.

Currency Exchange: Stazione Centrale has expensive 24hr. currency exchange. Smaller offices along C. Umberto I charge more reasonable fees, as do the banks along V. Toledo and in P. Municipio and P. Garibaldi. Decent rates at **Thomas Cook** in the airport. Open M-F 9:30am-1pm and 3-7pm. **Branch:** P. Municipio 70 (☎55 18 399).

> ▼ **LUG YOUR LUGGAGE.** The luggage store in Stazione Centrale is extremely unsafe; bring your luggage to your hostel locker or keep it with you!

LOCAL SERVICES

English-Language Bookstores: The university area around V. Mezzocannone teems with bookstores. **Feltrinelli,** V. San Tommaso d'Aquino 70/76 (☎55 21 436; www.lafeltrinelli.it), just north of the Municipio. Open M-F 9am-8pm, Sa 9am-2pm and 4-8:30pm. AmEx/MC/V. **Libreria Universal Books,** C. Umberto I 22 (☎25 20 069; unibooks@tin.it), in a *palazzo* off C. Umberto I by P. Bovio. Open daily 8:30am-1pm and 4-7pm. MC/V.

Laundromats: Onda Blu City, V. M. Zannotti 11/B, off C. Umberto I. Wash and dry from €7. **Internet** €1 per 30min. Open daily 8am-8pm. Cash only.

EMERGENCY AND COMMUNICATIONS

Police: ☎794 11 11. **Ambulance:** ☎75 28 282 or 75 20 696.

Tourist Police: Ufficio Stranieri, V. G. Ferrairis 131 (☎60 64 111), near Stazione Centrale. Helps tourist victims of crime and assists with passport problems.

Pharmacy: ☎26 88 81, at Stazione Centrale by Trenitalia ticket windows. Open 24hr., with a few exceptions on Su and holidays. **Farmacia Helvethia,** P. Garibaldi 111 (☎55 43 164; fax 081 554 19 20), across from station, is closed only 1-4pm daily.

Hospital: Cardarelli (☎74 72 859/848), north of town on R4 or OF bus line, or take the metro from P. Dante.

Internet Access: Available at **Onda Blu City** (see **Laundromats**). Internet places cluster around V. Mezzocannone. **Mouseclub,** V. Pignatelli 45 (☎55 10 763; www.mouseclub.it). Take V. Toledo from P. Municipio. Turn right at V. Capitelli. V. Pignatelli is the 2nd right after P. Gesù Nuovo. Bar, lounge, and Internet cafe. €1.50 per hr. Open daily 10am-6pm. **Internet Point,** V. de Sanctis 27, 20m from the Cappella San Severo. €2 per hr., 1hr. free after 10hr. Open daily 9am-9pm.

Post Office: ☎55 24 233. In P. Matteotti, at V. Diaz. Take the R2 line, a view into true Neapolitan life like nothing else. Also in Galleria Umberto I (☎55 23 467) and outside Stazione Centrale. Notoriously unreliable *fermoposta*. Open M-F 8:15am-6pm, Sa 8:15am-noon. **Postal Code:** 80100.

◪ ACCOMMODATIONS

Hotels litter the hectic and seedy area around **Stazione Centrale.** Don't trust anyone who approaches you in the station—people working on commission are happy to lead naïve foreigners to unlicensed, overpriced hotels. Stazione Centrale has several comfortable and inexpensive options that are quiet despite their bustling surroundings, but be especially careful when returning to them at night. The **centro** storico and **Piazza Plebiscito** areas are more expensive but also more relaxed. **Vomero,** albeit farther from the sights, provides views and tranquility. **Mergellina,** even farther from the hub, is even calmer. Be cautious when selecting a place to stay, and if possible, make reservations in advance. Don't surrender documents or passports before seeing a room, always agree on the price in writing before unpacking, and look for an intercom system or night attendants. Keep in mind that rooms with views of the city are rarely insulated from the noisy streets below. The tourist office distributes a helpful pamphlet of accommodations. For camping, check out nearby **Pozzuoli** (p. 578) and other small towns on the Bay of Naples.

STAZIONE CENTRALE

▨ **Hostel Pensione Mancini,** V. P. San Mancini 33, 2nd fl. (☎55 36 731; www.hostelpensionemancini.com), off far end of P. Garibaldi, 5min. walk to station. Friendly owners share their extensive knowledge of Naples. Clean and spacious rooms. New common room and kitchen. English spoken. Breakfast included. Free luggage storage, lockers, and Internet access. Reception 24hr. Check-in and check-out noon. Reservations suggested 1wk. in advance. Dorms €20; singles €35, with bath €45; doubles €55/60; triples €75/80; quads €90/100. 10% *Let's Go* discount. Cash only. ❷

Hotel Zara, V. Firenze 81 (☎28 71 25; www.hotelzara.it). Spacious, renovated rooms, all with TV, A/C, and bath; some with Internet access and radio. Breakfast €4. Internet €4 per hr. Reservations recommended. Singles €35; doubles €45, with bath €65; triples €75; quads €100. 5% *Let's Go* discount. AmEx/MC/V. ❸

Hotel Ginevra, V. Genova 116, 2nd fl. (☎/fax 28 32 10; www.hotelginevra.it). Exit P. Garibaldi on C. Novara, turn right on V. Genova. Short walk from the train station, good for late-night arrivals. Clean, comfortable, and family-run. Owners can reserve private tours of Naples for guests. English spoken. Internet €4 per hr. Reservations recommended. Singles €35, with bath €55; doubles €55/65; "superior" doubles, with minibar, safe, bath, TV, and A/C €80; triples €100. 10% *Let's Go* discount. AmEx/MC/V. ❸

Hotel Speranza, V. Palermo, 30/31 (☎26 92 86) by P. Garibaldi. Spacious rooms with city views, TV, phone, A/C, and bath. Breakfast included. Singles €40; doubles €60. ❹

CENTRO STORICO (SPACCANAPOLI)

6 Small Rooms, V. Diodato Lioy 18, 3rd fl. (☎79 01 378; www.6smallrooms.com). From P. Dante, turn left on V. Toledo, left on V. Senise, and right on V. Lioy. Owned by an Australian, hostel has larger rooms than the name suggests. Kitchen and English video collection available. Free lockers. Key deposit €5 to return after midnight curfew. Dorms €18; single €35; doubles €55, with private bath €65. Cash only. ❷

Hostel and Pensione Soggiorno Imperia, P. Miraglia 386, 6th fl. (☎45 93 47; www.soggiornoimperia.it). Take R2, exit at the University, take V. Mezzocannone through P. San D. Maggiore. Buzz 1st green doors to left on P. Miraglia. Climb 6 flights to reach this peaceful 16th-century *palazzo* and its 9 big, bright rooms. Reserve ahead, and confirm a few days before arrival. Dorms €20; singles €30; doubles €50, with bath €65; triples €90; quad €100. AmEx/MC/V. ❸

PIAZZA PLEBISCITO AND ENVIRONS

▨ **Hostel and Hotel Bella Capri,** V. Melisurgo 4 (☎55 29 494; www.bellacapri.it). Take R2 bus from station, exit at V. De Pretis. Top-notch hostel offers clean, safe, and fun accommodations for all. Laid-back atmosphere and helpful owner. All rooms have A/C and TV; some have bay views. Flat-screen satellite TV and DVDs in the common room;

CAMPANIA

common kitchen. English spoken. Breakfast included. Free lockers, luggage storage, and high-speed Internet access. Laundry €5. Reception 24hr. Dorms €20; singles €45-50, with bath €60-70; doubles €55-60/70-80; triples €80-84/90-100; quads €90-100/100-110. 10% *Let's Go* discount. AmEx/MC/V. ❷

■ **Hostel of the Sun,** V. Melisurgo 15 (☎42 06 393; www.hostelnapoli.com). Take R2 bus from station, exit at V. De Pretis. Buzz #51. Exuberant owner and staff provide free maps and advice. Spacious, clean rooms. Common room has satellite TV, DVDs, and library. Kitchen and fridge available. Breakfast included. Lockers and Internet free. Laundry €3, free load with 3-day stay. Dorms €20; singles €45, with bath €50; doubles €55/70; triples €80/90; quads €90/100. 10% *Let's Go* discount. MC/V. ❷

MERGELLINA

Ostello Mergellina (HI), V. Salita della Grotta 23 (☎76 12 346; fax 76 12 391). M: Mergellina. Make 2 sharp rights after Metro stop. After overpass, turn right onto driveway, which is unlit at night. Located in a beautiful part of the city, away from the commotion. Laundry €6. Lockout 9am-3pm. Curfew 12:30am. Reserve ahead July-Aug. Dorms €14; doubles €36; family rooms €16 per person. MC/V. ❶

VOMERO

■ **Hotel Cimarosa,** V. Cimarosa 29, 5th fl. (☎55 67 044; www.hotelcimarosa.it). Take the funicular from P. Plebiscito, exit at the station. Go around the corner to the right. Ring bell to enter (in the same building as the Centrale funicular station). Over 30 beautiful rooms that share spotless baths. Though a bit out of the way, it feels far from the bustle of Naples. Great views of harbor and the city. Check-out 11am. Curfew 1am. Singles €40, deluxe singles €60; doubles €50/90; triples €85/125. With bath, prices nearly double. MC/V. ❹

▸ FOOD

PIZZERIAS

If you ever doubted that Neapolitans invented pizza, Naples's pizzerias will take that doubt, beat it into a ball, throw it in the air, spin it on their collective finger, punch it down, cover it with sauce and mozzarella, and serve it *alla margherita*. The *centro storico* is full of excellent choices.

CENTRO STORICO

■ **Gino Sorbillo,** V. dei Tribunali 35 (☎339 19 12 760; www.accademiadellapizza.it), in the *centro storico* near Vco. San Paolo. The only pizzeria that boasts a grandfather who created both the *ripieno al forno* (calzone) and 21 pizza-making children. No reservations are taken, and both floors are always abuzz with customers; expect long waits. Basic *marinara* (€2.50), and *margherita* (€3) never tasted so good. Pizza €2.50-5. Service 10%. Open M-Sa noon-3:30pm and 7-11:30pm. MC/V. ❶

■ **Pizzeria Di Matteo,** V. dei Tribunali 94 (☎45 52 62), near V. Duomo. A brick oven churns out some of the best *marinara* around (€2.50). Pizzas burst with flavor and the building bursts with Neapolitans—get on the waiting list and try some of the fried zucchini while you wait. Pizza €2.50-6. Open M-Sa 9am-midnight. Cash only. ❶

Antica Pizzeria da Michele, V. Caesare Sersale 1/3 (☎55 39 204; www.damichele.net), at the corner of V. Colletta. From P. Garibaldi, take C. Umberto I and turn right. Huge line outside is an even better indication of quality than the legion of reviews. Serves only *marinara* and *margherita* pizzas. Chefs toss pies with superhuman grace and dexterity. Pizza €3.50-4.50. Open M-Sa 10am-11pm. Cash only. ❶

PIAZZA PLEBISCITO

Pizzeria Brandi, Salita Sant'Anna di Palazzo 1 (☎41 69 28; www.brandi.it), off V. Chiaia. In 1889, Raffaele Esposito invented the *margherita* for Queen Margherita in Brandi's ancient oven to symbolize Italy's flag with green basil, red tomato sauce, and white mozzarella. Famous patrons include Luciano Pavarotti, Isabella Rossellini, and Gérard Depardieu. *Margherita* €4.70. Cover €1.80. Service 12%. Open M and W-Su 12:30-3pm and 7:30pm-12:30am. Reservations recommended Sa-Su. AmEx/MC/V. ❶

RESTAURANTS AND TRATTORIE

Local fish and shellfish enjoy an exalted place in Neapolitan dishes. Devour plentiful *cozze* (mussels) with lemon or in soup. Savor *vongole* (clams) in all their glory, and don't miss their more expensive cousin, the *ostrica* (oyster). Try not to gawk as true Neapolitans suck the juices from the heads of *aragosta* (lobster) or devour *polipo* (octopus). For fresh fruits and seafood, the lively **market** on V. Soprammuro, off P. Garibaldi, is the place to go (open M-Sa 8am-1:30pm). Fruit stands, grocery stores, and pastry shops line V. Tribunali in *centro storico*, where smaller, cheaper shops cling to side streets. Fruit stands are often closed on Monday afternoons, while fishmongers generally close on Thursday afternoons. A large supermarket, **Supero,** is one block across the street from P. Dante, at Vico San Domenico Soriano 20. (Open M-Sa 8:30am-8pm, Su 8:30-1:30pm. MC/V.) The waterfront offers a combination of traditional Neapolitan fare and a change of culinary pace; take the Metro or C25 bus to P. Amedeo, on the Mergellina waterfront, for informal, hearty seafood.

CENTRO STORICO (SPACCANAPOLI)

▨ **Hosteria Toledo,** Vco. Giardinetto 78/A (☎42 12 57), in the Spanish Quarter. Prepare yourself for a long meal of Neapolitan comfort food. Tons of *antipasti*, pasta, and seafood options. If you can't decide, try the chef's surprise—it rarely disappoints. *Primi* and *secondi* €5-12. Cover €2. Service 10%. Open daily 8pm-midnight. MC/V. ❷

Ristorante Bellini, V. Santa Maria di Constantinopoli 79-80 (☎/fax 45 97 74), just off P. Bellini. Come for obliging service and an evening *al fresco*, surrounded by screens and fragrant flowers. Try the *linguine al cartoccio* (€11) or anything from the seafood menu. *Primi* €6.50-11, *secondi* from €8.50. Open daily 9am-4pm and 7pm-midnight. Closed Su evening in summer. MC/V. ❷

Antica Trattoria Campagnola, Piazzetta Nilo 22 (☎55 14 930). Heaping portions of regional cuisine at this outstanding trattoria, including an excellent rendition of the Neapolitan favorite *fritto di aliei* (fried seafood). Simple outdoor seating offers a calm alternative to the mobbed pizzerias nearby. Fast service and wide selection of local wines. *Menù* €12. Open daily 10am-midnight. MC/V. ❷

PIAZZA PLEBISCITO AND CHIAIA

▨ **Donna Margherita,** Vco. Il Alabardieri 4-6 (☎40 01 29). High quality food with a romantic flair. Also great for fun-loving youths due to location near great nightlife. Beautiful decoration inside displays the elegance and simplicity of the Neapolitan lifestyle. Pizza €3.50-€7. *Primi* €6-15. Open daily noon-3pm and 7pm-midnight. ❷

Zorba's, V. Martucci 5 (☎66 75 72). M: Mergellina. 2 blocks off P. Amedeo, to the right exiting the station. Turn left at the sign; it's 3 doors down. This delicious departure from the relentless pizza parade serves Greek cuisine. Go for fresh baklava (€3), or be bold and try *satanas* (devilishly spicy mini-sausages; €7). Open Tu-F and Su 8:30pm-1am, Sa 8:30pm-1am. Reservations recommended. Cash only. ❷

Ristorante Pizzeria 'a Taverna 'e zi Carmela, V. Niccolò Tommaseo 11-12 (☎76 43 35 81), on the corner of V. Partenope. On a breezy side street next to the waterfront. Known by locals for excellent seafood, especially *polipo* (octopus). Ask waiters for seafood sug-

gestions to get the best dishes of the day. *Primi* €3.50-12, *secondi* €5-12. Open in summer daily 11:15am-1:30pm and 7:30pm-1am. Cash only. ❷

Umberto, V. Alabardieri 30/31 (☎41 85 55; www.umberto.it). M: Mergellina. V. Alabardieri leads out of P. dei Martiri. In a nice area, this swanky but affordable locale serves Neapolitan fare with flair. House special is *tubettoni d' 'o treddeta* (tube pasta stuffed with seafood; €11). *Primi* €6-10, *secondi* €8.50-15. Open Tu-Su 12:30-3:30pm and 7:30pm-1am. Closed 3wk. in Aug. Reservations recommended. AmEx/MC/V. ❷

Castel Nuovo, P. Francese 42 (☎55 15 524). This restaurant, near the hostels in the Plebiscito area, offers high-quality food and an escape from the surrounding noise and craziness. The superb penne *con noci* (penne with walnuts; €6) and seafood are sure crowd-pleasers. Open Tu-Su 7:30-11:30pm. ❷

El Bocadillo, V. Martucci 50 (☎66 90 30). M: Mergellina. Authentic Brazilian-style barbecue, i.e. juicy slabs of name-your-animal. Delicious cuisine includes Mexican fare. Entrees €4-11. *Paella* €8.50. Sangria from €5 per L. Open daily 7pm-3am. MC/V. ❷

MERGELLINA

Cucina Casereccia e Pizzeria Zi Totonno a Mergellina, P. Sannazzaro 69 (☎66 65 64). All imaginable sea creatures are fried, sautéed, and stewed to perfection by a welcoming staff. *Zuppa di cozze* (mussel soup; €7) comes heaping with succulent mussels and octopus—good luck finishing the *zuppa di cozze super* (€9.50). Tempting heaps of *antipasti* in the counter window (€3.50). Open Tu-Su noon-6am. AmEx/MC/V. ❷

GELATERIE AND PASTICCERIE

Naples's most beloved pastry is *sfogliatelle*, filled with sweetened ricotta cheese, orange rind, and candied fruit. It comes in two forms: the popular *riccia*, a flaky-crust variety, and a softer, crumblier *frolla*. Look for creamy textures and muted colors for the most authentic tastes.

🔣 **Fantasia Gelati,** V. Toledo 381 (☎55 11 212), in the *centro storico*. Comes close to *gelato* perfection. The shop's fruit flavors, including heavenly *arancia* (orange) and tangy papaya, are made with real juices, yielding tart, refreshing results. Over 30 flavors and very generous scoops. Cones €1.50-3. Open daily 7am-11pm. Cash only. ❶

🔣 **Gay-Odin,** V. Vittoria Colonna 15/B (☎41 82 82; www.gay-odin.it), off P. Amedeo in Chiaia. Also at V. Toledo 214 (☎40 00 63) in the *centro storico*, and V. Benedicto Croce 61 (☎55 10 794) near P. Plebiscito.

Chocolate treats at this sweets shop include *foresta*, a sweet and crumbly chocolate stalk (from €1.70 for a small twig to €8.40 for a trunk best shared with friends). Also offers 12 flavors of gourmet chocolate *gelato*. Open M-Sa 9:30am-1:30pm and 4:30-8pm, Su 10am-2pm. AmEx/MC/V. ❶

Scaturchio, P. San D. Maggiore 19 (☎55 16 944; www.scaturchio.it), in the *centro storico*. Tucked quietly into a *piazza*, this is the perfect place to enjoy divine desserts and watch Neapolitans pass by. A contender for the city's best *sfogliatelle* (€1.30). The specialty is *ministeriale*, a chocolate and rum pastry (€1.50). Excellent *gelato* (cones from €1.50). Open M-Sa 9:30am-8pm, Su 9:30am-1:30pm. AmEx/MC/V. ❶

Pintauro, V. Toledo 275 (☎41 73 39). This tiny bakery invented *sfogliatelle* in 1785. Try it piping hot from €1.30. *Meringues* €1.50. Open in summer daily 8:30am-8pm; closed in winter Su. Cash only. ❶

◉ SIGHTS

The exquisite architecture that forms a backdrop to daily life in Naples is a narrative of successive conquests, featuring Greek, Roman, and Spanish styles. Excavations in situ can be found at the Museo Archeologico Nazionale or the Museo di Capodimonte. The Palazzo Reale's apartments center and the city's castles give a taste of 18th-century royal Neapolitan life.

> **BARGAINAPOLI.** The **Campania Artecard** is a worthwhile investment for those taking a few days to tour regional sights. It grants free admission to any 2 of 48 participating museums and sites in and around the city (including Pompeii), and half-price admission to the rest. Free public transportation, special transportation on weekends, and discounts on audio tours are also included. Artecards are available at the airport, train stations, travel agencies, and all the museums and sites included on the card throughout the region. (☎800 60 06 01; www.campaniartecard.it. Sights and transportation in Naples and Campi Flegrei €13 for 3 days, ages 18-25 €8. Sights and transportation in all of Campania for 3 days €25/18; 1 wk. €28/21.)

CENTRO STORICO (SPACCANAPOLI)

Naples's most renowned neighborhood is replete with brilliant architecture. The main sights get lost among ornate banks, *pensioni*, and *pasticcerie*, so watch for the shoebox-sized signs on buildings. To get to the historical center from P. Dante, walk through Pta. Alba and past P. Bellini before turning down V. dei Tribunali, the former route of a Roman road that now contains some of Naples's best pizzerias.

▨NAPOLI SOTTERRANEA (CATACOMBS AND UNDERGROUND OF NAPLES).

The underground of Naples, started by the Greeks in the 7th century BC, was used until the 60s; the catacombs of San Gennaro, San Gaudioso, and San Severo provide a glimpse of ancient Neapolis. Lasting more than an hour, fascinating guided tours of the city's subterranean alleys set visitors crawling through narrow underground passageways, grottoes, and catacombs. On your walk beneath the historical center, you'll spot Mussolini-era graffiti drawn when the area served as a bomb shelter, explore Roman aqueducts, and enter Neapolitan homes to see out how ancient Roman theaters have been incorporated into architecture over the ages. (*P. San Gaetano 68. Take V. Tribunali and turn left right before San Paolo Maggiore.* ☎29 69 44; www.napolisotterranea.org. *Tours in English, French, and German every 2hr. M-F noon-4pm, Sa-Su and holidays 10am-6pm. €9.30, students €8.*)

▨**MUSEO ARCHEOLOGICO NAZIONALE.** Situated in a 17th-century *palazzo*, this former seat of the University of Naples is one of Europe's oldest museums. A guidebook, audio tour, or guided tour is a worthy investment. The ground floor's Farnese Collection displays sculptures snatched from Pompeii and Herculaneum, as well as imperial portraits and colossal statues from Rome's Baths of Caracalla. The massive *Farnese Hercules* depicts the hero after his last labor—a diverging mythical account extends the traditional 12 labors to include a 13th: bedding 100 women in one night. Check out the ▨**Farnese Bull,** one of the largest existing ancient statues; sculpted from a single slab of marble, the figure was further worked on by none other than Michelangelo. The mezzanine contains a room filled with exquisite mosaics from Pompeii, most noticeably some delicious-looking fruits and the ▨**Alexander Mosaic,** which shows a young, fearless Alexander the Great routing a Persian army. Though most people have heard of the lovely Aphrodite, the *Gabinetto Segreto* (Secret Cabinet), introduces her lesser-known counterpart, Hermaphrodite, who was blessed with a curvy feminine form and handy masculine member. The collection, specializing in erotic paintings and objects from Pompeii, includes everything from images of godly love to phallic good luck charms. *(M: P. Cavour. Turn right from station, walk 2 blocks. ☎44 01 66; www.marketplace.it/ museo.nazionale. Open M and W-Su 9am-7:30pm. €6.50, EU students €3.25, under 18 or over 65 free. Included on Campania Artecard. Audio tour €4.)*

DUOMO. Naples's *duomo* lies on V. Duomo, its modest 19th-century facade hiding an ornate interior. Inaugurated in 1315 by Robert of Anjou, the *duomo* has been subject to many additions and renovations. Inside on the right, the main attraction is the **Cappella del Tesoro di San Gennaro,** decorated with Baroque paintings. A beautiful 17th-century bronze grille protects the high altar, with its reliquary containing the saint's head and two vials of coagulated blood. According to legend, disaster will strike the city if the blood does not liquefy on the day of the **Festa di San Gennaro** (**Entertainment and Festivals,** p. 571). Behind the main altar of the church lies the saint's **crypt,** decorated with Renaissance carvings in white marble. Visitors can also view the underground **excavation site,** which contains an intimate tangle of Greek and Roman roads constructed over several centuries. *(Walk 3 blocks up V. Duomo from C. Umberto I, or take the bus #42 from P. Garibaldi. ☎44 90 97. Open M-Sa 8:30am-noon and 4:30-6pm. Chapel free; excavation site €3.)*

CAPPELLA SAN SEVERO. The chapel, founded in 1590, is now a private museum. Several remarkable 18th-century statues inhabit its lovely corridors, including the ▨**Veiled Christ** by Giuseppe Sanmartino. Because the chapel's founder, Prince Raimondo of the San Severi, reached Grand Master status in the Free Masons, allusions to Masonry are laced throughout the Christian artwork. These include the swastika labyrinth design, which represents the exploration of universal mysteries. Three major symbols of Masonry can be found at the Veiled Christ's feet: a hammer, a compass, and pliers. Legend claims that the chapel's builder—an alchemist as well as a Grand Master—murdered his wife and her lover by injecting them with a poison that preserved their veins, arteries, and vital organs. *(V. De Sanctis 19, near P. San D. Maggiore. ☎55 18 470; www.museosansevero.it. Open M and W-Sa 10am-5:40pm, holidays 10am-1:30pm. Campania Artecard discount 20%. Admission €5, students under 26 €2.50, high school students €2, under 9 free.)*

CHIESA DI SANTA CHIARA. The bright and spacious Santa Chiara was built in the 1300s by the rulers of the house of Anjou. Since then, it has been renovated several times, most recently after a WWII bombing, which most visibly resulted in the broken floor on the left side. The church is littered with sarcophagi and tombs from the Middle Ages, including the 14th-century tomb of Robert of Anjou. The first chapel to the left is dedicated to Neapolitan-born Salvo D'Acquisto, who sacrificed his life during WWII. German troops, enraged at losing one of their own, rounded up 26 women and children to pay dearly for it—Salvo offered his life in the place of theirs, and the Germans conceded. Check out the garden, archaeological site, and monastery, adorned with Gothic frescoes and *majolica* (brightly painted clay) tiles. *(From P. Dante, take V. Toledo and turn left on V. B. Croce. The church is in P. Gesù Nuovo. ☎55 21 597; www.santachiara.info. M-F 9:30am-6:30pm, Su 9:30am-2:30pm.)*

CHIESA DI GESÙ NUOVO. Built for the Prince of Salerno in the 15th century, the church subsequently passed into the hands of the Jesuits. Though its facade is simple, the interior—from inlaid marble floors to colorful ceiling frescoes—is awash in opulent Baroque decor. The magnificent main altar, featuring a triumvirate of marble statues and a towering gold sun, is overwhelming. Outside the church, a spectacular spire glorifies the lives of Jesuit saints. *(Across from Chiesa di Santa Chiara. ☎55 18 613. Open daily 7am-12:30pm and 4-7:30pm. Modest dress required. Free.)*

PIO MONTE DELLA MISERICORDIA. This chapel was built by a group of nobles dedicated to helping the needy and sick, housing pilgrims, and ransoming Christian slaves held by infidels. The church has seven arches, each with an altar and painting, and the main archway holds Caravaggio's *Seven Works of Mercy*. In the *piazza* outside stands a spire dedicated to San Gennaro, who saved the city from plague in 1656. *(V. Tribunali 253, 1 block after V. Duomo, in a small piazza. ☎29 23 16; www.piomontedellamisericordia.it. Open M-Sa 9am-3pm. Tickets €5; EU students, over 65, and under 14 €3; with Campania Artecard €4. Call to book a tour Tu, Th, Sa 9:30am-1:30pm.)*

CHIESA DI SAN DOMENICO MAGGIORE. Several renovations on this 13th-century church have resulted in the 19th-century spiked Gothic interior present today. To the right of the altar in the Chapel of the Crucifix hangs the 13th-century painting that allegedly spoke to St. Thomas Aquinas when he lived in the adjoining monastery. Fine Renaissance sculptures decorate the side chapels, but many have been moved to the Capodimonte museum. *(P. San Domenico Maggiore. ☎45 91 88. Open daily 8:30am-noon and 4:30-7pm. Free.)*

PIAZZA PLEBISCITO AND CHIAIA

▧PALAZZO REALE. Statues of various Neapolitan rulers decorate this 17th-century *palazzo*, now home to the **Museo di Palazzo Reale.** Although the museum houses opulent royal apartments with original Bourbon furnishings, its artwork pales in comparison to its views of the Bay of Naples and Vomero, towering majestically in the distance. *(P. Plebiscito 1. ☎40 05 47; www.pierreci.it. Open M-Tu and Th-Su 9am-7pm. €4, EU students €2, under 18 and over 65 free. Included on Campania Artecard.)* The *palazzo* is also an intellectual mecca, housing the 1,500,000-volume **Biblioteca Nazionale,** which contains carbonized scrolls from the Villa dei Papiri (p. 576) in Herculaneum. *(☎78 19 231. Visits with reservation M-F 10am-1pm.)* Also in the *palazzo* is the famous **Teatro San Carlo,** built in 1737 and reputed to have better acoustics than La Scala in Milan. For info on performances, see **Entertainment and Festivals,** p. 571. *(Theater entrance on P. Trieste e Trento. ☎79 72 331; www.itineranapoli.com.)*

CASTELNUOVO O MASCHIO ANGIONO. It's impossible to miss this five-turreted landmark dominating the Neapolitan skyline. Built in 1286 by Charles II of Anjou as his residence in Naples, the fortress's most stunning feature is the high-ceilinged triumphal entrance marked by reliefs commemorating the arrival of Alphonse I of Aragon in 1443. Don't miss bullet holes left by WWII on the northern wall. Though actual exhibitions are limited—with the exception of a huge bronze helmet standing about 10ft. tall—the castle offers wonderful views of Naples. The splendid Cappella Palatina, also called the Chapel of St. Barbara, is a cool retreat from the castle's windy open churchyard. *(P. Municipio. Take the R2 bus from P. Garibaldi, or walk from centro storico.* ☎ *42 01 241. Open M-Sa 9am-7pm. €5.)*

CASTEL DELL'UOVO (EGG CASTLE). This massive Norman castle of yellow brick and odd angles was built on a large chunk of *tufa* rock. According to legend, Virgil—who was widely believed in medieval times to possess magical powers—put an enchanted egg in the foundation; if the egg breaks, the city will crumble. Once a monastery, the structure was converted to a fortress to defend against invaders in the end of the 5th century. It offers beautiful views, especially during sunset. *(Borgo Marinari. Take bus #1 from P. Garibaldi or P. Municipio to San Lucia and walk across the jetty.* ☎ *24 00 055. Open M-Sa 8:30am-6pm, Su 8:30am-2pm.)*

GALLERIA UMBERTO I. Although now a shopping mall complete with street vendors selling designer knock-offs, this 19th-century building is one of Naples's most beautiful. Designed by Emanuele Rocco and inspired by a similar gallery in Milan, this space became a meeting place for Allied soldiers toward the end of WWII—as remembered in John Horne Burns's *The Gallery* and Norman Lewis' *Naples '44. (P. Trieste e Trento. Most stores open daily 10am-1pm and 4-8pm.)*

CAPODIMONTE

▨**MUSEO DI CAPODIMONTE.** This museum is housed in a 16th-century royal *palazzo* inside a beautiful pastoral park where youngsters play soccer and lovers, well, play. As if its plush royal apartments were not reason enough to visit, the palace holds the Italian National Picture Gallery. The ▨**Farnese Collection** on the first floor is full of masterpieces, many of them removed from Neapolitan churches for safekeeping. Among these incomparable works are Bellini's *Trasfigurazione* (Transfiguration), Masaccio's *Crocifissione* (Crucifixion), and Titian's *Danae.* The 2nd floor traces the development of the Neapolitan realist style, from Caravaggio's visit to Naples (his *Flagellation* is on display) to Ribera and Luca Giordano's adaptations. *(Take bus #24, 110, M4, or M5 from Archaeological Museum and exit at the gate to the park, on the right. Park has 2 entrances, Pta. Piccola and Pta. Grande.* ☎ *74 99 111. Open M-Tu and Th-Su 8:30am-7:30pm. Museum €7.50, after 2pm €3.75. Park free.)*

VOMERO

MUSEO NAZIONALE DI SAN MARTINO. Once the monastery of St. Martin, the cloisters are now home to an excellent museum of Neapolitan history and culture. Collection highlights include Riberia's *Deposition of Christ,* held to be one of his finest works, and the *Nativity* by Guido Reni. In addition to extensive galleries, the monastery sports a lavish chapel festooned with Baroque marbles and statuary. Numerous balconies and a multi-level garden allow views of the city below, but couples monopolize most available benches. *(*☎ *55 85 942; www.pierreci.it. Open M-Tu and Th-Su 8:30am-7:30pm. €6, EU students €3. Included on Campania Artecard.)* The massive **Castel Sant'Elmo** next door was built to deter rebellion and hold political prisoners. The Castel is included on a ticket to San Martino, but does not otherwise warrant a visit. *(From V. Toledo, take the funicular to Vomero and turn right on V. Cimarosa. Continue straight up 2 flights of stairs, along V. Scarlatti, and then veer left, walking for about 10min., keeping left; Castel Sant'Elmo and Ple. San Martino emerge on the right.* ☎ *848 80 02 88; www.civita.it. Open M-Tu and Th-Su 9am-6:30pm. €3. Special exhibits around €6. Included on Campania Artecard. Free with entrance to Museo Nazionale di San Martino.)*

MUSEO DUCA DI MARTINA. Ceramics fans should visit this crafts gallery inside the lush gardens of the **Villa Floridiana** for 18th-century Italian and Asian porcelain—or just to stroll through the gardens. Though on the smaller side, this collection is thoughtfully presented and full of treasures. *(V. Cimarosa 77. Take funicular from V. Toledo to Vomero, turn right from the station, then left on V. Cimarosa. Enter the gardens and keep walking downhill. ☎57 88 418; www.pierreci.it. Open M and W-Su 8:30am-1:30pm. €2.50, EU students €1.25, EU citizens under 18 or over 65 free. Campania Artecard discount 20%.)*

MERGELLINA

VIRGIL'S TOMB. Unfortunately, this is just a tomb—only the most dedicated Latin scholars will find it interesting. Others can call ahead and arrange a translator to explain the inscriptions. Below lies the entrance to the now-closed **Crypta Neapolitana,** a tunnel built during Augustus's reign to connect ancient Neapolis to Pozzuoli and Baia. *(M: Mergellina, take 2 quick rights. Entrance between overpass and tunnel. ☎66 93 90. Open daily 9am-1hr. before sunset. Free. Guided tours upon request.)*

▊ SHOPPING

A thriving black market and low prices make Naples an enticing place for shopping—as long as you keep in mind that street vendors' lives depend on their craftiness, so if they can out-wit you, they will. If a transaction seems too good to be true, it is. **Never buy electronic products from street vendors!** Even brand-name boxes have been known to be filled with newspaper or rocks, and CDs and DVDs are often blank. Two words about bargaining: do it. In the dog-eat-dog world of unregulated transactions, bargaining is the law.

Via Santa Maria di Constantinopoli, south of the Archaeological Museum, has old books and antique shops. **Spaccanapoli** and its side streets near the Conservatorio house small music shops with inexpensive manuscripts. **Via Toledo, Corso Umberto I,** and **Via Duomo** provide high-class shopping for a lower budget, and the streets south of **San Lorenzo Maggiore** house Neapolitan craftsmen. For classy shopping, **Piazza Martiri** offers major Italian designers, and **Galleria Umberto** has plenty of higher-end stores. The most expensive shopping district is in the hills of **Vomero** along the perpendicular **Via Scarlatti** and **Via Luca Giordano.** Many artisans' workshops inhabit the streets nearby, hawking everything from wrought iron to delicate cameos. Most markets, such as one off **Porta Capuana,** are open Monday through Saturday (9am-2 or 5pm). Two weekends of every month (1 per month June-July), the **Fiera Antiquaria Neapolitana,** along V. Francesco Caracciolo on the waterfront, hosts flea markets filled with ancient artifacts. Though such items come with hefty price tags, hundreds wander through the stands browsing stamps, books, coins, and art. (☎62 19 51. Open daily 8am-2pm.) From early December to early January, Neapolitan artisans gather along the Spaccanapoli and surrounding streets to create hand-made fine porcelain nativity scenes renowned throughout Europe. This spectacle draws a huge international crowd.

♪ ▓ ENTERTAINMENT AND FESTIVALS

Once famous occasions for revelry, Naples's religious festivals are now excuses for sales and shopping sprees. On September 19 and the first Saturday in May, the city celebrates the **Festa di San Gennaro.** Join the crowd to watch the procession by the *duomo* in May and see the patron saint's blood miraculously liquefy in a vial. In July, P. San Domenico Maggiore holds concerts and the **Neapolis Festival** hosts pop concerts at

Arena Flegrea in Campi Flegrei. **Teatro San Carlo** (☎79 72 111) at Palazzo Reale hosts symphony (Oct.-May) and opera (Oct.-June) performances. Gallery tickets should be purchased in advance (from €12). Consult the ticket office and *Il Mattino* for schedules. Catch a soccer match at **Stadio San Paolo** in Fuorigrotta for a truly accurate portrait of Neapolitan life. **Napoli,** in Serie B (the 2nd division) attracts spectators for matches from August to June. (☎23 95 623. M: Campi Flegrei. Tickets from €20.)

▣ NIGHTLIFE

Travelers hoping to dance the night away may be surprised by the lack of discos, but Naples is not without nightlife. Come summer, Neapolitans, *gelato* and pizza in hand, pack the *piazze* by the hundreds, especially on Sundays. To maximize your enjoyment of the city's bustling nocturnal scene, follow this crash course in *piazza* personalities. At night, **Piazza Gesù Nuovo** and **Piazza Duomo** are crammed with university students who firmly believe in the "healing powers" of certain botanicals. Plentiful fast food satisfies their late-night munchies. Always packed, **Via Santa Maria La Nova** is frequented by sociable Neapolitans of all ages. Vendors sell hot dogs late into the night, and low priced liquor (beer usually €1) flows freely from local bars. The safer area around **Piazza dei Martiri,** including **Riviera di Chiaia** and Via dei Mille, offers the most bars, plus a cool atmosphere. Bars in the quieter **Piazza Bellini** host a relaxed mix of locals and tourists. Although these venues are often pricey, their low-key ambience just might provide the respite you crave after a hard day of sightseeing. The young and chic gather at **Piazza Vanvitelli,** just a short metro or funicular ride alongside V. Toledo or by the waterfront on V. Giuseppe Ferrigni. Don't bother showing up, however, unless you can pass for under 28 and don't mind weaving through couples. Beware: buses and funiculars may not run past 11pm. When the winter air blows through the *piazze* and students return to the university, Neapolitans run for warmth to the few clubs and pubs; they open around 11pm and remain open until everyone goes home around 4 or 5am. *Il Mattino, Qui Napoli,* and *Zero81* guides print decent club listings.

CENTRO STORICO

Keste, V. San Giovanni Maggiore Pignatelli 27 (☎55 13 984), near the university. Underground, alternative feel that attracts all strata of Neapolitan society. Enjoy eating outside by the garden or dancing inside to a live DJ. Beer €3. Open daily 9pm-2am.

Caffè Letterario Intra Moenia, P. Bellini 70 (☎29 07 20; www.intramoenia.it). Appeals to the intellectual crowd by keeping books out for skimming. Sit under umbrellas in the *piazza,* which is made even sweeter with a mixed drink (€6-7), beer (€3.50-6), or the *delizia caprese* (Caprisian delight; €8). Open daily 10am-2am.

Blue Moon Pizzeria, V. T. de Amicis 4, right in P. Gesù Nuovo. Supplies large bottles of Peroni beer to the masses for just €1.50, as well as all the food needed for a night of socializing in the *piazza.* Open daily 7pm to early morning.

Rising South, V. San Sebastiano 19 (☎333 653 42 73; www.risingsouth.it), near P. Gesù Nuovo. *Enoteca,* bar, cultural association, cinema—this club does it all. Plush, Oriental carpets, vintage chandeliers, and a sound-proof main hall carved from *tufa* set the scene at this student favorite for term-time fun. Mixed drinks €3-6. Open as a bar Sept.-May Tu-Su 10pm-3am (depending on weather); for special events in summer.

PIAZZA PLEBISCITO AND CHIAIA

Le Chandelier, Vco. Belledonne a Chiaia, 34/35 (☎333 25 28 177). Packed by young and fashionable Neapolitans, this place outdoes its surrounding competitors by providing a relaxed, Mediterranean ambience. Beer €4. Open daily 9pm-3am.

Farinella Music Hall, V. Alabardieri 10 (☎42 38 455). Enormous upscale bar and *discoteca,* packed in winter for live jazz concerts. In the summer, the hall is a relaxing prelude to a night on the *piazze.* A hip, young crowd drinks at the bar and watches sports on the big-screen TVs. Mixed drinks from €5, after 7:30pm from €7. AmEx/MC/V.

⚡ DAYTRIPS FROM NAPLES

POMPEII (POMPEI)   ☎081

On the morning of August 24, AD 79, a deadly cloud of volcanic ash from the eruption of nearby Mt. Vesuvius overtook Pompeii (pom-PAY), engulfing the city in black clouds. Many fled, but others—including the famous historian Pliny the Elder—unaware of the severity of the eruption or scared their property would be stolen, decided to stay. Mere hours after the eruption, stately buildings, works of art, and human bodies were sealed in casts of ash—natural tombs that would remain undisturbed for centuries. Today visitors to the site bear witness to an intimate record of the town's demise. Since excavation efforts began in 1748, archaeologists have continually turned up discoveries in their ongoing mission to understand life in the Roman era. Most of the interesting artifacts from Pompeii are in Naples' Museo Archeologico Nazionale (p. 568), meaning that the site itself consists mostly of buildings and streets. To get more out more out of your trip to Pompeii, preface it with a visit to the museum's extensive Pompeii collection and listen very attentively to the audio tour or buy one of the many useful books there.

> ❗ **SOME DON'T LIKE IT HOT.** The sites at Pompeii afford visitors few water fountains and little shade. Bring lots of water and keep cool to avoid heat stroke. Around 15 people per year die from heat-related illnesses at Pompeii. If you need medical attention, flag down a guide or call ☎113. Remember, you are walking a whole city! Don't think that because it's ancient, it's small.

🔳 ⚡ TRANSPORTATION AND PRACTICAL INFORMATION

The quickest route to Pompeii (25km south of Naples) is the Circumvesuviana **train** (☎77 22 444). Board at Naples's Stazione Centrale (dir.: Sorrento; 40min., 2 per hr. 5:40am-10:40pm, UnicoCampania Pass Fascia 3 €2.30) or from Sorrento's station. Get off at "Pompei Scavi." Eurail passes are not valid. The Porta Marina entrance to the city is downhill to the left. Trenitalia trains also leave from the Naples station, stopping at modern Pompeii en route to Salerno (30min., every hr., €2.20). The Trenitalia train station is a 10min. walk from the excavations' eastern entrance; to reach this entrance, walk to the end of V. Statale until it becomes V. Sacra and turn left on V. Roma.

The excavations stretch along an east-west axis, with the modern town (and its hotels and restaurants) at the eastern end. Stop by the **tourist office,** V. Sacra 1 (☎85 07 255; www.pompeiisites.org), or the info booth at the site, for an excellent free map. From the Pompei Scavi stop, take a right; follow the road down the hill to the **branch office** at P. Porta Marina Inferiore 12. (☎800 01 33 50. Both offices open M-F 8am-3:30pm, Sa 8am-2pm.) Free **luggage storage** is available at the entrance to the ruins. There is a **police station, info center,** and **post office** (☎85 06 164; open M-F 8:30am-1:30pm and Sa 8:30am-noon) at the site entrance, P. Esedra 1, and another police station at P. Bartolo Longo, where V. Roma ends.

🔵 SIGHTS

A comprehensive exploration of Pompeii takes all day. A popular tourist attraction year-round, Pompeii's ruins are most crowded in the spring when they are visited by

THE LOCAL STORY

POMPEII ROUND TWO?

Pompeii may be the most famous victim of Mt. Vesuvius, but the volcano—which has erupted more than 50 times since the famous AD 79 explosion—has since claimed many more lives, and threatens to strike again.

The last major eruption, in March 1944, added to the devastation already inflicted by WWII by destroying four villages and 88 U.S. B 25 bomber planes. After Mt. Etna in Sicily erupted for 24 days in July 2001, volcanologists started considering the possibility of another eruption at nearby Vesuvius. After all, a volcano that killed 20,000 people in ancient times—and now looms over 3,000,000—cannot be ignored without catastrophic consequences.

The current official evacuation plan is based on an eruption in 1631. It is a poor model for evacuation not only because there were far fewer people (not to mention no cars) in the 17th century, but also because the 1631 eruption did not actually affect the city. Predicting volcanic activity has proven difficult for scientists, who hope to be able to give a 27-day warning before an eruption, but predicting the response to such an announcement—stand-still traffic on the A1 highway—is not so difficult. With a major eruption approximately every 2000 years, Vesuvius is due for its next big blast.

throngs of school groups. A trip in early summer or fall is best for avoiding the crowds. (Open daily Apr.-Oct. 8:30am-7:30pm; Nov.-Mar. 8:30am-5pm. Last entry 1½hr. before close. Tickets €10, EU students €5, EU citizens under 18 or over 65 free. No re-entry.) The budget-conscious in search of an engaging tour should consider the excellent audio tours, available at the site's entrance, to supplement the free map. (€6.50, 2 tours for €10, children's tour €4.50.) A helpful pamphlet describes in detail the historical context of the most important sites. Independent guides gather solo travelers by the ticket office to form tour groups. Guided tours are crowded and expensive (2hr., €90 for 3 people) but can be informative.

NEAR THE FORUM. The **basilica** walls are to the right upon entering the ruins. Before the eruption, lawyers and prominent citizens fought legal battles on this floor. Walk farther down V. Marina to reach the **forum**, ringed by a marble colonnade. Once dotted with statues of emperors and gods, this site was the city's commercial, civic, and religious heart of the city. Glass display cases house gruesome body casts of Vesuvius's victims, contorted in surprise and agony. The **Templo di Giove**—largely destroyed by an earthquake 17 years before the eruption—stands at the upper end of the forum and offers a view of Mt. Vesuvius. To the left, the **Templo di Apollo** contains copies of the statues of Apollo and Diana (originals displayed in the **Museo Archeologico Nazionale**, p. 568) and a column topped by a sundial. With the Tempio di Giove behind you, the **Templo di Vespasiano** across the forum retains a delicate frieze depicting elaborate preparations for a sacrifice. To the right, the **Building of Eumachia** has a door frame carved with animals and insects.

NEAR HOUSE OF THE FAUN. At the **Forum Baths,** notice rooms allotted for servants who accompanied their patrons to watch their belongings. The **House of the Faun** has yielded stunning treasures, among them a dancing bronze faun and the spectacular Alexander Mosaic (originals in the **Museo Archeologico Nazionale**, p. 568). The building's opulence leads archaeologists to believe that it was the dwelling of one of the richest men in town. The **House of the Vettii** was the home of two brothers whose rivalry is apparent on every wall. A famous painting of the fertility god Priapus, flaunting his very ample endowment, is in the vestibule. Phalluses were considered lucky and believed to scare off evil spirits in ancient times. Notice ruts worn in the stone roads by chariot wheels passing through. *(Exit the forum through the upper end by the cafeteria; Forum Baths are on the*

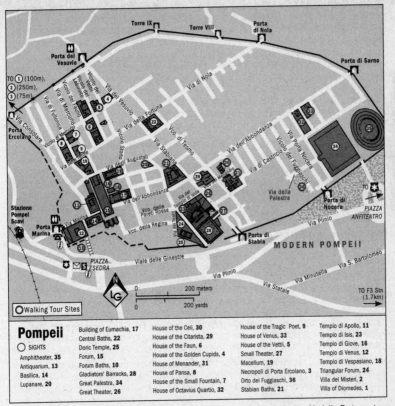

CAMPANIA

Pompeii

○ SIGHTS

Amphitheater, 35
Antiquarium, 13
Basilica, 14
Lupanare, 20

Building of Eumachia, 17
Central Baths, 22
Doric Temple, 25
Forum, 15
Forum Baths, 10
Gladiators' Barracks, 28
Great Palestra, 34
Great Theater, 26

House of the Ceii, 30
House of the Citarista, 29
House of the Faun, 6
House of the Golden Cupids, 4
House of Menander, 31
House of Pansa, 8
House of the Small Fountain, 7
House of Octavius Quartio, 32

House of the Tragic Poet, 9
House of Venus, 33
House of the Vettii, 5
Small Theater, 27
Macellum, 19
Necropoli di Porta Ercolano, 3
Orto dei Fuggiaschi, 36
Stabian Baths, 21

Tempio di Apollo, 11
Tempio di Isis, 23
Tempio di Giove, 16
Tempio di Venus, 12
Tempio di Vespasiano, 18
Triangular Forum, 24
Villa dei Misteri, 2
Villa di Diomedes, 1

left. A right on V. della Fortuna leads to the House of the Faun. Continuing on V. della Fortuna, turn left on Vco. dei Vettii to reach the House of the Vettii on the left.)

NEAR BROTHEL. The racier side of Pompeii can be found at the small brothel, or **Lupanare** (literally, dwelling of she-wolves). Beware if you've got young travelers in tow: the brothel is unsurprisingly covered in pornographic imagery. The **Stabian Baths** were privately owned and therefore fancier than the Forum Baths; the women's side has an impressive marine-creature mosaic. More body casts—some of the site's most gruesome and impressive—rest in dusty glass cases. *(From Vco. dei Vettii, cross V. della Fortuna over to Vco. Storto, and turn left on V. degli Augustali to reach Lupanare. Baths are on the main avenue, V. dell'Abbondanza.)*

NEAR GREAT THEATER. The **Great Theater,** built during the 2nd century BC, was already somewhat destroyed by the time of the volcanic eruption. Many stone-walled cells, thought to have been **Gladiators' Barracks,** line the edges of the field in front. The nearby **Small Theater** was used for music and poetry. North of the theaters stands the **Tempio di Isis,** Pompeii's monument to the Egyptian goddess of nature. At the end of the street, take a left to re-connect to the main road. The altar here was built to ward off evil spirits, which Romans believed gathered at crossroads. *(Across V dell'Abbondanza from the baths, V. dei Teatri leads to the theaters.)*

NEAR AMPHITHEATER. Red graffiti crowds the walls along V. dell'Abbondanza, expressing everything from political slogans to insults to declarations of love. At the end of the street await the **House of Octavius Quartio** and **House of Venus,** where gardens have been replanted according to modern knowledge of ancient horticulture. Nearby is the impeccably preserved **amphitheater** (70 BC), which once held crowds of 20,000. The spectators determined whether a gladiator would live or die during battle with a casual thumbs down or thumbs up. In the **Orto dei Fuggiaschi,** some of the body casts of fleeing victims display expressions and individual facial features. Also nearby, the **Great Palestra's** columns still surround a courtyard which once housed exercise sessions for local boys and now offers a great place to rest under the shadows of surrounding trees.

VILLA DEI MISTERI. Outside the city walls, the **Villa dei Misteri** is the best-preserved Pompeiian villa; gape at the extravagant atrium and the varied architecture—all "Four Styles" of Pompeii are displayed. The *Dionysiac Frieze* depicts a bride's initiation into the cult of Dionysus. Nearby, the famed **Cave Canem mosaic** still guards the entry to its master's villa, known as the **House of the Tragic Poet.** Head through the *porta* for a great view of the entire city. *(For the Villa go to western end of V. della Fortuna, turn right on V. Consolare, and walk up Villa delle Tombe.)*

▨ HERCULANEUM (ERCOLANO)

To reach Herculaneum, take a Circumvesuviana train from Naples's Stazione Centrale to "Ercolano Scavi" (dir.: Sorrento; 20min.). Walk 500m downhill to the ticket office. The Municipal Tourist Office, V. IV Novembre 82, is on the way (☎ 78 81 243; open M-Sa 9am-2pm). Archaeological site: ☎85 75 347; www.pompeiisites.org. Open Apr.-Oct. daily 8:30am-7:30pm; Nov.-Mar. 8:30am-5pm. Last entry 1½hr. before close. €11, EU students €5, EU citizens under 18 or over 65 free. Audio tours (in English, French, German, Italian, or Spanish) are especially enlightening. 1½-2hr.; €7, 2 for €11; under 18 €4/7. Grab an illustrated guidebook (€4-6) at the shops that flank the entrance, or pick up the free Brief Guide to Herculaneum and map at the entrance. Free mandatory bag check.

Neatly excavated and intact, the remains of this prosperous Roman town hardly deserve the term "ruins." Buried in superheated volcanic tuff instead of the ash that covered Pompeii, Herculaneum (in Italian, "ehr-co-LA-no") is much more intact—many buildings still have second stories—and better preserved than its larger and more famous neighbor. Exploring the houses—complete with frescoes, furniture, mosaics, small sculptures, wooden doors, and materials such as papyrus and fabric—can make a tourist feel more like a house guest; artifacts displayed in their original contexts lend to a very rewarding and informative experience.

Though archaeologists long held the opinion that most of Herculaneum's residents escaped the eruption that destroyed Pompeii, a 1982 discovery of skeletons huddled in a boathouse suggests that much of the population was buried while attempting to get away. Much of the city remains un-excavated, and only about a quarter of the city is open to the public. One of the more opulent buildings is the **House of Deer,** named for the grisly statues of deer being mauled by packs of dogs. Here, archaeologists also found the statues *Satyr with a Wineskin* and *Drunken Hercules,* a majestic marble representation of the hero struggling to relieve himself. The **palestra,** a gym and exercise complex, complete with a large vaulted swimming pool, still holds shelves once laden with massage oils and the *strigili* (back scrapers) used to clean skin after a rubdown. The **House of Neptune and Amphitrite** is famous for a breathtaking mosaic. The house is connected to a remarkably well-preserved **wine shop.** Dating back to the 2nd century BC, the **Samnite House** is one of the oldest buildings in Herculaneum. Down the street, the three-floored **House of the Wooden Partition** still has a door in its elegant courtyard and a clothes press around the corner. Outside the site lies the **theater,** perfectly preserved though buried underground. A well dug in 1709 unearthed the theater and catalyzed excavation of the rest of Herculaneum; unfortunately, the theater was soon stripped of its valuable decorations. (☎081 73 24 311. Occasionally open for visits; call to check.) The extravagant 250m-long **Villa dei Papiri,** 500m west of Herculaneum, earned its name in 1752 when papyrus scrolls were discovered in one of its rooms; the highly damaged works are still being studied and restored—thus far, no classics have been found. (Rarely open to the public; Campania Arte-card holders can view the site by special arrangement. Contact municipal tourist office at ☎78 81 243 for details. Scrolls on display at Biblioteca Nazionale, p. 569)

MOUNT VESUVIUS (MONTE VESUVIO)

Take Circumvesuviana train from Naples's Stazione Centrale to "Ercolano Scavi" (dir.: Sorrento; 20min.) Vesuvio Express buses (☎73 93 666) run from Herculaneum up to the crater of Vesuvius (every 30min. or as soon as van is filled, round-trip €10). Buy tickets next to the Ercolano Vesuviana station; buses leave from outside station. The "Vesuvius" stop is part way up the crater; it's a 20-30min. walk to the top. Open in summer 9am-5pm; in winter 9am-3pm. Wear proper footwear and bring water. Admission €6.50.

A semi-challenging hike to the top of the only active volcano on mainland Europe is completely worth it. From the top, enjoy great views of the Bay of Naples and impressive flora growing on the lava. In the good old days, visitors could clamber about in the crater to their hearts' content; the rules changed a little when a Belgian tourist accidentally took a fatal plunge in 1998. Now you'll have to settle for peering inwards from Vesuvius's steep lip. Each fiery belch (over 50 since the famous AD 79 eruption that buried Pompeii) has helped widen and deepen the aperture. Vesuvius hasn't blown its top since March 31, 1944—the longest it has lain dormant in several centuries. A geological station closely monitors tectonic rumblings, and local governments are always ready with a comprehensive evacuation plan. In the summer of 2003, a geological station near the site detected significant subterranean activity, prompting much speculation and concern; the next eruption is expected to be the most violent since 1631, when 3000 people died.

REGGIA DI CASERTA (PALACE OF CASERTA)   ☎0823

Caserta is easily accessible by trains to and from Naples (40min., 35 per day 4:50am-9:20pm). Buy the Fascia 4 Unico Campania pass (€5.50). The Caserta train station is also a major stop for local buses (€0.88). The Reggia is directly opposite the train station. EPT tourist offices operate inside the Reggia and at C. Trieste 43, at the corner of P. Dante. (☎32 11 37. Both offices open M-F 9am-1:40pm.) For Capua, take the train to "Santa Maria Capua Vetere," walk straight 1 block, and make the 1st left. Take the next left on V. Achille, walk 150m, and turn right on V. Eugenia Ricciardi, which becomes V. Amfiteatro. Or take the blue bus from the Caserta train station to P. Adriano near the ruins. Naples-bound buses leave from an intersection 1 block north of Capua train station.

Few palaces, no matter how opulent, hold a candle to Caserta's glorious royal palace, ■**La Reggia** (lah REH-jya), which was built over a period of 100 years with the purpose of rivaling Versailles. A world apart from Pompeii's brutality and Naples's quiet churches, the palace and its grounds resonate with a love of art and a passion for beauty that have earned it recognition as a UNESCO World Heritage site. Lovely grounds lead already impressed visitors up to the breathtaking palace. Completed in 1775, the expansive lawns, fountains, sculptures, and carefully pruned trees culminate in a 75m man-made waterfall—the setting of the final

CAMPANIA

scene of *Star Wars* (1977). On the 3km walk through the park, visitors can peer into the azure, fish-filled pools, from which royals and servants alike once caught their dinner. The impressive waterworks were made possible by an aqueduct from neighboring mountains made at the time of construction. Nearby, the lush **English Gardens,** complete with fake ruins inspired by Pompeii, are an excellent picnic spot. Instead of walking 30min. to the waterfall, consider taking a horse-and-buggy ride from the garden entrance (€10 per person) or a less-romantic trip on one of the park's mini-buses (€1). The **palazzo** itself boasts 1200 rooms, 1742 windows, and 34 staircases, yet somehow avoids arrogance. Frescoes and intricate marble floors adorn the royal apartments, some boasting beds guarded by sculptures of scary mythical beasts. (☎32 14 00. Open M and W-Su 9am-7:30pm; park open 9am-6:30pm. Gardens €2, *palazzo* and gardens €6. Included on Campania Artecard.)

CAMPI FLEGREI

SEPSA buses run from P. Municipio in Naples to the towns of Campi Flegrei (www.info-campiflegrei.it). Use the blue SEPSA bus (dir.: Monte di Procida/Torregaveta), or the yellow SEPSA bus #152. To Baia, take the blue or yellow SEPSA bus from M: Pozzuoli (30min.). Don't be confused by the outdated signs on the Ferrovia Cumana; this rail line no longer goes through Baia. In Baia, buy an Unico Napoli Fascia 1 ticket (€1.70) and ride any mode of transportation all day. To Cumae, take the SEPSA bus (dir.: Miseno-Cuma) from the train station at Baia to the last stop in Cumae (15min., €0.60), and walk to the end of the V. Cumae. The "Cuma" stop on the Ferrovia Circumflegrea is in the modern town, several kilometers from the archaeological sites. Get to Pozzuoli using the Ferrovia Cumana, Ferrovia Circumflegria, or Naples Metro.

The Campi Flegrei (CAM-pee fle-GREY), a group of tiny coastal towns west of Naples nestled among lakes and inactive volcanoes, were immortalized in Virgil's *Aeneid* as Aeneas's landing point in Italy (in Cumae). Their hot springs, intricate bath houses, and supposed gate to hell (according to the ancient Greeks) now form the backdrop for a residential center and beautiful bay away from the craziness of Naples.

Perched on a hill overlooking the bustling port center of **Baia,** where SEPSA buses drop passengers off, is Baia's central attraction: luxurious **Roman Baths,** remarkable for their well-preserved mosaics and detailed ceilings. At the base of the hill sits the gem of the bath houses, known as the **Tempio di Mercurio,** or the Temple of Echoes. (☎86 87 592. Open Tu-Su 9am-7pm. 2-day archaeological pass grants admission to the Baths, the Archaeological Museum in Baia, the *scavi* (caves) in Cumae, and the Amphitheater in Pozzuoli. €4. Sold at all participating sites. Included on Campania Artecard.) A short bus ride from the center of Baia runs to the **Museo Archeologico dei Campi Flegrei,** which contains a small collection of ancient artifacts, including many from the underwater city. (☎52 33 797. Open Tu-Sa 9am-1hr. before sunset, Su 9am-7pm. Entrance with archaeological pass or Campania Artecard.) For a cooler and less conventional view of ruins, try the glass-bottomed boat *Cymba* out of Baia's port to see the ⬛**Submerged Roman City.** (☎320 83 50 145. Departs Mar.-Nov. Sa noon, 3pm; Su 10am, 3pm. Does not run on days with murky water. €10, children 5-12 €7, under 5 free.)

The highlight of the excavations at **Cumae (Cuma)** is the **Antro della Sibilla,** a cave used as a pizza oven until 1932, when archaeologists realized what it actually was. Stroll through the cave and see where the mythical Sibyl, the most famous oracle this side of Delphi, gave her prophecies. Then gape at the **Augustan Tunnel,** a shaft used for transportation inland from the coast, and rumored to have been connected to Rome. According to legend, the **Tempio di Apollo** was constructed by Daedalus, who landed in Cumae after escaping captivity in Crete with his handcrafted wings. Little remains of the original temples, so the hike is really only worthwhile for visitors interested in seeing the view that captivated Daedalus.

Near the busy port of **Pozzuoli** is the famous volcanic crater **Solfatara,** accessed either by hiking from the center of Pozzuoli (following frequent signs) or by riding bus #152. Solfatara was believed by the ancients to be a portal to Hades, but nowadays there is not much to admire. (☎52 62 341; www.solfatara.it. Open daily Apr.-Nov. 8:30am-7pm; Dec.-Mar. 8:30am-1hr. before sunset. €5.50, children 5-10 €4.) **International Camping ❶,** offers a night's stopover in purgatory before you enter the underworld. (☎52 62 341. Reception 6am-11pm. Ring bell after hours. Camping €7.60 per person, €6.50 per student, €3.80 per child; high season €9.20/8/4.60. 2-person bungalows €46, 3-person €56, 4-person €66; high season €51/63/74. Campania Artecard discount 20%.) Beneath Solfatara, a short walk from both the waterfront and the train station, is the first-century ◪**Flavian Amphitheater,** the 3rd largest in Italy. The remarkably well-preserved structures below have given engineers an idea of how the Romans were able to raise a caged beast up to the floor of the stadium. (☎52 66 007. Open in summer M and W-Su 9am-8pm; in winter 9am-3pm. €4, EU students €2. Entrance with archaeological pass, or Campania Artecard.)

BAY OF NAPLES

The Bay of Naples could hardly seem farther away from the bustling city that shares its coast. Home to the pleasant islands of Capri, Ischia, and Procida, and the coastal town of Sorrento, the area offers peace and tranquility. On Capri, expensive shops and pristine waters are the playground of the rich and the envy of everyone else. Ischia's hot springs and therapeutic waters beckon those seeking health of mind and body. Procida, the quietest—but still touristed—island, has winding streets and empty shores that retain an unadulterated mystique. Merge with crowds at the famous villas and grottoes, but come back later to take a private dip. Above all, just take it easy. Back on solid ground, Sorrento is both a good base for island-hopping, or a coastal destination in its own right.

SORRENTO   ☎081

Built on cliffs above the glittering Bay of Naples, Sorrento (so-REN-toh; pop. 16,000) is a maze of tiny alleys and quiet side streets. Its *piazze* and roads are overrun with tourists strolling and window shopping in the old city and Marina Grande. At night, street music and majestic sunsets are the perfect end to a perfect day. Sorrento is a convenient base for daytrips, thanks to plentiful accommodations, swift transportation connections, and proximity to the Amalfi Coast.

▐ TRANSPORTATION

Circumvesuviana railway (☎77 22 484), just off P. Lauro, runs 39 **trains** per day (6:20am-11:55pm) to Herculaneum (45min., €1.80), Naples (1hr., €3.20), and Pompeii (30min., €1.80). **Ferries** and **hydrofoils** depart for the Bay of Naples islands. The port is accessible from P. Tasso by bus (€1). Linee Marittime Partenopee (☎80 71 812) runs ferries (40min., 5 per day 8:35am-4:55pm, €7.50) and hydrofoils (20min., 19 per day 7:20am-6:20pm, €12.50) to Capri. It also runs ferries to Positano (20min., 3 per day 8:50am-3:30pm, €7.50) and hydrofoils to Naples (35min., 8 per day 7:20am-8:25pm, €7.50). Caremar (☎80 73 077; www.caremar.it) runs ferries to Capri (50min., 4 per day 7:45am-7pm, €5). Metro del Mare (☎199 60 07 00) goes to Amalfi (30min., 4 per day 8:30am-6pm, €6). Ticket offices open just before boats depart. SITA **buses** leaving from Circumvesuviana station for the Amalfi Coast are the best way to travel south. From 6:30am-9:30pm, 21 buses head to Amalfi (1¼hr., €2.40) and to Positano (40min., €1.30). The city runs orange **local buses** (€1) every 20min. Buy tickets for SITA and local lines at a *bar, tabaccherie,* or at the hotel in P. Lauro. The Sorrento tourist office has ferry, bus, and train schedules. Rent **cars** and **scooters** at Rent A Car, C. Italia 253. Scooters start at €33 per day. (☎87 82 801. Insurance included. Driver's license and credit card required. 18+. Open daily 8:30am-9:30pm; last hire 7:30pm. AmEx/MC/V.)

◼🛈 ORIENTATION AND PRACTICAL INFORMATION

Most of Sorrento rests atop a flat shelf that descends steeply to the Bay of Naples. Festooned with flags from the home countries of its visitors, **Piazza Tasso** is at the town's center. Steep stairways and roads connect it to **Marina Piccola. Corso Italia** runs through P. Tasso; facing the sea, the train and bus stations are in **Piazza Lauro** to the right, and the old city is to the left. **Via San Cesareo** runs parallel to C. Italia on the old-city side of P. Tasso.

Tourist Office: V. Luigi De Maio 35 (☎80 74 033; www.sorrentotourism.com). From P. Tasso, take Luigi De Maio to the far end of P. San Antonio and continue toward the port. Office is to the right in the Circolo dei Forestieri compound. Free maps. Open M-Sa Apr.-Sept. 8:30am-6:30pm; Oct.-Mar. 8:30am-2pm and 4-6:15pm.

Currency Exchange: No-commission currency exchange is everywhere and easy to find. **Western Union** kiosk, V. San Cesareo 26 (☎87 73 552). Open in summer daily 10am-2pm and 4-10pm.

English-Language Bookstore: Libreria Tasso, V. San Cesareo 96 (☎80 71 639; www.libreriatasso.com). Stocks stellar classic texts, including the incomparable ▧**Let's Go,** along with thrillers and new fiction. Open M-Sa 9:30am-1pm and 5-9:30pm, Su 11am-1pm and 5:30-9:30pm. MC/V.

Laundromat: Wash and Dry, V. Fuoro 3. Wash and dry €8.50. Open daily 8am-8pm.

Police: (☎80 74 433), Vco. Terzo Rota. From the station, go right on C. Italia and turn left after V. Nizza.

Pharmacies: All along C. Italia.

Hospital: Ospedale Civile di Sorrento, C. Italia 129 (☎53 31 111).

Internet Access: IT.Sorrento, V. degli Aranci 49 (☎87 85 742). €5 per hr. Open M-F 10am-11pm, Sa 10am-8pm, Su noon-8pm.

Post Office: C. Italia 210 (☎87 81 495), near P. Lauro. Also has **ATM.** Open M-F 8am-6:30pm, Sa 8am-12:30pm. **Postal Code:** 80067.

▗ ACCOMMODATIONS AND CAMPING

Reasonably priced accommodations make Sorrento a convenient gateway to the Amalfi Coast or destinations farther south. Many visitors head to nearby beaches and towns during the day and return to Sorrento's hotels at night, a great way to avoid inflated prices for lodging and food on the Amalfi Coast. Reserve ahead in summer. To avoid being overcharged, ask hotel managers for an official price list.

Ostello Le Sirene, V. degli Aranci 160 (☎80 72 925). Centrally located yet protected from tourists, this hostel offers small dorms with private bath. The hostel is next to a bar, with some rooms right next to a railroad track. Also offers cheaper dorms (€14) in the nearby town of Sant'Angelo. Breakfast included. Kitchen. Dorms €18-22; doubles €60; triples €70. Cash only. ❶

Hotel Linda, V. degli Aranci 125 (☎87 82 916; www.hotellinda.com). Simple, comfortable rooms near the train station. Private bath. Breakfast €3. Singles €30-37; doubles €45-70. Cash only. ❸

Hotel Elios, V. Capo 33 (☎87 81 812), halfway to the Punta del Capo. Take bus A from in front of the flags of P. Tasso. The 14 rooms are ordinary, but 2 large terraces and a hilltop location make for great views. A 30min. walk from Sorrento's bus and train stations. Open Apr.-Oct. With *Let's Go* discount, singles €35-40; doubles €60-65; triples €90; quads €100. Cash only. ❸

Santa Fortunata Campeggio, V. del Capo 39 (☎80 73 579; www.santafortunata.com). Bus A from P. Tasso. Spacious, wooded seaside site with private beach, pool, hot showers, market, and restaurant. Laundry €4.50. No tent? No problem. Sites €16-25 with rented tent; dorms €19; 2- to 6-person bungalows €27-29 per person. Cash only. ❶

Nube D'Argento, V. Capo 21 (☎87 81 344; www.nubedargento.com). Comfortable, clean, intimate grounds for camping while still close to the town; bungalows also available. €8-10 per person, €5-10 per tent. 2-person bungalow €50-85; triples €60-95; quads €65-115. MC/V. ❶

◪ FOOD

Seek out Sorrento's restaurants for substantial portions of affordable Italian fare. Local favorites include *gnocchi alla Sorrentina* (potato dumplings in tomato sauce, mozzarella, and basil) and *cannelloni* (pasta stuffed with meat or cheese). **Fabbrica Liquori,** V. San Cesareo 51, provides free samples of *nocillo*, a dark walnut liqueur, and *limoncello*, its lemon cousin. (Open daily 9am-10pm.) Follow V. San Cesareo from P. Tasso for a **market** where sweet, ripe fruit awaits. Find organic lemon and orange *granita* (€2) at **ArancioLimone,** V. San Cesareo 57. (☎87 73 842. *Let's Go* discount 15%. Open daily 10am-11pm. AmEx/MC/V.) There's a giant **STANDA** supermarket on C. Italia 225. (Open M-Sa 8:30am-1:20pm and 5-9pm, Su 9:30am-1pm and 5-8:30pm. AmEx/MC/V.) There's also a small, individual **market** along C. Italia in front of the post office.

■ **Sedil Dominova,** (☎87 81 351), by V. San Cesareo. In front of a charming dome, this restaurant is true to its slogan: "good service with a smile." Street musicians add to the ambience. Savor a delicious *gnocchi alla sorrentina* for €7 or pizza for €5-8. Arrive early to avoid long lines. Open daily 7-11:30pm. ❶

■ **Ristorante e Pizzeria Giardiniello,** V. dell'Accademia 7 (☎87 84 616; ristoranteilgiardiniello@libero.it). Take 2nd left off V. Giuliani, which runs off C. Italia. Try Mamma Luisa's delightful *gnocchi* (€5) or *linguini al cartoccio* (linguini with mixed seafood; €7). Secluded seating surrounded by bamboo. Cover €1. Open Apr.-Nov. daily 11am-midnight; Dec.-Mar. M-W and F-Su 11am-midnight. AmEx/MC/V. ❷

Il Leone Rosso, V. Marziale 25 (☎80 73 089; www.theredlion.it). From P. Tazzo follow the signs and make a right onto V. Marziale. Low prices and roaring atmosphere, from fun backpackers to Italian vacationers. Packed every night; expect lines in summer, or reserve a day ahead. *Primi, secondi,* side, and dessert €14. Open daily noon-3:30pm and 7pm-12:30am. AmEx/MC/V. ❷

Pizzeria da Franco, C. Italia 265 (☎87 72 066). As one of the town's informal gathering spots, this pizzeria is always full. Instead of going for a pizza (€6-8), try the *panini* (€3-6) or Sorrento-renowned *antipasti* (€5-8). Open daily noon-11:30pm. ❷

CAMPANIA

CAMPANIA

👁 🔊 SIGHTS AND NIGHTLIFE

Sorrento's popularity among tourists is not unjustified, although neighboring towns offer more serenity. If you're willing to conquer the stairs (about 5min.; beach shoes are fine), the **Marina Grande,** far from the crowds swarming around P. Tasso, provides a pleasant setting for relaxing on a bench after a long day of walking or daytripping. A walk to **Punta del Capo** leads to the ruins of **Villa di Pollio Felice** clustered around a beautiful cove. Take bus A from P. Tasso to the end of the route, then take the footpath to the right of the stop. Bring a suit and a towel for a memorable swim in the turquoise pools, but do not expect much sand. Farther down the road on bus A in Massa Lubrense is **Puolo Beach,** a 300m stretch of sandy shore spread with umbrellas and chairs.

At night, don't miss the ■**sunset** from P. della Vittoria. After dark, the **old city** and the area around **Piazza Tasso** heat up. Hands-down the most stylish bar in Sorrento, **Photo Bar,** V. Correale 19, has a garden and creative interior with giant color photos. Sip creative mixed drinks (from €8) and munch on complimentary fresh *antipasti* while photography flashes on giant screens overhead. (☎87 73 686; www.photosorrento.com. Open daily 7pm-3am.) If you are feeling nostalgic for a good ol' beer and some Anglo-Saxon culture, try **The English Inn,** C. Italia 57, where a fun-loving crowd gathers after 10:30pm on summer nights to dance to blasting music. They return the next morning for a breakfast (€7) of eggs, sausages, and bacon—a hearty departure from Italian breakfast *cornetti,* or croissants. (☎80 74 357. Drinks €5-8. Open daily 9am-1am; later Sa-Su.)

PROCIDA   ☎ 081

Calmly rippling waters and bobbing fishing boats complete the perfect island serenity of Procida (PRO-chee-da; pop. 11,000), a setting so ideal that it was chosen for numerous films, including Italian favorite *Il Postino.* The flattest and smallest of the major islands in the Bay of Naples at just 10 sq. km, Procida is also the least touristed. From fresh seafood to tangy lemons, Procida will awaken your senses to life's simple pleasures. Surrounded by kind and generous islanders, it's almost possible to forget the throngs of tourists on the mainland.

▐ TRANSPORTATION

Ferries and hydrofoils: All boats dock at Marina Grande, near the ticket offices. Confirm times and prices at port ticket offices.

Caremar (☎89 67 280; www.caremar.it) runs to: **Ischia** (ferries: 35min., 10 per day 7:30am-11pm, €3.50; hydrofoils: 20min., 3 per day 10:35am-3:45pm, €4.50), **Naples** (ferries: 1hr., 5 per day 7:15am-8pm, €7.50; hydrofoils: 40min., 6 per day 6:50am-6:50pm, €9-11), and **Pozzuoli** (ferries: 50min., 3 per day 8:55am-6:05pm, €3.70; hydrofoils: 30min., 8:25am, €4.50).

Procida Lines (☎89 60 328). Hydrofoil to **Pozzuoli** (30min., 8 per day M-Sa 4am-7:15pm, €7.50).

SNAV (☎89 69 975; www.snav.it) runs hydrofoils to **Naples** (40min., 4 per day 7:35am-5:40pm, €9.50) and **Ischia** (40min., 8 per day 7:50am-9:10pm, €4).

Buses: SEPSA buses (€0.80 at *tabaccherie* or *bars* located near stops, €1.10 onboard) depart from the port and serve the entire island. Frequency and times vary by season; see schedules posted at many *tabaccherie* and hotels. All buses leave you nearby the different beaches.

L1 covers the middle of the island, running past hotels and campgrounds before stopping at the **Chiaiolella** port, the site of the liveliest restaurants and beaches. (Every 20min. 6:10am-11pm.)

C1 follows nearly the same route but also covers the less-populated northwestern part of the island. (Every 40min. 6:50am-8:25pm.)

C2 runs to the northeastern part of the island. (Every 40min. 6:55am-8:25pm.)

L2 serves the southeastern part. (Hourly 6:25am-8:25pm.) Bus drivers rarely call out stops; tell your driver where you want to get off and ask him to remind you when the stop approaches.

Taxis: ☎89 68 785. Taxi stand near the docks. Walking around Procida can be an adventure, as cars and scooters don't like to share the narrow streets with pedestrians. Flatten up against the nearest wall when they come speeding along.

⊠ PRACTICAL INFORMATION

Find an **ATM** at V. Roma 103, by the port. In an **emergency,** call the **carabinieri,** V. Libertà 70 (☎89 67 160), or take bus L1, L2, or C1 to the **emergency clinic,** V. Vittorio Emanuele 191 (☎89 69 058). Walk straight from the port to reach the **pharmacy, Madonna delle Grazie** (☎896 88 83). Access the **Internet** at **Bar Capriccio,** V. Roma 99, to the left of the ferry ticket office when facing away from the water (☎89 69 506; €3 per 30min., €5 per hr.; open daily 7am-2am), or at **Navigator,** V. Principe Umberto 33, on the way to Terra Murata, where **Western Union** services are available. (Open daily 10am-1pm and 5-8pm.) The **post office,** at the corner of V. V. Emanuele and V. Liberta, has an **ATM** outside. (☎89 60 740. Open M-F 8am-1:30pm, Sa 8am-12:30pm.) **Postal Code:** 80070.

⊓ ACCOMMODATIONS

Spending an inexpensive night on Procida is difficult, so non-camping budget travelers may want to make the island a daytrip from Naples. For the able or willing, however, Procida offers gorgeous options.

☒ **La Rosa dei Venti,** V. Vincenzo Rinaldi 32 (☎89 68 385; www.vacanzeaprocida.it). Take the C2 bus to V. Regina Elena. 20 cottages with kitchenette and dining area are surrounded by lush flowers and make busy Naples seem a world away. Private beach access. BBQ available. Breakfast included. Internet access €2.50 per hr. Refundable security deposit €100. 2-6 person cottage €35-45 per person. AmEx/MC/V. ❸

Hotel Residence Tirreno, V. Faro, 34 (☎89 68 341; www.tirrenoresidence.it). With two locations, one by V. Faro and another one right by the sea on V. Salette, this hotel offers exquisite beauty, gorgeous views, and relaxation. Huge lemon grove, free domestic calls, and free Internet access. €30-43 per person. AmEx/MC/V. ❸

Campeggio La Caravella (☎81 01 838) and **Campeggio Vivara** (☎89 69 242), adjacent to each other on V. IV Novembre. Take bus L1 or C1. Clean, pleasant grounds with snack bar and flowers. 15min. from beach at Ciraccio. Open June 15-Sept. 15. Reserve in June for Aug. €6 per person, €6 per tent. Hot shower €0.50. Cash only. ❶

Hotel Savoia, V. Lavadera 32 (☎89 67 616; hotelsavoiaprocida@virgilio.it). Take bus L2. Beautiful tiles, yellow rooms, private terraces, pool, great views, and friendly management make for an idyllic stay. Breakfast €4. Singles €60-75. AmEx/MC/V. ❺

◨ FOOD

Like accommodations, Procida's dining options are not designed for the budget-minded, but seek and you shall find. For snacks, try the small **Supermec SISA,** V. Libertà 72, across the street from the post office. (☎89 68 246. MC/V.) High quality—and expensive—restaurants can be found in the **Porto** and **Chiaiolella** parts of town. After dinner, ask for chilled *limoncello* made from Procidan lemons.

Il Galeone, V. Marina Chiaiolella 35 (☎89 69 622). Open-air seating, delicious cuisine, and attentive service distinguish this family-run restaurant from the more touristy ones along the port. Seafood *antipasti* €5-9. *Primi* €7-8, *secondi* €8-15. Daily *menù* €16. Cover €1.50. Open M-Tu and Th-Su noon-4pm and 7:30-11pm. AmEx/MC/V. ❸

La Locanda del Postino, V. Marina Corricella, 43 (☎810 18 87). This was the restaurant used in 1994 for *Il Postino* and its simple, relaxed beauty explains why. *Primi* and *secondi* €6-15. Open M and W-Su 1-3pm and 7-11:30pm. ❷

Graziella, V. Marina Corricella 14 (☎89 67 479). Escape the spotlight of La Locanda del Postino by heading here for delicious food. *Primi* €6-11. Open daily noon-midnight. ❷

Fishbone, V. Marina Chiaiolella 22 (☎89 67 422). Come to Fishbone for Procidan fare just above the water. Try the succulent rabbit (€8), a highlight of island cuisine. Pizza €2.50-8. *Primi* €4-9, *secondi* around €10. Cash only. ❷

Ristorante Lo Sfizicò, V. Roma 81 (☎89 69 931; www.ristorantesfizico.it). Enjoy fresh seafood while you watch the boats dock. Pizza €3.10-6.50. *Primi* €7-10, *secondi* €6-10. *Menù* €15. Open Tu-Su noon-3pm and 7:30-11pm. AmEx/MC/V. ❷

◉ ▣ SIGHTS AND ENTERTAINMENT

Procida has several **beaches,** most of which remain pleasantly uncrowded. The dark sand and calm waters of **Ciraccio** stretch across the western shore and are sprinkled with drink and snack stands. Ciraccio's western end, near Chiaiolella, is at the end of line L1. Another popular beach is **Chiaia,** on the southeastern cove, accessible by L1, L2, and C1. Perhaps the prettiest of them all, **Pozzo Vecchio** (a.k.a. *Il Postino* Beach, nicknamed after the movie was filmed here) rests amid striking layered cliffs. The Procida Diving Center, V. Giovanni da Procida, at Marina di Chiaiolella, runs scuba diving tours and lessons. (☎339 43 58 493; www.procidadiving.it. 1 dive and full equipment rental €28. Lessons €50. All levels welcome. Open M-Sa 9am-1pm and 3:30-7pm.) To reach the **Abbazia San Michele Arcangelo** (Abbey of St. Michael the Archangel), take bus #C2, or face a steep uphill trek. From the left of the port facing away from the water, take V. V. Emanuele and turn left on V. P. Umberto. The abbey is believed to have been founded exactly in the year 1000. Its plain yellow facade guards splendid 15th-century gold frescoes, while scroll work and stately archways prove a jarring contrast to the quiet, unassuming island outside the gates. Take a moment to admire the deeds of St. Michael emblazoned on the domes. (☎89 67 612; www.abbaziasanmichele.it. Open daily 9:45am-12:45pm and 3-5:30pm. Free.) En route to the abbey, the medieval walls of **Terra Murata** are downhill from the monastery, on V. San Michele. Procida's oldest settlement, this area's winding streets teem with speeding scooters. The lookout point outside the walls opens onto the idyllic marina of **Corricella;** pack a picnic and enjoy the breeze. The view is especially beautiful at night.

Lemons are everywhere you turn in Procida and are honored for their place in Procidan culture at the summertime **Festa del Limone** (around May 30-June 1). Besides delicious lemony treats, the festival features a fashion show and a debate on—what else—the lemon.

ISCHIA ☎081

Ischia's (EES-kya; pop. 60,000) combination of sea, sand, and sky presents a rich, earthy beauty so perfect you'll never want to leave. The island, once an active volcano, now houses hot springs, ruins, and lemon groves that give it a refreshing tranquility. Ischia first captivated Phoenicians 7000 years ago and later gained mention in both *The Iliad* and *The Aeneid;* the island's green waters have most recently been featured in the popular film *The Talented Mr. Ripley.* When tourists, particularly Germans, crowd the island in August, Italians turn to the therapeutic hot springs and thermal spas to cure their ailments. Whether or not you frequent its springs, the Ischia is sure to leave you refreshed.

TRANSPORTATION

Ferries: From Ischia, ferries and hydrofoils run to **Pozzuoli, Naples, Procida, Capri,** and **Sorrento.** Most ferries arrive and leave from **Ischia Porto,** generally known simply as "Ischia," where the main ticket offices are located. Ferries also arrive and depart from **Casamicciola,** on the northern side of the island, and from **Forio,** Ischia's largest town. Take the #1, 2, or CS bus from Ischia Porto to reach both departure points. Schedules and prices are subject to change. Call individual ferry lines for details or check online.

Caremar (☎98 48 18; www.caremar.it) runs to: **Naples** (ferries: 1½hr., 8 per day 6:45am-8:10pm, €10.50; hydrofoils: 1hr., 6 per day 6:50am-7:10pm, €16), **Pozzuoli** (ferries: 1hr., 3 per day 8:25am-6:55pm, €3.60), and **Procida** (ferries: 35min., 8 per day 6:45am-7:30pm, €3.10; hydrofoils: 20min., 3 per day noon-4:15pm, €4). Most Caremar ferries leave from Ischia Porto. Ticket offices open 30min. before departure of 1st boat.

Traghetti Pozzuoli (☎99 28 03; www.traghettipozzuoli.it) runs ferries to **Naples** (1½hr., 7 per day 6:40am-6:50pm, €8) and **Pozzuoli** (1hr., 6 per day 2:30am-7pm, €8). Ticket offices open 30min. before departure of 1st boat.

Alilauro (☎99 18 88; www.alilauro.it) runs hydrofoils to: **Capri** (40min., 10:40am, €12.20); Mergellina station in **Naples** (45min.; from Ischia Porto 11 per day 8am-7pm, €11.50; from Forio M and F-Su 4 per day 1-8:30pm, Tu-Th 3:40pm, €13); Molo Beverello station in **Naples** (45min.; from Ischia Porto 11 per day 6:35am-7pm, €16; from Forio 3 per day 12:50-6pm, €13); **Sorrento** (daily 5:20pm, €16.50).

Buses: Orange **SEPSA buses** depart from the intersection on V. Iasolino and V. Baldas-sarree Cossa. Take a right from Molo 1 or a left from Molo 2 and walk along the port, following the road as it curves away from the port. The main lines are CS, CD, and #1. **CS** circles the island counter-clockwise, hitting Ischia Porto, Casamicciola Terme, Lacco Ameno, Forio, Panza Cava Grado (Sant'Angelo), Serrara, Fontana, Buonopane, and Barano. **CD** follows the same route in a clockwise direction. (Both CS and CD every 15-30min., 4:20am-1am.) **Bus #1** follows the CS route as far as Cava Grado (Sant'Angelo) and then comes back (every 15-20min., in summer 5:05am-2:30am, in winter 5:05am-1am). Other routes are shorter, run less frequently, and stop earlier; use these for reaching specific sites or more remote locations. Don't expect breathing space; island buses are packed with passengers until the end of the night.

Taxis: The pricey **Microtaxi** fleet (☎99 25 50) and **taxis** (☎33 31 093) wait at a taxi stand in front of the ticket offices on V. Iasolino.

DAY TRIPPER. The Unicolschia Pass for all public transportation is a great deal for day-trippers or weekenders. (1hr. €1, 1¼hr. €1.20, 1 day €4, 2 day €7, 1 week €24.)

ORIENTATION AND PRACTICAL INFORMATION

Ischia's towns and points of interest lie largely on the coast, connected by the S.S. 270 (the main road), while the inner island is mainly mountainous wilderness. In **Ischia Porto,** the main harbor town, **Corso Vittorio Colonna** runs parallel to **Via de Luca** from the port, one block from the waterfront. Nearby **Ischia Ponte** is a small island connected by a footbridge. Counterclockwise, **Casamicciola, Lacco**

CAMPANIA

Ameno, and **Forio** continue along the coast. In the south, **Fontana,** reached by the CS and CD bus lines, is a good departure point for **Monte Epomeo.** An **AACST tourist office** is on V. Iasolino in Ischia Porto. Turn left from the port; the office is in the Terme Comunali. The staff provides local tour listings, free maps, and accommodations info. **Luggage storage** is €3 per 2hr. (☎50 74 231 or 50 74 211; www.ischiaonline.it. Open M-Sa 9am-2pm and 3-8pm.) In case of **emergency,** call the **police,** V. delle Terme 78, two blocks from V. de Luca in Ischia Porto. (☎507 47 11. Open M, W, and F 9am-noon, Tu and Th 9am-11am.) The **hospital, Ospedale Anna Rizzoli,** V. Fundera in Lacco Ameno, is accessible by bus #1, CS, or CD. (☎50 79 111 or 507 92 24.) **Internet** access is available at the **Pointel Store,** P. Trieste e Trento 9, right off the main bus stop near the port. (€3.60 per 30min., €6 per hr. Open M 4:30-8:30pm, Tu-Sa 9:30am-1pm and 4:30-8:30pm.) The **post office** is at V. Mazzella 446, with a branch at V. Alfredo De Luca 42. **Postal Code:** 80077.

ACCOMMODATIONS

Despite its immense popularity, Ischia has several budget options in Forio, making it the most affordable base for an island visit. Hotels in Ischia Porto, Casamicciola Terme, and Lacco Ameno tend to be very expensive, since many hotels have pools fed (allegedly) by hot springs, and views fit for a queen. Ischia's thriving tourist crowd ensures the presence of hotels everywhere, and among these, some truly fit the wallet of a budget-minded traveler.

FORIO

Ring Hostel, V. Gaetano Morgera 66 (☎98 75 46; www.ringhostel.com). Whether it's organizing midnight excursions to hot springs or planning dinners for over 20 people, the kind staff make sure this hostel is a second home for their guests. Housed in a 19th-century convent; some rooms have domed ceilings and tiled floors. Common room with guitar, Xbox, flat-screen satellite TV, foosball, and DVD collection. Don't miss the sunset from the roof. Breakfast included. Bar open 8pm-late. Free Internet access. Laundry €4. 12-bed dorm €17, 6-bed €19, 4-bed €21; singles €30; doubles from €28 per person. *Let's Go* discount 10%. ❶

Ostello Il Gabbiano (HI), Strada Statale Forio-Panza 182 (☎90 94 22), on the road between Forio and Panza. CS and #1 bus stop outside. The quiet yet fun atmosphere make this hostel a balanced choice, even if it is a bit secluded. Pool and easy, free beach access. Breakfast included. Lockout 10am-2pm; flexible. Open Apr.-Oct. Reserve 1 month in advance for Aug. 4-, 5-, and 6-person dorms €16.50. MC/V. ❶

Apartments in Ischia, V. Castello 4 (☎98 25 94 or 347 05 64 203; EDP1@interfree.it). Call English-speaking staff for directions. 6 well-maintained apartments (each hold up to 6) have terrace and easy beach access in a 300-year-old home full of antiques. With *Let's Go* discount, prices from €25 per person. Min 2-night. stay. Cash only. ❷

Pensione di Lustro, V. Filippo di Lustro 9 (☎/fax 99 71 63; www.pensionedilustro.com). Take the CS, CD, or #1 bus to Forio, exit at the seaside stop on V. Colombo, and make a slight left. Truman Capote slept here in 1949. This hotel has 10 airy, comfortable rooms with bath, A/C, and TV, all reached by ascending a winding staircase around an internal garden. Breakfast included. Reservations recommended 1 week in advance. Rooms in summer €40 per person. Half pension €45-60 per person. *Let's Go* discount €5 in winter. AmEx/MC/V. ❹

Hotel Villa Verde, V. Matteo Verde 34 (☎/fax 98 72 81; www.villaverdehotel.it). Follow directions to Pensione di Lustro, continuing on V. Filippo di Lustro and then taking left on V. Matteo Verde. Located in the center of Forio, yet still provides peaceful atmosphere with a rooftop patio, garden, and sweeping views of the port and Monte Epomeo. Clean, spacious rooms with A/C and TV. 10 rooms have terraces. Breakfast included. July rooms €40. Aug. €45. June and Sept. €35. Oct.-May €30. ❸

ISCHIA PORTO

Valery Hotel, V. Cossa 48 (☎99 10 94). From Ischia Porto bus station, ascend the main street and turn right; go upstairs to reception. Offers lovely terraces with the best view of the island. 15 basic rooms have bath, TV, fridge, and safe. With *Let's Go* discount, singles €30; doubles €50; triples €75; quads €100. MC/V. ❸

Albergo Fagianella, V. Mirabella 34 (☎98 19 91 256). Immaculate, spacious rooms with TV and private bath. Located in a relaxed residential area near the beach. €30-40 per person. MC/V. ❸

Albergo Macri, V. Iasolino 96 (☎99 26 03), along the docks, near where buses board. A quiet and conveniently located hotel, barely evading the hordes of tourists on V. Porto. 22 basic rooms have comfortable beds and spotless bath. Singles €45; doubles €66-75; triples €80-100. MC/V. ❸

Hotel Villa Ciccio, V. Quercia 26 (☎099 32 30; www.villaciccio.it). From Porto Ischia bus station, a short walk uphill to the right along V. Quercia. Small hotel offers the best for reasonable prices. Quiet, romantic, garden-surrounded thermal swimming pool and patio. All rooms with terrace or balcony, minibar, safe, and phone. Rooms €50-75, surcharge €5 to stay alone. Half pension €60-90, full pension €70-80. Cash only. ❹

🏕 **Eurocamping dei Pini,** V. delle Ginestre 34 (☎98 20 69). Take bus #13 from Ischia Porto. Ideal for the budget traveler, this clean and friendly campsite also has a popular restaurant. Many families camp here all summer, giving the site a community feel. Dogs not allowed. €7-10 per person, €6-10 per tent. Bungalows €12.50-25 per person. ❶

🍴 FOOD

Have fun exploring the delights of *cucina ischitana*. Seafood and fruit are excellent, but the local delicacy is *coniglio* (rabbit), served *all'ischitana* (with parsley). Besides the lip-smacking *limoncello*, also try *il rucolino* (a herbal liquor). Find all the provisions for a beach-side picnic at **Didi Supermercato,** V. Matteo Verde 33. (Open daily 8am-1:30pm and 5-9pm. Closed F morning. AmEx/MC/V.)

TOP TEN MUST-EATS IN CAMPANIA

1. Limoncello: Don't fall for fluorescent-yellow fakers. Find the authentic, syrupy sweet liqueur in small, family-owned restaurants where it's made using generations-old recipes passed down from *nonna* to *mamma.*

2. Pizza alla Margherita: The signature dish of Naples, made with fresh tomato, oozing mozzarella, and aromatic basil.

3. Granita: Remember that Italian ice you used to get at little league baseball games? This is it, but better. Think: fresh lemons.

4. Peperone: Find the hot, red peppers hanging from roadside stands all along the Amalfi Coast. Not to be confused with pepperoni sausage—much different.

5. Gnocchi alla Sorrentina: Typical of Sorrento, the *gnocchi* are smothered with crimson tomatoes and melted mozzarella.

6. Sfogliatelle: A soft, flaky, ricotta-filled pastry, invented in Naples in 1785. Best warm.

7. Pasta ai frutti di mare: Literally, "fruits of the sea," featuring octopus, mussels, and shrimp.

8. Scialatelli: A Neapolitan pasta, painstakingly handmade with egg and semolina grain.

9. Insalata caprese: A beautiful combo of tomatoes, basil, and mozzarella, drizzled with olive oil

10. Mozzarella di bufala: M and creamy, this mozzarella r from buffalo milk is abund dishes throughout the reg

Poggio del Sole, V. Baiola 193 (☎98 77 56), in Forio. Offers optimal food, a relaxing ambience, and friendly service. Pasta, seafood, and *limoncello* will not disappoint. Popular with tourists. *Spaghetti con cozze* (with mussels) €7. *Primi* and *secondi* €5-10. Open every day noon-3pm and 8pm-midnight. ❷

Castello de Aragona, (☎98 31 53), in Ischia Ponte. Right next to the entrance of the Castello Aragonese. This hidden spot offers amazing views, with tables so close to the beach that they're practically in the water. Fun atmosphere thanks to young clientele. Primi €7-10. Open daily 10am-3am. ❷

Pirozzi, V. Seminario 51/53 (☎98 32 17), in Ischia Ponte. Offers a gorgeous view of the marina from its terrace seats. Apart from its tasty seafood, this place boasts excellent pizza. Margherita €3.50. Cover €1. Open daily noon-3pm and 7pm-midnight. ❷

Vino&Co, C. Francesco Regine 26 (☎33 32 190), in Forio. Beautiful, spacious, romantic—ideal for a summer meal in paradise. Open everyday noon-3pm and 7-11pm. ❸

La Tinaia, V. Matteo Verde 39 (☎99 84 48), in Forio. Cheap food among a sea of expensive options. Crepes €2.60-3.40. Open daily 8:30am-midnight. Cash only. ❶

🔘 SIGHTS

MORTELLA GARDENS. Lady Suzanna Walton, wife of British composer Sir William Walton (1902-1983), planned and cultivated these exotic gardens, with over 800 rare and exotic plants. Named "Best Garden in Italy" in 2004, the park houses stately buildings, including a monolithic, modern sun temple and an incongruous Thai shrine nestled among vines, vivid blooms, and lily-covered pools. Allow at least an hour to fully absorb the beauty; the map given at the entrance will guide you. **Victoria House** has tropical plants and a gigantic Amazonian waterlily, one of the rarest flowers in the world. A fantastic panorama of Ischia's coast crowns the landscape just above the garden tea house. *(Take the CD or CS bus to the stop before San Francesco; ask driver for V. Calise. Walk downhill, following signs for "spiaggia." Garden entrance is on the right. V. Calise 39. ☎98 62 20; www.ischia.it/mortella. Concerts in summer; call for schedule and info. Open Tu, Th, and Sa-Su 9am-7pm. €10, ages 8-12 €8, ages 5-7 €6.)*

CASTELLO ARAGONESE. Perched atop its own tiny island called Ischia Ponte, the Castello sits in lofty isolation. Connected to the rest of the island by a 15th-century footbridge, this former stronghold hosts both the holy and the gruesome. The castle's **duomo,** largely destroyed by WWII bombing, revels in a heady mix of Roman and Baroque styles. Below, the **crypt** houses colorful 14th-century frescoes by craftsmen from the school of Giotto. The **nuns' cemetery** has a ghastly history: whenever a nun died, the order would prop her decomposing body up on a stone chair as a fragrant reminder to the other nuns of their own mortality. There is nothing of interest inside today—only empty torture chambers and abandoned rooms—yet its external beauty has appeared in many films, including *The Talented Mr. Ripley.* *(Bus #7 runs to Ischia Ponte from Ischia Porto. ☎99 28 34. Open daily 9am-7:30pm. €10, ages 9-14 €6.)*

BEACHES AND HOT SPRINGS. Nestled on an inlet and surrounded on three sides tall rock, the stunning **Citara** beach boasts coarse, white sands and azure Leave your frisbee at home; there won't be room for it on the crowded rby, the **Poseidon gardens** and hot springs offer a pleasant atmosphere. *om Ischia Porto.)* **Maronti,** on the island's south side, has calm water, and a great view. *(Take bus #5 from Ischia Porto.)* For a family-ori-aggia Cava dell'isola, north of Citara beach. Young crowds will enjoy **Lido di San Montano** and **Spiaggia degli Inglesi** *(between Ischia Porto and Ischia Ponte)*. For a steamier experience, the hot springs at **Sorgeto** in Forio on the far side of the island range from tepid to boiling. The beach is the perfect spot to lounge and soak aching feet. Locals claim that the lather formed by rubbing the light-green, porous rocks together is fantastic for the skin. Lacco Ameno and Casamicci-ola Terme are densely packed with the thermal baths that originally attracted visitors to Ischia. The springs are occasionally closed due to falling rocks, so ask the tourist office before setting out. *(Reach the beach from Panza by a 20min. hike.)*

▨ HIKING

A hike in the mountains of Ischia passes more than just greenery and exquisite flora. Scattered throughout the mountainside woods, centuries-old stone sculptures and over 30 ancient stone homes can be explored. Built as protection from frequent pirate attacks that led many Ischians to slavery, these rock houses were an exercise in creative design—improvising on the mountainous terrain, the locals built their homes directly into the hillside. To keep watch over those reckless pirates, the Ischian men guarded the *torrione* (towers), which are still visible along the waterfront in downtown Forio. Those not interested in the history will be rewarded for the fairly difficult climb with breathtaking views. For a more intense hike, head up the 788m to the top of **Monte Epomeo**. On clear days, the summit overlooks Capri and Terracina. *(Take bus CS or #1 from Forio to "Fontana." Take trail into woods; after 2hr. of hiking ruins begin to appear. If interested in going on horseback, contact different companies around Fiaiano, near Ischia Porto.)*

▨ NIGHTLIFE

Ischia's liveliest nocturnal scene is in Ischia Porto, along V. Porto and C. Vittorio Colonna. One of many options is the *discoteca* **New Valentino,** C. V. Colonna 97, where young Italians try to convince foreigners to dance with them. (☎99 26 53. Open F-Su 11pm-6am.) For something more low-key, head to any of the various piano bars in Forio and Ischia Porto, or go for a leisurely *passegiata* along the ocean front streets of Forio.

CAPRI AND ANACAPRI   ☎081

Nicknamed "the pearl of the Mediterranean," Capri (CA-pree; pop. 7000) has been a destination of the rich and famous for thousands of years. Augustus fell in love with Capri in 29 BC before trading its rocky cliffs for the fertile, volcanic Ischia. His successor Tiberius passed his last decade here, leaving scattered villas and a legacy of idyllic retirement homes. Today's royalty flits between ritzy boutiques and top-notch restaurants. Perched on the hills above Capri, the quaint Anacapri (AH-na-CA-pree; pop. 5000) is a relative oasis of budget hotels, lovely villas, and deserted mountain paths. If you can escape the tourists, take time to revel in the relaxed island life while enjoying a languid stroll along Capri's cobblestone paths, a breezy vista from Monte Solaro, or a dip in the Grotta Azzurra.

> **❗ DON'T GET RUN OVER.** Keep to the footpaths in Capri if you're planning on walking. The very narrow streets have no sidewalks and vehicles move at high speeds without watching for pedestrians. Walking on the major thoroughfares is strongly discouraged, so take the bus to faraway destinations.

⬛ TRANSPORTATION

Ferries and Hydrofoils: Capri's main port is **Marina Grande.** Naples and Sorrento are the main gateways to Capri; several different companies service these cities. Check ticket offices at Marina Grande for details.

> **Caremar** (☎83 70 700) runs to **Naples** (ferries: 1¼hr., 3 per day 5:45am-2:50pm, €7; hydrofoils: 40-50min., 4 per day 10:25am-10:20pm, €13) and **Sorrento** (hydrofoils: 25min., 4 per day 7am-6:15pm, €7.10).
>
> **SNAV** (☎83 77 577) runs hydrofoils to **Naples** (40-50min., 6 per day 9:10am-8:10pm, €15). Ticket office opens around time of 1st departure.
>
> **Linea Jet** (☎83 70 819) runs hydrofoils to **Naples** (40-50min., 11 per day 8:30am-6:25pm, €12) and **Sorrento** (25min., 15 per day 7:20am-6:20pm, €10). Ticket office opens right before 1st morning departure.

Public Transportation: SIPPIC buses (☎83 70 420) depart from V. Roma in Capri for Anacapri (every 15min. 6am-1:40am), Marina Piccola, and points in between. In Anacapri, buses depart from P. Barile, off V. Orlandi, for the Grotta Azzurra (Blue Grotto), the *faro* (lighthouse), and more. Direct line between Marina Grande and P. Vittoria in Anacapri (every hr. 5:45am-10:10pm; €1.30, day pass €6). Visitors rarely use the all-day pass enough to make it worthwhile, so buy individual tickets as needed. A **funicular** runs from Marina Grande to Capri (every 10min. 6:30am-1:30am, €1.30).

Taxis: At main bus stop in Marina Grande (☎83 70 543), at bus stop in Capri (☎83 70 543), or in P. Vittoria, in Anacapri (☎83 71 175). To avoid being overcharged, make sure the driver starts the meter when you get in.

> **KEEP THE CHANGE.** On Capri, tickets are generally bought onboard the bus (€1.30). Have exact change on hand to avoid holding up the bus, which won't leave until you pay. Drivers have few bills available.

✦ ❷ ORIENTATION AND PRACTICAL INFORMATION

There are two towns on the isle of Capri: **Capri** proper, near the ports, and **Anacapri,** higher up. Ferries dock at **Marina Grande,** below the town of Capri. To get to Anacapri, either wait for the funicular's long lines to subside, take the bus, or trek up the steep and winding 1hr. path past people's yards and up a stairway. Expensive boutiques and bakeries line the streets that radiate from **Piazza Umberto. Via Roma,** to the right exiting the funicular, leads to Anacapri. The bus to Anacapri passes through **Piazza Vittoria,** the main square; Villa San Michele and the Monte Solaro chairlift are nearby. **Via Giuseppe Orlandi,** running from P. Vittoria, leads past restaurants on the way.

Tourist Office: AAST (☎83 70 634; www.capritourism.com), in Capri, at the end of the dock at Marina Grande. Open daily 9am-1pm and 3:30-6:45pm. **Branches:** Capri, in P. Umberto (☎83 70 686), under the clock. Open M-Sa 8:30am-8:30pm, Su 8:30am-2:30pm. Anacapri, V. Orlandi 59 (☎83 71 524), right from bus stop. Open M-Sa 9am-⁀pm. To avoid tourists, head to the Anacapri branch. All provide detailed maps ⁀80), ferry and bus info, and the magazine *Capri è...*, with detailed info about the ⁀ accommodations and restaurants. Multilingual staff. Reduced hours Oct.-May.

⁀hange: V. Roma 31 (☎83 74 768), across from the main bus stop, and in ⁀nother agency in the center of Anacapri at P. Vittoria 2 (☎83 73 146). No ⁀⁀ in summer daily 8am-6pm; in winter hours vary.

⁀tside Capri's funicular. €2.85 per bag per 2hr. Open daily in sum-⁀ter 8:15am-6pm.

Bookstore: Librerie Studio La Conchiglia, V. Le Botteghe 12 (☎83 ⁀pri, off P. Umberto. Classics, new fiction, and beach trash. Open daily in

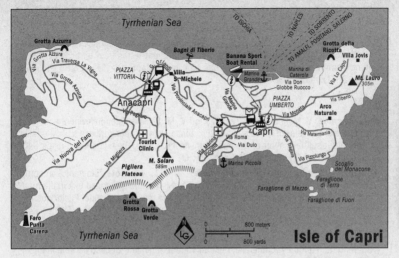

Isle of Capri

summer 9am-1:30pm and 3-10:30pm; in winter 9am-1:30pm and 3-9pm. Smaller branch in Anacapri, V. G. Orlandi 205 (☎83 72 646). Open daily in summer 9:15am-1:15pm and 4:30-9pm; in winter 9am-1pm and 4-8pm.

Emergency: ☎83 81 205. **Police:** V. Roma 70 (☎83 74 211), in Anacapri. **Ambulance:** ☎83 81 205.

Medical services: Ospedale Capilupi, V. Provinciale Anacapri 5 (☎ 83 81 111), a few blocks down V. Roma from P. Umberto. **Tourist Medical Clinic,** V. Caprile 30 (☎83 81 240), in Anacapri.

Internet Access: Capri Internet Point, P. Vittoria 3 (☎83 71 404), in Anacapri, has 2 fast computers. €5 per hr. Open daily 8am-7pm.

Post Office: Anacapri, Vle Tommaso de Tommaso 8 (☎83 71 015). Open M-F 8:30am-1:30pm, Sa 8:30am-noon. **Capri,** V. Roma 50 (☎97 85 211). Open M-F 8:30am-7pm, Sa 8:30am-1pm. **Postal Codes:** 80071 (Anacapri), 80073 (Capri).

ACCOMMODATIONS

Lodgings in Capri proper are pricey year-round and become even more expensive in the summer; opt to daytrip from Naples or Sorrento to save money. Anacapri offers a little more serenity; though cheaper by Capri's standards, it will dent anyone's budget. Call ahead for reservations.

> ❗ **DON'T PITCH A TENT.** Makeshift camping is illegal and heavily fined.

ANACAPRI

Bussola di Hermes, V. Traversa La Vigna 14 (☎83 82 010; www.bussolahermes.com). Call from P. Vittoria in Anacapri for pickup rather than navigate Anacapri's streets. By far the best budget lodging on the island. Recently renovated rooms and a complimentary drink. Breakfast included. Almost always full; reserve early. Dorms €27-30; singles €25-43; doubles €70-110; triples €85-130; quads €90-140. *Let's Go* discount 8% when booking via phone or email. MC/V. ❷

Villa Mimosa Bed and Breakfast, V. Nuova del Faro 48/A (☎83 71 752; villamimosa-capri@libero.it). 100m on the right past the last stop of the Marina Grande-Anacapri bus. Elegant rooms surround a terrace with flowering plants. All rooms with satellite TV, A/C, and bath. Breakfast included. Doubles €80-100. Cash only. ❹

Albergo Loreley, V. Orlandi, 16 (☎83 71 440; www.loreley.it). Tranquility and relaxation are the order of the day. Clean, huge rooms with great vistas from terraces at convenient location right by the funicular/bus stop in Anacapri. Singles €65-85; doubles €85-125. Extra bed €30. MC/V. ❺

CAPRI

Villa Palomba, V. Mulo 3 (☎83 77 322), off V. M. Piccola. Friendly owners and great vistas make this relaxed, private spot a nice place even for young travelers. Best deal in Capri, but it still falls short of the budget traveler's dream. Breakfast €5. Singles €40-75; doubles €60-90, Aug. €125. Cash only. ❹

Pensione 4 Stagioni, V. M. Piccola 1 (☎83 70 041; www.hotel4stagionicapri.com). From P. Umberto, walk 5min. down V. Roma. Turn left at the 3-pronged fork in the road, and look for green gate on the left. The 12 rooms are plain and pristine. Pricier doubles enjoy garden access and sea views. Breakfast included. Open Apr.-Nov. Singles €40-70; doubles €70-120. Extra bed €20. AmEx/MC/V. ❹

Vuotto Antonino, V. Campo di Teste 2 (☎/fax 83 70 230). Take V. V. Emanuele from P. Umberto, turn left on V. Camerelle, right on V. Cerio, then left. Housed in "Villa Margherita." Antique filled rooms devoid of modern distractions such as TV and A/C leave guests to contemplate the coastline from their terraces. Doubles €55-95. Cash only. ❸

🍴 FOOD

Savor creamy local mozzarella served with sweet red tomatoes, glistening olive oil, and zesty basil in an *insalata caprese*—the island's trademark, which many consider the *sine qua non* (a must-have) of summer dining. *Ravioli alla caprese* are hand-stuffed with a blend of local cheeses. Conclude with the indulgent *torta di mandorle* (chocolate almond cake), also known as *torta caprese*. Be discerning around P. Umberto, where restaurants can serve €3 sodas and equally overpriced stale pastries. Fruit stands around the island sell delectable goods at low prices. (Open daily 8am-1pm and 4-8pm.) In Anacapri, find fixings at the well-stocked **supermarket,** V. G. Orlandi 299. (☎83 71 119. Open M-Sa 8:30am-1:30pm and 5-8:30pm, Su 8:30am-noon.) Interestingly enough, it is often cheaper to buy *panini* at restaurants than at *salumerie*.

ANACAPRI

🍽 **Al Nido D'Oro,** Vle. T. de Tommaso 32 (☎83 72 148), on the way to the bus stop for the Grotta Azzurra. Probably the cheapest restaurant on the whole island, it is extremely popular with islanders for its high-quality Caprese dishes. Pizza and drink €7. Primi €5-8. Lunch *menù* €10. Open daily noon-3:30pm and 7-11:30pm. ❶

🍽 **Ristorante Il Cucciolo,** V. La Fabbrica 52 (☎83 71 917). Fresh food at low prices, such as *ravioli caprese* (€9). In the evening, watch the sunset on the seaside terrace. With *Let's Go* discount: *primi* and *secondi* €6-9. Service 12%. Open Mar.-Oct. daily noon-2:30pm and 7:30-11pm. AmEx/MC/V. ❷

Ristorante Materita Bar-Pizzeria, V. Orlandi 140 (☎83 73 375). Devour delicious pizza (from €4.50) on a terrace overlooking Anacapri's most fashionable *piazza*, and then linger over house-made *limoncello*. *Primi* and *secondi* from €7.50. Service 12%. Open daily 11:45am-3:30pm and 6:45pm-midnight; closed Tu Nov.-Mar. AmEx/MC/V. ❸

Caffé Orlandi, V. Orlandi 83 (☎83 82 138). The ideal spot for lunch before heading out to Monte Solaro or walking around Anacapri's *centro storico*. At just €10, their light lunch *menù* (salad, *primi*, drink, and *gelato*), is a great deal. Open daily noon-6pm. ❷

Vini e Bibite, P. Diaz (☎83 73 320). An oasis from the touristy tumult, tucked quietly away. *Primi* and *secondi* €7-12. Cover €2. Open daily noon-3pm and 7pm-midnight. ❸

La Rondinella, V. Orlandi 295 (☎83 71 223), near P. Vittoria, on the left. Enjoy a romantic, candlelit feast under a canopy. Fresh *antipasti* and seafood offerings, like the succulent *gamberoni* (prawns; €18). *Primi* €7-14, *secondi* €8-16. Cover €2. Service 11%. Open daily noon-2:30pm and 7-11:30pm. AmEx/MC/V. ❸

CAPRI

🖼 **Longano da Tarantino,** V. Longano 9 (☎83 70 187), just off P. Umberto. Possibly the best deal in town, featuring a sea view and a €15 *menù* (with *primo*, *secondo*, coffee, dessert, and *limoncello*). It is packed, but service is friendly and efficient. Pizza €4-9. Excellent grilled seafood €12. Cover €0.80. Open Mar.-Nov. M-Tu and Th-Su noon-3:30pm and 7pm-midnight. Reservations recommended. AmEx/MC/V. ❷

Villa Verde, Vico Sella Orta 6/A (☎83 77 024; www.villaverde-capri.com). To the left off V. V. Emanuele, off P. Umberto. Prices reflect the earning power of celeb guests whose pictures adorn the walls of this huge restaurant. Large portions of fresh fish, lobster, and vegetables. House specialties are *fusilli Villa Verde* (€15) and rich desserts (€5-7). Pizza €5.50-15. Daily specials €10-20. *Primi* €10-25, *secondi* €12-25. Service 15%. Open daily noon-4pm and 7pm-1am. AmEx/MC/V. ❹

Ristorante "Da Peppino," Marina Grande (☎83 70 344). Convenient for a quick bite before your boat back to the mainland. Reasonably-priced €16 *menù turistico* includes *primo*, *secondo*, salad, and *gelato*. Open daily 9am-11pm. ❸

Aurora Pizzeria, V. Fuorlovado 20-22 (☎83 70 181; www.auroracapri.com). This cozy establishment serves exactly what is expected of it: pizza (€8-9). Cover €2. Service 15%. Open daily Mar.-Dec. noon-3pm and 7pm-midnight. AmEx/MC/V. ❷

👁 🗻 SIGHTS AND OUTDOOR ACTIVITIES

CLIFFS. An exploration of the island's natural beauty can be a much-needed break from crowded *piazze* and commercial streets. For those who prefer land to sea, various trails starting in Capri lead to stunning panoramas. At the island's eastern edge, a 1hr. walk connects the **Arco Naturale,** a majestic stone arch, and the **Faraglioni,** the three massive rocks featured on countless post-cards. Parts of the path are unpaved dirt, so wear proper footwear. *(V. Tragara goes from Capri Centro to the Faraglioni, while the path to the Arco Naturale connects to the route to Villa Jovis through V. Matermania.)* Hike a steep uphill path 1½hr. to the ruins of Emperor Tiberius's magnificent **Villa Jovis.** Tiberius lived here, the largest of his 12 Capri villas, during his more eccentric final years. Always the gracious host, he was prone to tossing displeasing guests over the precipice. Sweeping views from the villa's **Cappella di Santa Maria del Soccorso** are unrivaled. *(Take V. Longano from P. Umberto. Don't miss the left on V. Tiberio, and follow the signs. Open daily 9am-6pm. €2.)*

COAST. Daily **boat tours** explore the gorgeous coast, including the Grotta Azzurra. *(Tickets and info at Grotta Azzurra Travel Office, V. Roma 53, across from the bus stop. ☎83 70 466; g.azzurra@capri.it. Ticket office open M-Sa 9am-1pm and 3:30-7pm, Su 9am-12:30pm. See below for info on Grotta Azzurra. Departures from Marina Grande at 9:30, 10:30, 11:30am. €13.)* Cavort in the clear water amid immense lava rocks, or rent a **motor boat** from

Banana Sport, in Marina Grande. (☎83 75 188 or 330 22 70 64. Open daily 9:30am-8:30pm. 2hr.; July €75, Aug. €100. AmEx/MC/V.) Many pebbly **beaches** surround the island. Take a boat (€5) from the port or descend between vineyards to **Bagni di Tiberio,** a bathing area within ruins of an imperial villa. A simple walk along **Marina Piccola** is also nice. (Take an internal bus. On foot, take V. Roma from P. Umberto to 3-pronged fork in road; take the left-most fork and head down the path to the left.)

VILLA SAN MICHELE. Henry James once declared this Anacapri enclave a clustering of "the most fantastic beauty, poetry, and inutility." The 20th-century estate displays Roman sculptures from a former Tiberian villa and glorious gardens, which host contemporary art shows and jammin' Friday night concerts from June to August. (Upstairs from P. Vittoria and to the left, past Capri Beauty Farm spa. ☎83 71 401. Open daily 9am-6pm. Concert info available at ticket desk and tourist offices. Villa €6.)

LA GROTTA AZZURRA (THE BLUE GROTTO). The walls of this water-filled cave shimmer vivid blue when sunlight radiates from beneath the water's surface (for this reason, the grotto is more impressive on sunnier days). Watch your head when entering. Some who visit find the water amazing; others don't think it's impressive enough to justify spending €9 on a 6min. guided tour (even if there's singing involved). Despite the narrowness of the cave opening and the sign warning that swimming is "strictly forbidden," some visitors take dips in the grotto for free after boats stop at 5pm. Check with the tourist office to make sure that the grotto is not closed due to choppy water. If you rent a boat, consider visiting the **Grotta Verde,** on the other side of the island. (Take the bus marked "Grotta Azzurra" from the intersection of Vle. T. De Tommaso and V. Catena in Anacapri. The grotto is accessible with the island boat tour as well, but the entrance charge still applies.)

OTHER SIGHTS. Capri's location makes it ideal for surveying southern Italy's topography. Viewed from the peak of ■**Monte Solaro,** the Apennines loom ahead to the east and the mountains of Calabria are to the south on the right. The vistas are so stunning that sky and sea actually seem to become one. A 12min. chairlift from P. Vittoria to the summit dangles from precipitous heights. (☎83 71 428. Chairlift open Mar.-Oct. daily 9:30am-4:45pm. Round-trip €7.) Alternately, take the difficult 45min. hike up V. Monte Solaro, which starts from the base near Villa San Michele. A bus from P. Vittoria leads to the **Faro Punta Carena,** Italy's 2nd-tallest lighthouse, and a fairly desolate swimming area. The pedestrian stretch of V. G. Orlandi, off P. Vittoria in Anacapri, leads to the least expensive (yet still pricey) **shopping.**

◧ NIGHTLIFE

Nocturnal action carries a hefty price tag, though Anacapri's prices are slightly lower. In typical Italian fashion, no one bothers heading out until around midnight. **Underground,** V. Orlandi 259, is one of the town's most popular night spots, thanks to no cover and €5 mixed drinks. In Capri try **BaraOnda,** V. Roma 8, which enjoys theme nights on many weekends. (☎83 77 147. Drinks around €7.) Both Capri clubs are open all night. Those sufficiently self-assured to hang with dressed-to-kill Italians should remember that buses stop running at 1:40am. For a more sophisticated night, attend a Friday night concert at Villa San Michele.

AMALFI COAST

It happens almost imperceptibly: after the exhausting tumult of Naples and the compact grit of Sorrento, the highway narrows to a two-lane road that zigzags down the coastline. Though the effortless simplicity and sophistication of Positano, Amalfi, and Praiano seduced Emperor Augustus, Ernest Hemingway, and Jacqueline Kennedy Onassis, the region's ultimate appeal rests in the tenuous balance it strikes between man and nature. Whitewashed homes cling defiantly to rock and crazy bus drivers tame even crazier roads. The coast's unassuming grandeur is a reminder to relax and simply enjoy life.

POSITANO ☎089

As birthplace of the modern bikini, Positano (po-zee-TA-no; pop. 4000) has quite a reputation to live up to. In the mid-1900s, the town was a posh haven for artists and literati, attracting visitors such as John Steinbeck, Jack Kerouac, and Tennessee Williams. Positano's classy reputation soon drew millionaires in addition to the writers, painters, actors, and filmmakers who made it famous, and today, its beachfront teems with a diverse crowd of vacationers. The nature of tourism has changed since Steinbeck sought solitude along Positano's coast, but the town remains a playground for the rich, and for the not-so-famous—ordinary travelers seeking its tranquility and beauty.

TRANSPORTATION

Over land, Positano is best reached by **bus.** Blue or green-and-white SITA buses run to Amalfi and Sorrento (June-Sept. 25 per day 7am-9pm, reduced hours Su and in winter; €1.30). There are two stops in Positano along V. Marconi, the main coastal road. Walk downhill from either stop to reach the *centro.* Tickets are sold at the friendly Bar Internazionale, by the Chiesa Nuova stop on V. Marconi, or at *tabaccherie.* Alternately, catch a **ferry** or **hydrofoil** from Spiaggia Grande. Linee Marittime Salernitane (☎81 11 64; www.amalficoastlines.com) runs ferries (50min., 8:45 and 10am, €11) and hydrofoils (30min.; 11am, 2:10, and 5:10pm; €14) to Capri. Travelmar (☎87 29 50) runs ferries to Amalfi (25min., 6 per day 10am-6:30pm, €5), Minori (30min., 4 per day noon-5:20pm, €5.50), and Salerno (1¼hr., 6 per day 10am-6:30pm, €6). Call ahead to confirm times and prices.

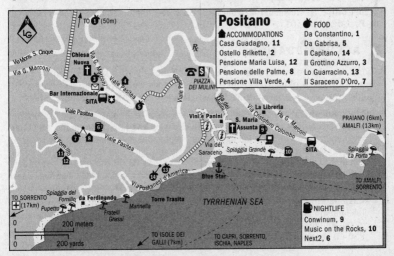

Positano

ACCOMMODATIONS
Casa Guadagno, **11**
Ostello Brikette, **2**
Pensione Maria Luisa, **12**
Pensione delle Palme, **8**
Pensione Villa Verde, **4**

FOOD
Da Constantino, **1**
Da Gabrisa, **5**
Il Capitano, **14**
Il Grottino Azzurro, **3**
Lo Guarracino, **13**
Il Saraceno D'Oro, **7**

NIGHTLIFE
Conwinum, **9**
Music on the Rocks, **10**
Next2, **6**

CAMPANIA

◆ 🛈 ORIENTATION AND PRACTICAL INFORMATION

Positano clings to two huge cliffs overlooking the Tyrrhenian Sea. Coming from Sorrento, **Chiesa Nuova** is the first SITA stop in town on **Via Marconi,** in front of Bar Internazionale. From here, if you don't mind the steep downhill walk, take **Viale Pasitea,** or wait for one of Positano's frequent **local buses** marked "Positano Interno" (every 15-30min. 7:15am-midnight, €1); the bus route ends downtown in **Piazza dei Mulini.** The 2nd SITA stop is at the intersection of V. Marconi and **Via Cristoforo Colombo;** internal buses don't run here, so walk 10min. downhill on V. C. Colombo to reach P. dei Mulini, where V. C. Colombo becomes Vle. Pasitea. Also from P. dei Mulini, **Via dei Mulini** winds through town, past the church of Santa Maria, and to **Spiaggia Grande,** the main beach. Take the footpath from Spiaggia Grande to get to the cozier **Fornillo** beach on the right.

Tourist Office: V. del Saraceno 4 (☎87 50 67; www.aziendaturismopositano.it), in a red building near the church. Provides a free map, hotel listings, and ferry and bus schedules. English spoken. Open in summer M-Sa 9am-2pm and 3-8pm; in winter M-Sa 9am-3pm. Branch: right off Spiaggia Grande. Open M-Sa 9am-3pm.

Currency Exchange: P. dei Mulini 6 (☎87 58 64), on the V. Mulini side of the *piazza.* Decent rates; €1 commission per traveler's check. Open daily in summer 9:30am-1:30pm and 4-9:30pm; in winter 9:30am-1pm and 3:30-7:50pm.

English Language Bookstore: La Libreria, V. C. Colombo 165 (☎81 10 77). Selection of classics, new fiction, and cookbooks. Open daily 10am-1:30pm and 5-8:30pm. Closed Nov.-Mar. AmEx/MC/V.

Carabinieri: (☎87 50 11), near top of the cliffs down the steps opposite Chiesa Nuova.

Hospital: (☎081 533 11 11), in Sorrento; a **tourist medical clinic** is in Amalfi.

Pharmacy: Vle. Pasitea 22 (☎87 58 63). Open in summer daily 9am-1pm and 5-9pm; in winter M-W and F-Sa 9am-1pm and 4-8pm.

Internet Access: Conwinum, V. Rampa Teglia 12 (☎81 16 87; www.positano.conwinum.it), below Buca di Bacco. Drinks available while you surf. €6 per hr. Open daily 9am-late (See p. 598).

Post office: V. Guglielmo Marconi 320. Open M-F 8am-1:30pm, Sa 8am-12:30pm. **Postal code:** 84017.

🏠 ACCOMMODATIONS

Budget travelers might consider making Positano a daytrip from Sorrento or Salerno. For those looking to stay in the village, however, there are a few very good budget options. The tourist office helps arrange *affittacamere* for longer stays.

Ostello Brikette, V. Marconi 358 (☎87 58 57; www.brikette.com). Accessible by orange Interno bus or SITA bus; exit at "Chiesa Nuova" stop and walk 100m to the left of Bar Internazionale; hostel is on the right. Clean, neat rooms and great views from terraces. Helpful English-speaking staff provides advice on sights and restaurants. Breakfast included. Laundry €10. Free Wi-Fi. Internet access €3.50 per hr. Lockout 11am-2:30pm. Lights-out M-Th and Su midnight. Reservation recommended July-Aug. Open late Mar. to Nov. Dorms €22-25; doubles €65-100. MC/V. ❷

Pensione Villa Verde, Vle. Pasitea 338 (☎87 55 06; www.pensionevillaverde.it). Take Interno bus to "Casale." 12 simple rooms by the valley overlooking Positano. All rooms with terrace and bath. TV and A/C available upon request. Breakfast included. €30-40 per person. AmEx/MC/V. ❸

Pensione delle Palme, Vle. Pasitea 252 (☎87 51 62; www.positanovilladelle-palme.com). In the same building as Saraceno d'Oro restaurant, with an easily accessible beach. Rooms full of quirky antiques; all with bath and terrace. Breakfast €5. Singles €55-60; doubles €80-90; triples €110-125. Cash only. ❹

Pensione Maria Luisa, V. Fornillo 42 (☎87 50 23; www.pensionemarialuisa.com). Take the Interno bus down Vle. Pasitea to V. Fornillo. 14 bright rooms with private baths and views from seaside terraces. Basic rooms are comfortable and quiet. Shared fridge. Singles €55; doubles €75. Cash only. ❹

Casa Guadagno, V. Fornillo 36 (☎87 50 42; fax 81 14 07). Take the Interno bus down Vle. Pasitea to V. Fornillo. Tiled floors and incredible views of the coast. Complimentary breakfast on the idyllic covered terrace. All rooms have bath, minifridge, and private terrace overlooking the sea. Reservation recommended. With *Let's Go* discount, doubles €85; Aug. €90. Cash only. ❹

FOOD

In Positano, high prices generally reflect high quality: homemade pasta, fresh produce, and excellent seafood are not hard to find. The well-stocked **Vini e Panini,** V. del Saraceno 29-31, near the tourist office, sells fresh sandwiches, cheese, and produce. (☎87 51 75. Open Mar.-Dec. daily 8am-2pm and 4:30-9pm. Cash only.)

Da Gabrisa, Vle. Pasitea 219 (☎81 14 98; fax 81 16 07). Bright, breezy dining room and great service. Savor the tender pumpkin in the grilled vegetable *antipasto* with plump mozzarella (€5). The simple *pasta alla norma* (pasta in tomato sauce with eggplant; €8) is a savory treat. *Primi* €6-10, *secondi* €8-15. Open daily 6-11pm. MC/V. ❸

Lo Guarracino, V. Positanesi d'America 12 (☎975 794). To avoid over-priced restaurants by Spiaggia Grande, take the stairs on the way to Fornillo Beach; this restaurant, complete with great views, will be to the right. Pizza €8, takeout €4. *Primi* and *secondi* €8-15. Open daily noon-3pm and 7pm-midnight. ❷

Da Constantino, V. Corvo 95 (☎87 57 38). From Ostello Brikette-walk up the stairs, and turn right when you hit the real road, or take the bus to "Nocelle." Amazing views, sea breezes, and occasional live music make this the spot to cap off a long day. Try the specialty *crespolini al formaggio* (crepes filled with cheese; €5.50). Pizza from €4. *Primi* €5-10, *secondi* €8-13. Open in summer daily noon-3:30pm and 7pm-midnight; in winter M-Tu and Th-Su noon-3:30pm and 7pm-midnight; closed Nov.-Jan. AmEx/MC/V. ❷

Il Grottino Azzurro, V. Marconi 304 (☎87 54 66), across from the "Chiesa Nuova" bus stop. Excellent fish and seafood priced right. Guests linger for hours in simple but inviting interior, or on the road outside. Excellent homemade white wine €8. Serves fresh seafood from €9, including delicious spaghetti with squid (€11). Homemade pasta dishes €8-10. Cover €2. Open M-Tu and Th-Su 12:30-2:30pm and 7:30-11pm. Closed Dec. to mid-Feb. Cash only. ❸

Il Saraceno d'Oro, Vle. Pasitea 254 (☎81 20 50). For a quick meal, enjoy delicious pizza to go (from €4.50; dinner only) or stay and enjoy the incredible *gnocchi alla sorrentina* (€8) while you listen to live music. Cover €1.50. Open in summer daily noon-3pm and 7-11:30pm; closed Nov.-Feb. Cash only. ❷

Il Capitano, Vle. Pasitea 119 (☎81 13 51). Perfect for a breezy romantic dinner and local wine (€8-12) overlooking the coast. *Primi* and *secondi* €10-20. Open daily 6pm-midnight. ❹

SIGHTS AND BEACHES

In Positano, the tragically chic spend entire days—or at least unbearably hot afternoons—in exorbitant boutiques or perusing sidewalk kiosks. Others take boat excursions along the coast and to neighboring islands, as well as the **Emerald** and **Blue Grottoes** (p. 593). For most, Positano's beaches are its main attraction; even these are not free. Your best bet for serene and secluded relaxation—and a waterside meal post-beach—is **Fornillo Beach,** hidden from the docks and downtown blitz by a shady, rocky walkway. Take **Via Positanese d'America,** a footpath that starts from the left side of the port facing away from the water and winds past **Torre Trasita.** Three other private beaches on this end are **Marinella, Fratelli Grassi,** and **Puppetto** (all €7). At the private **Lido L'Incanto** (☎81 11 77), guests revel in the fact that they are surrounded only by other people who shelled out €10 for a *lettino* (beach chair), umbrella, shower, and changing room. Outside the entrance, **Blue Star** (☎81 18 88; www.bluestarpositano.it) rents motorboats and rowboats, and provides boat tours of the Blue and Emerald Grottoes; call for prices and info. For a short, free boat ride, jump on any of the small, white boats off Spiaggia Grande, which will give you a tour of various restaurants that can only be reached by sea. The biggest, busiest, and priciest beach is **Spiaggia Grande** (about €12), in the main stretch by the docks.

Positano offers tremendous **hikes** for those with quads of steel. **Montepertuso,** a high mountain pierced by a large *pertusione* (hole), is one of three perforated mountains in the world (the other two are in India). Hike the 45min. trail up the hillside or take the bus, which leaves from P. dei Mulini near the port. From Montepertuso, take **The Path of the Gods** (4hr.), which explores the surrounding area. Ask the tourist office for a map. The three **Isole dei Galli,** peeking out of the waters off Positano's coast, were allegedly home to Homer's mythical Sirens, who lured unsuspecting victims with their spellbinding songs. While swimming around these beautiful islands is permitted, setting foot on them is not.

🎵 🎭 ENTERTAINMENT AND NIGHTLIFE

Positano's Art Festival includes fashion shows, art exhibitions, dance, and music concerts at different spots in the city (Apr.-Oct.; contact tourist office for more info). The swanky piano bar and disco, **Music on the Rocks,** on the far left side of the beach facing the water, packs well-dressed locals and visitors into a large cave with one side open to the water. Celebrities including Sharon Stone and Luciano Pavarotti have been known to drop in. (☎87 58 74. Mixed drinks from €12. Cover varies: M-Th and Su often free, Sa €25.) For less exclusive revelry, head to **Conwinum,** V. Rampa Teglia (p. 596) to meet young locals. No cover and €5 mixed drinks make this wine bar a fun spot to meet other travelers. Those looking to quench their thirst begin to arrive around 10pm, but the place opens at 9am as an Internet cafe. After grabbing a meal at **Next2,** Vle. Pasitea 242, stick around for a drink (around €8) and lounge music. (☎81 23 516. Open daily 7pm-midnight.)

PRAIANO   ☎089

The quiet town of Praiano (pry-AH-no; pop. 2000), a sparsely-populated expanse scattered over 10km of stunning coastline, is a welcome change from the rest of the heavily-touristed Amalfi Coast. Also unlike its neighbors, Praiano's cliff-side charm comes without an unreasonable price tag, making it a good base for trips along the coast. From crumbling towers to beautiful sunsets, unjustly-overlooked Praiano has a refreshingly authentic feel to it; come here to breathe some real sea air and take a vacation from your vacation.

✦ 🛈 ORIENTATION AND PRACTICAL INFORMATION

Praiano is less of a town than a loose conglomeration of hotels and restaurants. You can reach it by bus from Positano (15min.), or by a scenic 1hr. walk. The town is skirted to the south by **Via Gennaro Capriglione** which turns into **Via Roma; Via Giuglielmo Marconi** and **Via Umberto I** run parallel to their more southern counterparts. The **tourist office** (☎87 45 57) is at V. G. Caprigione. The nearest **hospital** is in Sorrento (☎081 533 11 11). Find an **ATM** on V. G. Capriglione. The **pharmacy** is at V. G. Capriglione 142 (☎874 846). For **Internet** access, go to **Dimensione Futuro,** V. G. Capriglione 27. (€4 per hr. Open M-F 9am-1pm and 5-9pm, Sa 9am-1pm.)

ACCOMMODATIONS AND CAMPING

There's no cheap hostel in Praiano, but the town does offer affordable housing options that are tranquil and intimate, especially if you're traveling with a friend.

Il Gelsomino, V. Roma 1 (☎87 44 68; www.ilgelsominopraiano.com). Impressive, nicely decorated, spacious, clean rooms and kind staff. 1-week min. stay in Aug. Breakfast included. Doubles €50-65, with private terrace €80-110. Extra bed €15. ❷

Casa Benvenuto Residence, V. Roma 60 (☎87 44 68). A kind owner runs 6 huge rooms with relaxing views of the Mar Tirreno. TV and huge bathrooms. Breakfast included. Doubles €70-90; made into triples or quads for same price. Cash only. ❸

La Conchiglia, V. Marina di Praia 17 (☎87 43 13). Family-run hotel offering beautiful, recently renovated rooms. Convenient location right on the beach, near restaurants and nightlife. Breakfast included. Doubles €60-100. Extra bed €25. Cash only. ❸

Camping La Tranquilità, V. Roma 21 (☎87 40 84). This cozy, sunny site has great vistas and a great location near Torre a Mare and Marina di Praia. Space for 10 tents; bring your own. No kitchen. Breakfast €5. €17.50 per person. ❶ Connected to **Hotel/ Restaurant Continental,** with rooms and bungalows. Singles €50; doubles €70. ❹

FOOD

Your palate won't know the difference between the food of Praiano and that of its pricier cousins, but your wallet will. For an especially cheap meal, try any of the four handy and delicious *alimentari* along V. Capriglione, which all share the same hours. (Open M-Sa 7:30am-1pm and 6-10pm.)

Il Pirata, V. Terramare (☎87 43 77). Tucked away to the right of Marina di Praia. Enjoy delicious food right on the edge of an impressive cliff overlooking fun-loving swimmers. *Primi* €7-10. Open daily noon-3:30pm and 7:30-11pm. ❷

Petit Restaurant Bar Mare, V. Marina di Praia 9 (☎87 47 06). Always delicious, this happening spot is especially popular among young partyers heading out to dance the night way. Spaghetti with squid €11. Cover €2. Open daily noon-3pm and 6:30-11:30pm. ❷

Open Gate, V. Roma (☎87 42 10), after the first tunnel. Connected to a nice hotel, this secluded spot—with killer vistas and delicious food—has the perfect ambience for either a romantic date or a fun gathering. Pizza €8-10. Spaghetti with clams €9. Service 10%. Open daily noon-2:30pm and 6:30-10:30pm. MC/V. ❷

SIGHTS AND NIGHTLIFE

Praiano's openness and natural beauty make it the coast's best spot for a scenic **scooter** ride, though the abundance of winding roads often makes rental companies hesitant to rent out scooters to first-time drivers. Inexperienced drivers especially should exercise caution while navigating the winding roads. The hotel **Casa di San Gennaro,** V. Capriglione 99, rents scooters from €30 per day. (☎97 42 93; www.ilsangennaro.it. AmEx/MC/V.) Don't miss **Torre a Mare,** a well-preserved tower that once protected against pirates, but now serves as an art gallery for the works of sculptor and painter Paolo Sandulli. (Open daily 9am-1pm and 3-7pm.) From Torre a Mare, descend the ramp that leads down V. Terramare to the **free beach** in **Marina di Praia.** Nearby, check out **La Boa Diving Center,** (☎81 30 34) which offers dives starting at €60. Marina di Praia, a 400-year-old fishing village, tucked in a tiny ravine, also hides restaurants, bars, and one of the Amalfi Coast's most popular clubs since the early 60s, **Africana.** Fish swim through the grotto under the glass dance floor, while music echoes off the dimly lit cave roof above, and boats dock at the stairwell right outside. (☎87 40 42. Africana mixed drink €8. Tu women free. No cover M and W-Th; 1-drink min. Cover Tu, F, Su €15-20; includes 1 free drink. Open mid-June to Sept. daily 10pm-3am.)

AMALFI   ☎089

Amalfi's (ah-MAL-fee; pop. 5500) location between the jagged rocks of the Sorrentine peninsula and the azure waters of the Tyrrhenian Sea make it picture-perfect. Monuments like the fanciful Arab-Norman *duomo* and medieval paper mills are the legacy of a long history of international prominence. Amalfi was the seat of Italy's first sea republic and the preeminent maritime powerhouse of the southern Mediterranean, thanks in part to the compass, invented here by Flavio Gioia. Sadly, Amalfi's universal appeal has lately rendered less appealing results: it is also responsible for the throngs of tourists, gaudy souvenir shops, and exorbitant prices that characterize the town today. Consider the town as a daytrip from Sorrento or Salerno to avoid the touristy prices.

▐ TRANSPORTATION

The **bus terminal** is in P. Flavio Gioia, on the waterfront. SITA **buses** (☎26 66 04; www.sitabus.it.) go to Positano (40min., 25 per day 6:30am-11pm, €1.30), Salerno (1¼hr., 20 per day 6am-10pm, €1.80), and Sorrento (1¼hr., 29 per day 5:15am-11pm, €2). Buy UnicoCampania tickets from *tabaccherie* (€5). **Ferry** and **hydrofoil** tickets and departures are at the dock off P. Flavio Gioia. Travelmar (☎87 31 90; www.coopsantandrea.it) runs hydrofoils to Minori (5min., 4 per day 12:45-6:20pm, €1.50), Positano (25min., 7 per day 9:20am-6pm, €5), and Salerno (35min., 6 per day 10:40am-7:10pm, €4). Metro del Mare (☎199 60 07 00; www.metrodelmare.com) runs ferries to Sorrento (30min., 4 per day 7:30am-3:25pm, €6). Rent **scooters** at Financial Tour Travel (p. 606). Call **taxis** at ☎87 22 39.

▐▌ ORIENTATION AND PRACTICAL INFORMATION

Amalfi is in the shape of an upside-down "T," with the top running along the shore. **Via Lorenzo d'Amalfi,** runs uphill from the shore past the white arch of **Piazza Flavio Gioia** and the town's main square, **Piazza Duomo. Piazza Municipio** is a 100m walk along the coast in the direction of Atrani, up **Corso Repubbliche Marinare** (on the left when facing the sea). Ferries and buses stop in P. F. Gioia, the intersection of the two roads. Go through the tunnel on C. Repubbliche Marinare to reach Atrani, 750m down the coast, or follow the public path through the restaurant just next to the tunnel, on the side facing the sea. The pleasant and easy walk takes 10min.

The **AAST tourist office,** C. delle Repubbliche Marinare, 27, is through a gate on the left on the road toward Atrani. Grab a free map along with hotel and restaurant listings. Ferry and bus timetables are also available. (☎87 11 07; www.amalfitouristoffice.it. Open M-Sa May-June 8:30am-1:30pm and 3:30-5pm; July-Oct. 8:30am-1:30pm and 3:30-6:30pm; Nov.-Apr. 8am-2pm.) To reach the **carabinieri,** V. Casamare 19 (☎87 10 22), follow V. Lorenzo D'Amalfi as it changes to V. Pietro Capuano and then V. Marino del Giudice; turn left to reach V. Casamare. For **medical assistance,** contact **American Diagnostics Pharmaceutics** (☎32 98 24 or 329 42 29

033), with doctors fluent in English, French, German, and medicinal Japanese on-call 24hr. For **Internet** access, head to **Financial Tour Travel,** V. Lorenzo D'Amalfi 29-31, which has three computers. It also offers **Western Union** services and rents **scooters.** (☎87 10 46. Internet €4 per hr. Scooters from €32 per day. Open daily 9am-2pm and 3-8pm.) The **post office,** C. Repubbliche Marinare 35, next to the tourist office, offers **currency exchange** for cash only with good rates. (☎83 04 811. Commission €2.58. Open M-F 8am-6:30pm, Su 8am-12:30pm.) **Postal Code:** 84011.

ACCOMMODATIONS

Lodgings fill up quickly in August, so reserve far ahead. Those on a budget should consider Salerno or Naples for excellent lodging at lower prices.

> **! NO-TELL MOTEL.** Don't accept tips from English-speaking solicitors at the Amalfi bus station waiting for gullible travelers. They hand out info on unregistered hostels. Such hostels—though inexpensive—are illegal, unregulated, often unsanitary, and very unsafe.

A'Scalinatella, P. Umberto 6 (☎87 14 92; www.hostelscalinatella.com), 15min. from Amalfi bus station in Atrani. Take C. Repubbliche Marinare through the tunnel, then the stairs immediately on the right down to the road to P. Umberto. Owners also rent rooms in Atrani, plus campsites and scenic rooms above Amalfi. Breakfast included. Dorms €21; doubles €50-60, with bath €73-83; quads €100. Cash only. ❷

Vettica House, V. Maestra dei Villaggi 96 (☎87 18 14; www.hostelscalinatella.com), shares management with A'Scalinatella. A haven of tranquility amid natural beauty, bright rooms with bath sit above lemon groves. Quick access to great hiking trails (not including the 270 stairs up from the road). Kitchen available. Dorms €15; singles with bath €50; doubles €60, with bath €83; quads €120. Call ahead. Cash only. ❶

Hotel Lidomare, V. Piccolomini 9 (☎87 13 32; www.lidomare.it), through alley across from *duomo*. 18 cozy rooms have terrace, satellite TV, phone, fridge, A/C, and fantastic bath. Small library and sitting room. Breakfast included. Free Internet access. In summer singles €65; doubles €130. In winter €55/100. Extra bed €20. AmEx/MC/V. ❺

Hotel Fontana, P. Duomo 7 (☎87 15 30; www.hotel-fontana.it). Comfortable, modern rooms in an optimal location overlooking both the *piazza* and the harbor. Spacious rooms all have high ceilings, bath, satellite TV,

Amalfi

🛏 ACOMMODATIONS
A'Scalinatella, **11**
Apartments in Amalfi, **7**
Hotel Fontana, **8**
Hotel Lidomare, **10**
Vettica House, **1**

🍴 FOOD
Al Teatro, **3**
Da Maria, **5**
Donna Stella Pizzeria, **2**
Il Chiostro, **6**
Porto Salvo, **9**
Trattoria La Perla, **4**

A/C, and minifridge. Breakfast included. May-Sept. singles €75; doubles €130. Extra bed €40. Oct.-Apr. €50/100/30. Suites available. AmEx/MC/V. ❺

Apartments in Amalfi, V. Sant'Andrea (☎87 28 04; www.amalfiapartments.com), next to the *duomo* at Suportico Sant'Andrea. Rents 2 small apartments with views of the sea and the *piazza.* The double apartment can fit 4 and the studio apartment is perfect for a couple; they share a fantastic terrace. Call or see website for more apartments in Amalfi. Reserve 1 month ahead and call for directions through the maze of stairs. 2-person €65; 4-person €90-110. Cash only. ❸

FOOD

Indulge in delicious seafood or *scialatelli* (a coarsely cut, fresh, local pasta). The town's many *paninoteche* are perfect for a tight budget, but so are some of its restaurants.

Il Chiostro, V. dei Prefetturi, (☎87 33 80). Hidden right next to the left of the *duomo,* this is the perfect place for a light lunch or a sumptuous dinner. Comfortable and private, the service, food, and ambience are the best Amalfi has to offer. Open daily noon-2:30pm and 7-11pm. ❷

Donna Stella Pizzeria, Salita Rascica 2 (☎338 35 88 483). The cool hang out for *amalfitani,* with a gorgeous terrace overlooking the city. Pizza to rival that of Naples. Full most of the time; make reservations or arrive early. Cover €1. Open Tu-Su 8-11pm. ❶

Da Maria, P. Duomo 14 (☎87 18 80). Daily seafood specials, as well as traditional favorites like *scialatelli* and delectable seafood risotto (€13). Live piano music. Pizza from €4.50. *Primi* from €10, *secondi* from €12. *Menù* from €20. Cover €3, for pizza €1.50. Wheelchair-accessible. Open M-Tu and Th-Su noon-3:30pm and 6:30-11:30pm. Reservations recommended. AmEx/MC/V. ❸

Al Teatro, V. E. Marini 19 (☎87 24 73). From V. L. d'Amalfi, turn left up Salita degli Orafi. Try the *scialatelli al Teatro* (local pasta with tomato and eggplant; €8). *Primi* and *secondi* from €6. *Menù* €15. Cover €1.50. Open M-Tu and Th-Su 11:30am-3pm and 7-11pm. Closed early Jan. to mid-Feb. AmEx/MC/V. ❷

Trattoria La Perla, Salita Truglio 5 (☎87 14 40), around corner from Hotel Amalfi. Excellent local cuisine in a quiet *piazza.* The specialty (homemade pasta with seafood), is served in a giant seashell. *Menù* with delightful desserts €17. Cover €2. Open Apr.-Oct. daily noon-3pm and 7pm-midnight; closed Nov.-Mar. AmEx/MC/V. ❸

Porto Salvo, P. Duomo 8 (☎338 18 81 800). This is the place for hanging out and eating great, ready-made pizza and sandwiches (both €3). Thick focaccia with toppings from €2. Order at the counter and enjoy its delicacies out on the beach. Mixed salads and vegetarian *panini* available. Open daily 8:30am-8:30pm. AmEx/MC/V. ❶

SIGHTS

The gorgeous AD 9th-century **Duomo di Sant'Andrea,** or Cathedral of Amalfi, is this small town's dominant feature. Its facade's intricate geometric designs of vividly contrasting colors, typical of the Arab-Norman style, will transport you to southern Spain. The **bronze doors,** crafted in Constantinople in 1066, are so handsomely wrought that they started a bronze door craze throughout Italy. (Open for prayer daily 7:30-10am, for visiting 10am-5pm. Modest dress required. Free.) To its left, the **Chiostro del Paradiso** (Cloister of Paradise), a 13th-century cemetery for Amalfitan nobles, has 120 striking marble columns and an intricate fresco of the Crucifixion. The elegant, interlaced arches of both the cloister and the church, like the bell tower in the square, reflect a Moorish influence. The modest church

museum houses mosaics, sculptures, and the church's treasury. Underneath, the newly restored **crypt** contains the body of the church's namesake, St. Andrew the Apostle, whose remains were brought to Amalfi during the Crusades. (☎87 13 24. Open daily in summer 9am-9pm; in winter 10am-5pm. Free multilingual guides available. Cloister, museum, and crypt €2.50.) In the center of the *piazza*, the **Fontana di Sant'Andrea** does its best to counteract the church's stately influence, featuring a marble female nude with water trickling from her nipples. Those who can put their Freudian complexes aside might venture a drink from the fountain, which was rebuilt in the 19th century according to an original medieval plan. The 9th-century waterfront contains relics of Amalfi's former maritime glory, including examples of Amalfitan currency (the *tari*), and early compasses by Flavio Gioia. The **Museo della Carta** (Paper Museum), V. delle Cartiere 24, portrays another component of Amalfi's past, as a major paper-producing powerhouse during the Middle Ages. The museum, in a 13th-century paper mill, showcases the history of paper production, including free paper samples made from pressed flowers and the water-powered machines. The ticket includes a 20min. tour with a multilingual guide. (☎83 04 561; www.museodellacarta.it. Open Mar.-Oct. daily 10am-6:30pm; Nov.-Feb. Tu-Su 10am-3:30pm. €3.50, students €2.60.)

🥾 HIKING

Amalfi is an excellent departure point for several ■**hikes,** which are of moderate difficulty and traverse a combination of trails and ancient staircases along the seaside mountains. Hikers often tackle paths from Amalfi and Atrani to the imposing **Monti Lattari,** winding through lemon groves and mountain streams. From Amalfi, the **Antiche Scale** lead past stalactite-heavy caves to the charming village of **Pogerola.** Trek through the **Valley of the Dragons,** named for the torrent of water and mist which plumes like smoke from a dragon and explodes out to sea each winter. However, if you only have time for one excursion, try the popular 4hr. ■**Path of the Gods,** from Bomerano (reachable by bus) to **Positano** (p. 595), with great views along the way. The beautiful hike from Atrani to **Ravello** (p. 604) runs through gently bending lemon groves, up secluded stairways, and down into green cliff valleys (1½-2hr.). From Ravello, it's only around 1hr. downhill to **Minori's** (p. 604) beautiful beaches, past quaint village churches and bountiful grapevines. SITA also runs frequent bus service from both Minori and Ravello to Amalfi, so you can ride back after a long walk. Hike past the old paper mills in **Valle delle Ferriere,** which begins from a staircase across the street from the paper museum. Naturally, the hikes can get steep, and a good map is essential (available at Amalfi's tourist office).

SERIOUSLY, DUDE. Take hikes on the Amalfi coast seriously: bring maps, water, and sturdy hiking boots. Be prepared to climb hundreds of stairs!

🏖 🎭 BEACHES AND NIGHTLIFE

Amalfi has two small **beaches;** one is sandy, the other rocky. The sandy beach, though not stunning, is a social stretch near the marina. Find better (and free) options in nearby **Atrani,** a 10min. walk away (see **Practical Information,** p. 600). With about 1000 inhabitants today, it's a quiet refuge from Amalfi's crowds during the day. At night, Atrani's P. Umberto offers lively bars and a casual atmosphere. Try **La Risacca,** P. Umberto 1, with friendly bartenders and a fun yet tourist-filled atmosphere. (☎87 28 66. Drinks from €1.50. Open daily 8pm-2am. MC/V.) Otherwise, head to nearby **Bar Birecto,** P. Umberto 2, with plentiful outdoor seating. (☎328 53 49 153. Open daily 7pm-3am. AmEx/MC/V.)

⚡ DAYTRIP FROM AMALFI: MINORI. With a decidedly low-key character and many pleasant sea front cafes, Minori (mee-NO-ree; pop. 3300) is serene and inviting. Smaller and less touristed than Amalfi or Positano, the town's large stretches of beautiful **free beaches** make it a perfect spot to relax. Sunbathers seeking the perfect day at the beach and hikers in search of the optimal trail-end spot (see **Hiking,** p. 603) can find peace and relaxation here. For a lunchtime *panino* (€3-6), try **Suzy Beach ❶,** P. California. (☎328 07 77 285. Open daily 8am-11pm. Cash only.) With plenty of breezy outdoor seating, this is the perfect place to reward tired feet after a long day's hike, or to extend your relaxed beach day into the evening. (SITA buses from Amalfi stop on V. G. Capone, which becomes V. G. Amendola as it heads 1km northwest to Amalfi.)

RAVELLO ☎089

Towering above the beach on its terraced cliff-top perch, Ravello (ra-VEH-lo; pop. 2500) caters mostly to music aficionados and wealthy vacationers. Founded by Romans in AD 500 and later invaded by Barbarians and Saracens, the town presides over a patchwork of villages and ravines that tumble into the sea. The gardens of Villa Rufolo inspired part of Boccaccio's *Decameron* and Wagner's *Parsifal;* to this day, Ravello's year-round performances have earned it the nickname *La Città della Musica.*

◨⚡ TRANSPORTATION AND PRACTICAL INFORMATION. Take the blue SITA **bus** marked "Ravello-Scala" from Amalfi (20min., 30 per day 6:30am-midnight, €1). For a gorgeous walk, hike along hills and lemon groves from Minori (1hr.), Atrani (1½hr., via Scala), or Amalfi (2hr., via Pontone). Ask at the tourist office in Amalfi for details. For a **taxi,** call ☎85 80 00. The **AAST tourist office,** V. Roma 18 bis, off P. Duomo, provides brochures, event and hotel listings, and a free map. (☎85 70 96; www.ravello-time.it. Open daily 9am-8pm.) Across from Cafe Calce is an **ATM;** another is at P. Duomo 5—look for a faded bronze sign to the left of the kiosk. **Public restrooms** are in P. Duomo. Find the **carabinieri** at V. Roma 1 (☎85 71 50), near P. Duomo. A **pharmacy** is at P. Duomo 14. (☎85 71 89. Open daily in summer 9am-1pm and 5-8:30pm; in winter 9am-1pm and 4:30-8pm. Closed Dec.) Access the **Internet** on V. Boccaccio near the bus stop. (€1.50 per 15min., €5 per hr.) The **post office** is at P. Duomo 15. (☎85 86 611. Open M-F 8am-1:30pm, Sa 8am-12:30pm.) **Postal Code:** 84010.

▞◖ ACCOMMODATIONS AND FOOD. Ravello offers mainly opulent options given that its main clientele is an older, wealthier crowd seeking relaxation. Among the more affordable options is **Palazzo della Marra ❸,** V. della Marra 3. This beautiful hotel offers four immaculate rooms with terraces. (☎85 83 02; www.palazzodellamarra.com. Breakfast included. Doubles €60-80. MC/V.) For a convenient spot by the bus station, head to the huge rooms of **A Due Passi ❹,** V. Boccaccio 1. All rooms have private bath and A/C. (☎320 84 07 605; www.aduepassi.it. Doubles €70-95. Extra bed €20.) To get to **Hotel Villa Amore ❹,** V. dei Fusco 4, follow V. San Francesco out of P. Duomo toward Villa Cimbrone, and take a left on V. dei Fusco. Twelve comfortable rooms share a quiet cliffside garden overlooking the sea. As its welcome sign says, "A stay at Villa Amore gives peace to the soul and joy to the heart." All rooms have terrace, bath, and ocean view. (☎/fax 85 71 35. Breakfast included. Reserve 1 month in advance. Singles €56; doubles €80-95. MC/V.)

For a snack, head to the inexpensive **alimentari** on V. Roma or Vle. della Rimembranza. (Open daily 8am-1pm and 4-8pm.) Ravello has few restaurants; one of the best is **Figli di Papa ❷**, V. della Marra 7. Beautiful views complement the affordable, high-quality food. (☎85 83 02; www.ristorantefiglidipapa.it. *Antipasto* €5-7. *Primi* €6-8. Cover €1.50. 10% discount for guests of Palazzo della Marra. Open daily 9am-11:30pm.) **Cumpà Cosimo ❸**, V. Roma 44, serves delicious food in a cozy dining room. The restaurant's atmosphere is laid-back and perfect for casual meals. The colorful *mista di pasta* (€14) mixes five delectable homemade pastas. (☎85 71 56. Cover €2. Open daily noon-4pm and 7pm-midnight. AmEx/MC/V.)

SIGHTS AND ENTERTAINMENT. The beautiful churches, ivy-covered walls, and meandering paths of the 13th-century **Villa Rufolo** inspired Wagner's magic garden, seen in the 2nd act of his opera *Parsifal*. The villa puts on a summer concert series with performances in some of its most picturesque spaces, and the main hall frequently exhibits works by big-name artists. Enter through the arch off P. Duomo near the tunnel. (☎85 76 57. Open daily in summer 9am-8pm; in winter 9am-6pm. €5, under 12 and over 65 €3.)

The Amalfi Coast's 3rd set of famous **bronze doors,** cast by Barisano of Trani in 1179, is in the portal of Ravello's **duomo.** The doors have 54 panels depicting detailed scenes from the Passion of Christ. Two pulpits with elaborate mosaics contrast the otherwise simple interior. In the **Cappella di San Pantaleone,** an image of the town's patron saint stands to the left of the altar, and San Pantaleone's blood has been preserved in a cracked vessel since he was beheaded on July 27, AD 290, at Nicomedia. Every year on this day the city holds a **religious festival,** during which the saint's congealed blood mysteriously liquefies. The small **museum** inside the church depicts the *duomo*'s history through pagan and Christian eras with ancient mosaics and sculptures. (Open daily 9am-7pm. €2.) Follow V. San Francesco out of P. Duomo to **Villa Cimbrone,** V. Santa Chiara 26. Renovated by Lord Greenthorpe in the 19th century, the villa is now an expensive hotel (€440-705 per night), made famous by guests such as D. H. Lawrence, T. S. Eliot, Virginia Woolf, Winston Churchill, Jacqueline Kennedy, and Hillary Clinton. Less famous travelers can still enjoy the floral walkways and majestic gardens, which offer magnificent views of the Amalfi coast. (☎85 74 59; www.villacimbrone.it. Gardens open daily 9am-sunset. €5.) If this isn't relaxing enough, head to the semi-sandy, free **Castiglione** beach.

Throughout the year, internationally-renowned musicians perform at classical music festivals. In warm weather, concerts can be heard in the gardens of Villa Rufolo; in winter they move inside the villa or *duomo*. Each season's festival is unified by a Wagnerian motif and includes screenings of films and panel discussions on a range of topics. Tickets are sold at the Ravello Festival Box Office, V. Richard Wagner 5. (☎85 84 22; www.ravellofestival.com. Tickets €20-100. Open daily 10am-8pm.)

SALERNO
☎089

As capital of the Norman Empire from 1077 to 1127 and home to Europe's 1st medical school, Salerno (sa-LEHR-no; pop. 144,000) once played host to a proud, powerful culture. During WWII, however, the city was blasted by Allied bombs and much of its medieval past was turned to rubble. Unlike the dreamy villages of the Amalfi Coast, Salerno is an urban reality with an industrial core and a famous university. A good, cheap base for visiting the Amalfi Coast and Paestum's ruins, Salerno is not wholly without charm of its own; side streets in the old city and the sea front promenade offer pleasant walks and views.

◰ TRANSPORTATION

Trains: (☎25 50 05), in P. V. Veneto. To: **Naples** (45min., 40 per day 3:41am-10:32pm, €5-10); **Paestum** (40min., 16 per day 5:52am-9:52pm, €2.70); **Reggia di Calabria** (3½-5hr., 16 per day, €17-35); **Rome** (2½-3hr., 22 per day, €21-33); **Venice** (9hr., 11 per day 2:54am-8:50pm, €36-43).

Buses: SITA buses leave from the train station for **Amalfi** (1¼hr., 24 per day 5:15am-10pm, €1.80) and **Naples** (1hr., 38 per day 5:05am-10:10pm, €3). Buy tickets from *tabaccherie*, and ask where your bus leaves (either P. Veneto or P. della Concordia). **CSTP** runs buses from P. della Concordia to **Paestum** (1½hr., 12 per day 6:30am-7:30pm, €2.70) and from P. Veneto to **Pompeii** (1hr., 14 per day 6:10am-9pm, €3.20).

Ferries and Hydrofoils: Most ferries leave from P. della Concordia, 2 blocks from the train station. Others leave from Molo Manfredi, up the waterfront. **Linee Marittime Salernitane** (☎23 48 92; www.amalficoastlines.com) runs hydrofoils from Molo Manfredi to **Capri** (2½hr.; after July 1 at 8:15, 11am, 5pm; €18). **Travelmar** (☎87 29 50) runs to **Amalfi** (35min., 6 per day 8:40am-3:30pm, €4), **Minori** (30min., 4 per day 7:50am-2:10pm, €4), and **Positano** (1¼hr., 6 per day 8:40am-3:30pm, €6).

Public Transportation: Orange **CSTP** buses connect the train station to the rest of the city. For routes and schedules, check the ticket booth in P. Veneto. 1½hr. tickets €1, day pass €5.

Taxis: ☎75 75 75.

Car Rental: Travel Car, P. Veneto 33 (☎22 77 22). Cars from €35 per day. 18+. Open daily 8am-1:15pm and 3-8pm. AmEx/MC/V. **Avis** and **Hertz** also have offices to the right as you exit the train station.

◪ ◰ ORIENTATION AND PRACTICAL INFORMATION

Salerno's **train station** is in **Piazza Vittorio Veneto**. The pedestrian **Corso Vittorio Emanuele** veers right out of the *piazza*, becoming **Via dei Mercanti** upon reaching the old quarter, the liveliest and most historically interesting part of Salerno. **Via Roma**, home to many of the city's best restaurants, runs parallel to C. V. Emanuele, one block toward the waterfront. Along the waterfront in front of the train station is **Piazza della Concordia**, from which many intercity buses depart, and **Lungomare Trieste**, which runs to Salerno's port, **Molo Manfredi**.

Tourist Office: EPT (☎23 14 32), in P. V. Veneto 1, to the right when leaving the station. Friendly staff provides free maps, brochures on hotels and restaurants, and bus and train info. Open M-Sa 9am-2pm and 3-8pm, Su 9am-1pm and 5-9:30pm.

English-Language Bookstore: La Feltrinelli, C. V. Emanuele 230. Decent selection of classics and new fiction. Open M-F 9:30am-2pm and 4-8:30pm, Sa 10am-2pm and 4-10pm, Su 10am-1:30pm and 5-9:30pm. MC/V.

Public restrooms: 2nd fl. of train station in P. Veneto.

Carabinieri: V. Duomo 17.

Hospital: G. da Procida, V. San Calenda (☎69 11 11).

Internet Access: Interlanguage Point, C. V. Emanuele (☎75 35 81), 1st fl. €4 per hr. Open M-Sa 9am-1pm and 3:30-9pm.

Post Office: C. Garibaldi 203 (☎25 72 111). Open M-Sa 8:15am-6:15pm. **Branch,** P. V. Veneto 9 (☎22 99 98). Open M-F 8am-1:30pm, Sa 8am-noon. **Currency exchange** at main office only. **Postal Code:** 84100.

ACCOMMODATIONS

Ostello Ave Gratia Plena, V. Canali (☎23 47 76; www.ostellodisalerno.it). Take C. Vittorio Emanuele into the old district, where it becomes V. dei Mercanti; then turn right on V. Canali. Amazing location in a former convent, close to restaurants and nightlife. Clean rooms, large showers, and a great indoor courtyard with music and cheap food. Book exchange. Private rooms have bath. Breakfast included. Towels €3.50. Laundry €3. Internet access €3.50 per hr. Curfew 2am. Single-sex 4- and 8-bed dorms €14; singles €26; doubles €45; triples €78. AmEx/MC/V. ❶

Albergo Koinè, V. A. Napolitano 10 (☎27 51 051; www.hostelkoine.it). 10min. walk from train station and port. Modern, clean, and cool, this hostel was recently renovated and even has an infirmary. Dogs welcome. Laundry €5. Internet access €2. Wheelchair-accessible bath available. Reception 24hr. 4-, 6-, and 10-bed dorms €12. MC/V. ❶

Albergo Santa Rosa, C. V. Emanuele 14, 2nd fl. (☎22 53 46; alb.srosa@tiscali.net), 1 block from the train station on the right. Fairly quiet for its central location. 12 clean, comfortable, pastel-toned rooms. A/C €5. Internet access €3 per hr. Singles €28; with bath €38; doubles €38-60; triples €51-81. Cash only. ❷

FOOD

Trattoria "da Peppe a Seccia," V. Antica Corte 5 (☎22 05 18). Large, yet quaint and intimate restaurant in the heart of the historical center serves cheap, delicious seafood. The fresh squid *antipasto* (€5) is a must. Pizza €2.50-6. *Primi* €4-8. Cover €1.50. Open Tu-Su noon-2:30pm and 8pm-midnight. ❶

Hosteria Il Brigante, V. Linguiti 4 (☎22 65 92). From P. Duomo, head up the ramp, look for sign on the left. Laid-back and as authentic as it gets: 1 menu, hand-written on brown paper. Try the *pasta alla sangiovannara* (€3), a hodge-podge of pasta, tomato, cheese, and sausage. Open Tu-Su 1:30-2:30pm and 9-11:30pm. Cash only. ❷

Santa Lucia, V. Roma 182/184 (☎22 56 96). Located in the main street of Salerno's historical center, this restaurant offers the same cool breeze, glamor, and laid-back ambience as its neighbors, but at cheaper prices. Try the spaghetti *alle vongole* (with clams; €6), or choose from a large array of cheap secondi €5-7. Open Tu-Su noon-2:30pm and 7-11:30pm. ❷

SIGHTS AND ENTERTAINMENT

To take in the evening air, take a stroll down C. V. Emanuele or sit in the lush gardens of the **Villa Comunale.** For a bit of historical flavor, explore the medieval section, starting at C. V. Emanuele; turn right off V. Mercanti or V. Roma on V. Duomo, which then runs uphill to **Duomo San Matteo.** First constructed in AD 845, the *duomo* was destroyed and rebuilt 200 years later by the Norman leader Robert Guiscard. If its beauty isn't enough of a draw, come to see a tooth from Evangelist Matthew, a hair from the Virgin Mary, and a splinter from the True Cross. (☎23 13 87. Open M-Sa 10am-6pm, Su 1-6pm. Modest dress required. Free.) To soak up some rays, take the bus along Lungomare Trieste and head to the sandy **beach** beyond the sailboat harbor. Though Salerno is right by the water, its beaches are not the nicest. Instead, hop on a bus and head to nearby **Vietri sul Mare,** home to hundreds of artisans and a pleasant beach. (Buses #4 and 9; 10min., €0.80.)

Through July, the **Salerno Summer Festival,** at the Arena del Mare near the Molo Manfredi, includes a concert series with jazz and blues. (☎66 51 76; www.comune.salerno.it. Concerts usually start 10pm. Prices vary.) At night,

CAMPANIA

younger crowds gather on the seaside promenade near **Bar/Gelateria Nettuno,** Lungomare Trieste 136-138. (☎22 83 75. Open daily 7am-2am.) Of the many bars along V. Roma, **Il Galleone** is the yuppies' favorite.

⚑ DAYTRIP FROM SALERNO

PAESTUM

The simplest way to get to Paestum is to take the train from Salerno (30min., 19 per day, round-trip €5.80). Exiting the Paestum station, walk straight under the stone arch for 7min. until you see the museum and entrance to temples on the right. CSTP buses also travel to Paestum from Salerno's P. della Concordia (1½hr., 12 per day 6:30am-7:30pm, round-trip €5.40), stopping at V. Magna Graecia, the main modern road in Paestum. The Paestum train station is abandoned, so buy tickets from tabaccherie. The tourist office in Salerno provides a list of return buses and trains from Paestum.

Not far from the Roman ruins of Pompeii and Herculaneum, Paestum's (peh-stoom) three ◪**Doric temples** rank among the best-preserved and most complete in the world, rivaling those of Sicily and Athens. Amazingly, these masterfully constructed temples were built without any mortar or cement, yet remained standing after the great earthquake of AD 62 reduced Pompeii's Temple of Jupiter to rubble. The town began as a Greek colony dedicated to sea god Poseidon, but was taken back by native Lucans and later conquered and expanded by the Romans. The city declined in the Middle Ages when a malaria epidemic ravaged its population. Today, many of the buildings have been reduced to crumbling foundations, but some still have intricate mosaics on their floors. The **Roman forum,** larger though more dilapidated than the one at Pompeii, lies on V. Sacra. More Roman ruins can be seen in the nearby **amphitheater** and **gymnasium.**

When excavators first uncovered the three temples in the 18th century, they attributed them to the wrong gods. Although recent scholarship has provided new info about the temples' true dedications, the 18th-century names have stuck. There are three entrances. The northernmost (closest to the bus stop) leads to the **Tempio di Cere** (actually built to honor Athena) built around 500 BC and later used as a church in the early Middle Ages. South of the forum lies the 5th-century BC **Tempio di Poseidon-Nettuno** (actually dedicated to Apollo). More sophisticated and complete than the Temple of Ceres, this temple incorporates many of the refinements found in Athens's Parthenon. Small lions' heads (now on display in the museum, see below) served as gargoyles on the temple roof. The southernmost temple, dubbed the **basilica** because it was believed to be a civil Roman building, is also the oldest, dating from the 6th century BC. Its unusual plan, with a main interior section split by a row of columns down the middle, has inspired the theory that the temple was dedicated to two gods, Zeus and Hera, rather than one, although most scholars contend that it was built solely to worship Hera. A ◪**museum** on the other side of V. Magna Graecia, will tell you everything you want to know about Paestum, and houses extraordinary pottery, paintings, and artifacts taken primarily from Paestum's tombs. The museum also holds samples of 2500-year-old honey and paintings from the famous **Tomb of the Diver,** dating from 475 BC. (Temples open daily in summer 9am-7:30pm; in winter 9am-4pm. Restoration work occasionally leaves temples fenced off or hidden. Museum open daily 9am-6pm. Last entry 1hr. before closing. Museum and temples closed 1st and 3rd M of each month for restoration. Museum €4, EU students €2, EU citizens under 18 or over 60 free. Ruins and museum €6.50, EU students €3.25, EU citizens under 18 or over 60 free. Included on Campania Artecard, p. 567.) The often overlooked, modern-day ◪**Paleo-Christian basilica,** right next to the tourist office, is a prime example of Christian incorporation of pagan architectural elements. The AAST **tourist office** in Paestum, V. Magna Graecia 887, is next to the museum. (☎0828 81 10 16. Open M-Sa June-Sept. 15 9am-7pm; Sept. 16-June 9am-1pm and 2-5pm.)

PUGLIA, BASILICATA, AND CALABRIA

HIGHLIGHTS OF PUGLIA, BASILICATA, AND CALABRIA

ENVISION yourself as a caveman when you stay in one of Matera's **sassi**—ancient homes carved into the rock, some dating back 7000 years (p. 632).

CRAWL into the **caves** of Castellana Grotte, once believed to be the gateway to the underworld (p. 614).

EXPLORE the cerulean waters of the grottoes of **Isola di Dino** in Praia a Mare (p. 646).

SCRUTINIZE ancient treasure at Reggio di Calabria's Museo Nazionale (p. 638).

PUGLIA

The often-overlooked Puglia (POOL-ya) region gives Italy its sun-baked southern kick—after all, what's a boot without a heel? Certainly not footwear befitting ever-fashionable Italy. Its ports are as animated and international today as they were hundreds of years ago when the Greeks and Romans used them as trade routes to the East, though now they tend to ferry tourists to Greece instead. Besides serving as a useful launching spot, the region harbors cultural treasures all its own: remote medieval villages, cone-roofed *trulli* houses, and ports with a distinct Middle Eastern flavor. Tourism has only recently begun to materialize in rustic, sunny Puglia, which remains a refreshing pause from Italy's more frequented destinations. Travelers to Puglia will welcome its passionate cultural heritage and distinctly southern zest for life.

BARI ☎ 080

Exquisite Puglian cuisine and nightlife, fueled by the city's university population, add to the complexity of Bari (BA-ree; pop. 329,000), the main Italian transportation hub for travel to Greece. On every street, clothing shops and *gelaterie* tempt pedestrians, and the sea is never more than a few blocks away. Amid the commotion, reckless drivers zoom about the modern city's wide avenues and pickpockets dart down alleys in the small medieval section. Although Bari does not figure prominently on most itineraries, its cosmopolitan vibe and urban grit make it a worthwhile divergence from southern Italy's more touristed cities, if only for a brief visit. Just ask the locals, who say Paris could be a *piccolo Bari* (little Bari) if it only had the sea.

◧ TRANSPORTATION

Flights: Palese Airport (☎800 94 99 44; www.seap-puglia.it), 8km west of the city. **Alitalia, Air France, British Airways,** and **Lufthansa** fly to major European cities from Bari. Shuttle bus #16 leaves from P. Aldo Moro (12 per day, 5:10am-8:10pm, €1).

Trains: Bari is connected to 4 railways running from **Bari Centrale** (☎52 40 148) in P. Aldo Moro. All regional (non-Trenitalia) trains have reduced or no service on Su. Make sure to double-check schedules, which change about every six months.

Puglia, Basilicata, and Calabria

Trenitalia (www.trenitalia.com), which serves large cities, runs trains to: **Brindisi** (1½-1¾hr., 22 per day 4:50am-11:11pm, €6-11); **Foggia** (1½-2hr., 39 per day 12:03am-11:55pm, €6.70-14); **Lecce** (2hr., 21 per day 4:50am-9:21pm, €7.50-13); **Milan** (9½-10hr., 13 per day 12:03am-10:56pm, €38-62); **Naples** (4½hr., 7 per day 12:13am-6:42pm, €20-28); **Reggio di Calabria** (7½-8hr., 6 per day 12:14am-10:44pm, €28-36); **Rome** (5-7hr., 7 per day 12:13am-6:42pm, €27-36); **Termoli** (2-3hr., 15 per day 12:03am-9:39pm, €11-22).

FSE (☎800 079 090; www.fseonline.it) runs trains from track 11 to **Alberobello** (1½hr., M-Sa 13 per day 6:28am-8:25pm, €4) and **Castellana Grotte** (50min., M-Sa 10 per day 7:07am-6:05pm, €2.30).

Ferrotramviaria Nord (☎57 89 542; www.ferrovienordbarese.it), to the left of Centrale, exit and re-enter the station. To **Ruvo** (45min., €2.30). On Su the Ruvo route is served by bus from P. Aldo Moro.

FAL (☎57 25 229; www.fal-srl.it), next door to Ferrotramviaria Nord station in P. Aldo Moro. Trains depart for **Matera** (1½hr., 8 per day 6:25am-7:05pm, €4) via **Altamura.**

Buses: SITA (☎52 16 004; www.sitabus.it), P. Aldo Moro.

Ferries: Obtain info and tickets at **Stazione Marittima** (☎52 19 140), individual company offices, or **Porto di Bari** (☎80 05 73 738; www.porto.bari.it). Take bus #20 to and from railway station. Some companies are listed below, but call ahead; schedules and prices vary, especially on weekends. Check-in at least 2hr. before departure. Visit www.greekferries.gr for more info on ferries to Greece. High season late July-Aug.

Marlines (☎52 31 824 or 52 75 409, reservations 52 10 206; www.marlines.com). To **Durres, Albania** (schedules vary weekly July-Sept., high season €62-130).

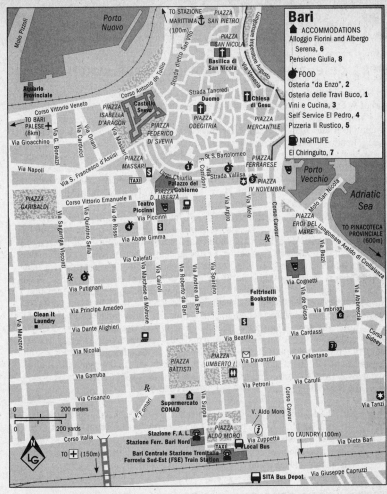

Bari

⌂ **ACCOMMODATIONS**
Alloggio Fiorini and Albergo
  Serena, **6**
Pensione Giulia, **8**

🍴 **FOOD**
Osteria "da Enzo", **2**
Osteria delle Travi Buco, **1**
Vini e Cucina, **3**
Self Service El Pedro, **4**
Pizzeria Il Rustico, **5**

🌙 **NIGHTLIFE**
El Chiringuito, **7**

PUGLIA, BASILICATA, CALABRIA

Superfast Ferries (☎52 41 527; www.superfast.com), offices outside in front of port terminal. Sails overnight to **Greece**. To **Corfu** (8hr.; odd days July and Sept. 1-9, even days in Aug.), **Igoumenitsa** (8½hr., M-Sa 1 per day 10pm), and **Patras** (14½hr., M-Th and Sa 10pm). The line to **Corfu** is operated by partner company **Blue Star Ferries**. High season €95-430, depending on seating. Discount for Eurail pass holders.

Ventouris Ferries, V. Piccinni 133, c/o P. Lorusso & Co. (☎52 17 609 to Greece, ☎52 75 499 to Albania; www.ventouris.gr). Windows #18-20 in Stazione Marittima. To **Corfu-Igoumenitsa, Greece** (10hr.; 2 per week Feb.-Apr., at least 5 per week May-Dec., daily in high season; shared cabin of four with bath €83-112) and **Durres, Albania** (13hr., €70-87).

Public Transportation: Local buses leave from P. Aldo Moro, in front of the train station. Tickets sold at *tabaccherie* or on the bus (€1). Bus #20 makes hourly trips between Stazione Marittima and train stations.

Taxis: RadioTaxi ☎53 46 666, leave voice message with departure location and destination. Taxi station ☎52 10 500.

ARRIVEDERCI, ITALIA. Bari is an important port for ferries to **Greece, Turkey, Albania, Croatia and Montenegro.**

ORIENTATION AND PRACTICAL INFORMATION

Via Sparano runs from the train station to **Piazza Umberto I,** Bari's main square. The end of V. Sparano intersects **Corso Vittorio Emanuele II** and the edge of the old city. To walk to the **port,** skirt the old city's winding streets by turning left on C. Vittorio Emanuele II and right at **Piazza della Libertà** onto **Via Giuseppe Massari.** Circle the castle, head right, and follow the coast. Otherwise, take the hourly bus #20 from the station. For a calmer route to the sea (not the port), turn right off V. Sparano on C. Vittorio Emanuele II, continuing past **Corso Cavour** to **Piazza Eroi del Mare.** Then turn right and enjoy a nice stroll down **Lungomare Araldo di Crollalanza.** Above all, make sure to see the beautiful **Piazza Ferrarese** and **Piazza Mercantile** in **Il Borgo Antico** (The Old Town) by walking down C. Cavour.

Right outside the trains station, find the **APT Tourist Office,** P. Aldo Moro 33/A. The office provides free maps, hotel listings, and bus schedules. (☎52 42 361; www.puglia-turismo.com. Open M-Sa 10am-1pm and 3pm-6pm, Su 10am-1pm.) For more maps and tourist info, try **Netcafe** (see below) or the small kiosk across from the station that gives out info about Bari from mid-July through early September. There is a **laundro-mat** at **Clean It,** V. Dante Alighieri 260. (☎52 37 096. **Internet** access €3 per hr. Wash €3.50 per 7.5kg; dry €3.50. Open M-F 11am-3:30pm and 6:30-9:30pm, Sa 11am-4pm.) For a **pharmacy,** try **San Nicola,** C. Cavour 53a. (Open M-F 8:30am-1pm and 4:30-8pm.) Late night pharmacy rotates; schedule posted outside. Check **Internet** and get helpful tourist info at **Netcafe,** V. Andrea da Bari 11. (☎52 41 756; www.netcafebari.it. €4 per hr. Open M-Sa 9am-11:30pm, Su 10am-1pm and 5-9:30pm. Cash only.) In case of **emer-gency,** dial the **carabinieri** (☎52 45 960). **Policlinino,** the local **hospital,** is at Ple. Giulio Cesare 11 (☎54 21 854). The **post office** is at P. Umberto I 33, to the right of P. Battisti, facing away from the train station. It has an **ATM** outside. (☎57 57 187; fax 57 57 053. Open M-F 8am-6:30pm, Sa 8am-12:30pm.) **Postal Code:** 70100.

BARESI, BEWARE. To keep intruders at bay, ancient citizens built the old city as a labyrinth in which to hide from surprise attacks. Today, the old city remains a maze for travelers and is safest when enjoyed in the light of day; turn to the many shop owners in P. Perrarese if you get lost. There is no need to ven-ture into the old city at night, but if you do, exercise caution.

ACCOMMODATIONS AND FOOD

Cheap accommodations in Bari are rare but can be found. Try **Alloggio Fiorini ❷,** V. Imbriani 69, #7, a time-tested hostel for students looking for a clean, neatly decorated place to stay just two blocks from the ocean. (☎55 40 788. Curfew midnight. Reception 7:30am-midnight. Singles €20; doubles €40, with bath €48. Cash only.) If the hostel is full, try **Albergo Serena ❷,** in the same building, #6. Each room is decorated with a different saint, but the prices do not vary according to holiness. (☎55 40 980. Singles €25; doubles €50, with bath €55.) For more options, try the three hotels on V. Crisanzio 12, nearby the train station. Of the three, **Pensione Giulia ❸,** on the 2nd floor, is the best value, with some country-style rooms equipped with A/C. (☎52 16 630. Breakfast included. Internet €1 per 10min. Extra-small singles €26; regular singles €45, with bath €55; doubles €60/70; triples €81/95; quads €102/120. AmEx/MC/V.)

Eating in the old city's restaurants can feel like a time warp; often restaurants offer neither menus nor itemized checks. The food, however, is inevitably excellent and the raucous atmosphere enjoyable. Follow *baresi* students and families to █**Pizzeria Il Rustico ❷**, V. Quintino Sella 95, a hidden gem for hungry travelers. With its extremely friendly staff and clientele, locals describe it as "genuine, simple, and honest." Fresh *antipasti* are offered in an amazing buffet. Come hungry, because the €9 *menù* includes an *antipasto*, *primo*, *secondo*, half-liter of local wine, and a *gelato*, biscotti, and liqueur to top it off. (Open M-Sa 7:30pm-midnight.) For a true Italian experience, head to cozy **Vini e Cucina ❷**, V. Vallisa 23, in a prime spot next to P. Ferrarese. Squeeze into a free seat, let the waiters tell you which of their daily specials you'll be receiving, then sit back and enjoy the authentic ambience and beauty of this *baresi* favorite. (☎330 43 30 15. *Antipasti* €2. *Primi* €4, *secondi* €6.50. Drinks €3. Open daily noon-3pm and 7pm-midnight; in winter closed Su. Cash only.) Hop over to **Osteria delle Travi Buco ❸**, Largo Chiurlia 12, at the end of V. Sparano in the old city, for fresh food, large portions, and an enthusiastic crowd. Help yourself to a plate of the *antipasti* buffet, and follow it with whatever fresh pasta and seafood the chef is preparing that day. (☎339 15 78 848. *Primi* €5, *secondi* €5-6. *Menù* with drink €18-20. Open Tu-Su 1:30-4pm and 7:30-11:30pm. Cash only.) For nice food, great wine, and a fun nautical interior, try **Osteria "da Enzo" ❷**, V. Vallisa 56. The kitchen is so close, one can't help but feel at home. (☎347 50 72 41. *Menù* from €10. Cover €1. Open daily noon-3pm and 7-10pm.) At **Self-Service El Pedro ❶**, V. Piccini 152, Italian food meets American buffet; the result is cheap and efficient albeit a departure from *la dolce vita*. Waiters carry your school-like tray to the chair they choose for you. (☎52 11 294. Closed Su.) Stock up on snacks at Supermercato **Conad,** V. Crisanzio 35. (Open M-Tu and Th-Su 7am-3pm and 5-8pm, W 8am-2pm. MC/V.)

◎ SIGHTS

Looks like Mom and Dad were wrong—there really is a Santa Claus, and the █**Basilica di San Nicola** proves it. Sixty *baresi* sailors stole St. Nicholas's remains from Turkey in 1087; the sailors initially refused to cede the body to local clergy but ultimately gave it up when the Church built this spartan basilica as Santa's final resting place. On the back wall, several paintings commemorate the jolly saint's good deeds, including his resurrection of three children who were sliced to bits and plunged into a brine barrel by a nasty butcher. (Open M-Sa 8:30am-6:30pm, Su 9:30am-7pm, except during mass. Free.) Just outside the old city, off C. Vittorio Veneto near the water, stands the colossal **Castello Svevo,** P. Federico di Svevia 4, built in the 13th century by Frederick II on Norman and Byzantine foundations. Visitors can't climb the jagged ramparts, but the medieval cellar displays art from the region's cathedrals and castles, and other areas display locally produced modern art. (☎52 86 111. Open M-Tu and Th-Su 9am-7pm. €2, ages 18-25 €1, under 18 and over 65 free.) Down Lungomare Nazario Sauro past P. Armando Diaz at V. Spalato 19, on the 4th floor, is the **Pinacoteca Provinciale.** Housed in a beautiful building with a tall clock tower, the gallery displays landscapes and works by Veronese, Tintoretto, Bellini, De Nittis, and Francesco Netti, an acclaimed hometown artist, as well as a vast collection of Greek art from the 1800s. (☎54 12 422. Open Tu-Sa 9am-7pm, Su 9am-1pm; Aug. open only in the morning. €3, students €1.)

♪ 🎭 ENTERTAINMENT AND NIGHTLIFE

Bari is Puglia's cultural nucleus. **Teatro Piccinni,** C. V. Emanuele 86, offers a spring concert season and year-round opera. Purchase tickets at the theater. (☎52 10 878; www.fondazioneliricabari.it. Open M-F 10:30am-12:30pm and 5-8pm.) Consult the ticket office, *La Gazzetta del Mezzogiorno* (the local newspaper), or the free newspapers *Leggo* and *City* for the latest info. From September through June, sports fans can catch **soccer matches** every Sunday. Tickets start at €15 and are available at the stadium or in bars. On May 7-9, *baresi* celebrate their stolen saint in the **Festa di San Nicola,** featuring traditional foods and a parade of children. There's also a huge **Summer Jazz Festival** in mid-July (☎45 55 696).

Bari does not have much of a club scene, but its bars are hopping. Most are open nightly from 8pm until 1 or 2am (3am on Sa) and generally close in August, when the town's university is on holiday. V. Sparano and P. Umberto are packed by night, and on weekends students cram into P. Ferrarese and other *piazze* along the breezy waterfront east of the old city. To avoid expensive drinks, try **El Chiringuito,** Molo San Nicola, next to P. Eroi del Mare, the main hangout for college students. (☎52 40 206. Open daily 11pm-4am.)

🌊 DAYTRIPS FROM BARI

CASTELLANA GROTTE

Take the FSE trains from Bari to "Grotte di Castellana Grotte" (1hr., about every 50min. 7:07am-5:05pm, €3). ☎49 98 211; www.grottedicastellana.it. Caves are across the parking lot and to the left. 50min. English tours in summer 1 and 4:30pm; €8, children €6.50. 2hr. tour 11am and 4pm, €13/10.50.

Superstitious locals once feared that these breathtaking natural caverns were an entrance to hell. The Castellana Grotte (CA-ste-LA-na GRO-tay), discovered in 1938, are famed for their impressive size and natural beauty. Over time, stalactites and stalagmites have developed into all sorts of whimsical shapes, including a miniature Virgin Mary, a camel, a wolf, and an owl. Even if the resemblances don't seem obvious, the formations invite the imagination to run wild. Visitors must take one of two **guided tours:** a short 1km jaunt (50min.) or a longer 3km trek (2hr.). Both start at **La Grave,** the enormous pit that was considered the opening to hell. The longer tour culminates in the stunning **Grotta Bianca** (White Cave), a giant cavern filled with white stalactites. No shoes, no go: be sure to wear proper footgear and perhaps bring a light jacket, since the grotto is chilly and damp year-round.

> **WHAT'S IN A NAME?** Not all trains heading for Castellana Grotte actually stop at the grottoes. The stop "Castellana Grotte" is for the city, 2km away. The next, unmarked stop is for the grottoes. Confirm with the conductor when boarding that the train actually stops at the grottoes.

ALBEROBELLO

Take the FSE train from Bari (1½hr., 13 per day M-Sa 6:28am-8:25pm, €4). To reach the trulli from the train station, bear left and take V. Mazzini, which becomes V. Garibaldi, to P. del Popolo. The Pro Loco Tourist Office, at V. Monte Nero 1, in the trulli district, can provide info on sights, directions, lodgings and guided tours. (☎0804 32 28 22. Open in summer daily 9am-9pm; in winter M-Sa 9am-9pm.) Visit www.alberobellonline.it for more info on the city.

The mere sight of *trulli*-covered hills—a sea of white limestone structures, strung together but each topped by its own neat conical roof—is well worth the trek out to Alberobello (AL-be-ro-BE-lo; pop. 11,000). The *trulli* are associated in Italian lore with magic and mystery—one glance at the fantastical landscape, populated by gnarled olive trees, rust-colored earth, and the homes themselves, and it's easy to understand why. Unfortunately, the origin of *trulli* in Alberobello proper is far less glamorous. A 17th-century count ordered the construction of these easy-to-dissemble dwellings; he planned to evade taxes by dismantling the houses when imperial inspectors came. Inhabitants inscribed symbols onto the stone roofs, reputedly to ward off evil spirits; many have unexpected meanings. For example, while the trident may seem like an obvious reference to Poseidon, it actually symbolized the Holy Trinity for the *trulli* inhabitants. Likewise, a heart struck by an arrow is not a victim of Cupid, but Mary's pierced heart. While some *trulli* remain occupied, more than 1000 *trulli* qualify as UNESCO World Heritage sights and currently house craftshops and restaurants, which are mostly open to the public.

To get a better idea of the lifestyle of the *trulli* residents before they were replaced by artisans hawking souvenirs, ask at **Casa d'Amore** (the local tourist office). From P. del Popolo, turn left at Eritrea store to P. XXVII Maggio to get to the **Museo del Territorio.** It exhibits artifacts from the town in a complex of 15 adjoining *trulli*. (Open mid-Sept. to mid-July Tu-Su 10am-1pm and 3:30-7pm; July 17-Sept.17 daily 10am-1pm and 3:30-7:30pm. Free. Tour €2.50.) **Sylva Tour** operates out of the museum, offering excursions into the countryside and guided walks around town. (☎43 21 838; www.sylvanet.it. Tours in English, French, and German.) To reach the **Trullo Sovrano,** P. Sacramento 10, take C. Vittorio Emanuele from P. del Popolo and continue past the church at the end. Built as the residence for the powerful family of a local priest in the 18th century, this two-story structure is still decorated with its original furniture and small homey details of a *trullo* household. It was declared an Italian national monument in 1923. (☎43 26 030. Open daily 10am-7:30pm. €1.50.) For a lunch break, escape the UNESCO district to find restaurants such as **Ristorante Terminal ❸,** V. Indipendenza 4. (☎43 25 103; www.ristoranteterminal.it. *Primi* and *secondi* €6.50-12. Cover €1.80. Service 15%. Open Tu-Su noon-3pm and 6:30pm-11pm. AmEx/MC/V.)

I LOVE YOU *TRULLI*. Most people visit Alberobello for its hills of *trulli*; however, the town's rural location also makes it an excellent starting point for a trip into the *bosco*, a small wooded park with winding paths running through the countryside past dilapidated but accessible *trulli*. Be sure to get a map from the tourist office no matter how far you intend to walk. To reach the park, head to the top of the hill of *trulli*, turn right, and follow signs for the *bosco*.

MARTINA FRANCA

Take the FSE train from track 11 in Bari (2hr., M-Sa 13 per day 6:28am-8:25pm, €4). A bus runs from the train station to Martina Franca's historic center (every 30min. 8am-8pm), but it might be quicker to walk. When you exit the train station, start walking uphill as you take a right on Vle. della Stazione and continue until you reach V. Alessandro Fighera. Take a left when you reach C. Italia and continue until P. XX Settembre to reach the old town.

Tucked in between the bigger cities of Bari and Taranto, Martina Franca (mar-TEE-nah FRAHN-kah; pop. 48,000) is often overlooked despite its impressive architecture and natural surroundings. With its optimal location near the Ionian and Adriatic Seas and overlooking the Valle d'Itria, this small town has a distinct Grecian vibe. To enter the old town, you'll pass under the impressive **Porta di San Stefano.** The 17th-century **Palazzo Ducale** in P. Roma, a standing legacy of the ruling Caracciolo family, still boasts frescoes by local painter Francavilla Fontana. **Basilica di San Martino,** in P. Plebiscito, displays a gorgeous facade and two different altars inside. During reconstruction in 2007, the original Romanesque foundation was found under the church; it was previously believed that only the campanile remained. Explore beautiful homes around P. Immacolata and find an example of the Greek influence in the **Chiesa di San Nicola dei Greci** near V. Metastasio. Once around there, swing around to V. Bellini for a pleasing vista of Valle D'Itria. From late July to early August, the **Festival della Valle D'Itria** hosts various events (jazz, classical symphonies, plays, etc.) in the Palazzo Ducale. (☎48 05 100; www.festivaldellavalleditria.it. Tickets €14-40.)

While in the old town, if you're hungry and not interested in a fancy restaurant, look into **Il Pranzo e Servito ❶**, V. Aprile 2 (☎48 05 339), right behind P. Roma.

The friendly tourist office, P. Roma 35 (☎48 05 702), in the old town, offers maps. (Open M-Sa 9am-1pm; Tu and Th also 4-7pm.) Nearest public baths are on V. Masaniello by Basilica di San Martino. Postal Code: 74015.

TRANI   ☎088

Trani (TRAH-nee; pop. 53,500), with its beautiful architecture, fresh seafood, and breezy seaside strolls, is Puglia's unsung hero. The contagious tranquility and local hospitality of this port town bring people back again and again, despite the local government's efforts to resist growth in size and attention. The only thing Trani is missing is a beautiful sandy beach. Although its history may be full of traders, Crusaders, and saints, Trani manages to live in the here and now, inviting its visitors to experience life in Italy.

⨎ TRANSPORTATION. Trains run from track 3 at Bari to Trani (45min., hourly M-Sa, €2.60) and from Trani to Foggia (45min., €5.10). **Buses** from Trani's P. XX Settembre, right outside the train station, run to Bari and Foggia (€3) and along the coast to towns like Barletta and Margherita di Savoia. Beware that schedules change frequently.

◪⨎ ORIENTATION AND PRACTICAL INFORMATION. From the train station, walk down **Via Cavour,** the first street perpendicular to the train station, through **Piazza della Repubblica** all the way to **Piazza Plebiscito,** which is right in front of the relaxing **Villa Comunale,** and turn left to get a view of the port. Walk down the street that borders the port all the way to the other end to **Piazza Trieste,** where you'll find **I.A.T tourist office,** P. Trieste 10, 2nd fl. (☎35 88 830). The office provides helpful guides, free detailed maps, a list of accommodations, and honest restaurant recommendations. (Open M-F 9am-1pm and 3:30-6pm. For winter hours, call ☎35 06 020). In an emergency, contact **Polizia Stradale,** Vle. Padre Pio (☎34 82 111); **Polizia Municipale,** C. Imbriani 119 (☎35 88 000); or the **carabinieri,** C. Imbriani 147 (☎35 80 400). **Pharmacies** are available throughout the city, including one right outside the train station by V. Cavour and another on P. della Repubblica. A **hospital** can be found on Vle. Padre Pio (☎34 82 111). **Internet** access, a phone center, and free maps are available at **Luciana,** V. Giovanni Bovio, by P. Gradenico (☎35 84 849; €3 per hr.). The **post office** is at V. Giovanni Bovio 115 (☎34 90 111; open M-F 8am-6:30pm and Sa 8am-12:30pm). **Postal Code:** 70059.

⨎⨎ ACCOMMODATIONS AND FOOD. Accommodations in Trani are varied and quite affordable. The best bet is **⨎Tre Re ❶,** V. Casale 58. This small hostel's cleanliness, location, and hospitable owner make it a great find. (☎34 03 328 or 34 07 25 534; www.trere.it. Breakfast included. Internet access available. Sept.16-May singles €16.50; doubles €38.50. June-15 Sept. €19/43.) Another excellent option is the charmingly personal 🖾Centro Storico ❸, V. Leopardi 29. This time capsule is a playground for historians and architects, as well as tourists enjoying cathedral views and the unique interior garden. Film directors have tried to use it as a setting various times, but the caring owner prefers to maintain its low-key publicity. (☎35 06 176; www.bbtrani.it. Breakfast included. Singles €30-35; doubles €50-75.)

When you're ready for a nice dinner outside, 🖾Carpe Diem ❶, V. Zanardelli 32, tucked between the busy P. Teatro and equally popular V. Statuti Marittimi, is the place to go. Its relaxed ambience caters to both long-established *tranese* families and hungry tourists. (☎34 85 464. *Antipasti* €5. Pizza €4.50. Open M-Tu and Th-Su 8pm-midnight. For a gorgeous view of the port and the cathedral without high prices, head to **Al Faro Pizzeria e Antipasteria ❶**, V. S. Marittimi 48/50. It's one of the few places open for lunch on weekdays. Avoid the cover (€1 for pizza, €2 for *antipasto*) by taking your food to go and eating on a bench by the harbor. (☎34 87 255. Open M-Tu and Th-Su noon-3pm and 7pm-midnight.) For a more private dining experience, the quaint **Nord-Est ❸**, P. Tiepolo 10/11, serves up fresh seafood at better prices than its neighbors. *Primo, secondo,* and wine cost €15. (☎34 81 114. Open M and W-Su noon-3:30pm and 8-11:30pm.)

◙ **SIGHTS.** Trani's main attraction is the **cathedral,** located on V. Archivo near P. Trieste. The sheer beauty of the structure, apart from its magnificent setting overlooking the Adriatic Sea, makes one want to stay in Trani and absorb the majestic serenity it resonates. The bones of Trani's patron saint, St. Nicholas the Pilgrim, are in a crypt under the church. (Open M-Sa 8:15am-12:15pm and 3:15-6:30pm, Su 9am-12:45pm and 4-7pm.) The other main monument is the nearby **castle;** make sure to enjoy the view along the way from the cathedral. Built by Frederick II, Holy Roman emperor from 1215-1250, the castle was most recently used as a prison; consequently, it is more impressive outside than in. Aside from its day job as an overrated tourist attraction, the castle is now used as a place for socialization and art displays. Don't use the clock at its entrance, which has been broken for years. (Open daily 8:30am-7pm. €2, ages 18-25 €1, under 18 and over 65 free.) The **Villa Comunale,** past P. Plebiscito, is often an undeservedly overlooked sight. It has a small park, pleasant gardens, a mini-aquarium, and most importantly, stunning views of the whole city.

🎵🎭 **ENTERTAINMENT AND NIGHTLIFE.** Trani is a beautiful city to walk around, and evening sunsets only add to its allure. Be sure to catch the sun drop between the cathedral and the castle. If you're looking for some fun, walk along the port or head to **Piazza Teatro** to enjoy *gelaterie,* pizzerias, and cool bars. If your drink of choice is beer, pizzerias offer a better deal than bars. The last weekend of July brings **Trani Film Festival,** when movies are shown in different historical buildings of the city, like the castle and the Monastero di Colonna.

SALENTO PENINSULA

Foreign tourists often overlook Italy's sun-baked heel, home to hidden grottoes, medieval fortresses, and the beautiful beaches of two seas. With roots stretching back to ancient Greece, the Salento modestly bears the laurels of centuries of history. Its art and architecture are some of the best preserved in Italy, its vistas pristine, and its scuba diving superb. Transportation within the peninsula can sometimes be complicated, but a sojourn along the varied coastline or inland among olive groves and vineyards is well worth the careful planning.

BRINDISI
☎ **0831**

As Italy's seaside gateway to the East, Brindisi (BREEN-dee-see; pop. 89,000) has always been more of a departure point than a destination. Pompey made his escape from Julius Caesar's army here in the first century BC, and crusaders used the port to sail for the Holy Land. As a port of industry and travel, the city is crowded with travelers who stay only long enough to pick up their ferry tickets. Whether you visit en route to Greece or as a base for a daytrip to beautiful Ostuni, you will find a mix of historic sights and modern Italian flavor.

◼ TRANSPORTATION

Trains: Stazione Brindisi Centrale at P. Crispi. Ticket office open daily 8am-8pm at Stazione Marittima. Trains go to: **Bari** (1½hr., 26 per day 4am-10:44pm, €6-13); **Lecce** (20-35min., 27 per day 6:01am-10:47pm, €2.32); **Milan** (9-12hr., 4 per day 7:26 am-7:30pm, €54-85); **Rome** (6-9hr., 6 per day 6:25am-10:45pm, €27-45); **Taranto** (1¼hr., 20 per day 4:45am-10:44pm, €4).

Buses: FSE, at the train station, handles buses throughout Puglia. **Marozzi** buses travel to **Rome** (7½-8½hr., 4 per day 11am-10pm, €36). **Miccolis** runs to **Naples** (5hr., 3 per day 6:35am-6:25 pm, €24). Be sure to ask where you should catch the bus, since neither Marozzi nor Miccolis buses leave from the *centro*. Buy tickets for both companies at the helpful, efficient **Grecian Travel,** C. Garibaldi 79 (☎56 83 33), which is also a CTS budget travel info point. Open M-F 9am-1pm and 4:30-8pm, Sa 9am-1pm.

Ferries: Ferries leave from **Costa Morena** to various destinations in Greece, including **Corfu** (8hr.); **Igoumenitsa** (10hr.); **Kephalonia** (16½hr.); **Patras** (17hr.); **Paxi** (13hr.). Catamarans operated by **Italian Ferries,** C. Garibaldi 96/98 (☎59 08 40), sail to **Corfu** (4hr.) and are only slightly pricier than ferries. Catamarans leave from **Stazione Marittima.** Prices for each ferry line are fixed by the transport authority so all agencies charge the same amount for tickets, but some agencies will book passages for a full or nonexistent ferry. To avoid getting scammed, use a reputable agency. Well-established ferry lines include **Med Link Lines,** C. Garibaldi 49 (☎52 76 67), **Fragline,** V. Spalato 31 (☎54 85 40), and **Hellenic Mediterranean Lines,** C. Garibaldi 8 (☎52 85 31), which offers discounts for Eurail pass holders. Port tax (€8) and the deck reservation fee (€5) are not included in ticket price. Most lines provide a **free shuttle** that runs from Stazione Marittima to Costa Morena. Check-in 2hr. before departure. Bring your own food to avoid the overpriced seagull fodder found in snack bars on board.

> **CIAO, BELLA!** Brindisi is a central port for passenger boats to Greece. To get to Athens, take the ferry from Brindisi to Patras and then a train or bus from Patras to Athens (2½hr.); you can buy these tickets at Brindisi's Stazione Marittima. Ferries also run to Çesme, Turkey (30hr.), and Durres, Albania (9hr.).

Public Transportation: City buses (☎54 92 45) run between the train station and port and to destinations around the city. **Local ferries** depart from the tourist office on V. Margherita every 10min., crossing Seno di Ponente and landing near Chiesa di Santa Maria del Casale. Purchase bus and ferry tickets at bars and *tabaccherie* for €0.80.

Taxis: (☎59 79 01). Make sure to take a licensed taxi (white with a bit of blue), as unofficial taxis tend to overcharge. Agree on a price before taking off; remember that drivers generally charge a supplementary fee after 9pm. Taxis from the train station to Costa Morena cost €12, and from there to Stazione Marittima cost €16.

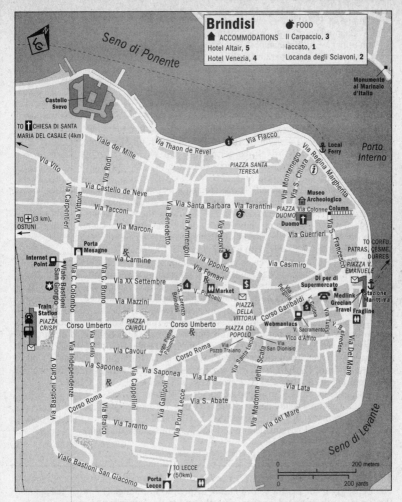

Brindisi

🏠 ACCOMMODATIONS
Hotel Altair, **5**
Hotel Venezia, **4**

🍴 FOOD
Il Carpaccio, **3**
Iaccato, **1**
Locanda degli Sciavoni, **2**

⚡ ℹ ORIENTATION AND PRACTICAL INFORMATION

Corso Umberto runs from the train station to **Piazza Cairoli** and through **Piazza del Popolo** and **Piazza della Vittoria**. At P. della Vittoria, it becomes **Corso Garibaldi,** which ends when it meets **Via Regina Margherita** at the port. A right onto V. R. Margherita leads to the **Stazione Marittima**. Keeping straight, the street becomes **Via Flacco** and then **Via Thaon de Revel**.

The **APT Information Office,** V. Regina Margherita 44, 2nd fl., provides a free **map** and advice about local services and sights. (☎56 21 26; www.pugliaturismo.com. Open July-Aug. daily 8:30am-1pm and 3-8pm; Sept.-June M-F 8:30am-1pm and 3-8pm, Sa 8:30am-1pm.) Reach the **carabinieri** at ☎15 29 11. A **hospital, Ospedale di Summa,** S.

Mesagne (☎53 75 10) offers emergency care. **Internet** access is available at **Internet Point,** V. Bastioni San Giorgio 20/22, to the right of the train station (€4 per hr.; open M-Sa 9am-9pm), or at **Webmaniacs,** Vico Sacramento 8, off C. Garibaldi. (☎52 15 32; www.webmaniacs.it. €3 per hr. Open M-Sa 9am-2pm and 4:30-8:30pm.) The **post office** is at P. Vittoria 10. (☎22 55 11. Open M-F 8am-6:30pm, Sa 8am-12:30pm.) Branch in the Stazione Marittima. (Open M-F 8am-1pm, Sa 8am-12:30pm.) **Postal Code:** 72100.

ACCOMMODATIONS AND FOOD

Close to the port and *centro*, the friendly, family-run **Hotel Altair ❷,** V. Giudea 4, offers rooms with TV, some with A/C. From Stazione Marittima, walk up C. Garibaldi, and take the 3rd left. Larger rooms have A/C for €10 extra; others have fans. (☎/fax 56 22 89; www.hotelaltair.191.it. Singles €25, with bath €35; doubles €50; triples with shower €60. AmEx/MC/V.) More affordable rooms can be found at **Hotel Venezia ❶,** V. Pisanelli 4, which is equidistant from the train station and Stazione Marittima. From the train station, pass the fountain and take a left off C. Umberto onto V. San Lorenzo da Brindisi, following the signs pointing right on V. Pisanelli. Twelve basic rooms have quirky decor and old beds; there is a smell of smoke throughout the hotel. Rooms with shared bath have a sink. (☎52 75 11. Singles €16; doubles €26, with bath €36; quads €52. Cash only.)

Avoid the restaurants and cafes on C. Garibaldi near the port, where the ubiquitous *menù turistico* yields small, bland portions and steep drink prices. Better options lie on nearby side streets. The fishermen's shack **Iaccato ❷,** V. Flacco 32, right on the water, has an unbeatable location. Iaccato is unmarked; look for the building with the green awning right by the water. (☎52 40 84. *Primi* €5-18, *secondi* €6-12. Cover €1.20. Open daily noon-3pm and 7-11pm. MC/V.) **Il Carpaccio ❷,** V. Marco Pacuvia 36, with outdoor seating and a laid-back atmosphere, is a popular family eatery. (☎328 80 26 322. Open Tu-Su 8pm-1am.) Great for both romantic dates and lively group gatherings, **Locanda degli Sciavoni ❷,** V. Tarantini 43, is a short walk from the *duomo*. The *spaghetti alle scampi* (€7) is just one of the many excellent fresh seafood dishes. (☎52 20 50. *Primi* €3-8, *secondi* €5-8. Cover €1.50. Open M-Sa 7pm-midnight. MC/V.) An ☎**open-air market,** off P. della Vittoria on V. Fornari, sells fresh fruit, vegetables, and dairy products. (Open M-Sa 7am-1pm.) Pick up supplies for your ferry ride at **Di per Di** supermarket, C. Garibaldi 106, one block from the port. (☎56 25 66. Open M-Sa 8am-1:30pm and 4:30-8:30pm, Su 9:30am-1pm.)

SIGHTS AND ENTERTAINMENT

Turning left at the seaside end of C. Garibaldi, V. R. Margherita passes a set of marble steps, great for restful *gelato*-eating or people-watching. The huge **column** at the top, recently restored, once marked the end of the **Appian Way.** Figures of Jove, Neptune, Mars, and tritons grace the marble capital. The column's twin, which once stood on the adjacent base, now resides in Lecce. V. Colonne runs behind the column to P. Duomo. Inside the 11th-century **duomo** (heavily restored in the 18th century), find relics and a mosaic floor. (Open daily 7am-noon and 4:30-7:30pm. Free.) Nearby, the **Museo Archeologico** traces Brindisi's history through pottery, statues, and other artifacts, although the display is currently limited to just a few rooms as the museum undergoes restoration. (☎56 55 01. Open Tu and Th 9am-1pm and 3:30-7:30pm, W and F 9am-1pm, Sa 3:30-7:30pm, Su 9am-12:30pm. Free.) Follow signs from the train station to the outskirts of town to see the **Chiesa di Santa Maria del Casale** and its 13th-century frescoes, including one of Mary blessing the Crusaders. (Open daily 7am-noon and 4-7pm. Free.)

PUGLIA, BASILICATA, CALABRIA

🔁 DAYTRIP FROM BRINDISI

OSTUNI

Ostuni is on the train line between Bari (1-1¼hr., 15 per day 6am-10:55pm, €4.10) and Brindisi (40min., 16 per day 4am-10:44pm, €2.30). From the train station (☎30 12 68), take the orange city bus 2.5km to P. della Libertà at the centro (15min.; M-Sa every 30min., Su hourly 7am-9:30pm). Buy tickets at the train station bar (€0.70) or onboard (€1.50). Buses are not numbered, so tell the driver your intended destination before boarding. The APT Tourist Office, (☎30 12 68) C. Mazzini 6, just off P. della Libertà, provides maps of the centro storico and a booklet of the town's historical info. Open June-Aug. M-F 8:30am-2:30pm and 3:30-8:30pm, Sa 8:30am-1:30pm and 6:30-8:30pm; Sept.-May M-F 8:30am-noon and 4-7pm.

Rising from a landscape of sea, dark-red earth, and olive trees, the *città bianca* (white city) of Ostuni (oh-STOO-nee; pop. 33,000) appears unworldly. The *centro storico*'s thick, whitewashed walls protect the city from the ocean wind and lend a fairy-tale touch to serpentine streets. The terrace at the top of C. V. Emanuele provides a view of the old city. Just off P. della Libertà, **Comune di Ostuni**—apart from being the city's administrative center—also displays the works of Onofrio Bramante, whose paintings provide a pictorial history of Puglia starting around 10,000 BC. (2nd floor. Open M-Sa 8am-2pm and 4-7pm. Free.) From P. della Libertà, V. Cattedrale runs through the *centro storico*, leading to the **Convento delle Monacelle** (Convent of Little Nuns), V. Cattedrale 15. Behind its Baroque facade and under its white-tiled dome, the convent houses an **archaeological museum** with a 24,500-year-old human skeleton. Crowning Ostuni's hill on V. Cattedrale, the **duomo** was among the last Byzantine buildings erected in southern Italy. The Spanish-Gothic facade, with its intricate rosette, contrasts sharply with Norman styles more common in Puglia. (Open daily 7:30am-12:30pm and 4-7pm.) Though several kilometers from the *centro*, Ostuni's praiseworthy **beaches,** accessible from P. della Libertà by STP bus, have free sections. (☎800 23 20 42; www.stpbrindisi.it. Take a bus toward "Torre Canne." 6 per day 5:50am-2:25pm, €0.90. *Tabaccherie* in the square post schedules. Ask bus driver to tell you when you have reached your destination.) The closest beach is **Villanova,** but the most popular is **Costa Merlata.** On August 26, Ostuni celebrates Sant'Oronzo—who saved them from a plague—with the **Cavalcata,** a parade of red-and-white costumed horses and riders.

Fresh seafood abounds in Ostuni. For lunch or dinner, try one of the many small taverns or *osterie* in the old city. The streets can be tricky to navigate, but signs everywhere point to restaurants. For reasonable prices and a friendly, family-oriented atmosphere, head to **Antony ❷,** C. Mazzini 35. (☎33 94 82. *Primi* €5-7. Open daily 12:30-3pm and 7pm-midnight.) Steep prices at **Porta Nova ❺,** V. Gaspare Petrarolo 38, are rewarded by fresh seafood and panoramic views of the surrounding land and seascapes from a plush dining room. (☎33 89 83; www.ristorporta-tanova.it. *Antipasto* €12. *Primi* €12-15, *secondi* from €20. Cover €3. Open in summer daily noon-3:30pm and 7pm-midnight; closed W in winter. AmEx/MC/V.)

LECCE   ☎0832

One of Italy's hidden pearls, Lecce (LEH-chay; pop. 90,000) is where Italians go when foreign tourists invade their country. Historical invaders have included Cretans, Romans, Saracens, and Swabians; Spanish Habsburg influence during the 16th and 17th centuries inspired beautiful Baroque buildings that now line Lecce's streets. Most of the city's churches and palaces are sculpted from *tufigna*—soft,

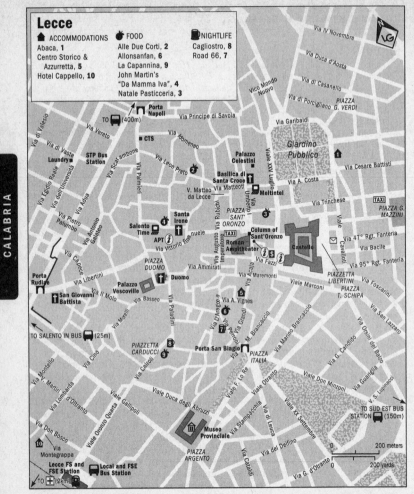

Lecce

♠ ACCOMMODATIONS
Abaca, **1**
Centro Storico &
   Azzurretta, **5**
Hotel Cappello, **10**

🍴 FOOD
Alle Due Corti, **2**
Allonsanfan, **6**
La Capannina, **9**
John Martin's
   "Da Mamma Iva", **4**
Natale Pasticceria, **3**

▮NIGHTLIFE
Cagliostro, **8**
Road 66, **7**

locally quarried "Lecce stone" that hardens when exposed to air. At night, the illuminated buildings make for a memorable *passeggiata* (promenade). Lecce, the "Florence of the South" and home to some of the country's best beaches, is a great starting point for a tour of the Salento Peninsula.

▮ TRANSPORTATION

Trains: Lecce is the southeastern terminus of the state railway. The **Trenitalia Station** (☎30 10 16) is in P. Massari. Buses #24 and 28 (€0.62) depart from front of the station on V. Oronzo Quarta to the *centro*. Trains to **Bari** (1½-2hr., 21 per day 5am-10:14pm, €6-13), **Brindisi** (20-40min., 23 per day 5am-10:14pm, €2.40-8.30), and **Rome** (6-9½hr.,

7 per day 6am-11pm, €30-44). **FSE** trains (☎66 81 11; www.fseonline.it) criss-cross the Salento Peninsula. Trains run M-Sa to **Gallipoli** (1hr., 11 per day 6:56am-8:50pm, €3.40) and **Otranto** (1¼hr., 11 per day 6:56am-8:50pm, €2.90) via **Maglie**. Schedules are subject to frequent change; consult www.salentointrenoebus.it for detailed schedules.

Buses: The **FSE Station** (☎34 76 34; www.fseonline.it), on V. Boito, is easily accessible by bus #4 (€0.70) from the train station. FSE buses depart daily from the **FSE Garage**, across from the train station on the left, and stop at the FSE station on their way out of town. Tickets are available in the train station bar. To **Gallipoli** (1hr., 5 per day, €2.90) and **Taranto** (2hr., 5 per day 7am-4pm, €4.58). **STP** (☎22 84 41), on V. San Nicola, heads to smaller towns of the Salento Peninsula. Pick up a schedule at the tourist office. In July-Aug., **Salento in Bus** (☎35 03 76; www.salentoinbus.it) is the most convenient way to traverse the peninsula, with green-line buses running to **Gallipoli** (1½hr., 7 per day 7:05am-9:53pm, €3.50) and red-line buses to **Otranto** (1hr., 9 per day 7:13am-12:23am, €3.50), and other peninsular towns such as Santa Maria di Leuca and Porto Cesareo. Buses stop on V. Pitagora, by the train station.

Taxis: (☎24 79 78), at the train station. (☎30 60 45), in P. Sant'Oronzo.

✈ 🛈 ORIENTATION AND PRACTICAL INFORMATION

Lecce lies 35km southeast of Brindisi. From the **train station,** take **Viale Oronzo Quarta** until it becomes V. Cairoli to get to the streets of the old city. Turn left on V. Paladini, and wind around the **duomo.** To the left, **Via Libertini** passes **Piazza Duomo** and Chiesa di San Giovanni Battista, eventually exiting the old city walls through Porta Rudiae. To the right lies **Via Vittorio Emanuele II,** which passes **Piazza Sant'Oronzo,** Lecce's main square containing the Roman amphitheater and *castello* beyond.

Tourist Office: APT Lecce, V. V. Emanuele 24 (☎24 80 92; www.pugliaturismo.it), near P. Duomo. Has good free maps and a comprehensive booklet on Lecce's numerous B&Bs. Open daily 9am-1pm and 5-8pm; closed in winter Su. Dozens of other tourist offices, both public and private, can be found around P. Sant'Oronzo.

Budget Travel: CTS, V. Palmieri 89 (☎30 18 62). From P. Sant'Oronzo, take V. V. Emanuele, and turn right onto V. Palmieri. Provides flight and train info and sells tickets. Open M-F 9am-1pm and 4-8:30pm, Sa 9am-noon.

Laundromat: Lavanderia Self-Service, V. dell'Università 47, between Pta. Rudiae and Pta. Napoli. Wash €3-7, dry €1.50 per 12min. Detergent €1. Open M-Sa 9am-9pm.

Public Bathrooms: In P. Sant'Oronzo, on the corner with V. Imperatore Augusto.

Carabinieri: V. Calabria (☎27 98 64).

Hospital: Ospedale Vito Fazzi (☎66 11 11 or 66 14 03), on V. San Cesario.

Internet Access: Salento Time, (☎30 36 86) by V. Regina Isabella, offers great advice. €2.50 per hr. Student discount. **Meltintel Phone Center,** V. Matteoti 23/B (☎30 71 67; www.meltintel.com), close to P. Sant'Oronzo. Has 6 fast computers. €0.50 for 1st 10min., €3.60 per hr., Su €2.50 per hr. Also has **money transfer** services. University student discount 15%. Open daily 9:30am-1:30pm and 4:30-9:30pm.

Post Office: ☎27 41 11. In Piazzetta Libertini, across from the *castello*. Open M-F 8am-6:30pm, Sa 8:30am-1:30pm. **Postal Code:** 73100.

🏠 ACCOMMODATIONS

Lecce lacks ultra-cheap accommodations, but B&Bs offer an alternative to impersonal hotels and the tourist office lists affordable *affittacamere* (rooms for rent).

▨ **Abaca,** V. Cavalloti 19 (☎24 05 48). Buses #24, 27, and 28 from the train station stop 1 block away. It's impossible to beat the prices of these simple, nice rooms. The owner's passion for ballet is reflected in the dainty decor. Nice views, a terrace, and a large communal kitchen and bathroom add to the appeal. Singles €20-25; doubles €40-50; triples €53-65; quads €65-75. Discounts for extended stays. ❷

Centro Storico, V. Andrea Vignes 2/B (☎24 27 27; www.bedandbreakfast.lecce.it). From P. S. Oronzo, take V. Augusto Imperatore till it becomes V. Federico D'Aragona; V. A. Vignes is on the left. Centrally located, this charming B&B boasts a sunroof with city views. 5 big rooms all have A/C, TV, and refrigerator. Breakfast included. Free Wi-Fi. Reservations recommended. Singles €35-40; doubles €52-57, with bath €70-80. Extra bed €20. AmEx/MC/V. ❸

Azzurretta, V. A. Vignes 2/B (☎24 22 11; www.bblecce.it). Shares management and 16th-century building with Centro Storico. 3 spacious rooms and 1 apartment with kitchen have big, sunny windows, A/C, TV, and balcony, and shared sunroof. Breakfast included. Free Wi-Fi. Reservations recommended. Singles €30-35; doubles €55-60; apartment €55-80. Extra bed €15. Cash only. ❸

Hotel Cappello, V. Montegrappa 4 (☎30 88 81; www.hotelcappello.it). From the station, take the 1st left off V. Quarta onto V. Don Bosco, and follow the signs. Conveniently located near the train station, this modern hotel has immaculate rooms, all with A/C, TV, and fridge. Bar in the lobby. Singles €35; doubles €50. AmEx/MC/V. ❸

◧ FOOD

Leccese food is a delight. Regional specialties range from hearty *cicerietria* (chickpeas and pasta) and *pucce* (sandwiches made with olive-bread rolls) to *confettoni* (traditional chocolate candies).

▨ **Alle Due Corti,** Corte dei Giugni 1 (☎24 22 23; www.alleduecorti.com), at the corner with V. Prato. Dedicated to the preservation of *leccese* culture through cuisine—it's so authentic, even Italians can't read some of the dialect on the menu, which changes every 10 days. The vegetable *antipasti* are excellent (€6). *Primi* €5-7, *secondi* €6-9.50. Cover €1.50. Open M-Sa noon-2pm and 8pm-12:30am. AmEx/MC/V. ❷

▨ **La Capannina,** V. Cairoli 13 (☎30 41 59), between the train station and P. Duomo. If you've ever dreamed of eating in the Parthenon, this is likely as close as you'll get. Attentive service in a nearly private *piazza* surrounded by columns, which are illuminated at night. Try the pasta specialty *orecchiette a casareccia* (with meat, tomato, and cheese sauce; €3.60). Pizza €2.60-5.20; dinner only. *Primi* €4-6, *secondi* €5-8. Cover €1.30. Open Tu-Su 1-3pm and 7:30pm-midnight. V. ❷

John Martin's "Da Mamma Iva," Vco. degli Alami (☎24 71 31), by V. Regina Isabella, behind Chiesa di Sant'Irene. Fish nets and paintings depicting life at sea set the tone for this restaurant's true asset: its delicious seafood. The generous *linguine allo scoglio* (linguini with seafood; €10) is truly filling. The owner, a fisherman, catches and carefully selects every ingredient. Open M-Tu and Th-Su 7:30pm-midnight. ❷

Allonsanfan, V. Federico D'Aragona 17 (☎24 39 29). French cuisine meets Italian flavor in this cool, sophisticated, and laid-back restaurant that has the best crepes and the best meat in town. Outdoor seating perfect for people-watching. Indoors, enjoy an international soundtrack of popular music as the owner prepares the perfect mojito (€4) in front of you. Open daily 8pm-2am. ❷

Natale Pasticceria, V. Trinchese 7 (☎25 60 60), off P. Sant'Oronzo. This copper-frosted pastry shop is full of so many pastries, candies, flavors of *gelato*, and eager customers that your head will spin. Take a number and try the pistachio if the crowds haven't already devoured it. Cones and *granita* €1.50-3. Local, cream-filled delights from €0.80. Open daily 8am-midnight. MC/V. ❶

⊙ SIGHTS

Lecce's close-knit *centro storico* is visually enchanting. Get an education in Baroque architecture by touring its churches and *palazzi*, which are a 10min. walk apart, but can take hours to enjoy.

BASILICA DI SANTA CROCE. Constructed between 1549 and 1695, this church is a masterpiece of *leccese* Baroque. Most of the area's architects contributed their skills to its ▉facade at some point. Inside, the lighting, artwork, and ambience are captivating; look closely to see the profile of Gabriele Riccardi, the basilica's original designer, hidden between the upper window and the column to its left. *(From P. Sant'Oronzo, head down V. Umberto I. Open daily 9am-noon and 5-8pm, except during mass. Modest dress required. Free.)*

DUOMO. Though its construction began in 1114, the duomo was "Zingarelloed" between 1661 and 1662. This means it was worked on by Giuseppe Zimbalo, nicknamed "Lo Zingarello" (The Gypsy) for his tendency to wander from one project to another. Except for two *leccese* altars, the stained-glass-bedecked interior dates from the 18th century. At night, when crowds flood the *piazza*, misty streams of light pour out of the **campanile** that rises from the left side of the cathedral. Opposite, the **Palazzo Vescovile** (Bishop's Palace) has been remodeled several times since its 1632 construction. On the right, with a Baroque well in its center, stands the **seminary,** designed by Cino in 1709. *(From P. S. Oronzo, take V. V. Emanuele. Duomo open daily 7am-noon and 5-7:30pm. Free.)*

ANCIENT ATTRACTIONS. The **Column of Sant'Oronzo** is one of two that marked the termination of the Appian Way in Brindisi (p. 620). Today, it is topped by a saint, and towers melodramatically over P. Sant'Oronzo. Nearby, the ruins of a 2nd-century **amphitheater** recede into the ground. In its prime, the structure held 20,000 spectators; these days, at least that many people seem to gather there on summer nights to flirt or just eat *gelato*. Near the station, the **Museo Provinciale** contains a large collection of Apulian ceramics and figurines from the 5th century BC, as well as rotating arts exhibits. *(V. Gallipoli 28. ☎24 70 25. Open M-Sa 9am-1:30pm and 2:30-7:30pm, Su 9am-1:30pm. Wheelchair-accessible. Free.)*

BEACHES. A relaxing daytrip of sand and sun at one of many beautiful beaches is just a short trip from Lecce. Try the small but beautiful **Torre dell'Orso**, a vacationer's hot spot with many free stretches. *(Blue line #101. 1 hr., 8 per day.)* Popular with beach-going Italians, **Santa Cesarea Terme** has a wide expanse of clear, pale blue ocean lapping against many caves and coves. *(Blue line, change in Maglie.)* At the tip of the peninsula, the rocky enclaves of **Santa Maria di Leuca** offer small, untouristed beaches. *(Blue line.)* North of Gallipoli, **Porto Cesareo's** coast is dotted with towers crumbling in to the sea. Bordered by tiny islands, the area is perfect for exploring with kayaks or boats. *(Pink line dir.: Gallipoli.)*

OTHER SIGHTS. The wildly intricate **Chiesa di San Giovanni Battista del Rosario** was Lo Zingarello's last work. The artist, who used dramatic Baroque norms as a basis for innovation, decorated the columns with unfettered glee. Inside the church, 15 altars surround a Roman cross design, testifying to Lo Zingarello's disdain for moderation. *(From P. Duomo, take V. Libertini. Open Tu-Su 9am-12:30pm and 4-7:30pm. Free.)* The ornate **Porta Napoli** once stood on the road to Naples. The arch was erected in 1548 in honor of Holy Roman Emperor Charles V, whose coat of arms adorns the front. *(From P. Duomo, take V. Palmieri.)*

NIGHTLIFE AND FESTIVALS

Don't be fooled by the quiet that takes over the city every afternoon; by night, Lecce wakes from a long siesta as people stroll its sidewalks and mingle in its many *piazze*. To join the fun, head to **Via d'Aragona,** which is crammed with young barhoppers on weekends. Major *piazze*, such as **Piazza Duomo** and **Piazza Sant'Oronzo,** often have live music on weekends. Most nightclubs, especially ones which open only for summer, are on the coast and are thus only accessible by car. For up-to-date info on the hottest nightlife options, chat with locals in the *piazze* or consult the monthly publication *Salento in Tasca*, available at local bars. Despite its private, exclusive feel, **Cagliostro,** V. Cairoli 25, has a chill interior and relaxed outdoor seating, making it a favorite among university students. (☎30 18 81. Draft beer and mixed drinks from €2. Open daily 8pm-3am.) Though lacking authentic Italian charm, **Road 66,** V. dei Perroni 8, near Pta. San Biagio, emulates American bars with its gas station decor. (☎24 65 68. Open daily 8pm-2am.)

  MedFest brings classical music concerts to the Castello Carlo V every summer. For info, call ☎24 23 68. The inner courtyard of **Palazzo Celestine,** next to Basilica di Santa Croce, hosts rock and classical music concerts in the summer. Keep an eye out for posters or ask at the AAST office for more info. During the third weekend in June, the **Festival Dei Musicisti di Strada** (www.festadellamusicalecce.org) brings street musicians from Europe, the Caribbean, and the Middle East to play great music out on the streets from about 10pm to 1am.

OTRANTO ☎0836

Although throngs of Italian tourists descend upon Otranto (OH-tran-toh; pop. 5300) and drive already high prices even higher in July and August, its winding streets, gorgeous coastline, and medieval sights merit a visit in any season. This town is testament to the power of faith; impressed by the piety of the 800 *Martiri d'Otranto* (Martyrs of Otranto) who chose to die rather than renounce their religion, Turkish pirates who had conquered the city in 1480 gave up Islam in favor of Christianity. Today, the martyrs' bones—and the mosaic-adorned cathedral that houses them—attract some visitors, but most make their pilgrimage to bathe in Otranto's warm, clear waters and bask in the town's laid-back atmosphere.

TRANSPORTATION AND PRACTICAL INFORMATION. Otranto is 40km southeast of Lecce. Rustic FSE **trains** run M-Sa from Lecce (1¼hr., 11 per day 6:56am-8:50pm, €2.90) to Maglie; take the awaiting bus or connecting train to Otranto. The FSE ticket to Lecce covers both. In July and August, the red line of **Salento in Bus** (☎0832 35 03 76; www.salentoinbus.it) runs straight from Lecce's V. Gallipoli (in front of Bar Rossa Nera) to Otranto's *castello* (2hr., €3.50). For a **taxi** to areas around Otranto, call ☎80 46 88 or 335 62 04 760.

  From the train station, walk straight ahead and bear left to reach the main beach, along the **Lungomare d'Otranto;** after the **public gardens,** V. Vittorio Emanuele leads to **Piazza de Donno** and the entrance to the *centro storico*. Enter through the city gate, and turn right on **Via Basilica** to reach the **duomo.** The **AIT Tourist Office,** across from the Castello Aragonese, offers advice on lodgings and transportation to towns on the peninsula, and provides free maps. (☎80 14 36. Open M-Sa 8:30-1pm and 4-8:30pm.) For the **carabinieri,** V. 800 Martiri 10, call ☎80 10 10. **Farmacia**

Ricciardi is at V. Lungomare 101. (☎80 10 36. Open M-Sa 8:30am-1pm and 4:30-8:30pm, Su 9am-noon and 6-8pm.) For **medical emergencies**, call ☎80 16 76. Stop by **Giardini Caffè,** V. V. Emanuele 9, for **Internet.** (☎338 64 88 100. €3.50 per hr. Open daily 7am-midnight.) The **post office** is by the stoplight on V. Pantaleone. (☎80 02 11. Open M-Sa 8:15am-6pm.) **Postal Code:** 73028.

▛▟ ACCOMMODATIONS AND FOOD. Lodgings in Otranto are very expensive, especially from mid-July to August when most hotels require that guests eat at their restaurants and all require reservations. The tourist office can help find *affittacamere.* **Hotel Miramare ❹,** V. Lungomare 55, across from the beach, has bold, impeccably clean, attractive bedrooms with fridge, phone, A/C, safe, and TV. Staff helps plan excursions and daytrips. Call in March to reserve a room with a sea view for August. (☎80 10 23; www.miramareotranto.com. Breakfast included. Free Internet access. Singles €55-80; doubles €80-140; triples €108-182. AmEx/MC/V.) The **Hotel Bellavista ❹,** V. V. Emanuele 19, directly across from the public gardens with a *bella vista* of the port, has large clean rooms with bath, TV, and A/C. (☎80 10 58; www.hotelbellavista.assovia.com. Breakfast included. Singles €50-100; doubles €75-130. Sea view extra €10. AmEx/MC/V.) In the center of town and close to both the station and the ocean, **Hotel Pietra Verde ❸,** V. P. Presbitero 62, has rooms with terrace, phone, TV, A/C, and bath. (☎/fax 80 19 01; www.hotelpietraverde.com. Singles €32.50-60; doubles €90-145. Extra bed €10. AmEx/MC/V.)

Facing the public gardens, **Boomerang Self-Service ❷,** V. V. Emanuele 13, serves tasty dishes cafeteria-style; take your meal outdoors and peer out at the gardens under the shade of your umbrella. (☎/fax 80 26 19. Pizza €3.10-7. *Primi* €4.50, *secondi* €4.50-7. Open Mar.-Sept. daily 12:15-3pm and 8:15pm-late. Cash only.) The true draw of **Acmet Pascià ❹,** on Lungomare degli Eroi, is the gorgeous harbor view and breezy outdoor dining area under a flower-covered trellis. (☎80 12 82. *Primi* €6-12, *secondi* from €20. Cover €2. Open in summer daily 12:30-2:30pm and 7:30pm-midnight; closed in winter M. AmEx/MC/V.) The public gardens sport numerous snack stands; try the delicious *noccioline zuccherate* (candy-coated nuts; €1). For essentials, visit the **market** by P. del Donno which sells fruit, meat, and fish (open daily 8am-1pm), or the **supermarket** on the way down the street from the train station to the beach.

◙ SIGHTS. The *centro storico,* which hosted Dante while he wrote parts of the *Divine Comedy,* guards many of Otranto's proudest historical sites. The first stop on a tour of the old city should be the ▧**duomo** (also called the cathedral), which is lined by a phenomenal 11th-century floor mosaic of the Tree of Life. The mosaic depicts religious and historical figures from Adam to Alexander the Great and King Arthur. Another section depicts the 12 zodiac signs and seasonal agricultural work. Equally impressive is the colorful gilded porcelain ceiling, which is well worth straining your neck to see. In the **Cappella dei Martiri,** a small chapel in the *duomo*'s crypt, to the right of the altar, three glass cabinets display the skulls and bones of all 800 *otrantini* who died for their faith at the hands of Turkish pirates. (*Duomo* open daily 8am-noon and 3-6:30pm, except during mass. Modest dress required. Free.) Take C. Garibaldi to P. del Popolo, and follow the signs up the stairs on the left to find aging frescoes of the Garden of Eden adorning the small, musty interior of the beautiful Byzantine **Chiesa di San Pietro,** on V. Martiri d'Otranto. (Open daily 10am-noon and 3-6pm.) The huge **Aragonese castle,** with its imposing walls and now-dry moat, may not be exciting inside, but it could still withstand a siege. (☎339 74 325 60. Open daily 9:30am-1pm and 4-10pm. €2, children and seniors €1.) A gate in the castle walls to the left of the main entrance leads to the refuge of Otranto's picturesque sailboat harbor. Every Wednesday a

market surrounding the castle sells local arts and foods. (Open 9am-1pm.) For a relaxing stroll, grab a friend and head to the **Santuario Santa Maria dei Martiri.** Walk straight out of the old city onto V. 800 Martiri, off P. Castello to the left (5min.). Peer into the church's Baroque interior and intricate white altar. This Baroque church, with stone steps, a freshly restored exterior, and a beautiful view of the surrounding seaside and landscape, provides a respite from the beach buzz. The peaceful sanctuary also memorializes one of the darkest moments in Otranto's history—the decapitation of the *martiri d'Otranto*.

◪ ⬛ BEACHES AND ENTERTAINMENT. In August, Otranto's **beaches** show less shore than skin as Italian vacationers stake claims to every patch of sand. For those seeking fewer crowds, the fine sand and azure waters are just as enjoyable in early summer. The **free** public strips interspersed along the *lungomare*, farther along V. degli Haethey, and all the way to the right on Lungomare Kennedy are the most accessible, but also the most crowded. Also consider the beaches north of Otranto, accessible by the red bus line. The beach closest to V. Pantaleone provides bathrooms and changing facilities (€5), as well as umbrellas and chairs (€10). While not actually a beach, one of the best places to swim is in the crystalline shallows off the concrete stretch in front of Lungomare degli Eroi. If exploring the depths of the briny blue sounds more appealing than sunbathing, **scuba diving** is available by appointment at V. San Francesco di Paola 43. (☎/fax 80 27 40; www.scubadiving.it. 1 dive €30. Open daily 9:30am-1pm and 4:30-8pm.)

After dark, Otranto's *lungomare* fills with people walking along the waterfront and hitting up the pubs, while those with cars head to the *discoteche* 5-6km away. Every year on August 13-15, Otranto enjoys fireworks, free concerts, and a lot of food for the **Festa dei Martiri d'Otranto,** a festival held in honor of the town's martyrs. On the first Sunday in September, the town celebrates the **Festa della Madonna dell'Altomare** (Festival of the Virgin of the High Seas).

GALLIPOLI   ☎ 0833

Ideal as a brisk daytrip from Lecce or a prolonged seaside vacation, Gallipoli (ga-LEE-po-lee; pop. 20,000) boasts a wealth of assets: gorgeous beaches, excellent seafood, and a charming maze of historical homes and churches. Gallipoli's old city is perched on a small island that juts into the sparkling Ionian Sea. Throughout its history, outsiders have coveted the island's strategic location; foreign remnants include a Greek fountain and an Aragonese Castle. Today, Gallipoli's friendly residents maintain a carefree island mentality, and the old city has retained an air of authenticity. Despite its growing popularity as a vacation spot (mostly for northern Italians) its whitewashed alleys and clear waters remain largely undiscovered.

◪ ⬛ TRANSPORTATION AND PRACTICAL INFORMATION. Gallipoli is southwest of Lecce, and is best reached by **train** from Lecce. FSE **trains** run M-Sa (1hr., 11 per day 6:56am-8:50pm, €3.40). In July and August, **Salento in Bus** (☎ 0832 35 03 76; www.salentoinbus.it) runs to the town hall in the *città nuova* (1hr., €3.40) on the green line; catch it in Lecce on V. Gallipoli, in front of Bar Rossa Nera. The train station is in the *città nuova*. To reach the *città vecchia*'s main *piazza*, **Piazza Imbriani,** from the train station, turn right on C. Roma, cross the bridge, and turn right. From there, the main road, **Via della Pace,** runs past the *duomo*, on the left, to the other side of the island. The **IAT Tourist Office,** P. Imbriani 10, offers advice on accommodations and travel around the Salento Peninsula, and has free maps. (☎ 26 25 29. Open daily 8:30am-1pm and 4-8:30pm.) In case of emergency, contact the **carabinieri,** P.

Malta 2 (☎26 74 00), or the **police** (☎26 61 05). **Farmacia Provenzano** is at V. della Pace 59. (☎26 64 12. Open M-Sa 8:30am-12:30pm and 4-8pm.) The **Ospedale Sacro Cuore di Gesù** (☎27 01 11) is at V. Alezio 12. The **post office**, V. Quartini 1, is on the 1st right after crossing the bridge from the *città vecchia* to the *città nuova*, and has an **ATM**. (Open M-F 8am-6:30pm, Sa 8am-12:30pm.) **Postal Code:** 73014.

⌐◻ ACCOMMODATIONS AND FOOD. Gallipoli's hotels are expensive, particularly in July and August. The seaside ◪**La Riviera Bed and Breakfast ❸**, Riviera Sauro 7, decorated with intricate frescoes, has six rooms all with A/C, phone, bath, and flat-screen TV. Five rooms each have a terrace with views of the Ionian sea, perfect for watching the sunset. (☎26 10 96; www.bedandbreakfastlariviera.com. Breakfast included. Single €30-50; doubles €65-80, in Aug. €100. Extra person €30. AmEx/MC/V.) **Hotel Al Pescatore ❹**, Riviera Colombo 39, to the right after crossing the bridge to the *città vecchia*, offers 16 impeccably clean, modern rooms, which branch off a stately inner courtyard. All rooms have phone, bath, flat-screen TV, and A/C. (☎26 36 56. Breakfast included. Singles €50-65; doubles €70-110. AmEx/MC/V.) **Trattoria L'Angolo Blu ❸**, V. Carlo Muzio 45, which is parallel to V. della Pace, offers local seafood specialties. Enjoy perfect *al dente* pasta in the cool, stone-walled interior. (☎348 38 60 129. *Primi* €6-8.50, *secondi* from €7. Cover €1.50. Open daily noon-3pm and 7pm-midnight. MC/V.) Find more seafood selections at **Trattoria Lu Tazziu ❷**, P. Imbriani 5, with a great location in part of an airy old market just inside the old city. The tasty *parmigiana ai frutti di mare* (eggplant parmesan with seafood; €7) is the house speciality. (☎347 484 82 35. *Antipasti* €5. *Primi* €7, *secondi* €9. Open daily noon-3pm and 7pm-midnight. Cash only.) For groceries, head to **Crai** supermarket on V. della Pace 35. (☎26 38 78. Open daily 8am-2:30pm and 6pm-midnight. MC/V.)

◖ BEACHES. By day, Gallipoli's cobbled streets are a colorful jungle of markets and produce vendors, its walls draped in fishing traps and fresh laundry. By night, the city is set aglow with lights. Residents make their evening *passeggiata* along the promenade encircling the *città vecchia;* the promenade passes by the port as well as the island's small, uncrowded, and completely **free beach: Seno della Purità.** The turquoise waters make for excellent swimming, although many residents also choose to just jump off Riviera Diaz's docks. Three miles down the coast, beaches encircle the emerald **Baia Verde,** with free sandy strips interspersed along private beaches. Three miles from Gallipoli's *città vecchia*, Baia Verde is accessible by bus #5 (€1) or by walking along the coastal seawall, bearing right after crossing the bridge. The walk passes many tiny beaches carved into the tufa, and offers excellent views of the coastline. For **scuba diving,** head to **DromiaSub,** off V. della Pace (☎347 46 56 533; www.divingcentergallipoli.it).

◉♫ SIGHTS AND ENTERTAINMENT. Aside from its beaches, the city contains many layers of historical relics. All the churches in the *città vecchia* are open daily in July and August 8am-12:30pm and 4-8pm (info ☎26 42 42). On V. Duomo, find the ornate exterior of the city's 17th-century Baroque **Cattedrale di Sant'Agata.** Its arched walls and ceilings are covered with intricate murals. Just before the *duomo* lies the **Museo Diocesano,** V. della Pace 51, containing religious art from the *duomo* and other churches in Gallipoli. Its large terrace offers great views of the *città vecchia* and harbor. (☎50 24 39. Open June-Sept. Tu-Su 5:30-11pm; Oct.-May Tu-F 9am-12:30pm, Sa-Su 9am-12:30pm and 3:30-6:30pm. €2.50, children and seniors €1.50, under 12 free.) Farther up the street on V. della Pace 108, the **Museo Civico** contains a variety of relics and artwork from the town's past. (Open M-F 10am-1pm and 4-8pm, Sa-Su 10am-1pm and 5-9pm. €1.) Before crossing the 17th-century bridge to the *città vecchia*, find the recently restored Greek fountain, also known as the **Fontana Ellenica,** to the left. In the evening, don't miss the ■sunset from Riviera Sauro, when the brilliant Salentino sun slips beneath the horizon in a thrilling finale of pink and orange.

From July 23-24, the city honors its patron saint with the **Festival of Santa Cristina.** To partake, head to C. Roma in the *città nuova* for more bands and lights in the evening. The Museo Diocesano, along with museums from Otranto and Lecce, also hosts **Arte Mare,** a series of concerts, art displays and discussions from the beginning of July to end of August.

BASILICATA

Mountainous and mostly land-locked, Basilicata (ba-zee-lee-CAHT-ah) retains a raw beauty. Considering the region's prehistoric *sassi* caves, refreshing vistas, lively culture, and smooth beaches, it's amazing that Basilicata remains largely untouristed and has never attained the economic prominence characteristic of booming port cities.

MATERA
☎ **0835**

Matera (ma-TEH-ra; pop. 60,000) is most famous for its ancient *sassi* (rock) homes. As restaurants, hotels, and offices creep into the cliffs, the once-dismal dwellings—previously reflecting some of the city's most miserable poverty—now ironically serve as one of Matera's most lucrative assets. The revitalized Matera is so beautiful and oddly captivating that its cliffside, sun-bleached buildings have served as a stand-in for ancient Jerusalem in major motion pictures, like the biblical epic *The Passion of the Christ* (2004). Matera's extraordinary sights, inexpensive accommodations, and engaging local culture certainly deserve a visit.

▟ TRANSPORTATION

The train station, **Matera Centrale,** is in P. Matteotti. FAL **trains** (☎33 28 61; www.fal-srl.it) run to Bari (1½hr., 15 per day M-Sa 5:10am-8:50pm, €4). FAL buses leave from P. Matteotti for Bari (1¾hr., Su 4 per day 1-9pm, €4). Buy tickets at the station. SITA **buses** (☎33 28 62; www.sitabus.it) leave from P. Matteotti and run to Metaponto (1hr.; 5 per day M-Sa 6:30am-6:10pm, reduced Su; €2.69) and Taranto (1½hr.; 5 per day M-Sa 6am-5:15pm, reduced Su; €4.60). Buy SITA bus tickets at the ticket office across the street. For a **taxi,** call ☎26 12 99.

▟ 🛈 ORIENTATION AND PRACTICAL INFORMATION

Matera's grottoes split into two small valleys that overlook a deep canyon in the **Parco della Murgia Materana.** From the **train** and **bus stations** at **Piazza Matteotti,** head down **Via Roma** or **Via Minzoni** to **Piazza Veneto,** the heart of the city and the entrance to the *sassi*. **Sasso Barisano,** the modern area located in the first valley, is straight ahead, through the stairway across from the Banco di Napoli. To reach the cavernous **Sasso Caveoso,** continue to the right along **Via del Corso,** which bears right on **Via Ridola,** then descend left at **Piazza Pascoli.** The more important *chiese rupestri* (rock churches) are on the other side of the ridge opposite the *Sasso Caveoso.* The tourist office and most hotels offer detailed maps of the *sassi.*

The **APT tourist office** is at V. Spine Bianche 22. From the train station, walk down V. Roma and take the 2nd right, then turn right again. (☎33 18 17; www.materaturismo.it. Open in summer daily 9am-1pm and 4-6:30pm; in winter M, W, F 9am-1pm,

Tu and Th 9am-1pm and 4-6:30pm.) The city also has an **information office,** on V. Madonna della Virtù, the road along the ridge in the *sassi* district. (Open Apr.-Sept. daily 9:30am-12:30pm and 3:30-6:30pm.) A helpful website about the town is www.sassiweb.it. **Banco di Napoli** is on V. Margherita. In case of **emergency,** call the **police,** V. Gattini 12 (☎26 71), or an **ambulance** (☎26 22 60). **Ospedale Madonna delle Grazie** (☎24 32 12) is on Centrada Cattedra Ambulante. For **Internet,** head to **Qui PC Net,** V. Margherita 52, to the left of the Banco di Napoli. (☎34 61 12. €1 per 15min. Open daily 4:30-8:30pm, Tu-Sa 8:30am-1pm.) The **post office,** V. Passerelli 15, is off P. Veneto. (☎24 55 49. Open M-F 8am-6:30pm, Sa 8am-noon.) **Postal Code:** 75100.

ACCOMMODATIONS

Matera has excellent budget accommodations, making it a great base for exploring other areas of Basilicata and Puglia.

■ **Le Monacelle (HI),** V. Riscatto 9/10 (☎33 65 41; www.lemonacelle.it). Facing the *duomo,* V. Riscatto borders the left side. This perfectly renovated 16th-century cloister is an ancient museum, modern hostel, hotel, conference center, and world-class concert venue all in one. Gorgeous view, gardens, a movie screening room, and chapel also inside. Spacious dorms all have A/C, domed ceilings and spotless bathrooms. Breakfast included for hotel, €1.70 extra for hostel. Free Internet access. All rooms with A/C and bath. Dorms €16; singles €43; doubles €86. AmEx/MC/V. Hostel ❶/Hotel ❹

Sassi Hostel/Hotel, V. San Giovanni Vecchio 89 (☎33 10 09). From the station, take V. Minzoni to P. Veneto and V. San Biagio to the church, where signs leading to the hostel appear on the right; the hostel is at the top of the staircase. Dorms are nice, but hotel rooms offer spectacular views of city and *sassi.* Anything but primitive, the cavernous prehistoric rooms are themselves renovated *sassi,* and all have bath. English spoken. Curfew midnight. Dorms €16; doubles €50-70. AmEx/MC/V. Hostel ❶/ Hotel ❹

Locanda di San Martino, V. Fiorentini 71 (☎25 66 00; www.locandadisanmartino.it). Offers the unique experience of sleeping inside what was once a Neolithic temple; 5000-year-old cisterns are preserved under the glass floor. Located in the *sassi,* many of the luxurious stone rooms offer impressive views. TV, free Wi-Fi, phone, A/C, and bath in all rooms add modern perks. Breakfast included. High season singles €88; doubles €109. Low season €68/86. Call ahead for seasonal changes. AmEx/MC/V. ❺

Bed and Breakfast Capriotti, P. Duomo 2 (☎33 39 97 or 329 61 93 757; www.capriotti-bed-breakfast.it). Facing the *duomo,* Capriotti is on the left. Three *sassi* cave-apartments with sleeping, cooking, and living nooks also have views of *Sasso Barisano.* All have bath, A/C, and fridge. Singles €50; doubles €67. Cash only. ❹

FOOD

Though small, Matera has managed to concoct several local specialties worth sampling, including *fave con cicoria* (a soup with beans, celery, chicory, and croutons mixed in olive oil) and *frittata di spaghetti* (pasta with anchovies, eggs, bread crumbs, garlic, and oil). Experience true Materan grit with *pane di grano duro,* made with extra-hard local wheat. Fruit can be found at the **open-air market** off V. Minzoni near P. Veneto. (Open daily 9am-1pm.)

■ **La Cola Cola,** V. Spartivento 20 (☎33 69 37; www.lacolacola.it). A local favorite, not only for its cheap prices, but for its phenomenal views of the *Sasso Barisano.* The waiters are extremely friendly and if you come in a big group, they might even open a free bottle of champagne for you. Open M-Tu and Th-Su noon-3pm and 8-11:30 pm. ❶

■ **Ristorante Nadi,** V. Fiorentini 1/3 (☎34 40 54), in the *sassi.* Serves huge portions of fantastic Basilicatan specialties amid authentic charm you won't find at its pricier counterparts. *Primi*

€4.50-6, *secondi* €6-9. Cover €1.50. Open Jan. and Mar.-Dec. M-Th and Sa-Su noon-3pm and 7-11:30pm. Reservations recommended for Aug. *Let's Go* discount 10%. AmEx/MC/V. ❷

Osteria U'Ciddar, V. Purgatorio Vecchio 25, in Sasso Caveoso. Near Savita Lucia alle Malve; look for the green handwritten signs. Like being invited to lunch at an old friend's *sassi* house. The combination of Materan cuisine, culture, and colorful locals make this hidden spot a unique experience. Enjoy full meals for about €15. Open daily 10:30am-4pm. Cash only. ❷

L'Osteria, V. Fiorentini 58. From P. Veneto entrance to *sassi,* head to the main street V. Fiorentini. Simple, Materan cuisine in sizable portions at low prices. The *capunti con cicerchie e funghi* (local pasta with beans and mushrooms; €5.50) is light and full of flavor. *Primi* €4-5.50, *secondi* €5-9. Cover €1.50. Open M-Tu and Th-Su noon-2:30pm and 7:30-10pm. MC/V. ❷

Trattoria Lucana, V. Lucana 48 (☎33 61 17), off V. Roma. Try the specialties *valvatelli alla lucana* (pasta with sausage and mushrooms; €7) and *bocconcini alla lucana* (veal with mushrooms; €7.50). Cover €1.50. Service 10%. Open M-Sa 12:30-3pm and 8-10:30pm. Closed mid-July and early Sept. AmEx/MC/V. ❷

Osteria Arti e Mestieri La Stalla, V. Roario 73 (☎24 04 55). From P. Veneto, take V. San Biagio, walk through archway on the right and down stairs for 20m. Perfect lunch break in the heart of the *sassi* after a day of trekking up stairs. Cool, rustic dining room. *Primi* €5, *secondi* €10. Open daily noon-4pm and 7pm-midnight. AmEx/MC/V. ❷

◎ SIGHTS

▨ THE CHURCHES. Rock-hewn churches periodically punctuate the *sassi* along V. Bruno Buozzi. The churches of **◪San Pietro Caveoso, Santa Maria d'Idris, Convicino di San Antonio, Santa Barbara,** and **Santa Lucia alle Malve** preserve beautiful 11th-century Byzantine frescoes in their caves. The Convicino di San Antonio abandoned its holy ways in the 16th century to become a rambunctious canteen instead—don't miss the play-on-words slogan: *"Prima Divino e Dopo Vino,"* meaning "First divine, and then after, wine." *(From P. Veneto, walk past Museo Ridola on V. Ridola and bear left until the end of P. Pascoli; descend stairs and head straight until hitting V. Bruno Buozzi on the left. Alternately, follow signs reading "Turistico Itinerario" and "Convicino di San Antonio" from the bottom of V. Bruno Buozzi. Follow path along cliffs to reach churches. Open daily 9am-1pm and 3-7pm. 1 church €2.50, 4 churches €5, all 7 churches €6.)* Farther along sits the multi-level structure containing houses and the churches **Madonna delle Virtù** and **San Nicola dei Greci**—where the Last Supper scene of the film *The Passion of the Christ* was filmed. The structure holds frescoes and modern sculptures by Leoncillo. *(Open daily 9am-9pm. English tours available. €2.50, students €1.25.)*

THE SASSI. These 7000-year-old homes sit amidst a maze of pathways; a detailed map, available at the tourist office, is necessary to negotiate them properly. Little is known about the people who first built and inhabited the *sassi.* The dwellings themselves are carved directly into the *tufa* stone of the city's *gravina* (ravine). The oldest *sassi*, inhabited around 7000 years ago, are the crumbling structures that line **Sasso Caveoso** (along V. Addozio). The valley east of the *duomo* around **Sasso Barisano** contains the 2nd type of *sassi;* these carved nooks date from around 2000 BC. The most elaborate *sassi* are also the newest—at a little more than 1000 years old—clustered near V. Bruno Buozzi (off V. Madonna delle Virtù near the *duomo*). Most of the 6th-century *chiese rupestri* (rock churches) remain unmodified, with remnants of original 12th-century frescoes. Until 1952, groups of up to 12 people still lived in these windowless caves, often sharing dwellings with the family livestock. In 1952, the Italian government declared these homes unsafe and unsanitary for the *materani* residents who had been living in them for millennia without electricity or running water, and inhabitants were moved to government-built suburban housing. Local children roam the *sassi* offering tours of the caves to visitors, but organized tours such as **Sassi Tourism** are more enlightening. *(V. B. Buozzi 141/143. ☎ 19 458; www.sassitourism.it.)* For a self-guided tour, buy a book at any magazine stand. In the *sassi*, the **Cooperative Amici Del Turistica** offers info and tours in English, French, German, and Italian. The **Sassi by Night** tour is a good one. *(V. Fiorentini 30. ☎ 33 03 01; www.amicidelturista.it. Open daily spring-summer 8am-1pm and 4-9pm; fall-winter 9am-noon and 4-7pm. €15 per person for groups of 4 or more.)* If you're really interested in the *sassi*, a few minutes is all it will take to see **La Casa Grotta;** these two small rooms are furnished as they were when occupied by 10 people and two horses. *(☎/fax 31 01 18. Open daily 9:30am-8:30pm. English tours available. €1.50, students €1.)* In a former Dominican monastery—converted to a nobleman's palace in the 16th century—lies the **MUSMA (Museum of Contemporary Sculpture Matera),** with an impressive array of artwork that covers over three millenia. *(Pomarici building by V. Giacomo in Sasso Caveoso. ☎ 33 05 82. Open Tu-Su 10am-2pm and 4-8pm. €4.50, students €3.50.)*

THE NEW(ER) CITY. Although Matera's ancient *sassi* have a timeless elegance, a trip to the 'modern' city is also worth your time. The towering spire and carved outer portals of the 13th-century Puglian-Romanesque **duomo** are certainly worth pausing to admire. Inside, the 15th-century carved choir stalls are just as intricate. *(From P. Veneto, take V. del Corso; immediately past Chiesa di San Francesco d'Assisi, turn left into P. Sedile and take V. Duomo. Open daily 8am-1pm and 3:30-6pm. Modest dress required. Free.)* Next, stop by the skeleton-and-skull-covered facade of **Chiesa del Purgatorio.** *(Retrace steps to Chiesa di San Francesco d'Assisi, make sharp left turn; church is on V. Ridola.)* Two hundred meters down, the **Museo Ridola** houses some of the region's finest archaeological treasures—many from the *sassi*. Five rooms hold excellent classical pottery and artwork and even contain a Neolithic skeleton. *(V. Ridola 24. ☎ 31 00 58. Open M 2-8pm, Tu-Su 9am-8pm. €2.50, students 18-25 €1.25, under 18 or over 65 free.)*

PARCO DELLA MURGIA MATERANA. The park straddles the ridge across the canyon from the *sassi* and offers some of the area's best **hiking.** The terrain, lush in some patches and bare in others, is dotted with over 150 *chiese rupestri* and the strange *jazzi*, caves built by shepherds to shelter flocks. *(Park entrance off Strada Statale, down V. Annunziatella then V. Marconi. 17km from the centro; best accessed by taxi. Tourist office has info on private tours.)*

🌿 FESTIVALS

From June 20 to the beginning of July, Matera celebrates the 🔲**Festa di Santa Maria della Bruna,** which features numerous musical and cultural events, nightly fireworks displays, and open-air markets selling everything from power tools to psychic readings by exceedingly gifted parakeets. The revelry culminates with the **Assalto al Carro** on July 2, when townspeople destroy an intricate papier mâché cart. The *sassi* house an **International Sculpture Exhibition** from June to October in the churches of Madonna delle Virtù and San Nicola dei Greci.

MARATEA ☎ 0973

The ancient city of Maratea (mah-rah-TEH-ah; pop. 5330), perched above the Gulf of Policastro on Mount San Biagio, was the site of an important fortress dating back to the Middle Ages. A French siege in 1806 led to the destruction of the fortress, but the *centro storico* survived. Today, the former site of the fortress is filled with an enormous statue of Christ, his arms outstretched, the port and sea-side town of Fiumicello at his back. While the Redeemer might shun the sea in favor of the hilly interior, holiday-makers pledge complete devotion to the 23km of Maratean coastline in July and August, sunbathing on local beaches and exploring paleolithic grottoes by day while passing nights in the shop-filled *centro storico*.

▐ ▐ TRANSPORTATION AND PRACTICAL INFORMATION. Transportation to and from Maratea is easiest by **train**. Trains stop in Marina di Maratea for the beach and at the main Maratea station. Trains depart from the main station for: Cosenza (2hr., 16 per day, €7.10); Napoli (3hr., 14 per day, €9); Reggio di Calabria (3½hr., 20 per day, €14); Rome (3-5 hr., 12 per day, €30). The station ticket office closes for a lengthy lunch break. (☎87 69 06. Open M-Sa 7am-12:15pm and 3:50-6:05pm, Su 8:30am-12:15pm and 3:50-6:05pm.) SITA orange **city buses** run approximately every hour and connect the main station to P. Biagio Vitolo, in the *centro storico*, and to Fiumicello (€0.60, purchase tickets onboard). Maratea is composed of three areas: Maratea itself, perched 2km up the mountain and home to the *centro storico;* **Fiumcello,** nearest to the train station; and the **port.** For bus schedules, maps, and other information on Maratea and its surroundings, visit the **A.P.T. tourist office,** P. del Gesù 40, off the main street in Fiumicello. Ask for ▐Elena, who speaks near-perfect English. (☎87 69 08. Open M-Sa 9am-2pm and 3:30-8pm, Su 9:30am-1:30pm and 5-8pm.) **San Paolo Banco di Napoli,** V. Santa Venere, is just across the street from A.P.T. (Open M-F 8:25am-1:25pm and 2:40-4:10pm.) **Farmacia Fortunato** is at V. San Pietro 5. (☎87 61 31. Open M-F 8:30am-1pm and 4:30-8pm.) In case of **emergency,** call the **carabinieri** (☎87 62 01). **Internet** is available at **Info Point,** V. Santa Venere 17, across from the gas station near Hotel Fiorella, in Fiumicello (€6 per hr.; open daily 9am-1pm and 5-8:30pm), or at **P.C. Online,** V. A. Mandarini 52, in the *centro storico.* (€4 per hr.; open M-F 9am-1pm and 4-8pm, Sa 9am-1pm.) The **post office,** V. A. Mandarini 15, also cashes traveler's checks. (☎87 64 98. Open M-F 8am-1:30pm, Sa 8am-12:30pm.) **Postal Code:** 85046.

▐ ▐ ACCOMMODATIONS AND FOOD. For a home-spun flavor, try the various *affittacamere* available for rent through the tourist office. **Talarico Giovanni ❷,** V. Santa Venere 29, is the best deal, with a great location in the center of Fiumicello and large simple rooms. Some rooms have private bath. (☎87 70 40. €25-35 per person. Cash only.) Lodging options in the *centro storico* are limited, though **Hotel La Dimora Del Cardinale ❺,** V. Cardinal Gennari 1, tempts travelers with two terraces overlooking P. B. Vitolo and peach-colored rooms outfitted with TV, A/C, bath, phone, and minibar. (☎87 77 12. Breakfast included. Reserve in advance for Aug. Singles €75-90; doubles €95-140; suites €135-170. AmEx/MC/V.) More affordable possibilities exist down the hill in Fiumicello, including **Hotel Fiorella ❹,** V. Santa Venere 21, which offers basic rooms with TV and bath. (☎/fax 87 65 14. Breakfast €5. Singles €40; doubles €70. AmEx/MC/V.) For camping, try **Villaggio-Camping Maratea ❶,** Contrada Castrocucco 72, 5km south of the Marina di Maratea train station, accessible by bus. (☎87 16 80; www.costadimaratea.com/campeggiomaratea. Minimarket, bar, and restaurant on premises. Open June-Sept. €10-12 per person. Tent rental €10-12. Free hot showers. AmEx/MC/V.)

Despite Maratea's proximity to the sea, the region is best known for its meats and cheeses, including *supressata* (pressed salami) from nearby Rivello and mozzarella from Massa. Pick up these specialties at shops in the *centro storico*. Locals seeking cheap eats usually head to ▐Pizzeria Bussola ❶, V. Santa Venere 43, in Fiumicello, where the service is snappy and the food delicious. (☎87 68 63. Pizza from €2.50. *Panini* from €4. *Primi* €4-6. Cover €1.10. Open daily 7:30-11pm.

AmEx/MC/V.) Dining in the *centro storico* is generally pricey, but **Pizzeria/Trattoria La Torre ❸**, with outdoor seating near the fountain in the *centro storico*, is the exception to the rule. (☎87 62 27. Wood-oven pizza from €3.50. *Primi* €7-9, *secondi* €8-10. Cover €1.50. Open daily noon-3:30pm and 7pm-midnight. AmEx/MC/V.) **Ristorante Pizzeria El Sol ❸**, V. Santa Venere 151, in Fiumicello, prepares fresh seafood on an outdoor grill. (☎87 74 10. Pizza from €3. *Primi* €6-9, *secondi* €7-13.50. Cover €1.50. Open daily noon-3pm and 7pm-midnight. AmEx/MC/V.) For more basic food items, stop at the **Pick-Up** supermarket across from the tourist office in Fiumicello. (Open M-Sa 8:30am-1:30pm and 5-8pm, Su 8:30am-1pm.)

◪ ▓ **SIGHTS AND FESTIVALS.** Maratea's **beaches** are the town's main draw. Though the black sands of Fiumicello are the most convenient for travelers lacking private transportation, the best beaches are at Marina di Maratea and Acquafredda. The latter is reachable by SITA bus #640/0, which runs from the *centro storico* in the direction of Sapri Scalo. Inquire at the tourist office for exact departure times. To escape the midday heat, head to **La Grotta delle Meraviglie**, off the road leading to Marina di Maratea. Discovered accidentally by highway workers in 1929, this underground cave contains 154 million-year-old stalactite, illuminated by artificial light. (Take the Rocco Maratea-Praia line from the *centro storico* or Fiumicello and ask to be let off at the *grotta*. Info ☎87 63 93. Open daily June-Sept. 9:30am-12:30pm and 4-7pm. Mandatory guided tours in English or Italian €3, children 5-15 €2.) Second in size only to the statue of Christ in Rio de Janeiro, the 21m ▓**Statua del Redentore**, crafted in 1965 by Bruno Innocenti, nonetheless offers first-rate views from its base. Visitors seeking a closer look can hire taxis through **Eurotravel**, in P. Biagio Vitolo. (☎87 60 77. Open M-Sa 10am-1pm and 5-8pm. Round-trip €15. AmEx/MC/V.) The only daily bus that runs to the statue departs from P. B. Vitolo leaves at 6:30pm and returns at 7:55pm (€0.60, purchase onboard). Bus riders will have just enough time to visit the 8th-century **Basilica Santuario di San Biagio,** which houses a silver bust of San Biagio, patron saint of Maratea, as well as a marble urn containing the saint's rib bones. (Open daily 9am-noon and 4-7pm. Free.) Every year, beginning on the 1st Sunday in May, Maratea hosts the **Festa di San Biagio,** which includes a procession of town residents carrying Saint Biagio's bust down Mount Biagio. The revelry does not end until one week later, when the bust is returned to its permanent home atop the hill.

CALABRIA

Sometimes called the last great oasis of the Mediterranean, Calabria (ca-LAH-bree-ah) is an undiscovered land of inspiring history and unspoiled natural beauty. Long stretches of beautiful beaches lie on the coast and untamed mountain wildnerness reigns in the interior. As one of Italy's less developed regions, it is one of the few places that has not become completely overrun with tourists touting cameras and maps. Two and a half millennia ago, when the northern cities that now belittle Calabria were but small backwaters, the region was of worldwide importance, home to leading philosophers, artists, and athletes. Fortunately for local pride, traces of this illustrious past remain in abundance, from the castles that dot the coast to the stunningly intact Greek bronze statues, *I bronzi di Riace*, that are still on display in Reggio di Calabria's Museo Nazionale della Magna Graecia. What Calabria lacks in urban bustle, she makes up in quiet natural beauty and a relaxed attitude that the North simply cannot match.

REGGIO DI CALABRIA   ☎ 0965

Though often regarded as merely a departure point for Sicily, Reggio and its environs actually comprise some of the finest landscapes and friendliest people in Italy. The provincial capital of Reggio di Calabria (REH-jo dee Ca-LA-bree-ya; pop. 190,000) was one of the earliest and proudest Greek settlements on the Italian mainland, but it slid into neglect and disarray following centuries of raids and natural disasters. After a devastating 1908 earthquake, a new city arose from the rubble, crowded with designer stores and turn-of-the-century *palazzi*. A vibrant and manageable city, Reggio offers magnificent sunsets, the amazing Riace Bronzes, and an evening stroll that the whole city partakes in along the *lungomare*. The nearby towns of Scilla and Locri offer one of Italy's most attractive beaches and fine archaeological treasures, respectively.

▛ TRANSPORTATION

Aeroporto dello Stretto (☎64 05 17) is 5km south of town. Orange buses #113, 114, 115, 125, or 131 run from P. Garibaldi outside Stazione Centrale to the airport (€1). Flights service Bologna, Florence, Milan, Rome, and Turin. Reggio's main **train station** is Stazione Centrale (☎27 120), on P. Garibaldi at the south end of town. The info office is open daily 7am-9pm. Trains run to: Cosenza (2½hr., 4 per day 5:05am-6:25pm, €13.60); Naples (4½hr., 12 per day 5:45am-11:40pm, €22); Rome (8hr., 11 per day 12:15am-10:21pm, €30); Scilla (30min., 20 per day 5:05am-8:35pm, €5.50); Tropea (2hr., 4 per day 6:16am-8:40pm, €11). Lirosi runs **buses** from P. Garibaldi to Florence (12hr.; M, W-F, Su 6:45pm; €47) and Rome (8hr.; 7am, 11:45am, 10pm; €35). Buy tickets at Agenzia Viaggi Simonetta, C. Garibaldi 521. (☎33 14 44. Open M-F 9am-8:15pm, Sa 9am-1pm. AmEx/MC/V.) Costaviola (☎75 15 86) runs buses from P. Garibaldi to Scilla (45min., 12 per day 7:20am-8:10pm, €3). Buy tickets onboard. **Ferries** depart from the port at the northern end of the city. Boats and hydrofoils serve Messina and the Aeolian Islands. Trenitalia (☎81 76 75), all the way to the left when facing the port, shares hydrofoil service with Ustica (☎090 66 25 06 or 090 36 40 44), to the right of Trenitalia. (Trenitalia office open daily 6:30am-8:15pm; Ustica office hours vary.) NGI (General Italian Navigation Line) is across from Onda Marina to the right of the port entrance. (☎335 84 27 784. Open M-F 12:20am-10:20pm, Sa 12:20am-8:20pm.)

▛ ▛ ORIENTATION AND PRACTICAL INFORMATION

Reggio's main thoroughfare is **Corso Garibaldi,** which runs parallel to the sea and to all the major sights. Facing away from **Stazione Centrale,** walk straight through **Piazza Garibaldi** to C. Garibaldi; a left turn leads to the *centro*. At the end of C. Garibaldi and down Vle. Genoese Zerbi is Reggio's **port,** from which hydrofoils and boats depart. One block to the left of the station, the twin roads **Corso Vittorio Emanuele III** and **Viale Matteotti** trace the *lungomare*. City buses run continuously up and down C. Garibaldi and northward along the two roads. At its center, C. Garibaldi becomes a pedestrian route, perfect for an evening *passeggiata* past the many bars and designer outlets that line the street. The APT **tourist office,** V. Roma 3, 1st fl., provides info and free maps. (☎21 171. Open M-W 7:30am-1:30pm and 2-4pm, Th-F 7:30am-1:30pm.) **Branches** are at Stazione Centrale (☎27 120) and airport (☎64 32 91). For **currency exchange,** head to **Banca Nazionale del Lavoro,** C. Garibaldi 431. (☎85 11. Open M-F 8:20am-1:20pm and 2:35-4pm.) **ATMs** and **pharmacies** line C. Garibaldi. In an **emergency,** call the **police** (☎53 991), near Stazione Centrale. The **hospital, Ospedale Riuniti** (☎39 111) is on V. Melacrino. **Internet Cafe,** V. De Nava 142, near the museum, provides fast connections on 14 computers. (☎23 902. €4 per hr., students €3. Open daily 9am-1pm and 4-8:30pm.) To reach the **post office,** V. Miraglia 14, turn left from P. Italia on C. Garibaldi. (☎31 52 68. Open M-F 8:30am-6:30pm, Sa 8am-12:30pm.) **Postal Code: 89127.**

ACCOMMODATIONS

Cheap, high-quality accommodations are nearly impossible to find in Reggio. **B&B La Pineta ❸,** Vle. G. Zerbi 13/B, is the diamond in the rough, with simply adorned rooms right on the *lungomare*. All rooms have bath and TV, and doubles have A/C. (☎59 37 13; www.bblapineta.info. Reserve ahead July-Aug. Singles €35; doubles €50-60. Cash only). **Hotel Mundial ❹,** V. Gaeta 9. offers relatively cheap rooms right near the train station. All rooms with bath, TV, A/C, and phone. (☎33 22 55; hotelmundial@virgilio.it. Singles €40; doubles €55; triples €60; quads €80. Cash only.) A fancier option is **Hotel Palace Masoanri's ❺,** V. V. Veneto 95. This three-star hotel next to Museo Nazionale offers rooms with bath, A/C, TV, phone, laundry service, minibar, and balcony. (☎26 433; www.montesanohotels.it. Breakfast included. Singles €90; doubles €120; triples €162. AmEx/MC/V.) If you're planning to stay in town for awhile, save money by staying outside the city at **B&B Villa Maria ❸,** V. Marina Arenile 3, in Gallico Marina. Take bus #110 from P. Garibaldi, walk to the waterfront (10min.), and turn right, or call to be picked up. The B&B is on V. Marina Arenile behind the "Ottica" shop. Offers rooms near the coast with terrace. (☎37 26 33. Singles €30, extra person €25. Cash only.)

FOOD

Chefs in Reggio serve *spaghetti alla calabrese* (pasta with pepper sauce), *capocollo* (a ham spiced with local hot peppers), and *pesce spada* (swordfish). Bars along C. Garibaldi often offer baked goods, so sweeten the day with a few of the region's beloved *biscotti*. For a good cheap meal, try **Cordon Bleu ❷,** C. Garibaldi 205. Despite chandelier lighting and a haughty French name, this versatile joint serves cheap *tavola calda* goodies from €1.50, as well as more sophisticated meat and vegetable entrees. (☎33 24 47. *Primi* €5-6, *secondi* €6-8. Open daily 6:30am-11pm. Kitchen open 11am-9pm. AmEx/MC/V.) **Le Palme ❸,** C. V. Emanuele III 25/C, serves

GIVING BACK

DIG IN

While ancient artifacts abound throughout Italy, chances are they're going to be inside a glass case. Those wanting a more in-depth experience with ancient pottery should consider volunteering with the **Mamertion Foundation,** a non-profit archaeological group. The group is currently excavating Monte Palazzi in southeastern Calabria, where a Greek fort stood from the 5th to 3rd centuries BC. While excavations have only just begun, Dr. Paolo Visona and his crew expect to find pottery, terra-cotta figures, and other treasure.

During minimum two-week sessions, volunteers learn how to excavate a site and sift dirt just like the pros. They work closely with Dr. Visona and his crew of students, gaining new information on the life of those who once called the fort home. The work is expected to be somewhat strenuous, but nothing that a budding archaeologist would find too hard.

While the job may be demanding, volunteers will enjoy the comfort of a three-star hotel with pool and all their meals will be included. Although its technically volunteer work, there is a US$1500 tax-deductible fee for each two-week session. Regardless of the price, the chance to become an actual archaeologist and work with artifacts, if only for two weeks, pays for itself.

For more information check out www.mamertiondig.org.

seafood and pizza on its palm-lined patio. (☎20 216. Pizza €4-7. *Primi* €9, *secondi* €10. Cover €1.50. Open daily noon-3pm and 7:30pm-midnight. MC/V). For cheaper pizza, head to **Pizzeria Rusty ❶,** V. Domenico Romeo, next to the museum. Double-folded Neapolitan slices, priced by weight (€7.75 per kg) and *tavola calda* favorites like *arancini* (€1.30) distinguish this pizzeria from the rest. (☎20 012. Open M-Tu and Th-Su 9am-1:30pm and 6pm-midnight. Cash only.) Stock up at **Di per Di** supermarket, past the museum where V. de Nava crosses V. Roma. (Both open M-Sa 8am-1:30pm and 5-8:30pm. MC/V.)

⑥ SIGHTS

The preeminence Reggio di Calabria enjoyed in antiquity as a great Greek *polis* may have passed, but the ■**Museo Nazionale** preserves the city's historical claim to fame with one of the world's finest collections of art and artifacts from *Magna Graecia* (Greater Greece). In the 1st floor galleries, a wealth of *amphorae* and *pinakes* (wine jars and votive tablets) depict scenes from mythology and daily life. The floor above the gallery has a large coin collection and a 2300-year-old novelty sarcophagus shaped like a huge, sandaled foot. Downstairs, treasures formerly submerged in the Ionian Sea, such as pottery and broken statues, comprise the **Sezione Subacquea** (Underwater Section). If the Subacquea is the centerpiece, ■**I Bronzi di Riace** are the crown jewels. Rescued from the sea in 1972, the Riace Bronzes are among the best (and arguably the most valuable) ancient Greek sculptures in the world. Dating from the 5th century BC, they depict nude male warriors in stunning detail. Muscular and assured, the bronzes share gallery space with the realistic **Head of the Philosopher,** which some cite as the Greek tradition's first life-like portrait. A display before entering the gallery documents the bronzes' restoration process. (P. de Nava, on C. Garibaldi toward the Stazione Lido. ☎89 69 72 or 31 62 42. Open Tu-Su 9am-8pm. Last entry 30min. before closing. €4, EU residents 18-25 €2, under 18 or over 65 free.) **Castello Aragonese** is said to date from 536 BC and has provided the city with protection ever since. It was greatly enlarged under the rule of Ferdinand of Aragon and Charles V, who sought to defend the city from Turkish invasions. Today the castle provides magnificent views of the city and Calabria's neighbor Sicily. (P. Castello, take V. degli Ottimati up from C. Garibaldi. ☎36 21 11. Open daily, hours vary.)

⦿ ♫ BEACHES AND ENTERTAINMENT

As the day cools, *reggiani* mingle on the ■**lungomare,** a long, narrow, botanical garden stretching along the seaside that Italian author Gabriele d'Annunzio immortalized as the "most beautiful kilometer in all of Italy." When they want to take a dip, travelers and locals head to the beach near **Lido Comunale.** Playgrounds, an elevated boardwalk, and monuments to the city's more famous citizens dot the *lungomare,* while the quiet beauty of a sunset behind the misty-blue mountains of nearby Sicily provides the final natural touch to a pleasant afternoon swim. Private beaches come alive at night and play host to Reggio's youth. Calabrians finish the summer with the **Festival of the Madonna della Consolazione.** The four-day festival, celebrated in mid-September, concludes with an elaborate fireworks display.

▣ DAYTRIPS FROM REGGIO DI CALABRIA

SCILLA

Scilla is accessible from Reggio by train (30min., 33 per day, €2.10) or by bus (20min., 12 per day, €1.30). Scilla's train station does not sell tickets, so purchase a round-trip ticket from Reggio or ask at nearby bars for regional train tickets.

Walk along the beach and listen for mermaids singing; local legend has it that mer-folk still dwell off the Scillan coast. Homer immortalized Scilla's (SHEEL-la; pop. 5163) great cliffs in *The Odyssey* as the home of the menacing Scylla, a terrible monster with six heads, 12 feet, and a fierce temper. Even fiercer was the monster's clever technique—as ships fled nearby Charybdis, a hazardous whirlpool in the straits where Sicily and Italy meet, Scylla would wait patiently and then devour the vessels as they sailed nearby. Travelers today can expect a more hospitable welcome. Only 23km from Reggio, this fishing-village-turned-resort's languorous pace and distinctive geography (it is built directly into cliffs which enclose a sandy beach) can make the real world seem far away—especially when the meteorological oddity *Fata Morgana* creates a natural magnifying glass out of the light over the sea, making the Sicilian city of Messina appear to be floating just above the water. For those craving seafood, **La Pescatora ❷**, V. Cristoforo Colombo 32, specializes in aquatic fare. (☎ 17 54 147. *Primi* €4-7.50, *secondi* €7-11.50. Open M-Tu and Th-Su noon-3:30pm, 8-11:30pm. AmEx/MC/V.)

THE IONIAN COAST AND ASPROMONTE NATIONAL PARK

Trains and buses along the Ionian Coast and to Aspromonte often have erratic schedules and multiple connections; allow ample travel time when planning an itinerary. Consult the tourist office in Reggio for more info. Those seeking hiking in Aspromonte should call the National Park ☎ 74 30 60 for park conditions and to arrange excursions.

From Reggio to Riace, the Ionian Coast (CO-sta Ee-YO-nee-ya) offers miles of beaches. White sands, rocks, and dunes cater to every taste and provide a contrast to the mountains visible in the distance. Though the ancient Greeks once made these shores as crowded as modern Tropea, it is now primarily locals who frequent these waters and relish their unexploited beauty. Even the more established sites at the villages of **Bianco, Bovalino Marina,** and **Soverato** are relatively unknown. Although it holds the title of the kidnapping capital of the world, **Aspromonte** provides miles of trails to get lost in natural wonder and not the trunk of someone's car. **Montalto,** the primary peak, is a 2hr. drive from Reggio then a 30min. hike. One can also visit the **Garibaldi Mausoleum,** which commemorates where Garibaldi was wounded by the *piedmontese*, enshrining the tree he leaned upon when injured.

TROPEA ☎ 0963

Resounding with the crash of waves against imposing rock faces, Tropea's (tro-PEY-ah; pop. 7000) coastline is truly dreamy. Poised at the edge of a severe precipice, the town's winding streets create a maze of hidden *piazze* and dignified churches. Though empty during the day when the beach's white sands beckon, these streets flood after sundown with a carnival-like procession of bronzed vacationers in skimpy designer wear. Tropea's traditional (if strange) dual claims to fame were its nobility and its *cipolle rosse* (red onions); the nobility has long since disappeared, but the onions remain as potent as the summer sun.

🖅🖪 TRANSPORTATION AND PRACTICAL INFORMATION. Trains run from the Reggio train station to Tropea (2hr., 10 per day, €11). There are three direct returns to Reggio; all others change at Rosarno. As the station has no ticket office, buy tickets at Valentour, P. Vittorio Veneto 17. (☎ 62 516. Open M-Sa 9am-1pm and 4-10pm, Su 6-10pm). FerSav (☎ 61 129) operates convenient *pullmini* (little blue buses) that pick up passengers on V. Stazione every 30min. The vans (€1) travel 27 routes, going as far as 24km afield; they are often the easiest way to access some of Tropea's more remote attractions. For exact stops, ask the English-speaking staff at the Pro Loco **tourist office,** down V. Stazione at P. Ercole. (☎ 61 475. Open June-Oct. daily 9am-1pm and 5-9pm; Nov.-May M-Sa 10am-noon and 4-7pm.) **Banca Carime,** on V. Stazione, has an **ATM** and a **currency-exchange** machine. (Open M-F

8:20am-1:20pm and 2:35-3:35pm.) In case of **emergency,** call an **ambulance** (☎61 366), the **carabinieri** (☎61 018), or the **police** (☎60 42 11). **Farmacia del Corso** is on C. Vittorio Emanuele (☎61 010: Open M-F 8:30am-1pm and 5-10pm. Posts after-hours rotation.) **Quellilà,** Largo Ruffo 5/6, offers **Internet** access. From Pro Loco, follow C. V. Emanuele through P. Ercole. If you've walked off the cliff and plummeted into the ocean, you've gone too far. (€6 per hr. Open M-Sa 10am-1pm and 5pm-midnight, Su 5pm-midnight.) The **post office** is on Vle. Coniugi Crigna, near P. V. Veneto. (☎60 44 49. Open M-F 8am-1:30pm, Sa 8am-12:30pm.) **Postal Code:** 89861.

⌂❒ ACCOMMODATIONS AND FOOD. A number of centrally-located *affitta- camere* rent rooms at prices that vary considerably by season. It's well worth it to spend a few extra euro for a prime location because the narrow roads that lead to and from the *centro* are not outfitted for pedestrians, and taxis are pricey. Ask for info at the Pro Loco tourist office. With ocean views from a rooftop terrace and a location just 5min. from the center, **Hotel la Porta del Mare ❶,** V. Liberta 52, offers rooms with bath, TV, and minibar. (☎60 70 41. Breakfast included. Doubles €35- 55, late Aug. €80. AmEx/MC/V.) For camping by the sea, look no farther than the shaded **Campeggio Marina dell'Isola ❶,** on V. Marina dell'Isola, at the bottom of the stairs leading to the beach. (☎61 970, in winter 60 31 28; www.maregrande.it. €6- 10 per person. 2-person tent €5. Electricity €3. Hot showers free. AmEx/MC/V.)

Tropea's *cipolle rosse* (red onions) and pepper-hot cheeses spice up local dishes, while the famous liquor *Vecchio Amaro del Capo* sweetens the palate. **La Boheme ❸,** V. Roma 21, boasts excellent prices and seating beneath the *duomo*. (☎60 30 53. Pizza from €4. *Primi* €7-9, *secondi* €7-14. Cover €1.50. Open daily 7pm-midnight. MC/V.) Head to elegant **Pimm's Restaurant ❹,** on Largo Migliarese next to the lookout at the end of C. V. Emanuele, to dine to the sound of crashing waves. (☎60 33 87. *Primi* €8-10, *secondi* €14-20. Cover €3. Open in summer Tu-Su 12:30-2:30pm and 7:30pm-midnight. MC/V.) For cheap pizza, head to **La Pizzeria Lupo Cattico ❶,** V. V. Emanuele 29, the first pizzeria to serve triangular pieces in Tropea. You can eat your fill for under €5. (☎328 83 40 974. Slices €1. Drinks including beer €1. Open daily 10am-midnight. Cash only.) Grab a freshly made sandwich at the almost century-old **Alimentari Pandullo Marco ❶,** Largo San Michele 20, on V. Stazione across from V. Umberto I. (Open daily 8am-10pm. Cash only.)

◉◪ SIGHTS AND BEACHES. The gleaming **Santuario di Santa Maria dell'Isola,** currently closed to the public, presides over the white cliffs at the edge of town. Featured on postcards sold from Reggio to Cosenza, the church's sequestered beauty and historical significance warrant the fierce local pride. To honor the Madonna, townsmen take the church's Holy Family statues out to sea every August 15 in a procession of hundreds of small boats. The naval parade tours nearby towns and ends with a display of fireworks in the evening. Up the cliff is Tropea's graceful **Norman cathedral.** Besides some elegant polychrome marble work and several sword-bearing dead *tropeani*, the interior houses two bombs that miraculously failed to destroy Tropea when an American warplane dropped them in 1943. To reach the absolutely flawless **beach,** take a winding set of stairs down the cliffs at the end of V. Umberto I and turn off C. V. Emanuele to the left.

COSENZA   ☎0984

One of the most important cultural and industrial centers of Calabria, Cosenza (co-SEN-za; pop. 70,185) is full of intrigue. From the plundered riches that King Alaric I supposedly buried in the city's Busento River in AD 410 to its Norman castle built by the Saracens, Cosenza's treasures mirror its unusual history. Though often ignored by tourists due to its inland location, Cosenza's charming *centro*

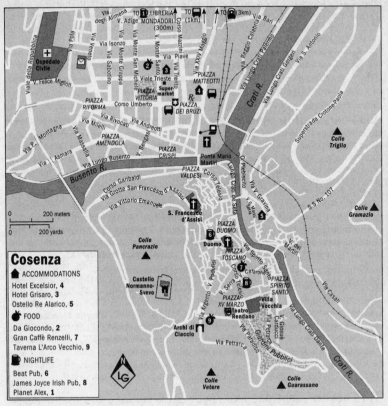

PUGLIA, BASILICATA, CALABRIA

Cosenza

🏠 ACCOMMODATIONS

Hotel Excelsior, **4**
Hotel Grisaro, **3**
Ostello Re Alarico, **5**

🍎 FOOD

Da Giocondo, **2**
Gran Caffè Renzelli, **7**
Taverna L'Arco Vecchio, **9**

🍸 NIGHTLIFE

Beat Pub, **6**
James Joyce Irish Pub, **8**
Planet Alex, **1**

storico, massive student population, and thriving nightlife make it worth a short stopover. The best time to visit is during the spring, when the university is in session, Teatro Rendano echoes with plays, and temperatures remain pleasant.

> **SUNDAY SERVICES.** Transportation options from Cosenza are severely reduced Su. City buses run less frequently, and Ferrovie della Calabria trains and buses do not run at all. Act like a local and lay low.

TRANSPORTATION. Trains depart from **Stazione Cosenza** (☎39 47 46), on V. Popilia, 4km north of the city center. The ticket office is open daily 6:10am-12:42pm and 1:50-8:22pm. Trains go to Naples (4½hr., 13 per day 4:35am-6:25pm, €17.30), and Reggio di Calabria (2½hr., 10 per day 6:10am-7:29pm, €13.60). Ferrovie della Calabria sends trains to Camigliatello (1½hr., M-Sa 9:18am, €3). It also sends regional blue **buses** to Camigliatello (45min., M-Sa 8 per day 6:50am-7:05pm, €2) and San Giovanni (2hr., M-Sa 10 per day, €3) from the station on V. Autostazione and the Stazione Cosenza. The ticket office is opposite the train ticket window and is open daily 6am-2:20pm and 4-7:30pm. All orange **city buses** stop at P. Matteotti. Tickets (€0.77) are sold at magazine kiosks (main kiosk at V. Trieste with C. Mazzini, near P. dei Bruzi) and at most *tabaccherie*. Buses #4T, 22, and 23 serve the *centro storico*, departing from P. Bruzi and stopping in P. Prefeturra (every 30min. 5:30am-11pm). Buses #17 and 27 run between P. Matteotti and the train station (every 7min. 5am-midnight). Routes are posted on yellow hanging street signs in P. Matteotti and at all bus stops. (Info ☎ 800 24 24 00.)

> ❗ Since none of the bus stops are marked, look for the yellow schedules posted roadside in order to distinguish one stop from another. If all else fails, ask the driver where you should get off.

▰◪ ORIENTATION AND PRACTICAL INFORMATION. The **Busento River** divides the city into two parts: the traffic-heavy new city, north of the Busento, and the relaxed *centro storico*, south of the river. **Corso Mazzini,** the main thoroughfare and shopping center, begins near the river at **Piazza dei Bruzi,** continues through **Piazza Kennedy,** and ends in **Piazza Bilotti.** To get to C. Mazzini, hop on any bus to **Piazza Matteotti** and, facing away from the bus stop, walk a block up **Corso Umberto** to P. dei Bruzi. The bus station is on **Via Autostazione,** to the right off P. Bilotti at the end of C. Mazzini, where the *corso* splits seven ways. Cosenza's *centro storico* lies across the **Ponte Mario Martiri.** A labyrinth of medieval stone buildings, the old city has winding streets and cobblestone staircases. The only discernible street, the narrow **Corso Telesio,** begins in **Piazza Valdesi,** near the Busento, and climbs to the statue of Telesio in the **Piazza XV Marzo** (also called **Piazza Prefettura**).

Since there is no tourist office in Cosenza, head to the town hall, P. dei Bruzi 1 (☎ 81 31), if you have any questions. In case of **emergency,** call the **police** in P. dei Bruzi, behind the town hall (☎ 25 422). **Farmacia Berardelli,** C. Mazzini 40, posts after-hours rotations. (☎ 26 452. Open M-F 8:30am-1pm and 4:30-8pm.) The **Ospedale Civile dell'Annunziata** (☎ 68 11) is on V. Felice Migliori. **Libreria Mondadori,** C. Mazzini 156, has a small selection of English-language best-sellers. (☎ 0983 79 58 14. Open M-F 9am-1pm and 4:30-8:30pm, Sa 9am-1pm. AmEx/MC/V.) For **Internet** access, head to **Web Point,** P. Campanella 32. (€2 per hr. Open daily 9am-1pm and 4:30-9pm.) The **post office,** V. Veneto 41, is at the end of V. Piave, off C. Mazzini. (☎ 22 162. Open M-F 8am-6:30pm, Sa 8am-12:30pm). **Postal Code:** 87100.

◪◪ ACCOMMODATIONS AND FOOD. Ostello Re Alarico ❶, Vico II Giuseppe Marini Serra 10, offers eight-bed rooms with ornate furniture. The hostel also has a bar, a kitchen, and courtyard. Across the Crati River from the old city, follow V. G. M. Serra and look for the sign for the small street where the hostel lies. This hostel is the perfect base for exploring the old city and the surrounding area. (☎ 79 25 70; www.ostellorealarico.com. Breakfast included. Dorms €17. AmEx/MC/V.) **Hotel Excelsior ❹,** P. Matteoti 14, lets recently renovated, high-ceilinged rooms with A/C, TV, and phone, right across from the old train station. (☎/fax 74 383. Breakfast included. Reception 24hr. Singles €40; doubles €60. AmEx/MC/V.) To reach **Hotel Grisaro ❸,** V. Monte Santo 6, walk one block up C. Mazzini from P. dei Bruzi, then turn left on V. Trieste to find V. Monte Santo. Rooms are spacious and comfortable, with fluffy beds, TV, and balcony. (☎ 27 952; fax 27 838. Wheelchair-accessible. Reservations recommended. Singles with exterior private bath €29, with interior bath €36; doubles €52; triples €67; quads €78. MC/V.)

Cosenza's cuisine is a crossroads of flavor, drawing on fresh prosciutto and rich mushrooms of the Sila forests, plentiful fish from the Tyrrhenian Sea, and the fruit of the region's orchards. For a proper meal, hike up the stone steps next to Teatro Rendano to reach **Taverna L'Arco Vecchio ❷,** P. Archi di Ciaccio 21. Done up in elegant wood, this versatile restaurant offers guests a range of salads

(€6-8), pizzas (€3-10), and entrees in a garden dining area. Enjoy the large wine selection and the marvelous location by the city's old arch. (☎72 564. *Primi* €4-8, *secondi* €3-6.50. Cover €1.50. Open M-Sa 1-3pm and 8-11pm. Reservations recommended. AmEx/MC/V.) Owned and operated by the same family since 1803, **Gran Caffè Renzelli ❶**, C. Telesio 46, specializes in homemade sweets; their *varchiglia alla mocale* is a chocolate-covered almond treat still made by nuns with a recipe from the 1300s. The *gran caffè* is as pretty as it is powerful, with steamed milk, cocoa, and *vov*, an egg liqueur. (☎26 814; www.grancafferenzelli.it. Mini *pizza rustica* €1. *Gelato* €2.60. Cover €0.52. Open daily 7am-midnight. Closed in winter Tu. Cash only.) An inexpensive but high-quality option in the new city is **Da Giocondo ❷**, V. Piave 53, near Hotel Grisaro. Fresh fish, regional specialties, and tasty fruit desserts complement a long wine list. (☎29 810. *Primi* €4-6, *secondi* €5-15. Cover €2. Open M-F noon-3pm and 7-10pm, Sa noon-3pm. AmEx/MC/V.) For fresh, juicy produce, stop at **Cooper Frutta**, Vle. Trieste 33, a block from C. Mazzini, and pick up everything else from **Cooperatore Alimentare**, next door at Vle. Trieste 35. (Open M-F 7am-8:30pm, Sa 7am-2:30pm.) Take a picnic to Villa Vecchia, at the end of C. Telesio in the old city.

◨◧ SIGHTS AND NIGHTLIFE. Cross Ponte Mario Martiri into the old city and head left up C. Telesio to reach the **duomo.** Alternatively, take bus #22 or 23 to P. Prefettura; facing away from P. del Governo, turn right down C. Telesio. Originally erected in 1140 with a Romanesque design, the church had to be entirely rebuilt in 1184 after an earthquake. When the *duomo* was reconsecrated in 1222 after yet another earthquake, Frederick II gave the city a gilt **Byzantine crucifix** containing a splinter said to be from the True Cross. Now the cross is in the Galleria Nazionale at the Palazzo Arnone; call ahead to see it. Inside the *duomo* is Cosenza's most prized work of art after the famed cross—*La Madonna del Pilerio*, a 12th-century painting in the Byzantine style. It is in a Baroque chapel, the first on the left side of the church entrance. (☎79 56 39. Open daily mornings and late afternoons.) Back in P. Prefettura, the **Teatro Rendano,** Calabria's most prestigious performance venue, was constructed in 1895 and destroyed by WWII bombing. It has since been restored to its former glory and its plush interior has even showcased the likes of José Carreras. Reservations for non-*calabresi* or unconnected foreigners are extremely difficult to get during the opera season (Oct.-Dec.); seats for the theater season (Jan.-May) may be somewhat easier to come by. The Rendano also hosts regional performance groups during the summer, with readily available tickets. (☎81 32 20. For plays, tickets may be available 10am-1pm and 5-8pm on day of performance. Tickets from €18, student discounts available.) To reach the fairy tale on a hill, **Castello Normanno-Svevo (Norman Castle),** walk up the stairs to the left of the *teatro* about 200m, going left at P. Archi di Ciaccio and continuing up the stairs opposite Taverna L'Arco Vecchio. Or take bus 4T to the elevated village and follow signs a steep 10-15min. climb uphill. The castle predates most of the *centro storico* and, in its ruined state, testifies to the city's tumultuous past. Originally built by the Saracens but refurbished by Frederick II after the *cosentini* tried to overthrow him, the castle offers views of the city. Now serene and barely visited, the *castello* has functioned as a barracks, a prison, and a seminary. (Open daily 8am-8pm. Currently undergoing renovations. Free.)

Partygoers from smaller, surrounding towns flock to Cosenza, as it is the center of action for the region. **◧Beat Pub,** P. Duomo 4/6, right next to the *duomo*, is huge, with more than 50 Belgian beers from which to choose. (☎29 548. Beers from €2. Open daily 7:30pm-3am. AmEx/MC/V). **Planet Alex,** P. XI Settembre 12, off C. Mazzini, is a disco-pub in the new city that blasts dance music. (☎79 53 37. Th-F live music in winter. Open M-Sa 7am-2am, Su 5pm-2am. AmEx/MC/V.) Get a taste of the Emerald Isle at the **James Joyce Irish Pub,** V. Cafarone 19, a lively bar that's packed on weekends. (☎22 799. Open daily from 8pm. AmEx/MC/V.)

> **SCHOOL'S OUT FOR SUMMER.** Cosenza's streets and pub echo silently during the summer when the university is not in session and the 15,000 students are not around. Consider planning your trip before the spring semester ends for a rowdy, good time.

CAMIGLIATELLO AND SILA MASSIF ☎0984

"Its nature will amaze you," states a billboard near the Sila Massif train station. Indeed, the 1850 sq. km plateau named Sila Massif is an untainted landscape of fertile, green mountains, dazzling lakes, and woods that burst with wildflowers in the spring. Covering the widest part of the Calabrian peninsula, Sila was once a huge forest, exploited from its earliest days to provide fuel and material for the buildings of Rome. Today, the area offers some of Italy's most spectacular natural settings and a wealth of activities to satisfy intrepid explorers. Camigliatello (cah-MEE-lyah-TEH-loh; pop. 700), a resort town within Sila, offers bus connections and access to hikes and ski slopes, making it the best base for exploring Sila.

TRANSPORTATION AND PRACTICAL INFORMATION. Trains to Sila run from Cosenza (1½hr., 9:18am, €2), but their schedules are fairly erratic; **buses** from Cosenza are usually more reliable (40min., 9 per day 6:30am-7pm, €2). Find bus schedules at the tourist office and buy tickets at Bar Pedace, the *bar* closest to the bus stop. Maps and info on Sila and surrounding attractions, events, and trails can be found at the Pro Loco **tourist office,** V. Roma 5, uphill from the train station and bus stop. (☎57 81 59. Open Tu-Su 9:30am-1pm and 3:30-7:30pm.) **Banca Carime** is at V. del Turismo 73. (☎57 80 27. Open M-F 8:30am-1:20pm and 2:35-3:35pm.) In case of **emergency,** call the **guardia medica** (☎57 83 28), near the bus stop. The **post office,** on V. Tasso, is at the intersection of V. del Turismo and V. Roma, next to Hotel Tasso. (☎57 80 76. Open M-F 8am-1:30pm, Sa 8am-12:30pm.)

ACCOMMODATIONS AND FOOD. Hotel Meranda ❸, V. del Turismo 29, offers modern rooms in a secluded area off the main road. Facilities include an elegant restaurant and *discoteca*. Prices rise during ski season. (☎57 80 22; fax 57 92 93. Singles €30-60; doubles with half pension €48-65, full pension €53-70. Extra bed €35-52. AmEx/MC/V.) **B&B Villa Guido ❸,** V. Napoli 19, in Moccone, is 1.5km up the road from V. Roma. At the intersection with Moccone, turn right and follow the signs—call ahead for pickup from Camigliatello. Four doubles and a four-bed suite for families all have bath and TV, and share a balcony and living room. (☎57 80 66; www.villaguido.it. Breakfast included. Doubles €70-80; suite €120-150. Cash only). Buses run from Camigliatello to **La Fattoria ❶** campground, 5km from Camigliatello. (☎57 83 64. Tent provided. €5.60 per person. Cash only.)

Le Tre Lanterne ❸, V. Roma 142, is a popular spot specializing in porcini mushrooms. (☎57 82 03. Pizza from €3.50. *Primi* 6-8, *secondi* 8-12. Cover €1.50. Open Tu-Su noon-3pm and 7-11pm. AmEx/MC/V.) Dine by lantern light at **Ristorante Hotel Lo Sciatore ❸,** V. Roma 128, where patrons savor creamy mushroom risotto in a dining room with a ski-lodge feel. (☎57 81 05. Wood-oven pizza from €2.60. *Primi* €6, *secondi* €7.50. Cover €1.60. Open daily 12:30-3pm and 7:30-10pm. AmEx/MC/V.) **La Casa del Fungo ❷,** on P. Misasil, just next door to Campanaro, sells locally-grown mushrooms. (Open daily 9am-8:30pm. Closed in winter Tu. Cash only.) Picnic grounds lie 10min. from the *centro*, up V. Tasso past the post office. There are also a number of *salumerie* that overflow with cheeses, cured meats, and marinated mushrooms, including **Antica Salumeria Campanaro,** P. Misasi 5, across from post office (☎57 80 15. Open daily 8:30am-9pm. MC/V.)

MENACING MUSHROOMS. When exploring the Parco Nazionale di Calabria, think twice before taking home any of the region's famous wild mushrooms. While the *funghi porcini* are both edible and delicious, other species range from mildly poisonous to lethally toxic. The safest way to enjoy Silan mushrooms is to purchase them in local shops or restaurants.

OUTDOOR ACTIVITIES AND SKIING. Want snow? Come winter, there's plenty of it at the **Tasso Monte Curcio Ski Trail,** 2km from town up V. Roma and left at Hotel Tasso. Go right at the fork in the road. In winter, minibuses leave for the trailhead from Camigliatello's bus stop. Buy tickets onboard. Though Tasso offers 35km of cross-country skiing, it has only 2km of downhill trails. (☎57 81 36 or 57 94 00. When snow is on the ground, lifts are open daily 9am-4:30pm. Round-trip lift ticket €4, weekends €5; day pass €15/20.) Getting to the **☒Parco Nazionale di Calabria** (☎57 97 57), 10km northwest, is more tricky; just two **Autolinee Scura** (☎31 324) buses head into the park daily, in the morning and afternoon, at varying times. **Altipiani,** V. Roma 146 (☎57 81 54 or 339 26 42 365; www.inaltipiani.it), offers guided tours of the park in English to large groups as well as moonlit bike trips. Arrange times and prices through reservation. Altipani also rents bikes. (Bikes €12 per half-day, €18 per day. Snowshoes €13 per day; cross-country skis €18 per day. *Let's Go* discount €3 on all full-day rentals. Cash only.)

PRAIA A MARE ☎0985

While Praia a Mare (PRY-ah A MAR-eh) may only have 6120 year-round residents, vacationing Italians cause this stunning beach town to surge come summer. Largely undiscovered by foreigners, this peaceful hamlet boasts beautiful beaches, cliff diving, and a southern Italian attitude of relaxation not found in any major northern city. Home to both the natural beauty of Isola Dino and the non-stop parties of the *Festa di Santa Maria della Grotta*, Praia seems to have something to offer for everyone. Those who make the trip to lovely Praia often end up staying longer than they expected—and then return as soon as they can.

WHAT'S IN A NAME? Praia a Mare also goes by the name Praja; both names show up on maps and train schedules.

TRANSPORTATION AND PRACTICAL INFORMATION. The best way to reach Praia is by train. **Trains** depart from the Praia station for: Cosenza (2hr., 16 per day, €7); Naples (3hr., 14 per day, €9); Reggio di Calabria (3½hr., 20 per day, €14); Rome (3-5hr., 12 per day, €30). For **taxis,** call ☎338 87 64 97 91. The best way to get around town is on **bikes,** which can be rented from Bike Motor Points, P. Italia. (☎72 126. €10 per day.) Praia basically consists of three main streets that run parallel to the ocean. **Via Roma** is the 1st street outside the train station; next is **Via C. P. Longo,** which becomes V. L. Giuguie and is the main avenue through town; after that is the **lungomare** which follows the ocean all the way to beautiful beaches of Fiuzzi. For maps and information on events in town head to the **IAT tourist office,** V. Amerigo Vespucci 12. (☎72 322. Open daily 8am-8pm.) For **currency exchange** and an **ATM** right off the main street, go to **Banco di Napoli,** V. della Libertà 14. (☎72 071. Open daily 7am-2pm.) In an **emergency,** call the **carabinieri** (☎72 020). A **pharmacy** can be found at V. C. P. Longo 51. (☎72 009. Open daily 8am-8pm.) Access the **Internet** with free Wi-Fi at the **Museo Communale** on V. Verdi. (Open M-F 8am-noon and 4-10pm, Sa 7pm-midnight.) The **post office** is located in P. Municipio near the town center (Open M-Sa 7am-1pm.) **Postal Code:** 87028.

⌂◻ ACCOMMODATIONS AND FOOD. While prices in Praia skyrocket in August, a few budget bargains still exist. With a fun community atmosphere, **▨The Onda Road Beach Hostel ❶,** V. Boccioni 13, is the best bet for backpackers. Martina, Papa, and their dog Sylla welcome foreigners with open arms. The hostel has simple dorms and two doubles. The real deals are their incredible discounts on attractions such as rafting, paragliding, bikes, and the beach clubs. (☎347 07 36 169; www.calabriahostel.com. Free pickup from the train station. Papa runs Isola di Dino boat tours for about €10 per person. Kitchen available. Breakfast and lunch included. Laundry €3 per load, free for stays longer than 3 nights. Reservations recommended. Dorms €19; doubles €25.) For slightly classier digs right in the center of town, head to **Le Arcata ❹,** V. Filippo Turati 25. This modern hotel has large marble-floored rooms, many with balcony overlooking the main street. All rooms with bath, TV, AC, and phone. (☎72 297. Breakfast included. Reservations recommended in Aug. Singles €45-75; doubles €60-150; triples €75-225. Full pension required in Aug.) Camping can be found a short walk from town near Fiuzzi at **La Mantinera ❶,** V. Giovanni Battista Falcone. With a pool, private beach, and restaurant, the campground truly deserves its self-proclaimed title of tourist village. (☎77 90 23; www.lamantinera.it. Reservations recommended Aug. €4.50-14 per person, €14-97 per tent. Bungalows €330-1350 per week. AmEx/MC/V).

While the tourist-geared eateries in Praia are generally overpriced, the restaurant at **Le Arcata ❷,** V. Filippo Turati 25, provides affordable upscale dining. Try their drink and pizza special for €5. (☎72 297. Pizza from €3.50; dinner only. *Primi* €4.50-8, *secondi* €6.20-14. Cover €1.50. Open 24hr. in summer. AmEx/ MC/V). There are five supermarkets within the city center, as well as numerous vegetable stands and fish markets that provide cheaper options. The most convenient is the **Sisa** supermarket located at V. L. Giuguie 37 right in the middle of town. (Open daily 9am-1:30pm and 4:30-8:30pm.)

◻◳ SIGHTS AND ENTERTAINMENT. Sitting just a few meters from the beaches at Fiuzzi, the massive **▨Isola di Dino** dominates the view with its lush forest and dramatic cliffs. The island is owned by the Ferrari family and sadly climbing to the top costs €7, but the grottoes underneath are easily accesible by kayak, paddle boat, or motorboat and are free of charge. There is even a spot where visitors can jump from 6m into the water below. After that warm up, the truly brave can venture to a natural arch 10min. away by boat that allows for jumps of 22m. Novices should not attempt this as serious injury can result. Those less inclined for wild leaps should try snorkeling in the startlingly clear water around the island. (Boat tours and all other rentals can be arranged at most of the beach clubs. Prices vary by season.) Home of the city's patron, the Blessed Madonna, the **Sanctuario Santa Maria della Grotta** is found in a large cave in the cliffs overlooking the city. Follow V. della Grotta up from V. L. Giuguie. The cave itself houses an ongoing archaeological dig, a modern church, and, of course, the statue of the Madonna which sits safely in a plexiglass case (you can only get up close and personal with the Virgin Mary by embarking on a guided tour). Legend goes that a 12th-century sea captain chose this cave as the refuge for the statue after his shipmates, stuck off the coast of Praia, deemed it a curse. The Madonna was later discovered by sheepherders who then founded Praia a Mare. The cave has been continually habituated for over 14,000 years and has provided archaeologists with a wealth of information regarding the lives and culture of the ancient inhabitants of Calabria. (For guided tours call ☎ 72 061. Open daily 8am-8pm.)

Beaches run the length of Praia all along the *lungomare*, though the nicest ones are located at **Fuizzi** nearest to Isola Dino. If you wish, you can rent chairs (from €5) and umbrellas (from €5) from any of the beach clubs. Don't feel intimidated; the beaches are free regardless of the presence of beach clubs. If sunbathing sounds too tame, **Parapendio** offers paragliding. After driving 600m up into the nearby mountains, you and a pilot take off for a 20min. flight over Praia and land directly on the beach right next to Fuizzi. (☎ 347 55 70 595. Flights €70, Onda Road Hostel guests €40. Reservations required. Cash only.) Although Praia fills up during the summer, it reaches critical mass August 15 for the **Festa di Santa Maria.** Locals bring the Madonna down from the church and at night parade it in a boat along the harbor with dozens of other boats following close by. When the Madonna passes revelers on the beach, they light their bonfires and ignite a week of festivities that brings thousands more visitors to the already overflowing town.

◪ DAYTRIP FROM PRAIA A MARE

▧ **LAO RIVER RAFTING.** The Lao River was once used by the ancient Greeks to bring messages quickly from Greece to Sicily, and today rafters can rush through the very same rapids, stopping only to gasp at the natural wonders. Located deep within the mountainous interior of Calabria, the Lao River Valley remains largely untouched by man and shimmers with the natural beauty of waterfalls, local wildlife, and ancient caves. While the river is cold, rafters will be outfitted with wetsuits and rubber shoes and can jump in and float along until the boat reaches the rapids. Rafters will brave some rapids but nothing too strenuous; just make sure you hang on to your paddle. **Rafting Yahoooooo,** V. Marconi 11, in Scalea, runs 5hr. tours of the river and will drive guests to the valley from anywhere in Scalea or Praia. Feel free to bring along your camera, as tour guides offer waterproof cases. (☎ 333 72 58 276; www.raftingcalabria.it. Wetsuits provided. Reservations required. €65 per person, €40 for Onda Road Hostel guests. Group rates available.) While the rafting itself is over an hour by van inland, most of the rafting companies are based in nearby Scalea which can easily be reached by train from Praia (10min., 16 per day, €1.80).

SICILY (SICILIA)

An island of contradictions, Sicily's (in Italian, "see-CHEE-lee-ya") complex culture emerges from millennia of diverse influences. Every great Mediterranean empire since the arrival of the Phoenicians in 900 BC has left its mark here. A string of Greek colonies followed Phoenician rule, and even today, the island sports more Greek temples than Greece itself. Roman theaters, Arab mosques, and Norman cathedrals round out the physical remnants of Sicily's past diversity. While Italian culture dominates in modern Sicily, the separation with the mainland is far greater than the narrow Straits of Messina would suggest. The ancient Greeks lauded the "golden isle" as the second home of the gods, but today it is known to many tourists as the home of Mt. Etna and *The Godfather*. The Mafia remains an unspoken presence in Sicilian society, but has lately been reduced largely to petty crime. Regardless of her connotations, Sicily overflows with the rich cultural, culinary, and natural wonders that its position at the center of the Mediterranean truly merits.

HIGHLIGHTS OF SICILY

BASK in the glow of **Byzantine gold** at Monreale Cathedral near Palermo (p. 655).

INTERACT with archaeologists restoring the world's largest intact mosaic at **Villa Romana del Casale** in Piazza Armerina (p. 690).

SCALE Mt. Etna (p. 688) in the morning and party all night in **Syracuse** (p. 698).

COMMUNE with the sultry splendors of Pantelleria's **azure-lapped shores** (p. 720).

TIP? **SCHEDULE? WHAT SCHEDULE?** Sleepy Sicilians fully embrace Italian life's relaxed pace. Taking their sweet time means that transportation seldom runs on time. Don't stress, be patient! Sit back, relax, and plan accordingly.

PALERMO

☎ 091

Both turbulent and exquisite, Italy's 5th largest city is a strangely alluring mix of beauty and decay. A smoggy, gritty metropolis with over 1,000,000 inhabitants, Palermo's (pa-LEHR-mo) pace of life dispels any myth of a sleepy Sicily; its racing stream of cars, buses, and scooters set the city's breakneck pace. Those who opt to slow down will be rewarded by Palermo's impressive sights and relics. While poverty, bombings, and centuries of neglect have taken their toll on Palermo, the city is slowly experiencing a revival. The 1993 election of an anti-Mafia mayor brought a temporary end to the Mob's knee-bashing control, and with political reform underway, Palermo is now at work restoring its architectural treasures.

✈ INTERCITY TRANSPORTATION

Flights: Falcone Borsellino Airport (☎ 70 20 111), at Punta Raisi, 30min. from central Palermo. **Prestia & Comande** (☎ 58 04 57) runs buses every 30min. from P. Castelnuovo (45min.) and Stazione Centrale (1hr., €4.65). **Taxis** (☎ 59 16 62) charge at least €30-50 to get to town and are parked outside the airport. For trains, look for the "shuttle to trains" sign. Free **shuttles** run every 30min. to and from the nearby train station at Punto Raisi. At the station, head left and down the escalator. Trains to **Stazione Centrale** run every hr. 5:40am-10:40pm (€4.85).

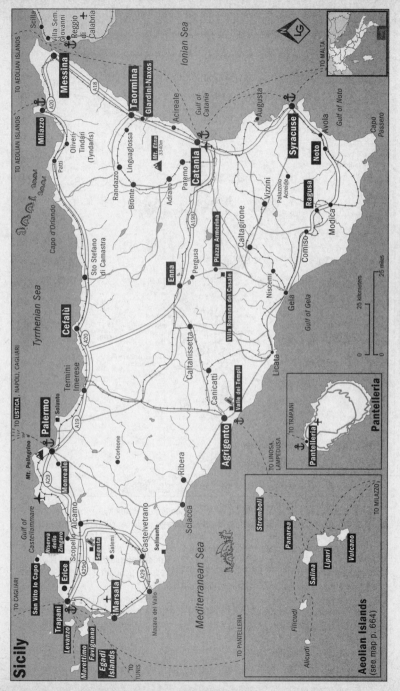

Sicily

SICILY

Tyrrhenian Sea

Ionian Sea

Mediterranean Sea

Messina
Milazzo
Taormina
Giardini-Naxos
Catania
Syracuse
Noto
Ragusa
Enna
Cefalù
Palermo
Monreale
Agrigento
Valle dei Templi
Piazza Armerina
Villa Romana del Casale
Trapani
Erice
San Vito lo Capo
Marsala
Segesta

Scilla
Villa Sem.
Giovanni
Reggio di Calabria

TO AEOLIAN ISLANDS
TO AEOLIAN ISLANDS
TO MALTA
TO USTICA, NAPOLI, CAGLIARI
TO CAGLIARI
TO TUNIS
TO PANTELLERIA
TO LIPANI
TO LIMOSA, LAMPEDUSA
TO MILAZZO

Gulf of Catania
Gulf of Noto
Capo Passero
Avola
Augusta
Acireale
Oliveri-
Tindari (Tyndaris)
Patti
Randazzo
Brónte
Linguaglossa
Mt. Etna 3340m
Adrano
Paternò
Vizzini
Palazzolo Acreide
Comiso
Modica
Cattagirone
Niscemi
Gela
Gulf of Gela
Licata
Pergusa
Canicattì
Ribera
Sciacca
Caltanissetta
Sto Stefano di Camastra
Capo d'Orlando
Termini Imerese
Solunto
Corleone
Castelvetrano
Selinunte
Salemi
Alcamo
Scopello
Riserva dello Zingaro
Gulf of Castellammare
Levanzo
Favignana
Marettimo
Egadi Islands
Mazara di Vallo
Mt. Pellegrino

A20
A18
A19
A29
A29
A19
4193

25 kilometers
25 miles
0

Pantelleria
Pantelleria

Aeolian Islands
(see map p. 664)
Stromboli
Panarea
Salina
Lipari
Vulcano
Filicudi
Alicudi

SICILY

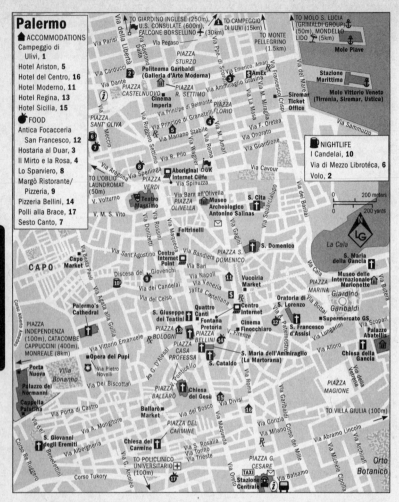

Palermo

ACCOMMODATIONS
Campeggio di
  Ulivi, **1**
Hotel Ariston, **5**
Hotel del Centro, **16**
Hotel Moderno, **11**
Hotel Regina, **13**
Hotel Sicilia, **15**

FOOD
Antica Focacceria
  San Francesco, **12**
Hostaria al Duar, **3**
Il Mirto e la Rosa, **4**
Lo Sparviero, **8**
Margò Ristorante/
  Pizzeria, **9**
Pizzeria Bellini, **14**
Polli alla Brace, **17**
Sesto Canto, **7**

NIGHTLIFE
I Candelai, **10**
Via di Mezzo Librotéca, **6**
Volo, **2**

Trains: Stazione Centrale (☎60 31 111; www.palermocentrale.it), in P. Giulio Cesare. Ticket office open daily 5:30am-9pm. **Luggage storage** available (**Practical Information,** p. 652). To: **Agrigento** (2hr., 14 per day 7:35am-8:15pm, €6.70); **Catania** (3½hr., 2 per day 8:15am and 2:45pm, €11.25); **Messina** (3½hr., 10 per day 4am-6pm, €10.55); **Milazzo** (3hr., 21 per day 4am-9:15pm, €9.20); **Falcone Borsellino Airport** (40min., every hr. 4:45am-10:10pm, €4.50); **Rome** (12hr., 6 per day 7:30am-9:50pm, €45); **Trapani** (2½hr., 11 per day 6:30am-6:40pm, €6.85).

Buses: All lines run along V. Paolo Balsamo, by the train station. Facing away from the tracks, turn right; exit with McDonald's on the left and the newsstands on the right; V. P. Balsamo is straight ahead, hidden by an army of buses. When purchasing tickets, ask exactly where the bus will be arriving and find out its logo.

> ★TIP★ **SPARE SOME CHANGE.** When purchasing train tickets at the Stazione Centrale, avoid using large bills if possible, as the machine only gives back change up to €4.50. If your change exceeds €4.50, you will receive a ticket credited to that amount can be used in the machine at a later date.

Cuffaro, V. P. Balsamo 13 (☎61 61 510; www.cuffaro.it). To **Agrigento** (2½hr.; M-Sa 7 per day 5:45am-8pm, Su 8am, noon, and 3:30pm; €7.20).

SAIS, V. P. Balsamo 16 (☎61 66 028; www.saisautolinee.it). To: **Catania** (3hr.) and **Catania Airport** (2½hr.; M-Th 14 per day, F 16 per day, Sa 13 per day 5am-8pm, Su 9 per day 8am-8pm; €12.50); **Messina** (3hr.; M-F 9 per day 5am-8pm, Sa-Su 4 per day 9am-8pm; €13.30); **Piazza Armerina** (2½hr.; M-F 8 per day 6:15am-8pm, Su 4 per day 9am-8pm; €7).

Segesta, V. P. Balsamo 14 (☎61 69 039; www.segesta.it). Buses marked "Sicilbus," "EtnaTransport," or "Interbus" to: **Alcamo** (1hr.; M-F 10 per day 6:30am-8pm, Sa 8 per day 6:30am-8pm, Su 11:30am and 8pm; €5.20, round-trip €7.90); **Rome** (12hr.; Th and Su from Politeama 6:30pm, Sa 7:45am; from Stazione Centrale 8am and 6:40pm; €45, round-trip €76.50); **Terrasini** (1hr.; M-Sa 6 per day 6:30am-8pm, Su 11:30am and 8pm; €2.60, round-trip €4.20); **Trapani** (2hr.; M-F 27 per day 6am-9pm, Sa every hr., Su 5, 9pm; €7.80).

Ferries and Hydrofoils:

Grimaldi Group, Calata Marinai d'Italia (seaport) on the waterfront (☎58 74 04; www.grimaldi.it), on V. del Mare, off V. Francesco Crispi. Ticket office open M-F 8:45am-1pm; departure M-F 2:15pm, Sa 9am-noon, Su 4:30pm. Ferries to **Civitavecchia** (12hr., €43-65) and **Genoa** (20hr., €63-100). Check ahead, as schedules are likely to change.

Siremar, V. Francesco Crispi 118 (☎58 24 03; www.siremar.it), on the last street before the waterfront, between V. Principe di Belmonte and V. Mariano Stabile. Ticket office open daily 8am-noon and 4-7pm. Reservation surcharge €1.50 per ticket. Ferries to **Ustica** (2½hr.; M-F 8:15am, Su 3:30pm; €19.90). Leaves from Stazione Marittima.

Tirrenia, V. Molo Vittorio Veneto (seaport) (☎60 21 111; www.tirrenia.it), 100m south of Grimaldi, next to the parking lot. Open M-F 8:30am-12:30pm and 3:30-8:45pm, Sa 3:30-8:45pm, Su 5-8:45pm. Ferries to **Naples** (10hr.; Oct.-May 8:15pm, June 8:45pm; €35-80) and **Cagliari** (14hr.; Oct.-July 15 Sa 7pm, July 15-Aug. Sa 5pm; €30-60).

Ustica, V. Cap. di Bartolo (☎84 49 002; www.usticalines.it), runs hydrofoils twice a day to the **Aeolian Islands.** Ticket office at end of Stazione Marittima. Open daily 9am-1pm and 5-7pm. All Hydrofoils to: **Alicudi** (2½hr.; €21.60, in winter €19.60), **Filicudi** (3hr., €27.10), **Lipari** (4hr., €33.30), **Salina** (3½hr., €32.40), **Vulcano** (4½hr.; summer daily 7am and 4:45pm, winter M, W, F 7am; €33.30).

■ ORIENTATION

Palermo's newer half follows a grid pattern, but older sections near the **train station** to the south form a tangled knot. The train station dominates **Piazza Giulio Cesare,** from which two primary streets define Palermo's central axis. **Via Roma** begins from the front of the station and runs the length of the old city, ending at V. Emerico Amari, to the right of the **Politeama.** On the left side of P. Giulio Cesare, running parallel to V. Roma, **Via Maqueda** meets **Via Vittorio Emanuele** at the **Quattro Canti,** and this intersection forms the *centro storico.* Continue up V. Maqueda to **Piazza Verdi** and **Teatro Massimo.** Turn right at P. Verdi on **Via Cavour** to go past V. Roma, out to the port. At P. Verdi, V. Maqueda becomes **Via Ruggero Settimo,** which leads to **Piazza Castelnuovo** and the Politeama. From there V. Ruggero Settimo becomes **Via della Libertà** and leads to the **Giardino Inglese.**

▣ LOCAL TRANSPORTATION

Public Transportation: Orange **AMAT city buses.** Main terminal in front of Stazione Centrale, under green awning. Tickets €1 per 2hr., €3.35 per day. Buy tickets from *tabac-*

SICILY

cherie, or ticket booths. Pick up a free **transit map** from the tourist office or AMAT info booth. Most bus stops are labeled and have route maps posted. Palermo also has the Metropolitana **subway** system, but it's usually faster to take a bus or walk.

Taxis: Station office ☎61 62 001. **Autoradio** ☎51 27 27. **RadioTaxi** ☎22 54 55, in front of Stazione Centrale, next to the bus stop.

⛷ PRACTICAL INFORMATION

TOURIST AND FINANCIAL SERVICES

Tourist Office: P. Castelnuovo 34, at the west end of the *piazza* (☎60 58 351; www.palermotourism.com). Maps, brochures, and *Agenda*, a seasonal info packet. Open M-F 10am-1pm, Tu also 3:30-6pm. **Branches** at train station (☎61 65 914) and airport (☎59 16 98). Open M-Sa 8:30am-2pm and 2:30-6pm.

Consular Services: UK, V. Cavour 117 (☎32 64 12). Open daily 9am-1pm, 4-7pm. **US,** V. Giovan Battista Vaccarini 1 (☎30 58 57). Open M-F 9am-12:30pm.

Currency Exchange: *Cambio* at the central post office. **Banca Nazionale del Lavoro,** V. Roma 201, and **Banco di Sicilia,** on V. Ruggero Settimo, both open M-F 8:20am-1:20pm. **ATMs** can be found on V. Roma and V. Maqueda; the Bancomat 3-plus ATMs are newer and more reliable.

American Express: G. Ruggieri and Figli Travel, V. Emerico Amari 38 (☎58 71 44). From P. Castelnuovo, follow V. E. Amari toward the water. Cashes **Travelers Cheques** for cardholders only. Open M-F 9am-1pm and 4-7pm, Sa 9am-1pm.

LOCAL SERVICES

Luggage Storage: In the train station, track #8. €3.80 per bag for 1st 5hr., €0.60 per each additional hr. up to 12hr., €0.20 per each additional hr. thereafter. Open daily 7am-11pm.

Laundromat: L'Oblio, V. Volturno 62 (☎333 80 32 82). 1 block west of Teatro Massimo, next to Porta Carini. Wash and dry €7. Detergent included. Open M-F 8:45am-7:30pm, Sa 8:45am-2:30pm.

EMERGENCY AND COMMUNICATIONS

Police: V. Dogali 29 (☎69 54 111).

Pharmacy: Lo Cascio, V. Roma 1 (☎61 62 117). Look for green cross near the train station. Open daily midnight-1pm and 4:30pm-midnight. **Di Naro,** V. Roma 207 (☎58 58 69), on the right, after V. V. Emanuele. Open M-F 8:30am-1pm and 4:30-8pm.

Hospital: Policlinico Universitario, V. del Vespro 147 (☎65 51 111).

Internet Access: Among a multitude of Internet points scattered around the city, the best is **Centro Internet Point,** V. V. Emanuele 304 (☎61 13 576), with 7 fast computers. €0.50 per 15min., €2 per hr.; 15min. minimum. **Aboriginal Internet C@fé,** V. Spinuzza 51 (☎66 22 229; www.aboriginalcafe.com), across P. Verdi from the Teatro Massimo. Look for the "Internet Point" sign. €1 per 15 min., €3.50 per hr. Student discount 20% before 8pm. Open daily 6pm-3am.

Post Office: V. Roma 322 (☎75 39 392). Massive white-columned building 5 blocks up V. Roma, past V. V. Emanuele. Open M-F 8am-1:30pm, Sa 8am-12:30pm. Branch at Stazione Centrale (☎80 31 60), next to track 1. Open M-F 8am-6:30pm, Sa 8am-12:30pm. **Postal Code:** 90100.

⚑ ACCOMMODATIONS

When it comes to finding a place to stay, Palermo is pricey. For the sake of comfort and, more importantly, safety, plan on spending a little more in Palermo and budget your trip accordingly.

⚑ Hotel Regina, V. V. Emanuele 316 (☎61 14 216; www.hotelreginapalermo.it), at the intersection of V. Maqueda and V. V. Emanuele, across from the larger Hotel Centrale. No-frills rooms at a reasonable price; some have balconies. Beach passes available. Curfew midnight. Credit card required for reservation. Singles €25; doubles €44, with bath €54; triples €66/75. AmEx/MC/V. ❷

⚑ Hotel Ariston, V. Mariano Stabile 139, 6th fl. (☎33 24 34; www.aristonpalermo.it). Take V. Roma 4 blocks past V. Cavour, or bus #122 from the station, and get off before V. E. Amari. Between Teatro Massimo and the Politeama. 7 bright rooms in minimalist modern style have bath, A/C, TV, and free Wi-Fi. Book in advance. 1st night paid with reservation. Singles €30-49; doubles €55-69. AmEx/MC/V. ❸

Hotel Sicilia, V. Divisi 99, 3rd. fl. (☎61 68 460). From P. Giulio Cesare, 5 blocks up V. Maqueda, on the right. Marble staircases lead to pastel-colored rooms, all equipped with bathroom, A/C, TV, balcony, and high arched ceilings. Breakfast included. Internet €2 per hr. Curfew 2am. Apr.-Oct. singles €45; doubles €72; triples €84. Nov.-Mar. €39/62/70. AmEx/MC/V. ❹

Hotel del Centro, V. Roma 72, 2nd fl. (☎61 70 376; www.hoteldelcentro.it). From the train station, 5 blocks up V. Roma. Rooms in this 3-star *albergo* feature towering ceilings and classy curtains. Bath, A/C, and Internet access. Breakfast included. Singles €52-100; doubles €72-120. Extra bed 35% more per person. MC/V. ❹

Hotel Moderno, V. Roma 276 (☎58 86 83 or 58 82 60; www.hotelmodernopa.com), at V. Napoli. Quiet rooms. Bath, A/C, and TV. Bar and communal TV room. Breakfast included. Singles €55; doubles €75; triples €95; quads €105. AmEx/MC/V. ❹

Campeggio di Ulivi, V. Pegaso 25 (☎/fax 53 30 21), 35min. outside Palermo. Take bus #101 from Palermo's central station to P. de Gasperi; then take bus #628 to V. Sferracavallo. Walk downhill and turn right on V. dei Manderini, just after the post office. Campground is on the right. Hot showers free. Tent rental €5 per day. €7 per person, €7.50 per motorist. 2-person bungalows €30; 4-person €45. Cash only. ❶

◨ FOOD

The best restaurants in town are between Teatro Massimo and the Politeama. Palermo's three bustling markets provide fresher and more interesting selections than most supermarkets. **Ballarò** dots V. Maqueda and V. V. Emanuele, while **Capo** covers the streets behind Teatro Massimo. **Vucciria,** in the area between V. V. Emanuele and P. San Domenico, complete the trio. All are open Monday through Saturday during daylight hours. Try *Palermitano* specialty *cassata*, a sweet ricotta pastry. If you don't feel like haggling, head to **Supermercato GS,** Salita Partanna 1. In P. Marina, with Villa Garibaldi on your left, walk straight toward Chiesa di. S. Maria dei Miracoli; turn right when you get there. (Open M-Sa 8:30am-8pm.)

⚑ Margò Ristorante/Pizzeria, P. Sant'Onofrio 3 (☎61 18 230). Follow Discesa dei Giovenchi, away from the intersection of V. Maqueda and V. Bari. Taste the best pizza in town (€4-8) or specialty *ravioli di cernia, spada, e crema di asparagi* (with grouper, swordfish, and cream of asparagus; €8.50). *Primi* €5.50-8.50, *secondi* €8-15. Cover €2. Open Tu-Su 8pm-midnight. AmEx/MC/V. ❸

Polli alla Brace, C. Tukory 54 (☎65 17 023). Follow C. Tukory from the train station and Polli will be on the left. Polli is the best bet in the area near the train station. For €5 they offer half of a rotisserie chicken and a heaping selection of Italian sides, more than enough for 2 people. Open daily 10am-10:30pm. Cash only. ❶

Il Mirto e la Rosa, V. Principe di Granatelli 30 (☎32 43 53; info@ilmirtoelarosa.com). Helpful owner serves traditional fare, including house specialty, *polpette di melanzane* (fried eggplant balls; €5). *Primi* €7-10, vegetarian *secondi* €6-7, fish and meat *secondi* €10-15. *Menù* €13-21. Open M-Sa 12:30-3pm and 7:30-11pm. AmEx/MC/V. ❷

Sesto Canto, V. Sant'Oliva 26 (☎33 68 36), from P. Sant'Oliva, walk away from P. Castelnuovo. Taking their restaurant's name from Dante's *Divina Commedia*, the Serafino sisters serve some hellishly-good cuisine. Sample sliced salmon and potatoes (€12) or steak filet topped with warm *caprese* cheese (€16). *Antipasti* €8-10. *Primi* €10-12, *secondi* €12-16. Cover €1.50. Open M-Sa 10am-2:30pm and 6:30-11pm. Closed Th in winter. AmEx/MC/V. ❹

Pizzeria Bellini, P. Bellini 6 (☎61 65 691), to the left of P. Pretoria. Outdoor seating among the ancient ruins of Palermo makes this restaurant an ideal spot for a romantic meal. Try their superb *granita* (€3). Pizza €4-8.50. *Primi* €5-15, *secondi* €7-15. Cover €2. Open Tu-Su noon-6pm and 7pm-midnight. AmEx/MC/V. ❸

Antica Focacceria San Francesco, V. Alessandro Paternostro 58 (☎32 02 64). From V. Roma, take V. V. Emanuele toward the port and turn right. This expansive *focacceria* has served delighted patrons in a secluded *piazza* since 1834. Behind the counter sits an infamous vat of *milza* (spleen). While the brave can try it in a *panino* or with *maritata* cheese (€2), the rest can choose from 2 separate menus: 1 features standard Italian fare, the other international cuisine. 19 salads from €4. *Primi* €5-10, *secondi* €6-25. Cover €1-4.Open M-W and F-Su 1-3pm and 8-11pm. AmEx/MC/V. ❷

Lo Sparviero, V. Sperlinga 23/25 (☎33 11 63), from Teatro Massimo, 1 block toward P. Verdi. Shrouded in antique decor, this local secret serves classic Sicilian cuisine. Varied salad options €4.50. Pizza from €4. *Primi* €7-8, *secondi* €7-16. Cover €1. Open daily 12:30-3pm and 7:30pm-midnight. AmEx. ❸

Hostaria al Duar, V. Ammiraglio Gravina 31 (☎0349 60 57 359). From V. Roma, walk 3 blocks toward the port. Mix of Sicilian and Arabic flavors served on bright picnic tables. *Primi* €5-8, *secondi* €6-20. Tunisian *piatti* €3-6.50. Cover €1. Service 15%. Open daily 10am-3:30pm and 7pm-midnight. Cash only. ❷

> **! SICILIAN STREET SMARTS.** Be careful in Palermo. The city can feel deserted at any time of the day, and some of the streets, particularly in the helter-skelter old city, south of Teatro Massimo, can be hard to navigate. When possible, stay on main streets: **Via Roma, Via Maqueda, Via Ruggero Settimo, Via della Libertà,** and **Via Vittorio Emanuele.** These straight thoroughfares will keep you on track, and the steady stream of traffic is reassuring.

◉ SIGHTS

Ancient glory, centuries of neglect, and heavy bombing during WWII have made Palermo a city of both splendor and deterioration, where ancient and modern ruins stand side-by-side. For much of the 20th century, corrupt politicians and Mafia activity diverted funds and attention from dilapidated landmarks, but recent political changes have made promising strides toward cleaning and rebuilding.

▓ TEATRO MASSIMO. Constructed between 1875 and 1897, the Neoclassical Teatro Massimo is the second-largest indoor stage in Europe. The stage is so big

> **PALERMO FOR POCKET CHANGE.** Sightseeing in Palermo can leave you with a bill that makes the Byzantine mosaics look cheap. If you're planning to visit several sights, consider an all-in-one pass from the ticket office of any major museum. These passes, which are good for 2 days, open the doors to multiple sights at reduced prices. For details on rates and specific deals, go to the tourist office and ask for the free guide, *Palermo e Provincia*.

that real horses and elephants were used in a production of *Aida*. After 30 years of renovation, the theater reopened for its 100th birthday in 1997. Rumor has it that the restoration was prolonged by Mafia feuding, not by artistic debates. (Incidentally, it was here that Francis Ford Coppola shot the climactic scene in *The Godfather: Part III*.) Guided tours allow visitors to repose in the VIP guest box and view the beautiful Morano flower light fixtures. Operas, plays, and ballets are performed here all year (student discounts available), while the **Festival della Verdura** brings famous performers in July. For this month only, shows move from the Massimo to nearby Villa Castelnuovo. *(On P. Verdi. From Quattro Canti walk up V. Maqueda. ☎ General info 800 65 58 58, tour info 60 90 831, box office 60 53 580; www.teatro-massimo.it. Open Tu-Su 10am-3pm. No entry during rehearsals. 20min. tours every 30min. in English, French, and German. €3, under 18 or over 65 €2, under 6 free.)*

▧ **MONREALE.** Palermo's greatest treasure isn't in Palermo, but in little Monreale, 8km from the city. The extraordinary Cattedrale di Monreale is an example of Sicilian Norman architecture, a mixture of Arabic and local styles on the northern template. The interior is a masterpiece of Byzantine design; the mystical flavor of the locale is emphasized by the minimal light from the cathedral's windows. Its walls glisten with 6340 sq. m of gold mosaics, the largest display of Byzantine religious art outside the Hagia Sofia. The series of panels over the main altar depicts the massive Christ Pantocrator. Every few minutes someone pays €1 to activate electric lighting in a portion of the church, and the sudden illumination is startling.

> **AVOID A WALLET CALAMITY.** The courtyard adjoining the Cattedrale di Monreale charges a steep €6 entry fee. Unless you're an architecture aficionado or especially interested in Doric, Corinthian, and Ionic columns, consider viewing the garden from the terrace of the Cathedral (€2).

The Old Testament narrative begins with Genesis at the upper left of the central aisle and continues clockwise with images of Adam and Eve. The quiet **cloister** offers a contrast to the cathedral's solemn shadows. The interior columns are ringed with 228 paired Sicilian columns, alternating with ones decorated by Arabic tiles. Each capital is constructed in Greco-Roman, Islamic, Norman, Romanesque, and Gothic styles. A balcony along the cathedral's apse looks over the cloisters to all of Palermo. Two doors down from the cloister is the entrance to tranquil **gardens**. *(Bus #389 leaves from Palermo's P. Indipendenza for Monreale's P. Vittorio Emanuele. 30min., 3 per hr., €1. To get to P. Indipendenza, take bus #109 or 318 from Palermo's Stazione Centrale. Tourist info (☎ 64 04 413) to the left of the church. Cathedral open M-Sa 8am-6:30pm, Su 8am-1pm and 3:30-7pm. Closed Nov.-Apr. 12:30-2:30pm. Modest dress required. Free. Balcony open daily 9am-5:30pm. €1.50. Cloister open daily 9am-6:30pm. €6.)*

CAPPELLA PALATINA. This chapel, in the monstrous **Palazzo dei Normanni,** houses a smaller version of the Monreale mosaics. While one corner to the far left of the altar was designed by local artisans, Norman kings imported artists from Constantinople to cover every inch of the remaining interior with gold and azure. Locally crafted Arabic mosaics complete the effect. Those who prefer this Christ Panto-crator over that of Monreale claim it is softer and more compassionate. *(Take V. V. Emanuele past the cathedral on the right and through the Porta Nuova; take a left just before you get to P. Indipendenza.* ☎ *70 56 001. Chapel open M-Sa 8:30am-5pm, Su 8:30am-12:30pm. Closed Easter M. Tu-Th entire palace €6, chapel €4; Under 18 or over 65 €3; M and F-Su special chapel-only rate not available. Tours of upstairs Sala di Ruggero every 20min. in Italian.)*

MUSEO ARCHEOLOGICO ANTONINO SALINAS. Housed in a quiet *palazzo* in the town center, this museum features an impressive collection of Sicilian archaeological treasures. Most impressive are several fine Greek and Roman works, including a large section of the **Punic Temple of Himera,** and the 3rd-cen-tury-BC Greek **Ram of Syracuse.** Also not to be missed is the recently restored **Mosaico delle Quattro Stagioni,** which depicts the four seasons in a haunting mosaic. Other temple remnants include fantastic renditions of Perseus beheading Medusa and Zeus courting Hera. *(P. Olivella 24. From Teatro Massimo, cross V. Maqueda and head down V. Bara all'Olivella.* ☎ *61 16 805. Open M, W, Sa 8:30am-1:45pm, Tu and F 8:30am-1:45pm and 3-6:45pm. €6, EU residents under 18 or over 65 free.)*

CATACOMBE CAPPUCCINI. Over the course of 350 years, the Cappuchin friars preserved remains of over 8000 men, women, and children. Hanging from niches by wires and nails and lying in glass-sided caskets, many are dressed in their finest and are in various stages of decay. Various notables are buried here, including sev-eral bishops and the painter Velázquez, but the most arresting remains are those of Rosalia, a three-year-old girl who lies in her own tiny glass box. *(P. Cappuccini 1. Take bus #109 from Stazione Centrale to P. Indipendenza. From there, hop on #327. Or, from V. V. Emanuele, pass P. Indipendenza, and turn right on V. Cappuccini, then right again on V. Ippolito Pindemonte.* ☎ *21 21 17. From P. Indipendenza, about a 20min. walk. Open daily in summer 9am-noon and 3-5:30pm; in winter 9am-noon and 3-5pm. €1.50.)*

PALERMO'S CATHEDRAL. As a part of their ongoing rivalry, the leaders of Pal-ermo and Monreale competed to construct the most beautiful church. Although many consider Monreale's mosaics to be superior, Palermo's cathedral is still awe-inspiring. Renovated from the 13th to the 18th centuries, this structure's exterior shows various styles of butting heads. Arabic columns, Norman turrets, and an 18th-century dome crowd the facade and walls. Note the inscription from the Qur'an on the first left column before the entrance; in 1185 the *palermitano* arch-bishop chose to plunk his cathedral down on top of a mosque, and this column was part of its stonework. The interior is dominated by saint-lined arches and carved rock walls. The neighboring **archbishop's palace** now serves as the Diocesan Museum of Palermo, and can be visited on the same ticket. *(On V. V. Emanuele.* ☎ *33 43 73. Cathedral open daily 9:30am-5:30pm. Closed Su during Mass. Treasury and crypt open M-Sa 9:30am-1:30pm and 2:30-5:30pm. Archbishop's museum open Tu-F 9:30am-1:30pm, Sa 10am-6pm, Su 9:30am-1:30pm. Admission €4.50, €2.50 for treasury and crypt only.)*

QUATTRO CANTI AND LA FONTANA PRETORIA. The intersection of V. Maqueda and V. V. Emanuele forms the center of the old city at the Quattro Canti (Four Screens). Dividing the old city into four districts, each sculpted corner of this 17th-century *piazza* has three levels. The lowest level has statues of the four seasons, on the middle level are the Spanish viceroys who commanded Sicily and Southern Italy, and on the top level are the city's patron saints. Covered in smog for decades, the sculptural works have recently benefitted from Palermo's city-wide restoration. P. Pretoria, down V. Maqueda, houses the Fontana della Vergogna (Fountain of Shame; also called Fontana Pretoria) adjacent to Teatro Bellini. The fountain got its name from irate churchgoers who didn't like staring at monsters and nude figures as they left Chiesa di San Giuseppe dei Teatini across the street. An even more shameful story explains its shameless size. In the early 16th century, a rich Florentine commissioned the fountain for his villa and sent his son to the marble quarries to ensure its safe delivery. In need of cash, the son sold the fountain to the senate of Palermo and shipped it to Sicily, bringing Albert Mobilio's words to mind: "Sicily is a world where deception is only frowned upon to the degree it lacks artfulness." *(630m down V. Maqueda from the train station.)*

PALAZZO ABATELLIS. Signs in P. Marina point toward this late 15th-century *palazzo*, which houses one of Sicily's best art museums, the **Galleria Regionale Siciliana.** Dozens of religious panel paintings and sculptures from the Middle Ages through the Baroque period culminate with Antonello da Messina's unusual *Annunciation.* The massive and morbid fresco *The Triumph of Death* claims a room of its own on the lower level. *(V. Alloro 4. From P. G. Cesare in front of train station, take V. Abramo Lincoln, turn left on V. Garibaldi and right on V. Alloro. ☎62 30 011. Open daily 9am-1pm, Tu-F also open 2:30-7pm. Ticket counter closes 30min. before museum. €6, EU students 18-25 and residents under 18 or over 65 free.)*

CHIESA DEL GESÙ (CASA PROFESSA). Nicknamed "Il Gesù," this green-domed church has a dazzling marble interior and Surrealist ceiling paintings of the Last Judgment, depicting figures with swords beating the unworthy into Hell and a black-clad man waving a pastel flag with "Jesus" written across it. WWII bombing damaged its courtyard and the Quartiere dell'Albergheria, filled with scarred buildings and bomb-blackened facades. *(In P. Casa Professa, on V. Ponticello, across V. Maqueda. Open daily 7-11:30am. No visits during mass.)*

PUPPETS. There are no small parts, only small wooden actors. For 300 years, Sicilian-made puppets have taken the stage at the **Museo Internazionale delle Marionette,** which showcases Sicilian stage culture. Galleries also display puppets from across the globe; it's a small world, after all. *(P. Niscemi 5. Follow signs from P. Marina. ☎32 80 60; fax 32 82 76. Open M-F 9am-1pm and 2:30-6:30pm. Closed 1 week around Aug. 15 for celebration of Ferragosto. €5, under 18 and over 65 €3. Demonstrations on request.)* Catch a puppet show at Vincenzo Argenti's **Opera dei Pupi.** Tall, armored puppets reenact the chivalric *Orlando e Ronaldo per la Bella Angelica. (V. Pietro Novelli 1. ☎32 91 94. Shows Sa-Su only, 5:30pm. €10, children €3.)*

GARDENS. The city's fresh gardens and parks provide relief from Palermo's smog-filled urban jungle. The large **Giardino Inglese,** off V. della Libertà, is not a stiffly organized British garden as its name might suggest, but a paradise harboring picnickers under its palms. In summer, the park hosts concerts and carnival rides for children. Down V. V. Emanuele toward the port, the **Giardino Garibaldi** in P. Marina features enormous banyan trees. The large Parisian-style **Villa Giulia,** at the end of V. A. Lincoln, has sand pathways, flower beds, and fountains. *(Open daily 8am-8pm.)*

MONTE PELLEGRINO. Monte Pellegrino, an isolated mass of limestone rising from the sea, is Palermo's principal natural landmark, separating the city from the beach at Mondello. Near its peak, the **Santuario di Santa Rosalia** marks the site where young Rosalia sought escape from her marriage and wandered into ascetic seclusion. After dying there, she appeared as an apparition to a woodsman and told him to carry her bones through the city in a procession. The procession is believed to have ended the plague that had been destroying Palermo. The bones of Rosalia, who is now the patron saint of the city, can be found in Palermo's cathedral or on parade display every year on July 15. *(☎54 03 26. Open daily 7am-7:30pm. Take bus #812 from P. Castelnuovo. Buses every 1½hr. 7am-8pm. Last bus back 7:30pm.)*

◈ NIGHTLIFE

Palermo's nightlife is as varied as the city's history. For info on cultural events, pick up *Un Mese a Palermo*, a monthly brochure available at any APT office, or in *News-News*. **Piazza Olivella**, in front of the Archaeological Museum, **Via dei Candelai**, off V. Maqueda to the left two streets past the Quattro Canti toward Teatro Massimo, and **Via Spinuzza**, across from Teatro Massimo and one street up from V. Bara all'Olivella, are popular nightlife hubs where mobs of young *palermitani* flood the outdoor bars and dance floors every night.

I Candelai, V. dei Candelai 65 (☎333 70 02 942; www.candelai.it). Picks up around midnight with one of central Palermo's few dance floors. Sip Carlsberg *alla spina* while listening to local cover bands do their best Chuck Berry impression, or to DJs spin Top 40 hits Th-Sa nights. Open daily noon-3:30pm and 6:30pm-2am. Closed M in winter.

Via di Mezzo Librotéca, V. Sant'Oliva 20/22 (☎60 90 090; viadmezzo@virgilio.it), from P. Sant'Oliva, walk toward Villa Fillipina, and Librotéca will be around the corner. The name stands for book+tea+coffee, and describes the vibe at this bistro. The conversation is as vibrant as the music is low-key. Coffee and tea €1.40-2.50. Beer €3.50-4. Wine €3. Mixed drinks €3.50-5. Service €1. Open daily in summer 9pm-1am; in winter 5pm-1am. AmEx/MC/V.

Volo, V. della Libertà 12 (☎61 21 284; www.volofood.it). 2 blocks up from P. Castelnuovo, after V. Giosuè Carducci on the left. Dress to impress at Volo, where the Euro-sleek interior and elegant garden exterior are equally perfect settings for young singles to flit about. Mixed drinks €5. Happy hour with free hors d'oeuvres 6-9pm. Open June-Oct. daily noon-3:30pm and 6:30pm-2am. Closed M Nov.-May. AmEx/MC/V.

◈ BEACHES

Mondello Lido is a beach for tourists by day and a playground of clubs and bars by night. All registered hotels provide tickets that must be shown at the entrance. Otherwise, beachgoers pay €8 to set up camp in the area near the Charleston—or sit for free directly on the shoreline. Take bus #101 or 102 from the station to reach the Politeama and V. della Libertà, and then bus #806 in the same direction to reach Mondello; the beach is beyond a tree-filled area known as *la Favorita*. Watch for the frequent vendors who wander around the sand with all types of goodies. *Ciambelle* (donuts caked in sugar; €1) are an essential beach treat.

◈ DAYTRIP FROM PALERMO

USTICA

Accessible by ferry or hydrofoil from Palermo. L'Agenzia Miletello, V. Capitano Vincenzo di Bartolo 15, right next to the church, is open daily 9am-1pm and 2:30-7pm (☎84 49 002; fax 84 49 457). It runs hydrofoils (1¼hr.; Sept.-May M-Th and Sa 8:15am and 3pm, F and Su 8:15am; July-Aug. daily 8:15am; Sept.-June 1 and 5:15pm; €20.30) and ferries (2½hr.; daily 5pm; Sept.-July €12.60, Aug. €13.60) to Palermo. For public transportation, orange minibuses run the entire perimeter of the island, a 30min. round-trip, from P. Vito Longo (every 30min., €0.80). Shops in P. Umberto I, the centro of Ustica, rent scooters for approx. €20 per day; helmet and gas included. To get to town from the hydrofoil port, turn right, and head up the road until you reach the staircase with an arrow marked "Centro" and follow that to P. Umberto I. With your back to the stairs, P. Capitano Vito Longo will be up and to the right. To reach the town from Cala Cimitero, the ferry port, take the road uphill, and turn left at the fork.

The self-proclaimed "diving capital of the world," Ustica (OOS-tee-ca; pop. 1300) has become a bustling tourist port with abundant outdoor and underwater activities to satisfy adventurous visitors. Hiking trails wind around the island's 9km scenic coastline and guided tours explore a prehistoric village and necropolis. Perhaps the island's most spectacular attractions are the ancient artifacts buried just below the water's surface, catalogued and labeled for divers to explore.

■**Boat tours** are a great way to explore the grottoes along the coastline, including the neon blue waters of **Grotta delle Barche** and **Grotta Azzurra,** a nautical graveyard filled with ancient vessels. Small boat owners advertise cheap rides that circle the island; find them at P. Umberto I or at the port. Set a price before embarking; women traveling alone should join a larger group. The island's most popular activity, **scuba diving** off rocky coasts, is quite affordable. **Alta Marea,** on V. Cristoforo Colombo, runs dives from May to October. (☎347 17 57 255; www.altamareaustica.it. Boats leave port daily 9:15am and 3:15pm. Single immersion €35, with full equipment €55; 6 dives €200; 10 dives €300. Diving class €330.) Once submerged, see the ■**underwater archaeological remains** of Roman lead anchors and *amphorae* (vases), part of Ustica's underwater archaeology experiment.

Satisfy the rumbling in your tummy at **Ristorante Al Clelia** ❸, V. Sindaco 1 at Hotel Clelia, provides views of the sea, the perfect setting to enjoy *gamberetto con fiori di zucca* (shrimp tucked into pumpkin flowers; €12), one of Chef Marino's masterpieces. (*Antipasti* €4-8. *Primi* €7-8, *secondi* €10. Open daily 1-2pm and 8-10:30pm. Evenings only in Aug.) The tiny **Market Caminita,** P. Umberto I 3, sells essentials. (☎84 49 474. Open M-Sa 8am-1pm and 4-8:30pm, Su 8am-1pm.) Relax at **Carpe Diem,** Largo Padiglione 1, which serves beer (€3.50), wine (€2.50), and mixed drinks. Visit their daily happy hour from 4:30-8:30pm, with beer for €2.50 at the bar. (Open Tu-Su 11am-3am.)

> :TIP: **RENAISSANCE MAN.** To get around Ustica, you need to know only one man: **Gigi Tranchina.** A lifelong resident of Ustica, Gigi is a one-man tourism bureau who knows everything about the island and will gladly coordinate hikes, scooter rentals, and diving trips. Head to **Trattoria da Umberto** to find Gigi himself, or check out his websites: www.usticatour.it and www.isoladiustica.it.

CEFALÙ ☎0921

The Sicilian proverb "good wine comes in small bottles" captures the timeless nature of Cefalù (che-fa-LOO; pop. 14,000), whose sleepy, seaside qualities were featured in the Academy Award-winning film *Cinema Paradiso.* Dominated by *La Rocca,* the imposing fortification rising 278m above the old town, Cefalù is a labyrinth of cobblestone streets. The city's aging terra-cotta and stone buildings cling to the water's edge, just as tourist crowds congregate along the expansive *lungomare* (seafront). Be aware, however, that Cefalù's charms do not come cheaply: the city's reputation as a beach resort and its proximity to Palermo allow *pensioni* to charge whatever they please.

▐ TRANSPORTATION

Cefalù is best accessed by train. Visitors can call the tourist office for a complete schedule. The **train station,** located in P. Stazione, offers service to: Messina (3hr., 14 per day 4:30am-10pm, €7.90); Milazzo (2½ hr., 21 per day, €6.45); and Palermo (1hr., 37 per day 5am-10:30pm, €4). **Sommatinese,** V. Cavour 2 (☎42

43 01), runs **buses** throughout the city (from €1.70). Schedules are posted at the train station bar's window and are also available in the tourist office. **Taxis** are available in P. Stazione or by calling ☎42 25 54.

⚡🛈 ORIENTATION AND PRACTICAL INFORMATION

From the **train station,** head right on **Via Aldo Moro,** which curves up to the city's biggest intersection. To the left, **Via Roma** cuts through the center of the new city. Straight and to the left, **Via Matteotti** leads into the old city, changing at the central **Piazza Garibaldi** into the boutique-lined **Corso Ruggero. Via Cavour,** across the intersection from V. A. Moro, leads directly to the *lungomare.*

Tourist Office: C. Ruggero 77 (☎42 10 50; fax 42 23 86), in the old city. English-speaking staff has brochures, maps, hotel listings, and schedules. English speakers should ask for Solaro Salvatore. Open June-Sept. M-Sa 8am-7:30pm, Su 9am-1pm; Oct.-May M-F 8am-7pm, Sa 9am-1pm.

Currency Exchange: Credito Siciliano (☎42 39 22), near train station, at the corner of V. Giglio and V. Roma. Open M-F 8:30am-1:30pm and 2:30-4pm. 24hr. **ATM** at the **Banca di Sicilia** (☎42 11 03 or 42 28 90), in P. Garibaldi.

Police: ☎92 60 11.

Guardia Medica: Vle. Mazzini 8 (☎42 36 23). Open nightly 8pm-8am.

Pharmacies: Dr. V. Battaglia, V. Roma 13 (☎42 17 89), in the new city. Open M-F 9am-1pm and 4:30-8:30pm. AmEx/MC/V. **Dr. Vacanti,** V. Vazzana 6 (☎42 25 66), across the street from the post office. Open M-F 9am-1pm and 4-8pm. AmEx/MC/V. Pharmacies alternate staying open Sa-Su.

Hospital: (☎92 01 11), on Contrada Pietra Pollastra, outside city limits.

Internet Access: La Galleria and **L'Arca di Noé** (see **Food**). **Capriccio Siciliano,** V. Umberto I 1 (☎42 05 50; capriccios@libero.it). €3 for 30min. Open daily 8:30am-1pm and 2:30-9pm. **Kefaonline,** P. San Francesco 1 (☎92 30 91), where V. Umberto I meets V. Mazzini. €5 per hr. Open M-F 9am-1pm and 3:30-7:30pm, Sa 9am-1pm.

Post Office: V. Vazzana 2 (☎92 55 40). In a modern concrete building on the right off the *lungomare,* 2 blocks off V. Roma. Open M-F 8am-6:30pm, Sa 8am-12:30pm. **Postal Code:** 90015.

🏠 ACCOMMODATIONS AND CAMPING

If you're planning on staying in one place for a week or more, consider renting an apartment from a local. Sealing the deal might take some haggling (and will often require a basic knowledge of Italian), but it usually pays off in the long run—especially when hotel rates peak during July and August. Look for "affittasi" signs in the desired area of residence.

Locanda Cangelosi, V. Umberto I 26 (☎42 15 91), off P. Garibaldi. This centrally located *affittacamere* is the best deal in the city. The private apartments are large, clean, and simply adorned. Some come with a balcony and other amenities. Laundry €5 per load. Reservations recommended. Apr.-Sept. singles €30; doubles €40; triples €60. Oct.-Mar. singles €25; doubles €35; triples €50. Cash only. ❸

Hotel Mediterraneo, V. Antonio Gramsci 2 (☎/fax 92 25 73; www.htlmediterraneo.it). Less than 1 block to the left of the train station, Mediterraneo has become pricier in recent years. 16 well-furnished rooms boast cloud-like beds, A/C, TV, hair dryer, minibar, and safe. Little English spoken. Full breakfast buffet included. Singles €65-90; doubles €80-140; triples €110-145; quads €130-165. MC/V. ❺

Camping Costa Ponente (☎42 00 85; fax 42 44 92), west of Cefalù, on Contrada Ogli-astrillo. A 45min. walk or short ride on the Cefalù-Lascari bus (round-trip €2.20) from P. Colombo. Swimming pool and hot showers included. July-Aug. €7 per person, €5.90 per tent, €4.50 per car. Sept.-June €5.90/4.90/3.80. ●

🔲 FOOD

Seafood is undoubtedly Cefalù's specialty, but delicious, formerly land-dwelling cuisine is also easily found. Just off the *lungomare*, next to the post office on V. Vazzana, an **IperSidis** supermarket sells basics, including bathing suits. (☎42 45 00. Open M-Sa 8:30am-1:30pm and 4:30-8:30pm, Su 9am-1pm.)

🔳 **Gelateria di Noto,** V. Bagno Cicerone 3 (☎42 26 54; www.gelateriadinoto.it), where the *lungomare* meets the old town. More than 40 flavors of some of Sicily's best *gelato*, with a terrace overlooking the beach. So good you'll probably come back for seconds. Some English spoken. Open Apr.-Sept. daily 9am-4am. Closed Oct.-Mar. Cash only. ●

Ristorante-Pizzeria Trappitu, V. di Bordonaro 96 (☎92 19 72; www.paginegialletrap-pitu.it). Offers filling food, including Sicilian sea bass (€13). An enormous olive press in the middle of the restaurant and seaside seating make for the best atmosphere in town. Some English spoken. Pizza €4-10. *Primi* €7-19, *secondi* €7-17. Open daily noon-3pm and 7pm-midnight; July-Aug. also open Th. Cover €1.50. AmEx/MC/V. ❷

Al Vicoletto, P. Duomo (☎42 01 81). Found in alley next to Il Caffè Duomo, Vicoletto offers a welcome respite from the crowds swarming in P. Duomo. Family style dining, animated staff, and large portions. No English spoken. Pizza €5-10. *Primi* €5-9, *secondi* €5-9. Service 10%. Open daily 10am-1:30pm and 6pm-11pm. AmEx/MC/V. ❷

La Vecchia Marina, V. V. Emanuele 73/75 (☎42 03 88). Seafood is the specialty at this popular and affordable restaurant, full of model ships and paintings of fishermen. Reserve ahead to get a table on the terrace overlooking the harbor. English spoken. *Primi* €8.50-12, *secondi* €10-18. Cover €1.60. Open daily noon-3pm and 7-11pm. In winter open M and W-Sa. Cash only. ❸

Ristorante-Osteria La Botte, V. Veterani 20 (☎42 43 15), off C. Ruggero. 2 blocks past P. Duomo. La Botte has a dim romantic atmosphere, perfect for the medieval old city. Best catch in town for those willing to forgo a seaside view. Outdoor seating available. English spoken. *Primi* €7-12, *secondi* €5.50-16. Cover €1.50. Open Tu-Su July-Aug. 7pm-midnight; Sept.-June 12:30-3pm and 7:30-11:30pm. AmEx/MC/V. ❷

La Galleria, V. XXV Novembre 1856 22/24 (☎14 20 211; www.caffeletterariolagalle-ria.it) Located in the heart of the old city, La Galleria opened in 2007. This "literary cafe" offers spacious courtyard dining, a full bar, an eclectic bookshop, local artwork on display and Internet access (€1 per 10min.). *Primi* €7-20, *secondi* €9-20. Service €1-3. Open M-Tu and Th-Su 11am-2am. Closed Nov. AmEx/MC/V. ❸

L'Arca di Noé, V. Vazzana 7/8 (☎92 33 51), across from the post office. Patrons crowd wooden booths docked among nautical maps, anchors, and ropes. A ship-shaped bar and *gelateria* serve those on the run, while outdoor seating and an extensive menu attracts those with some time to spare before heading out to sea. Pizza from €1.50. Internet access €2 per 30min. Open 24hr. AmEx/MC/V. ●

> **CAFFÈ, SICILIAN STYLE.** In an attempt to combat the sweltering summer heat, Sicilians have devised a cool alternative to traditional Italian coffee. Called *"caffè freddo"* and available in most cafes, this popular concoction is a mixture of espresso, raw sugar, and ice. Opt to drink it plain or with *panna* (whipped cream).

SICILY

◎ SIGHTS

La Rocca stands above Cefalù at the center of the city's history and offers breathtaking views. Take Salità Saraceni to Tempio di Diana, a 20min. uphill hike. From Diana, continue up for another, steeper, 20min. hike to Il Castello. From P. Garibaldi, follow the signs for *Pedonale Rocca* up V. G. Fiore to Vco. Macell between the fountain and Banco di Sicilia. Use caution, as the path is slippery when wet. Medieval fortifications lace the edges, while crumbling cisterns line forgotten avenues. The **Tempio di Diana** first acted as a place of sea worship and later as a defensive outpost. At the top of La Rocca is **Il Castello,** a military fort dating back to the Byzantines. Most remains date from the 12th and 13th centuries AD. (Gates closed 1hr. before sunset.)

Tucked away in Cefalù's narrow streets is the city's **duomo.** It was constructed in 1131 after King Ruggero II promised to build a monument to the Savior if he lived through a terrible shipwreck. The dramatic structure combines Arabic, Norman, and Byzantine styles, reflecting the cultures of the craftsmen hired for its construction. Once a potential fortress with towers and firing outposts, it now protects the king's remains and stunning Byzantine mosaics. An enormous **Christ Pantocrator** mosaic surveys with glistening calm all who enter. (Open daily in summer 8am-7pm; in winter 8am-5:30pm. Modest dress required.) Stuffed alligator cases and ancient urns get equal footing in the **Museo Mandralisca,** V. Mandralisca 13. Local 19th-century art connoisseur Baron Mandralisca bequeathed his collection to the city; this included an array of medieval and early Renaissance Sicilian paintings by anonymous artists, including the centerpiece, the **Ritratto di Ignoto,** by 15th-century Sicilian master Antonello da Messina. The image is inescapable in Cefalù—it smirks at tourists from every postcard rack—but the actual painting is surprisingly lively. Unfortunately, for every good painting there are hundreds of seashells and old books, as well as a half dozen lamps of questionable taste. (Opposite the *duomo.* ☎42 15 47. Open daily 9am-7pm. €5, €3 per person in groups of 10 or more.)

◎ ◉ BEACHES AND NIGHTLIFE

Mazzaforno and **Settefrati,** Cefalù's most attractive beaches, lie west of town. Take the Cefalù-Lascari bus (round-trip €2.75) from the train station or the Cefalù-Mazzaforno bus (round-trip €2.20) from P. Colombo. The popular beach off the *lungomare* boasting white sand, turquoise shallows, and free showers is crowded for good reason. The seven stones jutting out from the waves are said to have been placed in memory of seven brothers who died here while trying to rescue their sister from pirates. All beaches are free, though renting an umbrella and lounge chair costs €5. While nightlife is limited, there are a few good hangouts. Local favorite **Mas Que Nada Pub,** V. Discesa Paramura 5/7, just off P. Garibaldi and down the stairs, serves a variety of drinks (€2.40-5) and coffee (€1-2) on a palm tree-covered terrace. (☎338 90 30 347. Open Tu-Su 6:30pm-3am.) Head to the open-air garden at **Bar BeBop,** V. Nicola Botta 4, and share a few laid-back beverages (€2-5) beneath the oleander trees. From P. Duomo, head down C. Ruggiero, toward P. Garibaldi. V. Botta is two streets down on the right. (☎92 39 72. Karaoke Th and Su. Open daily 7:30pm-3am.) With a great seaside location, **Murphy's Pub,** Lungomare G. Giardina 5, offers a selection of draft beers (€2-4), a big-screen TV, and the ambience of an Irish pub. (☎42 25 88. *Panini* €3-4. Pizza €3.50-8. Live music or karaoke F and Su. Open Tu-Su noon-3pm and 6pm-3am.)

AEOLIAN ISLANDS (ISOLE EOLIE)

Homer believed this unspoiled archipelago to be a home of the gods; residents deem them Le Perle del Mare (Pearls of the Sea). Every summer, boatloads of visitors arrive from Milazzo and experience the magic of the rugged shores and pristine landscapes of the Isole Eolie (EE-so-leh Ey-OH-lee-yeh). Lipari, the central and largest island, has ancient ruins and is a perfect base for exploring the other islands. Visit nearby Stromboli for its restless volcano, Panarea for inlets and elitism, Salina for sheer cliffs over cerulean waters, and Vulcano for radioactive mud baths and the Great Crater, the long-extinguished home of Vulcan, god of fire. Far more affordable in the low season, the islands see a steep price increase in July and August. Reservations for this period should be made sooner rather than later, especially for more elite resorts.

◪ TRANSPORTATION

The islands lie off Sicily, north of Milazzo, the principal and least expensive departure point. **Trains** run to Milazzo from Messina (30min., 21 per day, €3.05) and Palermo (3hr., 13 per day, €11.20). **Giuntabus** (☎090 67 37 82/57 49) arrives in Milazzo's port from Messina (45min.; M-Sa 16 per day, Su daily; €3.40) and from the Catania airport (Apr.-Sept. daily 4pm, €10.33). From Milazzo's train station, the orange **AST bus** runs to the seaport (10min., every 30min., €1). **Hydrofoils** and **ferries** run regularly from mid-June through September to Lipari from Cefalù (3½hr., 8:15pm, €23.70); Messina (2-3hr., 5 per day 7:10am-6:20pm, €18.50); Naples (5½hr., 3pm, €85); Palermo (4½hr., 1-2 per day, €34); Reggio di Calabria (2hr., 4 per day, €19.50). Hydrofoils run twice as fast as fer-

> **SITTIN' ON THE DOCK OF THE BAY.** Give yourself extra time when planning travel in the Aeolian islands as ferry schedules change daily and are only on time about 30% of the time.

ries and more frequently, but for twice the price. Three major hydrofoil and ferry companies serve the islands, all with ticket offices in Milazzo on V. dei Mille, directly across from the docks in the port. High season (July-Aug.). Siremar, V. dei Mille 18, in Milazzo sends ferries and hydrofoils to the islands. (☎090 92 83 242; fax 090 92 83 243. Open daily 5:45am-6:30pm.) It also has offices in Lipari (☎090 98 12 193) and Naples (☎081 25 14 740). Ustica, V. dei Mille 23 (☎090 92 87 821), in Milazzo, sends hydrofoils to the islands, and it also has an office in Lipari (☎090 98 12 448). Ustica recently bought SNAV Lines, but some booths still say "SNAV." Navigazione Generale Italiana (NGI), V. dei Mille 26, is a 3rd option (☎090 92 84 091; fax 090 92 83 415); V. Mariano Amendola 14 (☎090 98 11 955), at Porto Sottomonastero in Lipari. The following table lists ferry and hydrofoil info for both Ustica and Siremar. There is a €1.50 fee to reserve in advance that is not included in the fees listed here. Schedules are subject to change, so call ahead. Both offices have convenient portable timetable booklets—just ask for an *orario*.

TO	FERRY FROM MILAZZO		HYDROFOIL FROM MILAZZO	
	TIME	HIGH SEASON	TIME	HIGH SEASON
Vulcano	1½hr.	7, 9am, 6:30pm; €6.30	45min.	16 per day 6:20am-6:20pm, €12.50
Lipari	2hr.	7, 9am, 6:30pm; €6.60	1hr.	17 per day 6:15am-6:10pm, €13.30
Salina	3hr.	7, 9am; €4	1½hr.	7 per day 6:15am-6:10pm, €14.80
Panarea	4hr.	M and W-Su 2:30pm, Tu and Sa 7am; €4.50	2hr.	5 per day 6:15am-4:20pm, €15.30

MILAZZO   ☎090

Visitors to Milazzo (mee-LAT-so; pop. 40,000) are all thinking the same thing: "What time does my boat leave?" Once upon a time, only a few boats a day sailed from Milazzo's port. Ferries and hydrofoils now zip to the Aeolian Islands and Italian mainland every hour. Welcome to Milazzo: get in, get your boat, and get out.

Milazzo gears itself toward travelers on the go, but food doesn't have to be rushed. Bars line the *lungomare*, and fruit vendors are along V. Regis in P. Natasi and at the intersection with V. del Sole. **Blue Pub ❶**, V. Alessandro Manzoni 4, serves pizza in air-conditioned, Tex-Mex splendor. (☎92 83 839. Pizza from €3.50. Cover €1. Open M-W and F-Su 7:30pm-midnight. MC/V.) For a relaxed meal, **Ristorante Al Gambero ❸**, V. Cavour 5/7, has a large, covered patio overlooking the water. (☎92 23 337. Pizza from €5.50. *Primi* €6.50-8.50, *secondi* €10-16.50. Cover €3. Open daily noon-3pm and 7pm-midnight. Closed in winter F. AmEx/MC/V.) A large **Despar** supermarket, V. del Sole 20, provides necessities. (Open M-Sa 8:30am-1pm and 5-8:30pm and Su 9am-1pm. AmEx/MC/V.)

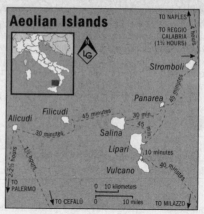

Aeolian Islands

Both city buses and Giuntabuses arrive in **Piazza della Repubblica** across from the Agip gas station close to the port; the train station is 10min. away by bus. **Lungomare Garibaldi** runs the length of the port. Turn left down V. Francesco Crispi and right into P. Caio Duilio; follow the signs to the **tourist office,** P. C. Duilio 20. (☎92 22 865; www.aastmilazzo.it. Open M-Sa 9:30am-1:30pm.) A **medical clinic** (☎92 81 158) is on V. F. Crispi, next to the **carabinieri** station. **Farmacia Vece**, P. C. Duilio 4, posts after-hours rotations. (☎92 81 181. Open M-F 9am-1pm and 4:30-8:30pm.)

LIPARI
☎090

Centuries ago, pirates ravaged Lipari's (LEE-pa-ree; pop. 10,000) shores. Today, boats and hydrofoils let loose packs of equally ravenous tourists, who pillage the island of overpriced T-shirts and other wares geared to the foreign masses. They descend in swarms upon its beaches and wallow in its waves like listless merpeople; those who prefer the colors of the sea and mountains to umbrellas and skimpy beachwear hike to nearby private beaches. Inexpensive hotels, divine sunbathing, and excellent archaeological museums make this island an ideal launching pad for further raids in this archipelago.

◪ TRANSPORTATION

Autobus Urso Guglielmo, V. Cappuccini 9 (☎98 11 262 or 98 11 026), operates **buses** on most of the island. Ticket office open daily 9am-7:30pm. (Tickets also available onboard; buses less frequent Su.) Island tours (€3.70) depart daily 9:30, 11:30am, and 5pm (reservations required). De. Sco., V. Stradale Pianoconte 5, at the end of C. Vittorio Emanuele, rents shiny **scooters,** lined up showroom-style. (☎98 13 288 or 368 75 35 590. €18-24 per day; Aug. €30-36. Gas extra. Open daily 9am-8pm. Cash only.) Steps away from De. Sco., Ditta Carbonaro Paola, C. V. Emanuele 21, also rents scooters. Prices are usually negotiable, especially if renting for more than one day. (☎98 11 994. €15 per day; Aug. €30. Open daily 8:30am-1pm and 2:30-8:30pm. Cash only.) For **taxis,** call ☎98 86 077 or 98 12 216.

◪ ☷ ORIENTATION AND PRACTICAL INFORMATION

The **hydrofoil** and **ferry port** are on the end of the promontory supporting the *castello* and museum. Restaurants and hotels cluster around **Corso Vittorio Emanuele,** the main thoroughfare, and **Via Garibaldi,** which runs mostly parallel to C. V. Emanuele around the base of the *castello*, and are accessible by large stone stairs; C. V. Emanuele ends at the docks. Purchase a map at a *tabaccheria*.

Tourist Office: AAST, C. V. Emanuele 202 (☎98 80 095; www.aasteolie.191.it). Info hub for all 7 islands. Ask for *Ospitalità in blu,* which contains helpful visitor info. Open M-F 8:30am-1:30pm and 4:30-7:30pm; July-Aug. also open Sa 8am-2pm and 4-9pm.

Currency Exchange: C. V. Emanuele is lined with banks and **ATMs.** Exchange money at **Banco Antonveneta** (☎98 12 117; open M-F 8:20am-1:20pm and 2:35-3:35pm) or at the **post office** (cash only). Some of the smaller Aeolian Islands have few or no ATMs; get cash on Lipari before visiting them.

Luggage Storage: At Ustica hydrofoil office (☎347 99 73 545). €3 per 12hr. €5 overnight surcharge. Open 8am-8pm.

English-Language Bookstore: Libreria Mimo Belletti, C. V. Emanuele 172 (☎98 11 282; mimmobelletti@tiscali.it). Small rack of varied English books, newspapers, and magazines. Open daily 8:30am-2pm and 4:30-11:30pm. AmEx/MC/V.

Laundry: Vico Storione 5 (☎98 13 177), off C. V. Emanuele. Wash and dry €4 per kg; min. 4kg. Open M-Sa 9am-1pm and 4:30-8:30pm. Cash only.

Ambulance: ☎98 95 267. **First Aid:** ☎98 85 467. **Carabinieri:** ☎98 11 333.

Pharmacies: Farmacia Internazionale, C. V. Emanuele 128 (☎98 11 583). Open in summer M-F 9am-1pm and 5-9pm; in winter 9am-1pm and 4-8pm. AmEx/MC/V. **Farmacia Cincotta,** V. Garibaldi 60 (☎98 11 472). Open M-F in summer 9am-1pm and 5-9pm; in winter 9am-1pm and 4-8pm. Posts after-hours rotation.

Hospital: (☎98 851), on V. Santana. At southern end of C. V. Emanuele, take side street between scooter rental places and turn right on V. Roma. V. Santana is the 2nd left. Open daily 8am-8pm. **Medical Clinic:** ☎98 85 226. Office 50m up V. Garibaldi from the waterfront. Open M, W, F 8:30am-1pm and Tu, Th 3:30-5:30pm.

Internet Access: Internet Point, C. V. Emanuele 185. 7 fast computers. €2 per 15min., €3 per 30min., €5 per hr. Open in summer M-Sa 9:30am-1pm and 5pm-midnight, Su 6pm-midnight; in winter M-Sa 9:30am-1:30pm and 4:30-9pm. **Net C@fe,** V. Garibaldi 61 (☎98 13 527). 3 computers. €3 per 30min., €5 per hr. Open daily 9am-1pm and 5pm-midnight; closed in winter F.

Post Office: Main branch for Aeolian Islands (☎98 10 051), on C. V. Emanuele. Open M-F 8am-6:30pm, Sa 8am-12:30pm. **Postal Codes:** 98052 (Canneto-Lipari); 98055 (Lipari); 98050 (all other islands).

▌ ACCOMMODATIONS AND CAMPING

As soon as you step off the hydrofoil exit ramp, you will be bombarded with offers for *affittacamere* (room rentals). These are often the most affordable way to enjoy the islands, and some of the best deals are listed below. Ask to see the room before accepting and always obtain a price quote in writing. Also, prices are often fairly negotiable outside of August, so try bargaining for a better rate.

Villa Rosa, V. Francesco Crispi 134 (☎98 80 280; www.liparivillarosa.it). From the port turn right away from the city center and walk until you reach a gas station. Relax on your private terrace away from the bustle of C. V. Emanuele. 8 rooms with bath, A/C, fridge, and kitchen. Doubles €30-60. ❶

Pensione Enzo Il Negro, V. Garibaldi 29, 3rd fl. (☎98 13 163 or 368 66 52 83; www.enzoilnegro.com), 20m from hydrofoil dock. Classy hotel has elegant archways, painted tiles, and 2 terraces with views of the harbor. 8 rooms have balcony, TV, fridge, A/C, and bath. Singles €60-70; doubles €90-130. AmEx/MC/V. ❹

Casa Vittorio di Cassara, Vico Sparviero 15 (☎/fax 98 11 523; www.casavittorio.com), off V. Garibaldi 22. Look for sign leading to the end of the alley and ring the bell to reach the owner. Ideal location near port and *centro*. Rooms vary from doubles to 5-person apartments; some have kitchen and sea-view terrace. Rooms €18-45 per person depending on season and length of stay. Cash only. ❷

Hotel Rocce Azzurre, V. Maddalena 69 (☎98 13 248; fax 98 13 247), on Porto delle Genti. Nestled in a quiet bay, this charming hotel has 33 rooms, all with bath, A/C, and fridge; many with balcony. Breakfast included. €68-74 per person. Aug. half pension €110; full pension €120. AmEx/MC/V. ❺

Affitacamere Marturano, V. Mavrolico 35 (☎368 32 24 997; www.enzamarturano.it), off C. V. Emanuele. 4 spacious rooms with bath, A/C, fridge, TV, kitchenette, and terrace. Reservations recommended. Doubles €50-90. Cash only. ❷

Baia Unci, V. Marina Garibaldi 2 (☎98 11 909; www.campeggitalia.it/sicilia/baiaunci). Campground near Canneto, 2km from Lipari. 10min. from beach. Self-service restaurant on grounds. Open Mar. 15-Oct. 15. €8-14 per person with tent. Cash only. ❶

◨ FOOD

Legions of lovers have sprinkled sauces, garnished salads, and spiced meats with the island's *capperi* (capers), renowned for their powers as aphrodisiacs. After following suit, complete a meal in style with local *Malvasia* dessert wine. Lipari's lip-smacking cuisine can get expensive, so head to **UPIM** supermarket, C. V. Emanuele 212, for a budget meal. (☎98 11 587. Open M-Sa 8am-9:30pm and Su 8am-2pm. AmEx/MC/V.) *Alimentari* along C. V. Emanuele sell cheap fruit every day.

▨ Da Gilberto e Vera, V. Garibaldi 22-24 (☎98 12 756; www.gilbertoevera.it). Famous for some of Italy's best *panini* with ingredients like prosciutto, capers, tomatoes, olives, mint, etc. Also carries tons of picnic supplies. *Panini* €4.50. Open daily Mar.-Jul. and Sept.-Oct. 7am-4am; Aug. 7am-6am; Nov.-Feb. 7pm-2am. AmEx/MC/V. ❶

La Cambusa, V. Garibaldi 72 (☎349 47 66 061). Husband and wife team makes this trattoria feel like home. Cluster around outdoor tables with *liparesi* or retreat indoors to enjoy authentic Sicilian flavors. Pasta from €5. Cover €1. Open daily Apr.-Oct. 10am-4pm and 6pm-midnight. Reservations recommended. Cash only. ❸

La Piazzetta, P. Luigi Salvatore d'Austria 13 (☎98 12 522; fax 98 13 761), off C. V. Emanuele, next to Pasticceria Subba. Walls and menus boast signatures of many famous, satisfied customers, including Audrey Hepburn. Elegant patio extends into a small *piazza*. Pizza €7.50. *Primi* from €5, *secondi* from €8.50. Cover €1. Service 10%. Open June-Oct. daily noon-2pm and 7:30-11pm; Nov.-May closed Tu. AmEx/MC/V. ❷

Ristorante Sottomonastero, C. V. Emanuele 232 (☎98 80 720; www.ritrovosottomonastero.it). This centrally located *ristorante* specializes in Aeolian sweets. Pizza from €4. *Primi* €5-8, *secondi* €5.50-15.50. *Menù* €13. Cover €1.80. Open daily 7am-midnight; late July-Aug. 24hr. Kitchen open noon-2:30pm and 7-11pm. AmEx/MC/V. ❷

Pasticceria Subba, C. V. Emanuele 92 (☎98 11 352). Pay by weight, in more ways than one, at the archipelago's oldest *pasticceria*. The ▨ **pasta paradiso** (€2.50), an almond paste dumpling, won a Gold Medal at the 1974 Milan Expo. Large pastries from €1.55. Open M-Th, Sa-Su May-Oct. 7am-1am; Nov.-Apr. 7am-9pm. Cash only. ❶

◉ SIGHTS

Lipari's best sights—aside from its beaches—are all in the *castello* on the hill, where a **fortress** with ancient Greek foundations dwarfs the surrounding town. In the vicinity is the **Museo Archeological Eoliano,** whose collection, explained in English and Italian, includes Liparite urns, galleries full of Greek and Sicilian figureware pottery from the 4th and 5th centuries BC, and treasures from underwater exploration. The geological and volcanic section is devoted to the island's natural history. Walk up the stone steps to the right off V. Garibaldi; turn left at the Church of San Bartolomeo. (☎98 80 174. Museum open daily 9am-1pm and 3-7pm. Last entry 1hr. before closing. €6, EU residents 18-25 €3, EU residents under 18 or over 65 free.) The **Chiesa di San Bartolomeo** is on the same hill. Built in the 12th century, it was sacked by Barbarossa the Turk in 1544. A new Baroque version, dedicated to St. Bartholomew, is done up in blue hues and topped by a painted ceiling. Stratified Greek, Roman, and Stone Age ruins encircle the building. The park's centerpiece is a contemporary Ancient-Greek-style **theater;** ask at the tourist office for programs and ticket prices. Continue walking past the church to find a walkway that leads to Lipari's harbor vistas. (Both sites are across from the museum. Open daily 9am-1pm and 3-7pm. Free.)

BEACHES AND FESTIVALS

From July to September, island **bus tours** (€3.70) run at 2pm from Autobus Urso Guglielmo (☎98 11 262/026) on V. Cappuccini. Reservations are required. A better way to see the coastline is from the water, aboard a rented boat from the hydrofoil port. For still better views, take the Lipari-Cavedi bus to the beaches of nearby **Canneto.** The pebbles are prickly and the sun scorching, so bring sunscreen and flip-flops. Rent a raft, kayak, or canoe along the beach at V. Marina Garibaldi (€3-5 per hr., €13-24 per day) to explore the coves flanking **Spiaggia Bianca.** A few kilometers north at **Pomiciazzo,** pumice mines line the road. Farther north at **Porticello,** people bathe at the foot of mines where flecks of stone float on the water's surface. A beach closer to the port is **Porto della Gente.** From the docks at the end of V. Garibaldi, turn left on the *lungomare*, and walk up the hill. Turn right up the stairs and take the first left away from the hotel. Turn right on the next road, and follow it to the shore. These beaches provide views of Salina, Panarea, and Stromboli. For the best vista, take the Lipari-Quattropani bus to **Pianoconte** and head to **Monte Sant'Angelo.** The mountain path is narrow and overgrown, so ask for directions to prevent getting lost. For a relaxed evening head to ▨**Bar Luna Quinta,** V. Francesco Crispi 44, a safe have for visiting mariners and local artists alike. With your back to the dock, V. F. Crispi runs along the water to your right. (Open daily 7:30pm-late.) Summer fever reaches its

IN RECENT NEWS

MAFIA JOCKEYS FOR POSITION

While chances are you won't wake to a horse's head in your bed, the Sicilian Mafia has created other equine complications. The Mafia has been staging illegal horse races on public roads in and around Messina, creating huge traffic problems for local officials. The races throng with roadside onlookers and a veritable motorcade of cars and motorbikes surrounding the horses. In addition to the congestion, local officials have to deal with the illegal gambling that accompanies the races and performance-enhancing drugs given to the horses.

These horse races are an anomaly, however, since Mafia activity in southern Italy has waned in recent years. The violence of the 80s and 90s has fallen dramatically, thanks to tougher law enforcement led by Palermo mayor Leoluca Orlando. The Mafia code of silence, or *omertà*, has begun to weaken as prominent members have agreed to divulge information in exchange for reduced sentences.

Although Orlando enforced tough anti-Mafia measures, in the May 2007 Palermo mayoral election, the two-time mayor lost to his opponent, Diego Cammarata. His defeat, along with new Mafia shenanigans, shows that while the Mafia has but a fraction of the power it once commanded, it continues to influence life in Sicily.

breaking point (and surpasses the island's capacity) on August 24 with the **Festa di San Bartolomeo,** when processions, parties, and pyrotechnics rule.

VULCANO   ☎090

Visitors can usually smell Vulcano (vool-CA-no; pop. 4000) before they see it. The pungent island was believed to be the home of the Greek blacksmiths' god, Vulcan, and the keeper of the winds, Aeolus. Thought to have been the gate to Hell, Vulcano is now known for its volcanic craters and savage landscapes. The largest volcano is the active and heavily touristed Fossa di Vulcano, which currently lies benign. However, geologists forecast an eruption within 20 years. Black beaches, bubbling seas, and natural sulfuric mud spas may make Vulcano seem abrasive, but these untamed natural phenomena usually end up winning over visitors.

▐ TRANSPORTATION. The island is accessible by **hydrofoil** and **ferry.** The Ustica ticket office (☎98 52 230) is directly off the port, next to Cantine Stevenson, while Siremar (☎98 52 149) sits atop a stone walkway at the Porto Levante intersection. **Hydrofoils** to: Lipari (10min., 17 per day 6:35am-8:05pm, €5.50); Milazzo (40min., 17 per day 7:20am-7:50pm, €17.50); Naples (6hr., 2:55pm, €79.40); Palermo (4 hr., 7:15am and 4:05pm, €34); Panarea (1¼hr., 7 per day 7:50am-6:30pm, €10.60); Reggio di Calabria (2¼hr., 4 per day 6:35am-6:30pm, €19.50); Salina (40min., 16 per day 7:15am-8:10pm, €10); Stromboli (2hr., 8 per day 7:50am-6:30pm, €17.60). NGI Biglietteria (☎98 52 401) sells ferry tickets for Milazzo and the Aeolian Islands under a blue awning on V. Provinciale, just off P. Levante. (Open daily 8am-2pm, 3pm-5:30pm, and 11:30pm-midnight.) Scaffidi Tindaro (☎98 53 073) runs **internal buses** off the port on V. Provinciale, next to Ritrovo Remigio. Infrequent buses run to Capo Grillo, Gelso Beach, Vulcanello, and Vulcano Piano from the port. Buy a ticket (€2) onboard. **Bikes** and **scooters** are available for rent at the two Sprint da Luigi shops, a block apart on V. Provinciale with almost identical prices. Multilingual owners provide maps and other tourist info. (☎98 52 208 or 347 76 00 275. Bikes €3-5 for 1st day, €3 per day thereafter. Tandem bike €8 per hr., €20 per day; minicar €15/45. Scooters in May €12.50-15 per day; June €15.50-18; July-Aug. €15-25; Sept. €15.50. 18+ for anything with a motor. Cash only.) Find **boat rental** at **Blob Oasi,** Baia di Ponente (☎338 89 69 690) on the Sabbie Nere. Rent motorboats ranging from two-person for €100 to 17-person for €350. (Open daily June-Oct. 9am-7:30pm. Cash only.) **Centro Nautico Baia di Levante** is on the beach behind Ritrovo Remigio, near the hydrofoil dock. (☎98 22 197 or 339 33 72 795. 8-person motorboat €100-200 per day. Gas extra. Open daily 8am-11pm. Cash only.) For a **taxi** from the port call ☎339 57 91 576 or 347 81 30 631.

▐▊ ORIENTATION AND PRACTICAL INFORMATION. Vulcano's casual atmosphere comes across in its lack of posted street names and address numbers. Frequent directional signs and arrows, however, make this pedestrian island easily navigable. Ferries and hydrofoils dock at **Porto di Levante,** on the eastern side of **Vulcanello,** the youngest of the island's three volcanoes. Facing away from the hydrofoil dock at the far left of the port, **Via Provinciale** heads toward the Fossa di Vulcane and its ▇**Gran Cratere** (Great Crater). Straight ahead and up a small hill is **Via Porto Levante,** a semicircular road that loops through town and reconnects to the ferry docks. At the small statue of Aeolus, V. Porto Levante bends and splits in three directions. The pharmacy is straight ahead, while the **acquacalda** and **Laghetto di Fanghi** are on the right. Continue along to the left of the pharmacy, passing green pastures on the way to the black shoreline of **Sabbie Nere.**

The **tourist office,** V. Provinciale 41, has info on *affittacamere*, though it is closed for most of the year. (☎98 52 028/142. Open Aug. daily 8am-1:30pm and 3-5pm.) All other info at AAST in Lipari. Head to Sprint da Luigi (see above) when the tourist office is closed for maps and other island info. Down V. Provinciale from the port, **Banco Sicilia** has an **ATM.** (☎98 52 335. Open M-F 8:30am-1:30pm and 3:45-4:45pm.) In case of **emergency,** call **first aid** (☎985 22 20) or the **carabinieri** (☎98 52 110). For a **pharmacy,** head to **Farmacia Bonarrigo,** V. Cesare Battisti 180, at the far end of the *piazza* where V. Provinciale breaks off. (☎71 75 89; emergency 338 56 56 260 or 98 52 616. Open daily Jan.-Sept. 9am-1pm and 4-8pm. Closed Oct.-May Sa afternoon and Su.) Two computers at **DeSpar market** on V. Lentia, 100m from Cafe Piazzetta, provide **Internet** access. (€4 per hr. Open daily 8am-1:30pm and 4-9pm.) The **post office** is at Vulcano Piano, down V. Provinciale. (Open M-F 8am-1:20pm, Sa 8am-12:20pm.) **Postal Code:** 98050.

⌂ ACCOMMODATIONS. Hotel Torre ❷, V. Favaloro 1, down V. Porto Levante from hydrofoil docks, is close to the *acquacalda.* Rooms have bath, A/C, TV, and kitchen; many offer great views. (☎/fax 98 52 342; www.hoteltorrevulcano.it. Doubles €40-80; triples €90-120; quads €120-160. Cash only.) Off V. Provinciale, **Residence Lanterna Bleu di Francesco Corrieri ❷,** V. Lentia 58, has tranquil apartments that come with bath, A/C, kitchenette, and terrace. Location is just 400m from *acquacalda* and mudbaths. (☎/fax 98 52 178. Doubles €50-90. Extra bed €18-25. Cash only.) On the opposite side of Vulcano's isthmus neck, 1.5km from hydrofoil dock and adjacent to the Sabbie Nere, **Campeggio Togo Togo ❶,** V. Porto Ponente, has an on-site pizzeria in summer. (☎/fax 98 52 303. Reservations recommended for Aug. Open Apr.-Sept. €11, includes tent and light. Larger bungalow with TV and kitchenette July-Aug. up to 4 people €85; 1st week in Sept. and Apr.-June €21 per person. Hot showers €1. AmEx/MC/V.)

◘ FOOD. *Granita* and *gelato* are in abundance at the port, but venture off the main roads for a good meal. The aromatic *Malvasia* wine is a delight. Popular with tourists and locals, **▣Remigio ❶,** V. Porto Levante 1, sells hot and cold sandwiches made to order (€3), delicious *gelato,* and many desserts. (☎98 52 085. Horseshoe *ciappe* €1.50. *Gelato* €2.50. Open daily 6am-2am. Cash only.) Down V. Provinciale from hydrofoil docks, **Cafe Piazzetta ❶,** in Piazzetta Faraglione, serves *gelato* from €3.80 and mixed drinks from €2.60, as well as the more substantial pizza for €5-7 or *basiluzzo panino* (with tomato, cheese, lettuce, olive oil, salt, and oregano) for €2.80. (☎98 53 267. Live music June-Sept. 10pm-1:30am. Service 10%. Open Apr.-Sept. daily 8am-2am. MC/V.) Restaurant meets nightlife gathering point at **Cantine Stevenson ❷,** on V. Porto Levante, where locals listen to classical music in a pub-like setting. Check out the 60-page wine list. (☎98 53 247. Occasional live music. Mixed drinks €5.50. Pizza from €6.50. *Primi* €6.50-12, *secondi* €8-14. Dessert €6. Open daily 7pm-3am. AmEx/MC/V.) The large and low-key **Ristorante Vincenzino ❸,** V. Porto Levante 25, serves Aeolian specialties including the expensive treat *gamberoni alla griglia* (grilled prawns) for €23. (☎98 52 016; fax 98 53 370. *Primi* €7-12, *secondi* €8-23. *Menù* including dessert and cover €17. Cover €1.50. Open daily 12:30-3pm and 7-11:30pm. AmEx/MC/V.) **Tridial Market,** on V. Porto Levante in the *piazza* before the pharmacy, has essentials, plus a sandwich counter. (Open daily 8am-8:30pm.) An **alimentari** on V. Provinciale, toward the crater from the port, sells produce. (Open daily 8am-1pm and 4-8pm.) A small **Conad** market is right below Hotel Torre. (Open daily 8am-8:30pm. AmEx/MC/V).

◙ SIGHTS. Anyone visiting Vulcano for more than a day should tackle the 1hr. hike to the **▣Gran Cratere** at the summit of Fossa di Vulcano (€3). The crater

SICILY

rewards trekkers with views of the island, sea, and volcanic landscape. The hike winds through yellow *fumaroli*, emissions of noxious smoke, and orange rock formations powdered with dust. Between 11am and 3pm, the sun transforms the volcano face into a furnace. Begin the climb during early morning or late afternoon, and bring a hat, sunscreen, sturdy climbing shoes, and plenty of water. Segments of the trail are quite strenuous and should be approached with caution. Obey the signs, and don't sit or lie down, as poisonous gases tend to accumulate close to the ground. To reach the volcano, face away from the port, turn left on V. Provinciale, and follow it until the path with *"Cratere"* signs appears. The notices point to a turn-off 300m on the left.

The murky gray-brown of the ■**Laghetto di Fanghi's** water blends with the surrounding volcanic rock formations, but the putrid smell makes this natural spa impossible to miss. Undeterred droves of visitors spread sludge over their bodies for its allegedly curative effects, especially for arthritis. (Up V. Porto Levante and to the right from the port. €2; showers €1.) Directly behind the mud pits at the **acqua-calda,** Vulcano's shoreline bubbles like a hot tub, courtesy of subterranean volcanic *fumaroli.* The sulfuric water has quite an effect on human blood circulation, creating a heavenly sensation upon emerging—although the mercilessly corrosive acid tends to destroy bathing suits. This is not the place to display the latest in swimwear fashion. Disposable suits are available nearby for €5.

> **IF EVERYONE JUMPED INTO A RADIOACTIVE MUDPIT, WOULD YOU?** Therapeutic or not, the mud is radioactive and high in corrosive sulfuric acid, which can cause severe burning or blistering. Remove all silver and leather accessories, and keep the mud away from your eyes.

If sulfur burns and radioactive mud don't sound appealing, join carefree sunbathers on Vulcano's best beach, **Sabbie Nere.** Black sands curl up against white-crested waves, and colorful umbrellas form a rainbow of relaxation. To get there, follow V. Provinciale, then take the road that veers to the left of the pharmacy. Continue along the pastures and past the Hotel Eolie until reaching the shore.

PANAREA   ☎090

As is apparent from the constant stream of white linen and Louis Vuitton luggage on the hydrofoil docks, petite Panarea (pa-na-RE-ah; pop. 200) is the island for chic repose. With simple, white buildings and a beguiling elegance, Panarea attracts an older, upscale crowd seeking an understated place to relax. In August, however, rambunctious youth overtake the *discoteche*, forcing the island's once-dignified, waterside bars to pump up the volume and party well into the morning.

▐▌ **TRANSPORTATION AND PRACTICAL INFORMATION.** Panarea is accessible by **ferry** and **hydrofoil.** The Ustica (☎98 33 44) and Siremar (☎98 30 07) offices are at the port. Hydrofoils to: Lipari (1hr., 26 per day 8:10am-6:15pm, €10); Milazzo (2hr., 9 per day 8:10am-6:15pm, €15.30); Naples (5hr., 1 per day 4:20pm, €66); Reggio di Calabria (2-4hr., 4 per day 9:25am-7:35pm, €21.60); Salina (½hr., 4 per day 9:25am-6:05pm, €9); Stromboli (45min., 8 per day 9:10am-7:35pm, €10.60); Vulcano (1hr., 8 per day 8:10am-6:05pm, €9.60). Panarea is a purely pedestrian island. All directional signs list distances by feet rather than kilometers, and street signs and numbers are very rare. The main road, **Via San Pietro,** runs past Chiesa San Pietro along a stone path to **Punta Milazzese. Banca Antonveneta** has an **ATM** on V. S. Pietro, on the left from the port, and **Banca di Sicilia** has one on Hotel Cincotta's patio. In case of **emergency,** call the **carabinieri**

(July-Aug. ☎98 31 81, Sept.-June ☎98 11 333 in Lipari) or the **medical clinic** (☎98 30 40). A 24hr. **golf cart taxi** service is run by Paola+Angelo (☎333 31 38 610), on V. S. Pietro. Passage to the beach costs around €8. A **pharmacy** is at V. Iditella 8. (☎98 31 48. Open in summer M-Sa 9am-1pm and 5-9pm; in winter M-Tu and Th-Su 9am-12:30pm.) The **post office** on V. S. Pietro **exchanges currency** and traveler's checks. (☎98 30 28. Open M-F 8am-1:30pm, Sa 8am-12:30pm.) **Postal Code:** 98050.

▐▌▐▌ ACCOMMODATIONS AND FOOD. Hotels are small and costly, and prices peak in July and August. Be sure to make reservations well in advance if you want to dole out the euro. Turn right from the docks and climb stairs to the white-and-blue houses of **Da Francesco/Pasqualina ➒**, on V. del Porto. All rooms have bath, fan, and sea view. (☎98 30 23. Breakfast included; trattoria on deck. Rooms €70-110 per person. MC/V.) **Quartara ➒**, V. S. Pietro 15, has the island's prettiest rooms, evident in each room's cream-colored canopy, balcony, A/C, TV, bath, hair dryer, and minibar. (☎98 30 27. Breakfast included. Restaurant on site; closed in winter until late Mar. Singles €120-250; doubles €180-320, with view €260-400; triples €252-448. Substantial discounts during low season. AmEx/MC/V.)

Near the port, at **Ristorante Da Pina ➒**, V. S. Pietro, swaths of gauze create an ethereal mood among the pillowed outdoor benches—guests don't sit, they lounge. *Gnocchi di melanzane* (with eggplant; €18) and *couscous di pesce e aragosta* (with fish and lobster; €18) are the house specialities. (☎98 30 32. Lobster €150 per kg. *Primi* €18, *secondi* €20. Reservations recommended. AmEx/MC/V.) Find *panini* (€5), *gelato* (€3.50), or another Sicilian sweet, at **Panea ➊**, V. S. Pietro. (☎98 31 88; www.panea.it. Open in high season 24hr.; in winter hours vary.) **Da Bruno** minimart is by the post office. (☎98 30 02. Open daily July-Aug. 7:45am-9pm; Sept.-June 8am-2pm and 5-9pm.) Locals line up at the **panificio** next door for focaccia and pizza slices. (☎98 32 84. Open daily Sept.-July 6:30am-1:30pm and 5-8pm; Aug. 6:30am-9pm.)

◢▐▌ BEACHES AND ENTERTAINMENT. The few who seek out Panarea's beaches do so precisely because most others do not. Tiny and free of umbrellas, these are some of the archipelago's more intimate coves. From Punta Milazzese, three small beaches extend along the coastline; gradually changing from rocks to sand. Two rights from the *centro* lead to **Calcara** (also known as Spiaggia Fumarole), near the thermal springs at **Acquacalda**. Reach the second beach by walking 30min. following V. S. Pietro's signs for **Spiagietta Zimmari**. Arrive early to find an empty patch of sand, and stop by the supermarket before heading out, as Spiagietta Zimmari's only food option is pricey. For views of coves and cliffs, embark on a **boat tour** with Eolie Mare, on V. Umberto I. The company also rents boats for private exploration. (☎98 33 28. 2-person tour €50. Open 24hr.) For **scuba diving**, Amphibia has an office on the *lungomare*, up the stairs next to the hotel Da Francesco. (☎335 61 38 529. Single immersion €36; 3 dives €100; 6 dives €190. Wetsuit rental €15. Office open daily May-Sept. 9am-1pm and 3-7pm. Cash only). Panarea comes alive in summer with disco fever. The spot to be is **Hotel RAYA**, V. S. Pietro, which pumps with energy and exclusivity until the first morning rays. Chatting up Italian soccer players, Milanese banking heirs, and actresses can be done at the RAYA, where mixed drinks and cover both run a steep €30-50. (☎98 30 13. Open July 22-Aug. Hotel guests free.)

SALINA   ☎090

Though close to Lipari in both size and distance, Salina (sa-LEE-na; pop. 2300) is far removed from its more developed neighbor. Untouched landscapes and the archipelago's most dramatic beaches make the island a tranquil paradise. Its most astounding rock formations are at Semaforo di Pollara, chosen as a backdrop for Massimo Troisi's film *Il Postino*. Some of Sicily's best restaurants hide on Salina's slopes and in dockside Santa Marina. Ultimately, Salina's tranquil simplicity is a welcome respite from the crowds on the other islands.

▆ TRANSPORTATION. Porto Santa Marina is Salina's main port, accessible from Lipari by **hydrofoil** (30min., 9 per day, €7.30) and **ferry** (50min., 3 per day, €3.20). The smaller port of **Rinella**, on the opposite side of the island, docks hydrofoils (45min., €6) and ferries (1½hr., €4). Hydrofoils run from Salina P. Santa Marina to: Messina (2½hr., 5 per day, €21.20); Milazzo (1½hr., 6 per day, €14.80); Panarea (25min., 5 per day, €8.10); Reggio di Calabria (1½-3 hr., 5 per day, €21.60); Stromboli (1hr., 6 per day, €13.20); Vulcano (45min., 8 per day, €9). Ustica (☎98 43 003) and Siremar (☎98 43 004) have offices on either side of Chiesa di Santa Marina, in front of the port in P. Santa Marina. Blue CITIS **buses,** V. Nazionale 10 (☎98 44 150), in Malfa, stop at the *chiesa*. Monthly schedules are posted outside the Siremar office. **Buses** run to Pollara (40min., 12 per day 7:30am-6:30pm, €2) via Malfa, and Gramignazzi, Leni, Lingua, Malfa, Rinella, and Valdichiesa (13-24 per day 7am-8:30pm). Rent **scooters** from Motonoleggio Bongiorno Antonio, V. Risorgimento 240, in Santa Marina. Facing away from the hydrofoil docks, turn left up the road that curves uphill. Turn right up the 1st side street just before a row of parked scooters to reach the office. Caution: Salina's roads are extremely narrow and curvy, and locals drive recklessly, so leave driving to the experts. If you do rent a scooter, absolutely wear a helmet. (☎98 43 409. Mountain bikes €2.50-3.50 per hr., €8-10.50 per day. Scooters €8-8.50 per hr., €26-31 per day. Gas extra. Open daily in summer 8:30am-7:30pm; in winter 8:30am-1:30pm. AmEx/MC/V.)

▆▟ ORIENTATION AND PRACTICAL INFORMATION. The main road, **Via Risorgimento,** runs parallel to the *lungomare*. **Banco di Sicilia,** V. Risorgimento 158-160, cashes traveler's checks, offers **currency exchange,** and has an **ATM.** (☎98 43 365. Open M-F 8:30am-1:30pm.) In case of **emergency,** call **first aid** (☎98 40 005), the **carabinieri** (☎98 43 019), or the **police** (☎98 43 021). A **pharmacy,** V. Risorgimento 211, is at the end of the street, behind the Ustica office. (☎98 43 098. Open M 5-8pm, Tu-F 9am-1pm and 5-8pm, Sa 9am-1pm.) Access **Internet** at **Salina Computer,** V. Risorgimento 110. (☎98 43 444. €6 per hr.) The **post office** is at V. Risorgimento 130. (☎98 43 028. Open M-F 8am-1:30pm, Sa 8am-12:30pm.) **Postal Code:** 98050.

▐▐ ACCOMMODATIONS AND FOOD. Unfortunately, Salina's accommodations are far from cheap. Get your money's worth at **Hotel Mamma Santina ❹,** V. Sanità 40, by the port. The hotel offers rooms with satellite TV, A/C, and Internet, overlooking a private swimming pool. Owner/chef (recently featured in *Cucina Italiana* Magazine) is known to give cooking lessons to inquisitive onlookers. (☎98 43 054; www.mammasantina.it. Breakfast included. Doubles €100-210. Half pension €30 extra per person. 15% surcharge for use of double as single. AmEx/MC/V). Salina's only true budget accommodation, **Campeggio Tre Pini ❶,** V. Rotabile 1, maintains a campground with a market, bar, and restaurant. (☎98 09 155, in winter 92 22 293. Take the bus to Rinella, then the hydrofoil to Salina Rinella. Reservations recommended July-Aug. €6-8 per person, €8-11 per tent. AmEx/MC/V.)

Restaurants crowd Santa Marina, the dockside town, and some meals can be pretty pricey. But given Salina's cuisine, it is inexcusable not to indulge in a meal. The finest is at ▨**Ristorante Mamma Santina ❸,** attached to the hotel, where chef Mario welcomes you to the terrace dining room and treats you to homemade specialties. *Spaghetti alla Mamma Santina* (€10), a family secret made with 14 fresh herbs and spices, is unbelievable. (*Primi* €5.50-10, *secondi* €8-12. Open daily noon-3pm and 8pm-midnight. AmEx/MC/V.) An exerting but rewarding 15min. uphill walk leads to **Ristorante da Franco ●**, V. Belvedere 8. From the *lungomare*, turn left just before the *carabinieri* station, then turn right at the 2nd major intersection. Follow signs to the restaurant, which offers supremely fresh local specialties and the best views in Salina. (☎98 43 287. Homemade wine €9.30 per bottle. *Primi* €9.30-12.50, *secondi* €13-16. Cover €2.60. Open daily 7:30pm-midnight. Closed Dec. 1-20. AmEx/MC/V over €150.) The cheapest way to eat is to assemble a beach picnic at any **alimentari** on V. Risorgimento.

🜨 OUTDOOR ACTIVITIES. Viewing Salina's finest sight involves a 1hr. bus ride from Santa Marina to the striking 🖼**Pollara**, a beach in the middle of a half-submerged volcanic crater, 100m below the town's cliffs. While there isn't much of a beach, black sand, crumbling boulders, sandstone walls, and blue water create a beautifully surreal scene. To the far right, a natural rock archway juts out from the water. On the other side of the island, **Valdichiesa** rests at the base of **Monte Fossa delle Felci,** the highest point of the Aeolians. Trails lead from the town 962m up the mountain. For less aerobic activity, relax at **Malfa's beach,** which offers equally tantalizing views—of the huge, sulfur bubbles known as *sconcassi*. On the 1st Sunday in June, the population of Salina heads to Pollara for the **Sacra del Cappero.** Each restaurant and volunteering family brings its own special dish in which the *cappero* (caper) is key. Visitors are invited to contribute their own treats, which is an easy way to make friends with the locals.

STROMBOLI   ☎090

In Italian geology, "strombolic activity" refers to the most violent type of volcanic eruption. In keeping with its title, the island of Stromboli (STROM-bo-lee; pop. 600) harbors the Aeolians' only active volcano—a fact that frightens residents and delights visitors. Though the great Stromboli is always rumbling, the island itself keeps quiet until summer. Sporadic volcanic activity scares away all but the most determined visitors, clearing out hotel rooms and turning the town into a deserted haven, albeit a dimly ominous one. The adventurous are drawn to nightly guided hikes up the mountain, but if the volcano's threat seems more intimidating than intriguing, renting a boat is also a great way to visit.

🮱 TRANSPORTATION. Along the *lungomare*, NGI (☎98 30 03), Siremar (☎98 60 16; open daily 9am-1pm, 3-8pm, and 8:30-10pm for service to Naples), and Ustica (☎98 60 03; open daily 8:30am-12:30pm and 4:15-8pm) run **ferries** and **hydrofoils.** Hydrofoils run to: Lipari (1hr., 9 per day 7:25am-5:25pm, €15.30); Messina (2hr., 3 per day 8:45am-8:15pm, €20.10); Milazzo (2½hr., 5 per day 7:25am-5:40pm, €18.20); Naples (4hr., 9:05am and 5pm, €62-70); Panarea (¾hr., 10 per day 7:25am-6:40pm, €9.60); Reggio di Calabria (1½hr., 3 per day 8:45am-8:15pm, €20.60); Salina (1hr., 6 per day 8:45am-6:40pm, €13.80); Vulcano (1½hr., 9 per day 7:25am-6:40pm, €16.60). **Boat rentals** are available from a number of companies at the port, including the Società Navigazione Pippo. (☎98 61 35. €70 per day. Gas extra. 3hr. boat tours daily 10:30am and 3:10pm; €20. Open daily 8am-10:30pm. Cash only).

🮱🮱 ORIENTATION AND PRACTICAL INFORMATION. On the calmer slopes of smoking Stromboli, the three villages of **Scari, Ficogrande,** and **Piscita** have melded into one stretch known as the town of Stromboli. From the ferry docks, the wide *lungomare* is on the right, continuing to the beach and two large hotels. The narrow **Via Roma** heads from the ticket offices to the *centro*. Twisting uphill to the left, V. Roma passes the island's only **ATM** next to the Alimentari da Maria, and finally the **pharmacy** (☎98 67 13; open M-Sa June-Aug. 8:30am-1pm and 4-8:30pm; Sept.-May 8:30am-1pm and 4-7:30pm), just before reaching **Piazza San Vincenzo.** Pick up an excellent map (€3) at **Totem Trekking,** across from the *duomo.* V. Roma then dips downhill, becoming **Via Vittorio Emanuele** which then leads to the trail up the mountain. In case of **emergency,** call the **medical clinic** (☎98 60 97) or the **carabinieri** (☎98 60 21). The **post office** is open Monday to Friday 8am-1:30pm and 8am-12:30pm on the weekend (☎98 60 27). **Postal Code: 98050.**

⚑❒ ACCOMMODATIONS AND FOOD. Unlike the more populated islands, the tourist deluge in Stromboli occurs in August, a time when *affittacamere* may be the best bet for lodging. Ask to see the room before paying, and don't be afraid to check for hot water and comfortable beds. Prices are considerably lower in low season. To reach **◨Casa del Sole ❷,** on V. Cincotta, follow the side street across from St. Bartholomew's church at the end of V. V. Emanuele. Big dorm rooms face a terrace and shared kitchen, while doubles populate the upstairs. Four bathrooms are downstairs. (☎/fax 98 60 17; casa-del-sole@tiscali.it. Dorms €27; doubles €60-70. Cash only.) **Albergo Brasile ❹,** up the street from Casa del Sole, offers simple rooms and home-cooked meals. (☎98 60 08; www.strombolialbergobrasile.it. Breakfast and either lunch or dinner included. Half-pension doubles €110-154; full-pension €166-190. AmEx/MC/V.) **La Lampara B&B ❸,** V. V. Emanuele 27, has five island-themed rooms with TV and large bath. (☎98 64 09; fax 98 67 21. Breakfast included; pizzeria attached. Rooms €35-50 per person. AmEx/MC/V.)

In order to admire the volcano's explosive activity from solid ground, head to **L'Osservatorio ❸,** in Punta Labronzo, the last establishment along V. V. Emanuele. The food is slightly overpriced, but the spectacular view of nighttime eruptions pays for itself. The restaurant is a serious trek away; bring a flashlight at night and wear sneakers. Taxis also depart for the restaurant from S. Bartolo hourly 5-11pm. (☎98 63 60 or 337 29 39 42. Pizza from €6.20. *Primi* from €7, *secondi* from €12. Cover €1.50. Open daily 9:30am-midnight. Cash only.) Locals say the best pizza on the island is at **La Lampara ❸,** V. V. Emanuele 27, on the left just after P. San Vincenzo. It shares management with La Lampara B&B. The freshly squeezed lemon *granita* (€2) is amazing. Sample the catch of the day caught by the owner by ordering the *frittura di pesce misto* (mixed fried fish) for €11. (Pizza from €5.50. *Primi* €6-10, *secondi* €10-14. Open Mar.-Nov. daily 6pm-midnight. AmEx/MC/V.) At **La Trottola ❷,** V. Roma 34, delve into the *pizza Strombolí,* a cone-shaped creation bursting with mozzarella, tomatoes, and olives. (☎98 60 46. Pizza from €4. Open daily noon-2:15pm and 6-10:30pm. AmEx/MC/V.) Stuff your knapsack with a pre-hike snack at **Alimentari da Maria,** V. Roma 191, just before the church. (☎98 61 49. Open daily 8:30am-1pm and 4:30-8:30pm, Su 9am-1pm. MC/V.)

◩ SIGHTS. ◨Strombolicchio, a gigantic rock with a small lighthouse, rises an inaccessible 2km in the distance from the beach at **Ficogrande.** The ravages of the sea have eroded the rock from 56m to a mere 42m in the past century. Beachgoers should check out the cove at the end of V. Giuseppe Cincotta, off V. V. Emanuele near Casa del Sole, where rocks encircle the stretch of black sand. At the **◨volcano,** rivers of orange lava and molten rock spill over the slope, lighting the **Sciara del Fuoco** (Trail of Fire) at roughly 10min. intervals. While it generally spews continuously, be forewarned that the volcano sometimes needs a rest; call Magmatrek (see below) ahead to check up on Stromboli's activity. An ordinance passed in

1990 made hiking the volcano without a guide illegal, and for good reason: a photographer was burned to death after getting too close to the volcanic opening, and in 1998, a Czech diplomat, lost in the fog, walked off the cliff's edge. If such an end is not in your stars, look into an escorted trip with **Magmatrek**, on V. V. Emanuele right past the church. (☎/fax 98 65 768. Open daily 10am-1pm and 4:30-6:30pm. Helmets required and provided. Tours offered in English. Departures daily Mar.-June and Sept.-Oct. 3:30pm; July-Aug. 5:30pm. €13.50 to 400m lookout point, €25 to the crater. Reserve at least 2-3 days in advance.) **Totem Trekking**, P. San Vincenzo 4, rents equipment and supplies, and offers Internet access for €2.50 per hr. (☎98 65 752. Open daily in summer 10am-1pm and 4:30pm-midnight; Dec. 15-Jan. 8 10am-1pm and 4-7pm. Call year-round to arrange rentals. AmEx/MC/V.) The **Società Navigazione Pippo** (☎98 61 35), at the port, runs a boat trip (1hr., 8:30 and 10pm, €15) for those wishing to view the volcano from the sea.

> ⚠ **STOP! IN THE NAME OF LAVA!** *Let's Go* does not recommend, advocate, or take responsibility for anyone hiking Stromboli's volcano, with or without a guide. Posted signs of red triangles with black vertical bars signify "danger."

◧ ENTERTAINMENT. The plateau of **Piazza San Vincenzo** is Stromboli's geographic center and its most exciting 46 sq. m (besides the crater itself). Each night around 10pm, islanders flock to **Ritrovo Ingrid** for *gelato* (€1.80-4.70) and drinks. (☎98 63 85. Open daily July-Aug. 8am-3am; Sept.-June 8am-1am. Cash only.) Its neighbor, **Ristorante-Pizzeria Il Conte Ugolino,** has a social seating area. The moon rising directly over the *piazza* with the volcano in the background is a spectacular sight. (☎98 65 765. Cover €3. Service 15%.)

EASTERN SICILY

MESSINA   ☎090

Messina (meh-SEE-na; pop. 240,000) is a transportation hub if ever there was one; better air-conditioning and a duty-free shop would turn this fast-paced town into an airport. While its role as a major port and the main commercial connection between Sicily and the mainland has brought prosperity, Messina has also weathered nonstop invasions, plagues, and earthquakes. Despite all obstacles, the town maintains its dignity in points of historical interest and beauty like the *duomo*, the allegorical clock tower, and the church of Santa Maria Annunziata dei Catalani.

▐ TRANSPORTATION

Trains: Stazione Centrale, in P. della Repubblica (☎67 97 95 or info 147 88 80 88). To: **Milazzo** (30min., €3); **Palermo** (3½hr., 15 per day, €11); **Rome** (9hr., 6 per day, €43); **Syracuse** (3½hr., 16 per day, €9); **Taormina** (40min., 27 per day, €3.15).

Buses: Messina has 4 bus carriers, many of which serve the same routes.

AST (☎66 22 44, ask for *"informazioni"*). Tickets sold in an orange minibus in P. del Duomo across from the cathedral, or simply buy tickets onboard. Serves small and less touristed areas all over southern Italy.

Giuntabus, V. Terranova 8 (☎67 37 82 or 67 57 49), 3 blocks up V. I Settembre, left on V. Bruno, right on V. Terranova. To **Milazzo** (45min.; M-Sa 16 per day 6am-8pm, Su 1 per day 7:15am; €3.40, €5.20 round-trip). Purchase tickets on bus.

Interbus, P. della Repubblica 6 (☎66 17 54), has blue offices next to SAIS. To: **Giardini-Naxos** (1½hr., 8 per day, €2.50); **Naples** (1 per wk., Su; €22); **Rome** (2 per day, €30); **Taormina** (1½hr., 12 per day, €2.50).

SAIS, P. della Repubblica 6 (☎77 19 14). Ticket office is immediately to the left when exiting the train station. To: **Catania airport** (1-2hr., 17 per day, €7.25); **Catania** (1½hr., 23 per day, €6.50); **Florence** (12½hr.; 1 per wk., Su; €50); **Naples** (22hr., 3 per wk., €25); **Palermo** (1½hr., 6 per day, €13.30).

Speedboats and Hydrofoils: From **BluVia** (☎67 86 51 7), the waterfront wing of Stazione Centrale, Trenitalia sends hydrofoils to **Reggio di Calabria** (25min.; M-F 13 per day 6:10am-7:40pm, Sa and Su 7 per day 7:30am-7:40pm; €2.80) and **Villa San Giovanni** (40min., 2 per hr., €1). From the station facing the *piazza*, turn right and walk toward the waterfront, then look for BluVia signs. Ticket office on the docks. MC/V. **Ustica** (☎36 40 44), has offices in a blue building on the waterfront side of V. V. Emanuele, 2km north of the train station off C. Garibaldi. Hydrofoils to: **Lipari** (5 per day, 7:10am-6:30pm, €18.50), **Panarea** (2hr., 3 per day 7:10am-3:25pm, €21.10), and **Salina** (2½hr., 6 per day 7:10am-6:20pm, €21.10). MC/V.

Public Transportation: Orange **Azienda Trasporti Milanesi buses** leave either from P. della Repubblica or from the bus station, 2 blocks up V. I Settembre from the station, on the right. **Bus #79** stops at the *duomo,* museum, and aquarium, and only runs from P. della Repubblica. **Trams** run from the station to the museum (10min., every 10min. 5am-10pm). The same ticket (€1, valid for 3hr.), available at any *tabaccheria* or newsstand, is good for both the ATM buses and the tram.

Taxis: Radiotaxi Jolly (☎65 05), to the right of the *duomo*.

 ## ORIENTATION AND PRACTICAL INFORMATION

Messina's transportation center is **Piazza della Repubblica,** in front of the **train station,** home to two tourist offices and several bus lines. The tram leaves from the *piazza,* and ferry and speedboats run from the port right next to the station. **Via Guiseppe la Farina** runs in front of the train station. Beyond the high rises to the left, **Via Tommaso Cannizzaro** leads to the *centro,* meeting palm-lined **Viale San Martino** at **Piazza Cairoli.** At the far right end begins **Via I Settembre,** which intersects **Corso Garibaldi,** which runs along the harbor to both the hydrofoil dock and **Corso Cavour.**

> **! MIDNIGHT MESSINA.** Women should not walk alone in Messina at night, and no one should roam the streets near the train station or the harbor after 10pm. Stay near the more populated streets around the *duomo* and the university. Be wary of pick-pockets and keep money in a secure place.

Tourist Office: Provincia Regionale, V. Calabria 301 (☎67 42 71; aptmeinfoturismo@virgilio.it), immediately to the right when exiting the train station. Well staffed and very helpful, with a deluge of maps and info on Messina, the Aeolian Islands, and Reggio di Calabria. Open M-Th 9am-1:30pm and 3-5pm, F 9am-1:30pm.

Currency Exchange: Frattelli Grosso, V. Garibaldi 58 (☎77 40 83). Open M-F 8:30am-1pm and 4:30-8pm.

ATMs: Outside the train station and to the right. Also at V. Tommaso Cannizzaro 24, and **Banco di Napoli** on V. V. Emanuele facing the port.

Pharmacy: Farmacia Abate, Vle. San Martino 39 (☎63 733, for info on all pharmacies in town 71 75 89). From the train station take V. del Vespro 4 blocks and turn left. All pharmacies open M-F 8:30am-1pm and 4:30-8pm. Posts after-hours rotation.

Hospital: Ospedale Piemonte (☎22 21), on Vle. Europa. **Medical Clinic:** V. Garibaldi 242 (☎34 54 22). Open M-F 8pm-8am, Sa 10am-Su 8am.

Internet Access: Punto Internet, V. Ghibellina 87, on the small street across V. T. Cannizzaro from Libreria Nunnari e Sfameri. 4 fast computers. €0.05 per min. Open daily 9:30am-1pm and 4-8pm.

Post Office: ☎66 86 415. In P. Antonello, off C. Cavour and across from Galleria. Open M-Sa 8:30am-6:30pm. **Postal Code:** 98100.

🛏🍴 ACCOMMODATIONS AND FOOD

Messina is definitely more fly-by than stop-over, and its handful of hotels caters not to cost-conscious travelers but to deep-pocketed businessmen. Cheaper hotels are found in the neighborhood by the station, but be careful at night. If you can afford it, make your stay in Messina short, and spring for a more expensive option. From the train station walk left past the buses and under the overpass and look for the sign for **Hotel Mirage ❷,** V. Nicola Scotto 3. Providing simple rooms at an affordable price, Hotel Mirage is perfect for those passing through. All rooms have TV, fan, sink, phone, and shared bath. (☎29 38 844. Singles €28; doubles €50, triples €70.) Rooms at the older **Hotel Cairoli ❹,** Vle. San Martino 63, off P. Cairoli, have bath, A/C, TV, and phone. (☎67 37 55. Ask front desk for free breakfast coupon. Singles €45; doubles €80. MC/V.)

Restaurants and trattorie line V. Risorgimento, reached by following V. Tomaso Cannizzaro two blocks past P. Cairoli. Messina is hooked on *pesce spada* (swordfish): baked, fried, or stewed. Another specialty is *caponata*, a dish of fried eggplant, onion, capers, and olives in a red sauce. For dessert, sugary *pignolata* is a decadent treat. 🍴**Osteria Etnea ❷,** Vle. San Martino 38, three blocks east of where C. Cavour intersects with V. T. Cannizaro, serves signature pasta and fish dishes (from €5). Try the *spaghetti etnea* (€5), a house specialty that packs a delicious shrimp-and-calamari, one-two punch. (☎67 260. Cover €1. Open M-Sa 11am-3:30pm and 8-11:30pm. MC/V.) At **Osteria del Campanile ❸,** V. Loggia dei Mercanti 7-13, behind the *duomo*, locals flood sidewalk tables and the subdued dining room for *fettuccine salmonate* (€8) and other staples. (☎/fax 71 14 18. *Primi* €5.50-11, *secondi* €7-15. Cover €2. Open M-Sa noon-3pm and 7pm-midnight. AmEx/MC/V.)

👁 SIGHTS

Though Messina has lost many of its monuments to both natural and man-induced calamities, the town still features a number of great sights. Churches on the outskirts of the town offer sweeping vistas of the city and port.

PIAZZA DEL DUOMO. Trees provide a shaded, relaxing respite from the city that surrounds this central *piazza*. The great 🏛**duomo,** built in Norman times and dedicated in 1197 to the Virgin Mary, dominates the square with an enormous marble facade that can be blinding in the afternoon sun. The long nave rolls past 14 niche sculptures of saints above sweeping tile floors and arrives at a massive altar dedicated to Madonna della Lettera, the city's patron saint. A statue of Archbishop Angelo Paino to the left of the altar commemorates the tireless efforts of the man who rebuilt the *duomo* twice, first after the earthquake of 1908 and again after WWII bombing destroyed half of the church. **Il Tesoro** (The Treasury) houses the church's most valuable possessions, including gold reliquaries and candlesticks. The highlight is the ornate **Manta d'Oro** (Golden Mantle), a special cover decorated with precious stones and jewels used to drape the picture of the Madonna and Child in the church's altar. It is on display after being locked away for three centuries and emerges from the church each year for an annual festival (see **Festivals**). Plans for

the **campanile** began in the early 16th century, and at 90m, it was intended to be Sicily's highest. After being struck by lightning in 1588, restorations continued until 1933, when the tower acquired its clock. At noon, a mechanized lion lets out a few roars and a creaky recording of the *Ave Maria* booms. Below the clock tower, ancient myth and local lore meet in stone at the ▓**Fontana di Orione,** designed in 1547 by Angelo Montorsoli, a pupil of Michelangelo. The intricate fountain glorifies Orion, the mythical founder of Messina. *(Duomo open daily 7am-7pm. Treasury open Apr.-Sept. M-Sa 9am-1pm and 3:30-6:30pm; Oct.-Mar. M-Sa 9am-1pm. Duomo free. Treasury €3, under 18 €2. Campanile €3.50/2. Combined ticket for treasury and campanile €5/3.50. Guided tours of treasury in English, French, German, and Spanish.)*

MUSEO REGIONALE. A converted spinning mill houses all that was salvaged from the monastery of St. Gregory and churches throughout the city after the devastating earthquakes of 1894 and 1908. Galleries around a quiet courtyard display the development of Messina's rich artistic tradition. Among more notable pieces are *The Polyptych of the Rosary* (1473) by local master Antonello da Messina; Andrea della Robbia's terra-cotta *Virgin and Child;* and Caravaggio's life-sized *Adoration of the Shepherds* (1608) and *Resurrection of Lazarus* (1609). Just past the entrance, door panels tell the story of the Madonna della Lettera. *(Take the tram from the station or catch bus #78 or 79 from P. Duomo; look for the museum and walk around to left to find the entrance. ☎36 12 92. Open June-Sept. M and F 9am-1:30pm, Tu, Th, Sa 9am-1:30pm and 4-6:30pm, Su 9am-12:30pm; Oct.-May M and F 9am-1:30pm, Tu, Th, Sa 9am-1:30pm and 3-5pm, Su 9am-12:30pm. Last entry 30min. before closing. €4.50, EU residents 18-25 €1.50, EU residents under 18 or over 65 and students free.)*

PORT. The port is more than a place to catch a hydrofoil; Messina's history and character largely center on its former naval prowess. The enormous **La Madonnina,** a 6m golden statue, surveys the city from a 60m column across the water in the port's center. On the city side, the gleaming **Fontana di Nettuno** graces the intersection of V. Garibaldi and V. della Libertà. The muscular marble god stands triumphant over the chained, muscle-bound she-beasts, Scylla and Charybdis. The port is dangerous after dark, so make this a daytime excursion.

❋ FESTIVALS

The **Festa di Madonna della Lettera** on June 3 celebrates Messina's guardian. Parades throughout the city end at the *duomo*, where the *Manta d'Oro* is restored to the altar for one day each year. Messina overflows with approximately 150,000 white-robed pilgrims during the nationally celebrated **Ferragosto Messinese** festival on August 13-15. During the first two days of Ferragosto, two huge human effigies called Mata and Grifone zoom around the city in the *Processione dei Gianti*.

TAORMINA ☎ 0942

Legend has it that Neptune wrecked a Greek boat off the eastern coast of Sicily in the 8th century BC and that the sole survivor, inspired by the spectacular scenery, founded Taormina (tah-or-MEE-na; pop. 10,000). Historians tell a different tale: the Carthaginians founded Tauromenium in the 4th century BC, only to have it wrested away by the Greek tyrant Dionysius. Disputed origins aside, Taormina's beauty is uncontested, with pines and mansions crowning a cliff above the sea. Disoriented, fanny-packed foreigners, hearty backpackers, and elite VIPs all come for a glimpse of what millions of photographic flashes and hyperbolic statements can't seem to dull—a vista that sweeps from boiling Etna to the straits of Messina.

▐ TRANSPORTATION

Taormina is accessible by bus from Messina or Catania. Although trains from Catania and Messina are more frequent than buses, the train station lies 5km below Taormina, next to neighboring Giardini-Naxos. Buses run from the train station to Taormina (every 30min. 7:35am-11pm, more frequently in summer) and Giardini-Naxos (7:50am-11:20pm, more frequently in summer).

Trains: (☎89 20 21). To **Catania** (50min., 35 per day 1:19am-10:36pm, €3.05), **Messina** (1hr., 25 per day 4am-11:32pm, €3.05), and **Syracuse** (2hr., 11 per day 4:20am-8:12pm, €9.70).

Buses: Interbus (☎62 53 01). Ticket office off C. Umberto I, at the end of V. L. Pirandello (open daily 6:20am-11:45pm). To **Catania** (M-Sa 16 per day 6:30am-8:45pm, Su 12 per day 8:45am-6pm; €4.20, round-trip €6.70) and **Messina** (M-Sa 5 per day 6:20am-5:40pm, Su 3 per day 8:50am-6pm; €3, round-trip €5.20). Same bus runs to **Giardini-Naxos** and **train station** (dir.: Recanti or Catania; M-F every 30min. 6:50am-midnight; €1.20, round-trip €2.20), **Gole Alcantara** (M-Sa 4 per day 9:15am-4:45pm, Su 9:15am; €2.50, round-trip €4.70), and **Isola Bella, Mazzaro,** and **Spisone** (M-Sa 14 per day 6:30am-7:40pm, Su 4 per day 8:40am-5:40pm; €1.50, round-trip €2.20). Pick up a helpful paper schedule at the Taormina bus terminal.

Taxis (☎23 000 or 23 800) run from the train station to downtown Taormina for €15. Within the city, don't pay more than €7. €3 surcharge 10pm-6am.

Car and Scooter Rental: Cundari Rent, Vle. Apollo Arcageta 12 (☎24 700), around corner from post office at the end of C. Umberto I. Scooters €15-40 per day. 21+. Cars available through **Budget Rent a Car.** Prices vary according to season and model. 21+. Gas extra. Open M-Sa 8:30am-1pm and 4-8pm, Su 8:30am-1pm.

✶ ▐ ORIENTATION AND PRACTICAL INFORMATION

To reach the city from the **train station,** hop on the blue Interbus that makes the trip uphill (10min., every 30min. 5am-11pm, €1.30). Cars are not allowed on Taormina's steep, narrow streets; automobiles can park in a small lot at the base of **Via Luigi Pirandello.** From the bus depot, a short walk left on V. L. Pirandello leads to the town's main street, **Corso Umberto I.** Beginning under a stone archway, the boutique-lined road runs left through four principal *piazze:* **Piazza Vittorio Emanuele II, Piazza IX Aprile, Piazza Duomo,** and **Piazza Sant'Antonio.** Small stairways and side streets wind downhill to a variety of more affordable restaurants, shops, and bars. Accurate and detailed maps are also posted on high brown signs throughout the city.

Tourist Office: AAST (☎23 243; www.gate2taormina.com), in the courtyard of Palazzo Corvaja, off C. Umberto I across from P. Vittorio Emanuele II. Friendly staff provides helpful pamphlets and a basic map. Visitors might also want to pick up the turquoise brochure "SAT Sicilian Airbus Travel." Open M-F 8am-2:30pm and 4-7pm.

Tours: CST, C. Umberto I 99-101, 1st fl. (☎62 60 88; csttao@tiscalinet.it), offers *Etna Tramonto,* a sunset trip up the volcano (June-Oct. F 4pm; €69) and runs tours to 3000m (June-Aug. M and W 3:45pm, Sept. 3:15pm, Oct. 2:15pm; €55) and to 2000m (year-round Tu and Th 8am; €25). AmEx/MC/V. **SAT,** C. Umberto I 73 (☎24 653; www.sat-group.it), operates day-long tours to Mt. Etna from €21.

Currency Exchange: Dozens of banks and **ATMs** line C. Umberto I and V. L. Pirandello, as do many currency exchange offices, including **Rocco Frisono,** C. Umberto I 224 (☎24 806), between P. Sant'Antonio and P. Duomo. Open M-Sa 9am-1pm and 4-8pm.

American Express: La Duca Viaggi, V. Don Bosco 39, 2nd fl. (☎62 52 55), in P. IX Aprile. Mail held. Open M-F Apr.-Oct. 9am-1pm and 4-7:30pm; Nov.-Mar. 9am-1pm and 2-6pm.

International Newsstand: Mr. Frank, C. Umberto I 9 (☎62 61 82). *International Herald Tribune, USA Today, Wall Street Journal,* and *Daily Mail,* as well as a small rack of English-language paperbacks (about €12). Open daily 8am-1pm and 4-8pm.

Emergency: ☎61 11 11. **Police:** ☎23 232. **First aid:** ☎62 54 19 or 57 92 97.

Pharmacy: Farmacia Ragusa, P. Duomo 9 (☎23 23). Open M-Tu and Th-Su 8:30am-1pm and 5-8:30pm. Posts after-hours rotations. AmEx/MC/V.

Hospital: Ospedale San Vincenzo (☎57 91), in P. San Vincenzo.

Internet Access: Service for Telecommunications, C. Umberto I 214 (☎62 88 39). 7 fast computers. **Western Union.** €2 per 20min., €5 per hr. Open daily Apr.-Sept. 9am-9pm; Oct.-Mar. 9am-1pm and 4-8pm. Cash only.

Post Office: ☎73 230. In P. Sant'Antonio at the very top of C. Umberto I. Cashes traveler's checks. Open M-Sa 8am-6:30pm. **Postal Code:** 98039.

▟ ACCOMMODATIONS

Taormina's popularity as a resort town makes cheap accommodations difficult to find. Those on a tight budget should consider staying in the hostel, or in nearby Mazzarò, Spisone, or Giardini-Naxos. Hike down steep trails to Mazzarò and Spisone or take the bus or cable cars; service stops around 1:30am.

▨ **Taormina's Odyssey Youth Hostel,** Traversa A di V. Galiano Martino 2 (☎24 533). A 15min. walk from the intersection of C. Umberto I and V. L. Pirandello. Take V. C. Patrizio to V. Cappuccini. When it forks, turn right onto V. Fontana Vecchia. Follow signs depicting a Greek ship. Renowned among backpackers. Friendly English-speaking employees, clean rooms, lockers, and a great price. 20 dorm-style beds. Kitchen open 10am-9pm. Breakfast included. Towel rental €2. Luggage storage €1. Reservations recommended. Dorms €18; 1 double €60. Cash only. ❶

La Campanella, V. Circonvallazione 3 (☎23 381; fax 62 52 48). Facing the archway at the intersection of C. Umberto I and V. L. Pirandello, turn left up V. Circonvallazione, and look for the "La Campanella" sign pointing up 3 flights of stairs. Stunning views from the breakfast salon and upper terrace compensate for the sparsely decorated rooms. Breakfast included. Singles €65; doubles €80. Cash only. ❺

Hotel Villa Nettuno, V. L. Pirandello 33 (☎23 797; www.hotelvillanettuno.it). Walk up stone steps toward the hotel's sign. Charming inn, complete with parlor and beautiful garden. All rooms with views and bath; some with A/C. Breakfast €4. Reservations recommended. Singles €40; doubles €74. Extra bed €16. Cash only. ❸

Pensione Svizzera, V. L. Pirandello 26 (☎23 790; www.pensionesvizzera.com), 3min. from the bus station. Luxury at a price worth every euro. Palm-laden patio and terrace. A/C, bath, and TV. Breakfast included. Internet access €6 per 30min., €18 per day. Reservations recommended May-Sept. Closed Jan. 10-Feb. 20. Singles €95; doubles €100; triples €135; quads €150. AmEx/MC/V. ❺

Inn Piero, V. L. Pirandello 20 (☎23 139; www.hotelinnpiero.com). Near base of C. Umberto I. Piero offers affordable rooms in a great location, all with bath and fan. Breakfast included. Reservations recommended. Singles €50; doubles €70. Student discount 10%, except in Aug. AmEx/MC/V. ❹

🗲 FOOD

Taormina's restaurants are of consistently high quality; prices tend to vary, though, so shop around. An **SMA** supermarket, V. Apollo Arcageta 21, is at the end of C. Umberto I, near the post office. (Open M-Sa 8am-9:30pm, Su 8:30-1pm.)

▨ **La Cisterna del Moro,** V. Bonifacio 1 (☎23 001), off C. Umberto I near P. IX Aprile. This pizzeria/restaurant serves incredible food on a secluded terrace. The pizza (€5-8.50) will leave you full while the view will keep you long after dessert. Try the *stuzzichini caserecci* (€10), an *antipasto* plate of vegetables, meats, and cheese. Cover €1.50. Open daily noon-3pm and 7pm-midnight, closes later in summer. AmEx/MC/V. ❷

Pigghia e Potta, V. Giovanni di Giovanni 23 (☎62 62 86), off P. V. Emanuele II. This brightly decorated and friendly hole-in-the-wall restaurant serves tasty and cheap food on the go. Pizza €2. Pasta €5. Open daily 11am-midnight. Cash only. ❶

Bella Blu, V. L. Pirandello 28 (☎24 239). One of the city's most unique views: cable cars glide down the mountain between clusters of cypress trees. Pizza and drink €7.50. *Primi* €4.50-10, *secondi* €6.50-11. Cover €1.50. Open daily 11am-5pm and 6-11pm. AmEx/MC/V. ❷

L'Arco dei Cappucini, V. Cappucini 1 (☎24 89 3), just up the hill from the intersection of C. Umberto I and V. L. Pirandello. The freshest seafood in Taormina. Don't miss the eggplant parmesan *antipasto* (€8). *Primi* €6-9, *secondi* €13-16. Cover €2. Open M-Tu and Th-Su 7:30pm-11:30pm. Call ahead to reserve an outdoor table. AmEx/MC/V. ❹

◆TIP◆ EAT SHELLFISH WITHOUT SHELLING OUT. For fresh yet cheap seafood, consider taking a short excursion outside the city. In nearby Forza D'Agro, a small hillside town 15km from Taormina, locals enjoy excellent fare for a fraction of the price. Though buses stop running early in the evening, a rental scooter or car will get you up the hill and back in under 45min. Ask for directions in the tourist office or at any hotel.

🗲 SIGHTS

From P. V. Emanuele II, walk up V. Teatro Greco to Taormina's best treasure: the well-preserved **Greek theater.** Although originally constructed by the Greeks in the

3rd century BC, it was rebuilt and enlarged by Romans in the AD 2nd century. It offers an unsurpassed view of Etna, whose sultry smoke and occasional eruptions rival even the greatest Sophoclean tragedies. In ancient times, the cliff-side arena seated 5000 spectators; that same number packs in for the summer-long festivals every year. (☎62 06 66. Open daily May-Aug. 9am-7pm; Apr. and Sept. 9am-6:30pm; Oct. and Mar. 9am-5pm; Nov.-Feb. 9am-4pm. €6, EU residents 18-25 €3, EU residents under 18 or over 65 free.) From P. V. Emanuele II, take C. Umberto I to reach the **duomo.** This 13th-century structure, rebuilt during the Renaissance, takes center stage in Taormina today. The Gothic interior shelters paintings by Messinese artists and a statue of the Virgin Mary. A two-legged female centaur, Taormina's mascot, crowns the fountain out front. (Hours vary; inquire at Museo Sacra next door.) Behind the tourist office, the **Chiesa di Santa Caterina** protects a small theater, the Roman **Odeon.** The short walk down V. Giovanni di Giovanni leads to Taormina's public gardens, the **Villa Comunale.** Filled with people relaxing under palms during summer's greatest heat, the gardens look out over Giardini-Naxos below and Etna in the distance. V. Circonvallazione leads away from the crowds to a small stairway that snakes up the mountainside to the **Piccolo Castello.** The **Galleria Gagliardi,** C. Umberto I 187a, debuts the latest in art. Exhibits change every 15 days. (☎62 89 02. Open daily 10am-1pm and 5-10pm.)

♫ ♪ ENTERTAINMENT AND BEACHES

In summer Taormina stays up late, as the beautiful people parade around and visit the chic bars along C. Umberto I well past midnight. Don't miss **Deja Vu,** P. Garibaldi 2, behind the post office. This exotic bar's mixed drinks (from €8) and Turkish coffee (€5-6) seduce partygoers both indoors and out. (☎62 86 94. Open Tu-Su 5pm-3am. MC/V.) **Re di Bastoni,** C. Umberto I 120, has a classy, laid-back vibe that goes well with live jazz on Friday and Sunday nights. (☎23 037; www.redibastoni.it. Open July-Aug. daily 11am-2am; closed Sept.-June M. AmEx/MC/V). **Tutti Ccà,** V. Fratelli Ingegneri 12, is right off C. Umberto I. Relax on the stairs outside, or head into the bar for an extensive list of alcohol (from €4) and a kitchen serving local specialties from €8. (Open Mar.-Oct. M and W-Su noon-3am. Cash only.)

Every summer brings ◨**Taormina Arte,** a theater, ballet, music, and film extravaganza with performances from June to August. Performances, held in the Greek Theater, have featured Bob Dylan and Ray Charles. (Box office in P. V. Emanuele II. ☎62 87 30; www.taormina-arte.com.) Cable cars take a breezy ride along the *funivia* from V. L. Pirandello to the beach. (☎23 605. Every 15min. M 8am-1:30pm, Tu-Su 8am-1:30am; €1.80, round-trip €3.) At the popular **Lido Mazzarò,** lounge-chair rentals (€7.50) from Lido La Pigna include shower, parasol and changing area—or just enjoy the view while drinking a coffee on the terrace upstairs. Five minutes to the right, there is a beautiful beach where sparkling waters surround the ◨**Isola Bella,** a nature preserve 100m offshore.

◨ DAYTRIP FROM TAORMINA: GIARDINI-NAXOS

Now the eastern coast's ultimate beach town and a watering hole for throngs of tourists, Giardini-Naxos (JAR-dee-nee NAX-ohs; pop. 9200) was the first Greek colony in Sicily in 734 BC. Excavations in the 60s unearthed traces of a Greek city built of lava blocks, founded in the shadow of the volcano. Visit the traces of the fortress, now overgrown with wildflowers, to escape the city. The nearby Museo Archeologico records the ancient city's earliest days and includes an inscribed ceramic cup, the colony's earliest surviving writing. (☎51 001. Open daily 9am-1hr.

before sunset. €2, ages 18-25 €1, EU citizens under 18 or over 65 free.) While there are some public beaches, private beaches provide umbrellas (€2), lounge chairs (€4), and cabanas (€8) and are much less crowded. Restaurants crowd the *lungomare* and offer sunbathers lots of pricey options. Consider heading off the beach for more budget options. Buy necessities at Sigma supermarket, V. Casarsa 15. Look for sign on V. Dalmazia, just off V. Naxos. (Open M-Sa 8:30am-1:30pm and 4:30-9pm, Su 8:30am-1pm.) Five kilometers from Taormina, Giardini-Naxos shares a train station with its neighbor. Interbus runs from Giardini to the train station and Taormina's bus station. (☎62 53 01. 40 per day 7:35am-11:35pm, €1.30.)

CATANIA   ☎095

Catania (ca-TA-nee-ya; pop. 500,000) is a modern transport hub that hasn't forgotten its ancient roots. From the stately grace of its *piazze* to the ancient history of Greek and Roman remains, the city merges tradition with youthful revelry, as university students funnel into its numerous cafes and bars. Leveled repeatedly, sometimes by invaders but mostly by nearby Mt. Etna, Catania has been rebuilt often since its founding in 729 BC. After the monstrous 1693 earthquake, Giovanni Battista Vaccarini recreated the city with his Baroque *piazze* and *duomo*.

▐ TRANSPORTATION

Flights: Fontanarossa (CTA), C. Sicilia 71 (☎34 05 05 or 800 60 56 56). Take Alibus #457 from the train station; purchase bus tickets in kiosk outside station or in *tabaccherie*. The 15min. cab ride to the airport costs about €20. 1 flight daily to Malta with **Air Malta** (☎34 53 11).

Trains: ☎53 27 19. In P. Papa Giovanni XXIII. To: **Agrigento** (3¼hr., 4 per day 5:45am-7:15pm, €10); **Enna** (1½hr., 7 per day 5:45am-7:15pm, €5); **Messina** (2hr., 28 per day 5:15am-8:50pm, €5.20); **Palermo** (3½hr., 3 per day 10:45am-7:15pm, €11.25); **Rome** (10hr., 6 per day 9:10am-10:50pm, €47); **Syracuse** (1½hr., 15 per day 5:10am-9pm, €5); **Taormina/Giardini-Naxos** (1hr., 39 per day 3:15am-8:50pm, €4).

Buses: All companies are on V. D'Amico, across the city-bus-filled *piazza* in front of the train station. Because service is significantly reduced on Su, weekend travelers may wish to take a train instead. Info office inside the train station.

SAIS Trasporti (☎53 62 01) to **Agrigento** (3hr., 22 per day 6:30am-9pm, €11) and **Rome** (14hr.; 8pm, 9:15pm via Naples; €45).

SAIS Autolinee (☎53 61 68) to **Enna** (1½hr.; M-Sa 8 per day 6:40am-8pm, Su 3 per day 9am-8pm; €6.40), **Messina** (1½hr.; M-Sa 25 per day 5:15am-8:30pm, Su 6 per day 7am-8:30pm; €6.70), and **Palermo** (3hr., 16 per day 5am-8pm, €12.50).

Interbus and **Etna** (☎53 27 16) both run to: **Brindisi** (8hr.; 10:30am, 10pm; €38.50); **Noto** (2½hr.; 2, 5:45, 7:15pm; €6.10); **Ragusa** (2hr., 10 per day 6am-8pm, €6.10); **Taormina/Giardini-Naxos** (1hr., 12 per day 7:15am-10pm, €4.20).

Ferries: La Duca Viaggi, P. Europa 1 (☎72 22 295). From train station, up Vle. Africa. To **Malta** (€85.22). Open M-F 9am-1pm and 4-7:30pm, Sa 9am-noon. **Traghetti Caronte** (☎53 77 97) to **Salerno** (daily 11:45pm). **Traghetti TTTLines** (☎28 13 88) to **Naples** (M-F 9:30pm, Sa-Su 7:30pm).

Public Transportation: AMT buses leave from train station in P. Papa Giovanni XXIII. **Alibus #27** to the beach. Tickets (€0.80; valid 1½hr.) are sold at the kiosk outside station and in *tabaccherie*.

Scooter Rental: Hollywood Rent by Motoservice, P. Cavour 12 (☎44 27 20). Scooter and cars €31 per day. 21+. AmEx/MC/V.

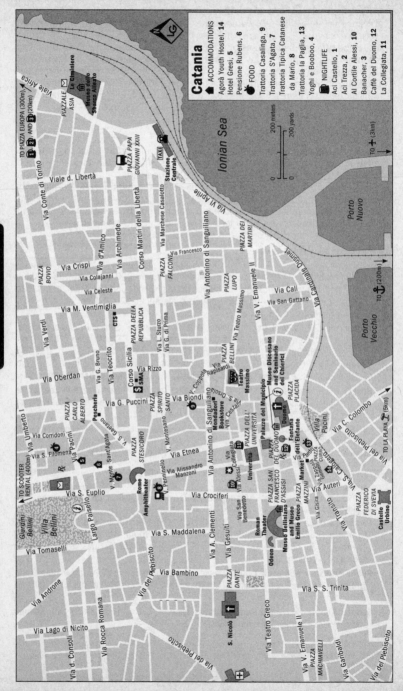

Catania

▲ **ACCOMMODATIONS**
Agorà Youth Hostel, 14
Hotel Gresi, 5
Pensione Rubens, 6

🍴 **FOOD**
Trattoria Casalinga, 9
Trattoria S'Agata, 7
Trattoria Tipica Catanese
  da Mario, 8
Trattoria la Paglia, 13
Yoghi e Booboo, 4

🎭 **NIGHTLIFE**
Aci Castello, 1
Aci Trezza, 2
Al Cortile Alessi, 10
Banacher, 3
Caffè del Duomo, 12
La Collegiata, 11

Ionian Sea

200 meters
200 yards

Porto Nuovo

Porto Vecchio

▄ 🔢 ORIENTATION AND PRACTICAL INFORMATION

Via Etnea, running from the *duomo* to the **Giardini Bellini,** is Catania's main street. Several main thoroughfares run perpendicular to V. Etnea from the waterfront. From north to south, these are **Via Umberto I,** which runs from **Piazza Galatea** on the water to **Villa Bellini** (Bellini Gardens); **Corso Martiri della Libertà,** which runs from the bus and train stations at **Piazza Papa Giovanni XXIII** before becoming **Corso Sicilia** at **Piazza della Repubblica** and bisecting V. Etnea at **Piazza Stesicoro; Via Antonino di Sangiuliano,** which runs past **Piazza Bellini** and the **Teatro Massimo** (Teatro Bellini); and **Via Vittorio Emanuele II,** which leads straight from the water to **Piazza Duomo.**

> ❗ **STREET SMARTS.** As with any city, travelers to Catania should be careful of petty thievery. Know where your things are at all times, don't walk around with a map glued to your face, and be wary of manufactured distractions. At night, stick to the populated and well-lit areas along V. Etnea and other main avenues.

Tourist Offices: Municipal Tourist Office, V. V. Emanuele II 172 (☎ 74 25 573 or 800 84 10 42). English-speaking staff provides maps, self-guided tours in English, theater schedules, and other useful info. Open M-F 8:15am-7pm. **AAPIT,** V. Cimarosa 10 (☎ 73 06 279 or 73 06 222), near the Giardini Bellini. From V. Etnea, turn on V. Pacini before the post office, and follow signs. Open M-F 8am-8pm, Sa-Su 8am-2pm. Branches at train station (☎ 73 06 255), V. Etnea 63 (☎ 31 17 78 or 73 06 233), and airport (☎ 73 06 266 or 73 06 277). Same hours as main office.

Tours: Acquaterra, V. Antonino Longo 74 (☎ 50 30 20; www.acquaterra.com). Company picks up clients from hotels in town and runs Jeep excursions up Mt. Etna. From €30.

Budget Travel: CTS, V. Monsignore Ventimiglia 153 (☎ 53 02 23; fax 53 62 46), off P. della Repubblica. Useful info on travel in Sicily, Italy, and beyond. Open M-F 9:30am-1pm and 4:30-7:30pm, Sa 9:30am-12:30pm.

American Express: La Duca Viaggi, P. Europa 1 (☎ 72 22 295), up Vle. Africa from train station. Mail held for 1 month. Open M-F 9am-1pm and 4-7:30pm, Sa 9am-12:30pm.

Luggage Storage: In train station. €3 per 12hr. Open daily 8am-8pm.

English-Language Bookstore: Libreria Mondadori, V. Antonino di Sangiuliano 223/225 (☎ 31 51 60), just down from Teatro Bellini. Brand-new branch of this national chain offers a selection of English titles and an in-store cafe. Open M and Sa 5pm-2am, Tu-F and Su 9am-2am.

Ambulance: ☎ 37 71 22. **Police:** ☎ 53 13 33.

Pharmacy: Crocerossa, V. Etnea 274 (☎ 31 70 53). **Croceverde,** V. Gabriele D'Annunzio 43 (☎ 44 16 62), at the intersection of C. Italia and C. della Provincia. Both open daily 8:30am-1pm and 4:30-8pm. AmEx/MC/V.

Hospital: Ospedale Garibaldi (☎ 75 91 111), in P. Santa Maria del Gesù. **Medical Clinic,** C. Italia 234 (☎ 37 71 22).

Internet Access: Internetteria, V. Penninello 44 (☎ 31 01 39). Hip young staff serve cappuccino, sandwiches, and couscous in a funky interior with cool music and 12 computers. Wi-Fi and Internet access €1 per 30min. Food €2-6. Open M-Sa 10am-midnight, Su hours vary.

Post Office: V. Etnea 215 (☎ 71 55 111), in the big building next to Giardini Bellini. Open M-F 8am-6:30pm, Sa 8am-12:30pm. **Postal Code:** 95125.

▌ ACCOMMODATIONS

A plethora of posh stores lining the streets suggests high hotel prices, but many *pensione* near V. Etnea are affordable. Reserve early for summer.

▨ **Agorà Youth Hostel,** P. Curro 6 (☎ 72 33 010; www.agorahostel.com). From the train station follow V. Dusmet until you pass the park (Villa Pacini), then walk uphill on V. Pardo until you reach P. Curro. Though loud music from the in-house bar, the nearby train tracks, and stuffy dorms make this place a bad choice for light sleepers, social types will enjoy the community atmosphere and central location. On-site grotto restaurant and underground wine bar serve food (*piatto unico*—all-in-one course—and drink; €5) and drinks (Happy hour 5-10pm; 2-for-1 mixed drinks and beer). Breakfast included. Towels €2. Laundry €4. Internet access €3 per hr. Sept.-July dorms €18; Aug. €20. Cash only. ❶

▨ **Hotel Gresi,** V. Pacini 28 (☎ 32 27 09; www.gresihotel.com), off V. Etnea before Villa Bellini and post office. Decorated hallways lead to an inviting salon, breakfast room, and spacious social bar. Spotless rooms with gorgeously painted ceilings all have bath, A/C, TV, and phone. Breakfast €5. Singles €50; doubles €80. AmEx/MC/V. ❹

Pensione Rubens, V. Etnea 196, 3rd fl. (☎ 31 70 73; fax 71 51 713). Amicable owners and attractive, well-kept rooms make this a comforting home away from home. All rooms have fridge, A/C, TV, and phone. Reservations recommended. Singles €60; doubles €80; triples €100; quads €120. AmEx/MC/V. ❹

▣ FOOD

When *catanesi* gather at the table, chances are they'll be dining on local favorites like eggplant- and ricotta-topped *spaghetti alla norma*, named for Bellini's famous opera. Another hit is the fresh *masculini*, or anchovies, rumored to be aphrodisiacs. The **market** off P. del Duomo and V. Garibaldi, features vendors with fish, fruit, and sweets. (M-Sa morning and early afternoon.) An **SMA** supermarket is at C. Sicilia 50. (☎ 32 60 699. Open M-Sa 8:30am-8:30pm.) **Bar Savia,** V. Etnea 304, across from Bellini Gardens, serves the best *granite di gelsi* (mulberry iced drinks; €1.60) in town. (Open M-Sa 8am-9:30pm.) Perhaps the best deal, however, is the *arancino*—a filling meat-stuffed fried rice ball, available for €1.30 at any bar with a sign reading "*tavola calda.*"

▨ **Trattoria la Paglia,** V. Pardo 23 (☎ 34 68 38), near P. Duomo. Brings the marketplace bustle indoors. This popular stop makes every effort to pack its customers in, so don't be surprised if you're sharing a table with strangers. Those tired of tomatoes can trade red sauce for black with *spaghetti al nero di seppia* (with squid ink; €4.65). *Primi* €4-9, *secondi* €6.50-12. Cover €1. Open M-Sa 10am-midnight. AmEx/MC/V. ❷

▨ **Trattoria Casalinga,** V. Biondi 19 (☎ 31 13 19). Popular with locals, theater-goers, and *casalinghe* (housewives), this little restaurant serves up traditional Italian *primi* (€6-8) and *secondi* (€8-12) on outdoor streetside tables. Cover €1.50. Open M-Sa noon-4pm and 8pm-midnight. MC/V. ❸

Trattoria S'Agata, V. Monte Sant'Agata 11-13 (☎ 31 54 53), off V. Etnea, just north of P. Stesicoro. Catanese charm accompanies risotto and other specialties listed on multi-language menus. *Primi* and *secondi* €7-8. Cover €2. Open in summer daily 11:30am-12:30am. AmEx/MC/V. ❸

Trattoria Tipica Catanese da Mario, V. Penninello 34 (☎ 32 24 61; www.catani-acity.com/trattoriamario), off V. Etnea near the amphitheater. Fish is the specialty at this family-run restaurant. Outdoor dining in summer. *Primi* €5-10, *secondi* €6-9. Cover €1.50. Open M-Sa 12:30-3pm and 6:30pm-midnight. MC/V. ❷

Yoghi e Booboo, V. Santa Filomena 48 (☎ 32 14 30; www.yoghiebooboo.it). The undisputed (if largely unchallenged) champion of Tex-Mex cuisine in Catania. If you're feeling more East than West, go for the sushi (€13). Pizza €6-8.50. Meal-sized salads €8.50-9. Entrees €12-18.50. Open daily 8pm-12:30am. AmEx/MC/V. ❸

◎ SIGHTS

PIAZZA DUOMO. Giovanni Battista Vaccarini's little lava ◪**Fontana dell'Elefante** (1736), commands the city's attention. Vaccarini carved his elephant (the symbol of the city) without visible testicles. When the statue was unveiled, horrified *catanesi* men, who construed from this omission an attack on their virility, demanded corrective measures. Vaccarini's acquiescence was, well, monumental. Residents claim that visitors may attain citizenship by smooching the elephant's nether regions, but the height of the pachyderm's backside precludes the fulfillment of such aspirations. Other buildings on the *piazza*, including the 18th-century Palazzo del Municipio on the left and the former Seminario dei Chierici on the right, are striped black and white to mirror the *duomo*'s side. Visit the **Museo Diocesano,** V. Etnea 8, next to the *duomo*, to see priestly vestments several centuries old. The 1950 restoration of the **duomo** revealed its interior predating the Baroque makeover. Restorators discovered stumps of columns and pointed arches of the original apses. The walls of the Norman **Cappella della Madonna** on the *duomo*'s right side surround a 15th-century statue of the Virgin Mary. The body of Catania's beloved priest, the Beato Cardinal Dusmet, lies nearby, his head and bony fingers protruding from his vestments. To the right of the main door is Bellini's tomb, guarded by a marble angel. The words and music from his *Sonnambula* are inscribed above the tomb and translate as "Ah, I didn't think I'd see you wilt so soon, flower." (☎ 28 16 35. Open M-Sa 9am-noon and 4-6pm, Su by appointment. Modest dress required. Free.)

GIARDINI BELLINI AND ENVIRONS. The centerpiece of Catania's restoration efforts sits on V. Etnea and is marked by a fountain and crooked cyprus trees. These gardens sprawl over small hills and around tiny ponds. Sunday afternoons half the city strolls here, *gelato* in hand. Below a Victorian bandstand, a plot displays the day's date in perfect grass figures, replanted daily. A few blocks away in P. Stesicoro, modern streets cradle a sunken pit holding ruins of a 2nd-century **Roman amphitheater,** with visible tunnels that gladiators used to enter the arena. Uphill from P. Duomo, at V. V. Emanuele 260, lies the entrance to the **Roman Theater,** built in the 2nd century on the grounds of an earlier Greek theater. Its passageways, lined with the remains of marble columns, spill out into the similar but smaller Odeon, with another entrance around the back. Mt. Etna's 1669 eruption coated the marble of both theaters with lava. (☎ 71 50 508. Open daily 9am-1:30pm and 3-7pm. €3, EU residents 18-25 €2, under 18 and over 65 free.)

LE CIMINIERE AND MUSEO STORICO. Near the train station on Vle. Africa, **Le Ciminiere,** a rescued factory complex has been restored as a cultural center with free art exhibits, concerts, and a cinema museum. In addition, the ◪**Museo Storico dello Sbarco Alleato in Sicilia-Estate 1943** (Historical Museum of the Allied Landing in Sicily—Summer 1943), Ple. Asia, skillfully showcases an oft-ignored aspect of WWII. Exhibits highlight the Allied bombing and subsequent invasion of Sicily by American, British, Canadian, and Australian troops, an event which immediately preceded the defeat of Mussolini and the end of the war with Italy. The museum depicts a typical Sicilian city square before and after bombing, as well as Axis and Allied propaganda. Also included are Italian postcards of various saints blessing the fascist troops marching under the fascist banner. (☎ 53 35 40. Open Tu-W 9:30am-12:30pm and 3-5pm, Th-Su 9:30am-12:30pm. €4, under 17 and over 65 €1).

BEACHES. The crowded **La Playa** offers a charming view of a nearby power plant. (Take bus *linea D Est*, which runs June-Sept.) Farther from the port is the more rugged **La Scogliera,** with fiery cliffs and a bathing area. (Take bus #534 or #535 from P. Borsellino; 30min.)

🎵 ENTERTAINMENT

From January to June, the **Teatro Massimo (Bellini),** V. Perrotta 12, off V. Antonino di Sanguiliano, mesmerizes audiences with its sumptuous setting during opera season. (☎71 50 921. Student discounts available for all tickets; contact tourist office. Tours in Italian available upon request. Box office open M-F 9:30am-12:30pm.) During cooler months, *catanesi* love their nightly *passeggiata* (stroll), circulating P. Duomo and near Teatro Bellini. Cafes pulsate with life on weekends, drawing a sometimes raucous crowd. Local university students and urban 30-somethings frequent local watering holes. In the late evening, university young-sters swarm the streets around P. Duomo. Catania's biggest feast day honors the city's patron, **Sant'Agata.** Fireworks and non-stop partying in the first five days of February salvage the city from winter gloom. In the summer, most *catanesi* leave town. Summer crowds typically scooter 20min. away to **Banacher** or **Aci Castello** and nearby **Aci Trezza,** nearly identical nightlife hubs with a variety of expensive bars and pretty seaside views. AAPIT's free monthly bulletin *Lapis*, available at the tourist office and in bars, details Catania's nightlife, concerts, and festivals.

La Collegiata, near P. dell'Università. A co-ed favorite, with live music and large crowds. Open daily 7pm-4am.

Al Cortile Alessi, V. Alessi 30, offers courtyard dining under swaying nespola trees and a welcome respite from the busy streets and buzzing nightlife nearby. Open Tu-Su 8pm-late. AmEx/MC/V.

Caffè del Duomo, (☎71 50 556), across from the elephant fountain. Offers *gelato* and coffee for a low-key night in Catania's main *piazza*. Open daily 5:30am-3am.

Banacher, V. XXI Aprile-S.S. 114 (☎27 12 57), a 15min. taxi ride from Catania's *centro*. Lights keep dancing crowds captive until the wee hours at what is reputed to be Europe's largest outdoor disco. Cover €10. Open Tu-Su 10pm-3am.

🔁 DAYTRIP FROM CATANIA

⛰ MOUNT ETNA

An 🚌 *AST bus leaves from Catania's central train station at 8:15am for a 2hr. ride to Rifugio Sapienza. The bus leaves Etna at 4:30pm (times subject to change; round-trip €5). Tours to Mt. Etna depart daily from Catania (p. 683) and Taormina (p. 679).*

Mount Etna's lava-seared wilderness is one of Italy's most compelling natural settings. Etna's history of volcanic activity is the longest documented of any volcano—the first recorded eruption was in 1500 BC, though it was probably active long before that. Also Europe's tallest active volcano (3350m), it has long held sway over the residents of eastern Sicily: the Greek poet Hesiod envisioned Etna as the home of Typhon, the last monster conceived by Earth to fight the gods before the dawn of the human race. The ancients also claimed its fires were the home of Vulcan, the blacksmith god. Apparently Typhon's aggressions aren't over yet: a 1985 eruption destroyed much of the summit tourist station, and eruptions in 2001 and 2002 sent lava rolling down slopes at

160km per hr. The most recent major eruptions occurred in the fall and winter of 2002-2003 and formed two new craters near the volcano's peak.

From parking lot at Rifugio Sapienza (1900m) where the AST bus stops, you can either take a 3hr. hike to the aptly named **Torre del Filosofo** (Philosopher's Tower; 2920m) or take the cable car and an off-road shuttle for €48 (includes a guided tour of the nearby craters; cable car and guided tour only, €25). Anyone with sturdy shoes can take a 30min. jaunt to explore the crater in front of the parking area. From the Philosopher's Tower, a 2hr. hike leads to the **craters** themselves. **Valle del Bove**, Etna's first volcanic crater, is on the way down. While the view of the hardened lava, huge boulders, and unearthly craters is incredible, the trail is so difficult and the volcanic activity so unpredictable that sightseers are allowed access only by guided tour. On a certified **tour**, hikers can hold molten rocks heated by subterranean activity or watch guides burn newspapers on exposed rifts in the rock. Those who brave the trip should take precautions: carry water and bring warm clothing, as winds are ferocious and pockets of snow linger even in mid-July. Windbreakers and hiking boots can be rented at the top of the cable car for €2 each.

DON'T BE A HERO. The trek up Mt. Etna is not for the faint of heart (or the faint of breath). Since you have 6hr. until the bus returns to Catania, you can take your time scaling the volcano. If you decide to bypass the hike for the comforts of the cable car, it's worth it to pay the extra €24 for the shuttle to the *Torre del Filosofo*. The hike to the towers is both steep and dusty, the latter due to passing shuttles.

CENTRAL SICILY

PIAZZA ARMERINA ☎0935

Perched in the Erei Mountains, the medieval city of Piazza Armerina (pee-YAT-sa ar-meh-REE-na; pop. 21,000) shows few signs of time's passing. Traditional Sicilian music still echoes from the green *duomo*, and the rhymes of the singing fruit-truck drivers resonate through town at mid-day. Locals are friendly and eager to welcome tourists into their peaceful town—over 30 new B&Bs have opened in the last two years alone. Many streets are little more than twisting stone staircases, but the foothills below contain the city's real attraction: the famed Villa Romana del Casale and its remarkably intact ancient mosaics, which are among the largest and most beautiful in the world.

⬛⁊ TRANSPORTATION AND PRACTICAL INFORMATION. Buses run to Piazza Armerina from Caltanissetta (1hr., 5 per day 6am-4:05pm, €4.65); Catania (1¾hr., 6 per day 7:45am-3:30pm, €7.40); Enna (35min., 8 per day 5:45am-5:10pm, €2.75); Syracuse (3½hr., M-Sa 1pm, €7.75). Buses arrive at the city's northern end in **Piazza Senatore Marescalchi.** Facing away from the Interbus office, walk two short blocks before turning left on **Via D'Annunzio,** which quickly becomes **Via Chiaranda,** then **Via Mazzini,** and finally arrives at **Piazza Garibaldi,** the *centro storico.* The **tourist office,** P. Rosalia 1, is in the courtyard of a *palazzo,* just off P. Garibaldi. (☎68 30 49. Open M-F 9am-1pm.) In P. Garibaldi, **Farmacia Quattrino** posts after-hour rotations. (☎68 00 44. Open M-F 9am-1pm and 4:30-8pm.) In case of **emergency,** call the **carabinieri** at ☎68 20 14. For **Internet,** visit **Wilma Wine Bar,** V. Garibaldi 89/91, which offers customers free Internet on a fast computer. (☎68 46

09. Open M-Sa 3:30pm-midnight.) The **post office** is at V. Salvatore La Malfa 1. (☎98 00 11. Open M-F 8am-6:30pm, Sa 8am-12:30pm.) **Postal Code:** 94015.

> **TIP** **BUS BUNGLE.** Before buying a round-trip bus ticket, check for a time limit on the return leg. Some tickets expire 1hr. after purchase or first use.

▐▌▐▌ ACCOMMODATIONS AND FOOD. Follow the signs to **Ostello del Borgo ❶**, Largo S. Giovanni 6, a renovated 14th-century monastery on V. Umberto I. This hostel offers rooms with dignified furniture and a friendly staff. All private rooms include bath and toiletries. Dorms have cramped but clean showers and toilets down the hall. Visitors must show an HI card at the dorm entrance. (☎68 70 19; www.ostellodelborgo.it. Wheelchair-accessible. Breakfast included. Internet access €2 per hr. Dorms €16.50; singles €43; doubles €57; triples €75; quads €91. AmEx/MC/V.) Located 1km from town, **Bed and Breakfast Pepito ❸**, Contrada da Centova, offers amenities few can match. Reasonably priced rooms all have A/C, TV and private bath, while the B&B offers a billiard table, a pool, bikes and horseback riding to all guests. (☎68 57 37; www.pepitoweb.it. Breakfast included. Horseback riding €15 per day. Singles €30-40; doubles €55-70. AmEx/MC/V.) **Hotel Villa Romana ❹**, P. de Gasperi 18, offers plain rooms with TV and A/C. Three dining rooms and two bars round out this splurge. (☎68 29 11; www.piazza-armerina.it/hotelvillaromana. Breakfast included. Mar.-Sept. singles €60; doubles €85; triples €115. Oct.-Feb. €50/75/105. AmEx/MC/V.)

A handful of restaurants sprinkle the streets of Piazza Armerina's historic district, though more options are available close to the bus station. ◧**Ristorante Pizzeria Pepito ❷**, V. Roma 140, serves Italian comfort food with a distinctly Spanish flair. Enjoy *agnello al forno* (baked lamb; €10) in the upstairs dining room with impressive views of the gardens across the street. (☎68 57 37; www.pepitoweb.it. *Primi* €6-7, *secondi* €7-11. Cover €1. Open daily noon-3pm and 7pm-midnight. AmEx/MC/V.) For great food at a great price, head to central **Café des Amis ❶**, V. Marconi 22. This tiny local hangout has outdoor seating and the best *arancini* (fried rice ball stuffed with meat or vegetables) and pizza in town (both €1.50). It is also open in the afternoon and evenings, when other restaurants are closed. (☎68 06 61; www.cafedesamis.net. Open daily 6am-11pm.) Savvy locals head to historic **Ristorante Pizzeria da Totó ❷**, V. Mazzini 29, near P. Garibaldi, for pizza and *insalata capricciosa* (a salad of mixed Sicilian ingredients; €3.60) served in a comfortable setting. (☎/fax 68 01 53. Pizza €3-6. *Primi* €5.50-7, *secondi* €6.50-12. Cover €1.50. Open Tu-Su 9am-4pm and 6pm-midnight. AmEx/MC/V.)

◙ SIGHTS. A fertile valley 5km southwest of town shelters the **Villa Romana del Casale**. This remarkable site, known locally as I Mosaici, is thought to have been constructed at the turn of the AD 4th century, but an AD 12th-century landslide kept it mostly hidden for another 800 years. In 1916, famed archaeologists Paolo Orsi and Giuseppe Culterra unearthed 40 rooms of **stone mosaics,** but there are rooms that have yet to be excavated. Glass walls and ceilings protect the mosaics but still allow for a sense of what the villa would have looked like at the height of its glory. Guidebooks from nearby vendors explain the finer points of the villa's construction and history. Enter first through the **baths,** then pass into a large hall on the left to find a mosaic depicting a chariot race; the flying legs are all that remain of the driver, believed to have been Maximenius Herculeus. His great wealth, fondness for the hunt, and side business as an importer of animals are part of the tiles' tale. One of the largest rooms shows the capture of bulls, tigers, and lions, while the floor of the **Triclinium** depicts the Battle of the Giants and the Feats of Hercules. The **Salle delle Dieci Ragazze** (Room of Ten Girls) showcases 10 scantily clad beauties in the most famous of the villa's mosaics. While the **Cubicolo Scena Erotica** is not quite as scandalous as its title suggests, the bare tush and intimate kiss depicted still make it the villa's raciest mosaic. A room off the great hall illustrates the battle between Odysseus and Polyphemus, though the artist fudged the finer narrative details, generously allowing the Cyclops three eyes instead of one. Restoration and excavations are ongoing and a prime opportunity for visitors to interact with real archaeologists. *(Buses leave from P. Marescalchi. The 5km walk is well marked with signs pointing to I Mosaici. City buses (€0.70) run hourly 9am-noon and 3-6pm. Return buses run hourly from 9:30am-12:30pm and 3:30-6:30pm. Villa ☎68 00 36. Tour office ☎68 70 27, www.guardalasicilia.it. Ticket office open daily 8am-6:30pm. €6, ages 18-25 €3, under 18 or over 65 free. Guided tours available for groups. Audio tours €5.)*

■ ※ **NIGHTLIFE AND FESTIVALS.** For an elegant but relaxed night on the town, head to **Pan e Vinu** wine bar in P. Garibaldi, where the friendly staff and laid-back atmosphere provide a nice complement to the dignified burgundy and darkwood interior. (☎347 74 38 344. Wine from €3 per glass and €10 per bottle. Free appetizers with wine. More elaborate fare €3-10. Open daily 11:30am-3pm and 7pm-1am.) Laid-back nightlife centers around cafes in P. Garibaldi and hot spots near the bus station. Activity of a speedier sort take place at the nearby **Autodromo di Pergusa** (☎256 60), which hosts **Grand Prix** auto races from March through October. The most important race is the **Formula 3** in May. Otherwise, the Autodromo acts as an all-purpose arena, hosting everything from motorcycle races to dog shows.

ENNA ☎0935

Dubbed *l'ombelico della Sicilia* (the belly button of Sicily), Enna (EN-na; pop. 30,000) is a mountaintop city of ancient castles, worn stone streets, and some of Sicily's most superb, far-reaching views. A self-proclaimed "island in the sun," Enna provides a welcome respite from the sun-soaked Sicilian interior.

■ ⁊ **TRANSPORTATION AND PRACTICAL INFORMATION. Trains** run to Enna from Agrigento (2hr., 4 per day 7am-3pm, €6), Catania (1¼hr., 8 per day 6am-8:30pm, €5) and Palermo (2½hr., 3 per day 3:30-8:30pm, €8). **Buses** run from the station to the *centro storico* (M-Sa 7 per day 6:25am-8:25pm, Su 8:45am, 1:10pm; €1.35 on board) and arrive on V. Diaz, just outside of Enna, from Catania (4 per day 6am-5pm, €6.10), Ragusa (10 per day 6am-8pm, €9), Syracuse (12 per day 6am-10pm, €8) and Taormina (8 per day 5am-3:30pm, €9). **Via Vittorio**

▌▌ ROLL OUT! Make sure to catch the last evening bus out of Enna. If you don't, you'll have to stay in town and pay an extravagant hotel rate or take a €20 taxi ride to Calascibetta or Pergusa.

Emanuele runs from the bus station to **Piazza Matteotti,** where **Via Roma** branches in two directions. V. Roma passes **Piazza Vittorio Emanuele** and the *duomo,* going toward Castello di Lombardia. The right fork of V. Roma cuts through residential areas to the **Torre di Federico II.** For info on the city, transportation, and lodgings, head to **AAST,** P. Cloajanni 6. (☎50 08 75. Open M-Tu and Th-F 8am-2:15pm, W 8am-2:15pm and 2:45-6:15pm.) **Banks** line V. Roma between P. V. Emanuele and P. Umberto I. In case of **emergency,** call the **carabinieri** at ☎50 12 67. **Farmacia del**

Centro, V. Roma 315, posts after-hours rotations. (☎50 06 50. Open daily 9am-1pm and 4-8pm.) Speedy **Internet access** is available at **Ciemme,** V. Lombardia 31, next to the Castello di Lombardia. (☎50 47 12. €3 per hr. Open M-Sa 9am-1pm and 4-8pm.) The **post office,** V. Volta 1, **exchanges currency.** (☎56 23 12. Open M-F 8am-6:30pm, Sa 8am-12:30pm.) **Postal Code:** 94100.

▐▐ ▐▌ ACCOMMODATIONS AND FOOD. Because accommodations are sparse in Enna, the budget-conscious may want to stay in nearby Piazza Armerina or B&Bs in the surrounding area that offer better deals. All rooms at **Affittacamere da Pietro ❸,** Contrada Longobardo da Pietro, have bath, TV, and A/C. (☎33 647. Singles €35; doubles €45. Cash only.) Luxuriously decorated rooms at **Hotel Sicilia ❺,** P. Colajanni 7, come complete with bath, TV, A/C, minibar, hair dryer, antiques, and Botticelli reproductions. (☎50 08 50; www.hotelsiciliaenna.it. Breakfast buffet included. Singles €62-72; doubles €91; triples €110. AmEx/MC/V.) Enna's relaxed character extends to its dining, making eating out an enjoyable and lengthy affair. Restaurants cluster along Vle. Marconi, behind V. Roma and P. Crispi. The dining terrace at **Ristorante La Fontana ❷,** V. Vulturo 6, overlooks the gorgeous valley below. The house specialty, *spaghetti alla donna concetta* (€6.20), mixes pasta and regional vegetables. (☎25 465. *Primi* from €5.20, *secondi* from €7.80. Cover €1.10. Service 15%. Open daily noon-4pm and 7-11pm. AmEx/MC/V.) Nibble from the extensive *antipasto* buffet (€7) and finish with delicious *panna cotta* (€3) at **San Gennaro da Gino ❷,** Vle. Marconi 6. (☎24 067. Pizza from €3.10. *Primi* €6-7, *secondi* €6-10. Cover €1.50. Open M-Tu and Th-Su 12:30-3pm and 8pm-12:30am. AmEx/MC/V.) Pick up picnic supplies at the **Sisa supermarket,** V. Lombardia 21. (Open M-Tu and Th-Sa 9am-2pm and 5-9pm, W 9am-2pm.)

◙ ♫ SIGHTS AND ENTERTAINMENT. Though more than a dozen religious orders have their own churches in Enna, all participated in creating the remarkable **duomo,** which combines as many architectural styles as there are brotherhoods. Note the detailed carvings in the ceiling and the lifelike statues above the altar. (Open daily 9am-1pm and 4-7pm. Free.) From the *duomo,* take left fork up V. Roma as it becomes V. Lombardia to the Norman **Castello di Lombardia.** Although grass and vines have overrun its courtyards, the walls and towers of this castle attest to a time when residents of Enna were more engaged in defending their environment than enjoying it. The tallest of the castle's towers, **La Pisana,** offers enviable views of the entire province after a steep climb. On clear days, the imposing silhouette of Mt. Etna shimmers in the distance. The weeping Demeter supposedly mourned the loss of her daughter Persephone to Hades at the **Rocca di Cerere,** on the path leading to the left of the castello. Turn left on V. IV Novembre for the **public gardens.** (☎50 09 62. Castello open daily Apr.-Oct. 8am-8pm; Nov.-Mar. 8am-5pm. Gates are often open later. Gardens open daily 9am-8pm. Free.) Take the right fork of V. Roma from the *duomo* to take cover at **Torre di Federico II,** on the other end of town from the castle. Once used as a hideout for Sicilian defenders during WWII, the tower is connected to the *castello* by an underground tunnel, the entrance of which is still visible from within the tower. (Open daily 8am-6pm. Free.)

Built onto the side of a hill between the castle and the Rocca di Cerere, **Azimut** serves up wine (from €2.50 per glass, from €10 per bottle) and offers patrons superb views of the valley below. At night things loosen up with a variety of live music shows. (☎333 98 76 159. Beer €3.50. Mixed drinks €4-5. Open Tu-Su 11am-3am.) On July 2, Enna floods the streets and celebrates the **Festa della Madonna** with the procession of three enormous votive statues through the streets of the city, followed by fireworks, music, and traditional *mastazzoli* (apple cookies).

The party continues through the summer with the feasts of **Sant'Anna** and **Madonna di Valverde** on the last Sundays of July and August respectively. Every Easter, the brothers of each religious fraternity parade through the streets.

SOUTHERN SICILY

SYRACUSE (SIRACUSA)   ☎0931

Mixing Baroque beauty with archaeological jewels, Syracuse (SEE-ra-COO-sa; pop. 125,000) combines the relics of an ancient Mediterranean powerhouse with the beauty of a seaside town. At its peak in the ancient world, Syracuse cultivated a selection of great contributors to Western culture, including Theocritus, Archimedes, and the Greek lyric poet Pindar. After many conquests, the city's fortunes waned and Syracuse receded from the spotlight. Although its sights are not particularly astounding, Syracuse has stepped confidently into the 21st century to become the flower of modern Sicily. Visitors join the nighttime crowds meandering near the stunning ruins of the Temple of Apollo and the ancient *duomo*.

⌷ TRANSPORTATION

Trains: ☎46 44 67. On V. Francesco Crispi. To: **Catania** (1½hr., 25 per day 5am-9:30pm, €4.80); **Florence** (14hr.; 3:30pm and 7:45pm; €44.31, bed extra €2); **Messina** (3hr., 19 per day 5am-9:30pm, €8.75); **Milan** (18hr.; 3:30 and 7:45pm; €50); **Noto** (30min., 18 per day 5:15am-8:05pm, €2.75); **Ragusa** (2-3hr., 6 per day 5:15am-2:50pm, €6.05); **Rome** (10-13hr., 6 per day 8am-9:30pm, €38); **Taormina** (2hr., 19 per day 5am-9:30pm, €6.70).

Buses: AST (☎46 27 11 or 44 92 15), on C. Umberto I near the train station. Reduced weekend service. To **Gela** (4hr., 7am and 1pm, €7.75), **Piazza Armerina** (3hr., 6:55am, €7.25), and **Ragusa** (3hr.; M-Sa 8 per day 7am-7:15pm, Su 2:20pm and 8:10pm). **Interbus**, V. Trieste 40 (☎66 710), 1 block from P. delle Poste toward center of Ortigia, 2nd street on left after stone bridge. To **Catania** (16 per day M-F 5:45am-7pm, Sa 4 per day 6:20am-1pm, Su 6 per day 6:40am-3pm; €4.40) and **Noto** (1hr.; M-Sa 5 per day 11am-6:30pm, Su 12:30, 8:30pm; €2.75).

Public Transportation: Orange **AST** buses depart from P. delle Poste. Buses #21 and 22 (in summer 27 and 28) run past Fontane Bianche every 2-3hr.; buses #23 and 24 do as well but much less frequently. Tickets (€0.80) sold in *tabaccherie*.

Taxis: ☎69 722 or 60 980. From the train station to Ortigia costs about €8.

✦ ℹ ORIENTATION AND PRACTICAL INFORMATION

Ponte Umbertino connects the island of Ortigia to mainland Syracuse. **Ponte Nuovo** (Ponte Santa Lucia), just to the left of Ponte Umbertino facing the mainland, is open even when Umbertino is closed to car traffic. On the mainland, **Corso Umberto I** links the bridge to the **train station** and passes through **Piazza Marconi**, from which **Corso Gelone** passes through town to the **Archaeological Park.** C. Umberto I continues past **Foro Siracusano** to the train station.

Tourist Office: AAT Office Ortigia, V. Maestranza 33 (☎46 42 55). After crossing Ponte Umbertino, turn right through P. Pancali to uphill C. Matteoti. Turn left on V. Maestranza

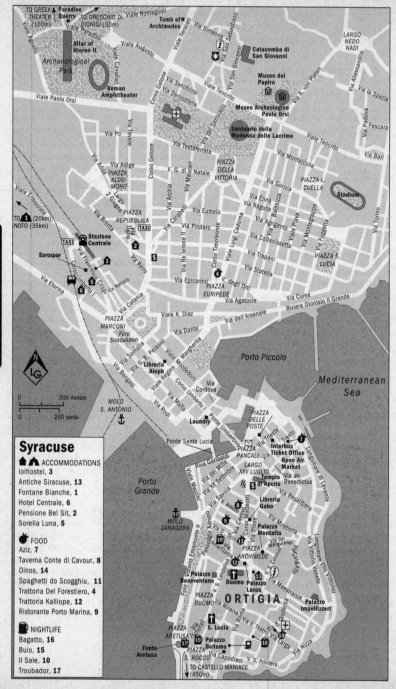

TO GREEK THEATER (100m)
Paradise Quarry
TO ORECCHIO DI DIONIGI (30m)
Viale Paradiso
Viale Agnello
Viale Romagnoli
Tomb of Archimedes
Via Teracati
Via Simeone
Via San Sebastiano
LARGO NEDO NADI
Altar of Hieron II
Viale Cavallari
Viale Augusto
Via San Giovanni
Catacomba di San Giovanni
Via A. von Platen
Via Allessandria
Archaeological Park
Roman Amphitheater
Viale Paolo Orsi
Corso Gelone
Via Senofonte
Via Demostene
Viale Teocrito
Museo del Papiro
Via la Spezia
Museo Archeologico Paolo Orsi
Via Po
Via del Santuario
Santuario della Madonna delle Lacrime
Viale Teocrito
Via Padova
Pescara
Via Bari
Via Tevere
Via Testaferrata
PIAZZA DELLA VITTORIA
Viale Montalcone
Via Torino
Via Adige
Via Adda
PIAZZA ALDO MORO
Corso Gelone
V. G. di Natale
Via Mauceri
Via Gorizia
PIAZZA L. CUELLA
Stadium
Largo 2 Giugno
PIAZZA REPUBBLICA
TAXI
Via Brenta
Via Oglio
Via Archia
Via Enna
Via Ragusa
Via Busizza
Viale Piave
Via Montegrappa
Via Tugenta
TO (20km); NOTO (35km)
Viale Ermocrate
Stazione Centrale
TAXI
Via Eumelo
Via Carabelli
Via Pindaro
Via Nerone II
Via Agrigento
Via Caltanissetta
PIAZZA S. LUCIA
Eurospar
Via Francesco Crispi
Via Reno
Via Luigi Cadorna
Via Trapani
Via Elorina
Via Epicarmo
Via Masana
PIAZZA EURIPEDE
Via degli Orti
Via Statella
Riviera Dionisio Il Grande
Via Cuma
Via Catania
Viale A. Diaz
Via Agatocle
PIAZZA MARCONI
Foro Siracusano
Via Dante
Via dell'Arsenale
Porto Piccolo
Mediterranean Sea
Via Somalia
Via G. B. Perasso
Viale Montedoro
Via Margherita
Via Bengasi
Viale Regina
Corso Umberto I
Via Cordova
Libreria Aleph
Via Malta
Via Rodi
MOLO S. ANTONIO
Laundry
Ponte Umberto I
PIAZZA DELLE POSTE
Via Trieste
Trento
Interbus Ticket Office
Open Air Market
Ponte Santa Lucia
PIAZZA PANCALI
Lungomare di Levante
Riva Garibaldi
Via della Maestranza
Via delle Mille
Via XX Settembre
LARGO XXV LUGLIO
Tempio di Apollo
Via de Benedictus
Porto Grande
MOLO ZANAGORA
Viale Mazzini
Via Savoia
Via V. Arangio
Via Resalibera
Libreria Gabo
Foro Vittorio Emanuele II
Passeggio Adorno
Corso Giacomo Matteotti
Via Dione
Via Mirabella
Lungomare Elio Vittorini
Via Roma
Via Cavour
Palazzo Montalto
Via de' Marguensi
Palazzo Beneventano
PIAZZA ARCHIMEDE
Via Maestranza
Lungomare Vittorio Veneto
PIAZZA DUOMO
Duomo
Palazzo Lanzo
Palazzo Impellizzeri
PIAZZA ARETUSA
S. Lucia
Via Roma
Via Minerva
ORTIGIA
Via della Giudecca
Fonte Aretusa
Palazzo Bellomo
PIAZZA S. ROCCO
Via Capodieci
V. S. Privitera
Via Larga
Via Nizza
TO CASTELLO MANIACE (450m)

200 meters
200 yards

Syracuse

♦ **ACCOMMODATIONS**
lolhostel, 3
Antiche Siracuse, 13
Fontane Bianche, 1
Hotel Centrale, 6
Pensione Bel Sit, 2
Sorella Luna, 5

🍴 **FOOD**
Aziz, 7
Taverna Conte di Cavour, 8
Oinos, 14
Spaghetti do Scogghiu, 11
Trattoria Del Forestiero, 4
Trattoria Kalliope, 12
Ristorante Porto Marina, 9

🍸 **NIGHTLIFE**
Bagatto, 16
Buio, 15
Il Sale, 10
Troubador, 17

SICILY

TIP **OLD TIME TOURS.** Ask at the APT tourist office about the **Val di Noto** train tour (€25), an all-day tour of southeastern Sicily with guided stops in either Noto and Modica or Ragusa and Scicli to admire the history, regional cuisine, and Baroque architecture, all from a historical steam locomotive.

at the fountain in P. Archimede; office is in courtyard of the *palazzo* across from the pharmacy. English spoken. Open M-F 8:30am-1:45pm and 3-5:30pm, Sa 8:30am-1:45pm. **APT,** V. San Sebastiano 45 (☎48 12 32). From the station, take V. Francesco Crispi to V. Catania, which becomes C. Gelone after the tracks. Turn right on Vle. Teocrito after 10min., then left on V. San Sebastiano; the office is across from the catacombs. Useful tourist map includes a mini-guide. Open M-F 8:30am-1:30pm and 3:30-6:30pm, Sa-Su 9am-1pm; July-Aug. also open Sa 3:30-6pm.

Luggage Storage: In train station. €4 per hr. Open daily 7:30am-1pm and 3-7pm.

English-Language Bookstores: Libreria Aleph, C. Umberto I 106 (☎46 32 82). Open M-Sa 9am-8:30pm. AmEx/MC/V. **Libreria Gabo,** C. Matteotti 38. (☎66 255). Internet access €1.50 per 15min. Open M-F and Su 9am-1pm and 4-8:30pm, Sa 5-8:30pm. AmEx/MC/V.

Laundry: Lavenderia ad Acqua, C. Umberto I 13, near the bridge to Ortigia. Wash €3.50, dry €1 per 6min. Detergent €1. Open M-Sa 8:30am-1:30pm and 3:30-8:30pm.

Carabinieri: ☎44 13 44. **Police:** ☎49 51 11.

Pharmacy: Mangiafico Farmacia, C. Matteotti 53 (☎65 643). Open M-Sa 8:30am-1pm and 4:30-8pm. After-hours rotations posted outside. AmEx/MC/V.

Hospital: Ospedale Generale Provinciale (☎68 555), a beige brick monstrosity on V. Testaferrata, off the end of C. Gelone. **Guardia Medica,** V. della Giudecca (☎48 46 39). Open daily 8am-8pm.

Internet Access: Libreria Gabo (see **English-Language Bookstores** above). **Internet Train,** V. Roma 122, in Ortigia. €1 for 10min., €4.30 per hr.; students under 26 €3.20 per hr. Open M-F 10am-2pm and 4-8pm, Sa 4-8pm.

Post Office: P. delle Poste 15, on Ortigia. Turn left crossing the bridge. **Currency exchange.** Open M-F 8:15am-6:30pm, Sa 8am-12:30pm. **Postal Code:** 96100.

ACCOMMODATIONS AND CAMPING

Many budget accommodations have staked out the area between the station and the bridge to Ortigia. While prices are good, quality is very uneven. Don't be fooled by big signs and a lot of flyers. This area is pretty run down, and at night, visitors should stick to the main, well-lit thoroughfares. Ortigia's options are more expensive, but generally of higher quality.

lolhostel, V. Francesco Crispi 92/96 (☎46 50 88; www.lolhostel.com). Opened in June 2007, this hostel is on its way to becoming a true Syracusan gem with its lively atmosphere and great prices. 4 dorm rooms and some doubles; all with A/C. Communal kitchen. Linens included. Internet access €3 per hr. June-July dorms€18; singles €35; doubles €60. Aug. €20/40/64. Sept.-May €17/33/50. Cash only. ❶

Sorella Luna, V. F. Crispi 23 (☎21 178; www.sorellalunasrl.it). This B&B retains the beautiful, wooden-beam ceilings of the convent here before, but everything else is brand-new. All rooms have phone, A/C, bath, wet bar with minifridge, and TV with some English-language channels. Breakfast included. Singles €50; doubles €80; triples €100. Extra bed €20. AmEx/MC/V. ❹

Hotel Centrale, C. Umberto I 141 (☎60 528; www.hotelcentralesr.com), near the train station. Sports newly renovated, sponge-painted rooms in modern style; some with views

EX(SYRA)CUSE ME, THERE'S NIGHTLIFE?

While Sicily often closes down early, Syracuse is the exception to the rule, buzzing with life from 10pm until the wee hours in these happening hot spots.

1 **Foro Vittorio Emanuele II:** Amble along this *lungomare*, *gelato* in hand, ogling the yachts that berth here.

2 **Via Amalfitana:** A courtyard home to threé bars and live music (in summer) sits on this late-night thoroughfare.

3 **Piazza Duomo:** Seemingly all of Syracuse floods this square at night. Don't miss the *duomo's* illuminated facade.

4 **Piazza Aretusa:** Definitely the most popular among the younger crowd, jam packed bars and teens on mopeds share space with a freshwater spring home to a group of swans.

5 **Castello Maniace:** While the castle is only open to visitors when the sun shines, different groups use it as an exclusive, invite-only party space.

of the sea (€5 extra). Rooms have bath, TV, and A/C. Breakfast included. Wi-Fi in the lobby. Singles €45-60; doubles €70-80; triples €90-110. AmEx/MC/V. ❹

Antiche Siracuse, V. Maestranza 12 (☎46 13 65), right next to P. Archimede. 3 beautiful rooms with bath, A/C, TV, and phone. Breakfast included at cafe downstairs. Book at least 2 weeks in advance. Singles €45; doubles €85; triples €110. AmEx/MC/V. ❹

Pensione Bel Sit, V. Oglio 5, 5th fl. (☎60 245; fax 46 28 82). Follow signs from C. Gelone, close to the train station in an older apartment building. If you make it past the crumbling lobby, hotel is manageable. Large, simply furnished rooms with colorful bedspreads have large windows, some with bath. Upstairs rooms also have A/C and TV. Reserve 1 week ahead July-Aug. Singles €20; doubles €34. Cash only. ❷

Fontane Bianche, V. dei Lidi 476 (☎79 03 33; fax 79 11 50), 20km from town. Take bus #21 or 22 (€0.80) from P. delle Poste in Ortigia. Showers included. Open May-Sept. €6 per person, €5 per tent. ❶

🄲 FOOD

While hotel prices can run fairly high, restaurants are affordable. On the mainland, the area around the station and the Archaeological Park offers some of the best deals. Ortigia has an **open-air market** on V. Trento, off P. Pancali, as well as several budget options on V. Savoia and V. Cavour. There is a **Eurospar** supermarket on C. Umberto I, right past the bus station.

▨ **Ristorante Porta Marina,** V. dei Candelai 35, (☎ 22 553), off V. Cavour. Elegant and affordable, Porta Marina offers a great selection of seafood in a sleek modern restaurant under an ancient stone archway. *Primi* €6.50-14, *secondi* €7-14. Open Tu-Su 12:30-3pm and 8-11:30pm. AmEx/MC/V. ❷

▨ **Trattoria Del Forestiero,** C. Timoleonte 2 (☎335 84 30 736), on the mainland. Walk 10min. out of touristy Ortigia and you'll find good, cheap food at this lively local favorite. Try their speciality, *pizza forestiero*. Takeout available. Pizza for dinner only from €2.50. *Primi* from €3.10, *secondi* from €4.20. Cover €1.10. Open M and W-Su noon-3:30pm and 7pm-midnight. Cash only. ❷

Aziz, V. Trento 10 (☎349 59 78 909), off of C. Umberto I, right before the Temple of Apollo. Serving up kebab (€7.50) and couscous (€6), Aziz is a great late-night, local hangout with outdoor seating and an upstairs dining room complete with pillows and hookah (€5). Open Tu-Su noon-3pm and 8:30pm-midnight. Cash only. ❷

Trattoria Kalliope, V. del Consiglio Regionale 26 (☎46 80 08; www.trattoriakalliope.com). In a small *piazza* filled with statues and jazz music, Kalliope serves appetizing pasta and seafood dishes. Perfect for a romantic rendezvous. *Primi* €6-12, *secondi* €8-18. Open M and W-Su noon-3pm and 7pm-midnight. AmEx/MC/V. ❷

Oinos, V. della Giudecca 69-75 (☎46 49 00). The elegance of this restaurant and *eno-teca* is matched only by its owner's eccentricity. 300+ wine varieties for sale. Sample a glass before finishing off one of many homemade desserts. Wine from €3 per glass, €12 per bottle. *Primi* €10-13, *secondi* €13-22. Desserts €4-6. Cover €2. Open Tu-Su 12:30-2:30pm and 7pm-midnight. AmEx/MC/V. ❹

Taverna Conte di Cavour, V. Cavour 67 (☎21 910). Kitchen specializes in traditional Sicilian fare, especially *pizza alla norma*. Caters to families and tourists. Listen to jazz amidst modern art and wine bottles. *Primi* and *secondi* from €5. Open M-Sa 10am-3pm and 8-11pm. AmEx/MC/V. ❷

Spaghetti do Scogghiu, V. Domenico Scinà 11, a tiny street off P. Archimede, in Ortigia. Over 20 varieties of spaghetti in a busy, hole-in-the-wall restaurant. *Primi* and *secondi* from €6. Cover €1.50. Open Tu-Su noon-3pm and 6-11pm. Cash only. ❷

◎ SIGHTS

MAINLAND SYRACUSE

▓**ARCHAEOLOGICAL PARK.** Syracuse's three centuries as a strategic city on the Mediterranean left behind a collection of immense monuments. The Greek ruins are the most impressive, but the Roman remains also attest to a rich heritage. Two theaters, an ancient quarry, and the remains of the world's largest altar share a fenced compound, viewable with a single ticket. The **Greek Theater** carved into the hillside in 475 BC showcases a view that makes it easy to understand why Syracuse became such a successful Greek colony. If the 15,000 spectators watching Aeschylus's original production of *The Persians* got bored, they could lift their eyes over the scenic ruins to scan the landscape. Original Greek inscriptions line the walls along the mid-level aisles, and the track for the *deus ex machina*, a large crane that made the gods "fly," is still in place. The **Paradise Quarry** next to the theater derives its name from the gardens that line the base of the chalky cliffs. These quarries provided most of the gray stone that built old Syracuse. Two large artificial caves, the **Orecchio di Dionigi** (Ear of Dionysius) and the **Grotta dei Cordari** (Ropemakers' Cave), were cut in the walls. The latter is closed to the public for safety reasons, but visitors can still hear the famous echoes that ricochet off the Orecchio di Dionigi's walls. Legend claims the tyrant Dionysius put his prisoners here so he could eavesdrop on their conversations. *(Open daily from 9am-2hr. before sunset. Free.)* Outside this area lies the site of the **Ara di Ierone II** (the altar of Hieron II, 241-215 BC), once used for public sacrifices. The altar was torn down in the 16th century by the Spanish, who used the stone to build the walls of Ortigia. The enormous steps of the altar's base are still intact. Up the hill is an AD 2nd-century Roman **amphitheater.** Visitors can see the tunnels through which gladiators and their prey entered the arena floor. *(Take C. Gelone to Vle. Teocrito. Park entrance down V. Augusto to the left; follow signs. Walk through the gauntlet of souvenir stands to reach the ticket office. Info ☎65 068. Park open daily in summer from 9am-2hr. before sunset; in winter 9am-3pm. Theater closed early May-June. Ticket office open daily in summer 9am-6pm; in winter 9am-2pm. €6, EU residents 18-25 €3, EU residents under 18 or over 65 free.)*

▓**CATACOMBA DI SAN GIOVANNI.** Dating from AD 415-460, this subterranean maze has over 20,000 tombs carved into the walls of what used to be a Greek aqueduct. No corpses linger—only ghostly frescoes, an occasional sarcophagus, and a few wall carvings. *(Across from the tourist office on V. San Giovanni, off Vle. Teocrito from C.*

Gelone. ☎ *64 694; www.kairos-web.com. Open daily 9:30am-12:30pm and 2:30-5:30pm. Mandatory guided tours every 30min. €5, under 15 and over 65 €3. AmEx/MC/V.)*

DUOMO. The 18th-century exterior of the cathedral looks like the standard Baroque compilation of architectural styles, but the interior holds a secret. A 5th-century BC Temple of Athena first stood on the site, and rather than demolishing the pagan structure, architects incorporated it into their construction. Fluted columns line the interior, recalling the structure's Classical origins. Large, shiny letters proclaim this the **first Christian church** in the West. Legend has it that the temple became a church with the arrival of St. Paul. The first chapel on the right is dedicated to Santa Lucia, the light-bearer and Syracuse's patron saint. Catch a glimpse of her left arm in the elaborate glass reliquary. Hidden from view above the reliquary is a masterpiece of Sicilian silver work, a life-sized statue of Lucia that parades through the streets on her feast day (see **Entertainment,** below). Lest people forget how she died, silversmiths thoughtfully included a dagger protruding from her throat, the punishment dealt the saint by the pagan government of AD 304. *(From P. Archimede, take V. Roma, and turn right on V. Minerva. Open daily 8am-7pm. Modest dress required. Free.)*

SANTUARIO DELLA MADONNA DELLE LACRIME. For three days in 1953, a mass-produced statuette of the Madonna reputedly began to weep in the home of the Iannuso family. Since then the number of pilgrims to the site has grown so large that the commanding spire of the **Basilica Madonna delle Lacrime** was built in 1994 to the plans of Frenchmen Michel Arnault and Pierre Parat. Whether you're a pilgrim or not, a stop at the sanctuary to admire the impressive architecture will be worth it. The **Museum of Lacrymation** and the **Museum of Liturgy** complement the basilica; timetables placed outside the sanctuary tell the statue's tale. *(On Vle. Teocrito, off V. del Santuario.* ☎ *21 446; www.madonnadellelacrime.it. Both museums open daily 9am-12:30pm and 4-6pm. Sanctuary open 8am-noon and 4-7pm. Museum of Lacrymation €1.55, Museum of Liturgy €1, both museums €2. Sanctuary free.)*

MUSEO ARCHEOLOGICO PAOLO ORSI. Named for the most famous archaeologist in Sicily, this museum has a collection of over 18,000 objects from prehistory through ancient Greece and early Christianity (roughly from 40,000 BC to AD 600). From the introductory room at the museum's core, hallways branch into chronologically arranged galleries. Exquisite *kouroi* torsos, grimacing Gorgons, elegant vases, and pygmy-elephant skeletons rest in dimly lit galleries. *(Vle. Teocrito 66.* ☎ *46 40 22. Open Tu-Sa 9am-7pm, Su 9am-2pm. Last entry 1hr. before closing. €6, EU residents 18-25 €3, EU residents under 18 and over 65 free.)*

🎵 🎭 ENTERTAINMENT AND NIGHTLIFE

Siracusani, like all Italians, fall prey in summer to ancestral instincts that force them from the cities to the beaches. **Fontane Bianche** is one such beach, well populated and with many discos. The campground there ensures a place to sleep when buses stop. Take bus #21 or 22 (30min., every 2-3hr., €0.80). In Ortigia, nightlife consists of a tour of the island, stopping at several bars along the way.

Piazzetta San Rocco is a nightlife hot spot; the two best bars there are the eclectic ■**Buio** ("darkness"), V. delle Vergini 16, where the elderly owner blares Tupac and other rap favorites well into the night (☎348 58 54 695), and the refined **Troubador,** Ronco 1 alla Fontana 4, off Piazzetta San Rocco. **Il Sale,** hidden away in the courtyard of an old building off V. Amalfitania, hosts live bands and revelers well past 3am (☎339 15 77 381). **Bagatto,** in the small P. San

Giuseppe, often features free, live music and is popular amongst locals for its prime location (☎22 040; show schedule available at www.bagattoilpub.it).

In May and June, the city stages **classical Greek drama** in ancient amphitheaters. The APT office has details. Tickets for **Istituto Nazionale del Dramma Antico** are available at the theater box office, in the Archaeological Park. (☎48 72 48; www.indafondazione.org. Open M-F 10am-7pm.) At the **Festa di Santa Lucia,** December 13, men shoulder the silver statue of the city's patron saint in a 6hr. procession from the *duomo* to Santa Lucia al Sepolcro on the mainland. After a week, the statue returns to the *duomo* on December 20.

■ DAYTRIP FROM SYRACUSE: NOTO

A haven of Baroque unity, Noto (NO-toh) is a pleasure to the eyes. After a 1693 earthquake shook Sicily's shore, the noble Landolina and Niccolaci families made Noto their favorite renovation project, restoring its elegance with monumental staircases, putti moldings, and pot-bellied balconies. Noto has a slower pace than coastal towns, making it a calm retreat from frenzied tourist destinations. In the 3rd week in May, artists work from Friday through Sunday for the **Infiorata,** decorating V. Niccolaci with big, bright flower petal murals. Toward the city center from C. Vittorio Emanuele and up four flights of giant steps stands the immense **Chiesa di San Francesco all'Immacolata,** which was built in 1704 and houses one of the bloodiest crucifixes in Sicily (open daily 8am-noon and 2-8pm). On C. V. Emanuele, stop at the **Teatro Comunale Vittorio Emanuele** to gaze up at its painted balconies and bright, red drapes. (☎896 655. Play season Nov.-May. Open Tu-Su 9am-1pm and 4-8pm. €1.50, show tickets €10-€25.) From C. V. Emanuele, turn right on V. Niccolaci for a view of the balconies of the **Palazzo Niccolaci,** supported by cherubs, griffins, and sirens. **La panoramica dal Campanile** affords a matchless view of the city from the top of the **Chiesa di San Carlo.** (Open daily 10am-1pm and 3-4pm. €1.50, under 18 and students €1.) The **Hall of Mirrors** at Palazzo Ducezio in P. Municipio on C. V. Emanuele is worth a look if you're into Baroque decorations. Dating from 1760, the frescoes of local history are interspersed with mirrors from which the hall takes its name. (Open Tu-Su 9am-1pm and 4-8pm.) Decent **beaches** are 7km away at **Noto Marina.** Buses depart from the Giardini Pubblici (July-Aug. M-Sa 8:30, 10am, 12:40, 4pm; €1.60). For hungry sightseers, **Pizzeria al Tarazzo ❷,** V. Baccarini 4, right off C. V. Emanuele, offers upscale outdoor dining at an affordable price. (☎839 710. Primi €5-7, secondi €6-10. Cover €1. AmEx/MC/V.) Noto is accessible by train from Syracuse (1 hr., 11 per day 5:15am-8:05pm, €2.75). The station is a 15min. walk from Ortigia. and can also be reached by Interbus (1hr.; 8 per day 7:05am-6pm, return 7 per day 6:55am-4:55pm; €2.75). To reach the *centro* from the train station, follow the road leading uphill and to the right until it ends, then walk through the park for a block. A left turn here and 5min. walk will put you at the far end of the town's main street, C. V. Emanuele.

RAGUSA ☎0932

The 1st thing you notice about the little town of Ragusa (ra-GOO-sa; pop. 68,000) is that it is actually two smaller towns: Ragusa Ibla, the old town, and higher up, Ragusa Superiore, the newer town, rebuilt after the earthquake of 1693. Ragusa Ibla and Superiore are divided by a breathtaking valley, which creates a scenic— albeit steep—hike between the two. Visitors will probably want to spend most of their time in Ragusa Ibla, where the combination of antique buildings and sweeping vistas create beautiful tours through the twisting streets and open *piazze.*

SICILY

THE LEG BONE'S CONNECTED TO THE KNEE BONE. Travelers to Sicily will undoubtedly come across the omnipresent **Trinacria**. The island's ancient symbol, an unusual combination of mythological references, consists of 3 legs bent at the knee, radiating equidistantly from Medusa's snake-haired head, adorned with wheat. Famous for turning men into stone with her fearsome gaze, Medusa was in charge of protecting the ends of the earth, which in the days of ancient Greece meant Sicily. The sheaves of wheat represent the cultivation of Sicily's fertile soil, and the 3 legs stand for the 3 corners of the triangular island: Capo Pallor at Messina, Capo Passer at Syracuse, and Capo Lille west of Marsala. The leg bent at the knee was a Spartan symbol of power. The Trinacria is most often represented in burnished gold, the color of the sun.

▐ TRANSPORTATION. The **train station** is at P. Stazione, above P. del Popolo and V. Dante in Ragusa Superiore, behind the bus stop. **Trains** run to Caltanissetta (3hr., 2 per day 2:58 and 4:50pm, €8.75), Gela (1¼hr., 6 per day 4:08am-8:20pm, €5), and Syracuse (2hr., 12 per day 7:45am-6:30pm, €6.05). **Etna Buses**, in P. del Popolo in Ragusa Superiore run to Catania (2hr.; M-F 10 per day 5:30am-7pm, Sa 6 per day 5:30am-5pm, Su 5 per day 8am-7pm; €6.60). Buy tickets at Caffè del Viale; from P. del Popolo with your back to the train station, turn left on Vle. Tenente Lena toward P. Libertà. AST, just off P. del Popolo (☎68 18 18), runs **buses** from P. del Popolo to: Chiaramonte (40min., 8 per day 7:10am-7:30pm, €2); Gela (1½hr.; M-Sa 9:45am and 3:15pm, €4.20); Noto (1½hr., 10 per day 6am-7pm, €4.20); Palermo (4hr.; M-Sa 4 per day 5:25am-5:25pm, Su 3:10 and 5:25pm; €11.35); Syracuse (2hr., 10 per day 6am-7pm, €6). Connections to Agrigento and Enna run via Gela.

▄▐ ORIENTATION AND PRACTICAL INFORMATION. The train station is in **Piazza Stazione** just above **Piazza del Popolo;** the buses stop in P. del Popolo and in nearby **Piazza Gramsci** (P. Pullman). To reach the *centro* of **Ragusa Superiore,** turn left on Vle. Tenente Lena, walk through **Piazza Libertà** and across Ponte Senatore F. Pennavaria, the first of three bridges spanning the Vallata Santa, at which point Vle. T. Lena becomes **Via Roma. Corso Italia,** off V. Roma, goes downhill for several blocks, passing the post office in **Piazza Matteotti** before becoming **Via XXIV Maggio.** It ends at Chiesa di Santa Maria della Scala. Here, stairs and roads wind down to **Ragusa Ibla,** the older section of town. City buses run a circuit of Ragusa Ibla and Ragusa Superiore (M-Sa 2 per hr., Su 1 per hr.).

Helpful staff has maps and brochures at **Pro Loco tourist office,** V. Largo Camerina 5, in Ragusa Ibla. Signs lead the way from P. Duomo. (☎24 44 73. Open Tu-Sa 10:30am-1pm and 3-7pm, Su 10:30am-1pm.) In an **emergency,** call the **police** (☎62 10 10) or **first aid** (☎62 14 10). For serious medical emergencies visit the hospital (☎24 51 84) on V. d. Vittorio in a peach building or call the **medical clinic** (☎62 39 46). **Ibl@cafe,** P. Marini 5, in Ragusa Ibla has 4 fast **Internet** terminals. (☎683 108. €3 per hr. Open daily 9:30am-10pm.) Two blocks down C. Italia from V. Roma. the **post office** in P. Matteotti closes at noon the last day of month. (☎23 21 11. Open M-Sa 8am-6:30pm.) **Postal Code:** 97100.

▐▐ ACCOMMODATIONS AND FOOD. From the train station, cross P. del Popolo to V. Sicilia and continue to the gas station and find **Hotel Jonio ❸** across the street at V. Risorgimento 49. The best deal in town, these plain rooms all have TV and bath, some with A/C. (☎62 43 22; fax 22 91 44. Breakfast included. Singles €30, with half pension €43; doubles €50/63; triples €66/79. AmEx/MC/V.) In nearby Marina, **Baia del Sole ❶** is a campground on Lungomare Andrea Doria. Tumino buses run from P. Gramsci in Ragusa to P. Duca degli Abruzzi in Marina (25min.; 13 per day 6am-8:30pm; €2.20, round-trip €3.60). Keeping water to the right, walk 1km from the main *piazza* on the *lungomare*. (☎23 98 44. Hot showers 7-9am and 5-7pm. Sept.-July €3 per person, €8 per tent. Aug. €6/13.)

Visitors to Ragusa during the winter months should try the specialty *panatigghie*, thin but savory pastries filled with the unlikely trio of cocoa, cinnamon, and ground meat. Purchase grocery essentials at **SMA**, a short walk from the station on V. Sicilia 14. (☎62 43 42. Open M-Sa 8:30am-8pm.) In Ragusa Ibla, a series of cafes and bars line C. XXV Aprile below P. Pola, offering *panini* and other cheap eats to university students. In Ragusa Ibla, **⬛Gelati Divini ❶**, P. Duomo 18/20, offers the best of both worlds with their *Moscato* (white wine) and *Brachetto* (red wine) ice-cream. (☎22 89 89; www.gelatidivini.it. Wine from €6.50 per bottle. *Gelato* €2-4. Open daily 10am-1am. Closed in winter Tu. AmEX/MC/V.) Located across from the Portale San Giorgio in Ragusa Ibla, the elegant but understated **⬛Ristorante da Candida ❷**, V. Valverde 95, serves fresh seafood on a vine-covered 2nd fl. terrace. (☎24 56 12. *Primi* €5.50-7, *secondi* €7-13. Cover €1.50. Open daily noon-3pm and 7:30pm-midnight. AmEx/MC/V.) **Ristorante Orfeo ❸**, V. Sant'Anna 117, off V. Roma in the *centro* of Ragusa Superiore, serves Sicilian specialties in a classy art deco atmosphere. (☎62 10 35. *Primi* €8, *secondi* €9-14. Fresh fish from €11. Cover €3. Service €1. Open M-Sa noon-3pm and 7-10pm. AmEx/MC/V.) **Pizzeria La Grotta ❶**, V. Giovanni Cartia 8, off V. Roma in Ragusa Superiore, dreams up original variations on standard *tavola calda* fare, including 31 *panini* choices. Wacky creations like pizza topped with french fries or Nutella are popular. (☎22 73 70. Pizza slices €1.40. Open M-Sa 5:30pm-12:30am.)

◨🎵 SIGHTS AND ENTERTAINMENT. The hilltops of Ragusa Superiore and Ragusa Ibla offer fantastic views of the countryside. Ragusa Ibla, the ancient section, is accessible by a steep but lovely 10min. hike down from the church at the bottom of C. Italia (V. XXIV Maggio) or by catching bus #1 or 3 (€1) from P. del Popolo. The buses return to the Ragusa Superiore from Largo Camerina, one block from the cathedral in Ibla. Purchase tickets on bus. The stairs at Santa Maria offer a stellar view, crowned by a monastery and the 18th-century dome of **San Giorgio,** which glows turquoise at night. (Modest dress required.) After the set of tricky steps to P. Repubblica, the road to the left circumvents the town, passing monasteries and farmland. P. del Duomo di San Giorgio sits at the top of the city. C. XXV Aprile runs downhill from the *piazza*, passes two churches, and ends at the **Giardini Iblei,** pleasant public gardens with views of the valley below, as well as a convent which organizes free art exhibits. (Park open in summer daily 9am-midnight.)

During the summer, Italians pack their swimsuits, rev up their Vespas, and spend the weekend baking their bodies and splashing in the crystal-blue waters at **⬛Marina di Ragusa.** Autolinee Tumino (☎62 31 84) runs **buses** from P. Gramsci (25min.; 15 per day, last bus returns 10pm; €2.20, round-trip €3.60). Ask the driver for a schedule with return times and clarification on where the bus returns for pick up. Since 1990 Ragusa Ibla has hosted to the annual **Ibla Grand Prize,** an international piano, voice, and composition competition that runs from late June to early July. Performances are held in the theater of the Palazzo Comunale.

AGRIGENTO ☎0922

Home to the father of modern medicine, Empedocle, and Nobel Prize-winning author Luigi Pirandello, Agrigento (AH-gree-JEN-toh; pop. 52,000) prides itself on integrating its historic monuments with a hillside metropolis. Visitors are treated to some of the Mediterranean's most impressive Greek ruins: a valley full of a series of intact, ancient Doric temples. Although Agrigento today takes great pride in its modernity, traces of its past still linger in the winding cobblestone streets and seemingly endless stairways.

▄ TRANSPORTATION

Trains: The **train station** is in P. Marconi, below P. Aldo Moro. Ticket office open daily 6:30am-8pm. Trains go to **Catania** (3¼hr.; 12:20pm, 6:50pm; €9.20) via **Enna** (2hr., €5.65) and **Palermo** (2hr., 11 per day 4:55am-8:10pm, €6.70).

Buses: Just beyond P. Vittorio Emanuele, buses depart from P. Roselli, behind the movie theater, where the ticket booth is located. **Cuffaro,** V. Balsamo 13 (☎091 61 61 510; www.cuffaro.info), runs buses to **Palermo** (M-Sa 9 per day 5:15am-6:30pm, Su 8:15am, 4:30, 6:30pm; €7.20); schedules and info available at the *bar* in P. Roselli. **SAIS Trasporti,** V. Ragazzi del 99 (☎59 59 33), runs buses to **Caltanissetta** (1hr., M-Sa 13 per day 4:30am-6:45pm, €4.40) and **Catania** (2¾hr., 13 per day, €11). **Lumia** (www.autolineelumia.it), runs buses to **Trapani** (M-Sa 6:30, 8:30am, 1:55pm; €10). Reduced service Su.

Public Transportation: Orange **TUA buses** depart from the train station. Tickets (€0.90) valid 1½hr. Available at *tabaccheria* in the train station. Buses #2 and 2/ run to the beach at **San Leone;** #1, 1/, 2, 2/, 3, and 3/ run to the **Valle dei Templi;** #1 runs to **Pirandello's house.**

Taxis: At train station, in P. Marconi (☎26 670). A trip to the temples (p. 704) should run about €15 on the meter—just make sure it's running.

✦ ❼ ORIENTATION AND PRACTICAL INFORMATION

Agrigento's **train station** is in **Piazza Marconi,** the main stop for all city buses. Walk up the stairs to find the town's lively park-like central square, **Piazza Aldo Moro.** From P. Aldo Moro, the posh **Via Atenea** leads to the *centro storico.* At the far side of P. Aldo Moro is **Piazza Vittorio Emanuele,** just beyond which is the **bus station.** The temples are a bus ride (#1, 1/, 2, 2/, 3, or 3/) or a long walk away, below the town.

Tourist Office: AAPIT kiosk in the train station and **AAST** (☎20 454), adjacent to P. Aldo Moro. English-speaking staff, maps, and brochures. AAST open M and W-Sa 8am-1pm and 3:30-7pm, Tu 8am-1pm and 2-6pm. AAPIT kiosk open daily in summer 9am-1pm and 3:30-7pm; in winter 9am-1pm. Another summer office is in **Valle dei Templi,** adjacent to parking lot. English spoken. Open daily 8:30am-1pm and 3pm-sunset.

English-Language Bookstore: Capalunga, V. Atenea 123 (☎22 338; www.capalunga.com). Art shows, hip decor and a modest selection of English books. Curl up in an egg-shaped window seat overlooking the sea. Customers enjoy free Internet access. Open daily 9:30am-1pm and 6-10pm; July-Aug. closed M.

Carabinieri: P. Aldo Moro 2 (☎59 63 22). **First Aid:** ☎40 13 44.

Pharmacy: Farmacia Averna Antonio, V. Atenea 325 (☎26 093) and **Farmacia Dr Patti,** V. Atenea 129 (☎20 591). Both open M-F 9am-1:30pm and 5-8:30pm. Both also post late-night and weekend rotations.

Hospital: Ospedale Civile (☎44 21 11), 6km from town center toward Palermo on Contrada Consolida, off V. San Michele. Take bus #4 from P. Roselli.

Internet Access: A.M. Servizi Internet Train, Cortile Contarini 7 (☎40 27 83; www.internettrain.it). 1 block before Chiesa del Purgatorio, make a right onto V. Ate-

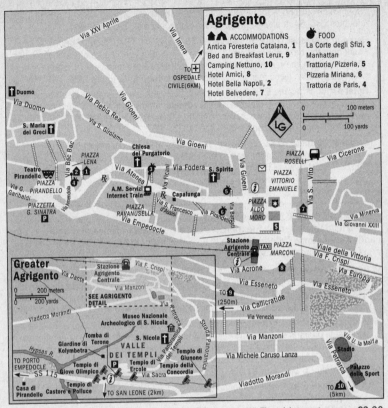

Agrigento

🏠🏠 ACCOMMODATIONS
Antica Foresteria Catalana, **1**
Bed and Breakfast Lerux, **9**
Camping Nettuno, **10**
Hotel Amici, **8**
Hotel Bella Napoli, **2**
Hotel Belvedere, **7**

🍴 FOOD
La Corte degli Sfizi, **3**
Manhattan
Trattoria/Pizzeria, **5**
Pizzeria Miriana, **6**
Trattoria de Paris, **4**

nea from P. Aldo Moro. 15 high-speed computers. Wi-Fi and Internet access €3.20 per hr. Open M-Sa 9:30am-1pm and 4-9pm.

Post Office: P. V. Emanuele (☎59 51 50; fax 22 926). Open M-Sa 8am-6:30pm. **Postal Code:** 92100.

🏠 ACCOMMODATIONS

Hotel Bella Napoli, P. Lena 6 (☎/fax 20 435; hotelbellanapoli@tin.it), off V. Bac Bac. Take V. Atenea 500m uphill, and turn right at the sign for Trattoria de Paris. Cheerful, yellow hallways lead to bright rooms with bath, A/C, phone and TV; some with balcony. Breakfast €3. Singles €35; doubles €65; triples €85. AmEx/MC/V. ❸

Antica Foresteria Catalana, P. Lena 5 (☎/fax 20 435; hotelbellanapoli@tin.it). Next door to Hotel Bella Napoli and under the same management. Large rooms with high, slanting ceilings and luxurious decor. All rooms with bath, A/C, phone and TV; some with balcony. Breakfast €3. Singles €45; doubles €75; triples €95. AmEx/MC/V. ❹

Hotel Belvedere, V. San Vito 20 (☎/fax 20 051). Follow clearly marked signs from train station. Friendly staff hosts guests in colorful classic rooms with fan, telephone, and TV.

Some rooms overlook the hotel's garden. Breakfast €3. Singles €35, with bath €49; doubles €45/64; triples €70/90. *Let's Go* discount 5%. Cash only. ❸

Bed and Breakfast Lerux, V. Callicratide 164 (☎27 203 or 333 20 59 606). A 5min. walk from the train station down V. Acrone. Owner Rugerro Casesa offers cheap apartment rooms in the residential district. Shared bath and communal TV room. Laundry €3. Reservations recommended. Singles €20; doubles €40; triples €60. Cash only. ❷

Hotel Amici, V. Acrone 5 (☎40 28 31; www.hotelamici.com). Down the stairs and next to the bingo parlor in P. Marconi. Offers 20 quiet rooms with bath, TV, and A/C; some with balcony and sea views. Parking and breakfast included. Singles €40-45; doubles €65-75; triples €75-85; quads €90-110. MC/V. ❹

Camping Nettuno, (☎41 62 68), on the beach, at V. l'Acquameno, by the bus stop. Take bus #2 or 2/ from the train station. Market, restaurant, bar, and pizzeria on premises. Free showers. €6 per person, €6 per tent, €3 per car. Cash only. ❶

🍴 FOOD

Alimentari cluster near P. Aldo Moro, and the small stairways tucked off V. Atenea lead to authentic, inexpensive trattorie. Indulge your sweet tooth at the candy stalls along V. della Vittoria. The *Sette Soli*, a smooth local wine, nicely complements most meals.

🍽 **Trattoria de Paris,** P. Lena 7 (☎25 413), beside Hotel Bella Napoli. Paris supplies locals with fresh pasta at a deliciously low price. Try the *cavatelli al cartoccio* (homemade pasta with eggplant, basil, ricotta cheese, and tomato sauce; €4.50). *Primi* €4.50, *secondi* €5-10. Service 15%. Open M-Sa noon-3pm and 7:30-10:30pm. AmEx/MC/V. ❷

🍽 **Manhattan Trattoria/Pizzeria,** Salita degli Angeli 9 (☎20 911), off V. Atenea. Sit inside or outside on terraced steps and enjoy regional specialties like *gnocchi al gorgonzola e pistacchio* (€7). The chef's specialty *ravioli* and tortellini options are excellent (€6-7). *Antipasto* buffet €5. Pizza from €3.50 (dinner only). *Primi* €5-7, meat *secondi* €5-7, fish *secondi* €6-15. Cover €1.50. Open M-Sa noon-3pm and 7-11pm. AmEx/MC/V. ❷

La Corte degli Sfizi, Cortile Contarini 4 (☎349 57 92 922), off V. Atenea. Classic Sicilian dishes served in a lush bamboo-enclosed garden. Pizza €4-7. *Primi* €5-8, *secondi* €6-12. Dinner *menù* €18-20. Cover €2, pizzeria service 20%. Open M and W-Su 11:30am-4pm and 6pm-1am. Cash only. ❷

Pizzeria Miriana, V. Pirandello 6 (☎22 828), off P. Aldo Moro. Simple takeout food for an unbeatable price. Pizza by the slice (€1.10) and pasta by the kilo (€2.50 per serving). Open M-Sa 8am-10pm. Cash only. ❶

👁 SIGHTS

VALLE DEI TEMPLI. Planted on a ridge below Agrigento's hilltop perch, the five temples revere the invincibility of Greek architecture. Having survived the ravages of time, earthquakes, vicious Punic Wars, and the rise of Christianity, the temples are official UNESCO World Heritage Sites. As sunlight transitions to moonlight, the temples cast eerie silhouettes across the countryside; after dark, they're illuminated by concealed lighting. From the ticket booth right off the road leading to Agrigento, an avenue heads uphill along the ridge, passing the **Tempio di Ercole.** You can climb amongst one row of solid, squat columns, which is all that remains of the earliest of the temples. Farther along, the perfectly intact pediment and columns of the **Tempio della Concordia** are the Valle's star attraction. Erected in the mid-5th-century BC from limestone, it owes its survival to its use by the Archbishop of Agrigento who, after kicking out the demons Eber and Ray, rededicated the temple to Saints Peter and Paul and transformed it into a Christian church. The road through the valley ends at the 5th-century BC **Tempio di Giunone.** During the ascent, hollows in the rock face to the left mark an early Christian burial site. Down the street lies the entrance to the eternally unfinished **Tempio di Giove Olimpico.** Had Carthaginian troops not interrupted its construction in 406 BC, it would have been one of the largest Greek temples ever built. The toppled partitioned columns and walls have challenged archaeologists for years, but the temple's most interesting sights are the gigantic *telamones*, 8m sculpted male figures meant to encircle the temple. One of these massive men has been reconstructed at the site. At the end of the path stand four columns of the long since destroyed **Tempio di Castore e Polluce,** also known as the Tempio dei Dioscuri, where sailors and athletes would offer sacrifice for good fortune in their endeavors.

The **Museo Nazionale Archeologico di San Nicola,** 1km uphill from the parking lot, has an enormous collection of red- and black-figure vases, terra-cotta votive figures, and funerary vessels from the area's necropolis. Escape from the sun, and go indoors to see an upright *telamon*, as well as model projections of how a completed Tempio di Giove Olimpico might have looked. The **Chiesa di San Nicola** near the museum displays the sarcophagus of Phaedra, one of the most impressive AD 3rd-century works of art. *(30min. walk from the train station. Starting on V. F. Crispi, follow signs downhill and left at the lower intersection. Buses #1/, 2, 2/, 3, or 3/ run from the train station and stop in a dirt parking lot with a snack bar. Make sure to bring lots of water, sunscreen, light clothes, and good walking shoes, as there is no break from the relentless Agrigento sun. Visiting when the park opens or right before it closes is a good way to avoid both heat and crowds. Temple ☎ 390 92 22 64 36, Museum ☎ 390 22 59 54 48. Lower temples open daily in summer 8:30am-7pm; in winter 8:30am-5pm. Upper temples open daily in summer 8:30am-7pm and 9pm-midnight; in winter 8:30am-7pm. Temples €6; museum €6; combined ticket €10; EU citizens 18-24 €5, under 18 or over 65 free. Parking €2 for 3hr., motorcycle €1.50.)*

GIARDINO DELLA KOLYMBETRA. Originally used as a garden and irrigation basin by the Greeks in 500 BC, the Gardens at Kolymbetra, translated roughly from Greek as "the place of giving waters," were used continually as an orchard until the 20th century. Given over to the FAI (Italian Environmental Agency) in the 1990s, the garden is now restored to its formal quiet splendor. Take a break from temple-gazing and enjoy a quiet walk through the shade. If you call ahead, a picnic lunch can be arranged for €1 per person. *(In a valley next to the Tempio di Castore e Polluce; follow the signs to the garden. ☎ 335 12 29 042; www.fondoambiente.it. Open daily July-Sept. 10am-7pm; Apr.-June 10am-6pm; Oct.-Mar. 10am-5pm. €2.)*

CHIESA DI SANTA MARIA DEI GRECI. First constructed by the Normans in the 1100s and remodeled by the Byzantines in the 1300s, Santa Maria dei Greci's real attraction is not what's inside, but what's beneath. Below the pews and through its glass floors, visitors can see a 5th-century BC ancient Greek temple dedicated to Athena and recently excavated ruins of Agrigento's first Christian church from the AD 5th century. The original Athenian sacrificial altar stands behind the Christian altar in the present church. Down below, pay special attention to the large hole in front of the temple's altar, where the entrance to a tunnel once led all the way to the Valle dei Templi. *(Follow the signs up the hill from V. Bac Bac, off V. Atenea. ☎ 333 87 02 111. Open M-Sa 9am-1pm and 3-6pm, Su upon request. Donations requested.)*

CHIESA DEL PURGATORIO (SAN LORENZO). The legendary craftsman Serpotta employed all of his wizardry to make this church's stucco sculptures look like marble. The statues of the Virtues were intended to help parishioners stay out of purgatory by reminding them of its unpleasantries. Church elders did a thorough job—it's pretty hard to ignore the reminders of eternal damnation, including the skull and crossbones on the confessionals and countless depictions of roasted sinners. *(In P. Purgatorio, off V. Atenea, in the* centro storico. *Open M-Sa 9:30am-7:30pm. €1.50.)*

TEATRO PIRANDELLO. Dedicated to Queen Margherita on its opening in 1880, the theater was renamed in honor of Agrigento's favorite son, playwright Luigi Pirandello, on the 10th anniversary of his death in 1946. After brief stints as a movie theater and playhouse, the building now hosts a variety of plays in the winter months, including many works by Pirandello. There are no plays in the summer, but the 19th-century building designed by local architect Dioniso Sciascia is worth a peek. Look for the four names on the dome ceiling of ancient *agrigentini* famous for the arts. *(☎59 02 22. Open M-F 8am-1pm, Tu and Th 3-6pm. Plays Nov.-May. Check the schedule posted at the theater or ask at the tourist office. €2.50, includes tour in English.)*

CASA NATALE DI LUIGI PIRANDELLO. Pirandello aficionados will enjoy a visit to his birthplace a few kilometers outside of the city. Treasures include a series of photographs, playbills, script drafts, and various letters to and from the master. A huge stone marks his gravesite. This site is best-suited for people with a strong interest in the life and work of Pirandello. *(Take the TUA bus #1 to P. Kaos. ☎51 11 02. Open daily 9am-1pm and 4-7pm. €2, under 18 or over 65 free.)*

🌸 🎭 FESTIVALS AND BEACHES

The hills surrounding the Valle dei Templi come alive with the sound of music every year on the first Sunday in February, when Agrigento hosts the **Almond Blossom Festival,** an international folk-dancing fest. The **Settimana Pirandelliana,** a week-long outdoor festival of plays, operas, and ballets in P. Kaos, pays homage to the town's beloved son in late July and early August. (Info ☎23 561.) During summer months, *agrigentini* abandon the town in search of the beach and nightlife at **San Leone,** 4km from Agrigento by bus #2. Just be careful not to tumble down the **Scala dei Turchi,** the beautiful natural steps that descend to **Lido Rossello,** another popular beach, after a night of carousing.

WESTERN SICILY

TRAPANI
☎0923

From ancient rooftops and buildings adorned with exquisite tilework to the colorful fishing boats and massive ferries plowing the waves just below the horizon, Trapani (TRA-pa-nee; pop. 75,000) is every bit the crossroads between Europe and North Africa it has been for centuries. Despite the town's appeal, most travelers only pass through. Reliable transportation and extensive lodgings make Trapani a good base for adventures to Marsala's monuments, Segesta's temple, the Egadi Islands' peaceful nature, Erice's medieval streets, San Vito Lo Capo's beaches, and the natural splendor of Riserva dello Zingaro reserve.

🚏 TRANSPORTATION

Flights: Vincenzo Florio Airport (☎84 25 02), in Birgi en route to Marsala, 16km outside of Trapani. Buses from P. Malta are timed to coincide with flights. Daily flights to **Rome** and **Pantelleria.** Not a heavily used airport.

Trains: (☎89 20 21), in P. Umberto I. Ticket office open daily 6am-7:50pm. To: **Castel-vetrano** (1½hr., 13 per day 6:05am-8:30pm, €4.40); **Marsala** (30min., 14 per day 6:05am-8:30pm, €2.75); **Palermo** (2hr., 12 per day 5am-8:25pm, €6.45).

Buses: AST (☎21 021). Station in P. Malta. From the front of the train station, turn left on V. Mazzini, then left again on V. Marinella. P. Malta will be to the left. To: **Erice** (45min.; M-Sa 11 per day 6:40am-5:30pm, Su 4 per day 9am-5pm; €2); **Marsala** (M-Sa 6:55, 10:45am, 12:50, 2:10pm; €2.75); **San Vito Lo Capo** (1½hr.; M-Sa 9 per day 6:45am-6pm, Su 4 per day 7:50am-6:30pm; €3.20). **Segesta** (☎21 754) runs buses to local towns and to **Rome** (15hr.; Th and Su 5:15pm, Sa 6am; €46).

Ferries: *Traghetti* (ferries) and *aliscafi* (hydrofoils) leave for the **Egadi Islands** (Levanzo, Favignana, and Marettimo), **Pantelleria, Sardinia** and **Tunisia.** Ferries leave from Stazione Marittima across from P. Garibaldi; hydrofoils depart from a dock farther along V. Ammiraglio Staiti, about 150m toward the train station. Buy tickets from the travel agents along V. A. Staiti, from ticket booths on the docks, and at Stazione Marittima. Chart below shows high-season (June-Aug.) times and rates; less frequent and less expensive in low season. Schedules change with weather and are available at all ticket offices and at tourist office.

Ustica (☎22 200; www.usticalines.it), in a yellow booth at the hydrofoil dock. AmEx/MC/V.

Siremar (☎54 54 55; www.siremar.it), with ticket offices at a blue-and-white striped waterfront booth, at the hydrofoil dock, and in Stazione Marittima. Open M-F 6:15am-noon, 3-6pm, and 9pm-midnight; Sa 6:15am-noon, 4:15-5:15pm, and 9:30pm-midnight; Su 6-10am, 5-5:45pm, and 9:30pm-midnight. AmEx/MC/V.

Tirrenia (☎54 54 55; www.tirrenia.it), in Stazione Marittima. Open M and W-F 9am-1pm and 3-6pm, Tu 9am-1pm and 6-9pm, Sa 9am-noon. AmEx/MC/V.

DESTINATION	COMPANY	DURATION	FREQUENCY	PRICE
Favignana (Egadi Islands)	Siremar (ferry)	1hr.	3 per day	€3.20
Favignana (E.I.)	Ustica (hydrofoil)	20min.	10 per day	€7.30
Favignana (E.I.)	Siremar (hydrofoil)	25min.	10 per day	€5.30
Levanzo (E.I.)	Siremar (ferry)	1hr.	3 per day	€3.20
Levanzo (E.I.)	Siremar (hydrofoil)	20min.	10 per day	€5.30
Levanzo (E.I.)	Ustica (hydrofoil)	30min.	10 per day	€7.30
Marettimo (E.I.)	Siremar (ferry)	3hr.	1 per day	€7.10
Marettimo (E.I.)	Siremar (hydrofoil)	40min.	3 per day	€11.80
Marettimo (E.I.)	Ustica (hydrofoil)	1hr.	2 per day	€13.80
Pantelleria	Siremar (ferry)	5¾hr.	midnight daily	€23.70
Pantelleria	Ustica (hydrofoil)	2½hr.	6pm daily	€36
Cagliari (Sardinia)	Tirrenia (ferry)	11½hr.	Tu 9pm	€40.65
Tunis, Tunisia	Ustica (ferry)	8hr.	M, W, F noon	€44

Public Transportation: Orange **SAU buses** have main terminal at P. Emanuele, 4 blocks up V. Scontrino from the train station. The SAU office will be on the right. Posts schedules of all routes. Complete schedules also available at the tourist office. Tickets (€0.80) sold at *tabaccherie*.

Taxis: in P. Umberto I, outside the train station (☎22 808). In V. Ammiraglio Staiti, near the port (☎23 233).

✈ 🛈 ORIENTATION AND PRACTICAL INFORMATION

Trapani sits on a peninsula 2hr. west of Palermo by bus or train. The old city began at the outer tip of the hook, growing backward from the peninsula until it spilled new streets and high-rises onto the mainland. The **train station** is in **Piazza Umberto I,** with the **bus station** just to the left and behind the train station in **Piazza Malta.** Via

Scontrino runs past the train station; a right from the station leads to an intersection with **Via Garibaldi** at **Piazza Emanuele,** where all the local buses stop. V. Garibaldi becomes **Via Libertà** and moves into the old city. The first left off V. Libertà is **Via Torrearsa,** home to the **AAPIT tourist office.** The next left off V. Libertà, **Via Roma,** leads down to the port. V. Libertà merges with **Corso Vittorio Emanuele,** which runs all the way to the **Torre di Ligny** at the end of the peninsula.

Tourist Offices:

AAPIT (☎29 000; www.apt.trapani.it), off V. Torrearsa. Eager-to-help staffer Mighali Augostino provides maps, helps with lodgings, and doles out info on attractions in and around town. Pick up a *Trapani Hotels* guide. Open M-Sa 8am-8pm, Su 9am-noon.

Provincial Tourism Office, V. San Francesco d'Assisi 27 (☎54 55 11; www.apt.trapani.it), off V. Verdi. Marked "APT" on maps. Serves the entire province of Trapani. Open M-Tu and Th-Sa 8am-2pm, W 8am-2pm and 2:30-6pm.

Currency Exchange: Banks line many of the city's streets, including C. Italia. They generally have better rates than the train station. The post office also changes money and traveler's checks. **ATMs** are at Stazione Marittima in the old city and along V. Scontrino in front of the train station.

Emergency: Police, P. Vittorio Veneto (☎59 02 98). **Carabinieri,** V. Orlandini 19 (☎27 122). **First Aid,** P. Generale Scio 1 (☎29 629). **Ambulance:** ☎180 94 50.

Pharmacy: Vle. Margherita 9, next to P. V. Veneto. All pharmacies open M-F 9am-1:30pm and 4:30-8pm. After-hours rotation posted outside. Look for bright green cross.

Hospital: Ospedale Sant'Antonio Abate, V. Cosenza 81 (☎80 91 11), far northeast of the city center.

Internet Access: Phone and Internet, V. Regina Elena 26/28 (☎28 866; www.trapaniservice.it). Right next to P. Garibaldi, along the *lungomare*, this business provides 3 computers for €5 per hr. as well as international phone services and fax. Open M-Sa 10am-1pm and 4-8:30pm.

Post Office: P. V. Veneto 3 (☎43 41 11). Huge building in P. V. Veneto on V. Garibaldi marked "Poste" on one tower and "Telegraph" on the other. **Currency exchange,** booth #18. Open M-Sa 8am-6:30pm. **Postal Code:** 91100.

⚡TIP **KA-CHING!** Before exchanging money, always ask if the bank or currency exchange charges a commission. Commissions can be as high as €10, and there is no Italian law requiring financial institutions to inform clients of exchange fees before finalizing transactions.

⌂ ACCOMMODATIONS AND CAMPING

Hotel Moderno, V. Genovese 20 (☎21 247; hotelmodernotrapani@virgilio.it). From P. Sant'Agostino on C. Vittorio Emanuele, turn right on V. Roma and left on V. Genovese. The *albergo* has an accommodating staff and modern, well-kept rooms, all with TV and bath. Reception 24hr. Singles €25; doubles €50; triples €67. AmEx/MC/V. ❷

Albergo Messina, C. V. Emanuele 71, 4th fl. (☎/fax 21 198). Run by an elderly couple, this tiny 9-room hotel is located near the port in the old city. High-ceilinged rooms have an antique atmosphere, but location and price couldn't get any better. All rooms have balcony, sink, fridge, and ceiling fan. Shared bath. Breakfast €4. Singles €20; doubles €35. Extra bed 35% of room cost. AmEx/MC/V. ❷

Hotel Vittoria, V. Francesco Crispi 4 (☎87 30 44; www.hotelvittoriatrapani.it), off P. V. Emanuele, near train station. 65 large, luxurious rooms offer modern comforts, including A/C, free Internet in lobby, and coastal views in some rooms. Inviting communal area. Breakfast included. Singles €60; doubles €95; triples €128. AmEx/MC/V. ❺

Nuovo Albergo Russo, V. Tintori 4 (☎22 166; fax 26 623), off C. V. Emanuele. Rooms are comfortable and centrally located with an eclectic mix of decorating styles. All with bath, A/C, and TV. Breakfast €7. Singles €43; doubles €77; triples €115; quads €145. AmEx/MC/V. ❹

Campeggio Lido Valderice, V. del Detince 15 (☎57 34 77), in the seaside town of Lido Valderice. Take bus for Bonegia or San Vito Lo Capo (€3.20). Follow flower-lined road opposite bus stop and perpendicular to the highway, and turn right at its end. Well-shaded campground near beaches. Hot showers €0.60. €5 per person, €4.50 per tent, €2.50 per car, €7-10 per camper. AmEx/MC/V. ❶

🍴 FOOD

Trapani's cuisine is an exotic blend of North African and Italian flavors. *Couscous* prepared with fish is one of the area's specialties as well as the *biscotti con fichi*, the Italian Fig Newton. If you're cooking your own meals, the old city has many *alimentari*, as well as a daily fish and fruit **market** along the northern *lungomare* at the intersection of V. Maggio and V. Garibaldi. In addition, **Supermercato Di per Di,** V. San Pietro 30, is two streets up from the port between Chiesa di Santa Maria del Gesù and Chiesa di San Pietro. (☎24 620. Open M-Tu and Th-Sa 8:30am-2pm and 4:30-8pm, W 8:30am-2pm.)

▨ Trattoria da Salvatore, V. Nunzio Nasi 19 (☎54 65 30), 1 street toward the port from C. V. Emanuele. Family-style restaurant serves regional pastas like *busiata con sarde* (€6.50) and spicy *couscous* (€8.50). *Primi* €4-8.50, *secondi* €7-8.50. Cover €1.50. Open daily noon-3:30pm and 6:30pm-midnight. In winter closed Su. AmEx. ❷

Ristorante Medina, Vle. Regina Margherita 19 (☎29 028). Just across the street from the main gate to the Villa Margherita Gardens. A popular teen hangout, Medina serves Middle Eastern cuisine and pizza in large portions at great prices. Pizza from €1.50 per slice. Kebabs €3.50. *Panini* €3.50. Open daily noon-3pm and 7pm-midnight. ❶

Cantina Siciliana, V. Giudecca 32 (☎28 673; www.cantinasiciliana.it). From the port, walk up V. XXX Gennaio. V. Giudecca is the 1st left past C. Italia. Specializes in Trapanese and Sicilian cuisine with decor resembling a ship's galley. *Primi* €6-12, *secondi* €8.50-12. Open daily 12:30-5pm and 7:30-11pm. MC/V. ❸

Ristorante Antichi Sapori, C. V. Emanuele 191 (☎22 866; www.gliantichisapori.it). Follow C. V. Emanuele until you reach P. Jolanda. A hearty mariner's meal of fresh fish awaits travelers coming into port at Sapori. Specialities include fresh fish straight from the lungomare market. Primi €6.50-17, secondi €7-13.50. AmEx/MC/V. ❷

Pizzeria Calvino, V. N. Nasi 77 (☎21 464), 100m from the *duomo*. With a line out the door every night, this pizzeria is widely considered the best in town. More than 30 delicious varieties cooked using handmade tomato sauce. Order to go or reserve 1-2hr. ahead for a table. Prepare for a potentially long wait. Delivery available. Pizza from €3.90. Open M and W-Su 7pm-12:30am. Cash only. ❶

Taverno Paradiso, Lungomare Dante Alighieri 22 (☎/fax 22 303). With vine-covered stone walls and cherub sculptures, Paradiso emits a romantic villa-like atmosphere. Serves seafood for the connoisseur not concerned with price. *Primi* from €9, *secondi* €9-13. Cover €3. Open M-Sa 12:30-3:30pm and 7:30-10:30pm. AmEx/MC/V. ❸

Poldo, P. Lucatelli 8 (☎347 03 23 231), off V. Turretta near the ferry station. Poldo serves delicious *panini* (€1.80-3) at modest prices with nicer service than most *bars*. Try a cheeseburger (€3) that puts most American burger joints to shame. *Primi* from €6, *secondi* from €7. Open daily 8:30am-11:30pm. Cash only. ❷

👁 SIGHTS

Delicate stone statues blend into the gray exterior of the 17th-century Baroque **Chiesa del Purgatorio,** 1 block up from P. Garibaldi. Inside, 20 nearly life-sized wooden sculptures, known as *I Misteri* ("The mysteries"), depict the passion and crucifixion of Christ. Every year on Good Friday, the sculptures, each requiring the strength of 14-30 men to move, are dressed up and paraded around the city. The sculptures' 18th-century artists constructed the Roman soldiers to resemble Spanish conquistadors, reflecting Spanish dominance in Sicily at the time. Several statues were damaged in WWII but have since been restored. (Open daily 9am-noon and 3:30-6:30pm. Free.) The main attraction in the modern part of town is the enormous and lavishly decorated **Sanctuario dell'Annunziata.** This church houses a 14th-century statue of the Madonna of Trapani. Legend has it that a boat carrying the statue got caught in a storm; the captain promised God that if he survived, he would leave it as a gift to the first port at which he arrived. In the same complex is the **Museo Nazionale Pepoli,** which features a collection of local sculpture and painting, coral carvings, and folk-art figurines, including a frightening portrayal of Herod's baby hunt. This area is 2 blocks to the right of the train station or an SAU bus ride (#24, 25, or 30) from P. V. Emanuele. (*Sanctuario* ☎53 91 84; museum ☎55 32 69 or 53 12 42. *Sanctuario* open M-Sa 8am-noon and 4-7pm, Su 8am-1pm and 4-7pm; museum open Tu-Sa 9am-1:30pm, Su 9am-12:30pm. Call to confirm hours. €4, ages 18-25 €2, under 18 or over 65 free.)

The picturesque **Torre di Ligny,** at the end of a wide jetty off a promontory, is visible from both of Trapani's ports. By day, the rock walls of the tower seem like outcroppings of the rocky surf, as the identically colored brick fortress rises over boulders. By night, the northern coastline appears as a vision of bright lights reflecting off the water. The tower houses the **Museo di Preistoria/Museo del Mare,** with shells, artifacts, and underwater excavation pieces. (☎22 300. Open M-Sa 9:30am-noon, Su 10:30am-12:30pm. €1.55.) At the cusp of the old and new cities, the **Villa Margherita's** gardens offer a change of pace from cobblestone and cement. Banyan trees, palms, and fountains surround avenues. In addition, playgrounds and a statuary complete the picture. Each July, the gardens host the **Luglio Musicale Trapanese,** a festival of opera, ballet, and cabaret that draws stars to the temporary stage amid shady trees. Other concerts occur almost every month of the year. (☎21 454. Shows 9pm. Info booth inside park gates.)

🔁 DAYTRIPS FROM TRAPANI

SAN VITO LO CAPO

AST buses leave Trapani's P. Malta for San Vito Lo Capo (depart 9 per day 6:45am-6pm, return 9 per day 6:45am-7:30pm; €3.35, round-trip €5.25). AST info ☎21 021. Buy tickets at station office or in the adjoining bar.

A popular vacation spot for Italians, Germans, and Spaniards, San Vito Lo Capo (pop. 3900) has largely remained under the radar of the English-speaking world. While sun worshippers flock to San Vito's 3km of flawless **beaches** in July and August, the annual **Couscous Fest,** held during the 3rd week of September, is the Super Bowl of multi-ethnic Mediterranean cuisine. For shade and seclusion, escape 10km away to the ☒**Riserva dello Zingaro,** Italy's first nature reserve, where rare Bonelli's eagles, mountain trails, and prehistoric caves abound. An unfinished four-lane highway came perilously close to marring the pristine reserve's isolation, but a 1981 environmental rally halted construction. Once in the reserve, follow the road to successive, secluded, pebble beaches that stretch along the coastline. Due to entrances on both sides of the reserve, the middle two beaches offer the most privacy. Although camping is illegal and motor vehicles are prohibited, the hiking is superb. **Bluvacanze**, V. Savoia 166, runs excursions (M, W, F 9am, return 4pm; €10), rents scooters, bikes, and cars. (☎62 10 85. Bikes €5 per day, scooters €30-35 per day, cars €42-54 per day. Cash only except for cars.)

For a taste of authentic Mediterranean cuisine, head to **Tha'am ❸**, V. Duca degli Abbruzzi 32, off V. Farina near the waterfront, where Sicilian and Tunisian flavors intermingle in an elegant Arabic-tiled dining area. (*Primi* €8-15, *secondi* €9-15. Cover €2.50. Open daily 12:30-3pm and 7pm-3am. MC/V.) The luxurious modern **Helios Hotel ❸**, V. Savoia 299, though far from the beach, offers fully-furnished rooms with balcony, A/C, phone, TV, minifridge, safe, and free shuttles to and from the beach. (☎97 44 18; www.sanvitoheli* oshotel.it. Breakfast included. 7-night min. July-Aug. €35-70 per person. AmEx/MC/V.)

MARSALA

Trains service Marsala from Trapani (30min., 14 per day, €2.65). AST buses (☎23 222) also run from Trapani (40min.; M-Sa 6:55, 10:45am, 12:50, 2:10pm; €2.75, round-trip €4.40) and back (M-Sa 7, 8:20am, 1:25, and 2:25pm). From the train station, a right facing V. A. Fazio and then a slight left on V. Roma leads to the centro storico. V. Roma turns into V. XI Maggio and then Vle. Vittorio Veneto. The Pro Loco Tourist Office is at V. XI Maggio 100, before Palazzo Comunale and the duomo. (☎71 40 97; www.prolocomarsala.org. Open M-Sa 8am-8pm, Su 9am-noon.)

An area of both ancient history and modern convenience, Marsala's (mahr-SA-lah; pop. 77,000) streets are worthy of a short visit. The city's lack of budget accommodations make it best suited for a daytrip from nearby Trapani. It was at Marsala that Garibaldi and his red-shirted revolutionaries landed in 1860 to launch the Risorgimento. Marsala celebrates this event with its **Porta Garibaldi**, an 18th-century gate erected where Garibaldi first entered the city. Additionally, in the San Pietro complex on V. XI Maggio, the **Museo Civico** features a variety of Garibaldi-related artifacts, including thousands of red shirts and Garibaldi's own ostentatious uniform. (Open daily 9am-1pm and 4-8pm. €2, under 18 €1, EU residents over 65 free.) The **Museo Archeologico Regionale Baglio Anselmi** guards the famed **Carthiginian warship.** This now skeletal vessel sank in the final battle of the First Punic War (241 BC), in which Rome defeated Carthage and established its naval supremacy. In addition to the ship, other galleries display objects from Lilybaeum and the Isle of Mozia, including pottery and two life-size sculptures. (☎95 36 14. Open daily 9am-6pm. €3, under 18 €2, EU residents over 65 free.)

Besides battles and revolutionaries, Marsala is famous for sweet Marsala wine. Samples are available at various *enoteche* scattered throughout the old city. For something to soak up all that wine, head to **Trattoria Garibaldi ❷**, P. Addolorata 5, fittingly across from Porta Garibaldi. This upscale trattoria serves vegetarian omelettes (€4) and a wide variety of Italian cuisine in a relaxed yet classy atmosphere. (*Primi* from €4.50, *secondi* from €6. Cover €1. Open M-F noon-3pm and 7:30-10:30pm, Sa 7-10pm, Su noon-3pm. AmEx/MC/V.) If you decide to spend the night, your best bet is **Hotel Acos ❹**, V. Mazara 14, with 37 rooms, along with a bar, restaurant, and swimming pool. All rooms have TV, bath, and A/C. (☎99 91 66; www.acoshotel.com. Breakfast €5. Singles €40-52; doubles €57-130.)

THE TEMPLE OF SEGESTA

Tarantola buses (☎31 020) leave P. Malta in Trapani for Segesta (depart 8am, noon, 2pm; return 1:10, 4:10pm; €3.05, round-trip €5). Temple open 9am-7pm; ticket office 9am-6pm. €6, EU residents ages 18-25 €3, EU residents under 18 or over 65 free.

The extraordinary Doric temple is one of the best-preserved relics of ancient Greek architecture. Isolated and untouched, it dominates a landscape of dramatic valleys and lush vineyards of Segesta (se-JEH-sta), a former Trojan colony. Roam among the 5th-century BC columns or take a Lilliputian seat on a pedestal and contemplate their majesty. A wealth of ruins, including a Greek theater, a castle, and a mosque, cluster nearby around Monte Barbaro. It's worth taking the bus (every 30min., €1.20) to avoid the steep uphill trek in the midday sun, but the 25min. walk to the top is quite pleasant on cooler days. The ◙**Greek theater** carved into the hilltop has a 4000-person capacity and holds performances from mid-July to August. Ask at the Trapani tourist office for details.

ERICE   ☎0923

Visitors to tiny Erice (EH-ree-chay; pop. 300) will be charmed by its quiet streets and awed by the panoramic views that stretch from Pantelleria to Mt. Etna. A center of worship since the fertility cults of the Phoenician goddess Tanit-Asarte, Erice is home today to a beautiful *duomo*—La Chiesa Madrice (the Mother Church). Once atop the *campanile* of the *duomo* or the peak of a Castello Normanno tower, it's easy to forget the bustling crowds below and understand why the people of Erice call their home "Il Monte del Dio" *(The Mountain of God)*.

◪⊅ TRANSPORTATION AND PRACTICAL INFORMATION. The **bus** from Trapani to Erice departs from P. Malta (40min.; M-Sa 10 per day 6:40am-7:50pm, last return to Trapani 7:30pm; Su 4 per day 9am-5:30pm, last return to Trapani 8:40pm; round-trip €3.05). Buses stop on **Via Conte Pepoli,** at the base of town and near the Castello Normanno. From the **Porta Trapani,** a left turn leads to the **duomo** and its hard-to-miss **campanile.** Straight through the Porta Trapani is **Via Vittorio Emanuele** and Erice's major *centro*, **Piazza Umberto I.** Back at the bus stop, following V. Conte Pepoli to its end leads to the **Giardino del Balio** (Balio Gardens) and the **Castello Normanno,** also known as the **Castello di Venere** (Castle of Venus). The **AAST Tourist Office** on V. Guarrasi 1, near P. Umberto I, provides colorful town maps and brochures. (☎86 93 88. Open M-F 9am-9pm.) **ATMs** can be found all over Erice, including one on V. V. Emanuele, near P. Umberto I.

▐▐ ACCOMMODATIONS AND FOOD. Finding reasonably priced accommodations in Erice may be difficult, so consider staying in nearby Trapani. One good option in Erice is ◙**Ulisse Camere ❸,** V. Santa Lucia 2, five blocks down V. Conte Pepoli from the bus stop. When reserving ahead, ask for a room with a view of the Egadi islands (no extra charge) or one that shares the quiet private courtyard. The best is Room 11, which includes a patio, entryway, and gorgeous view, in addition to the standard full bathroom and TV. (☎86 01 55; www.sitodiulisse.it. Singles €35, with breakfast €38; doubles €60/65; triples €70/79. Cash only.) **Villa San Giovanni ❸,** V. Nunzio Nasi 12, provides simple rooms with full bath, telephone, balcony, and panoramic views that make it worth every euro. (☎86 91 71; villas.giovanni@libero.it. Breakfast included. Singles €38-42; doubles €75-78; half pension €45-48; full pension €55-58.) At **La Vetta ❷,** V. Giuseppe Fontana 5, off P. Umberto I, savor Chef Mario's take on regional favorite *couscous* and *busiati*, Sicilian pasta hand-rolled into a narrow tube, both €7. (☎86 94 04. Pizza from €4.50. *Primi* €7, *secondi* from €6. Cover €1.50-2. Open M-W and F-Su noon-3:30pm and 7:30pm-midnight. Closed Oct.-Nov. AmEx/MC/V.) **Ristorante Monte San Giuliano ❸**, V. San Rocco 7. Offers a variety of regional cuisine on a seaside terrace tucked neatly under stone archways. (☎86 95 95; www.montesangiuliano.it. *Primi* €8-9, *secondi* €7-15. Cover €2. Open Tu-Su 12:15-3pm and 8-11pm. Closed Nov. 2-17 and Jan. 7-27. AmEx/MC/V.) In addition to the house specialty *morbido a coco* (almond-coconut candy; €30 per kg), **Pasticceria Tulipano ❶**, V. V. Emanuele 10-12, serves cheap, quick meals, including *tavola calda* (€2-5.50), pizza, and pasta. (☎86 96 72. Open daily 7:30am-midnight. AmEx/MC/V.)

◪ **SIGHTS.** Erice fits an impressive number of sights inside its 8th-century BC **Elymian walls.** The **Castello Normanno** (also known as Castello di Venere) was built on the site of ancient temples to fertility goddesses. It served as a prison until 1940, but the hollow tub against the wall farthest from the entrance, which was likely used for human sacrifice, indicates a more ominous legacy. Inquire at the tourist office about guided tours and winter hours. (Open daily 9am-7pm. Donations requested.) Next to the castle is a Spanish-style ◪**Torre Medievale** perched seemingly impossibly on a rock outcropping. At the castle's base, the **Giardini del Balio** spread green boughs over stone benches. The views from the gardens and castle are incomparable, and most of the countryside—the Egadi Islands, Pantelleria, and occasionally Etna and Tunisia—is visible over the horizon. Throughout Erice, 61 churches await exploration; all are accessible by a joint €5 ticket. The 14th-century Gothic **duomo** features ornate ceilings in the Arabian-influenced Neo-Gothic interior. The **campanile** (bell tower) offers broad views. (Open daily 10am-6pm; Aug. 10am-midnight. *Campanile* €2, with *duomo* €3.) In P. Umberto I, the **Museo Comunale di Erice**, inside the library, houses a small but varied collection primarily relating to the city's fertility goddesses. (Open M-F 8am-2pm, also M and Th 2:30pm-5:30pm. Free.)

EGADI ISLANDS (ISOLE EGADI)   ☎0923

The Egadi Islands (EE-zo-leh EH-ga-dee), inhabited since prehistoric times, offer some of the most peaceful relaxation in Sicily. Lying just off Trapani, the archipelago of Favignana, Levanzo, and Marettimo is easily accessible by ferry or hydrofoil. Favignana is the largest and most modern of the trio, with plenty of beaches—and tourists to pack them. In the port towns of Levanzo and Marettimo, mules and sheep share the plains with cacti, and rugged cliffs climb the coast.

▛ TRANSPORTATION

Siremar (☎92 13 68; www.siremar.it) and **Ustica** (☎92 12 77; www.usticalines.it) both run **hydrofoils** to the islands from Trapani (Favignana and Levanzo 25-45min., Marettimo 45-60min.; 11 per day 6:30am-8:20pm; Favignana €7.30, Marettimo €13.80, Levanzo €7.30). Ustica runs hydrofoils between the three islands (Favignana-Levanzo 6 per day 6:55am-9:30pm, €4.20; Favignana-Marettimo 10am, 2:35, and 4:50pm, €8.90). Siremar runs **ferries** from Trapani to Favignana (1hr.; M-Sa 7, 10am, and 5:15pm, Su 10am and 5:45pm; €3.20).

FAVIGNANA

Favignana's (fa-veen-YA-na; pop. 3800) ample and appealing beaches make it a summer playground for Italians enamored with island living. They build summer homes on the shoreline, while short-term vacationers arrive eager for a tan and expecting the modern conveniences the sister towns lack.

▐▐ TRANSPORTATION. Buses are necessary to reach the more remote beaches. Tarantola **buses** (☎92 19 44) run from Porto Florio: **Line 1** (10 per day 8am-7:30pm) to Calamone (5min.), Lido Burrone (8min.), Cala Azzurra (15min.); **Line 2** (8 per day 7:45am-7:40pm) to Calamone and Cala Rotonda (13min.); **Line 3** (7 per day 8:30am-6:50pm) to Cala Rossa (7min.), Lido Burrone, and Calamone. Buy tickets (€0.70) on the bus. **Francesca e Rocco,** Traversa Calamoni 7, runs **minibus** excursions around the island. (☎348 58 60 676. Available 24hr. €15 per person, 4-person min.) **Noleggio Isidoro,** V. Mazzini 40, rents **bikes** and **scooters.** (☎347 32 33 058. Bikes €3 per day, scooters €15. Driver's license required. Open daily 8am-8pm.)

> **▐▌ ALL ABOARD!** Make sure to board hydrofoils and ferries early. They usually leave exactly at the scheduled time, and tickets are non-refundable.

▐▌▐▌ ORIENTATION AND PRACTICAL INFORMATION. Hydrofoils and ferries run from **Porto Florio.** A right out of the port leads to **Piazza Europa** and **Via Vittorio Emanuele,** which connects P. Europa to the main plaza, **Piazza Madrice.** Running parallel to V. V. Emanuele, between the two *piazze*, is **Via Mazzini.** At P. Madrice, V. V. Emanuele becomes **Via Roma. Via Nicotera** also runs through P. Madrice. Off V. V. Emanuele, **Via Garibaldi** runs away from the *piazze* and eventually becomes **Via Libertà** as it heads into the countryside. The most beautiful beaches are about 1km away from the port. Agnese Lombardo happily provides brochures, schedules, maps, and accommodation help at **Pro Loco tourist office,** P. Madrice 68 (☎92 16 47; www.egadiweb.it/proloco. Open daily 9am-8pm.) **Banco di Sicilia,** P. Madrice 12/14, has an **ATM** and **currency exchange.** (☎92 13 47. Open M-F 8:20am-1:20pm and 2:50-3:50pm.) In case of **emergency,** the **carabinieri** (☎92 12 02) are on V. Simone Corleo, near P. Castello, and **first aid** (☎92 12 83) is on Contrada delle Fosse, off V. Calamoni. **Farmacia Barone** is at P. Madrice 64. (☎92 12 65. Open daily 8:30am-1pm and 5-8:30pm.) **Farmacia Dottore Abramo** is at P. Europa 41. (☎92 16 66. Open M-W and F-Su 8:30am-12:30pm and 5-8:30pm.) Both pharmacies post after-hours rotations outside. The **post office** is at V. Guglielmo Marconi 1, off P. Madrice. (☎92 12 09. Open M-F 8am-1:30pm, Sa 8am-12:30pm.) **Postal Code:** 91023.

▐▌▐▌ ACCOMMODATIONS AND FOOD. Rustic and rural, Favignana has better camping than hotels. However, the **Casa Vacanze Mio Sogno ❷,** V. Calamoni 2, is a real steal. Take V. Libertà and turn left on V. Dante. While somewhat out of the way, this establishment is couched in a castle-like structure. Rooms come with bath, kitchenette, A/C, TV, and patio, and are arranged around a small garden. The owner also rents scooters and bikes to guests. (☎92 16 76; www.miosogno.com. Bikes €3-5 per day, scooters €15-25 per day. Reservations recommended in summer. €20-40 per person. Cash only.) **Camping Egàd ❶,** Contrada Arena, is a comfortable choice for camping. Tents, bungalows with kitchenettes and bathrooms, and caravans with shared bathrooms are available. A scooter and bike rental shop, diving center, restaurant, market, and disco are all on-site. (☎/fax 92 15 55 or 92 15 67; www.campingegad.it. Look for the Camping Egàd shuttle at the port, or call to be picked up. Showers €0.30. July-Aug. €6.40 per person, €6.10 per tent; Sept.-June €5/4.60. 2-person bungalows €32-50; 2-person caravans €19-30.)

Alternative Pub ❶, P. Europa 4, serves a variety of salads amid a nautical decor. If you're thirsty, you can brave the Lanterna (€15), a very large, very colorful, very potent beverage made according to the owner's secret recipe and served in a gigantic beer stein. (Salads and *panini* from €3. Open daily 8:30am-3am.) **La Bettola ❷**, V. Nicotera 45, serves fish fresh out of the water to patrons in comfortable outdoor seating. From P. Madrice, walk down V. Nicotera; it will be toward the end of the street on the left. (☎/fax 92 19 88. *Primi* €5-14, *secondi* €4.50-15.50. Cover €2. Open daily 1-2:30pm and 8-11pm. Dec.-Jan. closed Th. AmEx/MC/V.) Tuna is a big part of Favignana's culinary tradition. A variety of tuna products are for sale at the **Antica Tonnara di Favignana ❶**, V. Nicotera 6. (☎/fax 92 16 10. Open daily June-Sept. 9am-midnight; Oct.-May 9am-1pm and 5-8pm. AmEx/MC/V.) Stock up for a demanding day lying on the beach at **San Paolo Alimentari**, V. Mazzini 24. (☎ 92 16 80. Open M-Tu and Th-Sa 8am-1pm and 5-8:30pm, W 8am-1pm.)

◨ ◙ BEACHES AND SIGHTS. The island's most popular beaches are the Lido Burrone, and the rockier Calamone, Cala Rossa, and Cala Azzurra. Lido Burrone is the best equipped, including places to change and shower. Both Cala Azzurra and the Cala Rossa are touted as the most beautiful. All beach areas can be reached by the public Tarantola buses (€0.70; p. 714). The tip of the island around Cala Rotonda and Galera makes a gorgeous boat trip, but is difficult to access from land. To hire a boat, inquire at the tourist office. With stints as a prison, an Arab lookout tower, and a Norman fortress, the **Castello di Santa Caterina** is a formidable sight on a hill overlooking the city. A funky cafe by day and a lively bar by night, **Camarillo Brillo,** V. V. Emanuele 18, is a favorite haunt of youth marooned on the island, offering a Happy hour (daily 6-10pm; drink and hors d'oeuvres €5) and nightly live music. (Wine €3.50 per glass, €10 per bottle. Breakfast buffet daily 8-10:30am. Open daily Easter-Sept. 8am-3am. Cash only.)

LEVANZO

Levanzo (LE-van-zo; pop. 220) is the smallest of the three Egadi Islands. Little more than a row of white-washed, blue-shuttered buildings, the *centro* is host to two bars above the docks which serve as the island's quiet social center. Head down the *lungomare* to visit the island's primary attraction, the **Grotta del Genovese,** a cave containing 14,000-year-old Paleolithic stone cuttings and slightly younger ochre-grease paintings of tuna fish rituals and dancing men. (www.grottadelgenovese.it. €6, ages 5-11 €3.) Tour guide **Natale Castiglione,** in the ceramics shop of Grotta del Genovese, offers info on the site. (☎ 92 40 32; nacasti@tin.it. Tour reservation required at least 1 day in advance. Boat or jeep excursions €13. Shop open daily 10:30am-1pm and 3:30-6pm, last tour leaves at 3pm.) A few kilometers along the coastal road, grottoes and beaches await. **Cala Tranate** and **Capo Grosso** (the end of the island where there is a lighthouse) are both about a 1½hr. walk. Be careful—the clear water between the rounded rock beach and the neighboring island has a ripping current when the wind picks up. Right from the harbor is **Albergo Paradiso ❺,** which keeps the island's best rooms, all with bath and A/C, many with sea view. The hotel's cozy restaurant serves traditional and regional specialties. (☎/fax 92 40 80. Reserve for Aug. by mid-Mar. Open Mar.-Nov. Half pension €60; full pension €80. AmEx/MC/V.) In the center, the bar on the right (when looking from the port), **Bar Arcobaleno,** V. Galvario 8, has homemade almond *gelato*, both for €2. (☎ 92 40 12. Cash only.) The **Ustica hydrofoil office** is on the dock, while the **Siremar office** is up an alley off the *lungomare*.

MARETTIMO

The most geographically remote of the Egadi Islands, subdued Marettimo (ma-RE-tee-mo; pop. 700) attracts fewer tourists but just as many nature-lovers as the others. Because there are few roads, a boat is the best way to see Marettimo's caves. They are available for rent, with a captain, from the port. Beyond the village, the only intrusion into the island's rugged environment is an outstanding set of hiking trails crossing the island. The 2½hr. hike to **Pizzo Falcone** (686m), the highest point on the Egadi Islands, starts at the sea road, past the Siremar office. Along the way, snuggled between cliffs and greenery, stand the **Case Romane,** ruins dating back to Roman domination. To the right of the little village and past a beach at **Punta Troia,** a **Spanish castle** tops the cliff. According to legend, when a prince married one of two sisters, the rejected one threw her sister off the cliff. The heartbroken prince tossed the offending sister down the same route and then followed himself. Locals say that at sunset, the ghosts of the two lovers find each other again at the castle.

A few *piazze* connect the town's maze-like streets. A left turn from the ferry port will lead you up to one of these town centers. From this *piazza,* V. Municipio becomes V. Umberto I, which leads all the way to the Old Port. The Siremar office will be on the right, the Ustica office 20m farther down on the left. There is a 24hr. **ATM** on V. Umberto I. A **cultural center** on V. Scalo Vecchio, along the fishing boat docks, has info on all three islands, as well as a local museum. (Open M-Sa 8am-noon and 3-8pm. Occasional closings.) From the fishing dock walk up V. Pepo then left on V. Chiusa to reach **Il Corallo ❷,** V. Chiusa 11. This quiet *pensione* rents furnished apartments with bath, patio, and kitchenette. (☎92 32 26. July 16-Aug. €25-30 per person; June-July 15 €20 per person; Apr. and Sept. €15 per person.) **Al Carrubo ❷,** Contrada Palosa, barbecues fish and serves pizzas on its large patio in a lush garden overlooking town. From the Old Port, walk up V. Pepo and continue until it ends at Contrada Palosa. Try the *pizza al carrubo* (€6.50), made with locally grown herbs. (☎92 31 32. Pizza €4.50-6.50. *Primi* €6-15, *secondi* €7.50-15.50. Open June-Sept. daily 7:30pm-3am. AmEx/MC/V.) For a peaceful afternoon, head to **Caffé Tramontana ❶,** V. Campi 11, where the outdoor tables above the *Scalo Vecchio* offer great views. (Coffee €1-2.50. Open daily 8am-3am. Cash only.) To stock up on supplies for your hike, you can head to **Alimentare Anastasi Clemente,** V. Mazzini 13. (Open M-Sa 8am-1:30pm and 5-10pm. AmEx/MC/V.)

PANTELLERIA   ☎0923

Known as *"La perla nera dell'Europa"* ("the black pearl of Europe"), Pantelleria (PAN-te-le-REE-ya; pop. 8000) is as African and Middle Eastern as she is European. A world of both stark contrasts and seamless integration, its main attractions are its natural beauty and tranquil isolation. Visitors come for thermal springs, Arab *dammusi,* and plump capers, but are quickly seduced by the island's breathtaking beauty of black lava rock against verdant vineyards.

⬛ TRANSPORTATION

Pantelleria is surprisingly expansive. Almost all tourists rent a car or scooter; public travel resources like buses are few and far between. The midnight ferry from Trapani may save money on a night's hotel, but if spending the night struggling to curl up in a straight-backed ferry chair doesn't sound appealing, opt for the hydrofoil and relax on the noon return ferry instead.

Flights: Contrada Margana (☎91 11 72), 2km from town. Flights from the largest Italian cities service the airport, including **Rome, Venice, Milan, Palermo,** and **Catania** (14 departures per day 8am-7:30pm).

Ferries and Hydrofoils: Ustica runs hydrofoils to **Trapani** (2½hr. 8:30am, €36.50). Tickets sold at **Agenzia Minardi,** V. Borgo Italia 15 (☎91 15 02), on the *lungomare,* and in

Isola di Pantelleria

⚓ ACCOMMODATIONS
Hotel Cossyra Mursia, 6
Hotel Khamma, 4
La Vela, 7

🍎 FOOD
La Risacca, 1
Ristorante-Pizzeria Castiglione, 3

🎵 NIGHTLIFE
Bar-Panineria U Friscu, 8
Il Goloso, 5
Tikirriki, 2

summer at a booth on the port. Open daily 7:30am-noon and 5:30-10:45pm. Cash only. Tickets also available at **La Cossira. Siremar,** V. Borgo Italia 65 (☎91 11 04), on the waterfront, runs ferries to **Trapani** (5hr., noon, €23.70). Open M-F 6:30am-1pm and 5-6:30pm, Sa-Su 6:30am-1pm. AmEx/MC/V.

Island Buses: Infrequent buses run M-Sa from P. Cavour to the airport and the 5 island towns of Khamma-Tracino, Scauri-Rekale, Bukkuram, Sibà, and Bugeber (€1). Check schedule posted outside the tourist office; times are subject to change.

Scooter and Car Rental:

Autonoleggio Policardo, V. Messina 31 (☎91 28 44 or 339 42 87 767; noleggiopolicar@tiscalinet.it), off the port, up the street to the right after the fenced-in scooter lot. Scooters €18-26 per day; Aug. €40 per day. Cars 21+. €35 per day, €196 per week; Aug. €55 per day. Open daily 8am-1:30pm and 4-8pm.

Autonoleggio Princioto Claudio, V. Ponte 8, Rekhale. (☎91 61 22 or 347 19 71 565). Cars only. Call when you arrive at the port for a driver to meet you. June €25 per day; July €35 per day; Aug. €45 per day. Reservations recommended in Aug. Open daily 8am-10pm. Cash only.

🔆🔟 ORIENTATION AND PRACTICAL INFORMATION

Ferries and **hydrofoils** arrive at the northwest tip of the teardrop-shaped island at Punta San Leonardo. The town of Pantelleria borders the curved **port.** The main street, **Via Borgo Italia,** changes to **Lungomare Paolo Borsellino** and stretches from the docks to the private sailboat moorings. At the end of Lungomare P. Borsellino beneath the **Castello, Piazza Almanza** becomes **Piazza Cavour.** Most services are here. Roads at either end of the *lungomare* lead along the coast to other towns. Facing away from the water, to the left are **Bue Marino, Lo Specchio di Venere, Cala Gadir,** and **Arco dell'Elefante.** The right road leads to the **airport,** the **Sesi, Scauri town,** and **Rekhale.** A road to the right of the sea highway inland from the Castello, past the Agip gas station, leads to **Sibà** and **Montagna Grande.**

Pantelleria

🏠 ACCOMMODATIONS
Hotel Khamma, **5**

🍴 FOOD
La Risacca, **1**
Ristorante-Pizzeria
Castiglione, **3**

🎵 NIGHTLIFE
Il Goloso, **2**
Tikirriki, **4**

Tourist Office: Pro Loco, P. Cavour 10 (☎91 18 38), at the corner of the municipal building closest to Banco di Sicilia. Look for country flags. Brochures, maps (€0.77), bus schedules, and hotel assistance. Open Apr.-Oct. M-Sa 9am-1pm, Su 9am-1pm.

Budget Travel: La Cossira, V. Borgo Italia 77 (☎91 10 78), left of Hotel Khamma, where V. Catania meets the *lungomare.* Cheap return flights can be organized from Pantelleria to Trapani and Palermo. Open daily 9am-1pm and 5:30-7:30pm. AmEx/MC/V.

Currency Exchange: Banca Nuova (☎91 27 32), up V. Catania from the *lungomare.* Open M-Sa 8:20am-1:20pm and 2:40-3:40pm, Su 8:20-11:50am. 24hr. **ATMs** located at Banca Nuova, across the street at **Monte dei Paschi di Siena** and **Banco di Sicilia,** in P. Cavour across from the municipal building.

Carabinieri: V. Trieste 13 (☎91 11 09).

First Aid: (☎91 02 55), at the end of the *lungomare.* Open M-F and Su 8am-8pm, Sa 10am-8pm.

Pharmacy: Farmacia Greco, P. Cavour 28 (☎91 13 10). Open M-Sa 8:30am-1pm and 4:30-8pm, Su 10am-12:30pm and 5-7:30pm.

Hospital: (☎91 01 11), in P. Nicolo Almansa, off the *lungomare.*

Internet: Internet Point Da Pietro, V. Dante 7 (☎91 13 67). €0.50 per 5min., €6 per hr., €10 per 2hr. Fax and copy available. Printing €0.15 per page. Open daily 9am-2pm and 4:30-9pm.

Post Office: V. Verdi 2 (☎69 52 32), behind the municipal building and across from Banco di Sicilia, off P. Cavour. **Exchanges currency** and **traveler's checks.** Open M-F 8am-1:30pm, Sa 8am-12:30pm. **Postal Code:** 91017.

🏠 ACCOMMODATIONS

Most visitors stay in *dammusi,* square-shaped, domed dwellings unique to the island. White roofs and thick lava-stone walls keep the interior cool, while cisterns catch rainwater that runs from the roof. Classic *dammusi* are whitewashed, simply furnished, and include a sleeping alcove. There are over 3000 *dammusi* on Pantelleria, and nearly every resident rents one out or knows someone who does. The town of Pantelleria also has reasonable *affittacamere.* Quality varies considerably, and finding a place requires perseverance. For both *dammusi* and rooms, inquire at the *bars* lining the beach or at the tourist office and look for flyers. Some *dammusi* require a minimum stay and most cost from €20-35. Be ready to haggle. Follow the sea road

10km south from Pantelleria town to Scauri's port, where 15 *dammusi* are for rent from ◙**La Vela ❸**, on Scauri Scalo. All have kitchen, bath, patio and A/C. A beach, private Turkish bath, and an upscale restaurant with sea view should seal the deal. (☎91 18 00 or 349 35 37 154. Reserve 4 months ahead for July-Aug. €30-40 per person. Cash only.) The **Hotel Khamma ❹**, V. Borgo Italia 79, right across the street from the dock, has more conventional accommodations. This hotel offers high-ceilinged rooms with harbor views and a great location right in port. Don't miss the breakfast from the roof-garden restaurant. All rooms have bathroom, A/C, TV, fridge, and phone. (☎91 26 80; hotelkhamma@libero.it. Airport pickup €5. Breakfast included. Single €40-60; doubles €70-110; triples €90-140. AmEx/MC/V.) You won't forgo modern luxuries at **Hotel Cossyra Mursìa ❺**, along the road from Pantelleria town to Scauri, before the *sesi* (huge funerary monuments erected during the Bronze Age). This resort-style hotel overlooking the sea has rooms resembling *dammusi*. Amenities include a deck, three swimming pools, TV lounges, a piano bar, tennis courts, archery ranges, scuba diving, and an acclaimed restaurant. (☎91 12 17; www.mursiahotel.it. Open Mar.-Oct. Rooms are divided into 3 classes. Full pension singles classic €118-200, comfort €128-210, superior €148-230; half pension doubles €90-170/100-180/120-200; full pension doubles €110-170/120-180/140-200. AmEx/MC/V.)

▐ FOOD

Arab domination in the 8th century AD turned Pantelleria away from fishing to the cultivation of its rich volcanic soil. A local specialty, *pesto pantesco*, is a sauce of tomato, capers, basil, garlic, and almonds, eaten with pasta or on *bruschetta*. The local *zibbibo* grape yields grape jelly and the amber *passito* and *moscato* dessert wines. **Ristorante-Pizzeria Castiglione ❸**, V. Borgo Italia 81, along the *lungomare*, serves 39 kinds of pizza (takeout €4-6) in a classic Italian dining room. Fish *secondi* are a particularly good deal. (☎91 14 48. *Primi* €7-15, *secondi* €8-13. Cover €1. Open daily 11am-3pm and 7:30pm-midnight. In winter closed W. AmEx/MC/V.) **La Risacca ❷**. is at V. Milano 65. From the port, head toward Sibà. La Risacca is above the port next to the hospital. Pizzas (€4-8), specialties like *spaghetti con gambero* (with shrimp; €9), and *ravioli panteschi* (ravioli stuffed with ricotta and mint, covered in a tomato or butter-herb sauce; €9) are served inside or on the terrace. (☎91 29 75. Open daily 12:30-2:30pm and 8-11pm. Oct.-May closed M. Cash only.) A **SISA** supermarket sits above the *lungomare* at V. Napoli 18. Hike up the stairs at the bend in the *lungomare*, passing the Banco Nuova sign on the right. (Open M-Tu and Th-Su 8:30am-1pm and 5:30-8:30pm, W 8:30am-1pm. MC/V.)

◉ SIGHTS

Pantelleria's natural beauty makes this island a Mediterranean jewel. Don't plan to hit more than two destinations in a day. Pantelleria's bus system is notoriously unreliable, frequently leaving travelers waiting in the sun for half a day, and many sights are at least an hour's walk from bus stops.

▓ BAGNO ASCIUTTO (LA GROTTA DI BENIKULÀ) AND MONTAGNA GRANDE.

Near the town of Sibà is a **rock sauna** and the summit of Pantelleria's highest mountain. Signs guide through and beyond Sibà to the sauna; the last 10min. or so must be traveled on foot. Visitors courageous enough to brave the well-behaved (read: rarely stinging) swarms of bees that guard the entrance lie face down in a deep, low cave. Bring water and a towel, and be prepared to leave and reenter several times due to the sauna's stifling heat. Farther along the sauna path, at the foot of Monte Gibele, the **Favara Grande** is a *fumarole* (crater) that emits clouds of hot smoke. Most of the trails that leave from the asphalt road are short, and a shady picnic area in a pine grove near the summit is the perfect place to relax after a dry bath or sauna. If the midday heat is already enough, head to Montagna Grande for the view. The road past Sibà leads almost to the top, with views stretching for miles. Watch for the lush Ghirlanda Plain. *(Take the Sibà bus from P. Cavour (M-Sa 6 per day 6:40am-7:40pm). Both the Bagno and the mountain are clearly marked. By car or scooter, follow signs from Pantelleria for Sibà. Note that on some maps and signs, the Bagno Asciutto is labeled as "Grotta di Benikulà." Free.)*

▨ LO SPECCHIO DI VENERE (THE MIRROR OF VENUS). Legend has it that Venus used this lake as a mirror before her dates with Bacchus. Mere mortals may also be lured by a glimpse into this startlingly aquamarine pool, fringed with firm, white mud and sunken into a bowl of green hillside. Sulfur springs warm the water and enrich the mud. Local practice recommends letting the sun dry the therapeutic mud to a white cake on the skin and then taking a long swim through the warm waters to wash it off. *(From P. Cavour take the bus to Bugeber; ask driver where to exit, and ask about return times. Buses depart Pantelleria M-Sa 7:40am and noon. By car or scooter, head to Bugeber, and follow signs for the turn-off. Free.)*

LA GROTTA DI SATARIA. At the Grotta di Sataria, stairs lead to a cave once thought to be the home of the nymph Calypso, with whom Ulysses resided for seven years of his odyssey. The 40°C (104°F) water in the thermal pools, only a jump away from the much cooler sea, is believed to cure aching joints. Be careful of the surf in the open water. *(Portions of this site may be blocked off due to falling rocks. Buses depart from Pantelleria (dir.: Rekale) M-Sa 7 times per day 6:40am-8:30pm. Be sure to inquire about return times. By car or scooter, follow the road from Pantelleria to Scauri. Free.)*

THE NORTHEASTERN COAST AND L'ARCO DELL'ELEFANTE. In the shadow of the black rock structures lining the coast, visitors crowd the best swimming holes off Pantelleria, located in three small inlets along the northeastern coast. The first, **Cala Gadir,** is one of the more popular *acqua calda* (hot water) spots on the island. Cement encloses the natural pool next to the sea. Even better swimming is down the coast at **Cala Tramontana** and **Cala Levante.** Perfect for sunbathing, these twin coves are actually one, split by a rocky outcropping. Cala Levante offers a view of the **Arco dell'Elefante,** off to the right. The unofficial symbol of the island, the unusual rock formation looks like a large elephant guzzling up the surf. *(All 3 inlets are on the Khamma-Tracino bus line. Buses leave P. Cavour M-F 6 per day 6:40am-5:20pm. Check return times, as they are subject to change. By car or scooter, follow signs for Khamma and Tracino, then signs for coastal roads.)*

LA PIANA DI GHIRLANDA (THE GARLAND PLAIN). Surrounded by a crumbled lip, this fertile crater makes a beautiful 2hr. hike from Tracino. On the way, scope out the terraces where peasants, working out of small, utilitarian *dammusi*, tend fruit orchards and caper fields. Follow signs to the **Byzantine tombs** at Gabbiana; surrounded by a vineyard, these tombs mark the resting place of a family of four from the early Middle Ages. *(By car, take the road leading out of Tracino's P. Perugio. Or take Tracino bus to the Byzantine tombs, then follow signs to trails.)*

LA GROTTA DEL BUE MARINO. This remarkable swimming area is 2km east of Pantelleria, along the *lungomare.* While snorkelers hug its coast, sunbathers drape towels over volcanic rock. Use extreme caution: the water is shallow in places, and the bottom is lined with jagged rocks. *(By car, follow road from Pantelleria toward Tracino. Or take the Pantelleria-Tracino bus.)*

I SESI. The Bronze Age people who inhabited Pantelleria 5000 years ago left behind the *sesi*, dome-shaped funerary monuments built around 1800 BC. Tunnels in the *sesi* gave access to chambers that stored kneeling corpses. Many have been torn down for building material, but the largest remaining congregation of *sesi* forms a cemetery with 70 tombs. *(On the road from Pantelleria to Scauri. Buses depart from Pantelleria in the Rekale direction. M-Sa 6:40am-8:30pm; M-F 5 times daily, M-Sa 7 times daily. Inquire about return times. Look for a sign indicating the "zona archeologica" to the left, past the Hotel Cossyra Mursìa.)*

🔓 NIGHTLIFE

Pantelleria's most vibrant nightlife is at the port. **Tikirriki,** V. Borgo Italia 7/9, and **Il Goloso,** V. Borgo Italia 35, both serve until about 2am and have tables outside by the water. Twelve kilometers away in Scauri is the lively **Bar-Panineria U Friscu,** C. da Scauri 54, which serves as the perfect pre-disco party stop. Try the local white wine. (☎91 83 40. Wine €3 per glass, €15 per bottle. Open daily 6am-4am. Cash only.)

SICILY

SARDINIA (SARDEGNA)

An old legend says that when God finished making the world, He had a handful of dirt left over, which He threw into the Mediterranean, stepped on, and—behold—created the island of Sardinia (in Italian, "Sar-DEN-ya"). Another myth claims that Sardinia was the land of Atlantis, covered by a tidal wave in the 2nd millennium BC. However it came to be, Sardinia has been bounced back and forth from country to country for centuries, leaving current citizens wary of any type of foreign investment or exploitation. Shuffled between the Phoenicians and the Carthusians, Sardinia got a break when the Romans made it an agricultural colony. But by the 13th century, it was again a theater for conflict between the Pisans, the Aragonese, the newly united Spanish, and the Piemontese. Until just decades ago, *padroni* (landlords) controlled the land, and farmers toiled under a system akin to serfdom. The architecture, language, and cuisine of traditional Sardinian life render it a cultural anomaly, a composite society of African, Italian, and Spanish influences. The latent independence movement, reflected in graffiti and Sardinian flags, speaks to the island's location on the border between many different peoples and cultures. Though a part of the Italy, Sardinians maintain a sense of independence, often beating their chests and saying "Sardegna" instead of "Italia."

HIGHLIGHTS OF SARDINIA

RIDE the sensational bus #8 from Nuoro to the top of **Monte Ortobene** where a magnificent statue of Christ the Redeemer seems to leap from the summit. (p. 754)

SOAK UP the sun on the **luxurious beaches** of L'Arcipelago della Maddalena. (p. 741)

SAIL from Alghero's busy waterfront to the luminescent **Grotte di Nettuno.** (p. 737)

MARVEL at the colorful streets of Orgosolo, where artists have been addressing social issues through enormous **murals** since 1975. (p. 755)

TRANSPORTATION

FLIGHTS. Alitalia flights link Alghero, Cagliari, and Olbia to major Italian cities. Though flights are faster than water travel, exorbitant fares discourage most air travelers. Recently, Ryanair and EasyJet have begun to serve Sardinia's airports. EasyJet (www.easyjet.com) flies from Olbia to Berlin, Geneva and London, and from Cagliari to Geneva and London. Ryanair (www.ryanair.com) flies from Cagliari to Barcelona, Milan, and Pisa and from Alghero to Barcelona, Dublin, Frankfurt, London, Milan, Pisa, and Stockholm.

FERRIES. The cheapest way to reach Sardinia is by ferry from **Civitavecchia, Genoa,** or **Livorno** to Olbia. Civitavecchia is easily reached by train from Rome's Termini station (80min., €4.50). The **ticket offices** and ferry info centers are in the ferry station. Expect to pay €23-75 each way, depending on the company, season, boat speed, and departure time (night trips, fast ferries, and summer ferries cost more). The cheapest fares are for daytime *posta ponte* (deck class) slots on slow-moving boats, but most ferry companies require that *poltrone* (reserved armchairs) be sold to capacity before they open *posta ponte*. In the price ranges below, the low number is the low-season *posta ponte* fare, and the high number is the high-season *poltrone* fare. Expect to pay €10-20 more for a *cabina* with a bed, plus €5-15 depending on the season, trip duration, and taxes. Travelers with vehicles, animals, or children should arrive 1½hr. before departure; everyone else should arrive 45min. beforehand.

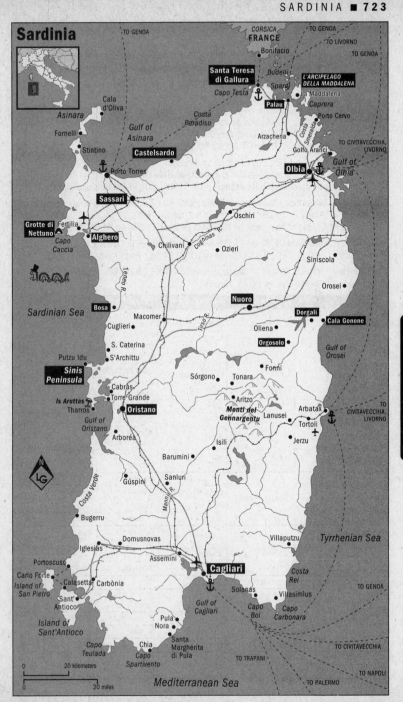

Sardinia

TO GENOA

CORSICA
FRANCE

TO GENOA

TO LIVORNO

TO GENOA

Bonifacio

Budelli

**Santa Teresa
di Gallura**

Spargi

L'ARCIPELAGO
DELLA MADDALENA

Capo Testa

Palau

la Maddalena

Caprera

Porto Cervo

Cala
d'Oliva

Asinara

Costa
Paradiso

Arzachena

Costa
Smeralda

Fornelli

Gulf of
Asinara

Golfo Aranci

TO CIVITAVECCHIA,
LIVORNO

Stintino

Castelsardo

Olbia

Gulf of
Olbia

Porto Torres

Sassari

Oschiri

**Grotte di
Nettuno**

Fertilia

Chilivani

Coghinas R.

Ozieri

Siniscola

Capo
Caccia

Alghero

Orosei

Sardinian Sea

Bosa

Macomer

Teneo R.

Tirso R.

Nuoro

Dorgali

Cala Gonone

Cuglieri

Oliena

Gulf of
Orosei

S. Caterina

Orgosolo

Putzu Idu

S'Archittu

Fonni

**Sinis
Peninsula**

Cabras

Sórgono

Tonara

Torre Grande

Monti del
Gennargentu

Is Aruttas

Oristano

Aritzo

Arbatax

TO
CIVITAVECCHIA,
LIVORNO

Tharros

Lanusei

Gulf of
Oristano

Arboréa

Isili

Tortolì

Jerzu

Barumini

Costa Verde

Gúspini

Sanluri

Mannu R.

Bugerru

Villaputzu

Tyrrhenian Sea

Domusnovas

Iglesias

Assemini

Cagliari

Costa
Rei

Portoscuso

Carlo Forte

Calasetta

Carbònia

Solanas

Villasimìus

Island of
San Pietro

Sant'
Antioco

Gulf of
Cagliari

Capo
Boi

Capo
Carbonara

TO GENOA

Island of
Sant'Antioco

Pula

Nora

Capo
Teulada

Chia

Santa
Margherita
di Pula

TO CIVITAVECCHIA

Capo
Spartivento

TO TRAPANI

TO NAPOLI

TO PALERMO

0

20 kilometers

0

20 miles

Mediterranean Sea

Transporting vehicles can cost €50-120, depending on the length of the voyage and the season. The ferry schedule below is for summer service. Winter ferries sell at lower prices and run overnight. Prices and times are extremely variable depending on time of day and the speed of the boat; call the companies for more info.

Tirrenia: (☎89 21 23; www.tirrenia.it). Offices in city harbors: **Arbatax** (☎07 82 66 78 41); **Cagliari** (☎07 06 66 065); **Civitavecchia** (☎07 66 58 19 25); **Fiumicino** (☎06 65 21 670); **Genoa** (☎01 02 69 81); **Olbia** (☎07 89 20 71 02); **Livorno** (☎05 86 42 47 30), on Calata Addis Abeba–Varco Galvani; **Naples,** Rione Sirignano 2 (☎08 15 51 90 96); **Palermo** (☎09 16 02 11 11), on Calata Marinai d'Italia; **Porto Torres,** V. Mare 38 (☎07 95 18 10 11).

Sardinia Ferries: (☎ 19 94 00 500; www.sardiniaferries.com). Offices in **Livorno** (☎05 86 88 13 80), at the Stazione Marittima; in **Civitavecchia** (☎07 66 50 07 14), at Terminal Autostrade del Mare; and **Golfo Aranci** (☎07 89 46 780), at the Stazione Marittima.

Moby Lines: (www.moby.it). Offices in **Olbia** (☎07 89 27 927), at the Stazione Marittima; **Livorno,** V. Veneto 24 (☎058 68 99 950); and **Genoa** (☎01 02 54 15 13), at the Terminal Traghetti. General help desk (☎19 93 03 040); in English (☎61 11 40 20).

Grandi Navi Veloci: (☎01 02 09 45 91; www.gnv.it). Offices in Civitavecchia (☎07 66 59 631); Olbia (☎07 89 20 01 26); Genoa (☎01 02 54 65); Porto Torres (☎0795 16 034).

SNAV: (www.snav.it). Offices in **Civitavecchia** (☎07 66 36 63 66), **Olbia** (☎07 89 20 00 84), and **Naples** (☎08 14 28 55 55).

ROUTE	COMPANY	DURATION	FREQUENCY	PRICE
Civitavecchia-Olbia		5-7hr.	M-F 8:30am and 11pm, Sa-Su 3pm	€22-33
Civitavecchia-Cagliari		12½hr.	M-Th and Sa 8:30am	€29-43
		14¾hr.	F and Su 6:30pm	
Genoa-Olbia	Tirrenia	13hr.	M and W-Su 11pm	€23-50
Genoa-Porto Torres		10hr.	Daily 8:30pm	€30-68
Naples-Cagliari		15½hr.	Th 7:15pm	€29-44
Fiumicino-Golfo Aranci		4½hr.	M and W 8:30am, Tu and Th-Sa 9am	€32-63
Fiumicino-Arbatax		3hr.	In Aug. M and W 7pm	€38-63
Civitavecchia-Golfo Aranci		7hr. (C. Shuttle)	8:15am	€17-38
	Sardinia Ferries	4¾hr. (C. Express)	2:15pm	€40-55
Livorno-Golfo Aranci		8hr.	11pm	€24-48
		6hr.	8:15am	€29-55
Livorno-Olbia		7-11hr.	Daily 8am, 9:30, and 11:30pm	€20-40
Civitavecchia-Olbia	Moby Lines	4¾-10hr.	Daily 3 and 10pm	€20-54
Genoa-Olbia		9½hr.	Daily 10pm	€20-59
Genoa-Porto Torres	Moby Lines	10hr	Daily 10pm	€20-59
Bonifacio-S.Teresa	Saremar	1hr.	Daily 8, 11am, 5pm	€8-10
Genoa-Palau	Enermar	11hr.	W and F 7pm	€58-72
			Su 9am	€47
Genoa-Olbia	Grandi Navi	9-10hr.	Daily, times vary	€31-38
Genoa-Porto Torres	Veloci	11hr.	Daily, 2-3 per day	€31-38
Genoa-Palau		12-13hr.	M, W, F-Sa 7pm	€16-70
Salerno-Olbia	Dimaio Lines	15hr.	M, W, F 6:30pm	€20-45

ROUTE	COMPANY	DURATION	FREQUENCY	PRICE
Piombino-Olbia	Linea dei Golfi	6½hr.	Aug. 2 per day; Sept.-July days and times vary	€18-23
Civitavecchia-Olbia	SNAV	7-8hr.	Daily 11am and 10pm	€30-40

⛵ **TICKET FOR TOMORROW.** If you buy your ferry ticket from Palau to Maddalena the day before, you can save 20% on EnerRmaR tickets. So, if you arrive late in Palau and are planning on visiting La Maddalena the following day, make sure to buy your round-trip tickets for €8 the day before instead of €10.

CAGLIARI ☎070

Since the Phoenicians founded the ancient port town of Korales over two millennia ago, several great civilizations have competed for domination of Cagliari (CAL-ya-ree; pop. 161,000), Sardinia's largest city and capital. In the 11th century, after defeating the Genoese, the Pisans built the fortified town of Castrum Kolaris, which became one of the most important artistic and cultural centers on the Mediterranean and was later renamed Cagliari. While the city maintains its rich history through its still-functioning Roman amphitheater, it also incorporates modern city designs like the Bastione di San Remy, which offers panoramic views of the port and surrounding territories. When the pulse of city life becomes too strong, a 20min. bus ride will bring you to the sparkling green water and bopping nightclubs of Il Poetto, one of the best beaches in Sardinia.

◰ TRANSPORTATION

Flights: In the village of Elmas. ARST buses run the 8km from the airport to the city terminal at P. Matteotti (30min., 32 per day 5:20am-10:30pm, €1).

Trains: (☎89 20 21), in P. Matteotti. Ticket office open daily 6:10am-8:45pm. 24hr. ticket machines. To: **Olbia** (4hr., 6:30pm, €14.60) via **Oristano** (1hr., 17 per day 5:33am-10:02pm, €5.15) or **Macomer; Porto Torres** (4hr., 2 per day, €14.60); **Sassari** (4hr., 4 per day 6:39am-4:38pm, €13.65). Other destinations include San Gavino, Iglesias, Decimomannu, and Carbonia.

Buses: 2 major bus companies serve Cagliari.

ARST, P. Matteotti 6 (☎40 98 324). Office open M-Sa 8-8:30am, 9am-2:15pm, and 5:30-7pm; Su 1:30-2:15pm and 5:30-7pm. Info in the front entrance area, ticket booth in the McDonald's. When office is closed, buy tickets onboard. To **Bosa** (3hr., M-F 2 per day, €11:50), **Nuoro** (2½hr., 3:30pm, €14.50), and **Oristano** (1½hr., M-F 2 per day, €6.50). Also serves local towns, including the beaches of **Chia** (1hr.; 9 per day 6:30am-7:35pm, last return 8pm; round-trip €7), **Villasimius** (5 per day 5am-8:10pm, €3).

FMS (☎800 04 45 53; www.ferroviemeridionalisarde.it). Buses leave from ARST station or P. Matteotti. Buses run to smaller towns. To: **Calasetta, Sant'Antioco-San,** and **Giovanni Suergiu** (6 per day 1:43-7:50pm); **Giba** and **Nuxis Santadi** (4:14, 6:19, 6:38pm); and **Iglesias** (14 per day 5:50am-8:47pm). Buy tickets at newsstand across from Farmacia Spanno on V. Roma or at the ticket booth in McDonald's at the ARST station.

Ferries: Tirrenia (☎66 60 65). Buy tickets from red building 1 block behind the ARST station. Ticket office open M-F 8:30am-12:30pm and 3:30-6:50pm, Sa 8:30am-12:20pm and 3:30-6pm, Su 4-6pm. **Linea dei Golfi** (☎65 84 13), V. Sonnino. Open daily 8am-7pm. Ferries leave from **Stazione Marrittima,** the large blue building near the water.

Local Buses: (☎20 911 or 20 91 200). Orange **CTM buses** run from P. Matteotti. Tickets sold in various *tabaccherie* and newsstands around P. Matteotti and V. Roma. €1 per 1hr., €1.50 per 2hr., €2.30 per day. **Buses P, PQ,** and **PF** go to Il Poetto 5:20am-

SARDINIA

> **EXTRA, EXTRA!** Sardinia's daily newspaper, *L'Unione Sarda*, publishes a page titled "Agenda" which lists departure times and contact info for all bus, airplane, train, and ferry routes serving Cagliari, Alghero, Oristano, Olbia, Arbatax, Porto Torres, Palau, Nuoro, Lanusei, and Sassari.

10:50pm, last return 11:25pm; in the summer, lines **3/P, 9/P, Yellow,** and **Arancio** run to Il Poetto. Pick up a map of the bus routes at the tourist office.

Taxis: Radiotaxi Quattro Mori (☎40 01 01), in front of the train station.

Car Rental: Auto Assistance, V. la Plaia 15 (☎68 48 874; www.autoassistance.it), in the garage beneath Iper Pan. Mountain bikes €10 per day; cars from €60 per day. 21+. Insurance included. Open M-F 9am-1pm and 4-7pm. AmEx/MC/V.

ORIENTATION AND PRACTICAL INFORMATION

Via Roma greets new arrivals to Cagliari, with the **harbor** and **Stazione Marittima** on one side and outdoor cafes on the other. **Piazza Matteotti,** between V. Roma, **Via Sassari,** and **Largo Carlo Felice,** contains the **train station,** the **ARST station,** and the **tourist office.** Across from P. Matteotti, **Largo Carlo Felice** climbs the steep hill leading to **Piazza Yenne,** then ascends even farther to the *centro storico,* also known as the **Castello district.**

Tourist Office: (☎66 92 55), in P. Matteotti, in park across from the train and bus stations. English-speaking staff has substantial info on local sights and lodgings. Open M-F 8:30am-1:30pm and 2-8pm, Sa-Su 8am-8pm; in winter hours vary. **EPT,** P. Deffenu 9 (☎60 42 41; enturismoco@tiscalinet.it). Open in summer M-Sa 9am-1pm and 5-8pm; in winter hours vary.

Currency Exchange: Banca di Roma, P. Yenne 5, at the corner of C. Vittorio Emanuele II. **ATM** outside. Open M-F 8:20am-4pm, Sa 8:30am-noon.

Luggage Storage: At ARST station. €1 per hr.

Laundry: Ghibli Lavanderia Self-Service, V. Sicilia 20 (☎56 55 21 or 349 43 31 129), off V. Baylle. Wash €4 per 6kg, €7 per 16kg; dry €4 per 20min. Detergent €1. Open daily 8am-10pm; last wash 9pm.

Police: ☎40 40 40. **Guardia medica:** V. Talente 6. Nights and weekends ☎50 29 31.

Pharmacy: Farmacia Dott. Spano, V. Roma 99 (☎65 56 83). Open in summer M-F 9am-1pm and 4:50-8:10pm, Sa 9am-1pm; in winter M-F 9am-1pm and 4:30-7:50pm, Sa 9am-1pm. AmEx/MC/V.

Hospital: Ospedale San Giovanni di Dio, V. Ospedale 54 (☎66 32 37), 5min. walk from Chiesa di San Michele. Open daily 8:30am-12:30pm.

Internet: Hay Service, V. Napoli 8 (☎320 18 19 727), off V. Roma. 5 fast computers; fax, photocopy, and Western Union money transfer also available. €2 per 30min., €3 per hr. Open M-F and Su 9am-1pm and 4-8pm.

Post Office: V. Carmine 27 (☎070 60 311). Take V. Sassari from P. Matteotti. *Fermo-posta,* phone cards, and **currency exchange.** Open M-F 8am-6:50pm, Sa 8am-1:15pm. **Postal Code:** 09100.

ACCOMMODATIONS

Budget accommodations dot the area just off V. Roma, between Largo Carlo Felice and Vle. Regina Margherita.

▨ **B&B Vittoria,** V. Roma 75, 2nd fl. (☎64 04 026 or 349 44 73 556). Airy, spacious rooms with antique decor, Murano glass chandeliers, clean bathrooms, A/C, and radio. Some rooms have TV. Be sure to sample the *Vernaccia,* a special wine produced by owner Luigi's family near Oristano, at the small bar in the breakfast room. Singles €48; doubles €78. *Let's Go* discount 10%. Cash only. ❹

▨ **Hotel aer Bundes Jack,** V. Roma 75 (☎/fax 66 79 70; hotel.aerbundesjack@libero.it). Run by the same couple as B&B Vittoria, this hotel's historic past has been docu-

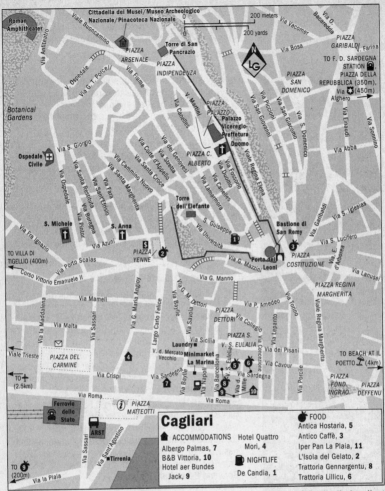

Cagliari

🏠 ACCOMMODATIONS
Albergo Palmas, **7**
B&B Vittoria, **10**
Hotel aer Bundes
Jack, **9**

Hotel Quattro
Mori, **4**

🍺 NIGHTLIFE
De Candia, **1**

🍴 FOOD
Antica Hostaria, **5**
Antico Caffè, **3**
Iper Pan La Plaia, **11**
L'Isola del Gelato, **2**
Trattoria Gennargentu, **8**
Trattoria Lillicu, **6**

mented in hand-written registers since 1938. It remains one of Cagliari's loveliest hotels. 20 rooms with Venetian chandeliers, Victorian molding, bath, phone, radio, and A/C. Check-in on 2nd fl. Breakfast €6. Reservations recommended. Singles €54; doubles €82, with sea view €86; triples €114. *Let's Go* discount 10%. Cash only. ❹

Hotel Quattro Mori, V. G. M. Angioj 27 (☎66 85 35; www.hotel4mori.it), offers 52 rooms with simple wood furnishings. Rooms have bath, A/C, TV, and fridge. Breakfast included. Reservations recommended. Singles €65; doubles €85; triples €115; quads €140. AmEx/MC/V. ❺

Albergo Palmas, V. Sardegna 14 (☎65 16 79). Cheaper option. Large no-frills rooms with sinks. Single €30; double €38, with shower €45; triples €60. MC/V. ❸

🍴 FOOD

Many small shops sell fruit, cheese, and bread along V. Sardegna. Try **Mini Market La Marina,** V. Sardegna 43, which also has a great bakery. (Open M-Sa 7am-1:30pm and 4:30-8:30pm. MC/V.) Find groceries and other essentials at the ◼**Iper Pan La Plaia** at V.

ON THE MENU

BREAD AND BOOZE

Sardinia may be known for its meat-heavy cuisine, yet the food and drink before and after, which are steeped in tradition and folklore, rarely receive the attention they deserve.

Bread has always been a central part of the Sardinian diet. In Sardinia, *pane carasau* was eaten for centuries by shepherds on their long treks. The thin, crisp pieces of bread are nicknamed *carta da musica* because their thinness resembles music paper. If funds are running low, pilfering the extra *carasau* bread from your basket in restaurants can provide a cheap meal during hikes up Sardinian peaks.

After meals, Sardinians swig alcoholic beverages to aid the digestive process. The most famous is *mirto*, a beverage made from myrtle berries only found on the island. The taste of this deep crimson liquor, which is normally 60 proof, resembles a mixture of blackberries and red licorice, with a bit of a kick. Sardinians generally sip the concoction from shot glasses, but there's no shame in opening up the hatch and downing it in one gulp. Diluted *mirto* is also readily available, but be on your guard when offered homemade *aqua vita* (water of life). Often illegally distilled, this very strong form of *grappa* can leave you face down in a ditch the next morning, with Dominic the Donkey licking your face.

la Plaia 15. (Open M-Sa 9am-9pm, Su 9am-2pm.) On Sunday mornings, there's a **market** on the far side of the stadium in Borgo Sant'Elia for fresh fruit and seafood.

L'Isola del Gelato, P. Yenne 35 (☎65 98 24). Friendly owner Giuseppe presides over this lively *gelateria*. A steady stream of customers flows over the artificial river running beneath the transparent floor. 50+ flavors, including low-fat options for those watching their beach figures. Cups from €1. Open Mar.-Nov. daily 9am-2am. Cash only. ❶

Trattoria Gennargentu, V. Sardegna 60/c (☎65 82 47). Join locals in this casual restaurant for the seasonal spaghetti with sea urchin and dried mullet fish (€8) or zesty *salsiccia arrosta* (roasted sausage; €5). *Primi* €4.50-8, *secondi* €5-15. Cover €1.60. Open M-Sa 12:30-3pm and 8-11pm. AmEx/MC/V. ❷

Antico Caffè, P. Costituzione 10/11 (☎65 82 06). Walls covered in collage of patrons who have come for over 150 years in search of appetizers and delicious desserts. Crepes €3.40-5.60. Sundaes €3.10-7.20. Service 20%. Open daily 7am-2am. Call to reserve a table outside. AmEx/MC/V. ❶

Trattoria Lillicu, V. Sardegna 78 (☎65 29 70). Family-run for 80 years. Small but impeccable selection of Sardinian dishes like *anguille* (grilled eels; €9) and snails with tomato sauce (€7). Dining room, with family-style seating, is loud and packed until late; if you're lucky, the guitar-playing owner just might serenade you. *Primi* €5-8, *secondi* €7-12. Cover €1.55. Open M-Sa 1-3pm and 8:30pm-midnight. Reservations strongly recommended. AmEx/MC/V. ❷

Antica Hostaria, V. Cavour 60 (☎66 58 70). This beautiful restaurant sports Art Nouveau decor and tuxedo-clad waiters. Start your meal off with a sparkling aperitif (€3). Try house favorite *fregola con arselle* (tiny semolina pasta in clam broth; €8) or veal in *Vernaccia* sauce (€9). *Primi* €7-12, *secondi* €9-13. Cover €2. Open M-Sa 1-3pm and 8-11:30pm. AmEx/MC/V. ❸

👁 SIGHTS

BASTIONE DI SAN REMY. Approaching **Piazza Costituzione,** an enormous arch encases a staircase that seems carved into the hillside. Climb up the graceful double stairway to the expansive terraces of the 19th-century *bastione* for a spectacular view of Cagliari below. Take note of the sometimes visible pink flamingoes, the **Golfo degli Angeli,** and the **Sella del Diavolo** (Devil's Saddle), a massive rock formation. The *bastione* divides the modern city and the medieval Castello district. For a stroll through medieval Cagliari, start at the top of the *bastione* and follow the narrow streets past the Aragonese churches and Piedmontese palaces. *(Take the stairway from P. Costituzione or enter through the elevator on Vle. Regina Elena. Open 24hr. Free.)*

■ **PALAZZO VICEREGIO.** Constructed by the Aragonese in 1216 and later used as a seat for Spanish and Savoyard viceroys, this beautiful *palazzo* serves as Cagliari's provincial capital. Portraits inside are by Sardinian masters like Giovanni Marghinotti, and the *palazzo* maintains its original Pisan marble floor and 18th-century furnishings. *(Next to the duomo in P. Palazzo. Open daily 9am-2pm and 3-7pm. Entrance only with tour in English or Italian. Free.)*

DUOMO (CATTEDRALE DI SANTA MARIA). The Pisans constructed this massive Gothic cathedral during the second half of the 13th century, dedicating it to the Virgin Mary and St. Cecilia, whose likenesses can be seen in mosaics above the doors. The *duomo* is modeled after the one in Pisa (p. 487) and filled with art by Pisan masters. Maestro Guglielmo carved the pulpits on either side of the main door in 1162, and Pisano sculpted the four lions at the base of the altarpiece in 1302. The ornate wood balcony to the left, in front of the altar, was constructed for the Piedmontese king, who refused to sit among the people for fear of regicide. Colorful marble inlays conceal 179 niches housing the remains of about 200 martyred saints from Cagliari. *(P. Palazzo 4. ☎ 16 63 837. Open M-F 8am-12:30pm and 4:30-8pm, Su 8am-1pm and 4-8pm. Altar and some chapels currently being restored. Modest dress required. Free.)*

MUSEUMS. The **Cittadella dei Musei** houses a modern complex of research museums, including the **Museo Archeologico Nazionale.** The extensive collection of Sardinian artifacts from the Nuraghic to Byzantine eras includes Mycenean pottery from 1600 BC; Barumini, jewelry and coins from the times of Punic control, Roman glass works and mosaics, and a 1000-year-old army of tiny bronze figurines. Comprehensive explanations, with wall-text displays in English and Italian, narrate the history of Sardinian occupation. The entire 2nd floor of the museum is devoted to the archaeological history of Cagliari from the Nuraghic to Roman ages. *(P. Arsenale. Take V. Buoncammino to P. Arsenale, go under the arch and turn left. ☎ 68 40 00. Open Tu-Su 9am-8pm. Wheelchair-accessible. €4, students 18-25 €2, under 18 or over 65 free. MC/V.)* The **Pinacoteca Nazionale,** in the same complex as the archaeological museum, displays medieval and Baroque religious paintings and altarpieces, including works by Pietro Cavaro who is regarded as the greatest Sardinian painter of all time. This labyrinthine museum is built around the remains of a 16th-century fortification, discovered during the reconstruction of the Citadel in 1966. The remains are visible on the ground floor. Be sure to visit the anonymously painted ■ **Madonna con Bambino** on the lower floor, which depicts Baby Jesus with flowing golden locks. *(☎ 68 40 00. Open Tu-Su 9am-8pm. Wheelchair-accessible. €2, students 18-25 €1, under 18 or over 65 free. Both museums €5, students €2.50. Get tickets at the Museo Archeologico Nazionale biglietteria. Ticket office open Tu-Su 8:30am-7:15pm.)*

ROMAN AMPHITHEATER. Constructed after the Carthaginians succumbed to the Roman juggernaut in 238 BC, this amphitheater lost its downhill side to the Pisans, who used the wall as a quarry to build their 13th-century monuments. Underground cages once held ferocious animals during the age of gladiators. Today, much of the original seating along the sides remains, and there are summer performances that are a just a bit more civilized than the ancient carnage. *(V. Fra Ignazio. ☎ 65 29 56; www.anfiteatroromano.it. 30min. guided tours Apr.-Sept. Tu-Sa 9:30am-1pm, Su 10am-1pm. €3.30, students €2.20, over 65 free.)*

TORRE DI SAN PANCRAZIO. As Cagliari's highest point, the tower was once used to watch out for ships and enemies during war, then converted into a medieval prison. Today, visitors can climb the steep stairs, blanketed in pigeon ploppings, to the top to view the city below. Although it is a great view, it is probably not worth the euro. *(€4, students €2.50. Guided visit €0.50. Open Tu-Su 9am-1pm and 3:30-7:30pm.)*

🎵 🎭 ENTERTAINMENT AND NIGHTLIFE

The **Roman amphitheater** continues to dazzle spectators with theater, dance performances, opera, and concerts in July and August on its large modern stage. Most shows start at 9:30pm and cost €18-50. Buy tickets at the amphitheater from 7pm on performance nights or at the box office, at Vle. Regina Margherita 43. (☎65 74 28. Open M-F 10am-1pm and 5-8pm, Sa 10am-1pm, Su when there's a show.) **Outdoor movies,** mostly dubbed American films, are screened in July and August around 9pm at the Marina Piccola off Spiaggia del Poetto. Buy tickets (€4) at the Marina. On Sunday mornings, merchants converge for **flea markets** in P. del Carmine and Bastione di San Remy, where visitors hone their haggling skills and find bargain antiques.

Most bars and clubs in the city are open from 9pm to 5am, but they shut down in the summer when students hit the beaches and the dancing moves outdoors. To dance the night away, either find a ride or rent one—most *discoteche* are on the beaches, 15-20km outside of Cagliari. The best night to go out is Friday. The crowd at **De Candia,** V. De Candia 1, enjoys DJ or live music and colorful mixed drinks, including *assenzio* (absinthe). The bar is one of several positioned on a terrace on top of the Bastione di San Remy that feature lounging leather couches and hammocks. (☎65 58 84. Mixed drinks €6-7. Open daily 7am-4am.) The area around P. Costituzione is usually hopping with street performers and window shoppers. On the first of May, Sardinians flock to Cagliari for the **Festival of Sant'Efisio,** honoring a deserter from Diocletian's army who saved the island from the plague but couldn't save himself from a beheading. A costumed procession escorts his effigy from the capital down the coast to the small church that bears his name.

🏖 BEACHES

Il Poetto, Cagliari's most popular stretch of beach, spans 10km from the Devil's Saddle to the Margine Rosso (Red Bluff). The beach was famous for its pure white sands until the government dumped several tons of coarse brown sand on top to prevent erosion. Locals claim it's ugly, but only because the gorgeous towns of **Villasimus** and **Chia** allow them to have high standards. The average traveler will be so focused on the crystal-clear waters that he'll hardly notice the slight imperfection. Behind Il Poetto, the salt-water **Stagno di Molentargius** (Pond of Molentargius) provides a habitat for flamingos. (City buses P, PQ, and PF, as well as the 3/P, 9/P, yellow, and *Arancio* run frequently to the beaches. 20min., €1.) Resist jumping off the bus at the first sight of sand; by remaining on the bus for a few extra stops, you'll avoid crowded areas. For a more remote sunning and swimming area, head to **Cala Mosca,** which is smaller and surrounded by dirt paths. Because some parts of the water contain submerged seaweed-covered rocks, water shoes might be a good idea for squeamish swimmers looking to avoid squishy surfaces. Take bus #5 to Stadio Amsicora, then bus #11 to the beach.

> 🌊 **DON'T GET BEACHED.** Prices for seaside hotels cover a vast range due to the hike that coincides with the national Italian vacation in August. It's best to avoid Sardinian coasts during the first three weeks of August, as beaches are crowded and prices doubled.

SASSARI ☎079

Founded as the first independent town of Sardinia in 1294, Sassari (SA-sa-ree; pop. 124,000) maintained its medieval wall perimeter until the late 1800s despite constant encroachment by Pisans, Genoese, Aragonese, and Austrians. In the last 400 years, Sassari has become the island's second-largest city and the home to its first university, popularly called "Culleziu." The university's presence has bolstered Sassari's cultural life, crowding its streets with bookstores, museums, tiny restaurants and shops, and plenty of students. Unfortunately, the strain of city life shows itself in the graffiti on Sassari's storefronts. However, through many ambitious public works projects, Sassari seeks to regain its former glory by renovating *piazze*, roads, and facades in a manner befitting its history.

▐ TRANSPORTATION

Trains: In P. Stazione (☎89 20 21), 1 block from P. Sant'Antonio. Take bus #8 from P. d'Italia. Tickets (€0.80) available at *bars*. To: **Alghero** (35min.; 11 per day 6am-8:55pm, reduced service Sa-Su; €2.20); **Cagliari** (3½hr.; 8 per day 6:36am-6:52pm, reduced service Sa-Su; €13.65); **Olbia** (2hr.; 4 per day 6am-5:08pm, reduced service Sa-Su; €6.35); **Porto Torres** (20min., 7 per day 7am-6:44pm, €1.40).

Buses:

ARST (☎263 92 06/03; www.arst.sardegna.it). Buses depart from V. Italia in the public gardens, and the bus station on V. XXV Aprile, in front of the train station. To: **Alghero-Fertilia Airport** (40min.; 9 per day 5am-6:50pm, 5 and 5:30am departs from the bus station at V. Turati; €4); **Castelsardo** (1hr.; 13 per day 7:20am-7:45pm, reduced service Sa-Su; €2.50); **Nuoro** (1¾hr., M-F 2 per day, €8); **Olbia** (1½hr., M-F 2:10pm); **Porto Torres** (20min., 1-2 per hr. 5:15am-9:15pm, €1.25); **Santa Teresa di Gallura** (3hr., 5 per day 7:20am-7:45pm, reduced service Sa-Su; €7.80). Tickets sold at Tonni's Bar, C. Savoia 11, and at the bus station. Cash only.

FDS (☎24 13 01; www.ferroviesardegna.it). Buses leave from V. XXV Aprile. Tickets sold at bus stop on C. Vico. To: **Alghero** (50min.; 14 per day 5:50am-8:15pm, reduced service Sa-Su; €3); **Bosa** (2½hr., 2 per day); **Castelsardo** (1hr., M-F 11:35am, €1.10); **Fertilia** (1hr.; 10 per day 6:30am-8:15pm, reduced service Sa-Su).

Taxis: RadioTaxi (☎26 00 60). 24hr.

Car Rental: Eurorent, V. Roma 56 (☎23 23 35; www.rent.it). Ages 18-20 pay a surcharge. Credit card required. Open M-F 8:30am-7pm, Sa 8:30am-noon. MC/V.

✦ ▐ ORIENTATION AND PRACTICAL INFORMATION

Many buses stop in the **giardini pubblici** (public gardens) before heading to the **bus station.** Since these gardens are close to Sassari's attractions, get off at **Via Italia** in the park. **Emiciclo Garibaldi** lies ahead, a small, semi-circular *piazza*, past **Via Margherita di Savoia.** To reach the *centro*, head straight through Emiciclo Garibaldi to **Via Carlo Alberto,** which spills into **Piazza d'Italia.** To the right, **Via Roma** runs to the tourist office and the Museo Sanna. To the left lies **Piazza Castello,** packed with people and restaurants. Two hundred meters away, **Corso Vittorio Emanuele,** a major thoroughfare, slices through the historical *centro storico*.

Tourist Office: V. Roma 62 (☎23 17 77; aastss@tiscali.it). Facing the provincial administration building, walk a few blocks to the right of P. d'Italia. Go through the gate and the doorway on the right. English-speaking staff provides maps and bus and train schedules. Also responds promptly to email requests for lodging and dining options. Open M-Th 9am-1:30pm and 4-6pm, F 9am-1:30pm.

Currency Exchange: Banca Commerciale D'Italia, P. Italia 22-23, has an **ATM** outside. Open M-F 8:30am-1:30pm and 2:45-4:15pm, Sa 8:30am-noon. 2 other banks in P. d'Italia as well.

Luggage Storage: In the bus station. €1.50 per bag per day. Open M-Sa 6am-9:15pm, Su 7am-2:15pm and 5:15-9:15pm. Cash only.

English-Language Bookstore: Giunta al Punto, V. Cavour 16 (☎20 13 118). Small selection on 1st fl. of mostly British classics. Open daily 9am-8pm. MC/V.

Pharmacy: Simon, P. Castello 5 (☎23 11 44). Open daily 9:10am-8:30pm. Posts after-hours rotations. MC/V.

Hospital: Ospedale Civile, V. Montegrappa 82/83 (☎20 61 000).

Internet Access: Net Gate, P. Università, 4 (☎23 78 94). 6 fast computers. €0.08 cents per min. Open M-F 9am-1pm and 3:30-8pm, Sa 9am-1pm.

Post Office: V. Brigata Sassari 11/13 (☎28 21 267), off P. Castello. **Currency exchange,** phone cards, and *fermoposta.* Open M-F 8am-6:50pm, Sa 8am-1:15pm. Branch located across the street from V. XXV Aprile's bus station. **Postal Code:** 07100.

ACCOMMODATIONS AND FOOD

■ **Casa Chiara ❸,** Vco. Matteo Bertolinis 7, a B&B located in the *centro storico*, has three large, tastefully decorated rooms, all with TV, as well as two clean, shared bathrooms and a kitchen. (☎20 05 052 or 333 69 57 118; www.casachiara.net. Breakfast included. Free Wi-Fi. €30 per person. Cash only.) Located close to the train and bus stations and the *centro*, **B&B Quattro Gatti ❸,** V. Sant'Eligio 5, has a kitchen, colorful modern rooms, and a young, sociable owner. Call to arrange free pickup from station. (☎23 78 19 or 349 40 60 481. Breakfast, locker, and laundry included. Wi-Fi free. €35 per person. Discounts for longer stays. Cash only.) **Hotel Leonardo da Vinci ❺,** V. Roma 79, is worth the splurge for a modern hotel with modern amenities. This hotel sweats class with oriental rugs, granite floors, a helpful staff, and hallways lit by chandeliers. Enormous rooms have bath, A/C, phone, minibar, TV, and hair dryer. (☎28 07 44; www.leonardodavincihotel.it. Breakfast included. Internet access available. Parking €8 per day. Singles €63; doubles €80, with two beds €92. AmEx/MC/V.)

At **Trattoria La Vela Latina ❸,** Largo Sisini 3, in a *piazza* off V. Arborea, owner Francesco loves his patrons as much as they love his food. Flavorful *cavallo* (horse meat) or *asino* (donkey meat; €10) win over even the most timid diners. For something less adventurous, try the fantastic lobster salad or the *riso alla pescatora* for €8. (☎23 37 37. *Primi* €6-12, *secondi* €7-13. Cover €2. Open M-Sa 1-2:30pm and 8-10:30pm. AmEx/MC/V.) **Il Senato ❹,** V. Alghero 36, is reputedly one of Sardinia's best restaurants and uses only first-rate seasonal ingredients. Don't miss the *dolce della suocera* ("the mother-in-law cake;" €6) with ricotta, almond, and a caramelized sugar crust. (☎27 77 88. *Primi* €10-15. Fish €8-15 per 100g. Meat €12-17 per 100g. Open M-Sa 1-2:30pm and 8-11pm. AmEx/MC/V.) To reach **Ristorante Trattoria L'Assassino ❸,** V. Ospizio Cappucini 1, from C. V. Emanuele, go down V. Rosello and take a right on V. Ospizio Cappucini. This comfortable local favorite serves Sardinian specialties, like *tripa* (tripe), *cavallo* (horsemeat), or roast suckling pig. (☎23 50 41. *Primi* €3.50-8, *secondi* €5-13. 3-course *menù* €20. Cover €2. Open M-Sa 12:30-3:30pm and 7:30pm-midnight. MC/V.) Fresh produce stands line V. Rosello from C. V. Emanuele. There is a **Multimarkets,** V. Cavour 64, on the corner with V. Manno. (☎23 72 78. Open M-Sa 8am-9pm.)

SIGHTS AND ENTERTAINMENT

The **Museo Giovanni Antonio Sanna,** V. Roma 64, is an informative and well-presented archaeological museum. Artifacts dating from the Neolithic Period to the Middle Ages, including arrowheads, tools, ceramics, bronze statuettes, and Romanesque sculptures, chronologically detail Sardinia's history. (☎27 22 03. Open Tu-Su 9am-8pm. €2, ages 18-25 €1, EU citizens under 18 or over 65 free.) From the *centro*, walk down C. V. Emanuele from P. Castello,and turn left on V. al Duomo to P. Duomo to reach Sassari's *duomo*, **Cattedrale di San Nicolò.** Reconstructed in Gothic-Catalán style in 1480, only the *campanile* remains from the original 13th-century structure. The impressive facade, covered with statues and engravings, conceals an unremarkable interior, but you may want to take a peak at some recently uncovered early frescoes that fill the side chapels. (Open daily 8:30am-noon and 4-7:30pm. Modest dress required. Free.)

If it weren't for the **University Pub**, V. Amendola 49/A (☎20 04 43), Sassari would be devoid of a hip youth scene. A favorite among locals, the subdued, three-tiered pub offers cheap drinks (beer from €1.80) and overflows with students when school is in session. Try the "Barman" (a mixed drink with unspecified ingredients; €5) or the potent, double malted *biere di demon* for €4.30. (Th karaoke night. Open Sept.-July M and W-Su 8:30pm-1am.) In the 3rd week of May, the lavish **Sardinian Cavalcade** is Sardinia's largest folk festival. The party includes a parade of costumed emissaries from local villages, a horse exhibition, singing, and dancing. On August 14th, **I Candelieri** brings worker's guilds carrying enormous candles through the streets. The medieval festival is one of the island's most colorful on the island. Each guild has its own costume and the candles are decked with flowers and streamers.

ALGHERO   ☎079

Limestone peaks and the 70-million-year-old Grotte di Nettuno are but a short trip from Alghero's (al-GEH-ro; pop. 45,000) palm-lined parks and cobblestone streets. The city has changed hands between everyone from native Sardinians to the Spanish Aragonese and the Ligurian Genoese. A distinctly Spanish flair still makes itself felt—in addition to Italian, a dialect of Catalán chimes in the streets. Today, Alghero is known for its dynamic nightlife, proximity to both the coast and the mountains, and its accessibility for tourists—the recent advent of Ryanair fights to Alghero-Fertilia airport has made Alghero a happening vacation spot.

▎ TRANSPORTATION

Flights: Fertilia Civil Airport (☎93 52 82), 6km north of the city. Buses run from *centro* every hr. Ryanair (www.ryanair.com) runs domestic flights year-round to **Barcelona, Frankfurt, London,** and **Rome.**

Trains: FDS (☎95 07 85) on V. Don Minzoni, in the northern part of the city. Take **AP** or **AF bus** from in front of Casa del Caffè in the park (3 per hr.) or walk 1km along port to the station. Taxis €7 from *centro*. Buy tickets at **Trenitalia stand** in the park, and ride the bus to the station for free, or buy from *biglietteria* in station. **Luggage storage** available (p. 726). To **Sassari** (35min.; 11 per day 6:01am-8:47pm; €2.20, round-trip €3.80). Reduced service Su.

Buses:

ARST (☎800 86 50 42) and **FDS** (☎24 13 01). Tickets at stand in the public gardens (☎95 01 79). Blue buses depart V. Catalogna, next to park. To: **Bosa** via Villanova Monteleone, mountain route (1¾hr., Sept.-June 2 per day 6:35am and 3:40pm, €4.50); **Bosa** via **Litoranea,** coastal route (1hr. to *centro* and Bosa Marina, 1½hr. to Bosa Stazione FDS; June-Sept. 9:55am and 7:30pm, Oct.-May 9am and 1:50pm; €3); **Porto Torres** (1hr.; up to 8 per day 4:45am-8:45pm, reduced service Sa-Su; €2.50); **Sassari** (1hr., 1-2 per hr. 5:35am-7:50pm, €3).

FDS also runs orange **city buses** (☎95 04 58). Buy tickets (€0.70) at *tabaccherie*. Buses run from P. della Mercede (in front of the church) before stopping at V. Cagliari (in front of Casa del Caffè) to the airport (20min., 13 per day 5am-10pm; schedule subject to monthly changes). **Line AF** runs between Fertilia and V. Cagliari, stopping at the port (40min.; from Alghero 7am, then every hr. from 8:40am-11:40pm, additional buses M-F 8:10am and 1:10am; from Fertilia 7:50am and then every hr. 9am-midnight, additional weekday buses at 8:30am and 1:30pm). **AP** buses run from Vle. della Resistenza to **train station** (every 30-60min., 6:20am-9pm). **AO** goes from V. Cagliari to the beach and the **hospital** (2 per hr. 7:15am-11:50pm). **AC** runs from V. Liguria to **Carmine** (2 per hr. 7:20am-7:50pm). Tourist office provides a complete schedule.

Taxis: V. Vittorio Emanuele (☎97 53 96), across from the BNL bank. Private taxi (☎98 92 028). From *centro* to airport about €20. Both stands and numbers are quite unreliable late at night–plan ahead.

Car Rental: Avis, P. Sulis 9 (☎97 95 77; www.avisautonoleggio.it), or at the airport (☎93 50 64). 25+. Credit card required. Open M-F 8:30am-1pm and 4-7pm, Sa

8:30am-1pm. AmEx/MC/V. **Europcar** (☎93 50 32; www.europcar.it), at the airport. Open daily 8am-11pm. AmEx/MC/V.

Bike and Scooter Rental: Cycloexpress di Tomaso Tilocca (☎98 69 50; www.cicloexpress.com), near the port at the intersection of V. Garibaldi and V. Spano. Bikes €7-13 per day; tandems €15 per day; electric scooters €15 per day; motor scooters €25-55 per day. Open M-Sa 9am-1pm and 4-8:30pm, Su 9am-1pm. AmEx/MC/V.

✦ ? ORIENTATION AND PRACTICAL INFORMATION

ARST and FDS buses stop at the corner of **Via Catalogna** and **Via Cagliari,** on the waterfront one block from the **port.** The tourist office, in **Piazza Porta Terra,** lies diagonally across the small park, on the right beyond the easily visible towers of the *centro storico.* The **train station** is a hike from the *centro* but accessible by local orange buses (lines AF and AP).

Tourist Office: P. Porta Terra 9 (☎97 90 54; infoturismo@comune.alghero.ss.it), on the right from the bus stop, toward the *centro storico.* Multilingual staff offers an indexed street map, bus and train schedules, tours of the city, and daytrips to local villages. Open M-Sa Apr.-Oct. 8am-8pm, Su 10am-1pm; Nov.-Mar. 8am-8pm.

Currency Exchange: Banca Nazionale del Lavoro (BNL), V. V. Emanuele 5 (☎98 01 22), across from the tourist office, has a 24hr. **ATM.** Open M-F 8:20am-1:20pm and 2:30-4pm, Sa 8:20-11:50am. Currency exchange also available at the **post office.**

Luggage Storage: In train station. €1 per bag per day.

English-Language Bookstore: Ex Libris Liberia, V. Carlo Alberto 2a (☎079 98 33 22), has a small selection of English-language novels. Open daily 9am-midnight. MC/V.

Police: P. della Mercede 7 (☎97 20 01). **First Aid:** ☎99 62 33.

Pharmacy: Farmacia Puliga di Mugoni, V. Sassari 8 (☎97 90 26). Posts after-hours rotations. Open May-Oct. M-Sa 9am-1pm and 5-9pm. AmEx/MC/V.

Hospital: Ospedale Civile (☎99 62 00), on V. Don Minzoni in Regione La Pietraia.

Internet Access: Bar Miramar, V. Gramisci 2. 3 computers. €1.60 per 15min., €5 per hr. Open daily 8am-noon and 3pm-3am. Cash only.

Post Office: V. Carducci 33/35 (☎97 20 231), has *fermoposta* and **currency exchange.** Open M-F 8am-6:50pm, Sa 8am-1:15pm. **Postal Code:** 07041.

🏠 🏨 ACCOMMODATIONS AND CAMPING

Hotel San Francesco, V. Ambrogio Machin 2/4 (☎98 03 30; www.sanfrancescohotel.com), in the heart of the *centro storico.* This converted 14th-century church cloister offers 21 rooms with bath, A/C, phone, and stone walls. Enjoy a drink in the small bar, which used to be a monk prison. The cloister hosts a classical music festival in the summer. Breakfast included. Reservation required June-Aug. Singles €60; doubles €96; triples €125. MC/V. ❹

Hotel La Margherita, V. Sassari 70 (☎97 90 06; hotel.margherita@tiscali.it), near P. Mercedes. 53 spacious rooms with A/C, minifridge, safe, phone, and TV. Breakfast served on rooftop, weather permitting. Social terrace with waterfront views, 2 treadmills, and 2 stationary bikes. Free beach umbrellas and lounge chairs. Breakfast included. Singles €50-85; doubles €80-125. Extra bed €20. AmEx/D/MC/V. ❹

Bed and Breakfast MamaJuana, Vco. Adami 12 (☎339 13 69 791; www.mamajuana.it), on a side street in the heart of the *centro storico,* parallel to V. Roma. 4 rooms with wooden ceilings. Check out 10am. Reception 9am-9pm; call ahead. Singles €50-65; doubles €80-90. Cash only. ❹

Hostal del'Alguer (HI), V. Parenzo 79 (☎/fax 93 20 39 or 93 04 78), in Fertilia. From the port, take bus AF to Fertilia (every hr., last bus 11:30pm). Turn right, and walk down the street; hostel is on right side of outdoor building complex. Cheapest option in area, but outside Alghero proper; Fertilia lacks Alghero's charm and bustle. Reception in building farthest from street. Fun-loving staff offers 100 simple beds, bike rental, bar, maps, and info on attractions. Cold showers, but large common room with TV and beach around the corner. Breakfast included; large lunch or dinner €9.50. Laundry €2.50 per 5kg. Internet access €5 per hr. Dorms €17; 4- to 6-bed dorms €18-20; doubles €21-25. HI-member discount €3. ❶

La Mariposa, V. Lido 22 (☎95 03 60; www.lamariposa.it). Campground right off the beach, 1.5km from Alghero toward Fertilia. Offers large grilling pit, restaurant, bar, market, bike rental, diving, and beach access. Laundry €5 per load. Reservations recommended. Open Mar.-Oct. €8-10.50 per person, €4-8.50 per child, €4-13 per tent, €2-4 per car. 2-person bunk-bed cabins €23-36. 2-person bungalows €26-31, 3-person €37-45, 4-person €45-75; must pay for full 4-person occupation in Aug. Electricity €2.50. Hot showers €0.50. Apr.-June tents and cars free. AmEx/MC/V. ❶

LIVE LIKE A LOCAL. Sardinia only has two youth hostels—one in Bosa Marino and one between Alghero and Fertilia. For a cheaper option, contact the local tourist office for B&Bs or *agriturismo* options. The lodging owners are usually friendly, travel-loving locals. Be sure to check out the rooms before booking.

🍴 FOOD

On Wednesday, there is an **open-air market** on V. Europa and V. Corsica. (Open 8:30am-1pm.) Walk 15min. from the *centro* to **Antiche Cantine del Vino Sfuso,** C. V. Emanuele 80, where you can sample and purchase local wholesale table wines for a mere €1.50 per L—bring your own tasting cup. (Open M-Sa 8:30am-1pm and 4:30-8pm. MC/V.) A **Sisa** supermarket is at V. Sassari 49. (☎97 31 067. Open M-Sa 8am-8:30pm, Su 8am-1:30pm.) Fresh **produce market** stalls also line the archways beneath V. Sassari 19-23. (Open M-Sa 7am-1:30pm and 4-8pm.)

Trattoria Maristella, V. Kennedy 9 (☎97 81 72). Slightly removed from the *centro storico*, this local haunt serves some of the best fish in town. Try the *fregola con cozze e vongole* (semolina pasta cooked with mussels and clams; €9) or the *maccarones de Busa* (macaroni with lobster sauce; €12). *Primi* €7.50-12, *secondi* €8-13. Service 5%. Open daily 12:15-2:30pm and 8-10:30pm. AmEx/MC/V. ❸

Osteria Taverna Paradiso, V. Principe Umberto 29 (☎97 80 01). Stone-vaulted ceilings and fine meats like the Argentina Angus filet (€6.50 per 100g) make for charming dining in the *centro storico*. Try the *Maestro Formaggiaio* (Cheese Master), owner Pasquale's renowned cheese platter (€16). *Primi* €8.30-12, *secondi* €13-20. Cover €1.50. Open daily noon-2pm and 8pm-midnight. AmEx/D/MC/V. ❹

Ristorante la Cueva, V. Gioberti 4 (☎97 91 83). From P. Porta Terra, take V. Simon, and turn right on V. Gioberti. Snug restaurant housed in an 8th-century building with arched stone ceilings. Savory fare includes *porcetto sardo* (roast suckling pig; €15), paella, and homemade *sebadas* (Sardinian ravioli; €4). *Primi* €7-20, *secondi* €9-20. Open M and W-Su 1-2:30pm and 7:30pm-midnight. AmEx/MC/V. ❸

Al Tuguri, V. Maiorca 113 (☎/fax 97 67 72; www.altuguri.it). Delicious variations on traditional cuisine give Al Tuguri its stellar reputation. Try the *triglie* (red mullet fish; €15.80) or the exceptional 5-course *menù* (€40), with a vegetarian option (€34). *Primi* €12-15, mandatory *secondi* €18.50-23. Open M-Sa 12:30-2pm and 8-10pm. Reservations recommended. MC/V. ❺

Schiaccineria La Buccia, V. Carlo Alberto 10 (☎349 31 81 575). The aroma of fresh pizza corrals customers into this tiny pizzeria, where slices are sold as soon as they come out of the oven. Try the delicious proscuitto and asparagus or opt for the sweeter *marmellata* pizza (€4.50). Slices €1.20-2.20. Open daily 11:30am-2:30pm and 5:30-11pm. ❶

SARDINIA

⚙ ⚠ SIGHTS AND OUTDOOR ACTIVITIES

A leisurely walk through the *centro storico* reveals tiny alleys, half-hidden churches, and ancient town walls. The old city is hard to navigate without a map, so stop by the tourist office first. The **Torre di Porta Terra** dominates the entrance to the town near the public gardens. Financed by the Jewish community in the 15th-century and consequently known as the **Torre degli Ebrei** (Tower of the Jews), it now offers panaromic views of the town. (Open M-Sa 9:30am-1pm and 5-9pm. €1.50.) Heading down V. Roma, Alghero's *duomo*, **La Cattedrale di Santa Maria,** is at the intersection with V. Principe Umberto. Begun in 1552, it took 178 years to construct, resulting in a stunning, motley Gothic-Catalán-Renaissance facade. Rebuilt in the 19th century, the cathedral has Gothic choirs, a mosaic of John the Baptist, and the original *porta petita* (small door) from the Catalán structure. One block from the *duomo*, down V. P. Umberto, are the 19th-century **Teatro Civico** and **Palazzo Machin,** classic examples of Gothic-Catalán architecture. Backtrack up V. Roma and take a right on V. Carlo Alberto to find **Chiesa di San Francesco.** The Neo-classical facade conceals a graceful Gothic interior with beautiful marble altar. (Open M-F 9:30am-noon and 5-6:15pm, Su 5-6:30pm. Modest dress required. Free.) Heading away from the harbor, take V. Carlo Alberto to reach the beautiful **Chiesa di San Michele** at P. Ginnasio, built between 1661 and 1675 and dedicated to the patron saint of Alghero. V. Carlo Alberto ends at P. Sulis and the **Torre dello Sperone,** where French soldiers were imprisoned in 1412 after failing to capture the Catalán fortress. In the 19th century, Sardinian patriot Vincenzo Sulis was a prisoner here, thus giving the *piazza* its name.

The countryside around Alghero is filled with spectacular nature reserves, inland mountains, and cliffs plunging into the sea, making it a popular destination for **trekking** and **bicycling.** Inquire at the tourist office for a comprehensive list of itineraries. One of the most popular parks, **Le Prigionette Nature Reserve,** lies at **Porto Conte,** off the Fertilia-Porto Conte highway on the road to Capo Caccia. Buses heading toward the Grotte di Nettuno (p. 737) pass by the reserve three times daily. Bike and hiking paths wind through mountains, past sloping valleys dotted with wild horses. The forestry house at the park entrance supplies good maps and advice. (☎94 90 60. Open daily 9am-5pm.) FDS buses also lead directly to Porto Conte (30min., 11 per day 7am-11:30pm, €1; returns 11 per day 7:30am-midnight), where a dirt road leads to **Punta Giglio Reserve.** The road is a difficult but popular route for bikers, ending after 3km at a ▧limestone peak on Punta Giglio. This point has the most impressive views in the region, as well as several semi-abandoned WWII barracks for war buffs or curious minds. For those not biking, get off at the Porto Conte stop, walk 300m down the road back toward town, and the entrance is on the right (45-60min.). The low-traffic seaside highway that heads away from Alghero to the Porto Conte area is also popular for biking. For the bike ride, follow the beachside road; V. Garibaldi turns into V. Lido, and then Vle. Maggio. Vle. Maggio leads to the dock at the end of Alghero's coast (8km); cross the bridge onto the highway to Fertilia. Continue along the bike path with the forest on one side and the highway on the other (3km). When the bike path ends, continue along highway for another 3km until Porto Conte. The **Nuraghi di Palmavera** is 3km past Fertilia, along the highway from Alghero to Porto Conte/Capo Caccia; follow the bike path next to the forest to its end and then go another 200m on the highway. A central tower surrounded by 50 huts forms a limestone complex dating from 1500 BC. (☎95 32 00; fax 98 87 65. Open daily Apr.-Oct. 9am-7pm; Nov.-Mar. 9:30am-4pm. €3, over 65 and children €2). The **S.I.L.T. cooperative,** V. Mattei 14, offers tours of *nuraghi* in English by request. (☎98 00 40; www.coopsilt.it. Tours run every hr. 9:15am-11:15am and 4-6pm. €2, audio tour €3.)

🎵 📻 ENTERTAINMENT AND NIGHTLIFE

Alghero comes alive at night. Revelers stream through the *centro storico*'s cramped streets and pour onto the promenade until the early morning hours. In summer months, locals in search of warm evening breezes and live music head to the open-air bars along **Lungomare Dante** and along the **waterfront** all the way to Fertilia. Both locals and tourists also enjoy **Poco Loco**, V. Gramsci 8, past P. Sulis, inland from Lungomare Dante. Famed for its pizza-by-the-meter (€17-27 per m; 0.5m also available), Poco has six bowling lanes (€3.50-6 per game) and Internet for €3 per hr. (☎97 31 034. Live music W in summer, F-Sa 11pm in winter. Beer from €2. Mixed drinks €5. Open in summer daily 7:30pm-3am or later. MC/V.)

📻 DAYTRIP FROM ALGHERO: GROTTE DI NETTUNO

Booming waves echo amidst stalactites and stalagmites in the wondrous 🏆**Grotte di Nettuno** (Neptune's Grottoes). These majestic caves, first discovered by fishermen, have been around for 60 to 70 million years and are one of Sardinia's most frequented tourist destinations. Thanks to modern lighting, the caves today seem magical—blue, green, and yellow light dances on the rocks. Well-run 30min. tours, conducted in English and Italian, point out whimsical rock formations like Christmas trees and pipe organs in the bowels of the caves. The caves are in Capo Caccia, a steep promontory that juts out from Porto Conte. Built in 1954, the steep Escala del Cabirol provides access to the grotto by land for those brave enough to walk down the 654 steps that plunge to the sea between massive white cliffs. (☎94 65 40. Open daily Apr.-Sept. 9am-7pm; Oct. 9am-5pm; Nov.-Mar. 9am-4pm. Groups admitted every hr. €10, children €5. FDS buses run to Capo Caccia. ☎95 01 79. 50min.; 3 per day 9:15am-5:10pm, last return 6:05pm; €2. Or take the pleasant Navisarda Grotte di Nettuno ferry tour. ☎97 62 02 or 95 06 03; www.navisarda.it. Guide in English and Italian. Boats Leave Alghero's Bastione della Maddalena. 2½hr. round-trip, with tour of caves; June-Sept. 9 per day 9am-5pm; Apr.-May and Oct. 9, 10am and 3pm. Round-trip €13, under 13 €7.)

> **⚡ TIP**
> **KILLING TIME.** Be advised that the FDS buses leaving at 9:15am, 3:10, and 5:10pm will arrive at Capo Caccia a few minutes past the hour, meaning that you will have to wait around 45min. until the next hourly tour of the Neptune's Grottoes. Also, if relying on public transportation, plan on taking either the 9:15am or 3:10pm buses since the 5:10 bus will leave you stranded in Capo Caccia.

CASTELSARDO   ☎079

When the Arabs invaded Sardinia in the 12th century, the conquerors founded Castelsardo (cah-stel-SAR-doh; pop. 5400) and left their mark on Sardinia's history forever in the form of the Sardinian flag—four Arab men in white bandanas. The flag still whips in the cool sea breeze atop the *castello*, which towers over zig-zagging streets that lead down to the pristine waters of the Mediterranean. Whether casting a line into the swirling sea or bronzing with the best of them on the white sand beaches, Castelsardo offers a respite from life's worries.

🚍 📻 TRANSPORTATION AND PRACTICAL INFORMATION. ARST **buses** run to Sassari (1hr., 11 per day 5:40am-8:50pm, €2.50) and Santa Teresa Gallura (1¾hr., 4 per day 8:23am-8:48pm, €5.50) via the *centro*. Tickets can be purchased La Nuova newsstand in P. Pianedda. From the *centro* bus stop, follow signs for the *centro storico* up **Via Nazionale** to **Via Bastione**, climbing up the large hillside to reach the **castello**. The **tourist office** is in P. del Popolo, right before the *castello*. (☎47 15 06; proloco.castel-

sardo@tiscali.it. Open M-Sa 10am-12:15pm and 5-7pm.) For a **taxi,** call ☎47 01 25. The **post office** is on V. Nazionale. (☎47 00 05. Open M-Sa 8am-1:15pm.) **Postal Code** 07031.

ACCOMMODATIONS AND FOOD. Casa Doria ❸, V. Garibaldi 10, is a beautiful B&B that offers spacious rooms. (☎349 35 57 882; www.casadoria.it. Breakfast included. 2 rooms with shared bath €60; double with private bath €70. Extra bed €20. Cash only.) Down the block, **B&B Smorfiosa e Calarina** ❸, V. Garibaldi 42, is spacious and clean, with large beds, private baths, and a terrace with a sea view. (☎347 86 12 095; www.bb-smorfiosaecalarina.it. Breakfast included. €35 per person. Cash only.) **B&B La Pianeddia** ❸, V. Mameli 9, is close to both the *centro* and the beach, and provides clean, colorful rooms with A/C, and TV above a ground-floor garden. (☎47 01 31 or 320 40 59 729. €30 per person. Cash only.) **Hotel Riviera** ❹, V. Lungomare Anglona 1, is worth the extra cost for its proximity to the sea. Its modern rooms have A/C, private bath, minifridge, safe, and TV. (☎47 01 43; www.hotelriviera.net. Complimentary umbrella and deck chair. Breakfast and parking included. Singles €50-70; doubles €100-130. Rooms with a sea view €15 extra. AmEx/MC/V.)

    Trattoria da Maria Giuseppa ❷, V. Nazionale 20, is a local favorite, serving an abundant selection of *primi* dishes like Sardinian *gnocchetti* (€7.50) and grilled calimari (€8). The trattoria sits off the main road, which winds up the hill from bus stop. (☎47 06 61. Fish €8-15 per 100g. *Primi* €6-9, *secondi* €7-14. Cover €1.50. Open daily noon-2:30pm and 7:30-11:30pm. Cash only.) For some nourishment and shade after the trying trek up to the *castlello,* dine at **Lu Scubili** ❸, V. Garibaldi 21, a pizzeria with pleasant, shaded tables dotting a cobblestone street. From P. del Popolo, walk all the way down the steps across from the tourist office, and turn left at the bottom. Try typical Sardinian fare, such as fish soup (€11), *cavallo* (horsemeat; €14), and large pizzas (dinner only) with a variety of toppings, including seafood, for €3.50. (☎47 05 11. Open M-Sa 12:30-2pm and 7:30pm-midnight. Cover €2. Service 20%. Cash only.) **Supermarkets** and fresh **produce stands** line the streets at the bottom of the hill, where the bus drops you off.

🄶🄲 SIGHTS AND BEACHES. The **castello**—for which Castelsardo is named—housed the town's *carabinieri* until the 90s. Today, the restored *castello* is home to a museum showcasing the town's long tradition of millinery and fishing through exhibits of historical and local artifacts as well as wicker crafts from Castelsardo. While the calm exhibits are short of exhilarating, the awe-inspiring view from the castle's terrace alone is worth the entrance fee. To reach the towering *castello,* walk to the top of the hill from the *centro*'s bus stop; from there, it's hard to miss. On the way back down, follow V. Bastione to the downhill path along the city walls that leads to grassy knolls, large rock formations, and yelping seagulls. (☎47 13 80. *Castello* open daily 9am-midnight. €2, children €1.) For your very own sample of Castelsardo wicker baskets, check out the artisanal shop, **Vecchio Mercato.** To reach the market from the *castello,* descend about 30 of the steps in front of the tourist office and it will be on the right. Visit the **beach** by winding down the curving roads from the *centro* and walking along V. Lungomare Anglona, following the signs for *la mare.* Or get off at the ARST bus stop on V. Lungomare Anglona. A 5min. bus ride away, the picturesque **Lu Bagnu** also offers sandy, white beaches and rolling waves perfect for bodysurfing. The private company **Spina Salvatore & Figli** runs orange shuttle buses between Castelsardo and Lu Bagnu. Buses leave from the ARST bus stop on V. Roma, near P. Pianedda (every 1½hr. 6:37am-6:17pm, last return 7pm; €0.70). Castelsardo also has a well-known, wind-swept rock, **la Roccia dell'Elefante,** so named because its profile resembles an elephant with his trunk curled up. The rock is on Strada Statale #134, the road between Castelsardo and Sedini. Check with tourist office for bus schedules.

PALAU   ☎0789

Situated on the luminous waters of Sardinia's northern coast, Palau (pa-LA-oo; pop. 4200) is both a gorgeous destination and an easy base for exploring La Maddalena. Palau's most famous sight is the Roccia dell'Orso, an enormous granite rock that the mistral winds have carved into the shape of a bear. It is immortalized in Homer's *Odyssey* with a warning about the ferocious *Lestrigoni* people that lived around it. Palau is now a heavily touristed town lined with pastel-colored modern buildings. Though the town does have some nice restaurants and a spectacular pair of camping facilities, its true attraction is the incomparable coastline nearby.

⊞⊠ TRANSPORTATION AND PRACTICAL INFORMATION. The port end of **Via Nazionale,** Palau's single major thoroughfare, contains a white building that houses a bar and ferry ticket offices, with bus stops outside. ARST **buses** run to Arzachena (13 per day 12:15am-9:30pm, €2); Olbia (13 per day, €2.50 to the *centro*); Porto Cervo (5 per day M-F 5:15am-5:05pm); Santa Teresa di Gallura (7 per day 7:50am-9:25pm, €2); and Sassari (4 per day M-F 5:15am-7pm, Sa-Su only 7pm). Tickets sold on buses. The **ferry** companies EneRmaR (☎70 84 84; www.enermar.it; 15min., every 30min. 6:15am-11:45pm; round-trip €10, cars €11.50-2.50, bikes €1) and Saremar Ferries (☎70 92 70 or 73 52 98; 15min.; every 30min. 7:30am-7:30pm; round-trip €10, ages 4-12 €8, cars €15.80-24) serve the island of La Maddalena. Nicos Buses runs **shuttles** to Porto Cervo. (☎079 67 06 13 or 079 63 41 42; www.nicosgroup.it. 45min., departs 9:58am and returns 6pm. Call for reservations and prices.) For an expensive **taxi,** call ☎70 92 18.

Palau's **◙tourist office,** P. Fresi, sits to the right of V. Nazionale when approaching from Stazione Maritime. English-speaking staff offers info on beaches, outdoor activities, and tours of neighboring islands, as well as a wealth of publications about Sardinia and the Palau region. (☎70 70 25; www.palau.it. Open daily 9am-1pm and 4:30-7:30pm.) **Banca di Sassari,** V. Roma 9, has **currency exchange** and **ATMs** in front. (Open M-F 8:20am-1:20pm and 2:30-3:30pm, Sa 8:20am-12:30pm.) In case of **emergency,** contact the **medical clinic** (☎70 93 96). **Farmacia Nicolai** is at V. delle Ginestre 19. (☎70 95 16, for urgent needs 70 83 53. Open M-Sa 9am-1pm and 5-8pm. AmEx/MC/V.) The **guardia medica turistica,** V. degli Achei, on the way toward Baia Saraceno from the port (follow signs for Baia Saraceno Camping), offers quick checkups and prescriptions for travelers' ailments. (☎70 93 96. Open 24hr.) Wi-Fi and **Internet** access are available at **Grillo's,** V. Fonte Vecchia 56. (€2 per 15min., €3 per 30min.) Follow the signs to the **post office** is at the intersection of V. Regina Margherita and V. La Maddalena. (☎70 85 27. Open M-Sa 8am-1:15pm, Sa 8:15am-12:45pm.) **Postal code:** 07020.

⌐ ACCOMMODATIONS. Accommodations in Palau are often prohibitively expensive. If you are desperate for A/C and a break from the beach, paying high prices at hotels will be necessary; otherwise, the campgrounds provide a stellar budget option. **Hotel La Roccia ❺,** V. dei Mille 15, has a lobby built around an enormous boulder and themed rooms, like *"Il Faro"* (the lighthouse). Sharing a lovely, small outdoor garden and large breakfast buffet room, all 22 rooms have balcony, A/C, phone, TV, and bath. (☎70 95 28; www.hotellaroccia.com. Breakfast and parking included. Reserve ahead. Singles €48-84; doubles €78-130. Extra bed additional 35%. AmEx/MC/V.) The same company operates two fantastically friendly, multilingual-staffed **◙campsites** in town. Of the two camping options, **Baia Saraceno ❶,** Località Puna Nera 1, is much larger, more self-contained, and farther away from the touristy center. Facing the water, turn right and follow the *lungomare* away from the port and the signs to Baia Saraceno (10-15min. walk). Across the docks from the port and behind a man-made forest, Baia Saraceno offers three picturesque beaches 500m outside Palau. This establishment has three clean, large shared bathroom areas, a restaurant, pizzeria, bar, minimarket, and laundry service. The facility has its own diving center and arranges water sports and trips to nearby islands. (☎70 94 03; www.baiasaraceno.com. Towels €1.50 per day. €8-17 per person, ages 4-12 €5.50-13. Electricity €3. 2-person bungalows €26-48, with bath €32-64; 4-person bungalows with kitchen €248-500. 4-person caravan €89. Final cleaning fee €6-25; price varies with accommodation. AmEx/MC/V.) On the other side of town and 10min. from the port, Mexican-themed, family-oriented **Acapulco ❶**, Località Punta Palau, has a private beach, a bar with nightly piano music, a pizzeria, and a restaurant. From port, walk up V. Nazionale two blocks to V. Maddalena. Turn right onto V. Maddalena, turn left at the end of the uphill block, and follow signs for camping. Alternatively, from the port, with the water to the right, follow the *lungomare* up the large hill and then the signs for camping. Extremely friendly and helpful English-speaking staff arrange underwater spear-fishing and excursions to La Maddalena Archipelago. (☎70 94 97; www.campingacapulco.com. Towels €2. Open Mar.-Oct. 15. Reservations recommended in summer. €8-17.50 per person, ages 4-12 €5.50-13. Electricity €3. Hot showers free. Single bungalows with mandatory half pension €52-64; 2-person bungalows with kitchen €90-170; 4-person bungalow with kitchen €240-500. 4-person caravans €45-90. Final cleaning fee €10-30. AmEx/MC/V over €50.)

BYOTP. If you're staying in a *tukul* (bungalows without private bath), camper, or tent without a private bath at Baia Saraceno or Acapulco, be aware that toilet paper is not provided in the restrooms. Grab a roll before walking from Palau to avoid a messy situation.

❒ FOOD. Numerous bakeries and stores line V. Nazionale, and a **market** every Friday (8am-1pm) crowds the harbor with fresh cheeses, meats, clothing, and crafts. **Sicily Creperie ❶**, V. Nazionale 45, is a Nutella haven, with Nutella crepes, Nutella and fruit crepes, Nutella and *gelato* brioches, and Nutella frappes for €2.50-4. (☎33 16 44 67 72. Open 9:30am-1pm and 4-10:30pm. Cash only.) The friendly waitstaff of **L'Uva Fragola ❶**, P. Fresi 4, serve a variety of refreshing salads (€5.50-10.50), spaghetti (€4.50-7), and 39 types of creative pizzas (€3.50-8) with toppings like octopus and egg. (☎70 87 65. Cover €1.50. Open daily noon-3pm and 7-11pm. MC/V.) **Ristorante da Robertino ❹**, V. Nazionale 20, a pricey but popular seafood restaurant, serves fresh fish and flavorful pasta, such as spaghetti with shellfish for €11. (☎70 96 10. *Primi* €6-14, *secondi* €15-25. Cover €1.50. Open Tu-Su 1-2:30pm and 8-10pm. Reserve 2-3 days in advance. MC/V.) **Ristorante Il Covo ❸**, V. Sportiva 10/12, serves seafood and traditional, meat-heavy Sardinian cuisine at reasonable prices. The *linguine del pescatore* (assorted seafood spaghetti; €10) is a good call for indecisive patrons, as is the Maine lobster salad, priced per 100g. (☎70 96 08. Pizza €3.70-7. *Primi* €6.80-10, *secondi* €5-14.50. 4-course dinner *menú* €30. Cover €2. Open M-Tu and Th-Su noon-2:30pm and 7-11:30pm. AmEx/MC/V.) If your sweet tooth is still aching, try the purple *mora*, an authentic black raspberry ice cream, at **La Gelateria dell' Angelo ❶**, V. Capo d'Orso 2, where V. Nazionale and Capo d'Orso meet. (Open daily 4pm-midnight.) **Supermercati SISA** is at V. Nazionale 104. (☎70 95 04. Open July-Aug. daily 8am-9pm). Fresh fruits and veggies are sold on V. Sportiva, across the street from **Grillo's**, V. F. Vecchia 56 .

◉ SIGHTS. The small **Spiaggia Palau Vecchia** is the beach to the left of the port as you face the water. Its shores are shaded most of the day, and therefore not the best for those set on tanning. However, Caramelli buses run to **Porto Pollo** (30min.; 5 per day 8:15am-6:45pm, last return 7:30pm; round-trip €2.50), a beach where Mediterranean seaweed sways under the water. Check out the **Roccia dell'Orso**, a rock that looks like a bear to some, from which you can enjoy stunning views of the countryside and port. (Buses to "Capo d'Orso"; 20min.; 4 per day 9:45am-6pm, last return 6:20pm; round-trip €1.50.) Bring proper footwear for the stair climb (10min.) and perhaps a picnic lunch and a good book, because the return bus doesn't come for roughly 3hr. If you want to see the Roccia without the exercise, look back toward Palau as you take the ferry to La Maddalena—it can sometimes be seen on the right side of the hill to the left of Palau.

L'ARCIPELAGO DELLA MADDALENA ☎ 0789

Corsica and Sardinia were once joined by a massive land bridge; L'Arcipelago della Maddalena (lar-chee-PEH-la-go DEL-la ma-da-LEH-na; pop. 12,000), Caprera, and the over 50 smaller islands that surround them are its fragmented remains. Though visitors crowd the streets and relax on calm, white-sand beaches, tourism has not spoiled the islands. The entire archipelago was declared Sardinia's first national park in 1996, and commercial development has been strictly regulated since. In addition, Italian patriots mob La Maddalena for their own reasons: their national hero and unifier, Giuseppe Garibaldi (1807-1882), made the nearby island of Caprera his home while he was in exile. The other main residents of La Maddalena are the members and families of a US Naval Station, located along V. Principe Amedeo, which explains why so much English is spoken on these small Sardinian islands. However, the base is expected to close in the near future.

▐▌ TRANSPORTATION AND PRACTICAL INFORMATION. EneRmaR (☎73 54 68 or 70 84 84; www.enermar.it; 15min.; every 30min. 5:45am-11pm; round-trip €10, cars €11.50-20.50, bikes €1) and Saremar (☎70 92 70; 15min.; every 30min., 7am-7pm; €10 per person, €15.80-24.60 per car, bikes €1) run **ferries** between Palau and La Maddalena. For a **taxi**, call ☎73 65 00 or 72 20 80. Rent **bikes** and **motor scooters** at Nicola, V. Amendola 18. (☎73 52 66. Bikes €10 per day. Motor scooters €20-50 per day. Open daily 9am-7:30pm.)

There is no tourist office, but Palau's tourist office usually has brochures featuring La Maddalena's major attractions. If still lacking direction, there is a map on a billboard in front of the bus stop at Maddelena's port. **Banco di Sardegna**, on V. Amendola off P. XXIV Febbraio, has **currency exchange** and a 24hr. **ATM.** (Open M-F 8:20am-1:20pm and 2:35-4:05pm.) A **laundromat, Azzura Lavanderia,** is at V. Dei Mille 3, off V. Principe Amedeo, one block past the public gardens. (☎38 99 72 40 27. Wash €4 per 6kg. Open M-Sa 9am-1pm and 4:30-8pm. Cash only.) In case of **emergency,** call the **carabinieri** (☎ 73 70 04 or 73 69 43) or the **hospital** (☎79 12 00). There is a **pharmacy** at the corner of P. Santa Maria Maddalena and V. Marsala. (Open M-F and Su 9am-1pm and 5-8:30pm.) **Patsi Net Internet Point,** V. Montanara 4, has three computers with fast connections; turn into the *piazza* to the left, off V. Principe Amedeo, across from the public gardens. Walk uphill and take a left. (☎72 31 04. €6 per hr. Open daily 9am-1pm and 5-9pm. AmEx/MC/V.) The **post office** is in P. Umberto 1, across the street from the main part of the *piazza.* (☎79 09 00. Open M-F 8am-6:50pm, Sa 8:15am-1:15pm.) **Postal Code:** 07024.

▐▌ ACCOMMODATIONS AND FOOD. Though a 20min. walk from the *centro*, **Hotel Arcipelago ❹**, V. Indipendenza 2, is a good deal. From P. Umberto, follow V. Mirabello along the water until the intersection with the stoplight. Turn left here, then take the first right on V. Indipendenza. Continue uphill, taking the first left onto a branch of the main road. The hotel is around the corner from the grocery store. The flower-lined entrance leads to a nautically themed lobby and 12 tastefully furnished rooms with TV, phone, and fan. (☎72 73 28. Breakfast included. Reservation required July-Aug. Singles €45-55; doubles €60-85. V.) Up V. Indipendenza before you turn left for the Archipelago, **Hotel La Conchiglia ❹,** V. Indipendenza 3, has seven spacious rooms that offer superb amenities, including A/C, bath, TV, phone, microwave, and minifridge. (☎72 80 90. Breakfast included. Singles €75; doubles €100. AmEx/MC/V.) Tourists and young locals flock to **Garden Bar ❸**, V. Garibaldi 65, for its tasty, varied cuisine, friendly owner Spike, and couches at the tables upstairs. After passing under the painting of the topless mermaid and the fountain with live turtles, try the *bruschetta* (€1.50-4) for a small snack or the vast selection of land and sea *primi* and *secondi*. (☎0787 73 88 25. Pizza €3.50-8. *Primi* €6-15, *secondi* €6-20. Cover €1.50. Open daily 11:30am-3pm and 5-11pm. MC/V.) For a bite to eat before catching the ferry back to Palau, stop in at **Pizzeria Pappa & Ciccia ❶**, V. Garibaldi, 47, for cheap, topping-heavy pizzas like the "Bad Girl" (€4.50), smothered in almost all possible toppings. (☎73 68 82. Pizzas €3.50-5.50; extra toppings €0.50 each. Open daily 6pm-midnight.) Pick up lunch at the **Despar** supermarket, V. Amendola 6, at the intersection with V. Italia. (☎73 90 05. Open daily 8am-1:30pm and 5:30-8:30pm. MC/V.) If staying at either of the hotels on V. Indipendenza, another Despar is less than a block away. (Open M-Sa 8am-1:30pm and 5-8pm, Su 8:30am-12:30pm.)

🏖️🏝️ BEACHES AND ISLANDS. The islands surrounding La Maddalena are paradises of well-preserved natural beauty. Their national park status protects them from over-development. Some claim that these waters, which radiate brilliant shades of green and blue, are the clearest in the world. The nearby island **Razzoli** has magnificent swimming holes, and sightseers can set out by boat to islands like **Santa Maria**, with its long, white sand cove, by boat. Santa Maria's **faro** (lighthouse), a 20min. stroll from the beach down a labeled trail, looks out over the surrounding islands, including nearby **Spargi**. The waters in Spargi's **Cala Verde** bay shimmer in stunning shades of green. On Spargi's western side, lovers canoodle on **Cala dell'Amore's** pristine shores. Around **Cala Corsara**, blustery rock formations reward the adventurous with spectacular vistas. Without a private yacht or powerboat, the only way to explore the archipelago is on a full-day ("spaghetti") **boat tour**, so nicknamed because of their pasta lunches. Companies like **🏝️Marinella IV** (☎33 92 30 28 42 or 33 37 41 95 28; www.marinellagite.it) send ticket sellers to the docks of Palau mornings and evenings. Packing between 50-80 people, the cruises are fun and informative, as guides point out the whimsical rock formations along the way. Tours cost €35 and typically include a pasta lunch, two or three 2hr. stops at beaches along the way, often at Spargi's Cala Corsara and **Cala Santa Maria**, and a picture-only stop at **Spiaggia Rossa**. Most boats leave between 10 and 11am and return between 5 and 6pm. Purchase tickets one day ahead; tours are usually less crowded on weekends.

Buses run from La Maddalena to Caprera's **Punta Rossa** (15 per day 7:10am-7pm, last return 7:30pm; round-trip €2, purchase on bus), giving travelers access to beaches along the eastern peninsula. Catch buses at the port (in P. Colonna Garibaldi; a large monumental column marks the *piazza*) for Caprera or the northern coast of La Maddalena island, towards Ornano. Sunbathers fill the shores of **🏖️Spiaggia del Relitto,** where a wide strip of white sand, calm waters, and an expansive swimming cove have made it one of Caprera's largest and most popular beaches. To reach it, follow the main road through Caprera to Punta Rossa or take the bus to the end of the Caprera line. Continue past beach Due Mare on the dirt road for about 1.5km and take a left when you see a sign for Spiaggia del Relitto. If Caprera still doesn't satisfy your quest for the perfect panorama, bike or motor along La Maddalena's **Panoramica dei Colmi,** about 25km of paved road circling the island. The road passes by marvelous sea views and attractive beach destinations, including **Cala Lunga** and the watersport-friendly **Cala Spalmatore.**

Buses also run to **🏖️Spiaggia Bassa Trinita** from P. Colonna Garibaldi (9 per day 9am-7pm, last return 7:25pm; round-trip €2). The bus ride (10-15min.) alone is worth the trip, as it winds around the coast of La Maddalena with the rocky cliffs to one side and the pristine aquamarine beaches of Cala Spalmatore, Porto Massimo, and M. d. Rena to the other. Resist the urge to get off at the first beach;

they get less and less full of tourists as you continue up the island. Bassa Trinita is the most beautiful, with a fine sandy beach, playful waves, and windswept rock formations jutting out from the waters. From the bus stop, walk down the road immediately to the right (there will be a sign pointing to Baia Trinita) for around 10min.; you will see Baia Trinita carved into a rock when you finally reach it. There are no lifeguards at the beaches, but the water remains shallow for over 50m out. Pick up a book from **La Liberia dell'Isola,** P. Umberto 3, to read before heading to the beach. La Liberia offers a small selection of classics and mindless beach reads. (☎ 73 52 92. Open daily 9am-midnight. AmEx/MC/V.)

SANTA TERESA DI GALLURA ☎ 0789

Perched on a hilltop, it is not immediately clear to new arrivals that Santa Teresa di Gallura (SAN-ta Te-RE-sa dee ga-LOO-ra; pop. 5000) is, in fact, near water. But as soon as you crest the hill in the middle of town, the sparkling blue sea will assure you that your bus ticket was worth the cash. With its narrow streets and social *piazze*, Santa Teresa is an ideal base for exploring Capo Testa, a peninsula of wind-sculpted granite with magnificent beaches. Santa Teresa boasts its own sandy beach, Rena Bianca, from which the hazy shores of Corsica are visible.

▐ TRANSPORTATION

ARST **buses** (☎ 55 30 00) depart from V. Eleonora d'Arborea, in the parking lot across from the post office, and run to Olbia's *centro* (1¾hr., 8 per day 6:10am-8:50pm, €4.50). Palau (40min., 8 per day 6:10am-8:50pm, €2), and Sassari (3hr., 5 per day 5:15am-7:15pm, €6.50). TURMO Travel Buses (☎ 21 487) run to: Cagliari (6hr., 2:30pm, €22.50); Nuoro (3hr., 2:30pm, €7.50); Olbia airport (1hr., 6 per day 6am-6:40pm, €7); Oristano (4¾hr., 2:30pm, €15); Palau (40min., 6 per day 6am-6:40pm, €2). DIGITUR runs to Porto Torres (2hr., 4pm, €15) and Alghero (2½hr., 4pm, €15). Buy tickets onboard or at Baby Bar, on V. Nazionale, 200m from the bus stop. (Open daily 8am-1pm and 4-6:30pm.) Saremar (☎ 75 41 56; 1hr., 3 per day 8am-5pm, €12-14 including port tax for Corsica) and Moby (☎ 75 14 49; 1hr., 4 per day 7am-7pm, €15) run **ferries** to Bonifacio, Corsica. Tickets are available at the office on V. del Porto. For a **taxi,** call ☎ 75 42 37, 75 44 07, or 74 10 24. **Car rentals** are available from Hertz, V. Nazionale 58. (☎ 75 56 89; www.gulpimmobiliare.it. Open M-Sa 9am-1pm and 4-7:30pm. Cash only.) **Scooters** and **bikes** can be rented from Global Noleggio, P. San Vittorio. (☎ 75 50 80; www.globalinformation.it. Mountain bikes €10 per day; scooters €25-50 per day. Open daily 9am-1pm, 3-8pm, and 9:30-11:30pm. AmEx/MC/V.) If motors aren't for you, go **horseback riding** with Li Nibbari, Località da Testa. (☎ 33 78 17 189. Guided excursions €18 per hr.)

> ▐ **MAKIN' A FUSS OVER THE BUS.** When traveling from Palau to Sassari, remember that every bus has to travel through either Santa Teresa di Gallura or Olbia. Consequently, it makes more sense to spend the night in either place when visiting Sassari instead of traveling all the way back to Palau.

▐ ▐ ORIENTATION AND PRACTICAL INFORMATION

The ARST bus stop is at the far end of the parking lot across the street from the post office. Hug the corner the post office is on, walk straight to the intersection, and turn right on **Via Nazionale.** Head for the church in **Piazza San Vittorio,** at the end of the street and turn right again to reach **Piazza Vittorio Emanuele.** The tourist office is on the opposite side of the *piazza.*

Tourist Office: P. Vittorio Emanuele 24, 2nd fl. (☎ 75 41 27). Provides a pocket-sized map of town and assists with accommodations. Ask about boat, horse, and moped rentals, as well as info about nearby archaeological attractions. Open M-Sa 9am-1pm and 5-7:30pm, Su 9am-11:30am.

Boat Tours: Consorzio delle Bocche, P. V. Emanuele 16 (☎ 75 51 12; www.consorziobocche.com), offers tours of the archipelago. Full-day tour daily 9:15am-5pm. Lunch included. €35-40, ages 4-12 €19. Office open daily 9am-1pm and 5pm-12:30am.

Medical Clinic: (☎ 75 45 92), on V. Carlo Felice, across from bus station. Open 9am-2pm and 4-10pm.

Internet Access: Bar Sport, V. Magnon 6, in between P. V. Emanuele and P. San Vittorio. €5 per hr. Open daily 10am-11pm.

Post Office: V. E. d'Arborea (☎ 73 53 24), near the bus stop. Open M-Sa 8am-1:15pm. **Postal Code:** 07028.

ACCOMMODATIONS

Hotel Bellavista, V. Sonnino 8 (☎/fax 75 41 62; www.hotelbellavista.stg@libero.it). Heading toward the ocean, take the 2nd left off P. Liberta onto V. Sonnino. Close to the beach. Airy rooms all have large, clean tiled bath, TV, phone, and A/C; many have balcony with sea view. Breakfast €5. Singles €40-45; doubles €60-75. AmEx/MC/V. ❸

Hotel Moderno, V. Umberto 39 (☎ 75 42 33; www.modernoweb.it), centrally located off V. Nazionale. 16 comfortable rooms with large clean baths, A/C, and balcony. Extremely friendly staff. Light fixtures, bedspreads, and serving dishes designed by Sardinian artist Franco Cassellati. Other Sardinian artifacts and crafts in hallways. Breakfast included. Open Apr.-Sept. Singles €45-65; doubles €55-120. AmEx/MC/V. ❹

Pensione Scano, V. Lazio 4 (☎ 75 44 47; www.albergoscano.it). Small rooms with TV and private bath. 1st fl. balconies. Breakfast €5. Doubles July €50-55, Aug. €72-78. Extra bed €10-15. AmEx/MC/V. ❸

FOOD

Shops line V. Aniscara, off P. V. Emanuele. A fruit and clothing **market** by the bus station opens Thursday morning and runs until the early evening. The **Sisa** supermarket, on V. Nazionale, next to Banco di Sardegna, packs the expected goods. (Open M-Sa 8am-1pm and 4:30-8pm, Su 9am-noon. MC/V.)

Papè Satan, V. Lamarmora 20/22 (☎ 75 50 48). Look for the sign off V. Nazionale. Neapolitan family cooks diabolically delicious pizza in a traditional brick oven in the courtyard. Try the rich *pizza alla Papè Satan* with cream, butter, mozzarella, and prosciutto (€7.50) or the well-presented *spaghetti alle cozze* (with mussels; €8). Cover €2. Open May-Oct. daily noon-3pm and 7-10pm. MC/V. ❷

Gastronomia Pizzeria, Vle. Tibula 13 (☎ 339 74 70 60 24). Walk down V. Val d'Aosta, and turn right; walk up hill. Farther away from the *centro*, this pizza shack has cheap slices sold by the kilo (about €1.50-2.80 per slice). Also offers seafood and pasta dishes priced by the kilo. Open M-Sa 11am-3:30pm and 7-11pm. Cash only. ❶

Da Thomas, V. Val d'Aosta 22 (☎ 75 51 33). Enjoy fresh fish and shellfish on a relaxed outdoor patio, away from touristy *centro*. *Primi* €5-15, *secondi* €10-15. Cover €2. Open daily 12:30-3pm and 7-11pm. AmEx/MC/V. ❸

Marlin, V. Garibaldi 4 (☎ 75 46 97; www.marlinristorante.it), off V. Imbriani towards the sea, to the left up the stairs. This elegant *enoteca* serves typical seafood pastas as well as creative plates like crayfish and green apple risotto (€12) to huge crowds. *Primi* €9-15, *secondi* €13-20. Pizza only available for dinner. Cover €1.65. Reservations recommended. Open daily noon-2:30pm and 7-11pm. AmEx/MC/V. ❹

Ristorante Azzurra, V. del Porto 19 (☎75 47 89). Friendly staff serves delicious fish and homemade pasta like *tagliatelle* with clams, tuna, eggs, and tomatoes (€9). Over 40 kinds of pizza (€4.80-8.50). *Primi* €7-13, *secondi* €10-18. Cover €2. Open Tu-Su noon-2pm and 7-11pm. AmEx/MC/V. ❹

👁 🕿 SIGHTS AND BEACHES

Long before tourists discovered it, Santa Teresa was home to **Lu Brandali,** one of the region's largest and least disturbed prehistoric villages. Follow V. Nazionale past the end of town, then turn right on the dirt road when you see the brown sign for "Tomba dei Giganti." From here, a narrow path leads to the massive Sardinian **Tomba dei Giganti,** communal village graves used between the 14th and 10th centuries BC. Due to their enormous dimensions and stone construction, the tombs were believed to hold legendary giants. Overgrown trails wind uphill past the old village dwellings and a pair of towers before culminating at the ruins of a *nuraghe* (prehistoric stone tower). The village is not labeled at all, so stop by the tourist office for historical information on the site. The whole walk takes about 35min.

V. XX Settembre, off P. V. Emanuele, leads toward the sea. As the road forks, bear left and continue past Hotel Miramar to reach P. Libertà. The Argonese **Tower of Longonsardo** (built 1358-1577), on the ruins of an ancient *nuraghe,* is framed by a stunning sea backdrop. Corsica's shore is visible through the mist. For a private, undisturbed swim in the sea, climb down the steep stone steps to reach the water—there's no sand, but the rocks are large enough to lie on. If you do desire a sandy spot, head to the popular **Spiaggia Rena Bianca.** Facing the tower, take a left, wind down the street, and walk down the stairs. (Chair €6, with umbrella €12. Paddle boats €10 per hr.; canoes €8 per hr.; kayaks €5-8 per hr. Open daily 8am-7pm. Cash only.)

Some of the town's most notable attractions lie 3km away on the rugged peninsula **Capo Testa.** Take the Sardabus from the post office (10min.; 3 per day; €0.67, round-trip €1.24). Plan accordingly, as the last bus returns immediately after it gets to Capo Testa, and a cab back to town will run you about €10. You can also bike or walk (45-60min.) along **Via Capo Testa,** off V. Tibula from V. Nazionale. If you're walking, take the opportunity to get off the busy highway and see some gorgeous vistas by going through the wooden gates on the right of the street; this is Sardinia's **Ente Forest,** which has trails for people and horses that wind through brush and boulders and crest onto views of the coastline that are truly breathtaking. The bus stops at an isthmus called **Spiaggia Rena di Ponente,** where two seas meet to form long parallel beaches ideal for water sports. (Two chairs and umbrella €15. Single canoes €5 per hr., doubles €8 per hr.; paddle boats €10 per hr.) Keep walking up the street that runs between the two beaches for 10min. Just before the road bends right at the crest of the hill, squeeze through a one-foot opening in the rocks on the left. Follow the dirt paths up and then down into the valley to reach the remote and stunning 📷**Valley della Luna.** Once an international hippie community, it is now home to some 20 dread-locked hangers-on who live in rock dwellings in the sides of the valley and hang out on the beach. The valley holds abandoned fire rings, rock paintings, and carved posts. Travelers may smell more than a bit of smoke—and, no, that's not tobacco.

OLBIA ☎0789

As the closest port to the mainland, Olbia (OL-bee-ya; pop. 51,045) is a major transportation hub that benefits from the thousands of tourists who come through the port and airport each day. A short distance from the Golfo Aranci, Olbia provides a stellar base for visiting other more interesting locations. It's not that there's anything wrong with the city itself, but it doesn't have much to offer and you'll quickly want to move on to bigger and better things. Take a quick

SARDINIA

stroll past the shops and restaurants, then head onto locales like Costa Smeralda, a lovely (albeit expensive) stop along the pristine Emerald Coast.

TRANSPORTATION

Flights: Local buses #2 and 10 run from **Olbia Costa Smeralda Airport** to the *centro* (€0.80).

Trains: Trenitalia (☎89 20 21) on V. Pala, just off C. Umberto. Open 6:05am-12:30pm and 1:50-8:15pm. Service to **Golfo Aranci** (25min., 7 per day, €2), **Sassari** (2hr., 3 per day, €6.35) with connections to: **Alghero, Cagliari, Oristano,** and **Porto Torres** (2¼hr., 2:08pm, €7.60). Buy tickets from the lobby's machine or in the station.

Buses:

ARST (☎55 30 00 www.arst.sardegna.it), bus stop located at V. Vittorio Veneto across the street from Bar della Caccia's yellow sign, where tickets are sold. To **Palau** (1hr., 12 per day 4:20am-11:15pm, €2.50), **Santa Teresa di Gallura** (2hr., 6 per day 6:15am-8:10pm, €4.50), and **Sassari** (3hr., 6:15am and 8:10pm, €6.50). Buses also run to **Arzachena** (40min., 11 per day 6:25am-11:15pm, €2), where you can catch a bus to **Porto Cervo, Costa Smeralda** (30min., 5 per day 9:10am-5:15pm). Buy tickets at the ticket office in the station (cash only).

Sun Lines, V. Pozzo 23 (☎50 885), the airport (☎348 26 09 881), and Stazione Marittima (☎20 20 82), run a shuttle service to **Porto Cervo** and **Palau** from the airport, Stazione Marittima, and P. Crispi (4 per day, €13).

Local buses have 6 useful lines: **Line 1** goes through the *centro* to V. Veneto and V. Aldo Moro, **Line 2** from the airport to the city center and suburban outskirts; **Line 10** is a faster loop from the airport to the *centro*. **Line 4** goes from *centro* to the beaches of the Gulf of Olbia. **Line 5** goes through the *centro* on V. Mameli to the beach in either direction (Porto Rotondo or Porto Istana). **Line 9** goes from the Stazione Marittima to the *centro* and train station. Tickets €0.80 at *tabaccherie*, €1.30 onboard.

Ferries: Tirrenia (☎24 691), in Stazione Marittima.

Taxi: At the airport (☎69 150) and in the *centro* (☎22 718). Extremely expensive, as everyone drives and taxis are considered a luxury service (10min. ride about €35).

Car Rental: Hertz, V. Regina Elena 34. Open M-F 8:30am-1pm and 3:30-7:30pm, Sa-Su 8:30am-1pm. AmEx/MC/V.

ORIENTATION AND PRACTICAL INFORMATION

Ferries arrive at **Stazione Marittima,** 1km east of the city center on **Viale Isola Bianca.** Be sure to pick up a **map** of Olbia in the information office at the port. ARST buses run from Stazione Marittima to the ARST station on **Via Vittorio Veneto,** as well as **Piazza Margherita. Viale Regina Elena** shoots off P. Margherita and leads to **Piazza Crispi.** On the other side of P. Margherita is **Via Porto Romano,** which is lined with shops and snack bars. The street winds across the train tracks and leads to the more industrial **Viale Aldo Moro,** which goes to northerly destinations like Golfo Aranci and Porto Rodolfo.

Currency Exchange: Banca Intesa, C. Umberto 191A. Has an **ATM.** Open M-F 8:30am-1:30pm and 2:45-4:15pm, Sa 8:30am-noon. Several other banks and ATMs around the *centro*.

Pharmacy: C. Umberto 134 (☎21 310). Open M-Sa 10am-5pm.

Hospital, V. Aldo Moro 22 (☎55 22 00).

Emergency: Carabinieri: ☎21 221. **Ambulance:** ☎55 22 01.

Internet Access: InterSmeraldo, V. Porto Romano 8/B (☎25 366; www.intersmeraldo.com). 9 fast computers in an air-conditioned room, with bean-bag chairs in the back and 3 DSL ports for laptops. Friendly, English-speaking staff. Fax and copy service available. €2.50 per 30min. Open M-Sa 10am-10pm, Su 5-10pm. Cash only.

Post Office: V. Bari 7 (☎20 74 00). Take V. Acquedotto from C. Umberto to the intersection of V. Acquedotto and V. Bari. Open M-Sa 8am-1pm. **Postal Code:** 07026.

ACCOMMODATIONS AND FOOD

Olbia is lacking in budget accommodations; your best bet is to head to your ultimate destination right away. For those who need to spend a night and can afford it, Olbia does have some very comfortable establishments. **Hotel Terranova ❹**, V. Garibaldi 3, offers renovated, wheelchair-accessible rooms with A/C, bath, and TV. Breakfast included. Try the homey seafood restaurant on the 1st fl. (☎22 395; www.hotelterranova.it. Parking €7. Singles €45-90; doubles €74-110; triples €90-150; quads €110-180. AmEx/MC/V.) Decorated with roosters and stenciled sunflowers, **Hotel Gallura ❹**, C. Umberto 145, lets rooms with A/C, TV, telephone, and bright baths. Some claim that the pricey restaurant downstairs is Olbia's best. (☎24 629 or 24 648. Breakfast included. Reservations recommended. Singles €65; doubles €85. AmEx/MC/V.)

Many restaurants along C. Umberto advertise overpriced tourist *menùs* and cater to a mostly foreign crowd. Head down the little side streets for a less expensive, more authentic meal. For stained-glass windows and massive portions of hearty Sardinian specialties, head to **⛰Antica Trattoria ❷**, V. G. Pala 6. Don't miss the spectacular *antipasti* bar (from €4) or the veal in lemon sauce (€6.80). Pizza (from €4.70) are only served at dinner. (☎24 053; www.anticatrattoria.net. *Primi* €7-9. Desserts €2-4. Cover €2. Open M 7:30-11pm, Tu-Sa 12:30-2:30pm and 7:30-11pm. AmEx/MC/V.) **Gelateria Smeralda ❶**, C. Umberto 124, has the best *gelato* in town. Try the local specialty *mirto* (myrtle) or the *pere alla grappa* for a change of pace. (☎26 443. Cones €1-3. Open daily M-Sa 4pm-midnight. Cash only.) **Super Pan Supermarket**, P. Crispi 2, is perfect for stocking up on supplies. Go to the end of V. Regina Elena, take a left, and walk through P. Crispi. (☎26 978. Open M-Sa 8:30am-9pm, Su 8:30am-1:30pm.)

ORISTANO   ☎0783

In the 7th century, the inhabitants of nearby Tharros repelled invasion after invasion until a band of merciless Moorish pirates forced them to abandon their homes. With nowhere else to go, they set up camp around Oristano (oh-rees-TA-no; pop. 35,000), which soon became an independent commercial port protected by Eleanora of Arborea, one of Sardinia's most important saints. The cheery, pastel-colored *centro storico* makes a good base for exploring the nearby Sinis Peninsula's Phoenician and Roman ruins at Tharros and the beaches of Is Aruttas and San Giovanni di Sinis.

TRANSPORTATION

Trains: In P. Ungheria (☎89 20 21), 1km from the *centro*. Ticket counter open 6:20am-8:15pm. **Luggage storage** available. To **Cagliari** (1-2hr., 27 per day 4:49am-9:26pm, €5.15), **Macomer** (1hr., 9 per day 6:38am-9:27pm, €3.30), and **Olbia** (2½hr., 1:20 and 7:46pm, €10) via **Ozieri, Chilivani,** or **Macomer.** To get to **Sassari,** connect via Macomer or Chivilani.

Buses: ARST, V. Cagliari 177 (☎71 185). Ticket office open daily 6am-8pm. To: **Bosa** via **Cuglieri** (2hr., 5 per day 8:05am-7:10pm, €5.50); **Cagliari** (2hr., 7:10am and 2:10pm, €6.50); **San Giovanni di Sinis** (dir.: Is Aruttas; 40min.; July-Oct. 5 per day, 8:25am-6:30pm, last return 7:45pm; round-trip €3); **Scano Montiferro** via **Santa Caterina** (40min., 7 per day 8:05am-7:10pm, round-trip €2.50).

Taxis: At P. Roma (☎70 280) and at the train station (☎74 328). Available 7am-1pm and 3-8:30pm. For 24hr. service, call ☎336 81 35 85.

Car Rental: Avis, V. Liguria 17 (☎31 06 38). 25+. Open M-F 9am-1pm and 4-7pm, Sa 9am-noon. AmEx/MC/V.

Scooter Rental: Marco Moto, V. Cagliari 99/101 (☎31 00 36). €30-50 per day. Insurance and helmet included. Open M-F 8:30am-1pm and 4-8pm, Sa 8:30am-1pm. AmEx/MC/V.

SARDINIA

⚡🔲 ORIENTATION AND PRACTICAL INFORMATION

To get to the *centro* from the **train station,** follow **Via Vittorio Veneto,** the street far-thest to the right, to **Piazza Mariano.** Then take **Via Mazzini** to **Piazza Roma,** the heart of the city. Walk down **Corso Umberto,** bear left at P. Eleanora d'Arborea, and take a right on **Via Ciutadela de Minorca** to reach the tourist office. From the **ARST bus station,** take the exit nearest the ticket office and turn left. You will see brown signs for the Pro Loco tourist office to the right, or you could continue past the *duomo* and up **Via De Castro** to P. Roma.

Tourist Office: Pro Loco, V. Ciutadella de Minorca 8 (☎ 70 621). Maps and info on local fes-tivals. Open M-F 9am-1pm and 4-8pm, Sa 9am-1pm. **EPT,** P. Eleonora 19 (☎ 36 831). Info on Oristano and province. Open M-Th 8:30am-1pm and 4:15-6:45pm, F 8:30am-1pm.

Luggage Storage: In ARST station. €1.50 per day. Open daily 6am-7:30pm.

English Language Bookstore: Libreria Canu, V. de Castro 20 (☎ 78 723). Small collec-tion of contemporary novels. Open M-Sa 9am-1pm and 5-10pm. MC/V.

First Aid: ☎ 74 333.

Pharmacy: C. Umberto 49/51 (☎ 70 338). Open M-F 9am-1pm and 5-10pm.

Hospital: V. Fondazione Rockefeller (☎ 31 71).

Internet Point: V. Verdi 4A and V. Tirso 13 (☎ 71 676). With the tower at your back facing P. Roma, look across the street for the arch in the buildings. Walk through the arch, turn right, and it's on the left. Internet €0.10 per min. Fax available. Open M-Sa 8am-1pm and 4-8:30pm.

Post Office: V. Mariano 4 (☎ 36 80 15). **Currency exchange** and fax available. Open M-F 8am-6:50pm, Sa 8am-1:15pm. **Postal Code:** 09170.

🔲 ACCOMMODATIONS AND CAMPING

Oristano caters primarily to travelers on their way to the beach, and low competition makes for high prices. Because B&Bs have lower prices and breakfast included, they offer a good alternative to hotels. For info on attractive *agriturismi,* ask at the tour-ist office or call the **Posidonia Society,** V. Umberto 64, in Riola, 10km from Oristano. (☎41 16 60; www.sardegnaturismo.net. Open daily 9am-1pm and 4-8pm.)

Eleonora B&B, P. Eleonora 12 (☎ 70 435 or 347 48 17 976; www.eleonora-bed-and-breakfast.com). Conveniently located in the *centro storico,* within 2 blocks of bus sta-tion and every major site. Friendly owners Paola and Andrea maintain this beautifully decorated Renaissance *palazzo,* which retains its original, 12th-century walls. Spacious rooms with private bath, A/C, and TV. Singles €35-40; doubles €65-70. Cash only. ❸

Palazzo Corrias, P. Eleonora 4 (☎ 78 194 or 349 56 81 703; www.palazzocorrias.com). Cen-trally located in P. Eleonora and housed in an old *palazzo.* Enormous rooms with A/C and *piazza* views. Clean shared bath. Breakfast included. Singles €35; doubles €60. Cash only. ❸

ISA, P. Mariano 50 (☎/fax 36 01 01). From ARST station, take exit nearest to the ticket office, turn left, then right on V. Ciutadela de Minorca. Go straight through P. Martini and follow V. La Marmora to the end. Turn right, then immediately left, and follow signs. Hotel with oriental rugs, chandeliers, and a frescoed elevator shaft. All rooms have bath, A/C, TV, phone, and minibar; some with balcony. Breakfast included. Singles €55; doubles €90; triples €105. AmEx/MC/V. ❹

Marina di Torregrande, V. Stella Maris 8 (☎/fax 22 228; www.campeggiotorre-grande.com), 200m from the beach and 7km from Oristano. Take the "azzurra" line of the orange local buses from V. Cagliari in front of ARST station (10min., 1-2 per hr. 7:30am-12:30am, €0.70) to the Stella Maris stop. Purchase tickets at *tabaccherie.* A cool, constant breeze sways the many trees at this well-shaded campground. An accom-modating staff presides over a small playground, bar, and market. Free parking and hot showers. Open Apr.-Sept. €5-6 per person, €3-5 per child, €9-12 per tent. Aging 5-person bungalows with bath €60-90. Electricity €2-3.50. Cash only. ❶

🍴 FOOD

The **Euro-Drink** market, P. Roma 22, sells inexpensive basics and Sardinian products like *mirto* (myrtle) and *sebadas*, a type of Sardinian ravioli. (Open M-Sa 8am-2pm and 5-9pm. MC/V.) A **Sisa** supermarket is at V. Amiscora 26. (Open M-Sa 8am-8pm. MC/V.)

🏆 **Ristorante Craf da Banana**, V. de Castro 34 (☎70 669). Pleasantly lit, low-arched brick ceilings and fine cuisine distinguish this restaurant from its peers. Try specialties like the delicious *ravioli della casa* with a meaty wild boar-and-mushroom sauce (€8). *Primi* €8, *secondi* €8-13. Cover €2. Open M-Sa 1-3pm and 8-11pm. Reserve ahead. AmEx/MC/V. ❸

Trattoria Da Gino, V. Tirso 13 (☎71 428). Locals love the cozy dining room and family feel. Menu features spaghetti, ravioli, fettuccini, *gnocchi*, and *risotti* in a variety of sauces. *Primi* €5.50-9, *secondi* €7.50-12. Fresh fish €8.50-13. Meats, including *cavallo* (horse meat) and lamb €9.50-12. Open M-Sa noon-3pm and 8-11pm. MC/V. ❸

Pizzeria La Grotta, V. Diego Contini 3 (☎30 02 06), off P. Roma. Pictures of the cooks during themed dinners reinforce the lighthearted atmosphere of this restaurant, which pumps out brick-oven pizzas. A popular favorite is the *pizza alla carciofi freschi e bottarga* (with artichoke hearts and fish eggs; €7.50). Pizzas €3-8.50. Cover €1.50. Open daily 7:30pm-12:30am. AmEx/MC/V. ❶

Antica Trattoria del Teatro, V. Parpaglia 11 (☎71 672). This restaurant's concise menu includes high-quality dishes like egg ravioli with artichokes and chives (€10). Fresh fish and meat €13-16. Cover €2. AmEx/D/MC/V. ❸

👁 SIGHTS

The whimsical **Chiesa di San Francesco**, in P. E. d'Arborea at the end of V. de Castro, complete with two small, brightly tiled domes, is the largest *duomo* in Sardinia. First built in 1250, it was heavily restructured in the 19th century, leaving little of the original interior intact. A notable remnant is the gruesome wooden crucifix with Christ's emaciated and tortured body. Constructed by a 16th-century Catalán teacher, the cross was once attributed to Nicodemus, a friend of Jesus; it was said that such a vivid depiction could only have been captured by an eyewitness. The sacristy houses a 16th-century polyptych, *St. Francis Receiving the Stigmata* and Nino Pisano's 14th-century marble statue of San Basilio. (Open M-Sa 7am-noon. Mass Su 9am. Free.) Adjacent to the cathedral on V. Vittorio Emanuele is the **Archiepiscopal Palace,** the seat of the Curia. Pope John Paul II was once a guest here. A distinctive, almost Oriental, tower, with a beautifully decorated dome, stands next to entrance. A short stroll up C. Umberto reveals the 13th-century **Tower of San Mariano II** in P. Roma. On summer evenings, young *oristanesi* gather in this *piazza* and the adjoining C. Umberto to flirt and sip Ichnusa (a Sardinian beer), while the elderly commandeer benches and enjoy the vivacity around them. The collection of Nuraghic, Punic, Phoenician, and Roman artifacts at **Antiquarium Arborense,** in P. Corrias, near P. E. d'Aborea, was unearthed at Tharros, and includes urns, cups, and earthenware of all shapes and sizes, some dating as far back as 5000 BC. A useful photo guide in English is provided to guide you from showcase to showcase. Also on display are tabletop models of the ancient port of Tharros and 11th-century Oristano. (☎79 12 62. Open daily 9am-2pm and 3-8pm. Wheelchair-accessible. €3, under 14 €1.50, students and seniors €1.)

SARDINIA

◢ DAYTRIP FROM ORISTANO

THE SINIS PENINSULA

For those without a car, the Sinis peninsula is best reached by bus from Oristano (5 per day from the ARST station). Ask for ticket to San Giovanni di Sinis for the beach (8:25am-6:30pm, last return 7:45pm; round-trip €3). Get off 1 stop earlier at Cabras for town center and archaeological museum. The Penisola del Sinis Isola di Mal di Ventre Info Center is located right in the piazza where the bus stops. The blue and white plastic signs next to the Info Center leads right out of the piazza onto the beach. A sign with an arrow points you in the direction of the ruins of Tharros, up the hill around 700m. Because Sinis Peninsula itself is a stretch of protected marine zones, all main commercial buildings are found in the town of Cabras.

Venture outside Oristano to see the impressive sights of the Marine Protected Area, the Sinis Peninsula. Decreed a natural preserve in 1997, some areas of the coast are accessible only for research and are off-limits to tourists. The Sinis Peninsula is most famous for its quartz sands, which have been eroded by the winds and broken granite of Mal di Ventre island. Ruins from the Roman and early-Christian period of Tharros can be found 700m up the hill from where the bus drops you off in San Giovanni di Sinis, at the **Tharros Archaelogical Site.** A large Aragonese tower marks the top of the hill. Call a day ahead to reserve a tour of the Tharros ruins in English. (☎37 00 19. Open in summer daily 9am-8pm. €5, includes 1hr. guided tour in Italian.) A ticket to the site also includes admission to the **Archaeological Museum,** V. Tharros, in Cabras, which contains the artifacts of the excavations at Tharros. (☎29 06 36. Open daily in summer 9am-1pm and 4-8pm; in winter 9am-1pm and 3-7pm.)

Located at the tip of the peninsula where the bus unloads, the beach **Spiaggia San Giovanni di Sinis** contains fine sands with bits of dark, volcanic rock. **Spiaggia Funtana Meiga's** sand is shielded by large dunes. The **Park of Seu,** a naturally preserved area of greenery, lies just up the coast. Farther up the coast, **Spiaggia Arutas** is most famous for its pebbly coastline. **Mare Morto,** on the other side of the peninsula from San Giovanni di Sinis, is famous for its wide, sandy, seaweed-littered shoreline. Along the curvy part of the coastline, in the Gulf of Oristano, is the **Laguna di Mistras,** where pink flamingos often strut about; bike from San Giovanni toward Cabras along the San Giovanni-Oristano road. Pink flamingos also inhabit the waters beneath the bridge crossing from the peninsula into Cabras. For **diving,** contact Aceti (☎53 747), Aquateam Diving (☎30 34 55), or 9511 Diving Team (☎335 60 59 412). For **scuba diving,** contact Ippocampos Scuba Team (☎348 80 58 001).

> **!** **CURRENT EVENTS.** Take caution when swimming at the lifeguardless Spaggia San Giovanni di Sinis and other beaches on the west coast. The waves and undertow are stronger here than on the more placid eastern coast.

BOSA ☎0785

Glowing with cheery pastels, Bosa (BO-sa; pop. 8,800) is half medieval village, half Riviera vacation hot spot. Situated on the banks of Sardinia's only navigable river, Bosa's castle overlooks the palm tree-lined streets of the Temo River Valley. Though the *centro storico* is generally a sleepy place, the newer Bosa Marina, 1km from the old city, boasts beautiful beaches, an assortment of seaside bars, and a hostel. If arriving from Oristano, be sure to look out the window at the small hill-towns along the way.

▐ TRANSPORTATION. ARST **buses** run from Bosa to Oristano (2hr., M-Sa 5 per day 5:25am-4:05pm, €5.50). Buy tickets at the *bar* or *tabaccheria* in P. Zanetti. FDS **buses** run to Alghero via Litoranea, the coastal route (1hr., 3 per day, €3), or via Villanove Monteleone, the mountain route (2 hr., 2 per day, €4.50); Nuoro (1¾hr.; 6 per day 6:06am-7:41pm, reduced service Sa-Su; €5.10); and Sassari (2hr.,

3 per day 8:20am-5:20pm, €5.50). Buy tickets at the FDS office in P. Zanetti. (Open daily 6:30pm-midnight.) Buses also run from Bosa to **Piazza Palmiro Togliatti** in Bosa Marina (5min., 22 per day, €1). For a **taxi,** call ☎336 81 18 00. To **rent cars, scooters,** or **bikes,** stop by Euroservice, V. Azuni 23. (☎37 34 79. 25+ for car or scooter. Bikes €10 per day; scooters €25-50; cars from €65. Open M-F 9am-1pm and 5-8pm.)

■ ▌ **ORIENTATION AND PRACTICAL INFORMATION. Bosa,** the city proper, lies across the **Temo River** from **Bosa Marina.** Buses stop in Bosa's **Piazza Angelico Zanetti,** from which **Via Azuni** leads to **Piazza Gioberti** at the base of the *centro storico.* The **Pro Loco tourist office,** V. Azuni 5, at the intersection with V. Francesco Romagna, provides maps and info on both the town and surroundings area. Ask for the handout, which contains a map, instead of purchasing their map for €2. (☎37 61 07; www.infobosa.it. Open M-Sa 10am-1pm.) The **tourist office** for Bosa Marina, Vle. Colombo, is on the *lungomare* about 5min. after the right turn off the main bridge. (☎37 71 08; www.agenziailponte.it or www.bosa.it. Open M-F 8:30am-12:30pm and 3:30-7:30pm.) For **currency exchange** and an **ATM,** head to **Unicredit Banca,** at the corner of V. Lamarmora and V. Giovanni XXIII. (☎37 31 18. Open M-F 8:20am-1:20pm and 2:35-4:05pm, Sa 8:20am-12:45pm.) In case of **emergency,** call the **carabinieri** (☎37 31 16), **Red Cross** (☎37 38 18), or **guardia medica** (☎22 53 18). **Internet Web Copy,** V. Gioberti 12, has six computers with fast connections (€0.07 per min.) and **fax** services. (☎37 20 49; web.copy@tiscali.it. Open M-Sa 9am-1pm and 5-9pm.) The **post office,** V. Pischedda 1, also has **currency exchange.** (☎0785 37 31 39. Open M-F 8:15am-6:50pm, Sa 8:15am-1:15pm.) **Postal Code:** 08013.

▐ ▍ **ACCOMMODATIONS AND FOOD.** Bosa Marina is home to one of Sardinia's two youth hostels, called simply **Youth Hostel (HI) ❶,** V. Sardegna 1. After crossing the bridge from the *centro,* take a right on the *lungomare.* V. Sardegna is about 5min. down on the left. Close to the beach, the hostel has clean rooms, with spacious communal bathrooms as well as a bar open until midnight. (☎/fax 37 50 09, 346 23 63 844, or 339 77 51 121. Breakfast included. A/C €3 per day. Reception 9am-1pm and 4pm-midnight. Curfew midnight. 5-bed dorms €16; doubles €40. Cash only.) **Albergo Perry Clan ❷,** V. Alghero 3, in Bosa, offers 12 simple rooms with TV, bath, and A/C. From the bus stop, follow V. Daniele Manin, and take 1st right on V. Giovanni XXIII; the hotel is on the left after P. Dante Alighieri. (☎37 30 74. July-Aug. Rooms €60 per person, including mandatory half pension. Sept.-June singles €20-25; doubles €45-50. Cash only.) **Hotel Al Gabbiano ❹,** on Vle. Mediterraneo, in Bosa Marina, directly across from the beach, offers large, comfortable rooms, all with bath, TV, A/C, phone, and minifridge; most have a balcony. (☎37 41 23; gabbiano-hotel@tiscali.it. Beach chair €5, beach umbrella €5. Breakfast included; restaurant downstairs. Singles €50-70; doubles €72-100. Extra bed €7. AmEx/D/MC/V.)

In a medieval building in the *centro storico,* **Ristorante Borgo Sant'Ignazio ❷,** V. S. Ignazio 33, serves delicacies like *nido dello chef* (egg pasta with tomato sauce and local lobster; €12 per 100g) and *azadda iscritta* (€10), a relative of shark. (☎37 41 29. *Primi* €8-15, *secondi* €7-15. Cover €2. Open in summer Tu-Su 1-3pm and 7:30-11pm. AmEx/MC/V.) Across the bridge from P. Duomo, on the other side of the river, **Sa Pischedda ❷,** V. Roma 8, has a garden patio and candlelit tables which are graced by delicious dishes like *razza alla bosana* (garlicky, sautéed flat fish; €7), *alisanzas al ragu di sorfano e basilico* (pasta with local fish, tomato, and basil; €8), and brick-oven pizza. (☎37 30 65. Pizza €4-11, dinner only. *Primi* €6.90-10.90, *secondi* €4.50-5 per 100g of fish. Open daily 1-2:30pm and 8-10:30pm. MC/V.) If near the beach and searching for a swashbuckling time, walk the plank down to the **S'Hardrock Cafe ❸,** which features S'Hardinian plates on the deck of a pirate ship. (Pizza €4-10. *Primi* €9-12, *secondi* €10-17. Open Tu-Su 12:30-3pm and 7pm-1am.) Head to **Sisa** supermarket, P. Gioberti 13, for groceries. (☎37 34 23. Open M-Sa 8am-1pm and 5:30-8:30pm, Su 9am-12:30pm.)

SARDINIA

⧈🏖 **SIGHTS AND BEACHES.** Bosa's principal museum, **Casa Deriu,** C. Vittorio Emanuele II 59, exhibits furnishings, tapestries, and family portraits from the wealthy Deriu family's 19th-century home. Examples of filet weaving, unique to Bosa, and traditional Sardinian dress and gold jewelry can be seen on the 1st floor. The 3rd floor holds a collection of ceramics, prints, and paintings by Melkiorre Melis, a leader in the applied and plastic arts. Landscapes of Bosa and surrealist works by Antonio Atza are housed in a permanent collection across the street. (Open Tu-Su 10:30-1pm and 8:30-11pm. €4.50, children €2.) The town's panoramic **Castello Malaspina** is a short hike uphill through the *centro storico;* take the flowery staircase or V. del Castello to see the castle that dates from 1112 and holds the early 14th-century **Chiesa Nostra Signora Regnos Altos.** On the 2nd weekend of September, residents celebrate the Virgin Mary by adorning their houses with flowers and small altars, dancing, and parading through the streets. The festival culminates with a mass in the courtyard of the castle. (☎333 54 45 675. Castle and church open daily 9:30am-1:30pm and 5:30-8:30pm. €2, under 12 €1.)

Local families fill a long stretch of sandy beach in Bosa Marina, where bars line the *lungomare* and surround the **Aragonese Tower.** The **Bosa Diving Center,** V. Colombo 2 (☎37 56 49; www.bosadiving.it), offers snorkeling, day and night scuba diving, and boat tours to nearby grottoes and beaches. Call for more info.

NUORO ☎0784

The architecture of this provincial capital is a mix of the Spanish-influenced buildings and block-style apartment complexes. Nuoro (noo-OH-ro; pop. 36,000) is known for its cultural value, boasting Sardinia's contemporary art museum, the Museo Arte Nuoro (MAN), and the only government-commissioned ethnographic museum. Once you've had your fill of museums, a stomach-churning bus ride or an arduous hike up Monte Ortobene will reveal a masterful statue of Christ the Redeemer and similarly spectacular views of the sea.

TIP **S.O.S.** At 8:30pm, buses stop running, and taxis are few and far between. If you are planning to be out past this time and are staying outside the *centro,* arrange for transportation home before you leave to avoid getting stranded. If you need a taxi in the early hours of the morning (before 9am), arrange for pick-up beforehand.

⌁ TRANSPORTATION

Trains: (☎30 115), on V. Lamarmora, in P. Stazione. Ticket office open M-Sa 7:30am-5:15pm. To **Cagliari** (3½hr., 5 per day 6:24am-6:51pm, €13.50) via **Macomer.**

Buses:

ARST (☎29 41 73). Buses stop at the ARST station on V. Toscana between Vle. Sardegna and V. Santa Barbara. Tickets available next door at Il Gusto Macelleria, Vle. Sardegna 21 (☎32 408). To: **Cagliari** (2½hr., 2:05pm, €14.50); **Olbia** (stops in port, airport, and city, although not all buses make all 3 stops; 1½hr., 7 per day 5:30am-5:40pm, €7.50); **Cala Ganone** (1hr., 7 per day 6:53am-7pm €3) via **Dorgali** (45min., 8 per day 6:53am-7pm, €2.50; reduced service Sa-Su); **Orgosolo** (30min.; 9 per day 5:50am-6:30pm, last return 7:05pm, reduced service Sa-Su; round-trip €2.50); **Sassari** (4:20 and 7:10pm; €7.50).

F. Deplano buses run from Vle. Sardegna, 1 block to the right of the ARST station, to the **Olbia airport** (☎29 50 30; 1½hr., 6 per day 4:15am-5:15pm, €10) and the **Alghero airport** (☎30 325; 2hr.; 11:25am, 3:20, 5pm; €18). Buses are scheduled around plane arrivals and departures.

Public Transportation: Buy tickets (€1.10) for the local buses at newsstands, *tabaccherie,* or in the train station. **Bus #2s** runs from P. Vittorio Emanuele through the *centro* to the train station and the hospital. **Bus #8** runs to the top of M. Ortobene. **Buses #3** and **#9** run between P. V. Emanuele and the ARST station.

Taxis: (☎335 39 91 74 or 368 90 94 71). At night it can be a very long wait, so call ahead. Reserve the night before for taxis before 9am.

Car Rental: Autonoleggio Maggiore, Vle. Monastir 116 (☎27 36 92; fax 20 80 536). 23+. Open M-F 8am-1pm and 4-7pm, Sa 8am-1pm and 4-6pm. AmEx/MC/V.

⚡🛈 ORIENTATION AND PRACTICAL INFORMATION

From the ARST **bus station,** turn right on Viale Sardegna. When you reach **Piazza Sardegna,** take a right on Via Lamarmora and follow it to **Piazza delle Grazie** and the *centro*. To get to the **tourist office** from P. delle Grazie, turn left and follow Via IV Novembre uphill through **Piazza Dante** to **Piazza Italia.** Brown signs will direct you to the rest of the way. Via Roma leads from P. Italia to **Piazza San Giovanni** and the town's social hub, **Piazza Vittorio Emanuele. Corso Garibaldi** is a major street with shops and cafes that runs out of P. V. Emanuele.

The enthusiastic, English-speaking staff at the **EPT tourist office,** P. Italia 19, has brochures, maps, and hiking info. (☎23 88 78. Open in summer daily 9am-7pm.) The 24hr. **guardia medica** is on V. Deffenu (☎24 08 48). There is a **pharmacy** at C. Garibaldi 65 (☎30 143). **Ospedale San Francesco,** V. Mannironi (☎24 02 49), is on the highway to Bitti. **Internet** access is available at **Smile Caffè,** V. Piemonte 3, off V. Veneto. (€3 per hr. Open in summer M-Sa 7am-10pm.) The **post office** is at P. Crispi 8, off V. Dante. (☎24 52 10. Open M-F 8am-6:50pm, Sa 8am-1:15pm.) Another **branch,** V. Santa Barbara 24, is near the ARST station. (☎23 28 07. Open M-F 8am-6:50pm, Sa 8am-1:15pm.) **Postal Code:** 08100.

🏠🍴 ACCOMMODATIONS AND FOOD

Inexpensive hotels are rare in Nuoro, and campgrounds are in distant towns. If you plan to stay in the area, consider B&Bs close to Nuoro or Monte Ortobene, or head to the smaller hamlets in the hills. ⬛**Casa Solotti ❸,** in Località Monte Ortobene, has five large rooms that share two bathrooms and a terrace with a mountain view that extends to the sea on clear days. Take bus #8 (every 50min. 8:15am-8pm) from P. V. Emanuele, which stops in front of the Casa at the "Solotti" stop. Welcoming multilingual owner, ⬛ **Mario,** serves homemade jam, yogurt, and pastries for breakfast. Mario also sometimes takes travelers on an excursion to his family's farm, where you can see an inhabited natural cave, pet domestic animals, and purchase organic cheese. (☎328 60 28 975; www.casasolotti.it. Call for free pickup from town. Singles €30-35; doubles €52-60, with bath €60-65. Cash only.)

For a local favorite, visit ⬛**Ristorante Tascusi ❷,** V. Apromonte 15, where high quality cuisine comes at surprisingly low prices. The ⬛ **menù** includes a *primo*, *secondo*, side dish, and 0.25L of wine or 0.5L of water for only €10. (☎37 287. Open M-Sa noon-3pm and 8-10:30pm. MC/V.) At **Canne Al Vento ❷,** V. Biasi 123, a half hour outside of town, high class and low prices dominate. Guests dine on classic *culurgiones* (ravioli stuffed with potatoes, cheese, and mint; €7) and sip compelling and rich espresso. (☎20 17 62. *Primi* €5-8.50, *secondi* €6.70-12.50. Open M-Sa 12:30-3pm and 8-10:30pm. AmEx/MC/V.) Don't miss the humble, local favorite, **Da Giovanni ❸,** V. IV Novembre 9, 2nd fl., where the *maccarones de busa* and *spaghetti alle arselle* (both €8) are delightful. (☎30 562. *Primi* €8, *secondi* €10-12. Open M-Sa 12:30-3pm and 8-10:30pm. AmEx/MC/V.) A quality bakery, **Antico Panificio Sardo,** V. Ferraciu 73 (☎36 275), off P. delle Grazie, sells hot rolls, *pane carasau* (€5 per kg), and scrumptious *panzerotti* (from €2) filled with cheese, tomato, and a choice of eggplant, mushroom, or ham. (Open M-F 8am-1:30pm and 4:30-8pm, Sa 8am-1:30pm.) **Pellicano** supermarket in P. Mameli has groceries. (☎23 26 66. Open M-Sa 8:30am-2pm and 5-8pm, Su 5-8pm. AmEx/MC/V.)

SARDINIA

LOCAL LEGEND

BEHIND THE MASK OF THE MAMUTHONES

In any souvenir shop on Sardinia's east coast, one can find imitations of the unusual, wooden masks of the Mamuthones. These often outrageously priced black masks frown in rigid, tragic expressions. But most travelers wonder, "Just who are these Mamuthones covered in black sheep skins? And why do they wear such scornful masks?"

Today, the march of the Mamuthones is celebrated in Mamoiada as a mixture of Catholic and pagan rituals. The exact meaning and origins of the procession remain a mystery to historians, but it is generally thought to be a dance associated with the cult of the god Dionysus. In the past, the Mamuthones may have represented mythical ox-men or captured enemies, but today they take the main stage during Carnavale. In the festival, 12 Mamuthones process through the town. Two parallel lines of actors march in a slow, solemn manner, craning their backs under the weight of heavy cowbells. It is quite a deviation from the otherwise joyous atmosphere of the festival, yet it remains the cornerstone of the celebration.

Carnavale is celebrated every year in February. Inquire at the Nuoro tourist office for further information, but be sure to check out this peculiar ritual.

👁 SIGHTS

▨ MUSEO DELLA VITA E DELLE TRADIZIONI POPULARI. Sardinia's largest ethnographic museum contains an extensive collection of traditional costumes, hand-woven rugs, musical instruments, and jewelry from around the island. The pieces are arranged in a series of stucco houses circling a flowered courtyard—a reconstruction of a typical Sardinian village. One house contains carnival masks shaped like devils, donkeys, pigs, cows, and goats; don't miss the creepy *Mamuthone* (traditional Sardinian costume masks) or your very own cutout *Mamuthone* mask in the museum's handout. *(V. Antonio Mereu 56. ☎ 25 70 35. Open daily July-Sept. 9am-8pm; Oct.-June 9am-1pm and 3-7pm. €3, under 18 and over 60 €1.)*

▨ MONTE ORTOBENE. The bronze ▨**Christ the Redeemer,** a 1905 statue of the town's symbol, beckons hikers to the peak of this hill, where a shady park and vivacious views await. After the hike to the statue, walk 20m down the road from the bus stop on Monte Ortobene to see Monte Corrasi, which dwarfs the neighboring town of Oliena. *(Take the sensational bus #8 from P. V. Emanuele 7km to the summit. 14 per day 8:15am-8pm, last return 8:15pm; €1.10. Or hike the 4.5km trail La Solitudine; start behind Chiesa della Solitudine at the beginning of V. Ortobene, and follow the red-and-white marked "Trail 101." Look for yellow sign saying "Redentore" to reach the statue.)*

MUSEO ARTE NUORO. Affectionately termed the "MAN," this striking white building contains a collection of 20th-century Sardinian art that incorporates both traditional and contemporary themes—a welcome change from the Nuraghic bronzes that crowd Sardinia's other museums. The middle two floors maintain a permanent collection of works by 20th-century Sardinian painters, while the 1st and 4th floors display rotating exhibits by contemporary artists. *(V. Satta 27. ☎ 25 21 10; www.museoman.it. Open Tu-Su 10am-1pm and 4:30-8:30pm. €3, students 18-25 €2, under 18 or over 60 free.)*

HOME OF GRAZIA DELEDDA. Locals are fiercely proud of Grazia Deledda, the first female Italian novelist to win a Nobel Prize (for literature; 1926). Nuoro is home to both the house where she was born and the church, Chiesa della Solitudine, where she is buried. Today, the house has transformed into Museo Casa Deledda, which will probably interest only those familiar with her work. *(V. Deledda. Church at base of hill of Monte Ortobene on Vle. La Solitudine. ☎ 24 29 00. Displays only in Italian. Open daily July-Sept. 8am-9pm; Oct.-June 9am-1pm and 3-7pm. Free.)*

▶ DAYTRIP FROM NUORO: ORGOSOLO

The bus ride alone merits a trip to picturesque **Orgosolo** (or-GO-zo-lo; pop. 5000) but the town itself is known for its impressive ▨**murals,** which range in style from Picasso replicas to controversial political themes. Both Sardinian and international influences appear in the murals, which cover the buildings along C. Repubblica. The *milanese* anarchist group, Gruppo Dioniso, created the first mural in 1969, and Francesco del Casino, a teacher from Siena, reinvented the mural-painting as an ongoing project in 1975. His works focus on social and political issues, including imperialism, fascism, and commercialism. Artists make new murals focused on modern themes like Sardinian independence; one chilling mural commemorates the terrorist attacks on the World Trade Center on September 11th, 2001. To eat a traditional meal in the mountains, contact **Cultura e Ambiente,** a local organization that operates excursions into the hills and organizes lunches in a field behind its restaurant, **Supramonte ❸,** in Località Sarthu Thithu, 3km uphill from town. Busloads of tourists come to devour smoked meats, cheese, fresh produce, and pastries off wooden platters. (☎40 10 15 or 349 17 75 877; www.supramonte.it. Tastings conducted for groups, but individuals may call ahead to join. Transportation provided on request. Lunch €18.) Though there is no tourist office, souvenir shop owners are quite helpful when navigating through town. Strolling leisurely along C. Repubblica and investigating side-streets will allow you to experience a jamboree of works. For those seeking more details about the paintings, shops sell an English-language picture guide (€12) to the murals. *(To arrive, take an ARST bus from the ARST station in Nuoro.)*

> **TIP**
> **THE RIGHT SIDE.** When taking the ARST bus from Nuoro to Orgosolo, make sure to sit on the right side of the bus. As the bus approaches Orgosolo, a few murals are visible, included one by Francesco Del Casino on 2 large boulders. The painting depicts the half-orange, half-white face of a native with wild eyes, reminding shepherds to always keep a watchful eye over their flocks.

DORGALI ☎0784

Nestled in mountains and ringed by pastures, pint-sized Dorgali (dor-GA-lee; pop. 8300) offers visitors relaxation and quiet among friendly locals. Since the tourist boom hit Sardinia in the 60s, travelers have trekked to Dorgali to admire craftsmen applying their trades or to indulge in Dorgali's renowned red wine. Though roads connect it to nearby Cala Gonone and archaeological sights, Dorgali's farmers and artisans maintain the town's isolated charm.

▣ **TRANSPORTATION AND PRACTICAL INFORMATION.** ARST **buses** stop at V. Lamarmora 59, at the intersection with C. Umberto. Buy tickets at the *tabaccheria* at the intersection of V. Lamarmora and V. Montessori. The schedule is posted at the tourist office and *tabaccherie*. Buses run to Cala Gonone (25min., 10 per day 6:20am-7:45pm, €1), Nuoro (45min., 9 per day 6:05am-7:25pm, €2.50), and Olbia port (3hr., 2 per day 6:35am and 5:25pm, €7.50). **Via Lamarmora,** which runs uphill from the bus stop, and **Corso Umberto** (perpendicular to V. Lamarmora) are the major streets. **Via Roma** descends past **Viale Kennedy,** which runs along the bottom of town. The **Pro Loco tourist office,** V. Lamarmora 108, provides maps and detailed info about Cala Gonone, Dorgali, and surrounding attractions. (☎96 243. Open M-Sa May-Sept. 9am-1pm and 4-8pm; Oct.-Apr. 9am-12:30pm and 3:30-7:30pm.) **Currency exchange** and **ATMs** are at **Banca Intesa,** at the intersection of V. Lamarmora and V. Fleming, and at the post office. (Open M-F 8:30am-1:30pm and 2:45-4:15pm, Sa 8:30am-noon.) In case of **emergency,** call the **carabinieri** (☎96 114) or the **medical clinic.** (☎93 150. Open M-F 10pm-8am, Sa-Su 24hr.) **Farmacia Mondula,** V. Lamarmora 55, at the intersection with V. Sardegna, posts the after-hours rotation. The closest hospital, **Ospedale Civile San Francesco** (☎24 02 49 37), is in Nuoro, on the highway toward Bitti. Go to **InformaticaMente,** V. Lamarmora 82, for **internet** access. (☎96 520. €6 per hr. Open M-Sa 9:30am-1pm and 4-8pm.) The **post office** is at the corner of V. Lamarmora and V. Ciusa, across the street from the bus stop. (☎94 712. Open M-F 8am-noon.) **Postal Code:** 08022.

⌐₪ ACCOMMODATIONS AND FOOD. Accommodations in Dorgali are generally less expensive than those in neighboring beach resorts. Although none of Dorgali's B&Bs are especially beautiful or outstanding, the clean, simple rooms in these family homes provide a cheap base for exploring Cala Gonone and the surrounding areas. **B&B di Bardilio Fancello ❷,** V. Azuni 5, keeps four rooms, all with bath, in the town center. A TV room, kitchen, delicious breakfast, and terrace shaded by grape vines make this B&B even more comfortable. (☎/fax 96 335; simfanc@inwind.it. Breakfast included. €25 per person. Cash only.) Surrounded by gardens and fruit trees, the friendly, family-owned **Il Querceto ❹,** V. Lamarmora 4, 10min. downhill from the *centro*, is reminiscent of a countryside retreat. The front entrance and restaurant feature rotating exhibitions by local artists. Forty enormous rooms all have tiled bath, satellite TV, phone, and mountain view; work on a pool will be completed by the summer of 2008. (☎96 509; www.ilquerceto.com. Breakfast included; restaurant downstairs. Singles €53-69; doubles €86-119; triples €111-147; quads €132-164. AmEx/MC/V.) Follow the signs off V. Lamarmora, 10min. uphill from *centro*, to **Hotel S'Adde ❸,** V. Concordia 38, another family-owned hotel with spacious rooms that have bath, A/C, TV, and phone. (☎/fax 94 412; www.hotelsadde.it. Breakfast included; restaurant downstairs. Wheelchair-accessible. Singles €40; doubles €70; triples €100; quads €110. AmEx/MC/V.)

For a small town, Dorgali has no shortage of snack bars, but the brick-oven pizzas at **█Il Giardino ❶,** V. Enrico Fermi 59, on the road to Cala Gonone, are a superb alternative to the all-too-prevalent pre-packaged *panini.* Try the delicious *giardino,* laden with grilled veggies (€8), a bountiful salad (€7.50), or an international selection of beers, including a refreshing white beer (from €2). The house tiramisu (€3.50) is to die for. (☎94 257. Pizza €4.50-8.50. *Primi* €6-10, *secondi* €8-16. Wheelchair-accessible. Open M and W-Su 8am-midnight. AmEx/MC/V.) Head to **Ristorante Colibri ❸,** V. Gramsci 14, for *penne alla dorgalese* (pasta with pork sauce; €7), the local specialty. From V. Lamarmora, take V. Cerere, which becomes V. Gramsci, to the intersection with V. Flores. (☎96 054. *Primi* €7, *secondi* €10.50-11.50. Cover €2. Open in summer daily 12:30-2:30pm and 7:30-10pm. MC/V.) **Deiana Dolci Sardi ❶,** V. Africa 3, serves handmade Sardinian sweets. Take V. Lamarmora to V. Cavalotti to P. Fancello. (☎95 096. Pastries €8-20 per kg, most around €10. Bag of 4 pastries approx. €1.50. Open M-Sa 8am-1pm and 4-8pm. Cash only.) Dorgali is also known for its heavy and flavorful red wine. Visit **Cantina Sociale,** V. Piemonte 11, to sample a wide selection of wines and *grappa.* (☎96 143. Bottles from €4.) **Supermarket Sia** is on V. Lamarmora 18. (Open M-Sa 8am-1pm and 4-9pm, Su 8am-1pm. AmEx/MC/V.)

◐◣ SIGHTS AND OUTDOOR ACTIVITIES. With the Supramonte mountains on one side and the Orosei Gulf on the other, Dorgali is an excellent center for embarking on **treks** through the Gorropu Canyon, hikes to the ancient Nuraghic villages of Tiscali and Serra Orrios, or swims along Cala Gonone's **beaches.** It is necessary to have a car to reach these natural sites. Consider renting one at **Prima Sardegna,** V. Lungomare Palmasera 32, in Cala Gonone, which offers rates from 4hr. to 7 days. (☎93 367 or 333 57 62 185; www.primasardegna.com. MC/V.) ▓**Atlan-**

tika, V. Lamarmora 195 (☎328 97 29 719; www.atlantika.it), arranges scuba diving, snorkeling, and guided excursions of the Tiscali's Nuraghic village and the Gorropu Canyon. Archaeological tours of the Supramonte of Dorgali, the murals of Orgosolo, and the coast of the Golfo di Orosei are also offered. (Arranges transportation and guide €30-60, depending on length and difficulty of excursions. Usually departs between 8:30 and 9am; returns between 4 and 5pm.) **Cooperative Ghivine,** V. La Marmora 69, arranges guided excursions, hikes, free-climbs and canyon-climbs of Tiscali, Gorropu, and the Supramonte mountains. (☎349 44 25 552 or 338 83 41 618; www.ghivine.com. Tours depart daily 9am-4pm; some available in English. Most tours €35, including transportation. Lunch usually €7.)

With 400m tall walls and canyons, the ◨**Goropu Canyon Gorge** is one of Europe's tallest and widest. Large, white limestone boulders, pink oleander trees, and an underground river that occasionally surfaces form breathtaking views and a spectacular hiking experience. The trip requires a car to reach the S'Abba Arva bridge where parking is available. From there, hike up the gorge (2hr.). Because there are no labeled paths or signs, a guided tour is the best way to explore S'Abba Arva.

A car is also required to reach the start of the ◨**Tiscali,** one of Italy's tallest mountains. From the bottom of the path, it is a 2hr. hike to the top. A Nuraghic village is hidden in a cave on the top of the mountain, where prehistoric people settled and hid from enemy invasions. The vault has since caved in and the top of the cave is open. (Hidden village open daily May-Sept. 9am-7pm; Oct.-Apr. 9am-5pm. €5, children and over 65 €2.) **Serra Orrios Village,** the largest Nuraghic settlement in Sardinia, is 10km away from Dorgali and only accessible by car. Once the island's most important religious center, Serra Orrios contains two small megaron temples and 70 huts. (Guided visits on the hr. 9am-noon and 4-6pm. Call Cooperativa Ghivine for info, reservations, and guided excursions that include transportation and lunch. €5, children and over 65 €3.) The **Ispingoli Cave** holds the longest stalagmite-stalactite column (38m high) in Europe and the second longest in the world. The cave is accessible by car along State Road #125 in the direction of Dorgali/ Orosei. Two hundred and eighty steps installed in the 70s descend to the base of the column. Used by prehistoric humans as shelter, the caves now showcase colorful stalagmites and stalactites. (For info and reservations, call Consorzio Atlantika at ☎328 97 29 719. Guided visits every hour 9am-noon and 3-5pm; additional tours June-Aug. 1, 6, and 7pm. €7, children and over 65 €3.50.)

▢ **SHOPPING.** Dorgali's craft stores are at the heart of its appeal. Tourists wander the tiny streets, observing artists weave, mold, and bake their wares. Stores along V. La Marmora and its side streets display the handmade *filigree* jewelry, *tappeti* (wool and cotton weavings), carvings, and pastries. Serafina and her mother weave beautiful *tappeti* at **Il Tapetto di Serafina Senette,** P. Asproni 22. (☎95 202. Pieces from €50. Open daily 8:30am-1pm and 4-8pm. MC/ V.) At **Ceramica di Tornino Loi,** V. Lamarmora 120, Giovanna sells both traditional plates featuring domesticated animals and other colorful works featuring cartoon characters and goblins. (☎340 12 68 238. Open M-Sa 9:30am-12:30pm and 6-10pm). For belts (from €13), pocketbooks, keychains, fanny packs, and other fine leatherworks, head to the pleasantly pungent **Pelleterie di Giovanni Ladu,** on V. Cavallotti, off V. Lamarmora (☎95 290. Open daily 8:30am-1pm and 3-11pm).

CALA GONONE ☎0784

Nestled between the sea and three mountains, Cala Gonone (CA-la go-NO-ne; pop. 1279) was once only accessible by boat. A tunnel now connects this town to Dorgali, though the contrast between the two is remarkable. As you emerge from the tunnel, the ocean appears as a vast expanse of hazy blue-gray. As word gets out of Cala Gonone's profound beauty, it is quickly becoming one of Sardinia's most popular tourist destinations. Its high mountains, archaeological wonders, postcard-perfect harbor, and secluded beaches—including the famed Cala Luna, where both versions of the film *Swept Away*, the 1975 original and 2001 Madonna remake, were filmed—make it an important stop on any trip to Sardinia.

TRANSPORTATION AND PRACTICAL INFORMATION. ARST **buses** run to Dorgali (20-25min., 10 per day 6:40am-8:10pm, €1), a bus hub. Buy tickets at Bar La Pinetta on Vle. C. Colombo. Deplano buses (☎29 50 30) leave Cala Gonone for the Olbia airport via Dorgali (4 per day 6:30am-1:15pm; €15, buy tickets onboard). Buses stop in front of the post office on **Via Cala Luna** and at the tourist office on **Viale del Bue Marino. Viale Cristoforo Colombo** leads downhill to the harbor; **Lungomare Palmesare** runs along the seafront. The **tourist office** is on Vle. del Bue Marino. (☎93 696. Open daily Apr.-Sept. 9am-1pm and 3:30-7:30pm; Oct.-Mar. 9am-1pm and 3:30-6:30pm.) An **ATM** is inside the yellow building in the center of the port. In case of **emergency,** call the **carabinieri** (☎96 114) or the **medical clinic** (☎92 00 32). **New Age Internet Point** is located in P. Verrazzano, off V. Magellano. (€5 per hr., €10 per 4hr. Open M-Sa 9am-12:30pm and 4:30-10pm.) The **post office,** at the corner of Vle. C. Colombo and V. Cala Luna, has **currency exchange.** (Open M-Sa 8:15am-1:15pm.) **Postal Code:** 08020.

ACCOMMODATIONS AND FOOD. **SOS Ozzastros B&B ②**, V. Vasco de Gama 7, has spacious, clean, sunny rooms, each with large double bed, private bath, A/C, and balcony. Common room has large TV and cozy wicker furniture. (☎93 145 or 339 13 78 510; www.miniresort2p.it. Breakfast included. Open Mar.-Nov. €20 per person; 4-person apartments with kitchen available for longer stays. AmEx/MC/V.) Just steps from the beach, **Hotel Bue Marino ④**, V. Vespucci 8, offers many rooms with balconies and views of the port and the beach. A/C, satellite TV, phone, minifridge, and deposit box in rooms; some even have massage tub. (☎92 00 78 or 347 77 13 099; www.hotelbuemarino.it. Breakfast included. Singles €55-95; doubles €75-150; junior suites €120-190. AmEx/MC/V.) **Camping Villaggio Calagonone ①**, V. Callodi 1, just off Vle. C. Colombo, is set back from the harbor in a mountain-ringed pine grove. The welcoming campground, which features a well stocked market, bar, swimming pool, and tennis court, is next to the info office along V. Bue Marino, near the Cala Gonone-Dorgali bus stop. (☎93 165; www.campingcalagonone.it. Reception 8am-8pm. Tent, parking, and hot showers free. €13-18.50 per person, €6.50-9 per child. 2-person campers €34-62, with toilet €38-67; 4-person €56-92/59-102. 4-person bungalows €64-140. Chalets with 2-4 beds €47-200. MC/V.) Most places along V. C. Colombo and the *lungomare* serve decent fare. Next to the post office, **Ristorante Self-Service L'Anphora ②**, V. Cala Luna, is a cafeteria-style restaurant with over 20 *primi*, including Sardinian *gulluriones*. (☎93 067. *Panini* €3. *Primi* €4-6.50, *secondi* €3-12. Takeout available. Open in summer daily 8:30am-midnight. AmEx/MC/V.) **Il Pescatore ③**, V. Acqua Dolce 7, serves flavorful favorites like *spaghetti alla bottarga* (€9) and *antipasto*. (☎83 174. *Primi* €7-14, *secondi* €10-18. Open daily 7-11pm. MC/V.) At the musically themed, **Pub Road House Blues ②**, V. Palmasera, next to the Prima Sardegna info office, enjoy rocking pizzas (€4.50-8.50), salads (€5.50-6), or beer. (☎93 187. *Secondi* €9.50-15. Open daily 8am-2am. AmEx/MC/V.) There is a **Sisa** supermarket on the corner of V. Cala Luna and V. C. Colombo (open M-Sa 7:30am-1:30pm and 4:30-8:30pm, Su 8am-1pm), and a **Sigma** supermarket on Vle. C. Colombo 18 (open M-Sa 7:30am-1pm and 4:30-8pm, Su 7:30am-1pm).

BEACHES AND OUTDOOR ACTIVITIES. Cala Gonone is ideally positioned to allow access to stunning beaches and adventure-sport venues. V. Bue Marino leads 3km along the waterfront, passing long stretches of beach before arriving at the resplendent **Cala Fuili** (cove). Treasured by Italians for its crystal-clear waters and tropical backdrop, and now infamous as the site of Madonna's *Swept Away* remake, ■**Cala Luna** is accessible by boat or foot. Sheltered by lime-stone cliffs and fuschia oleanders, the isolated cove has maintained its pristine beauty despite the boatloads of tourists that visit daily. To reach Cala Luna, hike a strenuous 2hr. on the 4km trail that departs from Cala Fuili or take the Consorzio Trasporti Marittimi ferry to Cala Luna. (☎93 305; port ticket booth 92 00 51. 8 per day 9am-5pm, last return 6:30pm; round-trip €15.)

Consorzio also runs ferries to the elusive **Bue Marino**, accessible only by sea. (Ferry fees include guided tour. Bue Marino: round-trip €16.50, ages 6-12 €10. Bue Marino and Cala Luna: €24, ages 6-12 €16.) Tour guides lead visitors through cave chambers that conceal natural curiosities, including the dripping stalactites of the **"Candle Room,"** and the **"Mirrors Room,"** in which a large pool of water reflects off the cave walls in a rainbow of colors, owing to variances in mineral composition. Fresh and salt water meet in the last room, where *bue marino* (sea cows) used to reproduce until moving away in the 80s. (30min. tours offered in English and Italian. July-Sept. 7 per day; May-June 2 per day. Photographs prohibited. €8.) **Atlantika**, V. Amerigo Vespucci or V. Lamarmora 195 in Dorgali (☎93 307 or 328 97 29 719; www.atlantika.it), organizes excursions and tours of the Bue Marino caves and beaches. Atlantika also arranges **scuba diving** and **snorkeling** with certified guides for €25-52.

Prima Sardegna, V. Lungomare Palmasera 32, rents cars (€78-89 per day), scooters (€40 per day), mountain bikes (€5-7 per hr., €16-24 per day, €73-90 per wk.), and kayaks (single €11 per hr., €24 per day €109 per wk.; double €18/42/150). Guides also lead excursions by boat, bike, or foot to natural and archaeological sites. (☎93 367 or 333 57 62 185; www.primasardegna.com. €30-160 per person. Open daily 9am-1pm and 4-8pm. AmEx/MC/V.) Alternatively, to enjoy the grottoes and secluded inlets of white, sandy beaches farther down the coast at your own leisure, rent a **dinghy** for the day from **Centro Informazioni Noleggio di Graziano Mereu**. (Cala Gonone Port, Box # 9. ☎93 048 or 380 32 15 448. Boats from €100 per day. MC/V.) From Cala Luna to Capo Monte Santu, there are several other beach inlets along the coast of the Golf di Orosei. The beach inlets are protected as UNESCO World Heritage sites, so no commercial traffic or building can damage the beautiful nature. One can also go **horseback riding** along the hills above the beaches. (Call Sebastiano ☎340 24 91 837 or Franco ☎349 61 12 850. €20 per hr., €70-80 per day.) **Dimensione Mare**, Vle. C. Colombo 2 (☎338 82 51 040; www.dimensionemare.com), also serves those interested in scuba diving.

APPENDIX

CLIMATE

Temperatures heat up throughout Italy in summer when the warm humid *sirocco* wind blows in from North Africa. While the ocean welcomes bathers from mid-May until October, the water can be nippy in the spring. In the Italian Alps, temperatures tend to be cooler. Wet weather hits from April to June. Consistent precipitation nurtures the fertile Po Valley in the northeast year-round, bringing rain in the sweltering summer and freezing fog, frost and snow in the winter. The south generally experiences mild winters and dry hot summers. In the far south, including Sicily and Sardinia, clouds shed few tears, letting the sun smile down more than anywhere else in Italy.

AVERAGE TEMPERATURE (HIGH/LOW) AND PRECIPITATION

	JANUARY			APRIL			JULY			OCTOBER		
	°C	°F	mm	°C	°F	mm	°C	°F	mm	°C	°F	mm
Milan	4/-2	39/28	64	17/7	63/45	81	29/17	84/63	69	18/8	64/46	99
Venice	6/-1	43/30	58	16/8	61/46	64	27/18	81/64	64	18/9	64/48	69
Turin	5/-1	41/30	31	13/6	55/43	91	24/16	75/61	46	14/9	57/48	74
Florence	10/1	50/34	74	18/7	64/45	79	31/17	88/63	41	21/10	70/50	89
Rome	13/3	55/37	81	18/8	64/46	56	28/18	82/64	15	22/12	72/54	94
Naples	12/3	54/37	104	18/8	64/46	76	29/18	84/64	25	22/11	72/52	130
Brindisi	12/6	54/43	61	18/10	64/50	36	28/20	82/68	10	21/14	70/57	71
Cagliari	14/6	57/43	46	18/9	64/48	38	29/18	84/64	3	23/13	73/55	56
Palermo	14/10	57/50	71	18/13	64/55	43	28/23	82/73	5	23/18	73/64	99

MEASUREMENTS

Italy uses the metric system. The basic unit of length is the **meter (m)**, which is divided into 100 **centimeters (cm)**, or 1000 **millimeters (mm)**. One thousand meters make up one **kilometer (km)**. Fluids are measured in **liters (L)**, each divided into 1000 **milliliters (ml)**. A liter of pure water weighs one **kilogram (kg)**, divided into 1000 **grams (g)**, while 1000kg make up one metric **ton**.

ENGLISH TO METRIC	METRIC TO ENGLISH
1 inch (in.) = 2.54cm	1 centimeter (cm) = 0.39 in.
1 foot (ft.) = 0.30m	1 meter (m) = 3.28 ft.
1 yard (yd.) = 0.914m	1 meter (m) = 1.09 yd.
1 mile (mi.) = 1.609km	1 kilometer (km) = 0.62 mi.
1 ounce (oz.) = 28.35g	1 gram (g) = 0.035 oz.
1 pound (lb.) = 0.454kg	1 kilogram (kg) = 2.205 lbs.
1 fluid ounce (fl. oz.) = 29.57mL	1 milliliter (mL) = 0.034 fl. oz.
1 gallon (gal.) = 3.785L	1 liter (L) = 0.264 gal.

APPENDIX

THE ITALIAN LANGUAGE
PRONUNCIATION

VOWELS

There are seven vowel sounds in standard Italian. **A**, **I**, and **U** each have one pronunciation. **E** and **O** each have two slightly different pronunciations, one open and one closed, depending on the vowel's placement in the word, the stress, and the regional accent. Below are approximate pronunciations.

VOWEL PHONOLOGY	
a	"a" as in father *(casa;* CAH-zah)
e: closed e: open	"ey" as in grey *(sera;* SEY-rah) "eh" as in wet *(sette;* SEHT-teh)
i	"ee" as in cheese *(vino;* VEE-no)
o: closed o: open	"o" as in bone *(sono;* SOH-noh) "oh" as in lord *(bocca;* BOH-kah)
u	"oo" as in moon *(gusto;* GOOS-toe)

CONSONANTS

C and G: Before a, o, or u, **c** and **g** are hard, as in *candy* and *goose* or as in the Italian *colore* (koh-LOHR-eh; color) or *gatto* (GAHT-toh; cat). Italians soften c and g into **ch** and **J** sounds, respectively, when followed by **I** or **e**, as in English *cheese* and *jeep* or Italian *cibo* (CHEE-boh; food) and *gelato* (jeh-LAH-toh; ice cream).

Ch and Gh: Adding an **h** after **c** and **g** returns the consonants to their "hard" sounds in front of **I** or **e**, as in the Italian *chianti* (kee-YAHN-tee; the Tuscan wine) and *spaghetti* (spah-GEHT-tee; the pasta).

Gn and Gli: Pronounce **gn** like the **ni** in *onion;* thus *bagno* (bath) is "BAHN-yoh." **Gli** is like the **lli** in *million,* so *sbagliato* (wrong) is pronounced "zbal-YAH-toh."

Sc and Sch: When followed by **a**, **o**, or **u**, sc is pronounced as **sk**. *Scusi* (excuse me) yields "SKOO-zee." When followed by an **e** or **I**, sc is pronounced **sh** as in *sciopero* (SHOH-pair-oh; strike). **H** returns **c** to its hard sound (sk) before **I** or **e**, as in *pesche* (PEHS-keh; peaches), not to be confused with *pesce* (PEH-sheh; fish).

Double consonants: When you see a double consonant, stress that consonant; failing to do so can lead to confusion. For example, *penne all'arrabbiata* (PEN-neh al ar-rahb-bee-AH-tah) is "short pasta in a spicy, red sauce," whereas *pene all'arrabbiata* (PEH-neh al ar-rahb-bee-AH-tah) means "penis in a spicy, red sauce."

STRESS

In Italian, the stress generally falls on the penultimate, or next-to-last, syllable. An accent indicates when it falls on the last syllable like *città* (cheet-TAH).

GENDER AND PLURALS

Italian nouns fall into two genders, masculine and feminine. The singular masculine ending is usually **o**, as in *duomo* (church), and the feminine is usually **a**, as in *donna* (woman). Words ending in an **a** in the singular (usually feminine) end with an **e** in the plural; *mela* (MEH-lah; apple) becomes *mele* (MEH-leh). Words ending in an **o** in the singular (usually masculine) generally end with an **I** in the plural; *conto* (KOHN-toh; bill) becomes *conti* (KOHN-tee). The exception: masculine words ending with **e** take an **I** in the plural; *cane* (KAH-neh; dog) becomes *cani* (KAH-nee). Words with a final accent, like *città* and *caffè,* and words that end in consonants, like *bar* and *sport,* do not change in the plural. Adjectives agree with their noun in gender and number. They are formed by adding the appropriate gender and number ending letter to the root.

ARTICLES

In Italian, the gender and number of a noun determine the article that precedes it. **Definite articles,** equivalent to the English "the," are **il, lo, l', la, i, gli,** and **le.** *Il* is used for most masculine singular nouns (*il gatto;* the cat), while those beginning with z or *s impura* (s plus any consonant) are preceded by the article *lo* (*lo zio,* the uncle; *lo stivale,* the boot). The article *la* is used with feminine singular nouns beginning with a consonant (*la capra;* the goat). For all singular nouns beginning with a vowel, *l'* is the appropriate article (*l'arte,* the art; *l'aereo,* the plane). In the plural, the article *i* is used for most masculine plural nouns (*i gatti;* the cats), while *gli* is used with masculine nouns beginning with a vowel, z, or *s impura* (*gli aerei,* the planes; *gli zii,* the uncles; *gli stivali,* the boots). *Le* precedes all plural feminine nouns (*le scarpe;* the shoes).

Indefinite articles, equivalent to the English "a/an," are **un, uno, una,** and **un'.** *Un* and *uno* behave like *il* and *lo,* respectively, except that *un* can precede a masculine noun beginning with a vowel: *un gatto* (a cat), *un uomo* (a man), *uno stivale* (a boot). For feminine nouns, *un'* is used before vowels and *una* is used everywhere else: *un'edicola* (a newsstand), *una ragazza* (a girl).

PHRASEBOOK

MONTHS*			
January	gennaio	July	luglio
February	febbraio	August	agosto
March	marzo	September	settembre
April	aprile	October	ottobre
May	maggio	November	novembre
June	giugno	December	dicembre

DAYS OF THE WEEK*	
Monday	lunedì
Tuesday	martedì
Wednesday	mercoledì
Thursday	giovedì
Friday	venerdì
Saturday	sabato
Sunday	domenica

NUMBERS			
1	uno	15	quindici
2	due	16	sedici
3	tre	17	diciassette
4	quattro	18	diciotto
5	cinque	19	dicianove
6	sei	20	venti
7	sette	30	trenta
8	otto	40	quaranta
9	nove	50	cinquanta
10	dieci	60	sessanta
11	undici	70	settanta
12	dodici	80	ottanta
13	tredici	90	novanta
14	quattordici	100	cento

*Note: In Italian, days of the week and months are not capitalized unless they come at the beginning of the sentence. Also, *domenica* (Sunday) is the only day of the week that is of the feminine gender.

ENGLISH	ITALIAN	PRONUNCIATION
GENERAL		
Hi/bye (informal)	Ciao	chow
Good day/Hello	Buongiorno	bwohn-JOHR-noh
Good evening	Buonasera	BWOH-nah-SEH-rah
Good night	Buonanotte	BWOH-nah-NOHT-teh
Goodbye	Arrivederci/ArrivederLa (formal)	ah-ree-veh-DAIR-chee/ah-ree-veh-DAIR-lah
Please	Per favore, Per piacere	pehr fah-VOH-reh, pehr pyah-CHEH-reh
Thank you	Grazie	GRAHT-see-yeh
How are you?	Come stai/Come sta (formal)?	COH-meh STA-ee/COH-meh stah
I am well	Sto bene	stoh BEH-neh
You're welcome/May I help you?/Please	Prego	PREH-goh
Excuse me	Scusi	SKOO-zee
I don't know	Boh	BOH
I'm sorry	Mi dispiace	mee dees-PYAH-cheh
My name is...	Mi chiamo...	mee kee-YAH-moh
I'm here on holiday	Sono qui in vacanza	SOH-noh qwee een vah-CAHN-zah
I'm American/British/Irish/Australian/New Zealander	Sono americano(a)/britan-nico(a)/irlandese/austra-liano(a)/neozelandese	SOH-noh ah-meh-ree-CAH-noh(nah)/bree-TAH-nee-coh(cah)/eer-lahn-DEH-zeh/au-strah-LYAH-noh(nah)/neh-oh-zeh-lahn-DEH-zeh
I live in...	Abito a...	AH-bee-toh ah
What's your name?	Come ti chiami? Come si chi-ama Lei? (formal)	COH-meh tee KYAH-mee/COH-meh see KYAH-mah lay
Yes/No/Maybe	Sì/No/Forse	see/no/FOHR-seh
I don't know	Non lo so	nohn loh soh
Could you repeat that?	Potrebbe ripetere?	poh-TREHB-beh ree-PEH-teh-reh
What does this mean?	Cosa vuol dire questo?	COH-za vwohl DEE-reh KWEH-stoh
I understand	Ho capito	oh kah-PEE-toh
I don't understand	Non capisco	nohn kah-PEES-koh
Do you speak English?	Parla inglese?	PAR-lah een-GLAY-zeh
I don't speak Italian	Non parlo italiano	nohn PARL-oh ee-tahl-YAH-noh
Could you help me?	Potrebbe aiutarmi?	poh-TREHB-beh ah-yoo-TAHR-mee
How do you say...?	Come si dice...?	KOH-meh see DEE-cheh
What do you call this in Italian?	Come si chiama questo in ital-iano?	KOH-meh see kee-YAH-mah KWEH-stoh een ee-tahl-YAH-no
this/that	questo/quello	KWEH-sto/KWEHL-loh
more/less	più/meno	pyoo/MEH-noh
How much does it cost?	Quanto costa?	KWAN-toh CO-stah
TIME		
At what time?	A che ora?	ah kay OHR-ah
What time is it?	Che ore sono?	kay OHR-eh SOH-noh
What time does it open/close?	A che ora apre/chiude?	ah kay OHR-ah AH-preh/KYOO-deh
It's noon/midnight	È mezzogiorno/mezzanotte	eh MEHD-zoh-DJOHR-noh/MEHD-zah-NOHT-eh
now	adesso/ora	ah-DEHS-so/OH-rah
Let's go now.	Andiamo adesso	Ahn-dee-AH-moh ah-DEHS-so
tomorrow	domani	doh-MAH-nee
today	oggi	OHJ-jee
yesterday	ieri	ee-YEH-ree

right away	subito	SU-bee-toh
soon	fra poco	frah POH-koh
after	dopo	DOH-poh
before	prima	PREE-mah
late/later	tardi/più tardi	TAHR-dee/pyoo TAHR-dee
early	presto	PREHS-toh
late (after scheduled arrival time)	in ritardo	een ree-TAHR-doh
daily	quotidiano	kwoh-tee-DYAH-no
weekly	settimanale	seht-tee-mah-NAH-leh
monthly	mensile	mehn-SEE-leh
vacation	le ferie	leh FEH-ree-eh

DIRECTIONS AND TRANSPORTATION

Where is...?	Dov'è...?	doh-VEH
How do you get to...?	Come si arriva a...?	KOH-meh see ahr-REE-vah ah
Do you stop at...?	Si ferma a...?	SEE FEHR-mah ah
at the center of town	in centro	een CHEHN-troh
at the consulate/the embassy	al consolato/ all'ambasciata	ahl kohn-so-LAH-toh/ ahl lahm-bah-SHAH-tah
the tourist office	l'ufficio turistico	loof-FEETCH-o tur-EES-tee-koh
the station	la stazione	lah staht-see-YOH-neh
the airport	l'aeroporto	LAYR-o-PORT-o
the bank/the exchange	la banca/il cambio	lah bahn-KAH/eel CAHM-bee-oh
the supermarket	il supermercato	eel SOO-pair-mehr-CAHT-oh
the post office	l'ufficio postale	loof-FEETCH-o pohs-TAL-eh
near/far	vicino/lontano	vee-CHEE-noh/lohn-TAH-noh
turn left/right	gira a sinistra/destra	JEE-rah ah see-NEE-strah/DEH-strah
straight ahead	sempre diritto	SEHM-preh DREET-toh
here	qui/qua	kwee/kwah
there	lì/là	lee/lah
the street address	l'indirizzo	leen-dee-REET-soh
the telephone	il telefono	eel teh-LEH-foh-noh
street	strada, via, viale, vico, vicolo, corso	STRAH-dah, VEE-ah, vee-AH-leh, VEE-koh, VEE-koh-loh, KOHR-soh
speed limit	limite di velocità	LEE-mee-teh dee veh-loh-chee-TAH
the taxi	il tassi	eel tahs-SEE
slow down	rallentare	rah-lehn-TAH-reh
one-way street	senso unico	SEHN-soh OOH-nee-coh
large, open square	piazza	pee-YAH-tzah
stairway	scalinata	scah-lee-NAH-tah
beach	spiaggia	spee-YAH-gee-ah
river	fiume	fee-YOO-meh
toilet, WC	gabinetto, bagno	gah-bee-NEH-toh, BAHN-yoh
What time does the... leave?	A che ora parte...?	ah kay OHR-ah PAHR-teh
From where does the... leave?	Da dove parte...?	dah DOH-veh PAHR-teh
next	prossimo	PROSS-ee-moh

the (city) bus	l'autobus	LAOW-toh-boos
the (intercity) bus	il pullman	eel POOL-mahn
the ferry	il traghetto	eel tra-GEHT-toh
the hydrofoil	l'aliscafo	la-lee-SCAH-foh
the plane	l'aereo	lah-EHR-eh-oh
the train	il treno	eel TRAY-noh
the ticket office	la biglietteria	lah beel-yeht-teh-RI-ah
How much does it cost?	Quanto costa?	KWAN-toh CO-stah
I would like to buy...	Vorrei comprare...	voh-RAY com-PRAH-reh
...a ticket	...un biglietto	oon beel-YEHT-toh
...a pass (bus, etc.)	...una tessera	OO-nah TEHS-seh-rah
one-way	solo andata	SO-lo ahn-DAH-tah
round-trip	andata e ritorno	ahn-DAH-tah ay ree-TOHR-noh
reduced price	ridotto	ree-DOHT-toh
student discount	lo sconto studentesco	loh SKOHN-toh stoo-dehn-TEHS-koh
the track/train platform	il binario	eel bee-NAH-ree-oh
the flight	il volo	eel VOH-loh
the reservation	la prenotazione	la preh-no-taht-see-YOH-neh
the entrance/the exit	l'ingresso/l'uscita	leen-GREH-so/loo-SHEE-tah
I need to get off here	Devo scendere qui	DEH-vo SHEN-dehr-eh qwee

EMERGENCY		
I lost my passport/wallet	Ho perso il passaporto/portafoglio	oh PEHR-soh eel pahs-sah-POHR-toh/por-ta-FOH-lee-oh
Where is my suitcase?	Dov'è la mia valigia?	doh-VEH lah mee-ah vah-LEE-jee-ah
I've been robbed	Sono stato derubato/a	SOH-noh STAH-toh deh-roo-BAH-toh/tah
Wait!	Aspetta!	ahs-PEHT-tah
Stop!	Ferma!	FEHR-mah
Help!	Aiuto!	ah-YOO-toh
Leave me alone!/Release me!	Lasciami stare!/Mollami!	LAH-shah-mee STAH-reh/MOH-lah MEE
Don't touch me!	Non mi toccare!	NOHN mee tohk-KAH-reh
I'm calling the police!	Telefono alla polizia!	tehl-LEH-foh-noh ah-lah poh-leet-SEE-ah
police/military police	polizia/carabinieri	po-leet-ZEE-ah/CAH-rah-been-YEH-ree
Go away, moron!	Vattene, cretino!	VAH-teh-neh creh-TEE-noh

MEDICAL		
the hospital	l'ospedale	los-peh-DAH-leh
the pharmacy	la farmacia	lah far-mah-CHEE-ah
the doctor	il medico	eel MEH-dee-koh
I have...	Ho...	OH
...allergies	...delle allergie	DEHL-leh ahl-lair-JEE-eh
...a cold	...un raffreddore	oon rahf-freh-DOH-reh
...a cough	...una tosse	OO-nah TOHS-seh
...the flu	...l'influenza	linn-floo-EN-zah
...a fever	...una febbre	OO-nah FEHB-breh
...a headache	...mal di testa	mahl dee TEHS-tah
My foot/arm hurts	Mi fa male il piede/braccio	mee fah MAH-leh eel pee-EHD-deh/BRAH-cho
I'm on the Pill	Prendo la pillola	PREHN-doh lah PEE-loh-lah

(3 months) pregnant	incinta (da tre mesi)	een-CHEEN-tah (dah TREH MEH-zee)

HOTEL AND HOSTEL RESERVATIONS		
hotel/hostel	albergo/ostello	al-BEHR-goh/os-TEHL-loh
I have a booking	Ho una prenotazione	oh oo-nah preh-no-taht-see-YOH-neh
Could I reserve a single room/double room (for the 2nd of August)?	Potrei prenotare una camera singola/doppia (per il due agosto)?	poh-TREY preh-noh-TAH-reh oo-nah CAH-meh-rah SEEN-goh-lah/DOH-pee-yah (pehr eel DOO-eh ah-GOH-stoh)
Do you have rooms available?	Ha camere libere?	ah CAH-mer-reh LEE-beh-reh
with bath/shower	con bagno/doccia	kohn BAHN-yo/DOH-cha
Is there a cheaper room without a bath/shower?	C'è una stanza più economica senza bagno/doccia?	cheh oo-nah STAN-zah pyoo eko-NOM-ika senzah BAHN-yo/DOH-cha
open/closed	aperto/chiuso	ah-PAIR-toh/KYOO-zoh
sheets/linens	i lenzuoli	ee lehn-SWO-lee
the blanket	la coperta	lah koh-PEHR-tah
the bed	il letto	eel LEHT-toh
Is there heating?	C'è riscaldamento?	cheh ree-skahl-dah-MEHN-toh
Is there air conditioning?	C'è aria condizionata?	cheh AH-ree-ah con-deet-syon-AH-tah
How much is the room?	Quanto costa la camera?	KWAHN-toh KOHS-ta lah KAM-eh-rah
Is breakfast included?	È compresa la prima colazione?	eh com-PREH-zah la PREEH-mah coh-laht-see-YO-neh
I will arrive (at 2:30pm)	Arriverò (alle due e mezzo)	ah-ree-veh-ROH (ah-leh DOO-eh eh MED-zoh)
You'll have to send a deposit/check	Bisogna mandare un anticipo/un assegno	bee-ZOHN-yah mahn-DAH-reh oon ahn-TEE-chee-poh/oon ahs-SEHN-yoh
What is that funny smell?	Che cos'è quest'odore strano?	kay kohz-EH kwest-oh-DOHR-eh STRAH-noh?

AMORE		
I have a boyfriend/girlfriend	Ho un ragazzo/una ragazza	oh oon rah-GAHT-soh/oo-nah rah-GAHT-sah
Let's get a room	Prendiamo una camera	Prehn-DYAH-moh oo-nah CAH-meh-rah
Voluptuous!	Volutuoso/a!	VOL-oot-oo-OH-zhoh/zhah
To be in love with	Essere innamorato/a di	Eh-seh-reh een-am-mo-rah-to/ta dee
Just a kiss	Solo un bacio	SOH-loh oon BAH-chyoh
Are you single?	Sei celibe?	SAY CHEH-lee-beh
You're cute (beautiful)	Sei carino/a (bello/a)	SAY cah-REEN-oh/ah (BEHL-loh/lah)
I love you, I swear	Ti amo, te lo giuro	Tee AH-moh, teh loh DJOO-roh
I'm married	Sono sposato/a	Soh-noh spo-ZA-to/ta
You're quite a babe	Sei proprio un figo/una figa	SAY PROH-pree-yo oon FEE-goh/oona FEE-gah
I only have safe sex	Pratico solo sesso sicuro	PRAH-tee-coh sohl-oh SEHS-so see-COO-roh
I am gay/a lesbian	Sono gay/lesbica	SOH-noh GAY-ee/lez-BEE-kah
Leave her alone, she's mine	Lasciala stare, è mia	LAH-shyah-lah STAH-reh, eh mee-ah
Leave right now!	Vai via subito!	VAH-ee VEE-ah SOO-beet-oh
I'll never forget you	Non ti dimenticherò mai	Nohn tee dee-men-tee-ker-OH mah-ee
I have a venereal disease	Ho una malattia venereale	oh oona mah-lah-TI-yah veh-ne-ree-AL-leh
Not if you're the last man on earth	Neanche se tu fossi l'unico uomo sulla terra	neh-AHN-keh seh too FOH-see LOO-nee-koh WOH-moh soo-LAH TEH-rah.

AT THE BAR		
May I buy you a drink?	Posso offrirle qualcosa da bere?	POHS-soh ohf-FREER-leh kwahl-COH-zah dah BEH-reh

a beer	una birra	OO-nah BEER-rah
a glass of wine	un bicchiere di vino	oon bee-kee-EHR-reh dee VEE-noh
liter of wine	litro di vino	LEE-troh di VEE-noh
I'm drunk	Sono ubriaco/a	SOH-noh oo-BRYAH-coh/cah
I don't drink	Non bevo	nohn BEH-voh
Cheers!	Cin cin!	cheen cheen
Do you have a light?	Mi fai accendere?	mee fah-ee ah-CHEN-deh-reh
No thank you, I don't smoke	No grazie, non fumo	noh GRAH-zyeh nohn FOO-moh
I was here first!	C'ero io prima!	CHEH-roh EE-oh PREE-mah
I feel like throwing up	Mi viene da vomitare	mee VYE-neh dah voh-mee-TAH-reh

RESTAURANTS		
food	il cibo	eel CHEE-boh
wine bar	l'enoteca	len-oh-TEK-ah
breakfast	la colazione	lah coh-laht-see-YO-neh
lunch	il pranzo	eel PRAHN-zoh
dinner	la cena	lah CHEH-nah
coffee	il caffè	eel kah-FEH
appetizer	l'antipasto	lahn-tee-PAH-stoh
first course	il primo	eel PREE-moh
second course	il secondo	eel seh-COHN-doh
side dish	il contorno	eel cohn-TOHR-noh
dessert	il dolce	eel DOHL-cheh
bottle	la bottiglia	lah boh-TEEL-yah
waiter/waitress	il/la cameriere/a	eel/lah kah-meh-ree-EH-reh/rah
the bill	il conto	eel COHN-toh
cover charge	il coperto	eel koh-PEHR-toh
tip	la mancia	lah MAHN-cha
vegetarian	vegetariano	veh-jeh-tar-ee-AN-oh
Kosher/Halal	Kasher/Halal	KA-sher/HA-lal

MENU READER

PRIMI (FIRST COURSES)	
pasta aglio e olio	pasta in garlic and olive oil
pasta all'amatriciana	pasta in a tangy tomato sauce with onions and bacon
pasta all'arrabbiata	pasta in a spicy tomato sauce
pasta alla bolognese	pasta in a meat sauce
pasta alla boscaiola	egg pasta, served in a mushroom sauce with peas and cream
pasta alla carbonara	pasta in a creamy sauce with egg, cured bacon, and cheese
pasta alla pizzaiola	pasta in a tomato-based sauce with olive oil and red peppers
pasta alla puttanesca	pasta in a tomato sauce with olives, capers, and anchovies
gnocchi	potato dumplings
ravioli	square-shaped pasta often stuffed with cheese or meat
tagliatelle	thin, flat pasta; the northern version of fettuccini
polenta	deep-fried cornmeal

PRIMI (FIRST COURSES)	
risotto	creamy rice dish, comes in nearly as many flavors as pasta sauce
PIZZA	
alla capricciosa	with ham, mozzarella, artichoke, olives and mushrooms
con rucola	with arugula (rocket for Brits)
marinara	with red sauce and no cheese
margherita	plain ol' tomato, mozzarella, and basil
pancetta/speck	bacon
pepperoni	bell pepper; be careful not to confuse the Italian bell pepper with the American pepperoni meat, which doesn't exist in Italy!
polpette	meatballs
quattro formaggi	four cheeses
quattro stagioni	four seasons; a different topping for each quarter of the pizza, usually mushrooms, *prosciutto crudo*, artichoke, and tomato
salsiccia	sausage
SECONDI (SECOND COURSES)	
agnello	lamb
animelle alla griglia	grilled sweetbreads
asino	donkey (served in Sicily and Sardinia)
bistecca	steak
cavallo (sfilacci)	horse (a delicacy throughout the South and Sardinia)
cinghiale	wild boar
coniglio	rabbit
cotoletta	breaded veal cutlet with cheese
cozze	mussels
fegato	liver
gamberetti/gamberi	shrimps/prawns
granchi	crab
maiale	pork
manzo	beef
merluzzo/baccalà	cod/dried salted cod
osso buco	braised veal shank
ostriche	oysters
pesce spada	swordfish
pollo	chicken
polpo	octopus
prosciutto	smoked ham, available cured (*crudo*) or cooked (*cotto*)
salsiccia	sausage
saltimbocca alla romana	slices of veal and ham cooked together and topped with cheese
sarde	sardines
scaloppina	cutlet
seppia	cuttlefish, usually served grilled in its own ink
sogliola	sole
speck	smoked raw ham, lean but surrounded by a layer of fat
tonno	tuna
trippa	tripe (chopped, sautéed cow intestines, usually in a tomato sauce)
trota	trout
vitello	veal

SECONDI (SECOND COURSES)	
vongole	clams

CONTORNI (SIDE DISHES)	
carciofe/carciofini	artichoke/artichoke hearts
carotte	carrots
cavolfiori	cauliflower
cavolo	cabbage
cetriolo	cucumber
cipolla	onion
fagioli	beans (usually white)
fagiolini	green beans
finocchio	fennel
funghi	mushrooms
insalata caprese	tomatoes with mozzarella cheese and basil, drizzled with olive oil
insalata mista	mixed salad with lettuce, cucumbers, and tomatoes
lenticchie	lentils
melanzana	eggplant
patate	potatoes
piselli	peas
pomodori	tomatoes
spinaci	spinach
tartufi	truffles

ANTIPASTI (APPETIZERS)	
bresaola	thinly sliced dried beef, served with olive oil, lemon, and *parmigiano*
bruschetta	crisp slices of garlic-rubbed, baked bread, often with raw tomatoes
caponata	mixed eggplant, olives, tomatoes, and anchovies
carpaccio	extremely thin slices of lean, raw beef
crostini	small pieces of toasted bread usually served with chicken liver or mozzarella and anchovies, though other toppings abound
fiori di zucca	zucchini flowers battered and lightly fried
insalata di mare	seafood salad
melanzane alla parmigiana	eggplant with tomato and parmesan cheese
peperonata	green and red peppers stewed in olive oil

FRUTTA (FRUIT)	
arancia	orange
ciliegia	cherry
fragola	strawberry
lampone	raspberry
mela	apple
pesca	peach
prugna	plum
uva	grape

DOLCI (DESSERTS)	
gelato	Italian-style ice cream
granita	ice-based fruit or coffee slushee
macedonia	fruit salad
panna cotta	flan
sfogliatelle	sugar-coated layers of flaky pastry filled with ricotta

APPENDIX

tiramisu	cake-like dessert drenched in *espresso*, layered with mascarpone

BIBITE (DRINKS)	
acqua con gas/selz minerale	soda water
acqua minerale	mineral water
aranciata	orangeade
bicchiere	glass
birra	beer
caffè	coffee
cioccolata calda	hot chocolate
ghiaccio	ice
latte	milk
limonata	lemonade
spremuta	fresh fruit juice
spumante	sparkling wine
succo	concentrated fruit juice with sugar
tè	tea
vino rosso/bianco/rosato/ secco/dolce	red/white/rosé/dry/sweet wine

PREPARATION	
al dente	firm to the bite (pasta)
al forno	baked
al sangue	rare
al punto	medium
ben cotto/a	well done
fritto/a	fried
crudo/a	raw
fresco/a	fresh
fritto/a	fried
piccante	spicy
ripieno	stuffed

APPENDIX

INDEX

ABOUT LET'S GO

NOT YOUR PARENTS' TRAVEL GUIDE

At Let's Go, we see every trip as the chance of a lifetime. If your dream is to grab a machete and forge through the jungles of Costa Rica, we can take you there. If you'd rather bask in the Riviera sun at a beachside cafe, we'll set you a table. We write for readers who know that there's more to travel than sharing double deckers with tourists and who believe that travel can change both themselves and the world—whether they plan to spend six days in Mexico City or six months in Europe. We'll show you just how far your money can go, and prove that the greatest limitation on your adventures is not your wallet, but your imagination.

BEYOND THE TOURIST EXPERIENCE

To help you gain a deeper connection with the places you travel, our fearless researchers scour the globe to give you the heads-up on both world-renowned and off-the-beaten-track attractions, sights, and destinations. They engage with the local culture only to emerge with the freshest insights on everything from local festivals to regional cuisine. We've also opened our pages to respected writers and scholars to hear their takes on the countries and regions we cover, and asked travelers who have worked, studied, or volunteered abroad to contribute first-person accounts of their experiences. In addition, we increased our coverage of responsible travel and expanded each guide's Beyond Tourism chapter to share more ideas about how to give back while on the road.

FORTY-EIGHT YEARS OF WISDOM

Let's Go got its start in 1960, when a group of creative and well-traveled students compiled their experience and advice into a 20-page mimeographed pamphlet, which they gave to travelers on charter flights to Europe. Four and a half decades later, we've expanded to cover six continents and all kinds of travel—while retaining our founders' adventurous attitude toward the world. Laced with witty prose and total candor, our guides are still researched and written entirely by students on shoestring budgets, experienced travelers who know that train strikes, stolen luggage, food poisoning, and marriage proposals are all part of a day's work.

THE LET'S GO COMMUNITY

More than just a travel guide company, Let's Go is a community. Our small staff comes together because of our shared passion for travel and our desire to help other travelers see the world the way it was meant to be seen. We love it when our readers become part of the Let's Go community as well—when you travel, drop us a postcard (67 Mt. Auburn St., Cambridge, MA 02138, USA), send us an e-mail (feedback@letsgo.com), or post on our forum (http://www.letsgo.com/connect/forum) to tell us about your adventures and discoveries.

For more information, visit us online: www.letsgo.com.

GET CONNECTED & SAVE WITH THE HI CARD

An HI card gives you access to friendly and affordable accommodations at over 4,000 hostels in over 60 countries, including across Italy. Members also receive complementary travel insurance, members-only airfare deals, and thousands of discounts on everything from tours and dining to shopping, communications and transportation.

Join millions of HI members worldwide who save money and have more fun every time they travel.

 Hostelling International USA

MAP INDEX

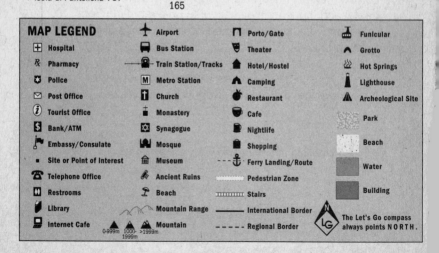

MAP LEGEND

- ⊞ Hospital
- ℞ Pharmacy
- ✪ Police
- ✉ Post Office
- ⓘ Tourist Office
- $ Bank/ATM
- ⚑ Embassy/Consulate
- ■ Site or Point of Interest
- ☎ Telephone Office
- ⊞ Restrooms
- Library
- Internet Cafe

- ✈ Airport
- 🚌 Bus Station
- Train Station/Tracks
- Ⓜ Metro Station
- ✝ Church
- ✟ Monastery
- ✡ Synagogue
- Mosque
- 🏛 Museum
- Ancient Ruins
- Beach
- Mountain Range
- Mountain
  0-999m 1000-1999m >1999m

- Π Porto/Gate
- Theater
- Hotel/Hostel
- Camping
- Restaurant
- Cafe
- Nightlife
- Shopping
- Ferry Landing/Route
- Pedestrian Zone
- Stairs
- International Border
- Regional Border

- Funicular
- Grotto
- Hot Springs
- Lighthouse
- Archeological Site
- Park
- Beach
- Water
- Building

The Let's Go compass
always points NORTH.